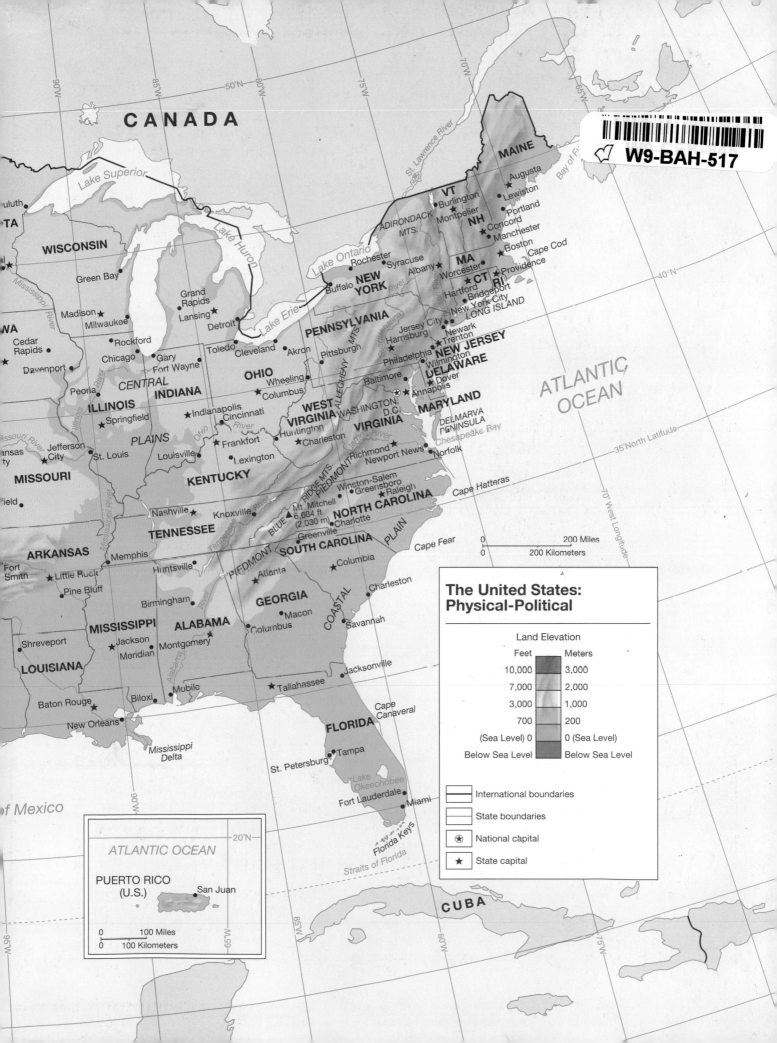

AMERICAN GOVERNMENT
Continuity and Change

2000 EDITION

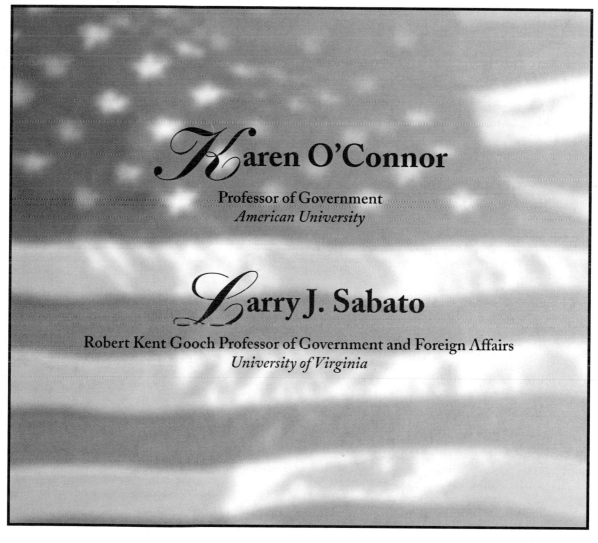

*K*aren O'Connor

Professor of Government
American University

*L*arry J. Sabato

Robert Kent Gooch Professor of Government and Foreign Affairs
University of Virginia

 LONGMAN

An imprint of Addison Wesley Longman, Inc.

New York • Reading, Massachusetts • Menlo Park, California • Harlow, England
Don Mills, Ontario • Sydney • Mexico City • Madrid • Amsterdam

Editor-in-Chief: Priscilla McGeehon
Acquisitions Editor: Eric Stano
Development Manager: Lisa Pinto
Senior Development Editor: Dawn Groundwater
Marketing Manager: Megan Galvin-Fak
Supplements Editor: Mark Toews
Full Service Production Manager: Eric Jorgensen
Project Coordination, Text Design, Art Studio, and Electronic Page Makeup: Electronic Publishing Services Inc., NYC
Cover Design Manager: Nancy Danahy
Cover Designer: Silvers Design
Cover Illustration Photos: Paula Bronstein/Tony Stone Images; Corbis Digital Stock; The Granger Collection; Mark Downey/Photodisc;
    Library of Congress; Ron Sherman/Tony Stone Images; Norman McGrath
Photo Research: PhotoSearch, Inc.
Senior Print Buyer: Hugh Crawford
Printer and Binder: Von Hoffman Press
Cover Printer: Von Hoffman Press

For permission to use copyrighted material, grateful acknowledgment is made to the copyright
holders on the pages where the material appears.

Library of Congress Cataloging-in-Publication Data

O'Connor, Karen, 1952-
    American government : continuity and change / Karen O'Connor, Larry J. Sabato.--
2000 ed.
        p. cm.
    Includes bibliographical references and index.
    ISBN 0-321-07033-x (hc.) -- ISBN 0-321-07689-3 (pb.)
        1. United States—Politics and government. I. Sabato, Larry. II. Title.

JK274 .O255 2000
320.473--dc21

                                                                    99-045630

Please visit our website at http://www.awlonline.com

ISBN 0–321–07033–X (hardcover)
ISBN 0–321–07689–3 (paperback)

12345678910—VH—02010099

To Meghan,
who grew up with this book

KAREN O'CONNOR

To my Government 101 students
over the years, who all know that
"politics is a good thing"

LARRY SABATO

BRIEF CONTENTS

CONTENTS

PART TWO   Institutions of Government

CHAPTER 7:   CONGRESS   214

CHAPTER 8:   THE PRESIDENCY   262

PART THREE   Political Behavior

CHAPTER 11:
PUBLIC OPINION AND POLITICAL
SOCIALIZATION   380

CHAPTER 12:
POLITICAL PARTIES   414

PART FOUR Public Policy

APPENDICES

PREFACE

*T*eaching introductory American government today requires special skills, sensitivity, and adaptability that many of us have only recently been forced to learn, as different movements and groups manifested a variety of attitudes toward their political leaders and even toward the political process itself. In 1992 we experienced the so-called "Year of the Woman" and the election of the first Democratic president in twelve years. While Bill Clinton's campaign operatives focused their message on the state of the economy, some pundits proclaimed the cardinal campaign principle of that election to be "It's abortion, Stupid," as women voters turned out in force to cast their votes for women candidates (most of whom were Democrats) and for Clinton. Studies showed that these voters were angry about a series of House banking scandals, the all-male Senate Judiciary Committee's treatment of Anita Hill during the Clarence Thomas hearings, and the specter of a conservative Supreme Court overruling *Roe* v. *Wade*. The nation watched the Thomas hearings on television and couldn't believe the manner in which the elected officials were conducting themselves and the country's business.

By 1994, however, the mood of the nation appeared to undergo a sea change. Women voters, lulled into believing that the right to abortion was secure and that the women legislators they had elected would act on their behalf, stayed home from the polls in record numbers. At the same time, those whom pundits nicknamed "Angry White Males" voted—and voted overwhelmingly Republican—ushering in the first Republican Congress in over a decade. These angry voters were perceived to want less government, particularly at the national level, and Republican lawmakers in Congress tried to respond as they sought to enact the varied proposals for sweeping governmental reform contained in what they termed their "Contract with America."

This return to divided government brought with it many changes in the way the national government operates. The swearing in of the Republican Congress also appeared to trigger a change in the way politics work in Washington, D.C. Conciliation was out; confrontation was in. The anger of many American voters was often echoed in the halls of Congress where civility was no longer a cherished virtue. Much of this rancor was duly, even gleefully, reported by the press and members of the mass media. Whether on call-in radio talk shows or from television news desks, the tone and subject of American political discourse changed.

This change in our political discourse intensified by a president who admitted to engaging in sexual relations with a White House intern in the Oval Office, by an Independent Counsel's report excruciatingly describing the intimate details of their encounters has led many of those who were angry in 1994 to become simply disillusioned with politics and politicians, especially those in our nations' capital.

In less than a decade, our perceptions of politics, the role of the media, and the utility of voting appear to have undergone tremendous change. Over the last four editions, this text has tried diligently to reflect those changes and to present information about politics in a manner to engage students actively—many of whom have little interest in politics when they come into the classroom. In this edition, we try to build on a solid-tried-and-true base and at the same time to present information about how politics now seems to be changing at an ever more rapid pace. Thus, we present new information that we hope will whet students' appetites to learn more about politics while providing them with all of the information they need to make informed decisions about their government, politics, and politicians. We very much want our students to make such decisions. We very much want them to *participate*. Our goal with this text is to transmit just this sort of practical, useful information while creating and fostering student interest in American politics despite growing national skepticism about government and government officials at all levels. In fact, we hope that this new edition of our text will explain the national mood about politics and put it in a better context for students to understand their important role in a changing America.

APPROACH

We believe that one cannot fully understand the actions, issues, and policy decisions facing the U. S. government, its constituent states, or "the people" unless these issues are examined from the perspective of how they have evolved over time. Consequently, the title of this book is *American Government: Continuity and Change*. In its pages we try to examine how the United States is governed today by looking not just at present behavior but also at the Framers' intentions and how they have been implemented and adapted over the years. For example, we believe that it is critical to an understanding of the role of political parties in the United States to understand the Framers' fears of factionalism, how parties evolved, and when and why realignments in party identification occurred.

In addition to questions raised by the Framers, we explore issues that the Framers could never have envisioned, and how the basic institutions of government have changed in responding to these new demands. For instance, no one more than two centuries ago could have foreseen election campaigns in an age when nearly all American homes contain television sets, and the Internet and fax machines allow instant access to information. Moreover, increasing citizen demands and expectations have routinely forced government reforms, making an understanding of the dynamics of change essential for introductory students.

Our overriding concern is that students understand their government as it exists today, so that they may become better citizens and make better choices. In spite of current voter apathy, we believe that by providing students with information about government, explaining why it is important, and why their participation counts, students will come to see that politics can be a good thing.

To understand their government at all levels, students must understand how it was designed in the Constitution. Each chapter, therefore, approaches its topics from a combination of perspectives which we believe will facilitate this approach. In writing this book, we chose to put the institutions of government (Part Two) before political behavior (Part Three). Both sections, however, were written independently, making them easy to switch for those who prefer to teach about the actors in government and elections before discussing its institutions. To test the book, each of us has taught from it in both orders, with no pedagogical problems.

WHAT'S CHANGED IN THIS EDITION?

In this 2000 edition of *American Government: Continuity and Change*, we have retained our basic approach to the study of politics as one of bedrock constants yet continual change. Recent changes in voter perceptions—from anger and frustration at government to alarm or apathy—are chronicled throughout every chapter. Since the last edition of this text, the president admitted to sexual misconduct in the White House, the nation's fascination with the O. J. Simpson trial was replaced by nightly television programs including "White House in Crisis," and some cable networks nearly became "All Monica TV." The Monica and Bill story has not been the only change. We could have never predicted how the use of the Internet would have so quickly changed the political landscape. Reports about the "White House intern" and the Linda Tripp tapes first appeared online; the 400-plus pages of the Starr Report and the White House rebuttal were instantaneously released on the Internet (ironically by a Congress otherwise devoted to keeping pornography off the Internet), candidates and political parties all have web pages, and information about government and politics is now much more accessible than ever before.

Many of these changes and others are reflected in this 2000 Edition, including **Chapter 1's** new sections on changes in family and family size, and voter apathy; **Chapter 3's** revised section on new federalism and the Reagan revolution, along with an updated section on violence against women; **Chapter 4's** history of state, local, and tribal governments; **Chapter 5's** new coverage of the Child Online Protection Act, the revised section on Congress and obscenity, and the updated section on drug testing and DNA sampling; **Chapter 7's** expanded discussion of filibusters and legislative oversight and congressional review; **Chapter 8's** updated section on the president and public opinion; **Chapter 9's** expanded coverage of judicial control of governmental agencies; **Chapter 12's** expanded coverage of minor and independent candidates, informal groups, and party campaign committees; **Chapter 13's** new coverage of crossover voting and raiding, along with expanded coverage of prospective voting, ballot initiatives, the effects of frontloading, and ticket-splitting; **Chapter 14's** new sections on Internet and campaign finance, soft money and issue advocacy advertisements, member-to-member candidate contributions and independent expenditures, along with updated coverage of negative advertising and PACs; **Chapter 15's** expanded coverage of media bias and the character issue in media coverage, along with updated coverage of the World Wide Web, covering the presidency, and media's influence; **Chapter 16's** new section on what makes an interest group successful, along with updated sections on the conservative backlash and organized labor; **Chapter 18's** updated section on recent environmental initiatives; and **Chapter 19's** changes in the state department and the Nuclear Non-Proliferation Treaty, along with updated coverage of U. S. exports and imports and the media's role in agenda setting.

We have also made a major effort to make certain that this edition contains the most up-to-date scholarship by political scientists, not only on how government works, but what they have said on contemporary debates.

In addition to chapter-by-chapter changes, we have developed several new features designed to enhance student understanding of the political processes, institutions, and policies of American government.

Global Politics Boxes

To put American government in perspective, these boxes compare and contrast some aspect of American politics to that of other industrial democracies, including Canada, France, Germany, Japan, Italy, and Great Britain. These boxes appear once per chapter on topics ranging from civil liberties in industrial democracies in Chapter 5, the power of the courts in Chapter 10, and campaigns in comparative perspective in Chapter 14.

Continuity and Change Sections

To reinforce the text approach, each chapter concludes with a section that looks at the evolution of a particular foundation, institution, behavior, or policy from three points in time: yesterday, today, and the future. Chapter 3, for example, examines the power of the states while Chapter 13 addresses the changing nature of voting. These sections conclude with a series of questions that ask students to apply what they learned in the chapter to the issues presented here. To further encourage student involvement, each section is also accompanied by a "Cast Your Vote" question, which prompts students to log onto the book specific web site (www.awlonline.com/oconnor) and offer their opinion on a particular issue—and to see how their opinions compare with fellow students from around the country.

Web Explorations and Try It Activities

Each chapter contains several links to the World Wide Web that prompt students to either explore or experience a particular process, topic, or issue in politics on our book specific web site. These links are of two types. Web Explorations, identified in the margins with an ![icon] icon, encourage the reader to learn more about a specific issue or concept (i.e., "For more about local gun initiatives, go to www.awlonline.com/oconnor) or guide them to primary sources. Try It activities, identified in the margins with an ![icon] icon, direct the reader to an interactive exercise or online simulation (i.e., "To try your hand at balancing the budget, go to www.awlonline.com/oconnor) where they can experience political processes and actions firsthand.

FEATURES

The *2000 Edition* has retained the best features and pedagogy from previous editions and added exciting new ones.

Historical Perspective

Every chapter uses history to serve three purposes: first, to show how institutions and processes have evolved to their present states; second, to provide some of the color that makes information memorable; and third, to provide students with a more thorough appreciation that government was born amid burning issues of representation and power, issues that continue to smolder today. A richer historical texture helps to explain the present.

Comparative Perspective

Changes in the Japanese economy, Russia, Eastern Europe, North America, and Asia all remind us of the preeminence of democracy, in theory if not always in fact. As new democratic experiments spring up around the globe, it becomes increasingly important for students to understand the rudiments of presidential versus parliamentary government and of multiparty versus two-party systems. To put American government in perspective, we continue to draw comparisons with Great Britain within the text discussion. As mentioned earlier, we have also developed new Global Politics boxes that compare U. S. politics and institutions with other industrialized democracies.

Enhanced Pedagogy

We have revised and enhanced many pedagogical features to help students become stronger political thinkers and to echo the book's theme of evolving change.

Preview and Review.   To pique students' interest and draw them into each chapter, we begin each chapter with a contemporary vignette. These vignettes, including how 18-year-olds acquired the vote, how special interests are lobbying Congress for laws to allow them to go after student debtors, and congressional efforts to deal with violence in public schools in the aftermath of the Littleton, Colorado shooting, frequently deal with issues of high interest to students, which we hope will whet their appetites to read the rest of the chapter. Each vignette is followed by a bridge paragraph linking the vignette with the chapter's topics and a roadmap previewing the chapter's major headings. Chapter Summaries restate the major points made under each of these same major headings.

Key Terms.   Glossary definitions are included in the margins of the text for all bold-faced key terms. Key terms are listed once more at the end of each chapter, with page references for review and study.

Special Features.   Each chapter contains several boxed features in keeping with its theme of continuity and change:

- *Roots of Government* These boxes highlight the role that a particular institution, process, or person has played in the course of American politics as it has evolved to the present. Chapter 11, for example, profiles George Gallup, the founder of modern polling, while Chapter 9 looks at Mary Anderson, the first head of the Federal Women's Bureau.
- *Global Politics* As described earlier, these boxes compare American politics with other industrialized democracies. Chapter 18, for example, contains a box on economic policy in a globalizing economy.
- *Politics Now* These boxes act as a counterpoint to the text's traditional focus on "roots." Based on current clippings, editorials, and moments in time, these boxes are designed to encourage students to think about current issues in the context of

the continuing evolution of the American political system. Chapter 10, for example, discusses the blurring line between state and federal prosecutions.

- *Highlight* These boxes focus on high student-interest material outside the stream of the text discussion. Chapter 6, for example, looks at professional sports team names coming under attack by ethnic groups. Another describes how one college student's term paper ended up with the ratification of a constitutional amendment.

- *Continuity and Change* These sections conclude each chapter. They encourage students to think critically and tie in with the book's theme of change in America. They focus on the possibilities of governmental, institutional, and citizen reform. In considering the role of the individual citizen, we hope to encourage students to reassess their roles in the political system and to explore ways to become more informed members of the electorate.

THE ANCILLARY PACKAGE

The ancillary package for *American Government: Continuity and Change, 2000 Edition*, reflects the pedagogical goals of the text: to provide information in a useful context and with colorful examples. We have tried especially hard to provide materials that are useful for instructors and helpful to students.

Supplements for Instructors

- *NEW! American Government Instructor's Resource CD-ROM* This complete presentation tool is certain to enliven your American Government classroom in a variety of ways. It contains video footage and still images that highlight important political concepts, presentation slides, the Instructor's Manuals that accompany Longman's American Government texts, and a variety of links to American Government websites.

- *PowerPoint Presentation CD-ROM* A set of PowerPoint presentation slides provides instructors with ready made lecture outlines and visuals for class presentations that they can adapt to suit their needs.

- *NEW! Active Learning Guide* This innovative guide provides instructors with a variety of thoughtful active learning projects for their classrooms. The exercises address important concepts in American government and follow the organization of the text. The simulations and group projects encourage students to get actively involved in course material and to evaluate different perspectives on American Government.

- *Instructor's Manual* The Instructor's Manual includes narrative lecture outlines, suggestions for class discussion, web activities, simulations, a list of websites, and an extensive list of sources for further study.

- *Test Bank* The Test Bank has been completely revised and contains hundreds of challenging multiple choice, true-false, short answer, and essay questions along with a page-referenced answer key.

- *Computerized Testing* The printed Test Bank is also available on a cross-platform CD-ROM through our fully networkable computerized testing system, TestGen-EQ. The program's friendly graphical interface enables instructors to view, edit, and add questions; transfer questions to tests; and print test in a variety of fonts and forms. Search and sort features help instructors locate questions quickly and arrange them in a preferred order. Six question formats are available, including short-answer, true-false, multiple-choice, essay, matching, and bimodal.

- *Transparencies* A set of four-color acetate transparencies includes figures, graphs and tables from the text.

- *Politics in Action Video or Laserdisc* Eleven "Lecture Launchers" covering broad topics such as social movements, campaigns, and the passage of a bill, are examined through narrated videos, interviews, edited documentaries and political ads. Politics in Action is accompanied by an extensive User's Manual, which provides background, links to topics in our American Government texts, and discussion questions.

- *NEW! Longman American Government Critical Thinking Video* This video includes twenty seven segments dealing with provocative issues in contemporary American politics. Topics include the school prayer amendment, welfare reform, the role of the internet in elections, and many more.

- *Longman American Government Video Archive* Longman offers a variety of videos covering a broad range of topics including famous debates, speeches, political commercials, and congressional hearings. We also offer acclaimed video series such as "Eyes on the Prize" and "The Power Game." Ask your local Addison Wesley Longman representative for more information.

Supplements for Students

- *NEW! Interactive Edition CD-ROM for Government in America* This unique CD-ROM takes students beyond the printed page, offering a complete multimedia learning experience. It contains the full text of the book on CD-ROM, with contextually placed media icons—audio, video, web links, activities, practice tests, primary sources, and more—that link students to additional content directly related to key concepts in the text. FREE when packaged with the text.

- *StudyWizard CD-ROM* This computerized student tutorial program, now available on a cross platform CD-ROM, helps students review and master key concepts in the text. Using chapter and topic summaries, practice test questions, and a comprehensive glossary, StudyWizard supplements the text by allowing students the opportunity to explore new topics and test their understanding of terms and ideas already presented in the reading assignments. Students receive immediate feedback on test questions in the form of answer explanations and page references to the text. In addition, the program allows students to print chapter outlines, difficult vocabulary, missed test questions, or a diagnostic report, which includes suggestions for further study.

- *Study Guide* The Study Guide reinforces the themes and concepts students encounter in the text. This edition includes a new section on study skills that helps students become more adept at reading, note-taking, testing, and avoiding common pitfalls when studying. The Study Guide also includes learning objectives, narrative chapter outlines, research ideas, websites of interest, and practice tests for each chapter.

- *Companion Website (CW+)* This online course companion provides a wealth of resources for both students and instructors using *American Government: Continuity and Change, 2000 Edition.* Students will find interactive simulations and exercises ties to text material, "Cast Your Vote"—where students can express their opinions in contemporary political issues, practice tests, links to related American government sites, a complete guide to conducting research on the Internet and more! Instructors will have access to lecture outlines, website links, and downloadable visuals from the text. Additionally, instructors can take advantage of Syllabus Builder, our comprehensive course management system.

- *NEW! Penguin-Putnam Paperback Titles at a Significant Discount* Longman is now offering 22 Penguin titles discounted more than 60% when packaged with *American Government: Continuity and Change.* It's a unique offer and a wonderful way to enhance students' understanding of concepts in American Government. Ask you local Addison Wesley Longman representative for a full listing of discounted Penguin titles and for information on how to order these books for your classes.

- *NEW! Discount subscription to Newsweek magazine* Available only through Longman, your students can receive 12 issues of *Newsweek* at more than 80% off the regular subscription price! Also included in this offer is an Instructor's Manual prepared by *Newsweek.* The reduced rate subscription cards come shrink-wrapped with *Amer-*

ican Government: Continuity and Change—ask your local Addison Wesley Longman representative how to take advantage of this offer.

- *Guide to the Internet for American Government, Second Edition* This guide introduces students and instructors to ways in which the Internet can be used to explore American government. It includes practical information about the Internet, critical thinking exercises to reinforce students' application of Internet-based skills, and a glossary of Internet terms. In addition, the guide offers dozens of relevant web sites that allow students to discover first-hand how the Web can be used as a resource for research. FREE when packaged with the text.

- *NEW! California State Supplement* This 64-page supplement on state and local issues in California was created for use in the American Government course. It introduces students to California's basic governmental structures and explores the political effects of California's Progressive tradition. FREE when packaged with the text.

- *NEW! Texas State Supplement* A brief primer on state and local issues in Texas for use in the American Government course, this supplement includes discussion of the constitution, the major branches of government, public policy, and other aspects of Texas politics. FREE when packaged with the text.

- *Getting Involved: A Student Guide to Citizenship* This practical handbook guides students through political participation with concrete advice and extensive sample material—letters, telephone scripts, student interviews, and real-life anecdotes. The aim of this exciting new guide is to generate student enthusiasm for political involvement and the help students to get connected, set goals and strategies, experiment with tactics, build networks, anticipate obstacles, and make a difference in their lives and communities. FREE when packaged with the text.

- *10 Things That Every American Government Student Should Read,* by Karen O'Connor, American University. American Government instructors across the country voted for the ten things beyond the text—essays, documents, articles—that they believed every American Government student should read. The top vote-getters in each of 10 categories were put into this unique and useful reader. FREE when packaged with the text.

- *NEW! Guide to Reading Tables, Graphs, and Charts* Developed as a guide for promoting visual literacy, this unique booklet helps students understand how tables, charts, and graphs are used to summarize and simplify political data. FREE when packaged with the text.

- *Writing in Political Science, Second Edition* Writing in political science requires a distinct set of skills, vocabulary, sources, and methods of inquiry. This guide takes students step-by-step through all the aspects of writing for political science courses. With an abundance of samples from actual students, the guide also features a section on how to address writing problems and a new section on how to evaluate and cite internet sources. Available at a significant discount when packaged with the text.

ACKNOWLEDGMENTS

Karen O'Connor thanks the thousand-plus students in her American Government courses at Emory and American Universities who, over the years, have pushed her to learn more about American government and to have fun in the process. She especially thanks her American University colleagues who offered books and suggestions for this most recent revision—Gregg Ivers, Ron Shaiko, and David Lublin. Her former professor and long-time friend and coauthor, Nancy E. McGlen, has offered support for more than two decades. Her former students, too, have contributed in various ways to this project, especially John R. Hermann, Paul Fabrizio, Bernadette Nye, Sue Davis, and Laura van Assendelft.

Over the last two editions of this book, Sarah Brewer, a third year graduate student at American, has taken on a growing role in the development and research done to update chapters and write new boxes and vignettes of interest to students. Her fresh perspective on politics and ideas about things of interest to students have greatly benefited these last two editions of the book. She has tracked down obscure citations, located relevant political science literature, and made this a much better book. These last two editions could not have been completed without her extraordinarily able assistance. Michael Fisher, an undergraduate student at American, was also a tremendous help in completing this edition. Fisher provided a student's perspective about what was interesting and what was not, which led us to revise, delete, or add several items. He also provided extraordinary assistance with finding and winnowing down useful web sites and simulations.

Larry Sabato would like to acknowledge the students, past and present in his University of Virginia Government 101 class, who have offered many valuable suggestions and much thoughtful feedback. He would also like to thank the staff and interns at the UVA Center for Governmental Studies who helped with this and previous editions of the textbook, including, but not limited to: Allison Barrett, Zene Colt, Whitney Duff, Howard Ernst, Brett Ferrell, Ed Fields, Emily Harding, Louisa Jilcott, Bruce Larson, Ade Patton, Dan Payne, Moshin Syed, and Matthew Wikswo. And finally, he extends his thanks to the faculty and staff of the Department of Government and Foreign Affairs at the University of Virginia, especially Nancy Rae, Lawrence Schack, and Shirley Mayes.

Particular thanks from both of us go to Steven G. Koven of the University of Louisville, who revised Chapters 17 (Social Welfare Policy), and 18 (Economic Policy); to Richard Cupitt at the Center for International Trade and Security at the University of Georgia, who coauthored Chapter 19 (Foreign and Military Policy); and to Dennis L. Dresang at the University of Wisconsin–Madison, who coauthored the Chapter 4 (State and Local Government). We also thank Jeffrey Anderson of Brown University, who helped provide comparisons between the American and British systems of government, and David Potter of the University of Northern Kentucky who prepared the Global Politics features.

In the now many years we have been writing and rewriting this book, we have been blessed to have been helped by many people at Macmillan, Allyn and Bacon, and now Longman. Bruce Nichols signed the project and nurtured us through writing our first drafts. Now, we have been lucky to have the new insights and help of our editor, Eric Stano, our development editor Dawn Groundwater, and our marketing manager Megan Galvin-Fak. We would also like to acknowledge the tireless efforts of the Longman sales force. In the end, we hope that all of these talented people see how much their work and support have helped us to write a better book.

Many of our peers reviewed past editions of the book and earned our gratitude in the process:

Danny Adkison
Oklahoma State University

Weston H. Agor
University of Texas at El Paso

Victor Aikhionbare
Salt Lake Community College

James Anderson
Texas A&M University

Judith Baer
Texas A&M University

Ruth Bamberger
Drury College

Christine Barbour
Indiana University

Jon Bond
Texas A&M University

Stephen A. Borrelli
University of Alabama

Ann Bowman
University of South Carolina

Robert C. Bradley
Illinois State University

Gary Brown
Montgomery College

John Francis Burke
University of Houston–Downtown

Greg Caldeira
Ohio State University

David E. Camacho
Northern Arizona University

Alan R. Carter
Schenectady County Community College

Steve Chan
University of Colorado

Richard Christofferson, Sr.
University of Wisconsin–Stevens Point

David Cingranelli
SUNY, Binghamton

Clarke E. Cochran
Texas Tech University

Anne N. Costain
University of Colorado

Cary Covington
University of Iowa

Stephen C. Craig
University of Florida

Lane Crothers
Illinois State University

Abraham L. Davis
Morehouse College

Robert DiClerico
West Virginia University

John Domino
Sam Houston State University

Keith L. Doughtery
St. Mary's College of Maryland

David F. Dupree
Victor Valley College

Craig F. Emmert
Texas Tech University

Walle Engedayehu
Prairie View A&M University

Alan S. Engel
Miami University

Frank B. Feigert
University of North Texas

Evelyn Fink
University of Nebraska

Scott R. Furlong
University of Wisconsin–Green Bay

James D. Gleason
Victoria College

Sheldon Goldman
University of Massachusetts, Amherst

Doris Graber
University of Illinois at Chicago

Jeffrey D. Green
University of Montana

Roger W. Green
University of North Dakota

Charles Hadley
University of New Orleans

William K. Hall
Bradley University

Robert L. Hardgrave, Jr.
The University of Texas at Austin

Chip Hauss
George Mason University/University of Reading

Stacia L. Haynie
Louisiana State University

John R. Hermann
Trinity University

Marjorie Hershey
Indiana University

Cornell Hooton
Emory University

Jon Hurwitz
University of Pittsburgh

Joseph Ignagni
University of Texas–Arlington

Susan M. Johnson
University of Wisconsin–Whitewater

Dennis Judd
University of Missouri–St. Louis

Carol J. Kamper
Rochester Community College

Kenneth Kennedy
College of San Mateo

Donald F. Kettl
University of Wisconsin

John Kincaid
University of North Texas

Karen M. King
Bowling Green State University

Jonathan E. Kranz
John Jay College of Criminal Justice

Nancy Kucinski
University of North Texas

Mark Landis
Hofstra University

Sue Lee
North Lake College

Brad Lockerbie
University of Georgia

Larry Martinez
California State University–Long Beach

Valerie Martinez
University of North Texas

Lynn Mather
Dartmouth College

Steve Mazurana
University of Northern Colorado

Clifton McCleskey
University of Virginia

James L. McDowell
Indiana State University

Mark C. Miller
Clark University

Joseph Nogee
University of Houston

Mary Alice Nye
University of North Texas

John O'Callaghan
Suffolk University

Bruce Oppenheimer
Vanderbilt University

Richard Pacelle
University of Missouri–St. Louis

Marian Lief Palley
University of Delaware

Richard M. Pious
Columbia University

David H. Provost
California State University–Fresno

Lawrence J. Redlinger
The University of Texas at Dallas

Leroy N. Rieselbach
Indiana University

David Robertson
Public Policy Research Centers, University of Missouri–St. Louis

David Robinson
University of Houston–Downtown

David W. Rohde
Michigan State University

Frank Rourke
Johns Hopkins University

Ronald Rubin
City University of New York Borough of Manhattan Community College

Bruce L. Sanders
MacComb Community College

Daniel M. Shea
The University of Akron

Mark Silverstein
Boston University

James R. Simmons
University of Wisconsin–Oshkosh

Andrea Simpson
University of Washington

Philip M. Simpson
Cameron University

Elliott E. Slotnick
The Ohio State University

Frank J. Sorauf
University of Minnesota

Gerald Stanglin
Cedar Valley College

C. S. Tai
University of Arkansas–Pine Bluff

Richard J. Timpone
SUNY–Stony Brook

Shirley Anne Warshaw
Gettysburg College

Rich Whisonant
York Technical College

Martin Wiseman
Mississippi State University

Finally, we'd also like to thank our peers who reviewed and aided in the development of the current edition:

Carl D. Cavalli
North Georgia College and State University

David E. DuPree
Victor Valley College

William K. Hall
Bradley University

Stacie L. Haynie
Louisiana State University

Steven Alan Holmes
Bakersfield College

Willoughby Jarrell
Kennesaw State College

Ted Lewis
Collin County Community College

Laurel A. Mayer
Sinclair Community College

Carl E. Meacham
SUNY–Oneonta

Kenneth F. Mott
Gettysburg College

David R. Penna
Gallaudet University

David H. Provost
California State University–Fresno

Denise Scheberle
University of Wisconsin–Green Bay

Gaye Lynn Scott
Austin Community College

Martin P. Sellers
Campbell University

John N. Short
University of Arkansas–Monticello

Michael W. Sonnleitner
Portland Community College

Brian Walsh
University of Maryland

Matt Wetstein
San Joaquin Delta College

Richard Whaley
Marian College

AMERICAN GOVERNMENT

(Photo courtesy: William S. Helsel/Tony Stone Images)

The Political Landscape

- **The Roots of American Government: Where Did the Ideas Come From?**
- **Characteristics of American Democracy**
- **The Changing Political Culture and Characteristics of the American People**
- **Political Culture and Views of Government**

e the People of the United States, in Order to form a more perfect Union, establish Justice, insure domestic Tranquility, provide for the common defense, promote the general Welfare, and secure the Blessings of Liberty to ourselves and our Posterity, do ordain and establish the Constitution for the United States of America.

So begins the Preamble to the United States Constitution. Written in 1787, this document has guided our nation, its government, its politics, its institutions, and its inhabitants for over 200 years.

Back when the Constitution was written, the phrases "We the People" and "ourselves" meant something very different than they do today. Although the Framers—the men who wrote the Constitution—probably intended to include nearly all white men and women, they still envisioned an electorate that was made up of less than half of those who lived in the thirteen original states. After all, voting was largely limited to property-owning white males. Indians, slaves, and women could not vote. Today, through the expansion of the right to vote, the phrase "the People" encompasses men and women of all races, ethnic origins, and social and economic status—a variety of peoples and interests the Framers could not have imagined, although most of those who are eligible to vote today do not.

In the goals it outlines, the Preamble to the Constitution describes what the people of the United States can expect from their government. But many Americans today are questioning how well the country and its government can deliver on these goals. Few Americans today would classify the Union as "perfect"; many feel excluded from "Justice" and the "Blessings of Liberty"; many more do not feel our domestic situation is particularly tranquil. Furthermore, judging from recent poll results and economic statistics, many Americans feel that their general welfare is not very well promoted by their government. Others simply do not care about government much at all.

Change. If there has been one constant in the life of the United States, it is change. The Framers would be astonished to see the forms and functions the institutions they so carefully outlined in the Constitution have taken on, and the number of additional political institutions that have arisen to support and fuel the functioning of the national government. The Framers would also be amazed at the array of services and programs the government—especially the national government—provides. They would be further surprised to see how the physical boundaries and the composition of the population have changed in more than 200 years. And they might well wonder, "How did we get here?"

It is part of the American creed that each generation should hand down to the next not only a better America, but an improved economic, educational, and social status. In general, Americans have long been optimistic about our nation, its institutions, and its future. Thomas Jefferson saw the United States as the world's "best hope"; Abraham Lincoln echoed these sentiments when he called it the "last, best hope of earth."[1] But during the 1990s, for the first time in decades, some of that optimism had faded. Many Americans were dismayed by the Clinton/Lewinsky affair, campaign finance abuses, and often even government in general. Nevertheless, most Americans report that their lives are better than their parents', although some fear that things will be worse for the next generation.

■ The "American Dream"—a house, a dog, two kids, a picket fence, the chance to realize one's dreams—has been part of the American political landscape for nearly as long as there has been a United States. Today's Americans are increasingly beginning to wonder whether their children's lives will continue to be better than theirs or their parents'. (Photo courtesy: Sue Ann Miller/Tony Stone Images)

Web Exploration

For more information on politics in general, see www.awlonline.com/oconnor.

In this text we present you with the tools you need to understand how our political system has evolved, and to prepare you to understand the changes that are yet to come. If you approach the study of American government and politics with an open mind, it should help you become a better citizen. We hope that you learn to ask questions, to understand how various issues have come to be important, and to see why a particular law was enacted and how it was implemented. With such understanding, we further hope you will learn not to accept everything you see on the television news, hear on the radio, or read in the newspaper at face value. Work to understand your government, and use your vote and other forms of participation to help ensure that your government works for you.

We recognize that the discourse of politics has changed dramatically in just the last few years, and even more recently as the president's indiscretions in the Oval Office were chronicled in minute detail on television, in the print media, and over the Internet. Just as Watergate changed Americans' perspectives on the presidency, the Clinton/Lewinsky affair and its ultimate conclusion are likely to have enormous short- and long-term consequences on how most Americans view politics, politicians, the presidency and future elections. We believe that a thorough understanding of the workings of government will allow you to question and think about the system—the good parts and the bad—and decide for yourself the advantages and disadvantages of possible changes and reforms. Equipped with such an understanding, we hope you will become better informed and more active participants in the political process.

Every long journey begins with a single step. In this chapter we'll examine the following topics:

■ First, we will look at *the roots of American government.* To understand how the U.S. government and our political system work today, it is critical to understand the philosophies that guided the American colonists as they created a system of governance different from those then in existence.

■ Second, we will explore the *characteristics of American democracy.* Several enduring characteristics have defined American democracy since its beginning and continue to influence our nation's government and politics today.

■ Third, we will explore the *changing political culture and characteristics of the American people.* Because government derives its power from the people it governs, an

■ In this image made from video, President Clinton responds to grand jury questions about his relationship with Monica Lewinsky during the third hour of his video-taped testimony at the White House. Ultimately, this led to impeachment in the House and trial and acquittal in the Senate. On February 12, 1999, efforts to remove the president from office failed when the Senate rejected two articles of impeachment by votes of 45 to 55 and 50 to 50, falling far short of the 67 votes needed. (Photo courtesy: APTV/AP/Wide World Photos)

understanding of who the American people are and how they are changing is critical to an understanding of American politics.

■ Fourth, we will discuss *political culture and Americans' views about government* and the role that government plays in their lives.

THE ROOTS OF AMERICAN GOVERNMENT: WHERE DID THE IDEAS COME FROM?

The current American political system did not spring into being overnight. It is the result of philosophy, trial and error, and yes, even luck. To begin our examination of why we have the type of government we have today, we look at the theories of government that influenced the Framers: those men who gathered in Philadelphia and drafted a new Constitution, thereby creating the United States of America.

From Aristotle to the Enlightenment

Aristotle (384–322 B.C.) and the Greeks were the first to articulate the notion of **natural law,** the doctrine that human affairs should be governed by certain ethical principles. Being nothing more nor less than the nature of things, these principles can be understood by reason. In the thirteenth century, the Italian priest and philosopher Thomas Aquinas (1225–74) gave the idea of natural law a new, Christian framework. He argued that natural law and Christianity were compatible because God created the natural law that established individual rights to life and liberty. In contradiction to this view, kings throughout Europe continued to rule as absolute monarchs, claiming this divine right came directly from God. Thus citizens were bound by the government under which they found themselves, regardless of whether they had a say in its workings: If government reflected God's will, who could argue with it?

In the early sixteenth century, a religious movement to reform the doctrine and institutions of Roman Catholicism began to sweep through Europe. In many cases these efforts at reform resulted in the founding of Protestant churches separate from their

natural law:

A doctrine that society should be governed by certain ethical principles that are part of nature and, as such, can be understood by reason.

Web Exploration

For more on Aristotle and natural law, see
www.awlonline.com/oconnor.

■ Headlines from newspapers around the country express the changing tenor of the Clinton/Lewinsky affair. (Courtesy: ©1998 by *The Los Angeles Times*. Reprinted by permission. © Chicago Tribune Company. All rights reserved. Reprinted with permission.)

Catholic source. During this period, known as Reformation, the resultant growth in the Protestant faith promoted the belief that people could talk directly to God without the intervention of a priest and altered the nature of government as people began to believe they could also have a say in their own governance.

During the Enlightenment period, the ideas of philosophers and scientists such as Isaac Newton (1642–1727) worked further to affect peoples' views of government. Newton and others argued that the world could be improved through the use of human reason, science, and religious toleration. He and other theorists directly challenged earlier notions that fate alone controlled an individual's destiny and that kings ruled by divine right. Together the intellectual and religious developments of the Reformation and Enlightenment periods encouraged people to seek alternatives to absolute monarchy and to ponder new methods of governing.

A Growing Idea: Popular Consent

In the late sixteenth century in England, "separatists" split from the Anglican Church. They believed that their ability to speak one-on-one to God gave them the power to participate directly in the governing of their own local assemblies. They established self-governing congregations, and were responsible for the first widespread appearance of self-government in the form of social compacts. When some separatists settled in America during the 1600s, they brought along their beliefs about self-governance. The Mayflower Compact, deemed sufficiently important to be written while that ship was still at sea, reflects this tradition. Although it addressed itself to secular government, the Pilgrims called it a "covenant" and its form was akin to other common religious covenants adopted by Congregationalists, Presbyterians, and Baptists.[2]

Two English theorists of the seventeenth century, Thomas Hobbes (1588–1679) and John Locke (1632–1704), built on conventional notions about the role of government and the relationship of the government to the people in proposing a **social contract theory**

social contract theory:

The belief that people are free and equal by God-given right and that this in turn requires that all people give their consent to be governed; espoused by John Locke and influential in the writing of the Declaration of Independence.

of government (see Roots of Government: The Philosophies of Thomas Hobbes and John Locke). They argued that, even before the creation of God-ordained governments theorized by Aquinas, all individuals were free and equal by natural right. This freedom, in turn, required that all men give their consent to be governed.

Hobbes and Locke.   In his now-classic political treatise, *Leviathan* (1651), in which he argued for King Charles's restoration to the throne (which finally occurred in 1661), Hobbes argued pessimistically that man's natural state was war. Government, Hobbes theorized, particularly a monarchy, was necessary to restrain man's bestial tendencies because life without government was a "state of nature." Without written, enforceable rules, people would live like animals—foraging for food, stealing, and killing when necessary. To escape the horrors of the natural state and to protect their lives, Hobbes argued, men must give up to government certain rights. Without government, Hobbes warned, life would basically be "solitary, poor, nasty, brutish, and short"—a constant struggle to survive against the evil of others. For this reason, governments had to intrude on people's rights and liberties to better control society and provide the necessary safeguards for property.[3]

Hobbes argued strongly for a single ruler, no matter how evil, to guarantee the rights of the weak against the strong. Leviathan, a biblical sea monster, was his characterization of an all-powerful government. Strict adherence to Leviathan's laws, however encompassing or intrusive on liberty, was but a small price to pay for living in a civilized society, or even for life itself.

In contrast, John Locke—like many other political philosophers of the era—took the basic survival of humanity for granted. He argued that government's major responsibility was the preservation of private property, an idea that ultimately found its way into the Constitution of the United States. In two of his works (*Essay Concerning Human Understanding* [1690] and *Second Treatise on Civil Government* [1689]), Locke responded to King James II's abuses of power, which were largely directed at the Anglican Church and Parliament. Locke not only denied the divine right of kings to govern, but argued that men were born equal and with natural rights that no king had the power to void. Under what Locke termed social contract theory, the consent of the people is the only true basis of any sovereign's right to rule. According to Locke, men form governments largely to preserve life, liberty, and property, and to assure justice. If governments act improperly, they break their contract with the people and therefore no longer enjoy the consent of the governed. Because he believed that true justice comes from laws, Locke argued that the branch of government that makes laws—as opposed to the one that enforces or interprets laws—should be the most powerful.

Locke believed that having a chief executive to administer laws was important, but that he should necessarily be limited by law or by the social contract with the governed. Locke's writings influenced many American colonists, especially Thomas Jefferson, whose original draft of the Declaration of Independence noted the rights to "life, liberty, and property" as key reasons to split from England.[4] This document was "pure Locke" because it based the justification for the split with England on the English government's violation of the social contract implicit in its dealings with the American colonies.

Devising a National Government

Although social contract theorists agreed on the need for government, they did not necessarily agree on the form that a government should take. Thomas Hobbes argued for a single leader; John Locke and Jean-Jacques Rousseau, a French philosopher (1712–78), saw the need for less centralized power.

The colonists rejected a system with a strong ruler, like the British **monarchy,** as soon as they had declared their independence. Most European monarchical systems gave hereditary rulers absolute power over all forms of activity. Many of the colonists had fled Great Britain to avoid religious persecution and other harsh manifestations of

Web Exploration

For more on Thomas Hobbes and John Locke, see www.awlonline.com/oconnor.

monarchy:

A form of government in which power is vested in hereditary kings and queens.

■ The title page from Thomas Hobbes's *Leviathan*, 1651. (Photo courtesy: Corbis/Bettmann)

oligarchy:

A form of government in which the right to participate is always conditioned on the possession of wealth, social status, military position, or achievement.

aristocracy:

A system of government in which control is based on rule of the highest.

democracy:

A system of government that gives power to the people, whether directly or through their elected representatives.

power wielded by George II, whom they viewed as a malevolent despot. They naturally were reluctant to put themselves in the same position in their new nation.

While some colonies, such as Massachusetts, originally established theocracies in which religious leaders eventually ruled claiming divine guidance, they later looked to more secular forms of governance. Colonists also did not want to create an **oligarchy,** or "rule by the few or an elite," in which the right to participate is conditioned on the possession of wealth, property, social status, military position, or achievement. Aristotle defined this form of government as a perversion of an **aristocracy,** or "rule of the highest." Again, the colonists were fearful of replicating the landed and titled system of the British aristocracy, and viewed the formation of a representative form of government as far more in keeping with the ideas of social contract theorists. But the **democracy** in which we live, as settled on by the Framers, is difficult to define. Nowhere is the word mentioned in the Declaration of Independence or the U.S. Constitution. The term comes from two Greek words: *demos* (the people) and *kratia* (power or authority). Thus democracy can be

 **IGHLIGHT 1.1**   **Taking Government for Granted**

Although many political polls show that Americans think that government no longer helps them, that just isn't so. Many of the critical functions performed by governments at all levels are forgotten, or simply taken for granted. But as federal government shutdowns and downsizing continue, and pet programs or projects are cut out or reduced, it's a good time to think about the diverse things government does. Is "less government" really better government?

Government sets the standard weights and measures that allow us to trade goods easily. Would you be assured of receiving three pounds of ground round if each farm and state computed "pound" differently? And what about a keg of beer? In colonial times the size of a "keg" varied by brewer and state. Now it is standardized by the government.

From cradle to grave, the government works to provide each of us with safety and security—from child-safety standards on cribs, infant car seats, bassinets, and toys to standards of care in nursing homes. The national government provides air traffic control and regulates the use of the skies as well as the public airwaves for radio and TV. Local governments issue zoning ordinances, which can prevent someone from putting a junk yard next to your home or an X-rated club next to an elementary school. They fund sidewalks, stoplights, crosswalks, and school crossing guards.

Local governments fluoridate water to prevent tooth decay. Governments inspect our food supplies and require safe handling of food from farms to restaurants. The federal government regulates food additives and standards, and periodically bans some considered harmful, like saccharin and red dye number 2. Federal regulators require food labeling so we can intelligently comparison shop to avoid fat and sodium and maximize nutritional value in our foods.

The government makes and enforces rules on compulsory education and provides funding and facilities for all levels of education. Government gets you to and from school on a bus. Colleges and universities, even private ones, receive huge amounts of federal funding through student aid programs, subsidies, research and development funding, and grants in aid. State universities would cost substantially more (as would private institutions) without large infusions of government monies.

One or more levels of government ensures job safety, maximum hours, and minimum wages, regulates benefits, provides income security and medical care in old age, and prevents child labor.

Government provides water, sewer systems, garbage collections, recycling programs, highways, and interstate roads. It provides mass transit to help you get to work and sets standards on car safety and emissions to make commuting safer and cleaner.

Government provides for the national defense by regulating customs and immigration, establishing borders and protecting them with military force.

The federal government issues passports and provides embassies and consulates to aid you if you have trouble in a foreign country. It provides information on necessary inoculations and health hazards while traveling, as well as travel advisories regarding safety hazards such as wars, riots, and dangerous levels of pollutants in air and water.

Without government and its research and development funding, we would not have cellular telephones, satellite communications, the Internet, silicon chips (and thus computers), cable TV, fax machines, Velcro, freeze-dried foods, or four-wheel drive, to name just a few modern inventions we encounter in our daily lives.

---

interpreted as a form of government that gives power to the people. The question, then, is how and to which people is this power given?

The Theory of Democratic Government

As evidenced by the creation in 1619 of the Virginia House of Burgesses as the first representative assembly in North America, and its objections to "taxation without representation," the colonists were quick to create participatory forms of government in which most men were allowed to take part. The New England town meeting, where all citizens gather to discuss and decide issues facing the town, today stands as a surviving example of a **direct democracy,** such as was used in ancient Greece when all free, male citizens came together periodically to pass laws and "elect" leaders by lot (see Politics Now: The Internet and Our Changing Society).

Direct democracies, in which the people rather than their elected representatives make political decisions, soon proved unworkable in the colonies. But as more and more

Web Exploration

To connect with others who are interested in politics, see www.awlonline.com/oconnor.

direct democracy:

A system of government in which members of the polity meet to discuss all policy decisions and then agree to abide by majority rule.

ROOTS OF GOVERNMENT

The Philosophies of Thomas Hobbes and John Locke

In almost any newspaper or TV news report, on any given day, you can find stories that show Americans grappling with questions about the proper role of government in their lives. These questions are not new. Centuries ago, Thomas Hobbes and John Locke both wrote extensively on these issues. Their ideas, however, differed remarkably. For Hobbes, who viewed humans as basically evil, a government that regulated all kinds of conduct was necessary. Locke, who was more optimistic, saw the need only for more limited government.

Hobbes

Thomas Hobbes was born in 1588 in Gloucestershire (Glouster), England, and began his formal education at the age of four. By the age of six he was learning Latin and Greek, and by the age of nineteen he had obtained his bachelor's degree from Oxford University. In 1608 Hobbes accepted a position as a family tutor with the earl of Devonshire, a post he retained for the rest of his life.

Hobbes was greatly influenced by the chaos of the English Civil War during the mid-seventeenth century. Its impact is evident in his most famous work, *Leviathan* (1651), a treatise on governmental theory that states his views on Man and Citizen. *Leviathan* is commonly described as a book about politics, but it also deals with religion and moral philosophy.

Hobbes characterized humans as selfishly individualistic and constantly at war with one another. Thus he believed that people must surrender themselves to rulers in exchange for protection from their neighbors.

Locke

John Locke, born in England in 1632, was admitted to an outstanding public school at the age of fifteen. It was there that he began to question his upbringing in the Puritan faith. At twenty he went on to study at Oxford, where he later became a lecturer in Aristotelian philosophy. Soon, however, he found a new interest in medicine and experimental science.

In 1666 Locke met Anthony Ashley Cooper, the first earl of Shaftesbury, and a politician who believed in individual rights and parliamentary reform. It was through Cooper that Locke discovered his own talent for philosophy. In 1689 Locke published his most famous work, *Second Treatise on Civil Government*, in which he set forth a theory of natural rights. He used natural rights to support his "social contract [theory]— the view that the consent of the people is the only true basis of any sovereign's right to rule." A government exists, he argued, because individuals agree, through a contract, to form a government to protect their rights under natural law. By agreeing to be governed, individuals agree to abide by decisions made by majority vote in the resolution of disputes.

Both men, as you can see, relied on wealthy royal patrons to allow them the time to work on their philosophies of government. While Hobbes and Locke agreed that government was a social contract between the people and their rulers, they differed significantly about the proper scope of government. Which man's views about government (and people) reflect your views?

---

indirect (representative) democracy:

A system of government that gives citizens the opportunity to vote for representatives who will work on their behalf.

republic:

A government rooted in the consent of the governed; a representative or indirect democracy.

settlers came to the New World, many town meetings were replaced by a system called an **indirect democracy** (this is also called *representative democracy*). This system of government, in which representatives of the people are chosen by ballot, was considered undemocratic by ancient Greeks, who believed that all citizens must have a direct say in their governance.[5] Later, in the 1760s, the French political philosopher Jean-Jacques Rousseau would also argue that true democracy is impossible unless all citizens participate in governmental decision making. Nevertheless, indirect democracy was the form of government opted for throughout most of the colonies.

Representative or indirect democracies, which call for the election of representatives to a governmental decision-making body, were formed first in the colonies and then in the new Union. Many citizens were uncomfortable with the term "democracy" and used the term "republic" to avoid any confusion between the system adopted and direct democracy. Historically, the term **republic** implied a system of government in which the interests of the people were represented by more educated or wealthier citizens who were responsible to those who elected them. Today, representative democracies are more

POLITICS NOW

The Internet and Our Changing Society

It is hard to believe that the Internet as we know it was not around when the first edition of this text was written in 1993. What began in 1969 as ARPANET, a communications network developed by the U.S. Department of Defense for its employees to maintain contact with defense contractors and universities in the case of a nuclear attack, has revolutionized how students write papers, people seek information, and even how some individuals date. The Internet is now a vast resource for those interested in politics and may have enormous consequences in the near future as it becomes as critical a part of our daily lives as televisions and telephones.

For the first decade of its existence, the Internet was largely used for e-mail and access to distant data bases, and to facilitate communication among governmental agencies, corporations, and universities.[a] During the early 1980s, all of the interrelated research networks converted to a new protocol that allowed for easy back-and-forth transfer of information; ARPANET became the backbone of the new system, facilitating by 1983 the birth of the Internet we know today.

Only a decade ago, HTML, a hypertext Internet protocol that allowed graphic information to be transmitted over the Internet, was devised. This allowed for the creation of graphic pages—called web sites—which then became "part of a huge, virtual hypertext network called the World Wide Web."[b] This new, improved Internet was then christened the web.

By 1998, over a third of adult Americans reported that they had used the Internet themselves, while 19 percent reported that they watched someone else use it.[c] Over three-fourths of those in Generation Y (see p. 21), however, had used the web. The U.S. Department of Education, however, estimated that more than 95 percent of all schools will be wired by the time you read this book.[d] Thus, given estimates that computer ownership and web access are increasing at

remarkable rates, the web's impact on democracy must be considered.

Near-universal usage of home telephones, for example, changed the way that public opinion was measured, and television eventually changed the way that candidates and their supporters reached potential voters. What kinds of changes can we foresee given the rise of the web?

- More reliance on candidate and party web sites to raise money and supporters
- A more informed electorate given easier access to information about candidates and issues
- A more effective grassroots mechanism for citizens to contact officials, policy makers, large corporations, and so on
- The eventual use of the Internet to conduct polling research

Today, however, a personal computer is still considered a luxury by many families in the way that telephones and televisions once were. Thus, if the Internet is to be used as a mechanism to advance or expand democracy and political participation, its heralders must be aware that this change may exacerbate economic divisions in the United States or overvalue the views or participation of those who can afford to be on-line.

[a]"Internet History," http://ww.tdi.uregina.ca/~ursc/internet/history.html
[b]"Internet History."
[c]Paul Eisenberg, "Half of Americans Aren't Even Newbies," The Freedom Forum Online, http://www.freedomforum.org/technology/1998/1/6/netpoll.asp
[d]Adam Clayton Powell, III, "Study Shows More African Americans Online than Previously Reported," http://www.freedomforum.org/technology/1998/4/1/17webuse.asp

commonly called "republics," and the words "democracy" and "republic" often are used interchangeably.

Why a Capitalist System?

In addition to fashioning a democratic form of government, the colonists also were confronted with the dilemma of what kind of role the government should play in the economy. Concerns with liberty, both personal and economic, were always at the forefront of their actions and decisions in creating a new government. They were well aware of the need for a well-functioning economy and saw that government had a key role in maintaining one. What a malfunction in the economy is, however, and what steps the government should take to remedy it, were questions that dogged the Framers and continue to puzzle politicians and theorists today.

free market economy:

The economic system in which the "invisible hand" of the market regulates prices, wages, product mix, and so on.

capitalism:

The economic system that favors private control of business and minimal governmental regulation of private industry.

mercantile system:

A system that binds trade and its administration to the national government.

The American economy is characterized by (1) the private ownership of property and (2) a **free market economy**—two key tenets of **capitalism,** a form of economic system that favors private control of business and minimal governmental regulation of private industry. In capitalist systems the laws of supply and demand, interacting freely in the marketplace, set prices of goods and drive production. Under capitalism, sales occur for the profit of the individual. Capitalists believe that both national and individual production is greatest when individuals are free to do with their property or goods as they wish. The government, however, plays an indispensable role in creating and enforcing the rules of the game.

In 1776, in the same year as the signing of the Declaration of Independence, Adam Smith (1723–90) argued that free trade would result in full production and economic health. These ideas were greeted with great enthusiasm in the colonies as independence was proclaimed. Colonists no longer wanted to participate in the mercantile system of Great Britain and other Western European nations. **Mercantile systems** bound trade and its administration to national governments. Smith and his supporters saw free trade as "the invisible hand" that produced the wealth of nations. This wealth, in turn, became the inspiration and justification for capitalism.

From the mid- to late eighteenth century, and through the mid-1930s in the United States and in much of the Western world, the idea of *laissez-faire* economics (from the French, "to leave alone") enjoyed considerable popularity. While most states regulated and intervened heavily in their economies well into the nineteenth century, the U.S. national government routinely followed a "hands-off" economic policy. By the late 1800s, however, the national government felt increasing pressure to regulate some aspects of the economy (often in part because of the difficulties states faced in regulating large, multistate industries such as the railroads, and from industry's desire to override the patchwork regulatory scheme produced by the states). Thereafter, the Great Depression of the 1930s forced the national government to take a much larger role in the economy. Afterward, any pretense that the United States was a purely capitalist sys-

■ While the traditional town meeting—where citizens meet, have their say, and vote on the town budget and other policy decisions—survives in certain communities as a modern-day embodiment of direct democracy, newer variations are broadcast on television and include more debating than voting. (Photo courtesy: Bob Daemmrich/The Image Works)

tem was abandoned. The worldwide extent of this trend, however, varied by country and over time. In post–World War II Britain, for example, the extent of government economic regulation of industry and social welfare was much greater than that attempted by American policy makers in the same period.

For most of U.S. history, capitalism and the American dream have been alive and well: Hard work has been rewarded with steady jobs and increased earning power and wages, and Americans have expected to hand down improved economic, social, and educational status to their children. In many ways World War II ushered in the era of the American dream: Men returned from the war and went to college, their tuition paid for by the G.I. Bill. Prior to the war, a college education was mainly the preserve of the rich; the G.I. Bill made it available to men from all walks of life. Many men got the education they needed to succeed and do much better than their parents before them. In addition, low-interest-rate mortgages were made available through the Veterans' Administration, and the American dream of owning a home became a reality for millions. Capitalism worked and made their efforts to preserve it worthwhile.

Other Economic Systems

Capitalism is just one type of economic system. Others include socialism, communism, and totalitarianism.

Socialism.   Socialism is a philosophy that advocates collective ownership and control of the means of economic production. Socialists call for governmental—rather than private—ownership of all land, property, and industry and, in turn, an equitable distribution of the income from those holdings. In addition, socialism seeks to replace the profit motive and competition with cooperation and social responsibility.

Some Socialists actually tolerate capitalism as long as the government maintains some kind of control over the economy. Others reject capitalism outright and insist on the abolition of all private enterprise.

Some Socialists, especially in Western Europe, have argued that socialism can evolve through democratic processes. Thus, in nations like Great Britain, certain critical industries or services such as health care or the coal industry have been *nationalized,* or taken over by the state, to provide for more efficient supervision and to avoid the major concentrations of wealth that occur when individuals privately own key industries.

socialism:
An economic system that advocates for collective ownership and control of the means of production.

Communism.   The german philosopher Karl Marx argued that government was simply a manifestation of underlying economic forces and could be understood according to types of economic production. In *Das Kapital* (1867), Marx argued that capitalism would always be replaced by Socialist states in which the working class would own the means of production and distribution and be able to redistribute the wealth to meet its needs.

Marx believed that it was inevitable for each society to pass through the stages of history: feudalism, capitalism, socialism, and then communism. When society reached communism, Marx theorized, all class differences would be abolished and government would become unnecessary. A system of common ownership of the means of sustenance and production would lead to greater social justice. In practice, most notably under Vladimir Ilyich Ulyanov, under the pseudonym Lenin, and the Soviet dictator Josef Stalin (also a pseudonym; his real name was Josif Vissarionivich Dzhugashvili), many of the tenets of Marxism were changed or modified.

Marx saw the change coming first in highly industrialized countries such as Britain and Germany, where a fully mature capitalism would pave the way for a Socialist revolution. But Lenin and the Bolshevik Party wanted to have such a revolution in underdeveloped Russia. So, instead of relying on the historical inevitability of the Communist future (as Marx envisioned), they advocated forcing that change. Lenin argued that by establishing an elite vanguard party of permanent revolutionaries and a dictatorship of

communism:
An economic system in which workers own the means of production and control the distribution of resources.

the proletariat (working class), they could achieve socialism and communism without waiting for the historical forces to work. In the 1940s China followed the Leninist path led by Mao Ze Dong (formerly transliterated as Mao Tse Tung).

In practice, the Communist states rejected free markets as a capitalist and exploitative way of organizing production and turned instead to planning and state regulation. In capitalist economies, the market sets prices, wages, product mix, and so on. Under a planned economy, government makes conscious choices to determine prices, wages, product mix, and so on.

totalitarianism:

An economic system in which the government has total control over the economy.

Totalitarianism.   A totalitarian system is basically a modern form of extreme authoritarian rule. In contrast to governments based on democratic beliefs, totalitarian governments have total authority over their people and their economic system. The tools of totalitarianism are secret police, terror, propaganda, and an almost total prohibition on civil rights and liberties. These systems also tend to be ruled in the name of an ideology or a personality cult organized around a supreme leader. The reign of Saddam Hussein in Iraq comes close to the total control of forms of production, the airwaves, education, the arts, and even sports implied by totalitarianism. Some Communist systems also approached totalitarianism.

CHARACTERISTICS OF AMERICAN DEMOCRACY

The United States, as created by the Framers, is an indirect democracy with several underlying concepts and distinguishing characteristics. Many of these characteristics are often in conflict, a factor that has led to some of the political discontent present in the population and simply turned off others. The political system, for example, is based on an underlying notion of the importance of balance among the legislative, executive, and judicial branches, between the state and federal governments, between the wants of the majority and the minority, between the rights of the individual and the best interests of the nation as a whole. The Framers built the system on the idea that there would be statesmen who would act for the good of the system. Without such statesmen, the system necessitates constant vigilance to keep a balance as the pendulum swings back and forth between various desires, demands, and responsibilities. To some, government may be a necessary evil; but a good government is less evil if it can keep things in balance as it operates in various spheres. The ideas of balance permeate many of the concepts and characteristics of American democracy presented below.

Popular Consent

popular consent:

The idea that governments must draw their powers from the consent of the governed.

Popular consent, the idea that governments must draw their powers from the consent of the governed, is one distinguishing characteristic of American democracy. Derived from Locke's social contract theory, the notion of popular consent was central to the Declaration of Independence. A citizen's willingness to vote represents his or her consent to be governed and is thus an essential premise of democracy. Growing numbers of nonvoters can threaten the operation and legitimacy of a truly democratic system.

Popular Sovereignty

popular sovereignty:

The right of the majority to govern themselves.

The notion of **popular sovereignty,** the right of the majority to govern themselves, has its basis in natural law: Ultimately, political authority rests with the people, who can create, abolish, or alter their governments. The idea that all governments derive their power from the people is found in the Declaration of Independence and the U.S. Constitution, but the term itself did not come into wide use until pre–Civil War debates over slavery. At that time, supporters of popular sovereignty argued that the citizens of new states seeking admission to the Union should be able to decide whether or not their states would allow slavery within their borders. (See Highlight 1.2: Who Makes Decisions in America? for some theories about who makes decisions about governing.) Today, public opinion polls are often used as instantaneous measures of the popular will.

Majority Rule

Majority rule, another basic democratic principle, means that the majority (normally) of citizens in any political unit should elect officials and determine policies (50 percent of the total votes cast plus 1). This principle holds for both voters and their elected representatives. Yet the American system also stresses the need to preserve minority rights, as evidenced by the myriad protections of individual rights and liberties found in the Bill of Rights.

The concept of the preservation of minority rights has changed dramatically in the United States. It wasn't until after the Civil War that slaves were freed and African Americans began to enjoy minimal citizenship rights. By the 1960s, however, rage at America's failure to guarantee minority rights in all sections of the nation fueled the civil rights movement, which ultimately led to congressional passage of the Civil Rights Act of 1964 and the Voting Rights Act of 1965, both designed to further minority rights. Today, attacks on affirmative action are often fueled by cries that majority rights are being trampled.

Concepts of majority rule today are threatened by a tradition of political apathy that has emerged slowly over time within the American electorate. Since 1960, the number of eligible voters who have cast ballots has continued to decline; in 1998 less than 50 percent of those eligible to vote did so. Although one in five of those who did not vote said they didn't do so because they couldn't take time off from work or were "too busy,"[6] others lay blame on the political process noting that low voter turnout is a message to politicians.[7] "Campaigns are the conversation of democracy," wrote one commentator discussing the 1994 campaign, "and the one that just concluded was angry, deeply personal, powerfully ideological, and exceedingly negative—sometimes all three at once."[8] That off-year congressional election drew only 39 percent of those eligible to the polls. Many of those same terms could be used to describe the 1998 elections, with frustration being substituted for anger. Whatever reasons are offered for nonvoting, however, it is an important phenomenon to keep in mind when we talk about majority rule. Most discussions of elections as the voice of the majority are really better cast as discussions of the wishes of the majority who voted.

majority rule:
The central premise of direct democracy in which only policies that collectively garner the support of a majority of voters will be made into law.

Individualism

Tremendous value is placed on the individual in American democracy and culture. All individuals are deemed rational and fair, and endowed, as Thomas Jefferson proclaimed in the Declaration of Independence, "with certain unalienable rights." Individualism, which holds that the primary function of government is to enable the individual to achieve his or her highest level of development, makes the interests of the individual more important than those of the state and is at the heart of our capitalistic system. It is also a concept whose meaning has changed over time. The rugged individualism of the western frontier, for example, was altered as more citizens moved westward, cities developed, and demands for government services increased.

Equality

Another key characteristic of our democracy is the American emphasis on political equality, the definition of which has varied considerably over time (as discussed in chapter 6). The importance of political equality is another reflection of American stress on the importance of the individual. Although some individuals clearly wield more political clout than others, the adage "One man, one vote" implies a sense of political equality for all.

HIGHLIGHT 1.2

Who Makes Decisions in America?

How conflicts are resolved is often determined by how the government is operated and by whom. All of these theories provide interesting ways to think about how policy decisions are made, whether we are looking at local, state, or national policies.

Elite Theory

Elite theory posits that all important decisions in society are made by the few, called the elite, so that government is increasingly alienated from the people and rarely responsive to their wishes. In *The Power Elite* (1956), American sociologist C. Wright Mills argued that important policies were set by a loose coalition of three groups with some overlap among each.[a] According to his elite theory, these three major influencers of policy—corporate leaders, military leaders, and a small group of key governmental leaders—are the true "power elite" in America. Other elite theorists have argued that the news media should be included as a fourth source of political power in the United States.

Another proponent of elite theory, political scientist Thomas R. Dye, contends that all societies are divided into elites and masses. The elite are the few who have power, and the masses are the many who don't.[b] This distribution of functions and powers in society is inevitable. Elites, however, are not immune from public opinion, nor do they by definition oppress the masses. Dye argues that in a complex society, such as ours, only a "tiny minority" actually make policy.

Bureaucratic Theory

Max Weber (1864–1920), the founder of modern sociology, argued that all institutions, governmental and nongovernmental, have fallen under the control of a large and ever-growing bureaucracy that carry out policy on a day-to-day basis using standardized procedures. Because all institutions have grown more complex, Weber concluded that the expertise and competence of bureaucrats allows them to wrest power from others, especially elected officials.

Interest Group Theory

David Truman argues that interest groups—not elites, sets of elites, or bureaucrats—control the governmental process.[c] He believes there are so many potential pressure points in the three branches of the federal government—as well as at the state level—that groups can step in on any number of competing sides. The government then becomes the equilibrium point in the system as it mediates between competing interests.

Pluralist Theory

According to some political scientists, the structure of our democratic government allows only for a pluralistic model of democracy.[d] Borrowing from Truman's work, Robert Dahl argues that resources are scattered so widely in our diverse democracy that no single elite group can ever have a monopoly over any substantial area of policy.

Adding to this debate, Theodore J. Lowi has described how political decision making takes place today in an era of what he terms "interest group liberalism." According to Lowi, participants in every political controversy get something; thus, each has some impact on how political decisions are made. Lowi also states that governments rarely say no to any well-organized interests. Thus, all interests ultimately receive some benefits or rewards. Lowi bemoans the fact that the public interest—that is, what is good for the public at large—often tends to lose in this system.[e]

[a]C. Wright Mills, *The Power Elite* (New York: Oxford University Press, 1956).
[b]Thomas R. Dye, *Who's Running America?* (New York: Prentice Hall, 1976).
[c]David B. Truman, *The Governmental Process* (New York: Knopf, 1951).
[d]Robert A. Dahl, *Preface to Democratic Theory* (Chicago: University of Chicago Press, 1956).
[e]Theodore J. Lowi, *The End of Liberalism* (New York: Norton, 1979).

Personal Liberty

personal liberty:

A key characteristic of U.S. democracy. Initially meaning freedom from governmental interference, today it includes demands for freedom to engage in a variety of practices free from governmental discrimination.

Personal liberty is perhaps the single most important characteristic of American democracy. The Constitution itself was written to assure "life" and "liberty." Over the years, however, our concepts of liberty have changed and evolved from "freedom *from*" to "freedom *to*." The Framers intended Americans to be free from governmental infringements on freedom of religion and speech, from unreasonable search and seizure, and so on (see chapter 5). The addition of the Fourteenth Amendment to the Constitution and its emphasis on equal protection of the laws and subsequent passage of laws guaranteeing civil rights, however, expanded Americans' concept of liberty to include demands for "freedom to" be free from discrimination. Debates over how much the government should do to guarantee these rights or liberties illustrate the conflicts that continue to occur in our democratic system.

THE CHANGING POLITICAL CULTURE AND CHARACTERISTICS OF THE AMERICAN PEOPLE

The concept **political culture** has been defined as the "attitudes toward the political system and its various parts, and attitudes toward the role of the self in the system." It is a set of orientations toward a special set of social objects and processes.[9] Where you live, how you were raised, and even your age or age cohort can affect how you view the government or a governmental program.

> **political culture:**
> Attitudes toward the political system and its various parts, and attitudes toward the role of the self in the system.

Americans are very divided on some issues; politicians, media commentators, and even the citizenry itself also tend to focus on how different Americans are. But before we explore some of those differences, which have profound implications on policy and individual preferences, we must note the similarities of Americans. Most Americans share a common language—English—and have similar aspirations for themselves and their families. Most agree that they would rather live in the United States than anywhere else; and that democracy, with all of its warts, is still the best system for most. Most Americans highly value education and want to send their children to the best schools possible, viewing an education as the key to success.

Since the 1994 elections, however, many politicians—especially many of those on the right—have tried to underscore how quickly and dramatically America is changing on a host of measures. But while it is true that America and its population are undergoing rapid change, this is not necessarily a new phenomenon. It is simply new to most of us. In the pages that follow, we take a look at some of the characteristics of the American population and its political culture. Because the people of the United States are the basis of political power and authority, these characteristics and attitudes have important implications for how America is governed and how and what policies are made.

Changing Size and Population

One year after the Constitution was ratified, less than 4 million Americans lived in the thirteen states. They were united by a single language and opposition to the king. Most shared a similar Protestant-Christian heritage, and those who voted were white male property owners. The Constitution mandated that each of the sixty-five members of the original House of Representatives should represent 30,000 citizens. However, due to rapid growth, that number often was much higher. Anti-Federalists, who opposed a strong national government during the founding period, at least took solace in the fact that members of the House of Representatives, who generally represented far fewer people than senators, would be more in touch with "the people."

As revealed in Figure 1.1, as the nation grew westward, the absolute population of the country also grew. Although the physical size of the United States has remained stable since the addition of Alaska and Hawaii in 1959, there are now more than 270 million Americans. A single member of the House of Representatives now represents as many as 870,000 people.

As a result of this growth, most citizens today feel far removed from the national government and their elected representatives. Members of Congress, too, feel this change. Often they represent diverse constituencies with a variety of needs, concerns, and expectations, and they can meet only a relative few of these people in face-to-face electioneering.

Changing Demographics of the U.S. Population

As the physical size and population of the United States have changed, so have many of the assumptions on which it was founded. Some of the dynamism of the American

Web Exploration
To get a minute by minute update on U.S. population see
www.awlonline.com/oconnor.

Figure 1.1   U.S. Population, 1790–2050

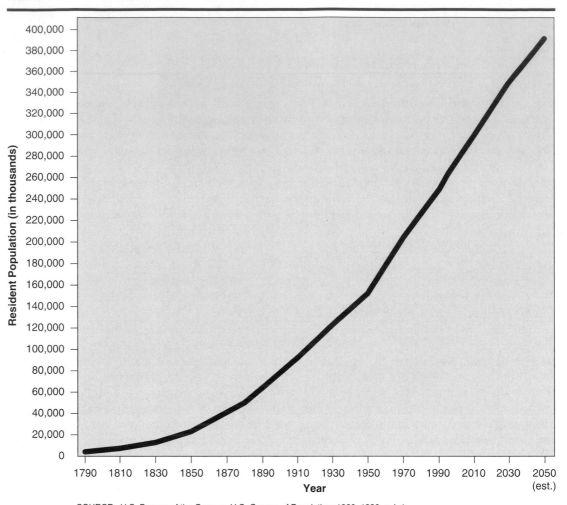

SOURCE: U.S. Bureau of the Census, *U.S. Census of Population: 1920–1990, vol. 1;*
Current Population Reports, 25–1097; www.census.gov/prod/1/pop/p25

system actually stems from the racial and ethnic changes that have taken place throughout our history, a notion that often gets lost in debates about immigration policy. Moreover, for the first time, the U.S. population is getting much older. This "graying" of America also will assuredly lead to changes in our expectations of government and in our public policy demands. The current debate over what to do with the budget surplus is illustrative of that phenomenon. Below, we look at some demographic facts (that is, information on characteristics of America's population), and then discuss some implications of these changes for how our nation is governed and what policy issues might arise.

Changes in Racial and Ethnic Distributions.   From the start, the population of America has been constantly changed by the arrival of various kinds of immigrants to its shores—Western Europeans fleeing religious persecution in the 1600s to early 1700s, Irish Catholics escaping the potato famine in the 1850s, Chinese laborers arriving to work on the railroads, Northern and Eastern Europeans from the 1880s to 1910s, and most recently, Southeast Asians, Cubans, Mexicans, and others.

Immigration to the United States peaked in the first decade of the 1900s, when nearly 9 million people, many of them from Eastern Europe, entered the country. The

United States did not see another major wave of immigration until the late 1980s, when nearly 2 million immigrants were admitted in one year, as illustrated in Figure 1.2. Unlike the arrivals in other periods of high immigration, however, these "new" Americans were often "nonwhite"; many were Southeast Asians or Latin Americans. In fact, in 1997, a poll commissioned by PBS revealed that 45 percent of Americans polled thought "too many" immigrants were entering the United States from Latin American countries.[10]

While immigration has been a continual source of changing demographics in America, race has also played a major role in the development and course of politics in the United States. As revealed in Figure 1.3, the racial balance in America is changing dramatically. In 1998, for example, whites made up 72.6 percent of the U.S. population, African Americans 12.1 percent, and Hispanics 11 percent. By 2050, it is estimated that Hispanics will become the largest minority group. The Asian population, too, is growing as a proportion of the total U.S. population.

Changes in Age Cohort Composition.   Just as the racial and ethnic composition of the American population is changing, so too is the average age of the population. "For decades, the U.S. was described as a nation of the young because the number of persons under the age of twenty greatly outnumber(ed) those sixty-five and older,"[11] but this is no longer the case, as Figure 1.4 shows. Due to changes in patterns of fertility, life expectancy, and immigration, the nation's age profile has changed drastically.[12] When the United States was founded, the average life expectancy was thirty-five years; by 1991, it was seventy-nine years for women and seventy-two years for men. As people live longer, the types of services and policies they demand from government differ dramatically. In Florida, for example, which leads the nation in the percentage of its population over age sixty-five,[13] citizens are far less concerned with the quality of public schools (especially if they are being taxed for those schools), than the citizens in states with far lower proportions of the elderly.

As the age profile of the U.S. population has changed, political scientists and others have found it useful to assign labels to various generations. Such labels can be useful in understanding the various pressures put on our nation and its government, because when people were born and the kinds of events they experienced can have important consequences on how they view other political, economic, and social events. For example, those 76.8 million people born after World War II (1946–1964) are often referred to as "Baby Boomers." These individuals grew up in a very different America than did

■ Immigrants have not often found American streets to be paved with gold, although letters back to the old country may have implied otherwise. (Photos courtesy: top, New York Public Library; bottom, Culver Pictures)

Figure 1.2   Legal Immigration 1901–1997

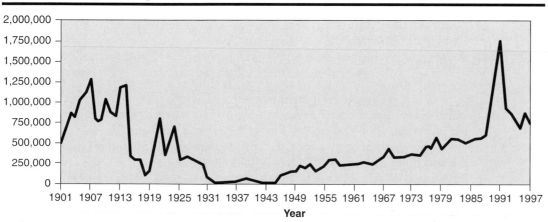

SOURCE: "Legal Immigration, Fiscal Year 1997," Office of Policy and Planning, U.S. Department of Justice *Annual Report* (January 1999),p1.

Figure 1.3   Race and Ethnicity in America: 1998 and Beyond

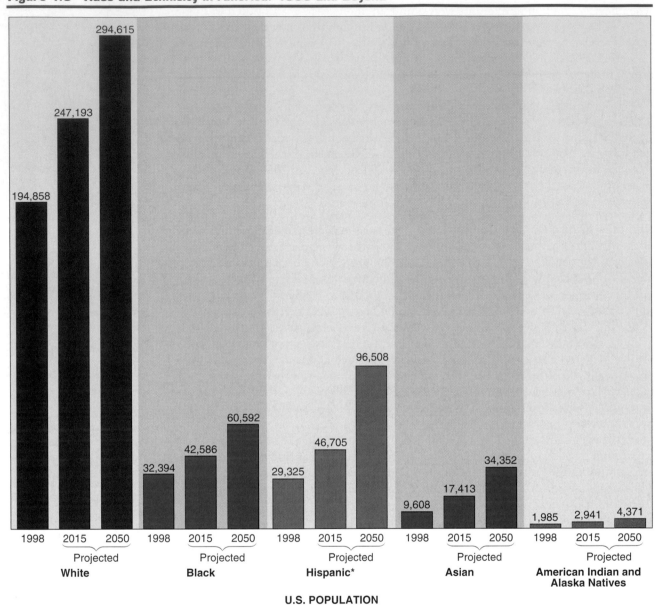

Projected U.S. Population, 2015
Projected U.S. Population, 2050
*Persons of Hispanic origin can be of any race.

SOURCE: U.S. Census Bureau, www.census.gov/population/projections

their parents and now are reaching retirement age, which will put a major strain on the already overburdened Social Security system.[14] In contrast, their children are often called Generation X-ers, a name of a early 1980s punk band and, later, a novel.[15] Soon, however, *Time* and *Newsweek* used the term to christen the 50 million who were born in the late 1960s and early 1970s to the Baby Boomers.

This group experienced the economic downturn of the 1980s. Jobs were scare when they graduated from college, and many initially had a hard time paying off their college loans. They overwhelmingly believe that political leaders ignore them, and they distrust the political process. X-ers work longer, are better educated, and are more

Figure 1.4   Changing Age Composition of the United States

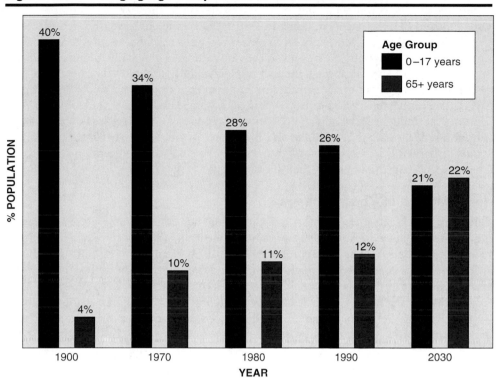

SOURCE: Susan A. McManus, *Young v. Old: Generational Combat in the 21st Century* (Boulder,CO: Westview Press, 1995),4.

grassroots oriented politically than their parents.[16] Moreover, it is a very libertarian generation. Says one commentator, "The difference between [Generation X-ers] and the liberal [Baby Boomer] generation that preceded [it] is that [X-ers] see capitalism as something that's not necessarily evil. [X-ers] see (they) can use capitalism for social change. It's one way to make government and big business stand up and take notice".[17]

In contrast, the fastest-growing group under age sixty-five is called "Generation Y," those aged ten to twenty-four. This group, unlike their Generation X predecessors, "has grown up in good times and [they] have nothing but optimism about their future".[18] This group is very Internet savvy and much more globally focused than any generation before it.

Changes in Family and Family Size.   Family size and household arrangements can be affected by several factors, including age at first marriage, divorce rates, economic conditions, longevity rates, and improvements in health care. In the past, large families were the norm (in part because so many children died early) and gender roles were clearly defined. Women did housework and men worked in the fields. Large families were imperative; children were the source of cheap farm labor.

Industrialization and knowledge of birth control methods, no matter how primitive, began to put a dent in the size of American families. No longer needing children to work for the survival of the household unit on the farm, couples began to limit the sizes of their families.

By 1949, 49 percent of those polled thought that four or more children was the "ideal" family size; in 1997, only 8 percent favored large families, and 54 percent responded that no children to two children were the "best".[19] As chronicled in the popular press as well as by the U.S. Department of Commerce, the American family no longer looks like *Leave*

Web Exploration

For more detail on population projections see www.awlonline.com/oconnor.

Web Exploration

To learn more about Generation Y, see www.awlonline.com/oconnor.

Web Exploration

For more information on families and household composition, see www.awlonline.com/oconnor.

It to Beaver or even the *Brady Bunch*. While the actual number of households in the United States grew from 93.3 million in 1970 to 101 million in 1997, what those households looked like has changed dramatically. In 1940, nine out of ten households were family households; by 1998, only seven out of ten were family households, as revealed in Figure 1.5.[20] Fewer than one-half of the family households had children under the age of eighteen. And the average number of people per household was 2.64.

In 1997, 76 percent of the families in America contained a married couple. Since 1970, the number of female-headed households has increased dramatically from 5.5 million to 12.8 million—a whopping 133 percent increase. These changes in composition of households, number of children, and prevalence of single-parent families affect the kinds of demands people place on government as well as their perceptions of the role that government should play in their lives.

Implications of These Changes

The varied races, ethnic origins, sizes of the various age cohorts, family types, and even gender roles of Americans have important implications for government and politics. Today, some believe that immigrants (legal and illegal) are flooding onto our shores with disastrous consequences. Such anti-immigration sentiments are hardly new—in fact, American history is replete with examples of "Americans" set against any new immigration. In the 1840s, for example, the Know Nothing Party arose in part to oppose immigration from Roman Catholic nations, charging that the pope was going to organize the slaughter of all Protestants in the United States. In the 1920s the Ku Klux Klan, which had over 5 million members, called for barring immigration to stem the tide of Roman Catholics and Jews into the nation.

Figure 1.5   Household Composition: 1997

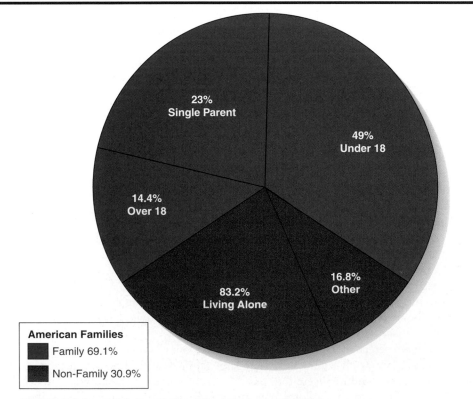

SOURCE: U.S. Bureau of the Census, Current Population Surveys, April 1998.

Today, even though almost all Americans have ancestors who emigrated to the United States, most Americans oppose unrestricted access to the United States and react negatively to reports that the foreign-born population is increasing. In the presidential campaign of 1996, immigration (legal and illegal) was a big issue. Many Americans believed (erroneously, for the most part) that floods of immigrants were putting Americans out of work and putting a strain on our already overburdened state and federal resources, especially school systems and welfare programs. During the presidential primary, Republican presidential hopeful Pat Buchanan tapped into the 1996 American public's frustration by reaching out to those who feared their jobs were being lost because of immigrants and international trade policies such as the General Agreement on Tariffs and Trade (GATT) and the North American Free Trade Agreement (NAFTA). He advocated banning *all* immigration to the United States for five years. He also suggested building a fence along the U.S./Mexico border to prevent illegal aliens from entering the United States. Another Republican challenger, Lamar Alexander, suggested building a new branch of the military to patrol our borders and enforce immigration laws.

Another indication of anti-immigrant sentiment was the most publicized initiative on the 1994 ballot, California's Proposition 187. This proposition was designed to stem the influx of illegal aliens to California, where 25.5 percent of all immigrants in 1997 settled. Proposition 187's purpose was to bar *illegal* aliens from using already strained taxpayer-subsidized services.[21] By 59 to 41 percent, Californians voted to ban the use of state funds for education, health, and social services for illegal aliens. Although federal courts voided the law and Congress appears to have retreated from its anti-immigration agenda, significant damage has been done to immigrant/governmental relations. More recently, in June 1998, California voters passed a referendum abolishing bilingual education programs in public elementary and secondary schools, a measure many view as anti-immigrant.

Hostility to immigrants manifests itself in a variety of ways in addition to those noted above. Some bemoan the fact that the nation is becoming "less white," or criticize those who refuse to adopt "American" ways as they cling to the customs, language, and

■ The size of the average American family is shrinking—but not the McCaugney's of Carlisle, Iowa. The birth of their septuplets was celebrated by one town shopkeeper. (Photo courtesy: John Gaps III/ AP/Wide World Photos)

traditions of their old country. Immigrants, too, often face blame from the citizenry or elected officials for lost jobs or depressed wages (because they are often willing to take low-wage jobs).

Changing racial, ethnic, and even age and family demographics also seem to intensify—at least for some—an "us" versus "them" attitude. For example, government affirmative action programs, which were created in the 1960s to redress decades of overt racial discrimination, are now under attack because some people believe that they give minorities and women unfair advantages in the job market, as well as easier access to higher education opportunities. Dramatic changes in educational and employment opportunities, revealed in Table 1.1, also underscore these tensions.

Sociologist James Davison Hunter defines the culture conflict that is the result of changing demographics as "political and social hostility rooted in very different systems of moral understanding."[22] These different worldviews—worker versus CEO; educated versus uneducated, young versus old, white versus black, native-born versus immigrant—create deep cleavages in society, as exemplified by the "polarizing impulses or tendencies" in American society.[23] Just as the two parties at times seem to be pushed to take extreme positions on many issues, so are many of those who speak out on those issues.

Demographics also affect politics and government because an individual's perspective often influences how he or she *hears* the debate on various issues. Thus, many African Americans viewed O. J. Simpson's acquittal as vindication for decades of unjust treatment experienced by blacks in the criminal justice system; the wealthy view proposals for a flat tax with much more enthusiasm than do many of the poor; and those who saw their jobs jeopardized by the North American Free Trade Agreement (NAFTA) were more likely to decry it than were their employers.

These cleavages and the emphasis many politicians put on our demographic differences play out in many ways in American politics. Baby Boomers and the elderly object to any changes in Social Security or Medicare, while those in Generation X vote for politicians who support change, if they vote at all. Many policies are targeted at one group or the other, further exacerbating differences—real or imagined—and lawmakers often find themselves the target of many different factions. All of this makes it difficult to devise coherent policies to "promote the general welfare," as promised in the Constitution.

The Ideology of the American Public

Political ideology is a term used by political scientists to refer to the more or less consistent set of values that historically have been reflected in the political system, economic order, social goals, and moral values of any given society. "It is the means by which the basic values held by a party, class, group or individual are articulated."[24] Most Americans espouse liberalism or conservatism, although a growing number call them-

political ideology:

An individual's coherent set of values and beliefs about the purpose and scope of government.

Table 1.1   Men and Women in a Changing Society

	Men	Women
Estimated life expectancy in 2010	74	81
% high school graduates	87	88
% with BA degrees	26	21
% of BAs in 1997	45	55
% of MAs in 1997	45	55
% of PhDs in 1997	61	39
Median earnings	$32,144	$23,710
% in legal profession	70	30
% in medical profession	74	26
# of single parents	1.9 million	9.9 million

SOURCE: "Census Bureau Facts for Features," U. S. Census Bureau, http://www.census.gov/Press-Release/ff98-03.html

Figure 1.6 Self-Identification as Liberal, Moderate, or Conservative, 1974–1999

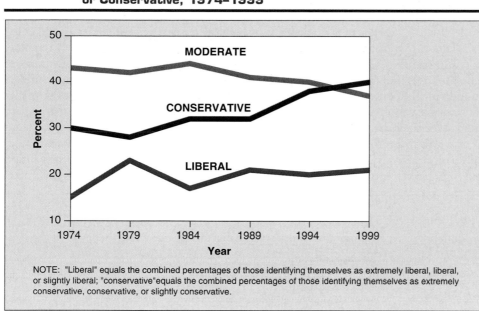

NOTE: "Liberal" equals the combined percentages of those identifying themselves as extremely liberal, liberal, or slightly liberal; "conservative" equals the combined percentages of those identifying themselves as extremely conservative, conservative, or slightly conservative.

SOURCE: Roper Center at the University of Connecticut, *Public Opinion Online*.

■ In the U.S. Senate, Barbara Boxer (D-Calif.) and Jesse Helms (R-S.C.) stand at polar opposites on the liberal (Boxer) and conservative (Helms) spectrum. (Photos courtesy: top, Bill Nation/Sygma; bottom, Ira Wyman/Sygma)

selves libertarians, who do not place themselves on traditional liberal/conservative continuums used by political scientists (see Figure 1.6).

You probably already have a good idea of what the terms liberal and conservative mean, but you may not be aware that the meaning of these terms has changed dramatically over time. During the nineteenth century, for example, conservatives supported governmental power and favored a role for religion in public life; in contrast, liberals supported freedom from undue governmental control. (See Table 1.2 for additional information about these terms.)

Conservativism. According to William Safire's *New Political Dictionary*, a **conservative** "is a defender of the status quo who, when change becomes necessary in tested institutions or practices, prefers that it come slowly, and in moderation."[25] Conservatives are thought to believe that a government is best that governs least, and that big government can only infringe on individual, personal, and economic rights. They want less government, especially in terms of regulation of the economy. Conservatives favor local and state action over federal action, and emphasize fiscal responsibility, most notably in the form of balanced budgets. Conservatives are likely to support smaller, less activist governments and believe that domestic problems like homelessness, poverty, and discrimination are better dealt with by the private sector than by the government. Less rigid conservatives see the need for governmental action in some fields

conservative:

One thought to believe that a government is best that governs least and that big government can only infringe on individual, personal, and economic rights.

Web Exploration

For more information on conservatives, see www.awlonline.com/oconnor.

Table 1.2 Liberal? Conservative? Libertarian? Chart Your Views on These Issues

	ISSUES						
	Abortion Rights	**Environmental Regulation**	**Organized School Prayer**	**Gun Control Laws**	**Anti-Discrimination Laws**	**Government Support of:**	
						Poor	**School Vouchers**
Conservative	Oppose	Oppose	Favor	Oppose	Oppose	Oppose	Favor
Liberal	Favor	Favor	Oppose	Favor	Favor	Favor	Oppose
Libertarian	Favor	Oppose	Oppose	Oppose	Oppose	Oppose	Oppose

and for steady change in many areas. They seek to achieve such change within the framework of existing institutions, occasionally changing the institutions when they show a need for it.

Liberalism. Liberalism is a political view held by those who "seek to change the political, economic, or social status quo to foster the development and well-being of the individual."[26] Safire defines a **liberal** as "currently one who believes in more government action to meet individual needs, originally one who resisted government encroachments on individual liberties."[27] Liberals now are considered to favor a big government that plays an active role in the economy. They also stress the need for the government to provide for the poor and homeless, to provide a wide array of other social services, and to take an activist role in protecting the rights of women, the elderly, minorities, and the environment. It is a political philosophy that has roots in the American Revolution and eighteenth-century liberalism. Today, many of its supporters refer to it as the "modern revival of classical liberalism."[28]

Libertarianism. Libertarianism is a political philosophy based largely on individual freedom and the curtailment of state power. **Libertarians** have long believed in the evils of big government and stress that government should not involve itself in the plight of the people or attempt to remedy any social ills. Basically, libertarians, although a very diverse lot, favor a free market economy and an end to governmental intrusion in the area of personal liberties. Generation X-ers are more libertarian in political philosophy than any other age cohort and credited with the success of libertarian Governor Jesse Ventura of Minnesota.

Liberals criticize libertarian calls for elimination of all government sponsored welfare and public works programs; conservatives bemoan libertarian calls for reductions in the defense budget and elimination of federal agencies such as the Central Intelligence Agency and the Federal Bureau of Investigation.

Problems with Political Labels

When considering what it means when someone identifies himself or herself as a conservative, liberal, libertarian, or some other political philosophy, it is important to remember that the labels such as "conservative" and "liberal" can be quite misleading and do not necessarily allow us to predict political opinions. In a perfect world, liberals would be liberal and conservatives would be conservative. Studies reveal, however, that many people who call themselves conservative actually take fairly liberal positions on many policy issues. In fact, anywhere from 20 percent to 60 percent will take a traditionally "conservative" position on one issue and a traditionally "liberal" position on another.[29] People who take conservative stances against "big government," for example, often support increases in spending for the elderly, education, or health care. It is also not unusual to encounter a person who could be considered liberal on social issues such as abortion and civil rights but conservative on economic or "pocketbook" issues. Moreover, libertarians, for example, often are against any governmental restrictions on abortion (a liberal view) but against any kind of welfare spending (a conservative view). Today, like libertarians, most Americans' positions on specific issues cut across liberal/conservative ideological boundaries to such a degree that new, more varied ideological categories may soon be needed to capture division within American political thought. (See Table 1.2 to see where your political views place you.)

POLITICAL CULTURE AND VIEWS OF GOVERNMENT

Americans' views about and expectations of government affect the political system at all levels. It has now become part of our political culture to expect negative campaigns,

---

liberal:

One considered to favor extensive governmental involvement in the economy and the provision of social services and to take an activist role in protecting the rights of women, the elderly, minorities, and the environment.

libertarian:

One who favors a free market economy and no governmental interference in personal liberties.

Web Exploration

For more information on liberals, see www.awlonline.com/oconnor.

Web Exploration

For more information on libertarians, see www.awlonline.com/oconnor.

TRY IT!

To find out your ideological stance, go to www.awlonline.com/oconnor.

dishonest politicians, and political pundits who make their living bashing politicians and the political process. How Americans view politics, the economy, and their ability to achieve the American dream is also influenced by their political ideology as well as by their social, economic, educational, and personal circumstances.

Since the early 1990s, the major sources of most individuals' on-the-air news—the three major networks (ABC, CBS, and NBC) along with CNN and C-SPAN—have been supplemented dramatically as the number of news and quasi-news outlets have multiplied like rabbits. First there were weekly programs including *Dateline* and *Primetime Live* on the regular networks. Then came the rapid expansion of cable programming beginning with CNN and C-SPAN, then the new FOX network, MSNBC, and CNBC—all competing for similar audiences. These networks' news programming was soon supplemented by the phenomenal development of the Internet as an instantaneous source of news as well as rumor about politics. One on-line newsletter, the *Drudge Report,* was actually the first to break the story about the president and Monica Lewinsky.

As more and more news programs developed, the pressure on each network or news program to be "the first" with the news—often whether it actually is verifiable or not—multiplied exponentially. So has their focus on political scandals. This phenomenon is well illustrated by the debate over whether *Newsweek* erred in delaying breaking the initial story of Bill Clinton's affair with Monica Lewinsky. For seven months the nation got a daily diet of speculation and conjecture about "Bill and Monica" until the president finally admitted to an "improper relationship."

The competition for news stories, as well as the instantaneous nature of these communications, often highlights the negative, the sensational, the sound bite, and usually the extremes. It's hard to remain upbeat about America or politics amidst the gloom and doom reported on the nightly news. It's hard to remain positive about the fate of Americans and their families if you listen to talk radio or watch talk shows like *Jerry Springer* or *Ricki Lake.* Revelations, and a litany of public scandals from Watergate (see chapter 8) to Whitewater to Paula Jones and Monica Lewinsky, have fed public cynicism about government. It is far easier for the press to focus on the Clinton/Lewinsky matter than to devote time and space to a story of a teenage mother who, aided by government programs, went to college, got a job, and became an involved parent and citizen. Those kinds of success stories are generally showcased only in State of the Union addresses or presidential nominating conventions.

This frustration and discontent with government and its institutions is a relatively new phenomenon in the United States. In the nineteenth and early twentieth centuries, immigrants who came to America lived in small, ethnic urban enclaves, but they made learning English and adopting American ways their first priority. At school, their children were taught pride in the United States and its symbols. Compulsory civics classes taught them about the Framers and how to be good citizens. The public schools, in essence, were engaged in state building, and there was general agreement about America and what it stood for.[30]

■ The year 1998 marked the beginning of a new era in how politics is reported. Matt Drudge, for example, started his on-line *Drudge Report,* which was the first "news outlet" to report on the Clinton/Lewinsky affair. (Photo courtesy: Thomas Dallal/Sipa Press)

High Expectations

In roughly the first 150 years of our nation's history, the federal government had few responsibilities, and its citizens had few expectations of it beyond national defense, printing money, collecting tariffs and taxes, and so on. The state governments were generally far more powerful than the federal government in matters affecting the everyday lives of Americans (see chapter 3).

As the nation and its economy grew in size and complexity, the federal government took on more responsibilities (such as regulating some businesses, providing poverty relief, and inspecting food). Then, in the 1930s, in response to the Great Depression, President Franklin D. Roosevelt's New Deal government programs proliferated in almost every area of American life (job creation, income security, aid to the poor, and

■ In spite of low unemployment rates, some workers still feel that government actions place their jobs at risk. Here, Austin, Texas, workers protest the North American Free Trade Agreement (NAFTA) as a threat to their livelihoods. (Photo courtesy: Bob Daemmrich/The Image Works)

so on). Since then, until recently, Americans have looked to the government for solutions to all kinds of problems.

Politicians, too, have often contributed to rising public expectations by promising far more than they or government could deliver. Although President Clinton's vow to end "welfare as we know it" was realized by the end of his first term, his ambitious promises to overhaul the health care system went nowhere. Similarly, several key provisions of the Republicans' highly ambitious Contract with America failed to see the legislative light of day. Term limits, for example, a battle cry of Republicans running for the 104th Congress in 1994, were not really so attractive to them once they took over control of Congress. These rising expectations about government's ability to reform itself, as well as to cure all social and economic ills, have led to cynicism about government and apathy, as evidenced in low voter turnout. It may be that Americans have come to expect too much from the national government and must simply readjust their expectations. Nevertheless, as revealed in Table 1.3, confidence in all institutions is up, although few have much confidence in Congress or the press.

A Missing Appreciation of the Good

During the Revolutionary period, average citizens were passionate about politics because stakes—the very survival of the new nation—were so high. Today the stakes aren't readily apparent to many, and the government is no longer perceived as central to the achievement of "the good life." If you don't have faith in America, its institutions, or symbols (and Table 1.3 shows that many of us don't), it becomes even easier to blame the government for all kinds of woes—personal as well as societal—or to fail to credit governments for the things governments do well. Many Americans, for example, enjoy a remarkably high standard of living and much of it is due to governmental programs, practices, and protections (see Table 1.4 for quality of life measures).

Even in the short time between when you get up in the morning and when you leave for classes or work, the government—or its rulings or regulations—pervades your life. The national or state governments, for example, set the standards for whether you wake up on Eastern, Central, Mountain, or Western Standard Time. The national government regulates the airwaves and licenses the radio or television broadcasts you might listen to or glance at as you eat and get dressed. States, too, regulate and tax telecommunications. Whether or not the water you use as you brush your teeth contains fluo-

Table 1.3   Faith in Institutions

	PERCENT OF AMERICANS DECLARING THEY HAD A "GREAT DEAL" OF CONFIDENCE IN THE INSTITUTION				
	1966	1975	1986	1996	1999
Congress	42%	13%	16%	8%	12%
Executive branch	41	13	21	10	17
The press	29	26	18	11	15
Business & industry	55	19	24	23	22
Colleges/universities	61	36	28	23	37
Medicine	73	51	46	45	39

SOURCE: *Newsweek* (January 8, 1996): 32; and *The Public Perspective* 8 (February/March 1994): 4. Data for 1999, Harris Poll, January 7–12, 1999.

■ Although we all complain about the government, we may lose sight of its invisible positive influence on almost every aspect of our lives. The fish you eat, for example, is inspected by federal agents for bacterial contamination. (Photo courtesy: Food and Drug Administration)

ride is a state or local governmental issue. The federal Food and Drug Administration inspects your breakfast meat and sets standards for the advertising on your cereal box, orange juice carton, and other food packaging. And states also set standards for food labeling. Are they really "lite," "high in fiber," or "fresh squeezed"? Usually, one or more levels of government is authorized to decide these matters (see Highlight 1.1: Taking Government for Granted).

Although all governments have problems, it is important to stress the good they can do. In the aftermath of the Great Depression in the United States, for example, the government created the Social Security program, which dramatically decreased poverty

Table 1.4 How Americans Are Really Doing

	1945	1970	1999
Population	132 million	203 million	272 million
Life expectancy	65.9	70.8	76.1[c]
Per capita income (1987 constant dollars)	$6,367	$9,875	19,241[d]
Adults who are high school grads	25%[a]	55%	82%[e]
Adults who are college grads	5%[a]	11%	24%[e]
Households with phones	46%	87%	94%[b]
Households with televisions	0%	95%	98%[e]
Households with cable TV	0%	4%	65.3%[c]
Households with computers	n/a	n/a	23.3%[e]
Women in labor force	29%	38%	67%[e]
Own their own home	46%	63%	65%[e]
Annual airline passengers	7 million	170 million	551 million[‡e]
Poverty rate	39.7%[†]	12.6%	13.3%[c]
Divorce rate (per 1,000 people)	3.5	3.5	9.9[a]
Children born out of wedlock	3.9%	16.7%	32%[d]

[a]1940 figure.   [†]1949 figure.   [b]1996 figure.   [‡]Estimate.   [c]1996 figure.   [d]1997 figure.   [e]1998 figure.

SOURCES: U.S. Census Bureau, Dept. of Economic Analysis, National Center for Health Statistics, Dept. of Education, Statistical Abstract, Bureau of Labor Statistics, the Air Transport Association.

among the elderly. Our contract laws and judicial system provide an efficient framework for business, assuring people that they have a recourse in the courts should someone fail to deliver as promised. Government-guaranteed student loan programs make it possible for many students to attend college. And even something as seemingly mundane as our uniform bankruptcy laws help protect both a business enterprise and its creditors when the enterprise collapses.

Mistrust of Politicians

It's not difficult to see why Americans might be distrustful of politicians. In August 1998 after President Clinton announced to the American public that he had misled them concerning his relationship with Monica Lewinsky, 45 percent said they were disgusted, 33 percent they were angry, but only 18 percent were surprised, according to a poll conducted by the *Washington Post*. Only 19 percent responded that the president had "high personal, moral and ethical standards," down from 45 percent two years earlier.[31]

The president isn't the only politician to incur the public's distrust. One 1998 poll conducted by the PEW Charitable Trust found that 40 percent of those polled thought that most politicians were "crooks."[32] The low levels of public confidence in Congress, the executive branch and the media revealed in Table 1.3 underscore this view. Character counts and the electorate has concluded—rightly or wrongly—that on this measure many elected officials can be found wanting.

Voter Apathy

"Campaigns are the conversation of democracy," an observer once said.[33] But a Gallup poll conducted after the 1988 presidential contest between George Bush and Michael Dukakis found that 30 percent of those who voted would have preferred to check off a "no confidence in either" box had they been given the choice.

Americans, unlike voters in most other societies, get an opportunity to vote on a host of candidates and issues, but some say those choices may just be too numbing. Respon-

Web Exploration

For more information on the American electorate, see www.awlonline.com/oconnor.

■ Source: *Los Angeles Times*, (August 21, 1998). Michael Ramires, Copley News Service.

sible voters may simply opt not to go to the polls, fearing that they lack sufficient information of the vast array of candidates and issues facing them.

A Census Bureau report examining the reasons that over 5 million eligible voters stayed home from the polls on election day in 1996 showed that "[t]ime constraints [were] the single biggest reason Americans" gave for not voting.[34] The head of the Committee for the Study of the American Electorate thinks that time is an excuse.[35] Instead, he faults the lack of real choices facing voters. Why vote, if your vote won't make much difference?

Other commentators have noted that nonvoting may not even be a sign of contentment. If things are good, or you perceive that there is no need for change, why vote?

Whatever the reason, declining voter participation is cause for concern. If information is truly a problem, it may be that the Internet and the access to information may have major consequences on the course of elections in the future and produce a more informed and, hence, motivated electorate.

There can be no doubt, however, that today, many citizens are disengaged from the political process. One 1999 poll found that 59 percent of those queried thought that "public officials don't care much what people like me think," and that only 28 percent believed that "having elections makes the government pay attention to what the people think."[36]

Redefining Our Expectations

Just as it is important to recognize that governments serve many important purposes, it is also important to recognize that government and **politics**—the process by which policy decisions are made—are not static. Politics, moreover, involves conflicts over different and sometimes opposing ideologies, and these ideologies are very much influenced by one's racial, economic, or historical experiences. These divisions are real and affect the political process at all levels. It is clear to most Americans today that politics and government no longer can be counted on to cure all of America's ills. Government, however, will always play a major role. True political leaders will need to help Americans come to terms with America as it is today—not as it was in the past—real or imaginary. Perhaps a discussion on how "community" is necessary for everybody to get along (and necessary for democracy) is in order. Some democratic theorists suggest that the citizen-activist must be ultimately responsible for the resolution of these divisions.

The current frustration and dissatisfaction about politics and government may be just another phase, as the changing American body politic seeks to redefine its ideas about government. This process is one that is likely to define politics well into the future, but the individualistic nature of the American system will have long-lasting consequences on how it can be accomplished. Americans want less government; but as they get older, they don't want less Social Security. They want lower taxes and better roads, but they don't want to pay for toll roads. They want better education for their children but lower expenditures on schools. Some clearly want less for others but not themselves, which puts politicians in the position of nearly always disappointing voters. This inability to please voters and find a middle ground undoubtedly led to the unprecedented retirements in the House and Senate in 1994 and 1996.

Politicians, as well as their constituents, are looking for ways to redefine the role of government, much in the same way that the Framers did when they met in Philadelphia to forge a solution between Americans' quest for liberty and freedom tempered by order and governmental authority. While citizens charge that it is still government as usual, a change is taking place in Washington, D.C. The federal government, like most American organizations, is downsizing. Sacrosanct programs like Social Security and welfare are being reexamined, and power is slowly being returned to the states. Thus the times may be different, but the questions about government and its role in our lives remain the same.

Although the Civil War and other national crises, such as the Great Depression and even the Watergate scandal (see chapter 8), created major turmoil, they demonstrated

politics:

The process by which policy decisions are made.

$\mathcal{G}$LOBAL POLITICS

Politics Around the World

One scholar of American politics recently published a book entitled *America the Unusual*.* That title speaks volumes about the American political experience when we compare it to those of other countries. Political institutions and practices in the United States really are different from politics elsewhere.

To give you a sense of how different, and in many cases how similar, politics in this country is to politics in other countries, each chapter will include a Global Politics box that compares some aspect of American politics to other countries. For the most part, comparisons will be to the G-7 countries, those seven whose economic and political leaders meet annually to consult about pressing international issues of common concern. Those seven—Canada, France, Germany, Italy, Japan, the United Kingdom and the United States—represent a variety of experiences within a

common framework: they are all industrial democracies. They have among the highest GNPs in the world, and enjoy a comparatively high standard of living, although there is also variation between them on specific indicators. Note, for example, the variations in country size. The United States is far larger than any of its counterparts except Canada. It has more than twice the population of Japan, the next most populous country in the group. More women are in the work force in this country, even as a proportion of total adult female population. The United States also has a low unemployment rate, especially compared to the European countries. Thus, they provide a pool of good cases for comparison of politics. Throughout this textbook, we will compare the United States to the other six.

*John W. Kingdon, *America the Unusual*. New York: Worth Publishers, 1999.

Vital Statistics Profiles of G-7 Countries

Country	Area (1000 km³)	Population (million, 1994)	GDP per Capita ($,1995)	Life Expectancy at Birth	Unemployment Rate (%, 1995)	Women in the Labor Force (% of Total Women 1994)
Canada	9,971	29.25	24,400	78.9	9.5	67.8
France	552	57.75	20,300	78.2	12.3	59.0
Germany	357	81.41	17,500	75.8	6.5	61.8
Italy	301	57.19	19,000	77.9	12.0	43.3
Japan	378	124.96	21,400	79.4	3.2	62.1
UK	244	58.09	19,500	76.2	8.8	65.3
USA	**9,364**	**260.65**	**27,600**	**75.9**	**5.6**	**70.5**

Sources: *Handbook of International Economic Statistics, 1996: OECD Country Trends.* URL http://wn.bilkent.edu.tr/prv/ftp/w . . . ov/cia/publications/hies96/d/d.htm. *Japan, 1997: An International Comparison.* Japan Institute for Social and Economic Affairs, 1997.

that our system can survive and even change in the face of enormous political, societal, and even institutional pressures. Often, these crises have produced considerable reforms. The Civil War led to the dismantling of the slavery system and to the passage of the Thirteenth, Fourteenth, and Fifteenth amendments (see chapter 6), which led to the seeds of recognition of African Americans as American citizens. The Great Depression led to the New Deal and the creation of a government more actively involved in economic and social regulation. In the 1970s, the Watergate scandal and resignation of President Richard M. Nixon resulted in stricter ethics laws that have led to the resignation or removal of many unethical elected officials. Even the aftermath of the Congress's investigation of President Clinton is likely in the long run to bring about a national discussion of what America needs her leaders to be.

Elections themselves, which often seem chaotic, help generation after generation remake the political landscape as new representatives seek to shake up the established order. Thus, while elections can seem like chaos, from this chaos comes order and often the explosive productivity of a democratic society.

*C*ONTINUITY and Change

The Face of America

When the original settlers came to what is now the United States, they did so for a variety of reasons. Still, they recognized the critical role that government could play for them in the New World. So even though the colonists considered themselves British subjects, they knew the importance of fashioning some form of governance, as illustrated by their signatures of agreement on the Mayflower Compact. Those who signed that historic document were largely British, male, and Caucasian. They expected the government to be best that governed least, but they also recognized the importance of order and protection of property and were willing to give up some rights in return for government preservation of those ideals.

Over time, young men in a variety of large and not so large wars fought for what they believed was the American ideal. At the same time, women often left their homes to work in hospitals or factories to help the war effort, generally forgoing their personal goals. Immigrants and native-born citizens alike all shared the American dream.

Today, the American dream is more difficult to see. A new wave of immigrants in the 1980s has changed the composition of many U.S. cities and states, often straining scare resources such as access to quality public education, which has always been at the forefront of the American political socialization process. Several states, especially California, have attempted to restrict the rights and privileges of aliens in recently unprecedented ways. It is a system of majority rule, where the rights of those newest to our borders often lose out.

As illustrated by Figure 1.3, however, the ethnic "look" of America is changing, and in some places such as California and Florida it is changing especially quickly. These changes prompt several questions.

1. What challenges do you believe national and state governments will face as the racial and ethnic composition of their citizenry changes dramatically?
2. What changes do you foresee as the nation's largest minority changes from African American to Latino, a group with a different language and culture?

Cast Your Vote.   What other challenges do you think national and state governments will face in the twenty-first century? To cast your vote, go to www.awlonline.com/oconnor.

SUMMARY

In this chapter we have made the following points:

1. THE ROOTS OF AMERICAN GOVERNMENT. WHERE DID THE IDEAS COME FROM?

The American political system was based on several notions that have their roots in classical Greek ideas, including natural law, the doctrine that human affairs should be governed by certain ethical principles that can be understood by reason. The ideas of social contract theorists John Locke and Thomas Hobbes, who held the belief that people are free and equal by God-given right, have continuing implications for our ideas of the proper role of government in our indirect democracy.

2. CHARACTERISTICS OF AMERICAN DEMOCRACY

Key characteristics of this democracy established by the Framers are popular consent, popular sovereignty, majority rule and the preservation of minority rights, equality, individualism, and personal liberty, as is the Framers' option for a capitalistic system.

3. THE CHANGING POLITICAL CULTURE AND CHARACTERISTICS OF THE AMERICAN PEOPLE

Several characteristics of the American electorate can help us understand how the system continues to evolve and change. Chief among these are changes in size and population, demographics, racial and ethnic makeup, family and family size, age patterns, and ideological beliefs.

4. POLITICAL CULTURE AND VIEWS OF GOVERNMENT

Americans have high and often unrealistic expectations of government. At the same time, they often fail to appreciate how much their government actually does for them. Some of this failure may be due to Americans' general mistrust of politicians, which may explain some of the apathy evidenced in the electorate.

KEY TERMS

aristocracy, p. 8
capitalism, p. 12
communism, p. 13
conservative, p. 25
democracy, p. 8
direct democracy, p. 9
free market economy, p. 12
indirect (representative) democracy, p. 10

liberal, p. 26
libertarian, p. 26
majority rule, p. 15
mercantile system, p. 12
monarchy, p. 7
natural law, p. 5
oligarchy, p. 8
personal liberty, p. 16
political culture, p. 17

political ideology, p. 24
politics, p. 31
popular consent, p. 14
popular sovereignty, p. 14
republic, p. 10
social contract theory, p. 6
socialism, p. 13
totalitarianism, p. 14

SELECTED READINGS

Almond, Gabriel A., and Sidney Verba. *Civic Culture: Political Attitudes and Democracy in Five Nations.* Princeton, NJ: Princeton University Press, 1963.

Craig, Stephen C., and Stephen Earl Bennett, eds. *After the Boom: The Politics of Generation X.* Lanham, MD: Rowman & Littlefield, 1997.

Dahl, Robert A. *Polyarchy: Participation and Opposition.* New Haven, CT: Yale University Press, 1971.

Elshstain, Jean Bethke. *Democracy on Trial.* New York: Basic Books, 1995.

Glendon, Mary Ann. *Rights Talk: The Impoverishment of Political Discourse.* New York: Free Press, 1991.

Grossman, Lawrence K. *The Electronic Republic: Reshaping Democracy in the Information Age.* New York: Viking, 1995.

Hobbes, Thomas. *Leviathan.* ed. Richard Tuck. New York: Cambridge University Press, 1996.

Hochschild, Jennifer, L. *Facing Up to the American Dream: Race, Class, and the Soul of the Nation.* Princeton NJ: Princeton University Press, 1995.

Hunter, James Davison, *Culture Wars: The Struggle to Define America.* New York: Basic Books, 1991.

Jamieson, Kathleen Hall. *Dirty Politics: Deception, Distraction, and Democracy.* New York: Oxford University Press, 1992.

Locke, John. *Two Treatises of Government,* ed. Peter Lasleti. New York: Cambridge University Press, 1988.

Lowi, Theodore J. *The End of Liberalism.* New York: Norton, 1979.

Samuelson, Robert J. *The Good Life and Its Discontents: The American Dream in the Age of Entitlement 1945–1995.* New York: Times Books, 1995.

Skocpol, Theda. *Protecting Soldiers and Mothers: The Political Origins of Social Policy in the United States.* Cambridge, MA: Harvard University Press, 1992.

Tolchin, Susan J. *The Angry American: How Voter Rage Is Changing the Nation.* Boulder, CO: Westview Press, 1996.

Truman, David B. *The Governmental Process.* New York: Knopf, 1951.

Verba, Sidney, Kay Schlozman, and Henry Brady. *Voice and Equality: Civic Volunteerism in American Politics.* Cambridge, MA: Harvard University Press, 1995.

NOTES

1. Thomas Byrne Edsall, "The Era of Bad Feelings," *Civilization* (March/April 1996): 37.

2. The English and Scots often signed covenants with their churches in a pledge to defend and further their religion. In the Bible, covenants were solemn promises made to humanity by God. In the colonial context, then, covenants were formal agreements sworn to a new government to abide by its terms.

3. The term "men" is used here because only males were considered fit to vote.

4. Jack C. Plano and Milton Greenberg, *The American Political Dictionary,* 6th ed. (New York: Holt, Rinehart and Winston, 1982).

5. Frank Michelman, "The Republican Civic Tradition," *Yale Law Journal* 97 (1988):1503.

6. Lynne Casper and Loretta Bass, "Hectic Lifestyles Make for Record-Low Election Turnout, Census Bureau Reports," *U.S. Census Bureau News* (August 17, 1998).

7. "Apathetic Voters? No, Disgusted," *Ledger* (July 12, 1998): A14.

8. Quoted in "Apathetic Voters? No, Disgusted,"

9. Gabriel A. Almond and Sidney Verba, *The Civic Culture: Political Attitudes and Democracy in Five Nations* (Princeton, NJ: Princeton University Press, 1963), 4.

10. "The USA's New Immigrants," *USA Today* (October 13, 1997): 11A.

11. Susan A. MacManus, *Young v. Old: Generational Combat in the 21st Century* (Boulder, CO: Westview Press, 1995), 3.

12. MacManus, *Young v. Old,* 4.

13. "Sixty-Five Plus in the United States," http://www.census.gov/socdemo/www/agebrief.html

14. See William Strauss and Neil Howe, *Generations: The History, of America's Future, 1984–2069* (New York: William Morrow, 1991), and Fernando Torres-Gil, *The New Aging: Politics and Generational Change in America* (New York: Auburn House, 1992).

15. William R. Buck and Tracey Rembert, "Not Just Doing It: Generation X Proves That Actions Speak Louder than Words: Age Group Born in Late 1960s and Early 1970s," *Earth Action Network* (September 19, 1997): 28.

16. Buck and Rembert, "Not Just Doing It."

17. Buck and Rembert, "Not Just Doing It."

18. Teresa Gubbins, "Teens Push Aside the Boomers, Emerge as New Kings of Cool," *Times-Picayune* (April 11, 1999): B3.

19. Kavita Varma, "Family Values," *USA Today* (March 11, 1997): 6D.

20. Lynne M. Casper and Ken Bryson, "Household and Family Characteristics, March 1998 (update) *Current Population Reports,* np.

21. "Californians Vote Against Illegal Aliens," *Agence France Presse* (November 9, 1994).

22. James Davison Hunter. *Culture Wars: The Struggle to Define America* (New York: Basic Books, 1991), 42.

23. Hunter, *Culture Wars,* 42.

24. Plano and Greenberg, *The American Political Dictionary,* 10.

25. William Safire, *Safire's New Political Dictionary* (New York: Random House. 1993), 144–45.

26. Jack C. Plano and Milton Greenberg. *The American Political Dictionary,* 9th ed. (Fort Worth, TX: Harcourt Brace. 1993). 16.

27. Safire, *Safire's New Political Dictionary.*

28. Plano and Greenberg, *The American Political Dictionary,* 16.

29. Philip E. Converse, "The Nature of Belief Systems in Mass Publics," in David E. Apter, ed., *Ideology and Discontent* (New York: Free Press, 1964), 206–21.

30. Ben J. Wattenberg, *Values Matter Most* (New York: Free Press, 1995); and Hunter, *Culture Wars,* chapter 8.

31. David Broder and Richard Morin, "Americans See 2 Distinct Bill Clintons," *Washington Post* (August 23, 1998): A10.

32. Howard Wilkinson and Patrick Crowly, "Campaign '98: Races Offer Definite Choices." *The Cincinnati Enquirer,* September 7, 1998, B1.

33. "Apathetic Voters? No, Disgusted," *Ledger*

34. Scott Shepard, "Non-voters Too Busy or Apathetic?" *Palm Beach Post* (August, 1998): 6A.

35. Shepard, "Non-voters."

36. 1999 Poll Questions on the Federal Government, National Journal's *Cloak Room Poll Track.* Questions from the Center of Policy Attitudes, conducted January 26–31, 1999.

(Photo courtesy: Michael Bryant/Woodfin Camp & Associates)

The Constitution

2

*A*t age eighteen, all American citizens today are eligible to vote in state and national elections. This has not always been the case. It took an amendment to the U.S. Constitution—one of only seventeen that have been added since the Bill of Rights in 1791—to guarantee the franchise to those under twenty-one years of age.

In 1942, during World War II, Rep. Jennings Randolph (D–W.Va.), proposed that the voting age be lowered to eighteen believing that since young men were old enough to be drafted to fight and die for their country, they should also be allowed to vote. He continued to reintroduce his proposal during every session of Congress, and in 1954 President Eisenhower endorsed the idea in his State of the Union message. Presidents Johnson and Nixon—both men who called upon the nation's young men to fight on foreign shores—also echoed his appeal.[1]

By the 1960s, the campaign to lower the voting age took on a new sense of urgency as hundreds of thousands of young men were drafted to fight in Vietnam and thousands of young men and women were killed. "Old Enough to Fight, Old Enough to Vote," was one popular slogan of the day. By 1970, four states—who under the U.S. Constitution are allowed to set the eligibility requirements for their voters—had lowered their voting ages to eighteen, and under considerable pressure from Baby Boomers, Congress passed legislation lowering the voting age in national, state, and local elections to eighteen.

The state of Oregon, however, challenged the constitutionality of the law in court arguing that Congress had not been given the authority to establish a uniform voting age in state and local government under the Constitution. The U.S. Supreme Court agreed.[2] The decision from the sharply divided Court meant that those under age twenty-one could vote in national elections but that the states were free to prohibit them from voting in state and local elections. The decision presented the states with a logistical nightmare in keeping two sets of registration books—one for those twenty-one and over, and one for those who were not.

Jennings Randolph, now the Senator from West Virginia, reintroduced his proposed amendment.[3] Within three months of the Supreme Court's decision, Congress sent the proposed Twenty-Sixth Amendment to the states for their ratification. The required three-fourths of the states ratified the amendment within three months of its proposal—making its adoption, on June 30, 1971, the quickest in the history of the constitutional amending process.

The Constitution was intentionally written to forestall the need for amendment, and the process by which it could be changed or amended was made intentionally time-consuming and difficult. Over the years, thousands of amendments—including those to prohibit child labor, provide equal rights for women, grant statehood to the District of Columbia, and balance the budget—have been debated or sent to the states for their approval, only to die slow deaths. Only twenty-seven amendments have successfully made their way into the Constitution. What the Framers came up with in Philadelphia has continued to work, in spite of continually increasing demands on and dissatisfaction with our national government. Perhaps Americans are happier with the system of government created by the Framers than they realize.

The ideas that went into the making of the Constitution and how the Constitution has evolved to address the problems of a growing and ever-changing nation are at the core of our discussion in this chapter.

- First, we will examine the *origins of the new nation* and the circumstances surrounding the break with Great Britain.
- Second, we will discuss the *Declaration of Independence* and the ideas that lay at its core.
- Third, we will discuss *the first American government* created by the *Articles of Confederation*.
- Fourth, we will examine the circumstances surrounding the drafting of a *new Constitution* in Philadelphia.
- Fifth, we will review the results of the Framers' efforts—The *U.S. Constitution*.
- Sixth, we will present the *drive for ratification* of the new government.
- Seventh, we will address the *process for amending the Constitution*.
- Eighth, we will explore the role of *judicial interpretation and cultural and technological change* in constitutional change.

THE ORIGINS OF A NEW NATION

Starting in the early seventeenth century, colonists came to the New World for a variety of reasons. Often it was to escape religious persecution. Others came seeking a new start on a continent where land was plentiful. The independence and diversity of the settlers in the New World made the question of how best to rule the new colonies a tricky one. More than merely an ocean separated England from the colonies; the colonists were independent people, and it soon became clear that the Crown could not govern the colonies with the same close rein used at home. King James I thus allowed some local participation in decision making through arrangements such as the first elected colonial assembly, the Virginia House of Burgesses, and the elected General Court that governed the Massachusetts Bay Company and that colony after 1629. Almost all the colonists agreed that the king ruled by divine right; but English monarchs allowed the colonists significant liberties in terms of self-government, religious practices, and economic organization. For 140 years, this system worked fairly well.[4]

By the early 1760s, however, a century and a half of physical separation, colonial development, and the relative self-governance of the colonies had led to weakening ties with—and loyalties to—the Crown. By this time, each of the thirteen colonies had drafted its own written constitution, which provided the fundamental rules or laws for each colony. Moreover, many of the most oppressive British traditions—feudalism, a rigid class system, and the absolute authority of church and king—were absent in the New World. Land was abundant. The restrictive guild and craft systems that severely limited entry into many skilled professions in England did not exist in the colonies. Although the role of religion was central to the lives of most colonists, there was no single state church, and the British practice of compulsory tithing (giving a fixed percentage of one's earnings to the state-sanctioned and -supported church) was nonexistent.

Trade and Taxation

Mercantilism, an economic theory based on the belief that a nation's wealth is measured by the amount of gold and silver in its treasury, justified Britain's maintenance of strict import/export controls on the colonies (see pp. 11–14 in Chapter 1 on Economic Systems). After 1650, for example, Parliament passed a series of navigation acts to prevent its chief rival, Holland, from trading with the English colonies. From 1650 until well into the 1700s, England tried to regulate colonial imports and exports, believing that it was critical to export more goods than it imported as a way of increasing the gold and silver in its treasury. These policies, however, were difficult to enforce and were widely ignored by the colonists, who saw little self-benefit in them. Thus, for years, an unwritten agreement existed. The colonists relinquished to the Crown and the British Parliament the authority to regulate trade and conduct international affairs, but they retained the right to levy their own taxes.

This fragile agreement was soon put to the test. The French and Indian War, fought from 1756 to 1763 on the "western frontier" of the colonies and in Canada, was part of a global war initiated by the British. The American phase of the Seven Years' War was fought between England and France with its Indian allies. In North America, its immediate cause was the rival claims of those two European nations for the lands between the Allegheny Mountains and the Mississippi River. The Treaty of Paris (signed in 1763) signaled the end of the war. The colonists expected that with the "Indian problem" on the western frontier now "under control," westward migration and settlement could begin in earnest. They were shocked when the Crown decreed in 1763 that there was to be no further westward movement by British subjects. Parliament believed that expansion into Indian territory would lead to new expenditures for the defense of the settlers, draining the British treasury, which had yet to recover from the high cost of waging the war.

To raise money to pay for the war as well as the expenses of administering the colonies, Parliament enacted the Sugar Act in 1764, which placed taxes on sugar, wine, coffee, and other products commonly exported to the colonies. A postwar colonial depression heightened resentment of the tax. Around the colonies the political cry "No taxation without representation" was heard. Major protest, however, failed to materialize until imposition of the Stamp Act by the British Parliament in 1765. This law required the colonists to purchase stamps for all documents, including newspapers, magazines, and commercial papers. To add insult to injury, in 1765 Parliament passed the Mutiny or Quartering Act, which required the colonists to furnish barracks or provide living quarters within their own homes for British troops.

Most colonists, especially those in New England, where these acts hit hardest, were outraged. Men throughout the colonies organized the Sons of Liberty, under the leadership of Samuel Adams (see Roots of Government: Samuel Adams) and Patrick Henry. Whereas the Sugar Act was a tax on trade—still viewed as being within the legitimate authority of the Crown—the Stamp Act was a direct tax on many items not traditionally under the control of the king, and protests against it were violent and loud. Riots, often led by the Sons of Liberty, broke out. They were especially violent in Boston, where the colonial governor's home was burned by an angry mob, and British stamp agents charged with collecting the tax were threatened. A boycott of goods needing the stamps as well as British imports was also organized.

First Steps Toward Independence

In 1765 the colonists called for the **Stamp Act Congress,** the first official meeting of the colonies and the first step toward a unified nation. Nine of the thirteen colonies sent representatives to a meeting in New York City, where a detailed list of Crown violations of their fundamental rights was drawn up. Attendees defined what they thought to be the proper relationship between the various colonial governments and the British Parliament; they ardently believed that Parliament had no authority to tax them without colonial representation in the British Parliament. In contrast, the British believed

Stamp Act Congress:

Meeting of representatives of nine of the thirteen colonies held in New York City in 1765, during which representatives drafted a document to send to the king listing how their rights had been violated.

ROOTS OF GOVERNMENT

Samuel Adams

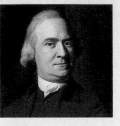

Although Samuel Adams (1722–1803) today perhaps is known best for the beer that bears his name, his original claim to fame was as a leader against British and loyalist oppressors (although he did bankrupt his family's brewery business). A second cousin of President John Adams, Samuel Adams was a signer of the Declaration of Independence and a member of Massachusetts's constitutional convention that ratified the U.S. Constitution. He served as governor of Massachusetts from 1794 to 1797.

Adams was heavily influenced by John Locke's belief in man's natural right to be self-governing and free from taxation without representation. As a member of the Massachusetts legislature, he advocated defiance of the Stamp Act. With the passage of the Townshend Acts in 1767, he organized a letter-writing campaign urging other colonies to join in resistance. Later, in 1772, he founded the Committees of Correspondence to unite the colonies.

(Painting by John Singleton Copely. Courtesy, Museum of Fine Arts, Boston. Reproduced with permission.©1999 Museum of Fine Arts, Boston. All Rights Reserved.)

Committees of Correspondence:

Organizations in each of the American colonies created to keep colonists abreast of developments with the British; served as powerful molders of public opinion against the British.

that direct representation of the colonists was impractical and that members of Parliament represented the best interests of all the English, including the colonists.

The Stamp Act Congress and its petitions to the Crown did little to stop the onslaught of taxing measures. Parliament did, however, repeal the Stamp Act and revise the Sugar Act in 1766, largely because of the uproar made by British merchants who were losing large sums of money as a result of the boycotts. Rather than appeasing the colonists, however, these actions emboldened them to increase their resistance. In 1767 Parliament enacted the Townshend Acts, which imposed duties on all kinds of colonial imports, including tea. Response from the Sons of Liberty was immediate. Another boycott was announced, and almost all colonists gave up their favorite drink in a united show of resistance to the tax and British authority.[5] Tensions continued to run high, especially after the British sent 4,000 troops to Boston. On March 5, 1770, English troops opened fire on a mob that included disgruntled dock workers, whose jobs had been taken by British soldiers, and members of the Sons of Liberty who were taunting the soldiers in front of the Boston Customs House. Five colonists were killed in what became known as the Boston Massacre. Following this confrontation, all duties except those on tea were lifted. The tea tax, however, continued to be a symbolic irritant. In 1772, at the suggestion of Samuel Adams, Boston and other towns around Massachusetts set up **Committees of Correspondence** to articulate ideas and keep communications open around the colony. By 1774 twelve colonies had formed committees to maintain a flow of information among like-minded colonists.

Meanwhile, despite dissent in England over the treatment of the colonies, Parliament passed another tea tax designed to shore up the sagging sales of the East India Company. The colonists' boycott had left that British trading house with more than 18 million pounds of tea in its warehouses. To rescue British merchants from disaster, in 1773 Parliament passed the Tea Act, granting a monopoly to the financially strapped East India Company to sell the tea imported from Britain. The company was allowed to funnel business to American merchants loyal to the Crown, thereby undercutting colonial merchants, who could sell only tea imported from other nations. The effect was to drive down the price of tea and to hurt colonial merchants, who were forced to buy tea at the higher prices from other sources.

When the next shipment of tea arrived in Boston from Great Britain, the colonists responded by throwing the Boston Tea Party. Similar "tea parties" were held in other colonies. When the news of these actions reached King George, he flew into a rage against the actions of his disloyal subjects. "The die is now cast," the king told his prime minister. "The colonies must either submit or triumph."

His first act was to persuade Parliament to pass the Coercive Acts in 1774. Known in the colonies as the Intolerable Acts, they contained a key provision calling for a total blockade of Boston Harbor until restitution was made for the tea. Another provision reinforced the Quartering Act, giving royal governors the authority to quarter in the homes of private citizens the additional 4,000 British soldiers sent to patrol Boston.

The First Continental Congress

The British could never have guessed how the cumulative impact of these actions would unite the colonists. Samuel Adams's Committees of Correspondence spread the word, and food and money were sent to the people of Boston from all over the thirteen colonies. The tax itself was no longer the key issue; now the extent of British authority over the colonies was the far more important question. At the request of the colonial assemblies of Massachusetts and Virginia, all but one colonial assembly agreed to select a group of delegates to attend a continental congress authorized to communicate with the king on behalf of the now-united colonies.

The **First Continental Congress** met in Philadelphia from September 5 to October 26, 1774. It was made up of fifty-six delegates from every colony except Georgia.

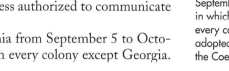

First Continental Congress:

Meeting held in Philadelphia from September 5 to October 26, 1774, in which fifty-six delegates (from every colony except Georgia) adopted a resolution that opposed the Coercive Acts.

■ Paul Revere's engraving of the Boston Massacre was a potent piece of political propaganda. Five men were killed, not seven, as the legend states, and the rioters in front of the State House (left) were scarcely as docile as Revere portrayed them. (Photo courtesy: The New-York Historical Society)

Web Exploration
For more information on the work of the Continental Congress, see www.awlonline.com/oconnor.

Second Continental Congress:

Meeting that convened in Philadelphia on May 10, 1775, at which it was decided that an army should be raised and George Washington of Virginia was named commander-in-chief.

■ After the success of *Common Sense,* Thomas Paine wrote a series of essays collectively entitled *The Crisis* to arouse colonists' support for the Revolutionary War. The first *Crisis* papers contain the famous words "These are the times that try men's souls." (Photo courtesy: Stock Montage, Inc.)

confederation:

Type of government in which the national government derives its powers from the states; a league of independent states.

The colonists had yet to think of breaking with Great Britain; at this point, they simply wanted to iron out their differences with the king. By October they had agreed on a series of resolutions to oppose the Coercive Acts and to establish a formal organization to boycott British goods. The Congress also drafted a Declaration of Rights and Resolves, which called for colonial rights of petition and assembly, trial by peers, freedom from a standing army, and the selection of representative councils to levy taxes. The Congress further agreed that if the king did not capitulate to their demands, they would meet again in Philadelphia in May 1775.

The Second Continental Congress

King George refused to yield, tensions continued to rise, and a **Second Continental Congress** was called. Before it could meet, fighting broke out early in the morning of April 19, 1775, at Lexington and Concord, Massachusetts, with what Ralph Waldo Emerson called "the shot heard round the world." Eight colonial soldiers, called Minutemen, were killed, and 16,000 British troops besieged Boston.

When the Second Continental Congress convened in Philadelphia on May 10, 1775, delegates were united by their increased hostility to Great Britain. The bloodshed at Lexington left no other course but war. To solidify colonial support, a Southerner, George Washington of Virginia, was selected as the commander of the new Continental Army, since up to that date, British oppression had been felt most keenly in the Northeast. That task complete, the Congress then sent envoys to France to ask its assistance against France's perennial enemy. In a final attempt to avert conflict, the Second Continental Congress adopted the Olive Branch Petition on July 5, 1775, asking the king to end hostilities. King George rejected the petition and sent an additional 20,000 troops to quell the rebellion. The stage was set for war.

In January 1776, Thomas Paine, with the support and encouragement of Benjamin Franklin, issued (at first anonymously) *Common Sense,* a pamphlet forcefully arguing for independence from Great Britain. In frank, easy-to-understand language, Paine denounced the corrupt British monarchy and offered reasons for breaking with Great Britain. "The blood of the slain, the weeping voice of nature cries 'Tis Time to Part,'" wrote Paine. *Common Sense,* widely read throughout the colonies, was instrumental in changing minds in a very short time. In its first three months of publication, the forty-seven-page *Common Sense* sold 120,000 copies, the equivalent of approximately 18.75 million books today (given the U.S. population today). One copy of *Common Sense* was in distribution for every thirteen people in the colonies—a truly astonishing number, given the low literacy rate.

THE DECLARATION OF INDEPENDENCE

Common Sense galvanized the American public against reconciliation with England. As the mood in the colonies changed, so did that of the Second Continental Congress. On May 15, 1776, Virginia became the first colony to call for independence, instructing one of its delegates to the Second Continental Congress to introduce a resolution to that effect. On June 7, 1776, Richard Henry Lee of Virginia rose to move "that these United Colonies are, and of right ought to be, free and independent States, and that all connection between them and the State of Great Britain is, and ought to be, dissolved." His three-part resolution—which called for independence, the formation of foreign alliances, and preparation of a plan of **confederation**—triggered hot debate among the delegates. A proclamation of independence from Great Britain was treason, a crime punishable by death. Although six of the thirteen colonies had already instructed their delegates to vote for independence, the Second Continental Congress was suspended to allow its delegates to return home to their respective colonial legislatures for final instructions. Independence was not a move to be taken lightly.

At the same time, committees were set up to consider each point of Lee's proposal. A committee of five was selected to begin work on a **Declaration of Independence.** The Congress selected Benjamin Franklin, John Adams, Robert Livingston, and Roger Sherman as members. Adams lobbied hard for a Southerner to add balance. Thus, owing to his Southern origin as well as his "peculiar felicity of expression," Thomas Jefferson was selected as chair.

On July 2, 1776, twelve of the thirteen colonies (with New York abstaining) voted for independence. Two days later the Second Continental Congress voted to adopt the Declaration of Independence penned by Thomas Jefferson. On July 9, 1776, the Declaration, now with the approval of New York, was read aloud in Philadelphia.[6]

A Theoretical Basis for a New Government

In simple but eloquent language, Jefferson set out the reasons for the colonies' separation from Great Britain. Most of his stirring rhetoric drew heavily on the works of seventeenth- and eighteenth-century political philosophers, particularly the English John Locke (see Roots of Government: Hobbes and Locke in chapter 1), who had written South Carolina's first Constitution, a colonial charter drawn up in 1663 when South Carolina was formed by King Charles II and mercantile houses in England. In fact, many of the words in the opening of the Declaration of Independence closely resemble passages from Locke's *Two Treatises of Government*.

Locke was a proponent of *social contract theory,* a philosophy of government that held that governments exist based on the consent of the governed. According to Locke, people leave the state of nature and agree to set up a government largely for the protection of property. In colonial times "property" did not mean just land. Locke's notion of property rights included life, liberty, and material possessions. Furthermore, argued Locke, individuals who give their consent to be governed have the right to resist or remove rulers who deviate from those purposes. Such a government exists for the good of its subjects and not for the benefit of those who govern. Thus, rebellion was the ultimate sanction against a government that violated the rights of its citizens.

Declaration of Independence:

Document drafted by Thomas Jefferson in 1776 that proclaimed the right of the American colonies to separate from Great Britain.

Web Exploration

For the text of the Declaration of Independence, see www.awlonline.com/oconnor.

■ American Renaissance man Thomas Jefferson (1743–1826)—author of the Declaration of Independence and the third president of the United States—voiced the aspirations of a new America as no other individual of his era. In the wake of scientific evidence proving he fathered at least one child by his slave, Sally Hemmings, historians are now reassessing his writings and political thought. Some of her descendants, right, gather at Monticello. (Photos courtesy: left, Corbis/Bettmann; right, Stephanie Gross)

It is easy to see the colonists' debt to John Locke. In ringing language the Declaration of Independence proclaims:

> We hold these truths to be self-evident, that all men are created equal, that they are endowed by their Creator with certain unalienable Rights, that among these are Life, Liberty and the pursuit of Happiness.

Jefferson and others in attendance at the Second Continental Congress wanted to have a document that would stand for all time, justifying their break with the Crown and clarifying their notions of the proper form of government. So, Jefferson continued:

> That to secure these rights, Governments are instituted among Men, deriving their just powers from the consent of the governed. That whenever any Form of Government becomes destructive of these ends, it is the Right of the People to alter or abolish it, and to institute new Government, laying its foundation on such Principles and organizing its Powers in such form, as to them shall seem most likely to effect their Safety and Happiness.

After this stirring preamble, the Declaration went on to enumerate the wrongs that the colonists had suffered under British rule. All pertained to the denial of personal rights and liberties, many of which would later be guaranteed by the U.S. Constitution through the Bill of Rights.

After the Declaration was signed and transmitted to the king, the Revolutionary War was fought with a greater vengeance. At a September 1776 peace conference on Staten Island (New York), British General William Howe demanded revocation of the Declaration of Independence. The Americans refused, and the war raged on while the Congress attempted to fashion a new united government.

THE FIRST ATTEMPT AT GOVERNMENT: THE ARTICLES OF CONFEDERATION

As noted earlier, the British had no written constitution. The colonists in the Second Continental Congress were attempting to codify arrangements that had never before been put into legal terminology. To make things more complicated, the delegates had to arrive at these decisions in a wartime atmosphere. Nevertheless, in late 1777 the **Articles of Confederation,** creating a loose "league of friendship" between the sovereign or independent states, were passed by the Congress and presented to the states for their ratification.

The Articles created a type of government called a confederation or confederacy. Unlike the unitary system of government in England, wherein all of the powers of the government reside in the national government, the national government in a confederation derives all of its powers directly from the states. Thus the national government in a confederacy is weaker than the sum of its parts, and the states often consider themselves independent states linked together only for limited purposes such as national defense. Key provisions in the Articles that created the confederacy included:

- A national government with a Congress empowered to make peace, coin money, appoint officers for an army, control the post office, and negotiate with Indian tribes.
- Each state's retention of its independence and sovereignty, or ultimate authority to govern within its territories.
- One vote in the Continental Congress for each state, regardless of size.
- The vote of nine states to pass any measure (a unanimous vote for any amendment).
- The selection and payment of delegates to the Congress by their respective state legislatures.

Thus the Articles—finally ratified by all thirteen states in March 1781—fashioned a government well reflective of the political philosophy of the times.[7] Although it had its flaws, the government under the Articles of Confederation saw the nation through the

---

Articles of Confederation:

The compact among the thirteen original states that was the basis of their government. Written in 1776, the Articles were not ratified by all the states until 1781.

Web Exploration
For a full text of the Articles of Confederation, see
www.awlonline.com/oconnor.

Revolutionary War. However, once the British surrendered in 1781 and the new nation found itself no longer united by the war effort, the government quickly fell into chaos.

Problems Under the Articles of Confederation

In today's America we ship goods, travel by car and airplane across state lines, make interstate phone calls, and more. Over 250 years ago, Americans had great loyalties to their states and often did not even think of themselves as Americans. This lack of national sentiment or loyalty in the absence of a war to unite the citizenry fostered a reluctance to give any power to the national government. Thus, by 1784, just one year after the Revolutionary Army was disbanded, governing the new nation under the Articles of Confederation proved unworkable.[8] Congress could rarely assemble the required quorum of nine states to conduct business. Even when it could, there was little agreement among the states. To raise revenue to pay off war debts and run the government, various land, poll, and liquor taxes were proposed. But since Congress had no specific power to tax, all these proposals were rejected. At one point Congress was even driven out of Philadelphia (then the capital) by its own unpaid army.

Although the national government could coin money, it had no resources to back up the value of its currency. Continental dollars were worth little, and trade between states became chaotic as some states began to coin their own money. Another weakness of the Articles was their failure to allow Congress to regulate commerce among the states and with foreign nations. As a result individual states attempted to enter into agreements with other countries, and foreign nations were suspicious of trade agreements made with the United States. In 1785, for example, Massachusetts banned the export of goods in British ships, and Pennsylvania levied heavy duties on ships of nations that did not have a treaty with the U.S. government.

Fearful of a chief executive who would rule tyrannically, moreover, the draftees of the Articles had made no provision for an executive branch of government that would be responsible for executing, or implementing, laws passed by the legislative branch. Instead, the "president" was merely the presiding officer at meetings. John Hanson, a former member of the Maryland House of Delegates and of the First Continental Congress, was the first person to preside over the Congress of the Confederation, as the new government under the Articles was called. Therefore he is often referred to as the first President of the United States.

In addition, the Articles of Confederation had no provision for a judicial system to handle the growing number of economic conflicts and boundary disputes among the individual states. Several states claimed the same lands to the west; Pennsylvania and Virginia went to war with each other; Vermont threatened to annex itself to Canada.

The Articles' greatest weakness, however, was their lack of creation of a strong central government. While states had operated independently before the war, during the war they acceded to the national government's authority to wage armed conflict. Once the war was over, however, each state resumed its sovereign status, and was unwilling to give up rights, such as the power to tax, to an untested national government. Consequently, the government was unable to force the states to abide by

■ With Daniel Shays in the lead, a group of farmers and Revolutionary War veterans marched on the court house in Springfield, Massachusetts, to prevent foreclosure on their mortgages. (Photo courtesy: Corbis/Bettmann)

the provisions of the Treaty of Paris, signed in 1783, which had officially ended the war. For example, states passed laws to stay the bills of debtors who owed money to Great Britain. They also failed to restore property to many who had remained loyal to Britain during the war. Both actions were in violation of the treaty.

The crumbling economy and a series of bad harvests that failed to produce cash crops, making it difficult for farmers to get out of debt quickly, took their toll on the new nation. George Washington and Alexander Hamilton, both interested in the questions of trade and frontier expansion, soon saw the need for a stronger national government with the authority to act to solve some of these problems. They were not alone. In 1785 and 1786, some state governments began to discuss ways to strengthen the national government. Finally, several states joined together to call for a convention in Philadelphia in 1787.

Before that meeting could take place, however, new unrest broke out in America. In 1780 Massachusetts adopted a state constitution that appeared to favor the interests of the wealthy. Property-owning requirements barred the lower and middle classes from voting and office holding. And, as the economy of Massachusetts worsened, banks foreclosed on farms to pay off debts to Massachusetts Continental Army veterans who were waiting for promised bonuses. The last straw came in 1786, when the Massachusetts legislature enacted a new law requiring the payment of all debts in cash. Frustration and outrage at the new law caused Daniel Shays, a former Revolutionary War army captain, and 1,500 armed, disgruntled, and angry farmers to march to Springfield. This group forcibly restrained the state court from foreclosing on mortgages on their farms.

The Congress immediately authorized the Secretary of War to call for a new national militia. A $530,000 appropriation was made for this purpose, but every state except Virginia refused the Congress's request for money. The governor of Massachusetts then tried to raise a state militia, but because of the poor economy, funds were unavailable in the state treasury. Frantic attempts at private support were made, and a militia was finally assembled. By February 4, 1787, this privately paid force put a stop to what was called **Shays's Rebellion.** The failure of the Congress to muster an army to put down the rebellion was yet another example of the weaknesses inherent in the Articles of Confederation.

THE MIRACLE AT PHILADELPHIA: WRITING A CONSTITUTION

On February 21, 1787—in the throes of economic turmoil and with domestic tranquility gone haywire—the Congress passed an official resolution. It called for a Constitutional Convention in Philadelphia for "the sole and express purpose of revising the Articles of Confederation." All states but Rhode Island sent delegates.

Twenty-nine individuals met in sweltering Philadelphia on May 14. Many at that initial meeting were intellectuals, others were shrewd farmers or businessmen, and still others were astute politicians. All recognized that what they were doing could be considered treasonous. Revising the Articles of Confederation was one thing; to call for an entirely new government, as suggested by the Virginia delegation, was another. So they took their work quite seriously, even to the point of adopting a pledge of secrecy. George Washington, who was unanimously elected the convention's presiding officer, warned:

> Nothing spoken or written can be revealed to anyone—not even your family—until we have adjourned permanently. Gossip or misunderstanding can easily ruin all the hard work we shall have to do this summer.[9]

So concerned about leaks were those in attendance that the delegates agreed to accompany Benjamin Franklin to all of his meals. They feared that the normally gregarious gentleman might get carried away with the mood or by liquor and inadvertently let news of the proceedings slip from his tongue.

Shays's Rebellion:

A 1786 rebellion in which an army of 1,500 disgruntled and angry farmers led by Daniel Shays marched to Springfield, Massachusetts, and forcibly restrained the state court from foreclosing on their farms.

The Framers

Fifty-five out of the seventy-four delegates ultimately chosen by their state legislatures to attend the Constitutional Convention labored long and hard that hot summer behind closed doors in Philadelphia. All of them were men; hence they are often referred to as the "Founding Fathers." Most of them, however, were quite young; many were in their twenties and thirties, and only one—Benjamin Franklin, at eighty-one—was very old as highlighted in Figure 2.1. Here we generally refer to those delegates as Framers because their work provided the framework for our new government. The Framers brought with them a vast amount of political, educational, legal, and business experience. Eight had signed the Declaration of Independence, thirty-nine had attended at least one Continental Congress, and seven were former governors. One-third were college graduates, and thirty-four were lawyers. Notably absent were individuals like Patrick Henry, who had proclaimed in the Virginia House of Burgesses before the Revolutionary War, "Give me liberty or give me death!" Now he stayed away because he "smelt a rat," fearing that the states could lose their powers. Also missing were Thomas Jefferson, author of the Declaration of Independence, and John Adams. Both were on ambassadorial stays in Europe. Although some scholarly debate continues concerning the motives of the Framers for shaping the new national government (see Highlight 2.1: The Motives of the Framers), it is clear that they were an exceptional lot who ultimately produced a brilliant document reflecting the best efforts of all present.

The Virginia and New Jersey Plans

The less populous states were concerned with being lost in any new system of government where states were not treated as equals regardless of population. It is not surprising that a large state and then a small one, Virginia and New Jersey, respectively weighed in with ideas about how the new government should operate.

Web Exploration
For demographic background on the Framers, see www.awlonline.com/oconnor.

Figure 2.1   The Framers

b. 1706
Oldest
delegate
Benjamin
Franklin (81)

Median age of
delegates in 1787
43 years

Last
survivor
James
Madison
d. 1836

Youngeast delegate
Jonathan Dayton (27)
b. 1760

1700   1720   1740   1760   1780   1787   1800   1820   1840

HIGHLIGHT 2.1   The Motives of the Framers

Debate about the Framers' motives filled the air during the ratification struggle and has provided grist for the mill of historians and political scientists over the years. Anti-Federalists, who opposed the new Constitution, charged that Federalist supporters of the Constitution were a self-serving, landed, and propertied elite with a vested interest in the capitalistic system that had evolved in the colonies. Federalists countered that they were simply trying to preserve the nation.

In his *Economic Interpretation of the Constitution of the United States* (1913), the highly respected political scientist and historian Charles A. Beard argued that the 1780s were a "critical period" (as the time under governance by the Articles of Confederation had come to be known) not for the nation as a whole, but rather for businessmen. These men feared that a weak, decentralized government could harm their economic interests. Beard argued that the merchants wanted a strong national government to promote industry and trade, protect private property, and most importantly, ensure payment of the public debt—much of which was owed to them. Therefore, according to Beard, the Constitution represents "an economic document drawn with superb skill by men whose property interests were immediately at stake."*

By the 1950s this view had fallen into disfavor when other historians were unable to find direct links between wealth and the Framers' motives for establishing the Constitution. In the 1960s, however, another group of historians began to argue that social and economic factors were, in fact, important motives for supporting the Constitution. In *The Anti-Federalists* (1961), Jackson Turner Main posited that while the Constitution's supporters might not have been the united group of creditors suggested by Beard, they were wealthier, came from high social strata, and had greater concern for maintaining the prevailing social order than the general public.

In 1969, Gordon S. Wood's *The Creation of the American Republic* resurrected this debate. Wood deemphasized economics to argue that major social divisions explained different groups' support for (or opposition to) the new Constitution. He concluded that the Framers were representatives of a class that favored order and stability over some of the more radical ideas that had inspired the Revolution.

*Quoted in Richard N. Current, *et al.*, *American History: A Survey*, 6th ed. (New York: Knopf, 1983), 170.

Virginia Plan:

The first general plan for the Constitution, proposed by James Madison. Its key points were a bicameral legislature, an executive chosen by the legislature, and a judiciary also named by the legislature.

The **Virginia Plan** called for a national system based heavily on the European nation-state model, wherein the national government derives its powers from the people and not from the member states.

Its key features included:

- Creation of a powerful central government with three branches—the legislative, executive, and judicial.
- A two-house legislature with one house elected directly by the people; the other chosen from among persons nominated by the state legislatures.

In general, smaller states felt comfortable with the arrangements under the Articles of Confederation. These states offered another model of government, the **New Jersey Plan.** Its key features included:

New Jersey Plan:

A framework for the Constitution proposed by a group of small states; its key points were a one-house legislature with one vote for each state, a multiperson "executive," the establishment of the acts of Congress as the "supreme law" of the land, and a supreme judiciary with limited power.

- Strengthening the Articles, *not* replacing them.
- Creating a one-house legislature with one vote for each state with representatives chosen by state legislatures.
- Giving the Congress the power to raise revenue from duties and a post office.

The Great Compromise

The most serious disagreement between the Virginia and New Jersey plans concerned representation in Congress. When a deadlock on this point loomed, Connecticut offered its own compromise. Each state would have an equal vote in the Senate. Again, there was a stalemate. As Benjamin Franklin put it:

The diversity of opinions turns on two points. If a proportional representation takes place, the small states contend that their liberties will be in danger. If an equality of votes is to be put in its place, large states say that their money will be in danger.

He continued:

When a broad table is to be made and the edges of a plank do not fit, the artist takes a little from both sides and makes a good joint. In like manner, both sides must part with some of their demands, in order that they both join in some accommodating position.[10]

A committee to work out an agreement soon reported back what became known as the **Great Compromise.** Taking ideas from both the Virginia and New Jersey plans, it recommended:

1. In one house of the legislature (later called the House of Representatives), there should be fifty-six representatives—one representative for every 40,000 inhabitants.
2. That house should have the power to originate all bills for raising and spending money.
3. In the second house of the legislature (later called the Senate), each state should have an equal vote, and representatives would be selected by the state legislatures.[11]

Still, a sticking point remained about how to determine state population. Slaves could not vote, but the Southern states wanted them included for purposes of determining population.

After considerable dissension, it was decided that population would be calculated by adding the "whole Number of Free Persons" to "three fifths of all other Persons." "All other Persons" was the delegates' "tactful" way of referring to slaves. Known as the **Three-Fifths Compromise,** this highly political deal assured that the South would hold 47 percent of the House—enough to prevent attacks on slavery but not so much as to foster the spread of slavery northward.

The Great Compromise ultimately met with the approval of all states in attendance. The smaller states were pleased because they got equal representation in the Senate; the larger states were satisfied with the proportional representation in the House of Representatives. The small states then would dominate the Senate while the large states, such as Virginia and New York, would control the House. But because both houses had to pass any legislation, neither body could dominate the other.

Unfinished Business

The Framers next turned to fashioning an executive branch. While they agreed on the idea of a one-person executive, they could not settle on the length of the term of office, nor on how the chief executive should be selected. With Shays's Rebellion still fresh in their minds, the delegates feared putting too much power, including selection of a president, into the hands of the lower classes. At the same time, representatives from the smaller states feared that the selection of the chief executive by the legislature would put additional power into the hands of the large states.

Amid these fears the Committee on Unfinished Portions, whose sole responsibility was to iron out problems and disagreements concerning the office of chief executive, conducted its work. The committee recommended that the presidential term of office be fixed at four years instead of seven, as had earlier been proposed. By choosing not to mention a period of time within which the chief executive would be eligible for reelection, they made it possible for a president to serve more than one term.

The Framers also created the electoral college and drafted rules concerning removal of a sitting president. The electoral college system gave individual states a key role, because each state would select electors equal to the number of representatives it had in the House and Senate. It was a vague compromise that removed election of the president and vice president from both the Congress and the people and put it in the hands

Great Compromise:

A decision made during the Philadelphia Convention to give each state the same number of representatives in the Senate regardless of size; representation in the House was determined by population.

Three-Fifths Compromise:

Agreement reached at the Constitutional Convention stipulating that each slave was to be counted as three-fifths of a person for purposes of determining population for representation in the U.S. House of Representatives.

of electors whose method of selection would be left to the states (see p. 478 for more on the electoral college).

In drafting the new Constitution, the Framers also were careful to include a provision for removal of the chief executive. The House of Representatives was given the sole responsibility of investigating and charging a president or vice president with "Treason, Bribery, or other high Crimes and Misdemeanors." A majority vote would then result in issuing Articles of Impeachment against the president. In turn, the Senate was given sole responsibility to try the chief executive on the charges issued by the House. A two-thirds vote of the Senate was required to convict and remove the president from office. The Chief Justice of the United States was to preside over the Senate proceedings in place of the vice president (that body's usual leader) in order to prevent any appearance of impropriety on the vice president's part.

THE U.S. CONSTITUTION

After the compromise on the presidency, work proceeded quickly on the remaining resolutions of the Constitution. The Preamble to the Constitution, the last section to be drafted, contains exceptionally powerful language that forms the bedrock of American political tradition. Its opening line, "We the People of the United States," boldly proclaimed that a loose confederation of independent states no longer existed. Instead, there was but one American people and nation. The original version of the Preamble opened with:

> We the people of the States of New Hampshire, Massachusetts, Rhode Island and the Providence Plantations, Connecticut, New Jersey, New York, Pennsylvania,

Web Exploration
For the full text of other nations' constitutions, see www.awlonline.com/oconnor.

■ The shootout at Ruby Ridge, the bombing of the federal building in Oklahoma City, and groups like the Freemen in Montana or "We the People" in Colorado, who believe that all forms of government, taxes, and licensing are illegal, provide an extreme example of the debate over the role of the federal government in the lives of American citizens, as well as in its control over the states. Here, a makeshift roadblock set up by the Freemen forewarns those who would trespass on "Justus township." (Photo courtesy: A. Lichtenstein/The Image Works)

Delaware, Maryland, Virginia, North Carolina, South Carolina and Georgia, do ordain, declare and establish the following Constitution for the government of ourselves and our Posterity.

The simple phrase "We the people" ended, at least for the time being, the question of whence the government derived its power: It came directly from the people, not from the states. The next phrase of the Constitution explained the need for the new outline of government. "[I]n Order to form a more perfect Union" indirectly acknowledged the weaknesses of the Articles of Confederation in governing a growing nation. Next, the optimistic goals of the Framers for the new nation were set out: to "establish Justice, insure domestic Tranquility, provide for the common defense, promote the general Welfare, and secure the Blessings of Liberty to ourselves and our Posterity"; followed by the formal creation of a new government: "do ordain and establish this Constitution for the United States of America."

On September 17, 1787, the Constitution was approved by the delegates from all twelve states in attendance. While the completed document did not satisfy all the delegates, of the forty-one in attendance, thirty-nine ultimately signed it. The sentiments uttered by Benjamin Franklin probably well reflected those of many others: "Thus, I consent, Sir, to this Constitution because I expect no better, and because I am not sure that it is not the best."[12]

The Basic Principles of the Constitution

The ideas of political philosophers, especially two political philosophers, the French Montesquieu (1689–1755) and the English John Locke (see Roots of Government: Hobbes and Locke in chapter 1), heavily influenced the shape and nature of the government proposed by the Framers. Montesquieu, who actually drew many of his ideas about government from the works of Greek political philosopher Aristotle, was heavily quoted during the Constitutional Convention.

The proposed structure of the new national government owed much to the writings of Montesquieu, who advocated distinct functions for each branch of government, called **separation of powers,** with a system of **checks and balances** between each branch. The Constitution's concern with the distribution of power between states and the national government also reveals the heavy influence of political philosophers, as well as the colonists' experience under the Articles of Confederation.[13]

Federalism.   Today, in spite of current calls for the national government to return power to the states, the question before and during the Convention was how much power states would give up to the national government. Given the nation's experiences under the Articles of Confederation, the Framers believed that a strong national government was necessary for the new nation's survival. However, they were reluctant to create a powerful government after the model of Britain, the country from which they had just won their independence. Its unitary system was not even considered by the colonists. Instead, they fashioned a system now known as the **federal system,** which divides the power of government between a strong national government and the individual states. This system, as the Court reaffirmed in 1995 in considering term limits, was based on the principle that the federal, or national, government derived its power from the citizens, not the states, as the national government had done under the Articles of Confederation.

Opponents of this system feared that a strong national government would infringe on their liberty. But James Madison argued that a strong national government with distinct state governments could, if properly directed by constitutional arrangements, actually be a source of expanded liberties and national unity. The Framers viewed the division of governmental authority between the national government and the states as a means of checking power with power, and providing the people with "double security" against governmental tyranny. Later, the passage of the Tenth Amendment, which stated that powers not given to the national government were reserved by the states or the people, further clarified the federal structure (see chapter 3).

separation of powers:

A way of dividing power among three branches of government in which members of the House of Representatives, members of the Senate, the president, and the federal courts are selected by and responsible to different constituencies.

checks and balances:

A governmental structure that gives each of the three branches of government some degree of oversight and control over the actions of the others.

federal system:

Plan of government created in the U.S. Constitution in which power is divided between the national government and the state governments and in which independent states are bound together under one national government.

Figure 2.2 Separation of Powers and Checks and Balances

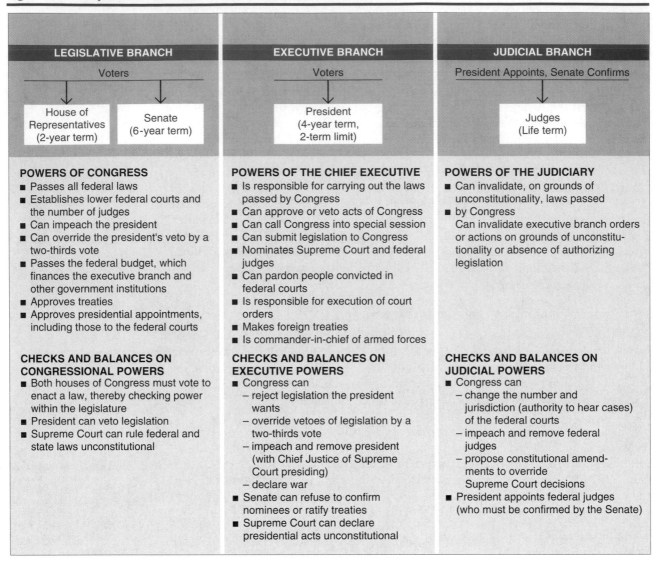

LEGISLATIVE BRANCH	EXECUTIVE BRANCH	JUDICIAL BRANCH
Voters	Voters	President Appoints, Senate Confirms
House of Representatives (2-year term) Senate (6-year term)	President (4-year term, 2-term limit)	Judges (Life term)

POWERS OF CONGRESS
- Passes all federal laws
- Establishes lower federal courts and the number of judges
- Can impeach the president
- Can override the president's veto by a two-thirds vote
- Passes the federal budget, which finances the executive branch and other government institutions
- Approves treaties
- Approves presidential appointments, including those to the federal courts

POWERS OF THE CHIEF EXECUTIVE
- Is responsible for carrying out the laws passed by Congress
- Can approve or veto acts of Congress
- Can call Congress into special session
- Can submit legislation to Congress
- Nominates Supreme Court and federal judges
- Can pardon people convicted in federal courts
- Is responsible for execution of court orders
- Makes foreign treaties
- Is commander-in-chief of armed forces

POWERS OF THE JUDICIARY
- Can invalidate, on grounds of unconstitutionality, laws passed
- by Congress
  Can invalidate executive branch orders or actions on grounds of unconstitutionality or absence of authorizing legislation

CHECKS AND BALANCES ON CONGRESSIONAL POWERS
- Both houses of Congress must vote to enact a law, thereby checking power within the legislature
- President can veto legislation
- Supreme Court can rule federal and state laws unconstitutional

CHECKS AND BALANCES ON EXECUTIVE POWERS
- Congress can
  - reject legislation the president wants
  - override vetoes of legislation by a two-thirds vote
  - impeach and remove president (with Chief Justice of Supreme Court presiding)
  - declare war
- Senate can refuse to confirm nominees or ratify treaties
- Supreme Court can declare presidential acts unconstitutional

CHECKS AND BALANCES ON JUDICIAL POWERS
- Congress can
  - change the number and jurisdiction (authority to hear cases) of the federal courts
  - impeach and remove federal judges
  - propose constitutional amendments to override Supreme Court decisions
- President appoints federal judges (who must be confirmed by the Senate)

Separation of Powers.   Madison and many of the Framers clearly feared putting too much power into the hands of any one individual or branch of government. His famous words, "Ambition must be made to counteract ambition," were widely believed at the Philadelphia convention.

Separation of powers is simply a way of parceling out power among the three branches of government. It has three key features:

1. Three distinct branches of government: the legislative, the executive, and the judicial.
2. Three separately staffed branches of government to exercise these functions.
3. Constitutional equality and independence of each branch.

As illustrated in Figure 2.2, the Framers were careful to create a system in which law-making, law-enforcing, and law-interpreting functions were assigned to independent branches of government. On the national level (and in most states), only the legislature has the authority to make laws; the chief executive enforces laws, and the judiciary interprets them. Moreover, members of the House of Representatives, members of the Senate, the president, and members of the federal courts are selected by and are therefore responsible to different constituencies. Madison believed that the scheme devised by the Framers would divide the offices of the new government and their methods of selection among many individuals, providing each office holder with the "necessary means and personal motives to resist encroachment" on his or her power.

The Framers could not have foreseen the intermingling of governmental functions that has since evolved. Locke, in fact, cautioned against giving a legislature the ability to delegate its powers. In Article I of the Constitution, the legislative power is vested in the Congress. But the president is also given legislative powers via his ability to veto legislation, although his veto can be overridden by a two-thirds vote in Congress. Judicial interpretation then helps to clarify the implementation of legislation enacted through this process.

So instead of a pure system of separation of powers, a symbiotic, or interdependent, relationship among the three branches of government has existed from the beginning. Or, as one scholar has explained, there are "separated institutions sharing powers."[14] While Congress is still entrusted with making the laws, most proposals for legislation originate with the president. And although the Supreme Court's major function is to interpret the law, its involvement in areas such as criminal procedure, abortion, and other fields has led many to charge that it has surpassed its constitutional authority and become a law-making body.

Separation of Power and Checks and Balances.   The separation of powers among the three branches of the national government is not complete. According to Montesquieu and the Framers, the powers of each branch (as well as the two houses of the national legislature and between the states and the national government) could be used to check the powers of the other two branches of government. The power of each branch of government is checked, or limited, and balanced because the legislative, executive, and judicial branches share some authority and no branch has exclusive domain over any activity. The creation of this system allowed the Framers to minimize the threat of tyranny from any one branch. Thus, for almost every power granted to one branch, an equal control was established in the other two branches. The Congress could "check" the power of the president, the Supreme Court, and so on, carefully creating "balance" among the three branches.

The Supremacy Clause.   Another key constitutional principle that some argue is the linchpin of the entire federal system is the notion of national supremacy. The supremacy clause contained in Article VI of the Constitution provides that the "Constitution, and the laws of the United States" as well as all treaties are to be the supreme law of the land. All national and state officers and officials are bound by oath to support the national Constitution above any state law or state constitution. As a result, any legitimate exercise of national power supersedes or preempts any conflicting state action. It is up to the federal courts to determine if such conflict exists. Where it does, national law is always to take precedence.

supremacy clause:

The law of the national government stands above any state law or state constitution.

The Articles of the Constitution

The document finally signed by the Framers condensed numerous resolutions into a Preamble and seven separate articles. The first three articles established the three branches of government, defined their internal operations, and clarified their relationships with one another. All branches of government were technically considered equal, yet some initially appeared more "equal" than others. It is likely that the order in which the articles appear, and especially the relative amount of detail in the first three articles, reflects the Framers' concern that the branches of the government might abuse their powers. The four remaining articles define the relationships among the states, declare national law to be supreme, and set out methods of amending the Constitution.

Article I: The Legislative Branch.   Article I vests all legislative powers in the Congress and establishes a bicameral legislature, consisting of the Senate and the House of Representatives. It also sets out the qualifications for holding office in each house,

■ Eagles on the backs of quarters are being replaced with designs from each of the fifty states. Five states will be featured each year from 1999 to 2008 as states get the opportunity to design the quarter based on the order that they ratified the Constitution or were admitted to statehood. (Photo courtesy: U.S. Treasury, U.S. Mint)

enumerated powers:

Seventeen specific powers granted to Congress under Article I, section 8, of the U.S. Constitution; these powers include taxation, coinage of money, regulation of commerce, and the authority to provide for a national defense.

elastic clause:

A name given to the "necessary and proper clause" found in the final paragraph of Article I, section 8, of the U.S. Constitution. It gives Congress the authority to pass all laws "necessary and proper" to carry out the enumerated powers specified in the Constitution.

the terms of office, methods of selection of representatives and senators, and the system of apportionment among the states to determine membership in the House of Representatives. Operating procedures and the officers for each house are also outlined and described.

Perhaps the most important section of Article I is section 8. It carefully lists the powers the Framers wished the new Congress to possess. These specified or **enumerated powers** contain many key provisions that had been denied to the Continental Congress under the Articles of Confederation. For example, one of the major weaknesses of the Articles was Congress's lack of authority to deal with trade wars. The Constitution remedied this problem by authorizing Congress to "regulate Commerce with foreign Nations, and among the several States." Congress was also given the authority to coin money.

Today, Congress often enacts legislation that no specific clause of Article 1, section 8, appears to authorize. Laws dealing with the environment, welfare, education, and communications, among others, are often justified by reference to a particular power plus the necessary and proper clause. After careful enumeration of seventeen powers of Congress in Article 1, section 8, a final, general clause authorizing Congress to "make all Laws which shall be necessary and proper for carrying into Execution the foregoing Powers" was added to Article I. Often referred to as the **elastic clause,** the necessary and proper clause has been a source of tremendous congressional activity never anticipated by the Framers, as definitions of "necessary" and "proper" have been stretched to accommodate changing needs and times. The Supreme Court, for example, has coupled Congress's authority to regulate commerce with the necessary and proper clause to allow Congress to ban prostitution (where travel across state lines is involved), regulate trains and planes, establish uniform federal minimum-wage and maximum-hour laws, and mandate drug testing for certain workers (see chapter 7).

Article II: The Executive Branch.   Article II vests the executive power, that is, the authority to execute the laws of the nation, in a president of the United States. Section 1 sets the president's term of office at four years and explains the electoral college. It also states qualifications for office and describes a mechanism to replace the president in case of death, disability, or removal.

The powers and duties of the president are set out in section 3. Among the most important of these are the president's role as commander-in-chief of the armed forces, the authority to make treaties with the consent of the Senate, and the authority to "appoint Ambassadors, other public Ministers and Consuls, the Judges of the supreme Court, and all other Officers of the United States." Other sections of Article II instruct the president to report directly to Congress "from time to time," in what has come to be known as the State of the Union Address, and to "take Care that the Laws be faithfully executed." Section 4 provides the mechanism for removal of the president, vice president, and other officers of the United States for "Treason, Bribery, or other high Crimes and Misdemeanors" (see chapter 8).

Article III: The Judicial Branch.   Article III establishes a Supreme Court and defines its jurisdiction. During the Philadelphia meeting, the small and large states differed significantly as to the desirability of an independent judiciary and on the role of state courts in the national court system. The smaller states feared that a strong unelected judiciary would trample on their liberties. In compromise, Congress was permitted, but not required, to establish lower national courts. Thus, state courts and the national court system would exist side by side with distinct areas of authority. Federal courts were given authority to decide cases arising under federal law. The Supreme Court was also given the power to settle disputes between states, or between a state and the national government.

Although some delegates to the convention had urged that the president be allowed to remove federal judges, ultimately judges were given appointments for life, presuming "good behavior." And, like the president's, their salaries cannot be lowered while they hold office. This provision was adopted to ensure that the legislature did not attempt to punish the Supreme Court or any other judges for unpopular decisions.

Judicial Review.   Perhaps the most important power of the Supreme Court, although it is not mentioned in the Constitution, is that of **judicial review,** the authority of a court to determine the constitutional validity of acts of the legislature. During the Constitutional Convention, the Framers debated and rejected the idea of a judicial veto of legislation or executive acts, and they rejected the Virginia Plan's proposal to give the judiciary explicit authority over Congress. They did, however, approve Article VI, which contains the supremacy clause discussed below.

In *Federalist No. 78,* Alexander Hamilton first publicly endorsed the idea of judicial review, noting, "whenever a particular statute contravenes the Constitution, it will be the duty of the judicial tribunals to adhere to the latter and disregard the former." Nonetheless, the actual authority of the Supreme Court to review acts of Congress to determine their constitutionality was an unsettled question. During its first decade, the Supreme Court (or justices riding circuit) had often reviewed acts of Congress, but it had not found any unconstitutional. But in *Marbury* v. *Madison* (1803), Chief Justice John Marshall claimed this sweeping authority for the Court by asserting the right of judicial review was a power that could be implied from the Constitution's supremacy clause.

Marbury v. *Madison* arose amidst a sea of political controversy. In the final hours of the Adams administration, William Marbury was appointed a justice of the peace for the District of Columbia. But in the confusion of winding up matters, John Marshall, Adams's Secretary of State, failed to deliver Marbury's commission. Marbury then asked James Madison, Thomas Jefferson's Secretary of State, for the commission. Under direct orders from Jefferson, who was irate over the Adams administration's last-minute appointment of several federal judges (quickly confirmed by the Federalist Senate), Madison refused to turn over the commission. Marbury and three other Adams appointees who were in the same situation then filed a writ of *mandamus* (a legal motion) asking the Supreme Court to order Madison to deliver their commissions.

Political tensions ran high as the Court met to hear the case. Jefferson threatened to ignore any order of the Court. Marshall realized that he and the prestige of the Court could be devastated by any refusal of the executive branch to comply with the decision. Responding to this challenge, in a brilliant opinion that in many sections reads more like a lecture to Jefferson than a discussion of the merits of Marbury's claim, Marshall concluded that although Marbury and the others were entitled to their commissions, the Court lacked the power to issue the writ sought by Marbury. In *Marbury* v. *Madison,* Marshall further ruled that the parts of the Judiciary Act of 1789, in which Congress had established the structure and operation of the federal court system and had extended the jurisdiction of the Court to allow it to issue writs, was inconsistent with the Constitution and therefore unconstitutional.

Although the immediate effect of the decision was to deny power to the Court, its long-term effect was to establish the rule articulated by Marshall in *Marbury* that "it is emphatically the province and duty of the judicial department to say what the law is." Through judicial review, a power that Marshall concluded could be implied from the

judicial review:

The authority of a court to review the acts of the legislature, the executive, or states to determine their constitutionality; enunciated by Chief Justice John Marshall in *Marbury* v. *Madison* (1803).

Marbury v. Madison (1803):

Supreme Court case in which the Court first asserted the power of judicial review in finding that a congressional statute extending the Court's original jurisdiction was unconstitutional.

Web Exploration
For the full text of *Marbury* v. *Madison,* see www.awlonline.com/oconnor.

Constitution, the Supreme Court can dramatically exert its authority to determine what the Constitution means. And since *Marbury,* the Court has routinely exercised the power of judicial review, an implied power, to determine the constitutionality of acts of Congress, the executive branch, and the states.

Articles IV through VII. Article IV begins with what is called the full faith and credit clause, which mandates that states honor the laws and judicial proceedings of the other states. Recently, for example, when it appeared that Hawaii might legalize same-sex marriages, the U.S. Congress passed the Defense of Marriage Act to allow states to disregard gay marriages even if they are legal in other states. Since no state has yet to legalize same-sex unions, this act has not been challenged in the federal courts. But, since the full faith and credit clause mandates that states recognize the laws of other states, some question about the legality of the federal law remains. Article IV also includes the mechanisms for admitting new states to the Union.

Article V specifies how amendments can be added to the Constitution. Article VI contains the supremacy clause. Mindful of the potential problems that could occur if church and state were too enmeshed, Article VI also specifies that no religious test shall be required for holding any office. The seventh and final article of the Constitution concerns the procedures for ratification of the new Constitution: Nine of the thirteen states would have to agree to, or ratify, its new provisions before it would become the supreme law of the land.

THE DRIVE FOR RATIFICATION

While delegates to the Constitutional Convention labored in Philadelphia, the Second Continental Congress continued to govern the former colonies under the Articles of Confederation. The day after the Constitution was signed, William Jackson, the secretary of the Constitutional Convention, left for New York City, then the nation's capital, to deliver the official copy of the document to the Congress. He also took with him a resolution of the delegates calling upon each of the states to vote on the new Constitution. Anticipating resistance from the representatives in the state legislatures, however, the Framers required the states to call special ratifying conventions to consider the proposed Constitution.

Jackson carried a letter from General George Washington with the proposed Constitution. In a few eloquent words, Washington summed up the sentiments of the Framers and the spirit of compromise that had permeated the long weeks in Philadelphia:

> That it will meet the full and entire approbation of every state is not perhaps to be expected, but each [state] will doubtless consider, that had her interest alone been consulted, the consequences might have been particularly disagreeable or injurious to others; that it is liable to as few exceptions as could reasonably have been expected, we hope and believe; that it may promote lasting welfare of that country so dear to us all, and secure her freedom and happiness is our ardent wish.[15]

The Second Continental Congress immediately accepted the work of the convention and forwarded the proposed Constitution to the states for their vote. It was by no means certain, however, that the new Constitution would be adopted. From the fall of 1787 to the summer of 1788, the proposed Constitution was debated hotly around the nation. State politicians understandably feared a strong central government. Farmers and other working-class people were fearful of a distant national government. And those who had accrued substantial debts during the economic chaos following the Revolutionary War feared that a new government with a new financial policy would plunge them into even greater debt. The public in general was very leery of taxes—these were the same people who had revolted against the king's taxes. At the heart of many of their concerns was an underlying fear of the massive changes that would be brought about by a new system. Favoring the Constitution were wealthy merchants, lawyers, bankers, and those who believed that the new nation could not continue to exist under the Articles of Confederation. For them, it all boiled down to one simple question offered by Madison: "Whether or not the Union shall or shall not be continued."

Federalists Versus Anti-Federalists

Almost as soon as the ink was dry on the last signature to the Constitution, those who favored the new strong national government chose to call themselves **Federalists.** They were well aware that many still generally opposed the notion of a strong national government. Thus they did not want to risk being labeled "nationalists," so they tried to get the upper hand in the debate by nicknaming their opponents **Anti-Federalists.** Those put in the latter category insisted that they were instead "Federal Republicans" who believed in a federal system. As noted in Table 2.1, Anti-Federalists argued that they simply wanted to protect state governments from the tyranny of a too-powerful national government.[16]

Federalists and Anti-Federalists participated in the mass meetings that were held in state legislatures to discuss the pros and cons of the new plan. Tempers ran high at public meetings, where differences between the opposing groups were highlighted. Fervent debates were published in newspapers. Indeed, newspapers played a powerful role in the adoption process. The entire Constitution, in fact, was printed in the *Pennsylvania Packet* just two days after the convention's end. Other major papers quickly followed suit. Soon articles on both sides of the adoption issue began to appear around the nation, often written under pseudonyms such as "Caesar" or "Constant Reader," as was the custom of the day.

One name stood out from all the rest: "Publius" (Latin for "the people"). Between October 1787 and May 1788, eighty-five articles written under that pen name routinely appeared in newspapers in New York, a state where ratification was in doubt. Most were written by Alexander Hamilton and James Madison. Hamilton, a young, fiery New Yorker born in the British West Indies, wrote fifty-one, Madison wrote twenty-six, and jointly they penned another three. John Jay, also of New York, and later the first Chief Justice of the United States, wrote five of the pieces. These eighty-five essays became known as *The Federalist Papers.*

Today *The Federalist Papers* are considered masterful explanations of the Framers' intentions as they drafted the new Constitution. At the time, although they were reprinted widely, they were far too theoretical to have much impact on those who would ultimately vote on the proposed Constitution. Dry and scholarly, they lacked the fervor of much of the political rhetoric that was then in use. *The Federalist Papers* did, however, highlight the reasons for the structure of the new government and its benefits. According to *Federalist No. 10*, for example, the new Constitution was called "a republican remedy for the disease incident to republican government." Moreover,

Federalists:
Those who favored a stronger national government and supported the proposed U.S. Constitution; later became the first U.S. political party.

Anti-Federalists:
Those who favored strong state governments and a weak national government; opposed the ratification of the U.S. Constitution.

The Federalist Papers:
A series of eighty-five political papers written by John Jay, Alexander Hamilton, and James Madison in support of ratification of the U.S. Constitution.

Table 2.1 Federalists and Anti-Federalists Compared

	Federalists	Anti-Federalists
Who were they?	Property owners, landed rich, merchants of Northeast and Middle Atlantic states	Small farmers, shopkeepers, laborers
Political philosophy	Elitist: saw themselves and those of their class as most fit to govern (others were to *be* governed)	Believed in the decency of the common man and in participatory democracy; viewed elites as corrupt; sought greater protection of individual rights
Type of government favored	Powerful central government; two-house legislature; upper house (six-year term) further removed from the people, whom they distrusted	Wanted stronger state governments (closer to the people) at the expense of the powers of the national government. Sought smaller electoral districts, frequent elections, referendum and recall, and a large unicameral legislature to provide for greater class and occupational representation
Alliances	Pro-British Anti-French	Anti-British Pro-French

■ James Madison (left), Alexander Hamilton (center), and John Jay (right) were important early Federalist leaders. Jay wrote five of *The Federalist Papers,* and Madison and Hamilton wrote the rest. Madison served in the House of Representative (1789–97) and as *secretary of state* in the Jefferson administration (1801–08). In 1808 he was elected fourth president of the United States and served two terms (1809–17). Hamilton became the first *secretary of the treasury* (1789–95) at the age of thirty-four. He was killed in 1804 in a duel with Vice President Aaron Burr, who was angered by Hamilton's negative comments about his character. Jay became the first *Chief Justice of the United States* (1789–95) and negotiated the Jay Treaty with Great Britain in 1794. He then served as governor of New York from 1795 to 1801. (Photos courtesy: left, Colonial Williamsburg Foundation; center, The Metropolitan Museum of Art, Gift of Henry G. Marquand, 1881 (81.11) copyright ©1987 by The Metropolitan Museum of Art; right, Corbis/Bettman)

TRY IT!

To compare the *The Federalist Papers* with the *Anti-Federalist Papers,* see www.awlonline.com/oconnor.

these musings of Madison, Hamilton, and Jay continue to be the best single source of the political theories and philosophies at the heart of our Constitution.

Forced on the defensive, the Anti-Federalists responded with their own series of "letters" written by Anti-Federalists adopting the pen names of "Brutus" and "Cato," two ancient Romans famous for their intolerance of tyranny. These "letters" (actually essays) undertook a line-by-line critique of the Constitution and were designed to counteract *The Federalist Papers.*

Anti-Federalists argued that a strong central government would render the states powerless.[17] They stressed the strengths the government had been granted under the Articles of Confederation, and argued that these Articles, not the proposed Constitution, created a true federal system. Moreover, they argued that the strong national government would tax heavily, that the Supreme Court would overwhelm the states by invalidating state laws, and that the president eventually would have too much power, as commander-in-chief of a large and powerful army.

In particular, the Anti-Federalists feared the power of the national government to run roughshod over the liberties of the people. They proposed that the taxing power of Congress be limited, that the executive be curbed by a council, that the military consist of state militias rather than a national force, and that the jurisdiction of the Supreme Court be limited to prevent it from reviewing and potentially overturning the decisions of state courts. But their most effective argument concerned the absence of a bill of rights in the Constitution. James Madison answered these criticisms in *Federalists Nos. 10* and *51.* (The texts of these two essays are printed in the Appendix.) In *Federalist No. 10,* he pointed out that the voters would not always succeed in electing "enlightened statesmen" as their representatives. The greatest threat to individual liberties would therefore come from factions within the government, who might place narrow interests above broader national interests and the rights of citizens. While recognizing that no form of government could protect the country from unscrupulous politicians, Madison argued that the organization of the new government would minimize the effects of political factions. The great advantage of a federal system, Madison maintained, was that it created the "happy combination" of a national government too large to be controlled by any single faction, and several state governments that would be smaller and more responsive to local needs. Moreover, he argued in *Federalist No. 51* that the proposed federal government's separation of powers would prohibit any one branch from either dominating the national government or violating the rights of citizens.

Debate continued in the thirteen states as votes were taken from December 1787 to June 1788, in accordance with the ratifying process laid out in Article VII of the proposed Constitution. Three states acted quickly to ratify the new Constitution. Two small states, Delaware and New Jersey, voted to ratify before the large states could rethink the notion of equal representation of the states in the Senate. Pennsylvania, where Federalists were well organized, was one of the first three states to ratify. Massachusetts assented to the new government but tempered its support by calling for an immediate addition of amendments including one protecting personal rights. New Hampshire became the crucial ninth state to ratify on June 21, 1788. This action completed the ratification process outlined in Article VII of the Constitution and marked the beginning of a new nation. But because New York and Virginia (which between them accounted for more than 40 percent of the new nation's population) had not yet ratified the Constitution, the practical future of the new nation remained in doubt.

Hamilton in New York and Madison in Virginia worked feverishly to convince delegates to their state conventions to vote for the new government. In New York, sentiment against it was high. In Albany, fighting broke out over the proposed Constitution, resulting in injuries and death. When news of Virginia's acceptance of the Constitution reached the New York convention, Hamilton was finally able to convince a majority of those present to follow suit by a narrow margin of three votes. Both states also recommended the addition of a series of structural amendments, and a bill of rights.

Two of the original states—North Carolina and Rhode Island—continued to hold out against ratification. Both had recently printed new currencies and feared that values would plummet in a federal system where the Congress was authorized to coin money. On August 2, 1788, North Carolina became the first state to reject the Constitution on the grounds that no Anti-Federalist amendments were included. Soon after Congress submitted a **Bill of Rights** in September 1789, North Carolina ratified the Constitution by a vote of 194 to 77. Rhode Island, the only state that had not sent representatives to Philadelphia, remained out of the Union until 1790. Finally, under threats from its largest cities to secede from the state, the legislature called a convention that ratified the Constitution by only two votes (34 to 32)—one year after George Washington became the first president of the United States (see Table 2.2).

Bill of Rights:

The first ten amendments to the U.S. Constitution.

Table 2.2   Ratification of the Constitution, by State

State	Date of Ratification	Vote
Delaware	Dec. 7, 1787	30–0
Pennsylvania	Dec. 12, 1787	43–23
New Jersey	Dec. 18, 1787	38–0
Georgia	Jan. 2 1788	25–0
Connecticut	Jan. 9, 1788	128–40
Massachusetts	Feb. 16, 1788	187–168
Maryland	April 26, 1788	63–11
South Carolina	May 23, 1788	149–73
New Hampshire	June 21, 1788	57–46
Virginia	June 25, 1788	89–79
New York	June 26, 1788	30–27
North Carolina*	Nov. 21, 1789	194–77
Rhode Island	May 29, 1790	34–32

*Ratification originally defeated in August, 1788.

FORMAL METHODS OF AMENDING THE CONSTITUTION

Once the Constitution was ratified, elections were held. When Congress convened, it immediately sent a set of amendments to the states for their ratification. An amendment authorizing the enlargement of the House of Representatives and another to prevent members of the House from raising their own salaries failed to garner favorable votes in the necessary three-fourths of the states. (See Highlight 2.2 The Twenty-Seventh (Madison) Amendment.) The remaining ten amendments, known as the Bill of Rights, were ratified by 1791 in accordance with the procedures set out in the Constitution (see Table 2.3). Sought by Anti-Federalists as a protection for individual liberties, they offered numerous specific limitations on the national government's ability to interfere with a wide variety of personal liberties, some of which were already guaranteed by many state constitutions (see chapters 5 and 6).

The Bill of Rights includes numerous specific protections of personal rights. Freedom of expression, speech, press, religion, and assembly are guaranteed by the First Amendment. The Bill of Rights also contains numerous safeguards for those accused of crimes.

In addition to guaranteeing these important rights, two of the amendments of the Bill of Rights were reactions to British rule—the right to bear arms (Second Amendment) and the right not to have soldiers quartered in private homes (Third Amendment). More general rights are also included in the Bill of Rights. The Ninth Amendment notes that these enumerated rights are not inclusive, meaning they are not the only rights to be enjoyed by the people, and the Tenth Amendment states that powers not given to the national government are reserved by the states or the people.

The Amendment Process

Article V of the Constitution creates a two-stage amendment process: proposal and ratification.[18] The Constitution specifies two ways to accomplish each stage. As illustrated in Figure 2.3, amendments to the Constitution can be proposed by:

1. A vote of two-thirds of the members in both houses of Congress; or
2. A vote of two-thirds of the state legislatures specifically requesting Congress to call a national convention to propose amendments.

Table 2.3   The Bill of Rights*

First Amendment	Freedom of religion, speech, press, and assembly
Second Amendment	The right to bear arms
Third Amendment	Prohibition against quartering of troops in private homes
Fourth Amendment	Prohibition against unreasonable searches and seizures
Fifth Amendment	Rights guaranteed to the accused; requirement for grand jury indictment; protections against double jeopardy, self-incrimination; due process guaranteed
Sixth Amendment	Right to a speedy and public trial before an impartial jury, to cross-examine witnesses, and to have counsel
Seventh Amendment	Right to a trial by jury in civil suits
Eighth Amendment	Prohibition against excessive bail and fines, and cruel and unusual punishment
Ninth Amendment	Rights not listed in the Constitution retained by the people
Tenth Amendment	States or people reserve those powers not denied to them by the Constitution or delegated to the national government

*For the full text of the Bill of Rights, see Appendix II.

HIGHLIGHT 2.2

On June 8, 1789, in a speech before the House of Representatives, James Madison stated.

[T]here is seeming impropriety in leaving any set of men without controul [sic] to put their hand into the public coffers, to take out money to put into their pockets. . . . I have gone therefore so far as to fix it, that no law, varying the compensation, shall operate until there is a change in the legislation.

When Madison spoke these words about his proposal, now known as the Twenty-Seventh Amendment, he had no way of knowing that more than two centuries would pass before it would become an official part of the Constitution.

Gregory Watson with a document that contains the first ten amendments to the Constitution, as well as the compensation amendment ("Article the second: No law varying the compensation for the services of the Senators and Representatives shall take effect until an election of Representatives shall have intervened"), which was finally ratified as the Twenty-Seventh Amendment in 1992. (Photo courtesy: Ziggy Kaluzny/*People* Weekly © 1993)

In fact, Madison deemed it worthy of addition only because the conventions of three states (Virginia, New York, and North Carolina) had demanded that it be included.

By 1791, when the Bill of Rights was added to the Constitution, only six states had ratified Madison's amendment, and it seemed destined to fade into obscurity. In 1982, however, Gregory Watson, a sophomore majoring in economics at the University of Texas-Austin, discovered the unratified compensation amendment while looking for a paper topic for an American government class. Intrigued, Watson wrote a paper arguing that the proposed amendment was still viable because it had no internal time limit and, therefore, should still be ratified. Watson received a "C" on the paper.

Despite his grade, Watson began a ten-year, $6,000 self-financed crusade to renew interest in the compensation amendment. Watson and his allies reasoned that the amendment should be revived because of the public's growing anger with the fact that members of Congress had sought to raise their salaries without going on the record as having done so. Watson's perseverance paid off, and on May 7, 1992, the amendment was ratified by the requisite thirty-eight states. On May 18, the United States Archivist certified that the amendment was part of the Constitution, a decision that was overwhelmingly confirmed by the House of Representatives on May 19 and by the Senate on May 20.

At the same time that the Senate approved the Twenty-Seventh Amendment, it also took action to ensure that a similar situation would never occur by declaring "dead" four other amendments that did not have internal deadlines.

Source: Fordham Law Review (December 1992): 497–539, and Anne Marie Kilday, "Amendment Expert Agrees with Congressional Pay Ruling." *The Dallas Morning News* (February 14, 1993): 13A.

Figure 2.3   Methods of Amending the Constitution

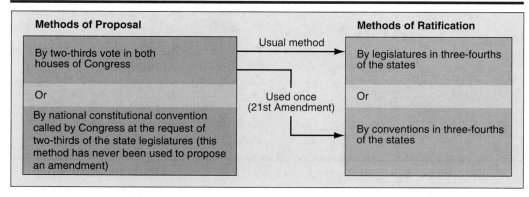

Methods of Proposal		Methods of Ratification
By two-thirds vote in both houses of Congress	Usual method →	By legislatures in three-fourths of the states
Or	Used once (21st Amendment)	Or
By national constitutional convention called by Congress at the request of two-thirds of the state legislatures (this method has never been used to propose an amendment)		By conventions in three-fourths of the states

■ For all its moral foundation in groups such as the Women's Christian Temperance Union (WCTU) (left), whose members invaded bars to protest the sale of alcoholic beverages, the Eighteenth Amendment was a disaster. Among its side effects were the rise of powerful crime organizations responsible for (among other things) the cache of over 3,000 bags of bottled beverages uncovered by federal agents (right). Once proposed, it took only ten months to ratify the Twenty-First Amendment, which repealed the Prohibition amendment. (Photos courtesy: left, Hulton Getty/Liaison Agency; right, AP/World Wide Photos)

Web Exploration

For the text of these failed amendments see
www.awlonline.com/oconnor.

The second method has never been used. Historically, it has served as a fairly effective threat, forcing Congress to consider amendments that might otherwise never have been debated. In the 1980s, for example, several states called on Congress to enact a balanced-budget amendment. To forestall the need for a special constitutional convention, Congress enacted the Gramm-Rudman-Hollings Act, which called for a balanced budget. When that act proved ineffective, the 104th Congress took up the issue of passage of a Balanced Budget Amendment as one of its planks in what Republicans term their "Contract with America."

Of the more than 10,000 amendments that have been introduced on one or both floors of the Congress, only thirty-three mustered the two-thirds vote required for them to be sent to the states for debate and ratification through 1999. Only six proposed amendments sent to the states failed to be ratified.

The ratification process is fairly straightforward. When Congress votes to propose an amendment, the Constitution specifies that the ratification process must occur in one of two ways:

1. A favorable vote in three-fourths of the state legislatures; or
2. A favorable vote in specially called ratifying conventions in three-fourths of the states.

The Constitution itself, however, was to be ratified by specially called ratifying conventions. The Framers feared that the power of special interests in state legislatures would prevent a positive vote on the new Constitution. Since ratification of the Constitution, however, only one ratifying convention has been called. The Eighteenth Amendment, which caused the Prohibition Era by outlawing the sale of alcoholic beverages, was ratified by the first method—a vote in state legislatures. Millions broke the law, others died from drinking homemade liquor, and still others made their fortunes

GLOBAL POLITICS

Comparing Constitutions

Americans are used to the idea of a durable written constitution. The U. S. Constitution stands out not only for being the first written constitution in the modern world (Poland followed soon after, in 1790), but because it remains the constitution of the United States today. In fact, the American case is rather anomalous, both in the number of constitutions it has had (two, if we count the Articles of Confederation) and in the continuity of the basic political rules it outlined. Among the G-7 countries, only Canada and the United Kingdom have had similar experience with a single constitution. Yet Canada's constitutional history is nearly a century shorter than that of the United States. Britain's single constitution is unwritten and has evolved over centuries (parts of it date to the Middle Ages), rendering it difficult to compare with a written constitution.

More typically, the European countries and Japan have had multiple constitutions. France is the extreme example, with fifteen constitutional regimes since 1789 (five in the first decade after the French Revolution). Most interesting for our purposes, those constitutions have established a wide range of political systems. Since 1789, France has had monarchies, republics, a commune, and a dictatorship in collaboration with a foreign occu-

pier. Germany's, Italy's, and Japan's first constitutions were anti-democratic monarchies. Italy and Germany had fascist constitutional systems in the 1930s and early 1940s. Germany, moreover, had two competing constitutional systems during the Cold War, with a parliamentary democracy in West Germany and a Soviet-style socialist political system in East Germany. In Germany and Japan, postwar occupations by outside powers led to new constitutions. In sum, the United States' constitutional history is rather remarkable for its continuity under a single written document.

Constitutions in the G-7 States

Country	Number of Constitutions	Year First Constitution Was Established
Canada	1	1867
France	15	1789
Germany	5	1870
Italy	3	1870
Japan	2	1890
United Kingdom	1	na
United States	**2**	**1777**

selling bootleg or illegal liquor. After a decade of these problems, Congress decided to act. An additional amendment—the Twenty-First—was proposed to repeal the Eighteenth Amendment. It was sent to the states for ratification, but with a call for ratifying conventions, not a vote in the state legislatures.[19] Members of Congress correctly predicted that the move to repeal the Eighteenth Amendment would encounter opposition in the statehouses, which were largely controlled by conservative rural interests. Thus, Congress's decision to use the convention method led to quick approval of the Twenty-First Amendment.

The intensity of efforts to amend the Constitution has varied considerably, depending on the nature of the change proposed. Whereas the Twenty-First Amendment took only ten months to ratify, an equal rights amendment (ERA) was introduced in every session of Congress from 1923 until 1972, when Congress finally voted favorably on it. Even then, years of lobbying by women's groups were insufficient to garner necessary state support. By 1982, the congressionally mandated date for ratification, only thirty-five states—three short of the number required—had voted favorably on the amendment.[20]

INFORMAL METHODS OF AMENDING THE CONSTITUTION

The Framers did not want to fashion a government that could respond to the whims of the people. The separation of powers and the checks and balances systems are just two indications of the Framers' recognition of the importance of deliberation and thought as a check against both government tyranny and the rash judgments of intemperate majorities. James Madison, in particular, wanted to draft a system of government that would pit faction against faction, and ambition against ambition,

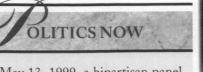

POLITICS NOW

Amending the Constitution

On May 13, 1999, a bipartisan panel brought together by Citizens for the Constitution, a project of the Century Foundation led by former members of Congress, "expressed dismay at the flurry of proposed constitutional amendments in recent years,"[a] ranging from those designed to overturn a Supreme Court decision allowing flag burning, to a balanced budget, to term limits. The Republicans' "Contract with America" and its 1996 party platform, in particular, called for several changes in the U.S. Constitution that would revolutionize the document. At no other time since the founding, when the Bill of Rights was added to the Constitution, have so many amendments been suggested.

In 1998, Congress began to act on some of those proposals. To reverse what its supporters called three decades of court rulings that have stifled religious expression, the House of Representatives voted 224–203 for what was called the religious freedom constitutional amendment. As drafted, it would have allowed prayer in public schools, religious icons on government land and property, and state support of parochial schools. The amendment, however, fell 65 votes short of the two-thirds needed to send it to the states for their ratification.

In April 1999, the Senate Judiciary Subcommittee's on the Constitution, Federalism, and Property Rights approved SJR 114 on a party line vote to override *Texas* v. *Johnson* (1989), in which the Supreme Court ruled that flag burning was a form of political speech protected by the First Amendment (see chapter 5). This was the third attempt by the Republican-led Congress to overrule the five to four Supreme Court decision.[b] In May 1999, however, supporters again fell short of the two-thirds vote needed to send the amendment to the states.

Interestingly, the proposed amendments appear to have public support. In 1999, 63 percent of those polled said that it was "worth it" to amend the Constitution to make flag burning illegal.[c] Nearly three-fourths of the men (74%) and 83.5% of the women polled believed that it should be illegal to burn the American flag.[d] In spite of these kinds of sentiments, the bipartisan panel believes that the Constitution should only be amended as a "last resort."[e] "We don't believe that the Constitution is a static document that should never be amended," said the director of the project. "But we do believe that the fundamentally conservative approach that the founders created is the right one."[f]

Among the panel's recommendations to prevent what it views as unnecessary changes to the Constitution are: (1) ratification periods should be fixed with no provisions for extension (as happened in the ERA effort); (2) only amendments presenting issues of "abiding importance" for future generations should be considered; and (3) "significant practical and legal obstacles" must make it nearly impossible to bring about the objectives by any other legal means.[g]

[a]Ben White, "Bipartisan Panel Urges Restraint on Constitutional Amendments," *The Washington Post* (May 14, 1999): A9.
[b]Molly Peterson, "Senate Panel Approves Constitutional Ban on Flag Desecration," LEGI-SLATE, http://www.legislate.com/xp/p-daily/i-19990422101/a-924733492/article.view
[c]The Washington Post Opinion Research Archive.
[d]The Washington Post Opinion Research Archive.
[e]White, "Bipartisan Panel."
[f]White, "Bipartisan Panel."
[g]White, "Bipartisan Panel."

to design a system of representation and policy making that would strengthen minority factions against possible encroachments by majority factions. Although it took a long time, the Constitution was eventually amended to protect the rights of African Americans through the addition of the Thirteenth, Fourteenth, and Fifteenth amendments.

The Framers also made the formal amendment process a slow one to ensure that amendments were not added lightly to the Constitution. But the formal amendment process is not the only way that the Constitution has been changed over time. Judicial interpretation and cultural and social change also have had a major impact on the way the Constitution has evolved.

Judicial Interpretation

As early as 1803, under the brilliant leadership of Chief Justice John Marshall, the Supreme Court declared that the federal courts had the power to nullify acts of the nation's government when they were found to be in conflict with the Constitution. Over the years, this check on the other branches of government and on the states has increased the authority of the Court and has significantly altered the meaning of various provisions of the Constitution, a fact that prompted Woodrow Wilson to call the Supreme Court "a con-

DOONESBURY

Garry Trudeau

stitutional convention in continuous session." (More detail on the Supreme Court's role in interpreting the Constitution is found in chapters 5, 6, and 10 especially, as well as in other chapters in the book.)

Today some argue that the original intent of the Framers, as evidenced in *The Federalist Papers* as well as in private notes taken by James Madison at the Constitutional Convention, should govern judicial interpretation of the Constitution.[21] Others argue that the Framers knew that a changing society needed an elastic, flexible document that could conform to the ages.[22] In all likelihood, the vagueness of the document was purposeful. Those in attendance in Philadelphia recognized that they could not agree on everything and that it was wiser to leave interpretation to those who would follow them.

Recently, law professor Mark V. Tushnet has offered a particularly stinging criticism of any kind of judicial review and exclusive reliance on the courts to say what the Constitution means.[23] He believes that we must create a "populist" constitutional law that allows people to believe that they have the right to enforce the Constitution and not leave it up to the courts. To give this power to the courts, says Tushnet, necessarily means that "We, the People," envisioned by the Framers, lose sight of the true meaning of the Constitution.

Social and Cultural Change

Even the most far-sighted of those in attendance at the Constitutional Convention could not have anticipated the vast changes that have occurred in the United States. For example, although many were uncomfortable with the Three-Fifths Compromise and others hoped for the abolition of slavery, none could have imagined the status of African Americans today, or that Colin Powell could serve as Chairman of the Joint Chiefs of Staff and have been frequently mentioned as a viable candidate for president or vice president in 1996. Likewise, few of the Framers could have anticipated the diverse roles that women would come to play in American society. The Constitution has often been bent to accommodate such social and cultural changes. Thus, although there is no specific amendment guaranteeing women equal protection of the law, the federal courts have interpreted the Constitution to prohibit many forms of gender discrimination, thereby recognizing cultural and societal change.

Social change has also caused changes in the way institutions of government act. Thus, as problems such as the Great Depression appeared national in scope, Congress took on more and more power at the expense of the states to solve the economic and social crisis. Today, however, Congress is moving to return much of that power to the states. The actions of the 104th and 105th Congresses to return powers and responsibilities to the states, for example, may be viewed as an *informal* attempt not necessarily to amend the Constitution but to return the balance of power between the national and state government to that which the Framers intended. Again, within the parameters of its constitutional powers, the Congress acted as the Framers intended without changing the document itself.

Advances in technology have also brought about constitutional change. Wiretapping and other forms of electronic surveillance, for example, are now regulated by the First and Fourth Amendments. Similarly, HIV testing must be balanced against constitutional protections. And all kinds of new constitutional questions are posed in the wake of congressional efforts to regulate what kinds of information can be disseminated on the Internet. Still, in spite of these massive changes, the Constitution still survives, changed and ever changing after more than 200 years.

CONTINUITY and Change

Counting Americans

The U.S. Constitution specifically requires that "representatives and direct Taxes shall be apportioned among the several States . . . according to their respective numbers. . . . The actual Enumeration shall be made within three Years after the first Meeting of the Congress of the United States, and within every subsequent Term of ten Years in such a Manner as they shall by Law direct." In response to this, the first national census was taken in 1790.[a] But, the process itself was very crude. U.S. Marshals and their assistants, providing their own paper, took eighteen months to collect all of the data. And, unlike today, when all personal census survey data is confidential, law required that all local reports be posted in at least two public places.

For years, census data were tabulated by hand. In 1890 a punch card tabulating system was created, revolutionizing the process and allowing for quicker tabulation of data. Over time, the compiling of the U.S. Census has become more and more complex in response to changing governmental needs and well as changing technology. And, as the national government has grown, so have the kinds of data collected by the Census Bureau.

By 1990 the nation had grown so large that even the Census Bureau admitted that, for the first time, its report was more inaccurate than the one before it.[b] Millions of people, especially the poor, homeless, and minorities, were undercounted. Since the allocation of federal dollars, as well as congressional representation, is based on the results of the diennial censuses, urban centers and the Democratic Party cried foul since they believed that they were the most hurt by the undercounting of as many as 5.3 million people. Lawsuits were filed even before the 1990 Census challenging its methods, and in 1991 Congress passed legislation to compel the Census Bureau to contract with the nonpartisan National Academy of Sciences to study more accurate means for the 2000 Census. One of the means suggested was to sample the population. Actually, the Census Bureau began to use sampling in 1940, asking only every fourth household some more detailed questions.

But this is not the kind of sampling that was suggested by the Clinton administration and subsequently rejected by the Supreme Court in 1999.[c] It wanted to be able to adjust the count to include people that the current system was likely to miss. The Court, however, ruled that sampling could not be used to count citizens for the purposes of reallocating congressional seats among the states, although it didn't prohibit the use of sampling-adjusted numbers when states draw their own congressional and legislative district lines.

The Census has far more political overtones than the Framers envisioned. Sampling is a well-recognized statistical technique, yet its use to "remedy" undercounting is highly contentious. In the future, the Census Bureau will continue to be challenged to come up with more accurate measures to count the population. With increasing use of multiple data bases, one might envision some sort of superdata base that could be combined and refigured to enhance the chances that everyone gets counted.

1. What kind of process might be developed to make sure that undercounting, particularly of certain populations with discrete interests, does not occur in the future?
2. How critical do you believe a totally accurate census is to the national government's ability to maintain a representative democracy?

Cast Your Vote.   Which method of census-taking do you prefer? To cast your vote, go to www.awlonline.com/oconnor.

[a]This box draws heavily on information provided by the U.S. Department of Commerce. See U.S. Bureau of the Census, "History and Organization," May 1988. Mimeo.
[b]Wisconsin v. City of New York, 517 U.S. 1 (1996) and Sheldon T. Bradshaw, Note, "Death, Taxes, and Census Litigation: Do the Equal Protection and Apportionment Clauses Guarantee a Constitutional Right to Census Accuracy?" George Washington University Law Review (1996) LEXIS.
[c]DOC v. United States House of Representatives, 119 S.Ct. 765 (1999)

SUMMARY

The U.S. Constitution has proven to be a remarkably enduring document. In explaining how and why the Constitution came into being, this chapter has covered the following points:

1. THE ORIGINS OF A NEW NATION

While settlers came to the New World for a variety of reasons, most remained loyal to Great Britain and considered themselves subjects of the king. Over the years, as new generations of Americans were born on colonial soil, those ties weakened. A series of taxes levied by the Crown ultimately led the colonists to convene a Continental Congress and to declare their independence.

2. THE DECLARATION OF INDEPENDENCE

The Declaration of Independence (1776), which drew heavily on the writings of John Locke, carefully enumerated the wrongs of the Crown and galvanized public resentment and willingness to take up arms against Great Britain in the Revolutionary War (1775–82).

3. THE FIRST ATTEMPT AT GOVERNMENT: THE ARTICLES OF CONFEDERATION

The Articles of Confederation (1781) created a loose league of friendship between the new national government and the states. Numerous weaknesses in the new government became apparent by 1784. Among the major flaws were Congress's inability to tax or regulate commerce, the absence of an executive to administer the government, and a weak central government.

4. THE MIRACLE AT PHILADELPHIA: WRITING A CONSTITUTION

When the weaknesses under the Articles of Confederation became apparent, the states called for a meeting to reform them. The Constitutional Convention (1787) quickly threw out the Articles of Confederation and fashioned a new, more workable form of government. The Constitution was the result of a series of compromises, including those over representation, questions involving large and small states, and over how to determine population. Compromises were also made about how members of each branch of government were to be selected. The electoral college was created to give states a key role in the selection of the president.

5. THE U.S. CONSTITUTION

The proposed U.S. Constitution created a federal system that drew heavily on Montesquieu's ideas about separation of powers. These ideas concerned a way of parceling out power among the three branches of government, and checks and balances to prevent any one branch from having too much power.

6. THE DRIVE FOR RATIFICATION

The drive for ratification became a fierce fight between Federalists and Anti-Federalists. Federalists lobbied for the strong national government created by the Constitution; Anti-Federalists favored greater state power.

7. FORMAL METHODS OF AMENDING THE CONSTITUTION

The Framers created a formal two-stage amendment process to include the Congress and the states. Amendments could be proposed by a two-thirds vote in Congress or of state legislatures requesting that Congress call a national convention to propose amendments. Amendments could be ratified by a positive vote of three-fourths of the state legislatures or specially called state ratifying conventions.

8. INFORMAL METHODS OF AMENDING THE CONSTITUTION

The formal amendment process is not the only way that the Constitution can be changed. Judicial interpretation and cultural and technological changes have also caused constitutional change.

KEY TERMS

Anti-Federalists, p. 57
Articles of Confederation, p. 44
Bill of Rights, p. 59
checks and balances, p. 51
Committees of Correspondence, p. 40
confederation, p. 42
Declaration of Independence, p. 43
elastic clause, p. 54

enumerated powers, p. 54
federal system, p. 51
The Federalist Papers, p. 57
Federalists, p. 57
First Continental Congress, p. 41
Great Compromise, p. 49
judicial review, p. 55
Marbury v. *Madison*, (1803) p. 55
New Jersey Plan, p. 48

Second Continental Congress, p. 42
separation of powers, p. 51
Shays's Rebellion, p. 46
Stamp Act Congress, p. 39
supremacy clause, p. 53
Three-Fifths Compromise, p. 49
Virginia Plan, p. 48

SELECTED READINGS

Bailyn, Bernard. *The Ideological Origins of the American Revolution.* Cambridge, MA: Belknap Press, 1992.

Beard, Charles Austin. *An Economic Interpretation of the Constitution of the United States.* (reissue edition) New York: Free Press, 1996.

Bernstein, Richard B., with Jerome Agel. *Amending America.* Lawrence: University of Kansas Press, 1995.

Bowen, Catherine Drinker. *Miracle at Philadelphia.* Boston: Little, Brown, 1986.

Brinkley, Alan, Nelson W. Polsby and Kathleen M. Sullivan, *New Federalist Papers: Essays in Defense of the Constitution.* New York: Norton, 1997.

Hamilton, Alexander, James Madison, and John Jay. *The Federalist Papers.* New York: Bantam Books, 1989 (first published in 1788).

Ketchman, Ralph, ed. *The Anti-Federalist Papers and the Constitutional Convention Debated.* New York: Mentor Books, 1996.

Kyvig, David E. *Explicit and Authentic Acts: Amending the U.S. Constitution, 1776–1995.* Lawrence: University of Kansas Press, 1996.

Levy, Leonard W., ed. *Essays on the Making of the Constitution,* 2d ed. New York: Oxford University Press, 1987.

Main, Jackson Turner. *The Social Structure of Revolutionary America.* Princeton, NJ: Princeton University Press, 1965.

Rossiter, Clinton. *1787: Grand Convention.* (reissue edition) New York: Norton, 1987.

Stoner, James R. Jr. *Common Law and Liberal Theory.* University Press of Kansas, Lawrence, Kan. 1992.

Vile, John R. *Encyclopedia of Constitutional Amendments, and Amending Issues, 1789–1995.* Santa Barbara, CA: ABC-CLIO, 1996.

Wood, Gordon S. *The Creation of the American Republic, 1776–1787.* (reissue edition) New York: Norton, 1993.

NOTES

1. See Richard B. Bernstein with Jerome Agel, *Amending America* (New York: New York Times Books, 1993), 138–140.

2. *Oregon* v. *Mitchell, 400* U.S. *112* (1970).

3. Bernstein with Agel, *Amending America,* 139.

4. For an account of the early development of the colonies, see D. W. Meining, *The Shaping of America,* vol. 1. *Atlantic America, 1492 1800* (New Haven, CT: Yale University Press, 1986).

5. For an excellent chronology of the events leading up to the writing of the Declaration of Independence and the colonists' break with Great Britain, see Calvin D. Lonton, ed., *The Bicentennial Almanac* (Nashville, TN: Thomas Nelson, 1975).

6. See Gary Wills, *Inventing America: Jefferson's Declaration of Independence* (New York: Random House, 1978). Wills argues that the Declaration was signed solely to secure foreign aid for the ongoing war effort.

7. See Gordon Wood, *The Creation of the American Republic, 1776–1787* (Chapel Hill: University of North Carolina Press, 1969).

8. For more about the Articles of Confederation, see Merrill Jensen, *The Articles of Confederation* (Madison: University of Wisconsin Press, 1940).

9. Quoted in Selma R. Williams, *Fifty-Five Fathers: The Story of the Constitutional Convention* (New York: Dodd, Mead, 1970), 10.

10. Quoted in Doris Faber and Harold Faber, *We the People* (New York: Charles Scribner's Sons, 1987), 31.

11. For more on the political nature of compromise at the convention, see Calvin C. Jillson, *Constitution Making: Conflict and Consensus in the Federal Constitution of 1787* (New York: Agathon, 1988).

12. Quoted in Richard N. Current, T. Harry Williams, Frank Freidel, and Alan Brinkley, *American History: A Survey,* 6th ed. (New York: Random House, 1983), 168.

13. Bernard Bailyn, *The Ideological Origins of the American Revolution* (Cambridge, MA: Harvard University Press, 1967).

14. Richard E. Neustadt, *Presidential Power: The Politics of Leadership from FDR to Carter* (New York: Macmillan, 1980), 26.

15. Quoted in Faber and Faber, *We the People,* 51–52.

16. Federal Republicans favored a republican or representative form of government (do not confuse this term with the modern Republican Party, which came into being in 1854; see chapter 12). Ultimately, the word *federal* came to mean the form of government embodied in the new Constitution, just as *confederation* meant the "league of states" under the Articles, and later came to mean the "Confederacy" of 1861–65.

17. See Ralph Ketcham, ed., *The Anti-Federalist Papers and the Constitutional Debates* (New York: New American Library, 1986).

18. See Alan P. Grimes, *Democracy and the Amendments to the Constitution* (Lexington, MA: Lexington Books, 1978).

19. David E. Kyvig, *Repealing National Prohibition* (Chicago: University of Chicago Press, 1978).

20. See Jane J. Mansbridge, *Why We Lost the ERA* (Chicago: University of Chicago Press, 1986).

21. Speech by Attorney General Edwin Meese III before the American Bar Association, July 9, 1985, Washington, D.C. See also Antonin Scalia and Amy Gutman, eds. *A Matter of Interpretation: Federal Courts and the Law* (Princeton, NJ: Princeton University Press, 1998).

22. Speech by William J. Brennan, Jr., at Georgetown University, Text and Teaching Symposium, October 10, 1985, Washington, D.C.

23. Mark V. Tushnet, *Taking the Constitution Away from the Courts* (Princeton, NJ: Princeton University Press, 1999).

(Photo courtesy: Mark Leffingwell/AP/Wide World Photos)

Federalism

■ The Roots of the Federal System
■ The Powers of Government in the Federal System
■ The Evolution and Development of Federalism
■ Federalism and the Supreme Court

A 1998 ruling by the U.S. Supreme Court brought an end to a long controversy between New York and New Jersey over title to Ellis Island, the home of the Statue of Liberty.[1] An 1834 compact between the two states set the boundary lines between them as the middle of the Hudson River and gave New York authority over the island even though Ellis Island was on the New Jersey side of the Hudson. New Jersey, however, retained rights to submerged lands on its side. In 1993, New Jersey finally filed suit to gain a final resolution of the issue.

Beginning in 1891, when the U.S. government decided to make Ellis Island the gateway to process the flood of immigrants coming to its shores, it also began to fill in around the island's natural shoreline. Eventually 24.5 acres were added to the original island, increasing its size considerably.

While the outcome of the lawsuit filed by New Jersey has little practical impact, prestige was on the line. Both states wanted bragging rights to this major tourist attraction that now houses a huge museum dedicated to those who passed through its buildings on the way to seeking the American dream.[2]

Because two states were involved, the U.S. Supreme Court had what is called original jurisdiction over the case, a term discussed in greater detail in chapter 9. A Special Master was appointed by the Court to investigate the dispute and to report back his findings to the justices. In 1998 the Court ultimately ruled that although New York claimed the land, New Jersey actual had all the rights to the "new lands" added by the federal government to the Island but New York retained title to the visitors center and museum.

The states didn't go to war over this boundary dispute; they went to court. When the Framers created the federal system, they were mindful that disputes might arise between the states. Thus they empowered the Supreme Court to serve as a trial court in these circumstances to provide each state with as fair of a hearing as possible.

Web Exploration

For a directory of federalism links, see www.awlonline.com/oconnor.

Web Exploration

For more on your state and local government, see www.awlonline.com/oconnor.

■ Among issues behind the move to return power to the states are government regulations affecting the environment. Swimming and fishing restrictions such as this one protect people from hazardous lake conditions. (Photo courtesy: Alan Reininger/Contact Press Images)

he Framers were mindful of the need for government as well as one unifying body of law, and that was the U.S. Constitution. Thus over 87,000 different state and local governments, including new Jersey and New York, are ultimately bound by its provisions (see Figure 3.1). This is not to say, however, that many citizens and their elected representatives have been working through legal channels to divest the national government of some of the enormous powers it has amassed over the years since the states initially ratified the Constitution. Many Americans simply believe that the national government takes far too great a role in issues such as welfare, education, land use, and health care.

According to a poll conducted in 1995 for *Time*/CNN, 75 percent of Americans support having the "states take over more responsibilities now performed by the federal government."[3] Many, however, have probably not considered all of the ramifications of such a devolution. What happens if one state allows companies to pollute waterways that flow into adjoining states? Are state governments and state bureaucracies better equipped to handle welfare, medical care, job training, or other problems associated with poverty? And with more responsibilities comes the need for more funds. Will states begin to raise taxes? It's unlikely. With states taking on more responsibilities but having less money to execute them, everyone may have to make do with fewer governmental programs, no matter how beneficial or laudatory their goals.

From its very beginning, the challenge for the United States of America was to preserve the traditional independence and rights of the states while establishing an effective national government. In *Federalist No. 51,* James Madison highlighted the unique structure of governmental powers created by the Framers:

> The power surrendered by the people is first divided between two distinct governments, and then . . . subdivided among distinct and separate departments. Hence, a double security arises to the rights of the people.

The Framers, fearing tyranny, divided powers between the state and the national governments. At each level, moreover, powers were divided among executive, legislative, and judicial branches.

Although most of the delegates to the Constitutional Convention favored a strong federal government, they knew that some compromise about the distribution of powers would be necessary. Some of the Framers wanted to continue with the confederate form of government defined in the Articles of Confederation; others wanted a more centralized system, like that of Great Britain. Their solution was to create the world's first federal system, in which the thirteen sovereign or independent states were bound together under one national government. The result was a system of government that was "neither wholly national nor wholly federal," as Madison explained in *The Federalist Papers.*

The nature of the federal relationship between the national government and the states, including their respective duties, obligations, and powers, is outlined in the U.S. Constitution, although the word "federal" does not appear in that document. Throughout history, however, this system and the rules that guide it have been continually stretched, reshaped, and reinterpreted by crises, historical evolution, public expectations, and judicial interpretation. All these forces have had tremendous influence on who makes policy decisions and how these decisions get made.

Issues involving the distribution of power between the national government and the states affect you on a daily basis. You do not, for example, need a passport to go from Texas to

Figure 3.1   Number of Governments in the U.S. in 1997

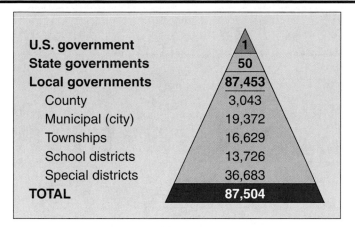

U.S. government	1
State governments	50
Local governments	87,453
County	3,043
Municipal (city)	19,372
Townships	16,629
School districts	13,726
Special districts	36,683
TOTAL	87,504

SOURCE: U.S. Bureau of the Census, http://www.cesus.gov/govs/www/gid.html

Oklahoma. There is one national currency and a national minimum wage. But many differences exist among the laws of the various states: The age at which you may marry is a state issue, as are laws governing divorce, child custody, and the purchase of guns.

Although some policies or programs are under the authority of the state or local government, others, such as air traffic regulation, are solely within the province of the national government.[4] In many areas, however, the national and state governments work together cooperatively. For example, you may receive national as well as state loans, grants, or other forms of assistance to finance your education. Similarly, many of the poor receive help from the national, state, and local governments. At times, the national government cooperates with or supports programs only if the states meet certain conditions. To receive federal funds for the construction and maintenance of highways, for example, states must follow federal rules about the kinds of roads they build.

To understand the current relationship between the states and the federal government and to better grasp some of the issues that arise from this constantly changing relationship, in this chapter, we'll examine the following topics:

- First, we will look at *the roots of the federal system* created by the Framers, and at their attempt to divide the power and the functions of government between one national and several state governments.
- Second, we will analyze the allocation of *the powers of government* between the national and state governments.
- Third, we will examine *the evolution and development of federalism*
- Fourth, we will explore the relationship between *federalism* and the Supreme Court.

THE ROOTS OF THE FEDERAL SYSTEM

The Framers worked to create a particular form of government: One that would be familiar to Americans yet unlike the unitary system found in Great Britain, and one that would remedy many of the problems experienced by the confederated government established by the Articles of Confederation (see chapter 2). (Figure 3.2 illustrates these different forms of government.) The relationship between the national and state governments, and their intertwined powers, are the heart of **federalism** (from the Latin *foedus*, or "covenant"), the philosophy that defines the allocation of power between the national government and the states. Ironically, as discussed in chapter 2, those who supported the government under the Articles of Confederation argued for what they called a federal system. But the fear of being labeled "nationalists" prompted supporters of the new Constitution to call themselves "Federalists," thus co-opting this popular term of

Web Exploration

For scholarly works on federalism, see www.awlonline.com/oconnor.

federalism:

The philosophy that describes the governmental system created by the Framers; see also federal system.

Figure 3.2   The Federal, Confederation, and Unitary Systems of Government

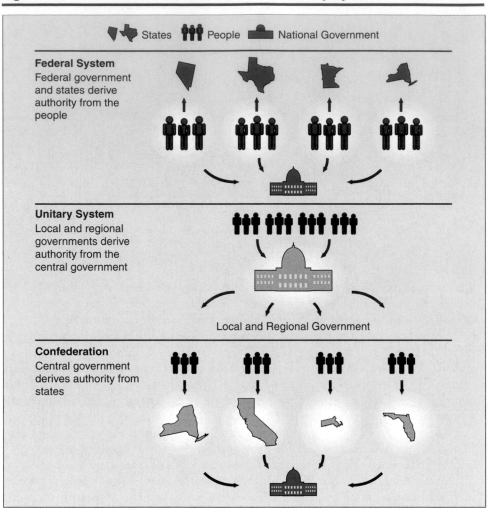

the day. Federalist supporters of the new Constitution articulated three major arguments for federalism: (1) the prevention of tyranny; (2) the provision for increased participation in politics; and (3) the use of the states as testing grounds or "laboratories" for new policies and programs.

The national government created by the Framers draws its powers directly from the people, so that both national and state governments are ultimately directly accountable to the public. While each government has certain powers in common with the other (such as the ability to tax) and has its own set of public officials, the Framers also envisioned each government to be supreme in some spheres, as depicted in Figure 3.3. In *Federalist No. 51*, James Madison explained what he perceived to be the beauty of this system: The shifting support of the electorate between the two governments would serve to keep each in balance. In fashioning the new federal system of government, the Framers recognized that they could not define precisely how all the relations between the national government and the individual states would work. But the Constitution makes it clear that separate spheres of government were to be at the very core of the federal system, with some allowances made for concurrent powers. The addition of Article VI to the federal Constitution underscored the notion that the national government was always to be supreme in situations of conflict between state and national law. It declares that the U.S. Constitution, the laws of the United States, and its treaties are to be "the supreme Law of the Land; and the Judges in every State shall be bound thereby."

Figure 3.3   The Distribution of Governmental Power in the Federal System

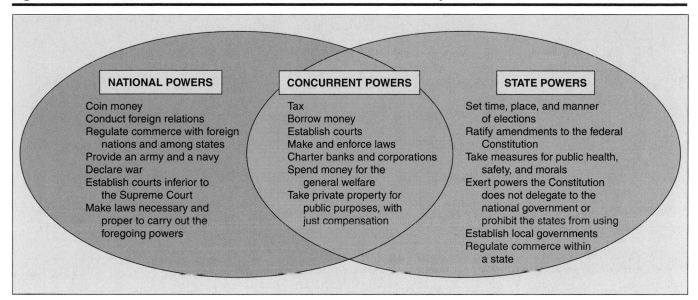

In spite of this explicit language, the meaning of what is called the **supremacy clause** has been subject to continuous judicial interpretation and reinterpretation. In 1920, for example, Missouri sought to prevent a U.S. game warden from enforcing the Migratory Bird Treaty Act of 1918, which prohibited the killing or capturing of many species of birds as they made their annual migration across the international border from Canada to parts of the United States.[5] Missouri argued that the Tenth Amendment, which reserved a state's powers to legislate for the general welfare of its citizens, allowed Missouri to regulate hunting. But the Court ruled that since the treaty was legal, it must be considered the supreme law of the land. Thus, when national law and state law come into conflict, national law (including treaties) is supreme. (See also *McCulloch v. Maryland* [1819].)

The federal government's right to tax was also clearly set out in the new Constitution. The Framers wanted to avoid the financial problems that the national government had experienced under the Articles of Confederation. To survive as a strong national government, the power of the national government to raise revenue had to be unquestionable.

The new Constitution left the qualifications of suffrage to the individual states, as noted in Roots of Government: U.S. Citizenship Rights and the Franchise. Thus, over time, the right to vote even in national elections has varied.

THE POWERS OF GOVERNMENT IN THE FEDERAL SYSTEM

The distribution of powers in the federal system is often described as two over-lapping systems, as illustrated in Figure 3.3. On the left are powers that were specifically granted to Congress in Article I. Chief among the exclusive powers delegated to the national government are the authorities to coin money, conduct foreign relations, provide for an army and navy, declare war, and establish a national court system. All of these powers set out in Article I, section 8 of the Constitution are called enumerated powers. Article I, section 8 also contains the **necessary and proper clause,** which gives Congress the authority to enact any laws "necessary and proper" for carrying out any of its enumerated powers. Thus, for example, Congress's power to charter a national bank was held to be an **implied power** derived from its enumerated power to tax and spend.[6]

The Constitution does not specifically delegate or enumerate many specific powers to the states. Because states had all the power at the time the Constitution was written,

supremacy clause:

Portion of Article VI of the U.S. Constitution that mandates that national law is supreme to (that is, supersedes) all other laws passed by the states or by any other subdivision of government.

necessary and proper clause:

The final paragraph of Article I, section 8 of the U.S. Constitution, which gives Congress the authority to pass all laws "necessary and proper" to carry out the enumerated powers specified in the Constitution: also called the "elastic" clause.

implied power:

A power derived from an enumerated power and the necessary and proper clause. These powers are not stated specifically but are considered to be reasonably implied through the exercise of delegated powers.

ROOTS OF GOVERNMENT

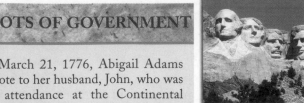

U.S. Citizenship Rights and the Franchise

On March 21, 1776, Abigail Adams wrote to her husband, John, who was in attendance at the Continental Congress. She urged him to "Remember the Ladies" in any "new Code of Laws" that was to be written, and to "be more generous . . . to them than [their] ancestors, . . ." She warned that ultimately, women would not consider themselves "bound by any Laws in which [they had] no voice, or Representation."* In spite of, or more likely simply ignoring, Abigail Adams's admonitions, neither the Articles of Confederation nor the Constitution even mentioned women. Article I, section 4, moreover, gave the states the authority to establish the "Time, Places, and Manner of holding Elections." Congress thus allowed the states to determine who would be eligible to cast their votes for their own representatives.

The Constitution begins with the ringing words "We the People," but it was silent on qualifications for citizenship and voting, noting only that the "Citizens of each State shall be entitled to all Privileges and Immunities of the Citizens of the several States." At the time the Constitution was ratified, while white women were considered citizens, *no* state allowed women to vote in their state elections. Nor could they hold state or national elective office.

It was not only women who were denied full participation in government. Most states had stringent land-owning or property requirements. Thus few poor white men could vote either. And in the Southern states, where slaves were not considered by the states to be citizens, they too could not vote.

Over the years states eliminated most of the restrictions on white male voting. Passage of the Fourteenth Amendment in 1868 defined U.S. citizenship—thereby making all former slaves citizens—noting that "All persons born or naturalized in the United States, and subject to the jurisdiction thereof, are citizens of the United States, and of the state wherein they reside." Passage of the Fifteenth Amendment specifically guaranteed the right to vote to newly freed male slaves—the first national statement of voter eligibility.

Women did not secure the right to vote nationally until 1920, with passage of the Nineteenth Amendment, although several states allowed women to vote before then. In 1971, the Twenty-sixth Amendment established eighteen as the legal age for voting throughout the United States.

Over time, the national government was forced to step in when some states tried to deny the right to vote to portions of their citizenry. First, the U.S. Supreme Court ruled that many state practices that acted to disenfranchise African Americans were unconstitutional. Later, the U.S. Congress enacted the Voting Rights Act of 1965 to make Southern states end their efforts to disenfranchise black voters.

*Quoted in H. L. Butterfield, *et al.*, eds., *The Book of Abigail and John* (Cambridge, MA: Harvard University Press, 1975), 21.

Web Exploration

For perspectives on the federal system, See
www.awlonline.com/oconnor

---

reserve (or police) powers:

Powers reserved to the states by the Tenth Amendment that lie at the foundation of a state's right to legislate for the public health and welfare of its citizens.

---

concurrent powers:

Powers shared by the national and state governments.

---

the Framers felt no need, as they did for the new national government, to list and restate the powers of the states. Article I, however, allows states to set the "Times, Places and Manner, for holding elections for senators and representatives," and Article II requires that each state appoint electors to vote for president. States were also given the power to ratify amendments to the U.S. Constitution. Nevertheless, the enumeration of so many specific powers to the national government and so few to the states is a clear indication of the Federalist leanings of the Framers. It was not until the addition of the Bill of Rights and the Tenth Amendment that the states' powers were better described: "The powers not delegated to the United States by the Constitution, nor prohibited by it to the States, are reserved to the States respectively, or to the people." These powers, often called the states' **reserve** or **police powers,** include the ability to legislate for the public health, safety, and morals of their citizens. The states' rights to legislate under their police powers today are used as the rationale for many states' restrictions on abortion, including twenty-four-hour waiting requirements and provisions requiring minors to obtain parental consent. Police powers are also the basis for state criminal laws. That is why some states have the death penalty and others do not. So long as the U.S. Supreme Court continues to find that the death penalty does not violate the U.S. Constitution, the states may impose it, be it by lethal injection, gas chamber, or the electric chair.

As revealed in Figure 3.3, national and state powers also overlap. The area where the systems overlap represents **concurrent powers**—powers shared by the national and state governments. States already had the power to tax; the Constitution extended this power to the national government as well. Other important concurrent powers include the right to borrow money, establish courts, and make and enforce laws necessary to carry out these powers.

Denied Powers

Article I also denies certain powers to the national and state governments. In keeping with the Framers' desire to forge a national economy, states are prohibited from entering treaties, coining money, or impairing obligation of contracts. States are also prohibited from entering into "compacts" with other states without express congressional approval. In a similar vein, Congress is barred from favoring one state over another in regulating commerce, and it cannot lay duties on items exported from any state.

Both the national and state governments are denied the authority to take arbitrary actions affecting constitutional rights and liberties. Neither national nor state governments may pass a **bill of attainder,** a law declaring an act illegal without a judicial trial. The Constitution also bars either from passing *ex post facto laws*, laws that make an act punishable as a crime even if the action was legal at the time it was committed.

Guarantees to the States

In return for giving up some of their powers, the states received several guarantees in the Constitution. Among them:

- Article I guarantees each state two members in the U.S. Senate and guarantees that Congress would not limit slavery before 1808.
- Article IV guarantees the citizens of each state the privileges and immunities of citizens of all other states; it also guarantees each state a "Republican Form of Government," meaning one that represents the citizens of the state; and it guarantees that the national government will protect the states against foreign attacks and domestic rebellion.

Relations Among the States

The Constitution was designed to improve relations among the squabbling states. To that end it provides that disputes between states are to be settled directly by the U.S. Supreme Court under its original jurisdiction to avoid any sense of favoritism (see chapter 10). Moreover, Article IV requires that each state give "Full Faith and Credit . . . to the public Acts, Records and judicial Proceedings of every other State." This clause ensures that judicial decrees and contracts made in one state will be binding and enforceable in another, thereby facilitating trade and other commercial relationships.

The Constitution requires states to extradite, or return, criminals to states where they have been convicted or are to stand trial. For example, Timothy Reed, an Indian-rights activist, spent five years in New Mexico fighting extradition to Ohio.[7] In 1998, the New Mexico Supreme Court ordered him released from custody in spite of an order from the New Mexico governor ordering his extradition to Ohio. Reed feared that his parole in Ohio would be revoked without due process, he would be returned to prison, and subject to bodily harm. The U.S. Supreme Court found that the Supreme Court of New Mexico went beyond its authority.[8]

States don't always get along however. As our opening vignette about Ellis Island illustrates, the U.S. Constitution gives the Supreme Court the final authority to decide controversies between the states.

THE EVOLUTION AND DEVELOPMENT OF FEDERALISM

The victory of the Federalists—those who supported a strong national government—had long-lasting consequences on the future of the nation. Over the course of our nation's history, the nature of federalism and its allocation of power between the

bill of attainder:
A law declaring an act illegal without a judicial trial.

ex post facto law:
Law passed after the fact, thereby making previously legal activity illegal and subject to current penalty; prohibited by the U.S. Constitution.

■ New Jersey sued New York, claiming it owned Ellis Island. In 1998, the Supreme Court ruled that most of the island, indeed, belonged to New Jersey, but New York was granted ownership of a small section of it. Although small, New York got the land that the visitors enter and the museum occupies. (Photo courtesy: Bernard Boutrit/Woodfin Camp & Associates)

national government and the states have changed dramatically. The debate continues today, too, as many Americans, frustrated with the national government's performance on a number of issues, look for a return of more power to the states. Because the distribution of power between the national and state governments is not clearly delineated in the Constitution, over the years the U.S. Supreme Court has played a major role in defining the nature of the federal system.

Early Pronouncements on Federalism

The first few years that the Supreme Court sat, it handled few major cases. As described in chapter 9, the Supreme Court was viewed as weak and many declined the "honor" of serving as a Supreme Court justice. The appointment of Chief Justice John Marshall, however, changed all of this. In a series of several decisions, he and his brethren carved out an important role for the Court, especially in defining the nature of the federal/state relationship as well as the power of the Court itself.

McCulloch v. Maryland (1819):

The Supreme Court upheld the power of the national government and denied the right of a state to tax the bank. The Court's broad interpretation of the necessary and proper clause paved the way for later rulings upholding expansive federal powers.

McCulloch v. *Maryland* **(1819).**   *McCulloch* v. *Maryland* was the first major decision of the Marshall Court to define the relationship between the national and state governments. In 1816 Congress chartered the Second Bank of the United States. (The charter of the First Bank had been allowed to expire.) In 1818 the Democratic-Republican-controlled Maryland state legislature levied a tax requiring all banks not chartered by Maryland (that is, the Second Bank of the United States) to (1) buy stamped paper from the state on which the Second Bank's notes were to be issued; (2) pay the state $15,000 a year; or (3) go out of business. James McCulloch, the head cashier of the Baltimore branch of the Bank of the United States, refused to pay the tax, and Maryland brought suit against him. After losing in a Maryland court, McCulloch appealed his conviction to the U.S. Supreme Court by order of the U.S. Secretary of the Treasury. In a unanimous opinion, the Court answered the two central questions that had been put to it: First, did Congress have the authority to charter a bank? And, second, if it did, could a state tax it?

Chief Justice Marshall's answer to the first question—whether Congress had the right to establish a bank or another type of corporation, given that the Constitution does not explicitly mention such a power—continues to stand as the classic exposition of the doctrine of implied powers, and as a reaffirmation of the propriety of a strong national government. Although the word "bank" cannot be found in the Constitution, the Constitution enumerates powers that give Congress the authority to levy and collect taxes, issue a currency, and borrow funds. From these enumerated powers, Marshall found, it was reasonable to imply that Congress had the power to charter a bank, which could be considered "necessary and proper" to the exercise of its enumerated powers.

Marshall next addressed the question of whether a federal bank could be taxed by any state government. To Marshall, this was not a difficult question. The national government was dependent on the people, not the states, for its powers. In addition, Marshall noted, the Constitution specifically calls for the national law to be supreme. "The power to tax involves the power to destroy," wrote Marshall.[9] Thus, the state tax violated the supremacy clause, because individual states cannot interfere with the operations of the national government, whose laws are supreme.

***Gibbons v. Ogden* (1824).**   Shortly after *McCulloch*, the Marshall Court had another opportunity to rule in favor of a broad interpretation of the scope of national power. *Gibbons v. Ogden* involved a dispute that arose after the New York State legislature granted to Robert Fulton the exclusive right to operate steamboats on the Hudson River. Simultaneously, Congress licensed a ship to sail on the same waters. By the time the case reached the Supreme Court, it was complicated both factually and procedurally. Suffice it to say that both New York and New Jersey wanted to control shipping on the lower Hudson River. But *Gibbons* actually addressed one simple, very important question: What was the scope of Congress's authority under the commerce clause? The states argued that "commerce," as mentioned in Article I, should be interpreted narrowly to include only direct dealings in products. In *Gibbons*, however, the Supreme Court ruled that Congress's power to regulate interstate commerce included the power to regulate commercial activity as well, and that the commerce power had no limits except those specifically found in the Constitution. Thus New York had no constitutional authority to grant a monopoly to a single steamboat operator, thereby interfering with interstate commerce.[10]

Web Exploration

For the full text of *McCulloch v. Maryland*, see www.awlonline.com/oconnor.

***Gibbons v. Ogden* (1824):**

The Court upheld broad congressional power over interstate commerce.

Web Exploration

For the full text of *Gibbons v. Ogden*, see www.awlonline.com/oconnor.

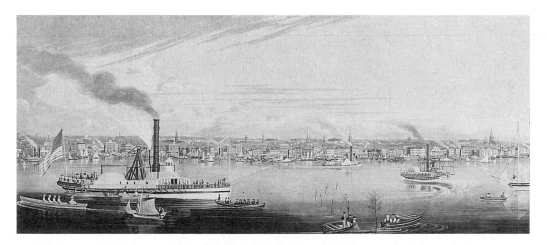

■ The *Gibbons v. Ogden* decision opened the waters to free competition; this is the New York waterfront in 1839. (Photo courtesy: I. N. Phelps Stokes Collection, Miriam and Ira D. Wallach Division of Art, Prints, and Photographs, The New York Public Library Astor, Lenox and Tilden Foundations)

Dual Federalism

In spite of these nationalist Marshall Court decisions, strong debate continued in the United States over national versus state power. It was under the leadership of Chief Justice Marshall's successor, Roger B. Taney (1835–63), that the Supreme Court articulated the notions of concurrent power, the belief that separate and equally powerful levels of government is the best arrangement; and **dual federalism,** which holds that the national government should not exceed its enumerated powers expressly set out in the Constitution.

dual federalism:
The belief that having separate and equally powerful levels of government is the best arrangement.

Federalism and Slavery.   During the Taney era, the comfortable role of the Court as the arbiter of competing national and state interests became troublesome when the Court found itself called upon to deal with the highly political issue of slavery. In cases such as *Dred Scott* v. *Sandford* (1857) and others, the Court tried to manage the slavery issue by resolving questions of ownership, the status of fugitive slaves, and slavery in the new territories. These cases generally were settled in favor of slavery and states' rights within the framework of dual federalism. In its treatment of slavery (see Highlight 3.1: The Dred Scott Saga) the Taney Court erred grievously and thereby contributed to the coming of the Civil War, since its decision seemed to rule out any political (legislative) solution to slavery by the national government.

The Civil War and Beyond

The Civil War (1861–65) forever changed the nature of federalism, but the Supreme Court continued to adhere to its belief in the concept of dual federalism. The importance and powers of the states were not diminished in spite of the addition of the Thirteenth, Fourteenth, and Fifteenth amendments to the Constitution, or by Abraham Lincoln's appointment of the first Republican Chief Justice, Salmon Chase (1864–73).

HIGHLIGHT 3.1

The Dred Scott Saga

Dred Scott, born into slavery around 1795, became the named plaintiff in a case that was to have major ramifications on the nature of the federal system. In 1833 Scott was sold by his original owners, the Blow family, to Dr. Emerson, an army surgeon in St. Louis, Missouri. The next year he was taken to Illinois and later to the Wisconsin Territory, returning to St. Louis in 1838.*

When Dr. Emerson died in 1843, Scott tried to buy his freedom. Before he could, however, he was transferred to Emerson's widow, who moved to New York leaving Scott in the custody of his first owners, the Blows. Some of the Blows (Henry Blow later founded the antislavery Free Soil Party) and other abolitionists gave money to support a test case seeking Scott's freedom: They believed that his residence in Illinois and later in the Wisconsin Territory, both of which prohibited slavery, in essence made him a free man.

After many delays, the U.S. Supreme Court ruled seven to two that Scott was not a citizen. "Slaves said the Court, "were never thought of or spoken of except as property"

At the urging of President James Buchanan, Chief Justice Roger B. Taney tried to fashion a broad ruling to settle the slavery question. In *Dred Scott* v. *Sandford* (1857), he concluded that the Congress of the United States lacked the constitutional authority to bar slavery in the territories. The decision narrowed the scope of national power while it enhanced that of the states. Moreover, for the first time since *Marbury* v. *Madison* (1803), the Court found an act of Congress—the Missouri Compromise—unconstitutional. And, by limiting what the national government could do concerning slavery, it in all likelihood quickened the march toward the Civil War.

(Photo courtesy: Missouri Historical Society)

*Don E. Ferenbacher, "The Dred Scott Case," in *Quarrels That Have Shaped the Constitution,* John A. Garraty, ed. (New York: Harper & Row, 1964), chapter 6.

Between 1865 (the end of the Civil War) and 1933 (when the next major change in the federal system occurred), the Court generally continued to support dual federalism along several lines. State courts, for example, were considered to have the final say on the construction of laws affecting local affairs.[11] Generally, the Court upheld any laws passed under the states' police powers, which allow states to pass laws to protect the general welfare of their citizens. These laws included those affecting commerce, labor relations, and manufacturing. After the Court's decision in *Plessy* v. *Ferguson* (1896), in which the Court ruled that state maintenance of "separate but equal" facilities for blacks and whites was constitutional, most civil rights and voting cases also became state matters, in spite of the Civil War amendments.[12]

The Court also developed legal doctrine in a series of cases that reinforced the national government's ability to regulate commerce. By the 1930s these two somewhat contradictory approaches led to confusion: States, for example, could not tax gasoline used by federal vehicles,[13] and the national government could not tax the sale of motorcycles to the city police department.[14] In this period the Court did recognize the need for national control over new technological developments, such as the telegraph.[15] And beginning in the 1880s, the Court allowed Congress to regulate many aspects of economic relationships such as outlawing monopolies, a type of regulation or power formerly thought to be in the exclusive realm of the states. Passage of laws such as the Interstate Commerce Act in 1887 and the Sherman Anti-Trust Act in 1890 allowed Congress to establish itself as an important player in the growing national economy.

Despite finding that most of these federal laws were constitutional, the Supreme Court did not consistently enlarge the scope of national power. In 1895, for example, the United States filed suit against four sugar refiners, alleging that their sale would give their buyer control of 98 percent of the U.S. sugar-refining business. The Supreme Court

■ This famous cartoon by noted political cartoonist Thomas Nast pokes fun at the myriad trusts that led to congressional passage of the Sherman Anti-Trust Act. (Photo courtesy: Corbis/Bettmann)

ruled that congressional efforts to control monopolies (through passage of the Sherman Anti-Trust Act) did not give Congress the authority to prevent the sale of these sugar-refining businesses, because manufacturing was not commerce. Therefore the companies and their actions were beyond the scope of Congress's authority to regulate.[16]

Cooperative Federalism

The era of dual federalism came to an abrupt end in the 1930s. Its demise began in a series of economic events that ended in the cataclysm of the Great Depression:

- In 1921 the nation experienced a severe slump in agricultural prices.
- In 1926 the construction industry went into decline.
- In the summer of 1929, inventories of consumer goods and automobiles were at an all-time high.
- Throughout the 1920s, bank failures had become common.
- On October 29, 1929, stock prices, which had risen steadily since 1926, crashed, taking with them the entire national economy.

Web Exploration

For more information on the Depression, see www.awlonline.com/oconnor.

The New Deal.   Rampant unemployment (historians estimate it was as high as 40 percent to 50 percent) was the hallmark of the Great Depression. To combat this unemployment and a host of other problems facing the nation, newly elected President Franklin D. Roosevelt (FDR) proposed in 1933 a variety of innovative programs under the rubric "the New Deal" and ushered in a new era in American politics. FDR used the full power of the office of president as well as his highly effective communication skills to sell the American public and Congress on a whole new ideology of government. Not only were the scope and role of national government remarkably altered, but so was the relationship between each state and the national government. It is, in fact, the growth in the federal government that began with the New Deal that many who urge less federal power bemoan today.

The New Deal period (1933–39) was characterized by intense government activity on the national level. It was clear to most politicians that to find national solutions to the Depression, which was affecting the citizens of every state in the Union, the national government would have to exercise tremendous authority.

In the first few weeks of the legislative session after FDR's inauguration, Congress and the president acted quickly to bolster confidence in the national government. Soon after, Congress passed a series of acts creating programs proposed by the president. These new agencies, often known by their initials, created what many termed an "alphabetocracy." Among the more significant programs were the Federal Housing Administration (FHA), which provided federal financing for new home construction; the Civilian Conservation Corps (CCC), a work relief program for farmers and homeowners; and the Agricultural Adjustment Administration (AAA) and the National Recovery Administration (NRA), both of which imposed restrictions on production in agriculture and many industries.

These programs tremendously enlarged the scope of the national government. Those who feared this unprecedented use of national power quickly challenged the constitutionality of New Deal programs in court. And, at least initially, the Supreme Court often agreed with them.

Through the mid-1930s, the Supreme Court continued to rule that certain aspects of the New Deal went beyond the authority of Congress to regulate commerce. In fact, many believe that the Court considered the Depression to be no more than the sum of the economic woes of the individual states and that it was a problem most appropriately handled by the states. The Court's *laissez-faire,* or "hands-off," attitude toward the economy was reflected in a series of decisions ruling various aspects of New Deal programs unconstitutional.

FDR and the Congress were outraged. FDR's frustration with the *laissez-faire* attitude of the Court prompted him to suggest what was ultimately nicknamed his

■ One of the hallmarks of the New Deal and FDR's presidency was the national government's new involvement of cities in the federal system. Here, New York City Mayor Fiorello La Guardia is commissioned as Director of Civil Defense by FDR. (Photo courtesy: AP/Wide World Photos)

"Court-packing plan." Knowing that he could do little to change the minds of those already on the Court, FDR suggested enlarging its size from nine to thirteen justices. This would have given him the opportunity to "pack" the Court with a majority of justices predisposed to the constitutional validity of the New Deal.

Even though Roosevelt was popular, the Court-packing plan was not. Congress and the public were outraged that he even suggested tampering with an institution of government. Nevertheless, the Court appeared to respond to this threat. In 1937 it reversed its series of anti-New Deal decisions, concluding that Congress (and therefore the national government) had the authority to legislate in areas that only *affected* commerce. Congress then used this newly recognized power to legislate in a wide array of areas, including maximum hour and minimum wage laws, and regulation of child labor. Moreover, the Court also upheld the constitutionality of the bulk of the massive New Deal relief programs, such as the National Labor Relations Act of 1935, which authorized collective bargaining between unions and employees in *NLRB* v. *Jones and Laughlin Steel Co.* (1937);[17] the Fair Labor Standards Act of 1938, which prohibited the interstate shipment of goods made by employees earning less than the federally mandated minimum wage;[18] and the Agriculture Adjustment Act of 1938, which provided crop subsidies to farmers.[19]

The New Deal programs forced all levels of government to work cooperatively with one another. Indeed, local governments—mainly in big cities—became a third partner in the federal system, as FDR relied on big-city Democratic political machines to turn out voters to support his programs. For the first time in U.S. history, in essence, cities were embraced as equal partners in an intergovernmental system and became players in the national political arena because many in the national legislature wanted to bypass state legislatures, where urban interests were usually significantly underrepresented.

The Changing Nature of Federalism: From Layer Cake to Marble Cake.

Before the Depression and the New Deal, most political scientists likened the federal system to a layer cake: Each level or layer of government—national, state, and local—had clearly defined powers and responsibilities. After the New Deal, however, the nature of the federal system changed. Government now looked something like a marble cake:

> Wherever you slice through it you reveal an inseparable mixture of differently colored ingredients. . . . Vertical and diagonal lines almost obliterate the horizontal ones, and in some places there are unexpected whirls and an imperceptible merging of colors, so that it is difficult to tell where one ends and the other begins.[20]

cooperative federalism:

A term used to characterize the relationship between the national and state governments that began with the New Deal.

This kind of "marble cake" federalism is often called **cooperative federalism,** a term that describes the relationship between the national, state, and local governments that began with the New Deal as a stronger, more influential national government was created in response to economic and social crises. States began to take a secondary, albeit important, "cooperative" role in the scheme of governance, as did many cities. Nowhere is this shift in power from the states *to* the national government more clear than in the growth of federal grant programs that began in earnest during the New Deal. The tremendous growth in these programs and in federal government spending in general, as illustrated in Table 3.1, changed the nature and discussion of federalism from that time to 1995: from "How much power should the national government have?" to "How much say in the policies of the states can the national government buy?" The national government initially imposed a national fifty-five-miles-per-hour speed limit on the states, for example, and forced states to adopt minimum-age drink restrictions in order to obtain federal transportation funds (see Highlight 3.2: Do You Have ID? Setting a National Alcohol Policy.)

Federal Grants.

As early as 1790, Congress appropriated funds for the states to pay debts incurred during the Revolutionary War. But it wasn't until the Civil War that Congress enacted its first true federal grant program, which allocated federal funds to the states for a specific purpose.

Most view the start of this redistribution of funds with the Morrill Land Grant Act of 1862, which gave each state 30,000 acres of public land for each representative in Congress. Income from the sale of these lands was to be earmarked for the establishment and support of agricultural and mechanical arts colleges. Sixty-nine land-grant

Table 3.1   Federal Grants-in-Aid, 1950–2000*

Year	Total (in Billions of Dollars)	GRANTS-IN-AID AS A PERCENTAGE OF	
		Federal Outlays	State and Local Outlays
1950	$ 2.3	5.3	—
1955	3.2	4.7	—
1960	7.0	7.6	19.0
1965	10.9	9.2	20.0
1970	24.1	12.3	24.0
1975	49.8	15.0	27.0
1980	91.4	15.5	31.0
1985	105.9	11.2	25.0
1990	135.3	10.8	21.0
1995	228.0	14.8	22.0
2000(est)	292.9	15.4	22.0

*1996 figure

SOURCE: Harold W. Stanley and Richard G. Niemi. *Vital Statistics on American Politics,* 5th ed. (Washington, DC: Congressional Quarterly, 1995). 299.

colleges—including Texas A&M University, the University of Georgia, and Michigan State University—were founded, making this grant program the single most important piece of education legislation passed in the United States up to that time.

Franklin D. Roosevelt's New Deal program increased the flow of federal dollars to the states with the infusion of massive federal dollars for a variety of public works programs, including building and road construction. These grants made the imposition of national goals on the states easier. No state wanted to decline funds, so states often secured funds for any programs for which money was available—whether they needed it for that specific purpose or not.

In the boom times of World War II, even more new federal programs were introduced; and by the 1950s and 1960s, federal grant-in-aid programs were well entrenched. They often defined federal/state relationships and made the national government a major player in domestic policy. Until the 1960s, however, most federal grant programs were constructed in cooperation with the states and were designed to assist the states in furthering their traditional responsibilities to protect the health, welfare, and safety of their citizens. Most of these programs were **categorical grants,** ones for which Congress appropriates funds for specific purposes. Funds are allocated by a precise formula and are subject to detailed conditions imposed by the national government, often on a matching basis, that is, states must contribute money to match federal funds, although the national government may pay as much as 90 percent of the total.

categorical grant:
Grant for which Congress appropriates funds for a specific purpose.

Creative Federalism

By the early 1960s, as concern about the poor and minorities rose, and as states (especially in the South) were blamed for perpetuating discrimination, those in power in the national government saw grants as a way to force states to behave in ways desired by the national government.[21] If the states would not cooperate with the national government to further its goals, it would withhold funds.

In 1964 the Democratic administration of President Lyndon B. Johnson (LBJ) (1963–69) launched its renowned "Great Society" program, which included what LBJ called a "War on Poverty." The Great Society program was a broad attempt to combat poverty and discrimination. In a frenzy of activity in Washington not seen since the New Deal, federal funds were channeled to states, to local governments, and even directly to citizen action groups in an effort to alleviate social ills that the states had been unable or unwilling to remedy. There was money for urban renewal, education, and poverty programs, including Head Start and job training. The move to fund local groups directly was made by the most liberal members of Congress in order to bypass not only conservative state legislatures, but also conservative mayors and councils in cities like Chicago, who were not frequently moved to help their poor, often African-American, constituencies. Thus these programs often pitted governors and mayors against community activists, who became key players in the distribution of federal dollars.

These new grants altered the fragile federal/state balance of power that had been at the core of most older federal grant programs. During the Johnson administration, the national government began to use federal grants as a way to further what federal (and not state) officials perceived to be national needs. Grants based on what states wanted or believed they needed began to decline, while grants based on what the national government wanted states to do in order to foster national goals increased dramatically. Soon states routinely asked Washington for help: "Pollution, transportation, recreation, economic development, law enforcement and even rat control evoked the same response from politicians: create a federal grant."[22] By 1970 federal aid accounted for 20 percent of all state and local government spending; this amount of money made the states ever more dependent on the national government.

■ Michigan Governor John Engler unfurls a scroll of nearly 3,000 federal antipoverty programs that several Republican governors wanted dismantled in favor of lump-sum block grants to allow the states to decide where federal dollars in the states are best spent. (Photo courtesy: Jym Wilson/Gannett News Service)

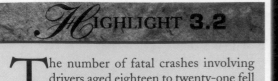

HIGHLIGHT 3.2   Do You Have ID? Setting a National Alcohol Policy

The number of fatal crashes involving drivers aged eighteen to twenty-one fell by 14.3 percent from 1983 to 1994. Why? In 1984, after years of often highly emotional lobbying by Mothers Against Drunk Drivers (MADD) and other concerned citizens groups, Congress passed an amendment to the Surface Transportation Act of 1982 designed to withhold 5 percent of federal highway funds from states that did not prohibit those under the age of twenty-one from drinking alcoholic beverages. Prior to that time, MADD had lobbied most state legislators to raise their state drinking ages with mixed success. Then, its leaders turned their eyes on Congress.[a]

In 1984 only sixteen U.S. senators voted against an amendment to the Surface Transportation Act of 1982, a provision designed to withhold 5 percent of federal highway funds from states that did not prohibit those under the age of twenty-one from drinking alcoholic beverages. Because the national government did not have the power to regulate the drinking age, it resorted to the carrot-and-stick nature of federalism, whereby the national government dangles money in front of the states but places conditions on its use. To force states to raise their drinking age to twenty-one by 1988, Congress initially decided to withhold 5 percent of all federal highway grants to the recalcitrant states. (This

was later raised to 10 percent.) In other words, no raised drinking age, no federal dollars. Even most conservative Republican senators—those most attached to the notion of states' rights—supported the provision, in spite of the fact that it imposed a national ideal on the states. After congressional action, the bill was signed into law by Ronald Reagan, another conservative long concerned with how the national government had trampled on state power. States still retain the power to decide who is legally drunk, however. In 1998, Mothers Against Drunk Driving pressured members of Congress to adopt a national blood alcohol level of .08 to indicate drunkenness, but that effort failed.[b] Thus, the blood alcohol content required for determining legal intoxication varies dramatically, from a low of .05 in Colorado to a high of .1 in several states.

In 1999, however, President Clinton signed legislation that contains incentives for states to lower their blood alcohol levels defining drunk driving to .08. Sixteen states and the District of Columbia have adopted that standard.

[a]Ruth Gastel, "Drunk Driving and Liquor Liability," *Insurance Issues Updates,* April 1999.
[b]Steve Piacente, "Blood Alcohol Limits Under Fierce Debate," *The Post and Courier,* May 27, 1998: B1.

New Federalism and the Reagan Revolution

In 1976 Jimmy Carter, a former governor of Georgia, successfully ran for president as an "outsider" opposed to big government and federal grants that mandated state spending for a variety of programs, including education and pollution-reduction programs. The unfunded mandates discussed later in the chapter were programs passed by Congress requiring state compliance but that came with no funds for the states to meet federal standards. Although Carter was the first president to reduce intergovernmental grant expenditures, the reforms in federal grant programs Carter introduced were insufficient to override the rest of his political woes, and in 1980 former California Governor Ronald Reagan was elected president. Reagan pledged to advance what he called a "New Federalism" and a return of power back to the states.

President Reagan's New Federalism had many facets. The Republican "Reagan Revolution" had at its heart strong views about the role of states in the federal system. Shortly after taking office, he proposed massive cuts in federal domestic programs (which had not become federal functions until the New Deal) and drastic income tax cuts.

The Reagan administration's budget and its policies dramatically altered the relationships among federal, state, and local governments. For the first time in thirty years, federal aid to state and local governments declined.[23] Reagan persuaded Congress to consolidate many categorical grants (for specific programs that often require matching funds) into far fewer, less restrictive **block grants**—broad grants to states for specified activities such as secondary education or health services, with few strings attached.

By 1992 most block grants fell into one of four categories—health, income security, education, or transportation; yet many politicians, including most state governors, urged

block grant:

Broad grant with few strings attached are given to states by the federal government for specified activities, such as secondary education or health services.

■ Dallas Cowboy and Head Start alum Deion Sanders helps children at a California Head Start Center. Sanders was there to launch an educational outreach program designed to provide computers, software, and staff training to selected Head Start centers on the West Coast. (Photo courtesy: Jill Connelly HO/AP/Wide World Photos)

the consolidation of even more programs into block grants. Calls to reform the welfare system—particularly to allow more latitude to the states in an effort to get back to the Hamiltonian notion of states as laboratories of experiment—seem especially popular with citizens and governments alike, as the New Federalism took hold.

The New "Republican" Federalism initially changed the nature of state politics. Many state governments—as well as cities within a single state—found themselves competing for funds. States were faced with revenue shortfalls caused by the recession of the early 1990s, legal requirements mandating balanced budgets, and growing demands for new social services and the replacement of some formerly provided by the federal government. Many governors around the nation found themselves in political trouble as they had to slash services and ask for tax increases. "A governor with over a 50 percent approval is more the exception than the rule now, and that just wasn't true three or four years ago," noted one pollster in 1991.[24] That same year legislators in forty-six states narrowly missed deadlines for their new budget authorizations because of rising costs. Many of these groups have either banded with others or set up individual offices in Washington to lobby for funds. Others hire full-time or part-time lobbyists to work solely on their behalf to keep abreast of funding opportunities or to lobby for programs that could be useful back home. Others lobby as well as litigate to make sure that their interests are represented before the courts.[25]

What scholars term the "Big Seven" are widely recognized as the premier **intergovernmental** lobbies (see Table 3.2). These groups, primarily founded from the turn of the century to the New Deal era, are well organized and well established.

Several of the Big Seven focus on state issues. The National Governors' Association (NGA) is composed of incumbent governors from each state. The governors meet twice a year but have a staff and standing committees that meet more regularly. Adoption of policy positions requires a quorum and vote of three-quarters of the governors. Small states tend to be more active within the group than larger states. The Council of State Governments (CSG), located in Washington, D.C., is an

intergovernmental lobby:

The pressure group or groups that are created when state and local governments hire lobbyists to lobby the national government.

umbrella organization designed to gather information and provide assistance to the states. The National Conference of State Legislatures (NCSL), headquartered in Denver, publishes a monthly magazine, *State Legislatures,* and uses its Washington office to monitor and publish information about the federal government that is useful to the states. It provides a variety of legislative services to all fifty state legislatures plus Puerto Rico.

Three other groups are often called the "urban lobby." The National League of Cities (NLC) represents medium and small cities, the U.S. Conference of Mayors (USCM) represents large cities, and the National Association of Counties (NAC) represents rural, suburban, and urban counties. The remaining member of the Big Seven is the International City/County Management Association (ICMA), which represents the country's appointed local chief executives.

The Devolution Revolution

In 1994 Republicans swept Congress, and no Republican governor who sought reelection was defeated, while some popular Democratic governors, such as Ann Richards of Texas, lost. In *Federalist No. 17,* Alexander Hamilton noted that "it will always be far more easy for the State government to encroach upon the national authorities than for the national government to encroach upon the State authorities." He was wrong. Today, some argue, the federal/state relationship has moved from "cooperation to coercion,"[26] a fact that in 1994 led many state governors and the Republican Party (remember, both increases in federal power—the New Deal and Great Society Program—were launched during Democratic administrations) to rebel openly against this growth of national power.

Preemption.   One method the federal government has used to cut into the authority of the states to set their own policy preferences derives from the Constitution's supremacy clause. This practice, known as **preemption,** allows the national government

preemption:

A concept derived from the Constitution's supremacy clause that allows the national government to override or preempt state or local actions in certain areas.

Web Exploration

For more on the Devolution Revolution, see www.awlonline.com/oconnor.

Table 3.2   The "Big Seven" Intergovernmental Associations

Association (Current Title)	Date Founded	Membership
National Governors' Association (NGA)	1908	Incumbent governors
Council of State Governments (CSG)	1933	Direct membership by states and territories; serves all branches of government; has dozens of affiliate organizations of specialists
National Conference of State Legislatures (NCSL)	1948	State legislators and staff
National League of Cities (NLC)	1924	Direct, by cities and state leagues of cities
National Association of Counties (NAC)	1935	Direct by counties; loosely linked state associations; affiliate membership for county professional specialists
United States Conference of Mayors (USCM)	1933	Direct membership by cities with population over 30,000
International City/County Management Association (ICMA)	1914	Direct membership by appointed city and county managers, and other professionals

SOURCE: Allan J. Cigler and Burdett A. Loomis, *Interest Group Politics* 4th ed. (Washington DC: CQ Press, 1995), 135.

■ President Clinton, himself a former governor, addresses the members of the National Governors' Association at their annual meeting. (Photo courtesy: Lennox McLendon/AP/Wide World Photos)

to override, or preempt, state or local actions in certain areas.[27] The Tenth Amendment expressly reserves to the states and the people all powers not delegated to the national government. The phenomenal growth of preemption statutes, laws that Congress has passed to allow the federal government to assume partial and/or full responsibility for traditional state and local governmental functions, began in 1965 during the Johnson administration. Since then, Congress routinely used its authority under the commerce clause to preempt state laws. These statutes not only took authority away from states, they often imposed significant costs on them in the form of unfunded mandates. In fact, the cost to the states—along with the perceived federal interference with local matters—is one reason that the electorate so willingly embraced the campaign message of the Republican Party in 1994.

The **Contract with America,** proposed by then House Minority Whip Newt Gingrich, was a campaign document signed by nearly all Republican candidates (and incumbents) for the House of Representatives in 1994. In it, Republican candidates pledged themselves to force a national debate on the role of the national government in regard to the states. A top priority was scaling back the federal government. Said House Budget Committee Chair John R. Kasich (R-Ohio). Congress wanted to "return money, power, and responsibility to the states," which some called the "devolution evolution."[28]

Republicans lambasted the growth of federal power over the states and were particularly critical of several features of the federal-state relationship that they believed robbed the states of their power to set policy for the health and welfare of their citizens. A key component of the Contract was a commitment to end unfunded mandates.

Web Exploration

For more on National Governors' Association, see
www.awlonline.com/oconnor.

Contract with America:

Campaign pledge signed by most Republican candidates in 1994 to guide their legislative agenda.

mandates:

National laws that direct states or local governments to comply with federal rules or regulations (such as clean air or water standards) under threat of civil or criminal penalties or as a condition of receipt of any federal grants.

Unfunded Mandates.   From the beginning, most categorical grants were matching grants that came with a variety of strings attached. As categorical grants declined, the national government continued to exercise a significant role in state policy priorities through **mandates**—laws that direct states or local governments to comply with federal rules or regulations (such as clean air or water standards) under threat of civil or criminal penalties or as a condition of receipt of any federal grants (a city might not get federal transportation funds, for example, unless the disabled have access to particular means of transportation).

Prior to 1995, the federal government required the states to shoulder the cost of federal programs it did not fund. Unfunded mandates often made up as much as 30 percent of a local government's annual operating budget. Between 1983 and 1990, it is estimated that the cumulative cost of unfunded mandates to state and local governments was between 8.9 and 12.7 billion dollars.[29]

As shown in Figure 3.4, the enactment of federal regulations requiring state and local spending increased tremendously through 1990. During the 1980s, for example, Congress added twenty-seven new programs requiring state spending, and many expensive unfunded provisions were attached to existing grant-in-aid programs. Columbus, Ohio, for example, with 633,000 residents, faced a $1 billion bill to comply with the federal Clean Water Act and the Safe Drinking Water Act at an estimated cost of $685 a year per household.

Unlike the national government, most states are required to have balanced budgets, and these federally mandated outlays were playing havoc with state budgets. In 1993 some state legislatures even passed laws summoning home their senators and representatives to explain why they were imposing costly national regulations on states without providing funds to implement these programs. It is not surprising, then, to understand why the Republican majority was able to secure passage of the Unfunded Mandates Reform Act of 1995 barring Congress from passing costly programs without debate on how to fund them.

By 1999 the cumulative impact of the federal government's moving some powers back to the states, an improved economy, and decreasing federal mandates produced record federal and state budget surpluses. The fifty states are now in the best fiscal shape they have been in since 1970s, before federal mandates hurt their abil-

Figure 3.4   The Growth of Regulatory Federalism: Enactments Added per Decade, 1931–1990

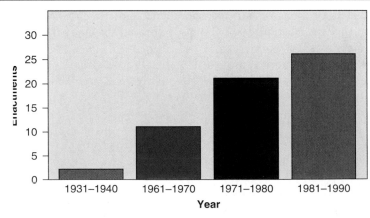

SOURCE: ACIR, *Regulatory Federalism,* Appendix Table 1.
Reprinted in Timothy J. Conlan and David R. Beam,
"Federal Mandates: The Record of Reform and Future Products,"
Intergovernmental Perspective (Fall 1992):9.

ity to prioritize spending. According to the National Conference of State Legislatures, total state budget surpluses in 1998 exceeded $30 billion. These kinds of surpluses are now allowing states to return money to taxpayers in the form of tax-cutting measures. But, the biggest chunk of these surpluses are going to educational reforms to help school districts keep up with enrollment growth caused by the "Baby Boomlet" generation.[30]

The federal government is also enjoying record surpluses. Federal surpluses will provide more opportunities for new federal programs. The new programs, however, are likely to reflect a greater sensitivity to the needs and desires of the fifty states.

FEDERALISM AND THE SUPREME COURT

Federal grants-in-aid and unfunded mandates forced the states to rethink their position in the federal system, and most were unhappy with it. Moreover, by 1996, Republicans controlled a sizable majority of the fifty state houses. Most Republicans, who generally favor a more limited role for the national government, attack many grants-in-aid programs as a way for the national government to exercise powers reserved to the states under the Tenth Amendment.

Some argue that one of the original reasons for federal grants—perceived overrepresentation of rural interests in state legislatures—has been removed, as the Supreme Court has ordered redistricting to ensure better representation of urban and suburban interests. Moreover, state legislatures have become more professional, state and local bureaucracies more responsive, and the delivery of services better. In fact, the greatest growth in government hiring has been in the state and local sectors. Poll after poll, moreover, reveals that Americans believe that the national government has too much power (48 percent) and that they favor their states assuming many of the powers and functions now exercised by the federal government (59 percent).[31]

While many argue that grants-in-aid are an effective way to raise the level of services provided to the poor, others attack them as imposing national priorities on the states. Policy decisions are largely made at the national level; and the states, always in search of funds, are forced to follow the priorities of the national government. States find it very hard to resist the lure of grants, even though many are contingent on some sort of state investment of matching or proportional funds.

Funds from the national government and changing presidential and congressional views about the federal-state relationship are not the only factors that have altered the nature of the federal system. The Supreme Court also has played an important role in the configuration of power between the national government and the states. From the days of Marshall's Federalist opinions, to *laissez-faire*, to the New Deal, the Supreme Court periodically has interjected itself into areas (most notably education and the electoral process) that the Framers intended to leave within the authority of the states.

Education

Through grants-in-aid programs like the Morrill Land Grant Act of 1862, and into the 1950s, Congress has long tried to encourage the states to develop their university and educational systems. Still, education was usually considered a function of the states under their police powers, which allow them to provide for public health and welfare. That tradition was shattered when the Supreme Court ruled in *Brown v. Board of Education of Topeka, Kansas* (1954) that state-mandated segregation has no place in the public schools (see chapter 6). *Brown* forced states to dismantle their segregated school systems and ultimately led the federal courts to play an important role in monitoring the efforts of state and local governments to tear down the vestiges of segregation.

 TRY IT!
To analyze where your state stands relative to other states, see
www.?oconnor?.com

GLOBAL POLITICS

Federalism in Comparative Perspective

All governments face the issue of how to divide political authority geographically. Of the variations presented in Figure 3.2, federal and unitary systems are the most prevalent throughout the world. The Commonwealth of Independent States (made up of most of the former republics of the Soviet Union) is the outstanding example of the rare confederation. The G-7, on the other hand, are split almost evenly between federal and unitary systems, with the latter slightly more common. While the federal systems listed above divide political authority between national and local government, the near balance suggests that there is nothing inherently better, or even more democratic, in a federal system.

Whether a country adopts one or the other tends to be the result of its political history. The United States and Germany were created out of existing confederacies, so the new governments accommodated theoretically strong state governments as the price of union. Canada was formed in 1867 out of three British provinces that voluntarily sought union. In France, Italy, and Japan, the creation of modern nation-states was driven by central authorities that imposed geographic political arrangements on their provinces. In all three cases, the subnational territories listed above were created by national governments intent on obliterating then-existing regional identities. The ability of the national government to alter local government at will remains a key feature of unitary systems. No better current example can be found than in the British Parliament's decision in 1998 to provide home parliaments for Scotland, Wales and

Northern Ireland. What the Parliament created in 1998 can be abolished by that body at any time.

Power is divided differently even among the federal systems. Canada has had a strong federal government with correspondingly weak provinces, although the latter have asserted their power in recent decades. Quebec is the clearest case, with its threat to separate from the rest of the country forcing the federal government to make concessions on issues like the national language and education. Unlike American states, German state governments cannot raise their own taxes, but they also retain sole control over state police forces, the highest level of regular law enforcement. In the original spirit of the American constitution, Canadian provincial governments and German state governments are represented in the upper houses of their respective federal parliaments.

Geographic Distribution of Authority

Country	System	Major Subnational Divisions
Canada	federal	10 provinces, 3 territories
France	unitary	96 departments
Germany	federal	16 states
Italy	unitary	20 regions
Japan	unitary	47 prefectures
United Kingdom	unitary	53 counties
United States	**federal**	**50 states**

The Electoral Process

A decade after *Brown*, the Supreme Court again involved itself in one of the most sacred areas of state regulation in the federal system—the conduct of elections. As a trade-off for giving the national government more powers, the Constitutional Convention allowed the states control over voter qualifications in national elections as well as over how elections were to be conducted. But in 1964 the Court began to limit the states' ability to control the process of congressional redistricting. In 1966, for example, the Supreme Court invalidated the poll tax, a state-imposed tax ranging from one to five dollars levied on those who wished to vote. The poll tax was widely used in the Southern states to curtail voting by the poor, who often were black.[32] Most Southern legislators assailed the Court's decision, viewing it as illegal interference with their powers to regulate elections under the Constitution, and as a violation of state sovereignty.

In 1995 the Supreme Court again reined in state power over the electoral process. In *U.S. Term Limits* v. *Thornton*, by a five to four margin, the Court struck down as unconstitutional state-imposed term limits on members of Congress.[33]

Web Exploration

For more about the state term limits issue, see
www.awlonline.com/oconnor.

■ The federal Violence Against Women Act was passed to help state and local law enforcement officials combat domestic violence and other forms of violence suffered by women. (Photo courtesy: T. Shumsky/The Image Works)

The Commerce Clause and the Performance of State Functions

After the constitutional revolution of 1937, the Supreme Court "upheld every New Deal statute that came before it," often basing its decision on an elastic reading of the commerce clause, which gives Congress the authority to regulate interstate commerce.[34] Since that time, the commerce clause has been the rationale for virtually any federal intervention in state and local governmental affairs. In *Garcia* v. *San Antonio Metropolitan Transit Authority* (1985), for example, which involved the constitutionality of applying federally imposed minimum wage and maximum hour provisions to state governments, the Court ruled that Congress has broad power to impose its will on state and local governments, even in areas that traditionally have been left to their discretion. The Court ruled that the "political process ensures that laws that unduly burden the states will not be promulgated" and that it should not be up to an "unelected" judiciary to preserve state powers.[35] Furthermore, the majority of the Court concluded that the Tenth Amendment, which ensures that any powers not given to the national government be reserved for the states, was—at least for the time being—essentially meaningless!

Of late, however, the U.S. Supreme Court has "begun to rein in the commerce clause" as there were indications that the Court believes that Congress has gone too far in interfering with functions best left to the states.[36] In *U.S.* v. *Lopez* (1995), which involved the conviction of a student charged with carrying a concealed handgun onto school property, a five-person majority of the Court ruled that Congress lacked constitutional authority under the commerce clause to regulate guns within 1,000 feet of a school.[37] The majority concluded that local gun control in the schools was a state, not a federal, matter.

Reproductive Rights

Mario M. Cuomo, the former liberal Democratic New York governor, has referred to the decisions of the Reagan-Bush Court as creating "a kind of new judicial federalism." According to Cuomo, this new federalism can be characterized by the Court's withdrawal of "rights and emphases previously thought to be national."[38] Perhaps most

Web Exploration

For more about local gun control initiatives, see www.awlonline.com/oconnor.

Web Exploration

For more information on state abortion restrictions, see www.awlonline.com/oconnor.

Figure 3.5 State-by-State Selected Abortion Restrictions, 1998

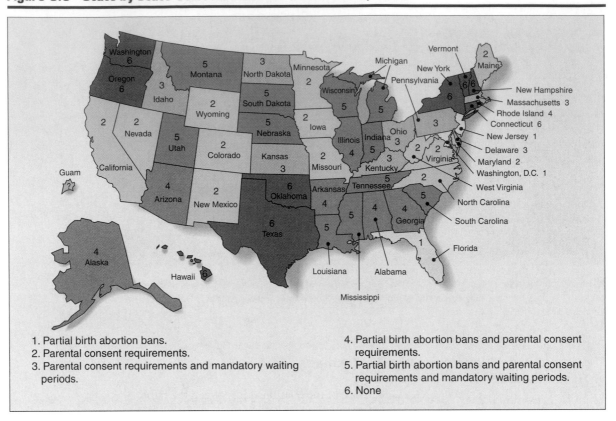

1. Partial birth abortion bans.
2. Parental consent requirements.
3. Parental consent requirements and mandatory waiting periods.

4. Partial birth abortion bans and parental consent requirements.
5. Partial birth abortion bans and parental consent requirements and mandatory waiting periods.
6. None

SOURCE: www.naral.org/publications/whod98summary. From *USA Today*, July 1, 1991, p. 2A. Reprinted by permission.

illustrative of this trend are the Supreme Court's decisions in *Webster* v. *Reproductive Health Services* (1989)[39] and *Casey* v. *Planned Parenthood of Southeastern Pennsylvania* (1992).[40] In *Webster* the Court first gave new latitude—and even encouragement—to the states to fashion more restrictive abortion laws. Since *Webster,* as illustrated in Figure 3.5, numerous states have enacted or are considering new restrictions. During the first five weeks of the 1997 legislative session, over 125 bills restricting abortion were introduced in state legislatures. Late-term abortion restrictions concerning what are often termed "partial birth abortions" were introduced in over half of the state legislatures.[41] Moreover, the Court has consistently upheld the authority of the individual states to limit a minor's access to abortion through imposition of parental consent or notification laws. And it has consistently declined to review other restrictions, including twenty-four-hour waiting period requirements.

Violence Against Women

In 1994, Congress passed the Violence Against Women Act (VAWA) to the near universal acclaim of legislators on both sides of the aisle. There was also substantial public support for the creation of a National Domestic Violence Hotline and millions in federal dollars to go to the states to fund rape crisis centers and domestic violence shelters, as well as to help local law enforcement officials combat violent crimes against women. Although Congress claimed the authority to enact the VAWA on its authority under the commerce clause, several federal courts have ruled the law unconstitutional in a variety of cases, including a lawsuit field by a Virginia Tech student who alleged that two university football players raped her.[42]

In that case a Court of Appeals, invoking earlier Supreme Court decisions holding that the federal government has enumerated and thus limited powers, ruled that sections of the VAWA were beyond the scope of Congress's authority to legislate under

Web Exploration

For more information on other important policies affected by federalism, see www.awlonline.com/oconnor.

the commerce clause. It was the first time that an appellate court struck down specific congressional action under the authority of *U.S.* v. *Lopez* (1995).

The appeals court decision concerning the constitutionality of VAWA reflects the increasing tendency of the federal courts, especially the U.S. Supreme Court, to rein in the authority of Congress to legislate in areas historically reserved to the states for their regulation.

In 1997, for example, the Supreme Court tried to redefine the relationship of the national government and the states by forcing the states to deal with issues such as physician-assisted suicide, and at the same time it struck down the Brady federal gun control law (see chapter 5). Both of these actions were seen as efforts by the Court to restore a better balance to the federal/state relationship.

CONTINUITY and Change

Power of the States

When the states ratified the U.S. Constitution they gave up considerable power to the untested national government. Under the Articles of Confederation, they had been a loose confederation of sovereign states; now they would be but one nation. In the beginning, however, the national government was quite small and the states gained economic stability and protection against internal and external aggression in exchange for giving the national government largely limited economic powers as well as authority over foreign affairs.

Over the years the U.S. Supreme Court often has been called upon to define and interpret the Constitution's careful delineation of the relationship between the national government and the states. And, over time, beginning with *McCulloch* v. *Maryland* (1803), the Court usually came down on the side of national power at the expense of the states. By the 1980s, a series of inconsistent Supreme Court decisions—on the one hand returning costly programs and problems to the states, while on the other hand continuing to order costly educational and penal programs—threatened the very sovereignty of the states. The Reagan administration attempted to clarify the federal/state relationship through an executive order in 1987, and several states even called for an amendment to the Constitution to return power to the states.

In 1995 Republicans regained control of both houses of Congress, intent on altering the delicate balance between the national and state governments. They immediately passed the Unfunded Mandates Reform Act of 1995 to prevent Congress from passing costly programs without debate on how to fund them. They also passed a series of reforms designed to give the states more control over their budgets and the day-to-day lives of their citizens. The total overhaul of the welfare system is but one example of the readjustment of power begun by the 104th Congress and continued today. The power of the states is clearly growing. In 1998 the Big Seven was instrumental in convincing the Clinton administration to postpone rewriting a Reagan executive order on federalism after initial drafts seemed to give the federal government broad powers over state affairs as discussed in Politics Now: The President and the Big Seven.

As more and more power is returned to the states, and the balance of the federal/state relationship is changed, it is likely that we will see tremendous diversity among the states on items including education, treatment of the poor and prisoners, and even issues of safety such as gun control.

1. Are there certain policy areas that are likely to need national standards?
2. What policy arenas are best left to the state legislatures?

Cast Your Vote.   Let us know what you think about the balance of power between the federal government and the states. To cast your vote, go to www.awlonline.com/oconnor.

POLITICS NOW

The President and the Big Seven

In 1999, President Clinton and the seven major state and local groups, the "Big Seven," finally agreed on a proposed executive order to substantially strengthen and develop the federal/state relationship.

A year earlier, President Clinton caused a political firestorm when he released Executive Order 13083 on federalism. Within months, pressure from Republicans in Congress and the Big Seven, including the National Governor's Association, forced him to withdraw that attempt to update two previous executive orders on federalism.[a] Their major objection was that the proposed order "contained vague wording that may have given the federal government broad powers over states' affairs."[b] The Clinton administration insisted that it wasn't trying to usurp power from the states; instead, officials claimed that they were only trying to clarify the federal government's relationship to the states in light of recent Supreme Court cases and the Unfunded Mandates Reform Act. This was the Clinton administration's third effort to draft a new executive order.[c] Both earlier versions were also opposed by the Big Seven, who claimed not to have been consulted before they were proposed.

In 1986, President Ronald Reagan, like Clinton a former state governor, issued Executive Order 12612, which stated several fundamental principles of federalism including assertions that (1) "political liberties are best assured by limiting the size and scope of the national government;" (2) "states are free, subject only to restrictions in the Constitution itself or in constitutionally authorized Acts of Congress, to define the moral, political, or legal character of their lives;" and, (3) "the presumption of sovereignty should rest with the individual states."[d] These ideas would not have been objectionable to the Framers but probably overstated the Supreme Court's view of federalism at the time. The new order directs agencies to access any federal actions that limit state and local discretion and construe federal laws that preempt state law only where direct conflicts with federal power exist.

[a]Executive Order 13095, suspending Executive Order 13083.
[b]Daniel Meisler, "State and Local Finance: White House Ready to Respond to Groups' Plea for Delay of Federalism Edict," *The Bond Buyer,* September 11, 1998, 5.
[c]Meisler, "State and Local Finance."
[d]Executive Order 12612.

SUMMARY

The inadequacies of the confederate form of government created by the Articles of Confederation led the Framers to create an entirely new, federal system of government. From the summer of 1776 until today, the tension between the national and state governments has been at the core of our federal system. In describing the origins of that tension and the renewed debate about the role of the national government in the federal system, we have made the following points:

1. THE ROOTS OF THE FEDERAL SYSTEM

The Framers created a federal system to replace the confederate form of government that had existed under the Articles of Confederation.

2. THE POWERS OF GOVERNMENT IN THE FEDERAL SYSTEM

The national government has both enumerated and implied powers, and also exercises concurrent powers with the states. Certain powers are denied to both the state and national governments. Certain guarantees concerning representation in Congress and protection against foreign attacks and domestic rebellion were made to the states in return for giving up some of their powers in the new federal system. Despite limitations, the national government is ultimately supreme.

3. THE EVOLUTION AND DEVELOPMENT OF FEDERALISM

Over the years, the powers of the national government have increased tremendously at the expense of the states. The Supreme Court, in particular, has played a key role in defining the relationship and powers of the national government through its broad interpretations of the supremacy and commerce clauses. For many years, however, it adhered to the notion of dual federalism, which tended to limit the national government's authority in areas such as slavery and, after the Civil War, civil rights. This notion of a limited role for the national government in some spheres ultimately fell by the wayside after the Great Depression.

The rapid creation of New Deal programs to alleviate many problems caused by the Depression led to a tremendous expansion of the federal government through the growth of federal services and grant-in-aid programs. This growth escalated during the Johnson administration and in the mid- to late 1970s. After his election in 1980, Ronald Reagan, upset by the growth of federal services, tried to reverse the tide through what he termed New Federalism. He built on earlier efforts by Richard M. Nixon to consolidate categorical grants into fewer block grant programs, and to give state and local governments greater control over programs. Since 1993 the national government and the states have been in a constant dialogue to reframe the structure of the federal-state relationship.

4. FEDERALISM AND THE SUPREME COURT

Over the years, the Supreme Court has been a major player in changing trends in the federal-state relationship. Its decisions in the areas of education, the electoral process, and the performance of state functions have given the federal government a wider role in the day-to-day functioning of the states, and have limited the scope of the states' police powers. Since the Reagan-Bush era, however, the Supreme Court has been willing to draw the line on congressional power and return some powers to the states. Recent cases on issues including abortion and crime cast doubt on the Court's willingness to expand congressional powers at the expense of the states.

KEY TERMS

bill of attainder, p. 77

block grant, p. 86

categorical grant, p. 85

concurrent powers, p. 76

Contract with America, p. 89

cooperative federalism, p. 84

dual federalism, p. 80

ex post facto law, p. 77

federalism, p. 73

Gibbons v. *Ogden* (1824), p. 79

implied power, p. 75

intergovernmental lobby, p. 87

mandates, p. 90

McCulloch v. *Maryland* (1819), p. 78

necessary and proper clause, p. 75

preemption, p. 88

reserve (or police) powers, p. 76

supremacy clause, p. 75

SELECTED READINGS

Bowman, Ann O'M., and Richard C. Kearney. *State and Local Government,* 2d ed. Boston: Houghton Mifflin, 1993.

Derthick, Martha. *The Influence of Federal Grants.* Cambridge, MA: Harvard University Press, 1970.

Elazar, Daniel J. *American Federalism: A View from the States,* 3d ed. New York: Harper & Row, 1984.

Feingold, Kenneth, and Theda Skocpol. *State and Party in America's New Deal.* Madison: University of Wisconsin Press, 1995.

Gillespie, Ed, and Bob Schellhas, eds. *Contract with America.* New York: Times Books, 1994.

Grodzins, Morton. *The American System.* Chicago: Rand McNally, 1966.

Kenyon, Daphne A., and John Kincaid, eds. *Competition among States and Local Governments.*

Washington, D.C.: The Urban Institute Press, 1991.

Phillips, Kevin. *The Politics of Rich and Poor: Wealth and the American Electorate in the Reagan Aftermath.* New York: Harper-Collins, 1990.

Riker, William H. *Federalism: Origin, Operation, Significance.* Boston: Little, Brown, 1964.

Rivlin, Alice M. *Reviving the American Dream: The Economy, the States, and the Federal Government.* Washington, D.C.: The Brookings Institution, 1993.

Walker, David B. *The Rebirth of Federalism.* Chatham, NJ: Chatham House, 1994.

Zimmerman, Joseph F. *Interstate Relations: The Neglected Dimension of Federalism.* New York: Praeger, 1996.

NOTES

1. *New Jersey* v. *New York,* 523 U.S. 767 (1998).

2. Linda Greenhouse, "Skeptical High Court Hears Case over Pride and Acreage on Ellis I," *New York Times,* (January 13, 1998): B1. See also Lisa Anderson, "Land of the Free, Home of the Silly Dispute," *Chicago Tribune,* (June 5, 1998): 8.

3. "How Much Government—Devolution," *The Public Perspective* (April/May 1995): 26.

4. In *City of Burbank* v. *Lockheed,* 411 U.S. 624 (1973), the U.S. Supreme Court ruled that the city could not impose curfews on plane takeoff or landing times. The Court said that one uniform *national* standard was critical for safety and the national interest.

5. *Missouri* v. *Holland,* 252 U.S. 416 (1920).

6. *McCulloch* v. *Maryland,* 4 Wheat. 316 (1819).

7. Nancy Plevin, "Ohio Frees Indian-Rights Activist 'Little Rock' Reed," *The Santa Fe New Mexican* (March 12, 1999): B1.

8. *New Mexico ex rel. Ortiz* v. *Reed,* 524 U.S. 151 (1998).

9. *McCulloch* v. *Maryland,* 4 Wheat. 316 (1819).

10. *Gibbons* v. *Ogden,* 22 U.S. 1 (1824).

11. *Lane County* v. *Oregon,* 74 U.S. 71 (1869).

12. 163 U.S. 537 (1896).

13. *Panhandle Oil Co.* v. *Knox,* 277 U.S. 71 (1928).

14. *Indian Motorcycle Co.* v. *United States,* 238 U.S. 570 (1931).

15. *Pensacola Telegraph* v. *Western Union,* 96 U.S. 1 (1877).

16. *United States* v. *E. C. Knight,* 156 U.S. 1 (1895).

17. 301 U.S. 1 (1937).

18. *United States* v. *Darby,* 312 U.S. 1 (1937).

19. *Wickard* v. *Filburn,* 317 U.S. 111 (1942).

20. Morton Grodzins, "Centralization and Decentralization in the American Federal System," in Robert A. Goldwin, ed. *A Nation of States* (Chicago: Rand McNally, 1963), 3–4.

21. Alice M. Rivlin, *Reviving the American Dream* (Washington, DC: Brookings Institution, 1992), 92.

22. Rivlin, *Reviving the American Dream,* 98.

23. Richard P. Nathan, *et al., Reagan and the States* (Princeton, NJ: Princeton University Press, 1987), 4.

24. Quoted in David E. Anderson, "Conservative Think Tanks Go Local," *UPI* (June 10, 1991).

25. Stephen G. Bragaw, "Federalism's Defense Fund: The Intergovernmental Lobby and the Supreme Court, 1982–1997," paper delivered at the 1999 annual meeting of the midwest Political Science Association.

26. John Kincaid, "From Cooperation to Coercion in American Federalism: Housing, Fragmentation, and Preemption, 1789–1992," *Journal of Law and Politics* 9 (Winter 1993): 333–430.

27. This discussion of preemption relies heavily on Joseph F. Zimmerman, *Contemporary American Federalism: The Growth of National Power* (New York: Praeger, 1992), 55–81.

28. The Close Up Foundation, "Federalism," http://www.closeup.org/federal.htm

29. Timothy J. Conlan and David R. Beam, "Federal Mandates: The Record of Reform and Future Prospects," *Intergovernmental Perspectives* (Fall 1992): 9.

30. Paul West, "Era of Big Government May Not Be Over After All," *Times-Picayune,* (January 13, 1998), A5.

31. "Devolutionary Thinking Is Now Part of a Larger Critique of Modern Governmental Experience," *The Public Perspective* (April/May 1995): 28.

32. *Harper* v. *Virginia Board of Elections,* 383 U.S. 663 (1966).

33. 115 S.Ct. 1842 (1995).

34. Wilfred M. McClay, "A More Perfect Union? Toward a New Federalism," *Commentary* (September 1995): 28.

35. 469 U.S. 528 (1985).

36. McClay, "A More Perfect Union?"

37. 115 U.S. 1624 (1995).

38. Marianne Arneberg, "Cuomo Assails Judicial Hodgepodge," *Newsday* (August 15, 1990): 15.

39. 492 U.S. 490 (1989).

40. 112 S.Ct. 931 (1992).

41. "Anti-Choice Onslaught Unleashed at Sate Level in '97 Session," *NARAL News* 2 (Spring 1997): 1.

42. *Brzonkala* v. *Virginia Polytechnic Institute* 132 F. 3d 949 (1997).

(Photo courtesy: Bob Daemmrich)

State and Local Government

- Evolution of State and Local Governments
- Relations with Indian Nations
- Grassroots Power and Politics
- State Governments
- Local Governments
- Finances

"*D*o you want to die?"

A fifteen-year-old member of a gang known as the TMC, or Tiny Man Crew, asked this question and then fired five shots at a thirteen-year-old who was a member of a rival gang, the Imperial Gangsters. This shooting was in retaliation for an earlier incident in which an Imperial Gangster was the victim. Fortunately, the thirteen-year-old, who was wounded, survived.

These shootings shocked the community of La Crosse, Wisconsin, a fairly typical medium-sized (75,000) city in mid-America. The community is commonly thought of as a friendly, safe, clean place in which to live and raise a family. Hood Park, the site of violent confrontations between these gangs, is in the middle of what had once been a blue-collar neighborhood, where children played without fear of violence and where doors to homes and cars were unlocked. But throughout the 1990s, the presence of youth gangs became increasingly evident. Some of the gangs are extensions of major regional and national organizations "headquartered" in Chicago or Los Angeles. Others are homegrown and referred to as "wannabes."

State and local governments are directly responsible for the health and safety of individuals and communities. Cities and counties hire and direct police, firefighters, paramedics, and other safety and emergency personnel. Local school boards run education programs and facilities. Local governments operate parks. States are responsible for courts, correctional programs, welfare, economic development, and other services related to issues of gangs and youth violence. A challenge is to get all these governing units to act as partners in addressing local issues. Luckily, these units came together in the community of La Crosse.

In response to the gang shootings, La Crosse formed an ad hoc task force made up local school, police, and community leaders. Soon after, the mayor became involved and neighbors came forth to volunteer their time and energy to design programs that might reduce youth violence, while the state provided technical and financial assistance to establish anti-gang projects. The formal authority and resources of government and the informal leadership and consensus in the community were essential. While La Crosse continues to face the challenges of gang activity, it has become a model of how state and local governments can collaborate to establish a wide variety of healthy alternatives for youth activity, intervention services for those who are at risk, and, where necessary, institutions to control those who are dangerous to themselves or others.[1]

*G*overnance in the United States is by multiple authorities, sometimes in conflict with one another and sometimes in harmony. It is easy for a school district, for example, to sidestep gang and youth violence issues and to define them as a problem for city police or for county social workers. The police might act only if a crime has actually been committed and refuse to get involved in prevention or intervention efforts, unless perhaps more money is put into their budget. Or, as happened in La Crosse, various agencies and governments might get together informally to address a problem, more out of a common concern than because of a requirement.

The relationships among the various governments in our country are dynamic. The legal authority, the financial resources, and the political will of the federal government, state and municipal governments, school districts, water districts, and all the other public bodies are constantly changing. On the one hand, this provides groups and individuals with many points of access to government. On the other hand, the multiple, changing jurisdictions that govern our society can be a challenging puzzle, so complex that in effect citizens will have very little access and influence.

This chapter will present the basic patterns and principles of state and local governance so that you might readily understand how public policies in your community are made and applied.

- First, we will review the *history of state and local governments.*
- Second, we will discuss relationships between federal and state governments and the Indian nations.
- Third, we will identify the nature of *power and politics in communities.*
- Fourth, we will describe the *development of state constitutions* and the major institutions of *state governments,* including trends in state elections.
- Fifth, we will examine the different types of *local governments* and explain the bases for their authority as well as the special traits of their institutions.
- Sixth, we will explain the budgeting process for state and local *finances.*

THE EVOLUTION OF STATE AND LOCAL GOVERNMENTS

As pointed out in chapter 3, the basic, original unit of government in this country was the state. The thirteen colonial governments became thirteen state governments and their constitutions preceded the U.S. Constitution. The states initially were loosely tied together in the Articles of Confederation, but then formed a closer union and more powerful national government.

State governments, likewise, determined the existence of local governments. As we will later discuss in more detail, in some cases—like counties and, for most states, school districts—state laws *create* local governments. In others, like towns and cities, states *recognize* and *authorize* local governments in response to petitions from citizens.

In other words, the history of governance in the United States is not one built from the bottom. Local communities do not form states, which then form the United States. Instead, states are the basic units, which on the one hand establish local governments and on the other hand are the building blocks of the federal government.

In the past, state and local governments were primarily part-time governments. This has changed somewhat, but it will never change entirely. Initially, almost all state and local elected officials were part-time. Except for governors and a handful of big-city mayors, people in office were farmers, teachers, lawyers, and shop owners who did public service during their spare time. This was true as well for many judges and local government bureaucrats.

As the responsibilities and challenges of government grew, more state and local officials became full-time. Increases in the need for urban services led to more full-time local governments. Likewise, states with high levels of urbanization, industrialization, and economic development needed larger, more professional, and full-time legislatures, courts, and administrators. These states did not, however, always get their needs met.

The boundaries of districts from which state legislators got elected did not change in response to population shifts in the post–Civil War period. As a result, state legislatures did not represent the character of their respective states. One legislator from a rural area might represent 50,000 people, whereas a legislator from an urban setting may represent as many as 500,000 constituents. Such a pattern led to low priority for urban needs.

This kind of misrepresentation remained in place until the 1960s. The 1962 ruling by the U.S. Supreme Court in *Baker* v. *Carr* became watershed in the evolution of state and local governments. The Court applied the Fourteenth Amendment to the U.S. Constitution and decreed that equal protection and the **one-person, one-vote** principles required that there be the same number of people in each of the legislative districts within a single state. As a result, state legislatures became more representative and the agendas of state governments became much more relevant than they had been. This in turn attracted more professional and serious individuals to seek administrative and elective positions in state governments.

The 1960s and 1970s were a period in which the federal government added both to the responsibilities and to the competence of state and local governments. Federal programs to combat poverty, revitalize urban areas, and protect the environment were designed to be administered by state and local officials rather than federal agencies. With this came assistance and sometimes mandates to improve the capacities of subnational governments.

In the past two decades, some trends in federalism have enhanced the importance of state and local governments. Conscious efforts since the Nixon administration were made to reverse the aggregation of power and authority in Washington, D.C. In part, this was philosophical, but it was also necessary. The federal government found itself unable to expand or even to maintain its presence in domestic policy areas. During the Reagan administration, the debt of the federal government more than tripled and there was no choice but to cut severely the flow of federal money and mandates that fueled much of the growth of state and local governments.

In 1995 the U.S. Supreme Court placed limitations on the federal government and reasserted the importance of state and local governments. This is best reflected in *U.S. v. Lopez*, where the Court ruled that Congress and the president did not have authority to require the establishment of gun-free zones around local schools and that it was a matter for state and local governments. The Court left open, however, the commonly used option of the federal government attaching conditions states had to meet to receive federal funds. This power had previously been affirmed in *South Dakota* v. *Dole* (1987), in which the Court said it was permissible for the federal government to require states that wanted transportation funds to pass laws setting twenty-one as the legal age for drinking. Congress and the President nonetheless seemed inclined to eliminate strings and to give state and local governments more discretion. For example they removed the requirement that states have certain speed limits in order to receive federal transportation funds and gave local governments more leeway in determining how they would meet clean water standards.

The twentieth century closed with many changes and uncertainties, but with a clear message that state and local governments will have roles and responsibilities of increasing importance. For the most part, these jurisdictions relish these developments. Some states and cities, for example, are taking bold initiatives and even establishing direct ties with other countries in order to spur economic growth.[2] Others, especially in smaller and medium-sized communities, are overwhelmed with all there is to do.

one-person, one-vote:
The principle that each legislative district within a state should have the same number of eligible voters so that representation is equitably based on population.

RELATIONS WITH INDIAN NATIONS

Treaties between the federal government and American Indian nations directly affect thirty-four states. Most of these states are west of the Mississippi River, but New York, Michigan, Florida, Connecticut, and Wisconsin are also included. Although the treaties were between two nations, the United States and an American Indian tribal nation,

domestic dependent nation:

A type of sovereignty that makes an Indian tribe in the United States outside the authority of state governments but reliant on the federal government for the definition of tribal authority.

compact:

A formal, legal agreement between a state and a tribe.

reservation land:

Land designated in a treaty that is under the authority of an Indian nation and is exempt from most state laws and taxes.

trust land:

Land owned by an Indian nation and designated by the federal Bureau of Indian Affairs as exempt from most state laws and taxes.

invariably the tribal leaders signed because of actual or threatened military defeat. Thus the legal status of the various tribes in the United States is that of a **domestic dependent nation,** where they retain their individual identity and sovereignty, but must rely on the U.S. federal government for the interpretation and application of treaty provisions. State and local governments are clearly affected by federal–tribal relations, but have little influence and virtually no legal authority over these relations.

The policy approach of the federal government toward Indians has varied widely. From 1830 to 1871, a major goal was to move all Indians to land west of the Mississippi. The policy between 1871 to 1934 was to assimilate Indians into the white culture of the United States. From 1934 until 1953 and then again from 1973 to today, the formal policy was to respect tribal customs, strengthen tribal governments, and promote economic self-determination. Between 1953 and 1973, the federal government terminated the legal status of various tribes, ended services to them, and refused to recognize their treaty rights. This generated protests and led to a resumption of the general policy begun in 1934.[3] While some would argue that the federal government has not been serious or effective enough in supporting treaty rights and self-determination, the current policy received new emphasis with the inclusion of tribes in steps to devolve responsibilities from Washington to states and local communities.

States are not parties to the treaties between the United States and American Indian nations and have no direct legal authority over tribes. The federal government has in several specific areas granted some powers to states. The Indian Gaming Regulatory Act of 1988, for example, gives state governments limited authority to negotiate agreements, called **compacts,** with tribes who wish to have casino gambling. Also, in 1953, Congress passed Public Law 280, which allows some states to pursue Indians suspected of criminal behavior even if they are on reservation land.

For the most part, however, federal–tribal relations provide given constraints and opportunities as states and communities engage in planning and problem solving. The two most important features of federal–tribal relations for state and local governments are land rights and treaty provisions for hunting, fishing, and gathering. Tribes have **reservation land** and **trust land,** neither of which is subject to taxation or regulation by state or local governments. The former was designated in the treaty. Tribes can acquire trust land by purchasing or otherwise securing ownership of a parcel and then seeking to have it placed in trust status by the Secretary of the Department of the Interior. Since a tribe can get trust land at any time and any place, there is the potential for some surprise and disruption of a community's development plans or tax base and an obvious challenge to cordial, working relationships between tribes, the federal government, and state or local government.

Hunting, fishing, and gathering activities have important cultural and religious significance for many American Indian nations. Treaty provisions giving rights to tribes to hunt, fish, and gather wild rice or berries on their own land and on public lands and waterways in land they once owned are key to tribal identity and dignity. These treaty rights supersede regulations enacted for environmental and recreational purposes.

Table 4.1   Federal Policies Toward Indian Nations

Up to 1830	Mixture of conquest and coexistence. Make treaties.
1830–1871	Force all tribes west of Mississippi. Make treaties.
1871–1934	Assimilate Indians into white culture.
1934–1953	Respect tribal customs and government. Encourage economic self-determination.
1953–1973	Terminate legal status of tribes. Ignore treaty provisions
1973–present	Recognize tribes and treaty rights. Encourage constitutions and self-determination.

Non-Indian anglers and hunters sometimes protest that Indians have special privileges. Environmental planners worry about the potential implications of unregulated Indian activity. In 1999, for example, the Makah tribe in the Northwest celebrated the successful capture and killing of a whale. While the tribe applauded the preservation of an important cultural tradition, wildlife advocates bemoaned the treaty rights that allowed this destruction of a valued animal. For some, the discord is more racial in nature than based in real environmental or recreational issues. For the states affected, the challenge is to promote harmony between groups and individuals and to deal effectively with any substantive issues that do materialize.

Since Congress passed the Indian Self-Determination and Education Assistance Act in 1975, the federal government has been trying to strengthen tribal governments by encouraging the adoption of constitutions. The Bureau of Indian Affairs offers assistance in writing the constitutions and other federal agencies, such as the Environmental Protection Agency, are willing to devolve some of their authority to tribes that have constitutions.

While a tribe may include some traditional patterns of governance in their constitutions, the basic concept of a constitution is alien to Indian tribes. The documents read very much like state constitutions, with preambles that espouse principles of democracy and provisions that provide for a familiar separation of powers among executive, legislative, and judicial branches. Not surprisingly, some nations struggle with the mandates of their constitutions and the informal but real power of their traditions.

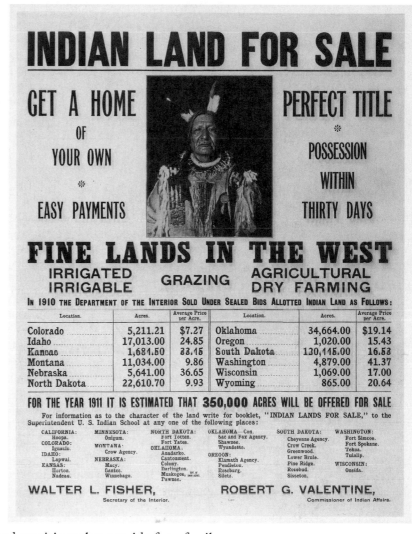

■ An advertisement from the Department of the Interior (c.1911) luring individuals to purchase land designated as surplus after tribal allotments were made to Indians. (Photo courtesy: Library of Congress)

Web Exploration
To learn more about American Indian nations and specific tribes, see www.awlonline.com/oconnor.

GRASSROOTS POWER AND POLITICS

The most powerful and influential people in a state or community are not necessarily those who hold offices in government. While there is always a distinction between formal and informal power, the face-to-face character of governance at the grass roots provides increased visibility to this dimension of politics. The part-time officials in particular have a more ambiguous identity than do full-time government officials.

In small to medium-sized communities especially it is common for a single family or a traditional elite to be the major decision maker, whether or not they have one of their members in a formal governmental position.[4] If you want to advocate for some improvements in a local park, a curriculum change in the schools, or a different set of priorities for the police department, it may be more important to get the support of a few key community leaders than the sympathy of the village president or the head of the school board. A newcomer interested in starting a business in a town likewise would be well advised to identify and court the informal elite and not just focus on those who hold a formal office.

Political participation in state and, especially, local politics is both more personal and more issue-oriented than at the national level. Much of what happens is outside the framework of political parties. Elections for some state and local government offices, in fact, are **nonpartisan elections,** which means parties do not nominate candidates and ballots do not include any party identification of those running for office. Access and approaches are usually direct. School board members receive phone calls at their homes. Members of the city council and county board bump into constituents while shopping for groceries or cheering their children in youth sports. The concerns that are communicated tend to be specific and neither partisan nor ideological. A particular grade school teacher is unfair and ineffective. Playground equipment is unsafe. It seems to be taking forever for the city to issue a building permit so that you can get started on a remodeling project.

In this setting, local news media invariably play a key role. The major newspaper in the state and what might be the only newspaper in a community can shape the agendas of government bodies and the images of government officials. The mere fact that a problem is covered makes it an issue. If the gang or cult activity is just a group of kids acting weird and dressing the same way, public officials might ignore it. News coverage of this or certainly of a violent incident, on the other hand, assures attention. Then the question is how the media define the issue—as an isolated and unusual event or as a signal that certain needs are not being met?

Ad hoc, issue-specific organizations are prevalent in state and local governments.[5] Individuals opposed to the plans of a state department of transportation to expand a stretch of highway from two to four lanes will organize, raise funds, and lobby hard to stop the project. Once the project is stopped or completed, that organization will go out of existence. Likewise, neighbors will organize to support or oppose specific development projects or to press for revitalization assistance, and then they will disband once the decision is made. The sporadic but intense activity focused on specific local or regional concerns is an important supplement to the ongoing work of parties and interest groups in state and local governments. A full understanding of what happens at the grass roots requires an appreciation of ad hoc, issue-specific politics as well as the institutions and processes through which state and local governments make and implement public policies.

STATE GOVERNMENTS

State governments have primary responsibility for education, public health, transportation, economic development, and criminal justice. States also are the unit of government that licenses and regulates various professions, such as doctors, lawyers, barbers, and architects. More recently, state governments have been active in welfare and the environment, in part as agents administering federal policies and programs and in part on their own.

State officials, in other words, have been and continue to be in charge of fundamental components of our society. They have also been challenged with problems that seem to defy solutions. Crime, for example, seems to be beyond our ability to do more than try to minimize it. Poverty is another such challenge. Likewise, we have not been fully satisfied with our efforts to educate everyone. Despite these awesome responsibilities, there has been a historic reluctance to make state governments fully capable institutions.

State Constitutions

Whereas a major goal of the writers of the U.S. Constitution in 1787 was to *empower* the national government, the authors of the original **state constitutions** wanted to *limit* government. The Constitutional Convention in Philadelphia was convened, as you recall from chapter 2, because of the perception that the national government under the Articles of Confederation was not strong enough. The debates were primarily over how strong the national, or federal, government should be.

---

nonpartisan election:

A contest in which candidates run without formal identification or association with a political party.

Web Exploration

To find statistics on any branch of government in the fifty states, see www.awlonline.com/oconnor.

state constitution:

The document that describes the basic policies, procedures, and institutions of the government of a specific state, much like the U.S. Constitution does for the federal government.

In contrast, the assumption of the authors of the first thirteen state constitutions, based on their backgrounds in the philosophy and experiences of monarchical rule, was that government was all-powerful, and so the question was how to limit it. The state constitutions were written and adopted before the Philadelphia Convention and included provisions that government may not interfere with basic individual liberties. These provisions, which were *integral* parts of each of the state constitutions, were *added* to the federal constitution as the first ten amendments, often called the Bill of Rights.

The first state constitutions provided for the institutions of government, such as governors, legislatures, and courts, with an emphasis on the limits of the authority of each institution.[6] These constitutions did not fully embrace the principle of checks and balances that is found in the U.S. Constitution. The office of governor was particularly weak. Not surprisingly, the most powerful institution was the legislature. In fact, initially only South Carolina, New York, and Massachusetts gave their governors the authority to veto legislation. After over 200 years, the state of North Carolina still does not let its governor use a veto.

The first state constitutions set the pattern for what was to come. In one of its last actions, the national Congress under the Articles of Confederation passed the Northwest Ordinance of 1781, which addressed how new states might join the Union. Lawmakers were responding primarily to settlers in what is now Ohio but extended coverage to the territory that includes Minnesota, Wisconsin, Iowa, Illinois, Michigan, and Indiana—which the people in the original states considered the "northwest." The basic blueprint included in the Ordinance was that a territory might successfully petition for statehood if it had at least 60,000 free inhabitants (slaves and American Indians did not count) and a constitution that was both similar to the documents of existing states and compatible with the national constitution. The first white settlers in the territory covered by the Northwest Ordinance were originally from New York and Massachusetts, with some individuals and families direct from Europe. Not surprisingly, the initial constitutions of these states were almost identical to those of New York and Massachusetts.[7]

The traumas of slavery and the Civil War had a profound impact on the constitutions of southern states. Events that led to the secession of Southern states included the Missouri Compromise of 1820–21, which simultaneously admitted Missouri and

---

 OOTS OF GOVERNMENT

The Northwest Ordinance of 1787

The Northwest Ordinance was the first national effort to create a system of governance for the territories, which ultimately became the basis for several state and local governments. It specifically set out some duties now reserved to the states, including the role of states in education and legislating for the morality of their citizens.

1. Congress shall appoint a governor, a secretary, and three judges for the Northwest Territory. These officials shall adopt suitable laws from the original states. When the territory has five thousand free male inhabitants of full age, they shall be allowed to elect representatives. These, together with the governor and a legislative council of five, shall form a general assembly to make laws for the territory.

2. The inhabitants shall be entitled to the benefits of trial by jury and other judicial proceedings according to the common law.
3. Religion, morality, and knowledge being necessary to good government and the happiness of mankind, schools and the means of education shall forever be encouraged.
4. There shall be formed in the said territory not less than three nor more than five States. . . . And, whenever any of the said States shall have sixty thousand free inhabitants therein, such State shall be admitted, by its delegates, into the Congress of the United States, on an equal footing with the original States.
5. There shall be neither slavery nor involuntary servitude in the said territory, otherwise than in the punishment of crimes whereof the party shall have been duly convicted.

Maine, the former with a constitution that legalized slavery and the latter as a "free state." The Missouri Compromise also included an agreement that no more states would be admitted that had constitutions allowing slavery. When, in 1854, that provision was violated by the admission of Kansas as a slave state and Nebraska as a free state, the confrontation between the two sides escalated.[8]

Slavery was a unique and very emotional issue. It raised the general question of the extent to which the national Congress could insist on specific clauses in state constitutions. The Civil War, of course, answered that question. That war also precipitated an era in which the states in the Confederacy wrote and discarded constitutions at a rapid pace and ended the process with documents that established state governments that were even weaker than those of the first thirteen states.

Southern states adopted new constitutions when they seceded and formed the Confederacy. After the Civil War, they had to adopt new constitutions acceptable to the Congress in Washington, D.C. These constitutions typically provided former slaves with considerable power and disenfranchised those who had been active in the Confederacy. These were not realistic constitutions. They divorced political power from economic wealth and social status, formal authority from informal influence. White communities simply ignored government and ruled themselves informally as much as possible. After less than ten years of this, whites reasserted political control and rewrote state constitutions.

The new documents reflected white distrust and provided for a narrow scope of authority for state governments and for weak, fragmented institutions. Governors could serve for only two-year terms. Legislatures could only meet for short periods of time and in some cases only once every other year. Law enforcement authority, both police and justices of the peace, rested squarely in local community power structures.

Western states entered the Union with constitutions that also envisioned weak governments. Here the central concerns were not slavery or national government interference, but rather political machines. In large cities in the Northeast and Midwest, machines based on bloc voting by new, non-English-speaking immigrants wrested political control and, sometimes in corrupt ways, began amassing economic wealth. New states in the West sought to keep machine politics from ever getting started in the first place.

Progressive Movement:

Advocates measures to destroy political machines and instead have direct participation by voters in the nomination of candidates and the establishment of public policy.

The most effective national anti-machine effort was the **Progressive Movement,** led by such figures as Woodrow Wilson, Theodore Roosevelt, Robert M. La Follette, and Hiram Johnson, who advocated changes that involved direct voter participation and bypassed traditional institutions.[9] These reforms included the use of primaries for nominating candidates instead of closed party processes, the initiative for allowing voters to enact laws directly and avoid legislatures and governors, and the recall for constituents to remove officials from office in the middle of their term. Progressives succeeded in getting their proposals adopted as statutes in existing states and in the constitutions of new states emerging from western territories.

Though weak state government institutions may have been a reasonable response to earlier concerns, they are inappropriate for current issues. The trend since the 1960s, throughout the United States, has been to amend state constitutions in order to enhance the capacity of governors, legislatures, and courts to address problems. In the 1970s alone, over 300 amendments to state constitutions were adopted. Most were to lengthen the terms of governors and provide chief executives with more authority over spending and administration, to streamline courts, and to make legislatures professional and full-time.[10]

Constitutional changes have also reflected some ambivalence. While there has been widespread recognition that state governments must be more capable, there is also concern about what that might mean in taxes and in the entrenchment of power. Thus, reforms have included severe restrictions on the ability of state and local governments to raise taxes and limits on how long legislators in some states might serve. Historic distrust of government continues.

 **IGHLIGHT 4.1**

The Hawaiian Constitution: A Special Case

Hawaii was a kingdom ruled by an absolute monarch through the reign of Kamehameha the Great (1782–1819). Out of deference to the traditions of this monarchy, when the federal government ruled Hawaii as a territory (1900–1959), it established an executive that was more powerful than is common in states. Also, the government did not foster local governments, but instead relied on the sugar and pineapple plantations to provide their own police and fire protection and other basic services.

As a legacy of this history, Hawaii's constitution provides for a more centralized governance than any of the other states. Public education, police and fire protection, library services, and health and welfare programs commonly run by local governments are operated directly by state government in Hawaii.

Another unique feature of Hawaii's constitution is the special attention to the welfare of native Hawaiians. Anyone who is at least 50 percent descended from the islands' indigenous inhabitants has land rights that are specially protected. Also the native Hawaiians benefit from income from certain land, originally designated by the federal government and now by state government. By contrast, other states may be affected by treaties agreed to by the federal government and Native American tribes. Hawaiians relate directly to the state for governance, whereas Native Americans continue to have their primary relationship with the federal government.

As compared with the U.S. Constitution, state constitutions are relatively easy to amend. Every state allows for the convening of a constitutional convention, and over 200 have been held. Also, every state has a process whereby the legislature can pass an amendment to the constitution, usually by a two-thirds or three-fourths vote, and then submit the change to the voters for their approval in a referendum. Seventeen states, mostly in the West, allow for amendments simply by getting the proposal on a statewide ballot, without involvement of the legislature or governor.

An implication of the relatively simple amendment processes is frequent changes. All but nineteen states have adopted wholly new constitutions since they were first admitted, and almost six-thousand specific amendments have been adopted. Another effect of the process is that state constitutions tend to be longer than the U.S. Constitution and include provisions that more appropriately should be statutes or administrative rules. The California constitution, for example, not only establishes state government institutions and protects individual rights, but also defines how long a wrestling match may be. Arkansas includes in its constitution what colors should be used for copies of registration documents. These are clear violations of the principle that constitutions are where the authority of government and its institutions is established and where policy-making processes are described.

Governors

Governors have always been the most visible elected officials in state governments. Initially, that visibility supported the ceremonial role of governors as their primary function. Now that visibility serves governors as they set the agenda and provide leadership for others in state governments.

The most important role that current governors play is in identifying the most pressing problems facing their respective states and proposing solutions to those problems. Governors first establish agendas when they campaign for office. After inauguration, the most effective way for the chief executive to initiate policy changes is when submitting the budget for legislative approval.

Budgets are critical to the business of state governments. The ways in which money is raised and spent say a lot about the priorities of decision makers. Until the 1920s, state legislatures commonly compiled and passed budgets and then submitted them for gubernatorial approval or veto. As part of the efforts to strengthen the capacities of state

governor:

Chief elected executive in state government.

Web Exploration

To learn about issues that governors nationwide deem most important, see www.awlonline.com/oconnor.

governments to deliberate and take action, governors were, like presidents, given the major responsibility for starting the budget process. Now all but four states have their governors propose budgets.

The role of governor as budget initiator is especially important when coupled with the governor's veto authority and executive responsibilities. Like presidents, governors in all states except North Carolina also have **package** or **general veto** authority, which rejects a bill in its entirety. In addition, governors in all but seven states may exercise a **line-item veto** on bills that involve spending or taxing. A line-item veto strikes only part of a bill that has been passed by the legislature. It allows a chief executive to delete a particular program or expenditure from a budget bill and let the remaining provisions become law. The intent of this authority is to enable governors to revise the work of legislators in order to produce a balanced budget.

Governor Tommy Thompson of Wisconsin has been the most extensive and creative user of the line-item veto. He has reversed the intent of legislation by vetoing the word "not" in a sentence and created entirely new laws by eliminating specific letters and numerals to make new words and numbers. Voters in Wisconsin were so upset with this free use of the veto pen that in 1993 they passed the "Vanna White amendment" to the state constitution, prohibiting the governor from striking letters within words and numerals within numbers. Not to be outmaneuvered, Governor Thompson then used his veto authority to actually *insert* new words and numbers in bills that had passed the legislature. The state supreme court, in 1995, upheld this interpretation of veto, as long as the net effect of the vetoes was not to increase spending.

While the Wisconsin case is extreme, it illustrates the significant power that veto authority can provide. Legislators can override vetoes, usually with a two-thirds vote in each of the chambers. But this rarely happens. Only 6 percent of gubernatorial vetoes are overturned,[11] and Governor Thompson has had enough support from his party to sustain all of his.

The executive responsibilities of governors provide an opportunity to affect public policies after laws have been passed. Agencies are then responsible for implementing the laws. That may mean improving a road, enforcing a regulation, or providing a service. The speed and care with which implementation occurs are often under the influence of the governor.[12] Likewise, governors can affect the many details and interpretations that must be decided. State statutes require drivers of vehicles to have a

package or general veto:

The authority of a chief executive to void an entire bill that has been passed by the legislature. This veto applies to all bills, whether or not they have taxing or spending components, and the legislature may override this veto, usually with a two-thirds majority of each chamber.

line-item veto:

The authority of a chief executive to delete part of a bill passed by the legislature that involves taxing and/or spending. The legislature may override a veto, usually with a two-thirds majority of each chamber.

■ State and local politics focus more closely on personal issues of concern to specific communities. Ultimately unsuccessful Democratic Louisiana gubernatorial candidate Cleo Fields (center) and Tipper Gore (right), wife of Vice President Al Gore, Jr., field questions on health care in a town meeting in New Orleans. (Photo courtesy: David Rae Morris/AP/Wide World Photos)

■ Specific issues arise from the grass roots to try to make their way onto the state and national political agendas. Sentiment among residents of the Mojave Desert town of Needles, California, obviously runs strongly against development of a nuclear waste dump in the Ward Valley, some twenty miles west of town. (Photo courtesy: Reed Saxon/AP/Wide World Photos)

license, but they typically let an agency decide exactly what one must do to get a license, where one can take the tests, and what happens if someone fails a test. Governors can influence these decisions primarily through appointing the heads of state administrative agencies.

One of the methods of limiting gubernatorial power was to curtail appointment authority.[13] Unlike the federal government, for example, states have some major agencies headed by individuals who are elected rather than appointed by the chief executive. Forty-three states, for example, elect their attorney general, a position that is part of the president's Cabinet. The positions of secretary of state, treasurer, and auditor are also usually filled by elected rather than appointed officials. Some states elect their head of education, agriculture, or labor. The movement throughout states to strengthen the institutions of their governments has included increasing the number of senior positions that are filled by gubernatorial appointments so that governors, like heads of major corporations, can assemble their own policy and management teams.

Another position that is filled by presidential appointment in the federal government but, in most cases, elected in state governments is judge. The structure of state courts and how judges are selected will be discussed later in the chapter. This is one more example of approaches that have been taken to restrict the authority of governors.

Nonetheless, governors are major actors in the judicial system. With the legislature, they define what is a crime within a state and attach penalties that should be meted out to those convicted of committing crimes. Once someone has been convicted, they will be institutionalized and/or supervised by an agency that is, in every state, headed by a gubernatorial appointment. Moreover, governors have authority to **pardon** someone who has been convicted, thereby eliminating all penalties and wiping the court action from an individual's record. Governors may also **commute** all or part of a sentence, which leaves the conviction on record even though the penalty is reduced.

In addition, governors grant **parole** to prisoners who have served part of their terms. Typically, governors are advised by a parole board on whether or not to grant a parole. Paroles usually have conditions that must be met, like staying in a certain area, avoiding contact with certain people or organizations, and participating in therapy or a work program. Violation of these conditions could mean a return to prison. Beginning in the mid-1990s, a number of states began eliminating parole and requiring convicts to serve their full sentences. This movement was known as "truth in sentencing."

Finally, under the U.S. Constitution, governors have the discretion to **extradite** individuals. This means that a governor may decide to send someone, against his or her will, to another state to face criminal charges. When Mario Cuomo, who opposed the death penalty, was governor of New York, he refused to extradite someone to a state

pardon:
The authority of a governor to cancel someone's conviction of a crime by a court and to eliminate all sanctions and punishments resulting from the conviction.

commute:
The authority of a governor to cancel all or part of the sentence of someone convicted of a crime, while keeping the conviction on the record.

parole:
The authority of a governor to release a prisoner before his or her full sentence has been completed and to specify conditions that must be met as part of the release.

extradite:
The authority of a governor to send someone against his or her will to another state to face criminal charges.

Figure 4.1   Party Control for State Governorships, 1999

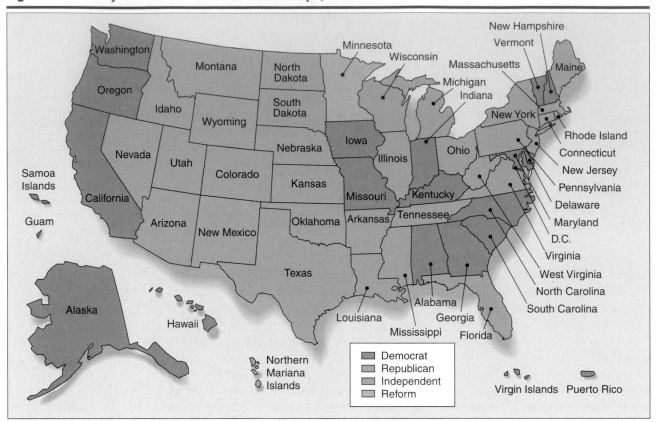

that used capital punishment. That refusal became an issue in Governor Cuomo's bid for reelection in 1994. Shortly after he was inaugurated, newly elected governor George Pataki ordered the extradition. In fact, with the support of Governor Pataki, New York itself adopted the death penalty.

Gubernatorial participation in the judicial process has led to some of the most colorful controversies in state politics. James E. Ferguson, as Governor of Texas, granted 2,253 pardons between 1915 and 1917. His successor, William P. Hobby, granted 1,518 during the next two years, and then Governor Miriam "Ma" Ferguson outdid her husband by issuing almost 3,800 during her term. Texans were used to shady wheeling and dealing in politics, but this volume of pardons seemed a bit excessive. The Texas constitution was amended to remove authority to grant pardons and paroles from the governor; this power was placed in the hands of a board. Governors of the Lone Star state now have the lowest amount of authority among the fifty state chief executives to check actions of the judiciary.[14]

The general trend since the 1960s, as has been noted, has been to increase rather than decrease the power and authority of governors.[15] Given the historic desire to have weak chief executives, some of the enhancement of gubernatorial powers has come at the cost of the prerogatives of other institutions. This is particularly the case with veto authority and the role in the budgetary process. Capacity, however, has both absolute and relative dimensions. Legislatures and courts have also developed into more capable institutions since the 1960s.

State Legislatures

The principles of representative democracy are embodied primarily in the legislature. Legislatures, as mentioned above, were initially established to be the most powerful of the institutions of state government. In over half of the original states, legislatures began without the check of a gubernatorial veto. Until the twentieth century, most state legislatures were responsible for executive chores such as formulating a budget and making administrative appointments.

These tasks were, even more than was envisioned for the U.S. Congress, to be done by "citizen–legislators" as a part-time responsibility. The image was that individuals would convene in the state capitol for short periods of time to conduct the state's business. State constitutions and statutes specified the part-time operation of the legislature and provided only limited compensation for those who served.

As mentioned earlier, the one-person, one-vote ruling of the U.S. Supreme Court in *Baker* v. *Carr* (1962) marked a turning point in the history of state legislatures, and state governments generally. Once legislatures more accurately represented their states, agendas became more relevant and policies were more appropriate.[16] State legislatures not only became more representative, they became more professional. Legislators worked more days—some of them full-time. In 1960, only eighteen state legislatures met annually. In 1995, forty-three met every year and only seven every other year. Moreover, the floor sessions were longer, and between sessions legislators and their staff increasingly did committee work and conducted special studies.[17]

Ideally, bills are drafted and votes are cast based on informed evaluations. Along with passing laws, legislatures must monitor and assess the activities of administrative agencies. Legislatures need to consider the many initiatives for policy change that come from agencies. To develop the capacity to provide oversight, conduct analyses, and serve constituents, state legislatures increased their staff by almost 130 percent between 1968 and 1974.[18] Growth since then has been at a rather steady 4 percent rate. Staff resources have been supplemented by the services of the National Conference of State Legislatures, established in 1973, and increasingly by computer technology and information sharing on the Internet. Like Congress, state legislatures have established library reference services and audit agencies to help serve their needs.

All states except Nebraska have two legislative houses. One, the senate, typically has fewer members than the other, usually called the "house" or the "assembly." The most common ratio between the two chambers is 1:3. In fourteen states the ratio is 1:2, and in New Hampshire it is 1:16. Another difference between the two bodies in thirty-four of the states is that senators serve four-year terms, whereas representatives in the larger house serve two-year terms. In eleven states everyone in both houses serves two-year terms, and in the remaining, including Nebraska, everyone serves for four years.

Although it has been common to have limits on how many terms someone may serve as governor, **term limits** for legislators is a development of the 1980s and 1990s. By 1999, twenty states had passed measures limiting the number of years one might be a state legislator. In thirteen states, the limit is eight consecutive years per house. In three states the limit is twelve years, and in the others the number varies with each house and ranges from six to twelve.

Proponents of term limits included minority party leaders who calculated—sometimes in error—that they stood a better chance of gaining seats if incumbents had to leave after a certain period of time. Others saw term limits as a way of making the ideal of citizen–legislator more probable. They saw intuitive appeal in the concept of having people being a legislator in addition to whatever else they did in life, as opposed to pursuing a career as an elected official.[19]

The movement to limit legislative service is a contrast to the pattern that evolved since the *Baker* v. *Carr* ruling. With an end to rural overrepresentation, state legislatures became relevant. Urban and economic development issues got serious attention. State budgets included a wider array of programs. The wider scope of state issues, enhanced when the federal government shed some of its responsibilities to the states, attracted individuals seriously interested in public service and required increased staff to help with analysis and evaluation.

State legislatures, although much more capable and serious institutions than they were prior to the early 1960s, are still primarily part-time, citizen bodies.[20] Every election puts new members in about one-fourth of the seats. Only a handful of legislators

Web Exploration

To learn about the policy issues being addressed in your state legislature, see www.awlonline.com/oconnor.

term limits:

Restrictions that exist in some states about how long an individual may serve in state and/or local elected offices.

Table 4.2 Time's Up for Some Politicians

By 1998, 206 state legislators in seven states became ineligible to run for reelection because of term limits.
By state:

Arkansas House **50 of 100** members

Maine House **11 of 151** members

California Assembly **16 of 80** members

Maine Senate **1 of 35** members

California Senate **11 of 40** members

Michigan House **67 of 110** members

Colorado House **18 of 65** members

Missouri Senate **1 of 34** members

Colorado Senate **9 of 35** members

Oregon House **22 of 60** members

STATES WITH TERM LIMITS
When each state's term limits affect the House and the Senate:

	HOUSE		SENATE	
	Takes effect	Limit (years)	Takes effect	Limit (years)
Maine	1996	8	1996	8
California	1996	6	1998	8
Colorado	1998	8	1998	8
Arkansas	1998	6	2000	8
Michigan	1998	6	2002	8
Oregon	1998	6	2002	8
Florida	2000	8	2000	8
Missouri[1]	2002	8	2002	8
Ohio	2000	8	2000	8
South Dakota	2000	8	2000	8
Montana	2000	8	2000	8
Arizona	2000	8	2000	8
Idaho	2004	8	2004	8
Oklahoma	2004	12	2004	12
Nevada	2008	12	2008	12
Utah	2006	12	2006	12
Wyoming	2006	12	2006	12
Louisiana	2007	12	2007	12

[1]Because of special elections, term limits are effective in 1998 for one senator and in 2001 for five House members.

SOURCE: *USA Today* (April 20, 1998): 2A. Reprinted by permission.

in each state envision careers as state lawmakers. Those with long-term political aspirations tend to view service in a state chamber as a step on a journey to some other office, in the state capitol or in Washington, D.C. For some, their goal is to don a black robe and preside in a courtroom.

State Courts

Almost everyone is in a courtroom at some point. It may be as a judge, a juror, an attorney, a court officer, or a litigant. It may also be for some administrative function like an adoption, a name change, or the implementation of a will. Few of us will ever be in a federal court; almost all of us will be in a state court.

The primary function of courts is to settle disputes, and most disputes are matters of state, not federal, laws. For the most part, criminal behavior is defined by state legislatures. Family law, dealing with marriage, divorce, adoption, child custody, and the like, is found in state statutes. Contracts, liability, land use, and much that is fundamental to everyday business activity and economic development also are part of state governance.

A common misunderstanding is that the courts in the United States are all part of a single system, with the U.S. Supreme Court at the head. In fact, state and federal courts are separate, with their own rules, procedures, and routes for appeal. The only time state and federal courts converge is when a case involves both federal and state laws or constitutions.

A famous example of overlap between state and federal courts was in 1994, when Los Angeles police officers arrested Rodney King for a traffic violation. An amateur photographer videotaped the arrest and captured shots of the police officers severely beating King. The officers were first tried in California state court for using excessive force. They convinced the jury that King was resisting and thus force was justified. Federal prosecutors nonetheless proceeded to try the officers for violating King's civil rights, a federal crime. In federal court, the jury came to a different conclusion and convicted the officers.

Although the state and federal courts had essentially the same facts, the laws that applied here were somewhat different. The central question posed by state law was whether the police officers used more force than professionally acceptable. The issue focused on professional standards. The federal law centered on racial discrimination and Rodney King's civil rights. Here the racial slurs and jokes made by police officers weighed more heavily and were more relevant than for the state issue of whether excessive force was used.

Sometimes federal and state laws are directly related. If there is a contradiction between the two, then federal law prevails. A state statute that allowed or encouraged racial hiring, for example, would directly conflict with the 1964 federal Civil Rights Act. Through a rule known as **inclusion,** state courts would be obliged to enforce the federal law.

The issue may be "more or less" rather than "either–or." Since the 1970s, the U.S. Supreme Court has generally taken the position that, especially with regard to individual rights protected in the Constitution, state courts should be encouraged to regard the federal government as setting minimums.[21] If state constitutions and laws provide additional protections or benefits, then state courts should enforce those standards.

State judges must incorporate **common law** as well as federal law into their analyses. Common law begins with the decisions made by judges in England in the thirteenth century; it has evolved with the interpretation and application of those rulings over the years. While some states and communities have made parts of common law into written laws, most of the rulings and rationale remain unwritten. Courts nonetheless are expected to apply traditional common law as they rule on family disputes, disorderly conduct, charges of indecency, and social conflicts in a community. Louisiana used to follow the Napoleonic Code of French tradition, but like other states now subscribes to fundamental edicts of Anglo-American common law and culture.

Another important distinction is between criminal law and civil law. **Criminal law** consists of instances where someone has been killed or injured or has suffered a loss or damage to property. These actions generally involve a victim, but they are considered to be crimes against society. A district attorney or state's attorney, representing society as a whole, prosecutes the alleged criminal. Penalties for those convicted include fines or incarceration or, in some states, death. **Civil law,** on the other hand, involves a dispute between two individuals and/or organizations. At issue may be a verbal or written contract. At stake is usually money. One party typically sues the other for compensation because of damages due to the violation of a contract or agreement. District attorneys or state's attorneys are not involved in civil law cases unless a state agency is suing or being sued.

Like other state government institutions, courts have modernized in the past few decades. Virtually extinct now is the justice of the peace, a judicial position that became

inclusion:

The principle that state courts will apply federal laws when those laws directly conflict with the laws of a state.

common law:

Legal traditions of society that are for the most part unwritten but based on the aggregation of rulings and interpretations of judges beginning in thirteenth-century England.

criminal law:

Codes of behavior related to the protection of property and individual safety.

civil law:

Codes of behavior related to business and contractual relationships between groups and individuals.

part of American lore, humor, and dismay. These were part-time judges. (Some of the ridicule aimed at justices of the peace identified their "other" job as the sheriff!) One might count on a justice of the peace for a quick wedding (or divorce), but rarely for consistent, impartial, well-reasoned rulings.

Many states reorganized their court systems in the 1970s to follow a model that relied on full-time, qualified judges, simplified appeal routes, and enabled state supreme courts to have a manageable workload. Figure 4.2 illustrates the court structure that is now common among the states.

Most court cases in urban areas begin in a court that specializes in issues like family disputes, traffic, small claims (less than $500 or $1,000), or probate (wills) or in a general jurisdiction municipal court. Small towns and rural areas usually do not have specialized courts. Cases here start in county-level courts that deal with the full array of disputes.

The specialized courts do not use juries. A single judge hears the case and decides. Other courts at this level do have juries if requested by the litigants. A major responsibility of the judges and juries that deliberate on cases when they are originated is to evaluate the credibility of the witnesses and evidence. Although mistakes can be made, judges and jurors have the opportunity to see and consider the demeanor and apparent confidence of witnesses. When cases are heard on appeal, the only individuals making oral presentations are attorneys.

Appellate courts have panels of judges. There are no juries in these courtrooms. An important feature of the court reorganizations of the 1970s is that a court of appeals exists between the circuit or county courts and the state supreme court. This court is to cover part of the state and is supposed to accept all appeals. In part, this appellate level is to allow supreme courts to decide whether or not it will hear a case. The basic principle is that all litigants should have at least one opportunity to appeal a decision. If the state supreme court is the only place where an appeal can be lodged, that court is almost inevitably going to have too heavy a caseload and unreasonable backlogs will develop.

Missouri Plan:

A method of selecting judges in which a governor must appoint someone from a list provided by an independent panel. Judges are then kept in office if they get a majority of "yes" votes in general elections.

Most state judges are elected to the bench for a specific term. The first states had their legislatures elect judges, and that is still the case in Connecticut, Rhode Island, South Carolina, Vermont, and Virginia. As Table 4.3 shows, in sixteen states, voters elect judges and use party identification. Another sixteen use nonpartisan elections. Only six states use gubernatorial appointments. The remaining states follow what is referred to as the **Missouri Plan,** in which the governor, who must select someone from

Figure 4.2   State Court Structure

	Jury or Bench Trials	Jurisdiction	Judges
STATE SUPREME COURT	Bench only	Appeal (limited)	Panel of judges, elected/appointed for fixed term
APPEALS COURTS	Bench only	Appeal (readily granted)	Panel of judges, elected/appointed for fixed term
CIRCUIT OR COUNTY COURTS	Jury and Bench	Original and appeal	One judge per court, elected/appointed for fixed term
MUNICIPAL AND SPECIAL COURTS	Bench only	Original	One judge per court, elected/appointed for fixed term

a list prepared by an independent panel, initially appoints judges for a specific term of years. If a judge wishes to serve for an additional term, he or she must receive approval from the voters, who express themselves on a "yes–no" ballot. If a majority of voters cast a "no" ballot, the process starts all over. Five states (California, Kansas, Missouri, Oklahoma, and Tennessee) use the Missouri Plan for some judicial positions and elections for the others.

Different selection processes can be expected to yield different results. Partisan elections and gubernatorial appointments would seem to emphasize patronage and politics, whereas the Missouri Plan and nonpartisan elections seem to suggest more independence. Studies, however, have found that selection processes do not seem to have any noticeable impact. The education, experience, and social backgrounds of judges are all similar, regardless of how they got to the bench. Likewise, there are no links between how judges were selected and whether their decisions favored criminal defendants, corporations, government agencies, or poor people.[22] In short, selection processes seem to be more important for how voters feel than for how courts behave.

Elections

Elections are the vehicle for determining who will fill major state government positions and who will direct the institutions of state government. Almost all contests for state government posts are partisan. The major exceptions are judicial elections in many states, as noted above, and the senate in Nebraska's unicameral legislature. Although

Table 4.3   Judicial Selection Patterns

Partisan Election	Nonpartisan Election
Alabama	Arizona
Arkansas	California
Georgia	Florida
Indiana	Idaho
Illinois	Kentucky
Kansas	Michigan
Louisiana	Minnesota
Mississippi	Montana
Missouri	Nevada
New Mexico	North Dakota
New York	Ohio
North Carolina	Oregon
Pennsylvania	Oklahoma
Tennessee	South Dakota
Texas	Washington
West Virginia	Wisconsin

Election by Legislature	Appointment by Governor
Connecticut	Delaware
Rhode Island	Hawaii
South Carolina	Maryland
Vermont	Massachusetts
Virginia	New Hampshire
	New Jersey

Missouri Plan

Alaska	Iowa	Oklahoma
California	Kansas	Tennessee
Colorado	Missouri	Utah
Indiana	Nebraska	Wyoming

SOURCE: *The Book of the States, 1996–1997* (Copyright, 1996), The Council of State Governments. Reprinted by permission.

party labels are not visible and political parties are not formally participants in nonpartisan races, the party identity of some candidates may be known and may have some influence.

Political parties have different histories and roles in the various states. The map in Figure 4.3 presents the states according to the level of competition between the two major national political parties. Most states have experienced significant competition between Republicans and Democrats since the Civil War. These states usually have party control split between the two houses of the legislature and the governor's office or have frequent changes in party control of state government.

The Democratic Party has been dominant in Arkansas, Louisiana, Mississippi, Alabama, and Georgia since 1865. This means Democrats have elected the governor and majorities in both houses of the legislature over 60 percent of the time. The Republican Party has occasionally won the governor's race in some of these states, and there have been small blocs of Republicans in state legislatures. No state has experienced long-term dominance by Republicans similar to the Democratic control of these five states.

States are classified as having "majority party rule" if a single party wins the governorship at least 40 percent of the time and both houses of the legislature over 50 percent of the time. Both parties in these states typically win at least 40 percent of the votes cast. There has been Republican majority rule in only two states, New Hampshire and South Dakota. The states of Hawaii, New Mexico, Texas, Oklahoma, Florida, South Carolina, North Carolina, Kentucky, Rhode Island, and Maryland have had Democratic Party majority rule.

Elections from 1994 through 1997 provided evidence that the Republican Party is acquiring significant, long-term strength that will enhance party competition generally

Figure 4.3 Patterns of Party Competition

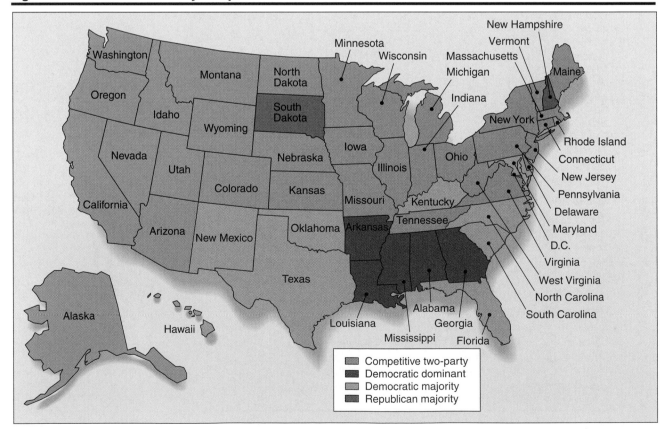

and perhaps lead to stable Republican dominance in some states. Republicans notched impressive victories throughout the country for federal and state offices. They gained control of the U.S. Senate and House of Representatives, won gubernatorial contests in populous states like New York, Texas, California, Florida, Illinois, and Pennsylvania, and secured the majority of seats in more state legislative chambers than ever before captured by the Republican Party. Democrats made somewhat of a comeback in 1998 and won the governor's race in California, but they lost Florida and generally had to concede that Republican gains in the 1990s are based on long-term changes in the political leanings of the population.

One of the reasons for Republican success is that voters in the South who had been voting for conservative Democrats began voting for conservative Republicans. Southerners have supported Republican presidential candidates since the Democratic Party began asserting leadership for civil rights following World War II. Alignment with Republicans in contests for state and congressional positions, however, has been much slower and more the exception than the rule. The 1994 elections may represent a threshold. After the votes were counted, six of the eleven Southern states had Republican governors. Republicans controlled the Florida state legislature and the house in North Carolina and came close in many chambers throughout the South. This pattern, with slight variations, continued through the rest of the decade. In short, Southerners no longer represent a significant minority within the national Democratic Party, but instead are part of the majority within the Republican Party—nationally and regionally.

It is easy to exaggerate the importance of partisanship in state politics. Whether at the state or the national level, the differences between Republicans and Democrats are important but not drastic. While party labels and organizations matter, campaigns are primarily centered on individual candidates. Voters usually have an opportunity to meet face-to-face with those contending for state government offices. A common strategy of candidates is to downplay their party identification, both to emphasize their strengths as an individual and to appeal to independent voters. After the election, party labels are important in determining who is in the majority and therefore who will control committees and who will preside in the legislature. That affects the agenda and the dynamics of policy making, but even here parties typically lack the homogeneity and the discipline to determine outcomes.

Direct Democracy

Ballots almost always include referenda and initiative questions, as well as the names of candidates. These questions are part of governance in states and communities. As mentioned earlier, a Progressive reform meant to weaken parties was to provide opportunities for voters to legislate directly, and not have to go through state legislatures and governors.[23] That process, known as the **direct initiative** and, as shown in Table 4.4, is available in nineteen states, most of them in the West. A disadvantage of the direct initiative is the possibility that a law may be passed solely because of public opinion, which might be shaped largely by thirty-second television commercials and short slogans.

An issue is placed on the ballot by securing enough signatures on a petition. There is no guarantee that those who sign the petition or those who cast votes have considered the issue thoroughly or secured all the relevant evidence. Direct initiatives do not allow for the debate and amendment process available in a legislature. Voters are presented with a simple yes or no question.

Sometimes initiatives are passed and then set aside by courts because they violate the state and/or federal constitution or because the federal government preempts the state. When California, for example, passed Proposition 187 in 1994 denying most public services to unregistered immigrants, federal courts kept the state from implementing the law because it trespassed on federal immigration policy and violated the U.S. Constitution.

Debate, deliberation, and amendment are included in the **indirect initiative.** In this process, legislatures first consider the issue and then pass a bill that will become law if

Web Exploration

To understand how campaigns are financed in state governments, see www.awlonline.com/oconnor.

direct initiative:

A process in which voters can place a proposal on a ballot and enact it into law without involving the legislature or the governor.

indirect initiative:

A process in which the legislature places a proposal on a ballot and allows voters to enact it into law, without involving the governor or further action by the legislature.

Table 4.4   Authority for the Initiative and Popular Referendum

State	Direct Initiative	Indirect Initiative	Popular Referendum
Alaska		X	X
Arizona		X	X
Arkansas	X		X
California	X		X
Colorado	X		
Florida	X		
Idaho	X		X
Illinois	X		
Kentucky			X
Maine		X	X
Maryland			X
Massachusetts		X	X
Michigan	X	X	X
Mississippi		X	
Missouri	X		X
Montana	X		X
Nebraska	X		X
Nevada	X	X	X
New Mexico			X
North Dakota	X		X
Ohio	X	X	X
Oklahoma	X		X
Oregon	X		X
South Dakota	X		X
Utah	X	X	X
Washington	X	X	X
Wyoming		X	X

SOURCE: *The Book of the States, 1996–1997* (Lexington, KY: Council of State Governments, 1996), 209. © 1996, Council of State Governments and Harold W. Stanley and Richard G. Niemi, *Vital Statistics on American Politics, 1997–1998* (Washington, D.C.: Congressional Quarterly 1998), 294–295.

approved by the voters. The governor plays no role. Of the eight states that have the indirect initiative, five also have the direct initiative.

Voters in twenty-four states have the opportunity to veto some bills. In these states, voters may circulate a petition objecting to a particular law passed in a recent session of the legislature. If enough signatures are collected, then an item appears on the next statewide ballot giving the electorate the chance to object and therefore veto the legislation. This is known as a **direct** or **popular referendum.**

All state and local legislative bodies may place an **advisory referendum** on a ballot. As the name implies, this is a device to take the pulse of the voters on a particular issue and has no binding effect. In addition, voter approval is required in a referendum to amend constitutions and, in some cases, to allow a governmental unit to borrow money through issuing bonds.

direct (popular) referendum:

A process in which voters can veto a bill recently passed in the legislature by placing the issue on a ballot and expressing disapproval.

advisory referendum:

A process in which voters cast nonbinding ballots on an issue or proposal.

LOCAL GOVERNMENTS

The institutions and politics of local governance are even more personalized than state governments. In part this is because officials are friends, neighbors, and acquaintances living in the communities they serve. Except in large cities, most elected officials fulfill their responsibilities on a part-time basis. In part, the personal nature of local governance is due to the immediacy of the issues. The responsibilities of local governments

■ Responsibilities of local governments are wide-ranging—from collecting the garbage in Minneapolis and filling potholes in Buffalo to patrolling the beach at Corpus Christi on spring break. (Photo courtesy: Bob Daemmrich/Stock Boston)

include public health and safety in their communities, education of children in the area, jobs and economic vitality, zoning land for particular uses, and assistance to those in need. Local government policies and activities are the stuff of everyday living.

Charters

Romantic notions of democracy in America regard local governments as the building blocks of governance by the people. Alex de Tocqueville, the critic credited with capturing the essence of early America, described government in the new country as a series of social contracts starting at the grass roots. He said, "the township was organized before the county, the county before the state, the state before the union."[24] It sounds good, but it's wrong.

A more accurate description comes from Judge John F. Dillon. In an 1868 ruling, known as **Dillon's Rule,** Dillon proclaimed:

> The true view is this: Municipal corporations owe their origins to and derive their power and rights wholly from the (state) legislature. It breathes into them the breath without which they cannot exist. As it creates, so it may destroy. If it may destroy, it may abridge and control.[25]

Dillon's Rule applies to all types of local governments.

There are many categories of local governments. Some of these are created in a somewhat arbitrary way by state governments. Counties and school districts are good examples. State statutes establish the authority for these jurisdictions, set the boundaries, and determine what these governments may and may not do and how they can generate funds.

Some local governments emerge as people and industries locate together and form a community. These governments must have a **charter** that is acceptable to the state legislature, much as states must have a constitution acceptable to Congress. Charters describe the institutions of government, the processes used to make legally binding decisions, and the scope of issues and services that fall within the jurisdiction of the governmental bodies. There are five basic types of charters:

1. **Special Charters.** Historically, as urban areas emerged, each one developed and sought approval for its own charter. To avoid inconsistencies, most state constitutions now prohibit the granting of special charters.
2. **General Charters.** Some states use a standard charter for all jurisdictions, regardless of size or circumstance.

Web Exploration

To learn more about the issues currently of concern to local government see www.awlonline.com/oconnor.

Dillon's Rule:

A court ruling that local governments do not have any inherent sovereignty, but instead must be authorized by state government.

charter:

A document that, like a constitution, specifies the basic policies, procedures, and institutions of a municipality.

3. **Classified Charters.** This approach classifies cities according to population and then has a standard charter for each classification.
4. **Optional Charters.** A more recent development is for the state to provide several acceptable charters and then let voters in a community choose from these.
5. **Home Rule Charters.** Increasingly, states are specifying the major requirements that a charter must meet and then allowing communities to draft and amend their own charters. State government must still approve the final product. Every state allows this process except Alabama, Indiana, Illinois, Kentucky, North Carolina, and Virginia.

An important feature of home rule is that the local government is authorized to legislate on any issue that does not conflict with existing state or federal laws. Other approaches list the subjects that a town or city may address.

In the early 1990s, Minnesota, California, and Colorado extended the concept of charters to public schools. They allowed teachers, parents, and/or community leaders to operate a school according to a charter instead of the standard rules and regulations of the state and the school district. To establish a **charter school,** a document would have to be approved that described the administration of the school, its curricula, admission policies, facilities, and general philosophy. States throughout the country have been authorizing charter schools as part of efforts to improve public education.

charter school:

Public schools sanctioned by a specific agreement that allows the program to operate outside the usual rules and regulations.

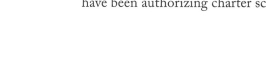 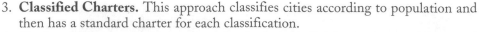 

POLITICS NOW   School Reforms

In 1999 Florida, Ohio, and Wisconsin had new programs that tested the boundaries between church and state. Parents in these states could get public funds to pay tuition at private schools, including religious schools. The intent of these programs is to satisfy a longtime, fundamental responsibility of state governments: to provide a quality educational opportunity to every child. The traditional approach has been to establish public schools where parents, regardless of their income or location, can send their children to school through the twelfth grade for little or no cost, other than the general taxes that they and everyone else pay. Parents who wanted to send their children to a private school, of course, may do so but must pay whatever extra costs are involved.

Advocates for reform contend that parents should be able to choose the school that best meets the needs of their children and that competition among schools will inevitably lead to higher quality. States like Minnesota, California, and Oregon have limited alternatives to public schools, and have not limited parents to the school in their neighborhood. These states have also allowed parents to educate their children at home. Only Florida, Ohio, and Wisconsin have extended the choice to religious schools,

contending that the taxpayer money is going to parents, not directly to the schools, so that technically the separation between church and state is maintained.

Those opposed to school choice argue that competitive market analogies don't apply when some parents cannot afford the time or money to transport children away from their neighborhood schools, and that attention and resources should be focused on providing good education for everyone. They regard public funds going indirectly to religious schools as a violation of the spirit of state and the U.S. constitutions, even if it can be argued as technically allowed.

The controversy over what, if any, choices parents should have is fueled by more than differences in philosophies. There is perennial conflict over whether schools should include subjects like sex education or creationism. Parents sometimes get very concerned about the quality of teachers their children have and the approaches taken to learning language and mathematical skills. They recognize how important schools are to the development of their children.

Education politics is typically intense and emotional. The issues of values and taxes are of fundamental importance, and the consequences are often immediate and personal.

Types of Local Governments

There are about 87,000 local governments in the United States. Table 4.5 presents the major categories.

1. **Counties.** Every state except Connecticut and Rhode Island has **counties,** although in Louisiana they are called parishes and in Alaska, boroughs. With few exceptions, counties have very broad responsibilities and are used by state governments as basic administrative units for welfare and environmental programs, courts, and the registration of land, births, and deaths. County and city boundaries may and do overlap, although state actions have merged city and county in New York, San Francisco, Denver, St. Louis, Nashville, and Honolulu.

2. **Towns.** In the first states and in the Midwest, "town" refers to a form of government in which everyone in a community is invited to an annual meeting to elect officers, adopt ordinances, and pass a budget. Another use of this term is simply to refer to a medium-sized city.

3. **Municipalities.** Villages, towns, and cities are established us **municipalities** and authorized by state governments as individuals congregate and form communities. Some of the most intense struggles among governments within the United States are over the boundaries, scope of authority, and sources of revenue for municipal governments.

4. **Special Districts. Special districts** are the most numerous form of government. A special district is restricted to a particular policy or service area. School districts are the most common form of special district. Others exist for library service, sewerage, water, and parks. Special districts are governed through a variety of structures. Some have elected heads and others, appointed. Some of these jurisdictions levy a fee to generate their revenues, whereas others depend on appropriations from a state, city, or county. A reason for the recent proliferation of special districts is to avoid restrictions on funds faced by municipalities, schools, or other jurisdictions. The creation of a special park district, for example, may enable the park to have its own budget and sources of funding and relieve a city or county treasury.

The reasons that an individual local government was established and given the authority it has are generally sound, but the multiple governments serving the same community and controlling the same area create incredible complexity and confusion. The challenge described in the opening vignette is to bridge the separation between cities, school districts, counties, and state agencies to address effectively the issue of

county:

A geographic district created within a state with a government that has general responsibilities for land, welfare, environment, and, where appropriate, rural service policies.

municipality:

A government with general responsibilities, such as a city, town, or village government, that is created in response to the emergence of relatively densely populated areas.

special district:

A local government that is responsible for a particular function, such as K–12 education, water, sewerage, or parks.

Table 4.5   Major Forms of Municipal Government

Population Group	FORM OF GOVERNMENT (NUMBER AND PERCENT)				
	All Cities	Mayor–council	Council–manager	Commission	Town meeting[a]
Over 1,000,000	8	6 (75%)	2 (25%)	0 (0%)	0 (0%)
500,000 to 1,000,000	16	13 (81%)	3 (19%)	0 (0%)	0 (0%)
250,000 to 499,999	39	16 (41%)	22 (56%)	1 (3%)	0 (0%)
25,000 to 249,999	1137	407 (36%)	681 (60%)	22 (2%)	27 (2%)
10,000 to 24,999	1602	676 (42%)	751 (47%)	52 (3%)	123 (8%)
2,500 to 9,999	3792	2192 (58%)	1240 (33%)	73 (2%)	287 (8%)
Total (all cities over 2,500)	6594	3310 (50%)	2699 (41%)	148 (2%)	437 (7%)

[a]Includes representative town meeting

Note: The mayor–council form of government is most popular in very large and very small cities. The council–manager form is most popular in medium-sized cities The commission form continues to lose popularity.

SOURCE: *The Municipal Year Book 1993* (Washington, DC:
International City/County Management Association, 1993), Table 2, xi. Reprinted by permission.

youth violence. A specific response may be to provide a youth center and/or skateboard rink for young people in a community to hang out in a safe and healthy setting. Such a project poses questions about which jurisdictions will provide funding and ensure staffing. Land may have to be rezoned and building permits acquired. Will a park district be involved? Will schools count on this facility for after-school programming? What will be the role and approach of the police department? Who will be in charge?

There are examples of formal and informal arrangements among local governments to cooperate and coordinate their work in a single community. Miami and Dade County in Florida have been an early and visible example. The two jurisdictions have merged their public health services, jointly administer parks, operate a unified mass transit system, and together plan for development and land use. Saint Paul and Minneapolis in Minnesota have also pioneered cooperative arrangements. The establishment of the 911 emergency service can be a catalyst for cooperation by various police, fire, and paramedical agencies in a metropolitan area. The norm, however, continues to be conflict and often a failure to even communicate. Local officials and citizens alike find the legacies of past actions creating local governments a serious challenge.

Executives and Legislatures

Except for the traditional New England **town meeting,** where anyone who attends has the authority to vote on policy and management issues, local governments have some or all of the following decision-making offices:

1. Elected executive, like a mayor, village president, or county executive
2. Elected council or commission, like a city council, school board, or county board
3. Appointed manager, like a city manager or school superintendent

town meeting:

Form of local government in which all eligible voters are invited to attend a meeting at which budgets and ordinances are proposed and voted on.

■ One type of informal local government body is the neighborhood association. Whether or not such associations succeed in communicating clearly and resolving their problems is an open question. (Photo courtesy: Kevin Jacobus/The Image Works)

Local government institutions are not necessarily bound to the principles of separation of powers or checks and balances that the U.S. Constitution requires of the federal government and most state constitutions require of their governments. School boards, for example, commonly have both legislative and executive authority. They make policies regarding instruction and facilities, and they do the hiring and contracting to implement those policies. School board members are, with few exceptions, part-time officials, so they hire superintendents and rely heavily on them for day-to-day management and for new policy ideas. The legislative and executive authority and responsibility, nonetheless, remains with the school board.

The patterns of executive and legislative institutions in local government have their roots in some of the most profound events in our history. The influx of non-English-speaking immigrants into urban areas in the North after the Civil War prompted the growth of political machines.[26] New immigrants needed help getting settled. They naturally got much of that help from ethnic neighborhoods, where, for example, a family from Poland would find people who spoke Polish, restaurants with Polish food, and stores and churches with links to the old country. Politicians dealt with these ethnic neighborhoods. If the neighborhood voted to help provide victory for particular candidates for **mayor** and **city council,** then city jobs and services would be provided. **Political machines** were built on these quid pro quo arrangements. The bosses of those machines were either the elected officials or people who controlled the elected officials.

As part of their efforts to destroy the political machines, Progressives sought reforms that minimized the politics in local government institutions.[27] Progressives favored local governments headed by professional **managers** instead of elected executives. Managers would be appointed by councils, the members of which were elected on a nonpartisan ballot, thus removing the role of parties.

As another way of sapping the strength of ethnic bloc voting, Progressive reformers advocated that council members be elected from the city at large rather than from neighborhood districts. The choice between **district-based** and **at-large elections** later raised concerns about discrimination against Hispanics and African Americans. A strategy for excluding these communities from influence and power would be to use at-large elections and keep them a minority, rather than to divide the city into districts that might have an ethnic group constitute a majority within a district. The at-large elections, in short, would have the same minimizing effect on these ethnic groups that was intended by Progressives on white ethnic groups.

Progressives argued that the **commission** form of government was an acceptable alternative to mayors and boss politics. The commission evolved as a response to a tidal wave in 1900 that killed over 5,000 people in southern Texas. After the disaster, a group of prominent business leaders in Galveston formed a task force, with each member of the force assuming responsibility for a specific area, such as housing, public safety, and finance. Task force members essentially assumed the roles of both legislators making policy and managers implementing policy. The citizens of Galveston were so impressed with how well this worked that they amended their charter to replace the mayor and city council with a commission, elected at-large and on a nonpartisan basis. The model spread quickly, and by 1917 almost 500 cities had adopted the commission form of government.

As Table 4.5 indicates, half of all U.S. cities have an elected mayor and a council. Mayors differ in how much authority they have. Some are strong and have the power to veto city council action, appoint agency heads, and initiate as well as execute budgets. The charters of other cities do not provide mayors with these formal powers. Except for the largest cities, mayors serve on a part-time basis.

Slightly more than 40 percent of the municipalities have the Progressive model of government, with an appointed, professional manager and an elected city council. This is the most common pattern among medium-sized cities, whereas the very large and the very small have mayors and councils. Some jurisdictions have both mayors and managers.

mayor:

Chief elected executive of a city.

city council:

The legislature in a city government.

political machine:

An organization designed to solicit votes from certain neighborhoods or communities for a particular political party in return for services and jobs if that party wins.

manager:

A professional executive hired by a city council or county board to manage daily operations and to recommend policy changes.

district-based elections:

Elections in which candidates run for an office that represents only the voters of a specific district within the jurisdiction.

at-large elections:

Elections in which candidates for office must compete throughout the jurisdiction as a whole.

commission:

Form of local government in which several officials are elected to top positions that have both legislative and executive responsibilities.

■ Chicago has long been home to many ethnic groups. Here African-American children celebrate their ancestry with a neighborhood parade. (Photo courtesy: Jean-Marc Giboux/Liaison Agency)

Only 2 percent of U.S. cities still use the commission form of government. Tulsa, Oklahoma, and Portland, Oregon, are the largest cities run by commissions. Galveston itself is one of the cities that has abandoned this structure.

Over 1,800 of the almost 3,000 county governments are run by boards or councils that are elected from geographic districts and without any executive. Committees of the county board manage personnel, finance, roads, parks, social services, and the like. Almost 400 counties elect an executive as well as a board, and thus follow the mayor–council model. Almost 800 hire a professional manager.

School districts, with very few exceptions, follow the council–manager model. Other special districts have boards, sometimes called **public corporations** or **authorities,** that are elected or appointed by elected officials. If the district is responsible for services like water, sewerage, or mass transit, the board is likely to hire and then supervise a manager.

public corporations (authorities):

Government organizations established to provide a particular service or to run a particular facility that are independent of other city or state agencies and supposed to be operated like a business. Examples include a port authority or a mass transit system.

FINANCES

State, tribal, and local governments must, of course, have money. Getting that money is one of the most challenging and thankless tasks of public officials. Unique to state and local governments is the requirement to balance budgets. Unlike the federal government, state and local units may not continually spend more money than they have. Unlike private businesses, state and local governments may not spend less money than they have. Whereas the goal of a private business is to have significantly more income than expenses, a governor, mayor, or other local public executive would be criticized for taxing too heavily if something akin to profits appeared on the books.

The budgeting process involves making projections of expenses and revenues. State and local officials face some special uncertainties when they make these guesses. One important factor is the health of the economy. If one is taxing sales or income, those will vary with levels of employment and economic growth. Moreover, the public sector faces double jeopardy when the economy declines. Revenues will go down as sales and incomes decline, and at the same time expenses go up as more families and individuals need assistance during harsh times.

Another important factor affecting state and local government budgets is the level of funding that governments give to one another. States have been getting about one-fourth of their funds from Washington, D.C. That level has varied over time and, especially with the pattern of deficit spending begun in the early 1980s, is likely to decline. The amount of the decline will depend as much on political dynamics as it will on the health of the national economy. Local governments do not receive as much, but water and sewerage districts have been getting about 15 percent of their funds from the federal government.

Local governments depend heavily on aid from state governments. The pattern varies from one state to another, but on the average school districts get slightly over half of their funds from state governments, counties get almost one-third, and cities about 20 percent.[28]

Different governments depend on different types of taxes and fees. Figure 4.4 presents the pattern of funding for state and local governments. Unlike the federal government, which relies primarily on the income tax, state governments rely almost equally on income taxes and sales taxes. States differ among themselves, of course. Alaska, Delaware, Montana, New Hampshire, and Oregon have no sales tax at all, whereas some of the Southern states have a double-digit sales tax. Likewise, Alaska, Florida, Nevada, South Dakota, Texas, Washington, and Wyoming do not tax personal incomes. Tax rates differ among those states that do have an income tax, but the levels are generally less than 10 percent.

■ In the aftermath of the devastating 1900 flood in Galveston, Texas, the commission form of city government came into being. Although Galveston has abandoned the commission form, the model spread quickly, and by 1917 almost 500 cities had adopted the commission form of government. (Photo courtesy: Corbis/Bettmann)

Figure 4.4   State and Local Government Revenues (percentage of total revenues)

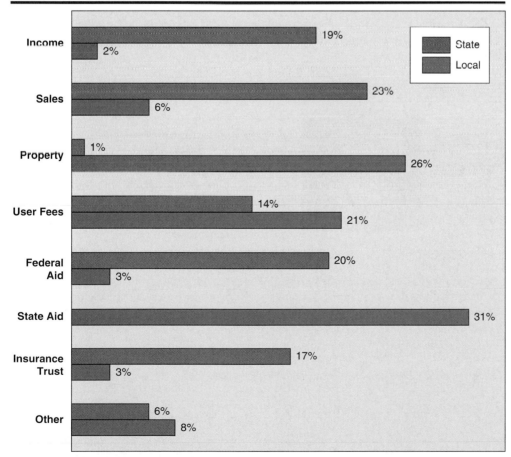

SOURCE: Adapted from Bureau of the Census, *Statistical Abstract of the United States: 1994* (Washington D.C.: Government Printing Office, 1994), 281-82.

Local governments rely primarily on property taxes, have little from levies on sales, and receive virtually nothing from income. Schools, in particular, depend on property taxes for funding. Both local and state governments levy user fees, such as admission to parks, licenses for hunting and fishing, tuition for public universities, and charges based on water use. States, more than local governments, administer retirement systems and insurance programs for public employees. Income from the investment of retirement funds is listed but is not generally available for any use other than paying retirement benefits. Similarly, user fees are typically placed in **segregated funds,** which means they can only be used to provide the service for which the fee was charged. Tuition must, in other words, be used by the university and cannot pay for prison costs or maintaining highways.

Most people accept user fees as the fairest type of taxation. The problem is that the income is both limited and segregated. In general, taxes can be evaluated according to how much money they can raise, whether the revenue is certain, and who bears the burden. Income taxes generate large sums of money, although there will be variations with how well the economy is doing, how many people are employed, and the like. Of all the taxes, those based on income are the most **progressive taxes,** which means that they are based on the ability to pay.

Sales taxes also generate money and they vary with how well the economy is doing. These are not based on earnings, but on purchases. Since those with a low income must spend virtually all that they earn in order to live, sales taxes are **regressive taxes.** To counter the regressive nature of sales taxes, some states exempt food, medicine, and other necessities.

The property tax varies with the value of one's property, not one's current income or spending. Thus farmers and those with a fixed income, like retired persons, might bear more of a burden than their current wealth suggests they should carry. The property tax can be a good revenue earner and is stable, since a jurisdiction can set a tax rate that virtually guarantees a certain level of revenue, regardless of economic trends. The local officials who set these rates invariably hear complaints about the regressive, arbitrary nature of property taxes.

segregated funds:

Money that comes in from a certain tax or fee and then is restricted to a specific use, such as a gasoline tax that is used for road maintenance.

progressive tax:

The level of tax increases with the wealth or ability of an individual or business to pay.

regressive tax:

The level of tax increases as the wealth or ability of an individual or business to pay decreases.

GLOBAL POLITICS

Local and Provincial Politics in Comparative Perspective

The United States has a long tradition of vigorous political activity at the state and local levels. This is not necessarily the case elsewhere. While the relationship between national and local government in the other G-7 countries shows a range of variation (in Britain's unitary system, there is no constitutional distinction made between national and local government; in Canada's federal system, local government is directly responsible only to provincial government, not to the federal government in Ottawa), national government and politics take center stage. Japanese textbooks on politics in that country, for example, include chapters on local autonomy (from national authority) rather than local politics *per se.* In the centralized political systems of Britain and France, devolution—the decentralization of government authority—has been an important trend in the last two decades, but the national government in each case has retained control over the scope and pace of the changes.

That is not to say that localities play no roles in these countries. Local and provincial governments have often been controlled by the parties out of power at the national level, and elections at the lower levels often act as barometers for upcoming national elections. In France, the far right National Front built up political support at the local level, from which it expanded to national significance in the 1990s. In the 1999 elections for the newly created Scottish home parliament, the Scottish Nationalist Party, a minor party in House of Commons, emerged with the second largest number of seats and denied the local Labour Party a majority. In France and Japan, local government has also been an important source of innovative policy later adopted at the national level.

The provinces and municipalities have also served as centers of citizen political participation. In the G-7 countries, environmental movements began as local organizations, and they remain largely that way in Japan. Those movements have used the local referendum, borrowed from American practice, to try to remove municipal officials or change their policies.

*C*ONTINUITY and Change

Increased Role of State, Local, and Tribal Governments

By design, state governments initially were weak. In response to the colonial experience, the founders established governments that were very limited in their powers, responsibilities, and abilities. Governors and the executive branch were especially limited. Likewise, governance at the local level was minimal. Officials were part-time, concerns were few, and funds were low. The federal government controlled Indian nations and gave them very little authority to make their own decisions. Tribes found themselves at the receiving end of federal policies that changed drastically, ranging from neglect to assimilation to some forms of self-determination.

The limitations of state, local, and tribal governments became a major problem as technological and economic developments made American society increasingly complex. Crises emerged in the middle of the twentieth century as urban areas emerged and basic government services were lacking. State legislatures commonly had more representatives from rural areas than from urban areas, and city issues got low priority on agendas. Finally, in a 1962 case, the U.S. Supreme Court declared that states had to adhere to the principle of one-person, one-vote and allocate legislative seats according to population. That decision, *Baker v. Carr*, marked a threshold. People had a more effective voice and demanded that their state and local governments develop the capacity to address major concerns and issues. On a parallel track, the federal government adopted a policy of promoting more self-governance for the Indian nations.

Subnational units of government today are considerably more competent and more responsive than their predecessors. The governments that provide the services that affect us most directly and regularly have more capable people and more efficient processes than they have ever had before. Although most state, local, and tribal elected officials are still part-time, increasingly professional, full-time staff serves them. Governments run by our neighbors, friends, and co-workers tend to be more accessible and more responsive to our needs.

The challenges of the future rest with reconciling the traditions of desiring a limited government and avoiding high taxes with the demands of a society that is increasingly complex. The federal government has shed much of its responsibilities and many of its programs for local and tribal communities, in part in recognition of the advantages of allowing problem solving by those most directly affected by issues. States, similarly, delegate considerable authority to their local governments. But federal and state funds do not always follow delegation. The health and vitality of local communities will depend greatly on the creativity of their leaders in meeting the challenges of increased responsibilities and limitations on funds.

1. What regulations and services that have affected you during the past week were the responsibilities of state and local government respectively?
2. In what ways can you influence elective and appointed officials in your state and local governments?

Cast Your Vote.   What kind of policies, if any, should the federal government impose on state, local, and tribal governments? To cast your vote, go to www.awlonline.com/oconnor.

SUMMARY

The expectations are that state and local governments are readily accessible to citizens and that they are likely to be responsive to the needs and wishes of a particular community. In this chapter we have examined the changing character of governance at the state and local levels in order to appreciate both the variation and the common patterns in subnational governments. In this chapter we have made the following points:

1. EVOLUTION OF SATE AND LOCAL GOVERNMENTS

The initial intent was to limit the capacity and scope of state and local governments. That changed with the increased complexity of our society and economy and with the ruling of the U.S. Supreme Court that legislative districts within a state must each have the same number of people. The trend since the 1960s has been for more representative and more professional state and local governments. These jurisdictions and the federal government are forming partnerships with each other and with the private sector to address issues and provide services.

2. RELATIONS WITH INDIAN NATIONS

American Indian nations obviously affect and are affected by the state and local governments. But, due to treaty rights and the domestic dependent sovereignty of the tribes, the Indian nations have a special relationship with the federal government. Tribes have important protections from the potential vagaries of state and local governments. Conversely, the special status of the tribes poses challenges to coherent and consistent policies in a community. Currently, the federal government is encouraging tribal governments to move to self-determination economically and politically and to enter into agreements with state and local governments on financial and policy matters.

3. GRASSROOTS POWER AND POLITICS

Those who wield the most influence over the making and implementation of public policy in a community are not always the ones elected to formal offices. Sometimes power is in the hands of a family, a small number of individuals, or the local media. Whether or not those who are most powerful are the ones in government offices, governance at the grass roots is face-to-face, between neighbors, friends, and former high school classmates.

4. STATE GOVERNMENTS

State governments have traditionally had primary responsibility for criminal justice, education, public health, and economic development. Recently, state officials have assumed a larger role in welfare and environmental policy. State constitutions, which reflect major historical developments in American society, provide the basic framework of institutions and values in which state governments fulfill their roles. Since the 1960s, these governments have dramatically become more competent, professional, and accessible to the general public.

5. LOCAL GOVERNMENTS

Local governance in the United States is conducted by a myriad collection of almost 87,000 units, most of which are run by part-time officials. These governments range from general jurisdictions covering densely urbanized areas to special districts functioning for a specific, narrow purpose. The forms of local governments also differ. There are town meetings in which all eligible voters in a community gather to conduct business, elected and appointed boards that have both executive and legislative powers, and governments with distinct legislative councils, elected executives, and professional managers. Local politics is frequently nonpartisan, thanks in part to conscious efforts to prevent control by political party machines.

6. FINANCES

Funding government is complex. Revenues are hard to project because governments tax personal and business incomes, sales, and property value—none of which governments can control. State, local, and tribal governments also rely heavily on money given to them by other jurisdictions, including the federal government. The challenge is, given these uncertainties and the general hostility toward taxes, to budget for required services and popular programs.

KEY TERMS

advisory referendum, p. 120

at-large elections, p. 125

charter, p. 121

charter school, p. 122

city council, p. 125

civil law, p. 115

commission, p. 125

common law, p. 115

commute, p. 111

compact, p. 104

county, p. 123

criminal law, p. 115

Dillon's Rule, p. 121

direct initiative, p. 119

direct (popular) referendum, p. 120

district-based elections, p. 125

domestic dependent nation, p. 104

extradite, p. 111

governor, p. 109

inclusion, p. 115

indirect initiative, p. 119

line-item veto, p. 110

manager, p. 125

mayor, p. 125

Missouri Plan, p. 116

municipality, p. 123

nonpartisan election, p. 106

one-person, one-vote, p. 103

package or general veto, p. 110

pardon, p. 111

parole, p. 111

political machine, p. 125

Progressive Movement, p. 108

progressive tax, p. 128

public corporations (authorities) p. 126

regressive tax, p. 128

reservation land, p. 104

segregated funds, p. 128

special district, p. 123

state constitutions, p. 106

term limits, p. 113

town meeting p. 124

trust land, p. 104

SELECTED READINGS

Banfield, Edward C. *The Unheavenly City.* Boston: Little, Brown, 1970.

Benjamin, Gerald, and Michael J. Malbin, eds. *Limiting Legislative Terms.* Washington, DC: Congressional Quarterly Press, 1992.

Burns, Nancy E. *The Formation of American Local Governments: Private Values in Public Institutions.* New York: Oxford University Press, 1994.

Crenson, Matthew A. *Neighborhood Politics.* Cambridge, MA: Harvard University Press, 1983.

Dahl, Robert A. *Who Governs? Democracy and Power in an American City.* New Haven, CT: Yale University Press.

Erie, Steven P. *Rainbow's End: Irish Americans and the Dilemmas of Urban Machine Politics,* 1840–1985. Berkeley: University of California Press, 1988.

Erikson, Robert S., Gerald C. Wright, and John P. McIver, *Statehouse Democracy: Public Opinion and Policy in the American States.* Cambridge, England: Cambridge University Press, 1993.

Jewell, Malcolm E., and Marcia Lynn Whicker. *Legislative Leadership in the American States.* Ann Arbor: University of Michigan Press, 1994.

Stone, Clarence N. *Regime Politics: Governing Atlanta, 1946–1988.* Lawrence: University of Kansas Press, 1989.

Woliver, Laura R. *From Outrage to Action: The Politics of Grass-Roots Dissent.* Urbana: University of Illinois Press, 1993.

NOTES

1. Wendy Kloiber, "Building This Plane as We Fly It: La Crosse's Response to Youth Violence and Gangs," *The La Follette Policy Report* 9 (Spring/Summer 1998): 4–7, and *www.lafollette.wisc.edu/gangs*.

2. Peter K. Eisinger, *The Rise of the Entrepreneurial State* (Madison: University of Wisconsin Press, 1988).

3. Sharon O'Brien, *American Indian Tribal Governments* (Norman: University of Oklahoma Press, 1989), 261–97.

4. Raymond Wolfinger, "Reputation and Reality in the Study of Community Power," *American Sociological Review* 25 (October 1960), 636–644; Nelson Polsby, *Community Power and Political Theory* (New Haven, CT: Yale University Press, 1963); and Robert E. Agger, Daniel Goldrich, and Bert Swanson, *The Rulers and the Ruled: Political Power and Impotence in American Communities* (New York: Wiley, 1964).

5. Laura R. Woliver, *From Outrage to Action: The Politics of Grass-Roots Dissent* (Urbana: University of Illinois Press, 1993); and Matthew A. Crenson, *Neighborhood Politics* (Cambridge, MA: Harvard University Press, 1983).

6. Albert L. Sturm, "The Development of American State Constitutions," *Publius* 12 (Winter 1982): 62–68.

7. Albert L. Kohlmeier. *The Old Northwest as the Keystone of the Arch of the American Federal Union* (Bloomington, IN: Principia Press, 1938); and *Pathways to the Old Northwest* (Indianapolis: Indiana Historical Society, 1988).

8. Theodore Clarke Smith, *Parties and Slavery* (New York: Harper and Brothers, 1906); and Arthur Charles Cole, *The Irrepressible Conflict, 1850–1865* (New York: Macmillan, 1934).

9. George E. Mowry, *The Progressive Era, 1900–20* (Washington, DC: American Historical Association, 1972).

10. Janice C. May, "Constitutional Amendment and Revision Revisited," *Publius* 12 (Winter 1982): 153–79.

11. Charles Wiggins, "Executive Vetoes and Legislative Overrides in the American States," *Journal of Politics* 54 (November 1980): 42. Also see Glenn Abney and Thomas Lauth, "The Line-Item Veto in the States," *Public Administration Review* 45 (January/February 1985): 66–79.

12. F. Ted Hebert, Jeffrey L. Brudney, and Deil S. Wright, "Gubernatorial Influence and State Bureaucracy," *American Politics Quarterly* 11 (April 1983): 37–52; and Abney and Lauth, "The Governor as Chief Administrator," *Public Administration Quarterly* 3 (January/February 1983): 40–49.

13. Thad L. Beyle and Robert Dalton, "Appointment Power: Does It Belong to the Governor?" *State Government* 54, no. 1 (Winter 1981): 6.

14. Leon W. Blevins, *Texas Government in National Perspective* (Englewood Cliffs, NJ: Prentice-Hall, 1987), 169.

15. James L. Garnett, *Reorganizing State Government: The Executive Branch* (Boulder, CO: Westview, 1980, 8 and 9; and Diane Kincaid Blair, "The Gubernatorial Appointment Power: Too Much of a Good Thing?" *State Government* 55 (Summer 1982): 88–91.

16. Timothy O'Rourke, *The Impact of Reapportionment* (New Brunswick, NJ: Transaction Books, 1980).

17. Alan Rosenthal, *Governors and Legislatures* (Washington, DC: Congressional Quarterly Press, 1990); and Malcolm E. Jewell and Marcia Lynn Whicker, *Legislative Leadership in the American States* (Ann Arbor: University of Michigan Press, 1994).

18. Gary T. Clarke and Charles R. Grezlak, "Legislative Staffs Show Improvement," *National Civic Review* 65 (June 1976): 292.

19. Gerald Benjamin and Michael J. Malin, eds. *Limiting Legislative Terms* (Washington, DC: Congressional Quarterly Press, 1992).

20. Diana Gordon, "Citizen Legislators—Alive and Well," *State Legislatures* 20 (January 1994): 24–27.

21. Earl M. Maltz, "Federalism and State Court Activism," *Intergovernmental Perspective* (Spring 1987): 23–26.

22. Bradley Cannon, "The Impact of Formal Selection Processes on Characteristics of

Judges—Reconsidered," *Law and Society Review* (May 1972): 570–93.

23. Thomas E. Cronin, *Direct Democracy* (Cambridge, MA: Harvard University Press, 1989); and David B. Magleby, *Direct Legislation* (Baltimore, MD: Johns Hopkins University Press, 1984).

24. Alex de Tocqueville, *Democracy in America,* ed. by Phillips Bradley (New York: Knopf, 1945), 40.

25. *City of Clinton* v. *Cedar Rapids and Missouri River Railroad Co.* (Iowa, 1868).

26. Steven P. Erie, *Rainbow's End: Irish-Americans and the Dilemmas of Urban Machine Politics, 1840–1985* (Berkeley: University of California Press, 1988); Alfred Steinberg, *The Bosses* (New York: New American Library, 1972); Seymour Mandelbaum, *Boss Tweed's New York* (New York: Wiley, 1955); and Milton Rakove, *Don't Make No Waves—Don't Back No Losers: An Insider's Analysis of the Daley Machine* (Bloomington, IN: Indiana University Press, 1975).

27. Samuel P. Hays, "The Politics of Reform in Municipal Government in the Progressive Era," *Pacific Northwest Quarterly* 55 (October 1964): 157–66.

28. U.S. Bureau of the Census, *Government Finances in 1993–94* (Washington, DC: Government Printing Office, 1994), 12–19.

(Photo courtesy: Corbis/Nik Wheeler)

Civil Liberties

5

- **The First Constitutional Amendments: The Bill of Rights**
- **First Amendment Guarantees: Freedom of Religion**
- **First Amendment Guarantees: Freedom of Speech and Press**
- **The Right to Keep and Bear Arms**
- **The Rights of Criminal Defendants**
- **The Right to Privacy**

*I*n July 1995, a Wyoming state trooper stopped a car driven by Dwight Young because it had a faulty taillight.[1] The officer noticed a hypodermic syringe in Young's pocket, and Young immediately admitted that he used it to take drugs.

Once Young made that admission, the officer immediately began to search the car for other drugs or drug paraphernalia. In the back seat of the car, in clear view of the officer, was passenger Sandra Houghton's pocketbook. The officer searched her purse, found methamphetamines, and placed her under arrest.

At trial, the officer admitted that he had no reason or "probable cause" to suspect Houghton of illegal activity. Nevertheless, he searched anyway and eventually Houghton was found guilty of possession of a controlled substance. Her conviction, however, was overturned by the Wyoming Supreme Court, which concluded that there must be probable cause to suspect illegal activity before an officer can search the belongings of an occupant in a car. Searches without probable cause, said the Wyoming Court, violate the Fourth Amendment's prohibition of unreasonable searches and seizures.

In 1999, a six-person majority of the U.S. Supreme Court disagreed with this analysis, making car passengers subject to warrantless searches for the first time. In significantly curtailing the rights of automobile passengers, the Court ruled that a police officer can search any passenger's belongings if he or she suspects that the *driver* has committed some illegal activity.[2] The dissenters voiced their fears that privacy rights of passengers would be trampled, echoing ACLU Legal Director Steven R. Shapiro's warning: "It shouldn't be true that whenever you get into a car as a passenger, you forfeit all your privacy rights."[3]

*W*hen the Bill of Rights, which contains many of the most important protections of individual rights, was written, its drafters were not thinking about issues such as abortion, gay rights, physician-assisted suicide, or many of the personal liberties discussed in this chapter. Civil liberties issues often present complex problems. Frequently, courts or policy makers are called on to balance competing interests and rights. As a society, for example, how much infringement on our personal liberties do we want to give the police? Do we want to have different rules in our homes, our lockers, our dorm rooms, and in our cars? Similarly, as we discuss later in this chapter, Congress and the courts are grappling with the scope of free speech rights on the Internet. Should citizens have unfettered discretion to write and print what they want, or should government impose limits? Even Congress's placing of the *Starr Report* and its graphic discussion of sex in the Oval Office drew critics about what information should be available over the Internet.

In most of the cases discussed in the chapter, there is a conflict between an individual or group of individuals seeking to exercise what they believe to be a right, and the government—local, state, or national—seeking to control the exercise of that right in an attempt to keep order and preserve the rights of others. It generally falls to the judiciary to balance those interests. And, depending on the composition of the Supreme Court and the times, the balance may lean toward civil liberties or toward the power of the government to limit those rights.

In this chapter we explore the various dimensions of civil liberties guarantees contained in the U.S. Constitution and the Bill of Rights. **Civil liberties** are the personal rights and freedoms that the federal government cannot abridge, either by law, constitution, or judicial interpretation. Civil liberties guarantees place limitations on the power of the government to restrain or dictate how individuals act. Thus, when we discuss civil liberties such as those found in the Bill of Rights, we are concerned with limits on what governments can and cannot do. Civil rights, in contrast, refer to the positive actions of the government taken to protect individuals against arbitrary or discriminatory treatment. Civil rights are discussed in chapter 6.

In this chapter we explore the various dimensions of civil liberties guarantees contained in the U.S. Constitution and the Bill of Rights:

- First, we will discuss the *Bill of Rights*, the reasons for its addition to the Constitution, and its eventual application to the states via the incorporation doctrine.
- Second, we will survey the meaning of *the First Amendment's freedom of religion clauses.*
- Third, we will discuss the meanings of *the free speech and press guarantees found in the First Amendment.*
- Fourth, we will discuss *the Second Amendment and its interpretation.*
- Fifth, we will analyze the reasons for many of *the criminal defendants' rights* found in the Bill of Rights and how those rights have been expanded and contracted by the U.S. Supreme Court.
- Sixth, we will discuss the meaning of *the right to privacy* and how that concept has been interpreted by the Court.

THE FIRST CONSTITUTIONAL AMENDMENTS: THE BILL OF RIGHTS

In 1787, most state constitutions explicitly protected a variety of personal liberties: speech, religion, freedom from unreasonable searches and seizures, trial by jury, and more. It was clear that the new Constitution would redistribute power in the new federal system between the national government and the states. Without an explicit guarantee of specific civil liberties, could the national government be trusted to uphold the freedoms already granted to citizens by their states?

Recognition of the increased power that would be held by the new national government led Anti-Federalists to stress the need for a bill of rights. Anti-Federalists

civil liberties:

The personal rights and freedoms that the federal government cannot abridge by law, constitution, or judicial interpretation.

Web Exploration

To view an original copy of the Bill of Rights, see www.awlonline.com/oconnor.

and many others were confident that they could control the actions of their own state legislators, but didn't trust the national government to be so protective of their civil liberties.

The notion of adding a bill of rights to the Constitution was not a popular one at the Constitutional Convention. When George Mason of Virginia proposed that such a bill be added to the preface of the proposed Constitution, for example, his resolution was defeated unanimously.[4] In the subsequent ratification debates, Federalists argued that a bill of rights was unnecessary. Not only did most state constitutions already contain those protections, Federalists believed it was foolhardy to list things that the national government had no power to do since the proposed Constitution didn't give the national government the power to regulate speech, religion, and the like.

Some Federalists, however, supported the idea. After the Philadelphia convention, for example, James Madison conducted a lively correspondence about the need for a national bill of rights with Thomas Jefferson. Jefferson was far quicker to support such guarantees than was Madison, who continued to doubt their utility because he believed that a list of "protected" rights might suggest that those not enumerated were not protected. Politics soon intervened, however, when Madison found himself in a close race against James Monroe for a seat in the House of Representatives in the First Congress. The district was largely Anti-Federalist. So to garner support, Madison, in an act of political expediency, issued a new series of public letters similar to the earlier *Federalist Papers,* in which he vowed to support a bill of rights.

Once elected to the House, Madison made good on his promise. He became the prime mover and author of the Bill of Rights, although he considered the Congress to have far more important matters to handle and viewed his labors on the Bill of Rights "a nauseous project."[5]

The insistence of Anti-Federalists on a bill of rights, the fact that some states conditioned their ratification of the Constitution on the addition of these guarantees, and the disagreement among Federalists about writing specific liberty guarantees into the Constitution led to prompt congressional action to put an end to further controversy. This was a time when national stability and support for the new government were particularly needed. Thus in 1789 the proposed Bill of Rights was sent to the states by Congress for ratification, which was finally achieved in 1791.

The **Bill of Rights,** the first ten amendments to the Constitution, contains numerous specific guarantees, including those of free speech, press, and religion (see Appendix II for the full text). The Ninth and Tenth amendments in particular highlight Anti-Federalist fears of a too-powerful national government. The Ninth Amendment, strongly favored by Madison, makes it clear that this special listing of rights does not mean that others don't exist; and the Tenth Amendment simply reiterates that powers not delegated to the national government are reserved to the states or the people.

The Incorporation Doctrine: The Bill of Rights Made Applicable to the States

The Bill of Rights was intended to limit the powers of the *national* government to infringe on the rights and liberties of the citizenry. And in *Barron* v. *Baltimore* (1833), the Supreme Court ruled that the federal Bill of Rights limited only the U.S. government and not the states.[6] In 1868, however, the Fourteenth Amendment was added to the U.S. Constitution. Its language suggested the possibility that some or even all of the protections guaranteed in the Bill of Rights might be interpreted to prevent state infringement of those rights. Section 1 of the Fourteenth Amendment reads: "No State shall . . . deprive any person of life, liberty, or property, without due process of law."

Until nearly the turn of the century, the Supreme Court steadfastly rejected numerous arguments urging it to interpret the **due process clause** found in the Fourteenth Amendment as making various provisions contained in the Bill of Rights applicable to the states. In 1897, however, the Court began to increase its jurisdiction over the states.[7] It began to hold states to a **substantive due process** standard whereby state laws had to

Bill of Rights:

The first ten amendments to the U.S. Constitution which guarantee specific rights and liberties.

due process clause:

Clause contained in the Fifth and Fourteenth Amendments. Over the years, it has been construed to guarantee to individuals a variety of rights ranging from economic liberty to criminal procedural rights to protection from arbitrary governmental action.

substantive due process:

Principle in which the Supreme Court has held that most, but not all, of the specific guarantees in the Bill of Rights limit state and local governments by making those guarantees applicable to the states through the due process clause of the Fourteenth Amendment.

■ Until *Gitlow* v. *New York* (1925), involving Benjamin Gitlow, the executive secretary of the Socialist Party, it was generally thought that the Fourteenth Amendment did not apply the protections of the Bill of Rights to the states. Here Gitlow is shown testifying before the Dees Committee, which was investigating un-American activities. (Photo courtesy: AP/Wide World Photos)

incorporation doctrine:

An interpretation of the Constitution that holds that the due process clause of the Fourteenth Amendments requires that state and local governments also guarantee those rights.

selective incorporation:

A judicial doctrine whereby most but not all of the protections found in the Bill of Rights are made applicable to the states via the Fourteenth Amendment.

be shown to be a valid exercise of the state's power to regulate the health, welfare, or public morals of its citizens. Interferences with state power, however, were rare. As a consequence, states continued to pass sedition laws (laws that made it illegal to speak or write any political criticism that threatened to diminish respect for the government, its laws, or public officials), expecting that the Supreme Court would uphold their constitutional validity. Then, in 1925 all of this changed dramatically. Benjamin Gitlow, a member of the Left Wing Section of the Socialist Party, was convicted of violating a New York law that—in language very similar to that of the federal Espionage Act—prohibited the advocacy of the violent overthrow of the government. Gitlow had printed 16,000 copies of a manifesto in which he urged workers to rise up to overthrow the U.S. government. Although Gitlow's conviction was upheld, in *Gitlow* v. *New York* (1925) the Supreme Court noted that the states were not completely free to limit forms of political expression:

> For present purposes we may and do assume that freedom of speech and of the press—which are protected by the First Amendment from abridgement by Congress—are among the *fundamental personal rights and "liberties"* protected by the due process clause of the Fourteenth Amendment from impairment by the states [emphasis added].[8]

Gitlow, with its finding that states could not abridge free speech protections, was the first step in the slow development of the **incorporation doctrine.** After *Gitlow*, it took the Court six more years to "incorporate" another First Amendment freedom—that of the press. *Near* v. *Minnesota* (1931) was the first case in which the Supreme Court found that a state law violated freedom of the press as protected by the First Amendment. Jay Near, the publisher of a weekly Minneapolis newspaper, regularly attacked a variety of groups—African Americans, Catholics, Jews, and labor union leaders. Few escaped his hatred. Near's paper was closed under the authority of a state criminal libel law banning "malicious, scandalous, or defamatory" publications. Near appealed the closing of his paper, and the Supreme Court ruled that "The fact that the liberty of the press may be abused by miscreant purveyors of scandal does not make any the less necessary the immunity of the press from previous restraint."[9]

As revealed in Table 5.1, not all the specific guarantees in the Bill of Rights have been made applicable to the states through the due process clause of the Fourteenth Amendment. Instead, the Court has selectively chosen to limit the rights of states by protecting the rights it considers most fundamental, and thus subject to the Court's most rigorous strict scrutiny review. This process is referred to as *selective incorporation* discussed below.

Selective incorporation requires the states to respect freedoms of press, speech, and assembly among other rights. Other guarantees contained in the Second, Third, and Seventh amendments, such as the right to bear arms, have not been incorporated because the Court has yet to consider them sufficiently fundamental to national notions of liberty and justice.

Selective Incorporation and Fundamental Freedoms

The rationale for **selective incorporation,** the judicial application to the states of only some of the rights enumerated by the Bill of Rights, was set out by the Court in 1937 in its decision in *Palko* v. *Connecticut*.[10] Frank Palko was charged with first-degree murder for killing two Connecticut police officers, found guilty of a lesser charge of second-degree murder, and sentenced to life imprisonment. Connecticut appealed. Palko was retried, found guilty of first-degree murder, and resentenced to death. Palko then appealed his second conviction on the grounds that it violated the Fifth Amendment's prohibition against double jeopardy because the Fifth Amendment had been made applicable to the states by the due process clause of the Fourteenth Amendment.

The Supreme Court upheld Palko's second conviction and the death sentence, thereby choosing not to bind states to the Fifth Amendment's double jeopardy clause. This decision set forth principles that were to guide the Court's interpretation of the incorporation doctrine for the next several decades. Some protections found in the Bill

Table 5.1 The Selective Incorporation of the Bill of Rights

Date	Amendment	Right	Case
1925	I.	Speech	*Gitlow* v. *New York*
1931		Press	*Near* v. *Minnesota*
1937		Assembly	*DeJonge* v. *Oregon*
1940		Religion	*Cantwell* v. *Connecticut*
	II.	Right to bear arms	*not incorporated* (Generally, the Supreme Court has upheld reasonable regulations of the right of private citizens to bear arms. Should a tough gun-control law be adopted by a state or local government and a challenge to it be made, a test of incorporation might be presented to the Court in the future.)
	III.	No quartering of soldiers	*not incorporated* (The quartering problem has not recurred since colonial times.)
1949	IV.	Unreasonable searches and seizures	*Wolf* v. *Colorado*
1961		The exclusionary rule	*Mapp* v. *Ohio*
1897	V.	Just compensation	*Chicago, B&O R.R. Co.* v. *Chicago*
1964		Self-incrimination	*Malloy* v. *Hogan*
1969		Double jeopardy	*Benton* v. *Maryland*
		Grand jury indictment	*not incorporated* (The trend in state criminal cases is away from grand juries and toward reliance on the sworn written accusation of the prosecuting attorney.)
1948	VI.	Public trial	*In re Oliver*
1963		Right to counsel	*Gideon* v. *Wainwright*
1965		Confrontation of witnesses	*Pointer* v. *Texas*
1966		Impartial trial	*Parker* v. *Gladden*
1967		Speedy trial	*Klopfer* v. *North Carolina*
1967		Compulsory trial	*Washington* v. *Texas*
1968		Jury trial	*Duncan* v. *Louisiana*
	VII.	Right to jury trial in civil cases	*not incorporated* (While Warren Burger was Chief Justice, he conducted a campaign to abolish jury trials in civil cases to save time and money, among other reasons.)
1962	VIII.	Freedom from cruel and unusual punishment	*Robinson* v. *California*
		Freedom from excessive fines or bail	*not incorporated*

of Rights were absorbed into the concept of due process only because they are so fundamental to our notions of liberty and justice that they cannot be denied by the states unless the state can show what is called a compelling reason for the liberties' curtailment. This is a very high burden of proof for the state. Thus abridgment of a fundamental right is not often sustained by the Court. Because the Court concluded that the protection against double jeopardy was *not* a fundamental right, Palko's appeal was rejected and he died in Connecticut's gas chamber one year later. Those rights deemed fundamental are not only those selectively drawn from the Bill of Rights and incorporated into the due process clause of the Fourteenth Amendment to apply to the states. Fundamental rights include not only less than the whole of the Bill of Rights, but more—that is, other un-enumerated rights, such as the right to privacy. The term *selective incorporation plus* suggests the reality of those rights recognized as fundamental and thus within the meaning of liberty protected by the due process clause of the Fourteenth Amendment.

Web Exploration

For groups with opposing views on
how the First Amendment should be
interpreted, see
www.awlonline.com/oconnor.

establishment clause:

The first clause in the First Amendment.
It prohibits the national government
from establishing a national religion.

free exercise clause:

The second clause of the First Amendment. It prohibits the U.S. government
from interfering with a citizen's right
to practice his or her religion.

FIRST AMENDMENT GUARANTEES: FREEDOM OF RELIGION

Today, many lawmakers bemoan the absence of religion in the public schools and voice their concerns that America is becoming a godless nation. Many of the Framers were religious men, but they knew what evils could arise if the new nation was not founded with religious freedom as one of its core ideals. Despite the fact that many colonists had fled Europe primarily to escape religious persecution, most colonies actively persecuted those who did not belong to their predominant religious groups. Pennsylvania, for example, was a "Quaker" colony. The Congregationalist Church of Massachusetts, a "Puritan" colony, taxed and harassed those who held other religious beliefs. Neverthe-less, the colonists were uniformly outraged in 1774 when the British Parliament passed a law establishing Anglicanism and Roman Catholicism as official religions in the colonies. The First Continental Congress immediately sent a letter of protest announc-ing its "astonishment that a British Parliament should ever consent to establish . . . a religion [Catholicism] that has deluged [England] in blood and dispersed bigotry, per-secution, murder and rebellion through every part of the world."[11]

This distaste for a national church or religion was reflected in the Constitution. Arti-cle VI, for example, provides that "no religious Test shall ever be required as a Qualifi-cation to any Office or Public Trust under the United States." This simple statement, however, did not reassure those who feared the new Constitution would curtail indi-vidual liberty. Thus, the First Amendment to the Constitution was ultimately ratified to lay those fears to rest.

The First Amendment to the Constitution begins, "Congress shall make no law respecting an establishment of religion, or prohibiting the free exercise thereof." This statement sets the boundaries of governmental action. The **establishment clause** ("Con-gress shall make no law respecting an establishment of religion") directs the national gov-ernment not to involve itself in religion. It creates, in Thomas Jefferson's words, a "wall of separation" between church and state. The **free exercise clause** ("or prohibiting the free exercise thereof") guarantees citizens that the national government will not inter-fere with their practice of religion. These guarantees, however, are not absolute. In the mid-1800s, Mormons traditionally practiced and preached polygamy, the taking of mul-tiple wives. In 1879, when it was first called on to interpret the free exercise clause, the Supreme Court upheld the conviction of a Mormon under a federal law barring polygamy. The Court reasoned that to do otherwise would provide constitutional pro-tections to a full range of religious beliefs, including those as extreme as human sacri-fice. "Laws are made for the government of actions," noted the Court, "and while they cannot interfere with mere religious belief and opinions, they may with practices."[12] Later, in 1940, the Supreme Court observed that the First Amendment "embraces two concepts—freedom to believe and freedom to act. The first is absolute, but in the nature of things, the second cannot be. Conduct remains subject to regulation of society."[13]

The Establishment Clause

Over the years, the Court has been divided over how to interpret the establishment clause. Does this clause erect a total wall between church and state, or is some govern-mental accommodation of religion allowed? While the Supreme Court has upheld the constitutionality of many kinds of church/state entanglements such as public funding to provide sign language interpreters for deaf students in religious schools,[14] the Court has held fast to the rule of strict separation between church and state when issues of prayer in school are involved. In *Engel* v. *Vitale* (1962), the Court first ruled that the recitation in public school classrooms of a twenty-two-word nondenominational prayer drafted by the New Hyde Park, New York, school board was unconstitutional.[15] In 1992 the Court continued its unwillingness to allow prayer in public schools by finding unconstitutional the saying of prayer at a middle school graduation.[16]

The Court has gone back and forth in its effort to come up with a workable way to deal with church/state questions. In *Lemon* v. *Kurtzman* (1971), the Court heard a case

■ In spite of the First Amendment's general ban on state entanglement with religion, prayer is still common at many public ceremonies. Here the president of the United States is shown praying at a graduation at West Point, a public institution. (Photo courtesy: Lisa Quinones/Black Star)

that challenged direct state aid to parochial schools, including the use of state funds to pay salaries of teachers at these schools.[17] In its decision, the Court tried—as it often does—to carve out a new "test" by which to measure the constitutionality of these types of laws. Under the **Lemon test,** to be constitutional a challenged law or practice must:

1. Have a secular purpose;
2. Have a primary effect that neither advances nor inhibits religion; and
3. Not foster an excessive government entanglement with religion.

State funding of parochial school teachers' salaries was found to fail this test and was therefore prohibited by the Constitution, said the Court in *Lemon.*[18] In 1980 the *Lemon* test was interpreted to invalidate a Kentucky law that required the posting of the Ten Commandments in public school classrooms. The Court ruled the posting had no secular purpose.[19] (See Highlight 5.1: Praying for Justice?)

Since 1980, however, the Supreme Court has appeared more willing to ignore the *Lemon* test and lower the wall between church and state as long as school prayer is not involved. In 1981, for example, the Court ruled unconstitutional a Missouri law prohibiting the use of state university buildings and grounds for "purposes of religious worship," which had been used to ban religious groups from using school facilities.[20]

This decision was taken by many members of Congress as a sign that this principle could be extended to secondary and even primary schools. In 1984 Congress passed the Equal Access Act, which bars public schools from discriminating against groups of students on the basis of "religious, political, philosophical or other content of the speech at such meetings." The constitutionality of this law was upheld in 1990 when the Court ruled that a school board's refusal to allow a Christian Bible club to meet in a public high school classroom during a twice-weekly "activity period" violated the act. According to the decision, the primary effect of the act was neither to advance religion nor to excessively entangle government and religion—even though religious meetings would be held on school grounds with a faculty sponsor. The important factor seemed to be that the students had complete choice in their selection of activities with numerous nonreligious options.[21] In 1993 the Court also ruled that religious groups must be allowed to use public schools after hours if that access is also given to other community groups.[22]

Lemon test:

A Court devised test designed to measure the constitutionality of state laws that appear to further a religion.

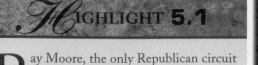

Ray Moore, the only Republican circuit court judge in Etowah County, Alabama, is well on his way to becoming a party to a major U.S. Supreme Court case—and it won't involve an appeal of a decision he made as a judge. Instead, it will involve his refusal to remove the handcrafted plaque of the Ten Commandments that he hung on his courtroom wall. Although the U.S. Supreme Court has ruled that the Ten Commandments cannot be displayed in a public school classroom, Moore says he is carrying on an Alabama tradition as he invites local Christian clergy to pray with him and others in his courtroom at the beginning of every jury organizing session.[a]

The ACLU filed suit against Moore on behalf of three county residents asking removal of the plaque and an end to the prayers, arguing that both practices violated the First Amendment's guarantee of separation of church and state. A state court judge ruled that the residents lacked standing to sue, even though they had served on juries in Moore's court. Even before that decision was announced, however, the governor and state attorney general filed a countersuit asking Circuit Court Judge Charles Price to declare Moore's practices constitutional.

Price ruled against the governor, attorney general, and judge, and ordered Moore to stop holding prayer vigils in the courtroom and to remove the Ten Commandments. (Price later won the John F. Kennedy Profiles in Courage Award in 1997 for his action.)

The governor and attorney general then appealed that decision to the state supreme court. Four justices excused themselves from the case; five others ruled that the governor and attorney general had no standing, thus voiding Price's lower court decision.[b] Moore, for the time being, is free to pray and display the Ten Commandments until civil liberties lawyers think of a way to have another go at him in court.

[a]Edith Stanley, "Alabama Judge Goes to Court in Religion Battle," *Los Angeles Times* (January 11, 1996): A5.
[b]Gita Smith, "Ruling Allows Judge to Pray with Juries," *Atlanta Journal and Constitution* (January 24, 1998): 2B.

Web Exploration

For more information on the *Agostini v. Felton* case, see
www.awlonline.com/oconnor.

■ Snake handling, once more common as part of certain fundamentalist Christian religious services, is banned by law in many parts of the South. (Photo courtesy: Corbis/Bettmann)

For another example of the current tendency to lower the wall between church and state, see Politics Now: Protecting the Children: Church Versus State.

Many believed that the 1993 replacement of Justice Byron White by Ruth Bader Ginsburg, a former attorney for the ACLU (see Highlight 5.2: The American Civil Liberties Union: Protector of First Amendment Rights), would halt the trend toward lowering the wall between church and state. But in 1995 the Court signalled that it was willing to lower the wall even further. Ironically, it did so in a case involving Thomas Jefferson's own University of Virginia. In a five to four decision, the majority held that the university violated the First Amendment's establishment of religion clause by failing to fund a religious student magazine written by a fundamentalist Christian student group even though it funded similar magazines published by 118 other student groups, some of which were religiously based.[23] In dissent, the importance of this decision was highlighted by Justice David Souter, who noted: "The Court today, for the first time, approves direct funding of core religious activities by an arm of the state."[24]

In 1997, in *Agostini* v. *Felton*, the Supreme Court overruled a twelve-year-old precedent.[25] Justices okayed a New York program that sent public school teachers into parochial schools during school hours to provide remedial education to disadvantaged students. The Court concluded that this was not an excessive entanglement of church and state and therefore was not a violation of the Establishment clause.[26]

The Free Exercise Clause

The free exercise clause of the First Amendment proclaims that "Congress shall make no law . . . prohibiting the free exercise [of religion]." Although the free exercise clause of the First Amendment guarantees individuals the right to be free from governmental interference in the exercise of their religion, this guarantee, like other First Amendment freedoms, is not absolute. When secular law comes into conflict with religious law, the right to exercise one's religious beliefs is often denied—especially if the reli-

POLITICS NOW

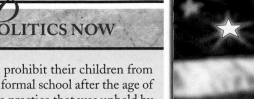

Protecting the Children: Church Versus State

The Amish prohibit their children from attending formal school after the age of fourteen, a practice that was upheld by the U.S. Supreme Court in 1972. In 1999, Congress took action to exempt Amish children from the protection of child labor laws.

Since the early 1900s in the United States there has been general agreement that many forms of child labor are wrong. Until around 1910, however, the children of immigrants and the poor aged ten to fifteen regularly worked long hours at low wages. Progressive groups including the National Child Labor Committee lobbied extensively for national legislation and even a constitutional amendment to allow Congress to ban the employment of underage children.

In 1938, Congress enacted (and the Supreme Court found constitutional) the Fair Labor Standards Act, which prohibited child labor. As a result, children aged fourteen and fifteen are allowed to work only three hours a day on school days and only from 7 A.M. to 7 P.M.

But what about Amish children, who are not in school at age fourteen? Even though the U.S. Department of Labor has visited several Amish shops where children are being trained in leatherwork, woodworking, and metal work, and labeled the conditions there "hazardous," Congress plans to exempt the Amish children because of their religion.[a] Proposed legislation will allow Amish children to work in "sawmills, the lumber industry, and other dangerous places," at the same time a national crackdown on child labor abuse is under way for non-Amish children.[b]

Said the chair of the Amish Steering Committee before Congress, "We believe that forced idleness in this age to be detrimental to our long-standing Amish way of raising our children and teaching them to become good, productive citizens."[c] The Clinton administration strongly opposes these kind of exemptions, arguing that this kind of religious preference was an unconstitutional violation of the establishment clause, as well as dangerous to children.[d] Supporters of the bill say it is a commonsense solution to protect the Amish way of life threatened by increasingly competitive markets. Should the government make an exception for Amish children? How can this bill be reconciled with the First Amendment?

[a]David Wastell, "Congress Moves to Let the Amish Use Child Labor," *Sunday Telegraph*, April 25, 1999, 26.
[b]Wastell, "Congress Moves."
[c]Wastell, "Congress Moves."
[d]Frank Swoboda, "Amish Child Labor Bill Has Few Foes," *The Washington Post*, April 2, 1999, A27.

gious beliefs in question are held by a minority or by an unpopular or "suspicious" religious group. State statutes barring the use of certain illegal drugs, snake handling, and polygamy—all practices of particular religious sects—have been upheld as constitutional when states have shown compelling reasons to regulate these practices. Nonetheless, the Court has made it clear that the free exercise clause requires that a state or the national government remain neutral toward religion.

Many critics of rigid enforcement of such neutrality argue that the government should do what it can to accommodate the religious diversity in our nation. In the early 1960s, for example, a South Carolina textile mill shifted to a six-day work week, requiring that all employees work on Saturday. When one employee—a Seventh-Day Adventist whose Sabbath was Saturday—said she could not work on Saturdays, she was fired. She sought to receive unemployment compensation and her claim was denied. She then sued to obtain her benefits.

The Supreme Court ordered South Carolina to extend benefits to the woman in spite of its law that required an employee to be available for work on all days but Sundays. The Court ruled that the state law was an unconstitutional violation of the free exercise clause because it failed to accommodate the worker's religious beliefs.[27]

In the same vein, the Court has interpreted the Constitution to mean that governmental interests can outweigh free exercise rights. In 1990, for example, the Supreme Court ruled that the free exercise clause allowed Oregon to ban the use of sacramental peyote (an illegal hallucinogenic drug) in some Native American tribes' traditional religious services. The focus of the case turned on what standard of review the Court should use. Should the Court use the compelling state interest test? In upholding the state's right to deny unemployment compensation to two workers who had been fired

HIGHLIGHT 5.2

The American Civil Liberties Union: Protector of First Amendment Rights

The American Civil Liberties Union (ACLU) was created in 1920 by a group that had tried to defend the civil liberties of those who were conscientious objectors to World War I. As the nation's oldest, largest, and premier nonpartisan civil liberties organization, the ACLU works in three major areas of the law: freedom of speech and religion, due process, and equality before the law. It lobbies for legislation affecting these areas and litigates to maintain these rights and liberties.

In its own words, the ACLU "has been a zealous advocate of the First Amendment and has steadfastly opposed government efforts to regulate either free speech or free thought, no matter how well-intentioned those efforts might be."* It regularly brings cases to court or files *amicus curiae,* or friend of the court briefs, in cases in which it is not lead counsel. *Amicus* briefs are a vehicle by which interested parties, usually interest groups or professional associations, can inform the Court of the policy and legal implications of its decision—from, of course, filing group's perspective. Among the major cases the ACLU has participated in are:

First Amendment rights:

- *The Scopes Case* (1945): Challenged a Tennessee law that made it a crime to teach evolution.

- *Tinker* v. *Des Moines Independent School Board* (1969): Upheld the right of students to wear black armbands in protest of the Vietnam War.
- *Lynch* v. *Donnelly* (1984): In a defeat for the ACLU, the Court held that a city's inclusion of a crèche in its annual Christmas display in a private park did not violate the establishment clause.

Criminal defendants' rights:

- *Mapp* v. *Ohio* (1961): Established that illegally obtained evidence can't be used at trial.
- *Gideon* v. *Wainwright* (1963): Granted indigents the right to counsel.
- *Miranda* v. *Arizona* (1966): Guaranteed all suspects a right to counsel.

Privacy rights:

- *Roe* v. *Wade* and *Doe* v. *Bolton* (1973): Established a woman's right to an abortion.
- *Bowers* v. *Hardwick* (1986): An unsuccessful challenge to Georgia's sodomy law.
- *Planned Parenthood* v. *Casey* (1992): An unsuccessful challenge to Pennsylvania's restrictive abortion regulations.

*Brief *Amicus Curiae, Wisconsin* v. *Mitchell,* October Term, 1992, LEXIS.

by a private drug rehabilitation clinic because they had ingested an illegal substance, a majority of the Court held that the state did not need to show a compelling interest to limit the free exercise of religion.[28] This decision prompted a dramatic outcry. Congressional response was passage of the Religious Freedom Restoration Act, which reinstated strict scrutiny as the required judicial standard of review to make it harder for states to interfere with how citizens practice their religion. In 1997, however, the Supreme Court ruled that the act was unconstitutional.[29]

In contrast, in 1993 the Supreme Court ruled that members of the Santería Church, an Afro-Cuban religion, had the right to sacrifice animals during religious services. In upholding that practice, the Court ruled that a city ordinance banning such practices was unconstitutionally aimed at the group, thereby denying its members the right to free exercise of their religion.[30]

Although conflicts between religious beliefs and the government are often difficult to settle, the Court has attempted to walk the fine line between the free exercise and establishment clauses. In the area of free exercise, the Court often has had to confront questions of "What is a god?" and "What is a religious faith?"—questions that theologians have grappled with for centuries. In 1965, for example, in a case involving three men who had been denied conscientious objector deferments during the Vietnam War because they did not subscribe to "traditional" organized religions, the Court ruled unanimously that belief in a supreme being was not essential for recognition as a conscientious objector. Thus the men were entitled to the deferments because their views paralleled those who objected to war and who belonged to traditional religions. In contrast, despite the Court's having ruled that Catholic, Protestant, Jewish, and Buddhist

" TODAY IN SCHOOL WE PRAYED FOR A TAX-CUT. "

■ (Photo courtesy: ©1999 Mick Stevens from cartoonbank.com. All rights reserved.)

prison inmates must be allowed to hold religious services,[31] in 1987 it ruled that Islamic prisoners could be denied the same right for security reasons.[32]

FIRST AMENDMENT GUARANTEES: FREEDOM OF SPEECH AND PRESS

Today some members of Congress criticize television talk shows, including *Ricki Lake* and *The Jerry Springer Show,* for pandering to the least common denominator of society. Other groups criticize popular performers, especially rap groups, for lyrics that promote violence in general and against women in particular. Despite the distastefulness of some talk show topics or rap lyrics, many civil libertarians have resisted even the suggestion that these things be regulated.

A democracy depends on a free exchange of ideas, and the First Amendment shows that the Framers were well aware of this fact. Historically, one of the most volatile areas of constitutional interpretation has been in the interpretation of the First Amendment's mandate that "Congress shall make no law . . . abridging the freedom of speech, or of the press." Like the establishment and free exercise clauses of the First Amendment, the speech and press clauses have not been interpreted as absolute bans against government regulation. In fact, over the years the Court has used a hierarchical approach, with some items getting greater protection than others. Generally, thoughts have received the greatest protection, and actions or deeds the least. Words have come somewhere in the middle, depending on their content and purpose.

In the United States, with few exceptions, thoughts are considered beyond the scope of governmental regulation. Although people may experience a negative reaction for revealing their thoughts, the government has no legal right to punish or sanction Americans for what they think. Words, or speech, which stand between thoughts and deeds, are subject to some forms of restraint. Speech that is obscene, libelous (false and causing someone disrepute), or seditious (advocating violent overthrow of the government), or that could incite or cause injury to those to whom they are addressed, has been interpreted as not protected by the First Amendment. Often, however, these exceptions to constitutional protection have troubled the Court. What is considered obscene in rural Mississippi, for example, may not offend someone in another part of the nation.

Actions, or deeds, are given the least constitutional protection. Thus actions are subject to the greatest governmental restrictions. For example, you may have a right to shoot a pistol in your back yard, but it is illegal to do so on most city streets. Over the years these competing rights have been balanced by the now classic observation that your "right to swing your arm ends at the tip of my nose."[33]

■ The popularity of Jerry Springer's nationally syndicated talk show is used by many to underscore declining morals and the need to regulate the airways. (Photo courtesy: Todd Buchanan/Black Star)

prior restraint:

Government prohibition of speech or publication before the fact, generally held to be in violation of the First Amendment.

When the First Amendment was ratified in 1791, it was considered to protect only against **prior restraint** of speech or expression, that is, to guard against the prohibition of speech or publication before the fact. As was the case in Great Britain concerning free speech, the First Amendment was not considered to provide absolute immunity from governmental sanction for what speakers or publishers might say or print. Thus, over the years, the meaning of this amendment's mandate has been subject to thousands of cases seeking judicial interpretation of its meaning.

Attempts to Limit Speech

Although the Supreme Court has allowed few governmental bans on most types of speech, some forms of expression are not protected. In 1942 the Supreme Court set out the rationale by which it would distinguish between protected and unprotected speech. According to the Court, obscenity, lewdness, libel, and fighting words are not protected by the First Amendment because "such expressions are no essential part of any exposition of ideas, and are of such slight social value as a step to truth that any benefit that may be derived from them is clearly outweighed by the social interest in order and morality."[34]

The Alien and Sedition Acts.

In 1798, soon after passage of the Bill of Rights, a constitutional crisis arose when the Federalist Congress enacted the Alien and Sedition Acts. Designed to ban any political criticism by the growing numbers of Jeffersonian Democratic-Republicans, these acts made publication of "any false, scandalous writing against the government of the United States" a criminal offense. Overtly partisan Federalist judges imposed fines and even jail terms on at least ten Democratic-Republican newspaper editors for allegedly violating the acts. The acts became a major issue in the 1800 presidential election campaign, which led to the election of Thomas Jefferson, a vocal opponent of the acts. He quickly pardoned all who had been convicted under their provisions, and the new Democratic-Republican Congress allowed the acts to expire before the Supreme Court had an opportunity to rule on the constitutionality of these serious infringements of the First Amendment.

Slavery, the Civil War, and Rights Curtailments.

After the public outcry over the Alien and Sedition Acts, the national government largely got out of the business of regulating speech, but in its place the states began to prosecute those who published articles critical of governmental policies. In the 1830s, at the urgings of abolitionists, the publication or dissemination of any positive information about slavery became a punishable offense in the North. In the opposite vein, in the South, supporters of the "peculiar institution" of slavery enacted laws to prohibit publication of any anti-slavery sentiments. Southern postmasters refused to deliver Northern abolitionist papers throughout the South, which amounted to censorship of the mails.

During the Civil War, President Abraham Lincoln effectively suspended the free press provision of the First Amendment (as well as many other sections of the Constitution) and even went so far as to order the arrest of the editors of two New York papers that were critical of him. Far from protesting against these blatant violations of the First Amendment, Congress acceded to them. Right after the war, for example, Congress actually prevented the Supreme Court from issuing a judgment on a case because members feared its decision would be critical of the powers Lincoln had taken on during the war.[35] William McCardle, a Mississippi newspaper editor, had sought to arouse sentiment against Lincoln and the Union occupation. Even though he was a civilian, McCardle was jailed by a military court without having any charges brought against him. He appealed his detainment to the U.S. Supreme Court, arguing that he was being held unlawfully. Congress, fearing that a victory for McCardle would prompt other Confederate newspaper editors to follow his lead, enacted a law barring the Supreme Court from hearing appeals of cases involving convictions for publishing statements critical of the Union. Because Article III of the Constitution gives Congress the power to determine the jurisdiction of the Court, the Court was forced to conclude that it had no authority to rule in the matter.

GLOBAL POLITICS

Civil Liberties in the Industrial Democracies

Since 1970, Freedom House, a civil liberties organization based in the United States, has measured the degree of political rights and civil liberties in the countries of the world. In measuring civil liberties, Freedom House investigates freedom of speech, assembly, religion, and movement, the ability to organize political organizations, existence of an independent judiciary and the rule of law, property rights, and freedom from arbitrary punishment. Countries are rated on a partly subjective scale from 1 (with the highest levels of political freedom) to 7 (no freedom). Countries are ranked as free, partly free, or not free based on their numerical rating.

The United States is in good company in terms of civil liberties. All G-7 countries are rated free, with limited restrictions on civil liberties. Each of the seven countries has some limitations on its citizens' freedom. In 1998, Germany, France, Japan, and Italy were cited for official policies that limit the rights of immigrants and foreign residents. In the United States, Germany, and the United Kingdom, law enforcement and criminal justice practices were cited as infringements on individual liberties. Reflecting the American bias toward written constitutions with explicit bills of rights as safeguards of civil liberties, Freedom House rated the United Kingdom at 2 because it has neither.

Civil Liberties Ratings for the G-7 Countries

Country	Score	Rating
Canada	1	Free
France	2	Free
Germany	2	Free
Italy	2	Free
Japan	2	Free
United Kingdom	2	Free
United States	1	**Free**

SOURCE: Freedom House, *Freedom in the World: 1997–1998*. (New Brunswick and London: Transaction Publishers, 1998).

After the Civil War, states also began to prosecute individuals for seditious speech if they uttered or printed statements critical of the government. Between 1890 and 1900, for example, there were more than one hundred state prosecutions for sedition in state courts.[36] Moreover, by the dawn of the twentieth century, public opinion in the United States had become exceedingly hostile to the preachings of groups such as socialists and communists who attempted to appeal to the thousands of new and disheartened immigrants. Groups espousing socialism and communism became the targets of state laws curtailing speech and the written word. By the end of World War I, over thirty states had passed laws to punish seditious speech, and more than 1,900 individuals and over one hundred newspapers had been prosecuted for violations.[37]

Anti-Governmental Speech. The next major national efforts to restrict freedom of speech and the press, however, did not occur until congressional passage of the Espionage Act of 1917. Nearly 2,000 Americans were convicted of violating its various provisions, especially those that made it illegal to urge resistance to the draft and prohibiting the distribution of anti-war leaflets. In 1919 the Supreme Court interpreted the First Amendment to allow Congress to restrict speech that was "of such a nature as to create a clear and present danger that will bring about the substantive evils that Congress has a right to prevent."[38] Under the **clear and present danger test,** which allowed Congress to ban speech that could cause a clear and present danger to society, the circumstances surrounding the incident count, according to the Court. Anti-war leaflets, for example, may be permissible in peacetime, but they pose too much of a danger in wartime to be allowed.

For decades, the Supreme Court wrestled with what constituted a "danger." Finally, in 1969, the Court fashioned a new test for deciding whether certain kinds of speech could be regulated by the government: the **direct incitement test.** Now the government could punish the advocacy of illegal action only if "such advocacy is directed to inciting or producing imminent lawless action and is likely to incite or produce such action."[39] The requirement of "imminent harm" makes it more difficult for the government to punish speech and is consistent with the Framers' notion of the special role played by speech in a democratic society.

clear and present danger test:

Test used by the Supreme Court to draw the line between protected and unprotected speech; the Court looks to see if there is an imminent danger that illegal action would occur in response to the contested speech.

direct incitement test:

A test used by the Court that holds that advocacy of illegal action is protected by the First Amendment unless imminent action is intended and likely to occur.

Libel and Slander.   Today, national tabloid newspapers such as the *National Enquirer* and the *Star* boast headlines that cause many just to shake their heads in disbelief. How can they get away with it, some may wonder. The Framers were very concerned that the press not be suppressed. The First Amendment works to allow all forms of speech, no matter how libelous. False or libelous statements are not restrained by the courts, yet the Supreme Court has consistently ruled that individuals or the press can be sued *after the fact* for untrue or libelous statements. **Libel** is a written statement that defames the character of a person. If the statement is spoken, it is **slander.** In many nations—such as Great Britain, for example—it is relatively easy to sue someone for libel. In the United States, however, the standards of proof are much more difficult. A person who believes that he or she has been a victim of libel, for example, must show that the statements made were untrue. Truth is an absolute defense against the charge of libel, no matter how painful or embarrassing the revelations.

It is often more difficult for individuals the Supreme Court considers to be "public persons or public officials" to sue for libel or slander. ***New York Times Co.* v. *Sullivan*** (1964) was the first major libel case considered by the Supreme Court.[40] An Alabama state court had found the *Times* guilty of libel for printing a full-page advertisement accusing Alabama officials of physically abusing African Americans during various civil rights protests (the ad was paid for by civil rights activists, including former First Lady Eleanor Roosevelt). The Supreme Court overturned the conviction, ruling that a finding of libel against a public official could stand only if there were a showing of "actual malice." Proof that the statements were false or negligent was not sufficient to prove "actual malice." The concept of actual malice (a burden of proof imposed on public officials and public figures suing for defamation and falsity requiring them to prove with clear and convincing evidence that an offending story was published with knowing falsehood or reckless disregard for the truth) can be difficult and confusing. In 1991 the Court directed lower courts to use the phrases "knowledge of falsity" and "reckless disregard of the truth" when giving instructions to juries in libel cases. Given the high degree of proof required, few public officials or public persons have been able to win libel cases.

More recently, the U.S. Supreme Court addressed the issue of whether a magazine could be sued for savage parody in *Hustler Magazine* v. *Falwell* (1988), a case popularized by the movie, *The People vs. Larry Flynt*.[41] A lower court, after dismissing a libel charge against Flynt, who had published a parody describing Moral Majority head, Rev. Jerry Falwell, and his mother engaged in a drunken incestuous encounter in an outhouse, ordered Flynt to pay damages for "intentional infliction of emotional distress." On appeal to the Supreme Court, the central issue was (in the absence of the kind of false statements purporting to be fact on which libel suits are based) this: Can a public figure such as Rev. Falwell win damages from a publication that intentionally causes emotional distress through public ridicule? Political cartoonists, in particular, were especially interested in the outcome of the case, and they and many newspaper associations lined up on Flynt's side. The justices upheld Flynt's First Amendment right to publish the parody, noting the need "to protect the free flow of ideas and opinions on matters of public interest and concern."[42]

Obscenity and Pornography. *   Although the Supreme Court has allowed few governmental bans on most types of speech, some forms of expression are not protected.

---

libel:

False statements or statements tending to call someone's reputation into disrepute.

slander:

Untrue spoken statements that defame the character of a person.

***New York Times Co.* v. *Sullivan* (1971):**

The Supreme Court concluded that "Actual malice" must be proved to support a finding of libel against a public figure.

■ The highly acclaimed movie *The People vs. Larry Flynt,* underscored the Constitutional doctrine that allows publishers tremendous leeway when writing about public figures. (Photo courtesy: Columbia Pictures/ Shooting Star)

---

*"Technically, obscenity refers to those things considered "disgusting, foul or morally unhealthy." Pornography, in contrast, is often broader in meaning and generally refers to "depictions of sexual lewdness or erotic behavior." While distasteful to many, pornography is not necessarily obscene. While the *Starr Report* contained sexual materials many say were pornographic, no one charged that its contents were obscene. See Donald Downs, "Obscenity and Pornography," in Kermit Hall, ed., *The Oxford Companion to the Supreme Court of the United States* (New York: Oxford University Press, 1992), 602.

In *Chaplinsky* v. *New Hampshire* (1942), the Supreme Court set out the rationale by which it would distinguish between protected and unprotected speech. According to the Court, obscenity, lewdness, libel, and fighting words are not protected by the First Amendment because "such expressions are no essential part of any exposition of ideas, and are of such slight social value as a step to truth that any benefit that may be derived from them is clearly outweighed by the social interest in order and morality."[43]

Through 1957, U.S. courts often based their decisions of what was obscene on an English common-law test that had been set out in 1868: "Whether the tendency of the matter charged as obscenity is to deprive and corrupt those whose minds are open to such immoral influences and into whose hands a publication of this sort might fall."[44]

In *Roth* v. *United States* (1957), the Court abandoned that approach and held that to be considered obscene, the material in question must be "utterly without redeeming social importance," and articulated a new test for obscenity: "whether to the average person, applying contemporary community standards, the dominant theme of the material taken as a whole appeals to the prurient interests."[45] In many ways the *Roth* test brought with it as many problems as it attempted to solve. Throughout the 1950s and 1960s, "prurient" remained hard to define, as the Court struggled to find a standard by which to judge actions or words. Moreover, it was very difficult to prove that a book or movie was "*utterly* without redeeming social value." In general, even some "hardcore" pornography passed muster under the *Roth* test, prompting some to argue that the Court fostered the increase in the number of sexually oriented publications designed to appeal to those living amidst what many called the "sexual revolution."

Richard M. Nixon made the growth in pornography a major issue when he ran for president in 1968, and he pledged to appoint to federal judgeships only those who would uphold "law and order" and stop coddling criminals and purveyors of porn. Once elected president, Nixon made four appointments to the Court, including Chief Justice Warren Burger. In *Miller* v. *California* (1973), the Supreme Court began to formulate rules designed to make it easier for states to regulate obscene materials and to return to communities a greater role in determining what is obscene.[46]

In *Miller* the Court set out a test that redefined obscenity. To determine whether or not material in question was obscene, the justices concluded that a lower court must ask "whether the work depicts or describes, in a patently offensive way, sexual conduct specifically defined by state law." Moreover, courts were to determine "whether the work, taken as a whole, lacks serious literary, artistic, political or scientific value." And in place of the contemporary community standards gauge used in earlier cases, the Court defined community standards to mean local, and not national, standards under the rationale that what is acceptable in Times Square in New York City might not be tolerated in Peoria, Illinois.

Local community standards still may not be the sole criterion of obscenity. In 1974 the Court overturned a decision of a Georgia state court that found *Carnal Knowledge* (a movie starring Jack Nicholson, Ann-Margret, and Art Garfunkel that included scenes of a partially nude woman) obscene. The Court concluded that the scenes were neither "patently offensive" nor designed to appeal to "prurient interest."[47] As Justice Potter Stewart had once announced, he couldn't define obscenity, but "I know it when I see it."[48] He did not see it in *Carnal Knowledge.*

Time and contexts clearly have altered the Court's and, indeed, much of America's perceptions of what is obscene. *Carnal Knowledge* is now often shown on television on Saturday afternoons with only minor editing. But through the early 1990s, the Court allowed communities greater leeway in drafting statutes to deal with obscenity and, even more important, forms of non-obscene expression. In 1991, for example, the Supreme Court voted five to four to allow Indiana to ban totally nude erotic dancing, concluding that its statute did not violate the First Amendment's guarantee of freedom of expression and that it furthered an important or substantial governmental interest (thereby adopting the intermediate standard of review).[49]

Congress and Obscenity.   While lawmakers have been fairly effective in restricting the sale and distribution of obscene materials, Congress has been particularly concerned with two obscenity and pornography issues: (1) federal funding for the arts; and (2) the distribution of obscenity and pornography on the Internet that has "embroiled it in constitutional struggles over the proper balance between free expression and the interests of the majority."[50]

In 1990 concern over the use of federal dollars by the National Endowment for the Arts (NEA) for works with controversial religious or sexual themes led to passage of legislation requiring the NEA to "tak(e) into consideration general standards of decency and respect for the diverse beliefs and values of the American public," when it makes its annual awards. In a challenge brought by several performance artists, the Supreme Court ruled that decency standards could be considered by the arts funder as instructed by Congress.[51] (See Figure 5.1 for the chronology of this challenge.)

Congress recently turned to a more difficult task: monitoring the Internet, which some charge has become a vehicle for easy distribution of obscenity and pornography

Web Exploration

For more information on the NEA, see www.awlonline.com/oconnor.

Figure 5.1 Free Speech Challenge

FREE SPEECH CHALLENGE

1989

National Endowment for the Arts funding for exhibits that included Robert Mapplethorpe's homoerotic photographs and Andres C. Serrano's "Piss Christ" incite controversy in Congress over federal arts funding and freedom of expression.

1990

Congress adopts a bill instructing the NEA to take "into consideration general standards of decency and respect for the diverse beliefs and values of the American public" when awarding grants.

1991

Four performance artists, including Karen Finley, known for smearing chocolate on her nude body, challenge the new provision in a lawsuit, claiming it violates constitutional free speech and due process protections.

1992

A federal judge in Los Angeles strikes down the decency provision as unconstitutionally vague because it does not clearly define the type of art that would be prohibited.

1993

Part of the lawsuit is settled after the NEA agrees to give $252,000 to the artists who claimed their applications for grants were rejected.

1996

The U.S. Court of Appeals for the 9th Circuit agrees that the "general standards of decency" clause is unconstitutionally vague and adds that it impermissibly restricts artistic content and viewpoint.

1998

The U.S. Supreme Court reverses the 9th Circuit and rules that the government can consider whether a project meets general standards of decency.

SOURCE: Figure by Adrianna Garcia from " 'Decency' Can Be Weighed In Arts Agency's Funding" by Joan Biskupic, *The Washington Post*, June 26, 1998, p. A18. © 1998,The Washington Post. Reprinted with permission.

as well as a means for young children to be exposed to these kinds of materials. In 1996 Congress overwhelmingly passed the Telecommunications Reform Act of 1996. It was then signed by President Clinton, even though he expressed some reservations about the constitutionality of some sections of the act. He wasn't alone. Civil libertarians and some computer communications experts were shocked by the scope of the Communications Decency Act provisions included in the final omnibus legislation.[52]

What did the act do? It maintains the same ban on obscene material that already applied to the media and criminalized the transmission of "indecent" speech or images to people younger than eighteen years of age. Indecency is defined as any communication that depicts or describes in patently offensive terms any sexual or excretory activities or organs as measured by contemporary community standards. This definition makes no exceptions for materials that have serious literary, artistic, scientific, or other redeeming social value as spelled out in *Miller* v. *California* (1973).

Supporters of the act believed that barring the distribution of certain materials to those under eighteen years of age would protect the act from constitutional challenge. Nevertheless, the act was immediately challenged by the American Civil Liberties Union (ACLU). In contrast, conservatives and the Christian Coalition claimed that the law did not go far enough because it penalized only those who post the materials, not the servers, such as America Online and Prodigy.[53]

The Supreme Court, however, agreed with the ACLU in finding that Congress violated freedom of speech rights when it tried to limit smut on the Internet.[54] To get around this Supreme Court ruling, Congress enacted the Child Online Protection Act in late 1998. It forced commercial web site operators to collect a credit card number as proof of age before allowing access to a site that could be considered "harmful to minors" without any sort of screening device that could render the material available only to adults. It also calls for fines of up to $150,000 a day per offense as well as jail time. A federal district court judge prevented the law from going into effect in 1999, and the Clinton administration has appealed that decision at this writing.[55]

What Types of Speech Are Protected?

Certain types of speech are protected, including symbolic speech, prior restraint, and hate speech.

Web Exploration

For more information on the *Reno* v. *ACLU* and *National Endowment for the Arts* v. *Finley* cases, see www.awlonline.com/oconnor.

■ Many Democrats criticized House Republicans when they released the full *Starr Report* online. (Photo courtesy: John Deering, *Arizona Democrat-Gazette/Creators Syndicate*)

symbolic speech:

Symbols, signs, and other methods
of expression generally also considered to be protected by the First
Amendment.

Symbolic Speech.   In addition to the general protection accorded pure speech, the Supreme Court has
extended the reach of the First Amendment to other
means of expression often called **symbolic speech**—symbols, signs, and the like—as well as to activities like pick-
eting, sit-ins, and demonstrations. In the words of Justice
John Marshall Harlan, these kinds of "speech" are part of
the "free trade in ideas."[56]

The Supreme Court first acknowledged that symbolic
speech was entitled to First Amendment protection in
Stromberg v. *California* (1931).[57] There the Court overturned the conviction of the director of a Communist
youth camp under a state statute prohibiting the display of
a red flag, a symbol of opposition to the U.S. government.
In a similar vein, the right of high school students to wear
black armbands to protest the Vietnam War was upheld in *Tinker* v. *Des Moines Independent Community School District* (1969).[58]

Burning the American flag has also been held to be a form of protected symbolic
speech. In 1989 a sharply divided Supreme Court (five to four) reversed the conviction
of Gregory Johnson, who had been found guilty of setting fire to an American flag during the 1984 Republican national convention in Dallas.[59] As a result, there was a major
public outcry against the Court. President George Bush and numerous members of
Congress called for a constitutional amendment to ban flag burning to overturn *Texas*
v. *Johnson.* Others, including Justice William J. Brennan, Jr., noted that if it had not
been for acts like that of Johnson, the United States would never have been created nor
would a First Amendment guaranteeing a right to political protest exist.

Instead of a constitutional amendment, Congress passed the Federal Flag Protection Act of 1989, which authorized federal prosecution of anyone who intentionally
desecrated a national flag. Those who originally had been arrested burned another flag
and were convicted. Their conviction was again overturned by the Supreme Court. As
they had in *Johnson,* the justices divided five to four in holding that this federal law "suffered from the same fundamental flaw" as had the earlier state law that was declared in
violation of the First Amendment.[60] Since that decision Congress has tried several times
to pass a constitutional amendment to allow it to ban flag burning. Those efforts, however, have yet to be successful, as discussed in chapter 2.

Prior Restraint.   With only a few exceptions, the Court has made it clear that it will
not tolerate prior restraint of speech. In 1971, for example, in *New York Times Co.* v.
United States (1971) (also called the "Pentagon Papers" case), the Supreme Court ruled
that the U.S. government could not block the publication of secret Defense Department documents illegally furnished to the *Times* by antiwar activists.[61] In 1976 the
Supreme Court went even further, noting that any attempt by the government to prevent expression carried "a 'heavy presumption' against its constitutionality."[62] In a
Nebraska case, a trial court issued a "gag order" barring the press from reporting the
lurid details of a crime. In balancing the defendant's constitutional right to a fair trial
against the press's right to cover a story, the trial judge concluded that the defendant's
right carried greater weight. The Supreme Court disagreed, holding the press's right to
cover the trial paramount. Still, judges are often allowed to issue gag orders affecting
parties to a lawsuit or to limit press coverage of a case.

Hate Speech.   "As a thumbnail summary of the last two or three decades of speech
issues in the Supreme Court," wrote the eminent First Amendment scholar Harry Kalven, Jr. in 1966, "we may come to see the Negro as winning back for us the freedoms
the Communists seemed to have lost for us."[63] Still, says noted African-American
scholar Henry Louis Gates, Jr., Kalven would be shocked to see the stance that some

■ Thatch was the name of this Brown University cartoon strip drawn and written by Jeff Shesol. In 1998, Shesol was hired by the Clinton White House as a speech writer. (From THATCH by Jeff Shesol. Copyright © 1991 by Jeff Shesol. Reprinted by permission of Random House, Inc.)

blacks now take toward the First Amendment, which once protected protests, rallies, and agitation in the 1960s: "The byword among many black activists and black intellectuals is no longer the political imperative to protect free speech; it is the moral imperative to suppress 'hate speech.'"[64]

In this decade a particularly thorny First Amendment area has emerged as cities and universities have attempted to prohibit what they view as offensive hate speech and Congress has moved to ban many forms of offensive speech on the Internet with passage of the Communications Decency Act. Since 1989, for example, hundreds of colleges and universities have banned a variety of forms of speech or conduct that creates or fosters an intimidating, hostile, or offensive environment on campus such as racial slurs directed at minority groups. Other college codes ban conduct or speech that causes emotional distress. The University of Connecticut, for example, banned "inappropriately directed laughter" and "conspicuous exclusion of students from conversations."

While many commentators poke fun at what they call the "politically correct," or "PC movement," any possible infringements with constitutional protections are a serious matter. Universities, however, believe that offensive speech, in the wake of rising incidents of racism and anti-semitism, require drastic measures. A series of court rulings, in fact, have found many state universities' speech codes to be unconstitutional; in contrast, private institutions can ignore public law rulings and enact whatever speech codes they desire. For example, at the University of Michigan in 1990, a student was accused of violating the university's regulation banning speech that stigmatizes individuals for their sexual orientation, when he said during a classroom discussion that he considered homosexuality to be a disease treatable with therapy. The university's code was challenged by the American Civil Liberties Union and found unconstitutional by a federal district court. In contrast, at Brown University, a private institution, a student was expelled for shouting anti-Semitic, anti-black, and anti-homosexual obscenities at students in their dorm rooms at 2:00 A.M.

Supporters of speech codes see them as "morally essential" to the resolution of the conflict between civil rights (freedom from harmful stigma) and civil liberties (freedom of speech). Today, many cities and towns are trying to limit hate speech, and PBS has even launched a program, "Not in Our Town" to help cities and schools stamp out hate speech and make citizens more sensitive to its effects.

THE RIGHT TO KEEP AND BEAR ARMS

The O. J. Simpson trial not only riveted many Americans to their televisions, it also brought with it tremendous attention to the criminal justice system, warts and all. That trial made Americans question some of the rights now guaranteed to defendants, the jury system, and many of the rules by which police, prosecutors, and the judicial system now work.

The O. J. Simpson case was not the only phenomenon that focused attention on the criminal justice system. Throughout the 1980s and into the early 1990s, most Americans cited crime as the most important issue facing the nation. Closely associated with the concern about crime is the issue of gun control.

While not traditionally thought of as a "civil liberties" issue by some, the right to keep and bear arms is a very hot topic in American politics. (It is also a controversy with considerable historical origins, as highlighted in Roots of Government: The Second Amendment and the Right to Keep and Bear Arms.") In the aftermath of the assassination attempt on President Ronald Reagan in 1981, many lawmakers called for passage of gun control legislation. At the forefront of that effort was Sarah Brady, the wife of James Brady, the presidential press secretary who was badly wounded and left partially disabled by John Hinkley, Jr., President Reagan's assailant. In 1993 her efforts helped to win passage of the so-called Brady Bill, which imposed a federal mandatory five-day waiting period on the purchase of handguns.

In 1994, in spite of extensive lobbying by the powerful National Rifle Association (NRA), Congress passed and President Clinton signed the $30.2-billion Violent Crime Control and Law Enforcement Act. In addition to providing money to states for new prisons and law enforcement officers, the act banned the manufacture, sale, transport, or possession of nineteen different kinds of semi-automatic assault weapons.

The NRA immediately targeted some of the act's sponsors for defeat in the 1994 congressional elections. They successfully beat several Democratic members of Congress, including Jack Brooks (D-Tex.), who had chaired the House Judiciary Committee that had authored many portions of the bill.

In 1997, a sharply divided five-to-four U.S. Supreme Court ruled that the section of the Brady Act requiring state officials to conduct background checks of prospective handgun owners violated principles of state sovereignty.[65] The background check provision, while important, is not critical to the overall goals of the Brady Act because a federal record-checking system went into effect in late 1998. School shootings in Littleton, Colorado, and Conyers, Georgia, heightened interest in gun control legislation. As detailed on page 217, in 1999 Congress failed to pass additional legislation designed to curb the availability of guns and to make them safer should they fall into the hands of children.

Web Exploration

To learn more about the gun control issue, see
www.awlonline.com/oconnor.

due process rights:

Procedural guarantees provided by the Fourth, Fifth, Sixth, and Eighth amendments for those accused of crimes.

THE RIGHTS OF CRIMINAL DEFENDANTS

The Fourth, Fifth, Sixth, and Eighth amendments provide a variety of procedural guarantees (often called **due process rights**) for those accused of crimes. Particular amendments, as well as other portions of the Constitution, specifically provide procedural

ROOTS OF GOVERNMENT

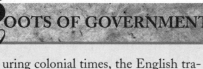

During colonial times, the English tradition of distrust of standing armies was evident: Most colonies required all white men to keep and bear arms, and all white men in whole sections of the colonies were deputized to defend their settlements against Indians and other European powers. These local militias were viewed as the best way to keep order and liberty.

The Second Amendment was added to the Constitution to ensure that Congress could not pass laws to disarm state militias. This amendment appeased Anti-Federalists, who feared that the new Constitution would cause them to lose the right to "keep and bear arms" as well as an unstated right—the right to revolt against governmental tyranny.

Through the early 1920s, few state statutes were passed to regulate firearms (and generally these laws dealt with the possession of firearms by slaves). And the Supreme Court's decision in *Barron* v. *Baltimore* (1833), which limited the application of the Bill of Rights to the actions of Congress alone, prevented federal review of those state laws. Moreover, in *Dred Scott* v. *Sandford* (1857) (see chapter 3), Chief Justice Taney listed the right to own and carry arms as a basic right of citizenship.

In 1934 Congress passed the National Firearms Act in response to the increase in organized crime that occurred in the 1920s and 1930s as a result of Prohibition (see chapter 2). The act imposed taxes on automatic weapons (such as machine guns) and sawed-off shotguns. In *United States* v. *Miller* (1939), a unanimous Court upheld the constitutionality of the Act by stating that the Second Amendment was intended to protect a citizen's right to own ordinary militia weapons and *not* unregistered sawed-off shotguns, which were at issue in the *Miller* case. *Miller* was the last time the Supreme Court directly addressed the Second Amendment. In *Quilici* v. *Village of Morton Grove* (1983), the Supreme Court refused to review a lower court's ruling upholding the constitutionality of a local ordinance banning handguns against a Second Amendment challenge.

■ James and Sarah Brady being applauded for their efforts to win congressional approval of the Brady Bill after it was signed into law by President Clinton. (Photo courtesy: John Ficara/Sygma)

guarantees to protect individuals accused of crimes at all stages of the criminal justice process. And as is the case with the First Amendment, many of these rights have been interpreted by the Supreme Court to apply to the states.

In interpreting the amendments dealing with what are frequently termed "criminal rights," the courts have to grapple not only with the meaning of the amendments, but also with how their protections are to be implemented. The Eighth Amendment, for example, prohibits "cruel and unusual punishments." The question of what is cruel and unusual, however, has vexed the Supreme Court for years. In 1972, for example, the Supreme Court—by a vote of five to four—for the first time struck down the death penalty under the cruel and unusual punishments clause of the Eighth Amendment.[66] Three justices for the majority concluded that the death penalty was imposed in an arbitrary and random pattern, and that this randomness was cruel and unusual. Two justices said it was always a violation. This decision sent the states back to the drawing boards to draft new, nonarbitrary death penalty laws. In 1976 the Court upheld Georgia's new, more specific standards and in 1999, thirty eight states had capital punishment statutes.[67]

Today a more conservative Court routinely allows executions to be carried out. Perhaps even more than in the area of First Amendment guarantees, prevailing thoughts about the rights of criminal defendants are changing quickly and dramatically not only as the public becomes more intolerant of crime but as more conservative and moderate justices have been appointed to the Supreme Court, causing it to move away from what some view as the "excesses" of the Warren Court (1953–69).

Over the years, many individuals criticized the liberal Warren Court's rulings, arguing that its rulings gave criminals more "rights" than their victims. The Warren Court made several provisions of the Bill of Rights dealing with the rights of criminal defendants applicable to the states through the Fourteenth Amendment. It is important to remember that most procedural guarantees apply to individuals *charged* with crimes, that is, before they have been tried. These rights were designed to protect those wrongfully accused, although, of course, they often have helped the guilty. But as Justice William O. Douglas once noted, "Respecting the dignity even of the least worthy citizen . . . raises the stature of all of us.[68]

Many continue to argue, however, that only the guilty are helped by the American system and that criminals should not go unpunished because of simple police error. The dilemma of balancing the rights of the individual against those of society permeates the entire debate, and often even judicial interpretations of the rights of criminal defendants.

The Fourth Amendment and Searches and Seizures

The Fourth Amendment to the Constitution declares:

> The right of the people to be secure in their persons, houses, papers, and effects, against unreasonable searches and seizures, shall not be violated, and no Warrants shall issue, but upon probable cause, supported by Oath or affirmation, and particularly describing the place to be searched, and the persons or things to be seized.

This amendment's purpose was to deny the national government the authority to make general searches. The English Parliament had often issued general "writs of assistance" that allowed such searches. These general warrants were often used against religious and political dissenters, a practice the Framers wanted banned in the new nation. But still, the language that they chose left numerous questions to be answered, including, what is an "unreasonable" search?

Over the years, in a number of decisions, the Supreme Court has interpreted the Fourth Amendment to allow the police to search:

1. The person arrested;
2. Things in plain view of the accused person; and
3. Places or things that the arrested person could touch or reach or are otherwise in the arrestee's "immediate control."

In 1995 the Court also resolved a decades-old constitutional dispute by ruling unanimously that police must knock and announce their presence before entering a house or apartment to execute a search. But, said the Court, there may be "reasonable" exceptions to the rule to account for the likelihood of violence or the imminent destruction of evidence.[69]

Warrantless searches often occur if police suspect that someone is committing or is about to commit a crime. In these situations, police may "stop and frisk" the individual under suspicion. In 1989 the Court ruled that there need be only a "reasonable suspicion" for stopping a suspect—a much lower standard than "probable cause."[70] Thus a suspected drug courier may be stopped for brief questioning but only a frisk search (for weapons) is permitted. The answers to these questions may shift "reasonable suspicion" to "probable cause," thus permitting the officer to search. But except at international borders (or international airports), a *search* requires probable cause.

Searches can also be made without a warrant if consent is obtained, and the Court has ruled that consent can be given by a variety of persons. It has ruled, for example, that police can search a bedroom occupied by two persons as long as they have the consent of one of them.[71]

In situations where no arrest occurs, police must obtain search warrants from a "neutral and detached magistrate" prior to conducting more extensive searches of houses, cars, offices, or any other place where an individual would reasonably have some expectation of privacy.[72] Police can't get search warrants, for example, to require you to undergo surgery to remove a bullet that might be used to incriminate you, since your expectation of bodily privacy outweighs the need for evidence.[73] But courts don't require search warrants in possible drunk driving situations. Thus, the police can require you to take a Breathalyzer test to determine whether you have been drinking in excess of legal limits.[74]

Homes, too, are presumed to be private. Firefighters can enter your home to fight a fire without a warrant. But if they decide to investigate the cause of the fire, they must obtain a warrant before their reentry.[75] In contrast, under the "open fields doctrine" first articulated by the Supreme Court in 1924,[76] if you own a field, and even if you post "No Trespassing" signs, the police can search your field without a warrant to see if you are illegally growing marijuana, because you cannot reasonably expect privacy in an open field.

Cars have proven problematic for police and the courts because of their mobile nature. As noted by Chief Justice William Howard Taft as early as 1925, "the vehicle can quickly be moved out of the locality or jurisdiction in which the warrant must be sought."[77] Over the years the Court has become increasingly lenient about the scope of automobile searches as highlighted in our opening vignette. Today, even the belongings of automobile passengers can be searched without probable cause.

Drug Testing and DNA Sampling.

Testing for drugs has become an especially thorny search-and-seizure issue. If the government can require you to take a Breathalyzer test, can it require you to be tested for drugs? In the wake of growing public concern over drug use, in 1986 President Ronald Reagan signed an executive order requiring many federal employees to undergo drug tests. In 1997 Congress passed a similar law authorizing random drug searches of all congressional employees. But, in *Chandler* v. *Miller* (1997), the U.S. Supreme Court refused to allow Georgia to require all candidates for state office to pass a urinalysis drug test thirty days before qualifying for nomination or election, concluding that its law violated the search-and-seizure clause.[78]

While many private employers and professional athletic organizations routinely require drug tests upon application or as a condition of employment, governmental requirements present constitutional questions about the scope of permissible searches and seizures. In 1989 the Supreme Court ruled that mandatory drug and alcohol testing of employees involved in accidents was constitutional.[79] And in 1995 the Court upheld the constitutionality of random drug testing of public high school athletes.[80]

Another thorny "testing" issue looms on the horizon: mandatory DNA sampling. In 1999, Attorney General Janet Reno asked the National Commission on the Future of DNA Evidence to "study the legality of taking DNA samples from everyone arrested instead of just the convicted sex offenders and violent felons currently permitted by law."[81] Taking DNA from those already convicted has been upheld by courts. DNA sampling is, however, another form of warrantless search.

The Fifth Amendment and Self-Incrimination

The Fifth Amendment provides that "No person shall be . . . compelled in any criminal case to be a witness against himself." "Taking the Fifth" is shorthand for exercising one's constitutional right not to self-incriminate. The Supreme Court has interpreted this guarantee to be "as broad as the mischief against which it seeks to guard,"[82] finding that criminal defendants do not have to take the stand at trial to answer questions,

Web Exploration

For more information on *Chandler* v. *Miller* see

www.awlonline.com/oconnor.

nor can a judge make mention of their failure to do so as evidence of guilt. Moreover, lawyers cannot imply that a defendant who refuses to take the stand must be guilty or have something to hide.

Use of "Voluntary" Confessions.   This right not to incriminate oneself also means that prosecutors cannot use as evidence in a trial any of a defendant's statements or confessions that were not "voluntary." As is the case in many areas of the law, however, judicial interpretation of the term "voluntary" has changed over time.

In earlier times, it was not unusual for police to beat defendants to obtain their confessions. In 1936, however, the Supreme Court ruled convictions for murder based solely on confessions given after physical beatings unconstitutional.[83] Police then began to resort to other measures to force confessions. Defendants, for example, were "given the third degree"—questioned for hours on end with no sleep or food, or threatened with physical violence until they were mentally "beaten" into a confession. In other situations family members were threatened. In one case a young mother was told that her welfare benefits would be terminated and her children taken away from her if she failed to talk.[84]

Miranda v. *Arizona* (1966) was the Supreme Court's response to these creative efforts to obtain confessions that were not truly voluntary. On March 3, 1963, an eighteen-year-old girl was kidnapped and raped on the outskirts of Phoenix, Arizona. Ten days later police arrested Ernesto Miranda, a poor, mentally disturbed man with a ninth-grade education. In a police-station lineup, the victim identified Miranda as her attacker. Police then took Miranda to a separate room and questioned him for two hours. At first he denied guilt. Eventually, however, he confessed to the crime and wrote and signed a brief statement describing the crime and admitting his guilt. At no time was he told that he did not have to answer any questions or that he could be represented by an attorney.

After Miranda's conviction, his case was appealed on the grounds that his Fifth Amendment right not to incriminate himself had been violated because his confession had been coerced. Writing for the Court, Chief Justice Earl Warren, himself a former district attorney and California State Attorney General, noted that because police have

Miranda v. Arizona (1966):

A landmark Supreme Court ruling that held the Fifth Amendment requires that individuals arrested for a crime must be advised of their right to remain silent and to have counsel present.

■ Even though Ernesto Miranda's confession was not admitted as evidence at his retrial, his ex-girlfriend's testimony and that of the victim were enough to convince the jury of his guilt. He served nine years in prison before he was released on parole. After his release, he routinely sold autographed cards inscribed with the Miranda rights now read to all suspects. In 1976, four years after his release, Miranda was stabbed to death in Phoenix in a bar fight during a card game. Two Miranda cards were found on his body, and the person who killed him was read his Miranda rights upon his arrest. (Photo courtesy: Howell/ Liaison Agency)

a tremendous advantage in any interrogation situation, criminal suspects must be given greater protection. A confession obtained in the manner of Miranda's was not truly voluntary; thus it was inadmissible at trial.

To provide guidelines for police to implement *Miranda,* the Court mandated that:

> Prior to any questioning, the person must be warned that he has a right to remain silent, that any statements he does make may be used as evidence against him, and that he has a right to the presence of an attorney, either retained or appointed.

In response to this mandate from the Court, police routinely began to read suspects their ***Miranda* rights,** a practice you undoubtedly have seen repeated over and over in movies and TV police dramas.

Although the Burger Court did not enforce the reading of *Miranda* rights as vehemently as had the Warren Court, Chief Justice Warren Burger, Warren's successor, acknowledged that they had become an integral part of established police procedures.[85] The Rehnquist Court, however, has been more tolerant of the use of coerced confessions and has employed a much more flexible standard to allow their admissibility. In 1991, for example, it ruled that the use of a coerced confession in a criminal trial does not automatically invalidate a conviction if its admission is deemed a "harmless error," that is, if the other evidence is sufficient to convict.[86]

The long-term prognosis for the continued viability of the Miranda rule is questionable. In 1999, a Fourth Circuit U.S. Court of Appeals allowed a voluntary confession made without the benefit of a *Miranda* warning to be admitted in court, a decision seemingly at odds with *Miranda.*[87]

The Fourth and Fifth Amendments and the Exclusionary Rule

In *Weeks* v. *United States* (1914), the U.S. Supreme Court adopted the **exclusionary rule,** which bars the use of illegally seized evidence at trial.[88] Thus, although the Fourth and Fifth Amendments do not prohibit the use of evidence obtained in violation of their provisions, the exclusionary rule is a judicially created remedy to deter constitutional violations. In *Weeks,* for example, the Court reasoned that allowing police and prosecutors to use the "fruits of a poisonous tree" (a tainted search) would only encourage that activity.

The Warren Court resolved the dilemma of balancing the goal of deterring police misconduct against the likelihood that a guilty individual would go free in favor of deterrence. In contrast, the Burger and Rehnquist Courts and, more recently, Congress have gradually chipped away at the exclusionary rule. In 1976 the Burger Court dramatically reduced the opportunities for defendants to appeal their convictions based on tainted evidence in violation of the Fourth Amendment.[89] The Court noted that the exclusionary rule "deflects the truth-finding process and often frees the guilty." Since then, the Court has carved out a variety of limited "good faith exceptions" to the exclusionary rule, allowing the use of "tainted" evidence in a variety of situations, especially when police have a search warrant, and "in good faith" conduct the search on the assumption that the warrant is valid—though it is subsequently found invalid. Since the purpose of the exclusionary rule is to deter police misconduct, and in this situation there is no police misconduct, the courts have permitted the introduction at trial of the seized evidence. Another exception to the exclusionary rule is "inevitable discovery." Evidence illegally seized may be introduced if it would have been discovered anyway in the course of continuing investigation.

The Sixth Amendment and the Right to Counsel

The Sixth Amendment guarantees to an accused person "the Assistance of Counsel in his defense." In the past this provision meant only that an individual could hire an attorney to represent him or her in court. Since most criminal defendants are impoverished, this provision was of little assistance to many who found themselves on trial.

Miranda rights:
Statements that must be made by the police informing a suspect of his or her constitutional rights protected by the Fifth Amendment, including the right to an attorney provided by the court if the suspect cannot afford one.

exclusionary rule:
Judicially created rule that prohibits police from using illegally seized evidence at trial.

Recognizing this, Congress required federal courts to provide an attorney for defendants too poor to afford one. This was first required in capital cases (where the death penalty is a possibility); eventually, attorneys were provided to the poor in all federal criminal cases.[90] In 1932 the Supreme Court directed states to furnish lawyers to defendants in capital cases.[91] It also began to expand the right to counsel to other state offenses, but did so in a piecemeal fashion that gave the states little direction. Given the high cost of providing legal counsel, this ambiguity often made it cost-effective for the states not to provide counsel at all.

These ambiguities came to an end with the Court's decision in *Gideon* v. *Wainwright* (1963).[92] As depicted in Anthony Lewis's book *Gideon's Trumpet* and in the made-for-television movie of the same name, Clarence Earl Gideon, a fifty-one-year-old drifter, was charged with breaking into a Panama City, Florida, pool hall and stealing beer, wine, and some change from a vending machine. At his trial he asked the judge to appoint a lawyer for him because he was too poor to hire one himself. The judge refused, and Gideon was convicted and given a five-year prison term for petty larceny. The case against Gideon had not been strong, but as a layperson unfamiliar with the law and with trial practice and procedure, he was unable to point out its weaknesses.

The apparent inequities in the system that had resulted in Gideon's conviction continued to bother him. Eventually, he borrowed some paper from a prison guard, consulted books in the prison library, and then drafted and mailed to the U.S. Supreme Court a petition asking it to overrule his conviction.

In a unanimous decision, the U.S. Supreme Court agreed with Gideon and his court-appointed lawyer, Abe Fortas, a future associate justice of the Supreme Court. Writing for the Court, Justice Hugo Black explained that "lawyers in criminal courts are necessities, not luxuries." Therefore, the Court concluded, the state must provide an attorney to poor defendants in felony cases. Underscoring the Court's point, Gideon was acquitted when he was retried with a lawyer to argue his case.

In 1972 the Burger Court expanded the *Gideon* rule, holding that "even in prosecutions for offenses less serious than felonies, a fair trial may require the presence of a lawyer."[93] Seven years later, the Court clarified its decision by holding that defendants charged with offenses where imprisonment is authorized but not actually imposed do not have a Sixth Amendment right to counsel.[94] But the right to counsel *is* constitutionally required where any prison or jail term is imposed.

The Sixth Amendment and Jury Trials

The Sixth Amendment (and, to a lesser extent, Article III of the Constitution) provides that a person accused of a crime shall enjoy the right to a speedy and public trial by an impartial jury—that is, a trial in which a group of the accused's peers act as a fact-finding, deliberative body to determine guilt or innocence. The Supreme Court has held that jury trials must be available if a prison sentence of six or more months is possible.

"Impartiality" is a requirement of jury trials that has undergone significant change, with the method of selecting jurors being the most frequently challenged part of the process. For example, whereas potential individual jurors who have prejudged a case are not eligible to serve, no groups can be systematically excluded from serving. In 1880, for example, the Supreme Court ruled that African Americans could not be excluded from state jury pools (lists of those eligible to serve).[95] And in 1975 the Court ruled that to bar women from jury service violated the mandate that juries be a "fair cross section" of the community.[96]

In the 1980s the Court expanded the requirement that juries reflect the community by invalidating various indirect means of excluding African Americans. For example, when James Batson, a black man, was tried for second-degree burglary, the state prosecutor used all his peremptory challenges to the jury to eliminate all four potential black jurors, leaving an all-white jury.[97] The state court judge overruled the contention of

DIVISION OF CORRECTIONS
CORRESPONDENCE REGULATIONS

MAIL WILL NOT BE DELIVERED WHICH DOES NOT CONFORM WITH THESE RULES

No. 1 -- Only 2 letters each week, not to exceed 2 sheets letter-size 8 1/2 x 11" and written on one side only, and if ruled paper, do not write between lines. Your complete name must be signed at the close of your letter. Clippings, stamps, letters from other people, stationery or cash must not be enclosed in your letters.

No. 2 -- All letters must be addressed in the complete prison name of the inmate. Cell number, where applicable, and prison number must be placed in lower left corner of envelope, with your complete name and address in the upper left corner.

No. 3 -- Do not send any packages without a Package Permit. Unauthorized packages will be destroyed.

No. 4 -- Letters must be written in English only.

No. 5 -- Books, magazines, pamphlets, and newspapers of reputable character will be delivered only if mailed direct from the publisher.

No. 6 -- Money must be sent in the form of Postal Money Orders only, in the inmate's complete prison name and prison number.

INSTITUTION _____ CELL NUMBER _____

NAME _____ NUMBER _____

In The Supreme Court of The United States
Washington D.C.
Clarence Earl Gideon
Petitioner | *Petition for a writ*
vs. | *of Certiorari Directed*
H.G. Cochran, Jr., as | *to The Supreme Court*
Director, Divisions | *State of Florida.*
of Corrections State | No.-- 890 Misc.
of Florida | OCT. TERM 1961
U.S. Supreme Court

To: The Honorable Earl Warren, Chief
Justice of the United States
Comes now The petitioner, Clarence
Earl Gideon, a citizen of The United States
of America, in proper person, and appearing
as his own counsel. Who petitions this
Honorable Court for a Writ of Certiorari
directed to The Supreme Court of The State
of Florida. To review the order and Judge-
ment of the court below denying The
petitioner a writ of Habeus Corpus.
*   Petitioner submits That The Supreme*
Court of The United States has The authority
and jurisdiction to review the final Judge-
ment of The Supreme Court of The State
of Florida the highest court of The State
Under sec. 344 (B) Title 28 U.S.C.A. and
Because the "Due process clause" of the

■ When Clarence Earl Gideon wrote out his petition for a writ of certiorari to the Supreme Court (asking the Court, in its discretion, to hear his case), he had no way of knowing that his case would lead to the landmark ruling on the right to counsel, *Gideon v. Wainwright*. Nor did he know that Chief Justice Earl Warren had actually instructed his law clerks to be on the lookout for a habeas corpus petition (literally, "you have the body," which argues that the person in jail is there in violation of some statutory or constitutional right) that could be used to guarantee the assistance of counsel for defendants in criminal cases. (Photo courtesy: The Supreme Court Historical Society)

Batson's lawyer that the exclusion of African Americans violated Batson's constitutional rights, and Batson was found guilty. The Supreme Court, however, overturned his conviction. While noting that lawyers historically used peremptory challenges to select juries they believed most favorable to the outcome they desired, the Court held that the use of peremptory challenges specifically to exclude African-American jurors violated the equal protection clause of the Fourteenth Amendment.[98]

In 1994 the Supreme Court answered the major remaining unanswered question about jury selection: Can lawyers exclude women from juries through their use of peremptory challenges? This question came up frequently because in rape trials and sex discrimination cases, one side or another often finds it advantageous to select jurors on the basis of their sex. At issue in *J. E. B.* v. *Alabama ex rel T. B.* (1994) was Alabama's use of peremptory challenge to exclude nine men from a group of potential jurors in a case brought by the state to establish that James Bowman, Sr., had fathered a child and was responsible for child-support payments.[99] Bowman was declared to be the father by a jury of twelve women. The Supreme Court ruled that the equal protection clause prohibits discrimination in jury selection on the basis of gender. Thus lawyers cannot strike all potential male jurors based on the belief that males might be more sympathetic to the arguments of a man charged in a paternity suit.

The Eighth Amendment and Cruel and Unusual Punishment

The Eighth Amendment prohibits "cruel and unusual punishments," a concept rooted in the English common-law tradition. In the 1500s, religious heretics and those critical of the Crown were subjected to torture to extract confessions, and then were condemned to an equally hideous death by the rack, disembowelment, or other barbarous means. The English Bill of Rights and its safeguard against "cruel and unusual punishments" was a result of public outrage against those practices. The same language found its way into the U.S. Bill of Rights. Prior to the 1960s, however, little judicial attention was paid to the meaning of that phrase, especially in the context of the death penalty.

The death penalty was in use in all the colonies at the time the Constitution was adopted, and its constitutionality went unquestioned. In fact, in two separate cases in the late 1800s, the Supreme Court ruled that deaths by public shooting[100] and electrocution were not "cruel and unusual" forms of punishment in the same category as "punishments which inflict torture, such as the rack, the thumbscrew, the iron boot, the stretching of limbs and the like."[101]

In the 1960s the National Association for the Advancement of Colored People (NAACP) Legal Defense Fund, believing that the death penalty was applied more frequently to African Americans than to members of other groups, orchestrated a carefully designed legal attack on its constitutionality.[102] Public opinion polls revealed that in 1971, on the eve of the NAACP's first major death sentence case to reach the Supreme Court, support for the death penalty had fallen to below 50 percent of the American public. With the timing just right, in *Furman* v. *Georgia* (1972), the Supreme Court effectively put an end to capital punishment, at least in the short run.[103] The Court ruled that because the death penalty was often imposed in an arbitrary manner, it constituted cruel and unusual punishment in violation of the Eighth and Fourteenth Amendments.

Following *Furman,* several state legislatures enacted new laws designed to meet the Court's objections to the arbitrary nature of the sentence. In 1976 in *Gregg* v. *Georgia,* Georgia's rewritten death penalty statute was ruled constitutional by the Supreme Court in a seven-to-two decision.[104] Troy Gregg had murdered two hitchhikers and was awaiting execution on Georgia's death row. Although his lawyers argued that to put him to death would constitute cruel and unusual punishment, the Court concluded that the death penalty "is an expression of society's outrage at particularly offensive conduct. . . . [I]t is an extreme action, suitable to the most extreme of crimes." Before he could be executed, however, Gregg escaped from death row using a hand-crafted hacksaw and a homemade prison guard uniform. He and three other inmates escaped to North Carolina, where Gregg was beaten to death before he could be recaptured by authorities.

Unless the perpetrator of a crime was fifteen years old or younger at the time of the crime, the Supreme Court is currently unwilling to intervene to overrule state courts' imposition of the death penalty. In *McCleskey* v. *Kemp* (1987), a five-to-four Court ruled that imposition of the death penalty—even when it appeared to discriminate against African Americans—did not violate the equal protection clause.[105] Despite the testimony of social scientists and evidence that Georgia was eleven times more likely to seek the death penalty against a black defendant, the Court upheld Warren McCleskey's death sentence. It noted that even if statistics show clear discrimination, there must be a showing of racial discrimination in the specific case. Five justices concluded that there was no evidence of specific discrimination against McCleskey proved at his trial. Within hours of that defeat, McCleskey's lawyers filed a new appeal, arguing that the informant who gave the only testimony against McCleskey at trial had been placed in McCleskey's cell illegally.

Four years later McCleskey's death sentence challenge again produced an equally, if not more important, ruling on the death penalty and criminal procedure from the U.S. Supreme Court. In the second McCleskey case, *McCleskey* v. *Zant* (1991), the Court found that the issue of the informant should have been raised during the first appeal,

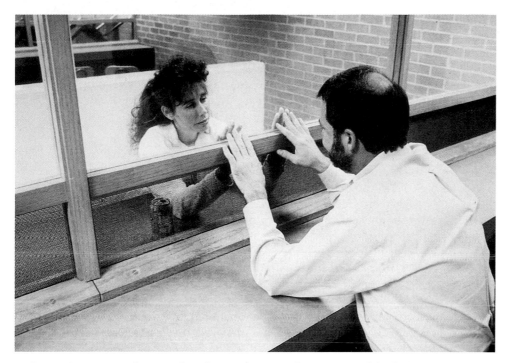

■ The prison conversion of convicted murderer Karla Faye Tucker (meeting with her husband in prison, before her execution), the wide support she got from many Christian groups, and the fact she was a woman, again focused national attention on the death penalty. In the end, however, Texas Governor George W. Bush refused to stop her execution by lethal injection. (Photo courtesy: Paul S. Howell/Liaison Agency)

in spite of the fact that McCleskey's lawyers were initially told by the state that the witness was not an informer. *McCleskey* v. *Zant* produced new standards designed to make it much more difficult for death-row inmates to file repeated appeals, a practice frequently decried by many of the justices.[106] Ironically, the informant against McCleskey was freed the night before McCleskey was electrocuted. Justice Powell, one of those in the majority, later said (after his retirement) that he regretted his vote and should have voted the other way.

By 1997 executions were commonplace in the United States. According to the Bureau of Justice Statistics, seventy-four persons in seventeen states were executed. Texas accounted for thirty-six of the executions. All were male; forty-five were white, twenty-seven were African American, one was an American Indian, and one was Asian. Sixty-eight were carried out by lethal injection and six by electrocution.[107]

THE RIGHT TO PRIVACY

To this point, the rights and freedoms we have discussed have been derived fairly directly from specific guaranties contained in the Bill of Rights. In contrast, the Supreme Court has also given protection to rights not specifically enumerated in the Constitution or Bill of Rights.

There is no mention of a **right to privacy** in either the main body of the Constitution or the Bill of Rights. Nevertheless, as Justice William O. Douglas noted in 1965, the notion of privacy is "older than the Bill of Rights." It is questionable, however, whether the Framers would ever have considered birth control, surrogate motherhood, in vitro fertilization, or euthanasia, all defended under "right to privacy" claims, proper subjects of constitutional protection.

Although the Constitution is silent about the right to privacy, the Bill of Rights contains many indications that the Framers expected that some areas of life were "off limits" to governmental regulation. The right to freedom of religion guaranteed in the First

right to privacy:

The right to be let alone; a judicially created doctrine encompassing an individual's decision to use birth control or secure an abortion.

Web Exploration

For other privacy issues, see
www.awlonline.com/oconnor.

Amendment implies the right to exercise private, personal beliefs. The guarantee against unreasonable searches and seizures contained in the Fourth Amendment similarly implies that persons are to be secure in their homes and should not fear that police will show up at their doorsteps without cause. As early as 1928, Justice Louis Brandeis hailed privacy as "the right to be left alone—the most comprehensive of rights and the right most valued by civilized men."[108] It was not until 1965, however, that the Court attempted to explain the origins of this right.

Birth Control

Today most Americans take access to many forms of birth control as a matter of course. Condoms are sold in the grocery store, and some television stations even air ads for them. Easy access to birth control, however, wasn't always the case. Many states often barred the sale of contraceptives to minors, prohibited the display of contraceptives, or even banned their sale altogether. One of the last states to do away with these kinds of laws was Connecticut. It outlawed the sale of all forms of birth control and even prohibited physicians from discussing it with their patients until the Supreme Court ruled its restrictive laws unconstitutional.

Griswold v. *Connecticut* (1965) involved a challenge to the constitutionality of an 1879 Connecticut law prohibiting the dissemination of information about and/or the sale of contraceptives.[109] In 1943 and again in 1961, groups seeking legislative repeal of the law had challenged its constitutionality. The Supreme Court refused to decide on the merits of the 1961 case, concluding that a doctor who had not been charged with violating the statute had no standing (legal right) to bring the lawsuit.[110] But because the Court's 1961 opinion had stressed the fact that the law had long gone unenforced, Planned Parenthood officials decided that they would need to create a test case. So Estelle Griswold, the executive director of Planned Parenthood League of Connecticut, and Dr. C. Lee Buxton opened a birth-control clinic and were arrested ten days later. With their arrest, Planned Parenthood had parties actually charged with violating the law. After Griswold and Buxton's conviction in the state courts, they appealed to the U.S. Supreme Court. In *Griswold*, seven justices decided that various portions of the Bill of Rights, including the First, Third, Fourth, Fifth, and Fourteenth amendments, cast what the court called "penumbras" (unstated liberties on the fringes or in the shadow of more explicitly stated rights), thereby creating zones of privacy, including a married couple's right to plan a family. Thus the Connecticut statute was ruled unconstitutional as a violation of marital privacy, a right the Court concluded could be read into the U.S. Constitution.

Later, the Court expanded the right of privacy to include the right of unmarried individuals to have access to contraceptives. "If the right of privacy means anything," wrote Justice William J. Brennan, "it is the right of the individual, married or single, to be free from unwarranted governmental intrusion into matters so fundamentally affecting a person as the decision to bear or beget a child."[111]

Abortion

In the early 1960s, two birth-related tragedies occurred: Severely deformed babies were born to women who had been given the drug thalidomide while pregnant, and a nationwide measles epidemic resulted in the birth of more babies with severe problems. The increasing medical safety of abortions and the growing women's rights movement combined with these tragedies to put pressure on the legal and medical establishments to enact laws that would guarantee a woman's access to a safe and legal abortion.

By the late 1960s, fourteen states had voted to liberalize their abortion policies, and four states decriminalized abortion in the early stages of pregnancy. But many women's rights activists wanted more. They argued that the decision to carry a pregnancy to term was a woman's fundamental constitutional right. In 1973, in one of the most controversial decisions ever handed down, seven members of the Court agreed with this position.

The woman whose case became the catalyst for pro-choice and anti-abortion groups was Norma McCorvey, an itinerant circus worker. The mother of one toddler she was unable to care for, McCorvey could not leave another child in her mother's care. So she decided to terminate her second pregnancy. Unable to secure a legal abortion and frightened by the conditions she found when she sought an illegal, back-alley abortion, McCorvey turned to two young Texas lawyers who were looking for a plaintiff to bring a lawsuit to challenge Texas's restrictive statute, which allowed abortions only when they were necessary to save the life of the mother. McCorvey, who was unable to obtain a legal abortion, later gave birth and put the baby up for adoption. Nevertheless, she allowed her lawyers to proceed with the case using her as their plaintiff, under the pseudonym Jane Roe, to challenge the Texas law as enforced by Henry Wade, the district attorney for Dallas County, Texas.

When the case finally came before the Supreme Court, Justice Harry A. Blackmun, a former lawyer at the Mayo Clinic, relied heavily on medical evidence to rule that the Texas law violated a woman's constitutionally guaranteed right to privacy, which he argued included her decision to terminate a pregnancy. Writing for the majority in *Roe v. Wade*, Blackmun divided pregnancy into three stages. In the first trimester, a woman's right to privacy gave her an absolute right (in consultation with her physician), free from state interference, to terminate her pregnancy. In the second trimester, the state's interest in the health of the mother gave it the right to regulate abortions—but only to protect the woman's health. Only in the third trimester—when the fetus becomes potentially viable—did the Court find that the state's interest in potential life outweighed the woman's privacy interests. Even in the third trimester, however, abortions to save the life or health of the mother were to be legal.[112]

Roe v. *Wade* unleashed a torrent of political controversy. Anti-abortion groups, caught off guard, scrambled to recoup their losses in Congress. Representative Henry Hyde (R Ill.) persuaded Congress to ban the use of Medicaid funds for abortions for poor women, and the constitutionality of the Hyde Amendment was upheld by the Supreme Court in 1977 and again in 1980.[113]

From the 1970s through the present, the right to an abortion and its constitutional underpinnings in the right to privacy have been under attack by well-organized anti-abortion groups. The Reagan and Bush administrations were strong advocates of the anti-abortion position, regularly urging the Court to overrule *Roe*. They came close to victory in *Webster* v. *Reproductive Health Services* (1989).[114] In *Webster* the Court upheld state-required fetal viability tests in the second trimester, even though these tests would increase the cost of an abortion considerably. The Court also upheld Missouri's refusal to allow abortions to be performed in state-supported hospitals or by state-funded doctors or nurses. Perhaps most noteworthy, however, were the facts that four justices seemed willing to overrule *Roe* v. *Wade*, and that Justice Antonin Scalia publicly rebuked his colleague Justice Sandra Day O'Connor, then the only woman on the Court, for failing to provide the critical fifth vote to overrule *Roe*.

After *Webster*, states began to enact more restrictive legislation. In the most important abortion case since *Roe*, *Planned Parenthood of Southeastern Pennsylvania* v. *Casey* (1992), Justices O'Connor, Anthony Kennedy, and David Souter, in a jointly authored opinion, wrote that Pennsylvania could limit abortions as long as its regulations did not pose "an undue burden" on pregnant women.[115]

The narrowly supported decision, which upheld a twenty-four-hour waiting period and parental consent requirements, did not overrule *Roe*, but clearly limited its scope by abolishing its trimester approach and substituting the "undue burden" standard. Since *Casey*, the Court has, for example, refused to find unconstitutional Mississippi's mandatory twenty-four-hour waiting period before an abortion. Mississippi has only three abortion clinics—all in Jackson. With this required waiting period, many women have to take time off work to drive over 100 miles, and then pay for a hotel. The number of abortions dropped 40 percent, and the clinics unsuccessfully argued that the waiting period posed an "undue burden." The U.S. Supreme Court refused to hear the appeal.[116]

TRY IT!

To compare the different sides of the abortion debate, see
www.awlonline.com/oconnor.

Roe v. Wade (1973):

The Supreme Court found that a woman's right to an abortion was protected by the right to privacy that could be implied from specific guarantees found in the Bill of Rights and the Fourteenth Amendment.

■ Anti-abortion group Operation Rescue has staged large-scale protests in front of abortion clinics across the nation. It now has a surprising new member—Norma McCorvey, the "Jane Roe" of *Roe* v. *Wade*, who announced in a 1995 press conference that she had become pro-life. (Photo courtesy: Tim Sharp/AP/Wide World Photos)

In 1993 newly elected President Clinton, who ran on a pro-choice platform, ended bans on fetal tissue research, abortions at military hospitals, federal financing for overseas population control programs, and lifted the "gag" rule, a federal regulation enacted in 1987 which barred public health clinics receiving federal dollars from discussing abortion.[117] He also lifted the ban on testing of RU-486, the so-called French abortion pill.

President Clinton used the occasion of his first appointment to the U.S. Supreme Court to select a longtime supporter of abortion rights, Ruth Bader Ginsburg, to replace Justice Byron White, one of the original dissenters in *Roe*. Most commentators believe that this was an important first step in shifting the Court away from any further curtailment of abortion rights, as was the later appointment of Justice Stephen Breyer in 1994.

While President Clinton was attempting to shore up abortion rights through judicial appointment, the newly elected Republican 104th Congress became the most active ever as it attempted to restrict abortion rights. There were nearly forty votes on reproductive choice taken in 1995, nearly double the next-highest year of anti-abortion legislative activity in Congress, 1977.[118] In fact, in March 1996 Congress passed and sent to President Clinton a bill that for the first time would ban a specific procedure used in late-term abortions.[119] The president vetoed the Partial Birth Abortion Act over the comments and pressure of the National Right to Life Committee, which had lobbied hard for the act. Many state legislatures, however, have passed their own versions of the act. The same measure was also vetoed by the president in late 1998, and the Senate, again, was unable to override that veto.

At this writing the right to an abortion is a constitutionally guaranteed right, although one no longer accorded the highest level of constitutional scrutiny. Its uncertain status underscores the role of politics in the civil liberties process. Change in composition of the Court, the partisan makeup of the Congress, and the political beliefs of the president all play an important role in the changing nature of civil liberties, including access to safe and legal abortions.

Homosexuality

Although the Supreme Court has ruled that the right to privacy includes the right to decide whether "to bear or beget a child," it has declined to interpret the right of privacy to include the right to engage in homosexual acts. In 1985 the Court, in a four-to-four decision (Justice Powell was ill), upheld a lower-court decision that found unconstitutional an Oklahoma law allowing the dismissal of teachers who advocate homosexual relations.[120] So the next year, when another case involving homosexual rights, *Bowers* v. *Hardwick* (1986), was argued before the Court, Lawrence Tribe, the lawyer representing Michael Hardwick, pitched his arguments toward Justice Powell, who he believed would be the crucial swing vote in this controversial area.[121] Tribe, a professor at the Harvard Law School, argued against the constitutionality of a Georgia law prohibiting consensual heterosexual and homosexual oral or anal sex.

In August 1982, in Atlanta, Georgia, Michael Hardwick was arrested in his bedroom by a police officer who was there to serve an arrest warrant on Hardwick for his failure to appear in court on another charge. One of his roommates let the officer in and directed him to Hardwick's room. After Hardwick's arrest on a sodomy charge, the local prosecutor decided not to prosecute. Nonetheless, Hardwick, a local gay activist, joined forces with the American Civil Liberties Union to challenge the constitutionality of the law under which he had been arrested. In a five-to-four decision, the Supreme Court upheld the law. At conference, Justice Powell reportedly seemed torn by the case. He believed that the twenty-year sentence that came with conviction was excessive, but he was troubled by the fact that Hardwick hadn't actually been (and never was) tried and convicted. Although he originally voted with the majority to overturn the law, Pow-

Web Exploration

For more on gay rights, see
www.awlonline.com/oconnor.

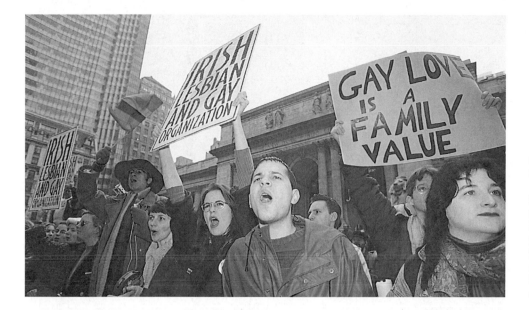

■ In a key First Amendment rights ruling, the Supreme Court held in 1995 that parade organizers had a free-speech right to ban gay marchers from Boston's annual St. Patrick's Day parade. The Court said that the organizers' free-speech rights took precedence over a state law barring discrimination in public places based on sexual orientation. (Photo courtesy: Lisa Quinones/Black Star)

ell was bothered by the broadness of Justice Blackmun's original draft of the majority opinion. Thus he changed his mind and voted with the minority view to uphold the law, making it the new majority.[122] And, like his change of heart in the *McCleskey* case, after his retirement Justice Powell confessed that he was wrong in *Bowers* and should have voted to overturn the Georgia law.

While the Court has refused to expand the right to privacy to invalidate state laws that criminalize some aspects of homosexual behavior, in 1996 it ruled that a state could not deny rights to homosexuals simply because they are homosexuals. Thus, as discussed in chapter 6, the Court ruled that the equal protection clause bars unreasonable state discrimination against gays and lesbians.[123]

The Right to Die

While the current Supreme Court is unlikely to expand the scope of the privacy doctrine to include greater protections for homosexuals in the near future, it is likely to continue to get more cases involving claims for personal autonomy. In 1990, for example, in *Cruzan by Cruzan* v. *Director, Missouri Department of Health,* the Supreme Court sided with the state against the privacy claims of the parents of Nancy Cruzan, a brain-injured woman living in a comatose state who, according to her doctors, could live like that for many more years. Her parents sued to remove her feeding tube, and the Bush administration and numerous anti-abortion groups filed briefs supporting the state against the Cruzans.

Writing for a five-person majority, Chief Justice Rehnquist rejected any attempts to expand the right of privacy into this thorny area of social policy. The Court did, however, note that individuals could terminate medical treatment if they were able to express, or had done so in writing via a living will, their desire to have medical treatment terminated in the event they became incompetent.[124]

States, too, have entered into this arena. Even before the *Cruzan* case, the New Jersey Supreme Court allowed the parents of a comatose woman to withdraw her feeding tube.[125] More recently, in a different but related vein, states have legislated to prevent what is often called "assisted suicide." Jurors, however, often appear unwilling to find loved ones or even Dr. Kervorkian guilty of helping the terminally ill carry out the decision to take their own lives. In 1999, however, after being acquitted in

Web Exploration

To learn about the right to die movement, see
www.awlonline.com/oconnor.

■ Dr. Jack Kevorkian was found guilty of second degree murder after airing this videotape on "60 Minutes" where he assisted the suicide of Thomas Youk, a 52-year-old man ravaged by Lou Gehrig's disease. (Photo courtesy: Sipa Press)

four other trials, Dr. Kevorkian represented himself and was found guilty of administering a lethal injection of chemicals to a fifty-two-year old man.

In 1997, the U.S. Supreme Court ruled unanimously that terminally ill persons do not have a constitutional right to physician-assisted suicide. The Court's action upheld the laws of New York and Washington state that make it a crime for doctors to give life-ending drugs to mentally competent but terminally ill patients who wish to die.[126] As revealed in Figure 5.2, state laws concerning assisted suicide vary considerably.

CONTINUITY and Change

Conceptions of Civil Liberties

When the new Constitution was adopted by the citizens in the states, it lacked a Bill of Rights. This absence was a glaring one in the eyes of many Americans. Their state constitutions often protected their civil liberties, and they feared that they already were giving up too many rights to an untested national government. So, when the first Congress met in 1789, one of the first items on its agenda was the passage of a Bill of Rights to prevent the national government from infringing the liberties of the citizenry.

In the late 1700s, issues of political speech, freedom of the press, and the right to gather and petition the government were among the rights most cherished. After all, without these rights, the colonists never would have been able to organize and mobilize effectively enough to make the successful break with Great Britain.

Today, our conceptions of civil liberties, as well as their need for protection, are quite different. Poll after poll shows that if Americans were to vote on the Bill of

Figure 5.2   Assisted-Suicide Laws in the USA

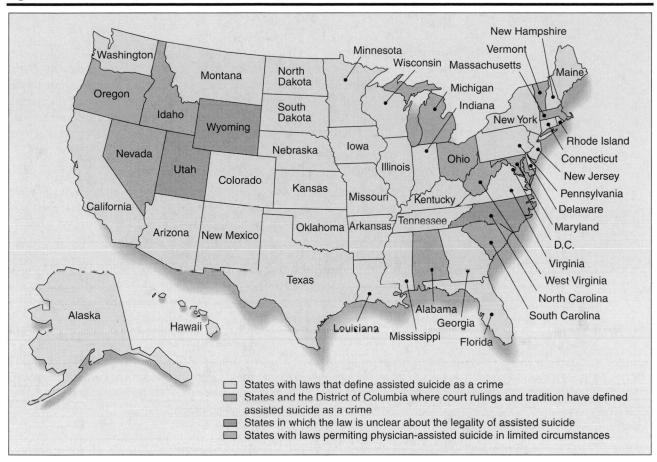

States with laws that define assisted suicide as a crime

States and the District of Columbia where court rulings and tradition have defined assisted suicide as a crime

States in which the law is unclear about the legality of assisted suicide

States with laws permiting physician-assisted suicide in limited circumstances

SOURCE: http://euthanasia.com/stlaws.html

Rights already contained in the Constitution, it would not garner enough votes in the states to be adopted. Over the years the role of the courts, especially the federal courts, in expanding the application of most of the Bill of Rights to the states, as well as in interpreting those provisions, has produced a panoply of rights never envisioned by the Framers. Moreover, the provisions of the Constitution and the Bill of Rights have been interpreted to protect a variety of rights, including protections for criminal defendants and liberties that are not explicitly stated, such as the right to privacy and reproductive rights.

Just think about how Americans' conceptions of rights have evolved in 200 years. The development of a variety of new technologies from cars (police searches) to telephones (wiretaps), to e-mail have created new laws dealing with issues of civil liberties. The development of the Internet will undoubtedly produce even more civil liberties issues than those already addressed by Congress dealing with pornography.

1. As it becomes easier and easier to get more and more information about all of us, what kind of civil liberties protections do you think the government should institute?
2. Conversely, in a Hobbesian sense, what kinds of practices and policies that curtail some rights, such as DNA testing, but may contribute the betterment of life for the majority, should be permitted?

Cast Your Vote.   Which civil liberties deserve protection? To cast your vote, go to www.awlonline.com/oconnor.

SUMMARY

In this chapter, we have made the following points:

1. THE FIRST CONSTITUTIONAL AMENDMENTS: THE BILL OF RIGHTS

Most of the Framers originally opposed the Bill of Rights. Anti-Federalists, however, continued to stress the need for a Bill of Rights during the drive for ratification of the Constitution, and some states tried to make their ratification contingent on the addition of a Bill of Rights. Thus, during its first session, Congress sent the first ten amendments to the Constitution, the Bill of Rights, to the states for their ratification. Later, the addition of the Fourteenth Amendment allowed the Supreme Court to apply some of the amendments to the states through a process called selective incorporation.

2. FIRST AMENDMENT GUARANTEES: FREEDOM OF RELIGION

The First Amendment guarantees freedom of religion. The establishment clause, which prohibits the national government from establishing a religion, does not, according to Supreme Court interpretation, create an absolute wall between church and state. While the national and state governments may generally not give direct aid to religious groups, many forms of aid, especially many that benefit children, have been held to be constitutionally permissible. In contrast, the Court has generally barred prayer in public schools. The Court generally has adopted an accommodationist approach when interpreting the free exercise clause by allowing some governmental regulation of religious practices.

3. FIRST AMENDMENT GUARANTEES: FREEDOM OF SPEECH AND PRESS

The First Amendment also guarantees freedom of speech and of the press. The Alien and Sedition Acts in 1798 were the first national efforts to curtail free speech, but they were never reviewed by the U.S. Supreme Court.

Some forms of speech were punished during the Civil War, and the Supreme Court refused to address their constitutionality directly. By the twentieth century, several states, and later the national government, passed laws restricting freedoms of speech and of the press. These curtailments were upheld by the Court, using the clear and present danger test. Later, the Court used the more liberal direct incitement test, which required a stronger showing of imminent danger before speech could be restricted.

Symbolic speech has been afforded the same protection as other forms of speech. Historically, the Supreme Court has disfavored any attempts at prior restraint of speech or press; thus, so called hate speech and politically correct speech requirements have come under constitutional challenge.

Libel, slander, and obscenity (as well as some forms of pornography) are not protected by the First Amendment and the Supreme Court has upheld the authority of Congress to legislate in these areas.

4. THE RIGHT TO KEEP AND BEAR ARMS

Initially, this right was envisioned as one dealing with state militias. Today, crime in the school in particular has led to a reexamination of this amendment's meaning with little Supreme Court interpretation as a guide.

5. THE RIGHTS OF CRIMINAL DEFENDANTS

The Fourth, Fifth, Sixth, and Eighth amendments provide a variety of procedural guarantees to individuals accused of crimes. In particular, the Fourth Amendment prohibits unreasonable searches and seizures, and the Court has generally refused to allow evidence seized in violation of this safeguard to be used at trial.

Among other rights, the Fifth Amendment guarantees that "no person shall be compelled to be a witness against himself." The Supreme Court has interpreted this provision to require that the government inform the accused of his or her right to remain silent. This provision has also been interpreted to require that illegally obtained confessions must be excluded at trial.

The Sixth Amendment's guarantee of "assistance of counsel" has been interpreted by the Supreme Court to require that the government provide counsel to defendants unable to pay for it in cases where prison sentences may be imposed. The Sixth Amendment also requires an impartial jury, although the meaning of impartial continues to evolve through judicial interpretation.

The Eighth Amendment's ban against "cruel and unusual punishments" has been held not to bar imposition of the death penalty.

6. THE RIGHT TO PRIVACY

The right to privacy is a judicially created right carved from the implications of several amendments, including the First, Third, Fourth, Fifth, and Fourteenth amendments. Statutes limiting access to birth control and abortion rights have been ruled unconstitutional violations of the right to privacy. In contrast, the Supreme Court has not expanded the right to privacy to invalidate state statutes criminalizing homosexual acts.

KEY TERMS

Bill of Rights, p. 137
civil liberties, p. 136
clear and present danger test, p. 147
direct incitement test, p. 147
due process clause, p. 137
due process rights, p. 154
establishment clause, p. 140
exclusionary rule, p. 159
free exercise clause, p. 140

incorporation doctrine, p. 138
Lemon test, p. 141
libel, p. 148
Miranda rights, p. 159
Miranda v. *Arizona* (1966), p. 158
New York Times Co. v. *Sullivan* (1971), p. 148
prior restraint, p. 146

right to privacy, p. 163
Roe v. *Wade* (1973), p. 165
selective incorporation, p. 138
slander, p. 148
substantive due process, p. 137
symbolic speech, p. 152

SELECTED READINGS

Abernathy, M. Glenn, and Barbara A. Perry, *Civil Liberties Under the Constitution.* Columbia: University of South Carolina Press, 1993.

Fiss, Owen M. *The Irony of Free Speech.* Cambridge, MA: Harvard University Press, 1996.

Friendly, Fred W. *Minnesota Rag: The Dramatic Story of the Landmark Case That Gave New Meaning to Freedom of the Press.* New York: Random House, 1981.

Gates, Henry Louis, Jr., ed. *Speaking of Race, Speaking of Sex: Hate Speech, Civil Rights, and Civil Liberties.* New York: New York University Press, 1995.

Greenawalt, Kent. *Fighting Words: Individuals, Communities, and Liberties of Speech.* Princeton: Princeton University Press, 1995.

Ivers, Gregg. *To Build a Wall: American Jews and the Separation of Church and State.* Charlottesville: University of Virginia Press, 1995.

Kalven, Harry, Jr. *A Worthy Tradition: Freedom of Speech in America.* New York: Harper & Row, 1988.

Lewis, Anthony. *Gideon's Trumpet.* (reissue edition) New York: Vintage Books, 1989.

———. *Make No Law: The Sullivan Case and the First Amendment.* New York: Random House, 1991.

Manwaring, David R. *Render Unto Caesar: The Flag Salute Controversy.* Chicago: University of Chicago Press, 1962.

O'Brien, David M. *Constitutional Law and Politics, Vol. 2: Civil Rights and Civil Liberties,* 3d ed. New York: Norton and Co., 1997.

O'Connor, Karen. *No Neutral Ground: Abortion Politics in an Age of Absolutes.* Boulder, CO: Westview Press, 1996.

Regan, Priscilla M. *Legislating Privacy: Technology, Social Values, and Public Policy.* Chapel Hill: University of North Carolina Press, 1995.

Weddington, Sarah. *A Question of Choice.* New York: Grosset/Putnam, 1993.

NOTES

1. This vignette draws heavily from Joan Biskupic, "High Court Expands Car Search Authority," *Washington Post* (April 16, 1999): A1, A12.

2. *Wyoming* v. *Houghton,* 1999 LEXIS 2347 (1999).

3. Quoted in Biskupic, "High Court."

4. The absence of a bill of rights led Mason to refuse to sign the proposed Constitution, noting that he "would sooner chop off his right hand than put it to the Constitution as

it now stands." (Quoted in Eric Black, *Our Constitution: The Myth That Binds Us* [Boulder, CO: Westview Press, 1988], 75.)

5. Quoted in Jack N. Rakove, "Madison Won Passage of the Bill of Rights but Remained a Skeptic," *Public Affairs Report* (March 1991): 6.

6. 7 Pet. 243 (1833).

7. *Allgeyer* v. *Louisiana,* 165 U.S. 578 (1897).

8. 268 U.S. 652 (1925).

9. 283 U.S. 697 (1931). For more about *Near,* see Fred W. Friendly, *Minnesota Rag* (New York: Random House, 1981).

10. 302 U.S. 319 (1937).

11. Continental Congress to the People of Great Britain, October 21, 1774, in Philip Kurland and Ralph Lerner, eds., *The Founders' Constitution,* vol. 5 (Chicago: University of Chicago Press, 1987), 61.

12. *Reynolds* v. *U.S.,* 98 U.S. 145 (1879).

13. *Cantwell* v. *Connecticut,* 310 U.S. 296 (1940).

14. *Zobrest* v. *Catalina Foothills School District,* 506 U.S. 813 (1992).

15. 370 U.S. 421 (1962).

16. *Lee* v. *Weisman,* 505 U.S. 577 (1992).

17. 403 U.S. 602 (1971).

18. 403 U.S. 602 (1971).

19. *Stone* v. *Graham,* 449 U.S. 39 (1980).

20. *Widmar* v. *Vincent,* 454 U.S. 263 (1981).

21. *Board of Education* v. *Mergens,* 496 U.S. 226 (1990).

22. *Lamb's Chapel* v. *Center Moriches Union Free School District,* 508 U.S. 384 (1993).

23. *Rosenberger* v. *University of Virginia,* 115 S. Ct. 2510 (1995).

24. *Rosenberger* v. *University of Virginia,* 115 S. Ct. 2510 (1995).

25. *Aguilar* v. *Fenton,* 473 U.S. 402 (1985).

26. - - -. 5221 U.S. 203 (1997).

27. *Sherbert* v. *Verner,* 374 U.S. 398 (1963).

28. *Employment Division, Dept. of Human Resources of Oregon* v. *Smith,* 494 U.S. 872 (1990).

29. *City of Boerne* v. *Flores,* 117 S.Ct. 2157 (1997).

30. *Church of the Lukumi Babalu Aye* v. *Hialeah,* 508 U.S. 525 (1993).

31. *Cruz* v. *Beto,* 405 U.S. 319 (1972).

32. *O'Lone* v. *Shabazz,* 482 U.S. 342 (1987).

33. See, for example, the opinion in *Boissonneault* v. *Flint City Council,* 392 Mich. 685 (1974).

34. *Chaplinsky* v. *New Hampshire,* 315 U.S. 568 (1942).

35. *Ex parte McCardle,* 74 U.S. 506 (1869).

36. David M. O'Brien, *Constitutional Law and Politics* vol. 2 (New York: Norton, 1991), 345.

37. See Frederick Siebert, *The Rights and Privileges of the Press* (New York: D. Appleton-Century, 1934), 886, 931–40.

38. *Schenck* v. *United States,* 249 U.S. 47 (1919).

39. *Brandenburg* v. *Ohio,* 395 U.S. 444 (1969).

40. 376 U.S. 254 (1964).

41. *Hustler* v. *Falwell,* 485 U.S. 46 (1988).

42. Edith Stanley, "American Album: Alabama Judge Goes to Court in Religion Battle," *Los Angeles Times* (January 11, 1996): A5.

43. 315 U.S. 568 (1942).

44. *Regina* v. *Hicklin,* L. R. 2 Q. B. 360 (1868).

45. 354 U.S. 476 (1957).

46. 413 U.S. 15 (1973).

47. *Jenkins* v. *Georgia,* 418 U.S. 153 (1974).

48. *Jacobellis* v. *Ohio,* 378 U.S. 184 (1964).

49. *Barnes* v. *Glen Theater,* 501 U.S. 560 (1991).

50. Joan Biskupic, "Decency Can Be Weighed in Arts Funding," *Washington Post* (June 26, 1998): A1, A18.

51. *National Endowment for the Arts* v. *Finley,* 118 S.Ct. 1550 (1998).

52. Harvey A. Silvergate, "Cyber Speech at Risk," *The National Law Journal* (March 4, 1996): A19.

53. Hiawatha Bray, "Stalled at the Gate: Confusion over New Law," *The Boston Globe* (February 24, 1996): 19.

54. *Reno* v. *ACLU,* 117 S.Ct. 2329 (1997).

55. Michael Rubinkam, "DOJ to (April 5, 1999) Appeal COPA Injunction," *Legal Intelligencer,* 5.

56. *Abrams* v. *United States,* 250 U.S. 616 (1919).

57. 283 U.S. 359 (1931).

58. 393 U.S. 503 (1969).

59. *Texas* v. *Johnson,* 491 U.S. 397 (1989).

60. *U.S.* v. *Eichman,* 496 U.S. 310 (1990).

61. 403 U.S. 713 (1971).

62. *Nebraska Press Association* v. *Stuart,* 427 U.S. 539 (1976).

63. Harry Klaven, Jr., *Negro and the First Amendment* (Chicago: University of Chicago Press, 1966).

64. Henry Louis Gates, Jr., "Why Civil Liberties Pose No Threat to Civil Rights," *New Republic* (September 20, 1993).

65. *Printz* v. *United States*, 117 S.Ct. 2365 (1997).

66. *Furman* v. *Georgia*, 408 U.S. 238 (1972).

67. *Gregg* v. *Georgia*, 428 U.S. 153 (1976).

68. *Stein* v. *N.Y.*, 346 U.S. 156 (1953).

69. *Wilson* v. *Arkansas*, 115 S. Ct. 1914 (1995).

70. *U.S.* v. *Sokolov*, 490 U.S. 1 (1989).

71. *U.S.* v. *Matlock*, 415 U.S. 164 (1974).

72. *Johnson* v. *U.S.*, 333 U.S. 10 (1948).

73. *Winston* v. *Lee*, 470 U.S. 753 (1985).

74. *South Dakota* v. *Neville*, 459 U.S. 553 (1983).

75. *Michigan* v. *Tyler*, 436 U.S. 499 (1978).

76. *Hester* v. *U.S.*, 265 U.S. 57 (1924).

77. *Carroll* v. *U.S.*, 267 U.S. 132 (1925).

78. *Chandler* v. *Miller*, 520 U.S. 305 (1997).

79. *Skinner* v. *Railway Labor Executives' Association*, 489 U.S. 602 (1989).

80. *Vernonia School District* v. *Acton*, 115 S. Ct. 2386 (1995).

81. Richard Willing, "Reno: Study Broad DNA Testing," *USA Today*, (March 1, 1999): A1.

82. *Counselman* v. *Hitchcock*, 142 U.S. 547 (1892).

83. *Brown* v. *Mississippi*, 297 U.S. 278 (1936).

84. *Lynumm* v. *Illinois*, 372 U.S. 528 (1963).

85. *Rhode Island* v. *Innis*, 446 U.S. 291 (1980).

86. *Arizona* v. *Fulminante*, 500 U.S. 938 (1991).

87. Gerald Walpin, "The Welcome Demise of Miranda," *New York Law Journal* (March 18, 1999): 2, discussing *U.S.* v. *Dickerson*, 166 F. 3d 667 (1999).

88. 232 U.S. 383 (1914).

89. *Stone* v. *Powell*, 428 U.S. 465 (1976).

90. *Johnson* v. *Zerbst*, 304 U.S. 458 (1938).

91. *Powell* v. *Alabama*, 287 U.S. 45 (1932).

92. 372 U.S. 335 (1963).

93. *Argersinger* v. *Hamlin*, 407 U.S. 25 (1972).

94. *Scott* v. *Illinois*, 440 U.S. 367 (1979).

95. *Strauder* v. *West Virginia*, 100 U.S. 303 (1880).

96. *Taylor* v. *Louisiana*, 419 U.S. 522 (1975).

97. Peremptory challenges are discretionary challenges. A lawyer representing an abortion clinic protester, for example, could use peremptory challenges to rid the jury of pro-choice advocates. "For cause" challenges, by contrast, are based on legal reasoning and not on an educated guess about the best persons to serve on the jury. In a capital case, for example, persons morally opposed to the death penalty could be removed "for cause."

98. *Batson* v. *Kentucky*, 476 U.S. 79 (1986).

99. 114 S. Ct. 1419 (1994).

100. *Hallinger* v. *Davis*, 146 U.S. 314 (1892).

101. *O'Neil* v. *Vermont*, 144 U.S. 323 (1892).

102. See Michael Meltsner, *Cruel and Unusual: The Supreme Court and Capital Punishment* (New York: Random House, 1973).

103. 408 U.S. 238 (1972).

104. 428 U.S. 153 (1976).

105. 481 U.S. 279 (1987).

106. 501 U.S. 1224 (1991).

107. All data in this paragraph are from "Prisoner Executions Rise Significantly," U.S. Department of Justice, December 14, 1997, press release.

108. *Olmstead* v. *United States*, 277 U.S. 438 (1928).

109. 381 U.S. 481 (1965).

110. *Poe* v. *Ullman*, 367 U.S. 497 (1961).

111. *Eisenstadt* v. *Baird*, 410 U.S. 113 (1972).

112. 410 U.S. 113 (1973).

113. *Beal* v. *Doe*, 432 U.S. 438 (1977) and *Harris* v. *McRae*, 448 U.S. 297 (1980).

114. 492 U.S. 490 (1989).

115. 502 U.S. 1056 (1992).

116. *Barnes* v. *Moore*, 506 U.S. 1013 (1992).

117. Karen O'Connor, *No Neutral Ground: Abortion Politics in an Age of Absolutes* (Boulder, CO: Westview Press, 1996).

118. The National Abortion and Reproductive Rights Action League, "Congressional Votes on Reproductive Choice, 1977–1995," February 1996.

119. "House Sends Partial Birth Abortion Bill To Clinton," *Politics USA* (March 28, 1996): 1.

120. *Board of Education of City of Oklahoma City* v. *National Gay Task Force*, 470 U.S. 903 (1985).

121. 478 U.S. 186 (1986).

122. Reported in O'Brien, *Constitutional Law and Politics*, 1223.

123. *Romer* v. *Evans*, 116 S. Ct. 1620 (1996).

124. 110 S. Ct. 2841 (1990).

125. *In re Quinlan*, 70 N.J. 10 (1976).

126. *Vacco* v. *Quill*, 117 S.Ct. 2293 (1997).

(Photo courtesy: Porter Gifford/Liaison Agency)

Civil Rights

- **Slavery, Abolition, and Winning the Right to Vote, 1800–90**
- **The Push for Equality, 1890–1954**
- **The Civil Rights Movement**
- **Other Groups Mobilize for Rights**
- **Affirmative Action**

6

n February 4, 1999, just as Amadou Diallo, a twenty-two-year-old unarmed African immigrant, stood in the vestibule of his apartment building in the Bronx, four white plainclothes police officers who were patrolling the neighborhood in an unmarked car opened fire on him, eventually firing forty-one shots. He died at the scene.[1] There were no witnesses. The four officers, who were eventually charged with second-degree murder, were members of the City's Street Crimes Unit, which was created by the New York City mayor to help lower the city's crime rate in the early 1990s. Known to have targeted black citizens, the unit admits to stopping and searching as many as 225,000 citizens since it was established.[2]

New York City's frightened minority community, African Americans and new immigrants alike, along with liberal activists and everyday citizens turned their anger on city police and Mayor Rudolph Guiliani, who they believe have used overly aggressive, and often racially biased, techniques to reduce crime. In the months after the shooting, citizens from all walks of life from actress Susan Sarandon to street cleaners protested at City Hall, and even marched from the federal courthouse over the Brooklyn Bridge into Manhattan in a procession reminiscent of many 1960s civil rights marches.[3] Over 1,500 protesters were arrested at one demonstration, the largest New York City has seen in 25 years.[4]

There is no question that in the 1980s, crime in the United States, and in particular New York City, was out of control and Americans demanded that their governments do something about it. Governments at all levels responded with more police and more prisons. But now that crime is on the wane and no longer even on Americans' list of top ten concerns, ordinary citizens are asking the question that troubled John Locke and Thomas Hobbes over three centuries ago: How much liberty should you give up to the government in return for safety? In the *Diallo* case, and many others, it is clear that black Americans, whether native- or foreign-born, are being targeted for civil rights deprivations at far higher rates than other identifiable groups. In 1999, for example, it was discovered that 40 percent of those strip-searched at the Chicago O'Hare airport by U.S. Customs officials were African-American women.[5] And, in New Jersey and other states, allegations of the use by state troopers of what is called racial profiling to stop black drivers is under legal challenge.[6] Even black college students recently filed suit when they were forced to pay higher room rates than white students in Daytona Beach during spring break.[7]

The Declaration of Independence, written in 1776, boldly proclaims: "We hold these truths to be self-evident, that all men are created equal, that they are endowed by their Creator with certain inalienable rights." The Constitution, written eleven years later, is silent on the concept of equality. Only through constitutional amendment and Supreme Court definition and redefinition of the rights contained in that document have Americans come close to attaining equal rights. Even so, as our opening vignette highlights, some citizens still have yet to experience full equality and the full enjoyment of civil rights many Americans take for granted.

The term civil rights refers to the positive acts governments take to protect individuals against arbitrary or discriminatory treatment by governments or individuals. The Framers considered some civil rights issues. But, as James Madison reflected in *Federalist No. 42*, one entire class of citizens—slaves—were treated in the new Constitution more like property than like people. Without the Three-Fifths Compromise, "No union could possibly have been formed" because the Southern states would not have agreed to join the union if slavery was prohibited by the national government.[8] In stipulating that slaves could be counted for purposes of fixing state population to determine congressional apportionment, slaves were counted as three-fifths of a person. The Constitution also stipulated that the importation of slaves could not be prohibited for twenty years. Delegates to the Constitutional Convention put political expediency before the immorality of slavery, and basic civil rights. Moreover, the Constitution considered white women full citizens for purposes of determining state population, but voting qualifications were left to the states and none allowed women to vote at the time the Constitution was ratified.

Since the Constitution was written, concepts of civil rights have changed dramatically. The addition of the Fourteenth Amendment, one of three amendments ratified after the Civil War, introduced the notion of equality into the Constitution by specifying that states could not deny "any person within its jurisdiction equal protection of the laws." The Fourteenth Amendment has generated more litigation to determine and specify its meaning than any other provision of the Constitution. Within a few years of its ratification, women—and later, African Americans and other minorities and disadvantaged groups—took to the courts to seek expanded civil rights in all walks of life. But the struggle to augment rights was not limited to the courts. Public protest, civil disobedience, legislative lobbying, and appeals to public opinion have all been part of the arsenal of those seeking equality. The *Diallo* case incorporates all of those actions. Ordinary citizens and celebrities took to the streets, legislators held hearings, police officers were put on trial, and the media reported it all.

Since passage of the Civil War amendments (1865–70), there has been a fairly consistent pattern of the expansion of civil rights to more and more groups. In this chapter we will explore how notions of equality and civil rights have changed in this country. To do so we'll discuss slavery, its abolition, and the achievement of voting rights for African Americans and women by examining the evolution of African-American rights and women's rights in tandem. To appreciate how each group has drawn ideas, support, and success from the other, throughout this chapter we discuss their parallel developments as well as those of other historically disadvantaged political groups.

- First, we will discuss *slavery, abolition, and the efforts of abolitionists, African Americans, and women to gain the vote* and expand **civil rights**.
- Second, we will examine these two groups' next *push for equality from 1885 to 1954*, using two of the Supreme Court's most famous decisions, *Plessy* v. *Ferguson* and *Brown* v. *Board of Education* as bookends for our discussion.
- Third, we will analyze *the civil rights movement* and the Civil Rights Act of 1964 and its effects, *including its facilitation of the development of a new women's rights movement* and its push for an equal rights amendment to the U.S. Constitution.

Web Exploration

For more on civil rights generally, see www.awlonline.com/oconnor.

---

civil rights:

Refers to the positive acts governments take to protect individuals against arbitrary or discriminatory treatment by governments or individuals based on categories such as race, sex, national origin, age, or sexual orientation.

- Fourth, we will present *the efforts of other groups*, including Native Americans, Hispanic Americans, homosexuals, and disabled Americans, to secure constitutional and statutory rights using methods often modeled after the actions of African Americans and women.

- Fifth, we will discuss *affirmative action* as a remedy for vestiges of discrimination and analyze its continued relevance in a time of *changing notions of civil rights guarantees*.

SLAVERY, ABOLITION, AND WINNING THE RIGHT TO VOTE, 1800–90

Today, we take the rights of women and blacks to vote for granted. Since 1980, in fact, women have outvoted men at the polls; and, in the 1990s, African Americans and women have become the core of the Democratic Party. But it wasn't always this way. The period from 1800 to 1890 was one of tremendous change and upheaval in America. Despite the Civil War and the freeing of the slaves, the promise of equality guaranteed to African Americans by the Civil War amendments failed to become a reality. Women's rights activists also began to make claims for equality, often using the arguments enunciated for the abolition of slavery, but they too fell far short of their goals.

Slavery and Congress

Congress banned slave trade in 1808, after the expiration of the twenty-year period specified by the Constitution. In 1820 blacks made up 25 percent of the U.S. population and were in the majority in some Southern states. By 1840 that figure had fallen to 20 percent. After the invention of the cotton gin (a machine invented in 1793 that separated seeds from cotton very quickly), the South became even more dependent on agriculture and cheap slave labor as its economic base. At the same time, technological advances were turning the Northern states into an increasingly industrialized region, which intensified the cultural and political differences and animosity between North and South.

Ever since the first Africans had been brought to the New World in 1619, slavery had been a divisive issue. But as the nation grew westward in the early 1800s, conflicts between Northern and Southern states intensified over the admission of new states to the Union with "free" or "slave" status. The first major crisis occurred in 1820, when the territory of Missouri applied for admission to the Union as a "slave state"—that is, one in which slavery would be legal. Missouri's admission would have weighted the Senate in favor of slavery and was therefore opposed by Northern senators. The resultant Missouri Compromise of 1820 allowed the admission of Missouri as a slave state, along with the admission of Maine (formed out of the territory of Massachusetts with the permission of Congress and Massachusetts) as a free state. Other compromises concerning slavery were eventually necessitated as the nation continued to grow and new states were added to the Union.

The Abolitionist Movement: The First Civil Rights Movement

The Compromise of 1820 solidified the South in its determination to keep slavery legal, but it also fueled the fervor of those who opposed slavery. In the early 1800s, some private charities purchased slaves and transported them to the west coast of Africa, where, in the 1820s, eighty-eight former slaves formed the independent nation of Liberia. But this solution to the slavery problem was not all that practical. Few owners were willing to free their slaves, and the trip to Africa and conditions there were dangerous. The abolitionist movement might have fizzled had it not been for William Lloyd Garrison, a white New Englander who became active in the movement in the early 1830s. Garrison, a newspaper editor, founded the American Anti-Slavery Society in 1833; by 1838

Web Exploration

For more on abolition, the American Anti-Slavery Society and its leaders, see www.awlonline.com/oconnor.

it had more than 250,000 members—given the U.S. population today, the National Association for the Advancement of Colored People (NAACP) would need 3.8 million members to have the same kind of overall proportional membership. (In 1998, it reported 500,000 members.)

The Women's Rights Tie-in.   Slavery was not the only practice that people began to question in the decades following adoption of the Constitution. In 1840, for example, Garrison and even Frederick Douglass, a well-known black abolitionist writer (see Roots of Government: Frederick Douglass), parted from the Anti-Slavery Society when it refused to accept their demand that women be allowed to participate equally in all its activities. Custom dictated that women not speak out in public, and most laws made women second-class citizens. In most states, for example, women could not divorce their husbands or keep their own wages and inheritances. And, of course, they could not vote.

Elizabeth Cady Stanton and Lucretia Mott, two women who were to found the women's movement, attended the 1840 meeting of the World's Anti-Slavery Society in London with their husbands. They were not allowed to participate because they were women. As they sat in the balcony apart from the male delegates, they paused to compare their status to that of the slaves they sought to free. They believed that women were not much better off than slaves, and resolved to address these issues. In 1848 they sent out a call for the first women's rights convention. Three hundred women and men, including Frederick Douglass, traveled to the sleepy little town of Seneca Falls, New York, to attend the first meeting for women's rights.

The Seneca Falls Convention (1848).   The Seneca Falls Convention attracted people from all over New York State who believed that all men and women should be able to enjoy all rights of citizenship equally. It passed resolutions calling for the abolition of legal, economic, and social discrimination against women. All of the resolutions reflected the attendees' dissatisfaction with contemporary moral codes, divorce and criminal laws, and the limited opportunities for women in education, the church, and in medicine, law, and politics. Only the call to extend the **franchise**—the legal right

franchise:

The right to vote.

ROOTS OF GOVERNMENT

Frederick Douglass

Frederick Douglass (1817–95), a leading advocate of civil rights for both blacks and women, was the son of a slave and an unidentified white man. Although born into slavery, Douglass learned how to read and write. Once he escaped to the North (where 250,000 free blacks lived), he became a well-known orator and journalist. He spoke to abolitionist groups about his experiences as a slave and included these experiences in his autobiography, *Narrative of the Life of Frederick Douglass.* His life was also romanticized in song.

In 1847 he started a newspaper, *The North Star,* in Rochester, New York, which quickly became a powerful voice against slavery. Douglass was a strong abolitionist, who urged President Abraham Lincoln to emancipate the slaves and helped recruit black soldiers for the Union forces in the Civil War. His home in Rochester was a station along the Underground Railroad. Douglass was also a firm believer in women's suffrage, and he attended the Seneca Falls Convention in 1848. He was a close friend of John Brown, whose raid at Harpers Ferry was a pivotal moment in the antislavery movement.

Douglass was appointed to several minor federal posts, including that of minister to Haiti from 1889 to 1891. He was considered the greatest black leader of his time. When he died in 1895, five states adopted resolutions of regret, and two U.S. senators and one Supreme Court justice were among honorary pallbearers.

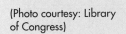

(Photo courtesy: Library of Congress)

to vote—to women failed to win unanimous approval. Most who attended the Seneca Falls meeting continued to press for women's rights along with the abolition of slavery.

The 1850s: The Calm Before the Storm. By 1850 much was changing in America—the Gold Rush had spurred westward migration, cities grew as people were lured from their farms, railroads and the telegraph increased mobility and communication, and immigrants flooded into the United States. Reformers called for change, the women's movement gained momentum, and slavery continued to tear the nation apart. Harriet Beecher Stowe's *Uncle Tom's Cabin,* a novel that showed the evils of slavery by depicting a slave family torn apart, further inflamed the country. *Uncle Tom's Cabin* sold more than 300,000 copies in a single year, 1852.

The tremendous national reaction to Stowe's work, which later prompted Abraham Lincoln to call Stowe "the little woman who started the big war," had not yet faded when a new controversy over the 1820 Missouri Compromise became the lightning rod for the first major civil rights case to be addressed by the U.S. Supreme Court. As discussed in chapter 3, in *Dred Scott* v. *Sandford* (1857), the Supreme Court bluntly ruled unconstitutional the 1820 Missouri Compromise, which prohibited slavery north of the geographical boundary at 36 degrees latitude on a map of the United States, also known as the Mason–Dixon Line for the surveyors who made maps of the region. Furthermore, in that case the Court found that slaves were not U.S. citizens and therefore could not bring suits in federal court, and concluded that "the Negro might justly and lawfully be reduced to slavery for his benefit." Ironically, after the case was decided, Scott's owner freed him.

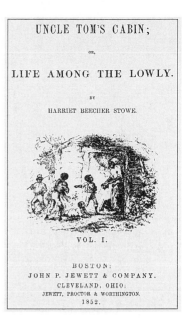

■ The original title page of *Uncle Tom's Cabin,* or *Life Among the Lowly,* by Harriet Beecher Stowe. (Photo courtesy: Library of Congress)

The Civil War and Its Aftermath: Civil Rights Laws and Constitutional Amendments

The Civil War had many causes, including (1) the political conflict between the North and the South over nullification, a doctrine allowing states to declare federal laws null and void, and secession, which involved the right of states to leave the Union; (2) the Northern states' increasing political strength in Congress, especially in the House of Representatives; (3) Southern agriculture versus Northern industry; and (4) the clash of conservative Southern culture with more progressive Northern ideas. Slavery, though, was clearly the key issue.

During the war (1861–65), abolitionists kept their antislavery pressure on. They were rewarded when President Abraham Lincoln issued the Emancipation Proclamation, which provided that all slaves in states still in active rebellion against the United States would automatically be freed on January 1, 1863. Designed as a measure to gain favor for the war in the North, the Emancipation Proclamation did not free all slaves—it freed only those who lived in the Confederacy. Complete abolition of slavery did not occur until congressional passage and ultimate ratification of the Thirteenth Amendment in 1865.

The Civil War Amendments. The **Thirteenth Amendment** was the first of the three so-called Civil War amendments. It banned all forms of "slavery [and] involuntary servitude." Although Southern states were required to ratify the Thirteenth Amendment as a condition of their readmission to the Union after the war, most of the former Confederate states quickly passed laws that were designed to restrict opportunities for newly freed slaves dramatically. These **Black Codes** prohibited African Americans from voting, sitting on juries, or even appearing in public places. Although Black Codes differed from state to state, all empowered local law-enforcement officials to arrest unemployed blacks, fine them for vagrancy, and hire them out to employers to satisfy their fines. Some state codes went so far as to require African Americans to work on plantations or to be domestics. The Black Codes laid the groundwork for Jim Crow laws, which would later institute segregation in all walks of life.

Thirteenth Amendment:

One of the three Civil War amendments; specifically bans slavery in the United States.

Black Codes:

Laws denying most legal rights to newly freed slaves; passed by Southern states following the Civil War.

The outraged Reconstructionist Congress enacted the Civil Rights Act of 1866 to invalidate some state Black Codes. President Andrew Johnson vetoed the legislation, but—for the first time in history—Congress overrode a presidential veto. The Civil Rights Act formally made African Americans citizens of the United States and gave the Congress and the federal courts the power to intervene when states attempted to restrict male African-American citizenship rights in matters such as voting. Congress reasoned that African Americans were unlikely to fare well if they had to file discrimination complaints in state courts, where judges were elected. Passage of a federal law allowed African Americans to challenge discriminatory state practices in the federal courts, where judges were appointed by the president.

Fourteenth Amendment:

One of the three Civil War amendments; guarantees equal protection and due process of the laws to all U.S. citizens.

Because controversy remained over the constitutionality of the act (since the Constitution gives states the right to determine qualifications of voters), the **Fourteenth Amendment** was proposed simultaneously with the Civil Rights Act to guarantee, among other things, citizenship to all freed slaves. Other key provisions of the Fourteenth Amendment barred states from abridging "the privileges or immunities of citizenship" or depriving "any person of life, liberty, or property without due process of law."

Unlike the Thirteenth Amendment, which had near-unanimous support in the North, the Fourteenth Amendment was opposed by many women. During the Civil War, women's rights activists, including Elizabeth Cady Stanton and Susan B. Anthony, put aside their claims for expanded rights for women, most notably the right to vote, and threw their energies into the war effort. They were convinced that once slaves were freed and given the right to vote, women similarly would be rewarded with the franchise. They were wrong.

In early 1869, after ratification of the Fourteenth Amendment (which specifically added the word "male" to the Constitution for the first time), women's rights activists met in Washington, D.C., to argue against passage of any new amendment that would extend suffrage to black males and not to women. The convention resolved that "a man's government is worse than a white man's government, because, in proportion as you increase the tyrants, you make the condition of the disenfranchised class more hopeless and degraded."

Fifteenth Amendment:

One of the three Civil War amendments; specifically enfranchised newly freed male slaves.

In spite of these arguments, the **Fifteenth Amendment** was passed by Congress in February 1869. It guaranteed the "right of citizens" to vote regardless of their "race, color or previous condition of servitude." Again, sex was not mentioned.

Women's rights activists were shocked. Abolitionists' continued support of the Fifteenth Amendment, which was ratified by the states in 1870, prompted many women's rights supporters to leave the abolition movement to work solely for the cause of women's rights. Twice burned, Anthony and Stanton decided to form their own National Woman Suffrage Association (NWSA) to achieve that goal. In spite of the NWSA's opposition, however, the Fifteenth Amendment was ratified by the states in 1870.

Civil Rights and the Supreme Court

While the Congress was clear in its wishes that the rights of African Americans be expanded and that the Black Codes be rendered illegal, the Supreme Court was not nearly so protective of those rights under the Civil War amendments. In the first two tests of the scope of the Fourteenth Amendment, the Supreme Court ruled that the citizenship rights guaranteed by the amendment applied only to rights of national citizenship and not to state citizenship. Ironically, neither case involved African Americans. In *The Slaughterhouse Cases* (1873), the Court upheld Louisiana's right to create a monopoly in the operation of slaughterhouses, despite the Butcher's Benevolent Association's claim that this action deprived its members of their livelihood and thus the privileges and immunities of citizenship guaranteed by the amendment.[9]

Similarly, in *Bradwell* v. *Illinois* (1873), when Myra Bradwell asked the U.S. Supreme Court to find that Illinois's refusal to allow her to practice law (although she had passed the bar examination) violated her citizenship rights guaranteed by the privileges and immunities clause of the Fourteenth Amendment, her arguments fell on deaf ears. In *Bradwell* one justice went so far as to declare that it was reasonable for the state to bar women from the practice of law because "the natural and proper timidity and delicacy which belongs to the female sex evidently unfits it for many of the occupations of civil life."[10]

The combined message of these two cases was that state and national citizenship were separate and distinct. In essence, the Supreme Court ruled that neither African Americans nor any others could be protected from discriminatory state action, because the Fourteenth Amendment did not enlarge the limited rights guaranteed by U.S. citizenship.

Claims for expanded rights and requests for a clear definition of U.S. citizenship rights continued to fall on deaf ears in the halls of the Supreme Court. In 1875, for example, the Court heard *Minor* v. *Happersett,* the culmination of a series of test cases launched by women's rights activists.[11] Virginia Minor, after planning with Anthony and other NWSA members, attempted to register to vote in her hometown of St. Louis, Missouri. When the registrar refused to record her name on the list of eligible voters, Minor sued, arguing that the state's refusal to let her vote violated the privileges and immunities clause of the Fourteenth Amendment. Rejecting her claim, the justices ruled unanimously that voting was not a privilege of citizenship. And, until 1999, the Supreme Court never again addressed the possible scope of the privileges and immunities clause as revealed in Politics Now: Poverty and the Revitalization of the Privileges and Immunities Clause.

In the same year, Southern resistance to African-American equality led Congress to pass the Civil Rights Act of 1875, designed to grant equal access to public accommodations such as theaters, restaurants, and transportation. The act also prohibited the exclusion of African Americans from jury service. After 1877, however, as Reconstruction was dismantled, national interest in the legal condition of African Americans waned. Most white Southerners had never believed in equality for "freedmen," as former slaves were called. Any rights freedmen received had been contingent on federal enforcement. Once federal troops were no longer available to guard polls and prevent whites from excluding black voters, Southern states moved to limit African Americans' access to the ballot. Other forms of discrimination were also allowed by judicial decisions upholding **Jim Crow laws,** which required segregation in public schools and facilities including railroads, restaurants, and theaters. Many Jim Crow laws also barred interracial marriage. All these laws, at first glance, appeared to conflict with the Civil Rights Act of 1875. In 1883, however, a series of cases decided by the Supreme Court severely damaged the vitality of the 1875 Act. The *Civil Rights Cases* (1883) were five separate cases involving the convictions of private individuals found to have violated the Civil Rights Act by refusing to extend accommodations to African Americans in theaters, a hotel, and a railroad.[12] In deciding these cases, the Supreme Court ruled that Congress could prohibit only state or governmental action and not private acts of discrimination. The Court thus seriously limited the scope of the Fourteenth Amendment by concluding that Congress had no authority to prohibit private discrimination in public accommodations.

The Court's opinion in the *Civil Rights Cases* provided a moral reinforcement for the Jim Crow system. Southern states viewed the Court's ruling as an invitation to gut the Thirteenth, Fourteenth, and Fifteenth Amendments.

In devising ways to make certain that African Americans did not vote, Southerners had to avoid the *intent* of the Fifteenth Amendment. This amendment did not guarantee suffrage; it simply said that states could not deny anyone the right to vote

Web Exploration
For more about the history of Jim Crow in the South, see www.awlonline.com/oconnor.

Jim Crow laws:
laws enacted by Southern states that discriminated against blacks by creating "whites only" schools, theaters, hotels, and other public accommodations.

Civil Rights Cases (1883):
Name attached to five cases brought under the Civil Rights Act of 1875. In 1883 the Supreme Court decided that discrimination in a variety of public accommodations, including theaters, hotels, and railroads, could not be prohibited by the act because it was private, not state, discrimination.

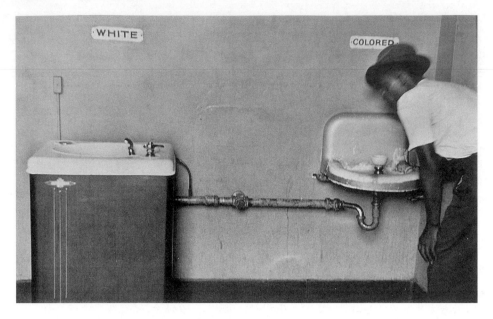

■ Throughout the South, examples of Jim Crow laws abounded. One such law required separate public drinking fountains, shown here. Notice the obvious difference in quality. (Photo courtesy: Corbis/Bettmann)

on account of race or color. So to exclude African Americans in a seemingly racially neutral way, Southern states used two devices before the 1890s: (1) poll taxes (small taxes on the right to vote that often came due when poor African-American sharecroppers had the least amount of money on hand) or some form of property-owning qualifications; and (2) "literacy" or "understanding" tests, which allowed local registrars to administer difficult reading-comprehension tests to potential voters whom they did not know.

These voting restrictions had an immediate impact. By the late 1890s, black voting fell by 62 percent from the Reconstruction period, while white voting fell by only 26 percent. To make certain that these laws didn't further reduce the numbers of poor or uneducated white voters, many Southern states added a **grandfather clause** to their voting qualification provisions, granting voting privileges to those who failed to pass a wealth or literacy test only if their grandfathers had voted before Reconstruction. Grandfather clauses effectively denied the descendants of slaves the right to vote.

While African Americans continued to face wide-ranging racism on all fronts, women also confronted discrimination. During this period married women, by law, could not be recognized as legal entities. Women often were treated in the same category as juveniles and "imbeciles," and in many states were not entitled to wages, inheritances, or custody of their children.

grandfather clause:

Laws that allowed only those whose grandfathers had voted before Reconstruction to vote unless they passed a wealth or literacy test.

THE PUSH FOR EQUALITY, 1890–1954

The **Progressive Era** (1889–1920) was characterized by a concerted effort to reform political, economic, and social affairs. Evils like child labor, the concentration of economic power in the hands of a few industrialists, limited suffrage, political corruption, business monopolies, and prejudice against African Americans were all targets of progressive reform efforts. Distress over the legal inferiority of African Americans was aggravated by the U.S. Supreme Court's decision in *Plessy* v. *Ferguson* (1896), a case that some commentators point to as the Court's darkest hour.

In 1892 a group of African Americans in Louisiana decided to test the constitutionality of a Louisiana law mandating racial segregation on all public trains. They convinced Homer Adolph Plessy, a man of seven-eighths Caucasian and one-eighth

Plessy v. Ferguson (1896):

Plessy challenged a Louisiana statute requiring that railroads provide separate accommodations for blacks and whites. The Court found that separate but equal accommodations did not violate the equal protection clause of the Fourteenth Amendment.

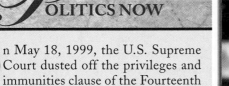

POLITICS NOW

Poverty and the Revitalization of the Privileges and Immunities Clause

On May 18, 1999, the U.S. Supreme Court dusted off the privileges and immunities clause of the Fourteenth Amendment, which had not been used by the Court to anchor a decision in 126 years. The Court's dramatic seven-to-two decision came in a case involving a challenge to a California law that allowed it to pay lower welfare benefits to new state residents.[a] Women who fled from abusive relationships in other states were ineligible for higher California state benefits although they still faced higher California cost of living expenses. Under the challenged provision, California paid new residents only the amounts that they were eligible for in the states that they left. So, if a person traveled from Oklahoma, they would get but $341 their first year in California. Former Alabamians were eligible for only $120, while long-time Californians could receive $631. "The states's legitimate interest in saving money provides no justification for its decision to discriminate among equally eligible citizens," said Justice John Paul Stevens writing for the Court.[b]

The Court said that this two-level benefits system violated citizens' constitutional right to travel and was the justices' first decision dealing with any of the new welfare reform efforts, which critics charge violate the constitutional rights of many of America's poor. The ruling is also important because of the Court's "revival of a constitutional doctrine making citizens of all states equal."[c] Scores of constitutional scholars immediately weighed in, speculating that the Court's use of the privileges and immunities clause could mean far greater protection for what the Court views as fundamental rights. For what other rights might the Court ground protection in the privileges and immunities clause of the Fourteenth Amendment?

[a] *Saenz* v. *Roe*, 1999 LEXIS 3174.
[b] *Saenz* v. *Roe*, 1999 LEXIS 3174.
[c] Joan Biskupic, "New-Resident Limits on Welfare Rejected," *The Washington Post*, May 18, 1999, A1.

African blood[13] to board a train in New Orleans and proceed to the "whites only" car. He was arrested when he refused to leave his seat and take one in the car reserved for African Americans. Plessy sued the railroad company, arguing that racial segregation was illegal under the provisions of the Fourteenth Amendment.[14]

The Supreme Court disagreed. After analyzing the history of African Americans in the United States, the majority concluded that the Louisiana law was constitutional. The justices based the decision on their belief that separate facilities for blacks and whites provided equal protection of the laws. After all, they reasoned, African Americans were not prevented from riding the train; the Louisiana statute required only that the races travel separately. Justice John Marshall Harlan (1877–1911) was the lone dissenter on the Court. He argued that "the Constitution is colorblind" and that it was senseless to hold constitutional a law "which, practically, puts the badge of servitude and degradation upon a large class of our fellow citizens."

Not surprisingly, the separate-but-equal doctrine enunciated in *Plessy* v. *Ferguson* soon came to mean only "separate," as new legal avenues to discriminate against African Americans were enacted into law throughout the South. The Jim Crow system soon became a way of life in the American South. In 1898 the Supreme Court upheld the constitutionality of literacy tests that were administered to African Americans and indicated its apparent willingness to allow the Southern states to define their own suffrage standards, whether or not they disproportionately affected blacks.[15] One year later, the Supreme Court upheld a school district's decision to maintain a whites-only high school but close a blacks-only high school to free up funds for a black elementary school.[16] The Supreme Court unanimously upheld the constitutionality of this disparate treatment.

By 1900, then, equality for African Americans was far from the promise first offered by the Civil War amendments. Again and again, the Supreme Court nullified the intent

of the amendments and sanctioned racial segregation while the states avidly followed its lead. While discrimination was widely practiced in many parts of the North, Southern states passed laws legally imposing segregation in education, housing, public accommodations, employment, and most other spheres of life. Miscegenation laws, for example, prohibited blacks and whites from marrying.

Jim Crow laws were not the only practices designed to keep African Americans in a secondary position. Indeed, these laws established a way of life with strong social codes as well. Journalist Juan Williams notes in *Eyes on the Prize:*

> There were Jim Crow schools, Jim Crow restaurants, Jim Crow water fountains, and Jim Crow customs— blacks were expected to tip their hats when they walked past whites, but whites did not have to remove their hats even when they entered a black family's home. Whites were to be called "sir" and "ma'am" by blacks, who in turn were called by their first names by whites. People with white skin were to be given a wide berth on the sidewalk; blacks were expected to step aside meekly.[17]

Notwithstanding these degrading practices, by the early 1900s a small group of African Americans (largely from the North) had been able to attain some formal education and were ready to push for additional rights. They found some progressive white citizens and politicians amenable to their cause.

■ William E. B. DuBois (second from right in the second row, facing left) is pictured with the original leaders of the Niagara Movement in this 1905 photo taken on the Canadian side of Niagara Falls. (Photo courtesy: Schomburg Center for Research in Black Culture/The New York Public Library)

Web Exploration

To learn more about the NAACP, see www.awlonline.com/oconnor.

The Founding of the National Association for the Advancement of Colored People

In 1909 a handful of individuals active in a variety of progressive causes—including women's suffrage and the fight for better working conditions for women and children— met to discuss the idea of a group devoted to the problems of "the Negro." Major race riots had recently occurred in several American cities, and progressive reformers who sought change in political, economic, and social relations were concerned about these outbreaks of violence and the possibility of others. Oswald Garrison Villard, the influential publisher of the New York *Evening Post*—and grandson of William Lloyd Garrison—called a conference to discuss the problem. This group soon evolved into the National Association for the Advancement of Colored People (NAACP). Along with Villard, its first leaders included Jane Addams of Hull House, vice president of the National American Woman Suffrage Association; Moorfield Storey, a past president of the American Bar Association; and W. E. B. DuBois, a founder of the Niagara Movement, a group of educated African Americans who took their name from their first meeting place in Niagara Falls, Ontario, Canada. (The Niagara reformers met in Canada because no hotel on the U.S. side of the falls would accommodate them.)

Key Women's Groups

The NAACP was not the only group getting off the ground. The struggle for women's rights was revitalized by the formation of the National American Woman Suffrage Association (NAWSA) in 1890, when the National and American Woman Suffrage Associations merged, with Susan B. Anthony as its president. Unlike the National Woman Suffrage Association, which had sought a wide variety of expanded rights for women, this new association was devoted largely to securing women's suffrage. Its task was greatly facilitated by the proliferation of women's groups that emerged during the Progressive era. In addition to the rapidly growing temperance movement—the move to ban the sale of alcohol, which many women blamed for a variety of social ills—women's groups were

■ Suffragettes demonstrating for the franchise. Parades like this one took place in cities all over the United States. (Photo courtesy: Library of Congress)

created to seek protective legislation in the form of maximum hour or minimum wage laws for women and to work for improved sanitation, public morals, education, and the like. Other organizations that were part of what was called the "club movement" were created to provide increased cultural and literary experiences for middle-class women. With increased industrialization, some women found for the first time that they had the opportunity to pursue activities other than those centered on the home.

One of the most active groups lobbying on behalf of women during this period was the National Consumers' League (NCL), which successfully lobbied for Oregon legislation limiting women to ten hours of work a day. When Curt Muller was then convicted of employing women more than ten hours a day in his small laundry and brought his appeal to the U.S. Supreme Court, the NCL sought permission from the state to conduct the defense of the statute.

At the urging of NCL attorney and future U.S. Supreme Court Justice Louis Brandeis, NCL members amassed an impressive array of sociological and medical data that were incorporated into what became known as the "Brandeis brief." This contained only three pages of legal argument, while more than a hundred pages were devoted to nonlegal, sociological data that were used to convince the Court that Oregon's statute was constitutional. In finding the law constitutional in *Muller* v. *Oregon* (1908), the Court relied heavily on these data to document women's unique status as mothers to justify their differential treatment.[18]

Women seeking the vote used reasoning reflecting the Court's opinion in *Muller*. Discarding earlier notions of full equality, NAWSA based its claim to the right to vote largely on the fact that women, as mothers, should be enfranchised. Furthermore, although many members of the **suffrage movement** were NAACP members, the new women's movement—called the suffrage movement because of its focus on the vote alone and not on broader issues of women's rights—took on racist overtones as women argued that if undereducated African Americans could vote, why couldn't women? Some NAWSA members even argued that "the enfranchisement of women would ensure immediate and durable white supremacy."

Diverse attitudes were clearly present in the growing suffrage movement, which often tried to be all things to all people. Its roots in the Progressive movement gave it an

suffrage movement:

Term used to refer to the drive for votes for women that took place in the United States from 1890 to 1920.

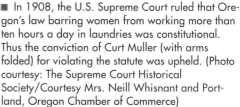

■ In 1908, the U.S. Supreme Court ruled that Oregon's law barring women from working more than ten hours a day in laundries was constitutional. Thus the conviction of Curt Muller (with arms folded) for violating the statute was upheld. (Photo courtesy: The Supreme Court Historical Society/Courtesy Mrs. Neill Whisnant and Portland, Oregon Chamber of Commerce)

exceptionally broad base that transformed NAWSA from a small organization of just over 10,000 members in the early 1890s to a true social movement of more than 2 million members in 1917. By 1920 a coalition of women's groups led by NAWSA was able to secure ratification of the **Nineteenth Amendment** to the Constitution. It guaranteed *all* women the right to vote—fifty-five years after African-American males had been enfranchised by the Fifteenth Amendment.

After passage of the suffrage amendment in 1920, the fragile alliance of diverse women's groups that had come together to fight for the vote quickly disintegrated. Women returned to their "home" groups, such as the NCL or the Women's Christian Temperance Union, to pursue their individualized goals. In fact, after the tumult of the suffrage movement, widespread, organized activity on behalf of women's rights did not reemerge until the 1960s. In the meantime, however, the NAACP continued to fight racism and racial segregation. In fact, its activities and those of others in the civil rights movement would later give impetus to a new women's movement.

Litigating for Equality

During the 1930s leaders of the NAACP began to sense that the time was right to launch a full-scale challenge in the federal courts to the constitutionality of *Plessy*'s separate-but-equal doctrine. The NAACP mapped out a long-range strategy that would first target segregation in professional and graduate education. Clearly, the separate-but-equal doctrine and the proliferation of Jim Crow laws were a bar to any hope of full equality for African Americans. Traditional legislative channels were unlikely to work, given blacks' limited or nonexistent political power. Thus the federal courts and a long-range litigation strategy were the NAACP's only hope. The NAACP often relied on Brandeis-type briefs, so-called because they relied heavily on sociological data to support their legal arguments. In fact, the NAACP eventually hired a statistician to help its lawyers amass data to help present evidence of discrimination to the courts.

Test Cases.   The NAACP opted first to challenge the constitutionality of Jim Crow law schools. In 1935 all Southern states maintained fully segregated elementary and

■ Lloyd Gaines was the subject of the major test case, *Missouri* ex rel. *Gaines* v. *Canada,* which contested the principle of segregated schools. Gaines chose to attend the University of Michigan, from which he strangely disappeared, never to be heard from again. (Photo courtesy: AP/Wide World Photos)

secondary schools. Colleges and universities were also segregated, but most states did not provide for postgraduate education for African Americans. NAACP lawyers chose to target law schools because they were institutions that judges could well understand, and integration there could prove less threatening to most whites.

Lloyd Gaines, a graduate of Missouri's all-black Lincoln University, sought admission to the all-white University of Missouri Law School in 1936. He was immediately rejected. In the separate-but-equal spirit, the state offered to build a law school at Lincoln (although no funds were allocated for the project) or, if he didn't want to wait, to pay his tuition at an out-of-state law school. Gaines lost his appeal of this rejection in the lower court, and the case was appealed to the U.S. Supreme Court.

Gaines's case was filed at an auspicious time. As you may recall from chapter 3, a "constitutional revolution" of sorts occurred in Supreme Court decision making in 1937. Before this time, the Court was most receptive to and interested in the protection of economic liberties. In 1937, however, the Court reversed itself in a series of cases and began to place individual freedoms and personal liberties on a more protected footing. Thus, in 1938, Gaines's lawyers pleaded his appeal to a far more sympathetic Supreme Court. NAACP attorneys argued that the creation of a separate law school of any less caliber than that of the University of Missouri would not and could not afford Gaines an *equal* education. The justices agreed with the NAACP's contention and ruled that Missouri had failed to meet the separate-but-equal requirements of *Plessy.* The Court ordered Missouri either to admit Gaines to the school or to set up a law school for him.[19]

Recognizing the importance of the Court's ruling, in 1939 the NAACP created a separate, tax-exempt legal defense fund to devise a strategy to build on the Missouri case to bring about equal educational opportunities for all African-American children. The first head of the NAACP Legal Defense and Educational Fund (LDF), as it was called, was Thurgood Marshall, who later became the first African American to serve on the U.S. Supreme Court (1967–91). Sensing that the Court would be more amenable to the NAACP's broader goals if it was first forced to address a variety of less threatening claims to educational opportunity, Marshall and the NAACP LDF brought a series of carefully crafted test cases to the Court.

The first case involved H. M. Sweatt, a forty-six-year-old African-American mail carrier, who in 1946 applied for admission to the all-white University of Texas Law School. Rejected on racial grounds, Sweatt sued. The judge gave the state six months to establish a law school or to admit Sweatt to the University of Texas. The university

Web Exploration

To learn more about the NAACP Legal Defense Fund, see www.awlonline.com/oconnor.

then rented a few rooms in downtown Houston and hired two local African-American attorneys to be part-time faculty members. (At that time there was only one full-time African-American law school professor in the United States.) The state legislature saw the handwriting on the wall and authorized $3 million for the creation of the Texas State University for Negroes. One hundred thousand dollars of that money was to be for a new law school in Austin across the street from the state capitol. It consisted of three small basement rooms, a library of more than 10,000 books, access to the state law library, and three part-time first-year instructors as the "faculty." Sweatt declined the opportunity to obtain an education there and instead chose to continue his legal challenge.

While working on the Texas case, the NAACP LDF and Marshall also decided to pursue another case. Thurgood Marshall chose to use the case of George W. McLaurin, a retired university professor who had been denied admission to the doctoral education program at the University of Oklahoma. Marshall reasoned that McLaurin, at sixty-eight years of age, would be immune from the charges that African Americans wanted integration in order to intermarry. After a lower court ordered McLaurin's admission, the university reserved a dingy alcove in the cafeteria for him to eat in during off-hours, and he was given his own table in the library behind a shelf of newspapers. And, in what surely "was Oklahoma's most inventive contribution to legalized bigotry since the adoption of the 'grandfather clause,' "[20] McLaurin was forced to sit outside classrooms while lectures were given and seminars were held.

The Supreme Court handled these two cases together.[21] The eleven Southern states filed an *amicus curiae* (friend of the court) brief, in which they argued that *Plessy* should govern both cases. The NAACP LDF received assistance, however, from an unexpected source—the U.S. government. In a dramatic departure from the past, the administration of Harry S. Truman filed a friend of the court brief urging the Court to overrule *Plessy*. Since the late 1870s, the U.S. government had never sided against the Southern states in a civil rights matter and had never submitted an *amicus* brief supporting the rights of African-American citizens. President Truman believed that because many African Americans had fought and died for their country in World War II, this kind of executive action was proper. The Court traditionally gives great weight to briefs from the U.S. government. The Court, however, again did not overrule *Plessy*, but the justices found that the measures taken by the states in each case failed to live up to the strictures of the separate-but-equal doctrine. The Court unanimously ruled that the "remedies" to each situation were inadequate to afford a sound education. In the *Sweatt* case, for example, the Court declared that the "qualities which are incapable of objective measurement but which make for greatness in a law school . . . includ(ing) the reputation of the faculty, experience of the administration, position and influence of the alumni, standing in the community, traditions and prestige" made it impossible for the state to provide an equal education in a segregated setting.

In 1950, after these decisions were handed down, the NAACP LDF concluded that the time had come to launch a full-scale attack on the separate-but-equal doctrine. The decisions of the Court were encouraging, and the position of the U.S. government and the population in general appeared to be more receptive to an outright overruling of *Plessy*.

Brown v. Board of Education (1954).

As discussed in Highlight 6.1: Why It's Called *Brown* v. *Board of Education*, *Brown* was actually four cases brought from different areas of the South, the border states, and others involving public elementary or high school systems that mandated separate schools for blacks and whites.[22]

In *Brown*, NAACP LDF lawyers, again headed by Thurgood Marshall, argued that *Plessy*'s separate-but-equal doctrine was unconstitutional under the **equal protection clause** of the Fourteenth Amendment, and that if the Court was still reluctant to overrule *Plessy*, the only way to equalize the schools was to integrate them. A major component of the NAACP LDF's strategy was to prove that the intellectual, psychological,

Brown v. Board of Education (1954):

U.S. Supreme Court decision holding that school segregation is inherently unconstitutional because it violates the Fourteenth Amendment's guarantee of equal protection; marked the end of legal segregation in the United States.

equal protection clause:

Section of the Fourteenth Amendment that guarantees that all citizens receive "equal protection of the laws"; has been used to bar discrimination against blacks and women.

and financial damage that befell African Americans as a result of segregation precluded any court from finding that equality was served by the separate-but-equal policy.

In *Brown,* the NAACP LDF presented the Supreme Court with evidence of the harmful consequences of state-imposed racial discrimination. To buttress its claims, the NAACP LDF introduced the now-famous "doll study," conducted by Kenneth Clark, a prominent African-American sociologist who had long studied the negative effects of segregation on African-American children. His research revealed that black children not only preferred white dolls when shown black dolls and white dolls, but that most liked the white doll better, many adding that the black doll looked "bad." This information was used to illustrate the negative impact of racial segregation and bias on an African-American child's self-image.

The NAACP LDF's legal briefs were supported by important *amicus curiae* briefs submitted by the U.S. government, major civil rights groups, labor unions, and religious groups decrying racial segregation. On May 17, 1954, Chief Justice Earl Warren delivered the fourth opinion of the day, *Brown* v. *Board of Education.* Writing for the Court, Warren stated:

> To separate [some school children] from others . . . solely because of their race generates a feeling of inferiority as to their status in the community that may affect their hearts and minds in a way very unlikely ever to be undone. We conclude, unanimously, that in the field of public education the doctrine of "separate but equal" has no place.

There can be no doubt that *Brown* was the most important civil rights case decided in the twentieth century.[23] It immediately evoked an uproar that shook the nation. Some called the day the decision was handed down "Black Monday." The governor of South Carolina decried the decision, saying, "Ending segregation would mark the beginning of the end of civilization in the South as we know it."[24] The NAACP LDF lawyers who had argued these cases and those cases leading to *Brown,* however, were jubilant.

Remarkable changes had occurred in the civil rights of Americans since 1890. Women had won the right to vote, and after a long and arduous trail of litigation in the federal courts, the Supreme Court had finally overturned its most racist decision of the era, *Plessy* v. *Ferguson.* The Court boldly proclaimed that separate but equal (at least in education) would no longer pass constitutional muster. The question then became how *Brown* would be interpreted and implemented. Could it be used to invalidate other Jim Crow laws and practices? Would African Americans be truly equal under the law?

THE CIVIL RIGHTS MOVEMENT

Our notion of civil rights has changed profoundly since 1954. First African Americans and then women have built upon existing organizations to forge successful movements for increased rights. *Brown* served as a catalyst for change, sparking the development of the modern civil rights movement. Women's work in that movement and the student protest movement that arose in reaction to the U.S. government's involvement in Vietnam gave women the experience needed to form their own organizations to press for full equality. As African Americans and women became more and more successful, they served as models for others who sought equality—Native Americans, Latino Americans, homosexuals, the disabled, and others.

School Desegregation After Brown

One year after *Brown,* in a case referred to as *Brown II,* the Court ruled that racially segregated systems must be dismantled "with all deliberate speed."[25] To facilitate implementation, the Court placed enforcement of *Brown* in the hands of appointed federal district court judges, who were considered more immune to local political pressures than were regularly elected state court judges.

The NAACP and its Legal Defense Fund continued to resort to the courts to see that *Brown* was implemented, while the South entered into a near-conspiracy to avoid

Web Exploration

To read the full text of *Brown,* see www.awlonline.com/oconnor.

HIGHLIGHT 6.1

Why It's Called *Brown v. Board of Education of Topeka, Kansas*

Seven-year-old Linda Brown of Topeka, Kansas, lived close to a good public school, but it was reserved for whites. So every day she had to cross railroad tracks in a nearby switching yard on her way to catch a run-down school bus that would take her across town to a school reserved for black students. Her father, Oliver Brown, concerned for her safety and the quality of her education, became increasingly frustrated with his youngster's having to travel far from home to get an education.

"The issue came up, and it was decided that Reverend Brown's daughter would be the goat, so to speak," recalled a member of the Topeka NAACP. "He

■ Linda Brown lived close to a good public school but her race precluded her attendance there. When the NAACP sought plaintiffs to challenge this discrimination, her father, a local minister, offered Linda to be one of several students named in the NAACP's case. (Photo courtesy: Carl Iwasaki/Life Magazine/Time Warner Inc.)

put forth his daughter to test the validity of the [law], and we had to raise the money."[a]

The NAACP continued to gather plaintiffs and test cases from around the nation. The Supreme Court first agreed to hear *Brown* and *Briggs v. Elliott* (South Carolina) in 1952. Two days before they were to be heard, the Court issued a postponement and added *Davis* v. *Prince Edward County* (Virginia) to its docket. Just a few weeks later, the Court added *Bolling v. Sharpe* from the District of Columbia and *Gebhart* v. *Belton* (Delaware). According to U.S. Supreme Court Justice Tom Clark of Texas, the Court "consolidated them and made *Brown* the first so that the whole question would not smack of being purely a Southern one."[b] Thus the case became known as *Brown* v. *Board of Education of Topeka, Kansas.*

[a]Quoted in Juan Williams, *Eyes on the Prize: America's Civil Rights Years, 1954–1965* (New York: Penguin, 1987), 21.
[b]Williams, *Eye on the Prize,* 31.

the mandates of *Brown II.* In Arkansas, for example, Governor Orval Faubus, facing a reelection bid, announced that he would not "be a party to any attempt to force acceptance of change to which people are overwhelmingly opposed."[26] The day before school was to begin, Faubus announced that he would surround Little Rock's Central High School with National Guardsmen to prevent African-American students from entering. While the federal courts in Arkansas continued to order the admission of African-American children, the governor remained adamant. Finally, President Dwight D. Eisenhower sent federal troops to Little Rock to protect the rights of the nine students who had attempted to attend Central High.

In reaction to the governor's outrageous conduct, the Court broke with tradition and issued a unanimous decision in *Cooper* v. *Aaron* (1958), which was filed by the Little Rock School Board asking the federal district court for a two-and-one-half-year delay in implementation of its desegregation plans. Each justice signed the opinion individually, underscoring his individual support for the notion that "no state legislator or executive or judicial officer can war against the Constitution without violating his undertaking to support it."[27] The state's actions were thus ruled unconstitutional and its "evasive schemes" illegal.

A New Move for African-American Rights

In 1955, soon after *Brown II,* the civil rights movement took another step forward—this time in Montgomery, Alabama. Rosa Parks, the local NAACP's Youth Council advisor, decided to challenge the constitutionality of the segregated bus system. First, Parks and other NAACP officials began to raise money for litigation and made speeches around town to garner public support. Then, on December 1, 1955, Rosa Parks made history when she refused to leave her seat on a bus to move to the back to make room for a white male passenger. She was arrested for violating an Alabama law banning integration of public facilities, including buses. After she was freed on bond, Parks and the NAACP decided to enlist city clergy to help her cause. At the same time, they distributed 35,000 handbills calling for African Americans to boycott the Montgomery bus system on the day of Parks's trial. Black ministers used Sunday services to urge their members to support the boycott. On Monday morning, African Americans walked, carpooled, or used black-owned taxicabs. That night, local ministers decided that the boycott should be continued. A twenty-six-year-old minister, Martin Luther King, Jr., was selected to lead the newly formed Montgomery Improvement Association. King was new to town, and church leaders had been looking for a way to get him more involved in civil rights work.

As the boycott dragged on, Montgomery officials and local business owners began to harass the city's African-American citizens. But King urged Montgomery's African-American citizens to continue their protest. The residents held out, despite suffering personal hardship for their actions, ranging from harassment to bankruptcy to job loss. In 1956 a federal court ruled that the segregated bus system violated the equal protection clause of the Fourteenth Amendment. After a year of walking, African Americans ended their protest as the buses were ordered to integrate. The first effort at nonviolent protest had been successful. Organized boycotts and other forms of nonviolent protest, including sit-ins at segregated restaurants and bus stations, were to follow.

Web Exploration

For more about the Montgomery Bus Boycott and Dr. Martin Luther King, Jr., see www.awlonline.com/oconnor.

Formation of New Groups

The recognition and respect that King earned within the African-American community helped him to launch the Southern Christian Leadership Conference (SCLC) in 1957, soon after the end of the Montgomery bus boycott. Unlike the NAACP, which had Northern origins and had come to rely largely on litigation as a means of achieving expanded equality, the SCLC had a Southern base and was rooted more closely in black religious culture. The SCLC's philosophy reflected King's growing belief in the importance of nonviolent protest.

On February 1, 1960, students at the all-black North Carolina Agricultural and Technical College participated in the first sit-in. Angered by their inability to be served at local lunch counters and heartened by the success of the Montgomery bus boycott, black students marched to the local Woolworth's and ordered cups of coffee. They were refused service. So they sat at the counter until police came and carted them off to jail. Soon thereafter, African-American college students around the South joined together to challenge Jim Crow laws. These mass actions immediately brought extensive attention from the national news media.

Over spring break 1960, with the assistance of an $800 grant from the SCLC, 200 student delegates—black *and* white—met at Shaw University in North Carolina to consider recent sit-in actions and to plan for the future. Later that year, two more meetings were held in Atlanta, Georgia, and the Student Nonviolent Coordinating Committee (SNCC) was formed.

Among SNCC's first leaders were Marion Barry, who would later serve as mayor of Washington, D.C. (1978–90, 1995–1999); John Lewis, a seven-term Democratic member of the House of Representatives and Chief Deputy Democratic Whip in the 106th Congress; and Marian Wright Edelman, who became first an NAACP lawyer and later the founder and head of the Children's Defense Fund. While the SCLC generally worked with church leaders in a community, the SNCC was much more of a grassroots organization. Always perceived as more radical than the SCLC, SNCC tended to focus its organizing activities on the young, both black and white.

In addition to joining the sit-in bandwagon, SNCC also came to lead what were called "freedom rides," designed to focus attention on segregated public accommodations. Bands of college students and other civil rights activists traveled by bus throughout the South in an effort to force bus stations to desegregate. Often these protesters were met by angry mobs of segregationists and brutal violence, as local police chose not

■ A prime objective of the protesters in Birmingham, Alabama was to focus national attention on their cause. For the first time in American history, a majority of the public owned television sets and could see the horrors of police brutality. But the print media continued to be a powerful tool. This picture was reprinted over and over again and even frequently mentioned on the floor of Congress during debates on the Civil Rights Act of 1964. (Photo courtesy: Charles Moore/Black Star)

to defend protesters' basic constitutional rights to free speech and peaceful assembly. African Americans were not the only ones to participate in freedom rides; increasingly, white college students from the North began to play an important role in the SNCC.

While the SNCC continued to sponsor sit-ins and freedom rides, in 1963 the Reverend Martin Luther King, Jr., launched a series of massive nonviolent demonstrations in Birmingham, Alabama, long considered a major stronghold of segregation. Thousands of blacks and whites marched to Birmingham in a show of solidarity. Peaceful marchers were met there by the Birmingham Police Commissioner, who ordered his officers to use dogs, clubs, and fire hoses on the marchers. Americans across the nation watched in horror as they witnessed the brutality and abuse heaped on the protesters. As the marchers hoped, these shocking scenes helped convince President John F. Kennedy to propose important civil rights legislation.

The Civil Rights Act of 1964

The older faction of the civil rights movement, as represented by the SCLC, and the younger branch, represented by the SNCC, both sought a similar goal: full implementation of Supreme Court decisions and an end to racial segregation and discrimination. The cumulative effect of collective actions including sit-ins, boycotts, marches, and freedom rides—as well as the tragic bombings and deaths inflicted in retaliation—led Congress to pass the first major piece of civil rights legislation since the post–Civil War era.

In 1963 President Kennedy requested that Congress pass a law banning discrimination in public accommodations. Seizing the moment and recognizing the potency of a show of massive support, the Reverend Martin Luther King, Jr., called for a monumental march on Washington, D.C., to demonstrate widespread support for legislation to ban discrimination in *all* aspects of life, not just public accommodations. The March on Washington for Jobs and Freedom was held in August 1963 only a few months after the Birmingham demonstrations. More than 250,000 people heard King deliver his famous "I Have a Dream" speech from the Lincoln Memorial. Before Congress had the opportunity to vote on any legislation, however, John F. Kennedy was assassinated on November 22, 1963, in Dallas, Texas.

It was clear that national laws outlawing discrimination were the only answer: Southern legislators would never vote to repeal Jim Crow laws. It was much more feasible for

African Americans to first seek national laws and then their implementation from the federal judiciary. But through the 1960s, African Americans lacked sufficient political power or the force of public opinion to sway enough congressional leaders. Their task was further stymied by loud and strong opposition from Southern members of Congress. Many of these legislators, because of the Democratic Party's total control of the South, had been in office far longer than most, and therefore held powerful committee chairmanships that were awarded on seniority. The Senate Judiciary Committee was controlled by a coalition of Southern Democrats and conservative Republicans. The House Rules Committee was chaired by a Virginian opposed to any civil rights legislation, who by virtue of his position could block such legislation in committee.

When Vice President Lyndon B. Johnson, a Southern-born former Senate majority leader, succeeded Kennedy as president, he put civil rights reform at the top of his legislative priority list and civil rights activists gained a critical ally. Thus, through the 1960s, the movement subtly changed in focus from peaceful protest and litigation to legislative lobbying. Its focus broadened from integration of school and public facilities and voting rights to issues of housing, jobs, and equal opportunity.

The push for civil rights legislation in the halls of Congress was helped by changes in public opinion. Between 1959 and 1965, Southern attitudes toward integrated schools changed enormously. The proportion of Southerners who responded that they would not mind their child's attendance at a half-black school doubled.

In spite of strong presidential support and the sway of public opinion, the Civil Rights Act of 1964 did not sail through Congress. Southern senators, led by South Carolina's Strom Thurmond, a Democrat who later switched to the Republican Party, conducted the longest filibuster in the history of the Senate. For eight weeks they held up voting on the civil rights bill until cloture (see chapter 7) was invoked and the filibuster ended. Once passed, the **Civil Rights Act of 1964:**

1. Outlawed arbitrary discrimination in voter registration and expedited voting rights lawsuits.
2. Barred discrimination in public accommodations engaged in interstate commerce.
3. Authorized the U.S. Justice Department to initiate lawsuits to desegregate public facilities and schools.
4. Provided for the withholding of federal funds from discriminatory state and local programs.
5. Prohibited discrimination in employment on grounds of race, color, religion, national origin, or sex.
6. Created the Equal Employment Opportunity Commission (EEOC) to monitor and enforce the bans on employment discrimination.

Other changes were sweeping the United States. Violence rocked the nation as ghetto riots broke out in the Northeast. Although Northern African Americans were not subject to Jim Crow laws, many lived in poverty and faced pervasive daily discrimination and its resultant frustration. Some, including Black Muslim leader Malcolm X, even argued that to survive, African Americans must separate themselves from white culture in every way. Given this growing "black power" movement and increased racial tension, it is not surprising that from 1964 to 1968, many Northern African Americans took to the streets, burning and looting to vent their rage.

Violence also marred the continued activities of civil rights workers in the South. During the summer of 1964 three civil rights workers—one black, two white—were killed in Neshoba County, Mississippi. In 1965 Martin Luther King, Jr., again led his supporters on a massive march, this time from Selma, Alabama, to the state capital in Montgomery, in support of a pending voting rights bill. Again, Southern officials unleashed a reign of terror in Selma as they used whips, dogs, cattle prods, clubs, and tear gas on the protesters. Again, Americans watched in horror as they witnessed this brutality on their television screens. This march and the public's reaction to it led to quick passage of the Voting Rights Act of 1965.

■ At this historic gathering on the Mall in Washington, D.C., in August, 1963, Rev. Martin Luther King, Jr., delivered his famous "I Have a Dream" speech. (Photo courtesy: Flip Schulke/Black Star)

Civil Rights Act of 1964:

Legislation passed by Congress to outlaw segregation in public facilities and racial discrimination in employment, education, and voting; created the Equal Employment Opportunity Commission

■ Court-ordered busing in the 1960s was frequently accompanied by police escorts. (Photo courtesy: Corbis/Bettmann)

de jure discrimination:

Racial segregation that is a direct result of law or official policy.

de facto discrimination:

Racial discrimination that results from practice (such as housing patterns or other social factors) rather than the law.

The Impact of the Civil Rights Act of 1964

Many Southerners were adamant in their belief that the Civil Rights Act of 1964 was unconstitutional because it went beyond the scope of Congress's authority to legislate under the Constitution, and lawsuits were quickly brought to challenge the act. The first challenge to the act was heard by the Supreme Court on an expedited review (which bypasses the intermediate courts). The Court upheld its constitutionality when it found that Congress was within the legitimate scope of its commerce power as outlined in Article I.[28]

Education.   One of the key provisions of the Civil Rights Act of 1964 authorized the U.S. Justice Department to bring actions against school districts that failed to comply with *Brown* v. *Board of Education.* In 1964, a full decade after *Brown,* fewer than 1 percent of African-American children in the South attended integrated schools.

After *Brown,* the Charlotte-Mecklenburg School District had assigned students to the school closest to their homes without regard to race, leaving over half of African-American students attending schools that were at least 99 percent black. In *Swann* v. *Charlotte-Mecklenburg School District* (1971), the Supreme Court ruled that all vestiges of state-imposed segregation, called **de jure discrimination,** or discrimination by law, must be eliminated at once and that lower federal courts had the authority to fashion a wide variety of remedies including busing, racial quotas, and the pairing of schools to end dual, segregated school systems.[29]

In *Swann* the Court was careful to distinguish *de jure* from **de facto discrimination,** unintentional discrimination often attributable to housing patterns and/or private acts. The Court noted that its approval of busing was a remedy for intentional, government-imposed or -sanctioned discrimination only.

Over the years, forced, judicially imposed busing has found less and less favor with the Supreme Court, even in situations where *de jure* discrimination had earlier been proven. In 1992 the U.S. Supreme Court even ruled that in situations where all-black schools still existed in spite of a 1969 court order to dismantle the *de jure* system, a showing that the persistent segregation was not a result of the school board's actions was sufficient to remove the district from court supervision. In 1995 the Court ruled five to four that city school boards can use plans to attract white suburban students to mostly minority urban schools only if both city and suburban schools still show the effects of segregation, thus reversing a lower court desegregation order.[30]

Employment.   Title VII of the Civil Rights Act of 1964 prohibits employers from discriminating against employees for a variety of reasons, including race, sex, age, and national origin. (In 1978 the act was amended to prohibit discrimination based on pregnancy.)

In 1971, in one of the first major cases decided under the act, the Supreme Court found that employers could be found liable for discrimination if the *effect* of their employment practices was to exclude African Americans from certain positions.[31] African-American employees were allowed to use statistical evidence to show that they had been excluded from all but one department of the Duke Power Company, because it required employees to have a high school education or pass a special test to be eligible for promotion.

The Supreme Court ruled that although the tests did not *appear* to discriminate against African Americans, their effects—that there were no African-American employees in any other departments—were sufficient to shift the burden of proving lack of discrimination on the employer. Thus the Duke Power Company would have to prove that the tests were "a business necessity" that had a "demonstrable relationship to successful performance" (of a particular job).

The notion of "business necessity," as set out in the Civil Rights Act of 1964 and interpreted by the federal courts, was especially important for women. Women had long been kept out of many occupations on the strength of the belief that customers preferred to deal with male personnel. Conversely, males were barred from flight-attendant positions because the airlines believed that passengers preferred to be served by young, attractive women. Similarly, many large factories, manufacturing establishments, and police and fire departments refused outright to hire women by subjecting them to arbitrary height and weight requirements, which also disproportionately affected Hispanics. Like the tests declared illegal by the Court, these requirements often could not be shown to be related to job performance and were eventually ruled illegal by the federal courts.

The Women's Rights Movement.   Just as in the abolition movement in the 1800s, women from all walks of life also participated in the civil rights movement. Women were important members of both the SNCC and more traditional groups like the NAACP and the SCLC, yet they often found themselves treated as second-class citizens. At one point Stokely Carmichael, chair of the SNCC, openly proclaimed: "The only position for women in the SNCC is prone."[32] Statements and attitudes like these led some women to found early women's liberation groups that were generally quite radical, small in membership, and not intended to use more conventional political tactics.

As discussed earlier, initial efforts to convince the Supreme Court to declare women enfranchised under the Fourteenth Amendment were uniformly unsuccessful. The paternalistic attitude of the Supreme Court, and perhaps society as well, continued well into the 1970s. As late as 1961, Florida required women who wished to serve on juries to travel to the county courthouse and register for that duty. In contrast, all men who were registered voters were automatically eligible to serve. When Gwendolyn Hoyt was convicted of bludgeoning her adulterous husband to death with a baseball bat, she appealed her conviction, claiming that the exclusion of women from juries prejudiced her case. She believed that female jurors—her peers—would have been more sympathetic to her and the emotional turmoil that led to her attack on her husband and her claim of "temporary insanity." She therefore argued that her trial by an all-male jury violated her rights as guaranteed by the Fourteenth Amendment. In rejecting her contention, Justice John Harlan (the grandson of the lone dissenting justice in *Plessy*) wrote in *Hoyt* v. *Florida* (1961):

> Despite the enlightened emancipation of women from the restrictions and protections of bygone years, and their entry into many parts of community life formerly considered to be reserved to men, a woman is still regarded as the center of home and family life.[33]

These kinds of attitudes and decisions (*Hoyt* was later unanimously reversed in 1975) were not sufficient to forge a new movement for women's rights. Shortly after *Hoyt*, however, three events occurred to move women to action. In 1961, soon after his election, President John F. Kennedy created the President's Commission on the Status of Women. The Commission's report, *American Women*, released in 1963, documented pervasive discrimination against women in all walks of life. In addition, the civil rights movement and publication of Betty Friedan's *The Feminine Mystique* (1963),[34] which led some women to question their lives and status in society, added to their dawning recognition that something was wrong. Soon after, the Civil Rights Act of 1964 prohibited discrimination based not only on race, but also on sex. Ironically, that provision had been added to Title VII of the Civil Rights Act by Southern Democrats. These senators saw a prohibition against sex discrimination in employment as a joke, and viewed its addition as a means to discredit the entire act and ensure its defeat. Thus it was added at the last minute and female members of Congress seized the opportunity to garner support for the measure.

In 1966, after the **Equal Employment Opportunity Commission** failed to enforce the law as it applied to sex discrimination, women activists formed the National Organization for Women (NOW). From its inception, NOW was closely modeled on the

Equal Employment Opportunity Commission:

Federal agency created to enforce the Civil Rights Act of 1964, which forbids discrimination on the basis of race, creed, national origin, religion, or sex in hiring, promotion, or firing.

Web Exploration

To learn more about NOW and the EEOC, see www.awlonline.com/oconnor.

Web Exploration

To learn more about the ERA, see www.awlonline.com/oconnor.

NAACP. Women in NOW were quite similar to the founders of the NAACP; they wanted to work within the system to prevent discrimination. Initially, most of this activity was geared toward two goals: achievement of equality through passage of an equal rights amendment to the Constitution, or by judicial decision. But because the Supreme Court failed to extend constitutional protections to women, the only recourse that remained was an amendment.

The Equal Rights Amendment (ERA).   Not all women agreed with the notion of full equality for women. Members of the National Consumers' League, for example, feared that an equal rights amendment would invalidate protective legislation of the kind specifically ruled constitutional in *Muller* v. *Oregon* (1908). Nevertheless, from 1923 to 1972, a proposal for an equal rights amendment was made in every session of every Congress. Every president since Harry S. Truman backed it, and by 1972 public opinion favored its ratification.

Finally, in 1972, in response to pressure from NOW, the National Women's Political Caucus, and a wide variety of other feminist groups, Congress passed the Equal Rights Amendment (ERA) by overwhelming majorities (84 to 8 in the Senate; 354 to 24 in the House). The amendment provided that:

- Equality of rights under the law shall not be denied or abridged by the United States or by any state on account of sex.
- The Congress shall have the power to enforce, by appropriate legislation, the provisions of this article.

Within a year twenty-two states had ratified the amendment, most by overwhelming margins. But the tide soon turned. In *Roe* v. *Wade* (1973), the Supreme Court decided that women had a constitutionally protected right to privacy that included the right to terminate a pregnancy. Almost overnight *Roe* gave the ERA's opponents political fuel. Although privacy rights and the ERA have nothing to do with each other, opponents effectively persuaded many people in states that had yet to ratify the amendment that the two were linked. If abortion was legal, why not marriages between and adoptions by homosexuals? They also claimed that the ERA and feminists were antifamily and that the ERA would force women out of their homes and into the workforce because husbands would no longer be responsible for their wives' support.

These arguments and the amendment's potential to make women eligible for the military draft brought the ratification effort to a near standstill. In 1974 and 1975, the amendment only squeaked through the Montana and North Dakota legislatures, and two states—Nebraska and Tennessee—voted to rescind their earlier ratifications.

By 1978, one year before the deadline for ratification was to expire, thirty-five states had voted for the amendment—three short of the three-fourths necessary for ratification. Efforts in key states such as Illinois and Florida failed as opposition to the ERA intensified.

Faced with the prospect of defeat, ERA supporters heavily lobbied Congress to extend the deadline. Congress extended the time period for ratification by three years, but to no avail. No additional states ratified the amendment and three more rescinded their votes.

What began as a simple correction to the Constitution turned into a highly controversial proposed change. Even though large numbers of the public favored the ERA, opponents needed to stall ratification in only thirteen states while supporters had to convince legislators in thirty-eight. The success that women's rights activists were having in the courts was hurting the effort. When women first sought the ERA in the late 1960s, the Supreme Court had yet to rule that women were protected by the Fourteenth Amendment's equal protection clause from any kind of discrimination, thus clearly showing the need for an amendment. But as the Court widened its interpretation of the Constitution to protect women from some sorts of discrimination, in the eyes of many the need for a new amendment became less urgent.

Litigation for Equal Rights. While several women's groups worked toward passage of the ERA, NOW and several other groups, including the Women's Rights Project of the American Civil Liberties Union (ACLU), formed litigating arms to pressure the courts. But women faced an immediate roadblock in the Supreme Court's interpretation of the equal protection clause of the Fourteenth Amendment.

The Equal Protection Clause and Constitutional Standards of Review

The Fourteenth Amendment protects all U.S. citizens from state action that violates equal protection of the laws. Most laws, however, are subject to what is called the rational basis or minimum rationality test. This lowest level of scrutiny means that governments must allege a rational foundation for any distinctions they make. Early on, however, the Supreme Court decided that certain rights were entitled to a heightened standard of review. As early as 1937, the Supreme Court recognized that certain rights were so fundamental that a very heavy burden would be placed on any government that sought to restrict those rights. As discussed in chapter 5, when fundamental rights such as First Amendment freedoms or **suspect classifications** such as race are involved, the Court uses a heightened standard of review called **strict scrutiny** to determine the constitutional validity of the challenged practices, as detailed in Table 6.1. Beginning with *Korematsu* v. *United States* (1944), which involved a constitutional challenge to the internment of Japanese Americans, Justice Hugo Black noted that "all legal restrictions which curtail the civic rights of a single racial group are immediately suspect," and should be given "the most rigid scrutiny."[35] In *Brown* v. *Board of Education of Topeka, Kansas* (1954), the Supreme Court again used the strict scrutiny standard to evaluate the constitutionality of race-based distinctions. In legal terms this means that if a statute or governmental practice makes a classification based on race, the statute is presumed

suspect classification:
Category or class, such as race, that triggers the highest standard of scrutiny from the Supreme Court.

strict scrutiny:
A heightened standard of review used by the Supreme Court to determine the constitutional validity of a challenged practice.

Table 6.1 The Equal Protection Clause and Standards of Review Used by the Supreme Court to Determine Whether It Has Been Violated

TYPES OF CLASSIFICATION (What kind of statutory classification is an issue?)	STANDARD OF REVIEW (What standard of review will be used?)	TEST (What does the court ask?)	EXAMPLE (How does the court apply the test?)
Fundamental freedoms: Religion, assembly, press, privacy, suspect classifications (including race)	Strict scrutiny or heightened standard	Is classification *necessary* to the accomplishment of a permissible state goal? Is it the least restrictive way to reach that goal?	*Brown* v. *Board of Education of Topeka, Kansas* (1954): Racial segregation not necessary to accomplish the slate goal of educating its students
Gender	Intermediate standard	Does the classification serve an important governmental objective, and is it substantially related to those ends?	*Craig* v. *Boren* (1976): Keeping drunk drivers off the roads may be an important governmental objective, but allowing eighteen- to twenty-one-year-old women to drink alcoholic beverages while prohibiting men of the same age from drinking is not substantially related to that goal.
Others (including age, wealth, and sexual preference)	Minimum rationality standard	Is there any rational foundation for the discrimination?	*Romer* v. *Evans* (1996): Colorado constitutional amendment precluding any legislative, executive, or judicial action at any state of local level designed to bar discrimination based on sexual preference is not rational or reasonable.

to be unconstitutional unless the state can provide "compelling affirmative justifications"—that is, unless the state can prove the law in question is necessary to accomplish a permissible goal and that it is the least restrictive means through which that goal can be accomplished.

Web Exploration

For more about the ACLU Women's Rights Project, see www.awlonline.com/oconnor.

During the 1960s and into the 1970s, the Court routinely struck down as unconstitutional practices and statutes that discriminated on the basis of race. "Whites-only" public parks and recreational facilities, tax-exempt status for private schools that discriminated, and statutes prohibiting racial intermarriage were declared unconstitutional. In contrast, the Court refused even to consider the fact that the equal protection clause might apply to discrimination against women. Finally, in a case brought in 1971 by Ruth Bader Ginsburg as Director of the Women's Rights Project of the ACLU, the Supreme Court ruled that an Idaho law granting male parents automatic preference over female parents as the administrator of their deceased children's estates violated the equal protection clause of the Fourteenth Amendment.

Reed v. *Reed* (1971), the Idaho case, turned the tide in terms of constitutional litigation. While the Court did not rule that sex was a suspect classification, it concluded that the equal protection clause of the Fourteenth Amendment prohibited unreasonable classifications based on sex.[36] And in 1976 the Court ruled that sex-discrimination complaints would be judged by a new, judicially created intermediate standard of review a step below strict scrutiny. In *Craig* v. *Boren* (1976), the owner of the Honk 'n' Holler Restaurant in Stillwater, Oklahoma, and Craig, a male under twenty-one, challenged the constitutionality of a state law prohibiting the sale of 3.2 percent beer to males under the age of twenty-one and to females under the age of eighteen.[37] The state introduced a considerable amount of evidence in support of the statute, including:

- Eighteen- to twenty-year-old males were more likely to be arrested for driving under the influence than were females of the same age.
- Youths aged seventeen to twenty-one were the group most likely to be injured or to die in alcohol-related traffic accidents, with males exceeding females.
- Young men were more inclined to drink and drive than females.

The Supreme Court found that this information was "too tenuous" to support the legislation. In coming to this conclusion, the Court carved out a new "test" to be used in examining claims of sex discrimination, "[T]o withstand constitutional challenge, . . . classifications by gender must serve important governmental objectives and must be substantially related to achievement of those objectives." According to the Court an intermediate standard of review was created within what previously was a two-tier distinction—strict scrutiny/rational basis.

As *Craig* demonstrates, men, too, can use the Fourteenth Amendment to fight gender-based discrimination. Since 1976, the Court has applied the intermediate standard of constitutional review to most claims that it has heard involving gender. Thus the following kinds of practices have been found to violate the Fourteenth Amendment:

- Single-sex public nursing schools.
- Laws that consider males adults at twenty-one years but females at eighteen years.
- Laws that allow women but not men to receive alimony.
- State prosecutors' use of preemptory challenges to reject men or women to create more sympathetic juries.
- Virginia's maintenance of an all-male military college, the Virginia Military Institute.

In contrast, the Court has upheld the following governmental practices and laws:

- Draft registration provisions for males only.
- State statutory rape laws that apply only to female victims.

The level of review used by the Court is crucial. Clearly, a statute excluding African Americans from draft registration would be unconstitutional. But because gender is not

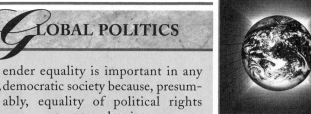

GLOBAL POLITICS

Civil Rights and Access to Political Power

Gender equality is important in any democratic society because, presumably, equality of political rights should to some extent translate into access to political power. By that criterion, the United States turns out to be below average when compared with the other G-7 countries. In terms of gender equality in the executive branch it is also a laggard. Canada, France, and the United Kingdom each have had women prime ministers. The relatively high percentage of women in Germany's parliament is a reflection of the majority coalition of leftist parties since 1998, which are committed to gender equality within their ranks. Japan's parliament, in contrast, has been dominated for the last fifty years by conservative parties with no interest in promoting gender equality. None of the G-7 countries, though, have parliamentary participation rates for women that even approach the rate of women employed in the economy.

The G-7 lag behind the Scandinavian countries, where representation of women in national legislatures exceeds 35%. The Scandinavian countries also have more female cabinet ministers: about one-third in 1994. They also have higher rates of female employment in the general economy.[a]

[a]United Nations Development Programme, *Human Development Report 1995*, 31–36.

Percentage of Women in Lower House of National Legislature

Country	Year of Last Election	Percentage of Women In Lower Chamber of Legislature
Canada	1997	19
France	1997	11
Germany	1998	31
Italy	1996	11
Japan	1996	5
United Kingdom	1997	18
United States	1998	12
Average(%)	-	15.2

Source: Election Data Resources on the Internet: Europe. http://pitt.edu/~ alvarez/europe.htm#DE; Election Data Resources on the Internet: The Americas. http://pitt.edu/~ alvaroz/amorica.htm#DE; colocted national govornmont sitos.

subject to the same higher standard of review that is used in racial discrimination cases, the exclusion of women from the requirements of the Military Selective Service Act was ruled permissible because the government policy was considered to serve "important governmental objectives."[38]

This history has perhaps clarified why women's rights activists continue to argue that until the passage of an equal rights amendment, women will never enjoy the same rights as men. An amendment would automatically raise the level of scrutiny that the Court applies to gender-based claims.

Statutory Remedies for Sex Discrimination. In part because of the limits of the intermediate standard of review and the fact that the equal protection clause applies only to *governmental* discrimination, women's rights activists began to bombard the courts with sex-discrimination cases. These cases have been filed under Title VII of the Civil Rights Act, which prohibits discrimination by private (and, after 1972, public) employers, or Title IX of the Education Amendments of 1972, which bars educational institutions receiving federal funds from discriminating against female students. Key victories under Title VII include:

- Consideration of sexual harassment as sex discrimination.
- Inclusion of law firms, which many argued were *private* partnerships, in the coverage of the act.
- A broad definition of what can be considered sexual harassment, which includes same-sex harassment.
- Allowance of voluntary affirmative action programs to redress historical discrimination against women.

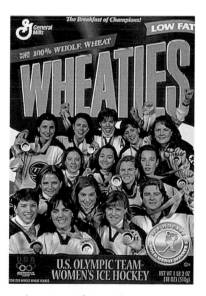

■ The success of American women at the most recent summer and winter Olympics highlighted the success of Title IX. (Photo courtesy: General Mills/AP/Wide World Photos)

Figure 6.1   EEOC Sexual Harassment Filings, 1990–1998

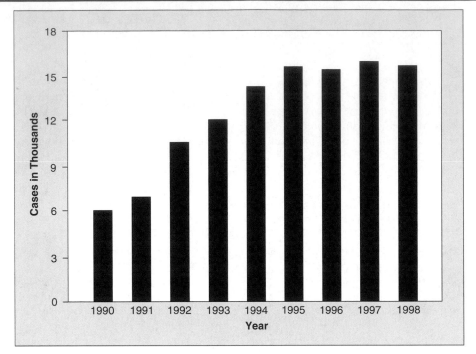

SOURCE: EEOC

After the Clarence Thomas hearings concerning whether or not he sexually harassed Anita Hill, sexual harassment claims skyrocketed until 1995 and then leveled off, as revealed in Figure 6.1. Claims more than doubled from 1990 to 1998. The EEOC was also able to reach record settlements with employers rising from $7.7 million in 1990 to over $27 million in 1997. In spite of all of the media attention to Paula Jones's claims that she was sexually harassed by Bill Clinton, complaints have begun to level off as more and more employers have begun education and training programs to avert workplace problems.

Title IX, which parallels Title VII, has also greatly expanded the opportunities for women in elementary, secondary, and postsecondary institutions. Since women's groups, like the NAACP before them, saw eradication of educational discrimination as key to improving other facets of women's lives, they lobbied for it heavily. Most of today's college students did not go through school being excluded from home economics or shop classes because of their sex. Nor, probably, did many attend schools that had no team sports for females. Yet this was commonly the case in the United States prior to passage of Title IX.[39] The 1996 and 1998 Olympics showed the impact of the law on women's participation in sport. Record numbers of women competed and won.

OTHER GROUPS MOBILIZE FOR RIGHTS

African Americans and women are not the only groups that have suffered unequal treatment under the law. Denial of civil rights has led many other disadvantaged groups to mobilize to achieve greater civil rights. And their efforts to achieve those rights have many parallels to the efforts made by African Americans and women. In the wake of the successes of those two groups in achieving enhanced rights, and sometimes even before, other traditionally disenfranchised groups have organized to gain fuller equality. Many of them have also recognized that litigation and the use of test-case strategies would be key to further civil rights gains. The Ford Foundation, which had heavily funded the NAACP LDF and some women's rights litigation, also helped interested

Mexican Americans to found the Mexican American Legal Defense and Education Fund (MALDEF). Established in 1968, and modeled after the NAACP LDF, MALDEF has played and continues to play a major role in expanding civil rights for Latinos. The Ford Foundation also facilitated the 1970 creation of the Native American Rights Fund to litigate for Indian rights.

Native Americans

Native Americans are the first "true" Americans, and their status under U.S. law is unique. Under the U.S. Constitution, "Indian tribes" are considered distinct governments, a situation that has affected Native Americans' treatment by the Supreme Court in contrast to other groups of ethnic minorities. And "minority" is a term that accurately describes American Indians. It is estimated that there were as many as 10 million Indians in the New World at the time it was discovered by Europeans in the 1400s, with 3 to 4 million living in what is today the United States. By 1900 the number of Indians in the continental United States had plummeted to less than 2 million.

Many commentators would agree that for years Congress and the courts manipulated Indian law to promote the westward expansion of the United States. The Northwest Ordinance of 1787, passed by the Continental Congress, specified that "the good faith should always be observed toward the Indians; their lands and property shall never be taken from them without their consent, and their property rights, and liberty, they shall never be invaded or disturbed, unless in just and lawful wars authorized by Congress." This is not what happened. Instead, over the years, "American Indian policy has been described as 'genocide-at-law' promoting both land acquisition and cultural extermination."[40] At first, during the eighteenth and nineteenth centuries, the U.S. government isolated Indians on reservations as it confiscated their lands and denied them basic political rights. Indian reservations were administered by the federal government and Native Americans often lived in squalid conditions.

With passage of the Dawes Act in 1887, however, the government switched policies to promote assimilation over separation. Each Indian family was given land within the reservation; the rest was sold to whites, thus reducing Indian lands from about 140 million acres to about 47 million. Moreover, to encourage Native Americans to assimilate, Indian children were sent to boarding schools off the reservation and native languages and rituals were banned. In 1924 Native Americans were made U.S. citizens and given the right to vote.

At least in part because tribes were small and scattered (and the number of Indians declining), they formed no protest movement in reaction to these drastic policy changes. It was not until the 1960s, at the same time that women were beginning to mobilize for greater civil rights, that Indians too began to mobilize to act. Like the civil rights and women's rights movements, it had a radical as well as a more traditional branch. In 1973, for example, national attention was drawn to the plight of Indians when members of the radical American Indian Movement took over Wounded Knee, South Dakota, the site of the massacre of 150 Indians by the U.S. Army in 1890. Just two years before the protest, the treatment of Indians had been highlighted in the best-selling *Bury My Heart at Wounded Knee,* which in many ways served to mobilize public opinion against the oppression of Native Americans in the same way *Uncle Tom's Cabin* had against slavery.[41]

At the same time, just as the growing number of women in the legal profession contributed to the push to secure greater rights for women through litigation, Indians, many attracted by the American Indian Law Center at the University of New Mexico, began to file hundreds of test cases in the federal courts involving tribal fishing rights, tribal land claims, and the taxation of tribal profits. Soon the Native American Rights Fund (NARF), founded in 1970, became the NAACP LDF of the Indian rights movement when the "courts became the forum of choice for Indian tribes and their members."[42]

Native Americans have won some very important victories concerning hunting, fishing, and land rights. Native American tribes all over America have begun to sue to

Web Exploration

For more about the Native American Rights Fund, see
www.awlonline.com/oconnor.

reclaim lands they say were stolen from them by the United States, often more than 200 years ago. One of the largest Indian land claims was filed in 1972 on behalf of the Passamaquoddie and the Penobscot tribes, who were seeking return of 12.5 million acres in Maine—about two-thirds of the entire state—and $25 billion in damages. The suit was filed by the Native American Rights Fund and the Indian Service Unit of a legal services office that was funded by the U.S. Office of Economic Opportunity. It took intervention from the White House before a settlement was reached in 1980, giving each tribe over $40 million.

Native Americans are also litigating to gain access to their sacred places. All over the nation they have filed lawsuits to stop the building of roads and new construction on ancient burial grounds or other sacred spots. "We are in a battle for the survival of our very way of life," said one tribal leader. "The land is gone. All we've got left is our religion."[43]

But Native Americans have not fared nearly so well in areas such as religious freedom, especially where tribal practices come into conflict with state law. As noted in chapter 5, the Supreme Court used the rational basis test to rule that a state could infringe religious exercise (use of peyote as a sacrament in religious ceremonies) by a neutral law, and limited their access to religious sites during timber harvesting. Congress, however, quickly acted to restore some of those rights through passage of the Religious Freedom Restoration Act, although the law was later ruled unconstitutional by the Supreme Court. Native Americans continue to fight the negative stereotypes that continue to plague their progress. Indians contend that even the popular names of thousands of high school, college and professional teams are degrading as discussed in Highlight 6.2: What's in a Name: Team Names Under Attack.

Latino Americans

Like women's efforts to garner expanded political rights, Latino Americans, too, can date their first real push for equal rights to 1965–75.[44] This civil rights movement included many tactics drawn from the African-American civil rights movement, including sit-ins, boycotts, marches, and other activities designed to attract publicity to their cause.[45] Like blacks, women, and Native Americans, Latino Americans have some radical militant groups, but the movement has been dominated by more conventional organizations. The more conventional groups have pressed for Chicano and Latino studies programs and have built up ties with existing, powerful mainstream associations, including unions and the Roman Catholic church.

Latinos have also relied heavily on litigation to secure greater rights. Key groups are the Mexican American Legal Defense and Educational Fund (MALDEF) and the Puerto Rican Legal Defense and Educational Fund.

MALDEF was founded in 1968 after members of the League of United Latin American Citizens (LULAC), the nation's largest and oldest Latino organization, met with NAACP LDF leaders and, with their assistance, secured a $2.2-million start-up grant from the Ford Foundation. It was created to bring test cases to force school districts to allocate more funds to schools with predominantly low-income minority populations, to implement bilingual education programs, to force employers to hire Latinos, and to challenge election rules and apportionment plans that undercount or dilute Latino voting power. Just as Native American and women's rights groups had depended on the legal expertise of their own constituents, MALDEF quickly drew on the talent of Latino attorneys to staff offices in San Antonio and Los Angeles. It also started a scholarship fund to train more Latino attorneys, and established a New Mexico branch office in conjunction with the New Mexico Law School.

MALDEF lawyers quickly moved to bring major test cases to the U.S. Supreme Court, both to enhance the visibility of their cause and to win cases. MALDEF has been quite successful in its efforts to expand voting rights and opportunities to Hispanic Americans. In 1973, for example, it won a major victory when the Supreme Court ruled that multimember electoral districts (in which more than one person represents

Web Exploration

To learn more about MALDEF, see www.awlonline.com/oconnor.

HIGHLIGHT 6.2

What's in a Name: Team Names Under Attack

In 1993 Ben Nighthorse Campbell (R–Colo.), the only Native American in Congress, introduced legislation to block approval of a $200-million stadium for the Washington Redskins unless the team changed its name. Campbell, who told a House panel that the word "redskin" was an offensive racial slur, failed to convince his colleagues. Still, Indian activists picketed football games, the World Series, and other sporting events to draw attention to racially insensitive team names such as the Atlanta Braves and the Cleveland Indians. Since the early 1990s, over 600 high schools and several universities have abandoned their Indian-themed names.[a]

Around the same time, Suzan Shown Hartjo, a Cheyenne, also tried to drum up support to change the name of the Redskins. Her work brought her to the attention of a trademark lawyer who asked her if she had considered challenging the team name under the provisions of the 1946 Lanham Act, which bars the federal government from registering trademarks that are "disparaging, scandalous, or contemptuous."[b]

After seven years of legal pleadings, in 1999 a three-judge trademark panel ordered that the Redskins had no legal right to trademark their name because it disparaged Native Americans. The team then filed suit on June 1, 1999 in U.S District Court challenging that decision. Challenges to the Atlanta Braves and Cleveland Indians trademarks are also pending.

The U.S. Justice Department is also investigating names. Recently, one North Carolina high school agreed to drop the term "squaws" in referring to its girls' sports teams. "At some point, there aren't going to be any Indian team names anymore. That's social change," said the dean of Northwestern University's Law School.[c]

[a]Brooke Masters, "Team Name Goes to Court," *Washington Post*, April 7, 1999, B1, B8.
[b]Masters, "Team Name Goes to Court," B1.
[c]Masters, "Team Name Goes to Court," B8.

---

a single district) in Texas discriminated against African Americans and Latino Americans.[46] In multimember systems, legislatures generally add members to larger districts instead of drawing smaller districts in which a minority candidate could get a majority of the votes necessary to win.

While enjoying greater access to elective office, Latinos still suffer discrimination. Language barriers and substandard educational opportunities continue to plague their progress. In 1973 the U.S. Supreme Court refused to find that a Texas law under which the state appropriated a set dollar amount to each school district per pupil, while allowing wealthier districts to enrich educational programs from other funds, violated the equal protection clause of the Fourteenth Amendment.[47] The lower courts had found that wealth was a suspect classification entitled to strict scrutiny. Using that test, the lower courts had found the Texas plan discriminatory. In contrast, a divided Supreme Court concluded that education was not a fundamental right (see chapter 5), and that a charge of discrimination based on wealth would be examined only under a minimal standard of review (the rational basis test).

Throughout the 1970s and 1980s, inter-school-district inequalities continued, and frequently had their greatest impact on poor Latino children, who often had inferior educational opportunities. Recognizing that the increasingly conservative federal courts (see chapter 10) offered no recourse, in 1984 MALDEF filed suit in state court alleging that the Texas school finance policy violated the Texas constitution. In 1989 it won a case in which a state district judge elected by the voters of only a single county declared the state's entire method of financing public schools to be unconstitutional under the state constitution.

MALDEF continues to litigate in a wide range of areas of concern to Latinos. High on its agenda today are affirmative action, the admission of Latino students to state colleges and universities, health care for undocumented immigrants, and challenging unfair redistricting practices that make it more difficult to elect Latino and Latina legislators. Its Census 2000 educational outreach campaign, moreover, seeks to make certain that all Latinos are counted in 2000.

Gays and Lesbians

Gays and lesbians have had an even harder time than African Americans, women, Native Americans, or Hispanics in achieving fuller rights.[48] Gays do, however, have on average far higher household incomes and educational levels than do these other groups. And they are beginning to convert these advantages into political clout at the ballot box. As discussed in chapter 5, the cause of gay and lesbian rights, like that of African Americans and women early in their quest for greater civil rights, did not fare well in the Supreme Court initially. In the late 1970s, the Lambda Legal Defense and Education Fund, the Lesbian Rights Project, and Gay and Lesbian Advocates and Defenders were founded by gay and lesbian activists dedicated to ending legal restrictions on the civil rights of homosexuals.[49] Although these groups have won important legal victories concerning HIV/AIDS discrimination, insurance policy survivor benefits, and even some employment issues, they generally have not been as successful as other historically legally disadvantaged groups.[50]

In *Bowers* v. *Hardwick* (1986), for example, the Supreme Court ruled that a Georgia law that made private acts of consensual sodomy illegal (whether practiced by homosexuals or by heterosexual married adults) was constitutional. Gay and lesbian rights groups had argued that a constitutional right to privacy included the right to engage in consensual sex within one's home, but the Court disagreed. Although privacy rights may attach to relations of "family, marriage, or procreation," those rights did not extend to homosexuals, wrote Justice Byron White for the Court. In a concurring opinion—his last written on the Court—Chief Justice Warren Burger called sodomy "the infamous crime against nature."[51]

The public's and Congress's discomfort with gay and lesbian rights can be seen most clearly in the controversy that occurred after President Clinton attempted to lift the ban on gays in the armed services. Clinton tried to get an absolute ban on discrimination against homosexuals, who were subject to immediate discharge if their sexual orientation was discovered. Military leaders and Senator Sam Nunn (D-Ga.), as head of the Senate Armed Services Committee, led the effort against Clinton's proposal. Eventually, Clinton and the Senate leaders compromised on what was called the "Don't ask, don't tell" policy. It stipulated that gays and lesbians would no longer be asked if they were homosexual, but barred them from revealing their sexual orientation (under threat of discharge from the service). But when the Senate finally voted on the "compromise," its version of the new policy labeled homosexuality "an unacceptable risk" to morale. In spite of gay and lesbian groups' labeling the new policy "lie and hide," the Clinton administration chose to back off on the issue, correctly sensing only minimal support in Congress.

The Supreme Court's unwillingness to expand privacy rights or special constitutional protections to homosexuals, and Congress's failure to end discrimination in the military, has led many gay and lesbian rights groups to other, potentially more responsive, political forums: state and local governments. Around the nation, such groups have lobbied for antidiscrimination legislation with mixed success. In 1992, for example, Colorado voters passed a state constitutional amendment that *rescinded* several local gay and lesbian rights ordinances and also prevented the adoption of any such measures. In 1996, however, the U.S. Supreme Court ruled that the amendment was unconstitutional. Although the Court used the rational basis test to invalidate the amendment, it was the first time ever that a majority of the justices applied the equal protection clause of the Fourteenth Amendment to prevent discrimination against homosexuals.[52]

Disabled Americans

Disabled Americans also have lobbied hard for antidiscrimination legislation. In the aftermath of World War II, many veterans returned to a nation unequipped to handle their disabilities. The Korean and Vietnam wars made the problems of disabled veterans all the more clear. These disabled veterans saw the successes of African

Web Exploration

For more on gay and lesbian rights groups, see
www.awlonline.com/oconnor.

Web Exploration

For more about disability advocacy groups, see
www.awlonline.com/oconnor.

Americans, women, and other minorities, and they too began to lobby for greater protection against discrimination.[53] In 1990, in coalition with other disabled people, veterans were finally able to convince Congress to pass the Americans with Disabilities Act. The statute defines a disabled person as someone with a physical or mental impairment that limits one or more "life activities," or who has a record of such impairment. It thus extends the protections of the Civil Rights Act of 1964 to all of those with physical or mental disabilities. It guarantees access to public facilities, employment, and communication services. It also requires employers to acquire or modify work equipment, adjust work schedules, and make existing facilities accessible. This means, for example, that buildings must be accessible to those in wheelchairs, and telecommunications devices be provided for deaf employees. In 1999, the U.S. Supreme Court issued a series of four decisions redefining and significantly limiting the scope of the ADA. The cumulative impact of these decisions is to dramatically limit the

number of people who can claim coverage under the act. Moreover, these cases "could profoundly affect individuals with a range of impairments—from diabetes and hypertension to severe nearsightedness and hearing loss—who are able to function in society with the help of medicines or aids but whose impairments—may still make employers consider them ineligible for certain jobs."[54] Thus, pilots who need glasses to correct their vision cannot claim discrimination when employers fail to hire them because of their correctable vision.

Simply changing the law, while often an important first step in achieving civil rights, is not the end of the process. Attitudes must also change. And, as history has shown, that can be a very long process and will be longer given the Court's decisions.

■ Senator Max Cleland (D-Ga.), shown here in a wheelchair, is a vocal proponent of the rights of those with disabilities. He knows firsthand the problems of noncompliance with the ADA; when he was first elected to the U.S. Senate, it took him several months to find housing to accommodate his wheelchair. (Photo courtesy: Mary Ann Chestain/AP/Wide World Photos)

AFFIRMATIVE ACTION

Since passage of major civil rights legislation in the mid-1960s, racial tolerance has increased, although discrimination still exists. In 1997, 77 percent of those surveyed by the Gallup organization said they approved of interracial marriage and 93 percent said that they would vote for a black president.[55] Nevertheless, while most Americans agree that discrimination is wrong, most whites—57 percent—today believe that affirmative action programs are no longer needed, although 86 percent thought that those programs were needed thirty years ago. As revealed in Figure 6.2, white men—in particular, 82 percent of them—believe that *qualified* minorities should *not* receive preference over equally qualified whites.

How did affirmative action come to be such a controversial issue? Attitudes, especially white attitudes, appear to be changing at the same time the federal courts and the national legislature is debating—and often siding against the continuance of—affirmative action programs. The civil rights debate has often centered on the question of equality of opportunity versus equality of results. Most civil rights and women's rights organizations argue that the lingering and pervasive burdens of racism and sexism can be overcome only by taking race or gender into account in fashioning remedies for discrimination. They argue that the Constitution is not and should not be blind to color

Web Exploration
For more on affirmative action, see www.awlonline.com/oconnor.

Figure 6.2   Affirmative Action: What Polls Show

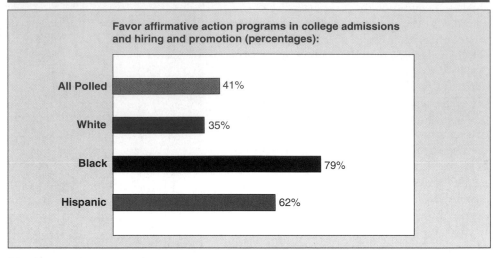

Favor affirmative action programs in college admissions
and hiring and promotion (percentages):

All Polled   41%

White   35%

Black   79%

Hispanic   62%

SOURCE: *Public Opinion Online*, Question 019, April 3, 1998; NEXIS.

affirmative action:

A policy or program designed to redress prior discrimination.

or sex. Therefore busing should be used to integrate schools and women should be given child-care assistance to allow them to compete equally in the marketplace.

The counter-argument holds that if it was once wrong to use labels to discriminate against a group, it should be wrong to use those same labels to help a group. Laws should be neutral or color-blind. According to this view, quotas and other forms of **affirmative action,** policies designed to give special attention or compensatory treatment to members of a previously disadvantaged group, should be illegal. As early as 1871, Frederick Douglass ridiculed the idea of racial quotas, arguing that they would promote "an image of blacks as privileged wards of the state." They were "absurd as a matter of practice" because some could use them to argue that blacks "should constitute one-eighth of the poets, statesmen, scholars, authors and philosophers."[61]

The debate over affirmative action and equality of opportunity became particularly intense during the Reagan years in the wake of two court cases that were generally decided in favor of affirmative action shortly before Reagan's election. In 1978 the Supreme Court for the first time fully addressed the issue of affirmative action. Alan Bakke, a thirty-one-year-old paramedic, sought admission to several medical schools and was rejected because of his age. He was wait-listed by the University of California at Davis. The Davis Medical School maintained two separate admissions committees—one for white students and another for minority students. Bakke was not admitted to the school, although his grades and standardized test scores were higher than those of all of the African-American students admitted to the school. In *Regents of the University of California* v. *Bakke* (1978), a sharply divided Court concluded that Bakke's rejection had been illegal because the use of strict quotas was inappropriate.[56] The medical school, however, was free to "take race into account."

Bakke was quickly followed in 1979 by another case in which the Court ruled that a factory and a union could voluntarily adopt a quota system in selecting black workers over more senior white workers for a training program. These kinds of programs outraged blue-collar Americans who had traditionally voted for the Democratic Party. In 1980 they abandoned the party in droves as they supported Ronald Reagan, an ardent foe of affirmative action.

For a while, the Court continued to uphold affirmative action plans, especially when there was clearcut evidence of prior discrimination, although it was by five-to-four votes. In 1987, for example, the Court for the first time ruled that a public employer could use a voluntary plan to promote women even if there was no judicial finding of prior discrimination.[57]

In all these affirmative action cases, the Reagan administration strongly urged the Court to invalidate the plans in question, but to no avail. With changes on the Court, however, including the 1986 elevation of William Rehnquist to Chief Justice, a strong opponent of affirmative action, the continued efforts of the Reagan administration finally began to pay off as the Court heard a new series of cases signaling an end to the advances in civil rights law. In a three-month period in 1989, the Supreme Court handed down five civil rights decisions limiting affirmative action programs and making it harder to prove employment discrimination.

The Legislative Response. In February 1990 the Democratic-controlled Congress and civil rights leaders passed legislation designed to overrule the Courts rulings, but it was vetoed by President Reagan's successor, George Bush. In late 1991, however, Congress and the White House reached a compromise on a weaker version of the civil rights bill, which was passed by overwhelming majorities in both the House (381 to 31) and Senate (93 to 5). The Civil Rights Act of 1991 overruled the Supreme Court rulings noted above, but specifically prohibited the use of quotas.

The Supreme Court, however, has not stayed silent on the issue. In 1995 the U.S. Supreme Court ruled that Congress, like the states, must show that affirmative action programs meet the strict scrutiny test noted on p. 197.[58] Today, in a decided retreat from its decisions in the late 1970s, the Court appears to allow race-based preferences only if they are narrowly tailored to meet unique circumstances.

■ Dr. John Hope Franklin, chair of the President's Race Advisory Board, greets President Clinton at a Washington hotel prior to the president's address before the board. The Board submitted its report to the president in September 1998, after meeting with experts and traveling around the United States to begin a dialogue on race. (Photo courtesy: Wilfredo Lee/AP/Wide World Photos)

In 1996, the 5th U.S. Circuit Court of Appeals ruled that the University of Texas Law School's affirmative action admissions program was unconstitutional, throwing college and university admissions programs in Texas, Oklahoma, and Mississippi (the three states in the 5th Circuit) into turmoil. Later that year, the U.S. Supreme Court refused to hear the case, thereby allowing the Court of Appeals decision to stand.[59] *Hopwood* v. *Texas* was filed on behalf of rejected white applicants who would automatically have been admitted (based on grades and LSAT scores) had they been African American or Mexican American. While Justices Ginsburg and Souter noted that "whether it is constitutional for a public college or graduate school to use race or national origin as a factor in its admission process is an issue of great national importance," all nine justices decided to wait for a better case to address the issue. The Court thought it had the "right" case when it accepted *Piscataway* v. *Taxman* in 1996 for review. At issue in *Piscataway* was a school board action that resulted in the firing of a white teacher who was alleged to have the same qualifications and experience as a black teacher.[60] However, fearing an adverse decision from the Court concerning affirmative action, civil rights groups actually negotiated a settlement between the two parties, making the case moot. Since the Supreme Court hears only cases that present actual cases and controversies, the case was removed from its docket and the issue of the constitutionality of affirmative action left for another day.

Affirmative action continues to be an issue of concern to many, including political candidates. In the 1996 presidential race, for example, Republican presidential candidate Bob Dole said he "opposes quotas, set-asides, and other preferences that favor individuals simply because they belong to a particular group." He even introduced legislation to end the federal government's practice of giving preference to individuals because they happen to belong to a particular group.[62] The Republican Party platform also came out squarely against affirmative action.

In contrast, Bill Clinton imposed a three-year moratorium on new affirmative action programs while they are reviewed. Unlike Dole, however, he promised not to end affirmative action programs favoring modest tinkering over elimination. The 1996 Democratic platform, in fact, stipulated, "When it comes to affirmative action, we should mend it, not end it."[63] The Supreme Court's recent nondecisions in affirmative action cases and a 1996 action by California voters outlawing most forms of state affirmative action have left their mark on state colleges and universities around the nation.[64] At Berkeley, 750 African-, Latino-, and Filipino-American applicants with 4.0 or better averages were rejected largely because of their low SAT scores, and there was a twelve percent drop in the number of minority students admitted to the California system.[65]

California and several other states where affirmative action is no longer permissible in hiring or educational admissions are exploring ways to enhance minority enrollment. California, for example, is exploring a policy that will guarantee admission to any student in the top four percent of their high school graduating class regardless of standardized test scores, which are frequently attacked as being race or gender biased.

Race- and gender-based remedies, initially designed by governments to allow them to redress the effects of decades of state-imposed discrimination, are now quickly going out of political favor—at least among whites, who still constitute a majority of legislators on all levels of government. If the Constitution is based on the premise of majority rule with protection of minority rights, is a governmental retreat on affirmative action a betrayal of minority interests or a validation that earlier programs designed to eliminate the vestiges of discrimination have worked?

CONTINUITY and Change

Race in America

When the Framers met in Philadelphia, they all recognized that the issue of slavery and how it was treated in the new Constitution could make or break their efforts to fashion a new nation and win acceptance in the Southern states. The Three-Fifths Compromise was their politically expedient solution. It got the Southern states on board, but only for a while. In 1861, the Civil War was fought largely over the issue of slavery. After slavery was abolished, the Southern states quickly acted to pass legislation to limit opportunities for newly freed slaves that persisted for nearly the next century.

Nearly one hundred years after the first shots rang out in the Civil War, African Americans and other civil rights supporters gained support for their efforts to attain fuller civil rights including the right to vote, attend desegregated schools, and be treated fairly in the workplace. Passage of the Civil Rights Act of 1964, which also protected women from discrimination, went a long way toward remedying the most onerous forms of discrimination, as did liberal Supreme Court decisions on a variety of issues protecting various classes including African Americans, women, Latinos, gays and lesbians, and the disabled.

Still, public opinion polls reveal that African Americans, in particular, believe that they are still discriminated against in a variety of subtle and not so subtle ways, as our opening vignette highlights. And, while African Americans clamor for ways to end this discrimination and fight off challenges to affirmative action, other groups seek expanded rights. Data presented in chapter 1 underscored how much change will occur in the racial composition of the United States as we move into the next century. While African American populations will increase substantially, Latino populations will skyrocket as a proportion of the total population. As the "color" of America changes, the United States will undoubtedly continually be reexamining its policies toward race.

1. What groups might seek further protection by the addition of new civil rights laws in the future?
2. Do you see the Supreme Court as a vehicle to seek expanded rights or one likely to be curtailing civil rights in the future?

Cast Your Vote. What groups do you think need protection? To cast your vote, go to www.awlonline.com/oconnor.

SUMMARY

While the Framers and other Americans basked in the glory of the newly adopted Constitution and Bill of Rights, their protections did not extend to all Americans. In this chapter we have shown how rights have been expanded to ever-increasing segments of the population. To that end, we have made the following points:

1. SLAVERY, ABOLITION, AND WINNING THE RIGHT TO VOTE, 1800–90

When the Framers tried to "compromise" on the issue of slavery, they only postponed dealing with a volatile question that was later to rip the nation apart. Ultimately, the Civil War was fought to end slavery. Among its results were the triumph of the abolitionist position and adoption of the Thirteenth, Fourteenth, and Fifteenth amendments. During this period women also sought expanded rights, especially the right to vote, but to no avail.

2. THE PUSH FOR EQUALITY, 1890–1954

Although the Civil War amendments were added to the Constitution, the Supreme Court limited their application. As Jim Crow laws were passed throughout the South, the NAACP was founded in the early 1900s to press for equal rights for African Americans. Women's groups were also active during this period, successfully lobbying for passage of the Nineteenth Amendment, which assured them the right to vote.

First women's groups such as the National Consumers' League (NCL), and then others, including NOW, began to view litigation as a means to their ends. The NCL was forced to court to argue for the constitutionality of legislation protecting women workers; in contrast, NOW sought the Court's help in securing equality under the Constitution.

3. THE CIVIL RIGHTS MOVEMENT

In 1954 the U.S. Supreme Court ruled in *Brown* v. *Board of Education* that state-segregated school systems were unconstitutional. This victory empowered African Americans as they sought an end to other forms of pervasive discrimination. Bus boycotts and sit-ins were common tactics. As new groups were formed, freedom rides, pressure for voting rights, and massive nonviolent demonstrations became common "lobbying" tactics. This activity culminated in the passage of the Civil Rights Act of 1964 and the Voting Rights Act of 1965. These acts gave African-American and women's rights groups two potential weapons in their legal arsenals: They could attack private discrimination under the Civil Rights Act, or state-sanctioned discrimination under the equal protection clause of the Fourteenth Amendment. Over the years the Supreme Court developed different tests to determine the constitutionality of various forms of discrimination. In general, strict scrutiny, the most stringent standard, was applied to race-based claims. An intermediate standard of review was developed to assess the constitutionality of sex discrimination claims.

4. OTHER GROUPS MOBILIZE FOR RIGHTS

Building on the successes of African Americans and women, other groups, including Native Americans, Latino Americans, gays and lesbians, and the disabled, organized to litigate for expanded civil rights as well as to lobby for antidiscrimination laws.

5. AFFIRMATIVE ACTION

Affirmative action for women and people of color has been under attack since the 1970s. Until recently, however, the Supreme Court was willing to find various remedial programs to be constitutional. The states are the hotbed of this controversy with states like Texas and California outlawing the use of affirmative action in admissions programs in educational programs.

KEY TERMS

affirmative action, p. 206
Black Codes, p. 179
Brown v. *Board of Education* (1954), p. 188
civil rights, p. 176
Civil Rights Act of 1964, p. 193
Civil Rights Cases (1883), p. 181
de facto discrimination, p. 194
de jure discrimination, p. 194

Equal Employment Opportunity Commission, p. 195
equal protection clause, p. 188
Fifteenth Amendment, p. 180
Fourteenth Amendment, p. 180
franchise, p. 178
grandfather clause, p. 182
Jim Crow laws, p. 181

Nineteenth Amendment, p. 186
Plessy v. *Ferguson* (1896), p. 182
Progressive Era, p. 183
strict scrutiny, p. 197
suffrage movement, p. 185
suspect classification, p. 197
Thirteenth Amendment, p. 179

SELECTED READINGS

Bacchi, Carol Lee. *The Politics of Affirmative Action: 'Women,' Equality and Category Politics.* Thousand Oaks, Calif.: Sage, 1996.

Bergmann, Barbara R. *In Defense of Affirmative Action.* New York: Basic Books, 1996.

Bowen, William G. and Derek C. Bok, *The Shape of the River.* Princeton: Princeton University Press, 1998.

Bullock, Charles III, and Charles Lamb, eds. *Implementation of Civil Rights Policy.* Pacific Grove, CA: Brooks/Cole, 1984.

Eastland, Terry. *Ending Affirmative Action: The Case for Colorblind Justice.* New York: Basic Books, 1997.

Edley, Christopher, Jr. *Not All Black and White: Affirmative Action, Race, and American Values.* New York: Hill and Wang, 1996.

Freeman, Jo. *The Politics of Women's Liberation.* New York: Longman, 1975.

Kluger, Richard. *Simple Justice.* New York: Vintage, 1975.

Knobel, Dale T. *'America for the Americans': The Nativist Movement in the United States.* Old Tappen, New Jersey: Twayne, 1996.

Mansbridge, Jane J. *Why We Lost the ERA.* Chicago: University of Chicago Press, 1986.

McClain, Paula D., and Joseph Stewart, Jr. *"Can We All Get Along?" Racial and Ethnic Minorities in American Politics,* 2nd ed. Boulder, CO: Westview Press, 1998.

McGlen, Nancy E., and Karen O'Connor. *Women, Politics and American Society* 2nd ed. Upper Saddle River, NJ: Prentice Hall, 1998.

Reed, Adolph, Jr., *Without Justice for All: The New Liberalism and our Retreat from Racial Equity.* Boulder, Colo.: Westview Press, 1999.

Rosales, Francisco A., and Arturo Rosales, eds. *Chicano! The History of the Mexican American Civil Rights Movement.* Houston, Texas: Arte Publico Press, 1996.

Verba, Sidney, and Gary R. Orren. *Equality in America: The View from the Top.* Cambridge, MA: Harvard University Press, 1985.

Williams, Juan. *Eyes on the Prize: America's Civil Rights Years, 1954–1965.* New York: Penguin, 1987.

NOTES

1. Michael Cooper, "Officers in Bronx Fire 41 Shots, and an Unarmed Man Is Killed," *New York Times,* February 5, 1999, A1.

2. Amy Wilentz, "New York: The Price of Safety in a Police State," *Los Angeles Times,* April 11, 1999, M1.

3. N. R. Kleinfield, "Veterans of 60's Protests Meet the Newly Outraged in a March," *New York Times,* April 16, 1999, B8.

4. Kleinfield, "Veterans of 60's Protests."

5. Lee, Jessica. Women Speak to House about unwarranted customs strip-searches. *USA Today.* May 21 1999. 10A.

6. Edward Walsh, "The Racial Issue Looming in the Rear-View Mirror, *Washington Post,* May 19, 1999, A3; and Ralph Siegel, "Turnpike Arrest Cases Explore Use of Racial Profiling Defenses," *The Record,* May 12, 1999, A3.

7. Judith Evans, "Suit Claims Race Bias at Fla. Hotel," *Washington Post,* May 21, 1999, A01.

8. Catherine Drinker Bowen, *Miracle at Philadelphia: The Story of the Constitutional Convention May to September 1787* (Boston: Little, Brown, 1986), 201.

9. 83 U.S. (16 Wall.) 36 (1873).

10. 83 U.S. (16 Wall.) 130 (1873).

11. 88 U.S. (21 Wall.) 162 (1875). See also Karen O'Connor, *Women's Organizations' Use of the Courts* (Lexington, MA: Lexington Books, 1980).

12. 109 U.S. 3 (1883).

13. Jack Greenburg, *Judicial Process and Social Change: Constitutional Litigation* (St. Paul, MN: West, 1976), 583–86.

14. 163 U.S. 537 (1896).

15. *Williams* v. *Mississippi.* 170 U.S. 213 (1898).

16. *Cummins* v. *Richmond County Board of Education.* 175 U.S. 528 (1899).

17. Juan Williams, *Eyes on the Prize: America's Civil Rights Years, 1954–1965* (New York: Penguin, 1987), 10.

18. 208 U.S. 412 (1908).

19. *Missouri* ex rel. *Gaines* v. *Canada,* 305 U.S. 337 (1938).

20. Richard Kluger, *Simple Justice* (New York: Vintage, 1975), 268.

21. *Sweatt* v. *Painter,* 339 U.S. 629 and *McLaurin* v. *Oklahoma,* 339 U.S. 637 (1950).

22. 347 U.S. 483 (1954).

23. But see Gerald Rosenberg, *Hollow Hope: Can Courts Bring About Social Change* (Chicago: University of Chicago Press, 1991).

24. Quoted in Williams, *Eyes on the Prize,* 10.

25. 349 U.S. 294 (1955).

26. Quoted in Williams, *Eyes on the Prize,* 37.

27. *Cooper* v. *Aaron,* 358 U.S. 1 (1958).

28. *Heart of Atlanta Motel* v. *United States,* 379 U.S. 241 (1964).

29. 402 U.S. 1 (1971).

30. *Missouri* v. *Jenkins,* 115 S. Ct. 2038 (1995).

31. *Griggs* v. *Duke Power Co.,* 401 U.S. 424 (1971).

32. Jo Freeman, *The Politics of Women's Liberation* (New York: David McKay, 1975), 57.

33. 368 U.S. 57 (1961).

34. Betty Friedan, *The Feminine Mystique* (New York: Dell, 1963).

35. 323 U.S. 214 (1944). This is the only case involving race-based distinctions applying the strict scrutiny standard where the Court has upheld the restrictive law.

36. 404 U.S. 71 (1971).

37. 429 U.S. 190 (1976).

38. *Rostker* v. *Goldberg,* 453 U.S. 57 (1981).

39. Joyce Gelb and Marian Lief Palley. *Women and Public Policies* (Charlottesville: University of Virginia Press, 1996).

40. Rennard Strickland, "Native Americans," in Kermit Hall, ed., *The Oxford Companion to the Supreme Court of the United States* (New York: Oxford University Press, 1992), 557.

41. Dee Brown, *Bury My Heart at Wounded Knee* (New York: Holt, Rinehart & Winston, 1971).

42. Strickland, "Native Americans," 579.

43. Hugh Dellios, "Rites by Law: Indians Seek Sacred Lands," *Chicago Tribune* (July 4, 1993): C1.

44. Ernesto B. Virgil, *The Crusade for Justice* (Madison: University of Wisconsin Press, 1999).

45. F. Chris Garcia, *Latinos and the Political System* (Notre Dame, IN: University of Notre Dame Press, 1988), 1.

46. *White* v. *Register,* 412 U.S. 755 (1973).

47. *San Antonio Independent School District* v. *Rodriguez.* 411 U.S. 1 (1973).

48. Diane Helene Miller, *Freedom to Differ: The Shaping of the Gay and Lesbian Struggle for Civil Rights.* (New York: New York University Press, 1998).

49. Sarah Brewer, David Kaib, and Karen O'Connor, "Sex and the Supreme Court: Gays, Lesbians, and Justice." *The Politics of Gay Rights,* Chicago: University of Chicago Press, 2000.

50. Evan Gerstmann, *The Constitutional Underclass: Gays, Lesbians, and the Failure of Class-Based Equal Protection* (Chicago: University of Chicago Press, 1999).

51. 478 U.S. 186 (1986).

52. *Romer* v. *Evans,* 116 S. Ct. 1620 (1996).

53. David Pfeiffer, "Overview of the Disability Movement: History, Legislative Record and Political Implications," *Policy Studies Journal* (Winter 1993): 724–742; and "Understanding Disability Policy," *Policy Studies Journal* (Spring 1996): 157–174.

54. Joan Biskupic, "Supreme Court Limits Meaning of Disability," *Washington Post,* June 23, 1999, A1.

55. "Poll: Whites, blacks differ on quality of race relations," June 17, 1997. CNN Interactive (http://cnn.com/US/9706/10/gallup.poll/index.html)

61. Frederick Douglass, *Frederick Douglass: Autobiography* (New York: Library of America, 1994), p. 28.

56. 438 U.S. 186 (1986).

57. *Johnson* v. *Santa Clara County,* 480 U.S. 616 (1987).

58. *Adarand Constructors Inc.* v. *Pena,* 115 S. Ct. 2097 (1995).

59. Cert. denied, *Texas* v. *Hopwood,* 116 S. Ct. 2581 (1996). See also Terrance Stutz, "UT Minority Enrollment Tested By Suit: Fate of Affirmative Action in Education Is at Issue," *Dallas Morning News* (October 14, 1995): 1A.

60. *Piscataway* v. *Taxman,* cert. dismissed 118 S.Ct. 595 (1997).

61. Frederick Douglass, *Frederick Douglass: Autobiography* (New York: Library of America, 1994), p. 28.

62. Politics USA, Issues '96 (www.RNC.org).

63. Democratic National Convention (www.DNCC96.org).

64. For interesting information about how college students have reacted to affirmative action restrictions, see Avis Alexandria Jones-DeWeever, "Affirmative Action in Higher Education: The Politics and Opinions of the NeXt Generation of American Voters," paper prepared for delivery at the 1999 annual meeting of the Midwest Political Science Association.

65. Michael Fletcher, "Civil Rights Groups File Suit over Calif. Admissions Policy, *The Washington Post,* February 3, 1999, A2.

(Photo courtesy: Terry Ashe/Liaison Agency)

Congress

- **The Roots of the Legislative Branch**
- **The Constitution and the Legislative Branch of Government**
- **The Members of Congress**
- **How Congress Is Organized**
- **The Lawmaking Function of Congress**
- **How Members Make Decisions**
- **Congress and the President**

*P*artisanship is alive and well in the U.S. Congress. Witness the political maneuverings that surrounded the ultimately unsuccessful attempts to enact gun control by Democrats in the 106th Congress. On April 21, 1999, two students dressed in long baggy black coats walked into their high school in Columbine, Colorado, unleashing a bombing and shooting spree that left fourteen students and one teacher dead and shocked the nation. It was the fifth episode since 1997 in which one or more students opened fire on other students in a public school.[1]

In the days after the Columbine massacre, Senate Majority Leader Trent Lott (R–Miss.) promised quick Senate action on a gun control measure. The Minority Leader, Thomas Daschle (D–S.D.), initially said more gun control is not the solution.[2] Disagreeing with his party leader, Representative Edward J. Markey (D–Mass.) "predicted the public, angered over 'the toxic cocktail of media violence and easy availability of guns,"' would be quick to demand that their elected representatives take some action on gun control.[3] Still, many wondered if Congress would bow to pressure from the powerful National Rifle Association (NRA), a 2.8-million-member group that spent over $3.4 million backing its preferred candidates in the 1998 congressional elections.[4] And the new House Speaker, J. Dennis Hastert (R–Ill.), as he expressed his condolences to the families of the dead and injured Columbine victims, called only for a National Conference on Youth and Culture, never mentioning possible legislation.

Less than a month later, the Republican-controlled Senate turned down a Democratic-sponsored bill to require background checks on all firearms sales at gun shows by a vote of 51 to 47.[5] It was a largely party-line vote, with 49 Republicans and 2 Democrats voting against the proposal. Republicans, however, underestimated the anger and concern of the American people over the gun control issue.

Within the week, in a "move that brought gun control forces their first big victory" since the Brady Bill five years earlier, with Vice President Al Gore, Jr., casting the tie-breaking vote, the Senate approved the measure requiring background checks on gun show purchases on a 51 to 50 vote.[6]

The Senate's schizophrenic action on the background check legislation mirrors many Americans' relationships with their representatives and their views of Congress.[7]

As each congressional representative pursues what appears to be his or her *individually* rational incentives to act on behalf of constituents, it can create centrifugal pressures that undermine Congress's *collective* capacity to get things done. Over the past three decades, changes both inside and outside Congress have enhanced the ability of congressional representatives to be somewhat more individualistic than in the past; this arguably has weakened the institution's collective capacities even more. Is it any wonder that, before the 1994 midterm elections, public confidence in Congress was at only eight percent? Although by February 1999, 41 percent of the public voiced approval about the way Congress was doing its job, in general, feelings about Congress as a whole are always much lower than the public's generally high level of support for individual representatives. Even one 1994 poll, for example, found that 59 percent of those polled believed that their own representatives deserved another term.[8] In 1999, that figure was 70 percent (see Figure 7.1 on page 223). Even more significant, the rate at which incumbents are reelected to the House continues to exceed 95 percent, despite the chamber's poor general standing with the public. Part of the public's strange split on these issues may stem from the dual roles that Congress plays—its members must combine and balance their roles as law and policy makers with their role as representatives selected to look after and serve the best interests of their constituents. Not surprisingly, this balancing act often results in role conflict. Moreover, recent studies by political scientists reveal many citizens hold Congress up to very high standards, which contributes to negative perceptions.[9] Increased media negativity doesn't help either.[10]

In this chapter we analyze the powers of Congress and the competing roles members of Congress play as they represent the interests of their constituents, make laws, and oversee the actions of the other two branches of government. We also see that, as these functions have changed throughout U.S. history, so has Congress itself.

- First, we will look at *the roots of the legislative branch* to better understand its place today.
- Second, we will examine what *the Constitution* has to say about Congress—the legislative branch of government. We also examine the *consequences of redistricting* on the House of Representatives and then look at the *constitutional powers* of Congress.
- Third, we will look at *the membership of Congress*, how members get elected, and how they spend their days.
- Fourth, we will describe *how Congress is organized*. We compare the two chambers and how their differences affect the course of legislation.
- Fifth, we will outline *how Congress makes laws*.
- Sixth, we will examine the various factors that influence *how members of Congress make decisions*.
- Seventh, we will discuss the ever-changing *relationship between Congress and the president*.

Web Exploration

To find out who your representative is and how he or she votes, see www.awlonline.com/oconnor.

THE ROOTS OF THE LEGISLATIVE BRANCH

As discussed in chapter 2, Congress's powers evolved from Americans' experiences in the colonies and under the Articles of Confederation. When the colonists came to the New World, their general approval of Britain's parliamentary system led them to adopt similar two-house legislative bodies in the individual colonies. One house was directly elected by the people; the other was a Crown-appointed council that worked under the authority of the colonial government.

The colonial assemblies were originally established as advisory bodies to the royal governors appointed by the king. Gradually, however, they assumed more power and authority in each colony, particularly over taxation and spending. The assemblies also legislated on religious issues and established quality standards for such colonial goods as flour, rice, tobacco, and rum. Before the American Revolution, colonists turned to their colonial legislatures (the only bodies elected directly by the "people") to represent and defend their interests against British infringement.

The first truly national legislature in the colonies, the First Continental Congress, met in Philadelphia in 1774 to develop a common colonial response to the Coercive Acts. All the colonies except Georgia sent a representative. Even though this Congress had no power to force compliance, it advised each colony to establish a militia and organized an economic boycott of British goods, among other things (see chapter 2).

By the time the Second Continental Congress met in Philadelphia in May 1775, fighting had broken out at Lexington and Concord. The Congress quickly helped the now-united colonies gear up for war, raise an army, and officially adopt the Declaration of Independence. During the next five years, the Congress directed the war effort and administered a central government. But it did so with little money or stability—because of the war, it had to move from city to city.

Although the Articles of Confederation were drafted and adopted by the Second Continental Congress in 1777, the states did not ratify them until 1781. Still, throughout the Revolutionary War, the Congress exercised the powers the Articles granted it: to declare war, raise an army, make treaties with foreign nations, and coin money. As described in chapter 2, however, the Congress had no independent sources of income; it had to depend on the states for money and supplies.

After the war the states began acting once again as if they were separate nations rather than parts of one nation, despite the national government that was created under the Articles of Confederation. The "national" government, moreover, was to serve the needs of the new nation. Discontent with the Articles and the government they created grew, and led eventually to the Constitutional Convention in Philadelphia in 1787.

THE CONSTITUTION AND THE LEGISLATIVE BRANCH OF GOVERNMENT

Article I of the Constitution created the legislative branch of government we know today. Any two-house legislature, such as the one created by the Framers, is called a **bicameral legislature.** All states except Nebraska, which has a one-house or *unicameral legislature,* follow this model. As discussed in chapter 2, the Great Compromise resulted in the creation of an upper house, the Senate, and a lower house, the House of Representatives. Each state is represented in the Senate by two senators, regardless of the state's population. The number of representatives each state sends to the House of Representatives, in contrast, is determined by that state's population.

The U.S. Constitution sets out the formal, or legal, requirements for membership in the House and Senate. House members must be at least twenty-five years of age; Senators, thirty. Members of the House must have resided in the United States for at least seven years; those elected to the Senate, nine. And representatives and senators must be legal residents of the states from which they are elected.

Members of each body were to be elected differently and would thus represent different interests and constituencies. Senators were to be elected to six-year terms by state legislatures, and one-third of them would be up for reelection every two years. Senators were to be tied to their state legislatures closely and were expected to represent those interests in the Senate. State legislators lost this influence with ratification of the Seventeenth Amendment in 1913, which provides for the direct election of senators by the voters.

In contrast to senators' six-year terms, members of the House of Representatives were to be elected to two-year terms by a vote of the eligible voters in each congressional district. It was expected that the House would be the more "democratic" branch of government because its members would be more responsible to the people (because they were directly elected by them) and more responsive to them (because they were up for reelection every two years).

Web Exploration

To see more about the legislative branch, see www.awlonline.com/oconnor.

bicameral legislature:

A legislature divided into two houses; the U.S. Congress and every state legislature are bicameral (except Nebraska, which is unicameral).

Apportionment and Redistricting

The U.S. Constitution requires that a census, which entails the counting of all Americans, be conducted every ten years. Until the first census could be taken, the Constitution fixed the number of representatives in the House at sixty-five. In 1790, then, one member represented 37,000 people. As the population of the new nation grew and states were added to the Union, the House became larger and larger. In 1910 it expanded to 435 members, and in 1929 its size was fixed at that number by statute.

Because the Constitution requires that representation in the House be based on state population, congressional districts must be redrawn by state legislatures to reflect population shifts, so that each member in Congress will represent approximately the same number of residents. This process of redrawing congressional districts to reflect increases or decreases in seats allotted to the states, as well as population shifts within a state, is called **redistricting**. The effects of redistricting are discussed in chapter 13.

Constitutional Powers of Congress

The Constitution specifically gives to Congress its most important power—the authority to make laws. (See Table 7.1: The Powers of Congress.) This lawmaking power is shared by both houses. For example, no **bill** (proposed law) can become law, without the consent of both houses. Examples of other constitutionally shared powers include the power to declare war, raise an army and navy, coin money, regulate commerce, establish the federal courts and their jurisdiction, establish rules of immigration and naturalization, and "make all Laws which shall be necessary and proper for carrying into Execution the foregoing Powers." As interpreted by the Supreme Court, the *necessary and proper clause*, when coupled with one or more of the specific powers enumerated in Article I, section 8, has allowed Congress to increase the scope of its

redistricting:

The redrawing of congressional districts to reflect increases or decreases in seats allotted to the states, as well as population shifts within a state.

bill:

A proposed law.

Table 7.1 The Powers of Congress

The Powers of Congress, found in Article I, section 8 of the Constitution, include the power to:

- Lay and collect taxes and duties
- Borrow money
- Regulate commerce with foreign nations and among the states
- Establish rules for naturalization (that is, the process of becoming a citizen) and bankruptcy
- Coin money, set its value, and fix the standard of weights and measures
- Punish counterfeiting
- Establish a post office and post roads
- Issue patents and copyrights
- Define and punish piracies, felonies on the high seas, and crimes against the Law of nations
- Create courts inferior to (that is, below) the Supreme Court
- Declare war
- Raise and support an army and navy and make rules for their governance
- Provide for a militia (reserving to the states the right to appoint militia officers and to train the militia under congressional rules)
- Exercise legislative Powers over the seat of government (the District of Columbia) and over places purchased to be federal facilities (forts, arsenals, dock-yards, and "other needful buildings")
- "Make all Laws which shall be necessary and proper for carrying into Execution the foregoing Powers, and all other Powers vested by this Constitution in the government of the United States" (Note: This "necessary and proper," or "elastic," clause has been expansively interpreted by the Supreme Court, as explained in chapter 2.)

authority, often at the expense of the states and into areas not necessarily envisioned by the Framers.

Congress alone is given formal lawmaking powers in the Constitution, but it is important to remember that presidents issue proclamations and executive orders with the force of law (see chapter 8), bureaucrats issue quasi-legislative rules (see chapter 9), and the Supreme Court renders opinions, as was the case with its redistricting decisions, which generate principles that also have the force of law (see chapter 10).

Reflecting the different constituencies and size of each house of Congress (as well as the Framers' intentions), Article I gives special, exclusive powers to each house in addition to their shared role in lawmaking. For example, as noted in Table 7.2, the Constitution specifies that all revenue bills must originate in the House of Representatives. Over the years, however, this mandate has been blurred, and it is not unusual to see budget bills being considered simultaneously in both houses, especially since each must approve all bills in the end, whether or not they involve revenues. In 1995, for example, when President Clinton submitted his budget deficit-reduction plan, both houses deliberated similar proposals simultaneously.

The House also has the power of **impeachment,** the authority to charge the president, vice president, or other "civil officers," including federal judges, with "Treason Bribery or other high Crimes and Misdemeanors." Only the Senate is authorized to conduct trials of impeachment, with a two-thirds vote being necessary before a federal official can be removed from office. (See The Impeachment Process, on p. 254.)

Until recently, only one president, Andrew Johnson, had been impeached by the House, but he was acquitted by the full Senate by a one-vote margin. Later, as we will discuss in greater detail in chapter 7, President Richard M. Nixon resigned from office in 1974 after the House Judiciary Committee voted to impeach him for his role in the Watergate scandal.

impeachment:
The power delegated to the House of Representatives in the Constitution to charge the president, vice president, or other "civil officers," including federal judges, with "Treason, Bribery, or other high Crimes and Misdemeanors." This is the first step in the constitutional process of removing such government officials from office.

Table 7.2 Key Differences Between the House and Senate

CONSTITUTIONAL DIFFERENCES

House	Senate
Initiates all revenue bills	Offers "advice and consent" on many major presidential appointments
Initiates impeachment procedures and passes articles of impeachment	Tries impeached officials
Two-year terms	Six-year terms (One-third up for reelection every two years)
435 members (apportioned by population)	100 members (two from each state)
	Approves treaties

DIFFERENCES IN OPERATION

House	Senate
More centralized, more formal: stronger leadership	Less centralized, less formal; weaker leadership
Rules Committee fairly powerful in controlling time and rules of debate (in conjunction with the Speaker)	No Rules Committee, limits on debate come through unanimous consent or cloture of filibuster
More impersonal	More personal
Power less evenly distributed	Power more evenly distributed
Members are highly specialized	Members are generalists
Emphasizes tax and revenue policy	Emphasizes foreign policy

CHANGES IN THE INSTITUTION

House	Senate
Power centralized in the Speaker's inner circle of advisors	Senate workload increasing and informality breaking down: filibusters more frequent
House procedures are becoming more efficient	Becoming more difficult to pass legislation
Turnover is relatively high	Turnover is moderate

■ Representative Henry Hyde (R–Ill.), chair of the House Judiciary Committee as it conducted impeachment hearings. Later, Hyde managed the case against President Clinton in the Senate. (Photo courtesy: Brad Markel/Gamma Liaison)

In October 1998 the House of Representatives again made history when a majority of its members voted to begin a broad impeachment inquiry against President Clinton. The House Judiciary Committee's chief investigative attorney used evidence submitted by the Independent Counsel Kenneth W. Starr to cite fifteen "events" that contained possible impeachable offenses. After a two-hour televised debate, lawmakers voted 258 to 176 to authorize the House Judiciary Committee to investigate "fully and completely" whether sufficient grounds exist to impeach the president. Only 31 Democrats joined in the resolution to investigate the president. Formal hearings began soon after the November 1998 elections.

The House and Senate share in the impeachment process, but the Senate has the sole authority to approve major presidential appointments, including federal judges, ambassadors, and Cabinet- and sub-Cabinet-level positions. The Senate, too, must approve by a two-thirds vote all treaties entered into by the president. Failure by the president to court the Senate can be costly. At the end of World War I, for example, President Woodrow Wilson worked long and hard to get other nations to accept the Treaty of Versailles, which contained the charter of the proposed League of Nations. He overestimated his support in the Senate, however, and that body refused to ratify the treaty, thereby dealing Wilson and his international stature a severe setback.

THE MEMBERS OF CONGRESS

Today, many members of Congress find the job exciting in spite of public criticism of the institution. But it wasn't always so. Until D.C. got air-conditioning and drained the swamps, Washington was a miserable town. Most representatives spent as little time as possible there, viewing the Congress, especially the House, as a stepping stone to other political positions. Thus, after spending a brief tour of duty in D.C., most representatives went home to run for local or state political office or were rewarded for their service by party bosses with a federal judgeship. It is only after World War I that House members, in particular, became what were termed "congressional careerists" who viewed their work in Washington as rewarding and long term.[11]

Table 7.3 A Day in the Life of a Member of Congress

TYPICAL MEMBER'S AT-HOME SCHEDULE[a]	TYPICAL MEMBER'S WASHINGTON SCHEDULE[b]
Monday, March 20	**Wednesday, April 10**

TYPICAL MEMBER'S AT-HOME SCHEDULE[a]

Monday, March 20

7:30 A.M.	Business group breakfast, 20 members of the business community leaders	(1 hour)
8:45 A.M.	Hoover Elementary School, 6th grade class assembly	(45 min)
9:45 A.M.	National Agriculture Day, speech, Holiday Inn South	(45 min)
10:45 A.M.	Supplemental Food Shelf, pass foodstuffs to needy families	(1 hour)
12:00 noon	Community College, student/faculty lunch, speech and Q & A	(45 min)
1:00 P.M.	Sunset Terrace Elementary School, assembly 4, 5, 6 graders, remarks/Q & A	(45 min)
(Travel Time: 1:45 P.M.–2:45 P.M.)		
2:45 P.M.	Plainview Day Care Facility, owner wishes to discuss changes in federal law	(1 hour)
4:00 P.M.	Town Hall Meeting, American Legion	(1 hour)
(Travel Time: 5:00 P.M.–5:45 P.M.)		
5:45 P.M.	PTA Meeting, speech, education issues before Congress (also citizen involvement with national associations)	(45 min)
6:30 P.M.	Annual Dinner, St. John's Lutheran Church Developmental Activity Center	(30 min)
7:15 P.M.	Association for Children for Enforcement of Support meeting discuss problems of enforcing child support payments	(45 min)
(Travel Time: 8:00 P.M.–8:30 P.M.)		
8:30 P.M.	Students Against Drunk Driving (SADD) meeting, speech, address, drinking age, drunk driving, uniform federal penalties	(45 min)
9:30 P.M.	State University class, discuss business issues before Congress	(1 hour)

TYPICAL MEMBER'S WASHINGTON SCHEDULE[b]

Wednesday, April 10

8:00 A.M.	Budget Study Group—Chairman Leon Panetta, Budget Committee, room 340 Cannon Building
8:45 A.M.	Mainstream Forum Meeting, room 2344 Rayburn Building
9:15 A.M.	Meeting with Consulting Engineers Council of N.C. from Raleigh about various issues of concern
9:45 A.M.	Meet with N.C. Soybean Assn, representatives re: agriculture appropriations projects
10:15 A.M.	WCHL radio interview (by phone)
10:30 A.M.	Tape weekly radio show—budget
11:00 A.M.	Meet with former student, now an author, about intellectual property issue
1:00 P.M.	Agriculture Subcommittee Hearing—Budget Overview and General Agriculture Outlook, room 2362 Rayburn Building
2:30 P.M.	Meeting with Chairman Bill Ford and southern Democrats re: HR-5, Striker Replacement Bill, possible amendments
3:15 P.M.	Meet with Close-Up students from district on steps on Capitol for photo and discussions
3:45 P.M.	Meet with Duke professor re: energy research programs
4:30 P.M.	Meet with constituent of Kurdish background re: situation in Iraq
5:30–7:00 P.M.	Reception—Sponsored by National Assn. of Home Builders, honoring new president Mark Tipton from Raleigh, H-328 Capitol
6:00–8:00 P.M.	Reception—Honoring retiring Rep. Bill Gray, Washington Court Hotel
6:00–8:00 P.M.	Reception—Sponsored by Firefighters Assn., room B-339 Rayburn Building
6:00–8:00 P.M.	Reception—American Financial Services Assn., Gold Room

[a]Craig Shultz, ed., *Setting Course. A Congressional Management Guide* (Washington, DC: The American University, 1994), 335.

[b]David E. Price. *The Congressional Experience: A View from the Hill* (Boulder, CO: Westview Press, 1992), 38.

Many members of Congress clearly relish their work, although there are indications that the high cost of living in Washington and maintaining two homes, political scandals, intense media scrutiny, the need to tackle hard issues, and a growth of partisan dissension is taking a toll on many members. Those no longer in the majority, in particular, often don't see their service in Congress as satisfying.

Members must attempt to appease two constituencies—party leaders, colleagues, and lobbyists in Washington, D.C., and constituents at home. As revealed in Table 7.3, members spend full days at home as well as in D.C. According to one study of House members in nonelection years, average representatives made thirty-five trips back home to their districts, and spent an average 138 days a year there.[12] Hedrick Smith, a Pulitzer Prize-winning reporter for the *New York Times,* has aptly described a member's days as a "kaleidoscopic jumble: breakfast with reporters, morning staff meetings, simultaneous committee hearings to juggle, back-to-back sessions with lobbyists and constituents, phone calls, briefings, constant buzzers interrupting office work to make quorum calls and votes on the run, afternoon speeches, evening meetings, receptions, fund-raisers,

casework:

The process of solving constituents' problems dealing with the bureaucracy.

all crammed into four days so they can race home for a weekend gauntlet of campaigning. It's a rat race."[13]

How do senators and representatives accomplish all that they must and also satisfy their constituents? They send newsletters to stay in touch, hold town meetings throughout their districts, and get important help from their staffs. **Casework,** although rarely indulged in by legislators themselves, is a major responsibility for selected staff members called caseworkers. Veterans who believe that they are getting the runaround at V.A. hospitals, retirees who experience delays in receiving Social Security checks, or entrepreneurs eager to start new businesses who need assistance from the Small Business Administration often seek help from their representative. Other citizens ask their legislators to intercede to overturn administrative decisions such as ones on eligibility for participation in a program or the receipt of benefits.

Increasingly, senators and representatives are placing most of their caseworkers back in their home district offices, where they are more accessible to constituents who can drop by and talk to a friendly face about their problems. In larger districts, caseworkers may "ride the circuit," taking the helping hand of the congressional office to county seats, crossroads, post offices, and mobile offices. The average House member has seventeen full-time staff members; the average size of a senator's office staff is forty-four, although this number varies with state population.[14]

Running for Office and Staying in Office

Despite the long hours, hard work, and sometimes even abuse, senators and representatives experience, thousands aspire to these jobs every year. Yet only 535 men and women actually serve in the U.S. Congress. Membership in one of the two major political parties is almost always a prerequisite for election, because election laws in various states often discriminate against independents (those without party affiliation) and minor-party candidates. And, as discussed in chapter 14, money is the mother's milk of politics—the ability to raise money is often key to any member's victory.

incumbency factor:

The fact that being in office helps a person stay in office because of a variety of benefits which go with the position.

The **incumbency factor** that helps members to stay in office once they are elected. Simply put, being in office helps you stay in office.[15] It's often very difficult for outsiders to win because they don't have the advantages (enumerated in Table 7.4) enjoyed by incumbents, including name recognition, access to media, and fund raising. As illus-

---

Table 7.4   The Advantages of Incumbency

- Name recognition gained through previous campaigns and repeated visits to the district to make appearances at various public events.
- Credit claiming for bringing federal money into the district in the form of grants and contracts.
- Positive evaluations from constituents earned by doing favors (casework) such as helping cut red tape and tracking down federal aid, and tasks handled by publicly supported professional staff members.
- Distribution of newsletters and other noncampaign materials free through the mails by using the "frank" (an envelope that contains the legislator's signature in place of a stamp).
- Access to media—after all, incumbents are news makers who provide reporters with tips and quotes.
- Greater ease in fund raising—their high reelection rates make them a good bet for people or groups willing to give campaign contributions in hopes of having access to powerful decision makers.
- Experience in running a campaign, putting together a campaign staff, making speeches, understanding constituent concerns, and connecting with people.
- Superior knowledge about a wide range of issues gained through work on committees, review of legislation, and previous campaigns.
- A record for supporting locally popular policy positions.

---

trated in Figure 7.1, which compares the way poll respondents feel about their own representatives to how they feel about the Congress as an institution, most Americans approve of their *own* members of Congress.

It is not surprising, then, that from 1980 to 1990, an average of 95 percent of the incumbents who sought reelection actually won their primary and general election races.[16] One study basically concluded that unless a member of Congress was involved in a serious scandal, his or her chances of defeat were minimal.[17] In 1998, the incumbency advantage reached new highs. Ninety-seven percent of the incumbents who ran won. However, voluntary retirements, regular district changes, and some defeats continue to make turnover in Congress substantial in spite of the benefits reaped by incumbents.

Term Limits

A **term-limits** movement began sweeping the nation in the late 1980s because of voter frustration with gridlock and ethics problems in Congress and in state legislatures. Citizens and citizens groups approved referenda limiting the elected terms not only of their state representatives, but also of members of Congress. Given the power of incumbency, proponents of term limits argued that election to Congress, in essence, equaled life tenure. The concept of term limits is a simple one that appeals to many who oppose the notion of career politicians.

Term limits aren't a new idea. In 1787 the Framers considered, but rejected, a section of the Virginia Plan, which called for members of the House to be restricted to one term. Still, many of the Framers believed in the regular rotation of offices among worthy citizens, and this was generally the practice in the early years of the republic.

Although the Contract with America called for congressional passage of federal term limits, in 1995 the U.S. Supreme Court ruled that state-imposed limitations on the terms of members of Congress was unconstitutional.[18] Thus any efforts to enact congressional term limits would necessitate a constitutional amendment—not an easy feat. In the 104th Congress, a term-limits amendment was brought to the floor for a vote. The proposal fell sixty votes short of the two-thirds vote needed to propose a constitutional amendment. The measure also failed in the Senate, where Republicans failed to muster enough votes to cut off a Democratic filibuster.

term limits:

Legislation designating that state or federal elected legislators can serve only a specified number of years.

 TRY IT!

To evaluate your own representative, see www.awlonline.com/oconnor.

Figure 7.1 Approval of Congress and District Representatives

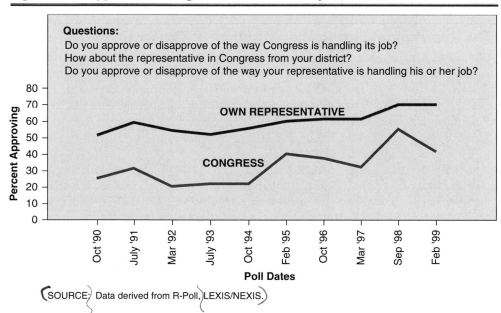

Questions:
Do you approve or disapprove of the way Congress is handling its job?
How about the representative in Congress from your district?
Do you approve or disapprove of the way your representative is handling his or her job?

OWN REPRESENTATIVE

CONGRESS

Percent Approving

Poll Dates: Oct '90, July '91, Mar '92, July '93, Oct '94, Feb '95, Oct '96, Mar '97, Sep '98, Feb '99

SOURCE: Data derived from R-Poll, LEXIS/NEXIS.

STILL THE BEST CONGRESSIONAL TERM-LIMITING DEVICE.

What Does Congress Look Like?

Congress is older, better educated, more white, more male, and richer than the rest of the United States. The Senate, in fact, is often called the "Millionaires' Club," and its members sport names like Rockefeller and DuPont.

As revealed in Figure 7.2, the 1992 elections, the first national elections after states redistricted congressional districts in response to the 1990 Census, saw a record number of women, African Americans, and other minorities elected to Congress. In 1992, for the first time ever, both senators elected from a single state—California—were women, democrats Dianne Feinstein and Barbara Boxer. With the 106th Congress, elected in 1998, the total number of women in Congress increased to sixty-seven; fifty-eight in the House and nine in the Senate. Two additional women serve as the elected (but nonvoting) delegates in the House. The first open lesbian (Tammy Baldwin, D–Wisc.) was also elected.

Similarly, record numbers of minorities also serve in the 106th Congress—thirty-nine African Americans, twenty Latinos, and eight Asian House members. Ben Nighthorse Campbell is the lone Native American in the U.S. Senate.

The Representational Role of Members of Congress

Questions of who should be represented and how that should happen are critical in a republic. Over the years, political theorists have enunciated various ideas about how constituents' interests are best represented in any legislative body. Does it make a difference if the members of Congress come from or are members of a particular group? Are they bound to vote the way their constituents expect them to vote even if they personally favor another policy? Your answer to these questions may depend on your view of the representative function of legislators.

British political philosopher Edmund Burke (1729–87), who also served in the British Parliament, believed that although he was elected from Bristol, it was his duty to represent the interests of the *entire* nation. He reasoned that elected officials were obliged to vote as they personally thought best. According to Burke, representatives should be **trustees** who listen to the opinions of their constituents and then can be trusted to use their own best judgment to make final decisions.

A second theory of representation holds that representatives are **delegates.** True delegates are representatives who vote the way their constituents would want them to,

trustee:

Role played by elected representatives who listen to constituents' opinions and then use their best judgment to make final decisions.

delegate:

Role played by elected representatives who vote the way their constituents would want them to, regardless of their own opinions.

Figure 7.2 Numbers of Women and Minorities in Congress

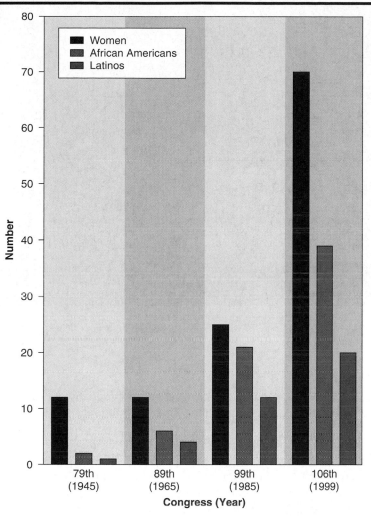

SOURCE: Harold W. Stanley and Richard G. Niemi, eds., *Vital Statistics on American Politics*, 1997-1998 (Washington D.C.: CQ Press, 1998), 197. Data updated by authors.

whether or not those opinions are the representative's. Delegates, therefore, must be ready and willing to vote against their conscience or policy preferences if they know how their constituents feel about a particular issue. Consider the case of Representative Sue Kelly (R–N.Y.). In 1994 she ran as an environmentalist, which set her apart in a crowded Republican primary. She then went on to win in the 1994 general election. When she voted against nine of the first ten environmental bills considered in the 104th Congress, many of her constituents were outraged. "Sue Kelly went down there to Washington and got caught up in all the excitement and forgot what her district wanted," said Robert F. Kennedy, Jr., a resident of her district and a lawyer for the Natural Resources Defense Council.[19] "But, she came home to a surprise—a lot of angry constituents who were saying they didn't send her there to gut our environmental laws."[20] Despite her campaign promises, as a freshman Republican Kelly felt obliged to vote for items in the Contract with America, including bills to sharply reduce protected wetlands and reduce the enforcement of several other environmental protection laws. In 1996 Kelly fended off a strong challenge and won her three-person race with 46 percent of the vote.

■ New members of the 106th Congress when it officially opened in January, 1999. (Photo courtesy: Brad Markel/Liaison Agency)

politico:

Role played by elected representatives who act as trustees or as delegates, depending on the issue.

Members of Congress often find themselves pulled in two directions that parallel the two worlds in which they often find themselves: the home district and the District of Columbia. Doing what's best for the district or what those back at home think is best for the district (or the nation, or the party leadership) pulls members in the direction of the delegate role; concern with national issues or looking at the bigger picture (or through the lens of party loyalty) moves the representative in the direction of the trustee role.

Not surprisingly, then, members of Congress and other legislative bodies generally don't fall neatly into either category. It is often unclear how constituents feel about a particular issue, or there may be conflicting opinions within a single constituency. With these difficulties in mind, a third theory of representation holds that **politicos** alternately don the hats of trustee or delegate, depending on the issue. On an issue of great concern to their constituents, representatives will most likely vote as delegates; on other issues, perhaps those that are less visible, representatives will act as trustees and use their own best judgment. Research by political scientists supports this view.[21]

How a representative views his or her role—as a trustee, delegate, or politico—may still not answer the question of whether or not it makes a difference if a representative or senator is male or female, African American or Latino or Caucasian, young or old, gay or straight. Burke's ideas about representation don't even begin to address more practical issues of representation. Can a man, for example, represent the interests of women as well as a woman? Can a rich woman represent the interests of the poor? The combinations are endless.

Female representatives historically have played prominent roles in efforts to expand women's rights. Studies reveal that female legislators are more likely than their male counterparts to sponsor legislation of concern to women.[22] One such study by the Center for the American Woman and Politics, for example, found that most women in the 103rd Congress "felt a special responsibility to represent women, particularly to represent their life experiences. . . . They undertook this additional responsibility while first, and foremost, like all members of Congress, representing their own districts."[23] Said Representative Nancy Johnson (R–N.J.). "We need to integrate the perspective of women into the policy-making process, just as we have now successfully integrated the perspective of environmental preservation, [and] the perspective of worker safety."[24]

■ Ben Nighthorse Campbell (R–Colo.). Campbell was elected as a Democrat in 1992 but changed political parties in 1995. (Photo courtesy: Karl Gehring/Liaison Agency)

Actions of the one Native American and one African American in the Senate underscore the representative function that can be played in Congress. Ben Nighthorse Campbell (R–Colo.), for example, is the only Native American who sits on the Senate Committee on Indian Affairs. Earlier, as a member of the House, he led the fight to change the name of Custer Battlefield Monument in Montana to Little Bighorn Battlefield National Monument to honor the Indians who died in battle. He also fought successfully for legislation to establish the National Museum of the American Indian within the Smithsonian Institution.

Before her defeat in 1998, the only African American in the Senate, Senator Carol Moseley Braun, also tried to sensitize her colleagues about issues of race. In 1993 Senator Jesse Helms (R–N.C.) sought to amend the national service bill in such a way to preserve the design patent held by the United Daughters of the Confederacy that included the Confederate flag. Most senators had no idea what they were voting on, and the amendment to the bill passed by a vote of 52 to 48. Then Senator Moseley-Braun took to the floor to express her outrage at Helms's support of a symbol of slavery: "On

■ The 1999 Congressional elections saw the first woman from Wisconsin, Tammy Baldwin, left, elected to the U.S. House of Representatives and the re-election of Senator Patty Murray of Washington, who held off a female Republican challenger. (Photos courtesy: left, Andy Manis/AP/Wide World Photos; right, John Froschauer/AP/Wide World Photos)

this issue there can be no consensus. It is an outrage. It is an insult."[25] Although Helms angrily insisted that slavery and race were not the issue, the Senate killed the Helms amendment by a vote of 75 to 25, as twenty-seven senators changed their votes. Said Senator Barbara Boxer (D–Calif.), "If there ever was proof of the value of diversity, we have it here today."[26]

HOW CONGRESS IS ORGANIZED

Every two years, a new Congress is seated. After ascertaining the formal qualifications of new members, the Congress organizes itself as it prepares for the business of the coming session. Among the first items on its agenda are the election of new leaders and the adoption of rules for conducting its business. As illustrated in Figure 7.3, each house has a hierarchical leadership structure.

Figure 7.3   Organizational Structure of the House of Representatives and the Senate during the 106th Congress (1999-2000)

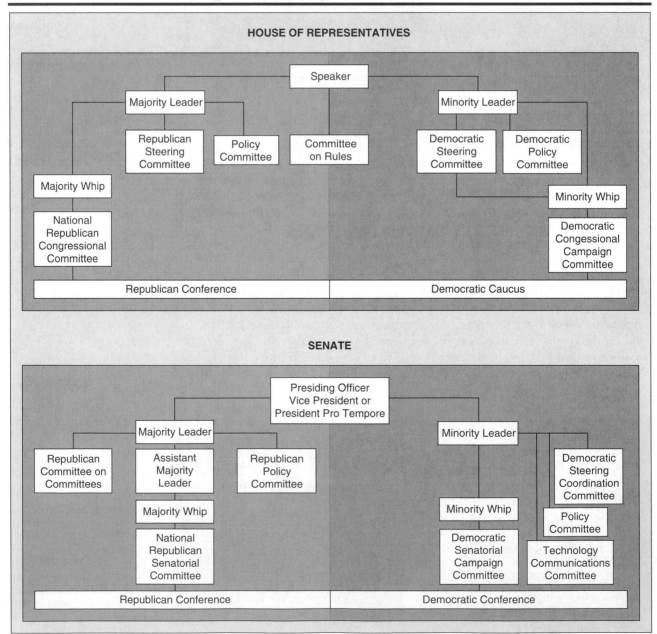

The House of Representatives

Even in the first Congress in 1789, the House of Representatives was almost three times larger than the Senate. It is not surprising then, that from the beginning the House has been more tightly organized, more elaborately structured, and governed by stricter rules. Traditionally, loyalty to the party leadership and voting along party lines have been more common in the House than in the Senate. House leaders also play a key role in moving the business of the House along. Historically, the Speaker of the House, the majority and minority leaders, and the majority and minority. House whips have made up the party leadership that runs Congress. This has now been expanded to include deputy minority whips of both parties.

The Speaker of the House.

The **Speaker of the House** is the only officer of the House of Representatives specifically mentioned in the Constitution. The office, the chamber's most powerful position, is modeled after a similar office in the British Parliament—the Speaker was the one who spoke to the king and conveyed the wishes of the House of Commons to the monarch.[27]

The Speaker is formally elected at the beginning of each new Congress by the entire House. Traditionally, the Speaker is a member of the **majority party,** the party in each house with the greatest number of members, as are all committee chairs. (The **minority party** is the major party with the second most members in either House.) While typically not the member with the longest service, the Speaker generally has served in the House for a long time and in other House leadership positions as sort of an apprenticeship. J. Dennis Hastert spent twelve years in the House, and his predecessor Newt Gingrich (R–Ga.) took sixteen years to work his way to the gavel and dais. Generally, a Speaker is reelected until he chooses to retire or his party ceases to be in the majority.

The Speaker presides over the House, oversees House business, is the official spokesperson for the House of Representatives, and is second in the line of presidential succession. Moreover, he is the House liaison with the president and generally has great political influence within the chamber. Through his parliamentary and political skills, he is expected to smooth the passage of party-backed legislation through the House.

The first "powerful" Speaker was Henry Clay. (See Roots of Government: Life on the Floor and in the Halls of Congress.) Serving in Congress at a time when turnover was high, he was elected to the position in 1810, his first term in office. He was Speaker of the House of Representatives for a total of six terms—longer than anyone else in the nineteenth century.

By the late 1800s, the House ceased to have a revolving door and average stays of members increased. With this professionalization of the House came professionalization in the Speakership. Between 1896 and 1910, a series of Speakers initiated changes that brought more power to the Speaker's office. Filibusters could be broken, and Speakers largely took control of committee assignments and appointing committee chairs. Institutional and personal rule reached its height during the tenure of Speaker Joseph Cannon (1903–10).

Negative reaction to those strong speakers eventually led to a revolt in 1910 and 1911 in the House and to a reduction of the formal powers of the Speaker. As a consequence, many Speakers between Cannon and Gingrich often relied on more informal powers that came from their personal ability to persuade.

Newt Gingrich, the first Republican Speaker in forty years, convinced fellow Republicans to return important formal powers to the Speaker. In return for a rule preventing Speakers from serving for more than eight years, the Speaker was given unprecedented authority, including the power to refer bills to committee, ending the practice of joint referral of bills to more than one committee, where they might fare better. These formal changes, along with his personal leadership skills, allowed Gingrich to exercise greater control over the House and its agenda than any other Speaker since the days of Joe Cannon.

■ Representative Barney Frank (D–Mass.) has been in the rare position of having fun while being in the minority party. Says Frank, "I'm a counterpuncher, happiest fighting on the defensive. Besides, I really dislike what the Republicans are doing. I think they are bad for the country and for vulnerable people. I feel, 'Boy, this is a moral opportunity—you've got to fight this.' Also, I'm used to being in a minority. Hey, I'm a left-handed gay Jew. I've never felt, automatically, a member of any majority. So, I started swinging from the opening bell of this Congress." (Photo courtesy: Corbis/AFP/Luke Frazza)

Speaker of the House:

The only officer of the House of Representatives specifically mentioned in the Constitution; elected at the beginning of each new Congress by the entire House; traditionally a member of the majority party.

majority party:

The political party in each house of Congress with the most members.

minority party:

Party with the second most members in either house of Congress.

Web Exploration

For more on the Speaker and his activities, see
www.awlonline.com/oconnor.

■ House Speaker Newt Gingrich stunned the nation when he announced that he would not seek reelection as Speaker. The architect of the Republican Revolution, Gingrich's brash methods and combative style never resonated well with much of the American public. (Photo courtesy: Dennis Brack/Black Star)

majority leader:

The elected leader of the party controlling the most seats in the U.S. House of Representatives or the Senate; is second in authority to the Speaker of the House and in the Senate is regarded as its most powerful member.

minority leader:

The elected leader of the party with the second highest number of elected representatives in either the House or the Senate.

Web Exploration

To get up-to-date data on House leaders, see
www.awlonline.com/oconnor.

In time, Gingrich's highly visible role as a revolutionary transformed him into a negative symbol outside the Beltway as his public popularity plunged. Exit polls conducted on election day 1996 revealed that 60 percent had an unfavorable opinion of the Speaker, although that dislike did not appear to translate into votes against incumbent House Republicans. But, in 1998, Republicans were stung when they failed to win more seats in the House and Senate. Gingrich's general unpopularity with large segments of the public simply worked to reinforce Republican's discontent with Gingrich. The 105th Republican Congress had few legislative successes; members were forced to accept a budget advanced by the White House, and Republicans running for office in 1998 lacked the coherent theme that had been so successful for them in 1994. These were but two of the myriad reasons that prompted several members to announce that they would run against the Speaker. And Gingrich, who could read the writing on the wall, opted to resign as Speaker (later he resigned altogether from the House) rather than face the prospect that he might not be reelected to the position that he so long had coveted.

Representative Bob Livingston (R–La.) quickly emerged as Gingrich's successor. But amidst the Clinton impeachment fervor, news of a long-time Livingston extramarital affair broke and Livingston stunningly announced that he would give up his expected speakership and resign from the House altogether. Scandal-weary Republicans then turned to someone largely unknown to the public: a well-liked and respected one-time high school coach and social studies teacher, J. Dennis Hastert.

Since coming into his "accidental Speakership," Hastert has shown himself to be a "pragmatic and cautious politician" as he tries to deal with his "whisker thin [ten-vote] majority."[28]

Other House Leaders.   After the Speaker, the next most powerful people in the House are the majority and minority leaders, who are elected in their individual party caucuses. The **majority leader** is the second most important person in the House; his counterpart on the other side of the aisle (the House is organized so that if you are standing on the podium, Democrats sit on the right side and Republicans on the left side of the center aisle) is the **minority leader.** Both work closely with the Speaker, and the majority leader helps the Speaker schedule proposed legislation for debate on the House floor.

■ House Minority Leader Richard Gephardt applauds the new speaker, Denis Hasert, as he talks over the House. (Photo courtesy: Robert Trippett/SIPA Press)

ROOTS OF GOVERNMENT

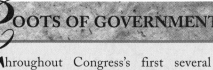

Life on the Floor and in the Halls of Congress

Throughout Congress's first several decades, partisan, sectional, and state tensions of the day often found their way onto the floors of the U.S. House and Senate. Many members were armed, and during one House debate thirty members showed their weapons. In 1826, for example, Senator John Randolph of Virginia insulted Henry Clay from the floor of the Senate, referring to Clay as "this being, so brilliant yet so corrupt, which, like a rotten mackerel by moonlight, shined and stunk." Clay immediately challenged Randolph to a duel on the Virginia side of the Potomac River. Both missed, although Randolph's coat fell victim to a bullet hole. Reacting to public opinion, however, in 1839 Congress passed a law prohibiting dueling in the District of Columbia.

Nevertheless, dueling continued. A debate in 1851 between representatives from Alabama and North Carolina ended in a duel, but no one was hurt. In 1856 Representative Preston Brooks of South Carolina, defending the honor of his region and family, assaulted Senator Charles Sumner of Massachusetts on the floor of the Senate. Sumner was disabled and unable to resume his seat in Congress for several years. Guns and knives were abundantly evident on the floor of both House and Senate, along with a wide variety of alcoholic beverages.

Today the House and the Senate are usually much more quiet. In 1984, however, a group of newly elected Republican representatives began taking over the House floor every day after the end of normal hours to berate their Democratic colleagues. The chamber was usually empty but, like all other action on the floor, these speeches were broadcast live on C-SPAN and often used by the members for distribution to local television stations back home. During a particularly strong attack on several Democrats' views on

Central America, Representative Newt Gingrich paused suggestively mid-speech, as though waiting for an objection or daring the Democrats to respond. No other House member was on the floor at the time, but since C-SPAN cameras at that time focused only on the speaker, viewers were unaware of that fact.

Democratic House Speaker Thomas P. O'Neill angrily reacted by ordering C-SPAN cameras to span the empty chamber to expose Gingrich's and other Republicans' tactics, but what Republicans labeled "CAMSCAM" ignited a firestorm on the floor. Incensed by remarks made by Gingrich, O'Neill dropped his gavel, left his spot on the dais, and took to the floor, roaring at Gingrich, "You challenged their [House Democrats'] patriotism, and it is the lowest thing that I have ever seen in my thirty-two years in Congress!" Trent Lott (R–Miss.) then demanded that the Speaker be "taken down," the House term to call someone to order for violating House rules prohibiting personal attacks. The House Parliamentarian looked in the dictionary to see if the word "lowest" was a slur. As a hush fell on the House, the presiding officer told O'Neill that he had violated House rules. Bristled O'Neill, "I was expressing my views very mildly because I think much worse than I said."

O'Neill's penalty? The rarely invoked enforced silence for the remainder of the day's debate. So uncomfortable with that action was the House minority leader that he asked Lott to make a motion exempting O'Neill from the penalty, to which Lott agreed. No other House Speaker has ever been so reprimanded.[a]

[a]Alexander Stanley, "Tip Topped: O'Neill Tangles with Some Republican Turks over Camera Angles," *Nation* (May 28, 1984): 36.

The Speaker and majority and minority leaders are assisted in their leadership efforts by the majority and minority **whips,** who are elected by party members in caucuses. The concept of whips originated in the British House of Commons, where they were named after the "whipper in," the rider who keeps the hounds together in a fox hunt. Party whips—who were first designated in the House in 1899 and in the Senate in 1913—do, as their name suggests, try to "whip" fellow Democrats or Republicans into line on partisan issues. They try to maintain close contact with all members on important votes,

whip:

One of several representatives who keep close contact with all members and take "nose counts" on key votes, prepare summaries of bills, and in general act as communications links within the party.

prepare summaries of content and implications of bills, get "nose counts" during debates and votes, and in general get members to toe the party line. Whips and their deputy whips also serve as communications links, distributing word of the party line from leaders to rank-in-file members and alerting leaders to concerns in the ranks. Whips can be extraordinarily effective. In 1998, for example, when President Clinton returned home from his trip to the Middle East amidst calls for his impeachment, he was stunned to learn that moderate Republicans that he had counted on to vote against his impeachment were "dropping like flies." The reason? Powerful House Whip Tom DeLay (R–Tex.) threatened Republicans that they would be denied coveted committee assignments and would even face Republican challengers in the next primary season unless they voted the party line.[29]

The Senate

The Constitution specifies that the presiding officer of the Senate is the Vice President of the United States. Because he is not a member of the Senate, he votes only in the case of a tie. Vice President Al Gore, Jr., for example, cast the tie-breaking vote in the Senate on the Budget Deficit Reduction bill in 1993.

The official chair of the Senate is the president pro tempore, who is selected by the majority party and presides over the Senate in the absence of the vice president. The position of president pro tempore is today primarily an honorific office that generally goes to the most senior senator of the majority party. Once elected, the pro tem, as he is called, stays in that office until there is a change in the majority party in the Senate. Since presiding over the Senate can be a rather perfunctory duty, neither the vice president nor the president pro tempore performs the task often. Instead, the duty of actually presiding over the Senate rotates among junior members of the chamber, allowing more senior members to attend more important meetings unless a key vote is being debated.

The true leader of the Senate is the majority leader, elected to the position by the majority party. Because the Senate is a smaller and more collegial body, operating without many of the more formal House rules concerning debate, the majority leader is not nearly as powerful as the Speaker of the House, a more overtly partisan body that requires more control by the Speaker. The majority and minority whips round out the leadership positions in the Senate and perform functions similar to those of their House counterparts. But leading and whipping in the Senate can be quite a challenge. Senate rules have always given tremendous power to individual senators; in most cases senators can offer any kind of amendments to legislation on the floor, and an individual senator can bring all work on the floor to a halt indefinitely through a filibuster unless two-thirds of the senators vote to cut him or her off.[30]

Because of the Senate's smaller size (see Figure 7.4), organization and formal rules have never played the same role in the Senate as they do in the House. Through the 1960s it was a "Gentlemen's Club" whose folkways—unwritten rules of behavior—governed its operation. One such folkway, for example, stipulated that political disagreements not become personal criticisms. A senator who disliked another referred to that senator as "the able, learned, and distinguished senator." A member who really couldn't stand another called that senator "my very able, learned, and distinguished colleague."

In the 1960s and 1970s, senators became more and more active on and off the Senate floor in a variety of issues and extended debates that often occurred on the floor—without the rigid rules of courtesy that had once been the hallmark of the body. These changes weren't accompanied by giving additional powers to the Senate majority leader, who now often has difficulty controlling "the more active, assertive, and consequently less predictable membership" of the Senate.[31] Thus, while the majority leader sets the agenda, there's often not much he can formally do to control the other members of the Senate.

■ Vermont Representative Bernie Sanders (I–Vt.) in a way falls into the third-party category; he is actually a socialist. Said Sanders of his election, "What Vermonters wanted is somebody to go down there and stand up and fight for ordinary people, rather than as the vast majority of members of Congress do—protect the interests of the wealthy and the powerful." (Photo courtesy: Glen Russell/SIPA Press)

Figure 7.4 Floor Plan of The Capitol Building

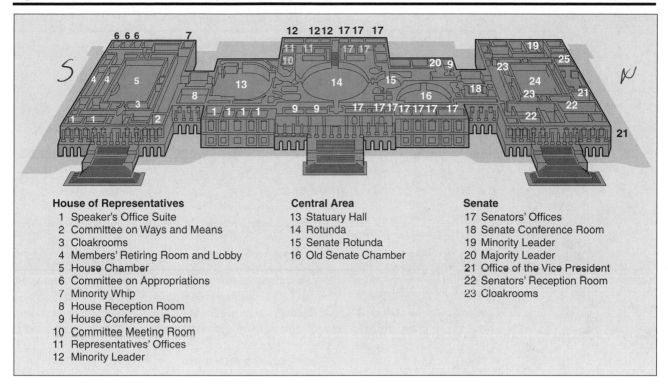

House of Representatives
1 Speaker's Office Suite
2 Committee on Ways and Means
3 Cloakrooms
4 Members' Retiring Room and Lobby
5 House Chamber
6 Committee on Appropriations
7 Minority Whip
8 House Reception Room
9 House Conference Room
10 Committee Meeting Room
11 Representatives' Offices
12 Minority Leader

Central Area
13 Statuary Hall
14 Rotunda
15 Senate Rotunda
16 Old Senate Chamber

Senate
17 Senators' Offices
18 Senate Conference Room
19 Minority Leader
20 Majority Leader
21 Office of the Vice President
22 Senators' Reception Room
23 Cloakrooms

The Role of Political Parties in Organizing Congress

When the first Congress met in 1789 in the nation's temporary capital in New York City, it consisted of only twenty-two senators and fewer than sixty representatives. Those men faced the enormous task of creating much of the machinery of government as well as that of drafting a bill of rights, for which the Anti-Federalists had argued so vehemently. During their debates, the political differences that divided Americans during the early years of the Union were renewed. For example, when Alexander Hamilton, the first Secretary of the Treasury and a staunch Federalist, proposed to fund the national debt and create a national bank, he aroused the ire of those who feared vesting the national government with too much power. This conflict led Hamilton's opponents to create the Democratic–Republican Party to counter the Federalists, creating a two-party system in Congress. Control of the political parties quickly gave Congress far more powers. The Democratic–Republican **party caucus** (the name for a formal gathering of all party members in the House) nominated Thomas Jefferson (1804), James Madison (1808 and 1812), and James Monroe (1816) for president, all of whom were elected.

party caucus:

A formal gathering of all party members.

The organization of both houses of Congress is closely tied to political parties and their strength in each House. For the party breakdowns in the 106th congress, see Figure 7.5. Parties play a key role in the committee system, an organizational feature of Congress that facilitates its lawmaking and oversight functions. The committees, controlled by the majority party in each House of Congress, often set the congressional agendas, although under Newt Gingrich's Speakership, this power eroded substantially in the House of Representatives as the Speaker's power was enhanced.[32]

At the beginning of each new Congress—the 106th Congress sits in two sessions, one in 1999 and one in 2000—the members of each party gather in its party caucus

Figure 7.5   Party Strength in the 106th Congress

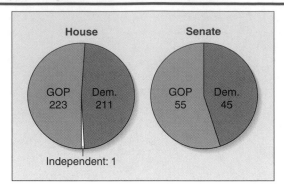

SOURCE: "Final Congressional Results", *Washington Post*, November 5, 1998, 1A.

or conference. Historically, these caucuses have enjoyed varied powers, but today the party caucuses—called "caucus" by House Democrats and "conference" by House and Senate Republicans and Senate Democrats—have several roles, including nominating or electing party officers, reviewing committee assignments, discussing party policy, imposing party discipline, setting party themes, and coordinating media, including talk radio. Conference and caucus chairs are recognized party leaders who work with others who are part of the House or Senate leadership.[33]

Each caucus or conference has specialized committees that fulfill certain tasks. House Republicans, for example, have a Committee on Committees that makes committee assignments. The Democrats' Steering Committee performs this function. Each party also has a Congressional Campaign Committee to assist members in their reelection bids.

The Committee System

The saying "Congress in session is Congress on exhibition, whilst Congress in its committee rooms is Congress at work" may not be as true today as it was when Woodrow Wilson wrote it in 1885.[34] Still, "The work that takes place in the committee and subcommittee rooms of Capitol Hill is critical to the productivity and effectiveness of Congress."[35] **Standing committees** are the first and last places that most bills go. It is usually committee members who play key roles in floor debate in the full House or Senate about the merits of the proposed bill. When different versions of a bill are passed in the House and Senate, a **conference committee** with members of both houses meets to iron out the differences.

Committees are especially important in the House of Representatives because its size makes organization and specialization key, as noted in Table 7.5. The establishment of subcommittees allows for even greater specialization.

An institutionalized committee system was created in 1816, and more and more committees have been added over time. So many committees resulted in duplication of duties and jurisdictional battles that the legislative process suffered. Changes were made to the committee system in the 103rd Congress. The growth of committees over the years greatly concerned House Republicans. Thus, when Republicans took control in 1995, they immediately targeted several committees and subcommittees (and the staffs of each of those committees) for cutting.

Types of Committees.   There are four types of congressional committees: (1) standing; (2) joint; (3) conference; and (4) ad hoc, special, or select.[36]

1. *Standing committees*, so called because they continue from one Congress to the next, are the committees to which proposed bills are referred for consideration. Fewer than

standing committee:

Committee to which proposed bills are referred.

conference committee:

Joint committee created to iron out differences between Senate and House versions of a specific piece of legislation.

Web Exploration

To get information on specific committees, go to
www.awlonline.com/oconnor.

10 percent of the more than 8,000 measures sent to committees are ever reported out. Standing committees also conduct investigations, such as the Senate Banking Committee's investigation of Whitewater. These are permanent committees.

2. *Joint committees* include members from both houses of Congress who conduct investigations or special studies. They are set up to expedite business between the houses and to help focus public attention on major matters, such as the economy, taxation, or scandals. A joint committee, for example, investigated the Iran-Contra scandal.

3. *Conference committees* are a special kind of joint committee that reconciles differences in bills passed by the House and Senate. The conference committee is made up of members from the House and Senate committees that originally considered the bill.

4. *Ad hoc, special,* or *select committees* are temporary committees appointed for specific purposes, generally to conduct special investigations or studies and to report back to the chamber that established them.

The House and Senate standing committees listed in Table 7.5 were created by statute. In the 106th Congress, the House had nineteen standing committees, each with an average of about thirty-one members. Together, they had a total of eighty-six subcommittees that collectively acted as the eyes, ears, and hands of the House. They considered issues roughly parallel to those of the departments represented in the president's

Table 7.5 Committees of the 106th Congress (with a Subcommittee Example)

STANDING COMMITTEES

House	Senate
Agriculture	Agriculture, Nutrition, and Forestry
Appropriations	Appropriations
Banking and Financial Services	Armed Services
Budget	Banking, Housing, and Urban Affairs
Commerce	Budget
Educational and the Workforce	Commerce, Science, and Transportation
Government Reform and Oversight	Energy and Natural Resources
House Oversight	Environment and Public Works
International Relations	Finance
Judiciary	Foreign Relations
National Security	Governmental Affairs
Resources	Indian Affairs
Rules	Judiciary *Judiciary Subcommittees:*
Science	Administrative Oversight and the Courts
Small Business	Antitrust, Business Rights, and Competition
Standards of Official Conduct (Ethics)	Constitution, Federalism, and Property Rights
Transportation and Infrastructure	Immigration
Veterans Affairs	Technology, Terrorism, and Government Information
Ways and Means	Youth Violence
	Labor and Human Resources
	Rules and Administration
	Small Business
	Veterans Affairs

SELECT AND SPECIAL COMMITTEES

House	Senate	JOINT COMMITTEES
Select Intelligence	Special Aging	Joint Committee on the Library
	Select Ethics	Joint Committee on Printing
	Select Intelligence	Joint Committee on Taxation
		Joint Economic Committee

Cabinet. For example, there were committees on agriculture, education, the judiciary, veterans affairs, transportation, and commerce.

Although most committees in one house parallel those in the other, the House Rules Committee, for which there is no counterpart in the Senate, plays a key role in the law-making process. Indicative of the importance of Rules, majority party members are appointed directly by the Speaker. This committee reviews most bills after they come from a committee and before they go to the full chamber for consideration. Perform-ing a "traffic cop" function, the House Rules Committee gives each bill what is called a *rule,* which contains the date the bill will come up for debate and the time that will be allotted for discussion, and often specifies what kinds of amendments can be offered. Bills considered under a *closed rule* cannot be amended.

Standing committees have considerable power. They can kill bills, amend them rad-ically, or hurry them through the process. In the words of Woodrow Wilson, once a bill is referred to a committee, it "crosses a parliamentary bridge of sighs to dim dungeons of silence from whence it never will return." Thus a committee reports out to the full House or Senate only a small fraction of the bills assigned to it. Bills can be "forced" out of a House committee by a **discharge petition** signed by a majority (218) of the House membership, but legislators are reluctant to take this drastic measure.

Until the 104th Congress, a House rule kept the names of those signing discharge petitions secret. In late 1993 the system was targeted by House Republicans who charged that the secrecy surrounding discharge petitions allowed members to claim that they supported legislation, yet assured that constituents could not learn whether a mem-ber indeed had tried to force a stalled bill out of committee. Under a new House rule, adopted in 1995, the clerk is required to publish the names of those who sign a dis-charge petition each week in the *Congressional Record* as well as to make that informa-tion available to the public electronically.

In the 106th Congress, the Senate had sixteen standing committees that ranged in size from twelve to twenty-eight members. It also had sixty-eight subcommittees, which allowed all majority party senators to chair one. For example, the Senate Judiciary Com-mittee had six subcommittees, as illustrated in Table 7.5.

In contrast to the House, whose members hold few committee assignments (an aver-age of 1.8 standing and three subcommittees), senators are spread more thinly, with each serving on an average of three to four committees and seven subcommittees. Whereas the committee system allows House members to become policy or issue spe-cialists, Senate members are often generalists. In the 106th Congress, Kay Bailey Hutchison (R–Tex.), for example, serves on four committees—Appropriations, Com-merce, Science, and Transportation, Environment and Public Works, and Rules and Administration. She also serves on thirteen subcommittees (Rules has no subcommit-tees) and chairs two of those subcommittees.

Senate committees enjoy the same power over framing legislation as do House com-mittees, but the Senate, being an institution more open to individual input than the House, gives less deference to the work done in committees. In the Senate, legislation is more likely to be rewritten on the floor, where all senators can participate and add amendments at any time.

Committee Membership.   Many newly elected members of Congress come into the body with their sights set on certain committee assignments. Others are more flex-ible. Many legislators seeking committee assignments inform their party's selection committee of their preferences. They often request assignments based on their own interests or expertise or on a particular committee's ability to help their prospects for reelection. Political scientist Kenneth Shepsle has noted that committee assignments are to members what stocks are to investors—they seek to acquire those that will add to the value of their portfolios.[37]

Representatives often seek committee assignments that have access to what is known as the **pork barrel.** Historically, pork barrel legislation has allowed representatives to

discharge petition:

Petition that gives a majority of the House of Representatives the author-ity to bring an issue to the floor in the face of committee inaction.

pork barrel:

Legislation that allows representatives to "bring home the bacon" to their districts in the form of public works programs, military bases, or other programs designed to benefit their districts directly.

"bring home the bacon" to their districts in the form of public works programs, military bases, or other programs designed to benefit districts directly. In the past a seat on the National Security Committee, for example, would allow a member to bring lucrative defense contracts back to his or her district, or discourage base closings within his or her district or state. The 1999 "emergency relief" bill for Kosovo well illustrates the pervasiveness of pork. The Senate version of that bill had something for everyone: In it was a $1-billion request for aid for ailing steel companies in Senator Byrd's West Virginia (Byrd is known as the "King of Pork."), $500 million in loans for faltering oil and gas interests, and a provision to prevent the Mississippi sturgeon in the Senate Majority Leader's home state, Mississippi, from being listed as an endangered species.[38]

Legislators who bring this kind of pork barrel back to their districts are hard to beat at the polls. But, ironically, these programs are the ones that attract much of the public criticism directed at the federal government in general and Congress in particular. Thus it is somewhat paradoxical that pork barrel improves a member's chances for reelection or for election to higher office. In 1984 Jesse Helms (R–N.C.), for example, turned down the chairmanship of the Senate Committee on Foreign Relations to stay on the less prestigious Committee on Agriculture, Nutrition, and Forestry, where he could better ensure continued support for the tobacco industry so vital to his home state's economy.

Pork isn't the only motivator for those seeking lush committee assignments. Some committees, such as Commerce, facilitate reelection by giving members influence over decisions that affect large campaign contributors. Other committees, such as Economic and Educational Opportunities or Judiciary, attract members eager to work on the policy responsibilities assigned to the committee even if the appointment does them little good at the ballot box. A third motivator for certain committee assignments is the desire to have power and influence within the chamber. The Appropriations and Budget Committees provide that kind of reward for some members.

In both the House and the Senate, committee membership generally reflects the party distribution within that chamber. For example, at the outset of the 106th Congress, Republicans held 52 percent of the House seats and claimed about that same share of the seats on several committees, including International Relations, Commerce, and Education and Workforce. On committees more critical to the operation of the House or to setting national policy, the majority often takes a disproportionate share of the slots. Since the Rules Committee regulates access to the floor for legislation approved by other standing committees, control by the majority party is essential for it to manage the flow of legislation. For this reason, no matter how narrow the majority party's margin in the chamber, it makes up at least two-thirds of Rules's membership.

Due to the smaller size of Senate committees, the majority party has a narrow margin on its committees. For example, in the 106th Congress, if one Republican joined a united Democratic contingent, then the Republicans would be unable to report legislation out of all but three committees. And, unlike the House, no Senate committees have a disproportionate number of majority party members.

Committee Chairs.   Before recent changes giving the Speaker more power, committee chairs long enjoyed tremendous power and prestige. Even today's chairs may choose not to schedule hearings on a bill to kill it. Chairs also carry with them the power to draft legislation, manage a million-plus dollar staff budget, and "hear pleas from lobbyists, Cabinet secretaries and even presidents who need something only a committee can provide."[39] Chairs may also convene meetings when opponents are absent, or they may adjourn meetings when things are going badly. Personal skill, influence, and expertise are a chair's best allies.

Historically, committee chairs have generally been the majority party member with the longest continuous service on the committee. In 1995 Speaker Gingrich ignored the seniority system and selected several committee chairs whom he trusted to move his reforms through the House.

In 1995 Republicans dramatically limited the long-term power of committee chairs. New rules prevent chairs from serving more than six years—three consecutive Congresses—or heading their own subcommittees. In return, committee chairs were, however, given some important powers. They are authorized to select all subcommittee chairs, call meetings, strategize, and recommend majority members to sit on conference committees. As the specter of the new term limits rules loom, many upset committee chairs plan to use their seniority to reclaim important posts on other committees. The House Armed Services Committee provides a good example. Chaired by Floyd Spence (R–S.C.), the next member in line to succeed him on the committee was Duncan Hunter (R–Calif.). However, Bob Stump (R–Ariz.), who was term-limited as chair of the Veterans Affairs Committee, traded up to the more prestigious committee, which upset Hunter, who was second to Spence on Armed Services, and had never been a committee chair. Thus, he had hoped to succeed Spence.[40]

THE LAWMAKING FUNCTION OF CONGRESS

The organization of Congress allows it to fulfill its constitutional responsibilities, chief among which is its lawmaking function. It is through this power that Congress affects the day-to-day lives of all Americans as well as sets policy for the future. Proposals for legislation—be they about education, V-chips, crime, or foreign aid—can come from the president, executive agencies, committee staffs, interest groups, or even private individuals. Only members of the House or Senate, however, can formally submit a bill for congressional consideration. Once a bill is proposed, it usually reaches a dead end. Of the approximately 9,000 bills introduced during the 105th Congress, fewer than 5 percent to 10 percent are enacted, or made into law. (See Highlight 7.1 "What's in a Name?")

It is probably useful to think of Congress as a system of multiple vetoes, which was what the Framers desired. They wanted to disperse power; and as Congress has evolved, it has come closer and closer to the Framers' intentions. As a bill goes through Congress, a dispersion of power occurs as roadblocks to passage must be surmounted at numerous steps in the process. In addition to realistic roadblocks, caution signs and other opportunities for delay abound. A member who sponsors a bill must get through *every* obstacle; in contrast, successful opposition means "winning" at only one of many stages, including: (1) the subcommittee, (2) the House full committee, (3) the House

ℋIGHLIGHT 7.1   What's in a Name?

Naming a bill has become a not-so-subtle art of late. In times past, Franklin D. Roosevelt could propose a Social Security Act without calling it the "Dignity in Old Age Act" or the "Keep Grandma Out of the Poorhouse Act."* Since Republicans took over control of Congress in 1995, bills have been named much more creatively and usually have value-laden names. A tax-cutting bill, for example, was named the "American Dream Restoration Act," and the Omnibus Budget Reconciliation bill's name was changed to the "Balanced Budget" bill to garner more favorable attention.

Representative Barney Frank (D–Mass.) wondered aloud on the House floor if the immigration bill entitled the "Immigration in the National Interest Act" should be renamed the "Statue of Liberty Was Wrong Act." One Republican representative, in an attempt to promote a bill requiring football, baseball, basketball, and hockey to use instant replays, named his proposal the "What Really Happened Bill" after he rejected his first choice, "It Wasn't a Touchdown, Stupid, Bill."

The names of bills such as the "Partial Birth Abortion Bill" can be particularly value laden and put opponents on the defensive. Can you think of other examples?

*This highlight draws heavily from Adam Clymer, "When 'Ketchup' Is 'Tomato Achievement,'" *New York Times* (March 24, 1996): section 4, 2.

Rules Committee, (4) the House, (5) the Senate subcommittee, (6) the full Senate committee, (7) the Senate, (8) floor leaders in both Houses, (9) the House-Senate Conference Committee, and (10) the president.

The story of how a bill becomes a law in the United States can be told in two different ways. The first is the "textbook" method, which provides a greatly simplified road map of the process to make it easier to understand. We'll review this method first. But real life, of course, rarely goes according to plan, as underscored in Highlight 7.2: How Legislation Follows Events. So we will next look at an actual example of how a particular bill became a law, and explore the true complexities of the process.

$\mathcal{H}$IGHLIGHT 7.2   How Legislation Follows Events

As the gun control legislation saga described in our opening vignette and How a Bill Really Becomes a Law underscore, the path a particular piece of legislation takes is often as varied as the content of the legislation itself. In the wake of so many school shooting tragedies, many Americans regard some form of gun control legislation as a must. Legislators, with their election campaigns always in sight, are mindful of this fact. With 64 percent of the American public responding that they would consider a candidate's position on gun control important when voting in the next election,[a] it is reasonable to expect Congress to act. In fact, as Figure 7.6 highlights, Congress frequently reacts to external stimuli that produces citizen demands for action. Still, gun control legislation was defeated in spite of public opinion perhaps underscoring the potency of the gun lobby.

[a]Gallup Poll, May 26, 1999.

Figure 7.6   Gun Control Legislation Following Publicized Shootings Since 1968

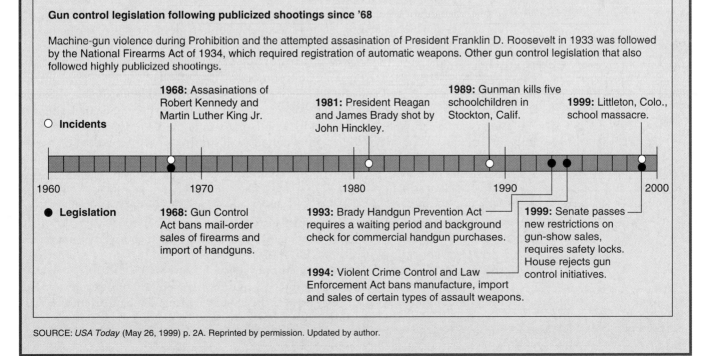

Gun control legislation following publicized shootings since '68

Machine-gun violence during Prohibition and the attempted assassination of President Franklin D. Roosevelt in 1933 was followed by the National Firearms Act of 1934, which required registration of automatic weapons. Other gun control legislation that also followed highly publicized shootings.

○ **Incidents**

1968: Assasinations of Robert Kennedy and Martin Luther King Jr.

1981: President Reagan and James Brady shot by John Hinckley.

1989: Gunman kills five schoolchildren in Stockton, Calif.

1999: Littleton, Colo., school massacre.

1960   1970   1980   1990   2000

● **Legislation**

1968: Gun Control Act bans mail-order sales of firearms and import of handguns.

1993: Brady Handgun Prevention Act requires a waiting period and background check for commercial handgun purchases.

1994: Violent Crime Control and Law Enforcement Act bans manufacture, import and sales of certain types of assault weapons.

1999: Senate passes new restrictions on gun-show sales, requires safety locks. House rejects gun control initiatives.

SOURCE: *USA Today* (May 26, 1999) p. 2A. Reprinted by permission. Updated by author.

How a Bill Becomes a Law: The Textbook Version

A bill must survive three stages before it becomes a law. It must be approved by one or more standing committees and both chambers, and, if House and Senate versions differ, a conference report resolving those differences must be accepted by each house. A bill may be killed during any of these stages, so it is much easier to defeat a bill than it is to get one passed. The House and Senate have parallel processes, and often the same bill is introduced in each chamber at the same time.

A bill must be introduced by a member of Congress, but it is often sponsored by a whole list of other members in an early effort to show support for it. Once introduced, the bill is sent to the clerk of the chamber, who gives it a number (for example, HR 1 or S 1—indicating House or Senate bill number one for the session). The bill is then printed, distributed, and sent to the appropriate committee or committees for consideration.

The first action takes place within the committee, after it is referred there by the Speaker. The committee usually refers the bill to one of its subcommittees, which researches the bill and decides whether to hold hearings on it. The subcommittee hearings provide the opportunity for those on both sides of the issue to voice their opinions. Most of these hearings are now open to the public because of 1970s sunshine laws, which require open sessions. After the hearings, the bill is revised, and the subcommittee votes to approve or defeat the bill. If the subcommittee votes in favor of the bill, it is returned to the full committee, which then either rejects the bill or sends it to the House or Senate floor with a favorable recommendation (see Figure 7.7).

The second stage of action takes place on the House or Senate floor. In the House, before a bill may be debated on the floor, it must be approved by the Rules Committee and given a rule and a place on the calendar, or schedule. (House budget bills don't go to the Rules Committee.) In the House, the rule given to a bill determines the limits on the floor debate and specifies what types of amendments, if any, may be attached to the bill. Once the Rules Committee considers the bill, it is put on the calendar.

When the day arrives for floor debate, the House may choose to form a Committee of the Whole. This allows the House to deliberate with only 100 members present to expedite consideration of the bill. On the House floor, the bill is debated, amendments are offered, and a vote ultimately is taken by the full House. If the bill survives, it is sent to the Senate for consideration if it was not considered there simultaneously.

Unlike the House, where debate is necessarily limited given the size of the body, bills may be held up by a hold or a filibuster in the Senate. A **hold** is a tactic by which a senator asks to be informed before a particular bill is brought to the floor. This request signals the Senate leadership and the sponsors of the bill that a colleague may have objections to the bill and should be consulted before further action is taken. Because any single member can filibuster a bill or other action to death, the Senate leadership is very reluctant to bring actions with a hold on them to the floor. Explained one Senate staffer, "Four or five years ago it started to mean that if you put a hold on something, it would never come up. It became, in fact, a veto."[41]

In the first sessions of the 103rd and 104th Congresses, for example, holds were placed on more than two-thirds of the 250 bills reported out of committee in the Senate. In the 105th Congress, holds were also used to prevent votes on many judicial nominees, prompting criticism from Chief Justice Rehnquist. Since holds were not made public, it was difficult to know how many were actually placed and who exercised the privilege. The secrecy attached to holds made them particularly powerful as a personal means to stall action. In March 1999, however, the Senate changed its rules. Senators who want to place a hold on legislation now must notify a bill or nomination's sponsor and the committee with jurisdiction over the issue in writing. "What this means," said Senator Ron Wyden (D–Oreg.), long a critic of holds, "is that the fog is starting to lift over the Senate."[42]

Historically, holds have been used as an advance warning of other delaying actions, such as filibusters.

hold:

A tactic by which a senator asks to be informed before a particular bill is brought to the floor. In effect, this stops the bill from coming to the floor until the "hold" is removed.

Figure 7.7 How a Bill Becomes a Law

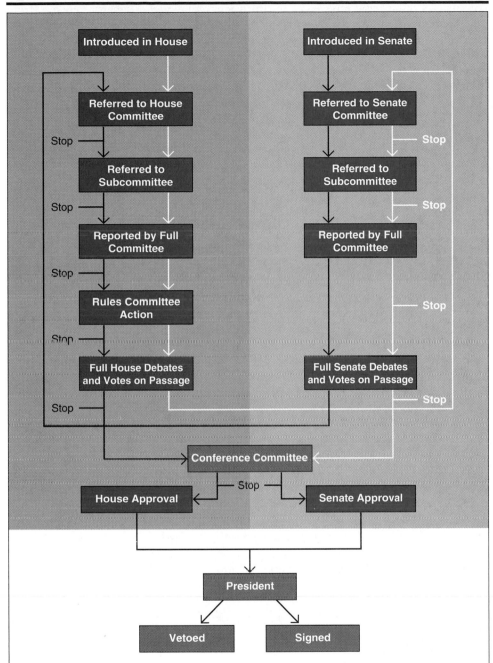

Filibusters, which allow for unlimited debate on a bill, grew out of the absence of rules to limit speech in the Senate and are often used to "talk a bill to death." In contrast to a hold, a filibuster is a more formal and public way of halting action on a bill by means of long speeches or unlimited debate in the Senate. The filibuster became an increasingly common feature of Senate life during the slavery debates. In 1917, eleven senators waged a filibuster against an important foreign policy matter supported by President Woodrow Wilson. The Senate then adopted a rule to avoid the potential disaster of tying the president's hands during World War I. Senate Rule 22 allows for

filibuster:

A formal way of halting action on a bill by means of long speeches or unlimited debate in the Senate.

cloture:

Motion requiring 60 Senators to cut off debate.

pocket veto:

If Congress adjourns during the ten days the president has to consider a bill passed by both houses of Congress, without the president's signature, the bill is considered vetoed.

line-item veto:

The power to veto specific provisions of a spending bill without vetoing the bill in its entirety.

unlimited debate on a motion before it is brought to a vote.[43] There are no rules on the content of a filibuster as long as the senator keeps on talking. A senator may read from a phone book, recite poetry, or read cookbooks in order to delay a vote. Often, a team of senators will take turns speaking to keep the filibuster going in the hope that a bill will be tabled or killed. In 1964, for example, a group of Northern liberal senators continued a filibuster for eighty-two days in an effort to prevent amendments that would weaken a civil rights bill. Since the 1950s, according to the Library of Congress, the average number of filibusters has risen from less than one a year to twenty a year.

To end a filibuster, **cloture** must be invoked. To cut off debate, sixteen senators must first sign a motion for cloture, then sixty senators must vote to end debate. If cloture is invoked, no more than thirty additional hours can be devoted to debate before the legislation at issue is brought to a vote.

The third stage of action takes place when the two chambers of Congress approve different versions of the same bill. When this happens, a conference committee is established to iron out the differences between the two versions of a bill. The president is not given a multiple choice and allowed to select which version he prefers. The conference committee, whose members are from the original House and Senate committees, hammers out a compromise, which is returned to each chamber for a final vote. No changes or amendments are allowed at this stage. If the bill is passed it is sent to the president, who either signs it or vetoes it. If the bill is not passed, it dies.

The president has ten days to consider a bill. He has five options: (1) He can sign the bill, at which point it becomes law. (2) He can veto the bill, which is more likely to occur when the president is of a different party than the majority in Congress. In the 103rd Congress, President Clinton became the first president in 140 years not to veto a single bill during a two-year Congress. He vetoed eight pieces of legislation passed by the 105th Congress, including a second veto of a proposed ban on partial birth abortions. Congress may override the president's veto with a two-thirds vote in each chamber, a very difficult task. (3) He can wait the full ten days, at the end of which time the bill becomes law without his signature if Congress is still in session. (4) If the Congress adjourns before the ten days are up, the president can choose not to sign the bill, and it is considered "pocket vetoed." A **pocket veto** figuratively allows bills stashed in the president's pocket to die. The only way for a bill then to become law is for it to be reintroduced in the next session and go through the process all over again. Because Congress sets its own date of adjournment, technically the session could be continued the few extra days necessary to prevent a pocket veto. Extensions are unlikely, however, as sessions are scheduled to adjourn close to the November elections or the December holidays. (5) For a short while, the last action that the president could take was to exercise a **line-item veto.**

Presidents since Ulysses S. Grant urged Congress to give them a line-item veto as a way to curb wasteful spending, particularly in pork barrel projects added to bills to assure member support. As adopted by Congress on Ronald Reagan's eighty-fourth birthday, the line-item veto allowed the president to strike or reduce any discretionary budget authority or eliminate any targeted tax provision (the line item) in any bill sent to him by the Congress. The president was then required to prepare a separate rescissions package for each piece of legislation he wished to veto and then submit his proposal to Congress within twenty working days. The president's proposed recisions were to take effect unless both houses of Congress passed a disapproval bill by a two-thirds vote within twenty days of receiving the rescissions.[44]

President Clinton used the line-item veto to reject a range of pork barrel provisions in legislation that was sent to him for his approval. In 1998, however, the U.S. Supreme Court struck down the line-item veto as unconstitutional. In a six-to-three decision, a majority of the Court concluded that the provision violates a constitutional provision that mandates that legislation be passed by both houses of Congress and then be sent to the president—in its entirety—for his signature or veto.[45] Allowing the president to pick and choose among budget authorizations submitted to it by Congress gives the president the power "to enact, to amend or to repeal statutes," said the Court, a constitutional power the Framers never intended the president to have. Clinton, who had used the power eighty-two times, bemoaned the Court's decision.[46]

How a Bill *Really* Becomes a Law: The Clean Air Act Amendments of 1990

The textbook version of a bill's life gives you an idea of the hurdles a bill must pass to become a law. But there is more to it than meets the eye. Republicans in the 104th Congress made several efforts to repeal sections of the Clean Air Act Amendments passed in 1990, and state and local legislators often were behind or in support of those efforts. While in theory everyone wants clean air, large corporations and localities are upset when costs of compliance with federal legislation reduce their profits or eat into their already strained budgets.[47]

As controversy over the Clean Air Act Amendments continues, it is useful to examine how they came to pass. The story is a good illustration of how the actual passage of laws deviates in complex and interesting ways from the textbook way described above. It also underscores the fact that even when these hard-fought battles appear to be complete, the real legislative process is never over—bills may be reconsidered, or appropriations to implement them fully may be reduced or eliminated altogether (see Figure 7.8).

Figure 7.8   How a Bill Really Becomes a Law: The Clean Air Act Amendments of 1990

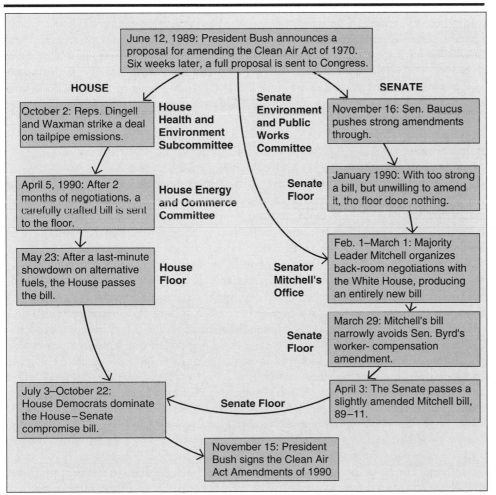

As with most major modern legislation, passage of the Clean Air Act Amendments of 1990 officially began at the White House. After campaigning for president in 1988 as an environmentalist, George Bush promised in his inaugural address to send Congress a major clean air legislative package. Over the next several months, he assembled an executive team: Robert Grady of the Office of Management and Budget (OMB); William Reilly, the head of the Environmental Protection Agency (EPA), and several aides; Roger Porter, the president's domestic policy adviser; and, in an unusual move, C. Boyden Gray, the White House chief counsel. Gray was a close adviser to the president and was considered by many to be the "real clean air nut" in the administration. Notably excluded were members of the Department of Energy.

After considerable discussion, study, and interviewing of academics and others, this team hammered together a vast proposal in Bush's name. Fully 140 representatives and twenty-five senators, led by Representative John Dingell (D–Mich.) and Senator John Chafee (R–R.I.), introduced it as a bill in each house.

In the Senate the bill was assigned to the Environment and Public Works Committee, which was considered extremely pro-environmentalist and out of sync with the rest of the Senate. When its version of the bill was reported back to the floor, the committee had stretched the proposed bill's provisions so much that the package was unacceptable to the full Senate. Automobile tailpipe emission standards, for example, were far too strict to win passage in the Senate. Instead of igniting a flurry of amendments and arguments, individual senators ignored the extreme bill entirely because they didn't want to touch it. Supporters knew that calling a vote would bring defeat.

George Mitchell (D–Me.), the Senate majority leader, then took over in a typical modern party-leadership maneuver. He called a series of closed-door negotiations that included representatives of the administration; Bob Dole (R–Kan.), the minority leader; and other key senators who were called in on those points in which they had a vested interest. After six long weeks of hard negotiating, this process produced an agreement among Democrats, Republicans, and the administration on every single point in the package, including tailpipe emissions and air-quality standards. As a group, the participants agreed to fight off every amendment that might be proposed from the floor, with the stipulation that any amendment successfully passed would free up any party to walk away from the deal.

This process, though extraordinary by historical standards, has become quite common on major bills as political parties have strengthened and the committees have proven unsuccessful at managing a more unruly Senate or House floor. Speaker Gingrich's formation of special task forces to formulate important legislation was thus the continuation of a trend. When the act was brought to the floor of the Senate, the powerful team led by Mitchell, Dole, and the White House succeeded in fending off all major amendments—only a few minor adjustments were allowed to pass—and the Senate proceeded to pass the resultant package by an overwhelming margin.

In the House, meanwhile, the Energy and Commerce Committees had much more say, partly because until recently, members of the House generally deferred to the typically greater expertise of the specialized committees, particularly when technical issues were involved. First, a rule was assigned to the bill so that no amendments could be offered without the approval of key committee members. Like representatives from tobacco-growing states, who for years have tried to prevent any legislation adverse to the tobacco industry, the powerful chair of the committee, John Dingell (D–Mich.), had long been trying to scuttle clean air legislation to protect his constituents, Detroit auto workers. The Environment and Health subcommittee of his panel, however, was chaired by Henry Waxman (D–Calif.), who for just as many years had championed clean air for his smog-ridden constituents in Los Angeles. Once Bush broke the legislative deadlock with a proposal, Dingell knew he would have to deal with Waxman and have the committee report out some kind of bill.

Taking a cue from the Senate, these two pulled back behind closed doors in informal negotiations that only indirectly involved other members of the committee. When they reached a deal on tailpipe emissions, their biggest sticking point, the official committee proceedings got back on track. Unlike what had occurred in the Senate, however, none of these behind-the-scenes or committee negotiations involved the White House. This was because House Republicans had become so ineffectual after so many years of Democratic control that the Democrats, in effect, could ignore them and their party leader in the White House. (It was this kind of arrogance that was to come back to haunt the Democrats when they lost power.) Dingell, Waxman, Speaker Thomas Foley, and their colleagues were much more willing to slam the door on those on the other side of the aisle than were their counterparts in the Senate.

Once both houses passed versions of the bill, the conference committee phase commenced. Because of House members' greater knowledge and expertise (they sit on fewer committees), they controlled the course of deliberations, making the bill stronger than the one originally proposed by the White House. President Bush was in no position to veto the stronger bill, however, because he had taken part (through his teammates) in the Senate's side of the deal making and had campaigned so loudly as a friend of the environment. In the end, therefore, the House crafters like Waxman who wanted a strong bill were able to carry the day.

HOW MEMBERS MAKE DECISIONS

As a bill makes its way through the labyrinth of the lawmaking process described above, members are confronted with the question: How should I vote? Members often listen to their own personal beliefs on many matters, but those views can often be moderated by other considerations. To avoid making any voting mistakes, members look to a variety of sources for cues.

Constituents

Constituents—the people who live and vote in the home district or state—are always in the member's mind when casting a vote.[48] It is rare for a legislator to vote against the wishes of his or her constituency regularly, particularly on issues of welfare rights, domestic policy, or other highly salient issues such as affirmative action, abortion, or war. Most constituents often have strong convictions on one or more of these issues. For example, during the 1960s, representatives from Southern states could not hope to keep their seats for long if they voted in favor of proposed civil rights legislation. But gauging how voters feel about any particular issue often is not easy. Because it is virtually impossible to know how the folks back home feel on all issues, a representative's *perception* of their preferences is important. Even when voters have opinions, legislators may get little guidance if their district is narrowly divided. Abortion is an issue about which many voters feel passionately; but a legislator whose district has roughly equal numbers of pro-choice and pro-life advocates can satisfy only a portion of his or her constituents.

If an issue affects their constituency, a representative often will try to determine how the people back home feel. Staff members often keep running tallies of the letters and phone calls for and against a policy that will be voted on soon. Only if a legislator has strong personal preferences will he or she vote against a clearly expressed desire of their constituents. Studies by political scientists show that members vote in conformity with prevailing opinion in their districts about two-thirds of the time.[49] And, on average, Congress passes laws that reflect national public opinion at about the same rate.[50] Legislators tend to act on their own preferences as trustees when dealing with topics that have come through the committees on which they serve or issues that they know about as a result of experience in other contexts, such as their vocation. On items of little concern to people back in the district or for which the legislator has little firsthand knowledge, the tendency is to turn to other sources for voting cues. The opinions of one's colleagues, especially those who belong to his or her party, often weigh heavily when casting a roll-call vote.

POLITICS NOW

Divided Government

For years, Republican presidents blamed the Democrats who controlled the Congress for legislative gridlock. Rarely could the two parties agree on any important pieces of legislation. Then in 1993, for the first time since 1980, both Houses of Congress and the presidency were controlled by the same political party. Several major presidential programs were passed, including bills previously passed by Congress but vetoed by President Bush. "Gridlock is gone," declared House Majority Leader Richard Gephardt (D–Mo.) after the end of the first session of the 103rd Congress, which was one of the most productive sessions in recent years.

The public, however, appeared either unimpressed or frustrated by Congress. In fact, immediately after the 1994 election that gave Republicans control of Congress, Americans told pollster Louis Harris that they liked divided government by a 48 percent to 36 percent margin.[a] After Republicans gained control of both houses, the partisan division that characterized most of the 1970s and 1980s returned. Efforts by congressional Republicans to slice deficits and eliminate social programs while spreading around tax cuts were impaled on President Clinton's veto pen. As a result of these basic disagreements over the role of the federal government, late in 1995 and again in early 1996, large portions of the U.S. government were forced to shut down when President Clinton vetoed budget and appropriations bills that he believed cut social programs too deeply.

The 1996 elections returned a Democrat to the White House and a Republican majority to the Congress, and both sides reached out to end gridlock. That promise was partially fulfilled when Clinton and Republican leaders hammered out a balanced budget. In 1998, however, the consequences of divided government again reared their ugly head. The president, under investigation in the Republican House, continually threatened to veto legislation and ill will between the two branches ran rampant as

best illustrated by the highly partisan impeachment hearings in the House.[b]

Agreeing on a budget, which in essence is often a statement of political priorities, can be a very difficult task in an era of *divided government*,[c] the term used to describe the political condition in which different political parties control the White House and Congress.[d] In fact, "in this era of divided government, the budget sent by a president from one party to a Congress controlled, at least nominally, by the other party must be viewed substantially and politically as an opening bid, not a final product."[d] In his proposed budget submitted in 1999, President Clinton committed 62 percent of the budget surpluses over the next fifteen years to Social Security and to paying down the federal debt. But Republicans wanted to use the surplus for tax cuts. The Republican Party, riddled with intraparty conflict in 1999 and an untested new Speaker, see themselves as fighting against a president who clearly enjoys far more popularity than congressional Republicans. It is the latest battle arising from the divided government that has been the norm for much of the modern era.

What consequences the fallout and lasting resentments of the impeachment process will have on the president and Congress's ability to hammer out future budget bills are yet to be seen. The Republican majority is razor thin and the specter of the 2000 elections looms large.

[a]Data from *National Journal 26* (December 17, 1994): 2996.
[b]For more on divided government, see Morris Fiorina, *Divided Government* 2d ed. (Boston: Allyn & Bacon, 1996); and Mark N. Franklin and Wolfgang Hirczy de Mino, "Separated Powers, Divided Government, and Turnout in U. S. Presidential Elections," *American Journal of Political Science* (January 1998): 316–326.
[c]Martha Phillips, "Clinton's Budget: A First Step, Not a Finished Product," *Nation's Cities Weekly* (March 29, 1999): 2
[d]Lawrence M. O'Rourke, "Crosscurrent Swirl as Congress Heads for Elections," *Sacramento Bee*, September 6, 1998, A17.

Colleagues

The range and complexity of issues confronting Congress means that no one can be up to speed on more than a few topics. When members must vote on bills about which they know very little, they often turn for advice to colleagues who have served on the committee that handled the legislation. On issues that are of little interest to a legislator, *logrolling*, or vote trading, often occurs. Logrolling often takes place on specialized bills targeting money or projects to selected congressional districts. A yea vote by an unaffected member often is given to a member in exchange for the promise of a future yea vote on a similar piece of specialized legislation.

Other appeals are of a more personal nature. During the Democrats' last-minute efforts to secure passage of the Omnibus Budget Reconciliation Act in 1993, President

Clinton and many of his aides did all they could to convince Senator Robert Kerrey (D–Neb.) to cast his critical vote for the act. At the request of the majority leader, Daniel Patrick Moynihan (D–N.Y.), Chair of the Senate Finance Committee, talked to Kerrey and even brought him home to talk to his wife. The next day, after Kerrey had again been courted by the president at a White House breakfast, Moynihan went to Kerrey's office and told him: "I need you on this one. If you give me this one, I promise I'll never ask you for anything else."[51] Sometimes a personal plea from a close colleague is what can ultimately win a vote. (In this case, without Kerrey's vote, Clinton's budget plan would have failed.)

Party

Political parties are another important source of influence.[52] The cohesion of the political parties in congressional floor votes has varied greatly over time. For example, during much of the period after World War II, congressional parties, and particularly the Democrats, often divided so that a conservative coalition consisting of Southern Democrats and Republicans frequently formed majorities on issues such as civil rights and social welfare issues. The growth of the role of a black electorate in the South's Democratic Party began in the early 1970s, after passage of the Voting Rights Act of 1965, and resulted in a gradual healing of the rift within the Democratic Party. After 1980 the conservative Southern Democrat/Republican coalition declined and clear-cut party voting became more common. From 1970 to the mid-1990s, the incidence of party votes in which majorities of the two parties took opposing sides roughly doubled to more than 60 percent of all roll-call votes, also underscoring the important role of the party whip system. In 1993 about two-thirds of the votes taken in each chamber broke along party lines. When the Republicans took control of Congress in 1995 with the Contract with America as its agenda, the parties divided on 73 percent of the House and 69 percent of the Senate roll-call votes, making 1995 the most partisan year in generations. In general, legislators are loyal to their parties about 80 percent of the time when issues divide the parties.[53]

Today, many members of Congress elected on a partisan ticket feel a degree of obligation to their party and to the president if he is of the same party. The national political parties have little say in who gets a party's nomination for the U.S. Senate or the House. But once a candidate has emerged successfully from a primary contest (see chapter 13), both houses have committees that provide campaign assistance. It is to each party's advantage to win as many seats as possible in each house. If a member is elected with the financial support or campaign visits from popular members and party leaders, they're much more inclined to toe the party line.

Caucuses

Special-interest caucuses were created to facilitate member communication—often across party lines—over issues of common concern. Caucuses also complement and counterbalance the informational roles played by the committee system.[54] By 1994 there were at least 140 special-interest caucuses, including many formed to promote certain industries, such as textiles, tourism, wine, coal, steel, mushrooms, and cranberries, or to advance particular views or interests.

Before 1995 twenty-seven caucuses enjoyed special status as legislative service organizations (LSOs). Included among these were the liberal Black Caucus, the Congressional Caucus for Women's Issues, and the Democratic Study Group. In 1995, the Republican majority voted to end the advantages given to LSOs, eliminating ninety-six staff positions and making sixteen offices available.[55] About one-third of the caucuses have died or just faded away without institutional support. Others have lost influence and members. Said Representative Charles Rangle (D–N.Y.) of the bipartisan Narcotics Abuse and Control Caucus, "We just couldn't keep it together."[56] Other new caucuses, however, continued to be formed. For example, in January 1996, nineteen Senators and eighty-one representatives founded the Internet Caucus, a bipartisan group devoted to helping educate members about the Internet. In order to join, members must agree to set up their own sites on the World Wide Web within ninety days.

State and regional caucuses are another important source of information exchange among members and across party lines. Large state delegations, such as those of California, New York, and Texas, often work together, regardless of party lines, to bring the bacon home to their states. Some state caucuses hold weekly meetings to assure that their interests are adequately represented on important committees and to keep abreast of pending legislation that might affect their states.

Interest Groups

The primary function of most interest group lobbyists is to provide information to supportive or potentially supportive legislators, committees, and their staffs.[57] It's likely, for example, that a representative knows the National Rifle Association's (NRA) position on gun control legislation. What the legislator needs to get from the NRA is information and substantial research on the feasibility and impact of such legislation. How could the states implement such legislation? Is it constitutional? Will it really have an impact on violent crime or crime in schools? Interest groups can win over undecided legislators or confirm the support of their friends by providing information that legislators use to justify the position they have embraced.

Pressure groups also use grassroots appeals to pressure legislators by urging their members in a particular state or district to call, write or fax, or e-mail their senators or representatives. Lobbyists can't vote, but voters back home can and do.

Political Action Committees

While a link to a legislator's constituency may be the most effective way to influence behavior, that is not the only path of interest group influence on member decision making.[58] The high cost of campaigning has made members of Congress—especially those without huge personal fortunes—attentive to those who help pay the tab for tens of thousands of dollars worth of television commercials that have become staples in contested elections. The 4,000 or so political action committees (PACs) organized by interest groups are a major source of most members' campaign funding. When an issue comes up on which the legislator has no strong opinion and which is of little consequence to constituents, there is, not surprisingly, a tendency to support the stand taken by those nice folks who helped pay for the last campaign. After all, who wants to bite the hand that feeds him or her? (Interest groups and PACs are discussed in detail in chapter 16.)

■ Organized labor has an impact on Congressional elections, with most unions contributing to Democratic candidates. (Photo courtesy: Charlyn Zlotnik/Woodfin Camp & Associates)

Staff

Members of Congress rely heavily on members of their staffs for information on pending legislation.[59] Staff members prepare summaries of bills and brief the representative or senator based on their research. If the bill is nonideological or one on which the member has no real position, staff members can be very influential. Staff members also do research on and even draft bills that a member wishes to introduce.

Table 7.6   Support Agencies

Congressional Research Service (CRS)

Created in 1914 as the Legislative Research Service (LRS), the CRS is administered by the Library of Congress and responds to more than a quarter of a million congressional requests for information each year. The service provides nonpartisan studies of public issues, compiling facts on both sides of issues, and it conducts major research projects for committees at the request of members. The CRS also prepares summaries of all bills introduced and tracks the progress of major bills.

General Accounting Office (GAO)

The GAO was established in 1921 as an independent regulatory agency for the purpose of auditing the financial expenditures of the executive branch and federal agencies. Today, the GAO performs four additional functions: It sets government standards for accounting, it provides a variety of legal opinions, it settles claims against the government, and it conducts studies upon congressional request.

Congressional Budget Office (CBO)

The CBO was created in 1974 to evaluate the economic effect of different spending programs and to provide information on the cost of proposed policies. It is responsible for analyzing the president's budget and economic projections. The CBO provides Congress and individual members with a valuable second opinion to use in budget debates.

Staff aides are especially crucial in the Senate. Because senators have so many committee assignments and are often spread so thin, they frequently rely heavily on aides. Every legislator has personal staff and other staff who work for each committee and subcommittee. The support personnel at the Congressional Budget Office and the Congressional Research Service at the Library of Congress are also considered to be staff working for Congress (see Table 7.6). Even with the reduction in House committee staffers enacted by Republicans in 1995, the ranks of the staffed total more than 15,000 (see Figure 7.9).

The next time you see a televised Senate hearing, notice how each senator has at least one aide sitting behind him or her, ready with information and often even with questions for the senator to ask. Some believe that staff members have become too important, too powerful, and that their bosses are too dependent on them. As Majority Leader, Bob Dole, for example, came under intense criticism by many conservative members of Congress for the alleged influence of his chief aide, Sheila Burke, a

Figure 7.9   Congressional Staff, 1930–97

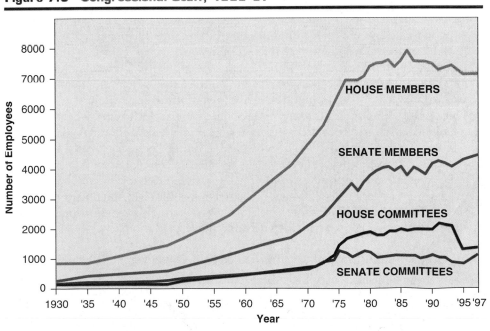

SOURCE: Norman J. Ornstein, *et al., eds., Vital Statistics on Congress, 1997–1998* (Washington D.C.: Congressional Quarterly, 1998), tables 5-2 and 5-5.

moderate Republican, who ultimately was the subject of a Sunday *New York Times Magazine* cover story about the woman behind the man.

CONGRESS AND THE PRESIDENT

The Constitution envisioned that the Congress and the president would have discrete powers and that one branch would be able to hold the other in check. Over the years, and especially since the 1930s, the president has often held the upper hand. In times of crisis or simply when it was unable to meet public demands for solutions, Congress has willingly handed over its authority to the chief executive. Even though the chief executive has been granted greater latitude, legislators do, of course, retain authority to question executive actions and can halt activities of the administration by cutting off funds. Congress also wields the ultimate oversight power—the power to impeach and even remove the president from office.

The Shifting Balance of Power

The balance of power between Congress and the executive branch has seesawed over time. The post–Civil War Congress attempted to regain control of the vast executive powers that President Abraham Lincoln, recently slain, had taken from it. Angered at the refusal of Lincoln's successor, Andrew Johnson, to go along with its radical "reforms" of the South, Congress passed the Tenure of Office Act, which prevented the president, under the threat of civil penalty, from removing any Cabinet-level appointments of the previous administration. Johnson accepted the challenge and fired Lincoln's secretary of war, who many believed was guilty of heinous war crimes. The House voted to impeach Johnson, but only the desertion of a handful of Republican senators prevented him from being removed from office. (The effort fell short by one vote.) Nonetheless, the president's power had been greatly weakened, and the Congress again became the center of power and authority in the federal government.

Beginning in the early 1900s, however, a series of strong presidents acted at the expense of congressional power. Theodore Roosevelt, Franklin D. Roosevelt, and Lyndon B. Johnson, especially, all viewed the presidency as carrying with it enormous powers.

Over the years, especially since the presidency of Franklin D. Roosevelt, Congress has ceded to the president a major role in the legislative process. Today, for example, Congress often finds itself responding to executive branch proposals. Critics of Congress point to its slow, unwieldy process and the complexity of national problems as reasons that Congress often doesn't seem to act on its own.

Individual members, especially if the president is popular with voters, often support White House initiatives. Legislators who are "on the fence" often find themselves targeted by the White House or inundated with invitations to state dinners.

During Bill Clinton's efforts to convince Congress to pass his budget deficit reduction plan and then NAFTA, he courted and cajoled numerous legislators and punished those who didn't go along. After Richard Shelby (D–Ala.) immediately criticized Clinton's tax plan, the White House retaliated by moving ninety federal jobs out of the Marshall Space Flight Center in Alabama and even denied Shelby an extra ticket to a White House South Lawn ceremony honoring his alma mater's champion football team.[60] It doesn't take many episodes like these to convince some legislators how to vote, although some may say that Shelby got in the last laugh when he switched to the Republican Party.

Congressional Oversight of the Executive Branch

According to political scientist Joel Aberbach, since 1961 there has been a substantial increase in the **oversight** activity by Congress.[61] Oversight subcommittees became particularly prominent in the 1970s and 1980s as a means of promoting investigation and program review,[62] to determine if an agency, department, or office is carrying out its responsibilities the way Congress intends. It also includes checking on possible abuses of power by governmental officials, including the president. In the 104th Congress,

oversight:

Congressional review of the activities of an agency, department, or office.

however, the House committee system was revamped by the new Republican leadership, which resulted in the elimination of more than half of the oversight subcommittees that existed in the 103rd.[63]

Key to Congress's performance of its oversight function is its ability to question members of the administration and the bureaucracy to see if they are enforcing and interpreting the laws passed by Congress as the members intended. These committee hearings, now routinely televised, are among Congress's most visible and dramatic actions. Millions, for example, tuned in to watch the House's investigation of Presidents Nixon and Clinton, the Senate's investigation of the Iran-Contra affair, and the Senate's trial of President Clinton. In contrast, despite the fact that 46 percent of those polled said they believed President Clinton and Vice President Gore broke campaign financing laws during the 1996 election, the Senate probe of campaign financing abuses drew little public interest.

By the late 1990s, a series of costly congressional investigations have led some to question the high cost of Senate oversight. Through January 1998 executive branch investigations have cost nearly $190 million since Republicans took control of Congress. In contrast, Congress allotted $98 million for the arts, $130 million for job training programs, and $100 million for UNICEF, the United Nations program to feed poor children.[64]

Reporting changes made by Republicans in the Senate now allow the public to keep track of the costs of investigations, including the Whitewater hearings chaired by Alfonse D'Amato (R.–N.Y.), campaign finance hearings chaired by Fred Thompson (R–Tenn.), the investigation of the FBI's conduct at Waco, Texas, and the abuse of taxpayers by the IRS. Congressional oversight is "one of the most important things that Congress does," said the president of the National Taxpayer's Union.[65] Depending on who controls Congress, however, there are always complaints that investigations are being used to pursue political goals, especially during times of divided government.

Hearings are not simply used to gather information. Rather, hearings that focus on the Bureau of Alcohol, Tobacco, and Firearms handling of the Branch Davidians in Waco, Texas, or the shootings of the Weavers in Ruby Ridge, Idaho, are clear signals that changes need to be made before the agency next comes before the committee to justify its budget. Thus it is easier to understand the go-slower approach the FBI took in 1996 when it chose to wait out the Freemen as opposed to taking more potentially violent action.

Hearings are also used to improve the administration of programs. Since most members of House and Senate committees and subcommittees are interested in the issues under their jurisdiction, they often *want* to help bureaucrats and not hinder them.

Recent research reveals that the more the legislative body sees the oversight committee as not representative of the House or Senate as a whole, the more likely it will allow the executive branch leeway in adopting regulations to implement congressional policy.[66]

Legislators augment their formal oversight of the executive branch by allowing citizens to appeal adverse bureaucratic decisions to agencies, Congress, and even the courts. **Congressional review,** a procedure adopted by the 104th Congress, by which agency regulations can be nullified by joint resolutions of legislative disapproval, is another method of exercising congressional oversight.[67]

In 1996 Congress adopted the Contract with America Advancement Act as part of its concern with regulatory reform. The Act provides Congress with sixty days to disapprove newly announced agency regulations, often passed to implement some congressional action. A regulation is disapproved if the resolution is passed by both chambers and signed by the president, or when Congress overrides a presidential veto of a disapproving resolution.

Congressional review differs from another form of legislative oversight called the legislative veto. The **legislative veto,** a procedure by which one or both houses of Congress can disallow an act of an executive agency by a simple majority vote, was first added to statutes in 1932, but the vetoes were not used frequently until the 1970s. They were usually included in laws that delegated congressional powers to the executive

congressional review:

The process by which Congress can nullify an executive branch regulation by a resolution jointly passed in both Houses within sixty days of announcement of the regulation and accepted by the president.

legislative veto:

A procedure by which one or both houses of Congress can disallow an act of the president or executive agency by a simple majority vote; ruled unconstitutional by the Supreme Court.

■ The War Powers Act, passed during the height of the Vietnam War, requires a president to obtain congressional approval before committing troops to a combat zone. (Photo courtesy: J.P. Fizet/Sygma)

branch while retaining the power of Congress to restrict their use. By 1981 more than 200 statutes contained legislative veto provisions.

In *Immigration and Naturalization Service* v. *Chadha* (1983), however, the U.S. Supreme Court ruled that the legislative veto as it was used in many circumstances was unconstitutional because it violated separation of powers principles.[68] The Court concluded that although the Constitution gave Congress the power to make laws, the Framers were clear in their intent that Congress should separate itself from executing or enforcing the laws. It is the president's responsibility to sign or veto legislation, not the Congress's. In spite of *Chadha*, however, the legislative veto continues to play an important role in executive-legislative relations. In signing the Omnibus Consolidation Recision and Appropriation Act in April 1996, for example, President Clinton noted that Congress had included a legislative veto that the Supreme Court would in all likelihood find unconstitutional under *Chadha*. Nevertheless, he signed the bill. The continued use by Congress, and the acceptance by the president, of the legislative veto, moreover, underscores the limits of judicial intervention without the cooperation of the other branches of government.

Through April 1999, only a few congressional reviews have been used and no regulations have been rejected by Congress. Nevertheless, it can be expected that Congress will opt for this procedure and abandon its use of legislative vetoes, which because they do not allow the president a role in the process, have been ruled unconstitutional.

Foreign Affairs Oversight. The Constitution divides foreign policy powers between the executive and the legislative branches. The president has the power to wage war and negotiate treaties, whereas the Congress has the power to declare war and the Senate has the power to ratify treaties. Throughout the twentieth century, the executive branch has become preeminent in foreign affairs despite the constitutional division of powers. This is partly due to the series of crises and the development of nuclear weapons in this century; both have necessitated quick decision making and secrecy, which are much easier to manage in the executive branch. Congress, with its 535 members, has a more difficult time reaching a consensus and keeping secrets.

After years of playing second fiddle to a series of presidents from Theodore Roosevelt to Richard M. Nixon, a "snoozing Congress" was "aroused"[69] and seized for itself the authority and expertise necessary to go head-to-head with the chief executive. In a delayed response to Lyndon B. Johnson's 1964–1969 conduct of the Vietnam War, Congress passed in 1973 the **War Powers Act** over President Nixon's veto. This Act requires any president to obtain congressional approval before committing U.S. forces to a combat zone and to notify Congress within forty-eight hours of committing troops to foreign soil. In addition, the president must withdraw troops within sixty days unless Congress votes to declare war. The president is also required to consult with Congress, if at all possible, prior to committing troops.

The War Powers Act has been of limited effectiveness in claiming a larger congressional role in international crisis situations. Presidents Ford, Carter, and Reagan never consulted Congress in advance of committing troops, citing the need for secrecy and swift movement, although each president did notify Congress shortly after the incidents. They contended that the War Powers Act was probably unconstitutional because it limits presidential prerogatives as commander-in-chief. When Congress does try to get into the foreign affairs area, it often seems to botch it. In 1999, for example, the House voted to bar President Clinton from deploying ground troops to Kosovo without its approval. But ultimately it took six often contradictory votes on intervention in Kosovo to formulate policy, as revealed in Table 7.7. With these kinds of confusing signals, it is not surprising that many presidents have insisted on quite a bit of autonomy in conducting foreign affairs, although President Clinton did pledge to consult Congress before he took action.

Confirmation of Presidential Appointments. The Senate plays a special oversight function through its ability to confirm key members of the executive branch, as well as presidential appointments to the federal courts. As discussed in chapters 9 and 10, although the Senate generally confirms most presidential nominees, it does not always do so. A wise president considers senatorial reaction before nominating potentially controversial individuals to his administration or to the federal courts. In the case of federal district court appointments, senators often have a considerable say in the nomination of judges from their states through what is called senatorial courtesy, a process by which presidents generally defer selection of district court judges to the choice of senators of their own party who represent the state in which a vacancy occurs (see chapter 10).

Presidential appointees during the Clinton administration faced a particularly hostile Congress. "Appointments have always been the battleground for policy disputes,"

War Powers Act:

Passed by Congress in 1973, the president was limited in his deployment of troops overseas to a sixty-day period in peacetime (which could be extended for an extra thirty days to permit withdrawal) unless Congress explicitly gave its approval for a longer period.

Table 7.7 Congressional Action on Kosovo: An Exercise in Foreign Affairs Oversight

House

Adopted 249–180	Bill that prohibits funds for ground forces in Yugoslavia without prior congressional approval
Rejected 290–139	Resolution to direct removal of U.S. armed forces from Yugoslavian conflict
Rejected 427–2	Declaration of war against Yugoslavia
Rejected 213–213	Senate-passed resolution authorizing air operations in Yugoslavia

Senate

Adopted 58–41	Resolution authorizing air operations in Yugoslavia
Tabled 78–22	Further debate on resolution allowing "all necessary force" in Yugoslavia

Source: "Congress Votes Both Ways," *USA Today* (May 5, 1999): 26A.

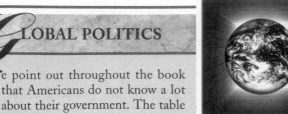

GLOBAL POLITICS

What Citizens Know About Their Legislatures

We point out throughout the book that Americans do not know a lot about their government. The table below provides some confirmation of that assertion. In surveys asking citizens to answer questions about their legislatures (including who their representative was) and issues currently before those bodies, Americans clearly knew less about the Congress than their Canadian and British counterparts know about their parliaments. Why is this the case?

One possible explanation has to do with the structure of American government. Americans tend to know more about the presidency than the Congress, reflecting the vis-ibility of the executive's "bully pulpit"; also, the separation of the executive and legislature into two branches likely makes keeping track of both more difficult for the average citizen. The combination of the executive and legislature in the Canadian and British parliamentary systems means that citizens in those countries have fewer "branches" to pay attention to.

Where citizens get their news also affects how much they know about their legislature. Americans tend to rely on television for their political news, which reinforces the visibility of the presidency. Congress does not have the kind of visual impact that medium requires. Canadian and British citizens rely more on newspapers, which are often associated with higher levels of political knowledge in general. Thus, the quality of media coverage of the legislature and how citizens use the media to gain information affect what they know.

Interestingly, researchers found that the more Americans know about the Congress, the less they approve of it. In contrast, the more Canadians know about their Parliament, the more likely they are to support it.

Citizens' Knowledge of Their Legislature in Three Countries

Country	Number of Questions About Legislature	Average Number of Correct Citizen Responses
Canada	11	9.8
United Kingdom	10	6.2
United States	10	2.99

SOURCE: John R. Baker, Linda Bennett, Stephen Bennett, and Richard Flickinger, "Citizens' Knowledge of Legislatures in Canada, Britain and the United States," *The Journal of Legislative Studies;* 2, (1996): 47–51. Canadian and British data are from 1988 polls, American data from 1992.

say political scientist G. Calvin MacKenzie, but now, "what's new is the rawness of it—all of the veneer is off," as the divided government discussed in Politics Now illustrates.[70]

The Impeachment Process.   The impeachment process is the Congress's ultimate oversight of the U.S. president (as well as federal court judges.) The U.S. Constitution is quite vague about the impeachment process and much of the debate about it of late concerns what is an impeachable offense. The Constitution specifies that a president can be impeached for treason, bribery, or other "high crimes and misdemeanors." Most commentators agree that this phrase was meant to mean significant abuses of power. The question for the U.S. House then was, were President Clinton's statements to the Grand Jury lies, and if so, did lying to a grand jury constitute a "high crime and mis-demeanor" deserving of possible removal from office? In *The Federalist Papers* Alexander Hamilton noted his belief that impeachable offenses "are of a nature which may with peculiar propriety be denominated POLITICAL, as they relate chiefly to injuries done immediately to society itself."

House and Senate rules control how the impeachment process itself operates. Yet, because the process is used so rarely, and under such disparate circumstances, there are few hard and fast rules. Until 1998, the U.S. House of Representatives had voted to impeach only sixteen federal officials—and only one of those was a president, Andrew Johnson. (Of those, seven were convicted and removed from office and three resigned before the process described below was completed.)

Until late 1998, only three resolutions against presidents had resulted in further action: (1) John Tyler, charged with corruption and misconduct in 1843; (2) Andrew Johnson, charged with serious misconduct in 1868; and, (3) Richard M. Nixon, charged with obstruction and the abuse of power in 1974. The House rejected the

■ Charged with serious misconduct in 1868, Andrew Johnson was acquitted by the Senate by a one-vote margin. (Photo courtesy: Corbis)

charges against Tyler; Johnson was acquitted by the Senate by a one-vote margin; and Nixon resigned before the full House voted on the articles of impeachment.

The impeachment process itself has eight distinct stages:

1. **The Resolution.** A resolution, called an inquiry of impeachment, is sent to the House Judiciary Committee. Members may also introduce bills of impeachment, which will be referred to the Judiciary Committee.

2. **The Committee Vote.** After the consideration of voluminous evidence, the Judiciary Committee votes on the resolution or bill of impeachment. A positive vote from the Committee indicates its belief that there is sufficiently strong evidence for impeachment in the House.

3. **The House Vote.** If the articles of impeachment are recommended by the House Judiciary Committee, the full House votes to approve (or disapprove) a Judiciary Committee decision to conduct full-blown impeachment hearings.

4. **The Hearings.** Extensive evidentiary hearings are held by the House Judiciary Committee concerning the allegations of wrongdoing. Witnesses may be called and the scope of the inquiry may be widened at this time. The Committee heard only from the Independent Counsel in the Clinton case.

5. **The Report.** The Committee votes on one or more articles of impeachment. Reports supporting this finding (as well as dissenting views) are forwarded to the House and become the basis for its consideration of specific articles of impeachment.

6. **The House Vote.** The full House votes on each article of impeachment. A simple majority vote on any article is sufficient to send that article to the Senate for its consideration.

7. **The Trial in the Senate.** A trial is conducted on the floor of the Senate with the House Judiciary Committee bringing the case against the president, who is represented by his own private attorneys. The Senate, in essence, acts as the jury, with the Chief Justice of the United States presiding over the trial.

8. **The Senate Vote.** The full Senate votes on each article of impeachment. If there is a two-thirds vote on any article, the president is automatically removed from office and the vice president assumes the duty of the president. Both articles issued against President Clinton were defeated in the Senate.

CONTINUITY and Change

Representatives—In or Out of Touch?

When the Framers met in Philadelphia, they were concerned that their representatives not get too far away from the American people. Thus the House of Representatives was created with members to stand for election every two years. The House was truly to be "the people's house." The Framers envisioned those elected to this body would well represent the interests of their constituents, go back home frequently, and not view the House as their ultimate career.

Over time, however, some members fell out of touch with their constituents. As House whip, Newt Gingrich was quick to realize that American voters were angry with Congress. People were simply fed up with congressional pay raises, check overdraft privileges, and freebies from special interests. The House, in particular, was intended to be responsive to the people, but how could members be in tune given their six-figure salaries, full medical insurance, and ability to skirt basic employment laws?

Gingrich effectively sensed this anger and was able to turn public anger against Congress into a Republican takeover of both Houses in 1994. Although incumbents still rarely get defeated, as party conflict in both houses grew, many members retired. Thus, by 1999, over half the members of Congress had served less than three terms. Members are now closer to the people who elect than at any other time in recent history.

As the nation continues to grow, however, one representative will represent more and more people so long as the number of House members stays the same. Yet, as technology like the Internet makes it easier to contact people and new on-line communities are created, it is difficult to foresee how citizens' expectations about their representatives may change. Regular virtual town halls may become the norm as people seek answers and accountability from their elected representatives.

1. In what other ways do you see representatives being closer to the people they serve?
2. How might the relationships between constituents and members of congress change in the future?

Cast your Vote. How long should House members stay in office? To cast your vote, go to www.awlonline.com/oconnor.

SUMMARY

The size and scope of Congress, and demands put on it, have increased tremendously over the years. In presenting the important role that Congress plays in American politics, we have made the following points:

1. THE ROOTS OF THE LEGISLATIVE BRANCH

Congress was molded after the bicameral British Parliament, but with an important difference. The U.S. Senate is probably the most powerful upper house in any national legislature. The Senate has unique powers to ratify treaties and to approve presidential nominees.

2. THE CONSTITUTION AND THE LEGISLATIVE BRANCH OF GOVERNMENT

The Constitution created a bicameral legislature with members of each body to be elected differently, and thus to represent different constituencies. Article I of the Constitution sets forth qualifications for office, states age minimums, and specifies how legislators are to be distributed among the states. The Constitution also requires seats in the House of Representatives to be apportioned by population. Thus, after every census, district lines must be redrawn to reflect population shifts. The Constitution also provides a vast array of enumerated and implied powers to Congress. Some, such as lawmaking and oversight, are shared by each house of Congress; others are not.

3. THE MEMBERS OF CONGRESS

Members of Congress live in two worlds—in their home districts and in the District of Columbia. Casework is one way to keep in touch with the district, since members, especially those in the House, never stop running for office. Incumbency is an important factor in winning reelection. Thus many have called for limits on congressional terms of office.

4. HOW CONGRESS IS ORGANIZED

Political parties play a major role in the way Congress is organized. The Speaker of the House is always a member of the majority party, and members of the majority party chair all committees. In 1995 Speaker Newt Gingrich became the most powerful Speaker of the House since the first decade of this century. Because the House of Representatives is large, the Speaker enforces more rigid rules on the House than exist in the Senate.

In addition to the party leaders, Congress has a labyrinth of committees and subcommittees that cover the entire range of government policies, often with a confusing tangle of shared responsibilities. Each legislator serves on one or more committees and multiple subcommittees. It is in these environments that many policies are shaped and that members make their primary contributions to solving public problems.

5. THE LAWMAKING FUNCTION OF CONGRESS

The road to enacting a bill into law is long and strewn with obstacles, and only a small share of the proposals introduced become law. Legislation must be approved by committees in each house and on the floor of each chamber. In addition, most House legislation is initially considered by a subcommittee and must be approved by the Rules Committee before getting to the floor. Legislation that is passed in different forms by the two chambers must be resolved in a conference before going back to each chamber for a vote and then to the president, who can sign the proposal into law, veto it, or allow it to become law without his signature. If Congress adjourns within ten days of passing legislation, that bill will die if the president does not sign it.

6. HOW MEMBERS MAKE DECISIONS

A multitude of factors impinge on legislators as they decide policy issues. The most important of the many considerations are constituents' preferred options and the advice given by better informed colleagues. When clear and consistent cues are given by voters back home, legislators usually heed their demands. In the absence of strong constituency preferences, legislators may turn for advice to colleagues who are experts on the topic or to interest group lobbyists, especially those who have donated to their campaigns.

7. CONGRESS AND THE PRESIDENT

The president can successfully twist arms or appeal to party loyalty when dealing with legislators who belong to his party. A president's influence both with fellow partisans and opponents is related to the chief executive's popularity with the public. Ronald Reagan, a popular president, succeeded in getting an economic package adopted by a House controlled by Democrats. Congressional oversight of the executive branch and the president takes many forms including hearings, appointments, and the ultimate weapon, impeachment.

KEY TERMS

bicameral legislature, p. 217

bill, p. 218

casework, p. 222

cloture p. 242

conference committee, p. 234

congressional review, p. 251

delegate, p. 224

discharge petition, p. 236

filibuster, p. 241

hold, p. 240

impeachment, p. 219

incumbency, p. 222

legislative veto, p. 251

line-item veto, p. 242

majority party, p. 229

majority leader, p. 230

minority party, p. 229

minority leader, p. 230

oversight, p. 250

party caucus, p. 233

pocket veto, p. 242

politico, p. 226

pork barrel, p. 236

redistricting, p. 218

Speaker of the House, p. 229

standing committee, p. 234

term limits, p. 223

trustee, p. 224

War Powers Act, p. 253

whip, p. 231

SELECTED READINGS

Aberbach, Joel D. *Keeping a Watchful Eye.* Washington, DC: Brookings Institution, 1990.

Davidson, Roger H., and Walter J. Oleszek. *Congress and Its Members,* 7th ed. Washington, DC: Congressional Quarterly Press, 1999.

Deering, Christopher J., and Steven S. Smith, *Committees in Congress,* 3d ed. Washington, DC: Congressional Quarterly Press, 1997.

Dodd, Lawrence C., and Bruce Ian Oppenheimer, eds. *Congress Reconsidered,* 6th ed. Washington, DC: CQ Press, 1997.

Fenno, Richard F., Jr. *Congressmen in Committees.* Boston: Little, Brown, 1973.

————. *Home Style: House Members in Their Districts.* Boston: Little, Brown, 1978.

Fox, Richard Logan. *Gender Dynamics in Congressional Elections:* Beverly Hills, CA: Sage, 1996.

Gill, Laverne McCain. *African American Women in Congress: Forming and Transforming History.* New Brunswick, NJ: Rutgers University Press, 1997.

Hammond, Susan Webb. *Congressional Caucuses in National Policy Making.* Baltimore MD: John Hopkins University Press, 1998.

Hibbing, John R., and Elizabeth Theiss-Morse. *Congress as Public Enemy: Public Attitudes Toward American Political Institutions.* New York: Cambridge University Press, 1996.

Kaptur, Marcy. *Women of Congress.* Washington, DC: CQ Press, 1996.

Mayhew, David R. *Congress: The Electoral Connection.* New Haven, CT: Yale University Press, 1986.

Oleszek, Walter J. *Congressional Procedures and the Policy Process,* 4th ed. Washington, DC: Congressional Quarterly Press, 1995.

Price, David E. *The Congressional Experience: A View from the Hill.* Boulder, CO: Westview Press, 1992.

Thurber, James A., and Roger Davidson, eds. *Remaking Congress: Change and Stability in the 1990s.* Washington, DC: Congressional Quarterly Press, 1995.

NOTES

1. Valerie Richardson, "A Massacre in Colorado; Students Killed, Injured in Blood Bath," *Washington Times* (April 21, 1999): A1.

2. Ceci Connolly, "Littleton Alters the Landscape of Debate on Guns," *Washington Post* (May 5, 1999): A3.

3. Connolly, "Littleton Alters the Landscape of Debate."

4. Connolly, "Littleton Alters the Landscape of Debate."

5. Helen Dewar, "Senate Turns Down Rules to Tighten Gun Show Sales," *Washington Post* (May 13, 1999): A1.

6. Helen Dewar and Juliet Eilperin, "Senate Backs New Gun Control, 51–50," *Washington Post* (May 21, 1999): A01

7. See Stephen J. Farnsworth, "Congress and Citizen Anger: Examining Political Support for the Institution, the Leadership and One's Own Representative," paper delivered at the 1999 annual meeting of the Midwest Political Science Association; and Robert H. Durr, John B. Gilmour, and Christina Wolbrecht, "Explaining congressional approval," *American Journal of Political Science* 41 (1), 1997: 175–207.

8. Humphrey Taylor, "Louis Harris Poll: Confidence in Leaders Down," Gannett New Service, March 6, 1994, NEXIS and Roper Center, *Public Opinion Online*, Question 005, 1998.

9. David C. Kimball and Samuel C. Patterson, "Living Up to Expectations: Public Attitudes toward Congress," *Journal of Politics* 59, (August 1997): 701–28.

10. John R. Hibbing and Elizabeth Theiss-Morse, "The Media's Role in Fomenting Public Disgust with Congress," *Extensions* (Fall 1996): 15–18.

11. Charles S. Bullock, III, "House Careerists: Changing Patterns of Longevity and Attrition," *American Political Science Review* 66 (December 1972): 1295–1300.

12. Richard F. Fenno, Jr., *Home Style* (Boston: Little, Brown, 1978), 32.

13. Hedrick Smith, *The Power Game* (New York: Ballentine Books, 1989), 108.

14. Norman Ornstein, ed. *Vital Statistics on Congress* (Washington, DC: CQ Press, 1998), 135.

15. Gary W. Cox and Jonathan N. Katz, "Why Did the Incumbency Advantage in U.S. House Elections Grow?" *American Journal of Political Science* 40 (May 1996): 478–497; and Kenneth N. Bickers and Robert M. Stein, "The Electoral Dynamics of the Federal Pork Barrel," *American Journal of Political Science* 40 (November 1996): 1300–1326.

16. Marjorie Randon Hershey, "Congressional Elections," in Gerald M. Pomper, *et al., The Election of 1992: Reports and Interpretations* (Chatham, NJ: Chatham House, 1993), 159.

17. Alan I. Abramowitz, "Incumbency, Congressional Spending, and the Decline of Competition in House Elections," *Journal of Politics* 53 (February 1991): 34–56.

18. *U.S. Term Limits, Inc. v. Thornton*, 115 U.S. 1842 (1995).

19. Andrew C. Revkin, "Back to Her Roots," *New York Times* (October 10, 1995): B1.

20. Revkin, "Back to Her Roots."

21. Warren E. Miller and Donald Stokes, "Constituency Influence in Congress," *American Political Science Review* 57 (March 1963): 45–57.

22. Sue Thomas, *How Women Legislate* (New York: Oxford University Press, 1994).

23. Center for the American Woman and Politics, *Voices, Views, Votes: The Impact of Women in the 103rd Congress* (New Brunswick, NJ: Eagleton Institute of Politics, Rutgers, 1995), 15.

24. Center for the American Woman and Politics, *Voices, Views, Votes,* 15.

25. Adam Clymer, "Daughter of Slavery Hushes Senate," *New York Times* (July 23, 1993): B6.

26. Clymer, "Daughter of Slavery Hushes Senate."

27. Barbara Hinckley, *Stability and Change in Congress,* 3d ed. (New York: Harper & Row, 1983), 166.

28. Katharine Seelye, "Congressional Memo; New Speaker, New Style, Old Problem," *New York Times* (March 12, 1999): A18.

29. Helen Thomas, "Clinton: Business as Usual," *United Press International* (December 18, 1998). NEXIS.

30. Barbara Sinclair, "The Struggle Over Representation and Lawmaking in Congress: Leadership Reforms in the 1990s," in James A. Thurber and Roger H. Davidson, eds., *Remaking Congress: Change and Stability in the 1990s* (Washington, DC: CQ Press, 1995), 105.

31. Quoted in Donald R. Matthews, *U.S. Senators and Their Worlds* (Chapel Hill, NC: University of North Carolina Press, 1960), 97–98.

32. Steven S. Smith and Eric D. Lawrence, "Party Control of Congress in the Republican Congress," in Lawrence C. Dodd and Bruce I. Oppenheimer, *Congress Reconsidered,* 6th ed. (Washington, DC: Congressional Quarterly, 1997), 163–164. For more on the role of parties in the organization of Congress, see Forrest Maltzman, *Competing Principals: Committees, Parties, and the Organization of Congress* (Ann Arbor: University of Michigan, 1997).

33. "A Short History of the Democratic Caucus," 1. Homepage; HillSource, House

Republican Conference, "Our Mission," 1 (www).

34. Woodrow Wilson, *Congressional Government: A Study in American Government* (New York: Meridian Books, 1956, originally published in 1885), 79.

35. Roger H. Davidson, "Congressional Committees in the New Reform Era: From Combat to the Contract," in Thurber and Davidson, *Remaking Congress,* 28.

36. See Steven Smith and Christopher J. Deering, *Committees in Congress,* 3d ed. (Washington, DC: CQ Press, 1997). For more about committees, see Christopher Deering and Steven Smith, Committees in Congress, 3d ed. (Washington, DC: CQ Press, 1997).

37. Kenneth A. Shepsle, *The Giant Jigsaw Puzzle: Democratic Committee Assignments in the Modern House* (Chicago: University of Chicago Press, 1978).

38. Jack Anderson, "Subcontractor Oversight Absent," *Press Journal* (May 17, 1999): A8.

39. Guy Gugliotta, "Term Limits on Chairman Shake Up House," *Washington Post* (March 22, 1999): A4.

40. Gugliotta, "Term Limits."

41. Barbara Sinclair, *The Transformation of the U.S. Senate* (Baltimore, MD: Johns Hopkins University Press, 1989).

42. Helen Dewar, "Senate Lifts Veil on Bill 'Holds'; Leaders Remove Anonymity from Long-Used Delay Tactic," *Washington Post* (March 4, 1999): A8.

43. Sarah A. Binder and Steven S. Smith, *Politics or Principle Filibustering in the United States: Filibustering in the United States* (Washington, DC: Brookings Institution, 1997).

44. James A. Thurber, "If the Game Is Too Hard, Change the Rules: Congressional Budget Reform in the 1990s," in Thurber and Davidson, *Remaking Congress,* 140.

45. *Clinton* v. *City of New York,* 118 S. Ct. 2091 (1998).

46. Quoted in Helen Dewar and Joan Biskupic, "Line-Item Veto Struck Down." *Washington Post* (June 26, 1998): A1.

47. For a lengthier account of passage of the Clean Air Act see Richard Cohen, *Washington At Work,* 2d ed. (New York: Macmillan, 1995).

48. See L. Martin Overby, "The Senate and Justice Thomas: A Note on Ideology, Race, and Constituent Pressures," *Congress & the Presidency* 21 (Autumn 1994): 131–136.

49. John W. Kingon, *Congressmen's Voting Decisions,* 3d ed. Ann Arbor: University of Michigan Press, 1989.

50. Kingon, *Congressmen's Voting Decisions* 1989. See also Lee Sigelman, Paul J. Wahlbeck, and Emmett H. Buell, Jr., "Vote Choice and the Preference for Divided Government: Lessons of 1992," *American Journal of Political Science* 41 (July 1997): 879–894.

51. Howard Fineman, *et al.,* "Whew!" *Newsweek* (August 16, 1993): 19.

52. See Joseph Cooper and Garry Young, "Partisanship, Bipartisanship, and Crosspartisanship in Congress Since the New Deal," in Lawrence C. Dodd, Bruce I. Oppenheimer eds., *Congress Reconsidered,* 6th ed., (CQ Press: Washington DC, 1997) 246–58.

53. Barbara Sinclair, *Congressional Realignment, 1925–1978.* (Austin: University of Texas Press, 1982).

54. Scott H. Ainsworth and Francis Akins. "The Informational Role of Caucuses in the U.S. Congress." *American Politics Quarterly* 25 (October 1997): 407–430.

55. Jonathan D. Salant, "LSOs are No Longer Separate, the Work's Almost Equal," *Congressional Quarterly* 53 (May 27, 1995): 1483.

56. A. B. Stoddard, "Caucuses Lose Influence after LSOs Abolished," *The Hill* (February 14, 1996):2.

57. Ken Kollman, "Inviting Friends to Lobby: Interest Groups, Ideological Bias, and Congressional Committees," *American Journal of Political Science* 41 (April 1997): 519–544.

58. Robert Beirsack, Paul Herrnson, and Clyde Wilcox, *After the Revolution: PACS, Lobbies and the Republican Congress* (Boston: Allyn and Bacon, 1999).

59. Barbara S. Romzek and Jennifer A. Utter, "Congressional Legislative Staff: Political Professionals or Clerks?" *American Journal of Political Science* 41 (October 1997): 1251–1279; and Susan Webb Hammond, "Recent Research on Legislative Staffs," *Legislative Studies Quarterly* (November 1996): 543–576.

60. Lloyd Grove, "White House Declares War on Upstart Senator," *Atlanta Constitution* (April 6, 1993): A15.

61. Joel D. Aberbach, *Keeping a Watchful Eye: The Politics of Congressional Oversight* (Washington, DC: The Brookings Institution, 1990).

62. William F. West, "Oversight Subcommittees in the House of Representatives, *Congress & the Presidency* 25 (Autumn 1998): 147–160.

63. West, "Oversight Subcommittees."

64. Jonathan D. Salant, "GOP Reveals the Cost of Senate Oversight," *Washington Post* (January 9, 1998): A19.

65. "National Poll Watch," *Bulletin's Frontrunner* (September 30, 1997).

66. Steven J. Balla, "Legislative Organization and Congressional Review of Agency Regulations," paper delivered at the 1999 annual meeting of the Midwest Political Science Association.

67. This discussion draws heavily on Balla, "Legislative Organization and Congressional Review."

68. 462 U.S. 919 (1983).

69. *Wall Street Journal* (April 13, 1973): 10.

70. Quoted in Stewart M. Powell, "Lee Fights Signals Tougher Battles Ahead on Nomination," *Commercial Appeal* (December 21, 1997): A15.

(Photo courtesy: Corbis/Reuters)

The Presidency

- **The Roots of the Office of President of the United States**
- **The Constitutional Powers of the President**
- **The Development of Presidential Power**
- **The Presidential Establishment**
- **The Role of the President in the Legislative Process: The President as Policy Maker**
- **The President and Public Opinion**

The shootings at Littleton and other schools around the nation. The bombing in Oklahoma City. The burning of churches throughout the South. The series of national floods, hurricanes, tornadoes, and other national disasters. The explosion of the space shuttle *Challenger*. The killing of 241 Marines in Beirut, Lebanon

What do all of these horrific disasters have in common? All allowed a sitting president to show his ability to heal and lead the nation. President Clinton, like President Reagan before him, has shown himself to be a master in bringing the nation together in times of personal crisis. Clinton is always quick to hop on a plane to console the affected families in private and then to lead the nation in prayer. The ability to act as a national unifier often transcends partisan politics, usually to the dismay of the party that does not control the White House.

Not all presidents have this kind of ability to mold national tragedies into celebrations of heroes and American spirit. Without the personal charisma exercised by Presidents Clinton and Reagan, the bombings in Oklahoma City and in Beirut, Lebanon, could have turned into indictments of executive branch misfeasance.

Similarly, the *Challenger* explosion could have been the fault of the Reagan administration's cost-cutting efforts, which led to faulty inspection procedures. That did not happen. But, when Americans were held hostage in Iran, President Jimmy Carter took personal blame.

The ability to heal the nation is a natural talent that likely cannot be taught. The ability to use the symbols of office, and how a president uses the power, scope, and gravity of his office often defines his administration. This critical dynamic also underscores the importance of understanding sources of a president's unwritten powers as well as his specific constitutional grants of authority.

The constitutional authority, statutory powers, and burdens of the presidency make it a powerful position and an awesome responsibility. Most of the men who have been president in the past two decades have done their best; yet, in the heightened expectations of the American electorate, most have come up short. Not only did the Framers not envision such a powerful role for the president, they could not have foreseen the skepticism with which many presidential actions are now greeted in the press, on talk radio, and on the Internet. These expectations have also led presidents into policy areas never dreamed of by the Framers. Imagine, for example, what the Framers might have thought about President Clinton's 1998 State of the Union message, which advocated eighteen as a national norm for class size in the lower grades.

At the same time the modern media has brought us "closer" to our presidents, it has also made them seem more human, a mixed blessing for those trying to lead. Only two photographs exist of Franklin D. Roosevelt in a wheelchair—his paralysis was a closely guarded secret. Five decades later, Bill Clinton was asked on national TV what kind of underwear he preferred (briefs). Later, revelations about his conduct with Monica Lewinsky made this exchange seem tame. This demythifying of the president, along with simultaneous increases in our general mistrust of government and in our expectations of it, have made governing a difficult job. A president does not rely only on the formal powers of office to lead the nation: Public opinion and public confidence are key components of his ability to get his programs adopted and his vision of the nation implemented. As political scientist Richard E. Neustadt has noted, the president's power often rests on his power to persuade.[1] And to persuade, he must not only be able to forge links with members of Congress, he must also have the support of the American people and the respect of foreign leaders.

The tension between public expectations and the formal powers of the president permeates our discussion of how the presidency has evolved from its humble origins in Article II of the Constitution to its current stature.

- First, we will examine *the roots of the office of president of the United States* and discuss how the Framers created a chief executive officer for the new nation.
- Second, we will discuss Article II and *the constitutional powers of the president*.
- Third, we will examine *the development of presidential power* and a more personalized presidency: How well a president is able to execute the laws often depends strongly on his personality, popularity, and leadership style.
- Fourth, to help you understand more fully the development of the office of the president as a central focus of power and action in the American political system, we will also discuss the development of what is called *the presidential establishment*. Myriad departments, special assistants, and a staff of advisers help the president, but also make it easier for a president to lose touch with the common citizen.
- Fifth, we will focus on *the role of the president in the legislative process*. Since the days of Franklin D. Roosevelt, most presidents have played major roles in setting the national policy agenda—a power that Congress is now trying to reclaim.
- Sixth, we will examine the role that public opinion plays on the American presidency as well as the role the president plays in molding public opinion.

■ President Clinton greeted by Monica Lewinsky on the White House lawn before news of their relationship became public. (Photo courtesy: CNN/Sygma)

THE ROOTS OF THE OFFICE OF PRESIDENT OF THE UNITED STATES

The earliest example of executive power in the colonies was the position of royal governor. The king of England appointed a royal governor to govern a colony. He was normally entrusted with the "powers of appointment, military command, expenditure, and—within limitations—pardon, as well as with large powers in connection with the powers of law making."[2] Royal governors often found themselves at odds with the colonists and especially with the elected colonial legislatures. As representatives of the Crown, the governors were distrusted and disdained by the people, many of whom had fled from Great Britain to escape royal domination. Others, generations removed from England, no longer felt strong ties to the king.

When the colonists declared their independence from England in 1776, their distrust of a strong chief executive remained. Most state constitutions reduced the office of governor to a symbolic post elected annually by the legislature. Governors were stripped of most rights we assume an executive must have today, including the right to call the legislature into session or to veto its acts. The constitution adopted by Virginia in 1776 illustrates prevailing colonial sentiment. It cautioned that "the executive powers of government" were to be exercised "according to the laws" of the state, and that no powers could be claimed by the governor on the basis of "any law, statute, or custom of England."[3]

Although most of the states opted for a more "symbolic" governor, some states did entrust wider powers to their chief executives. The governor of New York, for example, was elected directly by the people. And, perhaps *because* he was directly accountable to the people, he was given the power to pardon, the duty to execute the law faithfully to the best of his ability, and to act as "commander-in-chief" of the state militia.

The Constitutional Convention

As we saw in chapter 2, the delegates to the Philadelphia Convention quickly decided to dispense with the Articles of Confederation and fashion a new government composed of three branches—the legislative (to make the laws), the executive (to execute, or implement, the laws), and the judicial (to interpret the laws). The Framers had little difficulty in agreeing that executive authority should be vested in one person, although some delegates suggested multiple executives to diffuse the power of the executive branch. Under the Articles of Confederation, there had been no executive branch of government; and the eighteen different men who served as the president of the Continental Congress of the United States of America were president in name only—they had no actual authority or power in the new nation. Yet, because the Framers were so sure that George Washington—whom they had trusted with their lives during the Revolutionary War—would become the first president of the new nation, many of their deepest fears were calmed. They agreed on the necessity of having one individual speak on behalf of the new nation, and they all agreed that one individual should be George Washington.

The Framers also had no problem in agreeing on a title for the new office. Borrowing from the constitutions of Pennsylvania, Delaware, New Jersey, and New Hampshire, the Framers called the new chief executive the president. How the president was to be chosen and by whom was a major stumbling block. James Wilson of Philadelphia suggested a single, more powerful president, who would be elected by the people and "independent of the legislature." Wilson also suggested giving the executive an absolute veto over the acts of Congress. "Without such a defense," he wrote, "the legislature can at any moment sink it [the executive] into non-existence."[4]

The manner of the president's election haunted the Framers for a while, and their solution to the dilemma is described in detail in chapter 13. We leave the resolution of that issue—the creation of the electoral college—aside for now and turn instead to details of the issues the Framers resolved quickly.

Web Exploration

To learn more about specific presidents, see www.awlonline.com/oconnor.

Qualifications for Office.   The Constitution requires that the president (and the vice president, whose major function was to succeed the president in the event of his death or disability) be a natural-born citizen of the United States, at least thirty-five years old, and a resident of the United States for at least fourteen years. In the 1700s it was not uncommon for those engaged in international diplomacy to be out of the country for substantial periods of time, and the Framers wanted to make sure that prospective presidents spent some time on this country's shores before running for its highest elective office. Many presidents have prior elective experience, too, as revealed in Table 8.1.

Table 8.1   Personal Characteristics of the Men who Became President

President	Place of Birth	Higher Education	Occupation	First Political Office/ Last Political Office	Years in Congress	Years as Governor	Years as Vice President	Age at Becoming President
George Washington	Va.	None	Farmer/ surveyor	County surveyor/ military general	2	0	0	57
John Adams	Mass.	Harvard	Farmer/lawyer	Highway surveyor/ vice president	5	0	4	61
Thomas Jefferson	Va.	William & Mary	Farmer/lawyer	State legislator/ vice president	5	3	4	58
James Madison	Va.	Princeton	Farmer	State legislator/ secretary of state	15	0	0	58
James Monroe	Va.	William & Mary	Farmer/lawyer	State legislator/ secretary of state	7	4	0	59
John Quincy Adams	Mass.	Harvard	Lawyer	Minister to Netherlands/ secretary of state	0[a]	0	0	58
Andrew Jackson	S.C.	None	Lawyer	Prosecuting attorney/ U.S. Senate	4	0	0	62
Martin Van Buren	N.Y.	None	Lawyer	County surrogate/ vice president	8	0	4	55
William H. Harrison	Va.	Hampden	Military	Territorial delegate/ minister to Colombia	0	0	0	68
John Tyler	Va.	William & Mary	Lawyer	State legislator/ vice president	12	2	0	51
James K. Polk	N.C.	North Carolina	Lawyer	State legislator/ governor	14	3	0	50
Zachary Taylor	Va.	None	Military	None/military general	0	0	0	65
Millard Fillmore	N.Y.	None	Lawyer	State legislator/ vice president	8	0	1	50
Franklin Pierce	N.H.	Bowdoin	Lawyer	State legislator/ district attorney	9	0	0	48
James Buchanan	Pa.	Dickinson	Lawyer	County prosecutor/ minister to Great Britain	20	0	0	65
Abraham Lincoln	Ky.	None	Lawyer	State legislator/ U.S. House	2	0	0	52
Andrew Johnson	N.C.	None	Tailor	City alderman/ vice president	14	4	0	57
Ulysses S. Grant	Ohio	West Point	Military	None/military general	0	0	0	47
Rutherford B. Hayes	Ohio	Kenyon	Lawyer	City solicitor/governor	3	6	0	55
James A. Garfield	Ohio	Williams	Educator/ lawyer	State legislator/ U.S. Senate	18	0	0	50
Chester A. Arthur	Vt.	Union	Lawyer	State engineer/ vice president	0	0	1	51
Grover Cleveland	N.J.	None	Lawyer	District attorney/ governor	0	2	0	48

(continued)

Terms of Office. While many recent presidents seem to have had considerable difficulty being reelected to a second term, at one time, the length of a president's term was controversial. Four-, seven-, and eleven-year terms with no eligibility for reelection were suggested by various delegates to the Constitutional Convention. Alexander Hamilton suggested that a president serve during "good behavior." The Framers of the Constitution reached agreement on a four-year term with eligibility for reelection.

The first president, George Washington (1789–97), sought reelection only once, and a two-term limit for presidents became traditional. Although Ulysses S. Grant

Table 8.1 (continued)

President	Place of Birth	Higher Education	Occupation	First Political Office/ Last Political Office	Years in Congress	Years as Governor	Years as Vice President	Age at Becoming President
Benjamin Harrison	Ohio	Miami (Ohio)	Lawyer	City attorney/ U.S. Senate	6	0	0	56
Grover Cleveland	N.J.	None	Lawyer	District attorney/ governor	0	2	0	53
William McKinley	Ohio	Allegheny	Lawyer	Prosecuting attorney/ governor	14	4	0	54
Theodore Roosevelt	N.Y.	Harvard	Lawyer/ author	State legislator/ vice president	0	2	1	43
William H. Taft	Ohio	Yale	Lawyer	Prosecuting attorney/ secretary of war	0	0	0	52
Woodrow Wilson	Va.	Princeton	Educator	Governor/governor	0	2	0	56
Warren G. Harding	Ohio	Ohio Central	Newspaper editor	State legislator/ U.S. Senate	6	0	0	56
Calvin Coolidge	Vt.	Amherst	Lawyer	City council/ vice president	0	2	3	51
Herbert Hoover	Iowa	Stanford	Engineer	Relief administrator/ secretary of commerce	0	0	0	55
Franklin D. Roosevelt	N.Y.	Harvard	Lawyer	State legislator/ governor	0	4	0	49
Harry S Truman	Mo.	None	Clerk/Store owner	County judge/ vice president	10	0	0	61
Dwight D. Eisenhower	Texas	West Point	Military	None/military general	0	0	0	63
John F. Kennedy	Mass.	Harvard	Lawyer	U.S. House/ U.S. Senate	14	0	0	43
Lyndon B. Johnson	Texas	Southwest Texas State Teachers' College	Educator	U.S. House/ U.S. Senate	24	0	3	55
Richard Nixon	Calif.	Whittier/ Duke	Lawyer	U.S. House/ vice president	6	0	8	56
Gerald R. Ford	Neb.	Michigan/ Yale	Lawyer	U.S. House/ vice president	25	0	2	61
Jimmy Carter	Ga.	Naval Academy	Farmer/ business owner	Member, County Board of Education/governor	0	4	0	52
Ronald Reagan	Ill.	Eureka	Actor	Governor/governor	0	8	0	69
George Bush	Mass.	Yale	Business owner	U.S. House/ vice president	4	0	8	64
Bill Clinton	Ark.	Georgetown/ Yale	Lawyer	State attorney general/governor	0	12	0	46

[a]Adams served in the U.S. House for six years after leaving the presidency.

SOURCES: Adapted from *Presidential Elections Since 1789,* 4th ed. (Washington DC: Congressional Quarterly, 1987), 4; Norman Thomas, Joseph Pika, and Richard Watson, *The Politics of the Presidency,* 3d ed. (Washington, DC: CQ Press, 1993), 490; Harold W. Stanley and Richard G. Niemi, eds., *Vital Statistics on American Politics 1997–1998* (Washington, DC: CQ Press, 1998).

unsuccessfully sought a third term, the two terms established by Washington remained the standard for 150 years, avoiding the Framers' much-feared "constitutional monarch," a perpetually reelected tyrant. In the 1930s and 1940s, however, Franklin D. Roosevelt ran successfully in four elections as Americans fought first the Great Depression and then World War II. Despite Roosevelt's popularity, negative reaction to his long tenure in office ultimately led to passage (and ratification in 1951) of the Twenty-Second Amendment, which limited presidents to two four-year terms or a total of ten years in office, should a vice president assume a portion of a president's remaining term.

Removal.   During the Constitutional Convention, Benjamin Franklin was a staunch supporter of **impeachment,** a process for removing an official from office. He noted that "historically, the lack of power to impeach had necessitated recourse to assassination."[5] Not surprisingly, then, he urged the rest of the delegates to formulate a legal mechanism to remove the president and vice president.

Just as the veto power was a check on Congress, the impeachment provision ultimately included in Article II was adopted as a check on the power of the president. Each house of Congress was given a role to play in the impeachment process to assure that the chief executive could be removed only for "Treason, Bribery, or other high Crimes and Misdemeanors."

The Constitution gives the House of Representatives the power to conduct a thorough investigation in a manner similar to a grand jury proceeding to determine whether or not the president has engaged in any of those offenses (see chapter 7). If the finding is positive, the House is empowered to vote to impeach the president by a simple majority vote. The Senate then acts as a court of law and tries the president for the charged offenses, which are called **articles of impeachment.** (The Chief Justice of the United States presides over the vote on the articles and the Senate hearing.) A two-thirds majority vote in the Senate on any count contained in the articles of impeachment is necessary to remove the president from office. Only two presidents, Andrew Johnson and William Jefferson Clinton, were impeached by the House of Representatives. Neither man, however, was removed from office by the Senate. (For more on how the impeachment process works, see The Impeachment Process, p. 254.)

Succession.   Through 1996 eight presidents have died in office from illness or assassination. William Henry Harrison was the first president to die in office—he caught a cold at his inauguration in 1841 and died one month later. (John Tyler thus became the first vice president to succeed to the presidency.) In 1865 Abraham Lincoln became the first president to be assassinated. And in 1974, Richard M. Nixon, facing impeachment and likely conviction, became the first president to resign from office. The Framers were aware that a system of orderly transfer of power was necessary, so they created the office of the vice president. Moreover, the Constitution directs Congress to select a successor if the office of vice president is vacant. To clarify this provision, Congress passed the Presidential Succession Act of 1947, which lists—in order—those in line (after the vice president) to succeed the president:

1. Speaker of the House of Representatives
2. President pro tempore of the Senate
3. Secretaries of State, Treasury, and Defense, and other Cabinet heads in order of the creation of their department

The Succession Act has never been used because there has always been a vice president to take over when a president died in office. The Twenty-Fifth Amendment, in fact, was added to the Constitution in 1967 to assure that this will continue to be the case. Should a vacancy occur in the office of the vice president, the Twenty-Fifth Amendment directs the president to appoint a new vice president, subject to the approval (by a simple majority) of both houses of Congress.

The Twenty-Fifth Amendment has been used twice in its relatively short history. In 1973 President Richard M. Nixon selected the House Minority Leader, Gerald R.

---

impeachment:

Actual bringing of charges against a public official requiring a simple majority vote of the House of Representatives; not the hearings or trial on those charges.

 **Web Exploration**

For a chronology of the Clinton impeachment proceedings, see www.awlonline.com/oconnor.

articles of impeachment:

The specific charges brought against a president or a federal judge by the House of Representatives.

THE ASSASSINATION OF PRESIDENT LINCOLN.

■ When President Lincoln was shot by John Wilkes Booth, he became the first of four presidents to be assassinated in office. (Photo courtesy: Museum of the City of New York)

Ford, to replace Vice President Spiro T. Agnew after Agnew resigned in the wake of charges of bribe taking corruption, and income tax evasion. Less than a year later, when Vice President Ford became the thirty-eighth president after Nixon's resignation, he appointed (and the Senate approved) former New York Governor Nelson A. Rockefeller to vice president. This chain of events set up for the first time in U.S. history a situation in which neither the president nor the vice president had been elected to those positions.

Twenty-Fifth Amendment also contains a section that allows the vice president and a majority of the Cabinet (or some other body determined by Congress) to deem a president unable to fulfill his duties. It sets up a procedure to allow the vice president to become "acting president" if the president is incapacitated. The president can also voluntarily relinquish his power. In 1985, following the spirit of the amendment, President Ronald Reagan sent George Bush a letter that made Bush the acting president for the eight hours that Reagan was incapacitated as he underwent surgery for colon cancer.

The Vice President

The Framers paid little attention to the office of vice president beyond the need to have an immediate official "stand-in" for the president. Initially, for example, the vice president's one and only function was to assume the office of president in the case of the death of the president or some other emergency. After further debate, the delegates made the vice president the presiding officer of the Senate (except in cases of presidential impeachment). They feared that if the Senate's presiding officer was chosen from the Senate itself, one state would be short a representative. The vice president was given the authority to vote only in the event of a tie, however.

With so little authority, until recently, the office of vice president was considered a sure place for a public official to disappear into obscurity. When John Adams wrote to his wife, Abigail, about his position as America's first vice president, he said it was "the most insignificant office that was the invention of man . . . or his imagination conceived."[6]

Power and fame generally come only to those vice presidents who become president. Just "one heartbeat away" from the presidency, the vice president serves as a constant reminder of the president's mortality. In part, this situation has given rise to a trend of

■ In 1919 President Woodrow Wilson had what many believed to be a nervous collapse in the summer and a debilitating stroke in the fall that incapacitated him for several months. His wife, Edith Bolling Galt Wilson, refused to admit his advisors to his sickroom, and rumors flew about the "First Lady President," as many suspected it was his wife and not Wilson who was issuing the orders. (Photo courtesy: Stock Montage, Inc.)

Web Exploration

For more on the vice president, see
www.awlonline.com/oconnor.

uneasy relationships between presidents and vice presidents that began as early as Adams and Thomas Jefferson. As historian Arthur M. Schlesinger, Jr., once noted, "The Vice President has only one serious thing to do: that is, to wait around for the President to die. This is hardly the basis for a cordial and enduring friendship."[7]

In the past, presidents chose their vice presidents largely to "balance"—politically, geographically, or otherwise—the presidential ticket, with little thought given to the possibility of the vice president becoming president. Franklin D. Roosevelt, for example, a liberal New Yorker, selected John Nance Garner, a conservative Texan, to be his running mate in 1932. After serving two terms, Garner—who openly disagreed with Roosevelt over many policies, including Roosevelt's Court-packing plan (see chapter 10) and his decision to seek a third term—unsuccessfully sought the 1940 presidential nomination himself.

How much power a vice president has depends on how much the president is willing to give him. Although Jimmy Carter, a Southerner, chose Walter F. Mondale, a Northerner, as his running mate in 1976 to balance the ticket, he was also the first president to give his vice president more than ceremonial duties. In fact, Mondale was the first vice president to have an office in the White House. (It wasn't until 1961 that a vice president even had an office in the Executive Office Building next door to the White House!) Mondale—a former senator from Minnesota with Washington connections—became an important adviser to President Carter, a former governor who had run for office as a Washington "outsider."

The "Mondale model" of an active vice president set the expectations for what the influence, powers, and limitations of modern vice presidents should be. President Clinton expanded tremendously on the Mondale model. Al Gore, Jr., and Clinton forged a close working (and apparently personal) relationship when they traveled the country campaigning by bus in 1992. With more personal characteristics in common than many president/vice president teams (they're both Southerners, young, religious, fathers of teenage girls, and married to strong independent women, for example), Clinton made sure Gore was at his side in Arkansas when key early appointments were announced, and the two claim to consult on a daily basis. Moreover, Clinton placed Gore in charge of his effort to reform the bureaucracy (see chapter 9) and, because of Gore's long-standing interest in the environment, made him his point man on those issues. Unlike past vice presidents, Gore is often at Clinton's side when major policy initiatives are announced. In 1996, in what ABC News correspondent Cokie Roberts called a "remarkable laying on of hands," President Clinton allowed his vice president to speak in prime time, a day before Clinton accepted his party's nomination, at the Democratic National Convention. Never before had a sitting president so clearly indicated his support of his vice president as his successor. Clinton fund-raised and campaigned for Gore as he sought the Democratic Party's nod as its presidential candidate; it is clear that Clinton sees Gore's election as critical to extending his own legacy.

THE CONSTITUTIONAL POWERS OF THE PRESIDENT

Though the Framers nearly unanimously agreed about the need for a strong central government and a greatly empowered Congress, they did not agree about the proper role of the president or the sweep of his authority. In contrast to Article I's laundry list of provisions for authority of the legislative branch, Article II details few presidential powers. Distrust of a powerful chief executive led to the Constitution's intentionally vague prescriptions for the presidency. Nevertheless, it is these constitutional powers, when coupled with a president's own personal style and abilities, that allow him to lead the nation.

Despite the Framers' faith in George Washington as their intended first president, it took considerable compromise to overcome their continued fear of a too-powerful president. The specific powers of the executive branch that the Framers agreed on are enumerated in Article II of the Constitution. Perhaps the most important section of Article II is its first sentence: "The executive Power shall be vested in a President of the United States of America." Just what the Framers meant by "executive power" was left intentionally vague.

Over the years, the expected limits of these specific constitutional powers have changed as individual presidents asserted themselves in the political process. Some presidents are powerful and effective; others just limp along in office. Much of the president's authority stems from his position as the symbolic leader of the nation and his ability to wield power, whether those powers are specifically enumerated in the Constitution or not. When the president speaks—especially in the area of foreign affairs—he speaks for the whole nation. *But* the base of all presidential authority is Article II, which outlines only a limited policy-making role for the president. Thus, as administrative head of the executive branch, the president is charged with taking "Care that the Laws be faithfully executed," but he has no actual power to make Congress enact legislation he supports. Nonetheless, the sum total of his powers, enumerated below, allow him to become a major player in the policy process.

The Appointment Power

To help the president enforce the laws passed by Congress, the Constitution authorizes him to appoint, with the advice and consent of the Senate, "Ambassadors, other public Ministers and Consuls, judges of the supreme Court, and all other Officers of the United States, whose Appointments are not herein otherwise provided for, and which shall be established by Law." Although this section of the Constitution deals only with appointments, behind that language is a powerful policy-making tool. Not only does the president have the authority to make more than 3,000 appointments to his administration (technically more than 75,000, if military officers are included), many of those appointees are in positions to wield substantial authority over the course and direction of public policy. Although Congress has the authority "to make all laws," through the president's enforcement power—and his chosen assistants—he often can set the policy agenda for the nation. And, especially in the context of his ability to make appointments to the federal courts, his influence can be felt far past his term of office.

It is not surprising, then, that selecting the "right" people is often one of a president's most important tasks. Presidents look for a blend of loyalty, competence, and integrity. Identifying these qualities in people is a major challenge that every new president faces. Recent presidents, especially Bill Clinton, have also tried to appoint more women and minorities to top positions (see Table 8.2, for example). "Bad" appointments, moreover, can endanger an administration's ability to make policy.

In the past, when a president forwarded a nomination to the Senate for its approval, his selections were traditionally given great respect—especially those for the **Cabinet,** an advisory group selected by the president to help him make decisions and execute the laws. In fact, until recently, the vast majority (97 percent) of all presidential nominations were confirmed.[8]

President Clinton, however, has experienced significant difficulties in his efforts to see key policy makers, as well as federal court judges, confirmed. Even the conservative Chief Justice of the United States, William H. Rehnquist, warned that the "quality of justice" was being threatened by the Senate's failure to act on so many Clinton nominees

Cabinet:

The formal body of presidential advisers who head the fourteen executive departments. Presidents often add others to this body of formal advisers.

Table 8.2   Presidential Teams (Senior Administrative Positions Requiring Senate Confirmation)

	Total Appointments	Total Women	Percentage Women
Jimmy Carter	1,087	191	17.6%
Ronald Reagan	2,349	277	11.8%
George Bush	1,079	215	19.9%
Bill Clinton	1,257	528	42%

SOURCE: "Insiders Say White House Has Its Own Glass Ceiling," *Atlanta Journal Constitution* (April 10, 1995): A-4; and Judi Hasson, "Senate GOP leader Lott says he'll work with Clinton," *USA Today* (December 4, 1996): 8A.

Web Exploration

For more on President Clinton, see
www.awlonline.com/oconnor.

to the federal bench. Clinton's problems with the Republican majority's rejection of nominees or delay tactics are likely to increase as his term grows to a close. As Figure 8.1 reveals, moreover, the actual time it takes from inauguration to Senate confirmation of initial nominees has grown. More recent nominees have been waiting as long as three years for Senate approval. By May 1999, Senate Democrats complained that the Senate had acted on only 34 of President Clinton's 173 appointments made during the 106th Congress; one year ago, the Senate had acted on 29 nominees by this point. Moreover, no hearings had been held for any of Clintons' 38 nominees to the federal bench.[9]

Rejections of presidential nominees can have a major impact on the course of an administration. Rejections leave a president without first choices, have a chilling effect on other potential nominees, affect a president's relationship with the Senate, and affect how the president is perceived by the public. President Bill Clinton, for example, lost valuable policy-making time when key positions were unfilled; time after time he announced prospective nominees whose confirmation ran into trouble after press or other public revelations. Zöe Baird, for example, withdrew her name from Senate consideration for Attorney General after it became known that she had not paid Social Security taxes for her nanny and other household help. Lani Guinier's nomination to head the Civil Rights Division of the Justice Department was withdrawn by Clinton after he decided he could not support her views on race-based remedies. Other nominations have been held up because nominees are too liberal for the tastes of more conservative Republican senators.

The Power to Convene Congress

The Constitution requires the president to inform the Congress periodically of "the State of the Union," and authorizes the president to convene either or both houses of Congress on "extraordinary Occasions." In *Federalist No. 77*, Hamilton justified the latter by noting that because the Senate and the chief executive enjoy concurrent powers to make treaties, "It might often be necessary to call it together with a view to this object, when it would be unnecessary and improper to convene the House of Representatives." The power to convene Congress was important when Congress did not sit in nearly year-round sessions. Today this power has little more than symbolic significance.

The Power to Make Treaties

The president's power to make treaties with foreign nations is checked by the Constitution's stipulation that all treaties must be approved by at least two-thirds of the members

Figure 8.1   The Long and Winding (Possible) Road to Senate Confirmation

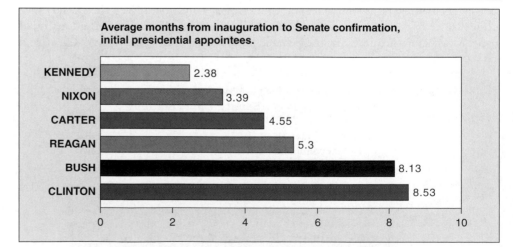

Average months from inauguration to Senate confirmation, initial presidential appointees.

KENNEDY	2.38
NIXON	3.39
CARTER	4.55
REAGAN	5.3
BUSH	8.13
CLINTON	8.53

SOURCE: From "Task Force Calls for Streamlined Political Appointments Process" by Stephen Barr, *Washington Post*, November 22, 1996, A29. © 1996, The Washington Post. Reprinted with permission.

of the Senate. The chief executive can also "receive ambassadors," wording that has been interpreted to allow the president to recognize the very existence of other nations.

Historically, the Senate ratifies about 70 percent of the treaties submitted to it by the president.[10] Only sixteen treaties that have been put to a vote have been rejected, often under highly partisan circumstances. Perhaps the most notable example of the Senate's refusal to ratify a treaty was its defeat of the Treaty of Versailles submitted by President Woodrow Wilson. The treaty was an agreement among the major nations to end World War I. At Wilson's insistence, it also called for the creation of the League of Nations—a precursor of the United Nations—to foster continued peace and international disarmament. In struggling to gain international acceptance for the league, Wilson had taken American support for granted. This was a dramatic miscalculation. Isolationists, led by Senator William Jennings Bryan (D-Neb.), opposed U.S. participation in the league on the grounds that the league would place the United States in the center of every major international conflict. Proponents countered that, league or no league, the United States had emerged from World War I as a world power and that membership in the League of Nations would enhance its new role. The vote in the Senate for ratification was very close, but the isolationists prevailed—the United States stayed out of the league, and Wilson was devastated.

The Senate also may require substantial amendment of a treaty prior to its consent. When President Carter proposed the controversial Panama Canal Treaties in 1977, for example, the Senate required several conditions to be ironed out between the Carter and Torrijos administrations before its approval was forthcoming.

When trade agreements are at issue, presidents are often also forced to be mindful of the wishes of Congress. The North American Free Trade Agreement (NAFTA) and the General Agreement on Tariffs and Trade (GATT) came to Congress after the president and his aides had negotiated these trade agreements under special rules referred to as "fast-track" procedures. These special rules are designed to protect a president's ability to negotiate with confidence that his accords will not be altered by Congress. The rules bar amendment and require an up or down vote in Congress within ninety days of introduction.

Presidents often try to get around the "advise and consent" requirement for ratification of treaties and the congressional approval required for trade agreements by entering into an **executive agreement,** which allows the president to enter into secret and highly sensitive arrangements with foreign nations without Senate approval. Presidents have used these agreements since the days of George Washington, and their use has been upheld by the courts. Although executive agreements are not binding on subsequent administrations, since 1900 they have been used far more frequently than treaties, further cementing the role of the president in foreign affairs.

executive agreement:

Secret and highly sensitive arrangements with foreign nations entered into by the president that do not require a positive Senate vote.

Veto Power

Presidents can also affect the policy process through the **veto power,** the authority to reject any congressional legislation. "Presidential vetoes have been vital to the development of the twentieth-century presidency."[11] The threat of a presidential veto often prompts members of Congress to fashion legislation that they know will receive presidential acquiescence, if not support. Thus just threatening to veto legislation often gives a president another way to influence law making.

veto power:

The formal, constitutional authority of the president to reject bills passed by both houses of Congress, thus preventing their becoming law without further congressional action.

Proponents of a strong executive at the Constitutional Convention argued that the president should have an absolute and final veto over acts of Congress. Opponents of this idea, including Benjamin Franklin, countered that in their home states the executive veto "was constantly made use of to extort money" from the legislatures. James Madison made the most compelling argument for a compromise on the issue:

> Experience has proven a tendency in our governments to throw all power into the legislative vortex. The Executives of the States are in general little more than Ciphers, the legislatures omnipotent. If no effectual check be devised for restraining the instability and encroachments of the latter, a revolution of some kind or other would be inevitable.[12]

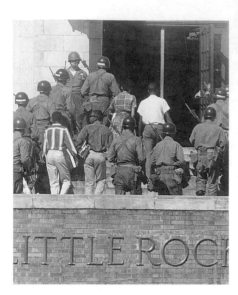

■ Chief law enforcer: National Guard troops sent by President Eisenhower enforce federal court decisions ordering the integration of public schools in Little Rock, Arkansas. (Photo courtesy: Wally McNamee/Folio, Inc.)

Leader of the party: Bill Clinton accepts his party's nomination for president at the 1996 Democratic National Convention. (Photo courtesy: Ted Soqui/Sygma)

Commander-in-Chief: President Bush and his wife, Barbara, with troops in the Persian Gulf. (Photo courtesy: Corbis/UPI)

The President's Many Hats

Shaper of domestic policy: President Lyndon B. Johnson confers with the Reverend Martin Luther King, Jr., and other black leaders about Johnson's War on Poverty. (Photo courtesy: Corbis/UPI)

Key player in the legislative process: Clinton proposes legislation to Congress and the nation. (Photo courtesy: Dirck Halstead/Liaison Agency)

Chief of State: President John F. Kennedy and his wife, Jacqueline, are greeted by the president of France and his wife during the Kennedys' widely publicized 1961 trip to that nation. (Photo courtesy: Corbis/UPI)

In keeping with the system of checks and balances, then, the president was given the veto power, but only as a "qualified negative." Although the president was given the authority to veto any act of Congress (with the exception of joint resolutions that propose constitutional amendments), Congress was given the authority to override an executive veto by a two-thirds vote in each House. The veto is a powerful policy tool because Congress cannot usually muster enough votes to override a veto. Thus, in over 200 years, there have been approximately 2,500 presidential vetoes and only about a hundred have been overridden.

President Bush was never reluctant to use his veto power: He often vetoed bills that were considered to enjoy wide popular support and had only one of his vetoes overridden. During Bill Clinton's first two years in office, he became the first president since James A. Garfield (1881) not to veto any act of Congress. But, beginning in August 1995, when he exercised his first veto involving Congress's passage of legislation to require the United States to lift its embargo of arms sales to Bosnian Muslims, Clinton found himself at odds with the Republican-controlled Congress and was forced to veto sixteen pieces of legislation through November 1996. He vetoed eight bills in the 105th Congress and only one was overridden.

The Line-Item Veto.   As early as 1873, in his State of the Union message, President Ulysses S. Grant proposed a constitutional amendment to give the president a line-item veto, a power enjoyed by many governors to disapprove of individual items within a spending bill and not just the bill in its entirety. Since then, over 150 resolutions calling for a line-item veto have been introduced in Congress. FDR, Eisenhower, Ford, Carter, Reagan, Bush, and Clinton supported the concept. In 1994 congressional passage of a line-item veto was a key item in the Contract with America.

Finally, in 1996, Congress enacted legislation giving the president the authority to veto specific spending provisions of a bill without vetoing the bill in its entirety. This move allowed the president to project his policy priorities into the budget by vetoing any programs inconsistent with his policy goals. It also allowed President Clinton to do away with more outrageous examples of "pork" (legislators' pet projects which often find their way into a budget) and to eliminate what the president viewed as needless fat in the budget. In 1998, however, the state of New York challenged the line-item veto law when the president used the line-item veto to stop payment of some congressionally authorized funds to the state. The Supreme Court then ruled that the line-item veto was unconstitutional because it gave powers to the president denied him by the U.S. Constitution. Those kinds of alterations of power, said the Court, require constitutional amendments.[13]

line-item veto:
The power to veto specific provisions of a bill without vetoing the bill in its entirely.

The Power to Preside over the Military as Commander-in-Chief

One of the most important constitutional executive powers is the president's authority over the military. Article II states that the president is "Commander-in-Chief of the Army and Navy of the United States." The Framers saw this power as consistent with state practices, and since the eighteenth century, it has proved to be wide-ranging. While the Constitution specifically grants Congress the authority to declare war, presidents since Abraham Lincoln have used the commander-in-chief clause in conjunction with the chief executive's duty to "take Care that the Laws be faithfully executed" to wage war (and to broaden various powers).

Modern presidents continually clash with Congress over the ability to commence hostilities. The Vietnam War, in which 58,000 American soldiers were killed and 300,000 were wounded, was conducted (at a cost of $150 billion) without a congressional declaration of war. In fact, acknowledging President Johnson's claim to war-making authority, in 1964 Congress passed—with only two dissenting votes—the Gulf of Tonkin Resolution, which authorized a massive commitment of U.S. forces in South Vietnam.

During that highly controversial war, presidents Johnson and then Nixon routinely assured members of Congress that victory was near. In 1971, however, publication of what were called *The Pentagon Papers* revealed what many had suspected all along—Lyndon B. Johnson had systematically altered casualty figures and distorted key facts to place the conduct of the war in a more positive light. In 1973 Congress passed the **War Powers Act** to limit the president's authority to introduce American troops into hostile foreign lands without congressional approval. President Nixon's veto of the act was overridden by a two-thirds majority in both houses of Congress.

Presidents since Nixon have continued to insist that the War Powers Act is an unconstitutional infringement of their executive power. Thus, over and over again, presidents—Democratic and Republican—have ignored one or more provisions of the act. In 1980, Jimmy Carter failed to inform members of Congress before he initiated the unsuccessful effort to rescue American hostages at the U.S. Embassy in Iran. In 1983, President Reagan ordered the invasion of Grenada. In 1990, President Bush ordered 13,000 troops to invade Panama. And, in 1993, President Clinton sent U.S. troops to Haiti to restore its president to power. On each of these occasions, members of Congress have criticized the president. Yet the president's actions in each case have been judged in terms of his success and not on his possible abuse of power.

In 1999, Congress attempted to reassert itself in the foreign affairs process but managed only to give the president mixed signals. The House of Representatives was divided down the middle on a resolution showing simple support for the air war in Yugoslavia. Then, six weeks after the bombings began, the House took another vote. This time, it barred the President from sending ground troops to the former Yugoslavia without prior approval.[14]

The Pardoning Power

Presidents can exercise a check on judicial power through their constitutional authority to grant reprieves or pardons. A **pardon** is an executive grant releasing an individual from the punishment or legal consequences of a crime before or after conviction, and restores all rights and privileges of citizenship. Presidents exercise complete pardoning power for federal offenses except in cases of impeachment, which cannot be pardoned. President Gerald R. Ford granted the most famous presidential pardon when he pardoned former President Richard M. Nixon—who had not been formally charged with any crime—"for any offenses against the United States, which he,

■ The president's foreign policy triumvirate—nicknamed ABC by White House staffers—meet at least once a week to discuss policy. Here, in February 1998, they took their show on the road to Ohio State University to rally public support for a possible military strike against Iraq. From right to left, "C" William Cohen (Secretary of Defense), "A" Madeleine Albright (Secretary of State), and "B" Sandy Berger (National Security Advisor) were shocked when White House policy was the subject of student protest during this televised meeting in Ohio. (Photo courtesy: Greg Sailor/AP/Wide World Photos)

Richard Nixon, has committed or may have committed while in office." This unilateral, absolute pardon, which prevented the former president from ever being tried for any crimes he may have committed, unleashed a torrent of public criticism against Ford and questions about whether or not Nixon had discussed the pardon with Ford before Nixon's resignation. Many attribute Ford's ultimate defeat in his 1976 bid for the presidency to that pardon.

In the waning days of his term, George Bush was showered with a torrent of criticism when he pardoned former Secretary of Defense Caspar Weinberger and five other administration officials on Christmas Eve 1992 for their conduct related to the Iran-Contra affair. Bush tried to place his pardons in the context of the historic use of the pardoning power to "put bitterness behind us and to look to the future."

Even though pardons are generally directed toward a specific individual, presidents have also used them to offer general amnesties. Presidents Washington, John Adams, Madison, Lincoln, Andrew Johnson, Theodore Roosevelt, Harry S Truman, and Jimmy Carter all used general pardons to grant amnesty to large classes of individuals for illegal acts. Carter, for example, incurred the wrath of many veterans' groups when he made an offer of unconditional amnesty to approximately 10,000 men who had fled the United States or gone into hiding to avoid being drafted to serve in the Vietnam War.

While the pardoning power is not normally considered a key presidential power, its use by a president can get him in severe trouble with the electorate. Three presidents defeated in their reelection bids—Ford, Carter, and Bush—all incurred the wrath of the electorate for unpopular pardons. Thus, just as members of Congress are always on the lookout for potentially disastrous votes, it may be that presidents should be equally as wary of using their pardoning power.

THE DEVELOPMENT OF PRESIDENTIAL POWER

Each one of the men who has served as president of the United States has brought with him some expectation about the use of presidential authority and some vision (often outlined by campaign promises) of how the country could be improved through his guidance and leadership. Through 1998, the forty-one men who have held the nation's highest office have been a diverse lot. (While there have been forty-two presidents, only forty-one men have held the office—Grover Cleveland served as the twenty-second and twenty-fourth presidents because he was elected to nonconsecutive terms in 1884 and 1892.) Yet most presidents have found accomplishing their goals much more difficult than they envisioned, even if they were elected with a sizable majority. After John F. Kennedy had been in office two years, for example, he noted publicly that there were "greater limitations upon our ability to bring about a favorable result than I had imagined."[15] Similarly, as he was leaving office, Harry S Truman mused about what surprises awaited his successor, Dwight D. Eisenhower, a former general: "He'll sit here and he'll say, 'Do this! Do that!' *And nothing will happen.* Poor Ike—it won't be a bit like the army. He'll find it very frustrating."[16]

A president's personal expectation of authority (and the public's expectations of him) are limited by the formal powers bestowed on the president by the Constitution and by the Supreme Court's interpretation of those constitutional provisions. These formal checks on presidential power are also affected by the times in which the president serves, by his selection of confidantes and advisers, and by the president's personality and leadership abilities. The postwar era of good feelings and economic prosperity presided over by the grandfatherly former war hero Dwight D. Eisenhower in the 1950s, for instance, called for a very different kind of leader from that needed by the Civil War–torn nation governed by Abraham Lincoln. Furthermore, not only do different times call for different kinds of leaders, they also often provide limits, or conversely, wide opportunities, for whoever serves as president at the time.

A president's authority can also be limited or expanded by the demands of the times in which he governs. Crises in particular have triggered expansions of presidential power. The danger to the Union posed by the Civil War in the 1860s required strong leaders to take up the reins of government. Because of his leadership during this crisis, Lincoln is generally ranked as the "best" president (see Table 8.3).

The First Three Presidents

The first three presidents, and their conception of the presidency, continue to have a profound impact on both the office and the public's expectations about the office and its inhabitants. When George Washington was sworn in as the first president of the United States on a cold, blustery day in New York City in April 1789, he took over an office and government that were really yet to be created. Eventually, a few hundred postal workers were hired and Washington appointed a small group of Cabinet advisers and clerks. During Washington's two terms, the entire federal budget was only about $40 million, or approximately $10 for every citizen in America. In contrast, in 1997 the federal budget was $1.6 trillion, or $6,065 for every man, woman, and child.

Like Washington (see Roots of Government: George Washington's Impact on the Presidency), the next two presidents, John Adams and Thomas Jefferson, also acted in ways that were critical to the development of the office of the chief executive and the president's role in the political system. Adams's poor leadership skills, for example, heightened the divisions between Federalists and Anti-Federalists and probably quickened the development of political parties (see chapter 12). Soon thereafter, Jefferson used the party system to cement strong ties with the Congress and thereby expand the role of the president in the legislative process. He also expanded on the concept of **inherent powers** by taking the opportunity to expand the size of the nation dramatically through the **Louisiana Purchase** in 1803.

Congressional Triumph: 1804–1933

The first three presidents made enormous contributions to the office of the chief executive and established important precedents to guide the conduct of those who came after them. But the very nature of the way government had to function in its formative years caused the balance of power to be heavily weighted in favor of a strong Congress. Americans routinely had intimate contacts with their representatives in Congress, while to most, the president seemed a remote figure. Members of Congress were frequently at home, where they could be seen by the voters; few ever even gazed on a president.

inherent powers:

Powers of the president that can be derived or inferred from specific powers in the Constitution.

Louisiana Purchase:

The 1803 land purchase authorized by Thomas Jefferson, which expanded the size of the United States dramatically.

Table 8.3   The Best and the Worst Presidents

Who was the best president and who was the worst? Many surveys of scholars have been taken over the years to answer this question, and virtually all have ranked Abraham Lincoln the best and Warren G. Harding the worst. A 1995 *Chicago Sun-Times* poll, for example, came up with these results:

Ten Best Presidents	Ten Worst Presidents
1. Lincoln (best)	1. Harding (worst)
2. Washington	2. Nixon
3. F. Roosevelt	3. Buchanan
4. Jefferson	4. Pierce
5. T. Roosevelt	5. Grant
6. Wilson	6. Fillmore
7. Truman	7. A. Johnson
8. Jackson	8. Coolidge
9. Eisenhower	9. Tyler
10. Polk (10th best)	10. Carter (10th worst)

SOURCE: Steve Neal, "Putting Presidents in Their Place; Longtime Favorites Top the List," *Chicago Sun-Times* (November 19, 1995): 30–1.

ROOTS OF GOVERNMENT

George Washington's Impact on the Presidency

In furtherance of his belief in the importance of the executive office to the development of the new nation, George Washington set several important precedents for future presidents:

- He took every opportunity to establish the primacy of the national government. In 1794, for example, Washington used the militia of four states to put down the Whiskey Rebellion, an uprising of 3,000 western Pennsylvania farmers opposed to the payment of federal excise tax on liquor. Leading those 1,500 troops was Secretary of the Treasury Alexander Hamilton, whose duty it was to collect federal taxes. Washington's action helped establish the idea of federal supremacy and the authority of the executive branch to collect the taxes levied by Congress.

- Washington began the practice of regular meetings with his advisers (called the Cabinet), thus establishing the Cabinet system.

- He asserted the prominence of the role of the chief executive in the conduct of foreign affairs. He sent envoys to negotiate the Jay Treaty with Great Britain. Then, over senatorial objection, he continued to assert his authority to negotiate treaties first and then simply submit them to the Senate for its approval. Washington made it clear that the Senate's function was limited to approval of treaties and did not include negotiation with foreign powers.

- He claimed the inherent power of the presidency as the basis for proclaiming a policy of strict neutrality when the British and French were at war. Although the Constitution is silent about a president's authority to declare neutrality, Washington's supporters argued that the Constitution granted the president inherent powers, that is, powers that can be derived or inferred from what is formally described in the Constitution. Thus, they argued, the president's power to conduct diplomatic relations could be inferred from the Constitution. Since neither Congress nor the Supreme Court later disagreed, this power was presumed added to the list of specific, enumerated presidential powers found in Article II.

By the end of Jefferson's first term, it was clear that the Framers' initial fear of an all-powerful, monarchical president was unfounded. The strength of Congress and the relatively weak presidents who came after Jefferson allowed Congress quickly to assert itself as the most powerful branch of government. In fact, with but few exceptions, most presidents from Jefferson to Franklin Roosevelt failed to exercise the powers of the presidency in any significant manner.

Andrew Jackson was the first president to act as a strong *national* leader, representing more than just a landed, propertied elite. By the time Jackson ran for president in 1828, eleven new states had been added to the Union, and the number of white males eligible to vote had increased dramatically as property requirements for voting were removed by nearly all states. When Jackson, a Tennessean, was elected the seventh president, it signaled the end of an era: He was the first president not to be either a Virginian or an Adams. His election launched the beginning of "Jacksonian democracy," a label that embodied the Western, frontier, egalitarian spirit personified by Jackson, the first "common man" to be elected president. The masses loved him, and legends were built around his down-to-earth image. Jackson, for example, once was asked to give a postmastership to a soldier who had lost his leg on the battlefield and needed the job to support his family. When told that the man hadn't voted for him, Jackson responded: "If he lost his leg fighting for his country, that is vote enough for me."[17]

Jackson used his image and personal power to buttress the developing party system by rewarding loyal followers of his Democratic Party with presidential appointments. He frequently found himself at odds with Congress, and made extensive use of the veto power. His veto of twelve bills surpassed the combined total of nine vetoes used by his six predecessors. Jackson also reasserted the supremacy of the national government (and the presidency) by facing down South Carolina's nullification of a federal tariff law.

Abraham Lincoln's approach to the presidency was similar to Jackson's. Moreover, the unprecedented emergency of the Civil War allowed Lincoln to assume powers that no president before him had claimed. Because Lincoln believed he needed to act quickly for the very survival of the Union, he frequently took action without first obtaining the approval of Congress. Among many of Lincoln's "questionable" acts:

- He suspended the writ of *habeas corpus*, which allows those in prison to petition to be released, citing the need to jail persons even suspected of disloyal practices.
- He expanded the size of the U.S. army above congressionally mandated ceilings.
- He ordered a blockade of Southern ports, in effect initiating a war without the approval of Congress.
- He closed the U.S. mails to treasonable correspondence.

Lincoln argued that the inherent powers of his office allowed him to circumvent the Constitution in a time of war or national crisis. Since the Constitution conferred on the president the duty to make sure that the laws of the United States are faithfully executed, reasoned Lincoln, the acts enumerated above were constitutional. He simply refused to allow the nation to crumble because of what he viewed as technical requirements of the Constitution. Noting the secession of the Southern states and their threat to the sanctity of the Union, Lincoln queried, "Are all of the laws *but one* to go unexecuted, and the Government itself go to pieces lest that one be violated?"[18]

Later, both Theodore Roosevelt (1901–9) and Woodrow Wilson (1913–21) expanded the powers of the presidency. Roosevelt worked closely with Congress, sending it several messages defining his legislative program. Roosevelt also followed the **stewardship theory** of executive-power, believing that Article II conferred on the president not only the power, but the duty to take whatever actions are deemed necessary in the national interest, unless prohibited by the Constitution or by law.[19] Wilson helped formulate bills and reinstated the practice of personally delivering the State of the Union message to Congress. World War I also forced him to take a pivotal role in international affairs.

Few presidents other than Jackson, Lincoln, Theodore Roosevelt, and Wilson subscribed to a broad and expansive interpretation of executive power prior to the administration of Franklin D. Roosevelt (1933–45), possibly because the nation was not ready to submit to a series of strong presidents and because the times and national events did not seem to call for strong, charismatic leaders. Instead, most other presidents adopted what is known as the **Taftian theory** of presidential power, which holds that the president is limited by the specific grants of executive power found in the Constitution.[20] President Taft argued explicitly for this literalist view of presidential power, a view shared by Presidents Harding and Coolidge, among others.

The Growth of the Modern Presidency

Before the days of instantaneous communication, the nation could afford to allow Congress, with its relatively slow deliberative processes, to make most decisions. Furthermore, decision making might have been left to Congress because its members, and not the president, were closest to the people. As times and technology have changed, however, so have the public's expectations of anyone who becomes president. For example, the breakneck speed with which the electronic media such as the Cable News Network (CNN) report national and international events have intensified the public's expectation that in a crisis the president will be the individual to act quickly and decisively on behalf of the entire nation. Congress is often just too slow to respond to fast-changing events—especially in foreign affairs.

In the twentieth century, the general trend has been for presidential—as opposed to congressional—decision making to be more and more important. The start of this trend can be traced to the four-term presidency of Franklin D. Roosevelt (FDR), who led the nation through several crises, including the Great Depression and World War II. This growth of presidential power and the growth of the federal government and its programs in general are now criticized by many. To understand the basis for many of the

stewardship theory:

The theory that holds that Article II confers on the president the power *and* the duty to take whatever actions are deemed necessary in the national interest, unless prohibited by the Constitution or by law.

Taftian theory:

The theory that holds that the president is limited by the specific grants of executive power found in the Constitution.

calls for reform of the political system being made today, it is critical to understand how the growth of government and the role of the president occurred.[21]

FDR took office in 1933 in the midst of a major crisis—the Great Depression—during which a substantial portion of the U.S. workforce was unemployed. Noting the sorry state of the national economy in his inaugural address, FDR concluded, "This nation asks for action and action now." To jump-start the American economy, FDR asked Congress for *and was given* "broad executive powers to wage a war against the emergency, as great as the power that would be given to me if we were in fact invaded by a foreign foe."[22]

Just as Lincoln had taken bold steps on his inauguration, Roosevelt also acted quickly. He immediately fashioned a plan for national recovery called the **New Deal,** a package of bold and controversial programs designed to invigorate the failing American economy. As part of that plan, Roosevelt:

- Declared a bank holiday to end public runs on the depleted resources of many banks
- Persuaded Congress to pass legislation to provide for emergency relief, public works jobs, regulation of farm production, and improved terms and conditions of work for thousands of workers in a variety of industries
- Made standard the executive branch practice of sending legislative programs to Congress for its approval; before, the executive branch had generally just reacted to congressional proposals
- Increased the size of the federal bureaucracy from fewer than 600,000 to more than 1 million workers

Throughout Roosevelt's unprecedented twelve years in office (he was elected to four terms but died shortly after beginning the last one), which saw the nation go from the economic "war" of the Great Depression to the real international conflict of World War II, the institution of the presidency changed profoundly and permanently. All kinds of new federal agencies were created to implement New Deal programs, and the executive branch became increasingly involved in implementing the wide variety of programs overseen by these agencies.

Not only did FDR create a new bureaucracy to implement his pet programs, he also personalized the presidency by establishing a new relationship between the presidency and the people. In his radio addresses—or "fireside chats," as he liked to call them—he spoke directly to the public in a relaxed and informal manner about serious issues. He opened his radio addresses with the words, "My friends . . . ," which made it seem as though he were speaking directly to each listener. In response to these chats, Roosevelt began to receive about 4,000 letters per day, in contrast to the forty letters per day received by his predecessor, Herbert Hoover. The head of the White House correspondence section remembered that "the mail started coming in by the truckload. They couldn't even get the envelopes open."[23] One letter that found its way to the White House was simply addressed "My Friend, Washington, D.C."

To his successors FDR left the "modern presidency," including a burgeoning (many would say bloated) federal bureaucracy (see chapter 9), an active and usually leading role in both domestic and foreign policy and legislation, and a nationalized executive office that used technology—first radio and then television—to bring the president closer to the public than ever before.

The communication and leadership styles of post-FDR presidents are very different from

New Deal:

The name given to the program of "Relief, Recovery, Reform" begun by President Franklin D. Roosevelt in 1933 designed to bring the United States out of the Great Depression.

■ President Franklin D. Roosevelt delivering one of his famous "fireside chats" to the American people. Roosevelt projected the voice and image of such a vigorous and active president that no one listening to him or seeing him in the newsreels would have guessed that he was confined to a wheelchair as a result of polio. (Photo courtesy: AP/Wide World Photos)

those of eighteenth- and nineteenth-century presidents. George Washington believed that the purpose of public appearances was to "see and be seen," and not to discuss policy issues. Abraham Lincoln was applauded for refusing to speak about the impending Civil War. Today, presidents use every opportunity to sell their economic, domestic, and foreign programs. In addition, the modes of communication have changed greatly. The rhetoric of early presidents was written, formal, and addressed principally to Congress. Today press conferences and speeches addressed directly to the public are the norm.

THE PRESIDENTIAL ESTABLISHMENT

Web Exploration

For more on the modern White House, see www.awlonline.com/oconnor.

As the responsibilities and scope of presidential authority have grown over the years, especially since FDR's time, so has the executive branch of government and the number of people working directly for the president in the White House itself. While the U.S. Constitution makes no special mention of a Cabinet, it does imply that a president will be assisted by advisers. Just think of the differences in governance faced by two Georges—Washington and Bush. George Washington supervised the nation from a temporary headquarters with a staff of but one aide—his nephew, paid out of Washington's own funds—and only four Cabinet members. In contrast, when George Bush left office in 1993, he had presided over a White House staff of 461, a Cabinet of fourteen members, and an executive branch of government that employed more than 3 million people. Today a president is surrounded by policy advisers of all types—from the attorney general, who advises him on legal issues, to the surgeon general, who advises him on health matters. The White House staff, the First Lady (see Highlight 8.1) and vice president and their staffs, the Cabinet, and the Executive Office of the President all help the president fulfill his duties as chief executive.

The Cabinet

The Cabinet, which has no basis in the Constitution, is an informal institution based on practice and precedent whose membership is determined by tradition and presidential discretion. By custom, this advisory group selected by the president includes the heads of major departments. Most presidents also include their vice presidents in Cabinet meetings, as well as any other agency heads or officials to whom he would like to accord Cabinet status.

As a body, the Cabinet's major function is to help the president execute the laws and assist him in making decisions. Although the Framers had discussed the idea of some form of national executive council, they did not include a provision for one in the Constitution. They did, however, recognize the need for departments of government and departmental heads.

As revealed in Table 8.4, over the years the Cabinet has grown as departments have been added to accommodate new pressures on the president to act in areas that were not initially considered within the scope of concern of the national government. As interest groups, in particular, pressured Congress and the president to recognize their demands for services and governmental action, they often were rewarded by the creation of an executive department. Since each was headed by a secretary who automatically became a member of the president's Cabinet, powerful groups including farmers (Agriculture), businesspeople (Commerce), workers (Labor), and teachers (Education) saw the creation of a department as increasing their access to the president.

The size of the president's Cabinet has increased over the years at the same time that most presidents' reliance on their Cabinet secretaries has decreased, although some individual members of a president's Cabinet may be very influential. Because the cabinet secretaries and high-ranking members of their departments are routinely subjected to congressional oversight and interest group pressures, they often have divided loyalties. In fact, Congress, through the necessary and proper clause, even has the authority to reorganize executive departments, create new ones, or abolish existing ones altogether.

HIGHLIGHT 8.1

First Ladies

From Martha Washington to Hillary Rodham Clinton, First Ladies (a term coined during the Civil War) have made significant contributions to American society. Until recently, the only formal national recognition given to First Ladies was an exhibit of inaugural ball gowns at the Smithsonian Institution. Not any more. Heightened interest—undoubtedly at least partially attributable to the highly visible role Hillary Rodham Clinton plays in the Clinton administration—led the Smithsonian to launch an exhibit that highlights the personal accomplishments of First Ladies since Martha Washington. The new exhibit is built around three themes: the political role of the First Ladies, including how they were portrayed in the media and perceived by the public; their contributions to society, especially their personal causes; and, still, of course, their inaugural gowns.

Although every action and even every haircut of Hillary Rodham Clinton is chronicled by the media, she is not the first First Lady to work for or with her husband.

- Martha Washington followed George to all the winter camps. At Valley Forge, she helped feed the troops and nursed the wounded.
- Abigail Adams was a constant sounding board for her husband. An early feminist, as early as 1776 she cautioned him "To Remember the Ladies" in any new code of laws.
- Edith Bolling Galt Wilson was probably the most powerful First Lady. When Woodrow Wilson collapsed and

was left partly paralyzed in 1919, Mrs. Wilson became his surrogate and decided who and what the stricken president saw. Her detractors dubbed her "Acting First Man."

- Eleanor Roosevelt also played a powerful and much criticized role in national affairs. Not only did she write a nationally syndicated daily newspaper column, she traveled and lectured widely, worked tirelessly on thankless Democratic Party matters, and raised six children. After FDR's death she shone in her own right as U.S. delegate to the United Nations, where she headed the commission that drafted the covenant on human rights. Later, she headed John F. Kennedy's Commission on the Status of Women.
- Rosalyn Carter also took an activist role by attending Cabinet meetings and traveling to Latin America as her husband's policy representative.

Given the times, Clinton is not all that much different than many of her predecessors. Public disapproval of her efforts to influence health care policy initially caused her to back off from controversial issues, however, and to champion more traditional women's issues including child care.

Following the Lewinsky scandal Hillary Clinton's approval ratings skyrocketed. This public support provided the impetus for her move to New York State and explore the political waters there. Her decision to seriously consider a run for public office is unprecedented.

For this reason most presidents now rely most heavily on members of their inner circle of advisers (the Executive Office of the President and the White House Office) for advice and information. (Chapter 9 provides a more detailed discussion of the Cabinet's role in executing U.S. policy.)

The Executive Office of the President (EOP)

The **Executive Office of the President (EOP)** was established by FDR in 1939 to oversee his New Deal programs. It was created to provide the president with a "general staff" to help him direct the diverse activities of the executive branch. In fact, it is a mini-bureaucracy of several advisers and offices located in the ornate Executive Office Building next to the White House on Pennsylvania Avenue, as well as in the White House itself, where his closest advisers often are located.

The EOP has expanded over time to include several advisory and policy-making agencies and task forces, each of which is responsible to the executive branch. Over time, the units of the EOP have become more responsive to individual presidents rather than to the executive branch as an institution. They are often now the prime policy makers in their fields of expertise as they play key roles in advancing the president's policy preferences. Two of the most important agencies are the National

Executive Office of the President (EOP):

Establishment created in 1939 to help the president oversee the bureaucracy.

Web Exploration

For more on First Ladies, see www.awlonline.com/oconnor.

Table 8.4 The U.S. Cabinet

Department	Date of Creation	Responsibilities
Department of State	1789	Responsible for the making of foreign policy, including treaty negotiation
Department of the Treasury	1789	Responsible for government funds and regulation of alcohol, firearms, and tobacco
Department of Defense	1789, 1947	Created by consolidating the former Departments of War, the Army, the Navy, and the Air Force; responsible for national defense
Department of Justice	1870	Represents U.S. government in all federal courts, investigates and prosecutes violations of federal law
Department of the Interior	1849	Manages the nation's natural resources, including wildlife and public lands
Department of Agriculture	Created in 1862; Elevated to Cabinet status in 1889	Assists the nation's farmers, oversees food-quality programs, administers food stamp and school lunch programs
Department of Commerce	1903	Aids businesses and conducts the U.S. Census (originally the Department of Commerce and Labor)
Department of Labor	1913	Runs labor programs, keeps labor statistics, aids labor through enforcement of laws
Department of Health and Human Services	1953	Runs health, welfare, and Social Security programs; created as the Department of Health, Education, and Welfare (lost its education function in 1979)
Department of Housing and Urban Development	1965	Responsible for urban and housing programs
Department of Transportation	1966	Responsible for mass transportation and highway programs
Department of Energy	1977	Responsible for energy policy and research, including atomic energy
Department of Education	1979	Responsible for the federal government's education programs
Department of Veterans' Affairs	1989	Responsible for programs aiding veterans

Security Council, the Council of Economic Advisers, and the Office of Management and Budget.

The National Security Council (NSC) was established in 1947 to advise the president on American military affairs and foreign policy. The NSC is composed of the president, the vice president, and the Secretaries of State and Defense. The president's national security adviser runs the staff of the NSC, coordinates information and options, and advises the president.

Although the president appoints the members of each of these bodies, they must still perform their tasks in accordance with congressional legislation. Thus, like the Cabinet, depending on who serves in key positions, these mini-agencies may not be truly responsible to the president.

White House Staff

Often more directly responsible to the president are the members of the White House staff: the personal assistants to the president, including senior aides, their deputies, assistants with professional duties, and clerical and administrative aides. As personal assistants, these advisers are not subject to Senate confirmation, nor do they have divided loyalties. Their power is derived from their personal relationship to the president and they have no independent legal authority.

George Washington's closest confidantes were Alexander Hamilton and Thomas Jefferson—both Cabinet secretaries—but that has often not been the case with modern presidents. As the size and complexity of the government grew, Cabinet secretaries had to preside over their own ever-burgeoning staffs, and presidents increasingly looked to a different inner circle of loyal informal advisers. By the 1830s Andrew Jackson had chosen to rely on his own inner circle, nicknamed his "Kitchen Cabinet," instead of his department heads to advise him. FDR surrounded himself with New York political operatives and an intellectual "brain trust"; Jimmy Carter brought several Georgians to

■ The president's National Security Team met after the 1998 bombings in Afghanistan and Sudan. (Photo courtesy AP/Wide World Photos)

the White House with him; and Ronald Reagan initially surrounded himself with fellow Californians.

Although each president organizes his staff in different ways, presidents typically have a chief of staff whose job is to facilitate the smooth running of the staff and the executive branch of government. Successful chiefs of staff have also protected the president from mistakes and helped implement their policies to obtain the maximum political advantage for the president. Other key White House aides include those who help plan domestic policy, maintain relations with Congress and interest groups, deal with the media, provide economic expertise, and execute political strategies.

As presidents have tried to consolidate power in the White House, and as public demands on the president have grown, so has the size of the White House staff—from fifty-one in 1943, to 247 in 1953, to a high of 583 in 1972. Since that time staffs have been trimmed, generally running around 400. During his 1992 presidential campaign, Bill Clinton promised to cut the size of the White House staff and that of the Executive Office of the President, and eventually he reduced the size of his staff by approximately 15 percent.

While White House staffers prefer to be located in the White House, in spite of its small offices, many staffers are relegated to the old Executive Office Building next door because White House office space is limited. In Washington, the size of the office is not the measure of power it often is in corporations. Instead, power in the White House goes to those who have the president's ear and the offices closest to the Oval Office. Figure 8.2 shows the offices of key presidential advisers.

THE ROLE OF THE PRESIDENT IN THE LEGISLATIVE PROCESS: THE PRESIDENT AS POLICY MAKER

When FDR sent his first legislative package to Congress, he broke the traditional model of law making.[24] As envisioned by the Framers, it was to be the *Congress* that made the laws. Now FDR was claiming a leadership role for the president in the legislative process. Said the president of this new relationship, "It is the duty of the President to propose and it is the privilege of the Congress to dispose."[25] With those words and the actions that followed, FDR shifted the presidency into a law- and policy-maker role.

Figure 8.2   Office Space at the White House, 1999

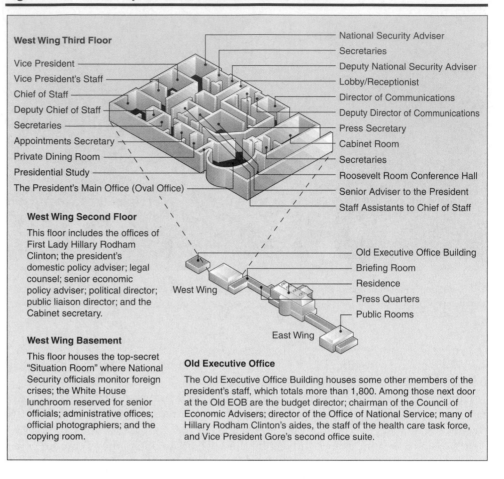

West Wing Third Floor

Vice President
Vice President's Staff
Chief of Staff
Deputy Chief of Staff
Secretaries
Appointments Secretary
Private Dining Room
Presidential Study
The President's Main Office (Oval Office)

National Security Adviser
Secretaries
Deputy National Security Adviser
Lobby/Receptionist
Director of Communications
Deputy Director of Communications
Press Secretary
Cabinet Room
Secretaries
Roosevelt Room Conference Hall
Senior Adviser to the President
Staff Assistants to Chief of Staff

Old Executive Office Building
Briefing Room
Residence
Press Quarters
Public Rooms

West Wing
East Wing

West Wing Second Floor

This floor includes the offices of First Lady Hillary Rodham Clinton; the president's domestic policy adviser; legal counsel; senior economic policy adviser; political director; public liaison director; and the Cabinet secretary.

West Wing Basement

This floor houses the top-secret "Situation Room" where National Security officials monitor foreign crises; the White House lunchroom reserved for senior officials; administrative offices; official photographiers; and the copying room.

Old Executive Office

The Old Executive Office Building houses some other members of the president's staff, which totals more than 1,800. Among those next door at the Old EOB are the budget director; chairman of the Council of Economic Advisers; director of the Office of National Service; many of Hillary Rodham Clinton's aides, the staff of the health care task force, and Vice President Gore's second office suite.

---

presidentialist:

One who believes that Article II's grant of executive power is a broad grant of authority and power allowing a president wide discretionary powers.

congressionalist:

A view of the president's role in the lawmaking process that holds Article II's provision that the president should ensure "faithful execution of the laws" should be read as an injunction against substituting presidential authority for legislative intent.

Now not only did the president and the executive branch *execute* the laws, he and his aides generally suggested them, too.

FDR's view of the role of the president in the lawmaking process of government is often called a **presidentialist** view. Thus a president such as FDR could claim that his power to oversee and direct the vast and various executive departments and their policies is based on the simple grant of executive power found in Article II that includes the duty to take care that the laws be faithfully executed. Presidentialists take an expansive view of their powers and believe that presidents should take a key role in policy making. For various reasons, Democratic presidents since FDR have tended to embrace this view of the president's role in law and policy making. In contrast, Republicans in the White House and in Congress have generally subscribed to what is called the **congressionalist** view, which holds that Article II's provision that the president should ensure "faithful execution of the 'laws" should be read as an injunction against substituting presidential authority for legislative intent.[26] These conflicting views of the proper role of the president in the lawmaking process should help you understand why presidents, especially Democratic presidents who have faced Republican majorities in the Congress or Republican presidents who have faced Democratic majorities, have experienced difficulties in governing in spite of public expectations.

From FDR's presidency to the Republican-controlled 104th Congress, the public routinely looked to the president to formulate concrete legislative plans to propose to Congress, which then adopted, modified, or rejected his plans for the nation. Although the public continues to look to the president to set the legislative and policy agenda for the nation, "merely placing a program before Congress is not enough," as President

■ President Johnson signs the long awaited Civil Rights Act of 1964. Immediately to his right is Senator Edward Brooke (D–Mass), the first African American Senator. On his left is Senator Walter Mondale (D–Minnesota) who later served as Vice President. (Photo courtesy: Corbis/Bettmann)

Lyndon B. Johnson (LBJ) once explained. "Without constant attention from the administration, most legislation moves through the congressional process at the speed of a glacier."[27] The president's most important power (and often the source of his greatest frustration), then, in addition to support of the public, is his ability to construct coalitions within Congress that will work for passage of his legislation. FDR and LBJ were among the best presidents at "working" Congress, but they were helped by Democratic majorities in both houses of Congress.[28]

On the whole, presidents have a hard time getting Congress to pass their programs.[29] Passage is especially difficult if the president presides over what is called a divided government, which occurs when the presidency and Congress are controlled by different political parties (see chapter 7). Recent research by political scientists, however, shows that presidents are much more likely to "win" on bills central to their announced agendas than to secure passage of legislation proposed by others.[30]

Presidents generally experience declining support for policies they advocate throughout their terms. That's why it is so important for a president to propose key plans early in his administration during the honeymoon period, a time when the goodwill toward the president often allows a president to secure passage of legislation that he would not be able to gain at a later period. Even LBJ, who was able to get about 57 percent of his programs through Congress, noted: "You've got to give it all you can, that first year . . . before they start worrying about themselves. . . . You can't put anything through when half the Congress is thinking how to beat you."[31] For example, during his honeymoon period, Bill Clinton saw several of his pet programs enacted into law with the support of a Democrat-controlled Congress. These included the National Service Education Plan, which revitalized national service and helped students pay for their education, and a crime bill, which included a federal waiting period for the purchase of guns, a ban on assault weapons, and more money to the states for police.

Presidential Involvement in the Budgetary Process

In addition to proposing new legislation or new programs, a president can also set national policy and priorities through his budget proposal. The budget proposal not only outlines the programs he proposes, it indicates the importance of each program by the amount of funding requested for each program and its associated agency or department. Because the Framers gave Congress the power of the purse, Congress had primary responsibility for the budget process until 1930. The economic disaster set off by the stock market crash of 1929, however, gave FDR the opportunity to assert himself in the congressional budgetary process, just as he inserted himself into the legislative

TRY IT!
To try your hand at balancing the budget, see
www.awlonline.com/oconnor.

process. In 1939 the Bureau of the Budget, which had been created in 1921 to help the president tell Congress how much money it would take to run the executive branch of government, was made part of the newly created Executive Office of the President. In 1970, President Nixon changed its name to the Office of Management and Budget (OMB) to clarify its function in the executive branch.

OMB works exclusively for the president and employs hundreds of budget and policy experts. Key OMB responsibilities include preparing the president's annual budget proposal, designing the president's program, and reviewing the progress, budget, and program proposals of the executive department agencies. It also supplies economic forecasts to the president and conducts detailed analyses of proposed bills and agency rules. OMB reports allow the president to attach price tags to his legislative proposals and defend the presidential budget. The OMB budget is a huge document, and even those who prepare it have a hard time deciphering all of its provisions. Even so, the expertise of the OMB directors often gives them an advantage over members of Congress.

The importance of the executive branch in the budget process has increased in the wake of the Balanced Budget and Emergency Deficit Reduction Act of 1985 (often called Gramm-Rudman, for two of the three senators who sponsored it). This act outlined debt ceilings and targeted a balanced budget for 1993. To meet that goal, the act required that the president bring the budget in line by reducing or even eliminating cost-of-living and similar automatic spending programs found in programs such as Social Security. It also gave tremendous power to the president's Director of the Office of Management and Budget, who was made responsible for keeping all appropriations in line with congressional understanding and presidential goals.

In 1990 Congress, recognizing that its goal of a balanced budget would not be met, gave OMB the authority to access each appropriations bill. Although this action gutted Gramm-Rudman, it "had the effect of involving [OMB] even more directly than it already is in congressional law-making."[32] Growing public (and even congressional) concern over the deficit thus has contributed to the president's and executive branch's increasing role in the budget process. As a single actor, the president may be able to do more to harness the deficit and impose order on the federal budget and its myriad programs than the 535 members of Congress, who are torn by several different loyalties.

Interestingly, many critics hail the joint efforts of the president and Congress in coming up with a balanced budget in 1998—a goal that long eluded Bill Clinton's predecessors and earlier Congresses. The feat of avoiding a deficit budget was achieved without benefit of a balanced budget amendment. Although both parties to the budget dance have sought to take credit for their thriftiness, much of the surplus that occurred is a result of savings brought about by the end of the cold war, which has led to much lower military spending, and a strong economy. Still, the president was happy to take credit for the balanced budget as he became the first president since Richard M. Nixon to sign a budget that had no red ink. By 1999, two years of budget surpluses, however, have led to fighting between Congress and the president over what to do with this money.

Winning Support for Programs

As we have seen, the job of the president is ever expanding, a trend that makes it more and more difficult for any one individual to govern well enough to meet the rising expec-

■ The president and vice president celebrate the first balanced budget in years. (Photo courtesy: J. Scott Applewhite/AP/Wide World Photos)

tations of the American public and their cynicism about politicians in general. Bill Clinton's lying to the public about his relationship with Monica Lewinsky didn't help his credibility with the public, either.

The ability to govern often comes down to a president's ability to get his programs through Congress. According to political scientist Thomas Cronin, a president has three ways to improve his role as a legislative lobbyist to get his favored programs passed.[33] The first two involve what you may think of as traditional political avenues. For example, he can use **patronage** (jobs, grants, or other special favors that are given as rewards to friends and political allies for their support) and personal rewards to win support. Invitations to the White House and campaign visits to members of Congress running for office are two ways to curry favor with legislators, and inattention to key members can prove deadly to a president's legislative program. House Speaker Thomas P. O'Neill reportedly was quite irritated when the Carter team refused O'Neill's request for extra tickets to Carter's inaugural. This did not exactly get the president off to a good start with the powerful Speaker.

A second political way a president can bolster support for his legislative package is to call on his political party. As the informal leader of his party, he should be able to use that position to his advantage in Congress, where party loyalty is very important. This strategy works best when the president has carried members of his party into office on his coattails, as was the case in the Johnson and Reagan landslides of 1964 and 1984, respectively. In fact, many scholars regard LBJ as the most effective legislative leader. Not only had he served in the House and as Senate majority leader, he also enjoyed a comfortable Democratic Party majority in Congress.[34]

Presidential Style.   The third way a president can influence Congress is a less "political" and far more personalized strategy. A president's ability to lead and to get his programs adopted or implemented depends on many factors, including his personality, his approach to the office, others' perceptions of his ability to lead, and his ability to mobilize public opinion to support his actions.

Some presidents have been modest in their approach to the office. Jimmy Carter, for example, adopted an unassuming approach to the presidency. During the energy crunch of the 1970s, he ordered White House thermostats set to a chilly 65 degrees and suggested that his advisers wear sweaters to work. Carter often appeared before the nation in cardigan sweaters instead of suits. He tried to build his "common man" image by carrying his own luggage and prohibiting the Marine band from playing the traditional fanfare, "Hail to the Chief," to signal his arrival on official occasions. In contrast, other presidents have been much more attuned to the trappings of office. Many believe that the Kennedys did it best.

Frequently, the difference between great and mediocre presidents centers on their ability to grasp the importance of leadership style. Truly great presidents, such as Lincoln and Franklin D. Roosevelt, understood that the White House was a seat of power from which decisions could flow to shape the national destiny. They recognized that their day-to-day activities and how they went about them should be designed to bolster support for their policies and to secure congressional and popular backing that could translate their intuitive judgment into meaningful action. Mediocre presidents, on the other hand, have tended to regard the White House as "a stage for the presentation of performances to the public" or a fitting honor to cap a career.[35]

■ During the thousand days the Kennedys lived in the White House, it became a trendsetting center of culture and style, a royal palace, a "Camelot." John F. Kennedy and his family had looks, youth, and wealth, and JFK was a witty and gifted speaker. (Photo courtesy: Corbis/Bettmann)

patronage:

Jobs, grants, or other special favors that are given as rewards to friends and political allies for their support.

Presidential Leadership. Leadership is not an easy thing to exercise, and it remains an elusive concept for scholars to identify and measure. Yet Americans demand that their presidents be great leaders, and ideas about the importance of effective leaders have deep roots in our political culture. The leadership abilities of the "great presidents"—Washington, Jefferson, Lincoln, and FDR—have been extolled over and over again, leading us to fault modern presidents who fail to cloak themselves in the armor of leadership. Americans have thus come to believe that "If presidential leadership works some of the time, why not all of the time?"[36] This attitude, in turn, directly influences what we expect presidents to do and how we evaluate them (see Highlight 8.2: The Character Issue). Research by political scientists shows that presidents can exercise leadership by increasing their public attention to particular issues. Analyses of presidential State of the Union Addresses, for example, reveal that mentions of particular policies translate into more Americans mentioning those policies as the most important problems facing the nation.[37]

The Power to Persuade. In trying to lead against long odds, a president must not only exercise the constitutional powers of the chief executive, but also persuade enough of the country that his actions are the right ones so that he can carry them out without national strife.[38] A president's personality and ability to persuade others are key to amassing greater power and authority.

Presidential personality and political skills often determine how effectively a president can exercise the broad powers of the modern presidency. To be successful, says political scientist Richard E. Neustadt, a president must not only have a will for power, he must use that will to set the agenda for the nation. In setting that agenda, in effect, he can become a true leader. According to Neustadt, "Presidential power is the *power to persuade*," which comes largely from an individual's ability to bargain. And, according to Neustadt, persuasion is key because constitutional powers alone don't provide modern presidents with the authority to meet rising public expectations.[39]

ℋIGHLIGHT 8.2 — The Character Issue

Not all discussions of presidential character center around lying, as was the case with Richard M. Nixon, or womanizing and draft evasion, as was the case with Bill Clinton. In an approach to analyzing and predicting presidential behavior criticized or rejected by many political scientists, political scientist James David Barber has suggested that patterns of behavior, many that may be ingrained during childhood, exist and can help explain presidential behavior.* Barber believes that there are four presidential character types, based on (1) energy level (whether the president is active or passive) and (2) the degree of enjoyment a president finds in his job (whether the president has a positive or negative attitude about his job). Barber believes that active and positive presidents are more successful than passive and negative presidents. Active-positive presidents generally enjoyed warm and supportive childhood environments and are basically happy individuals open to new life experiences. They approach the presidency with a characteristic zest for life and have a drive to lead and succeed. In contrast, passive presidents find themselves reacting to circumstances, are likely to take direction from others, and fail to make full use of the enormous resources of the executive office. Table 8.5 classifies presidents from Taft through Bush according to Barber's categories. Where would you place Bill Clinton?

Table 8.5 Barber's Presidential Personalities

	Active	Passive
Positive	F. D. Roosevelt	Taft
	Truman	Harding
	Kennedy	Reagan
	Ford	
	Carter[a]	
	Bush	
Negative	Wilson	Coolidge
	Hoover	Eisenhower
	L. B. Johnson	
	Nixon	

[a]Some scholars think that Carter better fits the active-negative typology.

*James David Barber, *The Presidential Character: Predicting Performance in the White House,* 4th ed. (Englewood Cliffs, NJ: Prentice Hall, 1992)

THE PRESIDENT AND PUBLIC OPINION

Presidents have long recognized the power of the "bully pulpit" and the importance of going public. Since the 1970s, however, the American public has been increasingly skeptical of presidential actions, and few presidents have enjoyed extended periods of the kind of popularity needed to help win support for programmatic change.

In 1974, President Richard M. Nixon resigned from office rather than face the certainty of impeachment, trial, and removal from office for his role in covering up details about a break-in at Democratic Party national headquarters in the Watergate office complex.

What came to be known simply as Watergate also produced a major decision from the Supreme Court on the scope of what is termed **executive privilege,** which later became an issue for Bill Clinton. In *United States* **v.** *Nixon* **(1974)** the Supreme Court ruled unanimously that there was no overriding executive privilege that sanctioned the president's refusal to comply with a court order to produce information to be used in the trial of the Watergate defendants.

Watergate forever changed the nature of the presidency. Because the president long had been held up as a symbol of the nation, the knowledge that corruption could exist at the highest levels of government changed how Americans viewed all institutions of government, and mistrust of government ran rampant. Watergate demystified the office and its occupant. As Richard M. Nixon toppled from office so did the prestige of the office itself. After Watergate, no longer was the president to be considered above the law or the scrutiny of the public or of the press.

Watergate not only forever changed the public's relationship to the president, it also spurred many reforms in how government and politics were run: Ethics and campaign finance laws were tightened up, and an independent counsel law, which allowed for independent investigation of the executive branch, was enacted as discussed in Politics Now: Independent Counsels and the Executive Branch. Perhaps even more than these changes, Watergate bruised Americans' optimism about what was good about America. Furthermore, intensive media attention to the president and the presidency brought him closer to the people (*and* to their intense public criticism) at the same time that the public expectations about the presidency itself increased. People began to look to the president rather than Congress to solve pressing and increasingly complex national problems even as their respect for the office—and often even its occupant—declined.

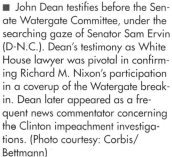

Web Exploration

For more details on Watergate, see
www.awlonline.com/oconnor.

executive privilege:

An assertion of presidential power that reasons that the president can withhold information requested by the courts in matters relating to his office.

United States v. Nixon (1974):

The Supreme Court ruled that there is no constitutional absolute executive privilege that would allow a president to refuse to comply with a court order to produce information needed in a criminal trial.

■ John Dean testifies before the Senate Watergate Committee, under the searching gaze of Senator Sam Ervin (D-N.C.). Dean's testimony as White House lawyer was pivotal in confirming Richard M. Nixon's participation in a coverup of the Watergate break-in. Dean later appeared as a frequent news commentator concerning the Clinton impeachment investigations. (Photo courtesy: Corbis/Bettmann)

POLITICS NOW

Independent Counsels and the Executive Branch

On June 30, 1999, the Independent Counsel Act that gave Kenneth Starr the authority to investigate President Clinton expired at midnight. Few tears were shed over its demise. The act, passed in response to Watergate, was enacted to remove politics from investigations of top officials in the executive branch, including the president. It called for a "nonpartisan" three judge panel to appoint an "independent" counsel to investigate charges of wrongdoing. It was hoped that transferring this authority from the Justice Department to the three judge panel would take partisan politics out of the process. The aura of nonpartisanship eroded over time and reached a new low when the three judge panel appointed the highly partisan former Republican U.S. Solicitor General Kenneth Starr.

When Independent Counsel Kenneth Starr asked to extend his probe of presidential wrongdoing to include allegations that the president lied about an involvement with a White House intern, he had no idea that his probe might ultimately give the president's popularity a boost *and* contribute to the demise of the act.

Starr was chosen to succeed the initial Whitewater Special Prosecutor in 1994. Starr's original charge was to investigate a failed Arkansas land deal that the Clintons had been involved with in the 1970s. By late 1997, the scope of his inquiry expanded to "include a bewildering range of accusations of fraud, obstruction of justice and abuse of power allegedly involving" the Clintons and some of their closest friends.[a]

In January 1998, after years of investigating both Clintons, Starr asked the court of appeals panel to expand his investigation because he had reason to believe that the president had lied under oath about his relationship with Monica Lewinsky during his deposition taken for the Paula Jones case. Starr's request was granted and subpoenas went out to scores of White House aides and Clinton friends. As the Grand Jury empaneled by Starr heard from witnesses, the president exerted the claim of executive privilege arguing that his lawyers and confidants in the White House could not be compelled to testify. Soon, Secret Service agents guarding the president were also called to testify. By June, a district court ruled that executive privilege could not be raised to block aides from testifying; the same month Starr challenged White House lawyer Bruce Lindsey's assertion that the attorney–client privilege blocked him from testifying about what he and his client, Bill Clinton, had discussed. The next month, Chief Justice William Rehnquist, long a staunch Republican before his appointment to the bench by Richard M. Nixon, refused to block Secret Service agents

from testifying, over their strong objections that the giving of compulsory testimony would impair their ability to guard the president. The same month, a federal court ruled that government lawyers such as Lindsey, could not invoke lawyer–client privilege to shield themselves or their clients from possible charges of criminal misconduct.

These victories in the courts emboldened the Independent Counsel, who then subpoenaed the president. On August 17, the president appeared before the Grand Jury via videotape from the White House. That evening, he appeared before the American people to admit to an "inappropriate relationship" with Lewinsky—a fact that he had vehemently denied earlier to the world, and even earlier in his Jones deposition.

In early September, 1998, the Special Prosecutor transmitted his 400-plus page report to the House of Representatives and it was quickly released on the Internet and disseminated in the nation's newspapers. The law calls on the Independent Counsel to advise the House of "any substantial and credible information . . . that may constitute grounds for an impeachment." Starr recommended eleven grounds for possible impeachment and testified against the President before the House in an unprecedented action by Independent Counsels.

After the Senate acquitted Clinton, Starr continued his on-going investigation of other actors in the Clinton saga. He interrogated Julie Hiatt Steele in reference to her statements about Kathleen Willey's sexual relationship with President and he negotiated a plea bargain with former Assistant Attorney General Webster Hubbell. Despite Starr's continued efforts at inquiry into the Clinton White House, the Independent Counsel Act was allowed to expire amidst much criticism of the act by members of Congress as well as former presidents.[b] The Clinton investigation was just one reason for Congress's failure to extend the act. Other reasons include the cost of these investigations (a total of $148.5 million through March 31, 1999), "lack of accountability and unchecked prosecutorial power."[c]

With the expiration of the act, the power to appoint special counsels returns to the Attorney General of the United States and no longer lies in the hands of a special three judge panel.

[a]Dan Froomkin, "Untangling Whitewater," Washingtonpost.com, October 5, 1998.
[b]Helen Dewar, "With Few Backers, Independent Counsel Law is Set to Lapse," *Washington Post*, June 5, 1999, A2.
[c]Dewar, "With Few Backers."

Writing in the 1940s, decades before Watergate, the great author John Steinbeck said, "We give the president more work than a man can do, more responsibility than a man should take, more pressure than a man can bear. We abuse him often, and rarely praise him. We wear him out, use him up, eat him up. And with all this, Americans have a love for the president that goes beyond party loyalty or nationality; he is ours, and we exercise the right to destroy him."[40]

The complex interaction of public opinion and the president are of considerable interest to scholars as well as members of the media and politicians. The president can mold public opinion and use public opinion to garner support for his favored programs. While all presidents try to manipulate public opinion to win support of their programs, they also are very mindful of their own standing in the polls.

Going Public

Even before the days of FDR's personal presidency, many others reached out to gain public support for their programs. Theodore Roosevelt (1901–9) referred to the presidency as a "bully pulpit" that he used to try to garner support for progressive programs.

■ Bill Clinton and China's Jiang Zemin at a welcoming ceremony at Tiananmen Square in June 1998 (Photo courtesy: Fritz Hoffman/The Image Works)

In this century, the development of commercial air travel and radio, news reels, television, and communication satellites have made direct communication to larger numbers of voters easier. Presidents no longer stay at home but instead travel all over the world to expand their views and to build personal support as well as support for their programs.

Direct, presidential appeals to the electorate like those often made by Bill Clinton are referred to as "going public."[41] Going public means that a president goes over the heads of members of Congress to gain support from the people, who can then place pressure on their elected officials in Washington. Ronald Reagan, for example, went directly to the American public to get support for his war on drugs. Similarly, President Gerald R. Ford went directly to the public to try to get support for his anti-inflation policies. Sporting a "WIN" button, Ford addressed the nation calling on them to rally Congress to "Whip Inflation Now."

Like most presidents, Clinton is keenly aware of the importance of maintaining his connection with the public. Beginning with his 1992 campaign, Clinton often appeared on Larry King's TV talk shown on CNN. Even after becoming president, Clinton continued to take his case directly to the people. He launched his health-care reform proposals, for example, on a prime-time edition of *Nightline* hosted by Ted Koppel. For an hour and a half, the president took audience questions about his health plan, impressing even those who doubted the plan with his impressive grasp of details. Moreover, at a black-tie dinner honoring radio and television correspondents, Clinton responded to criticisms levied against him for not holding traditional press conferences by pointing out how clever he was to ignore the traditional press. "You know why I can stiff you on the press conferences? Because Larry King liberated me from you by giving me to the American people directly," quipped Clinton.[42] In 1996, for example, President Clinton used the "bully pulpit" to convince television networks to get behind the idea of a rating system for television programs.

But some personal, direct appeals by a president appear to make no difference. In the case of health care, which the American public *seemed* to think was important in the 1992 presidential campaign, Clinton's personal approach had little apparent positive impact.

The "people" didn't *really* rank health-care reform as a priority, so his direct appeal was a complete failure and a media disaster, which ultimately made it more difficult for the president to get other programs passed by Congress. Clearly, going public—unless the public favors a policy not favored by Congress—is not a useful strategy.

Presidential Approval Ratings

Historically, a president has the best chances of convincing Congress to follow his policy lead when his public opinion ratings are up. Presidential popularity, however, generally follows a cyclical pattern. These "cycles" have occurred since 1938, when pollsters first began to track presidential popularity.

Typically, presidents enjoy their highest level of popularity at the beginning of their terms and try to take advantage of this honeymoon period to get their programs passed by Congress as soon as possible. Each action a president takes, however, is divisive—some people will approve, and others will disapprove. And disapproval tends to have a cumulative effect. Inevitably, as a general rule, a president's popularity wanes. As revealed in Figure 8.3, until the presidency of George Bush, the general trend has been increasingly

Figure 8.3   Presidential Approval Since 1938

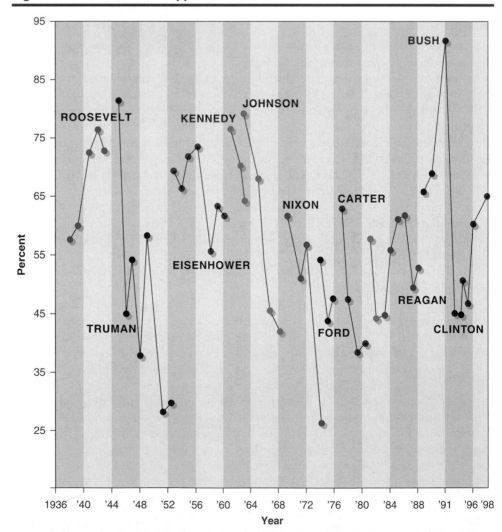

SOURCE: Harold W. Stanley and Richard G. Niemi, *Vital Statistics on American Politics,* 5th ed. (Washington D.C.: CQ Press, 1995), Figure 8-1; 1997–1998 data from *Washington Post-ABC News* polls.

lower rates of support for presidents. Many credit this trend to events such as Vietnam, Watergate, the Iran hostage crisis, and the Iran-Contra scandal, which have made the public increasingly skeptical of presidential performance. Both presidents Bush and Clinton, however, experienced increases in their presidential performance scores during the course of their presidencies. Bush's rapid rise in popularity occurred after the major and, perhaps more important, quick victory in the 1991 Persian Gulf War. His popularity, however, plummeted as the good feelings faded and Americans began to feel the pinch of recession. In contrast, Bill Clinton approval scores skyrocketed after the 1996 Democratic National Convention. More interestingly, Clinton's high approval ratings continued in the wake of allegations of wrongdoing in the Oval Office, his eventual admission of inappropriate conduct, and through his impeachment proceeding. Interestingly, as revealed in Figure 8.4, President Clinton's ratings stayed high during the House impeachment process. In fact, when Clinton went to the American public and admitted that he misled them about his relationship with Monica Lewinsky, an ABC poll conducted immediately after his speech showed a 10-point jump in his job approval rating.[43]

It was not until the Senate trial that Clinton's approval ratings began to fall. Then, as the U.S./NATO attacks on the former Yugoslavia continued and more and more reservists were called up for active duty, his ratings began to go into free fall. This is in contrast to the popular support other presidents have received during international crises.

Although surges in popularity caused by major international events do occur to bolster a president's popularity, they generally don't last long. As revealed in Table 8.6, each of the last ten presidents before Bill Clinton experienced at least one "rallying" point based on a foreign event. Rallies lasted an average of ten weeks, with the longest being seven months.[44] These popularity surges have allowed presidents to make some policy decisions that they believe are for the good of the nation, even though the policies are unpopular with the public. This phenomenon has led many to suspect a "Wag the Dog" effect. As the popular movie of that title depicted, do presidents, for example, launch bold international initiatives to distract critics of their personal (or domestic policy) problems and enhance their popularity with the public?

Presidential popularity in domestic or foreign affairs is likely to hold some sway on the president's ability to build support for programs, although some political scientists question direct linkages between presidential support and policy influence.[45] Still, it is critical to remember that the president—whether you voted for him, like him, or agree

Figure 8.4   Clinton's Job Rating Lowest Since 1996

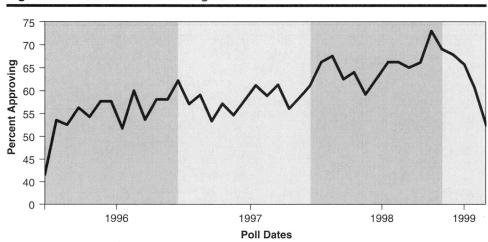

SOURCE: USA TODAY/CNN/Gallup nationwide telephone poll of 1,050 adults Sunday and Monday. Margin of error ±3 percentage points. (USA TODAY May 26,1999),8A.

Table 8.6 Temporary Rises in Presidential Popularity

Gallup poll measurements of the size and duration of the largest increase in each president's approval
rating before and after dramatic international events.

President	Event	Percentage Point Increase in Public Approval	Duration of the Increase in Weeks
Franklin D. Roosevelt	Pearl Harbor	12	30
Harry S Truman	Truman Doctrine;	12	N.A.[a]
	Korea invaded	9	10
Dwight D. Eisenhower	Bermuda Conf./Atoms for Peace speech	10	20
John F. Kennedy	Cuban Missile Crisis	13	31
Lyndon B. Johnson	Speech halting bombing of North Vietnam	14	19
Richard M. Nixon	Vietnam peace agreement	16	15
Gerald R. Ford	*Mayaguez* incident	11	25
Jimmy Carter	Hostages seized in Iran	19	30
Ronald Reagan	Beirut bombing/Grenada invasion;	8	N.A.[b]
	1st summit with Gorbachev	7	4
George Bush	Iraq invasion of Kuwait	18	30
William J. Clinton	1993 Air strike on Iraq	12	N.A.

[a]No polls conducted

[b]Overlapping events

SOURCE: *The New York Times* (May 22, 1991): A10, information from the Gallup Organization.

Information on Clinton from George C. Edwards III and Tami Swenson, "Who Rallies: The Anatomy of a Rally Event," *Journal of Politics* (February 1997): 200–12.

GLOBAL POLITICS

The Presidency in Comparative Perspective

Presidents and prime ministers, faced with the difficulties of leading governments, often wish they had those powers exercised by the other kind of executive. Is the president of the United States more powerful than the prime ministers of the parliaments of Europe, Canada, and Japan?

In some ways, the president has significant powers that prime ministers do not. First, presidents typically appoint 3,000 positions in the executive branch and judiciary, two to three times the number prime ministers appoint. Second, presidents have larger staffs than prime ministers, a significant information-gathering resource. And third, the separation of powers places the president at the center of the political system, which gives him the ability to focus popular attention on key issues and to appeal to the public.

Chief Executives in the G-7, 1999

Country	Chief Executive	Office
Canada	Jean Chretien	**Prime minister**
France	Jacques Chirac	**President**
Germany	Gerhard Schroder	**Chancellor**
Italy	Romano Prodi	**Prime minister**
Japan	Keizo Obuchi	**Prime minister**
United Kingdom	Tony Blair	**Prime minister**
United States	**Bill Clinton**	**President**

Presidents are harder to remove from office. Impeachment proceedings require that the president have committed "high crimes or misdemeanors." Prime ministers can be removed by a vote of no confidence, which requires only that a simple majority of the lower house of parliament agrees that it does not support the prime minister's leadership.

Prime ministers, on the other hand, have powers American presidents often wish they had. Prime ministers do not face formal term limits and, with the exception of Germany's chancellor, can call for elections whenever they choose (within limits). Unlike recent American presidents, prime ministers have long prior experience in the legislature (an informal requirement for the position) and cabinet: "Outsiders" do not take over the reins of government. Finally, because the majority party or coalition in the lower house of parliament elects the prime minister, the latter are virtually assured of support from the legislature. Unlike both the American and French presidents in 1999, for example, no prime minister in the G-7 faces a hostile majority in the parliament or Congress. As a result, prime ministers have a much easier time getting their legislative agendas passed into law; the success rate for cabinet-sponsored bills in the parliamentary systems is 80–90%, which no American president can match.

with him on any particular issue or philosophical debate—is the elected leader of the nation and a key player in the policy process. A president is many things to many people: a symbol of the nation, a political organizer, a moral teacher. As we discussed in chapter 1, until the 1960s most Americans looked up to their president. Watergate heightened cynicism about the president and government in general. Nevertheless, until the 1990s it was highly unusual to see a sitting president vilified in the press or on radio or television talk shows. Never before have Americans known so much about the activities of their presidents, their background, who they dated in high school and college, what affairs they've had, and what they eat. Unlike the U.S. Supreme Court, whose members deliberate in secret and wear long, black judicial robes, Bill Clinton's legs, his running shorts (and even his undershorts) were often the frequent objects of public attention and comment. In the wake of the Paula Jones and Monica Lewinsky affairs, even the presidential penis was considered fair game. Americans may need to step back and ask themselves if this is a good or a bad thing. While some feel this demystification has brought the president closer to the people, some argue that it has made it more difficult for the president to govern and a slave to public opinion. Think about your mental images of some presidents. The tendency of Americans to lionize former presidents—especially those in the distant past—makes it even more difficult for modern-day presidents to govern by comparison as the past looks better to many than the future.

CONTINUITY and Change

A Woman President?

When the Constitution was first adopted, women could not vote, let alone dream of being president. By the mid-1800s, however, some women had begun to mobilize for expanded rights and opportunities, and the right to vote in particular. As early as 1871, Victoria Woodhull, an outspoken proponent of "free love" and editor of a weekly newspaper, tried to convince women suffrage leaders to form their own political party, the Cosmo-Political Party.[46] Woodhull would then run for president in the 1872 elections. Susan B. Anthony soon vetoed the idea because she was distrustful of Woodhull and her motives.[47]

Campaigning for Woodhull in 1872 was Belva Lockwood, who founded the first D.C. franchise group, the Universal Suffrage Association in 1867. Lockwood was a strong believer in using publicity to serve the cause of women's rights. In 1884 Lockwood, along with a handful of other women, met in California and founded the National Equal Rights Party, which nominated Lockwood for president.[48] Her platform included equal rights for all, liquor restrictions, uniform marriage and divorce laws, and universal peace. Her run for the presidency was opposed by most women suffrage leaders; still, she received 4,149 votes in the six states where she was on the ballot. She ran again in 1888, but received even fewer votes.

In 1964 Senator Margaret Chase Smith (R–Me.), the only woman in the U.S. Senate, announced her candidacy for her party's nomination; her name was placed in nomination at the convention, but she garnered few votes. In 1984 the Democratic Party and its presidential candidate, former Vice President Walter Mondale, thought it could capitalize on its growing support from women voters and reenergize the party by nominating Geraldine Ferraro as his vice-presidential running mate.[49] Several women's groups, including the Women's Presidential Project, openly advocated that the Democrats add a woman to their party's ticket. The Mondale/Ferraro ticket was trounced by the popular incumbent Ronald Reagan. Still, women's hopes to have a woman president did not die. In fact, in 1998, a group called the White House Project was founded to change the political climate so that the public would be more receptive to the idea of a woman president.

Today, the idea of a woman president is becoming more and more accepted. In 1937, only 33 percent of those polled said they would vote for a woman for president.[50]

Web Exploration

For more on the White House Project, see www.awlonline.com/oconnor.

By 1999, when Elizabeth Dole announced her exploratory committee for president, 92 percent of those polled said that they could vote for a woman, up 10 percentage points since 1987.[51] To facilitate the election of a woman to the White House by the year 2004, the nonpartisan White House Project launched a campaign in 1998 with a straw ballot in women's magazines offering twenty women as potential nominees. Over 100,000 people responded; the top five winners were Hillary Rodham Clinton, Elizabeth Dole, Senator Dianne Feinstein, New Jersey Governor Christine Todd Whitman, and General Claudia Kennedy, the highest ranking woman in the U.S. military.[52]

Women today still have yet to reach parity in their representation in government at most levels. Over the years, however, the American public has clearly warmed to the idea of a female president.

1. Who do you see as emerging as likely candidates in the future?
2. Will the United States be willing to elect a woman as president by the year 2004? If not then, when?

Cast Your Vote. What female candidate would you elect as President of the United States? To cast your vote, go to www.awlonline.com/oconnor.

SUMMARY

Because the Framers feared a tyrannical monarch, they gave considerable thought to the office of the chief executive. Since ratification of the Constitution, the office has changed considerably—more through practice and need than from changes in the Constitution. In chronicling these changes, we have made the following points:

1. THE ROOTS OF THE OFFICE OF PRESIDENT OF THE UNITED STATES

Distrust of a too-powerful leader led the Framers to create an executive office with limited powers. They mandated that a president be at least thirty-five years old and opted not to limit the president's term of office. To further guard against tyranny, they also made provisions for the removal of the president and created an office of vice president to provide for an orderly transfer of power.

2. THE CONSTITUTIONAL POWERS OF THE PRESIDENT

The Framers gave the president a variety of specific constitutional powers in Article II, including the appointment power, the power to convene Congress, the power to make treaties, and the power to veto. The president also derives considerable power from being commander-in-chief of the military. The Constitution also gives the president the power to grant pardons.

3. THE DEVELOPMENT OF PRESIDENTIAL POWER

The development of presidential power has depended on the personal force of those who have held the office. George Washington, in particular, took several actions to establish the primacy of the president in national affairs and as true chief executive of a strong national government. But, with only a few exceptions, subsequent presidents often let Congress dominate in national affairs. The election of FDR, however, forever changed all that, as a new era of the modern presidency began. A hallmark of the modern presidency is the close relationship between the American people and their chief executive.

4. THE PRESIDENTIAL ESTABLISHMENT

As the responsibilities of the president have grown, so has the executive branch of government. FDR established the Executive Office of the President to help him govern. Perhaps the most key policy advisers are those closest to the president—the White House staff and some members of the Executive Office of the President.

5. THE ROLE OF THE PRESIDENT IN THE LEGISLATIVE PROCESS: THE PRESIDENT AS POLICY MAKER

Since FDR, the public has looked to the president to propose legislation to Congress. The modern president also plays a major role in the budgetary process. To gain support for his programs or proposed budget, the president can use patronage, personal rewards, his party connections, and direct appeals to the public. How the president goes about winning support is determined by his leadership and personal style, affected by his character and his ability to persuade.

6. THE PRESIDENT AND PUBLIC OPINION

Presidents have long recognized the power of the "bully pulpit" and the importance of going public. Since the 1970s, however, the American public has been increasingly skeptical of presidential actions, and few presidents have enjoyed extended periods of the kind of popularity needed to help win support for programmatic change.

KEY TERMS

articles of impeachment, p. 268
Cabinet, p. 271
congressionalist, p. 286
executive agreement, p. 273
Executive Office of the President (EOP), p. 283

executive privilege, p. 291
impeachment, p. 268
inherent powers, p. 278
line-item veto, p. 275
Louisiana Purchase, p. 278
New Deal, p. 281
pardon, p. 276
patronage, p. 289

presidentialist, p. 286
stewardship theory, p. 280
Taftian theory, p. 280
veto power, p. 273
War Powers Act, p. 276
Watergate, p. 291

SELECTED READINGS

Barber, James David. *The Presidential Character: Predicting Presidential Performance in the White House,* 4th ed. Englewood Cliffs, NJ: Prentice Hall, 1992.

Campbell, Karlyn Kohr, and Kathleen Hall Jamieson. *Deeds Done in Words: Presidential Rhetoric and the Genres of Governance.* Chicago: University of Chicago Press, 1990.

Corwin, Edwin S. *The Presidential Office and Powers,* 4th ed. New York: New York University Press, 1957.

Edwards, George, C. III., and Stephen J. Wayne. *Presidential Leadership: Politics and Policy Making.* New York: St. Martins, 1997.

Kellerman, Barbara. *The Political Presidency.* New York: Oxford University Press, 1986.

Kernell, Samuel. *Going Public: New Strategies for Presidential Leadership,* 3d ed. Washington, D.C.: CQ Press, 1997.

Levy, Leonard W., and Louis Fisher, eds. *Encyclopedia of the American Presidency.* Englewood Cliffs, N.J.: Prentice Hall, 1994.

Nelson, Michael, ed. *The Presidency and the Political System,* 6th ed. Washington, DC: CQ Press, 2000.

Neustadt, Richard E. *Presidential Power and the Modern Presidency.* New York: Free Press, 1991.

Pfiffner, James P. *The Modern President,* 2d ed. New York: St. Martins, 1998.

Pious, Richard M. *The Presidency.* Boston: Allyn and Bacon, 1996.

Ragsdale, Lyn. *Vital Statistics on the Presidency: Washington to Clinton.* Washington, DC: CQ Press, 1995.

Rossiter, Clinton. *The American Presidency.* Baltimore: Johns Hopkins University Press, 1987.

Skowronek, Stephen. *The Politics Presidents Make: Leadership from John Adams to Bill Clinton.* Cambridge, MA: Harvard University Press, 1997.

Walcott, Charles E., and Karen Hult. *Governing the White House.* Lawrence: University Press of Kansas, 1995.

Warshaw, Shirley Anne. *The Domestic Presidency: Policy Making in the White House.* Boston: Allyn and Bacon, 1996.

NOTES

1. Richard E. Neustadt, *Presidential Power: The Politics of Power from FDR to Carter* (New York: Wiley, 1980).

2. Edward S. Corwin, *The President: Office and Powers, 1787–1957,* 4th ed. (New York: New York University Press, 1957), 5.

3. F. N. Thorpe, ed., *American Charters, Constitutions, Etc.* (Washington, DC, 1909), VIII, 3816–17.

4. Quoted in Corwin, *The President,* 11.

5. Winston Solberg, *The Federal Convention and the Formation of the Union of the American States* (Indianapolis, IN: Bobbs-Merrill, 1958), 235.

6. Alfred Steinberg, *The First Ten: The Founding Presidents and Their Administrations* (New York: Doubleday, 1967), 59.

7. "Is the Vice Presidency Necessary?" *Atlantic* 233 (May 1974): 37.

8. Benjamin I. Page and Mark P. Petracca, *The American Presidency* (New York: McGraw-Hill, 1983), 262.

9. "Backlog of Nominations," *Washington Post* (May 27, 1999): A13.

10. Page and Petracca, *The American Presidency,* 268.

11. Todd Shields and Chi Huang, "Executive Vetoes: Testing Presidency Versus President Centered Perspectives of Presidential Behavior," *American Politics Quarterly* (October 1997): 431–432.

12. Quoted in Solberg, *The Federal Convention,* 91.

13. *Clinton* v. *City of New York,* 118 S.Ct. 2091 (1998).

14. Richard J. Newman, *et al.* "Making War from 15,000 ft." *U.S. News & World Report* (May 10, 1999): 32.

15. *Public Papers of the Presidents* (1963), 889.

16. Quoted in Richard E. Neustadt, *Presidential Power,* 9.

17. Quoted in Paul F. Boller, Jr., *Presidential Anecdotes* (New York: Penguin Books, 1981), 78.

18. Abraham Lincoln, "Special Session Message," July 4, 1861, in Edward Keynes and David Adamany, eds., *Borzoi Reader in American Politics* (New York: Knopf, 1973), 539.

19. "The Stewardship Presidency," in James Pfiffner and Roger Davidson, *Understanding the Presidency* (Boston: Allyn and Bacon, 1995), 29–30.

20. "The Strict Constructionist Presidency," in Pfiffner and Davidson, *Understanding the Presidency,* 27–28.

21. Lyn Ragsdale and John Theis, III, "The Institutionalization of the American Presidency, 1924–1992, *American Journal of Political Science* 41 (October 1997): 1280–1318.

22. Quoted in Page and Petracca, *The American Presidency,* 57.

23. Merlin Gustafson, "The President's Mail," *Presidential Studies Quarterly* 8 (1978): 36.

24. See Louis Fisher, *Constitutional Conflicts between Congress and the President,* 4th ed. (Lawrence: University of Kansas Press, 1997).

25. Franklin D. Roosevelt, Press Conference, July 23, 1937.

26. See, generally, Richard Pious, *The American Presidency* (Boston: Allyn and Bacon, 1996), 213, 254, 255.

27. Lyndon B. Johnson, *The Vantage Point* (New York: Holt, Rinehart and Winston, 1971), 448.

28. Morris Fiorina, *Divided Government* (New York: Macmillan, 1992).

29. See Lance LeLoup and Steven Shull, *The President and Congress: Collaboration and Conflict in National Policymaking* (Boston: Allyn and Bacon, 1999).

30. See Cary Covington, J. Mark Wrighton, and Rhonda Kinney, "A 'Presidency-Augmented' Model of Presidential Success on House Roll Call Votes," *American Journal of Political Science* 39 (November 1995): 1001–1024; and Wayne P. Steger, "Presidential Policy Initiation and the Politics of Agenda Control," *Congress & the Presidency* 24 (Spring 1997): 102–114.

31. Quoted in Thomas E. Cronin, *The State of the Presidency,* 2d ed. (Boston: Little, Brown, 1980), 169.

32. *Congressional Quarterly Weekly Report* (December 1, 1990): 4034.

33. Thomas Cronin, *The State of the Presidency* (Boston: Little, Brown, 1975).

34. Paul C. Light, *The President's Agenda: Domestic Policy Choice from Kennedy to Carter* (Baltimore: Johns Hopkins University Press, 1983).

35. George Reedy, *The Twilight of the Presidency* (New York: New American Library), 38–9.

36. Samuel Kernell, *New Strategies of Presidential Leadership,* 2d ed. (Washington, DC: CQ Press, 1993), 3.

37. Jeffrey Cohen, "Presidential Rhetoric and the Public Agenda," *American Journal of Political Science* 39 (February 1995): 87–107.

38. Reedy, *Twilight of the Presidency,* 33.

39. Neustadt, *Presidential Power,* 1–10.

40. Quoted in "Dear Abby," *The Atlanta Journal and Constitution* (March 13, 1996): D11.

41. Samuel Kernell, *Going Public: New Strategies of Presidential Leadership,* 3d ed (Washington, DC: CQ Press, 1996).

42. Dan Balz, "Strange Bedfellows: How Television and Presidential Candidates Changed American Politics." *Washington Monthly* (July 1993).

43. William E. Gibson, "Job approval ratings steady; personal credibility takes a hit," *News and Observer* (August 19, 1998): A16.

44. Michael R. Kagay, "History Suggests Bush's Popularity Will Ebb," *New York Times* (May 22, 1991): A10.

45. See Kenneth Collier and Terry Sullivan, "New Evidence Undercutting the Linkage of Approval with Presidential Support and Influence," *Journal of Politics* 57 (February 1995): 197–209; and George C. Edwards, III, "Aligning Tests with Theory: Presidential Approval as a Source of Influence in Congress," *Congress & the Presidency* 24 (Autumn 1997): 113–130

46. *Woodhull & Clafin's Weekly* (April 22, 1871).

47. Carol Hymowitz and Michaele Weissman, *A History of Women in America* (New York: Bantam Books, 1978), 172.

48. Louis Filler, "Belva Lockwood," in Edward T. James, ed., *Notable American Women,* vol. II (Cambridge, MA: Harvard University Press, 1971), 413–416.

49. Nancy E. McGlen and Karen O'Connor, *Women, Politics, and American Society,* 2d ed. (Upper Saddle River, NJ: Prentice Hall, 1998), 47–48.

50. Frank Newport, "Americans Today Much More Accepting of a Woman, Black, Catholic, or Jew as President," *Poll Releases,* The Gallup Organization, March 29, 1999.

51. Newport, "Americans Today Much More Accepting of a Woman."

52. Gloria Negri, "Liswood's Goal: A Woman in the White House," *Boston Globe* (May 2, 1999): *City Weekly,* 1.

(Photo courtesy: Dan Loh/AP/Wide World Photos)

The Bureaucracy

- **The Roots and Development of the Federal Bureaucracy**
- **The Modern Bureaucracy**
- **Policy Making**
- **Making Agencies Accountable**

On November 14, 1995, after learning that his brother in Italy was desperately ill, Sudjai Pattuma flew from St. Louis to Chicago, the only place in the Midwest that processes same-day passports. When he breathlessly arrived at the doors of the federal office building, he was told by guards on duty that the passport office was closed. Without the passport, he could not visit his brother.

The same day, Michelle Castillon went to her local Internal Revenue Service (IRS) office to obtain forms that she needed in order to be able to close the sale of her house, which was scheduled for the next day. The IRS office was closed.

In the Rocky Mountains, families who had dreamed of and saved for their vacation were turned away. The Rocky Mountain National Park was closed.

Karen O'Connor's American University American Politics class had a long-awaited tour of the Supreme Court canceled.

People calling the Social Security Administration were greeted with a recording: "Due to the shutdown of the government, our 800 number is temporarily closed."

People surfing the Internet could not reach Thomas, the computer service of the Library of Congress that allows the public to read legislation including the budget bill that was at the core of the 1996 budget impasse between Congress and the president.

Washington D.C.'s Department of Public Works was closed.

In Atlanta, Georgia, as the flu season began in earnest, 75 percent of the workers at the Centers for Disease Control and Prevention (CDC) were sent home. While flu rates weren't monitored, CDC Director David Satcher tried to reassure the public by telling a *New York Times* reporter, "I guess what we're trying to say is that we have tried to maintain employees who are in the front line and who have to respond most urgently to disease outbreaks."[1]

*L*ife-threatening problems? Probably not. Yet many Americans, some for the first time, were made painfully aware of the role that the federal government plays in their lives as many government agencies were closed as a result of the budget impasse in late 1995. While Americans in general rail against bureaucrats, the bureaucracy, and big government—especially the federal government—many were quick to learn that the national government provides services that they often take for granted.

Newspaper columnists, television commentators, and radio talk-show programs were abuzz with comments on the shutdown. They noted that congressional aides were still on the payroll, but that National Park Service rangers were closing the Statue of Liberty, D.C. tourist attractions, and national parks. They noted that gravediggers at Arlington National Cemetery continued to work, but federal health inspectors—who kept people alive—were not. Even the *New York Times* weighed in on the "essential" debate, reminding readers that what's essential today may not be tomorrow.[2]

The government shutdown made many citizens aware of the range of activities the U.S. government affects. Citizen anger over the 1995 government shutdown has played a major role in the Congress' more recent compromises with the president over budgets and budget priorities. Simply put, the slim Republican Congressional majority doesn't want to be blamed again for shutting down the government and the bureaucracy.

Often called the "fourth branch of government," because of the power agencies and bureaus can exercise, conservatives charge that the bureaucracy—the thousands of government agencies and institutions that implement and administer laws and programs established by Congress and the executive branch—is too liberal and that its functions constitute unnecessary government meddling in our lives. They argue that the bureaucracy is too large, too powerful, and too unaccountable to the people or to elected officials. In contrast, liberals view it as too slow, too unimaginative to solve America's problems, and too zealous a guardian of the status quo. Whether conservative, liberal, or moderate, most Americans think that the bureaucracy works poorly and is wasteful. Tales of bureaucratic agency payments for $640 toilet seats and $7,622 coffee makers (no matter how these costs are justified) do not help the public's image of the bureaucracy.

Candidates for public office, presidents, and Congress constantly criticize the bureaucracy and speak about it as though it were a foreign power to be conquered. Members of Congress joke that there is a game called "Bureaucracy" in which "There is only one rule. The first one to move loses." Even *Roget's Thesaurus* equates the term "bureaucracy" with officialism and red tape.[3] In fact, the **bureaucracy** consists of a set of complex hierarchical departments, agencies, commissions, and their staffs that exist to help a chief executive carry out his or her duty to enforce the law. As such, the bureaucracy is part of the executive branch of the federal government (the states and even local governments also have bureaucracies).

Harold D. Lasswell once defined political science as the "study of who gets what, when, and how."[4] It is by studying the bureaucracy that those questions can perhaps best be answered. To allow you to understand the role of the bureaucracy in the policy and governmental processes, this chapter explores the following issues:

- First, we will trace *the roots and development of the federal bureaucracy.*
- Second, we will examine *the modern bureaucracy* by discussing bureaucrats and the formal organization of the bureaucracy.
- Third, we will discuss *policy making,* including the role of rule making and adjudication.
- Fourth, we will analyze *how agencies are held accountable.*

THE ROOTS AND DEVELOPMENT OF THE FEDERAL BUREAUCRACY

In the American system, the bureaucracy can be thought of as the part of the government that makes policy as it links together the three branches of the national govern-

bureaucracy:

A set of complex hierarchical departments, agencies, commissions, and their staffs that exist to help a chief executive officer carry out his or her duty to enforce the law.

ment and the federal system. Although Congress makes the laws, it must rely on the executive branch and the bureaucracy to enforce them. Commissions such as the Equal Employment Opportunity Commission (EEOC) have the power not only to make rules, but also to settle disputes between parties concerning the enforcement and implementation of those rules. Often, agency determinations are challenged in the courts. And because most administrative agencies that make up part of the bureaucracy enjoy reputations for special expertise in clearly defined policy areas, the federal judiciary routinely defers to bureaucratic administrative decision makers.

German sociologist Max Weber believed bureaucracies were a rational way for complex societies to organize themselves. Model bureaucracies, said Weber, are characterized by certain features, including:

1. A chain of command in which authority flows from top to bottom
2. A division of labor whereby work is apportioned among specialized workers to increase productivity
3. A specification of authority where there are clear lines of authority among workers and their superiors
4. A goal orientation that determines structure, authority, and rules
5. Impersonality, whereby all employees are treated fairly based on merit and all clients are served equally, without discrimination, according to established rules
6. Productivity, whereby all work and actions are evaluated according to established rules[5]

This characterization more or less aptly describes the development of the federal bureaucracy since George Washington's time.

In 1999 the executive branch had over 2.6 million employees employed directly by the president or his advisers or in independent agencies or commissions. In 1789 conditions were quite different. George Washington's bureaucracy consisted of only three departments, which had existed under the Articles of Confederation: State (called Foreign Affairs under the Articles of Confederation), War, and Treasury. Soon, the head of each department was called its *secretary*. To help the president with legal advice, Congress created the office of attorney general. The original status of the attorney general, however, was unclear—was he a member of the judicial or executive branch? That confusion was remedied in 1870 with the creation of the Justice Department as part of the executive branch, with the attorney general as its head. From the beginning, individuals appointed as Cabinet secretaries (as well as the attorney general) were subject to approval by the U.S. Senate, but were removable by the president alone. Even the first Congress realized how important it was for a president to be surrounded by those in whom he had complete confidence and trust.

From 1816 to 1861, the size of the federal bureaucracy grew as increased demands were made on existing departments and new departments were created. The Post Office, for example, which Congress was constitutionally authorized to create in Article I, was forced to expand to meet the needs of a growing and westward-expanding population. In 1829 the Post Office was removed from the jurisdiction of the Treasury Department by Andrew Jackson, and the Postmaster General was promoted to Cabinet rank, thereby giving him greater control over the separate office and its immense number of employees.

The Civil War

The Civil War (1861–65) permanently changed the nature of the federal bureaucracy. As the nation geared up for war, thousands of additional employees were added to existing departments. The Civil War also spawned the need for new government agencies. A series of poor harvests and marketing problems led President Abraham Lincoln (who understood that one needs food in order to conduct a war) to create the Department of Agriculture in 1862, although it was not given full Cabinet-level status until 1889.

After the Civil War, the need for big government continued unabated. The Pension Office was established in 1866 to pay benefits to the thousands of Northern veterans who had fought in the war (more than 127,000 veterans were initially eligible for benefits). Justice was made a department in 1870, and other departments were added through 1900. Agriculture became a full-fledged department and began to play an important role in informing farmers about the latest developments in soil conservation, livestock breeding, and planting techniques. The increase in the types and nature of government services resulted in a parallel rise in the number of federal jobs, as illustrated in Figure 9.1. Many of the new jobs were used by the president or leaders of the president's political party for **patronage,** that is, jobs, grants, or other special favors given as rewards to friends and political allies for their support. Political patronage is often defended as an essential element of the party system because it provides rewards and inducements for party workers.

From Spoils to Merit

In 1831, describing a "rotation in office" policy for bureaucrats supported by President Andrew Jackson, Senator William Learned Marcy of New York commented, "To the victor belong the spoils." From his statement derives the phrase **spoils system** to describe the firing of public-office holders of the defeated political party and their replacement with loyalists of the new administration. Jackson, in particular, faced severe criticism for populating the federal government with his political cronies. But many presidents, including Jackson, argued that in order to implement their policies, they

patronage:

Jobs, grants, or other special favors that are given as rewards to friends and political allies for their support.

spoils system:

The firing of public-office holders of a defeated political party and their replacement with loyalists of the newly elected party.

Figure 9.1   Number of Federal Employees in the Executive Branch, 1792–1999

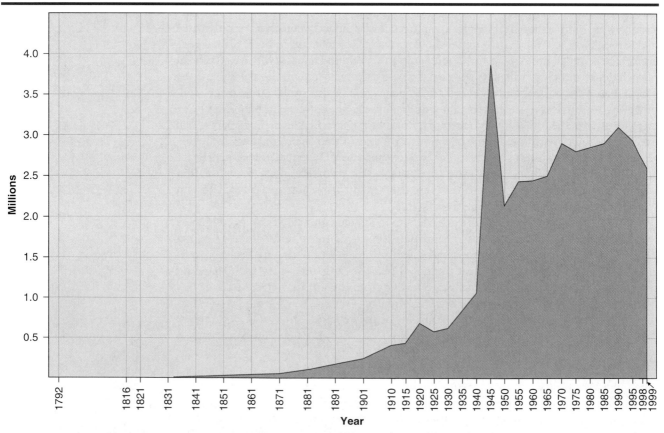

SOURCE: U.S. Department of Commerce, Bureau of the Census, *Historical State of U.S.: Colonial through 1970* (Washington: U.S. Government Printing Office, 1975): U.S. Bureau of Labor Statistics, *Monthly Labor Review*, November 1988, and U. S. Office of Personnel Management, *The Fact Book* http://www.opm.gov/feddata/factbook/html/fb-p08.htm
Note: The rapid increase in 1940 and subsequent decrease in 1945 was due to World War II.

had to be able to appoint those who subscribed to their political views.

The spoils system reached a high-water mark during Abraham Lincoln's presidency. By the time James A. Garfield, a former distinguished Civil War officer, was elected president in 1880, many reformers were calling publicly for changes in the patronage system. On his election to office, Garfield, like many presidents before him, was besieged by office seekers. Washington, D.C., had not seen such a demand for political jobs since Abraham Lincoln became the first president elected as a Republican. Garfield's immediate predecessor, Rutherford B. Hayes, had favored the idea of the replacement of the spoils system with a merit system based on test scores and ability. Congress, however, failed to pass the legislation he proposed. Possibly because potential job seekers wanted to secure positions before Congress had the opportunity to act on an overhauled civil service system, thousands pressed Garfield for positions. This siege prompted Garfield to record in his diary: "My day is frittered away with the personal seeking of people when it ought to be given to the great problems which concern the whole country."[6] Garfield resolved to reform the civil service, but his life was cut short by the bullets of an assassin who, ironically, was a frustrated job seeker.

Public reaction to Garfield's death and increasing criticism of the spoils system prompted Congress to pass the Civil Service Reform Act in 1883, more commonly known as the **Pendleton Act,** named in honor of its sponsor, George H. Pendleton (D-Ohio), to reduce patronage. It established the principle of federal employment on the

■ A political cartoonist's view of how President Andrew Jackson would be immortalized for his use of the spoils system. (Photo courtesy: Corbis/Bettmann)

Pendleton Act:

Reform measure that created the Civil Service Commission to administer a partial merit system. The act classified the federal service by grades, to which appointments were made based on the results of a competitive examination. It made it illegal for political appointees to be required to contribute to a particular political party.

■ An artist's interpretation of President Garfield's assassination at the hands of an unhappy office seeker. (Photo courtesy: Corbis/Bettmann)

civil service system:

The system created by civil service laws by which many appointments to the federal bureaucracy are made.

merit system:

The system by which federal civil service jobs are classified into grades or levels, to which appointments are made on the basis of performance on competitive examinations.

basis of open, competitive exams and created a bipartisan three-member Civil Service Commission, which operated until 1978. Initially, only about 10 percent of the positions in the federal **civil service system** were covered, but later laws and executive orders have extended coverage of the act to over 90 percent of all federal employees. This new system was called the **merit system.**

The civil service system as it has evolved today provides a powerful base for federal agencies and bureaucrats. Federal workers have tenure and the leverage of politicians is reduced. The good part is that the spoils system was reduced (but not eliminated). The bad part, however, is that federal agencies can and often do take on a life of their own making administrative law, passing judgments, and so on. With 90 percent of the federal workforce secure in their positions, some bureaucrats have been able to thwart reforms passed by legislators and wanted by the people. This often makes the bureaucracy the target of public criticism and citizen frustration.

National Efforts to Regulate the Economy

independent regulatory commission:

An agency created by Congress that is generally concerned with a specific aspect of the economy.

As the nation grew, so did the bureaucracy. In the wake of the tremendous growth of big business (especially railroads), widespread price fixing, and other unfair business practices that occurred after the Civil War, Congress created the Interstate Commerce Commission (ICC). It became the first **independent regulatory commission,** an agency outside of the major executive departments, generally concerned with particular aspects of the economy. Independent regulatory commissions such as the ICC are created by Congress to be independent of direct presidential authority. Commission members, although appointed by the president, hold their jobs for fixed terms and are not removable by the president unless they fail to uphold their oaths of office. In 1887 the creation of the ICC also marked a shift in the focus of the bureaucracy from service to regulation. Its creation gave the government—in the shape of the bureaucracy—vast powers over individual and property rights. In creating the ICC, Congress was reacting to public outcries over the exorbitant rates charged by railroad companies for hauling freight.

The 1900 election of Theodore Roosevelt, a progressive Republican, strengthened the movement toward governmental regulation of the economic sphere; the size of the bureaucracy was further increased when, in 1903, Roosevelt asked Congress to establish a Department of Commerce and Labor to oversee employer-employee relations. Roosevelt was motivated by the existence of intolerable labor practices, including low wages, long hours, substandard working conditions, the refusal of employers to recognize the rights of workers to join a union, and the fact that many businesses had grown so large and powerful that they could force workers to accept substandard conditions.

In 1913 President Woodrow Wilson divided the Department of Commerce and Labor and created a separate Department of Labor when it became clear that one agency could not well represent the interests of both employers and employees, factions with greatly differing perspectives. The creation of this department reflected the economic and societal changes that occurred as immigration increased and the economy became increasingly industrialized. One year later, in 1914, Congress created the Federal Trade Commission (FTC). Its function was to protect small businesses and the public from unfair competition, especially from big business. Agencies were also created to concentrate on women's crises. The Women's Bureau, as discussed in Roots of Government: Mary Anderson, is a good example of this type of program.

Web Exploration
For more about the Women's Bureau, see
www.awlonline.com/oconnor.

The ratification of the Sixteenth Amendment to the Constitution in 1913 also affected the size of government and the possibilities for growth. It gave Congress the authority to implement a federal income tax to supplement the national treasury and provided an infusion of funds to support new federal agencies, services, and governmental programs.

What Should Government Do?

During the early 1900s, while Progressives raised the public cry for governmental regulation of business, many Americans, especially members of the business com-

ROOTS OF GOVERNMENT

Mary Anderson: The First Head of the Federal Women's Bureau

After pressure from women's groups, the Women in Industry Service, a wartime bureau originally established within the Department of Labor, was converted into a permanent Women's Bureau within the Labor Department by an act of Congress in 1920. Its first director was Mary Anderson, who migrated from Sweden with her younger sister to Michigan in the late 1880s in steerage. She soon moved to Chicago and found work in a variety of factories. In 1899 she was elected president of the woman stitchers, which was part of the International Boot and Shoe Workers Union.

After years of union work, World War I brought a new role for Anderson when Samuel Gompers, labor's representative on the Advisory Commission on the U.S. Council of National Defense, appointed her to a subcommittee on women in industry. There she met Mary van Kleeck, who was chosen to head the women's branch in the Army's Ordnance Department; van Kleeck asked Anderson to join

her staff. "Six months later, the Department of Labor set up a wartime bureau, the Women in Industry Service, with van Kleeck as director and Anderson as assistant director."* Later, when van Kleeck resigned, Anderson took her place. A few months later, when the Service was converted into a permanent Woman's Bureau, President Woodrow Wilson appointed her as director.

Under Anderson's directorship, the Women's Bureau began its long tradition of fact-finding and advocacy on behalf of women workers. During World War II, Anderson, relying on her World War I experiences, established governmental procedures to facilitate the influx of women workers into the defense industry and to enhance women's access to jobs and job training. She retired in 1944.

*Edward T. James, "Mary Anderson," in Barbara Sicherman and Carol Hurd Green, eds. *Notable American Women: The Modern Period* (Cambridge, MA: Harvard University Press, 1980), 23.

---

munity, continued to resist such moves. They believed that any federal government regulation was wrong. Instead they favored governmental facilitation of the national economy through a commitment to *laissez-faire,* a French term that means to leave alone. In America, the term was used to describe a governmental hands-off policy concerning the economy. This philosophical debate about the role of government in regulating the economy had major ramifications on the size of government and the bureaucracy. A *laissez-faire* attitude, for example, implied little need for the creation of new independent regulatory commissions or executive departments. In many ways, this philosophy guided the current Republican Congress's efforts to downsize and deregulate the economy.

The New Deal and Bigger Government.

In the wake of the high unemployment and weak financial markets of the Great Depression, Franklin D. Roosevelt planned to revitalize the economy by creating hundreds of new government agencies to regulate business practices and various aspects of the economy. Roosevelt proposed and the Congress enacted far-ranging economic legislation. The desperate mood of the nation supported these moves, as most Americans began to change their ideas about the proper role of government and the provision of governmental services. Formerly, Americans had believed in a hands-off approach; now they considered it the government's job to get the economy going and get Americans back to work.

■ A political cartoonist satirizes President Roosevelt's criticisms of the Court's repeated rulings against the constitutionalizing of New Deal programs.(Photo courtesy: *Richmont-Times Dispatch*)

Within the first hundred days of Roosevelt's administration, Congress approved every new regulatory measure proposed by the president. Other measures that Congress approved were the National Industrial Recovery Act (NIRA), an unprecedented attempt to regulate industry, and the Agricultural Adjustment Act (AAA), to provide government support for farm prices and to regulate farm production to ensure market-competitive prices. Congress also created the Federal Deposit Insurance Corporation (FDIC) to insure bank deposits, and it passed the Federal Securities Act, which gave the Federal Trade Commission the authority to supervise and regulate the issuance, buying, and selling of stocks and bonds.

Until 1937 the Supreme Court refused to allow Congress or the president to delegate to the executive branch or the bureaucracy such far-ranging authority to regulate the economy. *Laissez-faire* was alive and well at the Court, and attempts to end the economic slump through greater governmental involvement were repeatedly stymied by the justices. In a series of key decisions made through 1937, the Supreme Court repeatedly invalidated key provisions in congressional legislation designed to regulate various aspects of the economy. The Court and others who subscribed to *laissez-faire* principles of a free enterprise system argued that natural economic laws at work in the marketplace control the buying and selling of goods. Thus advocates of *laissez-faire* believed that the government had no right to regulate business in any way.

In response, FDR, frustrated by the decisions of the Court, proposed his famous Court-packing plan (see chapter 10), which would have allowed him to add appointees to the Court. In the wake of that institution-threatening proposal, the Court quickly fell into sync with public opinion. In a series of cases, the Supreme Court reversed a number of its earlier decisions and upheld what some have termed the "alphabetocracy." For example, the Court upheld the constitutionality of the National Labor Relations Act of 1935 (NLRA), which allowed recognition of unions and established formal arbitration procedures for employers and employees.[7] Subsequent decisions upheld the validity of the Fair Labor Standards Act (FLSA) and the Agricultural Adjustment Act (AAA).[8]

Once these new programs were declared constitutional, the proverbial floodgates were open to the creation of more governmental agencies. And with the growth in the bureaucracy came more calls for reform of the system.

World War II and Its Aftermath.   During World War II, as revealed in Figure 9.1, the federal government grew tremendously to meet the needs of a nation at war. Tax rates were increased to support the war, and they never again fell to prewar levels. After the war, this infusion of new monies and veterans' demands for services led to a variety of new programs and a much bigger government. The G.I. Bill, for example, provided college loans for returning veterans and reduced mortgage rates to allow them to buy homes. The national government's involvement in these programs not only affected more people, it also led to its greater involvement in more regulation. Homes bought with Veterans' Housing Authority loans, for example, had to meet certain specifications. With these programs, Americans became increasingly accustomed to the national government's role in entirely new areas, such as middle-class housing.

After World War II, the civil rights movement and President Lyndon B. Johnson's War on Poverty (see chapter 6) produced additional growth in the bureaucracy. The Equal Employment Opportunity Commission (EEOC) was created in 1964, and the departments of Housing and Urban Development (HUD) and Transportation were created in 1966. These expansions of the bureaucracy corresponded to increases in the president's power and his ability to persuade Congress that new agencies would be an effective way to solve pressing social problems. Remember from chapter 8 that most major expansions in the power of the presidency have occurred during times of war or economic emergency. Similarly, most of the important changes that have occurred in the size of the bureaucracy through the 1970s occurred in response to war, economic, or social crises.

THE MODERN BUREAUCRACY

Critics continually lament that the national government is not run like a business. But the national government differs from private business in ways too numerous to cover here adequately. Governments exist for the public good, not to make money. Businesses are driven by a profit motive; government leaders, but not bureaucrats, are driven by reelection. Businesses get their money from customers; the national government gets its money from taxpayers. Another difference between a bureaucracy and a business is that it is difficult to determine to whom bureaucracies are responsible. Is it the president? Congress? The citizenry?

These kinds of differences have a tremendous consequence on the way the bureaucracy operates.[9] Because all of the incentive in government "is in the direction of not making mistakes," public employees view risks and rewards very differently than their private-sector counterparts.[10] The key to the modern bureaucracy is to understand how the bureaucracy is organized, who bureaucrats are, and how organization and personnel affect each other; but it is also key to understand that government cannot be run like a business. An understanding of these facts and factors can help in the search for ways to motivate positive change in the bureaucracy.

Who Are Bureaucrats?

Federal bureaucrats are career government employees who work in the executive branch, in the fourteen Cabinet-level departments and the more than sixty independent agencies that comprise more than 2,000 bureaus, divisions, branches, offices, services, and other subunits of the federal government. There are approximately 2.6 million federal workers in the executive branch. Nearly one-fourth of all civilian employees work in the Postal Service. The remaining federal civilian workers are spread out among the various executive departments and agencies throughout the United States. Most of these federal employees are paid according to what is called the "General Schedule" (GS). They advance within GS grades and onto higher GS levels and salaries as their careers progress.

As a result of reforms made during the Truman administration that built on the Pendleton Act, most civilian federal governmental employees today are selected by merit standards, which include tests (such as civil service or foreign service exams) and educational criteria. Merit systems protect federal employees from being fired for political reasons. (For a description of how a federal employee can be fired, see Table 9.1.)

Table 9.1 How to Fire a Federal Bureaucrat

Firing a bureaucrat can be very difficult. Civil service rules make it easier to fire someone for misconduct than poor performance. Incompetent employees must be given notice by their supervisors and given an opportunity for remedial training.

To fire a member of the competitive civil service, explicit procedures must be followed:

1. At least thirty days' written notice must be given to an employee in advance of firing or demotion for incompetence or misconduct.

2. The written notification must contain a statement of reasons for the action and specific examples of unacceptable performance.

3. The employee has the right to reply both orally and in written form to the charges, and has the right to an attorney.

4. Appeals from any adverse action against the employee can be made to the three-person Merit Systems Protection Board (MSPB), a bipartisan body appointed by the president and confirmed by the Senate.

5. All employees have the right to a hearing and to an attorney in front of the MSPB.

6. All decisions of the MSPB may be appealed by the employee to the U.S. Court of Appeals.

■ Who are the bureaucrats? Mulder and Scully, of Fox TV's *The X-Files*, a series about federal agents who investigate the paranormal, would be no one's idea of bureaucrats. But, as employees of the Federal Bureau of Investigation, that's exactly who they are supposed to be! (Photo courtesy: 20th Century Fox/Shooting Star)

TRY IT!

To examine the federal workforce by gender, race, and ethnicity, see www.awlonline.com/oconnor.

At the lower levels of the U.S. Civil Service, most positions are filled by competitive examinations. These usually involve a written test, although the same position in the private sector would not. Mid-level to upper ranges of federal positions don't normally require tests; instead, in the past, applicants had to fill out lengthy Form 171 job applications. Now, as a result of the national Performance Review's call for the reduction of paperwork, they can simply submit a resume, or even apply by phone. Personnel departments then evaluate potential candidates and rank candidates according to how well they fit a particular job opening. Only the names of those deemed "qualified" are then forwarded to the official filling the vacancy. This can be a time-consuming process; it is not unusual for it to take six to nine months before a position can be filled in this manner.

The remaining 10 percent of the federal bureaucracy is made up of persons not covered by the civil service system. These positions generally fall into three categories:

1. Appointive policy-making positions. About 600 persons are appointed directly by the president. Some of these, including Cabinet secretaries, are subject to Senate confirmation. These appointees, in turn, are responsible for appointing the high-level policy-making assistants who form the top of the bureaucratic hierarchy.
2. Independent regulatory commissioners. Although each president gets to appoint as many as one hundred commissioners, they become independent of his direct political influence once they take office.
3. Low-level, nonpolicy patronage positions. At one time, the U.S. Post Office was the largest source of these government jobs. In 1971, Congress reorganized the Post Office and removed positions such as local postmaster from the political patronage/rewards pool. Since then, these types of positions generally refer to secretarial assistants to policy makers.

Federal employees are stereotyped as "paper pushers," but more than 15,000 job skills are represented in the federal government and its workers are perhaps the best trained and most skilled and efficient in the world. Government employees, whose average age is 45.2 years, with an average length of service at 16.3 years, include forest rangers, FBI agents, foreign service officers, computer programmers, security guards, librarians, administrators, engineers, plumbers, lawyers, doctors, postal carriers, and zoologists, among others. The diversity of government jobs mirrors the diversity of jobs in the private sector. The federal workforce, itself, is also diverse. As revealed in Figure 9.2, the federal workforce largely reflects the racial and ethnic composition of the United States as a whole, although the employment of women lags behind that of men. Women also appear to hit the same glass ceiling in the federal workforce that they find in the private sector. Not only do women make up over 70 percent of the lowest GS levels, less than 25 percent of the positions at the highest levels of the federal General Service are held by women.

Only about 330,000 of the 2.6 million federal bureaucrats work in the nation's capital; the rest are located in regional, state, and local offices scattered throughout the country. The decentralization of the bureaucracy facilitates accessibility to the public. The Social Security Administration, for example, has numerous offices so that its clients may have a place nearby to take their paperwork, questions, and problems. Decentralization also helps distribute jobs and incomes across the country.

Many Americans also believe that the federal bureaucracy is growing bigger each year, but they are wrong. Efforts to reduce the federal workforce have had an effect.

Figure 9.2   Characteristics and Rank Distribution of Federal Civilian Employees, 1997

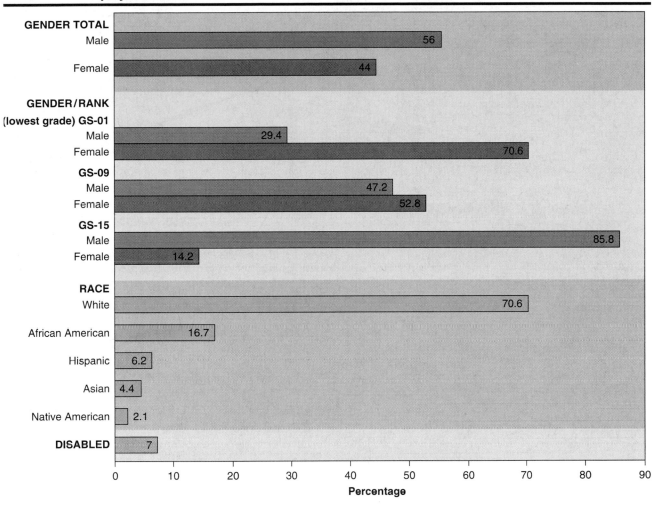

SOURCE: The Office of Personnel Management, *The Fact Book*, 1998 Edition (file:///A1/98FB-39.htm)

Although it is true that the number of total government employees has been increasing until lately, most growth has taken place at the state and local levels. And, as more federal programs are shifted back to the states, the size of state payrolls and state bureaucracies are likely to rise to reflect these new responsibilities.

Formal Organization

While even experts can't agree on the exact number of separate governmental agencies, commissions, and departments that make up the federal bureaucracy, there are probably more than 2,000.[11] A distinctive feature of the executive bureaucracy is its traditional division into areas of specialization. For example, one agency, the Occupational Safety and Health Administration, handles occupational safety, the Department of Education specializes in education, the State Department in foreign affairs, the Environmental Protection Agency in the environment, and so on. It is not unusual, however, for more than one agency to be involved in a particular issue or for one agency to be involved in myriad issues. In fact, numerous agencies often have authority in the same issue areas, making administration even more difficult. Agencies fall into four general types: (1) Cabinet departments, (2) government corporations, (3) independent agencies, and (4) regulatory commissions.

GOTTA HAND IT TO THESE NON-ESSENTIAL FEDERAL WORKERS... THEY HAVE AWESOME SURVIVAL SKILLS.

DEPARTMENT OF GOVERNMENT SHUTDOWNS

■ (Photo courtesy: The Chicago Tribune/©Tribune Media Services, Inc. All rights reserved. Reprinted with permission.)

department:

A major administrative unit with responsibility for a broad area of government operations. Departmental status usually indicates a permanent national interest in that particular governmental function, such as defense, health, or agriculture.

clientele agency:

Executive department directed by law to foster and promote the interests of a specific segment or group in the U.S. population (such as the Department of Education).

government corporation:

Business set up and created by Congress that performs functions that could be provided by private businesses (such as the U.S. Postal Service).

The Cabinet Departments. The fourteen Cabinet **departments** are major administrative units that have responsibility for conducting a broad area of government operations. Cabinet departments account for about 60 percent of the federal workforce.

As depicted in Figure 9.3, executive branch departments are headed by Cabinet members called secretaries (except the Justice Department, which is headed by the attorney general). The secretaries are responsible for establishing their department's general policy and overseeing its operations. As discussed in chapter 8, Cabinet secretaries are directly responsible to the president, but are often viewed as having two masters—the president and those affected by their department. Cabinet secretaries are also tied to Congress, from which they get their appropriations and the discretion to implement legislation and make rules and policy.

Although departments vary considerably in size, prestige, and power, they share certain features. Each department covers a broad area of responsibility generally reflected by its name. Each secretary is assisted by a deputy or undersecretary to take part of the administrative burden off the secretary's shoulders, as well as by several assistant secretaries, who direct major programs within the department. In addition, each secretary, like the president, has numerous assistants who help with planning, budgeting, personnel, legal services, public relations, and other key staff functions. Most departments are subdivided into bureaus, divisions, sections, or other smaller units, and it is at this level that the real work of each agency is done. Most departments are subdivided along function lines, but the basis for division may be geography, work processes (for example, the Economic Research Service in the Department of Agriculture), or clientele (such as the Bureau of Indian Affairs in the Department of the Interior). In addition to national offices in Washington, D.C., or its immediate suburbs, each executive department has regional offices to serve all parts of the United States.

Departmental status generally signifies a strong permanent national interest to promote a particular function. Moreover, departments are organized to foster and promote the interests of a given clientele—that is, a specific social or economic group. Such departments are called **clientele agencies.** The Departments of Agriculture, Education, Energy, Labor, and Veterans Affairs and the Bureau of Indian Affairs in the Department of the Interior are examples of clientele agencies/bureaus.

Because many of these agencies were created at the urging of well-organized interests to advance their particular objectives, it is not surprising that clientele groups are powerful lobbies with their respective agencies in Washington. The clientele agencies and groups are also active at the regional level, where the agencies devote a substantial part of their resources to program implementation. One of the most obvious examples of regional "outreach" is the Extension Service of the Department of Agriculture. Agricultural extension agents are scattered throughout the farm belt and routinely work with farmers on farm productivity and other problems. Career bureaucrats in the Agriculture Department know that farm interests will be dependable allies year in and year out. Congress and the president are not nearly so reliable, because they must balance the interests of farmers with those of other segments of society.

Government Corporations. **Government corporations** are the most recent addition to the bureaucratic maze. Dating from the early 1930s, they are businesses set up and created by Congress to perform functions that could be provided by private businesses. The corporations are formed when the government chooses to engage in activities that

Figure 9.3   Department of the Executive Branch

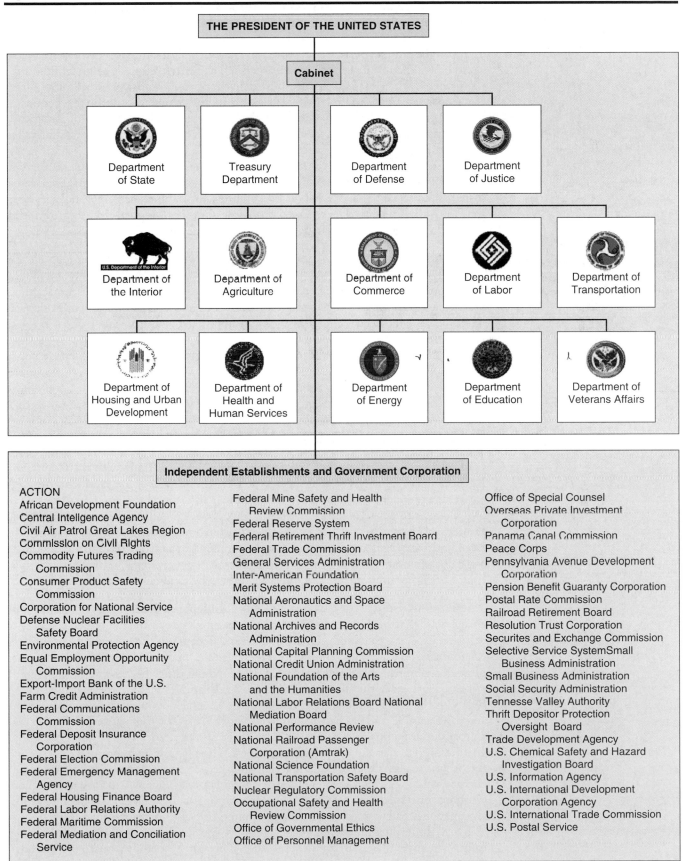

SOURCE: U.S. Government Agencies Directory. http://www.lib.lsu.edu/gov/fedgov.html

are primarily commercial in nature, produce revenue, and require greater flexibility than Congress generally allows regular departments. Some of the better-known government corporations include Amtrak and the Federal Deposit Insurance Corporation. Unlike other governmental agencies, government corporations charge for their services. For example, the largest government corporation, the U.S. Postal Service—whose functions could be handled by a private corporation, such as Federal Express or the United Parcel Service (UPS)—exists today to ensure delivery of mail throughout the United States at cheaper rates than those a private business might charge. Similarly, the Tennessee Valley Authority (TVA) provides electricity at reduced rates to millions of Americans in the Appalachian region of the Southeast, generally a low-income area that had failed to attract private utility companies to provide service there.

In cases like that of the TVA, where the financial incentives for private industry to provide services are minimal, Congress often believes that it must act. In other cases, it steps in to salvage valuable public assets. For example, when passenger rail service in the United States no longer remained profitable, Congress stepped in to create Amtrak and thus nationalized the passenger-train industry to keep passenger trains running.

independent executive agency:

Governmental unit that closely resembles Cabinet departments, these have narrower areas of responsibility (such as the Central Intelligence Agency), and are not part of any Cabinet departments.

Independent Executive Agencies.
Independent executive agencies closely resemble Cabinet departments, but have narrower areas of responsibility. Generally speaking, independent agencies perform service rather than regulatory functions. Many of these agencies are tied to the president and Congress as closely as executive departments because the heads of these agencies are appointed by the president and serve, like Cabinet secretaries, at his pleasure.

Independent agencies exist apart from executive departments for practical or symbolic reasons. The National Aeronautics and Space Administration (NASA), for example, could have been placed within the Department of Defense. That, however, could have conjured up thoughts of a space program dedicated solely to military purposes, rather than for civilian satellite communication or scientific exploration. Similarly, the Environmental Protection Agency (EPA) was created in 1970 to administer federal programs aimed at controlling pollution and protecting the nation's environment. It administers all congressional laws concerning the environment and pollution. Along with the Council on Environmental Quality, a staff agency in the Executive Office of the President, the EPA advises the president on environmental concerns. It also administers programs transferred to it along with personnel from the Departments of Agriculture, Energy, Interior, and Health and Human Services, as well as the Nuclear Regulatory Commission, among others. The expanding national focus on the environment, in fact, has brought about numerous calls to elevate the EPA to Cabinet-level status to reinforce a long-term national commitment to improved air and water and other environmental issues.

Independent Regulatory Commissions.
Independent regulatory commissions are agencies that were created by Congress to exist outside of the major departments to regulate a specific economic activity or interest. Because of the complexity of modern economic issues, Congress sought to create agencies that could develop expertise and provide continuity of policy with respect to economic issues because neither Congress nor the courts have the time or talent to do so. Examples include the National Labor Relations Board, the Federal Reserve Board, the Federal Communications Commission, and the Securities and Exchange Commission (SEC).[12] Congress started setting up regulatory commissions as early as 1887, recognizing the need for close and continuous guardianship of particular economic activities. Older boards and commissions, such as the Securities and Exchange Commission and the Federal Reserve Board, are generally charged with overseeing a certain industry. Regulatory agencies created since the 1960s are more concerned with how the business sector relates to public health and safety. The Occupational Safety and Health Administration (OSHA) promotes job safety.

Most of the older independent agencies were specifically created to be relatively free from immediate (partisan) political pressure. They are headed by a board composed of five to seven members (always an odd number, to avoid tie votes) who are selected by the president and confirmed by the Senate for fixed, staggered terms to increase the chances of a bipartisan board. Unlike executive department heads, they cannot be easily removed by the president. In 1935 the U.S. Supreme Court ruled that in creating independent commissions, the Congress had intended that they be independent panels of experts as far removed as possible from immediate political pressures.[13]

Newer regulatory boards lack this kind of autonomy and freedom from political pressures; they are generally headed by a single administrator who can be removed by the president. These boards and commissions, such as the EEOC, are therefore far more susceptible to political pressure and the political wishes of the president who appoints them.

Politics and Government Workers

As an increasing proportion of the American workforce came to work for the U.S. government as a result of the New Deal recovery programs, many began to fear that the members of the civil service would play major roles not only in implementing public policy but also in electing members of Congress and even the president. Consequently, Congress enacted the Political Activities Act of 1939, commonly known as the **Hatch Act,** which was designed to prohibit federal employees from becoming directly involved in working for political candidates.

Although presidents as far back as Thomas Jefferson had advocated efforts to limit the opportunities for federal civil servants to influence the votes of others, over the years many criticized the Hatch Act as too extreme. Critics argued that it denied millions of federal employees the First Amendment guarantees of freedom of speech and association, and discouraged political participation among a group of people who might otherwise be strong political activists. Critics also argued that civil servants *should* become more involved in campaigns, particularly at the state and local level, in order to understand better the needs of the citizens they serve.

In response to criticisms of the Hatch Act and at the urgings of President Bill Clinton, in 1993 Congress enacted the **Federal Employees Political Activities Act.** This liberalization of the Hatch Act among other things allows employees to run for public office in nonpartisan elections, contribute money to political organizations, and campaign for or against candidates in partisan elections. They still, however, are prohibited from engaging in political activity while on duty, soliciting contributions from the general public, or running for office in partisan elections. During the signing ceremony, Clinton said the law will "mean more responsive, more satisfied, happier, and more productive federal employees."[14] See Table 9.2 for more specifics about this new law.

Hatch Act:

Laws enacted in 1939 to prohibit civil servants from taking activist roles in partisan campaigns. This act prohibited federal employees from making political contributions, working for a particular party, or campaigning for a particular candidate.

Federal Employees Political Activities Act:

1993 liberalization of the Hatch Act. Federal employees are now allowed to run for office in nonpartisan elections and to contribute money to campaigns in partisan elections.

Table 9.2   The Liberalized Hatch Act

Here are some examples of permissible and prohibited activities for federal employees under the Hatch Act, as modified by the Federal Employees Political Activities Act of 1993.

Federal employees

- **May** be candidates for public office in nonpartisan elections
- **May** assist in voter registration drives
- **May** express opinions about candidates and issues
- **May** contribute money to political organizations
- **May** attend political fund-raising functions
- **May** attend and be active at political rallies and meetings
- **May** join and be active members of a political party or club
- **May** sign nominating petitions
- **May** campaign for or against referendum questions, constitutional amendments, and municipal ordinances
- **May** campaign for or against candidates in partisan elections
- **May** make campaign speeches for candidates in partisan elections
- **May** distribute campaign literature in partisan elections
- **May** hold office in political clubs or parties

- **May not** use their official authority or influence to interfere with an election
- **May not** collect political contributions unless both individuals are members of the same federal labor organization or employee organization and the one solicited is not a subordinate employee
- **May not** knowingly solicit or discourage the political activity of any person who has business before the agency
- **May not** engage in political activity while on duty
- **May not** engage in political activity in any government office
- **May not** engage in political activity while wearing an official uniform
- **May not** engage in political activity while using a government vehicle
- **May not** solicit political contributions from the general public
- **May not** be candidates for public office in partisan elections

SOURCE: U.S. Special Counsel's Office.

POLICY MAKING

One of the major functions of the bureaucracy is policy making—and bureaucrats can be, and often are, major policy makers.[15] When Congress creates any kind of department, agency, or commission, it is actually delegating some of its powers listed in Article I, section 8, of the U.S. Constitution. Therefore the laws creating departments, agencies, corporations, or commissions carefully describe their purpose and give them the authority to make numerous policy decisions, which have the effect of law. Congress recognizes that it does not have the time, expertise, or ability to involve itself in every detail of every program; therefore, it sets general guidelines for agency action and leaves it to the agency to work out the details. How agencies execute congressional wishes is called **implementation,** the process by which a law or policy is put into operation. (See chapter 17 for more detail on the policy-making process.) Much of the policy-making process occurs in the form of what some call iron triangles or issue networks.

Iron Triangles and Issue Networks

The relatively stable relationships and patterns of interaction that occur among an agency, interest groups, and congressional committees or subcommittees as policy is made are often referred to as **iron triangles,** or subgovernments (see Figure 9.4).

Policy-making subgovernments are "iron" because they are virtually impenetrable to outsiders and are largely autonomous. Even presidents have difficulty piercing the workings of these subgovernments, which have endured over time. Examples of iron triangles abound. Senior citizens' groups (especially the American Association of Retired Persons), the Social Security Administration, and the House Subcommittee on Aging all are likely to agree on the need for increased Social Security benefits. Similarly, the Department of Veterans' Affairs, the House Committee on Veterans' Affairs, and the American Legion and Veterans of Foreign Wars—the two largest organizations representing veterans—usually agree on the need for expanded programs for veterans.

The policy decisions made within these iron triangles often foster the interests of a clientele group and have little to do with the advancement of national policy goals. In part, subgovernmental decisions often conflict with other governmental policies and tend to tie the hands of larger institutions such as Congress and the president. The White House is often too busy dealing with international affairs or crises to deal with smaller issues like veterans' benefits. Likewise, Congress defers to its committees and subcommittees. Thus, these subgovernments decentralize policy making and make policy making difficult to control.[16]

implementation:

The process by which a law or policy is put into operation by the bureaucracy.

iron triangle:

The relatively stable relationship and pattern of interaction that occur among an agency, interest groups, and congressional committees or subcommittees.

Figure 9.4   An Iron Triangle

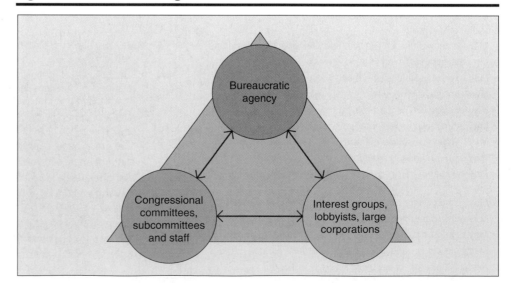

■ Senator Bob Kerrey (D Neb.) addresses former Vietnam era veterans. Kerrey is a highly decorated Vietnam veteran who earned the Congressional Medal of Honor. (Photo courtesy: Bob Daemmrich/ Stock Boston)

Today, iron triangles no longer dominate most policy processes for three main reasons: an increasingly complex society, issues that cut across several policy areas, and the phenomenal increase in number of Washington, D.C.–based interest groups. As these three changes have occurred, many iron triangles have become rusty, and new terms have been coined to describe the policy-making process and the bureaucracy's role in it. Hugh Heclo argues that this system of separate subgovernments is overlaid with an amorphous system of **issue networks,** that is, the fuzzy set of relationships among a large number of actors in broad policy areas.[17] In general, like iron triangles, issue networks are made up of agency officials, members of Congress (and committee staffers), and interest group lobbyists. But they also often include lawyers, consultants, academics, public relations specialists, and sometimes even the courts.[18] Unlike iron triangles, issue networks are constantly changing as members with technical expertise become involved in various issues.

Issue networks reflect the complexity of the issues that lawmakers and policy makers face. As an example, let's look at the plight of many American children. Lawmakers routinely call for new programs to make children's lives better, and the Clinton administration is sympathetic. First Lady Hillary Rodham Clinton, in fact, at one time chaired the board of the Children's Defense Fund, a national child advocacy group. But the plight of children isn't an easy problem to solve. All kinds of complex and interrelated issues are involved. It is, for example, a health issue, because many children don't have access to medical care; an education issue because many can't read, go to poor schools, or are dropouts; a labor issue because many have no job skills; and a drug and crime issue because many of these children live in drug-infested neighborhoods and often ultimately turn to crime, ending up in jail as a result. But given the segmented nature of policy making, how can the nation expect one coherent and encompassing policy to better the lives of American children to come from the Departments of Health and Human Services, Education, Labor, and Justice—plus all their associated House and Senate subcommittees, interest groups, and experts? And most of these agencies have to make do in the face of growing budget cutbacks.

issue network:

A term used to describe the loose and informal set of relationships that exist among a large number of actors who work in broad policy areas.

Policy making and implementation of the kind characterized by iron triangles or issue networks often take place on informal and formal levels. Practically, many decisions are left to individual government employees on a day-to-day basis. Justice Department lawyers, for example, make daily decisions about whether or not to prosecute someone. Similarly, street-level Internal Revenue Service agents make many decisions during personal audits.[19] These street-level bureaucrats make policy on two levels. First, they exercise wide discretion in decisions concerning citizens with whom they interact. Second, taken together, their individual actions add up to agency behavior.[20] Thus how bureaucrats interpret or apply (or choose not to apply) various policies are equally important parts of the policy-making process. Administrative discretion allows decision makers (whether they are in a Cabinet-level position or at the lowest GS levels) a tremendous amount of leeway.

Administrative Discretion

Essentially, bureaucrats make as well as implement policy. They take the laws and policies made by Congress, the president, and the courts, and develop rules and pro-

HIGHLIGHT 9.1

Enforcing Gender Equity in College Athletics

In 1972 Congress enacted legislation popularly known as Title IX, which prohibits discrimination against girls and women in federally funded education, including in athletics programs. This legislation mandates that "No person in the United States shall, on the basis of sex, be excluded from participation in, be denied the benefits of, or be subjected to discrimination under any education program or activity receiving federal financial assistance." It wasn't until December 1978—six years after passage of the Education Amendments—that the Office for Civil Rights in HEW released a "policy interpretation" of the law, dealing largely with the section that concerned intercollegiate athletics.[a] More than thirty pages of text were devoted to dealing with a hundred or so words from the statute. Football was recognized as unique, because of the huge revenues it produces, so it could be inferred that male-dominated football programs could continue to outspend women's athletic programs. The more than sixty women's groups that had lobbied for equality of spending were outraged, and turned their efforts toward seeking more favorable rulings on the construction of the statute from the courts.

Increased emphasis on Title IX enforcement has led many women to file lawsuits to force compliance. In 1991, in an effort to trim expenses, Brown University cut two men's and two women's teams from its varsity rosters. Several women on the downgraded gymnastics team filed a Title IX complaint against the school, arguing that it violated the act by not providing women varsity sport opportunities in relation to their population in the university. The women also argued that cutting the two women's program saved $62,000, whereas the men's cuts saved only $16,000.

Thus the women's varsity programs took a bigger hit, in violation of federal law.

A U.S. District Court refused to allow Brown to cut the women's programs. A U.S. Court of Appeals upheld that action, concluding that Brown had failed to provide adequate opportunities for its female students to participate in athletics.[b] In 1997, in *Brown University* v. *Cohen*, the U.S. Supreme Court declined to review the Appeals Court's decision.[c] This put all colleges and universities on notice that discrimination against women would not be tolerated, even when, as in the case of Brown University, the university had, since the passage of Title IX, tremendously expanded sports opportunities for women.

Women have made significant strides on all college campuses, but true equity in athletics is still a long way away at many colleges and universities. A survey compiled in 1999, based on a report filed pursuant to the mandates of the Equity in Athletics Disclosure Act, found that 40 percent of all NCAA Division I athletes were women, and that they received 40 percent of athletic scholarship budgets, although 53 percent of all students in those schools were female. On average, however, far less money goes to recruit women, and women's team coaches are only paid one-half to two-thirds of their male counterparts.[d]

[a]See Joyce Gelb and Marian Lief Palley, *Women and Public Policies* (Charlottesville: University of Virginia Press, 1996), chapter 5.
[b]*Cohen* v. *Brown University*, 101 F.3d 155 (1996).
[c]117 S.Ct. 1469 (1997).
[d]Joel Ozretich and Khan T. L. Tran, "PAC-10 Schools Still Come Up Short in Women's Athletics," *San Francisco Examiner* (May 22, 1999). eXaminer.com

cedures for making sure they are carried out. Most implementation involves what is called **administrative discretion,** the ability to make choices concerning the best way to implement congressional intentions. Administrative discretion is also exercised through two formal administrative procedures: rule making and administrative adjudication. This process is illustrated in Highlight 9.1: Enforcing Gender Equity in College Athletics.

Rule Making.   **Rule making** is a quasi-legislative administrative process that results in regulations and has the characteristics of a legislative act. **Regulations** are the rules that govern the operation of all government programs and have the force of law. In essence, then, bureaucratic rule makers often act as lawmakers as well as law enforcers when they make rules or draft regulations to implement various congressional statutes. Thus rule making is called a quasi-legislative process, and the process is illustrated in Figure 9.5. Some political scientists say that "[R]ulemaking is the single most important function performed by agencies of government."[21]

Because regulations often involve political conflict, the 1946 Administrative Procedure Act established rule-making procedures to give everyone the chance to participate in the process. The act requires that (1) public notice of the time, place, and nature of

> **administrative discretion:**
> The ability of bureaucrats to make choices concerning the best way to implement congressional intentions.

> **rule making:**
> A quasi-legislative administrative process that has the characteristics of a legislative act.

> **regulation:**
> Rule that governs the operation of a particular government program and has the force of law.

Figure 9.5 How a Regulation Is Made

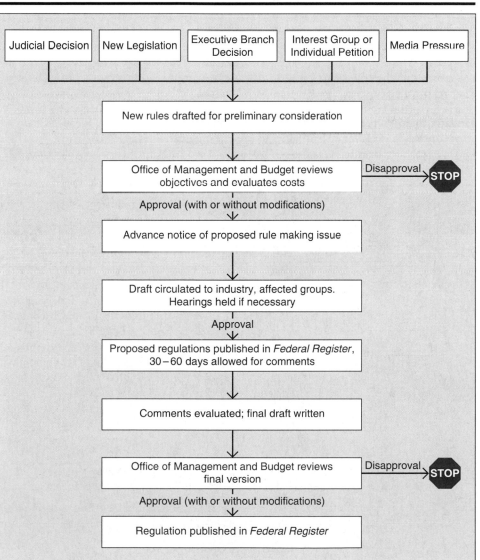

Web Exploration
To see federal agency rules and regulations of the *Federal Register,* see www.awlonline.com/oconnor.

administrative adjudication:

A quasi-judicial process in which a bureaucratic agency settles disputes between two parties in a manner similar to the way courts resolve disputes.

■ The Environmental Protection Agency (EPA) is a bureaucracy charged with administering all the government's environmental legislation. Here, EPA inspectors oversee the handling and storing of hazardous waste. (Photo courtesy: A. Ramey/Woodfin Camp & Associates)

the rule-making proceedings be provided in the *Federal Register;* (2) interested parties be given the opportunity to submit written arguments and facts relevant to the rule; and (3) the statutory purpose and basis of the rule be stated. Once rules have been written, thirty days must generally elapse before they take effect.

Sometimes an agency is required by law to conduct a formal hearing before issuing rules. Evidence is gathered, and witnesses testify and are cross-examined by opposing interests. The process can take weeks, months, or even years, at the end of which agency administrators must review the entire record and then justify the new rules. Although cumbersome, the process has reduced criticism of some rules and bolstered the deference given by the courts to agency decisions.

Administrative Adjudication.   **Administrative adjudication** is a quasi-judicial process in which a bureaucratic agency settles disputes between two parties in a manner similar to the way courts resolve disputes. Administrative adjudication, like rule making, is referred to as "quasi" (Latin for "seemingly") judicial, because lawmaking by any body other than Congress or adjudication by any body other than the judiciary would be a violation of the constitutional principle of separation of powers.

ℋIGHLIGHT 9.2

Can I Help You? Taming the IRS

Throughout 1997 and 1998, Congress held extensive hearings about abuses at the Internal Revenue Service (IRS), one of the most hated and feared federal agencies in America. Senate hearings in particular exposed abuses of ordinary citizens who found themselves in a nightmare of bureaucratic red tape and agency employee abuse of power. As a result of these hearings, Congress ordered the new IRS Commissioner to overhaul the way the IRS deals with the public.[a]

To do this, a computer "whiz kid" was appointed to totally reorganize the agency. "We're going to burn the house down and build it back from the foundation," said a member of the reorganization team that proposed dispatching IRS vans to neighborhoods, using e-mail to communicate with taxpayers, and setting up anonymous Internet chatrooms for taxpayers to engage in a give and take with the IRS on a range of problems that affect their tax status.[b] Other changes include twenty-four-hour customer service help lines, allowing use of credit cards to pay tax bills, and stepped up electronic filing and assistance.

Under the new reorganization, regional offices are being abolished and replaced with four operating divisions that will handle specific tax areas: (1) Wage and Investment Income; (2) Small Business and Self-Employed Income; (3) Large and Midsize Business; and (4) Tax Exempt. This will create a more specialized workforce and allow employees to learn more about a single area, cutting down on the transmission of misinformation. "Early reports are that the agency's workers as well as its leadership are taking seriously Congress's and the public's demand for good manners and pleasant service."[c] The moral? The bureaucracy can be tamed.

[a]Stephen Barr, "For IRS, a Deadline to Draft a Smile," *Washington Post* (January 31, 1999): H1.
[b]Barr, "For IRS, a Deadline."
[c]Albert B. Crenshaw, "Another Tax Year, A Whole New Attitude at the IRS; Overhaul Produces Nicer Treatment, Better Service," *Washington Post* (April 15, 1999): E9.

Agencies regularly find that persons or businesses are not in compliance with the federal laws the agencies are charged with enforcing, or that they are in violation of an agency rule or regulation. To force compliance, some agencies resort to administrative adjudication, which is generally less formal than a trial. Several agencies and boards employ administrative law judges to conduct the hearings. Although these judges are employed by the agency, they are strictly independent and cannot be removed except for gross misconduct. Congress, for example, empowers the Federal Trade Commission (FTC) to determine what constitutes an unfair trade practice.[22] Its actions, however, are reviewable in the federal courts.

MAKING AGENCIES ACCOUNTABLE

The question of to whom bureaucrats should be responsible is one that continually comes up in any debate about governmental accountability. Should the bureaucracy be answerable to itself? To organized interest groups? To its clientele? To the president? To Congress? Or to some combination of all of these? As illustrated in Highlight 9.2: Can I Help You? Taming the IRS, at times an agency becomes so removed from the public it serves that Congress must step in. While many would argue that bureaucrats should be responsive to the public interest, the public interest is difficult to define. As it turns out, several factors work to control the power of the bureaucracy, and, to some degree, the same kinds of checks and balances that operate among the three branches of government serve to check the bureaucracy (Table 9.3).

Many argue that the president should be in charge of the bureaucracy because it is up to him to see that popular ideas and expectations are translated into administrative action. But under our constitutional system, the president is not the only actor in the policy process. Congress creates the agencies, funds them, and establishes the broad rules of their operation. Moreover, Congress continually reviews the various agencies through oversight committee investigations, hearings, and its power of the purse. And the federal judiciary, as in most other matters, has the ultimate authority to review administrative actions.

Web Exploration
For more about the IRS and its modernization efforts, see www.awlonline.com/oconnor.

Table 9.3 Making Agencies Accountable

The president has the authority to:

- Appoint and remove agency heads and a few additional top bureaucrats.
- Reorganize the bureaucracy (with congressional approval).
- Make changes in an agency's annual budget proposals.
- Ignore legislative initiatives originating within the bureaucracy.
- Initiate or adjust policies that would, if enacted by Congress, alter the bureaucracy's activities.
- Issue executive orders.
- Reduce an agency's annual budget.

Congress has the authority to:

- Pass legislation that alters the bureaucracy's activities.
- Abolish existing programs.
- Investigate bureaucratic activities and compel bureaucrats to testify about them.
- Influence presidential appointments of agency heads and other top bureaucratic officials.
- Write legislation to limit the bureaucracy's discretion.

The judiciary has the authority to:

- Rule on whether bureaucrats have acted within the law and require policy changes to comply with the law.
- Force the bureaucracy to respect the rights of individuals through hearings and other proceedings.
- Rule on the constitutionality of all rules and regulations.

Executive Control

As the size and scope of the American national government in general, and of the executive branch and the bureaucracy in particular, have grown, presidents have delegated more and more power to bureaucrats. But most presidents have continued to try to exercise some control over the bureaucracy, although they have often found that task more difficult than they first envisioned. John F. Kennedy, for example, once lamented that to give anyone at the State Department an instruction was comparable to putting your request in a dead-letter box.[23] No response would ever be forthcoming.

Recognizing these potential problems, each president tries to appoint the best possible persons to carry out his wishes and policy preferences. Presidents may make thousands of appointments to the executive branch; in doing so, they have the opportunity to appoint individuals who share their views on a range of policies. And although presidential appointments make up less than 1 percent of all federal jobs, presidents usually fill most top policy-making positions.

Presidents can also, with the approval of Congress, reorganize the bureaucracy. They can also make changes in an agency's annual budget requests and ignore legislative initiatives originating within the bureaucracy. Several Presidents have made it a priority to try to tame the bureaucracy to make it more accountable. Thomas Jefferson was the first president to address the issue of accountability. He attempted to cut waste and bring about a "wise and frugal government." But it wasn't until the Progressive era (1890–1920) that calls for reform began to be taken seriously. Later, Calvin Coolidge urged spending cuts and other reforms. His Two Percent Club was created to cut staff, as its name implies, by 2 percent each year; his Correspondence Club was designed to reduce bureaucratic letter writing by thirty percent.[24]

All recent presidents since John F. Kennedy have tried to streamline the bureaucracy to make it smaller and thus more accountable. President Nixon, for example, proposed a plan to combine fifty domestic agencies and seven different departments into four large "super departments." But according to his former aide John Erlichman, this plan to "disrupt iron triangles" was dead on arrival. "Why? Because such a reorganization would have broken up the hoary congressional committee organization that corresponded to the existing departments and agencies." Said Erlichman, "A subcommittee chairman with oversight of the Agriculture Department would lose power, perks and status if we were authorized to fold Agriculture into a new Department of Natural Resources. The powerful farm lobbies were equally hostile to the idea."[25]

The Clinton administration has been especially bullish on reform. In 1993 Clinton created the President's Task Force on Reinventing Government, headed by Vice President Gore. He also signed executive orders to:

■ cut the size of the federal workforce by 252,000 people within five years.

■ cut in half the growing number of federal regulations within three years.

■ set customer service standards to direct agencies to put the people they serve first.

The National Performance Review, which recently changed its name to the National Program for Reinventing Government, is now "the longest running reform effort in U.S. history."[26] It lists major accomplishments that include:

■ savings of $137 million to the taxpayers.

■ elimination of 16,000 pages of governmental regulations.

■ reduction in thirteen of fourteen departments, for a total of 309,000 jobs eliminated.

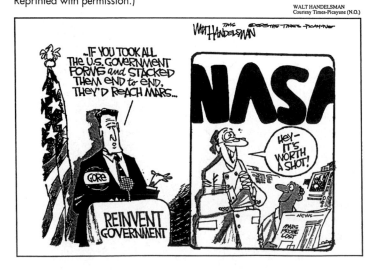

WALT HANDELSMAN
Courtesy Times-Picayune (N.O.)

■ creation of 325 reinvention labs to reengineer government processes and make better use of technology to "excite customers and employees alike with more flexible internal systems and improved services to the public."[27]

As some of Vice President Gore's initiatives have been implemented, both President Clinton and the Republican-controlled Congress have been making dramatic reforms in the bureaucracy not seen since the New Deal. See Politics Now: Downsizing the Bureaucracy for more about these efforts.

Another way presidents can shape policy and provide direction to bureaucrats is by issuing **executive orders.**[28] These are presidential directives to an agency that provide the basis for carrying out laws or for establishing new policies. Even before Congress acted to protect women from discrimination by the federal government, for example, the National Organization for Women convinced President Lyndon B. Johnson to sign Executive Order 11375 in 1967. This amended an earlier order prohibiting the federal government from discriminating on the basis of race, color, religion, or national origin in the awarding of federal contracts, by adding to it the category of "gender." Nevertheless, although the president signed the Order, the Office of Federal Contract Compliance (the executive agency charged with implementing the order) failed to draft

executive order:

Presidential directive to an agency that provides the basis for carrying out laws or for establishing new policies.

POLITICS NOW   Downsizing the Bureaucracy

In 1999 the size of the U. S. Civil Service was down to 1963 levels.[a] The Clinton administration has cut over 300,000 federal jobs. And, a variety of incentives are being used to convince older, higher-paid employees to retire. Since most of these workers are male, the White House is particularly eager to see them depart to shore up the Clinton administration's efforts to improve the proportion of women and minorities in the federal workforce.[b]

But simply the size of the workforce is not the only target of government downsizers. Americans want less government in general, and the Republican Congress wants to give it to them.

When Republicans took over control of both houses of Congress in 1995, they took it as a mandate from the public to cut wasteful spending and the duplication of government functions. The membership of the House Commerce Committee took this mandate to heart. The Commerce Department was one of its first targets. It had become an agency full of miscellaneous and unrelated functions, many of which duplicated programs in other departments and agencies. For example, Commerce housed the Office of the U.S. Trade Representative, the National Weather Service, the Census Bureau, the Bureau of Economic Analysis (which calculates the gross domestic product), the Coast Guard, the Patent and Trademark Office, the National Oceanic and Atmospheric Administration, and the U.S. Geological Survey.

The Clinton administration reacted angrily to the congressional hearings on legislation to disband the department. It claimed that dismantling the department would actually cost more money and not realize the savings that the Republicans claimed.

It's hard to figure out who is right because there are no precedents for closing a Cabinet-level department. To dismantle Commerce for example, the eleven authorizing committees with jurisdiction over the department would have to approve.

In the late 1990s, Senator Jesse Helms (R–N.C.), chairman of the Senate Foreign Relations Committee, led an effort to merge the U.S. Agency for International Development, the U.S. Information Agency, and the Arms Control and Disarmament Agency into the State Department. The Clinton administration believed it was not appropriate for the legislative branch to try to restructure how the executive branch conducts foreign affairs. Helms, however, was able to transfer one of the agencies, the Arms Control and Disarmament Agency, effectively ending its thirty-eight-year existence as an independent agency.[c]

Which agencies do you see as likely targets for the axe? Why?

[a]Mike Causey, "More Downsizing? There's Ample Opportunity," *Washington Post* (April 11, 1999): C9.
[b]Causey, "More Downsizing?"
[c]Charles A. Radin, "Top Aide Leaving: Cites Helms Rift," *Boston Globe* (May 19, 1999): A25.

appropriate guidelines for implementation of the order until several years later.[29] A president can direct an agency to act, but it may take some time for his orders to be carried out. Given the many "jobs" of any president, few can ensure that all their orders will be carried out or that they will like all the rules that are made.

Congressional Control

Congress, too, plays an important role in checking the power of the bureaucracy. Constitutionally, it possesses the authority to create or abolish departments and agencies as well as to transfer agency functions. It can also expand or contract bureaucratic discretion. And the Senate's authority to confirm (or reject) presidential appointments also gives Congress a "check" on the bureaucracy. Congress also exercises considerable oversight over the bureaucracy in several ways, as detailed in Table 9.4, which contains data from a study conducted by the Brookings Institution.

Political scientists distinguish between two different forms of oversight: *police patrol* and *fire alarm* oversight.[30] As their names might imply, police patrol oversight is proactive and allows Congress to set its own agenda for programs or agencies to review. In contrast, fire alarm oversight is reactive and generally involves a congressional response to a complaint filed by a constituent or politically significant actor. The range of congressional responses can vary from simple inquiries about an issue to full-blown hearings. As illustrated in Highlight 9.2, Congress at times even responds to constituent complaints about the bureaucracy. In that case, hearings resulted in total reorganization of the IRS.

Given the prevalence of iron triangles and issue networks, it is not surprising that the most frequently used form of oversight and the most effective is communication between house staffers and agency personnel. Various forms of program evaluations make up the next most commonly used forms of congressional control. Congress and its staff routinely conduct evaluations of programs and conduct oversight hearings.

Table 9.4   Frequency and Effectiveness of Oversight Techniques in a Single Congress

Oversight Technique	Number of cases in which Technique was used	Effectiveness Ranking
Staff communication with agency personnel	91	1
Member communication with agency personnel	86	2
Program reauthorization hearings	73	3
Oversight hearings	89	4
Hearings on bills to amend ongoing programs	70	5
Staff investigations	90	6
Program evaluations done by committee staff	89	7
Program evaluations done by congressional support agencies	89	8
Legislative veto	82	9
Analysis of proposed agency rules and regulations	90	10
Program evaluations done by outsiders	88	11
Agency reports required by Congress	91	12
Program evaluations done by the agencies	87	13
Review of casework	87	14

SOURCE: Joel Aberbach, *Keeping a Watchful Eye* (Washington, DC: Brookings Institution, 1990), 132, 135.

Congress also uses many of its constitutional powers to exercise control over the bureaucracy. These include its:

1. Investigatory powers. It is not at all unusual for a congressional committee or subcommittee to hold hearings on a particular problem, and then to direct the relevant agency to study the problem or find ways to remedy it. Representatives of the agencies also appear before these committees on a regular basis to inform members about agency activities, ongoing investigations, and so on.

2. Power of the purse. To control the bureaucracy, Congress dangles its ability to fund or not fund an agency's activities like the sword of Damocles over the heads of various agency officials.[31] The House Appropriations Committee routinely holds hearings to allow agency heads to justify their budget requests. Authorization legislation originates in the various legislative committees that oversee particular agencies (such as Agriculture, Veterans Affairs, Education, and Labor) and sets the maximum amounts that agencies can spend on particular programs. While some authorizations, such as Social Security, are permanent, others, including the State Department and Defense Department procurements, are watched closely and subject to annual authorizations.

Once funds are authorized, they must be appropriated before they can be spent. Appropriations originate with the House Appropriations Committee, not the specialized legislative committees. Often the Appropriations Committee allocates sums smaller than those authorized by the legislative committee. Thus, the Appropriations Committee, a budget cutter, has an additional oversight function.

To help Congress's oversight of the bureaucracy's financial affairs, in 1921 Congress created the General Accounting Office (GAO) at the same time that the Office of the Budget was created in the executive branch. With the establishment of the GAO, the Congressional Research Service, and later, the Congressional Budget Office (CBO), Congress essentially created its own bureaucracy to keep an eye on what the executive branch and *its* bureaucracy were doing. Today the GAO not only tracks how money is spent in the bureaucracy, it also monitors how policies are implemented. The CBO also conducts oversight studies. If it or the GAO uncovers problems with an agency's work, Congress is notified immediately.

Legislators also augment their formal oversight of the executive branch by allowing citizens to appeal adverse bureaucratic decisions to agencies, Congress, and even the courts. Congressional review, a procedure adopted by the 104th Congress, by which agency regulations can be nullified by joint resolutions of legislative disapproval also is another method of exercising congressional oversight. This form of oversight is discussed in greater detail in chapter 7.

Judicial Control

While the president's and Congress's control over the actions of the bureaucracy is very direct, the judiciary's oversight function is less so. The federal judiciary, for example, can directly issue injunctions or orders to an executive agency even before a rule is formally promulgated. The courts have also ruled that agencies must give all affected individuals their due process rights guaranteed by the U.S. Constitution. A Social Security recipient's checks cannot be stopped, for example, unless that individual is provided with reasonable notice and an opportunity for a hearing. On a more informal, indirect level, litigation, or even the threat of litigation, often exerts a strong influence on bureaucrats. Injured parties can bring suit against agencies for their failure to enforce the law, and can challenge agency interpretations of the law. In general, however, the courts give great weight to the opinions of bureaucrats and usually defer to their expertise.[32]

Research by political scientists also shows that government agencies are strategic. They often implement Supreme Court decisions "based on the costs and benefits of alternative policy choices."[33] Specifically, the degree to which agencies appear to respond to Supreme Court decisions is based on the "specificity of Supreme Court opinions, agency policy preferences, agency age, and *amicus curiae* support."[34]

The development of specialized courts has altered the relationship of some agencies with the federal courts, apparently resulting in less judicial deference to agency rulings.

■ Title IX of the Education Amendments of 1972 mandated nondiscrimination in women's sports. Since its passage, there has been a dramatic increase in the number of high school and college women competing in school sports—from 80,000 college women in 1982 to over 123,000 in 1996. (Photo courtesy: Karen O'Connor)

(Photo courtesy: Catherine Karnow/Woodfin Camp & Associates)

The Judiciary

- The Constitution and the Creation of the National Judiciary
- The American Legal System
- The Federal Court System
- How Federal Court Judges Are Selected
- The Supreme Court Today
- How the Justices Vote
- Judicial Policy Making and Implementation

hen the Framers drafted the Constitution, they never could have envisioned that the authority of the Supreme Court and other federal courts would grow to include issues as diverse as the right of married couples to use birth control, the right of parents to withdraw life-support systems from their children, and the question of whether a pregnant woman can be forced to undergo a caesarean section prior to going into natural labor. Personal injury lawsuits too, have exploded, especially since the 1980s, resulting in numerous calls for federal legislation to limit these kinds of lawsuits.

In January 1999, *A Civil Action* starring John Travolta and Robert Duvall opened in theaters nationwide. It depicted one of many lengthy personal injury suits filed each year in the United States. The movie, made from the book of the same name, is based on a tragedy.[1] In 1986, eight families sued two large companies, W. R. Grace and Beatrice Foods, charging that they polluted the city's drinking water by dumping chemicals near the Aberjona River, pollutants that eventually seeped into the town's water supply. The plaintiffs found twenty-eight instances of childhood leukemia in Woburn, Massachusetts, from 1964 to 1986—four times greater than would have been expected.[2] Five children and one adult died. After a costly and lengthy trial, one that had all of the trappings of David trying to best Goliath, Beatrice Foods was found not liable and W. R. Grace settled for 8 million dollars with no admission of guilt.

The tobacco industry has also been the target of all kinds of personal injury lawsuits. For example, in late March 1999, a twelve-member jury in Oregon ordered Philip Morris, the cigarette manufacturer, to pay $81 million to the family of Jesse Williams, a public school custodian and Marlboro smoker who died of lung cancer. Other large jury verdicts have followed and hundreds of other individual lawsuits are also pending against Philip Morris and other cigarette manufacturers.

These are but a few examples of large lawsuits settled, pending, or decided against huge corporations. The tobacco suit and others like it are separate from the lawsuits begun by forty state attorneys general against the tobacco industry on behalf of their citizens. In fact, in 1998, those states reached a $206-billion settlement of their lawsuits against the tobacco companies that had sought damages to compensate the states for the costs of smoking-related health problems of their citizens.

Over the years, the role of the courts—both state and federal—has evolved enormously. Courts at all levels have far greater latitudes in setting policy than ever before as illustrated by these examples. Moreover, as Congress and the states have enacted more and more federal and state laws, and Americans' understanding of rights has evolved, the courts on all levels now play a more important role in our daily lives than ever before.

*I*n 1787, when Alexander Hamilton wrote to urge support of the U.S. Constitution, he firmly believed that the judiciary was the weakest of the three departments of government. And in its formative years, the judiciary was, in Hamilton's words, "the least dangerous" branch. The judicial branch seemed so inconsequential that when the young national government made its move to the District of Columbia in 1800, Congress actually forgot to include any space to house the justices of the Supreme Court! Last-minute conferences with the Capitol architects led to the allocation of a small area in the basement of the Senate wing of the Capitol Building for a courtroom. No other space was allowed for the justices, however. Noted one commentator, "A stranger might traverse the darkest avenues of the Capitol for a week, without finding the remote corner in which justice is served in the American Republic."[3]

Today the role of the courts, particularly the U.S. Supreme Court, is significantly different from that envisioned in 1788, the year the national government came into being. The "least dangerous branch" is now perceived by many as having too much power.

During different periods of the judiciary's history, the role and power of the federal courts have varied tremendously. They have often played a key role in creating a strong national government and have boldly led the nation in social reform. Yet, at other times, the federal courts, especially the U.S. Supreme Court, have stubbornly stood as major obstacles to social and economic change.

In addition to being unaware of the expanded role of the federal judiciary, many Americans are also unaware of the political nature of the courts. They have been raised to think of the federal courts, especially the Supreme Court, as far above the fray of politics. That, however, is simply not the case. Elected presidents nominate judges to the federal courts and justices to the Supreme Court, often to advance their personal politics, and elected Senators ultimately confirm (or decline to confirm) presidential nominees. Not only is the selection process political, but the process by which cases ultimately get heard—if they are heard at all—by the Supreme Court is often political as well. Interest groups routinely seek out good test cases to advance their policy positions. Even the U.S. government, generally through the Justice Department and the U.S. solicitor general (another political appointee), seeks to advance its version of the public interest in court. Interest groups then often line up on opposing sides to advance their positions, much in the same way lobbyists do in Congress.

■ Pro-life protesters march before the Supreme Court. The Court has often been the target of interest group protests on account of its decisions on such controversial issues as abortion, affirmative action, and gay rights. (Photo courtesy: Richard Ellis/Sygma)

In this chapter we explore these issues and the scope and development of judicial power:

- First, we will look at *the creation of the national judiciary*. Article III of the Constitution created a Supreme Court but left it to Congress to create any other federal courts, a task it quickly took up, which resulted in passage of the *Judiciary Act of 1789*.
- Second, we will explore the structure and some rules of *the American legal system*. The American legal system contains parallel courts systems for the fifty states and the national government. Each court system has courts of original and appellate jurisdiction.
- Third, we will discuss *the federal court system*. The federal court system is composed of specialized courts, district courts, courts of appeals, and the Supreme Court, which is the ultimate authority on all federal law.
- Fourth, we will see *how federal court judges are selected*. All appointments to the federal district courts, courts of appeals, and the Supreme Court are made by the president and are subject to Senate confirmation.
- Fifth, we will take a look at *the Supreme Court today*. Only a few of the millions of cases filed in courts around the United States every year eventually make their way to the Supreme Court through the lengthy appellate process, as cases are filtered out at a variety of stages.
- Sixth, we will learn *how justices make decisions* and discuss how judicial decision making is based on a variety of legal and extra-legal factors.
- Seventh, we will discuss *how judicial policies are made and implemented*.

A note on terminology: When we refer to the "Supreme Court," the "Court," or the "high Court" here, we always mean the U.S. Supreme Court, which sits at the pinnacle of the federal and state court systems. The Supreme Court is referred to by the name of the chief justice who presided over it during a particular period (for example, the Marshall Court is the Court presided over by John Marshall from 1801 to 1835). When we use the term "courts," we refer to all federal or state courts unless otherwise noted.

THE CONSTITUTION AND THE CREATION OF THE NATIONAL JUDICIARY

The detailed notes James Madison took at the Philadelphia Convention make it clear that the Framers devoted little time to the writing of or the content of Article III, which created the judicial branch of government. The Framers believed that a federal judiciary posed little of the threat of tyranny that they feared from the other two branches. One scholar has even suggested that, for at least some delegates to the Constitutional Convention,

> provision for a national judiciary was a matter of theoretical necessity . . . more in deference to the maxim of separation [of powers] than in response to clearly formulated ideas about the role of a national judicial system and its indispensability.[4]

Alexander Hamilton argued in *Federalist No. 78* that the judiciary would be the "least dangerous branch of government." Anti-Federalists, however, did not agree with Hamilton. They particularly objected to a judiciary whose members had life tenure and the ability to interpret what was to be "the supreme law of the land," a phrase that Anti-Federalists feared would give the Supreme Court too much power.

The Framers also debated the need for any federal courts below the level of the Supreme Court. Some argued in favor of deciding all cases in state courts, with only appeals going before the Supreme Court. Others argued for a system of federal courts. A compromise left the final choice to Congress, and Article III, section 1, begins simply by vesting "The judicial Power of the United States . . . in one supreme Court, and in such inferior Courts as the Congress may from time to time ordain and establish." Although there some debate over whether the Court should have the power of

■ The justices of the Court pose annually for a formal portrait. Left to right are (bottom) Antonin Scalia, John Paul Stevens, Chief Justice William H. Rehnquist, Sandra Day O'Connor, Anthony Kennedy; (top) Ruth Bader Ginsburg, David Souter, Clarence Thomas, and Stephen Breyer.

Court filings—from 600 in 1890 to 275 in 1892.[32] As recently as the 1940s, fewer than 1,000 cases were filed annually. Since that time, filings have increased at a dramatic rate until the 1995–1996 term, as revealed earlier in Figure 10.4, although that does not mean the Court is actually deciding more cases. In fact, of the 7,692 petitions it received during the 1998–1999 term, it handed down opinions in only ninety-six. The process by which cases get to the Supreme Court is outlined in Figure 10.6.

Just as it is up to the justices to "say what the law is," they can also exercise a significant role in policy making and politics by opting *not* to hear a case. The content of the Court's docket is, of course, every bit as significant as its size. Prior to the 1930s, the Court generally heard cases of interest only to the immediate parties. During the 1930s, however, cases requiring the interpretation of constitutional law began to take a growing portion of its workload, leading the Court to take a more important role in the policy-making process. At that time only 5 percent of the Court's cases involved questions concerning the Bill of Rights. By the late 1950s, one-third of filed cases involved such questions; and by the 1960s, half did.[33] In 1990, however, only 30 percent of the Court's caseload dealt with constitutional questions.

The Supreme Court's Jurisdiction

The Court has two types of jurisdiction, as indicated in Table 10.2. Its original jurisdiction is specifically set out in the Constitution. The Court has original jurisdiction in "all Cases affecting Ambassadors, other public Ministers and Consuls, and those in which a State shall be a party." Most cases arising under the Court's original jurisdiction involve disputes between two states, usually over issues such as ownership of offshore oil deposits, territorial disputes caused by shifting river boundaries, or controversies caused by conflicting claims over water rights, such as when a river flows through two or more states.[34] The dispute between New York and New Jersey over ownership of Ellis Island discussed in chapter 3 is another example of a case involving the Court's exercise of its original jurisdiction. In earlier days, the Court would actually sit as a trial court and hear evidence and argument. Today, the Court usually appoints a Special Master—often a retired judge or an expert on the matter at hand—to hear the case in a district court on behalf of the Supreme Court and then report his or her findings and recommendations to the Court. It is rare for more than two or three of these cases to come to the Court in a year.

A second kind of jurisdiction enjoyed by the Court is appellate jurisdiction (see Table 10.2). The appellate jurisdiction of the Court can be changed by the Congress at any time, a power that has been a potent threat to the authority of the Court. The Judiciary Act of 1925 gave the Court discretion over its own jurisdiction, meaning that it does not have to accept all appeals that come to it. The idea behind the act was that the intermediate courts of appeals should be the final word for almost all federal litigants, thus freeing the Supreme Court to concentrate on constitutional issues, unless the Court decided that it wanted to address other matters. The Court, then, is not expected to exercise its appellate jurisdiction simply to correct errors of other courts. Instead, appeal

Figure 10.6 How a Case Goes to the United States Supreme Court

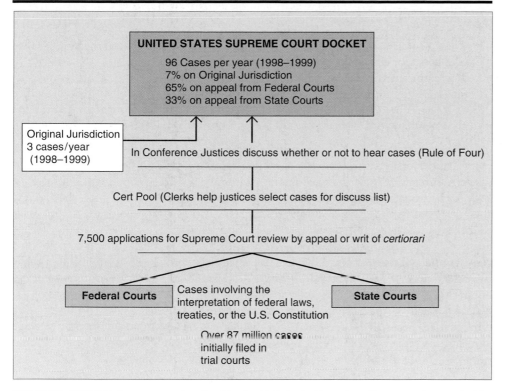

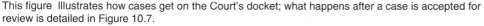

This figure Illustrates how cases get on the Court's docket; what happens after a case is accepted for review is detailed in Figure 10.7.

to the Supreme Court should be taken only if the case presents important issues of law, or what is termed "a substantial federal question." Since 1988, nearly all appellate cases that had gone to the Supreme Court arrived there on a petition for a **writ of *certiorari*** (from the Latin "to be informed"), which is a request for the Supreme Court—at its discretion—to order up the records of the lower courts for purposes of review.

About one-third of all Supreme Court filings involve criminal law issues.[35] Many of these, in fact more than half of all petitions to the Court, are filed *in forma pauperis* (IFP) (literally from the Latin, "as a pauper"), which is a way for an indigent or poor person to appeal a case to the Supreme Court. About 80 percent of these are filed by indigent prison inmates seeking review of their sentences. Permission to proceed *in forma pauperis* allows the petitioner to avoid filing and printing costs. Any criminal defendant who has had a court-appointed lawyer in a lower court proceeding is automatically entitled to proceed in this fashion.

In recent years, the Court has tended more and more to deny requests to file *in forma pauperis*. In *In re Sindram* (1991), for example, the Rehnquist Court chastised Michael Sindram for filing his petition *in forma pauperis* to require the Maryland courts to expedite his request to expunge a $35 speeding ticket from his record. Sindram was no stranger to the Supreme Court: During the previous three years, he had filed forty-two separate motions on various legal matters, twenty-four of them in the 1990 term. In denying Sindram's request to file as an indigent, the majority noted that "[t]he goal of fairly dispensing justice . . . is compromised when the Court is forced to devote its limited resources to the processing of repetitious and frivolous requests." Along with the order denying the petition, the Court issued new rules to provide for denial of "frivolous" or "malicious" IFP motions.[36]

writ of certiorari:

A request for the Court to order up the records from a lower court to review the case.

in forma pauperis:

Literally, "in the form of a pauper"; a way for an indigent or poor person to appeal a case to the U.S. Supreme Court.

The Rule of Four.   Unlike other federal courts, the Supreme Court controls its own caseload through the *certiorari* process, deciding which cases it wants to hear, and rejecting most cases that come to it. All petitions for *certiorari* must meet two criteria:

1. The case must come either from a U.S. Court of Appeals, a special three-judge district court, or a state court of last resort.
2. The case must involve a federal question. This means that the case must present questions of interpretation of federal constitutional law or involve a federal statute or treaty. The reasons that the Court should accept the case for review and legal argument supporting that position are set out in the petition (also called a brief).

The Clerk of the Court's office transmits petitions for writs of *certiorari* first to the chief justice's office, where his clerks review the petitions, and then to the individual justices' offices. All the justices on the Rehnquist Court except Justice John Paul Stevens participate in what is called the "*cert* pool."[37] As part of the pool, they review their assigned fraction of petitions and share their notes with each other. Those cases that the justices deem noteworthy are then placed on what is called the "discuss list"— a list of cases to be discussed—prepared by the chief justice's clerks and circulated to the chambers of the justices. All others are dead listed and go no further unless a justice asks that the case be removed from the dead list and discussed at conference. Only about 30 percent of submitted petitions make it to the discuss list. During one of the justices' weekly conference meetings, the cases on the discuss list are reviewed. The chief justice speaks first, then the rest of the justices, according to seniority. The decision process ends when the justices vote, and by custom, *certiorari* is granted according to the **Rule of Four**—when at least four justices vote to hear a case.

How Does a Case Survive the Process?

It can be difficult to determine why the Court decides to hear a particular case. The Court does not offer reasons, and "the standards by which the justices decide to grant or deny review are highly personalized and necessarily discretionary," noted former Chief Justice Earl Warren although sometimes individual justices publicly dissent from the Court's denial of *certiorari*. Moreover, he continued, "those standards cannot be captured in rules or guidelines that would be meaningful."[38] Political scientists have nonetheless attempted to determine the characteristics of the cases the Court accepts; not surprisingly, they are similar to those that help a case get on the discuss list. Among the cues are the following:

- The federal government is the party asking for review.
- The case involves conflict among the circuit courts.
- The case presents a civil rights or civil liberties question.
- The case involves ideological and/or policy preferences of the justices.
- The case has significant social or political interest, as evidenced by the presence of interest group ***amicus curiae*** briefs.

The Solicitor General.   One of the most important cues for predicting whether the Court will hear a case is the position the solicitor general takes on it. The **solicitor general,** appointed by the president, is the fourth-ranking member of the Justice Department and is responsible for handling all appeals on behalf of the U.S. government to the Supreme Court. The solicitor's staff is like a small, specialized law firm within the Justice Department. But because this office has such a special relationship with the Supreme Court, even having a suite of offices within the Supreme Court building, the solicitor general is often referred to as the Court's "ninth and a half member."[39] Moreover, the solicitor general, on behalf of the U.S. government, appears as a party or as an *amicus curiae* in more than 50 percent of the cases heard by the Court each term.

This special relationship with the Court helps explain the overwhelming success the solicitor general's office enjoys before the Supreme Court. The Court generally accepts 70 to 80 percent of the cases where the U.S. government is the petitioning party, com-

Rule of Four:

At least four justices of the Supreme Court must vote to consider a case before it can be heard.

amicus curiae:

"Friend of the court"; a third party to a lawsuit who files a legal brief for the purpose of raising additional points of view in an attempt to influence a court's decision.

solicitor general:

The fourth-ranking member of the Justice Department; responsible for handling all appeals on behalf of the U.S. government to the Supreme Court.

■ Kenneth Starr, the Independent Counsel who investigated President Clinton, served as Solicitor General from 1989–1993 during the Bush administration. (Photo courtesy: Spencer Tirey/Liaison Agency)

Web Exploration
To examine the recent filings of the office of Solicitor General, go to www.awlonline.com/oconnor.

pared with about 5 percent of all others.[40] But because of this special relationship, the solicitor general often ends up playing two conflicting roles: representing in Court both the president's policy interests and the broader interests of the United States. At times, solicitors find these two roles difficult to reconcile. Former Solicitor General Rex E. Lee (1981–85), for example, noted that on more than one occasion he refused to make arguments in Court that had been advanced by the Reagan administration (a stand that ultimately forced him to resign his position). Said Lee, "I'm not the pamphleteer general; I'm the solicitor general. My audience is not 100 million people; my audience is nine people. . . . Credibility is the most important asset that any solicitor general has."[41]

Conflict Among the Circuits.   Conflict among the lower courts is apparently another reason that the justices take cases. When interpretations of constitutional or federal law are involved, the justices seem to want consistency throughout the federal court system.

Often these conflicts occur when important civil rights or civil liberties questions arise. Political scientist Lawrence Baum has commented, "Justices' evaluations of lower court decisions are based largely on their ideological position."[42] Thus it is not uncommon to see conservative justices voting to hear cases to overrule liberal lower court decisions, or vice versa.

Interest Group Participation.   Another "quick" way for the justices to gauge the ideological ramifications of a particular case is by the amount of interest group participation. Richard C. Cortner has noted that "Cases do not arrive on the doorstep of the Supreme Court like orphans in the night."[43] Instead, most cases heard by the Supreme Court involve either the government or an interest group—either as the sponsoring party or as an *amicus curiae*. Liberal groups such as the ACLU, People for the American Way, the NAACP Legal Defense Fund, and conservative groups including the Washington Legal Foundation, Concerned Women for America, or Americans United for Life Legal Defense Fund routinely sponsor cases or file *amicus* briefs either urging the Court to hear a case or asking it to deny *certiorari*. Research by political scientists has found that "not only does [an *amicus*] brief in favor of *certiorari* significantly improve the chances of a case being accepted, but two, three and four briefs improve the chances even more."[44]

Clearly, it's the more the merrier, whether or not the briefs are filed for or against granting review.[45] Interest group participation may highlight lower court and ideological conflicts for the justices by alerting them to the amount of public interest in the issues presented in any particular case.

Starting the Case

Once a case is accepted for review, a flurry of activity begins (see Figure 10.7). If a criminal defendant is proceeding *in forma pauperis,* the Court appoints an expert lawyer to prepare and argue the case. Unlike the situation in many state courts, where appointed lawyers are often novices, it is considered an honor to be asked to represent an indigent before the Supreme Court even though such representation is on a *pro bono,* or no fee, basis.

Whether they are being paid or not, lawyers on both sides of the case begin to prepare their written arguments for submission to the Court. In these briefs, lawyers cite prior case law and make arguments as to why the Court should find in favor of their client.

More often than not, these arguments are echoed or expanded in *amicus curiae* briefs filed by interested parties, especially interest groups. (The vast majority of the cases decided by the Court in the 1990s had at least one *amicus* brief.)

Since the 1970s interest groups have increasingly used the *amicus* brief as a way to lobby the Court. Because litigation is so expensive, few individuals have the money (or time or interest) to pursue a perceived wrong all the way to the U.S. Supreme Court. All sorts of interest groups, then, find that joining ongoing cases through *amicus* briefs is a useful way of advancing their policy preferences. Major cases such as *Brown* v. *Board of Education of Topeka, Kansas* (1954), *Casey* v. *Planned Parenthood of Southeastern Pennsylvania* (1992), and *Harris* v. *Forklift Systems* (1993), which involved the degree of psychological damage a victim of sexual harassment must show, all attracted large numbers of *amicus* briefs as part of interest groups efforts to lobby the judiciary and bring about desired political objectives[46] (see Table 10.7).

Interest groups also provide the Court with information not necessarily contained in the major-party briefs, help write briefs, and assist in practice moot-court sessions. In these sessions the lawyer who will argue the case before the nine justices goes through a complete rehearsal, with prominent lawyers and law professors playing the roles of the various justices.

Oral Arguments.   Once a case is accepted by the Court for full review, and after briefs and *amicus* briefs are submitted on each side, oral argument takes place. The Supreme Court's annual term begins the first Monday in October, as it has since the late 1800s, and runs through late June or early July. In the early 1800s, sessions of the Court lasted only a few weeks twice a year. Today, justices hear oral arguments from the beginning of the term until early April. Special cases, such as *U.S.* v. *Nixon* (1974), have been heard even later in the year.[47] During the term, "sittings," periods of about two weeks in which cases are heard, alternate with "recesses," also about two weeks long. Oral arguments are usually heard Monday through Wednesday during two-week sitting sessions.

Figure 10.7   How Supreme Court Decisions Get Made

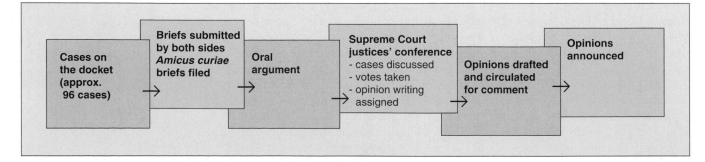

Table 10.7 *Amicus* **Briefs in Support of a Plaintiff**

■ Teresa Harris celebrates her victory after the Supreme Court ruled that her employer's conduct was illegal sexual harassment. (Photo courtesy: Fritz Hofmann/The Image Works)

In *Harris* v. *Forklift* Systems (1993), the U.S. Supreme Court unanimously ruled that federal civil rights law created a "broad rule of workplace equality." In *Harris,* the Court found that Title VII of the Civil Rights Act was violated when Teresa Harris was subjected to "intimidation, ridicule, and insults" of a sexually harassing nature by her supervisor. The following groups or governments filed *amicus* briefs:

In support of *Harris*

1. United States
   Equal Employment Opportunity Commission

2. National Conference of Women's Bar Associations
   Women's Bar Association of District of Columbia

3. National Organization for Women Legal Defense
      and Education Fund
   American Jewish Committee
   American Medical Women Association
   Asian-American Legal Defense and Education Fund
   Association for Union Democracy
   Center for Women's Policy Studies
   Chicago Women in Trades
   Illinois Coalition Against Sexual Harassment
   National Organization for Women
   Northern Tradeswomen's Network
   Northern New England Tradeswomen Institute
   Puerto Rican Legal Defense and Education Fund
   Women's Law Project

4. NAACP Legal Defense and Education Fund
   National Conference of Jewish Women

5. Women's Legal Defense Fund
   National Women's Law Center
   AFL-CIO
   Ayuda, Inc.
   Bar Association of San Francisco
   California Women Lawyers
   Center for Women Policy Studies
   Coalition of Labor Union Women
   Committee for Justice for Women of North Carolina
   Federally Employed Women, Inc.
   Federation of Organizations for Professional Women
   Institute for Women's Policy Research

Mexican American Women's National Association
National Association of Female Executives
National Association of Social Workers, Inc.
National Center for Lesbian Rights
National Council of Negro Women, Inc.
National Association of Working Women
9 to 5
Older Women's League
Trial Lawyers for Public Justice
Wider Opportunities for Women
Women Employed
Women's Action Alliance
Women's Bar Association of the District of Columbia
Women's Law Center of Maryland
YWCA of the U.S.A.

6. Employment Law Center
   California Women Lawyer's Committee
   Equal Rights Advocates

7. National Employment Lawyers Association

8. American Civil Liberties Union
   American Jewish Congress

9. Feminists for Free Expression

10. Southern States Police Benevolent Association
    North Carolina Police Benevolent Association

11. National Conference of Women's Bar Associations
    Women's Bar Association of the District of Columbia

In Support of *Forklift Systems*

1. Equal Employment Advisory Council

For Neither Party

1. American Psychological Association

WE'RE FILING AN AMICUS BRIEF WITH OPRAH WINFREY.

P. Steiner
THE WASHINGTON TIMES

■ Cartoon poking fun at lawsuit by cattle owners over Oprah Winfrey's negative comments about the safety of beef. (Photo courtesy: Reprinted by permission of Peter Steiner)

Oral argument is generally limited to the immediate parties in the case, although it is not uncommon for the U.S. solicitor general to appear to argue orally as an *amicus curiae*. Oral argument at the Court is fraught with time-honored tradition and ceremony. At precisely ten o'clock every morning when the Court is in session, the Court Marshal (dressed in a cutaway—a formal morning coat) emerges to intone "Oyez! Oyez! Oyez!" as the nine justices emerge from behind a reddish-purple velvet curtain to take their places on the raised and slightly angled bench. (From 1790 to 1972, the justices sat on a straight bench. Chief Justice Burger modified it so that justices at either end could see and hear better.) The chief justice sites in the middle with the justices to his right and left, alternating in seniority.

Almost all attorneys are allotted one-half hour to present their cases, and this allotment includes the time taken by questions from the bench. Justice John Marshall Harlan once noted that there was "no substitute for this method in getting at the heart of an issue and in finding out where the truth lies."[48] As the lawyer for the appellee approaches the mahogany lectern, a green light goes on, indicating that the attorney's time has begun. A white light flashes when five minutes remain. When a red light goes on, Court practice mandates that counsel stop immediately. One famous piece of Court lore told to all attorneys concerns a counsel who continued talking and reading from his prepared argument after the red light went on. When he looked up, he found an empty bench—the justices had quietly risen and departed while he continued to talk. On another occasion, Chief Justice Charles Evans Hughes stopped a leader of the New York bar in the middle of the word "if."

Although many Court watchers have tried to figure out how a particular justice will vote based on the questioning at oral argument, most find that the nature and number of questions asked does not help much in predicting the outcome of a case. Nevertheless, many believe that oral argument has several important functions. First, it is the only opportunity for even a small portion of the public (who may attend the hearings) and the press to observe the workings of the Court. Second, it assures lawyers that the justices have heard their case, and it forces lawyers to focus on arguments believed important by the justices. And last, it provides the Court with additional information, especially concerning the Court's broader political role, an issue not usually addressed in written briefs. For example, the justices can ask how many people might be affected by its decision or where the Court (and country) would be heading if a case were decided in a particular way. Justice Stephen Breyer also notes that oral arguments are a good way for the justices to try to highlight certain issue for other justices.

The Conference and the Vote.   The justices meet in closed conference on Fridays when the Court is hearing oral argument. Since the ascendancy of Chief Justice Roger B. Taney to the Court in 1836, the justices have begun each conference session with a round of handshaking. Once the door to the conference room closes, no others are allowed to enter. The justice with the least seniority acts as the doorkeeper for the other eight, communicating with those waiting outside to fill requests for documents, water, and so on.

Conferences highlight the importance and power of the chief justice, who presides over them and makes the initial presentation of each case. Each individual justice then discusses the case in order of his or her seniority on the Court, with the most senior justice speaking next. Most accounts of the decision-making process reveal that at this point some justices try to change the minds of others, but that most enter the conference room with a clear idea of how they feel. Although other Courts have followed different procedures, on the Rehnquist Court the justices generally vote at the same time they discuss the case with each justice speaking only once. Initial conference votes are not final, allowing justices to change their minds before final votes are taken later.

Writing Opinions.   There are basically five kinds of opinions that can be written:

1. A *majority opinion* is written by one member of the Court, and as such reflects the views of at least a majority of the justices. This opinion usually sets out the legal reasoning justifying the decision, and this legal reasoning becomes a precedent for deciding future cases.
2. A *concurring opinion* is one written by a justice who agrees with the outcome of the case but not with the legal rationale for the decision.
3. A *plurality opinion* is one that attracts the support of three or four justices. Generally, this opinion becomes the controlling opinion of the Court. Usually one or more justices agrees with the outcome of the decision in a concurring opinion, but there is no solid majority for the legal reasoning behind the outcome. Plurality opinions do not have the precedential value of majority opinions.
4. A *dissenting opinion* is one that is written by one or more justices who disagree with the opinion of a majority or plurality of the Court.
5. A *per curiam opinion* is an unsigned opinion issued by the Court. Justices may dissent from *per curiam* opinions but do so fairly rarely.

The chief justice, if he is in the majority, has the job of assigning the writing of the opinion. This privilege enables him to wield tremendous power. (If he is in the minority, the assignment falls to the most senior justice in the majority.)

The justice assigned to write the majority opinion circulates drafts of the opinion to all members of the Court. The Court must provide legal reasons for its positions. The reasoning behind any decision is often as important as the outcome. Under our system of *stare decisis*, both are likely to be relied on as precedent later by lower courts confronted with cases involving similar issues. The justice who drafts the opinion can have an important impact on how any legal issues are framed. Informal caucusing and negotiation then often take place, as justices may "hold out" for word changes or other modifications as a condition of their continued support of the majority opinion. At the same time, dissenting opinions and/or concurring opinions also circulate through the various chambers. The justices are often assisted in their writing of opinions by their clerks, who also can serve as intermediaries between the justices as they talk among themselves.

A good example of how politics can be involved at the opinion-writing stage is evident in *Bowers* v. *Hardwick* (1986), the Georgia consensual sodomy case discussed in chapters 5 and 6.[49] Justices White and Burger voted for *certiorari* believing that the Constitution doesn't protect homosexual acts. The liberal Justices Marshall and Brennan thought they had enough votes to overturn the law, but when Brennan perceived he would lose, he withdrew his vote for *certiorari,* albeit too late. Once the case was argued, coalitions quickly shifted. According to papers kept by Justice Marshall, Justice Powell originally indicated at conference that he would vote with the majority to find the law unconstitutional. After drafts of the majority and minority opinions were circulated, however, he changed his mind, thus changing a five-to-four majority to strike down the law into a five-to-four majority to uphold it.[50]

This kind of communal work can result in poorly written opinions, as was the case with *U.S.* v. *Nixon* (1974).[51] Although the opinion involving President Nixon's refusal to turn over tape recordings of his conversations was issued under Chief Justice Burger's name, many believe that it was a combination of several justices' contributions and additions. Sensing the need for the Court to speak unanimously in such an important opinion—one that pitted two branches of government against each other—Justice Burger apparently made concessions to get support.[52] This process led to some very confused prose in some sections of the opinion.

Recently, tensions have grown on the Court concerning some issues, and dissents or concurring opinions have become quite pointed. The protocol of the Court has always been characterized by politeness, but this has not stopped some justices from openly ridiculing their colleagues from the bench. Justice Scalia, for example, publicly criticized Justice O'Connor's opinion in *Webster* v. *Reproductive Health Services* (1989), saying that her "assertion that a fundamental rule of judicial restraint requires [the Court] to avoid reconsidering *Roe* [v. *Wade*] cannot be taken seriously."[53] This kind of ridicule was unprecedented and perhaps simply reflects how manners in politics are on the decline.

Not all cases result in split decisions from the justices. In *Clinton* v. *Jones,* which involved President Clinton's attempt to defer Paula Jones's action for civil damages against him, a unanimous Court affirmed the lower court ruling allowing the case to go forward. Justice Breyer, who concurred with the opinion of the other eight justices, did so only to underscore his belief that a federal judge could not schedule judicial proceedings that could interfere with the president's discharge of his public duties.[54] So here, in a decision that was to set the stage for debating articles of impeachment against the president, all nine justices—including two justices nominated by Clinton—were in agreement.

HOW THE JUSTICES VOTE

Justices are human beings, and they do not make decisions in a vacuum. Principles of *stare decisis* dictate that the justices follow the law of previous cases in deciding cases at hand. But more factors are usually operating. A variety of legal and extra-legal factors have been found to affect Supreme Court decision making.

Legal Factors

Legal scholars long have argued that judges decide cases based on the Constitution and their reading of various statutes. Determining what the Framers meant—if that is even important today—often appears to be based on an individual jurist's philosophy.

Judicial Philosophy and Original Intent.   One of the primary issues concerning judicial decision making focuses on what is called the activism/restraint debate. Advocates of **judicial restraint** argue that courts should allow the decisions of other branches to stand, even when they offend a judge's own sense of principles.[55] Restraintists defend their position by asserting that the federal courts are composed of unelected judges, which makes the judicial branch the least democratic branch of government. Consequently, the courts should defer policy making to other branches of government as much as possible.

Restraintists refer to *Roe* v. *Wade* (1973), the case that liberalized abortion laws, as a classic example of **judicial activism** run amok. They maintain that the Court should have deferred policy making on this sensitive issue to the states or to the other branches of the federal government—the legislative and executive—because their officials are elected and therefore are more receptive to the majority's will.

Advocates of judicial activism contend that judges should use their power broadly to further justice, especially in the areas of equality and personal liberty. Activists argue that it is the courts' appropriate role to correct injustices committed by the other branches of government. Explicit in this argument is the notion that courts need to protect oppressed minorities.[56]

Activists point to *Brown* v. *Board of Education of Topeka, Kansas* (1954) as an excellent example of the importance of judicial activism.[57] In *Brown*, the Supreme Court ruled that racial segregation in public schools violated the equal protection clause of the

judicial restraint:

A philosophy of judicial decision making that argues courts should allow the decisions of other branches of government to stand, even when they offend a judge's own sense of principles.

judicial activism:

A philosophy of judicial decision making that argues judges should use their power broadly to further justice, especially in the areas of equality and personal liberty.

■ Oregon voters defeated the attempted repeal of the Death with Dignity Law by 60%–40% margin. Oregon is the first state to legalize assisted suicide. (Photo courtesy: Don Ryan/AP/Wide World Photos)

Fourteenth Amendment. Segregation was nonetheless practiced after passage of the Fourteenth Amendment. An activist would point out that if the Court had not reinterpreted its provisions of the amendment, many states probably would still have laws or policies mandating segregation in public schools.

The debate over judicial activism versus judicial restraint often focuses on how the Court should interpret the meaning of the Constitution. Advocates of judicial restraint generally agree that judges should be strict constructionists; that is, they should interpret the Constitution as it was written and intended by the Framers. They argue that in determining the constitutionality of a statute or policy, the Court should rely on the explicit meanings of the clauses in the document, which can be clarified by looking at the intent of the Framers.

Precedent. Most Supreme Court decisions are laced with numerous references to previous Court decisions. Some justices, however, believe that *stare decisis* and adherence to precedent is no longer as critical as it once was. Chief Justice Rehnquist, for example, has noted that while "*stare decisis* is a cornerstone of our legal system . . . it has less power in constitutional cases."[58] In contrast, Justices O'Connor, Kennedy, and Souter explained their reluctance to overrule *Roe* v. *Wade* (1973) in *Planned Parenthood of Southeastern Pennsylvania* v. *Casey* (1992): "to overrule under fire in the absence of the most compelling reason to reexamine a watershed decision would subject this Court's legitimacy beyond any serious question."[59]

Interestingly, a 1990 study of the American public's knowledge and perceptions of the Court indicated that only 44 percent believed that the Court decides cases primarily on the basis of facts and law. Nearly 50 percent believe that the Court makes decisions based on other factors, including political pressures (28 percent), political/personal beliefs (18 percent), and religious beliefs (1 percent). Although *theoretically* the Framers envisioned the Court to be above these pressures, the American public does not appear to be particularly upset about the role of politics and personal beliefs in the decision-making process. In fact, those polled want the Court to take a more active role in the areas of discrimination against women and minorities.

Extra-Legal Factors

Most political scientists who study what is called judicial behavior conclude that a variety of forces shape judicial decision making. Of late, many have attempted to explain how judges vote by integrating a variety of models to offer a more complete picture of how judges make decisions.[60] Many of those models attempt to take into account justices' behavioral characteristics and attitudes as well as the fact patterns of the case.

Behavioral Characteristics.   Some political scientists argue that social background differences, including childhood experiences, religious values, education, earlier political and legal careers, and political party loyalties are likely to influence how a judge evaluates the facts and legal issues presented in any given case. Justice Harry A. Blackmun's service at the Mayo Clinic is often pointed to as a reason that his opinion for the Court in *Roe* v. *Wade* was so soundly grounded in medical evidence. Similarly, Justice Potter Stewart, who was generally considered a moderate on most civil liberties issues, usually took a more liberal position on cases dealing with freedom of the press. Why? It may be that Stewart's early job as a newspaper reporter made him more sensitive to these claims.

Ideology.   Critics of the social background approach argue that attitudes or ideologies can better explain the justices' voting patterns. Since the 1940s the two most prevailing ideologies in the United States have been conservative and liberal. On the Supreme Court, justices with "conservative" views generally vote against affirmative action, abortion rights, expanded rights for criminal defendants, and increased power for the national government. In contrast, "liberals" tend to support the parties advancing these positions.

Over time, scholars have generally agreed that identifiable ideological voting blocs have occurred on the Court. During Franklin D. Roosevelt's first term, for example, five justices, a critical conservative bloc, routinely voted to strike down the constitutionality of New Deal legislation. Traditionally, such voting blocs or coalitions have centered on liberal/conservative splits on issues such as states' rights (conservatives supporting and liberals opposing), economic issues (conservatives being pro-business; liberals, pro-labor), and civil liberties and civil rights (conservatives being less supportive than liberals). In death penalty cases, for example, Justices William Brennan, Jr., and Thurgood Marshall (sometimes joined by John Paul Stevens) consistently voted against the imposition of capital punishment.

The Attitudinal Model.   The attitudinal approach hypothesizes that there is a substantial link between judicial attitudes and decision making.[61] Simply stated, the attitudinal model holds that Supreme Court justices decide cases in light of the facts of the cases according to their personal preferences toward issues of public policy. Among some of the factors used to derive attitudes are a justice's party identification,[62] the party of the appointing president,[63] and the liberal/conservative leanings of a justice. To date, the attitudinal model is generally characterized as being the best at explaining Supreme Court decision making.[64]

Public Opinion.   Many political scientists also have examined the role of public opinion in Supreme Court decision making.[65] Not only do the justices read legal briefs and hear oral arguments, they also read newspapers, watch television, and have some knowledge of public opinion—especially on controversial issues. According to Chief Justice Rehnquist,

> Judges, so long as they are relatively normal human beings, can no more escape being influenced by public opinion in the long run than can people working at other jobs. And if a judge on coming to the bench were to decide to hermetically seal himself off from all manifestations of public opinion, he would accomplish very little; he would not be influenced by current public opinion, but instead would be influenced by the state of public opinion at the time he came to the bench.[66]

Web Exploration

To learn about ethics in the courts and view what some consider "outrageous" judicial rulings, go to www.awlonline.com/oconnor. Which rulings do you consider most "outrageous"?

Political scientist Thomas R. Marshall has discovered substantial variation in the degree to which particular justices' decisions were congruent with public opinion.[67] Whether or not public opinion actually influences some justices, public opinion can act as a check on the power of the courts as well as an energizing factor. Activist periods on the Supreme Court have generally corresponded to periods of social or economic crisis. For example, the Marshall Court supported a strong national government, much to the chagrin of a series of pro–states' rights Democratic–Republican presidents in the early crisis-ridden years of the republic. Similarly, the Court capitulated to political pressures and public opinion when, after 1936, it reversed many of its earlier decisions that had blocked President Roosevelt's New Deal legislation.

The courts, especially the Supreme Court, also can be the direct target of public opinion. During the spring of 1989, when the case of *Webster* v. *Reproductive Health Services* was about to come before the Supreme Court, the Court was subjected to unprecedented lobbying as groups and individuals on both sides of the abortion issue marched and sent appeals to the Court. Earlier, in the fall of 1988, Justice Harry A. Blackmun, author of *Roe* v. *Wade,* had warned a law school audience in a public address that he feared that the decision was in jeopardy. This in itself was a highly unusual move; until recently, it was the practice of the justices never to comment on cases or the Court.

Speeches like Blackmun's put pro-choice advocates on guard, and many took advantage of the momentum that had built around their successful campaign against the nomination of Robert H. Bork. In 1989, their forces mounted one of the largest demonstrations in the history of the United States—more than 300,000 people marched from the Mall to the Capitol building, just across the street from the Supreme Court. In addition, full-page advertisements appeared in prominent newspapers, and supporters of *Roe* v. *Wade* were urged to contact members of the Court to voice their support. Justice Sandra Day O'Connor, at the time the Court's lone woman, was targeted by many who viewed her as the crucial swing justice on the issue. Mail at the Court, which usually averages about 1,000 pieces a day, rose to an astronomical 46,000 pieces when *Webster* reached the Court, virtually paralyzing normal lines of communication. Several justices spoke out against this kind of "extra-judicial" communication and voiced their belief in its ineffectiveness. In *Webster* v. *Reproductive Health Services* (1989), Justice Scalia lamented,

> We can now look forward to at least another Term with carts full of mail from the public, and streets full of demonstrators, urging us—their unelected and life tenured judges who have been awarded those extraordinary, undemocratic characteristics precisely in order that we might follow the law despite the popular will—to follow the popular will.

But the fact remains that the Court is very dependent on the public for its prestige as well as for compliance with its decisions. In times of war and other emergencies, for example, the Court frequently has decided cases in ways that commentators have attributed to the sway of public opinion and political exigencies. In *Korematsu* v. *The United States* (1944), for example, the high Court upheld the obviously unconstitutional internment of Japanese-American citizens during World War II.[68] Moreover, Chief Justice Rehnquist himself has suggested that the Court's restriction on presidential authority in *Youngstown Sheet & Tube Co.* v. *Sawyer* (1952),[69] which invalidated President Harry S Truman's seizure of the nation's steel mills, was largely attributable to Truman's unpopularity and that of the Korean War.[70] And, as Table 10.8 reveals, the public and the Court often are in agreement on many controversial issues.

Public confidence in the Court, like other institutions of government, has ebbed and flowed. Public support for the Court was highest after the Court issued *U.S.* v. *Nixon* (1974). At a time when Americans lost faith in the presidency, they could at least look to the Supreme Court to do the right thing. Of late, however, the Court and the judicial system as a whole have taken a beating in public confidence. In the aftermath of the O. J. Simpson trial, many white Americans faulted the judicial system. This dissatisfaction was reflected in low levels of confidence in the judicial system, although

Table 10.8   The Court *Versus* the American Public

In recent years, the Court has agreed and disagreed with the public on various issues, such as:

Issue	Court	Public
Should TV and other recording devices be permitted in the Supreme Court?	No	Yes (59%)
Should a parent be forced to reveal the whereabouts of a child even though it could violate Fifth Amendment rights?	Yes	Yes (50%) No (39%) Don't know (11%)
Should a family be allowed to decide to end life-support systems?	Yes	Yes (88%)
Before getting an abortion, whose consent should a teenager be required to gain?	One parent	Both parents (38%) One parent (37%) Neither parent (22%)
Is the death penalty constitutional?	Yes	Yes (72% favor)
Should members of Congress be subject to term limits?	No	Yes (77% favor)

SOURCE: Table compiled from General Social Surveys, Gallup Poll data, and a Tarrance Group Poll.

the Supreme Court enjoys greater popular support than the other two branches of government. In 1998, 77 percent of those sampled by the Roper Center had a "favorable or mostly favorable opinion of the Supreme Court."

The Supreme Court also appears to affect public opinion. Political scientists have found that the court affects public opinion when it first rules in controversial cases such as those involving abortion or capital punishment but that subsequent decisions have little affect.[71]

JUDICIAL POLICY MAKING AND IMPLEMENTATION

Clearly, the American public regards the Supreme Court as a powerful policy maker. In a 1990 poll, most respondents said they believed that the Court was more powerful than the president (31 percent versus 21 percent), and that the Court was close to being as powerful as Congress (38 percent).

All judges, whether they like it or not, make policy. In 1996, when the U.S. Supreme Court ruled that Colorado could not prevent states and local governments from extending any constitutional protections to gay, lesbian, and bisexual citizens, the justices were making policy.[72] When the Court ruled that prayer at public school ceremonies was a violation of separation of church and state, the Court made policy.[73] It is through interpreting statutes or the Constitution that federal courts, and the Supreme Court in particular, make policy in several ways. Judges can interpret a provision of a law to cover matters not previously understood to be covered by the law, or they can "discover" new rights, such as that of privacy, from their reading of the Constitution. They can also affect lives, with the extreme being death penalty cases.

This power of the courts to make policy presents difficult questions for democratic theory, as noted by Justice Scalia in *Webster*, because democratic theorists believe that the power to make law resides only in the people or their elected representatives. Yet court rulings, especially Supreme Court decisions, routinely affect policy far beyond the interests of the immediate parties.

Policy Making

One measure of the power of the courts and their ability to make policy is that more than one hundred federal laws have been declared unconstitutional. Although many of these laws have not been particularly significant, others have. For example, in *Immigration and Naturalization Service* v. *Chadha* (1983) (discussed in chapter 7), the Court found that legislative vetoes were unconstitutional.[74]

Another measure of the policy making power of the Supreme Court is its ability to overrule itself. Although the Court generally abides by the informal rule of *stare decisis*, by one count it has overruled itself in more than 140 cases since 1810. *Brown* v. *Board of Education* (1954), for example, overruled *Plessy* v. *Ferguson* (1896), thereby reversing years of constitutional interpretation concluding that racial segregation was not a violation of the Constitution. Moreover, in the past few years, the Court has repeatedly reversed earlier decisions in the areas of criminal defendants' rights, affirmative action, and the establishment of religion, thus revealing its powerful role in determining national policy.

A measure of the growing power of the federal courts is the degree to which they now handle issues that, after *Marbury* v. *Madison* (1803), had been considered to be political questions more appropriately left to the other branches of government to decide. Prior to 1962, for example, the Court refused to hear cases questioning the size (and populations) of congressional districts, no matter how unequal they were.[75] The boundary of a legislative district was considered to be a political question. Then, in 1962, writing for the Court, Justice William Brennan, Jr., concluded that simply because a case involved a political issue it did not necessarily involve a political question. This opened up the floodgates to cases involving a variety of issues that the Court formerly had declined to address.[76]

Implementing Court Decisions

President Andrew Jackson, annoyed about a particular decision handed down by the Marshall Court, is alleged to have said, "John Marshall has made his decision; now let him enforce it." Jackson's statement raises a question: How do Supreme Court rulings translate into public policy? In fact, although judicial decisions carry legal and even moral authority, all courts must rely on other units of government to carry out their directives. If the president or Congress, for example, doesn't like a particular Supreme Court ruling, they can underfund programs needed to implement a decision or seek only lax enforcement. **Judicial implementation** refers to how and whether judicial decisions are translated into actual public policies affecting more than the immediate parties to the lawsuit.

How well a decision is implemented often depends on how well crafted or popular it is. Hostile reaction in the South to *Brown* v. *Board of Education* (1954) and the absence

judicial implementation:
Refers to how and whether judicial decisions are translated into actual public policies affecting more than the immediate parties to a lawsuit.

Table 10.9 The Future Composition of the Supreme Court

Justice	Age in 1999	Philosophy	Projected Year of Retirement*
Stevens	79	Moderate	2001
Rehnquist	75	Conservative	2005
O'Connor	69	Conservative to Moderate	2011
Scalia	63	Conservative	2017
Kennedy	63	Conservative to Moderate	2017
Souter	60	Moderate	2020
Thomas	51	Conservative	2029
Ginsburg	67	Moderate to Liberal	2009
Breyer	61	Moderate	2019

*This is based on the age of the last six justices (Brennan, Burger, Marshall, Powell, White, and Blackmun) when they retired from 1986 to 1994—eighty-one years of age.

of precise guidelines to implement the decision meant that the ruling went largely unenforced for years. The *Brown* experience also highlights how much the Supreme Court needs the support of both federal and state courts as well as other governmental agencies to carry out its judgments. For example, you may have graduated from high school since 1992, when the Supreme Court ruled that public middle school and high school graduations could not include a prayer. Yet your own commencement ceremony may have included one.

Charles Johnson and Bradley C. Canon suggest that the implementation of judicial decisions involves what they call an *implementing population* and a *consumer population*.[77] The implementing population consists of those people responsible for carrying out a decision. It varies, depending on the policy and issues in question, but can include lawyers, judges, public officials, police officers and police departments, hospital administrators, government agencies, and corporations. In the case of school prayer, the implementing population could include teachers, school administrators, or the school board. The consumer population consists of those people who might be directly affected by a decision, that is, students and parents.

For effective implementation of a judicial decision, the first requirement is that the members of the implementing population must act to show that they understand the original decision. For example, the Supreme Court ruled in *Reynolds* v. *Sims* (1964) that every person should have an equally weighted vote in electing governmental representatives.[78] This "one person, one vote" decision might seem simple enough at first glance, but in practice it can be very difficult to understand. The implementing population in this case consists chiefly of state legislatures and local governments, which determine voting districts for federal, state, and local offices (see chapter 7). If a state legislature draws districts in such a way that African-American voters are spread thinly across a number of separate constituencies, the chances are slim that any particular district will elect a representative who is especially sensitive to blacks' concerns. Does that violate "equal representation"? (In practice, through the early 1990s, courts and the Justice Department intervened in many cases to ensure that elected officials would include minority representation, only ultimately to be overruled by the Supreme Court.)

The second requirement is that the implementing population must actually follow Court policy. Thus, when the Court ruled that men could not be denied admission to a state-sponsored nursing school, the implementing population—in this case, univer-

■ Students and government workers around the nation celebrate May 5, 1994, as National Prayer Day. In spite of Supreme Court decisions ordering a wall of separation between church and state, celebrations like this one at a Georgia public high school are held all over America each May in public buildings or on public grounds. (Photo courtesy: Dianne Laakso/*Atlanta Journal and Constitution*)

sity administrators and the Board of Regents of the nursing school—had to enroll qualified male students.

Judicial decisions are most likely to be implemented smoothly if responsibility for implementation is concentrated in the hands of a few highly visible public officials, such as the president or a governor. By the same token, these officials can also thwart or impede judicial intentions. Recall from chapter 6, for example, the effect of Governor Orval Faubus's initial refusal to allow black children to attend all-white public schools in Little Rock, Arkansas.

The third requirement for implementation is that the consumer population must be aware of the rights that a decision grants or denies them. Teenagers seeking an abortion, for example, are consumers of the Supreme Court's decisions on abortion. They need to know that most states require them to inform their parents of their intention to have an abortion or to get parental permission to do so. Similarly, criminal defendants and their lawyers are consumers of Court decisions and need to know, for example, the implications of recent Court decisions for evidence presented at trial.

GLOBAL POLITICS — The Powers of the Courts

Judicial review is an American invention, and it reflects this country's concern with balancing the branches of government under a system of separation of powers. While most of the G 7 governments today give the courts the power of judicial review, how it is used varies.

The United Kingdom occupies one extreme; it stands out as the only country surveyed that does not give the courts the judicial review power. In fact, its highest court is the House of Lords, which combines a history of legislative and judicial functions. France occupies a middle position. Its Constitutional Council is not a court, but is composed of eminent persons appointed respectively by the president and the two houses of the parliament; it is given the power to rule only on the constitutionality of legislation.

Of the five countries that give their courts the judicial review power, four have parliamentary systems. In these systems, parliamentary supremacy is a defining feature of government organization. In Canada, Italy, and Japan, therefore, the courts have tended to defer to parliamentary authority on major issues that would be considered within the purview of American courts. Of the four, Germany is an exception, with a Federal Constitutional Court that is quite active. Since 1949, it has had an influential role, for example, in defining the limits of non-democratic political organizations' (i.e. neo-Nazi groups and the Communist Party) participation in democratic society.

Judicial Review in the G-7 Judiciaries

Country	Name of Highest Court	Power of the Courts
Canada	Supreme Court	judicial review
France	Constitutional Council	limited judicial review
Germany	Federal Constitutional Court	judicial review
Italy	Constitutional Court	judicial review
Japan	Supreme Court	judicial review
United Kingdom	House of Lords	no judicial review
United States	Supreme Court	judicial review

CONTINUITY and Change

Participation in the Judicial Process

At the time the Constitution was adopted, women and African Americans were largely excluded from the judicial process. Neither could vote, and largely on that basis, both groups were excluded from jury service. Similarly, no women or African Americans were lawyers or judges. A handful of black lawyers practiced in the North in the mid-1880s, and John Swett Rock was admitted to practice before the Supreme Court in 1861. The first women lawyers were admitted to practice in the late 1860s. When Belva Lockwood's petition to be admitted to the Supreme Court bar was denied in 1876, she energetically lobbied Congress, which passed a law requiring the Court to admit qualified women to practice. In 1879, she became the first woman admitted to practice before the Supreme Court.

Women and blacks were often excluded from jury service because many states selected jurors from those registered to vote. African Americans were systematically excluded from the voter rolls throughout the South until after passage of the Voting Rights Act of 1965 (VRA). They have only recently begun to be part of the judicial system as the VRA has been implemented. As early as 1880, however, the Supreme Court ruled that Negro citizens could not be barred from serving as jurors.[a] It was not until 1975 that the Supreme Court was to rule that states could not exclude women from jury service.[b]

As a result of the civil rights and women's rights movements detailed in chapter 6, the number as well as percentage of all women and minority lawyers and judges has grown tremendously. Today, 25 percent of all lawyers are women, and 4 percent are African American, Hispanic, or Native American. Similarly, beginning with President Carter's efforts to appoint more women and minorities to the federal courts, they have become a rising proportion of the federal judiciary, with African Americans holding 10 percent of all federal judgeships and white women another 15 percent (Hispanics hold 4 percent of the seats, Asians Americans less than 1 percent, and there are but two Native-American federal judges). While no state can bar African Americans or women from serving on a jury, it was not all that unusual, until recently, for lawyers to use their peremptory challenges (those made without a reason) to systematically dismiss women or African Americans if they believed that they would be more hostile jurors to their side. In two cases, however, the Supreme Court ruled that race or gender could not be used as reasons to exclude potential jurors.[c] Thus, today, juries are much more likely to be truly representative of the community and capable of offering any litigant in a civil or criminal matter a jury of their peers.

Many studies of the judicial process have concluded that male and female justices decide cases differently. Women and African American judges tend to be more liberal than their white male counterparts. Thus, the presence of more women and more minority judges could lead to enhanced public support for the judiciary. The O. J. Simpson case brought home to most Americans quite vividly that whites and blacks view the judicial process quite differently, often based on group treatment within that process.

1. Will greater participation by women and African-American judges have a difference on how cases are decided and the ways that laws are interpreted?
2. As we move into a society with more African-American and female jurists, lawyers, and jurors, what consequences will this have on public perceptions of the American legal system?

Cast Your Vote. What changes, if any, do you foresee in the judicial process? To cast your vote, go to www.awlonline.com/oconnor.

[a]*Strauder* v. *West Virginia,* 100 U.S. 303 (1888).
[b]*Duren* v. *Missouri,* 439 U.S. 357 (1979).
[c]*Batson* v. *Kentucky,* 476 U.S. 79 (1986) (African Americans) and *J. E. B.* v. *Alabama,* 511 U.S. 127 (1994) (women).

SUMMARY

The judiciary and the legal process—on both the national and state levels—are complex and play a far more important role in the setting of policy than the Framers ever envisioned. To explain the judicial process and its evolution, we have made the following points:

1. THE CONSTITUTION AND THE CREATION OF THE NATIONAL JUDICIARY

Many of the Framers viewed the judicial branch of government as little more than a minor check on the other two branches, ignoring Anti-Federalist concerns about an unelected judiciary and its potential for tyranny. The Judiciary Act of 1789 established the basic federal court system we have today. It was the Marshall Court (1801–35), however, that interpreted the Constitution to include the Court's major power, that of judicial review.

2. THE AMERICAN LEGAL SYSTEM

Ours is a dual judicial system consisting of the federal court system and the separate judicial systems of the fifty states. In each system there are two basic types of courts: trial courts and appellate courts. Each type deals with cases involving criminal and civil law. Original jurisdiction refers to a court's ability to hear a case as a trial court; appellate jurisdiction refers to a court's ability to review cases already decided by a trial court.

3. THE FEDERAL COURT SYSTEM

The federal court system is made up of constitutional and legislative courts. Federal district courts, courts of appeals, and the Supreme Court are constitutional courts.

4. HOW FEDERAL COURT JUDGES ARE SELECTED

District court and court of appeals judges are nominated by the president and subject to Senate confirmation. Senators often play a key role in recommending district court appointees from their home state. Supreme Court justices are nominated by the president and must also win Senate confirmation. Presidents use different criteria for selection, but important factors include competence, standards, ideology, rewards, pursuit of political support, religion, race, and gender.

5. THE SUPREME COURT TODAY

Several factors go into the Court's decision to hear a case. Not only must the Court have jurisdiction, but at least four justices must vote to hear the case, and cases with certain characteristics are most likely to be heard. Once a case is set for review, briefs and *amicus curiae* briefs are filed and oral argument scheduled. The justices meet after oral argument to discuss the case, votes are taken, and opinions are written and circulated.

6. HOW THE JUSTICES VOTE

Several legal and extra-legal factors affect how the Court arrives at its decision. Legal factors include judicial philosophy, the original intent of the Framers, and precedent. Extra-legal factors include public opinion and the behavioral characteristics and ideology of the justices.

7. JUDICIAL POLICY MAKING AND IMPLEMENTATION

The Supreme Court is an important participant in the policy-making process. The process of judicial interpretation gives the Court powers never envisioned by the Framers.

KEY TERMS

amicus curiae, p. 360
appellate court, p. 340
appellate jurisdiction, p. 340
brief, p. 346
constitutional court, p. 342
criminal law, p. 341
civil law, p. 341
in forma pauperis, p. 359
judicial activism, p. 366

judicial implementation, p. 371
judicial restraint, p. 366
judicial review, p. 336
Judiciary Act of 1789, p. 337
jurisdiction, p. 340
legislative courts, p. 343
Marbury v. *Madison* (1803), p. 340

original jurisdiction, p. 340
precedent, p. 346
Rule of Four, p. 360
solicitor general, p. 360
stare decisis, p. 346
strict constructionist, p. 354
trial court, p. 340
writ of *certiorari*, p. 359

SELECTED READINGS

Abraham, Henry J. *The Judicial Process,* 7th ed. New York: Oxford University Press, 1997.

Barrow, Deborah J., Gary Zuk, and Gerard S. Gryski, *The Federal Judiciary and Institutional Change.* Ann Arbor: University of Michigan Press, 1996.

Baum, Lawrence. *The Supreme Court,* 5th ed Washington, DC: CQ Press, 1995.

———. *The Puzzle of Judicial Behavior.* Ann Arbor: University of Michigan Press, 1997.

Clayton, Cornell and Howard Gillman eds. *Supreme Court Decision-Making: New Institutionalist Approaches.* Chicago: University of Chicago Press, 1999.

Epstein, Lee, *et al. The Supreme Court Compendium: Data, Decisions, and Developments,* 2d ed. Washington, DC: Congressional Quarterly Inc., 1996.

Goldman, Sheldon. *Picking Federal Judges: Lower Court Selection from Roosevelt Through Reagan.* New Haven: Yale University Press, 1997.

Hall, Kermitt L., ed. *The Oxford Companion to the Supreme Court of the United States.* New York: Oxford University Press, 1992.

Lazarus, Edward. *Closed Chambers: The First Eyewitness Account of the Epic Struggles Inside the Supreme Court.* New York: Times Books, 1998.

Maveety, Nancy. *Justice Sandra Day O'Connor: Strategist on the Supreme Court.* Lanham, MD: Rowman & Littlefield, 1996.

O'Brien, David M. *Storm Center: The Supreme Court in American Politics,* 5th ed. New York: Norton, 1999.

Perry, H. W. *Deciding to Decide: Agenda Setting in the United States Supreme Court.* Cambridge, MA: Harvard University Press, 1994.

Provine, Doris Marie. *Case Selection in the United States Supreme Court.* Chicago: University of Chicago Press, 1980.

Salokar, Rebecca Mae. *The Solicitor General: The Politics of Law.* Philadelphia: Temple University Press, 1992.

Slotnick, Elliot E. and Jennifer A. Segal. *Television News and the Supreme Court: All the News That's Fit to Air.* Boston: Cambridge University Press. 1998.

Sunstein, Cass R. *One Case at a Time: Judicial Minimalism on the Supreme Court.* Cambridge: Harvard University Press, 1999.

Woodward, Bob, and Scott Armstrong. *The Brethren: Inside the Supreme Court.* New York: Avon, 1996.

NOTES

1. Robert McCode, "Film reopens 'Woborn problems'; Chemical contamination becomes key focus of 'A Civil Action,'" *Houston Chronicle,* December 20, 1998, B-2.

2. See Campaign for Tobacco-Free Kids, http://www. tobaccofreekids.org/html/1998 _tobacco_settlement.html

3. Bernard Schwartz, *The Law in America* (New York: American Heritage, 1974), 48.

4. Julius Goebel, Jr., *History of the Supreme Court of the United States,* vol. 1: *Antecedents and Beginnings to 1801* (New York: Macmillan, 1971), 206.

5. 1 (Wheat.) 14 U.S. 304 (1816).

6. Quoted in Goebel, *History of the Supreme Court,* 280.

7. Schwartz, *The Law in America,* 11.

8. 2 Dall. 419 (1793).

9. 3 Dall. 171 (1796). In *Hylton* v. *United States* the Court ruled that a congressional tax on horse-drawn carriages was an excise tax and not a direct tax and therefore it need not be apportioned evenly among the states (as direct taxes must be, according to the Constitution).

10. 5 U.S. 137 (1803).

11. This discussion draws heavily on Jack C. Plano and Milton Greenberg. *The American Political Dictionary;* 10th ed. (Fort Worth, TX: Harcourt Brace, 1996), 247.

12. David W. Neubauer, *Judicial Process: Law, Courts and Politics* (Pacific Grove, CA: Brooks/Cole, 1991), 57.

13. Cases involving citizens from different states can be filed in state or federal court.

14. John R. Vile and Mario Perez-Reilly, "The U.S. Constitution and Judicial Qualifications: A Curious Omission," *Judicature* (December/January 1991): 198–202.

15. Sheldon Goldman and Elliot Slotnick, "Clinton's First Term Judiciary: Many Bridges to Cross," *Judicature* (May–June 1997): 254–55.

16. William H. Rehnquist, "The 1997 Year-End Report on the Federal Judiciary." http://www.uscourts.gov/cj97.htm. embargoed for release January 1, 1998, 12:01 A.M. EST.

17. "Rehnquist Sees Threat to Judicial System," *Washington Post* (January 2, 1998): A21.

18. Thomas B. Edsall, "Clinton Plans Judicial Offensive," *Washington Post* (January 16, 1998): A1.

19. Quoted in Edsall, "Clinton Plans."

20. Quoted in Nina Totenberg, "Will Judges Be Chosen Rationally?" *Judicature* (August/September 1976): 93.

21. Quoted in Judge Irving R. Kaufman. "Charting a Judicial Pedigree," *New York Times* (January 24, 1981): 23.

22. Quoted in Lawrence Baum, *The Supreme Court,* 3d. ed. (Washington. DC: CQ Press, 1989), 108.

23. See Barbara A. Perry, *A Representative Supreme Court? The Impact of Race, Religion and Gender on Appointments* (New York: Greenwood Press, 1991).

24. Clarence Thomas was raised a Catholic, but attended an Episcopalian church at the time of his appointment having been barred from Catholic sacraments because of his remarriage. He again, however is attending Roman Catholic services.

25. Saundra Torry, "ABA's Judicial Panel Is a Favorite Bipartisan Target," *Washington Post* (April 29, 1996): F7

26. Torry, "ABA's Judicial Panel."

27. M. A. Stapleton, "Judicial Selection Process Survives Flaws," *Chicago Daily Law Bulletin* (February 7, 1996): 1.

28. See Bruce Allen Murphy, *The Brandeis/ Frankfurter Connection* (New York: Oxford University Press, 1982).

29. Marcia Coyle, "How Americans View High Court," *National Law Journal* (February 26, 1990): 1.

30. John Brigham, *The Cult of the Court* (Philadelphia: Temple University Press, 1987).

31. Stephen L. Wasby, *The Supreme Court in the Federal Judicial System,* 4th ed. (Chicago: Nelson-Hall, 1988), 194.

32. Wasby, *The Supreme Court,* 194.

33. Wasby, *The Supreme Court,* 199. Much of this change occurred as the result of an increase in state criminal cases, of which nearly 100 percent concerned constitutional questions.

34. Neubauer, *Judicial Process,* 370.

35. William P. McLauchan, "The Business of the United States Supreme Court, 1971–1983: An Analysis of Supply and Demand," paper presented at the 1986 annual meeting of the Midwest Political Science Association.

36. 498 U.S. 177 (1991).

37. Justice Stevens chooses not to join this pool. According to one former clerk, "He wanted an independent review," but Stevens himself examines only about 20 percent of the petitions, leaving the rest to his clerks. Tony Mauro, "Ginsburg Plunges into the Cert Pool," *Legal Times* (September 6, 1993): 8.

38. "Retired Chief Justice Warren Attacks . . . Freund Study Group's Composition and Proposal," *American Bar Association Journal* 59 (July 1973): 728.

39. Kathleen Werdegar, "The Solicitor General and Administrative Due Process," *George Washington Law Review* (1967–1968): 482.

40. Rebecca Mae Salokar, *The Solicitor General: The Politics of Law* (Philadelphia: Temple University Press, 1992), 3.

41. Quoted in Elder Witt, *A Different Justice: Reagan and the Supreme Court* (Washington, DC: CQ Press, 1986), 133.

42. Lawrence Baum, *The Supreme Court,* 4th ed. (Washington, DC: CQ Press, 1992), 106.

43. Richard C. Cortner, *The Supreme Court and Civil Liberties* (Palo Alto, CA: Mayfield, 1975), vi.

44. Gregory A. Caldeira and John R. Wright, "*Amicus Curiae* Before the Supreme Court: Who Participates, When and How Much?" *Journal of Politics* 52 (August 1990): 803.

45. See also John R. Hermann, "American Indians in Court: The Burger and Rehnquist Years," Ph.D. dissertation, Emory University, 1996.

46. 510 U.S. 17 (1993).

47. 418 U.S. 683 (1974).

48. Quoted in Wasby, *The Supreme Court,* 229.

49. 478 U. S. 186 (1986).

50. "Justices' Files Show Struggle Over Georgia Sodomy Case," *Atlanta Journal and Constitution* (May 25, 1993): A9. The Marshall papers also reveal politics at the *certiorari* stage.

51. 418 U.S. 683 (1974).

52. Bob Woodward and Scott Armstrong, *The Brethren* (New York: Simon and Schuster, 1979), 65, 288–347.

53. 492 U. S. 490 (1989).

54. *Clinton* v. *Jones,* 520 U.S. 681 (1997).

55. Stanley C. Brubaker, "Reconsidering Dworkin's Case for Judicial Activism," *Journal of Politics* 46 (1984): 504.

56. Donald L. Horowitz, *The Courts and Social Policy* (Washington, DC: Brookings Institution, 1977), 538.

57. 347 U.S. 483 (1954).

58. *Webster* v. *Reproductive Health Services,* 492 U.S. at 518 (1989).

59. 112 S. Ct. 2791 (1992).

60. See, for example, Tracy E. George and Lee Epstein, "On the Nature of Supreme Court Decision Making," *American Political Science Review* 86 (1992): 323–37: Melinda Gann Hall and Paul Brace, "Justices' Responses to Case Facts: An Interactive Model," *American Politics Quarterly* (April 1996): 237–261; Lawrence Baum, *The Puzzle of Judicial Behavior* (Ann Arbor: University of Michigan Press, 1997); and Gregory N. Flemming, David B. Holmes, and Susan Gluck Mezey, "An Integrated Model of Privacy Decision Making in State Supreme Courts," *American Politics Quarterly* 26 (January 1998): 35–58.

61. Jeffrey A. Segal and Harold Spaeth, *The Supreme Court and the Attitudinal Model.* (Cambridge, England: Cambridge University Press, 1993).

62. Gerard Gryski, Eleanor C. Main, and William Dixon, "Models of State High Court Decision Making in Sex Discrimination Cases," *Journal of Politics* 48 (1986): 143–55; and C. Neal Tate and Roger Handberg. "Time Binding and Theory Building in Personal Attribute Models of Supreme Court Voting Behavior, 1916–1988," *American Political Science Review* 35 (1991): 460–80.

63. Donald R. Songer and Sue Davis, "The Impact of Party and Region on Voting Decisions in the U.S. Courts of Appeals, 1955–86," *Western Political Quarterly* 43: 830–44.

64. Hall and Brace, "Justices' Response to Case Facts." See also Lee Epstein and Jack Knight, *The Choices Justices Make* (Washington, DC: Congressional Quarterly Books, 1997).

65. Thomas R. Marshall, "Public Opinion, Representation and the Modern Supreme Court." *American Politics Quarterly* 16 (1988): 296–316.

66. William H. Rehnquist, "Constitutional Law and Public Opinion," paper presented at Suffolk University School of Law, Boston, April 10, 1986, 40–41.

67. Thomas R. Marshall, *Public Opinion and the Supreme Court* (Boston: Unwin and Hyman, 1989).

68. 323 U.S. 214 (1944).

69. 343 U.S. 579 (1952).

70. The Supreme Court ruled that President Truman's seizure and operation of U.S. steel mills in the face of a strike threat were unconstitutional, because the Constitution implied no such broad executive power. See Alan Westin, *Anatomy of a Constitutional Law Case* (New York: Macmillan, 1958); and Maeva Marcus, *Truman and the Steel Seizure Case* (New York: Columbia University Press, 1977).

71. Timothy R. Johnson and Andrew D. Martin, "The Public's Conditional Response to Supreme Court Decisions," *American Political Science Review* 92 (June 1998): 299–309.

72. *Romer* v. *Evans*, 116 S. Ct. 1620 (1996).

73. *Lee* v *Weisman*, 112 S. Ct. 2649 (1992).

74. 462 U.S. 919 (1983).

75. See *Colegrove* v. *Green*, 328 U.S. 549 (1946), for example.

76. *Baker* v. *Carr*, 369 U.S. 186 (1962).

77. Charles Johnson and Bradley C. Canon, *Judicial Policies: Implementation and Impact*, 2d ed. (Washington, DC: CQ Press, 1998), chapter 1.

78. 377 U.S. 533 (1964).

(Photo courtesy: Bob Daemmrich)

Public Opinion and Political Socialization

- ■ **What Is Public Opinion?**
- ■ **Early Efforts to Influence and Measure Public Opinion**
- ■ **Political Socialization and Other Factors That Influence Opinion Formation**
- ■ **How We Form Political Opinions**
- ■ **How We Measure Public Opinion**
- ■ **How Polling and Public Opinion Affect Politicians, Politics, and Policy**

*A*s soon as news of Independent Counsel's Kenneth W. Starr's efforts to wire Linda Tripp to get additional information about President Clinton from former White House intern Monica Lewinsky became public, the president did not issue a statement. Instead, he directed his pollsters to assess how much the Lewinsky controversy was damaging his stature with the American public. Immediately, Democratic pollsters Mark Penn and Doug Schoen began conducting a national poll paid for by the Democratic National Committee to help Clinton fashion a response to charges that he had an affair with Lewinsky.[1]

In the weeks and months leading up to the media frenzy surrounding the Lewinsky affair, after the President's first unpopular admission of wrongdoing, and later as he faced impeachment hearings in Congress, Bill Clinton proved himself to be extraordinarily dependent on polls to tap the pulse of the nation. In fact, to help him fashion the 1998 agenda that was ultimately announced in his State of the Union message, Clinton solicited 200 ideas from members of his administration and Congress. He then whittled the list to about forty proposals and commissioned a poll to find out which ideas were the most popular and resonated best with the American public.

According to *USA Today*, the poll tested solutions to "large and small problems from retirement benefits and child care to food safety and drunken driving."[2] It is commonly known that the Clinton administration makes "extensive and sophisticated use of polling to hone the president's proposals" and to assist his speechwriters by finding themes to help them as they seek to put the president's ideas into stirring language. Most White House aides, however, are unwilling to talk about the president's reliance on polling, fearing that the public will believe that the president is "driven by poll numbers rather than strongly held ideals."[3]

$\mathcal{T}$he president is not the only one in the United States looking at poll data. Professional pollsters routinely question Americans from all walks of life about their beliefs and opinions about a variety of things from washing detergent, to favorite television and radio programs, to their attitudes about government and democracy. Interestingly, Americans hold a variety of views on most issues presented to them by public opinion pollsters.

Over 200 years ago, in 1787, John Jay wrote glowingly of the sameness of the American people. He and other writers of *The Federalist Papers* believed that Americans had more in common than not. Wrote Jay in *Federalist No. 2,* we are "one united people—a people descended from the same ancestors, speaking the same language, professing the same religion, attached to the same principles of government, very similar in manners and customs." Many of those who could vote were of English heritage; almost all were Christian. Moreover, most believed that certain rights—such as freedom of speech, association, and religion—were unalienable rights. Jay also spoke of shared public opinion and of the need for a national government that reflected American ideals.

Today, however, Americans are a far more heterogeneous lot. Election after election and public opinion poll after poll reveal this diversity, but nonetheless, Americans appear to agree on many things. Most want less government, particularly at the national level. So did many citizens in 1787. Most want to leave a nation better for their children. So did the Framers. But the Framers did not have sophisticated public opinion polls to tell them this, nor did they have national news media to tell them the results of those polls. Today, many people wonder what shapes public opinion: poll results or people's opinions? Do the polls drive public opinion, or does public opinion drive the polls?

The role of public opinion in the making of policy is just one question we explore in this chapter. In analyzing the role of public opinion in a democracy, the development of polling, and how politicians respond to public opinion, in this chapter we'll look at the following issues:

- First, we will examine the question, *what is public opinion?* Here we offer a simple definition and then note the role of public opinion polls in determining public perception of political issues.
- Second, we will describe *early efforts to influence and measure public opinion.* From *The Federalist Papers* to the Republicans' Contract with America and the Democrats' Families First, parties and public officials have tried to sway as well as gauge public opinion for political purposes.
- Third, we will discuss *political socialization and other factors* that lead to the formation of opinions about political matters. We also examine the role of political ideology in public opinion formation.
- Fourth, we will examine *how Americans form opinions about political issues.*
- Fifth, we will analyze *how public opinion is measured* and note problems with various kinds of polling techniques.
- Sixth, we will look at *how polling and public opinion affect politicians* as well as how politicians affect public opinion.

public opinion:

What the public thinks about a particular issue or set of issues at any point in time.

public opinion poll:

Interviews or surveys with a sample of citizens that are used to estimate the feelings and beliefs of the entire population.

WHAT IS PUBLIC OPINION?

At first blush, **public opinion** seems to be a very straightforward term: It is what the public thinks about a particular issue or set of issues at a particular time. Since the 1930s, governmental decision makers have relied heavily on **public opinion polls**—interviews with a sample of citizens that are used to determine what the public is thinking. According to George Gallup, the founder of modern-day polling, polls have played a key role in defining issues of concern to the public, shaping administrative decisions, and helping "speed up the process of democracy" in the United States.[4] (See Roots of Government: George Gallup: The Founder of Modern Polling.)

According to Gallup, leaders must constantly take public opinion—no matter how short-lived—into account. Like the Jacksonians of a much earlier era, Gallup was distrustful of leaders who were not in tune with the "common man." According to Gallup,

> in a democracy we demand the views of the people be taken into account. This does not mean that leaders must follow the public's view slavishly; it does mean that they should have an available appraisal of public opinion and take some account of it in reaching their decision.[5]

Even though Gallup undoubtedly had a vested interest in fostering reliance on public opinion polls, his sentiments accurately reflect the feelings of many political thinkers concerning the role of public opinion and governance. Some, like Gallup, believe that the government should do what a majority of the public wants done. Others argue that the public as a whole doesn't have consistent opinions on day-to-day issues but that subgroups within the public often hold strong views on some issues. These *pluralists* (see chapter 1) believe that the government must allow for the expression of these minority opinions and that democracy works best when these different voices are allowed to fight it out in the public arena.

But, as we will see later in this chapter, what the public or even subgroups think about various issues is difficult to know with certainty, simply because public opinion can change so quickly. For example, two weeks before the United States bombed Iraq in January 1991, public opinion polls revealed that only 61 percent of the American public believed that the United States should engage in combat in Iraq. One week after the invasion, however, 86 percent reported that they approved of President Bush's handling of the situation.

EARLY EFFORTS TO INFLUENCE AND MEASURE PUBLIC OPINION

You can hardly read a newspaper or a news magazine or watch television without hearing the results of the latest public opinion poll on health care, crime, race and the president's performance or trustworthiness. But long before modern polling, politicians tried to mold and win public opinion. *The Federalist Papers* were themselves one of the first major attempts to change public opinion—in this case, to gain public support for the newly drafted U.S. Constitution. Even prior to publication of *The Federalist Papers*, Thomas Paine's *Common Sense* and later his *Crisis* papers were widely distributed throughout the colonies in an effort to stimulate patriotic feelings and increase public support for the Revolutionary War.

From the very early days of the republic, political leaders recognized the importance of public opinion and used all the means at their disposal to manipulate it for political purposes. By the early 1800s, the term "public opinion" was frequently being used by the educated middle class. As more Americans became educated, they became more vocal about their opinions and were more likely to vote. A more educated, reading public led to increased demand for newspapers, which in turn provided more information about the process of

■ As part of "the world's greatest adventure in advertising," the Committee on Public Information created a vast gallery of posters designed to shore up public support during World War I. (Photo courtesy: Corbis/Bettmann)

ROOTS OF GOVERNMENT

George Gallup: The Founder of Modern Polling*

George Gallup earned a Ph.D. in journalism from the University of Iowa with a dissertation that examined methods of measuring the readership of newspapers. He first became interested in polling when his mother-in-law ran for public office in 1932. She was running against a popular incumbent, and most observers considered her candidacy a lost cause. Nevertheless, because of the Democratic landslide of 1932, she was swept into office on Franklin D. Roosevelt's coattails.

Gallup's interest in politics, fostered by his experience in his mother-in-law's campaign and his academic background in journalism and advertising, led him to take a job at a New York advertising agency. In 1935 he founded the American Institute of Public Opinion, headquartered at Princeton University in New Jersey. At the institute, Gallup refined a number of survey and sampling techniques to measure the public's attitudes on social, political, and economic issues. Weekly reports called the Gallup Polls were sent to more than forty subscribing newspapers.

Gallup attracted considerable national attention when he correctly predicted the outcome of the 1936 presidential election. Recognizing many of the flaws of *Literary Digest's* poll, he relied on a sample of a few thousand people who represented the voting population in terms of important demographic variables, such as age, gender, political affiliation, and region.

*Benjamin Ginsberg, *The Captive Public* (New York: Basic Books, 1986).

(Photo courtesy: Corbis/Bettmann)

government. And as the United States grew, there were more elections and more opportunities for citizens to express their political opinions through the ballot box. As a result of these trends, political leaders were more frequently forced to try to gauge public opinion in order to remain responsive to the wishes and desires of their constituents.

An example of the power of public opinion is the public's response to the 1851–2 serialization of Harriet Beecher Stowe's *Uncle Tom's Cabin*. This novel was one of the most powerful propaganda statements ever issued about slavery. By the time the first shots of the Civil War were fired at Fort Sumter in 1861, more than one million copies of the book were in print. Even though Stowe's words alone could not have caused the public outrage over slavery that contributed to Northern support for the war, her book convinced the majority of the American people of the justness of the abolitionist cause and solidified public opinion in the North against slavery.

During World War I, some people argued that public opinion didn't matter at all. But President Woodrow Wilson (1913–21) argued that public opinion would temper the actions of international leaders. Therefore, only eight days after the start of the war, Wilson created a Committee on Public Information. Run by a prominent journalist, the committee immediately undertook to unite U.S. public opinion behind the war effort. It used all of the tools available—pamphlets, posters, and speakers who exhorted the patrons of local movie houses during every intermission—in an effort to garner support and favorable opinion for the war. In the words of the committee's head, it was "the world's greatest adventure in advertising."[6]

In the wake of World War I, Walter Lippmann, a well-known journalist and author who was extensively involved in propaganda activities during the war, openly voiced his concerns about how easily public opinion could be manipulated and his reservations about the weight it should be given. In his seminal work, *Public Opinion* (1922), Lippmann wrote, "Since Public Opinion is supposed to be the prime mover in democracies, one might reasonably expect to find a vast literature [examining it]. One does not find it."[7] By the 1920s, although numerous efforts had been made to manipulate public opinion, scientific measurement of public opinion had yet to occur.

Early Efforts to Measure Public Opinion

Public opinion polling as we know it today did not begin to develop until the 1930s. Researchers in a variety of disciplines, including political science, heeded Lippmann's call to learn more about public opinion. Some tried to use scientific methods to measure political thought through the use of surveys or polls. As methods for gathering and interpreting data improved, survey data began to play an increasingly important role in all walks of life, from politics to retailing.

Early Election Forecasting.   As early as 1824, one Pennsylvania newspaper tried to predict the winner of that year's presidential contest. Later, in 1883, the *Boston Globe* sent reporters to selected election precincts to poll voters as they exited voting booths, in an effort to predict the results of key contests. And in 1916, *Literary Digest*, a popular magazine, began mailing survey postcards to potential voters in an effort to predict election outcomes. *Literary Digest* drew its survey sample from "every telephone book in the United States, from the rosters of clubs and associations, from city directories, lists of registered voters [and] classified mail order and occupational data."[8] Using the data it received from the millions of postcard ballots sent out throughout the United States, *Literary Digest* correctly predicted every presidential election from 1920 to 1932.

Literary Digest used what were called **straw polls** to predict the popular vote in those four presidential elections. Its polling methods were widely hailed as "amazingly right" and "uncannily accurate."[9] In 1936, however, its luck ran out. *Literary Digest* predicted that Republican Alfred M. Landon would beat incumbent President Franklin D. Roosevelt by a margin of 57 percent to 43 percent of the popular vote. Roosevelt, however, won in a landslide election, receiving 62.5 percent of the popular vote and carrying all but two states.

Polling Matures.   Through the late 1940s, the number of polling groups and increasingly sophisticated polling techniques grew by leaps and bounds as new businesses and politicians relied on the information they provide to market products and candidates. In 1948, however, the polling industry suffered a severe, although fleeting, setback when Gallup and many other pollsters incorrectly predicted that Thomas E. Dewey would defeat President Harry S Truman.

What Went Wrong?   *Literary Digest* reached out to as many potential respondents as possible, with no regard for modern sampling techniques that require that respondents

SPEED BUMP   Dave Coverly

■ (Photo courtesy: Dave Covery/ *Boston Herald*/Creators Syndicate)

straw poll:
Unscientific survey used to gauge public opinion on a variety of issues and policies.

■ Not only did advance polls in 1948 predict that Republican nominee Thomas E. Dewey would defeat Democratic incumbent Harry S Truman, but based on early and incomplete vote tallies, some newspapers' early editions even on the day *after* the election declared Dewey to have won. Here a triumphant Truman holds aloft the *Chicago Tribune*. (Photo courtesy: Corbis/Bettmann)

be selected or sampled according to strict rules of cross-sectional representation. Respondents, in essence, were like "straws in the wind," hence the term "straw polls."

Literary Digest's sample had three fatal errors. First, its sample was drawn from telephone directories and lists of automobile owners. This technique oversampled the upper middle class and the wealthy, groups heavily Republican in political orientation. Moreover, in 1936, voting polarized along class lines. Thus the oversampling of wealthy Republicans was particularly problematic, because it severely underestimated the Democratic vote.

Literary Digest's second problem was timing: Questionnaires were mailed in early September. Thus the changes in public sentiment that occurred as the election drew closer were not measured.

Its third error occurred because of a problem we now call self-selection: Only highly motivated individuals sent back the cards—a mere 22 percent of those surveyed responded. Those who respond to mail surveys are quite different from the general electorate; they often are wealthier and better educated and care more fervently about issues. *Literary Digest*, then, failed to observe one of the now well-known cardinal rules of survey sampling: "One cannot allow the respondents to select themselves into the sample."[10]

At least one pollster, however, correctly predicted the results of the 1936 election: George Gallup. Gallup had written his dissertation on how to measure the readership of newspapers, and then expanded his methods to study public opinion about politics. He was so confident about his methods that he gave all of his newspaper clients a money-back guarantee: If his poll predictions weren't closer to the actual election outcome than those of the highly acclaimed *Literary Digest*, he would refund them their money. The *Digest* predicted Alf Landon to win; Gallup predicted Roosevelt. Although he underpredicted Roosevelt's victory by nearly 7 percent, the fact that he got the winner right was what everyone remembered, especially given *Literary Digest*'s dramatic miscalculation. And, as revealed in Figure 11.1, the Gallup Organization, now run by George Gallup's son, continues to be a successful predictor of elections.

Web Exploration

To learn more about the Gallup Organization and poll trends, see www.awlonline.com/oconnor.

Figure 11.1   The Success of the Gallup Poll in Presidential Elections, 1936–1996

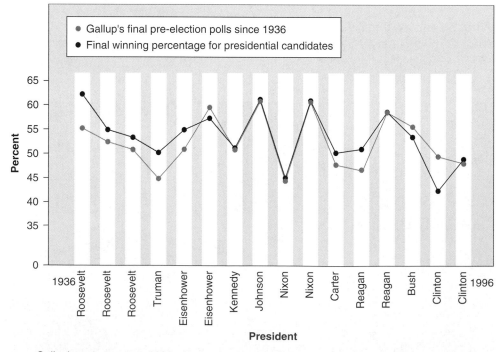

Gallup's average error: 1936–48, 4.3% 1952–63, 2.0% 1972–88, 1.6% 1992, 6.0% 1996, 1.0%

SOURCE: Marty Baumann, "How One Polling Firm Stacks Up," *USA Today* (October 27, 1992): 13A. 1996 data from Mike Mokrzycki, "Pre-election Polls' Accuracy Varied," *The Atlanta Journal/The Atlanta Constitution* (November 8, 1996): A12.

The American Voter, Public Opinion, and Political Socialization

The American Voter was published in 1960.[11] This book "intellectually contributed the dominant model for thinking about mass attitudes and mass behavior in the social science research that followed."[12] Drawing on data from the 1952 and 1956 presidential elections, *The American Voter* showed how class coalitions, which were originally formed around social-welfare issues, led to party affiliations—the dominant force in presidential elections. This book also led directly to the "institutionalization of regular surveys of the American electorate, through a biennial series now recognized as the National Election Study."[13] As discussed in Highlight 11.1, the National Election Study (NES) has given political scientists a long-term view of the political beliefs and attitudes of the American public. Indeed, the NES drives the research of many political scientists as they try to understand what drives public opinion, voting, and the course of elections. Work by political scientists has told us much about political socialization and how and when, as well as why, we form opinions about politics, government, and other political matters.

Web Exploration

To use NES data sets, see www.awlonline.com/oconnor.

POLITICAL SOCIALIZATION AND OTHER FACTORS THAT INFLUENCE OPINION FORMATION

Political scientists believe that many of our attitudes about issues are grounded in our political values. We learn these values through a process called **political socialization,** "the process through which an individual acquires his [or her] particular political orientations—his [or her] knowledge, feeling and evaluations regarding his [or her] political world."[14] Family, the mass media, schools, and peers are often important influences or agents of political socialization. For example, try to remember your earliest memory of the president of the United States. It may have been Ronald Reagan or George Bush (older students probably remember earlier presidents). What did you think of him? Of the Republican or Democratic Party? It's likely that your earliest feelings or attitudes

political socialization:

The process through which an individual acquires particular political orientations; the learning process by which people acquire their political beliefs and values.

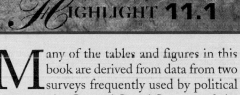

Doing Political Science: Social Science Surveys

Many of the tables and figures in this book are derived from data from two surveys frequently used by political scientists: the General Social Survey and the American National Election Studies.

The General Social Survey (GSS) The GSS is produced at the National Opinion Research Center (NORC) of the University of Chicago, which has been conducting national surveys since the 1930s. These surveys are conducted through interviews based on questionnaires that cover a broad range of social topics, including political issues. Because NORC often uses the same questions in different surveys for years, the GSS provides investigators with useful indicators of public opinion as it changes. The data produced by researchers in Chicago are made available to users through the Roper Public Opinion Research Center. For each of its surveys, NORC usually interviews roughly 1,500 randomly selected English-speaking people over the age of eighteen who live in noninstitutionalized settings.

The American National Election Studies (NES) The NES are conducted by social scientists at the Center for Political Studies of the Institute for Social Research at the University of Michigan. The Center's first major report was *The American Voter.*

NES surveys focus only on political attitudes and behavior of the electorate. Thus they include questions about how respondents voted, their party affiliation, and their opinion of the major political parties and candidates. These surveys also include questions about their interest in political matters, and their political participation, including participation in non-election-related activities, such as church attendance.

The surveys are conducted before and after midterm and presidential elections. A random sample of those eligible to vote on Election Day and living in the continental United States is used. Like the GSS, some of the same questions are used in each survey to compile long-term studies of the electorate to facilitate political scientists' understanding of how and why people vote and participate in politics.

■ Political values are shaped in childhood. (Photo courtesy: Nancy O'Connor Zeigler)

were shaped by what your parents thought about that particular president and his party. Similar processes also apply to your early attitudes about the flag of the United States, or even the police. Other factors, too, often influence how political opinions are formed or reinforced. These include political events; the social groups you belong to, including your church; demographic group, including your race, gender, and age; and even the region of the country in which you live.

The Family

The influence of the family can be traced to two factors: communication and receptivity. Children, especially during their preschool years, spend tremendous amounts of time with their parents; early on they learn their parents' political values, even though these concepts may be vague. One study, for example, found that the most important visible public figures for children under the age of ten were police officers and, to a much lesser extent, the president.[15] Young children almost uniformly view both as "helpful." But by the age of ten or eleven, children become more selective in their perceptions of the president. By this age children raised in Democratic households are much more likely to be critical of a Republican president than are those raised in Republican households. In 1988, for example, 58 percent of children in Republican households identified themselves as Republicans, and many had developed strong positive feelings toward Ronald Reagan, the Republican president. Support for and the popularity of Ronald Reagan translated into support for the Republican Party through the 1988 presidential election and also contributed to the decline of liberal ideological self-identification of first-year college students depicted in Figure 11.2.

The Mass Media

The media today is taking on a growing role as a socialization agent. Adult Americans spend nearly thirty hours a week in front of their television sets; children spend even more.[16] Television has a tremendous impact on how people view politics, government, and politicians. TV talk shows, talk radio, and now even on-line newsletters and magazines are important sources of information about politics for many, yet the information that people get from these sources is often skewed. One study, for example, found that 25 percent of all Americans learned about the 1996 presidential campaign from

Figure 11.2   Ideological Self-Identification of First Year College Students, 1970–1998

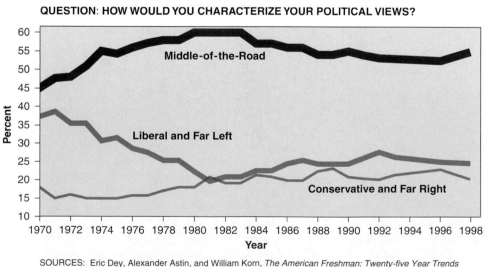

QUESTION: HOW WOULD YOU CHARACTERIZE YOUR POLITICAL VIEWS?

SOURCES: Eric Dey, Alexander Astin, and William Korn, *The American Freshman: Twenty-five Year Trends* (Los Angeles: Higher Education Research Institute, University of California, Los Angeles, 1991); *The American Freshman: National Norms for Fall 1991* (Los Angeles: Higher Education Research Institute, University of California, Los Angeles, 1991); *Fall 1992* (1992); *Fall 1993* (1993); *Fall 1994* (1994); *Fall 1995* (1995); *Fall 1996* (1996). Reprinted from: Howard W. Stanley and Richard G. Niemi, *Vital Statistics on American Politics*, 1997–1998 (Washington, DC: Congressional Quarterly, 1998), 113.

David Letterman and Jay Leno.[17] On those shows, emphasis was on Bob Dole's age and Bill Clinton's philandering and not on substance. Bob Dole, in particular, took it hard as his age was the subject of repeated barbs by comedians who appeal to younger audiences. In 1999 his position as the media spokesperson for erectile disfunction made him and his wife, Elizabeth, the target of more media barbs.

Television can often act to turn out the vote or turn voters on to particular candidates. For example, MTV continued its "Rock the Vote" campaign in 1996 and 1998 trying to galvanize young people to participate and vote.

Only 22 percent of those under age thirty report that they watch nightly news; for 13 percent, MTV was the major source of their information about politics.[18] MTV's election features are designed to spur those under twenty-five to vote and to increase their knowledge about issues and candidates.[19] In 1992 Bill Clinton and his running mate, Al Gore, Jr., appeared on MTV to discuss issues and answer questions. The under-twenty-five vote went overwhelmingly for the more liberal candidate, Clinton, in contrast to the presidential elections in 1984 and 1988.

All of the major candidates in the 1996 election also attempted to use another form of "media" to sway and inform voters: the Internet, a form of campaigning that was, believe it or not, still considered new in 1996. Republican presidential candidate Bob Dole even rattled off his campaign's Web site at the end of one presidential debate; unfortunately, he gave an incorrectly punctuated address. One resourceful "Virginia Web designer (even) registered two Internet domain names as a joke: www.dole-kemp.org and www.dole-kemp.com."[20] Dole's address was actually www.dolekemp96.org. The incorrect sites got over 40,000 hits providing a hot link to www.cg96.org, the official web site of the Clinton/Gore campaign.[21] While glitches like this are likely to continue, the 40,000 hits show the power of the Internet, which played a much more central role in the 1998 campaign, as candidates and their campaigns attempted to find new ways to sway voters and public opinion. America Online, for example launched "Talking Points," the first on-line political talk show, in 1998 and launched *Election 98: Politics on Your Terms* to allow subscribers to interact with candidates.

■ ABC Television's "Politically Incorrect with Bill Maher" brings together four-guest panels to debate hot-button issues of the day. (Photo courtesy: Patricia Schroeder/ABC, Inc.)

School and Peers

Researchers report mixed findings concerning the role of schools in the political socialization process. There is no question that, in elementary school, children are taught respect for their nation and its symbols. Most school days begin with the Pledge of Allegiance, and patriotism and respect for country are important, although subtle, components of most school curricula. The terms "flag" and the "United States" evoke very positive feelings from a majority of Americans. Support for these two icons serves the purpose of maintaining national allegiance and underlies the success of the U.S. political system in spite of relatively negative views about Congress, the courts, and the current government. In 1991, for example, few schoolchildren were taught to question U.S. involvement in the Persian Gulf. Instead, at almost every school in the nation, children were encouraged or even required to write servicemen and servicewomen stationed in the Gulf, involving these children with the war effort and implying school support for the war.

In 1994 the Kids Voting Program was launched nationwide. This civic education project was designed to have a short-term impact on student political awareness *and* lead to a higher voter turnout among their parents.[22] A study of the 2.3 million students who participated in 1994 revealed that the program met both goals.[23] Thus, a school-based program actually used children to affect their parents.

A child's peers—that is, children about the same age as a young person—also seem to have an important effect on the socialization process. Whereas parental influences are greatest during the tender years from birth to age five, a child's peer group becomes

POLITICS NOW

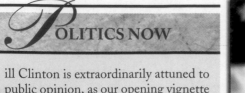

William Jefferson Clinton and Public Opinion

Bill Clinton is extraordinarily attuned to public opinion, as our opening vignette of this chapter highlights. Still, his standing in public opinion polls has continued to confound political scientists. Both his personal approval ratings and public trust in the office of the president did not falter during House impeachment proceedings against him. Traditionally, scandals hurt presidents and wars help them. This has not been the case with Clinton.

Public opinion polls throughout 1998 gave Bill Clinton his highest approval ratings since he took office.

More interestingly, several public opinion polls taken just before the Lewinsky scandal became public, Clinton's average job approval rating hovered around 60 percent. But, ten days later, after extensive media coverage of the then only alleged Lewinsky affair and the State of the Union message, Clinton actually received a 10 percent bump in his approval ratings.

As one noted student of public opinion notes, "The bounce in President Clinton's job ratings that occurred in the initial 10 days of the Lewinsky imbroglio may offer as much insight into the dynamics of public opinion as any single event in recent memory."[a] John R. Zaller speculates that it shows not only influence of a strong economy on presidential popularity, but also "the importance of political substance, as against media hype, in American politics."[b] He argues that those who study public opinion and the presidency have overlooked the role the economy, a nation at peace, and political moderation play in public attitudes toward the sitting president. "Peace, prosperity, and moderation," then, says Zaller, are much more important in influencing public opinion than the media or how a president uses the office symbolically or as a "bully pulpit."[c] However, once President Clinton initiated the 1999 bombings in Yugoslavia, his approval rating dropped, unlike the experience of most other presidents.

The longer-term effect of the Clinton administration on public opinion toward the office of the president, however, may prove to be the most important story of the Clinton presidency. Young people in grammar and high school appear to have formed very negative attitudes about the president and government in general, which may affect the course of politics and public opinion for years to come.[d] For example, only 26 percent of those in Generation Y aspire to become president of the United States.[e]

What factors do you see as contributing to positive public opinion toward the president? What factors do not appear to be that crucial? In your opinion, which factors should be the most important?

[a]John R. Zaller, "Monica Lewinsky's Contribution to Political Science," *PS: Political Science & Politics* (Summer 1998): 182.
[b]Zaller, "Monica Lewinsky's Contribution," 182.
[c]Zaller, "Monica Lewinsky's Contribution," 186.
[d]Diana Owen and Jack Dennis, "Kids and the Presidency: Assessing Clinton's Legacy," *Public Perspective* (April 1999): 41.
[e]Owen and Dennis, "Kids and the Presidency."

---

increasingly important as the child gets older, especially as he or she get into middle school or high school.[24]

High schools can also be important agents of political socialization. They continue the elementary school tradition of building good citizens and often reinforce textbook learning with trips to the state or national capital. They also offer courses on current U.S. affairs. Many high schools impose a compulsory community service requirement, which some studies report positively affects later political participation.[25] Although the formal education of many people in the United States ends with high school, research shows that better-informed citizens vote more often as adults. Therefore, presentation of civic information is especially critical at the high school level.

At the college level, teaching style often changes. Many college courses and texts like this one are designed in part to provide you with the information necessary to think critically about issues of major political consequence. It is common in college for students to be called on to question the appropriateness of certain political actions or to discuss underlying reasons for certain political or policy decisions. Therefore, most researchers believe that college has a liberalizing effect on students. Since the 1920s, studies have shown, students become more liberal each year they are in college. As we show in Figure 11.2, however, this trend appeared to decline in the 1980s, as more and more students with conservative views entered colleges and universities during the Reagan era. The 1992 and 1996 victories of Bill Clinton and his equally youthful running mate, Al Gore, Jr., who went out of their way to woo the youth vote, probably contributed to the small bump in the liberal ideological identification of first-year college students.

The Impact of Events

There is no doubt that parents—and, to a lesser degree, school and peers—play a role in a person's political socialization, but the role of key political events is also very important. You probably have some professors who remember what they were doing on the day that President John F. Kennedy was killed—November 22, 1963. This dramatic event is indelibly etched in the minds of virtually all people who were old enough to be aware of it. Similarly, most college students today remember where they were when the space shuttle *Challenger* exploded, or when they learned about the Oklahoma City bombing, or more recently JFK Jr.'s plane crash.

President Richard M. Nixon's fall from grace and forced resignation in 1974 also had a profound impact on the socialization process of all Americans. It made a particular impression on young people, who were forced to realize that their government was not always right or honest. This general distrust of politicians was reignited during the Starr investigation of the president and his subsequent impeachment.

One problem in discussing political socialization is that many of the major studies on this topic were conducted in the aftermath of Watergate and other crucial events, including the civil rights movement and the Vietnam War, all of which produced a marked increase in Americans' distrust of government. The findings reported in Table 1.3 on page 29, reveal the dramatic drop-off of trust in government that began in the mid-1960s and continued through the election of Ronald Reagan in 1980. In a study of Boston children conducted in the aftermath of the Watergate scandal, for example, one political scientist found that children's perception of the president went from that of a benevolent to a "malevolent" leader.[26] These findings are indicative of the low confidence most Americans had in government in the aftermath of Watergate and President Nixon's ultimate resignation from office to avoid impeachment. As discussed in Politics Now: The Clinton Presidency and Public Opinion, confidence in government remained high during 1998, although still down from the Watergate years. But the issues surrounding the Clinton impeachment have raised concerns about their impact on young people, especially Generation Y. Some studies show that their views toward the president and political affairs are significantly more negative than ever seen before—including during and immediately after Watergate.[27]

Social Groups

Group effects, that is, certain characteristics that allow persons to be lumped into categories, also affect the development and continuity of political beliefs and opinions. Among the most important of these groups are religion, education level, income, and race. More recently, researchers have learned that gender and age are becoming increasingly important determinants of public opinion, especially on certain issues. Region, too, while not a social group, per se, appears to influence political beliefs and political socialization.

Religion.   Today religion plays a very important role in the life of Americans. Although only one in five citizens in 1776 belonged to a church or synagogue, today 67 percent of all Americans report such membership.[28] Moreover, almost all Americans (96 percent) believe in God and 88 percent report that religion is "very" (61 percent) or "fairly" important in their own lives.[29] Nearly half of all Americans attend church regularly, and 62 percent believe that religion "can answer all or most of today's problems."[30]

In 1997, 58 percent of Americans identified themselves as Protestant, 27 percent as Catholic, 36 percent described themselves as born-again or evangelical Christians, 3 percent as Jewish, and 5 percent as other.[31] Only 9 percent claimed to have no religious affiliation.[32]* Over the years, analysts have found continuing ideological differences among these groups, with Protestants being the most conservative and Jews the most liberal, as shown in Figure 11.3.

---

* These numbers total more than 100 percent because some respondents view themselves, for example, as Protestants and born-again Christians.

Figure 11.3   The Ideological Self-Identification of Protestants, Catholics, and Jews

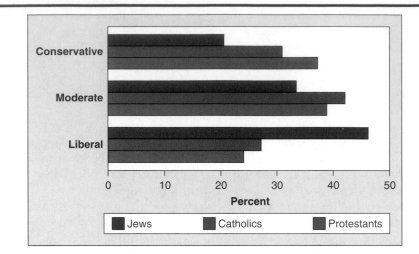

SOURCE: Data compiled by Sarah Brewer from the General Social Survey Cumulative File, 1999.

Shared religious attitudes tend to affect voting and stances on particular issues. Catholics tend to vote Democratic more than do Protestants, and they tend to vote for other Catholics. For example, in 1960 Catholics overwhelmingly cast their ballots for John F. Kennedy, who became the first Catholic president. Catholics as a group also favor aid to parochial schools, and many fundamentalist Protestants support organized prayer in public schools. Seventy-eight percent of regular church-attending evangelicals voted Republican in the 1994 elections, contributing substantially to the Republican Revolution in Congress in 1995.[33] Roman Catholics, in contrast, tend to vote more Democratic. In 1996, for example, Bill Clinton was the favorite candidate of Catholic men and women and of Catholics in all age groups (see Figure 11.4).

Recent research by political scientists reveals that a new religious cleavage is emerging, as defined by the "orthodoxy of religious beliefs, affiliations, and practices on religious behavior."[34] Thus conservative evangelical Christians are becoming increasingly Republican and more likely than less religious Protestants to vote for Republican candidates.[35]

As revealed in Figure 11.3, Jews continue to be the most liberal religious group. When political scientists have compared the attitudes of Jews with non-Jews on a variety of issues as revealed in Figure 11.5, Jews display very liberal attitudes on a range of issues from abortion to domestic spending on social programs.[36]

Race.   Differences in political socialization of African Americans and whites appear at a very early age. Young black children, for example, show "great affection for the national political community, [but] this attachment becomes seriously undermined with maturation."[37] Black children fail to hold the president in the esteem accorded him by white children; indeed, older African-American children in the 1960s viewed the government primarily in terms of the U.S. Supreme Court.[38] These differences continue through adulthood.

During the O. J. Simpson trial, public opinion poll after public opinion poll revealed in stark numbers the immense racial divide that continues to exist in the nation. Blacks distrust governmental institutions far more than do whites, and are much more likely to question police actions. Not surprisingly, then, while a majority of whites believed that Simpson was guilty, a majority of blacks believed that he was innocent.

Race is an exceptionally important factor in elections and in the study of public opinion. The direction and intensity of African-American opinion on a variety of hot-button

Figure 11.4   Whom Catholics Said They Would Vote For, 1996

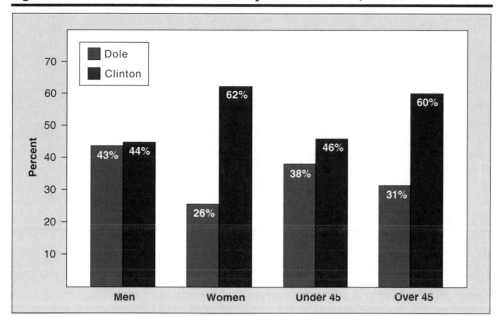

NOTE: Numbers may not add up to 100 due to rounding.
SOURCES: Pew Center for the People and the Press, NBC/*Wall Street Journal* poll. *Washington Post*
(October 20, 1996): A18.

**Figure 11.5   Percent with Liberal Attitudes on Specific Issues Among Jews
and Non-Jews**

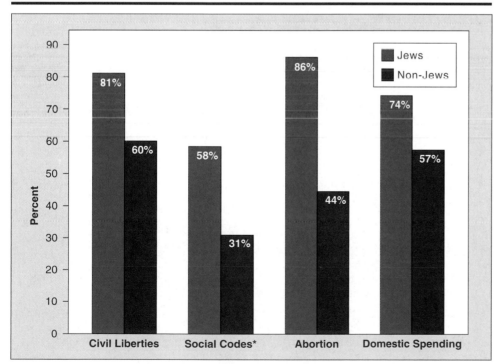

*Social codes include support for liberal divorce laws, homosexual marriage, and premarital sex.
SOURCE: Adapted from Steven M. Cohen and Charles S. Liebman, "American Jewish Liberalism: Unraveling the Strands,"
Public Opinion Quarterly 61 (1997): 417.

issues is often quite different from that of whites. As revealed in Figure 11.6, whites oppose affirmative action plans at significantly higher levels than do African Americans or Latinos. Likewise, significant differences can be seen in other areas, including abortion and support for the death penalty, and even support for Bill Clinton after release of the Starr report. Other issues, however, such as gun control, show much smaller racial dimensions.

Latinos, Asians/Pacific Islanders, and Americans Indians are other identifiable ethnic minorities in the United States (see Figure 1.3) who often respond differently to issues than do whites. Generally, Latinos and American Indians hold similar opinions on many issues largely because many of them have low incomes and find themselves targets of discrimination. Within the Hispanic community, however, existing divisions often depend on national origin. Generally, Cuban Americans who cluster in Florida (and in the Miami-Dade County area in particular) are more likely to be conservative. They fled from communism and Fidel Castro in Cuba, and they generally vote Republican. In the 1976 presidential election, for example, only 40.2 percent of the Cuban Americans in the Miami-Dade area voted for Jimmy Carter.[39] In contrast, Chicanos (people of Mexican origin) voting in California, New Mexico, Arizona, Texas, and Colorado cast 83.1 percent of their votes for Carter that year.[40]

Gender.   Poll after poll continues to reveal that women hold very different opinions from men on a variety of issues, as shown in Table 11.1. From the time that the earliest public opinion polls were taken, women have been known to hold more negative views

Figure 11.6   Racial Attitudes on Selected Issues

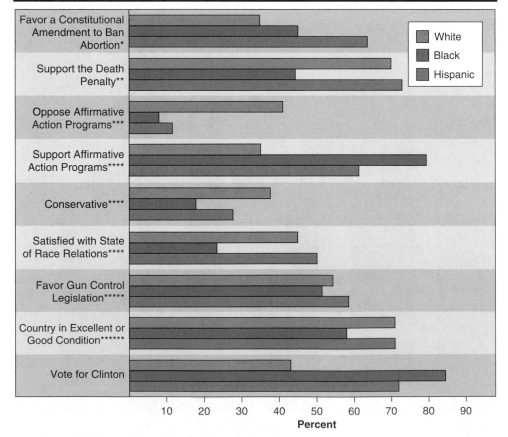

SOURCE: Compiled by authors from 1988 National Election Study.

Questions from the Roper Center, Public Opinion Online.
* December 1996   ** August 1997   *** March 1998   **** April 1998   ***** December 1998   ****** January 1999

Table 11.1   Gender Differences on Political Issues

Favored or Supporting	Males	Females
Initial sending of troops to Gulf (1991)	62	41
Contract with America (1994)	72	54
Approve of Bill Clinton's handling of the presidency (1998)	60	66
Favor affirmative action for women and minorities (1998)	49	63
Favor the death penalty (1998)	71	63
Favor gun control legislation (1999)	53	75

SOURCE: Data from CNN/*USA Today* (December 28–30, 1994); *The Public Perspective* (June/July 1995) 38; and (April/May 1996): 39; Roper Center, *Public Opinion Online,* 1998; and PEW Charitable Trusts (1999).

about war and military intervention than do men, and more strongly positive attitudes about issues touching on social-welfare concerns, such as education, juvenile justice, capital punishment, and the environment. Some suggest that women's more "nurturing" nature and their prominent role as mothers lead women to have more liberal attitudes on issues affecting the family or the safety of their children. Research by Pamela Johnson Conover and Virginia Sapiro, however, finds no support for a maternal explanation.[41]

These differences on political issues have often translated into substantial gaps in the way women and men vote. Women, for example, are more likely to be Democrats, and they often provide Democratic candidates with their margin of victory.[42] This is one of the reasons that Republican presidential candidate Bob Dole asked then-Representative Susan Molinari (R-N.Y.) to be the keynote speaker at the Republican National Convention. The selection of Molinari, a pro choice mother of an infant, was one way Dole tried to attract more women voters to the GOP.

The public's reaction to the Monica Lewinsky affair reveals especially interesting gender differentials. Women polled by the *Washington Post* in January 1998, for example, were less likely than men to believe that the president had an affair with Monica Lewinsky (60% vs. 46%) or sexually harassed Paula Jones (35% vs. 29%).[45] But, interestingly, polls showed no gender gap when respondents were asked if Bill Clinton should be impeached.[46]

The historic gender gap on military issues appears to be closing. In 1999, public opinion polls on Kosovo showed no more than a 10-point gap. And one NBC *News/Wall Street Journal* poll showed only a 4-point difference.[43] Experts offer several reasons for this shrinking gap, including the increased participation of women in the workforce and in the military, the "sanitized nature of much of the war footage" shown on TV, and the humanitarian reasons offered for NATO involvement in Yugoslavia.[44]

Age.   As Americans live longer, senior citizens are becoming a potent political force. In states such as Florida, to which many Northern retirees have flocked seeking relief from cold winters and high taxes, the elderly have voted as a bloc to defeat school tax increases and to pass tax breaks for themselves. As a group, senior citizens are much more likely to favor an increased governmental role in the area of medical insurance and to oppose any cuts in Social Security benefits.

In the future, the "graying of America" will have major social and political consequences. As we discuss in chapter 13, the elderly under age seventy vote in much larger numbers than do their younger counterparts. Moreover, the fastest-growing age group in the United States is that of citizens over the age of sixty-five. Thus not only are there more people in this category, but they are more likely to be registered to vote, and often vote conservatively.

The elderly continue to be a potent voting bloc with high concern about particular issues, but the youth vote that was mobilized in 1992 appeared to have burned itself out by 1996. Young voters are least likely to follow campaigns, with only 15 percent of those under thirty years of age reporting that they followed campaigns "very closely" compared with 43 percent for those over sixty years of age.[47] One 1996 poll found that only 28 percent think that "keeping up with politics" was "important"; in 1966, 57 percent believed it was important.[48]

Polls and focus groups conducted for MTV find that younger voters believe that "politics and real life are not in sync. Their main beef is that the candidates are not talking about issues, they're talking about politics."[49] The under-thirty generation, or Generation X, also holds strong views on certain issues, as revealed in Figure 11.7. The vast majority want stronger environmental laws, a higher minimum wage, and a balanced budget amendment.

Age also seems to have a decided effect on one's view of the proper role of government, with older people continuing to be affected by having lived through the Depression and World War II. One political scientist predicts that as baby boomers age, the age gap in political beliefs about political issues, especially governmental programs, will increase.[50] Young people, for example, resist higher taxes to fund Medicare, while the elderly resist all efforts to limit it or Social Security.

Region.   Regional and sectional differences have been important factors in the development and maintenance of public opinion and political beliefs since colonial times. As the United States grew and developed into a major industrial nation, waves of immigrants with different religious traditions and customs entered the United States and often settled in areas they viewed as hospitable to their way of life. For example, thousands of Scandinavians settled in cold, snowy, rural Minnesota, and many Irish settled in the urban centers of the Northeast, as did many Italians and Jews. All brought with them unique views about many issues, as well as about the role of government. Many of these regional differences continue to affect public opinion today and sometimes result in conflict at the national level.

Recall, for example, that during the Constitutional Convention most Southerners staunchly advocated a weak national government. Nearly a hundred years later, the Civil War was fought in part because of basic differences in philosophy toward government (states' rights in the South versus national rights in the North). As we know from the results of modern political polling, the South has continued to lag behind the rest of the nation on support for civil rights, while continuing to favor return of power to the states at the expense of the national government.

The South is also much more religious than the rest of the nation, as well as more Protestant. Sixty-four percent of the South is Protestant (versus 39 percent for the rest of the nation), and 45 percent identify themselves as born-again Christians. Nearly half

Figure 11.7   Generation X on Political Issues

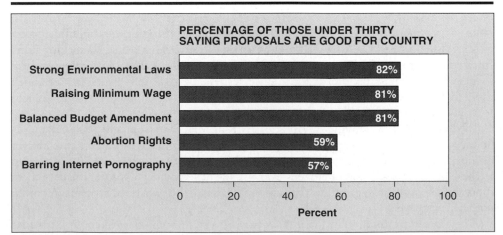

SOURCE: Paul Leavitt, "In Some States It's Beginning to Look A lot Like Election Day," *USA Today,* (October 16, 1996): 7A.

of all Southerners believe that "the United States is a Christian country, and the government should make laws to keep it that way."[51] Church attendance is highest in the South, where 38 percent report weekly visits. In contrast, only 26 percent of those living in the Midwest and 19 percent of those residing in the West go to church or synagogue on a weekly basis.[52] Given the South's higher churchgoing rates, it is not surprising that the Christian Coalition has been very successful at mobilizing voters in that region.

Southerners also are much more supportive of a strong national defense. They accounted for 41 percent of the troops in the Persian Gulf in the early days of the war, even though they make up only 28 percent of the general population.

The West, too, now appears "different" from other sections of the nation. Some people have moved there to avoid city life; other residents have an anti-government bias. And many who have sought refuge there are staunchly against any governmental action, especially on the national level.

■ The Amish are a religious group with distinct political views. (Photo courtesy: Dan Loh/AP/Wide World Photos)

Political Ideology and Public Opinion About Government

As discussed in chapter 1, an individual's coherent set of values and beliefs about the purpose and scope of government is called his or her **political ideology.** Americans' attachment to strong ideological positions has varied over time. In sharp contrast to spur-of-the-moment responses, these sets of values, which are often greatly affected by political socialization, can prompt citizens to favor a certain set of policy programs and adopt views about the proper role of government in the policy process.

Conservatives are generally likely to support smaller, less activist governments, limited social welfare programs, and reduced government regulation of business. In contrast, liberals generally believe that the national government has an important role to play in a wide array of areas, including helping the poor and disadvantaged. Unlike most conservatives, they generally favor activist governments. Most Americans today, however, identify themselves as moderates.

Political scientists and politicians often talk in terms of conservative and liberal ideologies, and most Americans believe that they do hold a political ideology. When asked by the Roper Center in April 1999, most Americans (42 percent) responded that their political beliefs were moderate, although a substantial number called themselves conservatives (39 percent) with 17 percent describing themselves as liberal. Only 2 percent of those polled "didn't know" or refused to label themselves.

political ideology:

An individual's coherent set of values and beliefs about the purpose and scope of government.

Web Exploration

For the most recent Roper Center polls, see
www.awlonline.com/oconnor.

HOW WE FORM POLITICAL OPINIONS

Many of us hold opinions on a wide range of political issues, and our ideas can be traced to our social group and the different experiences each of us has had. Some individuals (called ideologues) think about politics and vote strictly on the basis of liberal or conservative ideology. Others use the party label. Most people, however, do neither. Most people—those who are not ideologues—filter their ideas about politics through the factors discussed above; but they are also influenced by (1) personal benefits, (2) political knowledge, and (3) cues from various leaders or opinion makers.

Personal Benefits

Most polls reveal that Americans are growing more and more "I" centered. This perspective often leads people to choose policies that best benefit them personally. You've probably heard the adage, "People vote with their pocketbooks." Taxpayers generally favor lower taxes; hence, the popularity of candidates pledging "No new taxes." Similarly, an elderly person is likely to support Social Security increases, while a member of Generation X, worried about the continued stability of the Social Security program, is not likely to be very supportive of federal retirement programs. Those born in what is now being called Generation Y, or Generation X, appear even less willing to support retirement programs. Similarly, an African American is likely to support strong civil rights laws and affirmative action programs, while a majority of nonminorities will not, as revealed in Figure 11.6.

Some government policies, however, don't really affect us individually. Legalized prostitution and the death penalty, for example, are often perceived as moral issues that few citizens experience. Individuals' attitudes on these issues are often based on underlying values they have acquired through the years.

When we are faced with policies that don't affect us personally and don't involve moral issues, we often have difficulty forming an opinion. Foreign policy is an area in which this phenomenon is especially true. Most Americans often know little of the world around them. Unless moral issues such as ethnic cleansing in Kosovo are involved, American public opinion is likely to be volatile in the wake of any new information.

Political Knowledge

TRY IT!

To test your own political knowledge see www.awlonline.com/oconnor.

Americans enjoy a relatively high literacy rate, and most Americans (82 percent) graduate from high school. Most Americans, moreover, have access to a range of higher education opportunities. In spite of that access to education, however, Americans' level of actual political knowledge is low. As illustrated in Table 11.2, Americans generally don't know much about politics. In 1996, for example, 94 percent couldn't identify the Chief Justice of the United States and nearly 50 percent didn't know that Newt Gingrich was the Speaker of the House. Moreover, only 33 percent of people surveyed could correctly identify their representative in Congress. Americans, alas, don't know much about foreign policy, and some would argue that many Americans are geographically illiterate. One Gallup study done in 1988, for example, found that 75 percent of all Americans were unable to locate the Persian Gulf on a map. Two-thirds couldn't find Vietnam. Americans age eighteen to twenty-four scored the lowest, with two-thirds not being able to point to France on an outline map.[53]

In 1925 Walter Lippmann critiqued the American democratic experience and highlighted the large but limited role the population plays. Citizens, said Lippmann, cannot know everything about candidates and issues but they can, and often do, know enough to impose their views and values as to the general direction the nation should take.[54] This generalized information often stands in contrast and counterbalance to the views held by more knowledgeable political elites "inside the Beltway."

Table 11.2 American Political Knowledge

Percentage Unable to Identify

Party with most members in Senate (1996)	38
Name of vice president (1996)	40
Name of the Speaker of the House (1996)	47
Both senators from their state (1996)	54
Chief Justice of United States (1996)	94

SOURCE: Richard Morin, "Who's in Control: Many Don't Know or Care," *Washington Post* (January 29, 1996): A1, A6.

As early as 1966, V. O. Key argued in his book *The Responsible Electorate* that voters "are not fools."[55] Since then, many political scientists have argued that generalizable knowledge is enough to make democracy work. Research, for example, shows citizens' perception "of the policy stands of parties and candidates were considerably more clear and accurate when the stands themselves were more distinct: in the highly ideological election of 1964, for example, as opposed to that of 1957, or in the primaries rather than the general election of 1968."[56] In elections with sharper contrasts between candidates, voters also seemed to pay more attention to issues when they cast their ballots, and to have more highly structured liberal–conservative belief systems.[57] In addition, the use of more sophisticated analytical methods involving perceived issue distances between candidates and voters seems to reveal more issue voting in general than had previously been discovered.[58]

Cues from Leaders

Low levels of knowledge, however, can lead to rapid opinion shifts on issues. The ebb and flow of popular opinion can be affected dramatically (some might say "manipulated") by political leaders. Given the visibility of political leaders and their access to the media, it is easy to see the important role they play in influencing public opinion. Political leaders, members of the news media, and a host of other experts have regular opportunities to influence public opinion because of the lack of deep conviction with which most Americans hold many of their political beliefs.[59]

The president, especially, is often in a position to mold public opinion through effective use of the "bully pulpit," as discussed in chapter 8.[60] Political scientist John E. Mueller concludes, in fact, that there is a group of citizens—called *followers*—who are inclined to rally to the support of the president no matter what he does.[61]

According to Mueller, the president's strength, especially in the area of foreign affairs (where public information is lowest), derives from the "majesty" of his office and his singular position as head of state. Recognizing this phenomenon, presidents often take to television in an effort to drum up support for their programs.[62] President Clinton, like Reagan before him, clearly realizes the importance of mobilizing public opinion. He frequently takes his case directly to the public, urging the people to support his programs and to convey that support to their elected officials. He has used his wife, Hillary Rodham Clinton, to mobilize public opinion in support of his efforts to ward off being removed from office.

HOW WE MEASURE PUBLIC OPINION

Public officials at all levels use a variety of measures as indicators of public opinion to guide their policy decisions. These measures include election results; the number of telephone calls, faxes, or e-mail messages received pro and con on any particular issue; letters to the editor in hometown papers; and the size of demonstrations or marches. But the most commonly relied-on measure of public sentiment continues to be the public opinion survey, more popularly called a public opinion poll.

Traditional Public Opinion Polls

The polling process most often begins when someone says, "Let's find out about X and Y." Xs and Ys can be many things. Potential candidates for local office may want to know how many people have heard of them (the device used to find out is called a *name recognition survey*). Better-known candidates contemplating running for higher office might want to know how they might fare against an incumbent. Polls can also be used to gauge how effective particular ads are or if a candidate is being well (or negatively) perceived by the public. Even incumbent presidents use polls. According to the Federal Election Commission, in 1993 alone, President Clinton spent $1,986,410 on polling. Remember, this is money for polls taken while in office—not for running for office. These polls and others have several key phases,

THE LATEST POLL SHOWS THE PEOPLE DON'T TRUST STATISTICAL SAMPLING. OF COURSE, THE LATEST POLL IS STATISTICAL SAMPLING.

■ (Photo courtesy: Peter Steiner/© Tribune Media Services. All rights reserved. Reprinted with permission.)

including (1) determining the content and phrasing the questions; (2) selecting the sample; and, (3) contacting respondents.

Determining the Content and Phrasing the Questions.   Once a candidate, politician, or news organization decides to use a poll to measure the public's attitudes, special care has to be taken in constructing the questions to be asked. For example, if your professor asked you, "Do you think my grading procedures are fair?" rather than asking, "In general, how fair do you think the grading is in your American Politics course?" you might give a slightly different answer. The wording of the first question tends to put you on the spot and personalize the grading style; the second question is more neutral. Even more obvious differences appear in the real world of polling, especially when interested groups want a poll to yield particular results. Responses to highly emotional issues such as abortion, busing, and affirmative action are often skewed depending on the wording of a particular question. As Highlight 11.2. Question the Numbers and Check the Wording suggests, answers to questions about all kinds of controversial issues appear to differ considerably depending on how the questions are worded.

Selecting the Sample.   Once the decision is made to take a poll, pollsters must determine the *universe,* or the entire group whose attitudes they wish to measure. This universe could be all Americans, all voters, all city residents, all women, or all Democrats. Although in a perfect world each individual would be asked to give an opinion, this kind of polling is simply not practical. Consequently, pollsters take a sample of the universe in which they are interested. One way to obtain this sample is by **random sampling.** This method of selection gives each potential voter or adult the same chance of being selected. In theory, this sounds good, but it is actually impossible to achieve because no one has lists of every person in any group. This is why the method of poll taking is extremely important in determining the validity and reliability of the results.

random sampling:

A method of selection that gives each potential voter or adult the same chance of being selected.

Nonstratified Sampling.   *Literary Digest* polls suffered from an oversampling of voters whose names were drawn from telephone directories and car registrations; this group was hardly representative of the general electorate in the midst of the Depression. Thus the use of a nonstratified or non representative sample led to results that could not be used to predict accurately how the electorate would vote.

Perhaps the most common form of unrepresentative sampling is the kind of straw poll used today by local television news programs or on-line services. Many have regular features asking viewers to call in their sentiments (with one phone number for pro and another for con) or asking those logged on to indicate their preferences. The results of these unscientific polls vary widely because those who feel very strongly about the issue often repeatedly call in their votes or "vote" more than once. One poll taken by *Mother Jones* magazine on-line, for example, recorded a slightly different outcome than the 1996 general presidential election. Libertarian candidate Harry Browne led the field with 35 percent of the vote, followed by Green Party candidate Ralph Nader at 28 percent. Bill Clinton drew only 21 percent of the vote, as compared with his ultimately victorious 49 percent. The *Mother Jones* on-line poll wasn't the only one predicting a Browne win. Over half of those casting their ballots on CNN/*Time's* AllPolitics Web site voted for Browne, often more than once, a practice known as "virtual stuffing."[63]

Web Exploration

To see an example of a nonstratified poll, see

www.awlonline.com/oconnor.

HIGHLIGHT 11.2 — Question the Numbers and Check the Wording

Opinion polls are big news—especially during an election year. But even the most accurate polls can be very deceiving. In the past 60 years, polls have improved so much that we may be dazzled—and fooled—by their statistical precision.

Polls, however, can often mislead. "Slight differences in question wording or in the placement of the questions in the interview can have profound consequences," says David Moore, vice president of the Gallup Organization. He points out that poll findings "are very much influenced by the polling process itself."

Consider, for instance, what researchers discovered in a 1985 national poll: Only 19 percent of the public agreed that the country wasn't spending enough money on "welfare." But when the question contained the phrase "assistance to the poor" instead of "welfare," affirmative responses jumped to 63 percent.

That 44 percent shift explains how people can make opposite—and equally vehement—claims about what "polls show." The truth is that, at best, polls offer us flat snapshots of a three-dimensional world.

At worst, when they're funded by partisans, polls may be purposely deceptive. In those cases, faulty polling can come back to haunt those who initially seemed to benefit from it.

In autumn 1994, Republican pollster Frank Luntz declared that each provision of the ten-point Contract with America had overwhelming support. Luntz failed to mention that he'd only surveyed responses to GOP slogans. When public support for many items in the Contract appeared to falter, an editor at *Congressional Quarterly*, Philip Duncan, noted: "The revelation that there are gaps in the Contract's appeal might have come sooner if the media had pressed Luntz during the 1994 campaign to document his claim of public support. But all too often, reporters simply pass along results of polls

that were designed to influence voter sentiment, not merely measure it."[a]

Regardless of their quality, polls that depict public opinion end up altering it. Poll data "influence perceptions, attitudes and decisions at every level of our society," David Moore writes in *The Superpollsters*.[b]

Some polls are skewed by intensive efforts to sway the electorate. For example, in times of crisis, many presidents have been able to orchestrate publicity that spikes the numbers—which are then cited as proof that the White House is in sync with the popular will.

While polling seems to offer choices, it also limits them. Author Herbert Schiller says that opinion-polling is commonly "a choice-restricting mechanism." Why? "Because ordinary polls reduce, and sometimes eliminate entirely, the. . . true spectrum of possible options." Schiller aptly describes poll responses as "guided" choices.[c]

To make matters worse, the narrow range of options presented by pollsters is far from random. "Those who dominate governmental decision-making and private economic activity are the main supporters of the pollsters," Schiller observes. "The vital needs of these groups determine, intentionally or not, the parameters within which polls are formulated."[d]

We become overly impressed with polls when we pay too much attention to the answers and not enough to the questions.

[a]Quoted in Norman Solomon, "Question the Numbers," *Atlanta Journal and Constitution* (May 17, 1995): A23.

[b]David W. Moore, *The Superpollsters: How They Measure and Manipulate Public Opinion in America*, 2d ed. (New York: Four Walls Eight Windows, 1995).

[c]Quoted in Solomon, "Question the Numbers."

[d]Quoted in Solomon, "Question the Numbers."

A more reliable nonprobability sample is a quota sample, in which pollsters draw their sample based on known statistics. Assume that a citywide survey has been commissioned. If the city is 30 percent African American, 15 percent Hispanic, and 55 percent white, interviewers will use those statistics to determine the proportion of particular groups to be questioned. These kinds of surveys are often conducted in local shopping malls. Perhaps you've wondered why the man or woman with the clipboard has let you pass by but has stopped the next shopper. Now you know it is likely that you did not match the profile of the subjects that the interviewer was instructed to locate. Although this kind of sampling technique can produce relatively accurate results, the degree of accuracy falls short of those surveys based on probability samples. Moreover, these surveys generally oversample the visible population, such as shoppers, while neglecting the stay-at-homes who may be glued to the Home Shopping Network or prefer to buy on-line.

■ A typical polling instrument.
(Photo courtesy: Stephen
Savios/AP/Wide World Photos)

```
                              NATIONAL STUDY

INTERVIEWER_____           STUDY #__5483____
TARRANCE & ASSOCIATES                 CODING_____
GREENBERG-LAKE                        COMPUTER_____
PERSONAL/CONFIDENTIAL                 FINANCE_____
                                      INTERVIEWING_____


Hello, I'm _____ of Tarrance & Associates, a national
research firm.  We're calling from our national telephone center.
We're talking to people in the nation today about public leaders
and issues facing us all.

A.   Are you registered to vote
     in your state and will you be
     able to vote in the election
     for President that will be
     held in 1992?


     IF "NO", ASK:  Is there someone
     else at home who is registered
     to vote?  (IF "YES", THEN ASK:
     MAY I SPEAK WITH HIM/HER?)
                              Yes (CONTINUE)

                              No  (THANK AND TERMINATE)
```

stratified sampling:

A variation of random sampling;
census data are used to divide a
country into four sampling regions.
Sets of counties and standard metropolitan statistical areas are then randomly selected in proportion to the
total national population.

Stratified Sampling.   Most national surveys and commercial polls use samples of from 1,000 to 1,500 individuals and use a variation of the random sampling method called **stratified sampling.** Simple random, nonstratified samples aren't very useful at predicting voting because they may undersample (or oversample) key populations that are not likely or particularly likely to vote.

To avoid these problems, reputable polling organizations use stratified sampling based on census data that provides the number of residences in an area and their location. Researchers divide the country into four sampling regions. They then randomly select a set of counties and standard metropolitan statistical areas in proportion to the total national population. Once certain primary sampling units are selected, they are often used for many years, because it is cheaper for polling companies to train interviewers to work in a fixed area.

About twenty respondents from each primary sampling unit are selected to be interviewed. Generally four or five city blocks or areas are selected, and then four or five target families from each district are used. Large, sophisticated surveys like the National Election Study and General Social Survey, which produce the data commonly used by political scientists, attempt to sample from lists of persons living in each household. The key to the success of the stratified sampling method is not to let people volunteer to be interviewed—volunteers as a group often have different opinions from those who don't volunteer.

Stratified sampling (the most rigorous sampling technique) is generally not used by those who do surveys reported in the *New York Times* and *USA Today* or on network news programs. Instead, those organizations or pollsters working for them randomly survey every tenth, hundredth, or thousandth person or household. If those individuals are not at home, they go to the home or apartment next door.

Contacting Respondents.   After selecting the methodology to conduct the poll, the next question is how to contact those to be surveyed. Television stations often ask people to call in, and some surveyors hit the streets. Telephone polls, however, are becoming the most frequently used mechanism by which to gauge the temper of the electorate.

Doonesbury

BY GARRY TRUDEAU

Telephone Polls.   The most common form of telephone polls are random-digit dialing surveys, in which a computer randomly selects telephone numbers to be dialed. Because it is estimated that as many as 95 percent of the American public have telephones in their homes, samples selected in this manner are likely to be fairly representative.

In spite of some problems (such as the fact that many people don't want to be bothered, especially at dinner time), most polls done for newspapers and news magazines are conducted this way. Most polls, in fact, contain language similar to that used by the Gallup Organization in reporting its survey results:

> The current results are based on telephone interviews with a randomly selected national sample of 1,008 adults, conducted _____ to _____. For results based on a sample of this size, one can say with 95 percent confidence that the error attributable to sampling and other random effects could be plus or minus 3 percentage points. In addition to sampling error, question wording and practical difficulties in conducting surveys can introduce error or bias into the findings of public opinion polls.[64]

In-Person Polls.   Individual, in-person interviews are conducted by some groups, such as by the University of Michigan for the National Election Studies. Some analysts favor such in-person surveys, but others argue that the unintended influence of the questioner or pollster is an important source of errors. How the pollster dresses, relates to the person being interviewed, and even asks the questions can affect responses. (Some of these factors, such as tone of voice, can also affect the results of telephone surveys.)

Political Polls

As polling has become increasingly sophisticated and networks, newspapers, and magazines compete with each other to report the most up-to-the-minute changes in public opinion on issues or political candidates, new types of polls have been suggested and put into use. Each type of poll has contributed much to our knowledge of public opinion and its role in the political process.

Tracking Polls.   During the 1992 presidential elections, **tracking polls,** which were taken on a daily basis by some news organizations (see Figure 11.8), were first introduced to allow presidential candidates to monitor short-term campaign developments and the effects of their campaign strategies.

Tracking polls involve small samples and are conducted every twenty-four hours (usually of registered voters contacted at certain times of day). They are usually combined with some kind of a moving statistical average to boost the sample size and therefore the statistical reliability.[65] Even though such one-day surveys are fraught with reliability problems, many major news organizations continued their use as they reported on the 1996 presidential campaign.

Exit Polls.   **Exit polls** are polls conducted at selected polling places on Election Day. Generally, large news organizations send pollsters to selected precincts to sample every

tracking poll:

Continuous surveys that enable a campaign to chart its daily rise or fall in support.

exit poll:

Poll conducted at selected polling places on Election Day.

Figure 11.8   A Daily Update Tracking Poll of the 1996 Presidential Election

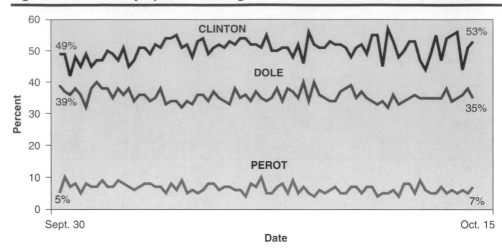

SOURCE: Copyright 1996, *USA Today*. Reprinted with permission.

tenth voter as he or she emerges from the polling place. The results of these polls are used to help the television networks predict the outcome of key races, often just a few minutes after the polls close in a particular state and generally before voters in other areas—sometimes in a later time zone—have cast their ballots. They also provide an independent assessment of why voters supported particular candidates "free from the spin that managers and candidates alike place on the 'meaning of an election'."[66]

In 1980 President Jimmy Carter's own polling and the results of network exit polls led him to concede defeat three hours before the polls closed on the West Coast. Many Democratic Party officials and candidates criticized Carter and network predictions for harming their chances at victories, arguing that with the presidential election already "called," voters were unlikely to go to the polls. In the aftermath of that controversy, all networks agreed not to predict the results of presidential contests until all polling places were closed. Exit polls have also been faulted because it appears that not all voters are willing to reply truthfully to pollsters' questions, especially in biracial contests.[67]

Deliberative Polls.   From January 18 to 21, 1996, a new experiment in polling and American democracy began in Austin, Texas. Six hundred Americans, selected by the National Opinion Research Center (NORC) through rigorous random sampling methods, came together for intensive briefings, discussions, and presentations about three large clusters of issues: foreign affairs, the status and needs of the American family, and the U.S. economy.

The **deliberative poll** is different from any others used by pollsters in the United States. "Ordinary polls model what the public is thinking, even though the public may not be thinking very much or paying much attention. A deliberative poll attempts to model what the public would think, had it a better opportunity to consider the question at issue."[68]

The idea of a deliberative poll, while novel, was quite simple. The logistics of bringing one off, however, were daunting. A random national sample of the electorate was transported from all over the United States to Austin, Texas. There they were administered one poll that included opinion and information questions. Then the attendees were bombarded with issue discussions and briefing papers in a carefully balanced manner. Vice President Al Gore, Jr., joined, but only one of the six invited Republican presidential candidates showed up.

The three days of talk and debate were broadcast on PBS for six hours. The deliberative poll thus marries "two technologies, polling and television, that have given us a

---

deliberative poll:

A new type of poll to bring a representative sample of people together to discuss and debate political issues in order to provide considered policy suggestions to lawmakers.

Web Exploration

For information on the Center for Deliberative Polling, see www.awlonline.com/oconnor.

superficial form of mass democracy, and harnesses them to a new and constructive purpose—giving voice to the people under conditions where the people can think,"[69] says the poll's creator, James S. Fishkin, a University of Texas political scientist.

The deliberative poll cost $4.5 million (more than any one news organization budgeted for its whole slate of preelection polls[70]) and was hailed by Fishkin, his colleagues, and those who attended as a great success.[71] But what was the overall import of the poll? Its organizers did not mean for the poll to be able to help describe and predict public opinion. Instead, they viewed the poll as prescriptive in nature because a deliberative poll allows a microcosm of the country to think about issues and make recommendations to the country as a whole.

Shortcomings of Polling

In 1990 the networks consolidated their polling operations under the umbrella of Voter Research and Surveys (VRS), which was a major cost-saving measure for all involved. But the construction of a single questionnaire and one data set meant that problems could arise. In 1992 the VRS data significantly overpredicted the support for Republican candidate Patrick Buchanan in the New Hampshire primary, and showed President Bush to be in much more trouble than he was. Armed with these erroneous survey results, commentator after commentator (all relying on the same data) predicted a narrow victory for Bush—who actually went on to win by a healthy sixteen-point margin. Nevertheless, "[M]any Americans went to bed believing that the president had been badly damaged."[72] This kind of reporting based on inaccurate polls can skew the rest of a campaign, particularly in an era when campaigns are viewed as horse races and everyone wants to know who's winning and by how much. Thus polls and the way they are reported can affect election outcomes; they are a powerful tool that gives the media additional sway in the democratic process.

■ Former African American Virginia Governor L. Douglas Wilder's election in 1989 demonstrated some of the difficulties of polling. Despite advance surveys and exit polls that indicated a comfortable lead, Wilder's actual margin of victory was razor thin. Either the preelection polls were widely inaccurate, or some voters were unwilling to admit that they had voted against an African American. (Photo courtesy: Corbis/Bettmann)

Sampling Error. The accuracy of any poll depends on the quality of the sample that was drawn. Small samples, if properly drawn, can be very accurate if each unit in the universe has an equal opportunity to be sampled. If a pollster, for example, fails to sample certain populations, his or her results may reflect that shortcoming. Often the opinions of the poor and homeless are underrepresented because insufficient attention is given to making certain that these groups are representatively sampled. And, in the case of tracking polls, if you choose to sample only on weekends or from 5 P.M. to 9 P.M., you may get more Republicans, who are less likely to have jobs that require them to work in the evening or on weekends. There comes a point in sampling, however, where increases in the size of the sample have little effect on a reduction of the **sampling error** (also called **margin of error**), the difference between the actual universe and the sample.

All polls contain errors. Standard samples of approximately 1,000 to 1,500 individuals provide fairly good estimates of actual behavior (in the case of voting, for example). Typically, the margin of error in a sample of 1,500 will be about 3 percent. If you ask 1,500 people "Do you like ice cream?" and 52 percent say "yes" and 48 percent say "no," the results are too close to tell whether more people like ice cream than not. Why? Because the margin of error implies that somewhere between 55 percent (52 + 3) and 49 percent (52 - 3) of the people like ice cream, while between 51 percent (48 + 3) and 45 percent (48 - 3) do not. The margin of error in a close election makes predictions very difficult.

The introduction of tracking polls into the 1992 election scenario brought more critics of political polling. According to one political scientist, their advent "played upon

sampling error or margin of error:

A measure of the accuracy of a public opinion poll.

the worst tendencies of journalists to focus almost entirely upon who is ahead and by how much."[73] Moreover, the one-day polls were fraught with other problems. Sampling is conducted with limited or no callbacks and may be skewed because certain groups may not be at home at certain times. The CNN/Gallup poll, for example, used two different time periods—weekdays 5 P.M. to 9 P.M. and all day on the weekends. Thus midweek surveys produced candidate distributions that disproportionately favored Bush, while weekend surveys showed the reverse.

This problem was exacerbated by two shifts in the way data was collected. First, pollsters moved from surveying "registered" voters to surveying "likely" voters[74]; second, Gallup changed the way it allocated "undecided" voters. All of these methodologies created the impression that the race was closer than it was and gave a boost to Bush, the Republican candidate. Thus, some argue that the danger of tracking polls needs to be highlighted and discussed before more emphasis is placed on them.

Limited Respondent Options.   Polls can be inaccurate when they limit responses. If you are asked, "How do you like this class?" and are given only like or dislike options, your full sentiments may not be tapped if you like the class very much or feel only so-so about it.

Lack of Information.   Public opinion polls may also be "off" when they attempt to gauge attitudes about issues that some or even many individuals don't care about or about which the public has little information. For example, few Americans probably care about the elimination of the electoral college. If a representative sample were polled, many would answer pro or con without having given much consideration to the question.

Most academic public opinion research organizations, such as the National Election Study, use some kind of filter question that first asks respondents whether or not they have thought about the question. These screening procedures generally allow surveyors to exclude as many as 20 percent of their respondents, especially on complex issues like the federal budget. Questions on more personal issues such as moral values, drugs, crime, race, and women's role in society get far fewer "no opinion" or "don't know" responses.

Intensity.   Another shortcoming of polls concerns their inability to measure intensity of feeling about particular issues. Whereas a respondent might answer affirmatively to any question, it is likely that his or her feelings about issues such as abortion, the death penalty, or support for U.S. troops in the Gulf are much more intense than are his or her feelings about the electoral college.

Elitism.   The deliberative poll has brought another set of criticisms to polling. Critics charge that the poll is elitist and that it created "an agenda and the setting for a discussion of [participants'] issues that meets *their* criteria for deliberation."[75] Opinion formation, moreover, in any election year, is "more of an evolution than an epiphany."[76] It is a rolling process as issues gel, candidates come and go, and new events occur that require public and candidate responses. Critics of deliberative polls argue that no issues are static and events—no matter what the setting—can't begin to mirror the actual deliberative process that goes on in the formation of a personal opinion about political issues or candidates.

HOW POLLING AND PUBLIC OPINION AFFECT POLITICIANS, POLITICS, AND POLICY

As our opening vignette illustrates, President Clinton recognizes the importance of public support. Much earlier, the authors of *The Federalist Papers* noted that "all government rests on public opinion," and, as a result, public opinion inevitably influences the actions of politicians and public officials. The public's perception of crime as a problem, for example, was the driving force behind the comprehensive crime bill President Clinton submitted to Congress in 1994 and congressional passage of the Brady

GLOBAL POLITICS

Public Opinion on Government Responsibilities

The notions of limited government and individual liberty are two major components of political culture in the United States. The public opinion effects of these notions is clear in the table below: In a 1990 survey, the percentage of American respondents who definitely agreed that their government is responsible for providing health care and full employment was well below that of citizens polled in Germany, Italy, and Britain.

The difference can be traced to two related phenomena. First, Americans tend to agree with the Jeffersonian dictum that small government is better than big government. While Americans may not distrust government any more than

Europeans do (polls show that Italians trust their government less than citizens in other European governments, and even a significant number of British citizens do not trust theirs), they have been less willing to put up with what they perceive as big government to the extent that Europeans and Japanese have. Unlike the United States, Canada, and Britain, the countries of continental Europe and Japan have had modern histories in which the state has taken a major role in shaping national society and has actively competed with the private sector.

Second, these public predispositions have affected what governments have actually been able to do. While the size of government in every G-7 country has grown since World War II, it has grown less in important policy areas in the United States than it has in the G-7 counterparts. In particular, the postwar welfare state (of which healthcare and employment are a part) in the United States has not developed to the extent that it has in Japan, Canada, and Europe.

Citizen Attitudes About Appropriate Government Services

Country	Agree Government Is Responsible for Health Care (%)	Agree Government Is Responsible for Jobs (%)
Germany	57	30
Italy	88	38
United Kingdom	85	24
United States	40	16

Source: Frank Wilson, *European Politics Today,* 3d ed. (Upper Saddle River, New Jersey: Prentice-Hall 1999), 84.

gun control bill in 1993. The public's concern with crime skyrocketed to an all-time high in 1994, when 37 percent of the public rated crime as the nation's most important problem, and politicians at all levels were quick to convert that concern into a campaign issue. In 1996 during the presidential campaign, Bill Clinton even called for the addition of a constitutional amendment to protect crime victims' rights. But action by Clinton and Congress and dropping crime rates actually have pushed concern with crime way down; in 1999, only 13 percent of those polled thought it was the most important problem.[77]

Politicians and government officials spend millions of dollars each year taking the "pulse" of the public. Even the federal government spends millions annually on polls and surveys designed to evaluate programs and to provide information for shaping policies. But, as political scientist Benjamin Ginsberg noted, "the data reported by opinion polls are actually the product of an interplay between opinion and the survey instrument." They interact with each other and, in essence, often change the "character of the views receiving public expression."[78] Polls can thus help transform public opinion.

We know that politicians rely on polls, but it's difficult to say to what degree. Several political scientists have attempted to study whether public policy is responsive to public opinion, with mixed results.[79] As we have seen, public opinion can fluctuate, making it difficult for a politician or policy maker to assess. Some critics of polls and of their use by politicians argue that polls hurt democracy and make leaders weaker. Ginsberg, one of these critics, argues that these polls weaken democracy.[80] He claims that these polls allow governments and politicians to say they have considered public opinion even though polls don't always measure the intensity of feeling on an issue or might overreflect the views of the responders who lack sufficient information to make educated choices. Ginsberg further argues that democracy is better served by politicians' reliance on telephone calls and letters—active signs of interest—than on the passive voice of public opinion. Some say that politicians are simply driven by the results of polls that do not reflect a serious debate of issues. In response to this argument, George Gallup retorted, "One might as well insist that a thermometer makes the weather."[81]

Polls can clearly distort the election process by creating what are called "bandwagon" and "underdog" effects. In a presidential campaign, an early victory in the Iowa caucuses or the New Hampshire primary, for example, can boost a candidate's standings in the polls as the rest of the nation begins to think of him or her in a more positive light. New supporters jump on the bandwagon. A strong showing in the polls, in turn, can generate more and larger donations, the lifeblood of any campaign. Political scientist Herbert Asher has noted that "bad poll results, as well as poor primary and caucus standings, may deter potential donors from supporting a failing campaign."[82]

Election Forecasting

The first attempts to measure public opinion were quite crude.* While politicians attempted to influence how Americans would vote, as well illustrated by the Federalist/Anti-Federalist debates that played themselves out in local newspapers and in political tracts circulated among the thirteen states, the true test of public opinion was the election results. It wasn't until the development of more sophisticated methods of communication such as mass-circulation magazines and a reliable mail service that organizations such as the *Literary Digest* even attempted to tap the pulse of American voters in any systematic fashion.

The development of the telephone truly revolutionized the polling industry. While social scientists still recognize the value of face-to-face interviews with respondents, as more and more households in all regions of the nation got telephone service, the ability to use sampling techniques to draw representative samples, and quickly administer surveys and polls, proved a real boon to the political polling industry. The telephone changed fundamentally how most political polls were conducted. And, since their widespread use in the 1970s, "telephone polls, on the whole, have proved to be remarkably accurate predictors of voter behavior—the gold standard of all polling research."** Problems with telephone polls are rapidly increasing, however. Over 40 percent of those contacted now refuse to participate, and such polls get more and more costly each year.***

In the 1990s, American pollsters and social scientists began to experiment with a variety of other kinds of polls, often spurred on by news agencies desire to be the "first" with the "news." Sophisticated exit polls, often conducted to allow a network to be the first on the air with a prediction, and tracking polls, often conducted to make political races seem closer than they are thereby enhancing their "newsworthiness," are particularly popular today. While these polls utilized new techniques, they didn't utilize a new medium.

A second revolution may be on the horizon. Many social scientists are now advocating the Internet as a platform for conducting political polls. One study used an Internet data base of more than one million respondents in sixteen states to complete three polls in 1998—one in mid-October, the second the week before the election, and the third an exit poll. As of this writing, the results of that experiment had yet to be released. Internet polls will require social scientists to forgo random sampling in favor of a system of using much larger samples coupled with sophisticated weighting processes that will undoubtedly take a while to devise. Still, the potential uses of Internet polling must be addressed.

1. What other potential problems do you see with Internet polling?
2. Can huge sample sizes reduce polling problems regardless of the way the sample was drawn?

Cast Your Vote. Will the Internet serve as an effective and accurate tool for political polling? To cast your vote, go to www.awlonline.com/oconnor.

*For an interesting discussion of measuring public opinion before surveys, see Karen Hoffman, "Going Public in the Eighteenth and Nineteenth Centuries: Measuring the Influence of Public Opinion Before Surveys," paper prepared for delivery at the 1999 annual meeting of the Midwest Political Science Association.
**Gordon S. Black and George Terhanian, "Using the Internet for Election Forecasting," http://www.pollingreport.com./internet.htm.
***Black and Terhanian, "Using the Internet."

SUMMARY

Public opinion is a subject constantly mentioned in the media, especially in presidential election years or when important policies (such as health care, balancing the budget, race, or crime) are under consideration. What public opinion is, where it comes from, how it's measured, and how it's used are aspects of a complex subject. To that end, this chapter has made the following points:

1. WHAT IS PUBLIC OPINION?

Public opinion is what the public thinks about an issue or a particular set of issues. Public opinion polls are used to estimate public opinion.

2. EARLY EFFORTS TO INFLUENCE AND MEASURE PUBLIC OPINION

Almost since the beginning of the United States, various attempts have been made to influence public opinion about particular issues or to sway elections. Modern-day polling did not begin until the 1930s, however. Over the years, polling to measure public opinion has become increasingly sophisticated and more accurate because pollsters are better able to sample the public in their effort to determine their attitudes and positions on issues. Pollsters recognize that their sample must reflect the population whose ideas and beliefs they wish to measure.

3. POLITICAL SOCIALIZATION AND OTHER FACTORS THAT INFLUENCE OPINION FORMATION

The first step in forming opinions occurs through a process called political socialization. The family, school, peers, the impact of events, the social group of which one is a member—including religion, race, gender, and age—as well as where one lives all affect how one views political events and issues, as do the major events themselves. Our political ideology—whether we are conservative, liberal, or moderate—also provides a lens through which we filter our political views, as does our level of personal benefit from and our political knowledge of issues and events. Even the views of other people affect our ultimate opinions on a variety of issues, including race relations, the death penalty, abortion, and federal taxes.

4. HOW WE FORM POLITICAL OPINIONS

Myriad factors enter our minds as we form opinions about political matters. These include a calculation about the personal benefits involved, degree of personal political knowledge, and cues from leaders.

5. HOW WE MEASURE PUBLIC OPINION

Measuring public opinion can be difficult. The most frequently used measure is the public opinion poll. Determining the content, phrasing the questions, selecting the sample, and choosing the right kind of poll are critical to obtaining accurate and useful data.

6. HOW POLLING AND PUBLIC OPINION AFFECT POLITICIANS, POLITICS, AND POLICY

Knowledge of the public's views on issues is often used by politicians to tailor campaigns or to drive policy decisions. Polls, however, have several shortcomings including sampling error and inadequate respondent information.

KEY TERMS

deliberative poll, p. 404
exit poll, p. 403
margin of error, p. 405
political ideology, p. 397

political socialization, p. 387
public opinion, p. 382
public opinion poll, p. 382
random sampling, p. 400

sampling error, p. 405
stratified sampling, p. 402
straw poll, p. 385
tracking poll, p. 403

SELECTED READINGS

Asher, Herbert. *Polling and the Public: What Every Citizen Should Know,* 4th ed. Washington, DC: CQ Press, 1998.

Bennet, W. Lance, and David L. Paletz. ed. *Taken by Storm: The Media, Public Opinion, and U.S. Foreign Policy in the Gulf War.* Chicago: University of Chicago Press, 1994.

Brace, Paul, and Barbara Hinckley. *Follow the Leader: Opinion Polls and Modern Presidents.* New York: Basic Books, 1992.

Carmines, Edward G., and James A. Stimson. *Issue Evolution.* Princeton, NJ: Princeton University Press, 1990.

Crespi, Irving. *Public Opinion, Polls, and Democracy.* Boulder, CO: Westview Press, 1989.

Erikson, Robert S., and Kent L. Tedin. *American Public Opinion: Its Contents, Origins and Impact.* Englewood Cliffs, NJ: Prentice Hall, 1995.

Fishkin, James S. *The Voice of the People: Public Opinion and Democracy.* New Haven, CT: Yale University Press, 1996.

Ginsberg, Benjamin. *The Captive Public.* New York: Basic Books, 1986.

Herbst, Susan. *Numbered Voices: How Opinion Polling Has Shaped American Politics.* Chicago: University of Chicago Press, 1993.

Jennings, M. Kent, and Richard Niemi. *Generations and Politics: A Panel Study of Young Adults and Their Parents.* Princeton, NJ: Princeton University Press, 1981.

Key, V. O., Jr. *Public Opinion and American Democracy.* New York: Alfred E. Knopf, 1961.

MacManus, Susan A. *Young v. Old: Generational Combat in the 21st Century.* Boulder, CO: Westview Press, 1995.

Rubenstein, Sondra Miller. *Surveying Public Opinion.* Belmont, CA: Wadsworth Publishing, 1994.

Shafer, Bryon E., and William J. M. Claggett. *The Two Majorities: The Issue Context of Modern American Politics.* Baltimore: Johns Hopkins University Press, 1995.

Stimson, James A. *Public Opinion in America: Moods, Cycles, and Swings.* 2nd ed. Boulder, CO: Westview Press, 1998.

Yeric, Jerry L., and John R. Todd. *Public Opinion: The Visible Politics,* 3d ed. Itasca, IL: Peacock, 1994.

Zaller, John. *The Nature and Origins of Mass Opinions.* New York: The University Press, 1992.

NOTES

1. John E. Harris, "White House Assessing Damage," *Washington Post* (January 26, 1998): A1.

2. William M. Welch, "President's Proposals Could Face Problems," *USA Today* (January 27, 1998): A2.

3. Mimi Hall, "Partial to Polls and Unpopular Ideas." *USA Today* (January 27, 1998): A2.

4. Allan M. Winkler, "Public Opinion," in Jack Greene, ed., *The Encyclopedia of American Political History* (New York: Charles Scribner's Sons, 1988), 1038.

5. Quoted in *Public Opinion Quarterly* 29 (Winter 1965–66): 547.

6. Winkler, "Public Opinion," 1035.

7. Quoted in Winkler, "Public Opinion," 1035.

8. *Literary Digest* 122 (August, 22 1936): 3.

9. *Literary Digest* 125 (November, 14 1936): 1.

10. Robert S. Erikson, Norman Luttbeg, and Kent Tedin, *American Public Opinion: Its Origin, Content and Impact* (New York: Wiley, 1980), 28.

11. Angus Campbell, Philip Converse, Warren Miller, and Donald Stokes, *The American Voter* (New York: Wiley, 1960).

12. Byron E. Shafer and William J. M. Claggett, *The Two Majorities: The Issue Context of Modern American Politics* (Baltimore, MD: The Johns Hopkins University Press, 1995), 12.

13. Shafer and Claggett, *The Two Majorities*, 13.

14. Richard Dawson, *et al. Political Socialization*, 2d ed. (Boston: Little, Brown, 1977), 33.

15. Robert D. Hess and David Easton, "The Child's Changing Image of the President," *Public Opinion Quarterly* 14 (Winter 1960): 632–42; and Fred I. Greenstein, *Children and Politics* (New Haven, CT: Yale University Press, 1965).

16. *Statistical Abstract of the United States, 1997*, 117th ed. (Washington, DC, 1997), 1011.

17. Sandor M. Polster, "Bad News for Much TV News," *Bangor Daily News* (May 18, 1996), NEXIS.

18. Polster, "Bad News for Much TV News."

19. David Buckingham, "News Media, Political Socialization and Popular Citizenship: Towards a New Agenda," *Critical Studies in Mass Communication* 14:1 (December 1997): 344–366.

20. Lisa Greim, "PC 'Pirates' Sail the Web," *Rocky Mountain News* (October 13, 1996): 8B.

21. Greim, "PC 'Pirates' Sail the Web."

22. Miranda Yates and James Youniss, "Communication and Age in Childhood Political Socialization: An Interactive Model of Political Development," *Journalism and Mass Communication Quarterly* (Winter 1998): 699–718.

23. Yates and Youniss, "Community and Age."

24. James Simon and Bruce D. Merrill, "Political Socialization in the Classroom Revisited: The Kids Voting Program," *Social Science Journal* 35 (1998): 29–42.

25. Simon and Merrill, "Political Socialization."

26. F. Christopher Arterton, "The Impact of Watergate on Children's Attitudes Toward Political Authority," *Political Science Quarterly* 89 (June 1974): 273.

27. Diana Owen and Jack Dennis, "Kids and the Presidency: Assessing Clinton's Legacy," *Public Perspective* (April 1999), NEXIS.

28. "Church Membership Trend," http://www.gallup.com/POLL_ARCHIVES/970329.htm.

29. "Church Membership Trend."

30. "Basic Religious Beliefs," *Public Perspective* (October/November 1995): 4–5.

31. "America's Religious Makeup," http://www.gallup.com/POLL_ARCHIVES/970329.htm.

32. "America's Religious Makeup."

33. Lyman A. Kellstedt, *et al.,* "Has Godot Finally Arrived? Religion and Realignment," *Public Perspective* (June/July 1995): 19.

34. Geoffrey C. Layman, "Religion and Political Behavior in the United States: The Impact of Beliefs, Affiliations, and Commitment from 1980 to 1994," *Public Opinion Quarterly* 61 (1997): 288.

35. Layman, "Religion and Political Behavior in the United States."

36. Steven M. Cohen and Charles S. Liebman, "American Jewish Liberalism," *Public Opinion Quarterly* 61 (1997): 405–30.

37. Edward S. Greenberg. "The Political Socialization of Black Children," in Edward S. Greenberg, ed., *Political Socialization* (New York: Atherton Press, 1970), 181.

38. Greenberg, "The Political Socialization of Black Children."

39. Alejandro Portest and Rafael Mozo, "The Political Adaptation Process of Cubans and Other Ethnic Minorities in the United States: A Preliminary Analysis," in F. Chris Garcia, ed., *Latinos and the Political System* (Notre Dame, IN: University of Notre Dame Press, 1988), 161.

40. John A. Garcia and Carlos H. Arce, "Political Orientations and Behaviors of Chicanos: Trying to Make Sense Out of Attitudes and Participation," in Garcia, *Latinos and the Political System,* 125–51.

41. Pamela Johnson Conover and Virginia Sapiro, "Gender, Feminist Consciousness and War," *American Journal of Political Science* 37 (November 1993): 1079–99.

42. Margaret Trevor, "Political Socialization, Party Identification, and the Gender Gap," 63: Public Opinion Quarterly (Spring 1999): 62–89.

45. "Number Crunching," *Washington Post* (March 22, 1998):C2.

46. "Newsweek."

43. Alexandra Marks, "Gender Gap Narrows over Kosovo," *Christian Science Monitor* (April 30, 1999): 1.

44. "*Newsweek:* No Gender Gap on Impeachment Question," *Hotline* (December 14, 1998).

47. William Booth, "Younger Voters Reflect Rise in Apathy, Discontent with Politics," *Washington Post* (November 5, 1996): A10.

48. Tanya Bricking, "Young Voters May Not," *Cincinnati Enquirer* (October 19, 1996): A1.

49. Booth, "Younger Voters Reflect Rise in Apathy."

50. Susan A. MacManus, *Young v. Old: Generational Combat in the 21st Century* (Boulder, CO: Westview Press, 1995).

51. Richard Morin, "Southern Exposure," *Washington Post* (July 14, 1996): A18.

52. "Church Pews Seat More Blacks, Seniors, and Republicans," http://www.gallup.com/POLL_ARCHIVES/970329.htm.

53. "Geography: A Lost Generation," *Nation* (August 8, 1988): 19.

54. Quoted in Everett Carl Ladd, "Fiskin's 'Deliberative Poll' Is Flawed Science and Dubious Democracy," *Public Perspective* (December/January 1996): 41.

55. V. O. Key, Jr. *The Responsible Electorate: Rationality in Presidential Voting, 1936–1960* (Cambridge, MA: Belknap Press of Harvard University, 1966).

56. Gerald M. Pomper, *The Performance of American Government,* (New York: Free Press, 1972); and Benjamin I. Page, *Choices and Echoes in Presidential Elections* (Chicago: University of Chicago Press, 1978).

57. Norman H. Nie, Sidney Verba, and John R. Petrocik. *The Changing American Voter* (Cambridge, MA: Harvard University Press, 1976).

58. Ladd, "Fiskin's 'Deliberative Poll,'" 42.

59. Richard Nodeau, *et al.,* "Elite Economic Forecasts, Economic News, Mass Economic Judgments and Presidential Approval," *Journal of Politics* 61 (February 1999): 109–135.

60. Micheal Towle, review of Jeffrey E. Cohen's "Presidential Responsiveness and Public Policy-making: The Public and the Policies," *Journal of Politics* 61 (February 1999): 230–232.

61. John E. Mueller, *War, Presidents and Public Opinion* (New York: Wiley, 1973), 69.

62. Roderick P. Hart, *The Sound of Leadership: Presidential Communication in the Modern Age* (Chicago: University of Chicago Press, 1987).

63. Alejandro Bodipo-Memba, "Clinton? Dole? Hah! Polls Show Harry Browne is Virtual Shoo-In," *Wall Street Journal* (October 29, 1996): B1.

64. David W. Moore, "Public Opposes Gay Marriages," The Gallup Organization, April 4, 1996.

65. Michael W. Traugott, "The Polls in 1992: Views of Two Critics: A Good General Showing, but Much Work Needs to Be Done," *Public Perspective* 4 (November/December 1992): 14–16.

66. Michael W. Traugott, "The Polls in 1992: It Was the Best of Times, It Was the Worst of Times," *Public Perspective* (December/January 1992): 14.

67. Adam Berinsky, "A Tale of Two Elections: An Investigation of Pre-election Polling in Biracial Contests," paper presented at the

1999 annual meeting of the Midwest Political Science Association.

68. James S. Fishkin, *The Voice of the People: Public Opinion and Democracy* (New Haven, CT: Yale University Press, 1995), 161.

69. James S. Fishkin, "Bringing Deliberation to Democracy," *Public Perspective* (December/January 1996): 1.

70. Warren J. Mitofsky, "It's Not Deliberative and It's Not a Poll," *Public Perspective* (December/January 1996): 6.

71. Fishkin, "Bringing Deliberation to Democracy," 1.

72. Traugott, "The Polls in 1992."

73. Traugott, "The Polls in 1992."

74. Michael W. Traugott and Clyde Tucker, "Strategies for Predicting Whether a Citizen Will Vote and Estimation of Electoral Outcomes," *Public Opinion Quarterly* (Spring 1984): 330–43.

75. Mitofsky, "It's Not Deliberative," 4.

76. Mitofsky, "It's Not Deliberative."

77. "Most Important Problem," The Gallup Organization, 6/19/99.

78. Benjamin Ginsberg, "How Polls Transform Public Opinion," in Michael Margolis and Gary A. Mauser, eds., *Manipulating Public Opinion* (Pacific Grove, CA: Brooks/Cole, 1989), 273.

79. See, for example, Benjamin Page and Robert Shapiro, "Effects of Public Opinion on Policy," *American Political Science Review* 57 (March 1983): 175–90.

80. Benjamin Ginsberg, *The Captive Public* (New York: Basic Books, 1986), chapter 4.

81. Quoted in Pace, "George Gallup Is Dead at 82," New York Times, July 28, 1984, A-1.

82. Herbert Ascher, *Polling and the Public: What Every Citizen Should Know* (Washington, DC: CQ Press, 1988), 109.

Corbis/Wally McNamee

Political Parties

*N*o election in the midterm contest of 1998 received more attention than Reform Party candidate Jesse Ventura's election as governor of Minnesota. It was a guaranteed media spectacle: a clownish former wrestling star who traveled the state reminding people about his mediocre Hollywood roles and his semifamous line, "I don't have time to bleed."

At the same time, Ventura was greatly underestimated by his opponents, Democrat Hubert H. Humphrey III, the state's attorney general, and Republican Norman Coleman, mayor of St. Paul. Right up to election day, the polls showed that Humphrey was likely to win, with Coleman second, and Ventura a fairly distant third. But like all successful modern politicians, Ventura ran a shrewd campaign that used the mass media as much as they used him, thereby securing for himself substantial free media exposure and coverage. He also ran a series of clever ads, depicting children playing with Jesse Ventura dolls fighting government bureaucrats, and made extensive use of the Internet. All in all, it was a high-tech, unconventional campaign that suited both Ventura's style and the voters' mood.

In the end, Ventura garnered 37 percent of the popular vote, with 28 percent for Humphrey and 34 percent for Coleman. It was a stunning upset that gained Ventura immediate and extensive attention, not only as a hopeful symbol of a new and viable alternative to "politics as usual," but also more specifically as a potential Reform Party candidate for the presidency. However, Ventura has kept his distance from the party's other presidential candidate, Ross Perot, whom he considered an eccentric billionaire unable to help him win a plurality. It is unlikely that Ventura will run at the national level until he has succeeded in at least one term as governor. It remains to be seen how his administration will play out—so far the results are mixed, although Ventura's popularity remains high. If nothing else, his election has clearly put the Reform Party on the map for the immediate political future.

*I*t is difficult to reject the assertion that we are now entering a new, more fluid era of party politics. But, while some maintain that our two-party system is likely to be replaced by a chaotic multiparty system, or that a system in which presidential hopefuls bypass party nominations altogether and compete on their own is on the horizon, it is important to remember that political parties have been staples of American life since the late 1700s and, in one form or another, they will most likely continue to be. As this chapter explains, political scientist E. E. Schattschneider was not exaggerating when he wrote, "Modern democracy is unthinkable save in terms of the parties."[1]

The chapter addresses contemporary party politics and attempts to help you understand political parties by examining them from many vantage points. Our examination of political parties traces their development from their infancy in the late 1700s to today:

- First, we will discuss *what a political party is.*
- Second, we will look at *the parties' evolution* through U.S. history.
- Third, we will examine *the roles of the American parties* in our political system.
- Fourth, we will analyze the phenomena of *one-partyism and third-partyism.*
- Fifth, we will present *the basic structure of American political parties.*
- Sixth, we will explore *the party in government,* the office holders and candidates who run under the party's banner.
- Seventh, we will examine *the modern transformation of the parties,* paying special attention to how political parties have moved from the labor-intensive, person-to-person operations of the first half of the century toward the use of technology and communication strategies.
- Eighth, we will look at *the party-in-the-electorate,* showing that a political party's reach extends well beyond the relative handful of men and women who are the party-in-government.
- Finally, we will discuss independent and third-party candidates and the history of party alignment.

WHAT IS A POLITICAL PARTY?

Any definition of "political party" must be kept general because there are so many kinds of parties in the United States. In some states and localities, party organizations are strong and well entrenched, whereas in other places the parties exist more on paper than in reality. A definition of "party" might also be shaped by what people expect of parties. Some people expect parties to seek policy changes, while others expect them to win elections. This distinction flavors some of the debate over the effectiveness of political parties. If you expect parties to help candidates win office, then you might conclude that they are healthy. But if you believe that the main goal of political parties should be to promote and accomplish policy changes, then you might believe they frequently fail. We will be concerned here primarily with the electoral functions served by political parties, but it is important to remember these distinctions.[2]

At the most basic level, a **political party** is a group of office holders, candidates, activists, and voters who identify with a group label and seek to elect to public office individuals who run under that label. Notice how pragmatic this concept of party is. The goal is to win office, not just compete for it. This objective is in keeping with the practical nature of Americans and the country's historical aversion to most ideologically driven, "purist" politics (as we discuss later in this chapter). Nevertheless, the group label, also called party identification for the voters who embrace the party as their own, can carry with it clear messages about ideology and issue positions. Although this is especially true of minor, less broad-based parties that have little chance of electoral success, it also applies to the national, dominant political parties in the United States, the Democrats and the Republicans.

political party:

A group of office holders, candidates, activists, and voters who identify with a group label and seek to elect to public office individuals who run under that label.

■ The major national parties are not always recognized as progressive forces, but in fact many advances in suffrage and voting rights have been spearheaded by the parties as they search for new sources of support. Although still seriously underrepresented, women in recent years have made inroads as delegates, candidates, and office holders. (Photo courtesy: Terry Ashe/Liaison Agency)

When it comes to providing a formal definition of political parties, however, political scientists have often disagreed.[3] Some political scientists, for example, conceive of political parties as being made up of three separate but related entities: (1) the office holders and candidates who run under the party's banner (the **governmental party**), (2) the workers and activists who staff the party's formal organization (the **organizational party**), and (3) the voters who consider themselves to be allied or associated with the party (the **party-in-the-electorate**).[4] Other political scientists take issue with this definition, arguing that, especially in the American political system, voters should not be included in the definition of political parties. Voters, they note, are not part of the parties but choosers among them, in much the same way that fans of a sports team are not actually part of the team.[5] In this chapter, we examine all three components of political parties—the governmental party, the organizational party, and the party-in-the-electorate—including voters if only because they are so important in driving the actions of the other two components. First, however, we turn to the history and development of political parties in the United States.

governmental party:
The office holders and candidates who run under a political party's banner.

organizational party:
The workers and activists who staff the party's formal organization.

party-in-the-electorate:
The voters who consider themselves to be allied or associated with the party.

THE EVOLUTION OF AMERICAN PARTY DEMOCRACY

It is one of the great ironies of the early republic that George Washington's public farewell, which warned the nation against parties, marked the effective end of the brief era of partyless politics in the United States (see Figure 12.1). Washington's unifying influence ebbed as he stepped off the national stage, and his vice president and successor, President John Adams, occupied a much less exalted position. Adams was allied with Alexander Hamilton. To win the presidency in 1796, he narrowly defeated

Figure 12.1 American Party History at a Glance

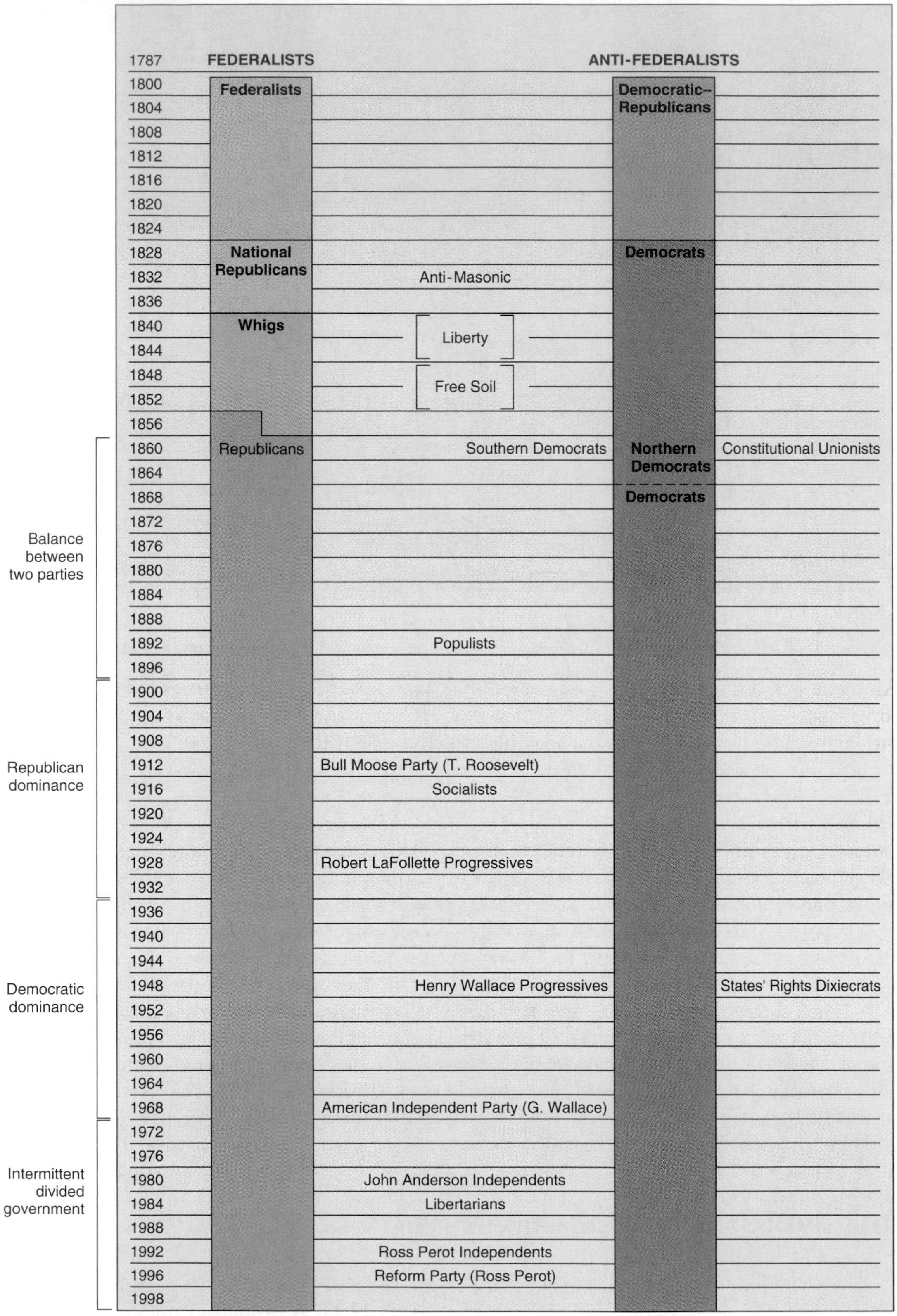

Year	Federalists		Anti-Federalists	
1787	FEDERALISTS		ANTI-FEDERALISTS	
1800	Federalists		Democratic–Republicans	
1804				
1808				
1812				
1816				
1820				
1824				
1828	National Republicans		Democrats	
1832		Anti-Masonic		
1836				
1840	Whigs			
1844		Liberty		
1848				
1852		Free Soil		
1856				
1860	Republicans	Southern Democrats	Northern Democrats	Constitutional Unionists
1864				
1868			Democrats	
1872				
1876				
1880				
1884				
1888				
1892		Populists		
1896				
1900				
1904				
1908				
1912		Bull Moose Party (T. Roosevelt)		
1916		Socialists		
1920				
1924				
1928		Robert LaFollette Progressives		
1932				
1936				
1940				
1944				
1948		Henry Wallace Progressives		States' Rights Dixiecrats
1952				
1956				
1960				
1964				
1968		American Independent Party (G. Wallace)		
1972				
1976				
1980		John Anderson Independents		
1984		Libertarians		
1988				
1992		Ross Perot Independents		
1996		Reform Party (Ross Perot)		
1998				

Left-margin era labels:
- Balance between two parties
- Republican dominance
- Democratic dominance
- Intermittent divided government

This table shows the transformations and evolution of the various parties that have always made up the basic two-party structure of the American political system.

Thomas Jefferson, Hamilton's former rival in Washington's Cabinet. Before ratification of the Constitution, Hamilton and Jefferson had been leaders of the Federalists and Anti-Federalists, respectively (see chapter 2). Over the course of Adams's single term, two competing congressional party groupings (or caucuses) gradually organized around these clashing men and their principles: Hamilton's Federalists supported a strong central government; the Democratic–Republicans of Thomas Jefferson and his ally James Madison inherited the mantle of the Anti-Federalists and preferred a federal system in which the states were relatively more powerful. (Jefferson actually preferred the simpler name "Republicans," a very different group from today's party of the same name, but Hamilton insisted on calling them "Democratic–Republicans" to link them to the radical democrats of the French Revolution.) In the presidential election of 1800, the Federalists supported Adams's bid for a second term, but this time the Democratic-Republicans prevailed with their nominee, Jefferson, who became the first U.S. president elected as the nominee of a political party.

Jefferson was deeply committed to the ideas of his party, but not nearly as devoted to the idea of a party system. He regarded his party as a temporary measure necessary to defeat Adams and Hamilton. Neither Jefferson's party nor Hamilton's enjoyed widespread "party identification" among the citizenry akin to that of today's Democrats and Republicans. Although Southerners were overwhelmingly partial to the Democratic–Republicans and New Englanders to the Federalists, no broad-based party organizations existed on either side to mobilize popular support. Rather, as political scientist John H. Aldrich observes, the congressional factions organized around Hamilton and Jefferson were primarily governmental parties designed to settle the dispute over how strong the new federal government would be.[6] Just as the nation was in its infancy, so, too, was the party system, and attachments to both parties were weak at first.

The Early Parties Fade

After the spirited confrontations of the republic's early years, political parties faded somewhat in importance for a quarter of a century. The Federalists ceased nominating presidential candidates by 1816, having failed to elect one of their own since Adams's victory in 1796, and by 1820 the party had dissolved. James Monroe's presidency from 1817 to 1825 produced the so-called Era of Good Feelings, when party politics was nearly suspended at the national level. Even during Monroe's tenure, though, party organizations continued to develop at the state level. Party growth was fueled in part by the enormous increase in the electorate that took place between 1820 and 1840, as the United States expanded westward and most states abolished property requirements as a condition of white male suffrage. During this twenty-year period, the number of votes cast in presidential contests rose from 300,000 to more than 2 million.

At the same time, U.S. politics was being democratized in other ways. By the 1820s all the states except South Carolina had switched from state legislative selection of presidential electors to popular election of electoral college members. This change helped transform presidential politics. No longer just the concern of society's upper crust, the election of the president became a matter for all qualified voters to decide.

The party base broadened along with the electorate. Small caucuses of congressional party leaders had previously nominated candidates, but after much criticism of the process as elitist and undemocratic, this system gave way to nominations at large party conventions. The country's first major national presidential nominating convention was held in 1832 by the Democratic Party,[7] the successor to the old Jeffersonian Democratic-Republicans (the shortened name had gradually come into use in the 1820s). Formed around the charismatic populist President Andrew Jackson, the Democratic party attracted most of the newly enfranchised voters, who were drawn to Jackson's style. His strong personality helped to polarize politics, and opposition to the president coalesced into the Whig Party. The Whig Party was descended from the Federalists; its early leaders included Henry Clay, the Speaker of the House from 1811 to 1820. The incumbent Jackson defeated Clay in the 1832 presidential contest. He became the

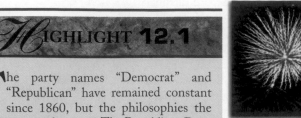
first chief executive who won the White House as the nominee of a truly national, popularly based political party.

The Whigs and the Democrats continued to strengthen after 1832, establishing state and local organizations almost everywhere. Their competition was usually fierce and closely matched, and they brought the United States the first broadly supported two-party system in the Western world.[8] Unfortunately for the Whigs, the issue of slavery sharpened the many existing divisive internal party tensions that led to its gradual dissolution and replacement by the new Republican Party. Formed in 1854 by antislavery activists, the Republican Party set its sights on the abolition (or at least the containment) of slavery. After a losing presidential effort for John C. Fremont in 1856, the party was able to assemble enough support primarily from the Whigs and antislavery Northern Democrats to win the presidency for Abraham Lincoln in a fragmented 1860 vote. In that year the South voted solidly Democratic, beginning a habit so strong that not a single Southern state voted Republican for president again until 1920.

It should also be recognized that, between 1838 and 1890, many minor parties engaged in the political activities developed by the major parties. Minor parties, that is, organized themselves, nominated candidates, and attempted to mobilize the support of voters.[9] Thus, despite the self-imposed "outsider" image of minor parties in this era, they clearly adhered to the tactics and strategies deployed by the major parties.

The British political system, which has been characterized by competition between two main political parties with significant third-party activity, provides an interesting contrast to the American case. In Britain the massive extension of suffrage in 1867 prompted the emergence of two modern, mass political parties (the Liberals and the Conservatives), which were needed to organize and mobilize the now unwieldy electorate. In the aftermath of World War I, the Liberals gave way to the Labour Party as the Conservatives' principal contender for power.

Democrats and Republicans: The Golden Age

From the presidential election of 1860 to this day, the same two major parties, the Republicans and the Democrats, have dominated elections in the United States, and control of an electoral majority has seesawed between them. The dominance of the Republicans (now often called the Grand Old Party, or GOP) in the post–Civil War Reconstruction era eventually gave way to a closely competitive system from 1876 to 1896, in part because the Democrats were more successful at integrating new immigrants into U.S. society in port cities like New York, Boston, and Chicago. In the later years of the nineteenth century, however, the Republicans skillfully capitalized on fears of a growing antiestablishment, anti–big business sentiment in the Democratic Party. They fashioned a dominant and enduring majority of voters that essentially lasted until the early 1930s, when the Great Depression created the conditions for a Democratic resurgence.

President Franklin D. Roosevelt's New Deal coalition of 1932 consisted of the South, racial and ethnic groups, organized labor, farmers, liberals, and big-city "machines," as well-oiled party organizations are sometimes called. This coalition characterized both the Democratic Party and the prevailing national majority until at least the late 1960s. Since 1970, neither party has been clearly dominant, as more and more voters have seemed to be less committed to either of the two parties. In this same period, the Republicans have dominated presidential elections and Democrats have won most congressional contests, a pattern that was broken in 1994 when the Republicans won control of both congressional houses. (The development of a "divided government" is discussed later in this chapter.)

The Modern Era Versus the Golden Age

The modern era seems very distant from the "golden age" of parties that existed from the 1870s to the 1920s. Emigration from Europe (particularly from Ireland, Italy, and Germany) fueled the development of big-city party organizations that ruled their domains with an iron hand. Party and government were virtually interchangeable, and the parties were the providers of much-needed services, entertainment, and employment. These big-city party organizations were called **machines.** A political machine is a party organization that recruits its members with tangible incentives—money, political jobs, an opportunity to get favors from government—and that is characterized by a high degree of leadership control over member activity. Machines were a central element of life for millions of people: They sponsored community events, such as parades and picnics, and provided social services, such as helping new immigrants settle in and giving food and temporary housing to those in immediate need, all in exchange for votes.

The parties offered immigrants not just services, but also the opportunity for upward social mobility as they rose in the organization. Because they held the possibility of social advancement, the parties engendered among their supporters and office holders intense devotion that helped to produce startlingly high voter turnouts—75 percent or better in all presidential elections from 1876 to 1900, compared with only about 50 percent to 55 percent today.[10] They also fostered the greatest party-line voting ever achieved in Congress and many state legislatures[11] (see Roots of Government: Plunkitt of Tammany Hall).

As several political scientists have observed, political machines have not been exclusive to urban areas.[12] Although the most prominent and colorful political machines existed in cities, political machines could be found in some rural and suburban areas as well. Even today, for example, a traditional, machine-style Republican party organization continues to exist in Nassau County, New York—a wealthy suburb of New York City situated on Long Island.[13]

Is the Party Over?

The heyday of the political party—at least this kind of party—has passed. In the twentieth century, many social, political, technological, and governmental changes have contributed to party decline. Historically, the government's gradual assumption of important functions previously performed by the parties, such as printing ballots, conducting elections, and providing social welfare services, had a major impact. Social services began to be seen as a right of citizenship rather than as a privilege extended in exchange for a person's support of a party. Also, as the flow of immigrants slowed dramatically in the 1920s, party organizations gradually withered in most places.

machine:
A party organization that recruits its members with tangible incentives and is characterized by a high degree of control over member activity.

ROOTS OF GOVERNMENT

Plunkitt of Tammany Hall

Tammany Hall was a powerful New York City political organization during the mid-nineteenth and early twentieth centuries. Originally formed as a social club in 1797, it had been transformed into an influential political machine by 1850, with membership including most of the city's prominent Democrats.

Of all the organization's politicians, one of the most renowned at the turn of the twentieth century was ward boss George Washington Plunkitt. Starting as a teenager, this son of Irish immigrants worked his way up through the ranks of the organization to become the leader of the city's Fifteenth Assembly District. (An assembly district is made up of many smaller units, called election districts.) He is remembered as one of the shrewdest politicians of his time. Plunkitt was born poor but died a millionaire, acquiring most of his wealth through what he called "honest graft," a term best described in his own candid words:

> My party's in power in the city, and its goin' to make a lot of public improvements. Well, I'm tipped off, say, that they're going to lay out a new park at a certain place.
>
> I see my opportunity and I take it. I go to that place and I buy up all the land I can in the neighborhood. Then the board of this or that makes it public, and there is a rush to get my land, which nobody cared particular for before.
>
> Ain't it perfectly honest to charge a good price and make a profit on my investment and foresight? Of course, it is. Well, that's honest graft.

For Plunkitt there was a difference between dishonest and honest graft, "between [dishonest] political looters and [honest] politicians who make a fortune out of politics by keepin' their eyes wide open":

> The looter goes in for himself alone without considerin' his organization or his city. The politician looks after his own interests, the organization's interests, and the city's interests all at the same time.

Plunkitt certainly looked after his constituents' interests. During Tammany's reign, the population of New York City was made up predominantly of poor immigrants, mostly Irish, for whom Plunkitt and his fellow district leaders served as a bridge between the Old and New Worlds and also as a way out of the slums. Besides assimilating these newcomers to life in the United States and acquainting them with the processes of self-government, the ward bosses used the patronage at their disposal to provide tangible benefits. Be it a job, liquor, a pushcart license, or even cash, the ward boss was always happy to help out a needy constituent—in exchange, of course, for loyalty at the ballot box during election time.

In contrast to the issue-oriented or image-appeal politics we know today, Plunkitt's politics were *personal*. As Plunkitt put it, "[I] learned how to reach the hearts of the great mass of voters. I don't bother about reaching their heads." Plunkitt understood the value of this personalized, community-oriented politics to both voters and leaders. His advice to aspiring politicians was simply to know and study the members of their communities and to "study human nature and act accordin'."

Plunkitt's brand of politics had all but disappeared by the mid-twentieth century. First, a drastic decline of immigration during the 1920s strangled the fuel line that fed the fires of city machines. Second, many of the services the parties provided gradually came to be viewed as rights of citizenship rather than as rewards for supporting a particular party; therefore, government replaced party organizations as the dispensers of benefits. Most important, however, and much to the chagrin of Plunkitt himself, were the new civil service laws passed by reformers in the 1920s to combat the alleged corruption of machine politics. These laws, which struck at the heart and soul of machine politics—patronage and the spoils system—induced Plunkitt to deem the civil service laws "the biggest fraud of the age" and the ruin of the nation:

> There can't be no real patriotism while it lasts. How are you goin' to interest our young men in their country if you have no offices to give them when they work for their party? . . . I know more than one man in the past years who worked for the ticket and was just overflowin' with patriotism, but when he was knocked out by the civil service humbug he got to hate his country and became an anarchist.

For better or worse, however, the reformers prevailed, and by the mid-twentieth century, civil service had come to dominate government at every level, consigning Plunkitt's brand of politics to America's past.

SOURCE: William L. Riordon, ed., *Plunkitt of Tammany Hall* (New York: Dutton, 1963), 11, 89.

The **direct primary,** whereby party nominees were determined by the ballots of qualified voters rather than at party conventions, was widely adopted by the states in the first two decades of the twentieth century. The primary removed the power of nomination from party leaders and workers and gave it instead to a much broader and more independent electorate, thus loosening the tie between the party nominee and the party organization. **Civil service laws** also removed much of the patronage used by the parties to reward their followers. Civil service laws require appointment on the basis of merit and competitive examinations, whereas **patronage**—also called the **spoils system**—awards jobs on the basis of party loyalty. These changes were encouraged by the Progressive movement (consisting of politically liberal reformers), which flourished in the first two decades of the twentieth century.

In the post–World War II era, extensive social changes led the movement away from strong parties. Broad-based education gave rise to **issue-oriented politics,** politics that focuses on specific issues, such as civil rights, tax cutting, environmentalism, or abortion, rather than on party labels. Issue politics tends to cut across party lines and encourages voters to **ticket-split,** that is, to vote for candidates of different parties for various offices in the same election. Another post–World War II social change that has affected the parties is the shift in the population. Millions of people have moved out of the cities, which are easily organizable because of population density, and into the sprawling suburbs, where a sense of privacy and detachment can deter the most energetic organizers.

Politically, many other trends have contributed to the parties' decline. Television, which has come to dominate U.S. politics, naturally emphasizes personalities rather than abstract concepts such as party labels. In addition, the modern parties have many rivals for the affections of their candidates, including **political consultants,** the hired guns who manage campaigns and design television advertisements. Both television and

direct primary:
The selection of party candidates through the ballots of qualified voters rather than at party nomination conventions.

civil service laws:
These acts removed the staffing of the bureaucracy from political parties and created a professional bureaucracy filled through competition.

patronage:
Jobs, grants, or other special favors that are given as rewards to friends and political allies for their support.

spoils system:
The firing of public-office holders of a defeated political party and their replacement with loyalists of the newly elected party.

issue-oriented politics:
Politics that focuses on specific issues rather than on party, candidate, or other loyalties.

ticket-split:
To vote for candidates of different parties for various offices in the same election.

political consultant:
Professional who manages campaigns and political advertisements for political candidates.

■ Mary Matalin, Deputy Campaign Manager in 1992 for Bush–Quayle campaign, is seen here with her husband and political rival James Carville, President Clinton's 1992 campaign manager. This unlikely couple was married in 1993 and has since co-authored the best-selling political campaign book, *All's Fair: Love, War, and Running for President.* (Photo courtesy: Larry Downing/Sygma)

consultants have replaced the party as the intermediary between candidate and voter. It is little wonder that many candidates and office holders who have reached their posts without much help from their parties remain as free as possible of party ties.

The Parties Endure

The parties' decline can easily be exaggerated, however. Viewing parties in the broad sweep of U.S. history, it becomes clear that first, although political parties have evolved considerably and changed form from time to time, they usually have been reliable vehicles for mass participation in a representative democracy. In fact, the gradual but steady expansion of suffrage itself was orchestrated by the parties. As political scientist E. E. Schattschneider concluded, "In the search for new segments of the populace that might be exploited profitably, the parties have kept the movement to liberalize the franchise well ahead of the demand. . . . The enlargement of the practicing electorate has been one of the principal labors of the parties, a truly notable achievement for which the parties have never been properly credited."[14]

Second, the parties' journey through U.S. history has been characterized by the same ability to adapt to prevailing conditions that is often cited as the genius of the Constitution. Flexibility and pragmatism are characteristics of both and help ensure their survival and the success of the society they serve.

Third, despite massive changes in political conditions and frequent dramatic shifts in the electorate's mood, the two major parties have not only achieved remarkable longevity, but they also have almost consistently provided strong competition for each other and the voters at the national level. Of the twenty-nine presidential elections from 1884 to 1996, for instance, the Republicans won fifteen and the Democrats fourteen. Even when calamities have beset the parties—the Great Depression in the 1930s or the Watergate scandal of 1973–74 for the Republicans (see chapter 8), and the Civil War or left-wing McGovernism in 1972 for the Democrats—the two parties have proved tremendously resilient, sometimes bouncing back from landslide defeats to win the next election. After losing the presidential election badly in 1988, for example, the Democrats managed to win the presidency in 1992 and 1996, demonstrating again that the only constant in politics is change. Indeed, political scientist Philip A. Klinkner argues that the national committees have been at their most innovative in adapting to changing political conditions precisely when they are responding to electoral defeat.[15]

Perhaps most of all, history teaches us that the development of parties in the United States (outlined in Figure 12.1) has been inevitable, as James Madison feared. Human nature alone guarantees conflict in any society; in a free state, the question is simply how to contain and channel conflict productively without infringing on individual liberties. The Founders' utopian hopes for the avoidance of partisan faction, Madison's chief concern, have given way to an appreciation of the parties' constructive contributions to conflict definition and resolution during the years of the American republic.

THE ROLES OF THE AMERICAN PARTIES

For 150 years the two-party system has served as the mechanism American society uses to organize and resolve social and political conflict. Although political parties are arguably less popular today than in previous times, it is important both to remember that political parties often are the chief agents of change in our political system and to discuss the vital services to society the parties provide and how difficult political life would be without them.

Mobilizing Support and Gathering Power

Party affiliation is enormously helpful to elected leaders. They can count on disproportionate support among their partisans in times of trouble and in close judgment calls. Therefore the parties thus aid office holders by giving them room to develop their policies and by mobilizing support for them. When the president addresses the nation and

Web Exploration

To evaluate how the "Big Two" political parties portray their platform issues and use political language to present their policies, go to www.awlonline.com/oconnor.

requests support for his policies, for example, his party's activists are usually the first to respond to the call, perhaps by flooding Congress with telegrams urging action on the president's agenda.

Because there are only two major parties, pragmatic citizens who are interested in politics or public policy are mainly attracted to one or the other standard, creating natural majorities or near-majorities for party office holders to command. The party creates a community of interest that bonds disparate groups over time into a **coalition.** This continuing mutual interest eliminates the necessity of creating a new coalition for every campaign or every issue. Imagine the constant chaos and mad scrambles for public support that would ensue without the continuity provided by the parties.

coalition:

A group of interests or organizations that join forces for the purpose of electing public officials.

A Force for Stability

As mechanisms for organizing and containing political change, the parties are a potent force for stability. They represent continuity in the wake of changing issues and personalities, anchoring the electorate in the midst of the storm of new political policies and people. Because of its unyielding, practical desire to win elections (not just to contest them), each party in a sense acts to moderate public opinion. The party tames its own extreme elements by pulling them toward an ideological center in order to attract a majority of votes on Election Day.

Another aspect of the stability the parties provide is found in the nature of the coalitions they forge. There are inherent contradictions in these coalitions that, oddly enough, strengthen the nation even as they strain party unity. Franklin D. Roosevelt's Democratic New Deal coalition, for example, included many African Americans and most Southern whites, opposing elements nonetheless joined in common political purpose. This party union of the two groups, as limited a context as it may have been, provided a framework for acceptance of change and contributed to reconciliation of the races in the civil rights era. Nowhere can this reconciliation be more clearly seen than in the South, where most state Democratic parties remained predominant after the mid-1960s by building on the ingrained Democratic voting habits of both whites and blacks to create new, moderate, generally integrated societies.

Unity, Linkage, and Accountability

Parties provide the glue that holds together the disparate elements of the fragmented U.S. governmental and political apparatus. The Framers designed a system that divides and subdivides power, making it possible to preserve individual liberty but difficult to coordinate and produce action in a timely fashion. Parties help compensate for this drawback by linking all the institutions of power one to another. Although rivalry between the executive and legislative branches of U.S. government is inevitable, the partisan affiliations of the leaders of each branch constitute a common basis for cooperation, as any president and his fellow party members in Congress usually demonstrate daily. Each time President Bill Clinton proposed a major new program (such as health care and crime control), for instance, Democratic members of the Congress were the first to speak up in favor of the program and to orchestrate efforts at its passage. Furthermore, political scientist Kelly D. Patterson shows that presidential candidates continue to advocate policies similar to those advocated by their party's congressional leaders, suggesting that the diminished power of party elites in the presidential nomination process has not weakened parties' linkage function.[16]

Even within each branch there is intended fragmentation, and the party once again helps narrow the differences between the House of Representatives and the Senate, or between the president and his chiefs in the executive bureaucracy. Similarly, the division of national, state, and local governments, while always an invitation to conflict, is made more workable and easily coordinated by the intersecting party relationships that exist among office holders at all levels. Party affiliation, in other words, is a basis for mediation and negotiation laterally among the branches and vertically among the layers.

■ Clinton shaking hands with a representative of the Chinese government during his well publicized trip to China. Chinese-American relations were strained in the later half of Clinton's second term due to disagreements over foreign policy and other matters. (Photo courtesy: Brad Markel/Liaison Agency)

The party's linkage function does not end there. Party identification and organization are natural connectors and vehicles for communication between the voter and the candidate, as well as between the voter and the office holder. The party connection is one means of increasing accountability in election campaigns and in government. Candidates on the campaign trail and elected party leaders in office are required from time to time to account for their performance at party-sponsored forums, nominating primaries, and conventions.

Political parties, too, can take some credit for unifying the nation by dampening sectionalism. Because parties must form national majorities in order to win the presidency, any single, isolated region is guaranteed minority status unless it establishes ties with other areas. The party label and philosophy build the bridge that enables regions to join forces; and in the process, a national interest, rather than a merely sectional one, is created and served.

The Electioneering Function

The election, proclaimed author H. G. Wells, is "democracy's ceremonial, its feast, its great function," and the political parties assist this ceremony in essential ways. First, the parties funnel eager, interested individuals into politics and government. Thousands of candidates are recruited each year by the two parties, as are many of the candidates' staff members—the people who manage the campaigns and go on to serve in key governmental positions once the election has been won.

This function is even more crucial in the British parliamentary system. In the postwar period, the only avenue to national power (that is, the prime minister's office or a choice seat on the Cabinet) has been through either the Conservative Party or the Labour Party. Ambitious politicians must work their way up through the party hierarchy and build a supporting coalition along the way.

Elections can have meaning in a democracy only if they are competitive, and in the United States they probably could not be competitive without the parties. Even in the South, traditionally the least politically competitive U.S. region, the parties today regularly produce reasonably vigorous contests at the state (and, increasingly, the local) level.

Party as a Voting and Issue Cue

A voter's party identification acts as an invaluable filter for information, a perceptual screen that affects how he or she digests political news. Therefore party affiliation provides a useful cue for voters, particularly for the least informed and least interested, who can use the party as a shortcut or substitute for interpreting issues and events they may not fully comprehend. But even better-educated and more involved voters find party identification helpful. After all, no one has the time to study every issue carefully or to become fully knowledgeable about every candidate seeking public office.

Policy Formulation and Promotion

U.S. Senator Huey Long (D–La.), one of the premier spokesmen for "the people" of this century, was usually able to capture the flavor of the average person's views about politics. Considering an independent bid for president before his assassination in 1935, Long liked to compare the Republican and Democratic parties to the two patent medicines offered by a traveling salesman. Asked the difference between them, the salesman explained that the "High Populorum" tonic was made from the bark of the tree taken from the top down, while "Low Populorum" tonic was made from bark stripped from the root up. The analogous moral, according to Long, was this: "The only difference I've found in Congress between the Republican and Democratic leadership is that one of 'em is skinning us from the ankle up and the other from the ear down!"[17]

Long would certainly have insisted that his fable applied to the **national party platform,** the most visible instrument by which parties formulate, convey, and promote public policy. Every four years, each party writes for the presidential nominating conventions a lengthy platform explaining its positions on key issues. Most citizens in our own era undoubtedly still believe that party platforms are relatively undifferentiated, a mixture of pabulum and pussyfooting. Yet political scientist Gerald M. Pomper's study of party platforms from 1944 through 1976 has demonstrated that each party's pledges were consistently and significantly different, a function in part of the varied groups in their coalitions.[18] Interestingly, about 69 percent of the specific platform positions were taken by one party but not the other. The trend observed by Pomper continues: on abortion, for example, the Democrats are strongly for abortion rights while the Republicans are firmly against them in their most recent platforms.

Granted, then, party platforms are quite distinctive. Does this elaborate party exercise in policy formulation mean anything? One could argue that the platform is valuable, if only as a clear presentation of a party's basic philosophy and as a forum for activist opinion and public education. But platforms have much more impact than that. About two-thirds of the promises in the victorious party's presidential platform have been completely or mostly implemented; even more astounding, one-half or more of the pledges of the

national party platform:

A statement of the general and specific philosophy and policy goals of a political party, usually promulgated at the national convention.

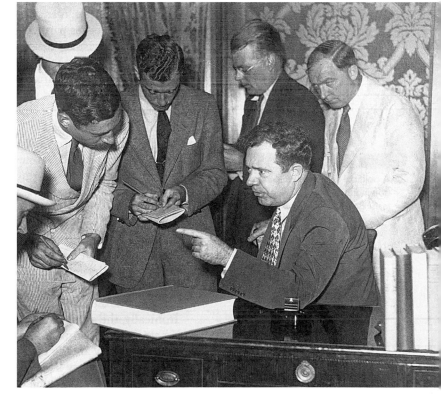

■ Senator Huey Long (D–La.) campaigned for the presidency in 1935 on a populist platform, arguing in fiery speeches that neither of the major parties' policies had the people's best interests at heart. (Photo courtesy: Corbis/Bettmann)

to the First Family. When many of the Democratic senators and representatives elected on his presidential coattails were endangered in the 1966 midterm election, LBJ canceled a major campaign trip on their behalf lest his policies get tied too closely to their possible defeats. Democrats lost forty-seven House seats, three Senate seats, and eight governorships in the 1966 debacle.

In 1972 Richard M. Nixon discouraged the GOP from nominating candidates against conservative Southern Democrats in order to improve his own electoral and congressional position, since the grateful unopposed legislators would presumably be less likely to cause Nixon trouble on the campaign trail or in Congress. Nixon also subordinated the party's agenda almost wholly to his own reelection. Shunting aside the Republican National Committee, Nixon formed the Committee to Re-Elect the President, which became known by the acronym CREEP. So removed were party leaders from the Committee's abuses (see the coverage on Watergate in chapter 8) that the Republican Party organization itself escaped blame during the Watergate investigations.

Jimmy Carter also showed little interest in his national party. Elected as an outsider in 1976, Carter and his top aides at first viewed the party as another extension of the Washington establishment they had pledged to ignore. Carter and his DNC chairmen failed to develop the Democratic Party organizationally and financially in order to keep it competitive during a critical period, while the Republicans were undergoing a dramatic revitalization stimulated by their desire to recover from the Watergate scandal. Later, during his unsuccessful 1980 reelection campaign, Carter was properly criticized for diverting DNC personnel and resources to his presidential needs, such as travel and Christmas cards, rather than permitting them to pursue essential partywide electoral tasks.

Clearly, then, some presidents have taken their party responsibilities more seriously than have others. In general, argues political scientist Sidney Milkis, most presidents since (and including) Franklin D. Roosevelt have been less supportive of their respective political parties than have been earlier presidents.[47]

The Parties and the Judiciary

Many Americans view the judiciary as "above politics" and certainly as nonpartisan, and many judges are quick to agree. Yet not only do members of the judiciary sometimes follow the election returns and allow themselves to be influenced by popular opinion, but they are also products of their party identification and possess the same partisan perceptual screens as all other politically aware citizens.

Legislators are much more partisan than judges, but it is wrong to assume that judges reach decisions wholly independent of partisan values. First, judges are creatures of the political process, and their posts are considered patronage plums. Judges who are not elected are appointed by presidents or governors for their abilities but also as members of the executive's party and increasingly as representatives of a certain philosophy of or approach to government. In this century every president has appointed judges overwhelmingly from his own party; Jimmy Carter and Ronald Reagan, for instance, drew 95 percent or more of their judicial choices from their respective parties. Furthermore, Democratic executives are naturally inclined to select for the bench liberal individuals who may be friendly to the welfare state or critical of some business practices. Republican executives generally lean toward conservatives for judicial posts, hoping they will be tough on criminal defendants, anti-abortion, and restrained in the use of court power. During the Clinton administration when Republicans were in charge of both Houses of Congress, the GOP strongly opposed many of President Clinton's judicial nominations and refused to confirm a fair number of them or even to bring the nominations to a vote. As a result, there were many judicial vacancies across the country. Unfortunately, this was an inevitable result of divided government in a very partisan and ideologically polarized era marked by a mutual lack of trust. Even the strongly Republican Chief Justice, William H. Rehnquist, was moved to criticize the Republican Senate's failure to confirm Clinton nominees.

Research has long indicated that party affiliation is in fact a moderately good predictor of judicial decisions, at least in some areas.[48] In other words, party matters in the judiciary just as it does in the other two branches of government, although it certainly matters less on the bench than in the legislature and in the executive.

Many judges appointed to office have had long careers in politics as loyal party workers or legislators. Supreme Court Justice Sandra Day O'Connor, for example, was an active member of the National Republican Women's Club and is a former Republican state legislator. Some jurists are even more overtly political, since they are elected to office. In a majority of states at least some judicial positions are filled by election, and seventeen states hold outright partisan elections, with both parties nominating opposing candidates and running hard-hitting campaigns. In some rural counties across the United States, local judges are not merely partisanly elected figures; they are the key public officials, controlling many patronage jobs and the party machinery itself.

Clearly, in many places in the United States, judges by necessity and by tradition are not above politics but are in the thick of it. Although election of the judiciary is a questionable practice in light of its specially sanctioned role as impartial arbiter, partisan influence exerted both by jurists' party loyalties and by the appointment (or election) process is useful in retaining some degree of accountability in a branch often accused of being arrogant and aloof.

The Parties and State Governments

Most of the conclusions just discussed about the party's relationship to the legislature, the executive, and the judiciary apply to those branches on the state level as well. The national parties, after all, are organized around state units, and the basic structural arrangement of party and government is much the same in Washington and the state capitals. Remarkably, too, the major national parties are the dominant political forces in all fifty states. This has been true consistently; unlike Great Britain or Canada, the United States has no regional or state parties that displace one or both of the national parties in local contests. Occasionally in U.S. history a third party has proven locally potent, as did Minnesota's Farmer-Labor Party and Wisconsin's Progressives, both of which elected governors and state legislative majorities earlier in this century. But over time, no such party has survived,[49] and every state's two-party system mirrors national party dualism, at least as far as labels are concerned.

Parties and Governors.   Currently the partisan makeup of governors in the United States is heavily Republican, with Republicans in 1999 controlling the executive office in thirty-two states, Democrats in seventeen, and independents in two (Maine and Minnesota).

The powerful position of governor is a natural launching pad for a presidential candidacy. Just in the twentieth century, Woodrow Wilson, Franklin D. Roosevelt, Jimmy Carter, Ronald Reagan, and Bill Clinton went from a statehouse to the White House. In 2000, at least one Republican governor may throw his or her hat in the ring for president: Texas Gov. George W. Bush, son of the former president. Governors in many states tend to possess even greater influence over their parties' organizations and legislators than do presidents. Many governors have more patronage positions at their command than does a president, and these material rewards and incentives give governors added clout with activists and office holders. In addition, tradition in some states permits the governor to play a role in selecting the legislature's committee chairs and party floor leaders, and some state executives even attend and help direct the party legislative caucuses, activities no president would ever undertake. Moreover, forty-three governors possess a power denied the national executive until 1997: the line-item veto, which permits the governor to veto single items (such as individual pork barrel projects) in appropriations bills. Whereas many presidents prior to Clinton accepted objectionable measures as part of a bill too urgent or important to be vetoed, a governor could gain enormous leverage with legislators by means of the line-item veto. A Republican-sponsored measure in the 104th Congress gave the president this potent tool, beginning in January 1997.

■ Newly sworn-in Arizona legislators wave at the end of the swearing-in ceremony at the State Capitol in Phoenix Monday, Jan. 4, 1999. From left are, Governor Jane D. Hull, Secretary of State Betsey Bayless, Attorney General Janet Napolitano, Treasurer Carol Springer, and Superintendent of Public Instruction Lisa Graham Keegan. (Photo courtesy: Roy Dabner/AP/Wide World Photos)

Subsequently, however, the presidential line-item veto was ruled unconstitutional in federal court.

Parties and State Legislatures. Unlike the partisan makeup of state executives, state legislatures are nearly evenly split with neither party having a significant advantage. Similar to state executives, however, the party role in the legislature itself tends to be more high-profile and effective at the state level. Most state legislatures surpass the U.S. Congress in partisan unity and cohesion. Even though fewer than half of congressional roll calls in the post–World War II era have produced majorities of the two parties on opposite sides, a number of state legislatures (including Massachusetts, New York, Ohio, and Pennsylvania) have achieved party voting levels of 70 percent or better in some years. Not all states display party cohesion of this magnitude, of course. Nebraska has a nonpartisan legislature, elected without party labels on the ballot. In the South the lack of two-party competition has left essentially one-party legislatures split into factions, regional groupings, or personal cliques. As real interparty competition reaches the legislative level in Southern states, however, party cohesion in the legislatures is likely to increase.

One other party distinction is notable in many state legislatures. Compared with the Congress, state legislative leaders have much more authority and power; this is one reason party unity is higher in the state capitols.[50] The strict seniority system that usually controls committee assignments in Congress is less absolute in most states, and legislative leaders often have considerable discretion in appointing the committee chairs and members. The party caucuses, too, are usually more active and influential in state legislatures than in their Washington counterparts. In some legislatures, the caucuses meet weekly or even daily to work out strategy and count votes, and nearly one-fourth of the caucuses bind all the party members to support the group's decisions on key issues (such as appropriations measures, tax issues, and procedural questions).

Not just the leaders and caucuses but the party organizations as well have more influence over legislators at the state level. State legislators are much more dependent than their congressional counterparts on their state and local parties for election assistance. Whereas members of Congress have large government-provided staffs and lavish perquisites to assist (directly or indirectly) their reelection efforts, state legislative candidates need party workers and, increasingly, the party's financial support and technological resources at election time.

THE MODERN TRANSFORMATION OF PARTY ORGANIZATION

Political parties have moved from the labor-intensive, person-to-person operations of the first half of the century toward the utilization of modern high technologies and communication strategies. Nevertheless, the capabilities of each party's organization vary widely.

Republican Strengths

Until 1992 the modern Republican Party thoroughly outclassed its Democratic rival in almost every category of campaign service and fund raising. There are a number of explanations for the disparity between the two major parties: From 1932 until 1980, the Republicans were almost perennially disappointed underdogs, especially in congressional contests; they therefore felt the need to give extra effort. The GOP had the willingness, and enough electoral frustrations, to experiment with new campaign technologies that might hold the key to elusive victories. Also, since Democrats held most of the congressional offices and thus had most of the benefits of incumbency and staff, Republican nominees were forced to rely more on their party to offset built-in Democratic advantages. The party staff, in other words, compensated for the Democratic congressional staff, and perhaps also for organized labor's divisions of election troops, which were usually at the beck and call of Democratic candidates. Then, too, one can argue that the business and middle-class base of the modern GOP has a natural managerial and entrepreneurial flair demonstrated by the party officers drawn from that talented pool.

Whatever the causes, the contemporary national Republican Party has organizational prowess unparalleled in American history. The Republicans have surpassed the Democrats in fund raising by large margins in recent election cycles—never by less than two to one and usually by a considerably higher ratio (see Figure 12.4). Democrats must struggle to raise enough money to meet the basic needs of most of their candidates, while, in the words of a past chairman of the Democratic Senatorial Campaign Committee, "The single biggest problem the Republicans have is how to legally spend the money they have."[51] Republican presidential candidate Bob Dole benefited from this large GOP war chest in the spring of 1996. After he had spent the maximum allowed by law in his successful presidential nomination bid, the Republican party opened its coffers to fund some of Dole's operation until the August GOP convention.

Most of the Republican money is raised through highly successful mail solicitation. This procedure started in the early 1960s and accelerated in the mid-1970s, when postage and production costs were relatively low. From a base of just 24,000 names in 1975, for example, the national Republican Party has expanded its mailing list of proven donors to several million in the 1990s. Mailings produce about three-fourths of total revenue, and they do so with an average contribution of less than $35. In this fashion

Figure 12.4 Political Party Finances, 1976–1998: Total Receipts

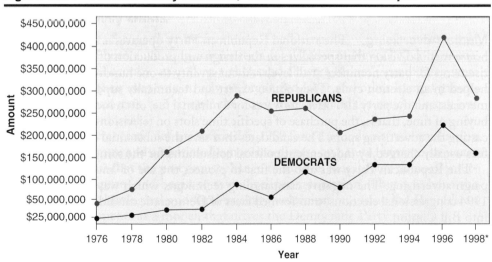

Note how the Republican Party has consistently taken in substantially higher receipts than their Democratic competitors— especially during the 1980s, when the Republican party consolidated and prospered during Ronald Reagan's administration. Not until 1996 did Democrats reach levels long enjoyed by the Republicans.

* Numbers represent total monies raised between January 1, 1997 and December 31, 1998. Includes total for national senatorial and congressional committees as well as all other reported national, state, and local spending.

SOURCE: Federal Election Commission.

By 1996, the gender gap of 1994 had become a gender chasm. Women, by anywhere between a 14 and 20 percent margin in polls taken during the summer leading up to the Democratic and Republican conventions, favored President Clinton over his Republican challenger, Bob Dole. This difference was not offset by men who, prior to the conventions, tended to split their support evenly between the two candidates.

Hoping to bridge this gap, Republicans attempted to use their convention to woo women voters back into the fold. By moderating their message and their tone, Republicans did gain a brief post-convention boost in the polls, but following the Democratic convention, the pre-convention polling numbers returned. Two months later, the largest gender gap in the nation's history was recorded. While men split their vote evenly between the two candidates (Dole received 45 percent of the male vote and Clinton 44 percent), according to exit polls women supported Clinton by a 54 to 37 margin! One of the biggest challenges then facing Republicans is how to gain the support of women without alienating their male base. Besides abortion and women's rights issues, female concerns for peace and social compassion may provide much of the gap's distance. For instance, women are usually much less likely than men to favor American military action, and they are less inclined to support cuts in government funding of social welfare programs.

Race and Ethnicity.   African Americans are the most dramatically different population subgroup in party terms. The 80-percent-plus advantage they offer the Democrats dwarfs the edge given to either party by any other segment of the electorate, and their proportion of strong Democrats (about 40 percent) is three times that of whites. African Americans account almost entirely for the slight lead in party affiliation that Democrats normally enjoy over Republicans, since the GOP has recently been able to attract a narrow plurality of whites to its standard. Perhaps as a reflection of the massive party chasm separating blacks and whites, the two races differ greatly on many policy issues, with blacks overwhelmingly on the liberal side and whites closer to the conservative pole. An exception, incidentally, is abortion, where religious beliefs may lead African Americans to the more conservative stance. The much smaller population group of Hispanics supplements this group as a Democratic stalwart; by more than three to one, Hispanics prefer the Democratic label. An exception is the Cuban-American population, whose anti–Fidel Castro tilt leads to Republicanism.

Age.   Young people are once again becoming more Democratic. Polls in 1972 indicated that the group of eighteen- to twenty-four-year-olds, and particularly students, was the only age group to support Democratic presidential nominee George McGovern. But by the 1990s the eighteen-to-thirty-four-year-old age group was the most Republican of all. Much of this margin was derived from strong student affiliation with the Republicans. Perhaps because of the bad economy from 1990 to 1992, which limited job availability for college graduates, young people swung back to the Democrats in 1992. Bill Clinton ran strongly among eighteen- to twenty-four-year-olds, and they were among his best groups in the electorate. In 1996, Clinton again carried the under-30s, with approximately the same margin as he attained nationwide across the board.

Social and Economic Factors.   Some traditional strengths and weaknesses persist for each party by occupation, income, and education. The GOP remains predominant among executives, professionals, and white-collar workers, whereas the Democrats lead substantially among blue-collar workers and the unemployed. Labor union members are also Democratic by two-and-a-half to one. The more conservative, retired population leans Republican. Women who do not work outside the home are less liberal and Democratic than those who do. Occupation, income, and education are closely related, of course, so many of the same partisan patterns can be detected in all three classifications. Democratic support usually drops steadily as one climbs the income scale. Similarly, as years of education increase, identification with the Republican Party climbs; in graduate school, however, the Democrats rally a bit and only narrowly trail GOP partisans.

Religion. The party preferences by religion are also traditional, but with modern twists. Protestants—especially Methodists, Presbyterians, and Episcopalians—favor the Republicans, whereas Catholics and, even more so, Jews are predominantly Democratic in affiliation. Decreased polarization is apparent all around, though.[58] Democrats have made inroads among many Protestant denominations over the past three decades, and Republicans can now sometimes claim up to 25 percent of the Jewish population and nearly 40 percent of the Catholics. The "born again" Christians, who have received much attention in recent years, are somewhat less Republican than commonly believed. The GOP usually has just about a 10 percent edge among them, primarily because so many blacks classify themselves as members of this group.

Marital Status. Even marital status reveals something about partisan affiliation. People who are married, a traditionally more conservative group, and people who have never married, a segment weighted toward the premarriage young who currently lean toward the Republicans, are closely divided in party loyalty. But the widowed are Democratic in nature, probably because there are many more widows than widowers; in this, the gender gap is again expressing itself. The divorced and the separated, who may be experiencing economic hardship and appear to be more liberal than the married population, are a substantially Democratic group.

GLOBAL POLITICS

Political Parties in Parliamentary Democracies

The United States has a limited range of political parties at the national level. While there are many parties in this country, the Reform Party is currently the most prominent "third party." Since the Civil War, the Republican and Democratic parties have always controlled the federal government. Currently, there are only two members of Congress, Bernie Sanders and Robert Smith, who are not members of the two dominant parties.

Election rules offer a partial explanation for this. The "winner-take-all" single-member district system found here tends to produce a two-party system. Yet Canada and the United Kingdom also use the winner-take-all election rule, with two parties dominating their parliaments, but other parties also have at least a few members representing them in the legislature. In Britain's House of Commons, for

example, even the Sinn Fein, the political arm of the Irish Republican Army, now has two seats (currently vacant because the party opposes British government policy in Northern Ireland). Canada and the United Kingdom are thus better described as two-plus party systems.

The European countries and Japan have multiparty systems. Typically, there are several parties that can expect to control the executive branch, and a coalition of parties in the cabinet is a frequent feature of these systems. Again, election rules tend to produce such a party configuration. Germany, Italy, and Japan all have two-ballot elections in which voters elect part of the legislature from single-member districts and part by proportional representation based on party lists. Proportional representation tends to benefit smaller parties, because their electoral bases are not confined to districts. Not only do these countries' parliaments have several medium-sized parties (Japan is a bit different because the conservative party is far larger than any of its rivals), but they have parties that span the political spectrum. On the left, social democratic parties are represented in every legislature. France, Germany, and Japan have communist parties (a reformed one in Germany's case). In France, the reactionary National Front has emerged in the last decade as a powerful alternative to the mainstream conservative Union for French Democracy and the Rally for the Republic.

Number of Political Parties in the Lower House of National Legislatures, 1999

Country	Number of Parties
Canada	5
France	6
Germany	6
Italy	8
Japan	8
United Kingdom	11
United States	**3**

for president the previous year. In 1965 two Southern House Democrats lost all their committee seniority because of their 1964 endorsement of GOP presidential nominee Barry Goldwater, as did another Southerner in 1968 for backing George Wallace's third-party candidacy. In early 1983 the House Democratic Caucus removed Texas Representative Phil Gramm from his Budget Committee seat because of his "disloyalty" in working more closely with Republican committee members than with his own party leaders. (Gramm resigned his seat in Congress, changed parties, and was reelected as a Republican. He then used the controversy to propel himself into the U.S. Senate in 1984.)

40. David W. Rohde, (Chicago: University of Chicago Press, 1991). *Parties and Leaders in the Postreform House.* John A. Aldrich and David W. Rohde, "The Transition to Republican Rule in the House: Implications for Theories of Congressional Politics," *Political Science Quarterly* 112 (1997–98), pp 541–67.

41. Joseph A. Schlesinger, "The New American Political Party," *American Political Science Review* 79 (1985): 1168.

42. Kevin M. Leyden and Stephen A. Borrelli, "An Investment in Goodwill: Party Contributions and Party Unity Among U.S. House Members in the 1980s," *American Politics Quarterly* 22 (1994): pp. 421–52.

43. Richard A. Clucas, "Party Contributions and the Influence of Campaign Committee Chairs on Roll-Call Voting," *Legislative Studies Quarterly* XXII (1997): pp. 179–94. David M. Cantor and Paul S. Herrnson, "Party Campaign Activity and Party Unity in the U.S. House of Representatives," *Legislative Studies Quarterly* XXII (1997): pp 393–415.

44. Rhodes Cook, "Reagan Nurtures His Adopted Party to Strength," *Congressional Quarterly Weekly* 43 (September 28, 1985): 1927–30.

45. George C. Edwards III, *Presidential Influence in Congress* (New York: Freeman, 1980); and Herbert M. Kritzer and Robert B. Eubank, "Presidential Coattails Revisited: Partisanship and Incumbency Effects," *American Journal of Political Science* 23 (1979): 615–26.

46. Lyn Ragsdale, "The Fiction of Congressional Elections as Presidential Events," *American Politics Quarterly* 8 (1980): 375–98; and Thomas E. Mann and Raymond E. Wolfinger, "Candidates and Parties in Congressional Elections," *American Political Science Review* 74 (1980): 617–32.

47. Sidney M. Milkis, *The President and the Parties: The Transformation of the American Party System Since the New Deal* (New York: Oxford University Press, 1993).

48. See S. Sidney Ulmer, "The Political Party Variable on the Michigan Supreme Court." *Journal of Public Law* 11 (1962): 352–62; Stuart Nagel, "Political Party Affiliation and Judges' Decisions," *American Political Science Review* 55 (1961): 843–50; David W. Adamany, "The Party Variable in Judges' Voting: Conceptual Notes and a Case Study," *American Political Science Review* 63 (1969): 57–73; Sheldon Goldman, "Voting Behavior on the United States Courts of Appeals, 1961–1964," *American Political Science Review* 60 (1966): 374–83; and Robert A. Carp and C. K. Rowland, *Policymaking and Politics in the Federal District Courts* (Knoxville: University of Tennessee Press, 1983).

49. The Farmer-Labor Party did survive in a sense; having endured a series of defeats, it merged in 1944 with the Democrats, and Democratic candidates still officially bear the standard of the Democratic-Farmer-Labor (DFL) Party. At about the same time, also having suffered severe electoral reversals, the Progressives stopped nominating candidates in Wisconsin. The party's members either returned to the Republican Party, from which it had split early in the century, or became Democrats.

50. Morehouse, "Legislatures and Political Parties," 19–24.

51. Senator George J. Mitchell (D–Me.), as quoted in *The Washington Post* (February 9, 1986): A14.

52. As quoted in a speech to the RNC by the Associated Press, January 24, 1987, and in *The Washington Post* (January 24, 1987): A3.

53. Tim Kenworthy, "Collaring Colleagues for Cash," *Washington Post* (14 May 1991): p. A17.

54. Jennifer Babson and Beth Donovan, "GOP Fundraiser Raises Sights and Tightens Belt," *Congressional Quarterly Weekly Report* (2 April 1994): pp. 809–11.

55. Larson, "Ambition and Money in the U.S. House of Representatives: Analyzing Campaign Contributions from Incumbents' Leadership PACs and Reelection Committees." Herrnson, "Money and Motives: Spending in House Elections." Bibby, "Party Networks: National-State Integration, Allied Groups, and Issue Activists."

56. See Steven E. Finkel and Howard A. Scarrow, "Party Identification and Party Enrollment: The Difference and the Consequence," *Journal of Politics* 47 (May 1985): 620–42.

57. Martin P. Wattenberg, *The Decline of American Political Parties, 1952–1994* (Cambridge, MA: Harvard University Press, 1996).

58. The presidential election of 1960 may be an extreme case, but John F. Kennedy's massive support among Catholics and Nixon's less substantial but still impressive backing by Protestants demonstrates the polarization that religion could once produce. See Philip E. Converse, "Religion and Politics: The 1960 Election," in Angus Campbell *et al.*, *Elections and the Political Order* (New York: Wiley, 1966), 96–124.

59. Richard Benedetto, "Fed-Up Voters in Search of a Better Candidate," *USA Today* (August 11, 1995): A4.

(Photo courtesy: Bob Daemmrich)

Voting and Elections

*S*imply put, elections matter, and the career of Bill Clinton proves it. The little-known governor from Arkansas could never have been elected in 1992 had the national economy been reasonably good. The slogan, "It's the economy, stupid!" summed up the entire election, and Clinton promised to "focus like a laser" on fixing the economy. However, having won on the economy, Clinton became distracted by issues such as health care and gays in the military, and in 1994 was punished by the voters for not fulfilling his pledge of 1992. In national elections marked by debate on both economic and moral issues, Republicans took control of both houses of Congress for the first time since the early 1950s. Clinton had to defend the relevancy of his presidency until he could retrieve his footing, concentrate on the economy, and use his rhetorical skills to best the congressional Republicans in a dramatic showdown on government spending in 1995. By 1996, Clinton was in a position to benefit from an economy on the upswing, though again he won his presidential election without securing a majority of the popular vote.

By election-time 1998, the Clinton/Lewinsky story had broken, and while the public disapproved strongly of Clinton's relationship with a twenty-something intern, they did not want him thrown out of office on that account. But House Republicans were clearly pushing for impeachment, and the public was unhappy that their wishes were not being taken into account. In the 1998 Congressional elections, the president's party actually gained seats in the House of Representatives for the first time since 1934; the Republican majority was cut from eleven to six; and ironically enough, Clinton was able to claim a "moral" victory. The House did manage an act of impeachment after the election, but it failed in the Senate, and the public disgust with the political circus taught the Republican party a bitter lesson at the polls about defying the will of the people.

ecall for a moment Election Day, November 5, 1996. A plurality of the voting electorate, simply by casting ballots peacefully across a continent-sized nation, reelected or replaced politicians at all levels of government—from the President of the United States, to members of the U.S. Congress, to state legislators. Other countries do not have the luxury of a peaceful transition of political power. We tend to take this process for granted, but in truth it is a marvel. Fortunately, most Americans, though not enough, understand why and how elections serve their interests. Elections take the pulse of average people and gauge their hopes and fears; the study of elections permits us to trace the course of the American revolution over 200 years of voting.

Today the United States of America is a democrat's paradise in many respects, because it probably conducts more elections for more offices more frequently than any nation on earth. Moreover, in recent times the U.S. electorate (those citizens eligible to vote) has been the most universal in the country's history; no longer can one's race or sex or creed prevent participation at the ballot box. But challenges still remain. After all the blood spilled and energy expended to expand the suffrage (as the right to vote is called), little more than half the potentially eligible voters bother to go to the polls!

This chapter focuses on the purposes served by elections, the various kinds of elections held in the United States, and patterns of voting over time. We concentrate in particular on presidential and congressional contests, both of which have rich histories that tell us a great deal about the American people and their changing hopes and needs. We conclude by returning to contemporary presidential elections and addressing some topics of electoral reform.

- First, we will examine *the purposes served by elections,* pointing out that they confer a legitimacy on regimes better than any other method of change.
- Second, we will analyze *different kinds of elections,* including the many different types of elections held at the presidential and congressional levels.

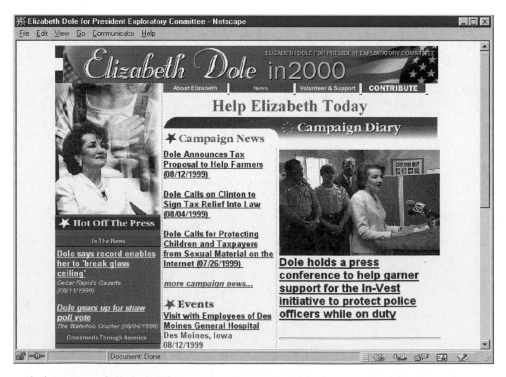

■ The home page of Elizabeth Dole's presidential campaign website. Campaign websites were substantially more widespread and more sophisticated in 1999 than they were when they first appeared in 1996. (Photo courtesy: Elizabeth Dole For President Exploratory Committee)

- Third, we will take a closer look at the elements of *presidential elections,* including primaries, conventions, and delegates.
- Fourth, we will explore how *congressional elections,* although they share similarities with presidential elections, are really quite different.
- Fifth, we will discuss *how voters behave* in certain distinct ways and exhibit unmistakable patterns each election cycle.
- Finally, we will present arguments for *reforming the electoral process* for the most powerful official in the world, the president of the United States.

THE PURPOSES SERVED BY ELECTIONS

Both the ballot and the bullet are methods of governmental change around the world, and surely the former is preferable to the latter. Although the United States has not escaped the bullet's awful effects, most change has come to this country through the election process. Regular free elections guarantee mass political action and enable citizens to influence the actions of their government. Election campaigns may often seem unruly, unending, harsh, and even vicious, but imagine the stark alternatives: violence and social disruption. Societies that cannot vote their leaders out of office are left with little choice other than to force them out by means of strikes, riots, or coups d'état.

Popular election confers on a government the legitimacy that it can achieve no other way. Even many authoritarian and Communist systems around the globe recognize this. From time to time, they hold "referenda" to endorse their regimes or one-party elections, even though these so-called elections offer no real choice that would ratify their rule. The symbolism of elections as mechanisms to legitimize change, then, is important, but so is their practical value. After all, elections are the means to fill public offices and staff the government. The voters' choice of candidates and parties helps to organize government as well. Because candidates advocate certain policies, elections also involve a choice of platforms and point the society in certain directions on a wide range of issues, from abortion to civil rights to national defense to the environment.

Regular elections also ensure that government is accountable to the people it serves. At fixed intervals the **electorate,** citizens eligible to vote, is called on to judge those in power. If the judgment is favorable, and the incumbents are reelected, the office holders may continue their policies with renewed resolve. Should the incumbents be defeated and their challengers elected, however, a change in policies will likely result. Either way, the winners will claim a **mandate** (literally, a command) from the people to carry out their platform.

Sometimes the claim of a mandate is suspect because voters are not so much endorsing one candidate and his or her beliefs as rejecting his or her opponent. Frequently, this occurs because the electorate is exercising **retrospective judgment;** that is, voters are rendering judgment on the performance of the party in power. This judgment makes sense because voters can evaluate the record of office holders much better than they can predict the future actions of the out-of-power challengers.

At other times, voters might vote using **prospective judgment,** that is, they vote based on what a candidate pledges to do about an issue if elected. This forward-looking approach to choosing candidates voters believe will best serve their interests requires that the electorate examine the views that the rival candidates have on the issues of the day and then cast a ballot for the person they believe will best handle these matters. Unfortunately, prospective voting requires lots of information about issues and candidates. Voters who cast a vote prospectively must be willing to spend a great deal of time seeking out information and learning about issues and how each candidate stands on them. As the authors of a classic study on the American electorate note, three requirements exist in order for voters to engage in prospective voting: (1) voters must have an opinion on an issue, (2) voters must have an idea of what action, if any, the government is taking on the issue, and (3) voters must see a difference between the two parties on the issue.[1] Only a

electorate:

Citizens eligible to vote.

mandate:

A command, indicated by an electorate's votes, for the elected officials to carry out their platforms.

retrospective judgment:

A voter's evaluation of the performance of the party in power.

prospective judgment:

A voter's evaluation of a candidate based on what he or she pledges to do about an issue if elected.

small minority of voters, the authors concluded, could meet these requirements, although scholars studying more recent elections have found voters better equipped to engage in prospective voting.[2] Consider for a moment how voters retrospectively and prospectively judged recent presidential administrations in reaching their ballot decisions:

- *1968:* No one could know what Richard M. Nixon's promised "secret plan to end the Vietnam War" really was, but the electorate knew that President Lyndon B. Johnson had failed to resolve the conflict. Result: Voters retrospectively voted against the nominee of the party in power, Hubert H. Humphrey, and prospectively for Richard Nixon and his "secret plan."

- *1972:* The American people were satisfied with Nixon's stewardship of foreign affairs, especially his good relationship with the Soviet Union, the diplomatic opening of China, and the "Vietnamization" of the war. Thus they retrospectively judged his administration to have been a success and looked to the future, believing that he, rather than Democrat George McGovern, could best lead the country. The Watergate scandal (involving Nixon's coverup of his campaign committee's bugging of the Democrats' national headquarters) was only in its infancy, and the president was rewarded with a forty-nine-state sweep.

- *1976:* This year retrospective judgments clearly prevailed over prospective considerations. Despite confusion about Jimmy Carter's real philosophy and intentions, the relatively unknown Georgia Democrat was elected president as voters held President Gerald R. Ford responsible for an economic recession and deplored his pardon of Richard M. Nixon for Watergate crimes.

- *1980:* Burdened by difficult economic times and the Iranian hostage crisis (one year before Election Day, Iranian militants had seized fifty-three Americans, whom they held until January 20, 1981, Inauguration Day), Carter became a one-term president as the electorate rejected the Democrat's perceived weak leadership. At age sixty-nine, Ronald Reagan was not viewed as the ideal replacement by many voters, and neither did a majority agree with some of his conservative principles. But the retrospective judgment on Carter was so harsh and the prospective outlook of four more years under his stewardship so glum that an imperfect alternative was considered preferable to another term of the Democrat.

- *1984:* A strong economic recovery from a midterm recession and an image of strength derived from a defense buildup and a successful military venture in Grenada combined to produce a satisfied electorate that retrospectively and prospectively decided to grant Ronald Reagan four more years. The result: A forty-nine-state landslide reelection for Reagan over Jimmy Carter's vice president, Walter Mondale.

- *1988:* Continued satisfaction with Reagan, a product of strong economic expansion and superpower summitry, produced an electoral endorsement of Reagan's vice president, George Bush. Bush was seen as Reagan's understudy and natural successor; the Democratic nominee, Michael Dukakis, offered too few convincing reasons to alter the voters' considered retrospective judgment.

- *1992:* A prolonged economic recession and weak growth in jobs plus Ross Perot's candidacy, which split the Republican base, denied a second term to George Bush, despite his many significant triumphs in foreign policy (the Persian Gulf War victory and arms control agreements, for example). In the end, voters decided to vote retrospectively, gambling on a little-known governor, Bill Clinton, rather than order up more of the same by reelecting Bush.

- *1996:* Similar to 1984, only with the party labels reversed, a healthy economy prompted Americans to retrospectively support President Bill Clinton in his quest for reelection. Voters also looked prospectively at the two candidates and again registered their support for President Clinton. Clinton then received relatively high marks by voters both for his stewardship during the first four years of his administration and his vision for the country's future.

■ Geraldine A. Ferraro earned her place in history as the first woman vice-presidential candidate on a national party ticket. In 1998, her attempt at a political comeback failed when she lost in her bid to become the New York state Democratic Party's nominee for the U.S. Senate. Here she speaks to the press after voting in 1998. (Photo courtesy: Jeff Geissler/AP/Wide World Photos)

Whether one agrees or disagrees with these election results, there is a rough justice at work here. When parties and presidents please the electorate, they are rewarded; when they preside over hard times, they are punished. A president is usually not responsible for all the good or bad developments that occur on his watch, but the voters nonetheless hold him accountable, not an unreasonable way for citizens to behave in a democracy.

On rare occasions, off-year congressional elections can produce mandates. In 1974 a tidal wave for Democrats produced a mandate to clean up politics after Watergate, while in 1994 Republicans enjoyed a similar wave and claimed a mandate for limiting government.

DIFFERENT KINDS OF ELECTIONS

So far we have referred mainly to presidential elections, but in the U.S. system, elections come in many varieties.

Primary Elections

In **primary elections,** voters decide which of the candidates within a party will represent the party's ticket in the general elections. The primaries themselves vary in kind. For example, **closed primaries** allow only a party's registered voters to cast a ballot, and **open primaries** allow independents and sometimes members of the other party to participate. (Figure 13.1 shows the states with open and closed primaries for presidential delegate selection.) Closed primaries are considered healthier for the party system ballot because they prevent members of one party from influencing the primaries of the opposition party. Studies of open primaries indicate that **crossover voting**—participation in the primary of a party with which the voter is not affiliated—occurs frequently.[3] On the other hand, little evidence exists that much **raiding** occurs—an *organized*

primary elections:

Elections in which voters decide which of the candidates within a party will represent the party in the general election.

closed primary:

A primary election in which only a party's registered voters are eligible to vote.

open primary:

A primary in which party members, independents, and sometimes members of the other party are allowed to vote.

crossover voting:

Participation in the primary of a party with which the voter is not affiliated

raiding:

An organized attempt by voters of one party to influence the primary results of the other party

Figure 13.1 Methods of Selecting Presidential Delegates

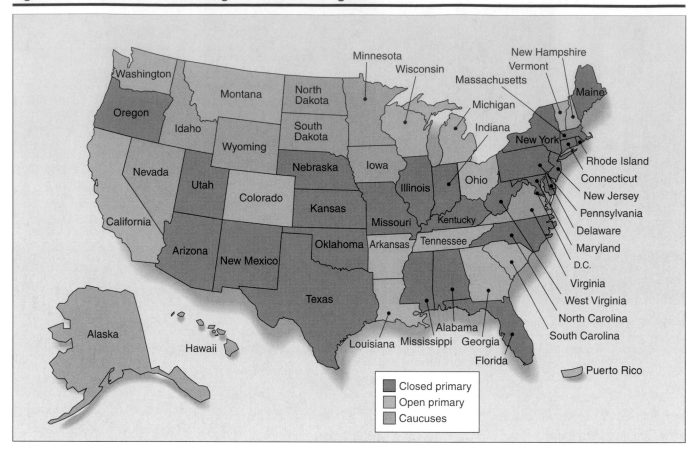

blanket primary:

A primary in which voters may cast ballots in either party's primary (but not both) on an office-by-office basis.

runoff primary:

A second primary election between the two candidates receiving the greatest number of votes in the first primary.

general election:

Election in which voters decide which candidates will actually fill elective public offices.

attempt by voters of one party to influence the primary results of the other party.[4] In the **blanket primary,** voters are permitted to vote in either party's primary (but not both) on an office-by-office basis. When none of the candidates in the initial primary secures a majority of the votes, there is a **runoff primary,** a contest between the two candidates with the greatest number of votes.

General Elections

Once the party candidates for various offices are chosen, general elections are held. In the **general election,** voters decide which candidates will actually fill the nation's elective public offices. These elections are held at many levels, including municipal, county, state, and national. While primaries are contests between the candidates within each party, general elections are contests between the candidates of opposing parties.

General elections come in many varieties, because Americans perceive the various offices as substantially different from one another. In sizing up presidential candidates, voters look for leadership and character, and they base their judgments partly on foreign policy and defense issues that do not arise in state and local elections. Leadership qualities are vital for gubernatorial and mayoral candidates, as are the nuts-and-bolts issues (such as taxes, schools, and roads) that dominate the concerns of state and local governments. Citizens often choose their congressional representatives very differently than they select presidents. Knowing much less about the candidates, people will sometimes base a vote on simple name identification and visibility. This way of deciding one's vote obviously helps incumbents and therefore to some degree explains the high reelection rates of incumbent U.S. representatives: Since World War II, 92 percent of all U.S. House members seeking another term have won, and in several recent election years the proportion has been above 95 percent. In 1994 the percentage of those members reelected dipped a little, to 90 percent. But in 1996, it again approached recent election averages when fully 94 percent of the lawmakers who sought reelection won. Still, as political scientist Gary Jacobson observes, greater name recognition *per se* is probably not the most important factor driving the incumbency advantage. More important is that incumbents are typically able to cultivate more favorable public images than are challengers.[5]

Initiative, Referendum, and Recall

Three other types of elections are the initiative, the referendum (plural, referenda), and the recall. Used in twenty-four states and the District of Columbia, initiatives and referenda involve voting on issues (as opposed to voting for candidates). An **initiative** is a process that allows citizens to propose legislation and submit it to the state electorate for popular vote, as long as they get a certain number of signatures on petitions supporting the proposal. Ballot initiatives have been the subject of growing controversy in the past decades, as critics charge that the process—which was intended to give citizens more direct control over policy-making—is now unduly influenced by interest groups and "the initiative industry" —"law firms that draft legislation, petition management firms that guarantee ballot access, direct-mail firms, and campaign consultants who specialize in initiative contests . . . ."[6]

For example, Proposition 209, one of the more famous and controversial initiatives, passed in 1996. This initiative eliminated state and local affirmative action programs in California for women and minorities in the areas of education, public employment, and contracting that give preferential treatment on the basis of sex, race, color, ethnicity, or national origin. A **referendum** is a procedure whereby the state legislature submits proposed legislation to the state's voters for approval. Although both of these electoral devices provide for more direct democracy, they are not problem-free. In the 1990 elections, for instance, California had so many referenda and initiatives on its ballot that the state printed a lengthy two-volume guide in an attempt to explain them all to voters.

The third type of election (or "deelection") found in many states is the **recall**, whereby an incumbent can be removed from office by popular vote. Recall elections are very rare, and sometimes they are thwarted by the official's resignation or impeachment prior to the vote. For example, Arizona Governor Evan Mecham was impeached and ousted in 1988 by the state legislature for mishandling campaign finances (among other offenses) just a few weeks before a recall election had been scheduled.

PRESIDENTIAL ELECTIONS

Variety aside, no U.S. election can compare to the presidential contest. This spectacle, held every four years, brings together all the elements of politics and attracts the most ambitious and energetic politicians to the national stage. The election itself, though altered by a front-loaded primary season, remains a collection of fifty separate state elections within each party in which delegates to each party's national convention are allotted. The election of delegates is followed in midsummer by the parties' grand national conventions and then by a final set of fifty separate state elections all held on the Tuesday after the first Monday in November. This lengthy process exhausts candidates and voters alike, but it allows the diversity of the United States to be displayed in ways a shorter, more homogeneous presidential election process could not. Every state has its moment in the sun, every local and regional problem a chance to be aired, every candidate an opportunity to break away from the pack.

Web Exploration

Select, evaluate, and debate upcoming referendum or initiatives currently under consideration in California, the "Referendum State". Go to www.awlonline.com/oconnor.

initiative:

A process that allows citizens to propose legislation and submit it to the state electorate for popular vote.

referendum:

A procedure whereby the state legislature submits proposed legislation to the state's voters for approval.

recall:

Removal of an incumbent from office by popular vote.

Web Exploration

To see how presidential candidates present themselves in the technology age of the 2000 race, go to www.awlonline.com/oconnor.

The state party organizations use a number of methods to elect national convention delegates:

1. *Winner-take-all:* Under this system the candidate who wins the most votes in a state secures all of that state's delegates. The Democrats moved away from this mode of delegate selection in 1976 and no longer permit its use because of the arguable unfairness to all candidates except the primary winner. Republicans do not prohibit winner-take-all contests, thus enabling a GOP candidate to amass a majority of delegates more quickly.

2. *Proportional representation:* Under this system, candidates who secure a threshold percentage of votes (usually around 15 percent) are awarded delegates in proportion to the number of popular votes won. This system is now strongly favored by the Democrats and is used in many states' Democratic primaries. Although proportional representation is probably the fairest way of allocating delegates to candidates, its downfall is that it renders majorities of delegates more difficult to accumulate and thus can lengthen the contest for the nomination.

3. *Proportional representation with bonus delegates; beauty contest with separate delegate selection; delegate selection with no beauty contest:* Used rarely, the first of these awards delegates to candidates in proportion to the popular vote won and then gives one bonus delegate to the winner of each district. The second serves as an indication of popular sentiment for the conventions to consider as they choose the actual delegates. Finally, under the "delegate selection with no beauty contest" system, the primary election chooses delegates to the national conventions who are not linked on the ballot to specific presidential contenders.

4. *The caucus:* The caucus is the oldest, most party-oriented method of choosing delegates to the national conventions. Traditionally, the caucus was a closed meeting of party members in each state that selected the party's choice for presidential candidate. In the late nineteenth and early twentieth centuries, however, these caucuses came to be viewed by many people as elitist and antidemocratic, and reformers succeeded in replacing them with direct primaries in most states. While there are still presidential nominating caucuses today, as in Iowa, they are now more open and attract a wider range of the party's membership. Indeed, political scientists Elaine Ciulla Kamarck and Kenneth M. Goldstein note that the new participatory caucus more closely resembles primary elections than they do the old, exclusive party caucuses.[7]

Web Exploration
To learn about the functions of the Federal Election Commission, the government agency that monitors and enforces campaign finance and election laws, go to www.awlonline.com/oconnor.

Primaries Versus Caucuses

The mix of preconvention contests has changed over the years, with the most pronounced trend being the shift to primaries: Only seventeen states held presidential primaries in 1968, compared with thirty-eight in 1992 and forty-two in 1996. Figure 13.1 shows which states use primaries (open and closed) and which use caucuses to select presidential delegates.

The increase in the number of primaries is supported by some people who claim that this type of election is more democratic. The primaries are open not only to party activists, but also to anyone, wealthy or poor, urban or rural, Northern or Southern, who wants to vote. Theoretically, then, representatives of all these groups have a chance of winning the presidency. Related to this idea, advocates argue that presidential primaries are the most representative means by which to nominate presidential candidates. They are a barometer of a candidate's popularity with the party rank and file. Finally, the proponents of presidential primaries claim that they constitute a rigorous test for the candidates, a chance to display under pressure some of the skills needed to be a successful president.

Critics of presidential primaries, however, see the situation somewhat differently. First, they argue that although it may be true that primaries attract more participants than do caucuses, this quantity is more than matched by the quality of caucus participation. Compared with the unenlightening minutes spent at the primary polls, caucus attendees spend several hours learning about politics and the party, listening to speeches by candidates or their representatives, and taking cues from party leaders and elected officials. Moreover, voters may not know very much about any of the field of candidates in a primary, or they may be excessively swayed by popularity polls, television ads, and other media presentations, such as newspaper and magazine coverage.

Critics also argue that the scheduling of primaries unfairly affects their outcomes. For example, the earliest open primary is in the small, atypical state of New Hampshire, which is heavily white and conservative, and it receives much more media coverage than it warrants simply because it is first. Such excessive coverage undoubtedly skews the picture for more populous states that hold their primaries later. The critics also argue that the qualities tested by the primary system are by no means a complete list of those a president needs to be successful. For instance, skill at playing the media game is by itself no guarantee of an effective presidency. Similarly, the exhausting schedule of the primaries may be a better test of a candidate's stamina than of his or her brain power.

The primary proponents have obviously had the better of the arguments so far, though the debate continues, as do efforts to experiment with the schedule of primaries. From time to time, proposals are made for **regional primaries.** Under this system, the nation would be divided into five or six geographic regions (such as the South or the Midwest). All the states in each region would hold their primary elections on the same day, with perhaps one regional election day per month from February through June of presidential election years. This change would certainly cut down on candidate wear and tear. Moreover, candidates would be inspired to focus more on regional issues. On the other hand, regional primaries would probably cost candidates at least as much as the state-by-state system, and the system might needlessly amplify the differences and create divisive rifts among the nation's regions.

Occasionally, a regional plan is adopted. In 1988, for instance, fourteen Southern and border South states joined together to hold simultaneous primaries on "Super Tuesday" (March 8) in order to maximize the South's impact on presidential politics. This was an attempt by conservative Democrats to influence the choice of the party nominee. Their effort failed, however, since the two biggest winners of Super Tuesday were liberals Jesse Jackson (who won six Southern states) and Michael Dukakis, who carried the megastates of Texas and Florida. This outcome occurred because, in general, the kinds of citizens who vote in Democratic primaries in the South are not greatly different from those who cast ballots in Northern Democratic primaries—most tend toward the liberal side of the ideological spectrum. This trend was repeated in 1996 with the construction of the so-called "Yankee Primary," with five of the six New England states holding their contests on March 5 (Massachusetts, Connecticut, Rhode Island, Vermont, and Maine) plus New York on March 7, and the continuation of a scaled-down Super Tuesday on March 12.

The primary schedule has also been altered, as we saw earlier in the chapter, by a process called **front-loading,** the tendency of states to choose an early date on the primary calendar. Seventy percent of all the delegates to both party conventions are now chosen before the end of March. This trend is hardly surprising, given the added press emphasis on the first contests and the voters' desire to cast their ballots before the competition is decided. The focus on early contests (such as the Iowa caucus and the New

■ Pat Buchanan announcing his third run for the Presidency, March 1999. Buchanan has no realistic chance to win the Presidency, but his longevity as a candidate ensures national attention for his political platform. (Photo courtesy: Rick Friedman/Black Star)

regional primary:

A proposed system in which the country would be divided into five or six geographic areas and all states in each region would hold their presidential primary elections on the same day.

front-loading:

The tendency of states to choose an early date on the primary calendar.

Hampshire primary), coupled with front-loading, can result in a party's being saddled with a nominee too quickly, before press scrutiny and voter reflection are given enough time to separate the wheat from the chaff. Front-loading has also had other important effects on the nomination process. First, a front-loaded primary schedule generally benefits the front-runner, since opponents have little time to turn the contest around once they fall behind. Second, front-loading advantages the candidate who can raise the bulk of the money *before* the nomination season begins, since there will be little opportunity to raise money once the process begins and since candidates will need to finance campaign efforts simultaneously in many states. Finally, front-loading has amplified the importance of the "invisible primary"—the year or so prior to the start of the official nomination season when candidates begin raising money and unofficially campaigning.[8]

THE PARTY CONVENTIONS

The seemingly endless nomination battle does have a conclusion: the national party convention held in the summer of presidential election years. The out-of-power party traditionally holds its convention first, in late July, followed by the party holding the White House in mid-August. Preempting some of prime-time television for four nights, these remarkable conclaves are difficult for the public to ignore; indeed, they are pivotal events in shaping the voters' perceptions of the candidates.

Yet the conventions once were much more: They were deliberative bodies that made actual decisions, where party leaders held sway and deals were sometimes cut in "smoke-filled rooms" to deliver nominations to little-known contenders called "dark horses" (see Roots of Government: The Party Conventions of 1920). But this era predated the modern emphasis on reform, primaries, and proportional representation, all of which have combined to make conventions mere ratifying agencies for preselected nominees.[9]

The first national convention was held in 1831 by the Anti-Masonic Party. In 1832 Andrew Jackson's nomination for reelection was ratified by the first Democratic National Convention. Just four years later, in 1836, Martin Van Buren became the first nonincumbent candidate nominated by a major party convention (the Democrats) to win the presidency.

From the 1830s to the mid-twentieth century, the national conventions remained primarily under the control of the important state and local party leaders, the so-called bosses or kingmakers, who would bargain within a splintered, decentralized party. During these years, state delegations in the convention consisted mostly of *uncommitted delegates* (that is, delegates who had not pledged to support any particular candidate). These delegates were selected by party leaders, a process that enabled the leaders to broker agreements with prominent national candidates. Under this system, a state party leader could exchange delegation support for valuable political plums—for instance, a Cabinet position or even the vice presidency—for an important state political figure.

Today the convention is fundamentally different. First, its importance as a party conclave, at which compromises on party leadership and policies can be worked out, has diminished. Second, although the convention still formally selects the presidential ticket, most nominations are settled well in advance. New preconvention political processes have lessened the role of the convention in three areas.

Delegate Selection.   The selection of delegates to the conventions is no longer the function of party leaders but of primary elections and grassroots caucuses. Moreover, recent reforms, especially by the Democratic Party, have generally weakened any remaining control by local party leaders over delegates. A prime example of such reform is the Democrats' abolition of the **unit rule,** a traditional party practice under which the majority of a state delegation (say, twenty-six of fifty delegates) could force the minority to vote for its candidate. Another new Democratic Party rule decrees that a state's delegates be chosen in proportion to the votes cast in its primary or caucus (so that, for example, a candidate who receives 30 percent of the vote gains about 30 percent of the convention delegates). This change has had the effect of requiring delegates

unit rule:

A traditional party practice under which the majority of a state delegation can force the minority to vote for its candidate.

Roots of Government

The Party Conventions of 1920

The national party convention of the present day is a different animal from that of the past. No longer is it a deliberative forum for choosing the party presidential nominee; rather, the convention now merely ratifies the choices of the preconvention state caucuses and primaries. A look at the Republican and Democratic Party conventions of 1920 illuminates the contrast between the old-style and new-style conventions.

The 1920 Republican convention featured a rift in the party. On one side was the party's old presidential faction, moderate and internationalist, with Abraham Lincoln and Theodore Roosevelt serving as its models. On the other side stood the more conservative wing of the party, with Senator Henry Cabot Lodge of Massachusetts at the helm and including most if not all of Capitol Hill's GOP leadership.

The "presidential" party during those days usually exerted more influence in presidential nominations than did the congressional party. But this changed in 1920, because Lodge's congressional party had garnered more power and influence during the latter part of Democratic President Woodrow Wilson's White House tenure (1913–21), when Wilson was seriously ill and his policies were under attack. Could the two wings of the party compromise on a presidential candidate for 1920? Any such compromise would undoubtedly be difficult to come by, because most potential candidates were aligned firmly with one wing of the party or the other.

Senator Warren G. Harding of Ohio was one possible compromise candidate. A small-town politician and one-time editor of a staunchly Republican Ohio newspaper, Harding had a reputation in the Senate based primarily on his ability to win allies in all factions of the Republican Party. But Harding's chances appeared bleak at the outset of the convention, and after the first ballot, he was considerably behind a number of other Republican hopefuls. Yet several frontrunners continued to deadlock in ballot after ballot, testing the patience of the delegates, who were baking in the hot Chicago summer.

The weather, combined with the seemingly unresolvable convention impasse, spurred a group of influential Senate leaders to meet at a nearby hotel room to attempt to hammer out a compromise—the classic gathering of party leaders behind the closed doors of a smoke-filled room. At the meeting, Harding's name continued to be floated.

Although most of the party leaders questioned the Ohioan's convictions and leadership abilities, he did have some attractive qualities: He was handsome (it was said that Harding "looked like a president"), he hailed from a politically important state, and he could be expected to work with leaders of both party factions. The GOP kingmakers therefore decided to test the waters with Harding, but agreed to reconvene later in the more likely event that the delegates rejected him. Harding soon went to work to ensure that no new meeting would be needed, however; he campaigned vigorously for his candidacy throughout the evening, roaming the halls and trying to convince any delegate he could find of his credibility as a candidate.

The deadlock at the convention continued for a few more ballots, but the frazzled delegates gradually realized that Harding perhaps was the only candidate with the potential to secure a majority. This realization sent frontrunners scurrying around the convention to build a coalition to stop Harding. They failed, however, and dark-horse candidate Harding—on the tenth ballot—secured enough votes to win the nomination.

The Democrats also needed a candidate to unite the party in 1920, one who could emphasize Wilson's successes yet downplay his failures. After thirty-eight ballots at the Democratic National Convention, no majority candidate had yet emerged, instilling in Wilson a hope that the party might again turn to him as the nominee, despite his deteriorated physical condition. It was one thing for the Democrats to remain loyal to Wilson—which they did by endorsing his policies and paying him homage in the party platform—and another for the party to nominate him for a third term. A return to Wilson was ultimately unnecessary, as Ohio Governor James M. Cox finally secured the nomination on the forty-fourth ballot.

Conditions are very different today. Nominations are no longer decided in smoke-filled back rooms at the conventions; instead, the critical moments occur well beforehand in the highly visible primary-and-caucus obstacle course that creates not dark horses but wornout horses by convention time.

to indicate their presidential preference at each stage of the selection process. Consequently, the majority of state delegates now come to the convention already committed to a candidate. Again, this diminishes the discretionary role of the convention and the party leaders' capacity to bargain.

In sum, the many complex changes in the rules of delegate selection have contributed to the loss of decision-making powers by the convention. And even though many of these changes were initiated by the Democratic Party, the Republicans were carried

■ The 1996 presidential candidates and their running mates. On the left, Vice President Al Gore, Jr., and President Bill Clinton. On the right, Republican presidential candidate Bob Dole and running mate Jack Kemp. (Photo courtesy: left, Dennis Brack/Black Star; right, Dave Zapotosky/AP/Wide World Photos)

superdelegate:

Delegate slot to the Democratic Party's national convention that is reserved for an elected party official.

along as many Democrat-controlled state legislatures enacted the reforms as state laws. There have been new rules to counteract some of these changes, however. For instance, since 1984 the number of delegate slots reserved for elected Democratic Party officials—called **superdelegates**—has been increased in the hope of adding stability to the Democratic convention. Before 1972 most delegates to a Democratic National Convention were not bound by primary results to support a particular candidate for president. This freedom to maneuver meant that conventions could be exciting and somewhat unpredictable gatherings, where last-minute events and deals could sway wavering delegates. Superdelegates are supposed to be party professionals concerned with winning the general election contest, not simply amateur ideologues concerned mainly with satisfying their policy appetites. All Democratic governors and 80 percent of the congressional Democrats, among others, are now included as voting delegates at the convention.

National Candidates and Issues.   The political perceptions and loyalties of voters are now influenced largely by national candidates and issues, a factor that has undoubtedly served to diminish the power of state and local party leaders at the convention. The national candidates have usurped the autonomy of state party leaders with their preconvention ability to garner delegate support. And issues, increasingly national in scope, are significantly more important to the new, issue-oriented party activists than to the party professionals, who, prior to the late 1960s, had a monopoly on the management of party affairs.

The News Media.   The mass media have helped to transform the national conventions into political extravaganzas for the television audience's consumption. They have also helped to preempt the convention, by keeping count of the delegates committed to the candidates; as a result, the delegates and even the candidates now have much more information about nomination politics well before the convention. From the strategies of candidates to the commitments of individual delegates, the media cover it all. Even the bargaining within key party committees, formerly done in secret, is now subject to some public scrutiny, thanks to open meetings. The business of the convention has been irrevocably shaped to accommodate television: desirous of presenting a unified image to kick off a strong general election campaign, the parties assign impor-

■ Elizabeth Dole delivered an extraordinarily popular speech at the 1996 Republican National Convention. The success of the speech has led to Elizabeth Dole's viability as a candidate in the year 2000 presidential race. (Photo courtesy: Brooks Kraft/Sygma)

tant roles to attractive speakers, and most crucial party affairs are saved for prime-time viewing hours.

Extensive media coverage of the convention has its pros and cons. On the one hand, such exposure helps the party launch its presidential campaign with fanfare. On the other hand, it can expose rifts within a party, as happened in 1968 at the Democratic convention in Chicago. Dissension was obvious when "hawks," supporting the Vietnam War and President Lyndon B. Johnson, clashed with the antiwar "doves" both on the convention floor and in street demonstrations outside the convention hall. Whatever the case, it is obvious that saturation media coverage of preelection events has led to the public's loss of anticipation and exhilaration about convention events.

Some reformers have spoken of replacing the conventions with national direct primaries, but it is unlikely that the parties would agree to this. Although its role in nominating the presidential ticket has often been reduced to formality, the convention is still a valuable political institution. After all, it is the only real arena where the national political parties can command a nearly universal audience while they celebrate past achievements and project their hopes for the future.

Who Are the Delegates?   In one sense, party conventions are microcosms of the United States: every state, most localities, and all races and creeds find some representation there. (For some historic "firsts" for women and the conventions, see Table 13.1: Women and the Conventions.) Yet delegates are an unusual and unrepresentative collection of people in many other ways. It is not just their exceptionally keen interest in politics that distinguishes delegates. These activists also are ideologically more pure and financially better off than most Americans.

In 1996, for example, both parties drew their delegates from an elite group that had income and educational levels far above the average American's. The distinctiveness of each party was also apparent. Democratic delegates tended to be younger and were more likely to be African American, female, divorced or single, and a member of a labor union. Republicans drew their delegates more heavily from people over forty-five years

Table 13.1   Women and the Conventions

Since 1980, Democratic Party rules have required that women comprise
50 percent of the delegates to its national convention. The Republican Party
has no similar quotas. Nevertheless, both parties have tried to increase the role
of women at the convention. Some "firsts" for women at conventions include:

1876	First woman to address a national convention
1890	First women delegates to conventions of both parties
1940	First woman to nominate a presidential candidate
1951	First woman asked to chair a national party
1972	First woman keynote speaker
1984	First major party woman nominated for vice president (Democrat Geraldine Ferraro)
1996	Wives of both nominees make major addresses

SOURCE: Center for the Study of American Women in Politics.

old, whites, married men, and Protestants. GOP conventioneers were also more likely to be elected or appointed officials and to have attended previous party conventions.

The contrast in the two parties' delegations is no accident; it reflects not only the differences in the party constituencies, but also conscious decisions made by party leaders. After the tumultuous 1968 Democratic National Convention (which, as noted, was torn by dissent over the Vietnam War), Democrats formed a commission to examine the condition of the party and to propose changes in its structure. As a direct consequence of the commission's work, the 1972 Democratic convention was the most broadly representative ever of women, African Americans, and young people, because the party required these groups to be included in state delegations in rough proportion to their numbers in the population of each state. (State delegations failing this test were not seated.) This new mandate was very controversial, and it has since been watered down considerably. Nonetheless, women and blacks are still more fully represented at Democratic conventions (as Table 13.2 shows) than at Republican conventions. GOP leaders have placed much less emphasis on proportional representation, and instead of procedural reforms, Republicans have concentrated on strengthening their state organizations and fund-raising efforts, a strategy that has clearly paid off at the polls in the elections of 1980, 1984, and 1988, which saw Republicans elected as president.

The delegates in each party also exemplify the philosophical gulf separating the two parties (see Table 13.3). Democratic delegates are well to the left of their own party's voters on most issues, and even further away from the opinions held by the nation's electorate as a whole. Republican delegates are a mirror image of their opponents—considerably to the right of GOP voters and even more so of the entire electorate. Although it is sometimes said that the two major parties do not present U.S. citizens with a "clear choice" of candidates, it is possible to argue the contrary. Our politics are perhaps too polarized, with the great majority of Americans, moderates and pragmatists overwhelmingly, left underrepresented by parties too fond of ideological purity.

The philosophical divergence is usually reflected in the party platforms, even in years such as 1996, when both parties attempted to water down their rhetoric and smooth over ideological differences (see Highlight 13.1: Selected Contrasts in the 1996 Party Platforms). (The Democrats did so in 1996; the Republicans have done so in earlier years, as in 1968.)

The Electoral College: How Presidents Are Elected

Given the enormous amount of energy, money, and time expended to nominate two major-party presidential contenders, it is difficult to believe that the general election could be more arduous than the nominating contests, but it usually is. The actual campaign for the presidency (and other offices) is described in chapter 14, but the object of

Table 13.2   A Comparison of Delegates to the 1996 Presidential Nominating Conventions*

Ideology	Democratic Delegates	Republican Delegates	All Voters in Nov. 1996 Presidential Election
Liberal	36%	1%	21%
Moderate	47	19	46
Conservative	3	74	31
Age			
18–29	4%	2%	16%
30–39	12	14	21
40–59	60	52	38
60 and older	24	31	25
Race/Ethnicity			
White	67%	92%	81%
Black	21	2	11
Hispanic	6	2	4
Other	6	3	3
Labor Union			
Member	34%	2%	11%
Not a member	66	98	89
Sex			
Male	43%	61%	48%
Female	57	39	52

*Margin of sampling error is plus or minus 4.5 percentage points when figures do not include those who declined to answer the question; the margin of error is plus or minus 2 percentage points for all others. Other totals may not add up to 100 percent because of rounding.

SOURCE: Figures in the first two columns are from a *Washington Post* telephone poll of 511 Republican delegates from July to August 1996, and 496 Democratic delegates from June to July. Figures in the last column are adapted from the Voter Research & Surveys (VRS) poll of 15,232 Americans as they exited from their voting booths on November 5, 1996. VRS is an association of ABC News, CNN, CBS News, and NBC News.

the exercise is clear: winning a majority of the **electoral college.** This uniquely American institution consists of representatives of each state who cast the final ballots that actually elect a president.

The electoral college was the result of a compromise between Framers like Roger Sherman and Elbridge Gerry, who argued for selection of the president by the Congress, and those such as James Madison, James Wilson, and Gouverneur Morris, who favored selection by direct popular election. The electoral college compromise, while not a perfect solution, had practical benefits. Since there were no mass media in those days, it is unlikely that common citizens, even reasonably informed ones, would know much about a candidate from another state. This situation could have left voters with no choice but to vote for someone from their own state, thus making it improbable that any candidate would secure a national majority. On the other hand, the **electors** (members of the electoral college) would be men of character with a solid knowledge of national politics who were able to identify, agree on, and select prominent national statesmen. There are three essentials to understanding the Framers' design of the electoral college: (1) It was meant to work without political parties, (2) it was designed to cover both the nominating and electing phases of presidential selection, and (3) it was constructed to produce a nonpartisan president.

The machinery of the electoral college was somewhat complex. Each state designated electors (through appointment or popular vote) equal in number to the sum of

electoral college:
Representatives of each state who cast the final ballots that actually elect a president.

elector:
Member of the electoral college chosen by methods determined in each state.

Table 13.3 Comparison of the Views of the Public with Those of Delegates to the 1996 Presidential Nominating Conventions*

Question: "I am going to read a few statements. After each, please tell me if you agree with the statement or disagree with it, or if, perhaps, you have no opinion about the statement." (Figures show percentage who agreed with the statement.)

	All Voters	Democratic Delegates	Democratic Voters	Republican Delegates	Republican Voters
A. A constitutional amendment to require a balanced federal budget	82%	32%	77%	88%	87%
B. The death penalty for people convicted of murder.	76	48	67	88	88
C. Cut off public assistance payments a poor person can receive after a maximum of live years.	73	38	67	88	81
D. Ban the sale of most assault weapons.	73	93	78	47	67
E. Impose a five-year freeze on legal immigration.	59	15	57	29	65
F. Reduce spending on social programs	55	20	44	84	71
G. Reduce spending on defense and the military.	44	65	47	11	29
H. Amend the U.S. Constitution to allow organized prayer in public schools.	66	19	66	50	73
I. Cancel affirmative action programs giving preference to women, blacks and other minorities.	45	11	31	83	63
J. Bar illegal immigrants from public schools, hospitals, and other state run social services.	48	16	36	65	61

*Margins of sampling error are plus or minus 5 percentage points for figures based on delegates (Republicans and Democrats) and 3 points for figures based on all voters.

SOURCE: Figures are from a *Washington Post* telephone poll of Republican delegates August 11, 1996; Democratic delegates, August 25, 1996.

its representation in the House and Senate. Figure 13.2 shows a map of the United States drawn in proportion to their electoral college votes. The electors met in their respective states. Each elector had two votes for president, an attempt by the Founders to ensure that at least one candidate would secure a majority of electoral votes needed for victory. The candidate with the most votes, providing he received votes from a majority of the total number of electors, won the presidency; the candidate securing the second greatest number of votes won the vice presidency. If two candidates received the same number of votes and both had a majority of electors, the election was decided in the House of Representatives, with each state delegation acting as a unit and having one vote to cast. In the event that no candidate secured a majority, the election would also be decided in the House, with each state delegation having one vote to cast for any of the top five electoral vote-getters. In both of these scenarios, a majority of the total number of states was necessary to secure victory.

But the Framers' idea of nonpartisan presidential elections lasted barely a decade, ending for the most part after George Washington's two terms. In 1796 their arrangement for presidential selection produced a president and vice president with markedly different political philosophies, a circumstance much less likely in modern times.

The Election of 1800

The republic's fourth presidential election revealed a flaw in the Framers' plan. In 1800 Thomas Jefferson and Aaron Burr were, respectively, the presidential and vice-presidential candidates advanced by the Democratic–Republican Party, and supporters of the Democratic-Republican Party controlled a majority of the electoral college. Accordingly, each Democratic–Republican elector in the states cast one of his two votes for Jefferson and the other one for Burr, a situation that resulted in a tie for the presidency

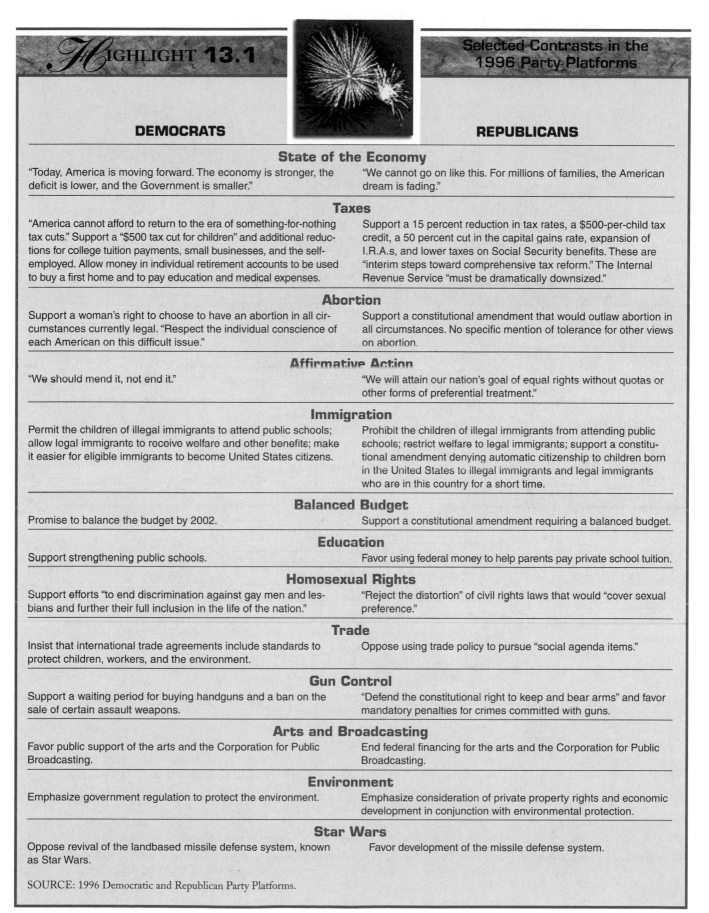

HIGHLIGHT 13.1 — Selected Contrasts in the 1996 Party Platforms

DEMOCRATS	REPUBLICANS

State of the Economy

"Today, America is moving forward. The economy is stronger, the deficit is lower, and the Government is smaller."

"We cannot go on like this. For millions of families, the American dream is fading."

Taxes

"America cannot afford to return to the era of something-for-nothing tax cuts." Support a "$500 tax cut for children" and additional reductions for college tuition payments, small businesses, and the self-employed. Allow money in individual retirement accounts to be used to buy a first home and to pay education and medical expenses.

Support a 15 percent reduction in tax rates, a $500-per-child tax credit, a 50 percent cut in the capital gains rate, expansion of I.R.A.s, and lower taxes on Social Security benefits. These are "interim steps toward comprehensive tax reform." The Internal Revenue Service "must be dramatically downsized."

Abortion

Support a woman's right to choose to have an abortion in all circumstances currently legal. "Respect the individual conscience of each American on this difficult issue."

Support a constitutional amendment that would outlaw abortion in all circumstances. No specific mention of tolerance for other views on abortion.

Affirmative Action

"We should mend it, not end it."

"We will attain our nation's goal of equal rights without quotas or other forms of preferential treatment."

Immigration

Permit the children of illegal immigrants to attend public schools; allow legal immigrants to receive welfare and other benefits; make it easier for eligible immigrants to become United States citizens.

Prohibit the children of illegal immigrants from attending public schools; restrict welfare to legal immigrants; support a constitutional amendment denying automatic citizenship to children born in the United States to illegal immigrants and legal immigrants who are in this country for a short time.

Balanced Budget

Promise to balance the budget by 2002.

Support a constitutional amendment requiring a balanced budget.

Education

Support strengthening public schools.

Favor using federal money to help parents pay private school tuition.

Homosexual Rights

Support efforts "to end discrimination against gay men and lesbians and further their full inclusion in the life of the nation."

"Reject the distortion" of civil rights laws that would "cover sexual preference."

Trade

Insist that international trade agreements include standards to protect children, workers, and the environment.

Oppose using trade policy to pursue "social agenda items."

Gun Control

Support a waiting period for buying handguns and a ban on the sale of certain assault weapons.

"Defend the constitutional right to keep and bear arms" and favor mandatory penalties for crimes committed with guns.

Arts and Broadcasting

Favor public support of the arts and the Corporation for Public Broadcasting.

End federal financing for the arts and the Corporation for Public Broadcasting.

Environment

Emphasize government regulation to protect the environment.

Emphasize consideration of private property rights and economic development in conjunction with environmental protection.

Star Wars

Oppose revival of the landbased missile defense system, known as Star Wars.

Favor development of the missile defense system.

SOURCE: 1996 Democratic and Republican Party Platforms.

Figure 13.2 The States Drawn in Proportion to their Electoral College Votes

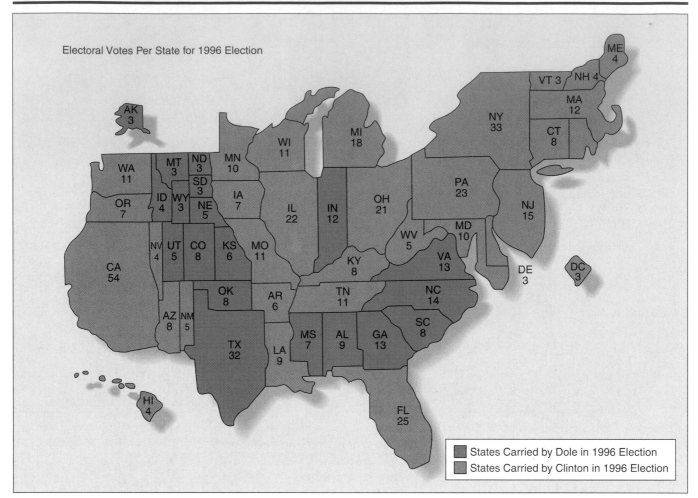

Electoral Votes Per State for 1996 Election

■ States Carried by Dole in 1996 Election
■ States Carried by Clinton in 1996 Election

This table visually represents the electors "weight" of the 50 states.

Note: States drawn in proportion to number of electoral votes. Total electoral votes: 538

between Jefferson and Burr, since there was no way under the constitutional arrangements for electors to earmark their votes separately for president and vice president. And even though most understood Jefferson to be the actual choice for president, the Constitution mandated that a tie be decided by the House of Representatives. And so it was, of course, and in Jefferson's favor, but only after much energy was expended to persuade lame-duck Federalists not to give Burr the presidency.

The Twelfth Amendment, ratified in 1804 and still the constitutional foundation for presidential elections, was an attempt to remedy the confusion between the selection of vice presidents and presidents that beset the election of 1800. The amendment provided for separate elections for each office, with each elector having only one vote to cast for each. In the event of a tie or when no candidate received a majority of the total number of electors, the election still went to the House of Representatives; now, however, each state delegation would have one vote to cast for one of the three candidates who had received the greatest number of electoral votes.

The electoral college modified by the Twelfth Amendment has fared better than the college as originally designed, but it has not been problem-free. For example, in the 1824 election between John Quincy Adams and Andrew Jackson, neither presidential candidate secured a majority of electoral votes, once again throwing the election into the House. Despite the fact that Jackson had more electoral and popular votes than Adams, the House voted for the latter as president. On two other occasions in the nineteenth century, the presidential candidate with fewer popular votes than his opponent won the presidency. In the 1876 contest between Republican Rutherford B. Hayes and Democrat Samuel J. Tilden, no candidate received a majority of electoral votes; the House decided in Hayes's favor even though he had only one more (disputed) electoral vote and 250,000 fewer popular votes than Tilden. In the election of 1888, President Grover Cleveland secured about 100,000 more popular votes than did Benjamin Harrison, yet Harrison won a majority of the electoral college vote, and with it the presidency.

The Electoral College in the Twentieth Century.

Although generally more stable than the previous two centuries, the twentieth century has also witnessed a number of near-crises pertaining to the electoral college. For instance, in the turbulent year of 1968, the possibility that the presidential election would be decided in the House increased considerably with the entrance into the race of third-party candidate George Wallace. And the election of 1976 was almost a repeat of those nineteenth-century contests in which the candidate with fewer popular votes won the presidency: Even though Democrat Jimmy Carter received about 1.7 million more popular votes than Republican Gerald Ford, a switch of some 8,000 popular votes in Ohio and Hawaii would have secured for Ford enough votes to win the electoral college, and hence the presidency. Had Ross Perot stayed in the 1992 presidential contest without his summer hiatus, it is possible that he could have thrown the election into the House of Representatives. His support had registered from 30 percent to 36 percent in the polls for much of the spring and early summer of 1992. When he reentered the race, some of that backing had evaporated, and he finished with 19 percent of the vote and carried no states. However, Perot drained a substantial number of Republican votes from George Bush, thus splitting the GOP base. This enabled Clinton to win many normally GOP-leaning states such as Georgia, Nevada, and Montana, although he carried them with well less than a majority of the votes.

Patterns of Presidential Elections

The electoral college results reveal more over time than simply who won the presidency. They show which party and which region(s) are coming to dominance and how voters may be changing party allegiances in response to new issues and generational changes.

Party Realignments.

Usually such movements are gradual, but occasionally the political equivalent of a major earthquake swiftly and dramatically alters the landscape. During these rare events, called **party realignments**,[10] existing party affiliations are subject to upheaval: Many voters may change parties, and the youngest age group of voters may permanently adopt the label of the newly dominant party. Until recent times, at least, party realignments have been spaced about thirty-six years apart in the U.S. experience.

A major realignment is precipitated by one or more **critical elections,** which may polarize voters around new issues and personalities in reaction to crucial developments, such as a war or an economic depression. In Britain, for example, the first postwar election held in 1945 was critical, since it ushered the Labour Party into power for the first time and introduced to Britain a new interventionist agenda in the fields of economic and social welfare policies.

In the entire history of the United States, there have been six party realignments; three tumultuous eras in particular have produced significant critical elections (see Figure 13.3). First, during the period leading up to the Civil War, the Whig Party gradually dissolved and the Republican Party developed and won the presidency. Second, the populist radicalization of the Democratic Party in the 1890s enabled the Republicans to greatly strengthen their majority status and make lasting gains in voter attachments. Third, the Great Depression of the 1930s propelled the Democrats to power, causing large numbers of voters to repudiate the GOP and embrace the Democratic Party. In each of these cases, fundamental and enduring alterations in the party equation resulted.

The last confirmed major realignment, then, happened in the 1928–36 period, as Republican Herbert Hoover's presidency was held to one term because of voter anger about the Depression. In 1932 Democrat Franklin D. Roosevelt swept to power as the

Web Exploration
To access the most up-to-date, high-quality data on voting, public opinion, and political participation, go to www.awlonline.com/oconnor.

party realignment:

A shifting of party coalition groupings in the electorate that remains in place for several elections.

critical election:

An election that signals a party realignment through voter polarization around new issues.

Figure 13.3   Electoral College Results for Three Realigning Presidential Contests

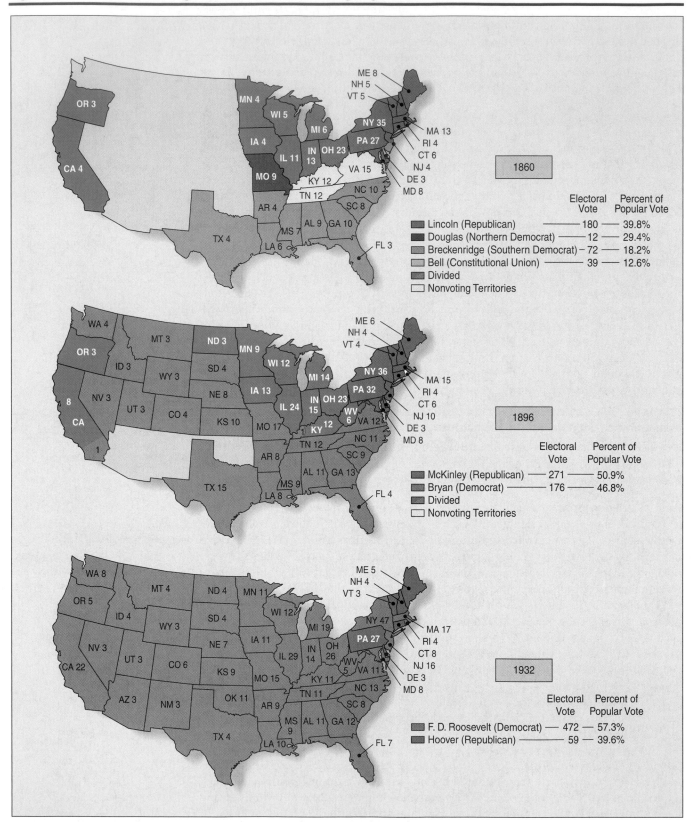

This figure shows the electoral votes in three crucial elections of our century.

electorate decisively rejected Hoover and the Republicans. This dramatic vote of "no confidence" was followed by substantial changes in policy by the new president, who demonstrated in fact or at least in appearance that his policies were effective. The people responded to his success, accepted his vision of society, and ratified their choice of the new president's party in subsequent presidential and congressional elections.

Simultaneously, the former majority party (Republican) reluctantly but inevitably adjusted to its new minority role. So strong was the new partisan attachment for most voters that even when short-term issues and personalities that favored the Republican Party dislodged the Democrats from power, the basic distribution of party loyalties did not shift significantly. In 1952, 1956, 1968, and 1972, then, Republicans won the presidency, but the New Deal Democratic coalition was still visible in the voting patterns, and it survived to emerge again in future elections.

With the aid of timely circumstances, realignments are accomplished in two main ways.[11] Some voters are simply converted from one party to the other by the issues and candidates of the time. New voters may also be mobilized into action: Immigrants, young voters, and previous nonvoters may become motivated and then absorbed into a new governing majority. However vibrant and potent party coalitions may be at first, as they age, tensions increase and grievances accumulate. The majority's original reason for existing fades, and new generations neither remember the traumatic events that originally brought about the realignment nor possess the stalwart party identifications of their ancestors. New issues arise, producing conflicts that can be resolved only by a breakup of old alignments and a reshuffling of individual and group party loyalties. Viewed in historical perspective, party realignment has been a mechanism that ensures stability by controlling unavoidable change.

A critical realigning era is by no means the only occasion when changes in partisan affiliation are accommodated. In truth, every election produces realignment to some degree, since some individuals are undoubtedly pushed to change parties by events and by their reactions to the candidates. Recent research suggests that partisanship is much more responsive to current issues and personalities than had been believed earlier, and that major realignments are just extreme cases of the kind of changes in party loyalty registered every year.[12]

Secular Realignment.   Although the term *realignment* is usually applied only if momentous events such as war or depression produce enduring and substantial alterations in the party coalitions, political scientists have long recognized that a more gradual rearrangement of party coalitions could occur.[13] Called **secular realignment,** this piecemeal process depends not on convulsive shocks to the political system, but on slow, almost barely discernable demographic shifts—the shrinking of one party's base of support and the enlargement of the other's, for example—or simple generational replacement (that is, the dying off of the older generation and the maturing of the younger generation). A recent version of this theory, termed "rolling realignment,"[14] argues that in an era of weaker party attachments (such as we currently are experiencing), a dramatic, full-scale realignment may not be possible. Still, a critical mass of voters may be attracted for years to one party's banner in waves or streams, if that party's leadership and performance are consistently exemplary.

Some scholars and political observers also contend that the decline of party affiliation has in essence left the electorate dealigned and incapable of being realigned as long as party ties remain tenuous for so many voters.[15] Voters shift with greater ease between the parties during dealignment, but little permanence or intensity exists in identifications made and held so lightly. If nothing else, the obsolescence of realignment theory may be indicated by the calendar; if major realignments occur roughly every thirty-six years, then we are long overdue. The last major realignment took place between 1928 and 1936, and so the next one might have been expected in the late 1960s and early 1970s.

secular realignment:

The gradual rearrangement of party coalitions, based more on demographic shifts than on shocks to the political system.

As the trends toward ticket-splitting, partisan independence, and voter volatility suggest, there is little question that we have been moving through an unstable and somewhat "dealigned" period at least since the 1970s. The foremost political question today is whether dealignment will continue (and in what form) or whether a major realignment is in the offing. Each previous dealignment has been a precursor of realignment,[16] but realignment need not succeed dealignment, especially under modern conditions.

Clearly, major changes in the U.S. electorate have been occurring, but these changes may or may not constitute a major critical realignment of party balance. The Democrats are not the dominant party they once were, but the GOP has not obtained majority status, either. The struggle between the parties for dominance continues, and the outcome is as yet uncertain.

CONGRESSIONAL ELECTIONS

Many similar elements are present in different kinds of elections: Candidates, voters, issues, and television advertisements are constants. But there are distinctive aspects of each kind of election as well. Compared with presidential elections, congressional elections are a different animal.

First, most candidates for Congress labor in relative obscurity. While there are some celebrity nominees for Congress—television stars, sports heroes, even local TV news anchors—the vast majority of party nominees are little-known state legislators and local office holders. For them, just getting known, establishing name identification, is the biggest battle. No major-party presidential nominee need worry about this elementary stage because so much media attention is focused on the race for the White House. This is not so for most congressional contests; elections for spots in the House of Representatives receive remarkably little coverage in many states and communities.

POLITICS NOW

Senate Race Steals Spotlight

Every now and then, a race for a governorship or U.S. Senate seat becomes the headline race of an election season, defining the political year or providing an exceptionally memorable match-up. It was clear from the moment that First Lady Hillary Rodham Clinton expressed interest in an open New York Senate seat that 2000 would be such a year and the contest in the Empire State would be the race. It was not simply that a First Lady had never in American history run for any public office, nor that her likely opponent, New York City mayor Rudolph Giuliani, was almost as well known as Clinton and an exceptionally feisty campaigner. Rather, the Senate contest would top the charts because it would inevitably encapsulate all of the important current issues and personalities in American politics today, from President Clinton and his scandals to splits within the Republican party and the voracity of the press.

In early 1999, just as the Clinton impeachment was drawing to a close, a rumor wafted up from the White House that Mrs. Clinton might consider the Senate contest. Most people discounted the rumors as totally incredible. Very quickly, however, Clinton aides and political consultants began to be approached for advice, and no sooner had they hung up the phone than they appeared on cable TV talk shows to discuss what they knew or suspected. In fact, the Clintons really had decided to live in New York, and Mrs. Clinton would make a dramatic departure from her past. No longer would she labor to support her husband's career and cover up his foibles—now she would strike out on her own.

The immediate question was whether or not New York would support a carpetbagger. In fact, in an earlier headline race that helped define an election year, New Yorkers had already done so, by voting former U.S. Attorney General Robert Kennedy to a handy victory over a Republican incumbent in 1964. One difference between the two cases is that Kennedy was revered as the inheritor of his assassinated brother's political legacy, whereas Mrs. Clinton presumably hopes not to inherit many parts of Bill Clinton's baggage.

Nevertheless, the press are likely to tear into a candidate in a New York minute and are certain to review and revive all the issues of the Clinton era. Giuliani's prominence, however, will ensure that all the events of his own two mayoral terms come in for scrutiny as well. Whatever the outcome, the race will be sure to satisfy anyone's taste for political drama!

The Incumbency Advantage

Under these circumstances the advantages of **incumbency** (that is, already being in office) are enhanced, and a kind of electoral inertia takes hold: Those people in office tend to remain in office. Every year, the average member of the U.S. House of Representatives expends about $750,000 in taxpayer funds to run the office. Much of this money directly or indirectly promotes the legislator by means of mass mailings and *constituency services,* the term used to describe a wide array of assistance provided by a member of Congress to voters in need (for example, tracking a lost Social Security check, helping a veteran receive disputed benefits, or finding a summer internship for a college student). Indeed, one political scientist found that constituents for whom a House incumbent did casework gave the incumbent considerably higher evaluations than constituents who did not benefit from such casework.[17] In addition to these institutional means of self-promotion, most incumbents are highly visible in their districts. They have easy access to local media, cut ribbons galore, attend important local funerals, and speak frequently at meetings and community events. Nearly a fourth of the people in an average congressional district claim to have met their representative, and about half recognize their legislator's name without prompting. This spending and visibility pay off: reelection rates for sitting House members range well above 90 percent in most election years, and research shows district attentiveness is at least partly responsible for incumbents' electoral safety.[18]

Frequently, the reelection rate for senators is as high, but not always. In a "bad" year for House incumbents, "only" 88 percent will win (as in the Watergate year of 1974), but the senatorial reelection rate can drop much lower on occasion (to 60 percent in the 1980 Reagan landslide, for example). There is a good reason for this lower senatorial reelection rate. A Senate election is often a high-visibility contest; it receives much more publicity than a House race. So while House incumbents remain protected and insulated in part because few voters pay attention to their little known challengers, a Senate-seat challenger can become well known more easily and thus be in a better position to defeat an incumbent.

The 1994 congressional elections are yet another example of the power of incumbency. The press focused on the Republican takeover of both houses of Congress, naturally enough, but another perspective is provided by the reelection rates for incumbents. More than 90 percent of the sitting representatives and senators who sought reelection won another term, despite electoral conditions that were termed a tidal wave.

Despite the attention from the media, which suggested a more dramatic change than really occurred, approximately 98 percent of incumbent senators and congressmen sought reelection successfully in 1998. The biggest concern to incumbents that year, especially to Republicans, was a frequently reduced mandate. While still enough to give them the necessary majority, the closer margins of victory indicated a significant degree of voter dissatisfaction.

Redistricting, Scandals, and Coattails

For the relatively few incumbent members of Congress who do lose their reelection bids, three explanations are paramount: redistricting, scandals, and coattails. Every ten years, after the census, all congressional

incumbency:

The condition of already holding elected office.

■ Mary Bono, center right, wife of the late U.S. Congressman and recording star Sonny Bono, celebrating with her family and supporters after winning a special election for the seat vacated by her husband. (Photo courtesy: Susan Sterner/AP/Wide World Photos)

district lines are redrawn (in states with more than one congressperson) so that every legislator represents about the same number of citizens. The U.S. Constitution requires that a census, which entails the counting of all Americans, be conducted every ten years. Until the first census could be taken, the Constitution fixed the number of representatives in the House at sixty-five. In 1790, then, one member represented 37,000 people. As the population of the new nation grew and states were added to the Union, the House became larger and larger. In 1910 it expanded to 435 members, and in 1929 its size was fixed at that number by statute.

Because the Constitution requires that representation in the House be based on state population, congressional districts must be redrawn by state legislatures to reflect population shifts, so that each member in Congress will represent approximately the same number of residents. This process of redrawing congressional districts to reflect increases or decreases in seats allotted to the states, as well as population shifts within a state, is called **redistricting.** When shifts occur in the national population, states gain or lose congressional seats. For example, in the 1990 Census (as in most censuses since 1960), many Northeastern states showed a population decline and lost congressional seats, whereas states in the South, Southwest, and West (the sunbelt) showed great population growth and gained seats. For example, California picked up seven seats in 1990 for a total of fifty-two seats. In contrast, Alaska, Delaware, Montana, North Dakota, South Dakota, Vermont, and Wyoming, the least populous states, have only one representative each (but two senators).

Through redistricting, the political party in each statehouse with the greatest number of members tries to assure that the maximum number of its party members can be elected to Congress. This redistricting process, which has gone on since the first census in 1790, often involves what is called **gerrymandering** (see Figure 13.4).

Creative redistricting and the actions of state legislators have often created problems that have ended up in litigation. Over the years, the Supreme Court has ruled that:

- Congressional as well as state legislative districts must be apportioned on the basis of population.[19]
- Purposeful gerrymandering of a congressional district to dilute minority strength is illegal under the Voting Rights Act of 1965.[20]
- Redrawing of districts for obvious racial purposes to enhance minority representation is unconstitutional because it denies the constitutional rights of white citizens.[21]

Redistricting inevitably puts some incumbents in the same districts as other incumbents, and weakens the base of other congresspersons by adding territory favorable to the opposition party. In 1992 ten incumbents were paired together—five therefore lost—and about a dozen more incumbents were defeated in part because of unfavorable redistricting. The number of incumbents who actually lose their reelections because of redistricting is lessened by the strategic behavior of redistricted members—who often choose to retire rather than wage an expensive (and likely unsuccessful) reelection battle.[22]

Scandals come in many varieties in this age of the investigative press. The old standby of financial impropriety (bribery and payoffs, for example) has been supplemented by other forms of career-ending incidents, such as personal improprieties (sexual escapades, for instance). As with redistricting, the number of incumbents who actually lose their reelections because of a scandal is reduced by the propensity of implicated members to retire rather than seek reelection.[23] The power of incumbency is so strong, however, that many legislators survive even serious scandal to win reelection. Congressman Barney Frank (D–Mass.), for instance, an acknowledged homosexual, hired a male prostitute who ran a prostitution service out of Frank's apartment in Washington. This situation became public knowledge in 1989. Though Frank claimed ignorance of the man's activities, he admitted having some of his parking tickets "fixed." Despite the sordid nature of this arrangement, most of Frank's constituents were satisfied with his representation of them and easily reelected him in 1990 and continued to reelect him.

redistricting:

The redrawing of congressional districts to reflect increases or decreases in seats allotted to the states, as well as population shifts within a state.

gerrymandering:

The legislative process through which the majority party in each statehouse tries to assure that the maximum number of representatives from its political party can be elected to Congress through the redrawing of legislative districts.

Figure 13.4   Gerrymandering

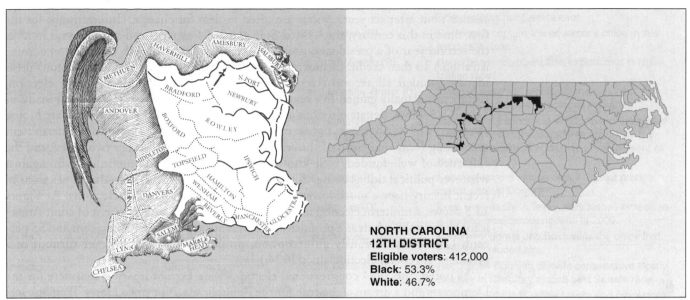

The Original "Gerrymander" Cartoon, 1812   Contested 1990 North Carolina Gerrymander

**NORTH CAROLINA
12TH DISTRICT
Eligible voters:** 412,000
Black: 53.3%
White: 46.7%

Two drawings—one a mocking cartoon, the other all too real—showing the bizarre geographical contortions involved in gerrymandering.

SOURCE: From "Snakes or Ladders?" by David Van Biema, *Time*, July 12, 1993. © 1993 Time Inc. Reprinted by permission.

Sometimes the scandal factor comes into play because of national rather than local conditions. In 1998 the accumulation of many scandals in the Clinton administration resulted in the appointment of seven separate independent counsels. These scandals and the investigations they spawned energized at least a few Republican campaigns, while damaging strong Democratic defenders of Clinton. This was most clearly the case in states where Clinton is weak (for example, Idaho and Texas).

The defeat of a congressional incumbent can also occur as a result of the presidential coattail effect. As Table 13.4 shows, successful presidential candidates usually carry into office congressional candidates of the same party in the year of their election. Notice the overall decline in the strength of the coattail effect in modern times, however, as party identification has weakened and the powers and perks of incumbency have grown. Whereas Harry S Truman's party gained seventy-six House seats and nine additional Senate seats in 1948, George Bush's party actually lost three House seats and one Senate berth in 1988, despite Bush's handsome 54 percent majority. The gains can be minimal even in presidential landslide reelection years, such as 1972 (Nixon) and 1984 (Reagan). Occasionally, though, when the issues are emotional and the voters' desire for change is strong enough, as in Reagan's original 1980 victory, the coattail effect can still be substantial.

Off-Year Elections

Elections in the middle of presidential terms, **off-year elections**, present a different threat to incumbents. This time it is the incumbents of the president's party who are most in jeopardy. Just as the presidential party usually gains seats in presidential election years, it usually loses seats in off years. The problems and tribulations of governing normally cost a president some popularity, alienate key groups, or cause the public to want to send the president a message of one sort or another. An economic downturn or a scandal can underline and expand this circumstance, as the Watergate scandal of 1974 and the recession of 1982 demonstrated.

off-year election:

Election that takes place in the middle of a presidential term.

■ In 1992, MTV and Rock the Vote, a Santa Monica–based voter registration campaign, registered approximately 350,000 college students. In 1996, the campaign sported a red, white, and blue bus covered with quotes from President Harry S Truman to Snoop Doggy Dog. "Choose or Lose" was also in evidence at the Republican National Convention in August. (Photo courtesy: Piet van Lier/Impact Visuals)

part. Some nations try to get around the effects of voter attitudes with compulsory voting laws (Australia and Belgium), or by taxing citizens who do not vote. Not surprisingly, voter turnout rates in Australia and Belgium are often greater than 95 percent.

As noted previously, alienation afflicts some voters, and others are just plain apathetic, possibly because of a lack of pressing issues in a particular year, satisfaction with the status quo, or uncompetitive (even uncontested) elections. Furthermore, many citizens may be turned off by the quality of campaigns in a time when petty issues and personal mudslinging are more prevalent than ever. Finally, perhaps turnout has declined due to rising levels of distrust of government. More and more people are telling pollsters that they lack confidence in political leaders. In the past, some scholars argued that there is no correlation between distrust of political leaders and nonvoting. But as the levels of distrust rise, these preliminary conclusions might need to be revisited.

Weak Political Parties.   Political parties today are no longer as effective as they once were in mobilizing voters, ensuring that they are registered, and getting them to the polls. As we discussed in chapter 12, the parties once were grassroots organizations which forged strong party-group links with their supporters. Today these bonds have been stretched to the breaking point for many. Candidate-centered campaigns and the growth of expansive party bureaucracies have resulted in a somewhat more distant party with which most people do not identify very strongly.

How Can the United States Improve Voter Turnout?

Reformers have suggested many ideas to increase voter turnout in the United States. Always on the list is raising the political awareness of young citizens, a reform that inevitably must involve our nation's schools. Political scientists Steven J. Rosenstone and John Marc Hansen's research show that the rise in formal education levels among Americans played a significant role in preventing an even greater decline in voter turnout.[29] No less important, and perhaps simpler to achieve, are the institutional reforms, though many of these reforms, if enacted, may result in only a marginal increase in turnout.

Easier Registration and Absentee Voting.   Registration laws vary by state; but in every state except North Dakota, registration is required in order to vote. Many observers believe that voter turnout could be increased if registering to vote were made simpler for citizens. The typical thirty-days-before-an-election registration deadline could be shortened to a week or ten days. After all, most people become more interested in voting as Election Day nears. Indeed, one political scientist calculated that allowing citizens to register on the same day as they vote would boost national turnout by five percentage points.[30] Better yet, all U.S. citizens could be registered automatically at the age of eighteen. Absentee ballots could also be made easier to obtain by eliminating the in-person requirement.

In 1993 a major advance toward easier registration was achieved with the passage by Congress of the so-called motor-voter bill, which required states to permit individuals to register by mail, not just in person. The law, strongly backed by President Clinton, also allows citizens to register to vote when they visit any motor vehicles office, public assistance agency, or military recruitment division. Proponents of the law say it will result in the registration of the roughly 49 million Americans of voting age with driver's licenses or identification cards but who have failed to register to vote. Opponents claim the new law is yet another in a long line of intrusive and costly federal mandates that do not appropriate money to pay for the costs involved in implementing the programs. The motor-voter bill took effect in 1995, so it will be some time before we know how many people it will add to the registration rolls. However, research on motor voter laws passed by states prior to the passage of federal legislation indicates that such laws indeed have a positive impact on voter registration levels.[31]

Make Election Day a Holiday.

Besides removing an obstacle to voting (the busy workday), making Election Day a holiday might focus more voter attention on the contests in the critical final hours.

Strengthen Parties.

Reformers have long argued that strengthening the political parties would increase voter turnout, because parties have historically been the organizations in the United States best suited for and most successful at mobilizing citizens to vote. During the late 1800s and early 1900s, the country's "Golden Age" of powerful political parties, one of their primary activities was getting out the vote on Election Day. And even today, the parties' Election Day get-out-the-vote drives increase voter turnout by as many as several million in national contests.

■ A state registry of motor vehicles worker displays the form that makes it easy for those visiting the registry also to register to vote. (Photo courtesy: Dennis Brack/Black Star)

Other Suggestions.

Other ideas to increase voter turnout are less practical or feasible. For example, holding fewer elections might sound appealing, but it is difficult to see how this could be accomplished without diluting many of the central tenets of federalism and separation of powers that the Founders believed essential to the protection of liberty.

Does Low Voter Turnout Matter?

Some political observers have argued that nonvoting is not a critical problem. For example, some feel that the preferences of nonvoters are not much different from those who do vote. If this is true, the results would be about the same if everyone voted. Others contend that since legal and extralegal denial of the vote to previously disfranchised groups—African Americans, women, Hispanics, people over eighteen—have now been outlawed, nonvoting is voluntary. By choosing not to vote, these individuals are said to be indicating their acceptance of things as they are. Therefore we should not attempt to make it easier for these people, often characterized as apathetic and lazy, to vote. Finally, some even claim that low voter turnout is a positive benefit, based on the dubious supposition that less-educated people are more easily swayed. Thus low turnout supposedly increases the stability of the system and discourages demagogic, populist appeals.

We should not be too quick to accept these arguments, which have much in common with the early nineteenth-century view that the Nineteenth Amendment to the Constitution (which enfranchised women) need not be passed because husbands could protect the interests of their wives. First, the social makeup and attitudes of present-day nonvoters are significantly different from those of voters. Nonvoters tend to be low income, younger, blue collar, less educated, and more heavily minority. Even if their expressed preferences about politics do not look very distinctive, their objective circumstances as well as their need for government services differ from the majority of those who do vote. These people—those who require the most help from government—currently lack a fair share of electoral power. A political system that actively seeks to include and mobilize these people might well produce broader-based policies that differ from those we have today.

A New Voting Pattern: Ticket-Splitting

There is an important voting trend that cannot be ignored among citizens who do cast their ballots. Citizens have been increasingly deserting their party affiliations in the

GLOBAL POLITICS   The Trouble with Turnout

The problem of declining voter turnout over the last two decades has been a cause of concern across the industrial democracies. Nowhere is the issue seen as more acute than in the United States, which has the lowest voter turnout of any G-7 country (state, local, and midterm Congressional election turnouts are even lower). Why do the other member countries have higher voter turnouts?

One explanation has to do with when elections are held. Every other G-7 government holds elections on weekends, usually on Sunday, when voters are not at work. Another explanation is that parliamentary systems require their voters to vote less often. Elections for the parliament typically happen every three to four years. Prime ministers are elected by the lower house of parliament, so a vote for a legislature candidate is also an indirect vote for a chief executive. By definition, moreover, there are no midterm legislative elections, when turnout in the United States drops from presidential election levels.

Most important, voter registration is automatic, or nearly so, in the other countries. Voters are placed on the election rolls when they register their at the local government office. The Canadian government actively canvasses citizens of voting age to ensure their inclusion on the rolls. This is significant because the percentage recorded for the United States in the table above shows voter turnout as a proportion of the voting-age population (including people ineligible to vote); the proportion of actual voters to registered voters in 1996 was nearly two-thirds, close to the other G-7 levels. Automatic registration would undoubtedly increase the number of registered voters, and therefore turnout, as it does in Europe, Canada, and Japan.

Voter Turnout in Recent National Elections

Country	Year, Election	Turnout (%)
Canada	1997, parliamentary	69.6
France	1997, parliamentary	71.4
Germany	1998, parliamentary	82.2
Italy	1996, parliamentary	82.9
Japan	1996, parliamentary	59.6
United Kingdom	1997, parliamentary	71.5
United States	**1996, presidential**	**49.0**

Sources: Election Data Resources on the Internet: Europe. http://pitt.edu/alvarez/europe.htm#DE; Election Data Resources on the Internet: The Americas. http://pitt.edu/alvarez/america.htm#DE; and selected national government sites.

the political landscape. At least every other presidential election brings a change of administration and a focus on new issues. Every other year at least a few fresh personalities and perspectives infuse the Congress, as newly elected U.S. senators and representatives claim mandates and seek to shake up the established order. Each election year the same tumult and transformation can be observed in the fifty states and in thousands of localities.

The welter of elections may seem like chaos, but from this chaos comes the order and often explosive productivity of a democratic society. For the source of all change in the United States, just as Hamilton and Madison predicted, is the individual citizen who goes to the polls and casts a ballot.

CONTINUITY and Change

Election Technology—Past, Present, Future

In the last century, the political parties themselves ran the elections, supplying not only ballots, but also many of the poll-watchers and judges. This was a formula for fraud, of course, and there was no truly secret ballot, as people voted on different colored ballot forms depending on their choice of party!

Election practices and technology have changed dramatically in this century. To clean up elections, the states now oversee the election process, with official state boards of elections in all fifty states. From paper ballots, we also progressed to sophisticated automatic ballot machines in the middle decades of the century. Voting machines were nearly universal in America by the 1970s, except in some isolated rural localities, and permitted truly secret voting through the use of electronic controls and curtains that conceal the voter's motions when choosing a candidate. This helped secure the integrity of the election process; fraud was reduced, though not eliminated.

The "motor-voter" law of 1993 helped to liberalize the integral process of registering to vote by making it possible to register when renewing a driver's license or visiting various government offices. The law was intended to reduce some of the physical obstacles along the way to voting on Election Day, but while it has made a substantial difference in the number of registered voters, it has had no significant impact on the actual number of votes cast. While advances like secret ballots and relaxed registration can only help bring more people to the polls, technology and convenience will never be cure-alls for apathetic democratic participation.

We are probably headed for a very different system of voting in the future. Oregon is only one of several places to have permanently instituted a vote-by-mail program whereby registered voters are mailed a ballot and given several weeks to vote before returning their ballot by mail. It may also be that in the next century, we are each assigned a voting security code and enabled to vote over the Internet. As with all voting practices, the main concern is the privacy and security of the voting act and ballot return, though it will also be important to pay attention to any changes in the campaign process that might attend such highly private and decentralized voting and a protracted election period.

1. Speaking statistically, if less than 50 percent of eligible Americans vote, then voting becomes an "abnormal" act. Since voter turnout in recent national elections has indeed been well below that threshold, what does it mean if our national leaders are elected by a process that could fairly be called "abnormal" for most Americans? Is such an election meaningful? What does it mean for the entire nation to be governed by leaders who represent no more than half of the electorate?
2. We tend to take fair elections and private voting for granted in the United States, but in many countries such conditions are still not widespread. What do the lessons of election reform in America teach us about ways of improving the integrity of elections in other nations? What can a country without a long stable democratic tradition do to ensure fraud-free elections and private voting?

Cast Your Vote. How can America improve voter turnout? To cast your vote, go to www.awlonline.com/oconnor.

SUMMARY

The explosion of elections we have experienced in over 200 years of voting has generated much good and some harm. But all of it has been done, as Hamilton insisted, "on the solid basis of the consent of the people." In our efforts to explain the complex and multilayered U.S. electoral system, we covered these points in this chapter:

1. THE PURPOSES SERVED BY ELECTIONS

Regular elections guarantee mass political action and governmental accountability. They also confer legitimacy on regimes better than any other method of change.

2. DIFFERENT KINDS OF ELECTIONS

When it comes to elections, the United States has an embarrassment of riches. There are various types of primary elections in the country, as well as general elections, initiatives, referenda, and recall elections. In presidential elections, primaries are sometimes replaced by caucuses, in which party members choose a candidate in a closed meeting, but recent years have seen fewer caucuses and more primaries.

3. PRESIDENTIAL ELECTIONS

Variety aside, no U.S. election can compare to the presidential contest. This spectacle, held every four years, brings together all the elements of politics and attracts the most ambitious and energetic politicians to the national stage.

4. THE PARTY CONVENTIONS

No longer closed affairs dominated by deals cut in "smoke-filled rooms," today's conventions are more open made-for-television events in which the party platform is drafted and adopted, and the presidential ticket is formally nominated.

5. CONGRESSIONAL ELECTIONS

Many similar elements are present in different kinds of elections: Candidates, voters, issues, and television advertisements are constants. But there are distinctive aspects of each kind of election as well. Compared with presidential elections, congressional elections are a different animal.

6. VOTING BEHAVIOR

Whether they are casting ballots in congressional or presidential elections, voters behave in certain distinct ways and exhibit unmistakable patterns to political scientists who study them.

KEY TERMS

blanket primary, p. 470
closed primary, p. 469
critical election, p. 483
crossover voting, p. 469
elector, p. 479
electoral college, p. 479
electorate, p. 467
front-loading, p. 473
general election, p. 470
gerrymandering p. 488
incumbency, p. 488

initiative, p. 471
mandate, p. 467
off-year election, p. 489
open primary, p. 469
party realignment, p. 483
primary election, p. 469
prospective judgment,
p. 467
raiding, p. 469
recall, p. 471
redistricting, p. 488

referendum, p. 471
regional primary, p. 473
retrospective judgment,
p. 467
runoff primary, p. 470
secular realignment, p. 485
superdelegate, p. 476
ticket-splitting, p. 500
turnout, p. 493
unit rule, p. 474

SELECTED READINGS

Bartels, Larry M. *Presidential Primaries and the Dynamics of Public Choice.* Princeton, NJ: Princeton University Press, 1988.

Berelson, Bernard R., Paul F. Lazarsfeld, and William N. McPhee. *Voting: A Study of Opinion Formation in a Presidential Campaign.* Chicago: University of Chicago Press, 1954.

Burnham, Walter Dean. *Critical Elections and the Mainsprings of American Politics.* New York: Norton, 1970.

Campbell, Angus, Philip E. Converse, Warren E. Miller, and Donald E. Stokes. *The American Voter.* New York: Wiley, 1960.

Carroll, Susan J. *Women as Candidates in American Politics.* Bloomington: Indiana University Press, 1994.

Conway, M. Margaret. *Political Participation in the United States,* 2d ed. Washington, DC: CQ Press, 1990.

Darcy, Robert, Susan Welch, and Janet Clark. *Women, Elections, and Representation,* 2d ed. Lincoln: University of Nebraska Press, 1994.

Fiorina, Morris P. *Retrospective Voting in American National Elections.* New Haven, CT: Yale University Press, 1981.

Herrnson, Paul S. *Congressional Elections: Campaigning at Home and in Washington.* Washington, DC: Congressional Quarterly Press, 1995.

Jacobson, Gary C. *The Politics of Congressional Elections,* 3rd ed. New York: Harper Collins, 1992.

———. *The Electoral Origins of Divided Government.* Boulder, CO: Westview Press, 1990.

Key, V. O., Jr., with the assistance of Milton C. Cummings. *The Responsible Electorate.* Cambridge, MA: Harvard University Press, 1966.

Nie, Norman H., Sidney Verba, and John R. Petrocik. *The Changing American Voter.* Cambridge, MA: Belknap Press of Harvard University, 1976.

Polsby, Nelson W., and Aaron Wildavsky. *Presidential Elections: Strategies and Structures of American Politics,* 7th ed. Chatham, NJ: Chatham House, 1996.

Sundquist, James L. *Dynamics of the Party System: Alignment and Realignment of Political Parties in the United States.* Washington, DC: Brookings Institution, 1983.

Teixeira, Ruy. *The Disappearing American Voter.* Washington, DC: Brookings Institution, 1992.

Verba, Sidney, Norman H. Nie, and Jae-on Kim. *Participation and Political Equality.* Cambridge, England: Cambridge University Press, 1978.

Verba, Sidney, Kay Lehman Schlozman and Henry E. Brady, *Voice and Equality: Civic Voluntarism in American Politics.* Cambridge, MA: Harvard University Press, 1995.

Wayne, Stephen J. *The Road to the White House,* 6th ed. New York: St. Martin's Press, 1997.

Weisberg, Herbert F., ed. *Democracy's Feast: Elections in America.* Chatham, NJ: Chatham House, 1995.

NOTES

1. Angus Cambell, Philip E. Converse, Warren E. Miller, and Donald E. Stokes, *The American Voter* (New York: Wiley, 1960).

2. Paul Abramson, John H. Aldrich, and David W. Rohde, *Change and Continuity in the 1996 Elections* (Washington DC, Congressional Quarterly Press, 1998).

3. Paul Allen Beck, *Party Politics in America,* Eight Edition (New York: Longman, 1998). David Adamany, "Cross-over Voting and the Democratic Party's Reform Rules," *American Political Science Review* 70 (1976): pp. 536–41. Ronald Hedlund and Meredith W. Watts, "The Wisconsin Open Primary: 1968 to 1984," *American Politics Quarterly* 14 (1986) 55–74. Gary D. Wekkin, "The Conceptualization and Measurement of Crossover Voting," *Western Political Quarterly* 41 (1988):105–14.

4. Beck, *Party Politics in America.* Alan Abromowitz, John McGlennon, and Ronald Rapoport, "A Note on Strategic Voting in a Primary Election," *Journal of Politics* 43 (1981): 899–904. Gary D. Wekken, "Why Crossover Voters Are Not 'Mischievous' Voters," *American Politics Quarterly* 19 (1991): 229–47.

5. Gary C. Jacobson, *The Politics of Congressional Elections* (New York: Longman, 1997), pp. 107–108.

6. Shaun Bowler, Todd Donovan, and Caroline Tolbert, editors, *Citizens as Legislators: Direct Democracy in the United States* (Columbus, OH: Ohio State University Press, 1998).

7. Elaine Ciulla Kamarck and Kenneth M. Goldstein, "The Rules Matter: Post-Reform Presidential Nominating Politics," in L. Sandy Maisel, *The Parties Respond: Changes in American Parties and Campaigns* (Boulder: Westview Press, 1994), p. 174.

8. Larry J. Sabato, "Presidential Nominations: The Front-loaded Frenzy of 1996," in Larry J. Sabato, editor, *Toward the Millennium: The Elections of 1996* (New York: Allyn and Bacon, 1997).

9. Byron Shafer, *Bifurcated Politics: Evolution and Reform in the National Party Convention* (Cambridge, Mass: Harvard University Press, 1988).

10. On the subject of party realignment, see Walter Dean Burnham, *Critical Elections and the Mainsprings of American Politics* (New York: Norton, 1970); Kristi Andersen, *The*

Creation of a Democratic Majority (Chicago: University of Chicago Press, 1979); and John R. Petrocik, "Realignment: New Party Coalitions and the Nationalization of the South," *Journal of Politics* 49 (May 1987): 347–75.

11. Barbara Farah and Helmut Norpoth, "Trends in Partisan Realignment, 1976–1986: A Decade of Waiting," paper prepared for delivery at the annual meeting of the American Political Science Association, Washington, DC, August 27–31, 1986.

12. Morris P. Fiorina, *Retrospective Voting in American National Elections* (New Haven, CT: Yale University Press, 1981); and Charles H. Franklin and John E. Jackson, "The Dynamics of Party Identification," *American Political Science Review* 77 (1983): 957–73.

13. See, for example, V. O. Key, Jr., "A Theory of Critical Elections," *Journal of Politics* 17 (February 1955): 3–18.

14. The less dynamic term "creeping realignment" is also sometimes used by scholars and journalists.

15. Everett Carl Ladd, "Like Waiting for Godot: The Uselessness of 'Realignment' for Understanding Change in Contemporary American Politics," in Byron Shafer, editor, *The End of Realignment? Interpreting American Electoral Eras* (Madison: Wisconsin, 1991).

16. See Paul Allen Beck, "The Dealignment Era in America," in Russell J. Dalton, *et al.*, *Electoral Change in Advanced Industrial Democracies: Realignment or Dealignment?* (Princeton, NJ: Princeton University Press, 1984), 264. See also Philip M. Williams, "Party Realignment in the United States and Britain," *British Journal of Political Science* 15 (January 1985): 97–115.

17. George Serra, "What's in it for Me? The Impact of Congressional Casework on Incumbent Evaluation," *American Politics Quarterly* 22 (1994): pp. 403–420.

18. Glenn R. Parker and Suzanne L. Parker, "Correlates and Effects of Attention to District by U.S. House Members," *Legislative Studies Quarterly* 10 (May 1985), pp. 223–42.

19. *Wesberry* v. *Sanders*, 376 U.S. 1 (1964).

20. *Thornburg* v. *Gingles*, 478 U.S. 30 (1986).

21. *Shaw* v. *Reno*, 113 S. Ct. 2816 (1993).

22. Sunhil Ahuja, Staci L. Beavers, Cynthia Berreau, Anthony Dodson, Patrick Hourigan, Steven Showalter, Jeff Waltz, and John Hibbing, "Modern Congressional Election Theory Meets the 1992 House Elections," *Political Research Quarterly* 47 (1994): pp. 909–21. Paul S. Herrnson, *Congressional Elections: Campaigning at Home and in Washington*. Second Edition (Washington DC: Congressional Quarterly Press, 1998).

23. Gary C. Jacobson and Michael A. Dimock, "Checking Out: The Effects of Bank Overdrafts on the 1992 House Elections," *American Journal of Political Science* 38 (1994): pp. 601–24. Herrnson, *Congressional Elections: Campaigning at Home and in Washington*.

24. The Kennedy-Johnson years (1961–69) and the Nixon-Ford years (1969–77) are each considered an eight-year unit for our purposes here.

25. Gary C. Jacobson, "The 1994 House Elections in Perspective," *Political Science Quarterly* 111 (1996): pp. 203–223.

26. Richard E. Cohen, Campaigning for Congress: The Echo of '94," in Larry J. Sabato, editor, *Toward the Millennium: The Elections of 1996* (New York: Allyn and Bacon, 1997).

27. Abramson, et al., *Change and Continuity in the 1996 Elections*.

28. See, for example, Laura Stoker and M. Kent Jennings, "Life-Cycle Transitions and Political Participation: The Case of Marriage," *American Political Science Review* 89 (1995): pp. 421–36, and Abramson, et al., *Change and Continuity in the 1996 Elections*.

29. Steven J. Rosenstone and John Marc Hansen, *Mobilization, Participation, and Democracy in America* (New York, McMillan, 1993).

30. Mark J. Fenster, "The Impact of Allowing Day of Registration Voting on Turnout in U.S. Elections from 1960 to 1992: A Research Note," *American Politics Quarterly* 22 (January 1994), pp. 74–87.

31. Stephen Knack, "Does 'Motor Voter' Work? Evidence from State-Level Data," *Journal of Politics* 57 (1995): pp. 796–811.

32. Cited in Everett Carl Ladd, Jr., "On Mandates, Realignments, and the 1984 Presidential Election," *Political Science Quarterly* 100 (Spring 1985): 23.

33. Morris P. Fiorina, *Divided Government* (Boston: Allyn and Bacon, 1996).

34. Martin P. Wattenberg, *The Decline of American Political Parties, 1952–1994* (Cambridge, MA: Harvard University Press, 1996).

35. Thomas E. Mann and Raymond E. Wolfinger, "Candidates and Parties in Congressional Elections," *American Political Science Review* 74 (September 1980): 617–32; Albert D. Cover, "One Good Term Deserves Another: The Advantage of Incumbency in Congressional Elections," *American Journal of Political Science* 21 (August 1977): 535; and Gary C. Jacobson, *The Politics of Congressional Elections,* 2d ed. (Boston: Little, Brown, 1987), 86.

(Photo courtesy: Bob Daemmrich)

The Campaign Process

*S*erious presidential candidates do not simply materialize out of thin air. On the contrary, they are the product of a lifetime's work in careful strategy and campaign planning, and the case of Elizabeth Dole proves the point perfectly. Until recently, Dole was best known as the wife of 1996 Republican presidential candidate Bob Dole, a longtime U.S. senator from Kansas, though in fact, she has long been an accomplished political figure in her own right. Even before she had met Bob Dole, she had served in the Nixon White House as a presidential assistant, and after her marriage, she campaigned alongside her husband when he was Gerald Ford's vice-presidential nominee in 1976.

Dole held various other government positions through the 1970s, and was ultimately selected for two separate positions in Ronald Reagan's and George Bush's cabinets: Secretary of Labor and Secretary of Transportation. Following her government service, Dole became head of the International Red Cross, a prestigious position that enabled her to travel the globe and direct one of the world's great humanitarian agencies. In 1996, acting in her capacity as loyal spouse to her candidate–husband, Dole gave an overwhelmingly popular speech at the Republican National Convention, which many read even then as a passport to a spot on the national presidential ticket in 2000.

Though her husband, at over seventy years of age, proved not to be a viable presidential candidate in 1996, Elizabeth Dole definitely was, and, as it turned out, she wanted the job. The news came as no surprise. Dole had dropped hints in the press for several years prior to her formal announcement in 1999, and many had also read her resignation from the Red Cross in January 1999 as a sure sign that she was considering a bid for national executive office. By March 1999, she announced the formation of her "exploratory committee"—the formal term for the organization, legally registered with the Federal Election Commission, that works to develop a candidate's campaign, including polling, financing, and fund raising. The exploratory committee paid for her travel around the country, the hiring of key campaign staffers, and various advertising expenses such as Dole's sophisticated web site.

Realistically, Dole's chances as a presidential candidate are slim. She has a most impressive list of appointments in her credentials, but they lack one important distinction: actual election by the public to an office at any level of government. Many, however, have seen her as outstandingly qualified for the position of vice president, and believed that she would make a popular addition to the Republican national ticket. Regardless of the final outcome, her campaign illustrates one thing clearly: the actual competition for public office begins years before the election itself.

*U*p to this point in the book, we have focused on the election decision itself and have said little about the campaign conducted prior to the balloting. Many today denounce electioneering and politicians for their negative use of the airwaves and the perceived disproportionate influence of a few wealthy donors and a handful of well-endowed and well-organized political action committees and interest groups. Nonetheless, the basic purpose of modern electioneering remains intact: one person asking another for support, an approach unchanged since the dawn of democracy.

The art of campaigning involves the science of polls, the planning of sophisticated mass mailings, and the coordination of electronic telephone banks to reach voters. More importantly, it also involves the diplomatic skill of unifying disparate individuals and groups to achieve a fragile but election-winning majority. How candidates perform this exquisitely difficult task is the subject of this chapter, in which we discuss the following topics:

Web Exploration

To compare the development of presidential candidates, go to www.awlonline.com/oconnor.

- First, we will explore *the structure of a campaign,* the process of seeking and winning votes in the run-up to an election, which consists of five separate components: the nomination campaign, the general election campaign, the personal campaign, the organizational campaign, and the broadcast media campaign.

- Second, we will look at the question of *which we vote for: the candidate or the campaign.* Although campaign methods have clearly become very sophisticated, in most cases the candidate wins or loses the race according to his or her abilities, qualifications, communication skills, issues, and weaknesses.

- Third, we will see how the modern candidate faces two major *modern campaign challenges:* communicating through the media and raising the money needed to stay in the race.

- Fourth, we will see where campaign contributions come from and how those funds are spent.

- Fifth, we will discuss *the 1996 presidential campaign and election.* No liberal Democrats stepped forward to challenge a rejuvenated and popular President Clinton; the Republicans, despite protestations from party activists, nominated a moderate Washington insider—former Senate Majority Leader Bob Dole. Surprisingly, Dole's primary battle turned out to be a little more exciting than expected. But in the end he prevailed, securing the right to face Clinton in the general election for president.

- Sixth, we will look at *campaign finance laws,* exploring ways that these might be changed so that their effect can be strengthened.

■ *"Next time, why don't you run? You're a well-known figure, people seem to like you, and you haven't had an original idea in years."* (Reproduced by Special Permission of *Playboy* magazine. Copyright © 1992 by Playboy.)

THE STRUCTURE OF A CAMPAIGN

A campaign for high office (such as the presidency, a governorship, or a U.S. Senate seat) is a highly complex effort akin to running a multimillion-dollar business, while campaigns for local offices are usually less complicated. But all campaigns, no matter what their size, have certain aspects in common. Indeed, each campaign really consists of several campaigns run simultaneously:

1. The **nomination campaign.** The target is the party elite, the leaders and activists who choose nominees in primaries or conventions. Party leaders are concerned with electability, while party activists are often ideologically and issue oriented, so a candidate must appeal to both bases.

2. The **general election campaign.** A farsighted candidate never forgets the ultimate goal: winning the general election. Therefore the candidate tries to avoid taking stands that, how-

ever pleasing to party activists in the primary, will alienate a majority of the larger general election constituency.

3. The **personal campaign.** This is the public part of the campaign. The candidate and his or her family and supporters make appearances, meet voters, hold press conferences, and give speeches.

4. The **organizational campaign.** Behind the scenes, another campaign is humming. Volunteers telephone voters and distribute literature, staffers organize events, and everyone raises money to support the operation.

5. The **media campaign.** On television and radio the candidate's advertisements (termed *paid media*) air frequently in an effort to convince the public that the candidate is the best person for the job. Meanwhile, campaigners attempt to influence the press coverage of the campaign by the print and electronic news reporters—the *free media*.

British election campaigns are very different from those in the United States. In the first place, candidate selection is controlled by local party organizations, not by any sort of primary system. Second, the national parties control key facets of the campaign. For example, they provide all the financing, which is regulated by national statute, and execute the campaign strategy. As a result, national party platforms—not candidate personalities—play a dominant role in British campaigns. Finally, the power of the prime minister to call elections at his or her discretion—literally at a moment's notice—produces campaigns of a mere four to five weeks in duration instead of the two-year (for a Senate seat) to four-year campaigns (for president) we endure in the United States.

To better comprehend the various campaigns, let's examine a few aspects of each, remembering that they must all mesh successfully for the candidate to win.

The Nomination Campaign

New candidates get their sea legs early on, as they adjust to the pressures of being in the spotlight day in and day out. This is the time for the candidates to learn that a single careless phrase could end the campaign or guarantee a defeat. This is also the time to seek the support of party leaders and interest groups and to test out themes, slogans, and strategies. The press and public take much less notice of shifts in strategy at this time than they will later in the general election campaign.

At this time there is a danger not widely recognized by candidates: Surrounded by friendly activists and ideological soulmates in the quest to win the party's nomination, a candidate can move too far to the right or the left and become too extreme for the November electorate. Conservative Barry Goldwater, the 1964 Republican nominee for president, and liberal George McGovern, the 1972 Democratic nominee for president, both fell victim to this phenomenon in seeking their party's nomination, and they were handily defeated in the general elections by Presidents Lyndon B. Johnson and Richard M. Nixon, respectively.

The General Election Campaign

Once the choice between the two major-party nominees is clear, both candidates can get to work. Most significant interest groups are courted for money and endorsements, although the results are mainly predictable: liberal, labor, and minority groups usually back Democrats, while conservative and business organizations support Republicans. The most active and intense groups are often coalesced around emotional issues such as abortion and gun control, and these organizations can produce a bumper crop of money and activists for favored candidates. Race and class divisions can often play an important role in general elections, although this tends not to be true in the United States.

Virtually all candidates adopt a brief theme, or slogan, to serve as a rallying cry in their quest for office. The first to do so was William Henry Harrison in 1840, with the slogan "Tippecanoe and Tyler, Too." Tippecanoe was a nickname given to Harrison, a reference to his participation in the battle of Tippecanoe, and Tyler was Harrison's vice-presidential candidate, John Tyler of Virginia. Some presidential campaign slogans have entered national lore, like Herbert Hoover's 1928 slogan "A chicken in every pot, a car

nomination campaign:

That part of a political campaign aimed at winning a primary election.

general election campaign:

That part of a political campaign following a primary election, aimed at winning a general election.

personal campaign:

That part of a political campaign concerned with presenting the candidate's public image.

organizational campaign:

That part of a political campaign involved in fund raising, literature distribution, and all other activities not directly involving the candidate.

media campaign:

That part of a political campaign waged in the broadcast and print media.

in every garage." President Clinton has used two memorable slogans: "Time for a change" and "Building a bridge to the twenty-first century." Most slogans can fit many candidates ("She thinks like us," "He's on our side," "She hears you," "You know where he stands"). Candidates try to avoid controversy in their selection of slogans, and some openly eschew ideology. (An ever-popular one of this genre: "Not left, not right—forward!") The clever candidate also attempts to find a slogan that cannot be lampooned easily. In 1964 Barry Goldwater's handlers may have regretted their choice of "In your heart, you know he's right" when Lyndon B. Johnson's supporters quickly converted it into "In your guts, you know he's nuts." (Democrats were trying to portray Goldwater as a warmonger after the Republican indicated a willingness to use nuclear weapons in Vietnam and elsewhere under some conditions.)

The Personal Campaign

In the effort to show voters that they are hard-working, thoughtful, and worthy of the office they seek, candidates try to meet personally as many citizens as possible in the course of a campaign. A candidate for high office may deliver up to a dozen speeches a day, and that is only part of the exhausting schedule most contenders maintain. The day may begin at 5 A.M. at the entrance gate to an auto plant with an hour or two of handshaking, followed by similar gladhanding at subway stops until 9 A.M. Strategy sessions with key advisers and preparation for upcoming presentations and forums may fill the rest of the morning. A luncheon talk, afternoon fund raisers, and a series of television and print interviews crowd the afternoon agenda. The light fare of cocktail parties is followed by a dinner speech, perhaps telephone or neighborhood canvassing of voters, and a civic-forum talk or two. More meetings with advisers and planning for the next day's events can easily take a candidate past midnight. Following only a few hours of sleep, the candidate starts all over again. After months of this grueling pace, the candidate may be functioning on automatic pilot and unable to think clearly.

Beyond the strains this fast-lane existence adds to a candidate's family life, the hectic schedule leaves little time for reflection and long-range planning. Is it any wonder that under these conditions many candidates commit gaffes and appear to have foot-in-mouth disease?

It's not all drudgery, however. The considerable rewards to be had on the campaign trail can balance the personal disadvantages. A candidate can affect the course of the government and community, and in so doing become admired and respected by peers. Meeting all kinds of people, solving problems, gaining exposure to every facet of life in one's constituency—these experiences help a public person live life fully and compensate for the hardships of campaigning.

The Organizational Campaign

If the candidate is the public face of the campaign, the organization behind the candidate is the private face. Depending on the level of the office sought, the organizational staff can consist of a handful of volunteers or hundreds of paid specialists supplementing and directing the work of thousands of volunteers. The most elaborate structure is found in presidential campaigns. Tens of thousands of volunteers dis-

■ Right-wing 1964 Republican candidate Barry Goldwater's famous slogan, "in your heart, you know he's right" was quickly lampooned by incumbent Democratic opponent President Lyndon B. Johnson's campaign as "in your guts, you know he's nuts." (Photo courtesy: Corbis/Bettman)

tribute literature and visit neighborhoods. They are directed by paid staff that may number 300 or more, including a couple of dozen lawyers and accountants.

At the top of the organizational chart is the **campaign manager,** who coordinates and directs the various aspects of the campaign. Beside the manager is the **political consultant,** whose position is one of the most important developments in campaigning for office in this century. The political consultant is a private-sector individual (or, more often now, a team of individuals or a firm) who sells to a candidate the technologies, services, and strategies required to get that candidate elected to his or her office of choice. The number of consultants has grown exponentially since they first appeared in the 1930s, and their specialties and responsibilities have increased accordingly, to the point that they are now an obligatory part of campaigns at almost any level of government. Candidates hire generalist consultants to oversee their entire campaign from beginning to end, which often include responsibilities ranging from defining campaign objectives to formulating strategy, developing tactics, and fighting individual battles alongside the candidate. Alongside the generalist consultant, or perhaps hired by the generalist in turn, are more specialized consultants who focus on the new and complex technologies for only one or two specialties such as fund raising, polling, mass mailings, media relations, advertising, and speech writing.

The best-known consultants for any campaign are usually the **media consultant,** who produces the candidate's television and radio advertisements; the **pollster,** who takes the public opinion surveys that guide the campaign; and the **direct mailer,** who supervises direct-mail fund raising. After the candidate, however, the most important person in the campaign is probably the **finance chair** who is responsible for bringing in the large contributions that pay most of the salaries of the consultants and staff.

Many critics claim that consultants strip campaigns of substance and reduce them to a clever bag of tricks for sale, even blaming the degeneration of American politics in the latter half of this century on the rise of the political consultant. Disappointed office seekers sometimes blame their loss entirely on their consultants, while successful candidates often retain their consultants after the election as political advisers, thereby lending even more credibility to the claim that politics now is all about appearance and not about issues. And candidates, always busy with making public appearances and canvassing, often entrust the entire management of campaigns to their consultants without understanding entirely what those consultants do. Sometimes, as in the notable case of Mary Matalin and James Carville (see chapter 12, p. 423), the consultants become media stars in their own right.

Yet there are others who insist that despite the consultants, running for office is still about the bread and butter of campaigns: shaking hands, speaking persuasively, and listening to the voters. Voters, they say, are smart enough to tell the difference between a good candidate and a bad one, regardless of the smoke and mirrors erected by their consultants. Nevertheless, consultants do make a difference. Recent research on political consultants conducted by political scientists indicates that consultants have a significant impact in elections. In campaigns for the U.S. House, for example, the use of professional campaign consultants has been shown to have a positive impact on candidates' fund-raising ability[1] and on candidates' final vote shares.[2]

In addition to raising money, the most vital work of the candidate's organization is to get in touch with voters. Some of this is done in person by volunteers who walk the neighborhoods, going door to door to solicit votes. Some is accomplished by volunteers who use computerized telephone banks to call targeted voters with scripted messages. (See Politics Now: High-Tech Campaigning for a discussion of the types of technologies contemporary campaigns rely on.) Both contact methods are termed **voter canvass.** Most canvassing takes place in the month before the election, when voters are paying attention. Close to Election Day, the telephone banks begin the vital **get-out-the-vote (GOTV)** effort, reminding supporters to vote and arranging for their transportation to the polls if necessary.

TRY IT!

To find out what Americans have to say on a range of political issues and to experience poll taking firsthand, go to www.awlonline.com/oconnor.

campaign manager:

The individual who travels with the candidate and coordinates the many different aspects of the campaign.

political consultant:

A hired individual, team, or firm that advises the campaign on strategies and techniques to win an election.

media consultant:

A professional who produces political candidates' television, radio, and print advertisements.

pollster:

A professional who takes public opinion surveys that guide political campaigns.

direct mailer:

A professional who supervises a political campaign's direct-mail fund-raising strategies.

finance chair:

A volunteer who coordinates the fund-raising efforts for the campaign.

voter canvass:

The process by which a campaign gets in touch with individual voters: either by door-to-door solicitation or by telephone.

get-out-the-vote (GOTV):

A push at the end of a political campaign to encourage supporters to go to the polls.

paid media:

Political advertisements purchased for a candidate's campaign.

free media:

Coverage of a candidate's campaign by the news media.

positive ad:

Advertising on behalf of a candidate that stresses the candidate's qualifications, family, and issue positions, without reference to the opponent.

negative ad:

Advertising on behalf of a candidate that attacks the opponent's platform or character.

contrast ad:

Ad that compares the records and proposals of the candidates, with a bias toward the sponsor.

spot ad:

Television advertising on behalf of a candidate that is broadcast in sixty-, thirty-, or ten-second duration.

inoculation advertising:

Advertising that attempts to counteract an anticipated attack from the opposition before the attack is even launched.

The Media Campaign

What voters actually see and hear of the candidate is primarily determined by the **paid media** (such as television advertising) accompanying the campaign and the **free media** (newspaper and television coverage). The two kinds of media are fundamentally different: Paid advertising is completely under the control of the campaign, whereas the press is independent. Great care is taken in the design of the television advertising, which takes many approaches. (See Roots of Government: The Television Advertising Campaign of 1952 for information on the first national political ad campaign.) **Positive ads** stress the candidate's qualifications, family, and issue positions with no direct reference to the opponent. These are usually favored by the incumbent candidate. **Negative ads** attack the opponent's character and platform and (except for a brief, legally required identification at the ad's conclusion) may not even mention the candidate who is paying for their airing. In 1996 Steve Forbes made extensive use of negative ads prior to the Iowa caucus and the New Hampshire primary, spending millions denouncing then front-runner Bob Dole. These attacks prompted Dole to tag Forbes "the king of negative advertising," before unleashing some negative ads of his own. These ads contributed to the generally held belief that the early stages of the 1996 Republican nomination battle was one of the most vicious ever witnessed. In the 1996 presidential campaign, National Republican Party ads persistently impugned Bill Clinton's personal integrity because of his misleading statements concerning marijuana use and draft-dodging. Meanwhile, Democratic ads repeatedly featured House Speaker Newt Gingrich as much as they did the actual presidential candidate, Bob Dole, in an attempt to tar Dole with the brush of Gingrich's unpopularity—all to an ominous score reminiscent of a sequel to the horror film *Halloween*. **Contrast ads** compare the records and proposals of the candidates, with a bias toward the sponsor. And whether the public likes them or not, all three kinds of ads can inject important (as well as trivial) issues into a campaign. Incidentally, some of the negative ads aired in modern campaigns are sponsored *not* by candidates but by interest groups. These ads usually focus on issues and are independent of the actual campaigns, though it may be easy to tell which candidate the interest group favors.

Occasionally, advertisements are relatively long (ranging from four-and-one-half-minute ads up to thirty-minute documentaries). Usually, however, the messages are short **spot ads,** sixty, thirty, or even ten seconds long.

While there is little question that negative advertisements have shown the greatest growth in the past two decades, they have been a part of American campaigns for some time. In 1796 Federalists portrayed Thomas Jefferson, a Founding Father and one of the chief authors of our Constitution, as an atheist and a coward. In 1800 Federalists again attacked Jefferson, spreading a rumor that Jefferson was dead! Clearly, although negative advertisements are more prevalent today, they are not solely the function of the modern media. Furthermore, their effects are well documented. While voters normally need a reason to vote for a candidate, they also frequently vote *against* the other candidate—and negative ads can provide the critical justification for such a vote.

Before the 1980s well-known incumbents usually ignored negative attacks from their challengers, believing that the proper stance was to be above the fray. But after some well-publicized defeats of incumbents in the early 1980s in which negative television advertising played a prominent role,[3] incumbents began attacking their challengers in earnest. The new rule of politics became "An attack unanswered is an attack agreed to." In a further attempt to stave off brickbats from challengers, incumbents even began anticipating the substance of their opponents' attacks and airing **inoculation advertising** early in the campaign to protect themselves in advance of the other side's spots. (Inoculation advertising attempts to counteract an anticipated attack from the opposition before the attack is even launched.) For example, a senator who fears a broadside about her voting record on Social Security issues might air advertisements featuring senior citizens praising her support of Social Security.

POLITICS NOW

High-Tech Campaigning: The Changing Nature of Running for Office

The age of modern technology has brought many changes to the traditional campaign. Labor-intensive community activities have been replaced by carefully targeted messages disseminated through the mass-media, and candidates today are able to reach voters more quickly than at any time in our nation's history. Consequently, the well-organized party machine is no longer essential to winning an election. The results of this technological transformation are candidate-centered campaigns in which candidates build well-financed, finely tuned organizations centered around their personal aspirations.

At the heart of the move toward today's candidate-centered campaigns is an entire generation of technological improvements. Contemporary campaigns have an impressive new array of weapons at their disposal: faster paper printing technologies; instantaneous Internet publishing and mass email; fax machines and video technology; and enhanced telecommunications and teleconferencing. As a result, candidates can gather and disseminate information better than ever.

One outcome of these changes is the ability of candidates to employ "rapid-response" techniques: the formulation of prompt and informed responses to changing events on the campaign battlefield. In response to breaking news of a scandal or issue, for example, candidates (as well as journalists) can conduct background research; implement an opinion poll and tabulate the results; devise a containment strategy and appropriate "spin"; and deliver a reply. This makes a strong contrast with the campaigns of the 1970s and early 1980s, which were dominated primarily by radio and TV advertisements, which took much longer to prepare and had little of the flexibility enjoyed by contemporary campaigners.

The first widespread use of the Internet in national campaigning came in 1996. Republican presidential candidate Bob Dole urged voters to log onto his website, and many did. According to one source, 26 percent of the public regularly logged on to the Internet to get campaign and election information.* Similarly, CNN's AllPolitics site reported an estimated 50 million hits on election night 1996—a number expected to pale in comparison to that of 2000. All the candidates for the 2000 presidential campaign have maintained a website—and did so even when their candidacies were only in the exploratory stage, before their formal declarations. These sites have always presented platforms, offered easily accessible information on how to get involved in the campaign, and, for the very enthusiastic web-surfer, information on how to contribute money.

As bandwidth on the Internet continues to improve, real-time video clips enable web-users to view speeches, press conferences, state-of-the-nation addresses, and other typically "live" events at their own convenience, independent of the schedule of the original television coverage or rebroadcast. Campaign sites often offer the text of the speech as well as multiple video and audio versions of the real public event. Whatever the real benefit of such an embarrassment of riches, the goal is to suggest a candidate's technological mastery, sophistication, and depth of resources. The new media appear to be serving the current paradigm of mass-media, candidate-centered campaigns, but it is possible that with time it may reshape the campaign landscape. One possibility is that political parties might use new technologies to organize and manage massive voter bases, in an effort to return to an older mode of campaign that supports the party, rather than just one individual candidate. Another possible outcome is that with increasing ease of public access, the number of candidates or parties might increase, while elections and voting become increasingly private, solitary events.

*The Public Perspective (December/January 1997): 42.

There has been significant debate among political scientists about the impact of negative advertising on American electoral politics. Particularly prominent have been studies investigating the influence of negative advertising on voter turnout. In an important study, political scientists Stephen Ansolabehere and Shanto Iyengar concluded that negative advertising decreases voter turnout (especially among political independents), and, worse yet, that political consultants use negative advertising precisely for such purposes.[4] However, this study by no means constitutes the last word on the subject. Indeed, several studies have cast doubt on the demobilizing effect of negative advertising.[5] Hence the only conclusion we can arrive at here is that there is presently little consensus among scholars regarding the impact of negative advertising on voter turnout.

ROOTS OF GOVERNMENT

The Television Advertising Campaign of 1952

Forty-four years—and a world of difference—separate the presidential campaigns of 1952 from that of 1996 when viewed through the camera lens of television advertising.

The initial, landmark year for political television was 1952. Television had become truly national, not just regional, and portions of the political parties' national conventions were telecast for the first time. With 45 percent of the nation's households owning television sets, the presidential campaign was forced to take notice. Republican presidential nominee Dwight D. Eisenhower's advisers were particularly intrigued with the device, seeing it as a way to counter Eisenhower's stumbling press-conference performances and to make him appear more knowledgeable.

Eisenhower's advertising campaign was a glimpse of the future. The three primary themes of the commercials (corruption, high prices, and the Korean War) were chosen after consultation with pollster George Gallup. There was an extraordinarily large number of spots (forty-nine produced for television, twenty-nine for radio). Most spots were twenty seconds in length; the rest, sixty seconds. They played repeatedly in forty-nine selected counties in twelve non-Southern states as well as in a few targeted Southern states. The GOP's media strategy appeared to have been successful, and the Nielsen ratings showed that Eisenhower's telecasts consistently drew higher ratings than those of his Democratic opponent, Adlai Stevenson.

The commercials themselves were simplistic and technically very primitive in comparison with modern fare. Eisenhower had a peculiarly stilted way of speaking while reading cue cards, and his delivery was amateurish, albeit sincere and appealing. If nothing else, the GOP commercials from 1952 reveal that the issues in U.S. politics never seem to change. Eisenhower's slogan, "It's Time for a Change," for example is a perennial production. One advertisement was a clever adaptation of the "March of Time" newsreel series that preceded the main features in U.S. movie theaters of the period, and various news clips of Eisenhower accompanied the audio.

Narrator: The man from Abilene. Out of the heartland of America, out of this small-frame house in Abilene, Kansas, came a man, Dwight D. Eisenhower. Through the crucial hours of historic D-Day, he brought us to the triumph and peace of VE-Day. Now, another crucial hour in our history. The big question . . .

Man's voice: General, if war comes, is this country really ready?

Eisenhower: It is not. The administration has spent many billions of dollars for national defense. Yet today we haven't enough tanks for the fighting men in Korea. It is time for a change.

Narrator: The nation, haunted by the stalemate in Korea, looks to Eisenhower. Eisenhower knows how to deal with the Russians. He has met with Europe's leaders, has got them working with us. Elect the number-one man for the number-one job of our time. November fourth, vote for peace, vote for Eisenhower.

Yet this spot had an odd ring to it, perhaps because the approach ignored the intimate nature of television, which reaches its viewers in the home's cozy quarters as opposed to the blare of a newsreel in an auditorium.

By the best estimates, this first media blitz cost the Republicans close to $1.5 million. During that campaign, the Democrats spent only about $77,000 on television, and the new spots they produced played on New Deal themes and Republican responsibility for the Great Depression: "Sh-h-h-h. Don't mention it to a soul, don't spread it around . . . but the Republican party was in power back in 1932 . . . 13 million people were unemployed . . . bank doors shut in your face . . . ." The Democrats, who had wanted to run an ad blitz but could not raise the money to pay for it, turned instead to broadsides about the GOP's "soap campaign." Stevenson's supporters charged that the Republican ad managers conceived a multimillion-dollar production designed to sell a political party ticket to the American people in precisely the way they sell soap.

The poet Marya Mannes was moved to write "Sales Campaign" in reaction to the Eisenhower advertising effort. Her poem read, in part: "Phillip Morris, Lucky Strike, Alka Seltzer, I Like Ike." For better or worse, the pattern was set for future campaigns.

■ Media consultants arrange every-thing from paid advertising to daily photo opportunities, such as this "candid" Oval Office setting for President Clinton. (Photo courtesy: Corbis/Reuters)

THE CANDIDATE OR THE CAMPAIGN: WHICH DO WE VOTE FOR?

Much is said and written about media and organizational techniques during the campaign, and they are often presented as political magic. Despite their sophistication, however, the technologies often fail the candidates and their campaigns. The political consultants who develop and master the technologies of polling, media, and other techniques frequently make serious mistakes in judgment. Despite popular lore and journalistic legend, few candidates are the creations of their clever consultants and dazzling campaign techniques. Partly, this is because politics always has been (and always will be) much more art than science, not subject to precise manipulation or formulaic computation. Of course, campaign techniques can enhance the candidate's strengths and downplay his or her weaknesses, and in that respect, technique certainly matters. In the end—in most cases—the candidate wins or loses the race according to his or her abilities, qualifications, communication skills, issues, and weaknesses. Although this simple truth is warmly reassuring, it has been remarkably overlooked by election analysts and reporters seemingly mesmerized by the exorbitant claims of consultants and the flashy computer lights of their technologies.[6]

The voter deserves much of the credit for whatever encouragement we can draw from this candidate-centered view of politics. Granted, citizens are often inattentive to politics, almost forcing candidates to use empty slogans and glitz to attract their attention. But it is also true that most voters want to take the real measure of candidates, and they retain a healthy skepticism about the techniques of running for office. Political cartoonist Tom Toles suggested as much when he depicted the seven preparatory steps the modern candidate takes: (1) Set out to discover what voters want, (2) conduct extensive polling, (3) study

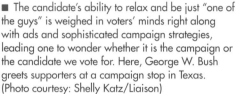
■ The candidate's ability to relax and be just "one of the guys" is weighed in voters' minds right along with ads and sophisticated campaign strategies, leading one to wonder whether it is the campaign or the candidate we vote for. Here, George W. Bush greets supporters at a campaign stop in Texas. (Photo courtesy: Shelly Katz/Liaison)

demographic trends, (4) engage in sophisticated interpretation of in-depth voter interviews, (5) analyze results, (6) discover that what the voters want is a candidate who doesn't need to do steps one through five, and (7) pretend you didn't. The chastened politician then tells his assembled throng, "I follow my conscience."[7]

MODERN CAMPAIGN CHALLENGES

The modern candidate faces two major challenges: communicating through the media and raising the money needed to stay in the race. We consider each challenge in turn.

The News Media

The news media present quite a challenge to candidates. Although politicians and their staffs cannot control the press, they nonetheless try to manipulate press coverage. They use three techniques to accomplish this aim. First, the staff often seeks to isolate the candidate from the press, thus reducing the chances that reporters will bait a candidate into saying something that might damage the candidate's cause. Naturally, the media are frustrated by such a tactic and insist on as many open press conferences as possible.

Second, the campaign stages media events—activities designed to include brief, clever quotes called *sound bites* and staged with appealing backdrops so that they are all but irresistible, especially to television news (see Highlight 14.1: Famous Sound Bites from Presidential Campaigns). In this fashion the candidate's staff can successfully fill the news hole reserved for campaign coverage on the evening news programs and in the morning papers.

Third, the handlers and consultants have cultivated the technique termed *spin*—that is, they put the most favorable possible interpretation for their candidate on any circumstance occurring in the campaign, and they work the press to sell their point of view or at least to ensure that it is included in the reporters' stories. An example of spin can be seen in the early 1996 Republican presidential primaries. Those candidates who did not win the primary or caucus but placed better than expected were portrayed by their handlers as the real winners of the contest. Pat Buchanan, Steve Forbes, and Lamar Alexander all practiced this strategy. On the other hand Bob Dole, the winner of the

Iowa caucus, failed in the expectations game by not winning the contest by more than 5 percentage points, the amount political pundits agreed on as the threshold for the Republican front-runner. This allowed Pat Buchanan, who finished second in the caucus, to claim victory and establish the momentum he needed to carry him to victory in the New Hampshire primary one week later. **Candidate debates,** especially the televised presidential variety, are also showcases for the consultants' spin patrol, and teams of staffers from each side swarm the press rooms to declare victory even before the candidates finish their closing statements.

candidate debates:

Forums in which political candidates face each other to discuss their platforms, records, and character.

Televised Debates.   Candidate debates are media extravaganzas that are a hybrid of free and paid media. As with ads, much of the candidate dialogue (jokes included) is canned and prepackaged. Yet spontaneity cannot be completely eliminated, and gaffes, quips, and slips of the tongue can sometimes be revealing. President Gerald Ford's insistence during an October 1976 debate with Jimmy Carter that Poland was not under Soviet domination may have cost him a close election. Ronald Reagan's refrain, "Are you better off today than you were four years ago?" neatly summed up his case against Carter in 1980. Moreover, Reagan's easygoing performance reassured a skeptical public that wanted Carter out of the White House but was not certain it wanted Reagan in.

Senator John F. Kennedy's visually impressive showing in the first 1960 presidential debate dramatically reduced the edge that experience gave two-term Vice President Richard M. Nixon. Not only was Nixon ill at the time, but he also was poorly dressed and poorly made up for television. Interestingly, most of those who heard the debate

---

ℋIGHLIGHT 14.1

Famous Sound Bites from Presidential Campaigns

1996

"I ask for your help and if you really want to get involved, just tap into my homepage, www.dolc/kcmp96.org."
—*Senator Robert Dole (R), speaking during the second presidential debate.*

1992

"Message: I care"
—*George Bush (R), attempting to connect with New Hampshire's economically devastated voters.*

"Let's clean out the barn!"
—*Ross Perot (I)*

"Who am I? Why am I here?"
—*Retired Adm. James Stockdale, Ross Perot's 1992 vice-presidential running mate, during a televised debate.*

1988

"Read my lips: no new taxes."
—*George Bush (R)*

"Stop lying about my record!"
—*Senator Robert Dole (R–Kans.), speaking to George Bush during their campaign for the Republican nomination.*

"I knew Jack Kennedy; he was a friend of mine. And, Senator, you're no Jack Kennedy."
—*Democratic vice-presidential nominee Lloyd Bentsen (D–Tex.), responding in an October debate to Republican nominee Dan Quayle's comparison of himself to John F. Kennedy.*

"Follow me around . . . [you'll] be very bored."
—*Gary Hart (D–Colo.) to a reporter shortly before his May 1987 weekend with model Donna Rice.*

1984

"Where's the beef?"
—*Walter Mondale to his Democratic rival Gary Hart, who claimed to have "new ideas."*

1980

"There you go again . . . ."
—*Ronald Reagan (R) to President Jimmy Carter (D), in response to some of Carter's charges against Reagan in a debate.*

"Are you better off today than you were four years ago?"
—*Reagan's oft-repeated question to the voters.*

on radio—and therefore could not see the contrast between the pale, anxious, sweating Nixon and the relaxed, tanned Kennedy—thought that Nixon had won.

The importance of debates can easily be overrated, however. A weak performance by Reagan in his first debate with Walter Mondale in 1984 had little lasting effect, in part because Reagan did better in the second debate. And most of the debates in 1960, 1976, 1980, and 1988 were unmemorable and electorally inconsequential. Debates usually just firm up voters' predispositions and cannot change the fundamentals of an election (the state of the economy, scandal, and presidential popularity, for example). This is what appeared to happen in 1992 and 1996 when none of the three presidential debates and one vice-presidential debate changed the underlying pro-Clinton trends in the election. Nonetheless, because debates are potentially educational and focus the public's mind on the upcoming election, they are useful. Since they have been held in every presidential campaign since 1976, debates are now likely to be an expected and standard part of the presidential election process. They are also an established feature of campaigns for governor, U.S. senator, and many other offices.

Can the Press Be "Handled"?   Candidates and their consultants constantly try to "spin" (or influence) the thinking of the press. For example, campaigns today will often fax a dozen or more statements or releases a day to key journalists. Whether in these fax wars or elsewhere, efforts by candidates to manipulate the news media often fail because the press is wise to their tactics and determined to thwart them. Not even the candidates' paid media are sacrosanct anymore. Major newspapers throughout the country have taken to analyzing the accuracy of the television advertisements aired during the campaign—a welcome and useful addition to journalists' scrutiny of politicians.

Less welcome are some other news media practices in campaigns. Many studies have shown that the media are obsessed with the horse race aspect of politics—who's ahead, who's behind, who's gaining—to the detriment of the substance of the candidates' issues and ideas. Public opinion polls, especially tracking polls, many of them taken by the news outlets themselves, dominate coverage, especially on network television, where only a few minutes a night are devoted to politics. (Tracking polls were discussed in chapter 11.)

Related to the proliferation of polls is the media's expectations game in presidential primary contests. With polls as the objective backdrop, journalists set the margins by

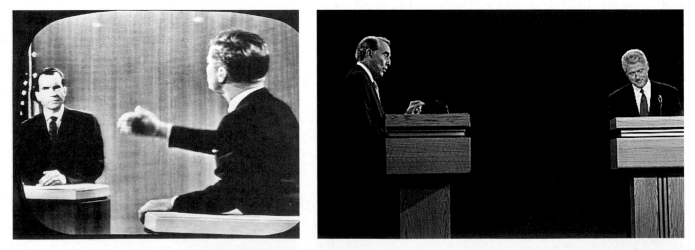

■ Presidential debates have come a long way—at least in terms of studio trappings—since the ill-at-ease Richard M. Nixon was visually bested by John F. Kennedy in the first televised debate. In the first of the 1996 debates, Robert Dole's rapid eye blinks were taken by many analysts as a sign of unease in the face of incumbent Clinton's comfortable position. (Photos courtesy: left, Corbis/Bettman; right, Wally McNamee/Folio, Inc.)

which contenders are expected to win or lose—so much so that even a clear victory of 5 percentage points can be judged a setback if the candidate had been projected to win by 12 or 15 points. Finally, the news media often overemphasize trivial parts of the campaign, such as a politician's minor gaffe, and give too much attention to the private lives of candidates. This superficial coverage and the resources needed to generate it are displacing serious journalism on the issues. These subjects are taken up again in the next chapter, which deals with the news media.

Web Exploration
To get an insider's look at the detail and urgency with which campaigns are now covered, go to www.awlonline.com/oconnor.

Campaign Financing

To run all aspects of a campaign successfully requires a great deal of money. In 1996 alone, more than $765 million was raised and spent in U.S. House and Senate races.[8] This amount was an increase of greater than 40 percent over the 1990 elections. On average, an incumbent Democrat in the House spent nearly $525,000; Republican incumbents in the House spent an average of $700,000. Their challengers in contrast, spent an average of $100,000. In contests with open seats, usually the most expensive races, over 80 percent of the candidates spent in excess of $400,000. As humorist Will Rogers once remarked early in the twentieth century, "Politics has got so expensive that it takes lots of money even to get beat with."

All this political money is regulated by the federal government under the terms of the Federal Election Campaign Act of 1971, first passed in 1971 and substantially strengthened after Watergate in 1974 and again in 1976. (Still more amendments were passed in 1979.) Table 14.1 summarizes some of the important provisions of this law, which limits what individuals, interest groups, and political parties can give to candidates for president, U.S. senator, and U.S. representative. These limits on contributions are discussed in the passages that follow, but the goal of all limits is the same: to prevent any single group or individual from gaining too much influence over elected officials, who naturally feel indebted to campaign contributors.

Given the cash flow required by a campaign and the legal restrictions on political money, raising the funds necessary to run a modern campaign is a monumental task. Consequently, presidential and congressional campaigns have squads of fund raisers on staff. These professionals rely on several standard sources of campaign money.

Individual Contributions.   Individual contributions are donations from individual citizens. The maximum allowable contribution under federal law for congressional and presidential elections is $1,000 per election to each candidate, with primary and general elections considered separately. Individuals are also limited to a total of $25,000 in

Table 14.1   Current Contribution Limits for Congressional Candidates (under the Federal Election Campaign Act)

Contributions From	Given to Candidate (Per Election)[a]	Given to National Party (Per Calendar Year)	Total Allowable Contributions (Per Calendar Year)
Individual	$1,000	$20,000	Limited to $25,000
Political action committee[b]	$5,000	$15,000	No limit
Any political party committee[c]	$5,000	No limit	No limit
All national and state party committees taken together	To House candidates: $30,000 plus "coordinated expenditures"[d] To Senate candidates: $27,500 plus "coordinated expenditures"[d]		

[a]Each of the following is considered a *separate* election: primary (or convention), runoff, general election.

[b]Multicandidate PACs only. Multicandidate committees have received contributions from at least fifty persons and have given to at least five federal candidates.

[c]Multicandidate party committees only. Multicandidate committees have received contributions from at least fifty persons and have given to at least five federal candidates.

[d]Coordinated expenditures are party-paid general election campaign expenditures made in consultation and coordination with the candidate.

gifts to all candidates combined in each calendar year. Most candidates receive a majority of all funds directly from individuals, and most individual gifts are well below the maximum level.

Political Action Committee (PAC) Contributions.   Donations from **political action committees (PACs)** are those from interest groups (labor unions, corporations, trade associations, and ideological and issue groups). Under federal law these organizations are required to establish officially recognized fund-raising committees, called PACs, in order to participate in federal elections. (Some but not all states have similar requirements for state elections.) Approximately 4,000 PACs are registered with the Federal Election Commission—the governmental agency charged with administering the election laws. In 1994 all PACs together gave $179 million to Senate and House candidates. (By contrast, individual citizens donated nearly $336 million.) In 1998 PACs contributed $207 million to Senate and House candidates, while individuals donated $420 million. On average, PAC contributions account for 32 percent of the war chests (campaign funds) of House candidates and 17 percent of the treasuries of Senate candidates. (Interest groups are treated in more detail in chapter 16.)

Political Party Contributions.   Candidates also receive donations from the national and state committees of the Democratic and Republican parties. As mentioned in chapter 12, political parties can give substantial contributions to their congressional nominees. In 1996 both the Republicans and the Democrats funneled over $25 million to their standard-bearers. In competitive races, the parties may provide 15 percent to 17 percent of their candidates' total war chests.

Member-to-Candidate Contributions.   In Congress and in state legislatures, well-funded, electorally secure incumbents now often contribute campaign money to their party's needy incumbent and nonincumbent legislative candidates.[9] This activity has long occurred in some state legislatures (notably California), but it has recently become increasingly important at the congressional level.[10] Generally, members contribute to other candidates in one of two ways. First, some members have established their own PACs—informally dubbed "leadership" PACs—through which they distribute campaign support to candidates. For example, Republican Majority Leader Dick Armey's PAC—The Majority Leader's Fund—contributed $718,352 to 144 Republican House general election candidates during the 1995–96 election cycle. Second, members also make contributions to other candidates directly from their own reelection accounts. Either way, members are limited in what they may contribute to other candidates: $1,000 per candidate per election to federal candidates from their reelection committees, and $5,000 per candidate per election to candidates through a leadership PAC.

Collectively, these contributions can add up. For example, in 1996 fifty-four House Republicans contributed a total of $111,242 to the campaign of Randy Tate, an electorally vulnerable Republican House incumbent running for reelection in Washington State's Ninth congressional district. Astonishingly, the amount contributed to Tate by his colleagues was $41,167 *greater* than that contributed in cash and coordinated expenditures by the National Republican Congressional Committee (NRCC), the primary fund-raising arm of the House Republican Conference. In general, members give their contributions to the same candidates who receive the bulk of congressional campaign committee resources. As such, member contributions at the congressional level have emerged as a major supplement to the campaign resources contributed by the party campaign committees.[11] In an interesting twist on member-to-candidate contribution activity in congressional elections, it now appears that some leadership PACs are raising and spending soft money.[12]

Candidates' Personal Contributions.   Candidates and their families may donate to the campaign. The Supreme Court ruled in 1976 in *Buckley* v. *Valeo* that no limit could be placed on the amount of money candidates can spend from their own families' resources, since such spending is considered a First Amendment right of free

political action committee (PAC):

Federally mandated, officially registered fund-raising committee that represents interest groups in the political process.

speech.[13] For wealthy politicians such as U.S. Senators John D. Rockefeller IV (D–W. Va.) or Herbert H. Kohl (D–Wisc.), this allowance may mean personal spending in the millions. Most candidates, however, commit much less than $100,000 in family resources to their election bids. Ross Perot, who publicly committed to spend millions, was not the usual candidate. In 1994 House and Senate candidates loaned or contributed almost $123 million to their own campaigns. In 1996 House and Senate candidate contributions to their own campaigns was $107 million, a decrease due mostly to 1996 senatorial candidates spending less of their own funds. Steve Forbes, though, did not follow the lead of the senatorial candidates. He spent more than $30 million of his own money on his bid for the Republican presidential nomination.

Public Funds.   **Public funds** are donations from general tax revenues. Only presidential candidates (and a handful of state and local contenders) receive public funds. Under the terms of the Federal Election Campaign Act of 1971 (which first established public funding of presidential campaigns), a candidate for president can become eligible to receive public funds during the nominating contest by raising at least $5,000 in individual contributions of $250 or less in each of twenty states. Once the receipt of this money is certified, the candidate can apply for federal **matching funds,** whereby every dollar raised from individuals in amounts less than $251 is matched by the federal treasury on a dollar-for-dollar basis. This assumes there is enough money in the Presidential Election Campaign Fund to do so. The fund is accumulated by taxpayers who designate $3 of their taxes for this purpose each year when they send in their federal tax returns. (Only about 20 percent of taxpayers check off the appropriate box, even though participation does not increase their tax burden.)

For the general election, the two major-party presidential nominees are given a lump-sum payment in the summer before the election ($62 million each in 1996), from which all their general election campaign expenditures must come. A third-party candidate receives a smaller amount proportionate to his or her November vote total if that candidate gains a minimum of 5 percent of the vote. Note that in such a case the money goes to third-party campaigns only *after* the election is over; no money is given in advance of the general election. The only third-party candidate to qualify for general election funds before Ross Perot did so was John Anderson, the Independent candidate for president in 1980, who garnered 7 percent of the national vote. While Ross Perot chose not to take public funds for his campaign in 1992, a campaign which was largely self-financed, in 1996 Perot did accept public funding. He qualified for this funding by securing 19 percent of the popular vote in the 1992 presidential election.

Independent Expenditures. In the landmark case of *Buckley* v. *Valeo* (1976), the Supreme Court ruled that it is unconstitutional for Congress to limit the amount of money that an individual or a political committee may spend supporting or opposing a candidate *if the expenditures are made independently of the candidate's campaign.* (see Figure 14.1)[14] In a 1996 case, *Colorado Republican Federal Campaign Committee* v. *Federal Election Commission,* the Supreme Court extended

public funds:

Donations from the general tax revenues to the campaigns of qualifying presidential candidates.

matching funds:

Donations to presidential campaigns from the federal government that are determined by the amount of private funds a qualifying candidate raises.

■ Steve Forbes reaches out to campaign supporters during his 1996 presidential bid. Critics have suggested that Forbes' political presence is sustained only by large campaign expenditures drawn from his personal fortune, and that such campaigns have an adverse effect on modern American politics by giving an unfair advantage to the super-rich. (Photo courtesy: AP/Wide World Photos)

Figure 14.1 Expenditures by PACs in 1996

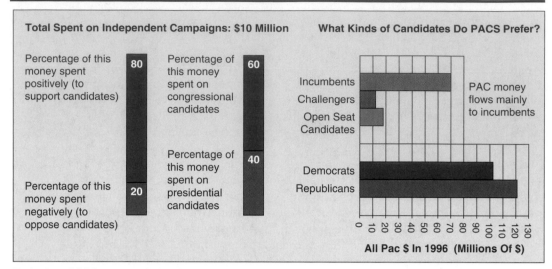

Notice how PACS use a majority of their expenditures to support congressional candidates positively, and only a small fraction to attack opponents in presidential campaigns. Notice how PAC spending has a slight bias towards Republican candidates and a strong bias toward incumbents.

SOURCE: Federal Election Commission.

hard money:

Legally specified and limited contributions that are clearly regulated by the Federal Election Campaign Act and by the Federal Election Commission.

soft money:

The virtually unregulated money funneled by individuals and political committees through state and local parties.

this ruling to political parties.[15] Hence, individuals, PACs—and now political parties as well—may spend unlimited amounts of money directly advocating the election or defeat of a candidate as long as these expenditures are not made in coordination with the candidate's campaign. Often, when a group spends independently of candidate, it will do so for television advertisements urging voters to support or defeat a particular candidate. However, because independent expenditure advertisements expressly advocate the election or defeat of a specific federal candidate, they must be paid for with **hard money**—that is, with money raised under the guidelines of the Federal Election Campaign Act (see Table 14.1). This stands in direct contrast to *Soft money—financed issue advocacy ads,* which are considered next.

Soft Money/Issue Advocacy Advertisements. **Soft money** is campaign money raised and spent by political parties and interest groups that is not subject to the regulations of the Federal Election Campaign Act. In a 1978 advisory opinion, the Federal Election Commission ruled that political parties could raise these unregulated funds in order to pay for expenses—such as overhead and administrative costs—and grassroots activities that did not directly influence campaigns for federal elections.[16] In 1979 Congress passed an amendment to the Federal Elections Campaign Act allowing parties to *spend* unlimited sums on these same activities.[17] In the years immediately following the rule changes, the national parties began raising five- and six-figure sums from individuals and interest groups to pay for expenses such as rent, employee salaries, and building maintenance. The national parties also began transferring large sums of soft money to state parties in order to help pay for grassroots activities (such as get-out-the-vote drives) and campaign paraphernalia (such as yard signs and bumper stickers).

However, the line separating expenditures that influence federal elections from those that do not has proved to be quite blurry, and this blurriness has resulted in a significant campaign finance loophole. The largest controversy has come in the area of campaign advertisements. The federal courts have ruled that only campaign advertisements that use explicit words—for example, "vote for," "vote against," "elect," or "support"—qualify as *express-advocacy* advertisements. Political advertisements that do not use these words are considered *issue-advocacy* advertisements.[18] The distinction here is crucial. Because express-advocacy advertisements are openly intended to influence federal elections, they must be paid for with strictly regulated hard money. Issue-advocacy advertisements, on the other hand, can be paid for with unregulated soft money. The parties' response to these rules has been to create issue-advocacy advertisements that very much resemble express-advocacy ads. Typically, for example, such advertisements call attention to the voting record of the candidate supported or opposed and are replete with images of the candidate. However, the parties ensure that the magic words "vote for" or "vote against" are never uttered in the advertisements, allowing them to be paid for with soft rather than hard money.

The national parties have not been the only groups to exploit the soft-money loophole; interest groups have increasingly joined the fray by running their own "issue"-advocacy ads and conducting other soft money–financed campaign activities. For example, in the 1996 congressional elections, the AFL–CIO spent in the neighborhood of $35 million in soft money on "voter education"—direct-mail and media advertisements attacking the legislative record of House Republicans. These efforts played a significant role in the defeat of many GOP freshmen.[19] Interestingly, in 1999 House Republican leaders started their own soft money–financed voter education fund—called the Republican Majority Issues Campaign—to counter the AFL–CIO's ongoing efforts.[20] Whether or not parties and interest groups may coordinate issue-advocacy campaigns with candidates is a matter yet to be decided by the Federal Election Commission.[21] In any case, the introduction of huge sums of soft money into federal campaigns has the potential to transform campaigns from candidate-centered to interest group–and party-centered affairs.[22]

Some argue that the recent proliferation of soft money (in 1996, the Republican and Democratic party committees raised $138 million and $124 million respectively in soft money—a 178 percent increase for the Republicans and 242 percent increase for the Democrats in total soft money from 1992) is not to be lamented. They maintain that political parties deserve more fund-raising freedom, which would give these critical institutions a more substantial role in elections. But when individual contributors are able to donate as much money as they like via the soft money route, they at least theoretically gain a heightened level of access to politicians not enjoyed by the electorate as a whole. The money itself has been the cause of great concern during the 1996 presidential campaign and has been the subject of a series of congressional and legal investigations. Government watchdog groups such as Common Cause and Public Campaign believe that the soft-money/issue-advocacy loophole has created a complete meltdown of federal campaign laws, and they argue that political parties should be banned from raising soft money.

The Internet and Campaign Finance

The Internet has the potential to alter radically the way candidates raise funds for their campaigns. After all, making an on-line appeal for campaign contributions costs significantly less than raising funds through expensive direct-mail campaigns or pricey fund-raising events—the standard means of raising campaign resources. Still, it's not clear that on-line fund-raising appeals would be all that successful. The Internet, veteran political consultant Hal Malchow reminds us, is a self-directed medium, and "it is not human nature to seek out places to give money."[23] Nevertheless, the potential weaknesses of Internet fund raising are unlikely to stop candidates from experimenting with it. Indeed, several candidates for the 2000 presidential contest are attempting to raise contributions from their campaign's web site.

The Internet also promises to create headaches for the Federal Election Commission. Already, the FEC has been forced to rule on issues such as whether a business site link to a campaign site constitutes in-kind contribution from the business to the campaign, and whether funds raised on-line by presidential candidates are eligible to be matched with public funds from the Presidential Election Campaign Fund. (In the first case, the FEC ruled yes; in the second case, it ruled no.) And clearly, these issues are only the beginning of a seemingly limitless plethora of concerns regarding the

Internet and campaign finance that the FEC will be asked to address. "Every day," noted former FEC Chair Trevor Potter, "I'm running into people in my practice who are saying, 'This is what I want to do on the Internet—are there any Federal Election law implications?'"[24] Indeed, campaign finance experts have wondered aloud whether the agency has the resources to regulate and monitor the newly unfolding campaign activity on the Internet.[25]

Are PACs a Good or Bad Part of the Process?

Of all these forms of spending, probably the most controversial is that involving PAC money. Some PACs, due to the amount of money they are able to raise and their ability to get their supporters to the polls on Election Day, are more influential than others; but there are few poor, noninfluential PACs. Some observers claim that PACs are the embodiment of corrupt special interests that use campaign donations to buy the votes of legislators. Furthermore, they argue that the less affluent and minority members of our society do not enjoy equal access to these political organizations.

These charges are serious and deserve consideration. Although the media relentlessly stresses the role of money in determining policy outcomes, the evidence that PACs buy votes is less than overwhelming.[26] Political scientists have conducted a multitude of studies regarding the impact of interest group PAC contributions on legislative voting, and the conclusions reached by these studies have varied widely.[27] Whereas some studies have found that PAC money affects members' voting behavior, other studies have uncovered no such correlation. It may be, of course, that interest group PAC money has an impact on members' behavior at earlier stages of the legislative process. Along these lines, one innovative study found that PAC money had a significant effect on members' participation in committee on legislation important to the contributing group.[28] Thus, interest group PAC money may mobilize something more important than votes—the valuable time and energy of members themselves.

Also serious is the charge that some interests are significantly better represented by the PAC system than are others. This view was put forth most recently by political scientist Thomas Gais, who argues that laws regulating PAC activity inherently favor PACs with parent organizations—corporate, labor, and trade PACs—over citizen-based PACs without parent organizations.[29] Although Gais's argument is complex, a simple example of the biases of federal law illustrates his point. As Gais points out, federal campaign finance law allows corporate, labor, and trade PACs to use general treasury funds from the PAC's parent organization to pay for the (often formidable) overhead and administrative costs of running the PAC, whereas PACs without parent organizations are forced to rely on voluntary contributions to pay their overhead and administrative costs. The result of these laws, argues Gais, is that citizen-based PACs have a more difficult time organizing than do PACs with a well-established, wealthy parent organization. Consequently, the PAC system, in Gais's view, aids some interests more than others. Gais argues that any campaign finance reform should raise substantially the limits on the amount of money an individual may contribute to a PAC—to the point where a single person could underwrite a citizen group's formation and maintenance costs.

Still, for all their faults, many political scientists view PACs as a natural manifestation of interest group politics in a diverse democracy. Also, many political scientists point out that a person need not belong to a PAC to wield electoral and political influence. The Democrats' best-known external resources—and the ones that most pain Republicans—are the PACs associated with organized labor, and minority groups as a whole. While organized labor has for decades provided Democrats with an army of volunteers and huge amounts of financial support, minorities have been the single most loyal Democratic voting bloc—in raw vote terms even more indispensable to the Democrats than labor.

Although a good number of PACs of all persuasions existed prior to the 1970s, it was during this decade—the decade of campaign reform—that the modern PAC era began.

Spawned by the Watergate-inspired revisions of the campaign-finance laws, PACs grew in number from 113 in 1972 to 4,599 by the late 1990s (see Figure 14.2), and their contributions to congressional candidates multiplied almost eighteenfold, from $8.5 million in 1971 and 1972 to $206 million in 1996 and 1998 (see Figure 14.3). But these numbers should not obscure a basic truth about the PAC system: that a very small group of PACs conducts the bulk of total PAC activity. Indeed, as political scientist Paul Herrnson

Figure 14.2 Growth in Total Number of PACs[a]

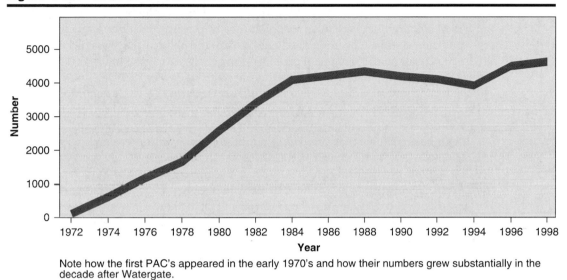

Note how the first PAC's appeared in the early 1970's and how their numbers grew substantially in the decade after Watergate.

[a]As of December 31st of every other year, starting in 1972.

SOURCE: Federal Election Commission.

Figure 14.3 Growth in Total Contributions by PACs to House and Senate Candidates[a]

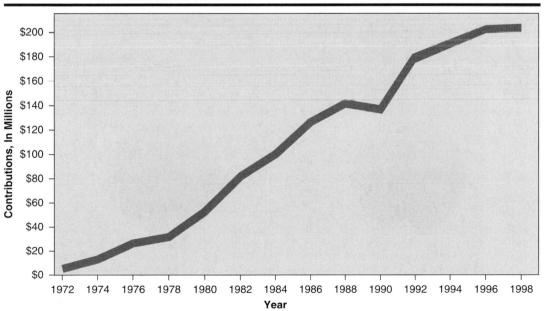

The growth of campaign spending by PAC's has roughly paralleled the increasing number of PAC's over their 30-year history.

[a] For two-year election cycles ending in years shown.

SOURCE: Federal Election Commission.

observes, a mere 4 percent of all PACs contributed a full 57 percent of the total dollars given to congressional candidates by PACs during the 1995–96 election cycle.[30]

Some people argue that PACs are newfangled inventions that have flooded the political system with money. Although the widespread use of the PAC structure is new, the fact remains that special-interest money of all types has always found its way into politics. Before the 1970s it did so in less traceable and much more disturbing and unsavory ways, because little of the money given to candidates was regularly disclosed to public inspection. And although it is true that PACs contribute a massive sum to candidates in absolute terms, it is not clear that there is proportionately more interest group money in the system than before. The proportion of House and Senate campaign funds provided by PACs has certainly increased since the early 1970s; but individuals, most of whom are unaffiliated with PACs, together with the political parties, still supply more than 60 percent of all the money spent by or on behalf of House candidates, 75 percent of the campaign expenditures for Senate contenders (see Figure 14.4), and 85 percent of the campaign expenditures for presidential candidates. So while the importance of PAC spending has grown, PACs clearly remain secondary as a source of election funding and therefore pose no overwhelming threat to the system's legitimacy.

It can be argued that contemporary political action committees are another manifestation of what James Madison called "factions." Through the flourishing of competing interest groups or factions, said Madison in *Federalist No. 10,* liberty would be preserved. In any democracy, and particularly in one as pluralistic as that of the United States, it is essential that groups be relatively unrestricted in advocating their interests and positions (see Highlight 14.2: Women's PACs Continue to Make a Difference). Not only is unrestricted political activity by interest groups a mark of a free society, it also provides a safety valve for the competitive pressures that build on all fronts in a democracy and supplies a way to keep representatives responsive to legitimate needs.

The election outlays of PACs, like the total amount expended in a single election season, seem huge. But the cost of elections in the United States is less than or approximately the same as in some other nations, measured on a per-voter basis.[31] Moreover,

**Figure 14.4   Campaign for Senate, 1996: A "Typical" Candidate's Budget
of $2 Million**

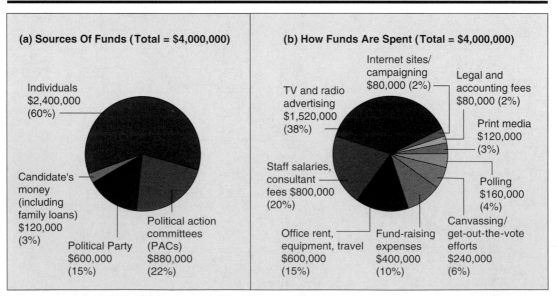

The breakdown of a sample budget for a typical Senate campaign. Note how most of the revenue comes from individual contributions, and how the greatest expense is media advertising.

HIGHLIGHT 14.2 — Women's PACs Continue to Make a Difference

Women's political action committees made a real difference in the 1990 and 1992 elections. In 1990, women's PACs contributed over $2.6 million to candidates and in 1992 nearly triple that.

EMILY's List, which stands for Early Money Is Like Yeast (it makes the dough rise), is the largest contributor to women's campaigns. Founded in 1985, its members contributed nearly $1.5 million to female candidates in 1990. Ann Richards, who ran a hotly contested race for the Texas governorship in 1990, credits EMILY's List with providing crucial funding at a key time. In 1992, EMILY's List provided $6.2 million to fifty-five pro-choice Democratic woman candidates, of whom twenty-five won. It spent more than that to support thirty-eight candidates in the 1994 election cycle.

In 1996, it was again a major player in the state and congressional elections. A study released by the Federal Election Commission in late September 1996, for example, reported that EMILY's List led all PACs raising $9.4 million; to that time, no other PAC had raised more than $7 million. Similarly, the WISH LIST, which stands for Women in the House and Senate and backs Republican candidates, spent $325,000 and the Susan B. Anthony List, a nonpartisan PAC, raised $250,000 for the twelve anti-abortion women candidates it backed for House election. In 1998, EMILY's List contributed $7.5 million to elect seven new pro-choice women to the House.

SOURCE: Center for the American Woman and Politics, *CAWP News & Notes* (Winter 1991): 10–11; *The Times-Picayune*, "EMILY's List Dough Helps Women Rise," (January 26, 1994): A1; and EMILY's List.

---

the cost of all elections in the United States taken together is less than the amount many individual private corporations spend on advertising cereals, dog food, cars, and toothpaste. These days it is expensive to communicate, whether the message is political or commercial. The costs of television time, polling, consultants, and other items have soared over and above the inflation rate.

A SUMMARY OF CONTRIBUTIONS AND EXPENSES

Figure 14.4 gives an idea of where all the money comes from and goes to. A typical U.S. Senate campaign candidate in 1996 received most of his or her war chest (about 60 percent) from relatively small individual donations. PACs supplied about 22 percent, the political party committees 15 percent, and the candidates about 3 percent.

The single greatest outlay (40 percent of the total) was for television advertising; the next-largest item, staff and consultant salaries, was half television's cost (20 percent). The other 40 percent of the budget was spent on everything from polls to travel expenses. Keep in mind that in a large state with a dozen or more media markets (concentrated population centers with many television and radio stations), expenditures often balloon to $5 million, $10 million, and even more.

Some candidates have more difficulty than others in raising the necessary dollar amounts. Those in power—the incumbents—have the least trouble, although challengers who face incumbents weakened by scandal can also find the task of financing the campaign relatively easy. The size of a challenger's war chest is really the key variable. There is a point of diminishing returns for incumbent spending, since most office holders are already well known to the voters. But the challenger's name and platform are likely to be obscure. If the challenger can raise and spend enough to get his or her basic message across, there is a reasonable chance that the election will be at least moderately competitive. As is more common, though, if the challenger is starved for funds, the contest will probably turn into a romp for the well-heeled incumbent.

BRINGING IT TOGETHER: THE 1996 PRESIDENTIAL CAMPAIGN AND ELECTION

Roughly a year before the November 1996 presidential election, it looked to be a somewhat uneventful affair. No liberal Democrats stepped forward to challenge a rejuvenated and popular President Clinton, who had rebounded from his party's 1994 midterm congressional electoral defeats. Republicans, despite vehement protestations from party activists, seemed poised to nominate a moderate Washington insider—Senate Majority Leader Bob Dole. Although Dole's primary battle turned out to be a little more exciting than expected, in the end he prevailed, securing the right to face Clinton in the general election for president.

As it turned out, Dole was no match for Clinton. Buoyed mainly by a healthy economy (unemployment and interest rates were down, economic productivity and growth were up), voters revived the time-honored tradition of voting their pocketbooks, returning Clinton to the Oval Office for four more years.

The Party Nomination Battle

President Clinton's hopes for an uncontested renomination were realized when Democrats decided to coalesce around their embattled party leader. Afraid that an intra-party squabble would open the door for Republicans both to build upon their congressional advantage and secure the presidency, Democratic liberals and moderates alike decided early on to pledge their support to the sitting president. They hoped for a repeat of 1948, when Democrats, after losing control of Congress in 1946, rallied behind Democratic President Harry Truman, returning him to the White House for another term and recapturing Congress from a Republican congressional majority that was regularly criticized during that period for flirting with extremism in domestic legislation.

Republicans, on the other hand, sponsored an unusual free-for-all for the presidential nomination in 1996 that was reminiscent of many former Democratic nomination battles. The leading announced candidate from the beginning was Senator Robert Dole of Kansas. Despite some weak straw poll showings in the latter months of 1995 against the more conservative GOP candidates, Dole, buttressed by strong financial support and the endorsement of virtually every GOP stalwart, seemingly had the nomination wrapped up. But after conservative television commentator Patrick J. Buchanan single-handedly ended Phil Gramm's candidacy in Louisiana and came within 5 percentage points of winning the Iowa caucus, other Republican candidates—most notably the multimillionaire publisher of *Forbes* magazine, Malcolm S. "Steve" Forbes, and the former Secretary of Education and Governor of Tennessee, Lamar Alexander—began to press Dole as well. A week later at the New Hampshire primary, Buchanan bested Dole, with Alexander and Forbes close behind. But after some lackluster performances by Buchanan, Forbes, and Alexander in South Carolina and the "Yankee" primary (Forbes did win the Delaware and Arizona contests, but these victories were not unexpected), the well-financed Dole campaign began to generate unstoppable momentum. By mid-March Dole had managed to outlast all his rivals, becoming the presumptive Republican presidential nominee. Many political observers believe that Dole won largely because of the front-loaded GOP primary (see chapter 12)—which gives advantage to the initial front-runner.[32]

Republicans, like Democrats in 1992, seemed more resigned than enthusiastic as they looked to a Dole candidacy. Dole trailed Clinton in the polls by anywhere between 10 and 20 percentage points (some polls had him in the 30s in a two-way race and some even had him in the 20s in a three-way contest with Texas billionaire and 1992 independent presidential candidate Ross Perot). But on May 16 Dole, in a stunning move, relinquished the Senate seat he had held for twenty-seven years to campaign for the presidency in earnest. Stating that his campaign was "about telling the truth, it's about doing what is right, it's about electing a president who's not attracted to the glories of the office but rather to its difficulties," Dole placed his future in the hands of the American electorate with but two possible destinations: the White House or back to Kansas.

The Third Force: Ross Perot

Though many names surfaced, most notably Colin Powell, the former Chairman of the Joint Chiefs of Staff, Ross Perot in 1996 remained the only major third-party challenger for the presidency. (Other independent or third-party candidates did join the 1996 presidential race, for example, author Harry Brown of the Libertarian Party and Ralph Nader of the Green Party, but none of them were able to generate the levels of support necessary to offer a realistic threat to either Clinton or Dole.)

Perot again made use of his favorite medium—television—and his favorite forum—*Larry King Live*—to announce his intention to run for president "if the voters want me to." His announcement followed on the heels of the news that former Colorado Governor and Democrat Richard Lamm would be seeking the nomination of Ross Perot's Reform Party. Though he had previously remained coy regarding whether or not he would join the 1996 presidential race, Richard Lamm's entry seemed to ignite Perot's interest.

Perot's hold on the Reform Party proved too strong for Lamm to overcome. After an accounting firm had tabulated the votes (though over 1 million ballots were mailed out to Reform Party members, only about 50,000 were filled out and mailed back, a 5 percent return), Perot had secured the support of two-thirds of those Reform Party members who chose to participate in the mail-in election.

Three weeks later, Perot announced that his running mate would be economist Pat Choate, a Perot confidant and adviser during the 1992 presidential election effort, and the man regarded by many as the chief architect of Perot's thoughts concerning taxes, the economy, the budget, and deficit reduction. Though virtually unknown outside of economic and political circles, it was thought that Choate would prove to be a more capable running mate than Perot's 1992 choice, political novice Admiral James Stockdale. (Who can forget the image of Stockdale during the 1992 vice-presidential debate beginning his opening remarks with the comment "Who am I? Why am I here?")

While the impact of Perot and Choate on the 1996 presidential election did not approach Perot's 19 percent of the popular vote showing in 1992, their presence did help ensure that difficult domestic policy issues such as deficit reduction, and tax and campaign finance reform would be addressed. The true value of third-party and independent candidates has been not so much their effect on the actual outcome of the election as it has been their ability to force the two major political parties to address issues they might otherwise have chosen to ignore. When looked at in this perspective, one can understand why many an attentive voter and well-informed citizen, though they might intend to vote Republican or Democratic, welcome presidential campaigns that include these party crashers.

The Party Conventions

Republicans and Democrats, as well as the fledgling Reform Party, each held conventions in the month of August.

The Reform Party Convention.   The Reform Party kicked off convention month, meeting in Long Beach, California, on August 11. After announcing one week earlier that Ross Perot had defeated Richard Lamm for the party's nomination, this convention, like those of the two major parties, was more of an infomercial that touted the accomplishments of Perot and the correctness of his vision for America than anything else. Shorter in duration than its four-day counterparts, and covered extensively only by CNN and C-SPAN, the Reform Party convention did not even contain the drama reserved for most conventions featuring a challenge to the present administration—the party's vice-presidential selection and the introduction of that selection to the country.

■ Joe Lockhart, White House Press Secretary, speaks to the press. Lockhart was Deputy Press Secretary under Mike McCurry, whom he succeeded at Presidential requests after McCurry resigned in the wake of the Lewinsky scandal. (Photo courtesy: David Burnett/Contact Press Images)

(Perot had not yet settled on a nominee and was also unsure about the reception he would receive from his top choices.) By the close of the weekend, the Reform Party had attempted to make its case to the American people. In a pattern that would be repeated during the Republican and Democratic conventions, few were listening.

The Republican Party Convention. The very next day, Republicans kicked off their convention in San Diego, California, gathering to officially nominate Robert Dole. While many felt that the convention itself contained little real news, as Republicans attempted to put their own spin on the proceedings without any interference from what they view as an unsympathetic and sometimes hostile liberal-leaning media, the days leading up to the convention were just the opposite. First, Dole announced that his economic agenda would include a 15 percent across the board income tax cut as well as a 50 percent reduction in the capital gains tax. This announcement, one which championed supply-side economics (supply-side economics is based on the belief that lower tax levels result in increased revenue and capital, which in turn spurs economic growth) over Dole's deficit reduction instincts, was followed by his announcement that supply-side champion Jack Kemp, a former professional football player, congressman, and Secretary of Housing and Urban Development, would be his running mate. This move surprised many, some of whom recalled a widely reported "joke" attributed to Dole earlier in his career: "Did you hear the good news? A bus load of supply-siders just went over a cliff. Did you hear the bad news? Jack Kemp wasn't on it."

The uniting of Dole, a self-described deficit hawk who throughout his career placed deficit and spending reductions ahead of tax cuts and was always wary of supply-side economic theories, with Kemp, a man thirteen years his junior whose view on the economy as well as immigration and affirmative action could not have been more different from Dole's before he joined the Republican presidential ticket, showed once again that politics can make strange bedfellows.

While Dole was introducing Jack Kemp to the country, behind the scenes, moderate and conservative Republicans vied for control of the party platform. While moderate Republicans demanded that language including toleration for the views of those Republicans who did not support the passage of a constitutional amendment banning abortion be added to the platform, conservative Republicans demanded that any language that hinted at tolerance on this issue be stricken from the platform. In the end, the two sides struck a compromise that temporarily satisfied the opponents and helped to avoid a fight over the issue on the convention floor, an outcome that all Republicans hoped to avoid.

The convention itself contained a number of highlights. On the opening night, Republicans led off with former Presidents Gerald R. Ford and George Bush. They were followed by a stirring video tribute to former President Ronald Reagan, which brought many in the convention hall to tears. Afterward, Nancy Reagan appeared on stage and offered an emotional speech on behalf of her ailing husband. She was followed by the night's keynote speaker, retired General Colin Powell. Making the case for a "big tent" party, one that was big enough to include social conservatives and those whose views were more moderate, Powell gave a rousing speech, offering us a glimpse of a possible future Powell candidacy. Bob Dole's wife, Elizabeth Dole, made her first significant campaign appearance at the convention. Moving from the podium to the convention floor during her address, Elizabeth Dole discussed her husband's accomplishments in a manner that endeared her to the convention delegates as well as the viewing audience. After her unexpectedly stunning performance, many openly wondered how the Democratic Party and Hillary Clinton would respond.

On the convention's final night, Bob Dole gave what many considered to be his best speech of the campaign. Offering himself up as a bridge to America's future as well as its past, Dole went on the offensive, attacking President Clinton and many of his "liberal" supporters, most notably the teachers' union, touting his economic agenda, and promising to renew and reinvigorate efforts to crack down on crime and drug use. By convention's end, some polls showed that Dole had received anywhere between a 10 and 20 percent post-convention "bounce" in the polls, narrowing his gap with Bill Clinton considerably. For all the criticism then heaped on the Republican convention by journalists and some political pundits who felt the GOP had offered up a carefully crafted political spectacle, one devoid of real news that generated dismal television ratings, Republicans claimed they had accomplished their major goals—erase memories of the contentious 1992 convention in Houston, paint a picture of a unified Republican party, and rally support for the Dole/Kemp ticket. Indeed, "the most remarkable feature of the 1996 Republican convention," observed political scientist William Keefe, "was its preoccupation with conformity and unity."[33]

The Democratic Party Convention.   Two weeks later, Democrats gathered in Chicago, home of the infamous 1968 Democratic convention in which Vietnam war protesters and Chicago police repeatedly clashed in the city parks and streets. Unlike the Republican convention, the days leading up to the Democratic gathering contained few significant developments. But, while the Democrats might have seemed like a unified party, beneath the surface fissures in the foundation could be detected. A week earlier, President Clinton signed a bill that ended the federal guarantee of welfare, transferring all responsibility for managing welfare to the states. This move, though popular with the majority of Americans, angered many Democrats, especially Democratic delegates, who tend to be more liberal than both Democrats and the country as a whole. This convention though, like the Republican gathering, was designed to showcase unity, not division. The welfare debate then was not highlighted by convention organizers.

Similar to the Republican gathering, the Democratic convention contained some highlights. Former Ronald Reagan Chief of Staff James Brady and his wife Sarah Brady appeared on stage to thank President Clinton for championing the passage of the Brady Bill, a bill that called for a waiting period before an individual could purchase a gun, which Republicans found difficult to support in the past due to their close affiliation with the National Rifle Association. Seeing Jim Brady, who has been confined to a wheelchair and undergone untold amounts of physical and speech therapy since he was shot during an assassination attempt on President Reagan, both address the convention hall and do so standing, was an emotional moment. Vice President Gore also gave a moving speech, discussing his sister's fight against lung cancer—a fight she eventually lost—in an effort to crystallize the Democrat's opposition to tobacco use by teenagers. Democrats did also decide to feature Hillary Clinton, a decision that became a necessity after Elizabeth Dole's performance at the Republican convention. Mrs. Clinton deftly responded to her conservative critics, all the while touting the achievements of the first four years of her husband's administration. In the end, Hillary Clinton's convention performance, though not as well received as Elizabeth Dole's, was praised rather than panned, an outcome that relieved many Democratic operatives who had pre-convention jitters because of the First Lady's somewhat negative poll ratings. Finally, President Clinton closed the convention with a speech that outlined his accomplishments during his first four years as president and sketched out his agenda for the next four years, an agenda that promised "more of the same." Marred only by the untimely resignation of

Dick Morris, President Clinton's chief political adviser, this convention, like the Republican one before it, received criticism for being more a staged event than real news. But in spite of this criticism and continued low viewer ratings, much like the Republicans before them Democrats achieved their overriding goals, painting a picture of a unified Democratic party that had put their differences aside, and embraced the opportunity to champion the Clinton/Gore ticket.

One measure of the Democrats' success can be seen in the public opinion polling. Polls the next day showed that Clinton's post-convention bounce had placed him again anywhere from 10 to 20 percentage points ahead of Dole, and that both Clinton and Dole held substantial leads over Ross Perot. Overall, while all three conventions were a success as judged by their organizers, the dramatic bounce we have sometimes seen occur after previous conventions, where one candidate trailing badly in the polls makes a sudden and sustained jump following their convention, failed to occur in 1996. By month's end, each of the three major presidential candidates saw poll ratings similar to those they enjoyed before the first convention was held. Whether or not this is a trend we will continue to see as these affairs become more tightly organized and orchestrated remains to be seen.

The Debates

After weeks of discussion, the Commission on Presidential Debates, a bipartisan panel of five Republicans and five Democrats, brokered a deal with Republican presidential candidate Bob Dole and Democrat Bill Clinton, agreeing on a debate schedule that included two presidential debates along with one vice-presidential debate. The format of the first presidential debate, held in Hartford, Connecticut, on October 6, was a traditional one, 90 minutes in length and moderated by a single individual—Jim Lehrer, the host of public television's evening news program. The second debate, held in San Diego, California, made use of the popular "town-hall" style first used at the presidential level in the 1992 presidential contest, with those in attendance asking questions of the candidates.

The big early news was the debate commission's decision to bar Reform Party presidential candidate Ross Perot and vice-presidential candidate Pat Choate from the debates. In addition to several objective guidelines, such as whether or not Perot or Choate were on enough ballots in enough states to win, the debate commission examined whether or not Perot and Choate stood a "realistic chance" of winning.

■ Hoping for media attention, Clinton supporters stage a march outside a California bookstore where Republican presidential hopeful Bob Dole was signing copies of his book *Unlimited Partners.* (Photo courtesy: Damian Dovarganes/AP/Wide World Photos)

The debate commission's decision to exclude Perot and Choate was quickly followed by a lawsuit. Demanding that the Federal Election Commission (FEC) or the debate commission halt the scheduled debates unless he and his running mate were allowed to participate, Perot alleged that the debate commission violated recent FEC regulations, first by including President Clinton and Republican Bob Dole solely because of their major-party affiliation and, second, by then using subjective standards for admitting any other debaters. Two days before the first presidential debate, a panel of federal appeals court judges turned Perot down, citing the fact that Perot needed to take his arguments through the months-long FEC complaint process instead of jumping straight to court.

Going into the first presidential debate, the stakes were high and the goals of each of the two major-party candidates clear. Republican challenger Dole hoped to use the debates to kick off a campaign turnaround. Trailing President Clinton by roughly 15 percent in most polls, Dole wanted to reintroduce himself to voters and demonstrate that despite his age, he was upbeat, vigorous, and sharp. Aiming simply to avoid substantive blunders and nonverbal gaffes (in 1992, a camera caught then President George Bush glancing down at his watch, giving many viewers the impression he thought he had better places to be), Clinton's goal was much simpler—to do no harm to his own successful campaign.

During the generally civil first presidential debate, both Bob Dole and Bill Clinton took steps toward accomplishing their debate goals. While Dole took great care to draw a picture of a nation lacking in leadership and establish himself as a man to lead the country into the twenty-first century, Clinton's oft-repeated reply echoed his basic theme—"It is not midnight in America, Senator. We are better off than we were four years ago." Offering contrasting views of the twenty-first century, the basic difference that emerged from the debate was Clinton's contention that government should provide people with the tools necessary to make the most out of their own lives and Dole's response that in most cases, it is better to reduce the reach and cost of the federal government and trust the people to make their own way.

Post-debate polls gave Clinton the edge, although almost two thirds of the respondents contacted within the first half-hour after the debate for a CNN/*Newsweek* poll replied that Bob Dole had won the expectations game, doing better than they expected prior to the debate. Two polls, one by ABC news and the other by *Newsweek,* conducted immediately after the debate had Clinton winning the contest by a 50 to 28 percent margin and a 55 to 38 percent margin, respectively. But it should be remembered that debates usually reinforce rather than change opinions, and that was mainly what happened on October 6. Among those who supported Clinton before the debate, 82 percent thought he won it, and 95 percent still supported him after it. Among viewers who supported Bob Dole before the debate, 63 percent thought he won it, and 94 percent still supported him after it.

Vice President Al Gore, Jr., and Republican vice-presidential candidate Jack Kemp squared off October 9 in St. Petersburg, Florida. Focusing on the familiar issues that differentiated their top-of-the-ticket running mates just three days earlier, both Gore and Kemp cast the election as a referendum on the country's direction. Gore, characterizing Dole's 15 percent across the board tax cut proposal as a risky scheme, argued that the Republicans' plan would "blow a hole" in the deficit, sending the nation's economy over "Niagara Falls" in a barrel. Kemp shot back that "the only hole it would blow is a hole in the plans of this administration to tinker with the tax code." While a post-debate poll conducted by ABC News showed that sampled voters preferred Gore's performance to Kemp's by a 50 to 27 percent margin (with 21 percent calling it a tie), the big story was how few voters watched the debate. As with the August 1996 conventions, when television ratings hit an all-time low, viewership for this debate as well as the first presidential debate was down over 20 percent from four years ago.

In the final presidential debate, an audience of 113 San Diego citizens who had been selected by the Gallup Organization (a well-known national polling organization) because they had supposedly not yet made up their minds about whom they intended to vote for in November posed questions to President Clinton and Senator Dole. Still trailing Clinton in the polls by a double-digit margin, Dole turned his attention to more personal issues, raising doubts both about the personal and public character of Clinton and his administration. An extremely comfortable Clinton—Clinton has always been at his best in settings like the one in San Diego—responded to none of the accusations, instead displaying an easygoing attitude in a setting that allowed him to sympathize with voters one minute and display a mastery of policy the next. Having made use of the town meeting format since his days as governor of Arkansas, Clinton realized early on in his political career that audience members want to be part of a civil enterprise more than a pro wrestling match. His instincts proved correct this night. In an ABC

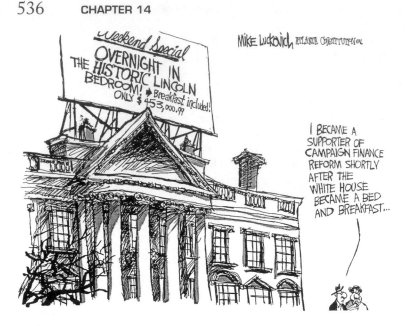

News post-debate poll, while 14 percent of viewers called the contest a tie, 55 percent thought Clinton won, while 28 percent viewed Bob Dole as the winner. Again though, in a pattern similar to the first presidential debate, 97 percent of those people surveyed who supported either Clinton or Dole prior to the debate still supported the same candidate after it, proving once again how little the 1996 presidential debates did to change the attitudes of a largely uninterested electorate.

The Fall Campaign and General Election

As the campaign developed in the months following the August conventions, all of the pre-election public opinion polls showed President Clinton well in front of his GOP challenger. Without question, he again ran a superb campaign. His strategy, targeted television advertising, use of the media, and energetic stumping proved to be largely on target. Fielding a strong Democratic campaign team that included many familiar faces from 1992, Clinton was again able to successfully project a moderate, centrist image that appealed to a wide range of voters. Keeping his message focused on the relatively strong economy, Clinton secured the support of many so-called "Reagan Democrats"—registered Democrats who had voted for Republican candidates in the 1980s. Clinton also

■ (Photo courtesy: By permission of Mike Luckovich and Creators Syndicate.)

Figure 14.5   Landmarks in the 1996 Campaign

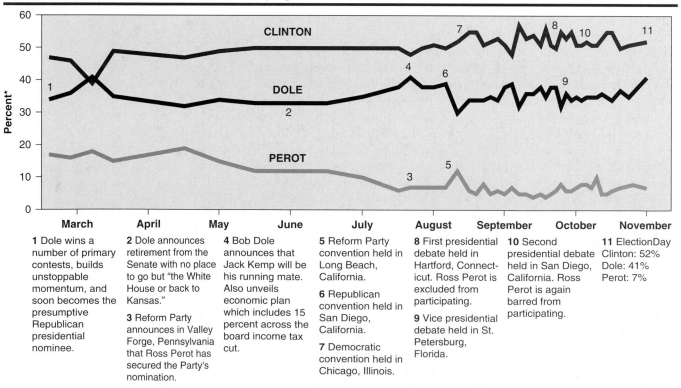

*Percentages indicate percentage of registered voters sampled by the Gallup poll who said they would vote for the candidates.
SOURCE: The Gallup Poll

appealed directly and effectively to young voters, senior citizens, minorities, and women, securing the strong support of each of these voting groups.

Dole's campaign, in contrast, was slow to organize and even slower to focus on consistent themes. Finding his voice only late in the campaign, the Dole campaign hopped, skipped, and jumped from one topic to another before finally settling on trust and character issues just a few weeks prior to Election Day. Reminding many of the inept campaign efforts of former President Bush in 1992 and Michael S. Dukakis in 1988, even Republicans were quick to criticize their presidential nominee.

Although the differences between the two campaigns was certainly a factor in the outcome of the election, as we have seen, it is also true that any election involving an incumbent president is essentially a referendum on his incumbency. In 1980 Ronald Reagan hit on this point when he asked voters to consider whether they were better off today than they were four years ago. The electorate decided it was not and voted accordingly.

To illustrate this point, in 1992 a number of reasons beyond George Bush's lackluster campaign drove voters to Bill Clinton, the most important of which was the state of the U.S. economy. The most basic of all forces in presidential elections, the economy suffered a serious recession in 1990–91 and began to recover only fitfully and painfully in the months leading up to the 1992 election. In many ways relating to their pocketbooks, voters simply did not believe they were better off in 1992 than four years earlier, which predisposed them to change the status quo. In contrast, in 1996 Clinton was fortunate enough to have presided over four years of relatively stable economic growth. This general optimism about the economy spilled over into a general sense of well-being. Over half of those voters surveyed said the country was on the right track. This represented a reversed scenario from 1992, when only 39 percent said the country was on the right track while 56 percent said it was on the wrong track. As the election approached its conclusion, voters looked back to 1992 and concluded that in fact they were better off than four years earlier.

Election Results

Capping a remarkable comeback just two years after voters soundly rejected his policies and threw the Democrats out of power in Congress, Clinton became the first Democrat since Franklin D. Roosevelt to win reelection. Clinton stitched together a victory by winning the vast majority of the black and Hispanic vote and splitting the white vote with Dole. Clinton also defeated Dole in all age categories (18–29; 30–44; 45–59; 60+)—from Generation X-ers to seniors, with his biggest margin among young voters (53 to 35 percent). Clinton's grand prize, however, was the women's vote: He beat Dole 54 to 37 percent among women. Among white women, the 1996 gender chasm narrowed somewhat—49 to 42 percent. Having split the male vote with Dole (44 percent for Clinton, 45 percent for Dole), Clinton's edge among women proved to be the difference in the 1996 election.

Voter turnout was down in 1996. Just an estimated 48.8 percent of those Americans eligible to vote did so. These numbers represent a sharp decline from 1992, when about 55 percent of Americans aged eighteen and over turned up at the polling places. In fact, voter turnout in 1996 was the lowest since 1924. As one study of the 1996 elections pointed out, more Americans chose not to vote than voted for Clinton.[34]

Clinton's Electoral College victory (379 for Clinton, 159 for Dole, and 0 for Perot) was much broader than his popular vote plurality (49 percent for Clinton, 41 percent for Dole, and 9 percent for Perot) (see Table 14.2). He was thus again to be a "minority president"—elected by less than half of the popular vote*—but one whose win was nonetheless impressive.

The Democrats won states in every region of the country. As in 1992, they swept the Northeast, again winning even reliably Republican New Hampshire. Except for Indiana, the Midwest was solidly Democratic, as was the Pacific Coast.

---

* Fifteen of our forty-two chief executives were elected with less than a majority. The most recent, prior to Clinton's 1996 and 1992 elections, was Richard Nixon, who garnered 43 percent of the popular vote in 1968's three-way race.

Table 14.2   1996 Election Results

State	Clinton	Dole	Perot	State	Clinton	Dole	Perot
Alabama	43%	51%	6%	Montana	41%	44%	14%
Alaska	33	51	11	Nebraska	35	53	11
Arizona	47	44	8	Nevada	44	43	9
Arkansas	54	37	8	New Hampshire	50	40	10
California	51	38	7	New Jersey	53	36	9
Colorado	44	46	7	New Mexico	49	41	6
Connecticut	52	35	10	New York	59	31	8
Delaware	52	37	11	North Carolina	44	49	7
District of Columbia	85	9	2	North Dakota	40	47	12
Florida	48	42	9	Ohio	47	41	11
Georgia	46	47	6	Oklahoma	40	48	11
Hawaii	57	32	8	Oregon	47	37	11
Idaho	34	52	13	Pennsylvania	49	40	10
Illinois	54	37	8	Rhode Island	60	27	11
Indiana	42	47	10	South Carolina	44	50	6
Iowa	50	40	9	South Dakota	43	46	10
Kansas	36	54	9	Tennessee	48	46	6
Kentucky	46	45	9	Texas	44	49	7
Louisiana	52	40	7	Utah	33	54	10
Maine	52	31	14	Vermont	54	31	12
Maryland	54	38	7	Virginia	45	47	7
Massachusetts	62	28	9	Washington	51	36	9
Michigan	52	38	9	West Virginia	51	37	11
Minnesota	51	35	12	Wisconsin	49	39	10
Mississippi	44	49	6	Wyoming	37	50	12
Missouri	48	41	10				

SOURCE: *The Associated Press* (Wednesday, November 6, 1996).

Bob Dole achieved a respectable showing only in the South, the Plains states, and the Rocky Mountains. But even in the South, which had long been solidly Republican, Florida went to Bill Clinton, as did Kentucky, Louisiana, as well as Clinton's Arkansas and Gore's Tennessee.

By the standards of recent history, Clinton's Electoral College majority (an improvement from his 370 Electoral College votes in 1992) was the most impressive and diverse for a Democrat since Lyndon Johnson's landslide election in 1964. Dole fared worse than Bush, who in 1992 won 168 Electoral College votes, but did better than former President Jimmy Carter, who in his 1980 reelection bid captured just forty-nine Electoral College votes, the post–World War II record for the most decisive defeat of an incumbent.

CAMPAIGN FINANCE LAWS

In response to growing concerns about the amounts of money spent on federal elections, both Republicans and Democrats have sponsored major campaign finance reform bills in Congress. But changing the rules of the game can alter the results of elections. Not surprisingly, Democratic proposals tend to favor Democratic candidates while Republican proposals tend to favor Republican candidates. For many years now, as a consequence, Congress has created more smoke than fire on campaign reform.

Prior to the 1994 congressional elections, Democrats supported setting a limit on the amount of money congressional candidates could spend in an effort to win office. (For the House, a candidate would have been limited to $600,000; the Senate limit

■ Republican Senator Fred Thompson of Tennessee (left) is seen here presiding over the Senate's campaign finance hearings. (Photo courtesy: R. Ellis/Sygma)

would have depended on each state's population, with a more heavily populated state having a higher limit.) Republicans, long the congressional minority, were adamantly against these spending caps. They argued that the limits mainly hurt challengers who are not as well known as incumbents and who need to spend more money to increase their name identification. For example, from 1978 to 1988, only seven of the thirty-two winning Senate challengers remained within the spending limits proposed by the Democrats. The Democrats responded that without limits on total campaign spending, personally wealthy candidates, like Steve Forbes, have an advantage over less affluent candidates. This advantage results from the present federal contribution limits and the Supreme Court decision in *Buckley* v. *Valeo*, which ruled that limits on a candidate's spending of personal funds violates his or her Constitutional right to free speech. In the spring of 1992, the proposed legislation was passed by the Democratic legislative majority only to be vetoed by then Republican President George Bush.

In the time since President Bush's veto, Democratic President Bill Clinton and Republican lawmakers have championed campaign finance reform only to later renege on their pledges. Prior to the 1992 presidential election, then candidate Bill Clinton pledged to support and sign strong campaign finance reform legislation. Once in office, this promise fell by the wayside. In 1994 Democratic legislators were swept out of office and replaced with Republicans, who had also campaigned on the promise of change. Yet campaign finance reform was conspicuously absent from the Republican Contract with America. In June 1995, President Clinton and Republican Speaker of the House of Representatives Newt Gingrich, in a joint appearance, were asked by an audience member whether they would support the formation of a commission to reform the campaign finance system. Both men said yes—shaking hands in mutual agreement for the cameras. Finally, after months of stalling by the House Republican leadership, the House passed the Shays–Meehan campaign finance reform bill in the 105th Congress (1995–96), which, among other provisions, banned the national parties from raising soft money. Unfortunately for reform proponents, however, senators could not muster enough votes to stop a filibuster on the Senate version of the Shays–Meehan bill (authored by Senators John McCain and Russ Feingold), and campaign finance reform died still another death. As of this writing, reform proponents in the House and Senate were preparing for yet another battle in the 106th Congress.[35]

TRY IT!

To get involved and find out what you can do about campaign reform, go to www.awlonline.com/oconnor.

The impasse continues, despite all the additional scandals and alleged scandals connected to the campaign financing of the 1996 presidential campaign. Congress has remained resistant to the various schemes produced for reform of the political system. Extensive efforts by members of both parties in 1998, for example, were unsuccessful, though the debate itself was well publicized and may have furthered the cause of reform in the longer term. Of course, both parties' positions on this issue are rooted in self-interest. The Republicans are usually more successful than are Democrats at raising money, and the Democrats want to limit that advantage. Moreover, the cost to either party of conceding too much on this issue is the possibility of relinquishing control of Congress. This makes campaign spending an issue that does not easily lend itself to compromise.

While most discussions of campaign finance reform focus on spending and contribution limits, many experts inside and outside of Congress argue that there are other ideas concerning campaign finance that would create a more wholesome system without resorting to limits. One idea is to limit the influence of political action committees (PACs). Critics charge that PACs reduce political competition by giving overwhelmingly to incumbents—usually about two-thirds to three-quarters of their war chests—while at the same time they corrupt the system by indebting legislators to the special interests that form PACs. Supporters argue that PACs better represent the "little guys" in American politics by allowing them to pool their funds and have a greater impact on campaigns and elections. Abolishing PACs altogether, however, is probably unconstitutional, since doing so would violate the First Amendment's guarantee of free political association. Restricting their contribution limits too greatly would only divert their money into other forms of political spending that are not easily revealed (such as funneling cash to state and local parties in states that do not require full campaign finance disclosure). As reformers through the years have discovered, it is nearly impossible to dam the flow of political money in a free and open democratic system in which participation is encouraged.

A better way to control PACs and special-interest groups is to increase the influence and level of spending by political parties. This would limit PACs indirectly by augmenting the power of a rival source of campaign funds. As is discussed in chapter 12, parties can be strengthened in many ways, especially by loosening or eliminating current restrictions on what citizens may give to a party or what a party may donate to its candidates. In addition, parties ought to receive some free broadcast time on all television and radio stations. This air time could then be allocated to the most needy nominees—incumbents who are in trouble, as well as promising challengers. Since candidates spend a major portion of their campaign funds for media advertising time—up to 60 percent in some Senate races—such a reform could conceivably help to cut the burgeoning costs of campaigns. And it would aid challengers and less wealthy candidates in particular, balancing some of the advantages of incumbency. Of course, this reform also has First Amendment problems because, along with the "free" air time, candidates would likely be required to agree on total television advertising time. The United States, incidentally, is the only major democratic country that does not provide some free media time to parties or candidates. Moreover, while increasing party spending limits may augment party power, it is unlikely to cleanse the campaign finance system of interest group influence. After all, parties would presumably raise much of the money they spend from interest groups, which—in return for their contributions—would likely have the ear of party leaders who set the legislative agenda.[36]

There is one other possible workable solution to the campaign finance ills, one that takes advantage of both current realities and the remarkable self-regulating tendencies of a free-market democracy. Consider the American stock market. Most government oversight simply makes sure that publicly traded companies accurately disclose vital information about their finances. The philosophy is that buyers, given the information they need, are intelligent enough to look out for themselves. There will be winners and losers, of course, both among companies and the consumers of their securities, but it is

GLOBAL POLITICS

Campaigns in Comparative Perspective

Nowhere is the American political system more unusual than in the way that it elects its leaders. Election campaigns in the United States have the distinction of being the longest and most expensive of any in the G-7. Institutions like PACs, the "horse race" media coverage of presidential campaigns, and the concentration on "momentum" in presidential primaries are unknown in the other six democracies.

Just how different are American campaigns? First, consider that no other G-7 political system has primaries. Candidates are selected by the political party organizations, not the rank-and-file voters in those parties. The public does not have to go to the polls twice in a year to elect a government. Second, parliamentary general election campaigns typically last less than a month (Japan's 1996 parliamentary election campaign lasted 11 days), and, except for Germany and France, occur whenever the prime minister calls for them (the French president has that power). The campaign season is therefore short. Moreover, the parliament elects the prime minister, so direct election of the executive (except for the president in France) is not possible.

Short campaign seasons mean cheaper campaigns. Not only are parliamentary campaigns cheaper, but in almost all the G-7 parliamentary systems (Japan until recently was an exception) the parties are the candidates' major source of funding. Sympathetic interest groups channel their campaign contributions through the parties. Not only do PACs not exist, but pronouncements such as that by U.S. Senator Russ Feingold that one way to lessen the expense of campaigns is to refuse "soft money" from the national parties and their committees* would be unintelligible to a candidate in any of the other six countries.

Observers in the European countries have worried in recent years about the "Americanization" of parliamentary campaigns, by which they mean in particular the growing use of television as a campaign tool. In the most recent rounds of parliamentary elections in Britain and Germany, the winning parties' campaign teams closely studied how the Clinton campaign had used media techniques to deliver effective messages. In 1998, Gerhard Schroder's winning team used focus groups and speeches deliberately geared to television during the campaign for the German Bundestag. It is not clear, however, how far American-style campaigning can go; in France and Japan, the government carefully regulates media coverage of campaigns, and candidates are prohibited from buying television and radio time.

*Russ Feingold, "Running and Winning a 'Restrained' Campaign," *Extensions* (Spring 1999): 4.

not the government's role to guarantee anyone's success. The notion that people are smart enough—and indeed have the duty—to think and choose for themselves also underlies our basic democratic arrangement. There is no reason that the same principle cannot be successfully applied to a free market for campaign finance. In this scenario, disclosure laws would be broadened and strengthened, and penalties for failure to disclose would be ratcheted up, while rules on other aspects—such as sources of funds and sizes of contributions—could be greatly loosened or even abandoned altogether.

Call it *deregulation plus.* Let a well-informed marketplace, rather than a committee of federal bureaucrats, be the judge of whether someone has accepted too much money from a particular interest group or spent too much to win an election. Reformers who object to money in politics would lose little under such a scheme, since the current system has already utterly failed to inhibit special-interest influence. On the other hand, reform advocates might gain substantially by bringing all financial activity out into the open where the public can see for itself the truth about how campaigns are conducted.

Campaign finance reform is a favorite Washington topic; but for all the good (and bad) ideas that are proposed, little legislation is ever passed. Many incumbents prefer not to alter the system that—whatever its faults—elected them. Democrats and Republicans are also at loggerheads over the partisan effects of various reforms. The American people also remain skeptical of political parties, and little popular support can be found for strengthening them. The last set of campaign finance reforms passed in the wake of Watergate, and it may take more scandal to generate enough momentum to pass a successor package of reforms in the Congress.

As the analysis of the 1996 election suggests, the campaign process in the United States is far from perfect. Campaigns seem to stretch out interminably. Moreover, trivialities rather than the important issues of the day often determine the success or failure of campaigns, voters cast many ballots for the lesser of two evils, and some contenders for lower office never raise enough money to get a fair hearing. But those who follow campaigns would also do well to remember the wise words of one of this century's greatest political scientists, V. O. Key, Jr. Key's central observation was simple but powerful: "Voters are not fools." Not every citizen devotes enough time to politics, and many people are woefully uninformed at times. But virtually all voters know their basic interests and cast their ballots accordingly. They are not always right in their judgments, yet over time there is a rough justice to election results. Parties and office holders who produce a measure of prosperity and happiness for the electorate are usually rewarded, and those who do not keep the home folks satisfied may be forced to find another line of work (see chapter 13).

̸ONTINUITY and Change

Campaign Ethics in American Politics

American politics has never been particularly clean or ethical, and even the Founders were much maligned in their campaigns. The rumors about Jefferson's black mistress, Sally Hemings, first came to prominence during his presidential campaign in 1800, and Jefferson's campaigns were the subject of much acrimonious and partisan strife in newly emerging American newspapers.

When Andrew Jackson campaigned for president in 1828, his opponents widely published the fact that the divorce of his wife's first marriage had not been finalized by the time of their marriage many years ago, though this was unbeknownst to her or Jackson at the time. Rachel Jackson was completely humiliated by the ensuing public scandal, and historians have read this as a major contribution to the physical and emotional breakdown that took her life between the time of Jackson's election and his swearing-in as president.

America did not leave campaign corruption behind in the nineteenth century. The country's greatest political scandal, Watergate, is still well within the nation's living memory. The Watergate scandal centered precisely around Richard Nixon's flagrantly illegal measures to investigate anti-Vietnam activists and to ensure his reelection in 1972—including misusing the CIA, FBI, and IRS; accepting huge concealed campaign contributions; and bugging and breaking into the Democratic National Committee, headquartered in the Watergate Building that gave the scandal its name. Laws passed after Watergate to compel campaign finance reform have had some limited success in cleaning up the campaign process in America, although the disguising and misreporting of fund raising inevitably continues in new forms.

Personal political attacks, especially in TV advertising, are still par for the course today. The most infamous egregious example of negative campaigning occurred in 1988, when George Bush ran the infamous "Willie Horton ad." This ad featured the face of Willie Horton—a convicted African-American criminal who had escaped from a Massachusetts prison and committed a rape while on a weekend furlough program advocated by Bush's Democratic presidential opponent, Massachusetts Governor Michael Dukakis. The advertisement was extremely effective in casting doubt on some of Dukakis's policies, though many criticized it for brazenly exploiting racial and cultural prejudices to asperse Dukakis himself.

Push-polling, the dissemination of negative and often inaccurate information about a candidate under the guise of asking opinion-poll questions, is a dirty but increasingly popular campaign tactic that remains unregulated and can only worsen in upcoming campaigns. In push-polling, a pollster for Candidate Y might make a phone call and ask the respondent, "Would you be less likely to vote for [Candidate X] if you found out that she had voted for six consecutive tax increases?" (Notice how the question implies that Candidate X actually has voted for six increases whether she really has or, more likely, has not voted for them.) As Americans become increasingly immersed in the Internet, it is not hard to imagine how push-polling might rear its ugly head in the form of e-mail messages.

Some candidates will always push the letter of the law, and sometimes even break it, in their attempts to win elected office—it will always be true that campaign ethics is an oxymoron for many. The public can only keep a close eye on their antics and do its best to keep the political arena as clean as possible.

1. Campaign finance reform is a perennially popular topic for congressional debate, but little action has resulted from recent discussions of the issue. What reasons, if any, do politicians have to pass laws regulating their own campaign behavior? What do they stand to gain (or lose) by policing their own activity? What is the role of party affiliation in supporting campaign finance reform? How can one ethically justify a partisan vote opposing another party's proposal for reform legislation?

2. Debate the specific merit of the "no-limits, full-disclosure" system of campaign finance, in which unlimited campaign contributions are allowed if they are fully declared in a publicly accessible manner. Will it ever be possible to close all the loopholes in laws governing campaign ethics? What would be the particular advantages and disadvantages of such an open system—not only to politicians, but to PACs and other lobbyists, and to the interest of the general public? Do you believe that the general public is smart enough to track political contributions and take them into account when voting for a candidate?

Cast Your Vote. Should there be a limit on campaign contributions, or should there be no limits, but full-disclosure on the contributors? To cast your vote, go to www.awlonline.com/oconnor.

SUMMARY

With this chapter we switched our focus from the election decision itself and turned our attention to the actual campaign process. What we have seen is that while modern campaigning makes use of dazzling new technologies and a variety of strategies to attract voters, campaigns still tend to rise and fall on the strength of the individual candidate. In this chapter we have stressed the following observations:

1. THE STRUCTURE OF A CAMPAIGN

Campaigns, the process of seeking and winning votes in the run-up to an election, consist of five separate components: the nomination campaign or "invisible primary," in which party leaders and activists are courted to ensure that the candidate is nominated in primaries or conventions; the general election campaign, in which the goal is to appeal to the nation as a whole; the personal campaign, in which the candidate and his or her family make appearances, meet voters, hold press conferences, and give speeches; the organizational campaign, in which volunteers telephone voters, distribute literature, organize events, and raise money; and the broadcast media campaign waged on television and on the radio.

Campaign staffs combine volunteers, a manager to oversee them, and key political consultants—including media consultants, a pollster, and a direct mailer. In recent years media consultants have assumed greater and greater importance, partly because the cost of advertising has skyrocketed, so that campaign media budgets consume the lion's share of available resources.

2. THE CANDIDATE OR THE CAMPAIGN: WHICH DO WE VOTE FOR?

Despite the dazzle of technology and the celebrity of well-known consultants, the candidate remains the most important component of any campaign. The candidate's strengths, weaknesses, and talents are central to the success or failure of the campaign.

3. MODERN CAMPAIGN CHALLENGES

Candidates tell their story directly in paid broadcast media advertising. They are much less successful in managing and directing their press coverage.

4. A SUMMARY OF CONTRIBUTIONS AND EXPENSES

Receiving the majority of their financial war chest from individuals, and spending most of these funds for television advertising, today's senatorial candidates struggle to keep pace with the rising costs associated with campaigning for a seat in the U.S. Senate.

5. BRINGING IT TOGETHER: THE 1996 PRESIDENTIAL CAMPAIGN AND ELECTION

After an uncontested Democratic nomination, and a relatively straightforward Republican nomination, Bill Clinton rebounded from the rebuke of the 1994 congressional elections and handily defeated Bob Dole for the presidency of the United States, largely on the basis of a very healthy U.S. economy. While Ross Perot collected a smaller portion of the vote than he did in 1992, it was still enough to deny Clinton a straight majority for the second time.

6. CAMPAIGN FINANCE LAWS

Campaign finance is regularly a reform issue because candidates who outspend their opponents tend to win, and raising money is easier for some candidates than for others. Incumbents enjoy a fund-raising edge as well as advantages related to name recognition and some of the perks of office, such as mailing privileges.

KEY TERMS

campaign manager, p. 513
candidate debates, p. 519
contrast ad, p. 514
direct mailer, p. 513
finance chair, p. 513
free media, p. 514
general election campaign, p. 511
get-out-the-vote (GOTV), p. 513
hard money, p. 524
inoculation advertising, p. 514

matching funds, p. 523
media campaign, p. 511
media consultant, p. 513
negative ad, p. 514
nomination campaign, p. 511
organizational campaign, p. 511
paid media, p. 514
personal campaign, p. 511
political action committee (PAC), p. 522
political consultant, p. 513

pollster, p. 513
positive ad, p. 514
public funds, p. 523
soft money, p. 524
spot ad, p. 514
voter canvass, p. 513

SELECTED READINGS

Abramson, Paul R., John H. Aldrich, and David W. Rohde. *Change and Continuity in the 1992 Elections.* Washington, D.C.: CQ Press, 1995.

Ansolabehere, Stephen, and Shanto Iyengar. *Going Negative: How Attack Ads Shrink and Polarize the Electorate.* New York: Free Press, 1995.

Ceaser, James W., and Andrew E. Busch. *Losing to Win: The 1996 Elections and American Politics.* Lanham, MD: Rowman & Littlefield Publishers, 1997.

Fenno, Richard F. *Senators on the Campaign Trail: The Politics of Representation.* Norman: University of Oklahoma Press, 1996.

Goldenberg, Edie, and Michael W. Traugott. *Campaigning for Congress.* Washington, D.C.: CQ Press, 1984.

Greive, R. R. Bob. *The Blood, Sweat, and Tears of Political Victory—and Defeat.* Lanham, MD: University Press of America, 1996.

Herrnson, Paul S. *Congressional Elections: Campaigning at Home and in Washington.* Washington, DC: CQ Press, 1995.

Hertzke, Allen D. *Echoes of Discontent: Jesse Jackson, Pat Robertson, and the Resurgence of Populism.* Washington, DC: CQ Press, 1993.

Holbrook, Thomas M. *Do Campaigns Matter?* Thousand Oaks, CA: Sage Publications, 1996.

Jackson, Brooks. *Honest Graft: Big Money and the American Political Process.* Washington, D.C.: Farragut, 1990.

Kern, Montague. *30-Second Politics: Political Advertising in the Eighties.* New York: Praeger, 1989.

Mayer, William G., ed. *In Pursuit of the White House: How We Choose Our Presidential Nominees.* Chatham, NJ: Chatham House Publishers, 1996.

Nelson, Michael, ed. *The Elections of 1996.* Washington, DC: CQ Press, 1997.

Orren, Gary R., and Nelson W. Polsby, eds. *Media and Momentum: The New Hampshire Primary and Nomination Politics.* Chatham, NJ: Chatham House, 1987.

Patterson, Thomas E. *The Mass Media Election.* New York: Praeger, 1980.

Pika, Josepha A. and Richard A. Watson. *The Presidential Contest,* 5th ed. Washington, DC: CQ Press, 1995.

Pomper, Gerald M., ed. *The Election of 1992: Reports and Interpretations.* Chatham, NJ: Chatham House, 1993.

Sabato, Larry J., ed. *Campaigns and Elections: A Reader in Modern American Politics.* Glenview, IL: Scott, Foresman, 1989.

———. *PAC Power: Inside the World of Political Action Committees.* New York: Norton, 1985.

———. *Paying for Elections: The Campaign Finance Thicket.* New York: Priority Press for the Twentieth Century Fund, 1989.

———. *The Rise of Political Consultants: New Ways of Winning Elections.* New York: Basic Books, 1981.

———. *Toward the Millennium: The Elections of 1996.* Boston: Allyn and Bacon, 1997.

Sabato, Larry J., and Glenn R. Simpson. *Dirty Little Secrets: The Persistence of Corruption in American Politics.* New York: Times Books, 1996.

Salmore, Barbara G., and Stephen Salmore. *Candidates, Parties, and Campaigns,* 2d ed. Washington, DC: CQ Press, 1989.

Sorauf, Frank J. *Inside Campaign Finance.* New Haven, CT: Yale University Press, 1992.

Troy, Gil. *See How They Ran: The Changing Role of the Presidential Candidate.* Cambridge, MA: Harvard University Press, 1996.

NOTES

1. Paul S. Herrnson, "Campaign Professionalism and Fundraising in Congressional Elections." *Journal of Politics* 54 (1992): 859–70.

2. Stephen K. Medvic and Silvo Lenart, "The Influence of Political Consultants in the 1992 Congressional Elections," *Legislative Studies Quarterly* 22 (February 1997): 61–77.

3. Five liberal Democratic U.S. senators, including George McGovern of South Dakota, were defeated in this way in 1980, for example.

4. Stephen Ansolabehere and Shanto Iyengar, *Going Negative: How Political Advertisements Shrink and Polarize the Electorate* (New York: The Free Press, 1995).

5. See, for example, Steven E. Finkel and John G. Geer, "A Spot Check: Casting Doubt on the Demobilizing Effect of Attack Advertising," *American Journal of Political Science* 42 (1998): 573–95.

6. See Larry J. Sabato, ed., *Campaigns and Elections: A Reader in Modern American Politics* (Glenview, IL: Scott, Foresman, 1989), 3–4.

7. From a 1987 cartoon by Tom Toles, copyrighted by the *Buffalo News*.

8. Data provided by the Federal Election Commission.

9. Amy Keller, "Helping Each Other Out: Members Dip into Campaign Funds for Fellow Candidates," *Roll Call*, June 15, 1998, 1.

10. For member contribution activity at the state level, see Jay K. Dow, "Campaign Contributions and Intercandidate Transfers in the California Assembly," *Social Science Quarterly* 75 (1994): 867–80. For member contribution activity at the congressional level, see Bruce A. Larson, "Ambition and Money in the U.S. House of Representatives: Analyzing Campaign Contributions from Incumbents' Leadership PACs and Reelection Committees" (Ph.D. dissertation, University of Virginia, 1998). For a briefer account, see Paul S. Herrnson, "Money and Motives: Spending in House Elections," in *Congress Reconsidered*, Lawrence C. Dodd and Bruce I. Oppenheimer, eds. 6th ed. (Washington, DC: Congressional Quarterly Press, 1997).

11. Larson, "Ambition and Money in the U.S. House of Representatives."

12. Susan B. Glasser and Julie Eilperin, "A New Conduit for Soft Money: Critics Decry Big, Largely Untraceable Donations to Lawmakers' 'Leadership PACs,'" *Washington Post*, May 16, 1999, A1.

13. 424 U.S. 1 (1976).

14. 424 U.S. 1 (1976).

15. 116 S.Ct. 2309 (1996).

16. Anthony Corrado, "Party Soft Money," in Anthony Corrado, et al., eds., *Campaign Finance Reform: A Sourcebook* (Washington DC: Brookings, 1997).

17. Corrado, "Party Soft Money."

18. Trevor Potter, "Issue Advocacy and Express Advocacy," in Anthony Corrado, et al., eds., *Campaign Finance Reform: A Sourcebook* (Washington DC: Brookings, 1997).

19. Gary Jacobson, "The Effect of the AFL-CIO's 'Voter Education' Campaigns on the 1996 House Elections," *Journal of Politics* 61 (1999): 185–94.

20. Julie Eilperin, "In Divided House, All Eyes on 2000," *Washington Post*, June 3, 1999, A3, A11.

21. Potter, "Issue Advocacy and Express Advocacy."

22. David Magleby and Marianne Holt, "The Long Shadow of Soft Money and Issue Advocacy Ads," *Campaigns and Elections* (May 1999): 22.

23. Michael Cornfield, "The On-Line Campaigner: Interacting for Campaign Dollars," *Campaigns and Elections* (June 1999): 31.

24. Amy Keller, "Experts Wonder about FEC's Internet Savvy: Regulating Web Is a Challenge for Watchdog Agency," *Roll Call*, May 6, 1999, 1, 21.

25. Keller, "Experts Wonder about FEC's Internet Savvy."

26. Frank Sorauf, *Inside Campaign Finance: Myths and Realities* (New Haven, CT: Yale University Press, 1992), Chapter 6.

27. Richard A. Smith, 1995, "Interest Group Influence in the U.S. Congress," *Legislative Studies Quarterly* 20 (1995): 89–139. See also Janet Grenzke, "PACs and the Congressional Supermarket: The Currency Is Complex." *American Journal of Political Science* 33 (1989): 1–24.

28. Richard L. Hall and Frank W. Wayman. "Buying Time: Moneyed Interests and the Mobilization of Bias in Congressional Committees." *American Political Science Review* 84 (1990): 797–820.

29. Thomas Gais, *Improper Influence: Campaign Finance Law, Political Interest Groups, and the Problem of Equality* (Ann Arbor: University of Michigan Press, 1996).

30. Paul S. Herrnson, *Congressional Elections: Campaigning at Home and in Washington*, 2nd ed., (Washington, DC: Congressional Quarterly Press, 1998), p. 105.

31. See Howard Penniman, "U.S. Elections: Really a Bargain?" *Public Opinion* (June/July 1984): 51.

32. Paul R. Abramson, John H. Aldrich, and David Rohde, *Change and Continuity in the 1996 Elections* (Washington DC:

Congressional Quarterly Press, 1998), 21; and Larry J. Sabato, "Presidential Nominations: The Frontloaded Frenzy of '96," in Larry J. Sabato, ed., *Toward the Millennium: The Elections of 1996* (Boston: Allyn and Bacon), p. 58.

33. William J. Keefe, *Parties, Politics, and Public Policy in America*, 8th ed. (Washington DC: Congressional Quarterly Press, 1998), 112.

34. Paul R. Abramson, John H. Adrich, and David Rohde, *Change and Continuity in the 1996 Elections*, 65.

35. Amy Keller, "Campaign Finance Reform in Turmoil," *Roll Call* (May 13, 1999), 1, 21.

36. Frank J. Sorauf, "Political Parties and Campaign Finance," in L. Sandy Maisel, ed., *The Parties Respond: Changes in American Parties and Campaigns* (Boulder, CO: Westview Press, 1998): 238–239.

(Photo courtesy: Brooks Kraft/Sygma)

The News Media

15

- The American Press of Yesteryear
- The Contemporary Media Scene
- How the Media Cover Politicians and Government
- The Media's Influence on the Public
- How Politicians Use the Media
- Government Regulation of the Electronic Media

he difference between the coverage of the Persian Gulf War of 1990–91 and that of the NATO–Yugoslav conflict of 1999 aptly demonstrates the dramatic changes that have taken place in news coverage in the decade of the 1990s. During the Persian Gulf War, television coverage was extensive on the major commercial networks and CNN, but the coverage was primarily factual and centered on the military activities of the moment. Commentary at that time was provided mostly by retired military officers hired by the networks to explain weapons systems and military terminology unfamiliar to both journalists and the general public.

By 1999, however, the talk-show mentality of television had taken over even the coverage of military conflict. The networks certainly covered the facts of the Yugoslav war, but the recent additions of cable networks such as the Fox News Channel, MSNBC, and CNBC, combined with the usual extensive coverage on CNN, meant that the long-standing talk shows such as Chris Matthew's *Hardball, Geraldo Live,* and John Hockenberry's program on MSNBC ran almost full-time coverage of the war. With only a limited supply of hard breaking news, the networks and cable channels filled the remainder of their airtime with constant speculation and second guessing of the military strategy, even when they lacked sound or certain knowledge of the proceedings from either the battlefield or the war room.

Furthermore, the commentary conspicuously came from journalists whose experience extended little further than running talk shows, let alone military operations. Such televised discussion, which sometimes approaches kibitzing, makes it exceedingly difficult for public leaders to control the presentation and reception of military operations and their outcomes. Some would argue that this keeps leadership open and accountable; others would argue that it interferes with the government's ability to conduct its appointed business with the required security. President Clinton spoke for the second opinion during the Yugoslav war when he criticized the current state of affairs with a touch of sarcastic humor: on May 1, he attended a dinner of the White House Correspondents' Association and, referring to prominent journalistic commentator and lawyer-by-training Howard Fineman, said he would not know what to do without the "second-guessing" and "continual critiquing of Retired General Howard Fineman."

The media have the potential to exert enormous influence over Americans. Not only does the press tell us what is important by setting the agenda for what we will watch and read, but they can also influence what we think about issues through the content of the news stories. The simple words of the Constitution's First Amendment, "Congress shall make no law . . . abridging the freedom of the speech, or of the press" have shaped the American republic as much as or more than any others in the Constitution and its amendments. With the Constitution's sanction, as interpreted by the Supreme Court over two centuries, a vigorous and highly competitive press has emerged. This freedom has been crucial in facilitating the political discourse and education necessary for the maintenance of democracy. But does this freedom also entail responsibility on the part of the press? Has the press, over the years, met its obligation to provide objective, issue-based coverage of our politicians and political events, or does the media tend to focus on the trivial and sensational, ignoring the important issues and contributing to voter frustration with their government and their politicians? How this freedom evolved, the ways in which it is manifested, and whether press freedom is used responsibly, are subjects we examine further in this chapter.

The chapter reviews the historical development of the press in the United States, and then explores the contemporary media scene. Does the press go too far in their coverage of public figures and issues, and are they biased in their reporting? Does the press really influence public opinion, and does the press allow itself to be manipulated by skilled politicians? We also explore the ways in which the government controls the organization and operation of the press, attempting to promote a balance between freedom and responsibility on the one hand, and competitiveness and consumer choice on the other. In discussing the changing role and impact of the media, we will address the following:

- First, we will discuss *the evolution of the press,* from the founding of the country up to modern times.
- Second, we will examine the *current structure and role of the media.*
- Third, we will discuss the *contemporary trends in media attention* toward investigative journalism during the Watergate era and, more recently, toward character issues and intrusive examination of the private lives of public figures.
- Fourth, we will investigate *the media's influence on the public,* and whether public opinion is significantly swayed by media coverage.
- Fifth, we will observe *the ways politicians use the media* and attempt to influence press coverage for their own ends.
- Sixth, we will explain how *the government regulates the electronic media,* and identify the motivations for and evolution of such control.

THE AMERICAN PRESS OF YESTERYEAR

Journalism—the process and profession of collecting and disseminating the news (that is, new information about subjects of public interest)—has been with us in some form since the dawn of civilization (see Table 15.1 for a history of the media in the United States).[1] Yet its practice has often been remarkably uncivilized, and it was much more so at the beginning of the American republic than it is today.

The first newspapers were published in the American colonies in 1690. The number of newspapers grew throughout the 1700s, as colonists began to realize the value of a press free from government oversight and censorship. Thus it was not surprising that one of the most important demands made by Anti-Federalists (see chapter 2) during our country's constitutional debate was that an amendment guaranteeing the freedom of the press be included in the final version of the Constitution.

During his presidency, George Washington escaped most press scrutiny but detested journalists nonetheless; his battle tactics in the Revolutionary War had been much criticized in print, and an early draft of his "Farewell Address to the Nation" at the end of his presidency (1796) contained a condemnation of the press that has often been described as savage.[2] Thomas Jefferson was treated especially harshly by elements of

Table 15.1 Landmarks of the American Media

1960	First newspaper published	1960	First televised presidential campaign debates
1789	First party newspapers circulated	1979	The Cable Satellite Public Affairs Network (C-SPAN) is founded, providing live round-the-clock coverage of politics and government.
1833	First penny press		
1890	Yellow journalism spreads		
1900	Muckraking in fashion		
1928	First radio broadcast of an election	1980	Cable News Network (CNN) is founded by media mogul Ted Turner, making national and international events available instantaneously around the globe.
1948	First election results to be covered by television		
1952	First presidential campaign advertisements aired on television		

1992	Talk-show television circumvents the news, allowing candidates to go around journalists to reach the voting public directly.
1996	Official candidate home pages containing, among other things, candidate profiles, issue positions, campaign strategy and slogans, and e-mail addresses appear on the World Wide Web.

the early U.S. press. For example, one Richmond newspaper editor, angered by Jefferson's refusal to appoint him as postmaster, printed a rumor that started a debate that continues to this day: that Jefferson kept a slave as his concubine and had several children by her.[3] One can understand why Jefferson, normally a defender of a free press, commented that "even the least informed of the people have learned that nothing in a newspaper is to be believed." Jefferson, of course, probably did not intend that statement literally, since he himself was instrumental in establishing the *National Gazette,* the newspaper of his political faction and viewpoint.

The partisan press eventually gave way to the penny press. In 1833 Benjamin Day founded the *New York Sun,* which cost a penny at the newsstand. Because it was not tied to one party, it was politically more independent than the party papers. The *Sun* was the forerunner of the modern press built on mass circulation and commercial advertising to produce profit. By 1861 the penny press had so supplanted partisan papers that President Abraham Lincoln announced that his administration would have no favored or sponsored newspaper.

The press thus became markedly less partisan but not necessarily more respectable. Mass-circulation dailies sought wide readership, and readers were clearly attracted by the sensational and the scandalous. The sordid side of politics became the entertainment of the times. One of the best-known examples occurred in the presidential campaign of 1884, when the *Buffalo Evening Telegraph* headlined "A Terrible Tale" about Grover Cleveland, the Democratic nominee.[4] In 1871, while sheriff of Buffalo, the bachelor Cleveland had allegedly fathered a child. Even though the woman in question had been seeing other men, Cleveland willingly accepted responsibility since all the other men were married, and he had dutifully paid child support for years. Fortunately for Cleveland, another newspaper, the *Democratic Sentinel,* broke a story that helped to offset this scandal: Republican presidential nominee James G. Blaine and his wife had had their first child just three months after their wedding.

In the late 1800s and early 1900s, the era of the intrusive press was in full flower. First yellow journalism and then muckraking were in fashion. Pioneered by prominent publishers such as William Randolph Hearst and Joseph Pulitzer, **yellow journalism**[5] featured pictures, comics, and color designed to capture a share of the burgeoning immigrant population market. These newspapers also oversimplified and sensationalized many news developments. The front-page editorial crusade became common, the motto for which frequently seemed to be, "Damn the truth, full speed ahead."

After the turn of the century, the muckrakers—so named by President Theodore Roosevelt after a special rake designed to collect manure[6]—took charge of a number of newspapers and nationally circulated magazines. **Muckraking** journalists such as Upton Sinclair and David Graham Phillips searched out and exposed real and apparent misconduct by government, business, and politicians in order to stimulate reform.[7] There was no shortage of corruption to reveal, of course, and much good came from these efforts. But an unfortunate side effect of the emphasis on crusades and investigations was the frequent publication of gossip and rumor without sufficient proof.

Web Exploration
For examples of nineteenth-century yellow journalism, go to www.awlonline.com/oconnor.

yellow journalism:

A form of newspaper publishing in vogue in the late nineteenth century that featured pictures, comics, color, and sensationalized, oversimplified news coverage.

muckraking:

A form of newspaper publishing, in vogue in the early twentieth century, concerned with reforming government and business conduct.

■ "Uncle Sam's Next Campaign—the War Against the Yellow Press." In this 1898 cartoon in the wake of the Spanish-American War, yellow journalism is attacked for its threats, insults, filth, grime, blood, death, slander, gore, and blackmail, all of which are "lies." The cartoonist suggests that, after winning the foreign war, the government ought to attack its own yellow journalists at home. (Photo courtesy: Stock Montage, Inc.)

The modern press corps may also be guilty of this offense, but it has achieved great progress on another front. Throughout the nineteenth century, payoffs to the press were not uncommon. Andrew Jackson, for instance, gave one in ten of his early appointments to loyal reporters;[8] and during the 1872 presidential campaign, the Republicans slipped cash to about 300 newsmen.[9] Wealthy industrialists also sometimes purchased editorial peace or investigative cease-fire for tens of thousands of dollars. Examples of such press corruption are exceedingly rare today, and not even the most extreme of the modern media's critics believe otherwise.

As the news business grew, its focus gradually shifted from passionate opinion to corporate profit. Newspapers, hoping to maximize profit, were more careful to avoid alienating the advertisers and readers who produced their revenues, and the result was less harsh, more objective reporting. Meanwhile, media barons such as Joseph Pulitzer and William Randolph Hearst became pillars of the establishment; for the most part, they were no longer the antiestablishment insurgents of yore.

Technological advances had a major impact on this transformation in journalism. High-speed presses and more cheaply produced paper made mass-circulation dailies possible. The telegraph and then the telephone made news gathering easier and much faster, and nothing could compare to the invention of radio and television. When radio became widely available in the 1920s, millions of Americans could hear national politicians instead of merely reading about them. With television—first introduced in the late 1940s, and nearly a universal fixture in U.S. homes by the mid-1950s—citizens could see and hear candidates and presidents. The removal of newspapers and magazines as the foremost conduits between politicians and voters had profound effects on the electoral process, as we discuss shortly.

print press:

The traditional form of mass media, comprising newspapers, magazines, and journals.

electronic media:

The newest form of broadcast media, including television, radio, cable, and the internet.

THE CONTEMPORARY MEDIA SCENE

The editors of the first partisan newspapers could scarcely have imagined what their profession would become more than two centuries later. The number and diversity of media outlets existing today are stunning: The **print press**—many thousands of daily and weekly newspapers, periodicals, magazines, newsletters, and journals; and the **electronic media**—radio and television stations and networks, computerized information services, and the Internet. In some ways the news business is more competitive now than at any time in history; yet, paradoxically, the news media have expanded in some ways and contracted in others, dramatically changing the ways in which they cover politics.

The growth of the political press corps is obvious to anyone familiar with government or campaigns. Since 1983, for example, the number of print (newspaper and magazine) reporters accredited at the U.S. Capitol has jumped from 2,300 to more than 4,100; the gain for broadcast (television and radio) journalists was equally impressive and proportionally larger, from about 1,000 in 1983 to an average of 3000 by 1999.[10] On the campaign trail, a similar phenomenon has been occurring. In the 1960s a presidential candidate in the primaries would attract a press entourage of at most a couple of dozen reporters, but in the 1990s a hundred or more print and broadcast journalists can be seen tagging along with a front-runner. Consequently, a politician's every public utterance is reported and intensively scrutinized and interpreted in the media.

Although there are more journalists, they are not necessarily attracting a larger audience, at least on the print side. Daily newspaper circulation has been stagnant for twenty years at 60 million to 62 million papers per day (see Figure 15.1). On a per-household basis, circulation has actually fallen 47 percent from 1976 to 1998.[11] Barely half of the adult population reads a newspaper every day. Among young people age eighteen to twenty-nine, only one-third are daily readers—a decline of 50 percent in two decades.

Along with the relative decline of readership has come a drop in the overall level of competition. In 1880, 61 percent of U.S. cities had at least two competing dailies, but by 1990 a mere 2 percent of cities did so. Not surprisingly, the number of dailies has declined significantly, from a peak of 2,600 in 1909 to around 1,500 today.[12] Most of the remaining dailies are owned by large media conglomerates called chains such as Gannett, Hearst, Knight-Ridder, and Newhouse. In 1940, 83 percent of all daily newspapers were independently owned, but by 1990 just 24 percent remained independent of a chain. Chain ownership usually reduces the diversity of editorial opinions and can result in the homogenization of the news.

Part of the cause of the newspapers' declining audience has been the increased numbers of television sets and cable subscribers (see Figure 15.2) and the increased popularity of television as a news source. At the dawn of the 1960s, a substantial majority of Americans reported that they got most of their news from newspapers; but by the latter

Figure 15.1   Circulation of Daily Newspapers, 1850–1998 (Selected Years)

Year	Number Of Daily Newspapers	Circulation (In Thousands)	CIRCULATION AS A PERCENTAGE OF POPULATION
1850	254	758	3.3%
1890	1,610	8,387	13.3%
1909	2,600	24,212	26.2%
1919	2,441	33,029	31.0%
1927	2,091	41,368	35.7%
1937	2,065	43,345	34.1%
1947	1,854	53,287	37.0%
1958	1,778	58,713	33.6%
1970	1,748	62,100	30.3%
1991	1,586	60,687	23.9%
1993	1,556	59,812	22.8%
1996	1,520	56,990	21.1%
1998	1,509	56,728	20.7%

Over the last fifty years the percentage of Americans reading daily newspapers has steadily declined. This trend may suggest that Americans have become increasingly passive consumers of news, accepting news as it is handed to them from television or online sources rather than actively pursuing more detailed print information.

SOURCE: Adapted from Harold W. Stanley and Richard G. Niemi, *Vital Statistics on American Politics, 1997-1998 (6th ed.)*. (Washington, D.C.: Congressional Quarterly, Inc., 1998), Table 4-2, pp.163-164. *The Editor & Publisher Yearbook 1998*.

Figure 15.2   Television in the American Home

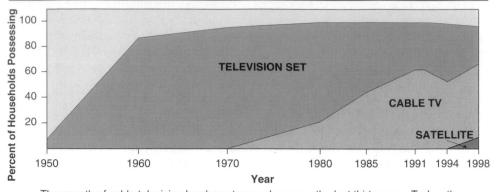

The growth of cable television has been tremendous over the last thirty years. Today, the majority of American households posses access to cable television. Moreover, satellite television, bring literally hundreds of channels to viewers, is also on the rise. Smaller satellite dishes and lower prices are sure to make satellite television a more attractive media source in the future.

SOURCE: Adapted from Harold W. Stanley and Richard G. Niemi, *Vital Statistics on American Politics, 1997-1998 (6th ed.)*. (Washington, D.C.: Congressional Quarterly, Inc.,1998), Table 4-1, p.162. Television Bureau of Advertising.

half of the 1980s, television was the people's choice by an almost two-to-one margin.[13] Moreover, by a margin of 55 percent to 21 percent, Americans now say that they are inclined to believe television over newspapers when conflicting reports about the same story arise. Of course, most individuals still rely on both print *and* broadcast sources,[14] but there can be little question that television news is increasingly important. Despite its many drawbacks (such as simplicity, brevity, and entertainment orientation), television news is "news that matters."[15] Although not totally eclipsing newspapers, television frequently overshadows them, even though it often takes its agenda and lead stories from the headlines produced by print reporters (especially those working for the print elite—papers such as *The New York Times, The Washington Post,* and the *Wall Street Journal;* wire services such as the Associated Press and United Press International; and journals such as *Time, Newsweek,* and *U.S. News & World Report*). Regrettably, busy people today appear to have less time to review the printed word, and consequently they rely more on television's brief headline summaries to stay in touch. Perhaps over time, the Internet will nudge Americans back to the printed word—not in newspapers but on web sites sponsored by the major news organizations.

The television news industry differs from its print counterpart in a variety of ways. The number of outlets has been increasing, not declining, as with newspapers. The three major networks now receive broadcast competition from Cable News Network (CNN), *Headline News,* Cable Satellite Public Affairs Network (C-SPAN), and PBS's *News-Hour/Jim Lehrer.* Although the audiences of all the alternative shows are relatively small compared with those of the network news shows, they are growing while the networks' audience shares contract. The potential for cable expansion is large: nearly half of all U.S. households are currently wired for cable. In addition, the rise of cable has had important implications for the political system. For instance, political scientists Matthew Baum and Samuel Kernell suggest that the splintering of television audiences caused by cable makes it much more difficult for the president to drum up support for his favored policies. Whereas the president could at one time command the attention of all television consumers by appearing on network television, this is no longer possible.[16]

Adding to television's diversity, the national television news corps is often outnumbered on the campaign trail by local television reporters. Satellite technology has provided any of the 1,300 local stations willing to invest in the hardware an opportunity to beam back reports from the field. On a daily basis, local news is watched by more people (67 percent of adults) than is network news (49 percent), so increased local attention to politics has some real significance.

The decline of the major networks' audience shares and the local stations' decreasing reliance on the major networks for news—coupled with stringent belt tightening ordered by the networks' corporate managers—resulted in severe news staff cutbacks at NBC, CBS, and ABC during the 1980s and 1990s. These economy measures have affected the quality of broadcast journalism. Many senior correspondents bemoan the loss of desk assistants and junior reporters, who did much of the legwork necessary to get less superficial, more in-depth pieces on the air. As a consequence, stories requiring extensive research are often discarded in favor of simplistic, eye-catching, "sexy" items that increasingly seem to dominate campaign and government coverage.

There has also been a substantial increase in the number of media mergers in recent years, so that each national television network now is only a piece of a massive corporation. These mergers have had at least two important effects. One effect is that the large corporations have their financial bottom line as the alpha and the omega of their existence. As a consequence, if news shows cannot be profitable, the corporate executives will either cut the news divisions back or force the news divisions to do virtually anything to expand the audience. Unfortunately, what expands the audience is sleazy, tabloid coverage of gossip, innuendo, and sex. (see Highlight Box: The Punditocracy)

HIGHLIGHT 15.1

The Punditocracy

The Constitution specifies three branches of government, but many observers of modern American politics would add an informal fourth branch—the news media. Within the world of the media, the role of so-called pundits (media commentators who dissect and interpret daily political affairs) is increasingly controversial as the media, especially television, becomes even more pervasive and influential.

The pundits appearing in the media today come in many forms. Some are relatively neutral academics who have studied American history, government, and politics. Others come from the partisan and ideological world, where they have worked for candidates and parties for years prior to becoming media experts.

Once limited to a handful of key reporters and television anchors, the punditocracy now numbers in the hundreds. This is largely due to the expansion of cable television. The advent of CNN, MSNBC, Fox News Network, and other cable outlets, as well as the proliferation of network news magazines such as *20/20*, *Dateline*, and *60 Minutes*, has created an ever-growing platform from which pundits operate. Today, the pundits are everywhere, all the time. Although only a relatively small fraction of the American public watches any particular channel at any particular time, another audience, small but loyal, made up of politicians and fellow opinion-shapers, pays a great deal of attention to pundits.

Bias in the punditocracy is often assumed, since so many of the pundits come from a particular partisan or ideological background. In many cases, the pundits' most important objective is to project their side's spin—the interpretation of real events and issues in the light most favorable for their preferred party or ideology. Spin is a constant fixture on TV, as partisan operatives battle to frame issues in a way that benefits their political objectives.

Many of us will recognize the dramatic displays of punditry that occur on organized shouting matches such as CNN's *Crossfire* and *The Capital Gang*. These programs deliberately produce talk-show fireworks by pairing up hosts and guests of different political orientations to debate current and controversial issues. While it is often difficult to hear the guests, the points made in this process have an undeniable impact. (For more information, check out http://www.cnn.com/CNN/Programs/crossfire/ and http://www.cnn.com/CNN/Programs/capital.gang/)

The cacophony of competing perspectives can confuse and even mislead the average citizen. Negativity and intense partisanship within the punditocracy may actually contribute to the public's apathetic and skeptical view of politics.* Some argue that the spectacle of pundits picking fights can easily disillusion thoughtful citizens and cheapen political discourse, while others claim that pundits offer important insights and opinions that would otherwise go unreported by traditional news coverage.

*James Fallows, *Breaking the News: How the Media Undermine American Democracy* (New York: Vintage Press, 1997).

Web Exploration
To see how media is diversifying and repackaging itself through the use of pundits, go to
www.awlonline.com/oconnor.

network:

An association of broadcast stations (radio or television) that share programming through a financial arrangement.

affiliates:

Local television stations that carry the programming of a national network.

wire service:

An electronic delivery of news gathered by the news services' correspondents and sent to all member news media organizations.

Another suspected effect is that the media megacorporations are censoring news that reflects badly on products created by the nonnews divisions of those corporations.[17] While conservative critics say that media bias is mainly liberal—and in coverage of politics this criticism may well be valid—it is also true that another form of bias in the news media is conservative since these corporations are making sure that the coverage of their own products stays positive.

Every newspaper, radio station, and television station is influential in its own area, but only a handful of media outlets are influential nationally. The United States has no nationwide daily newspapers to match the influence of Great Britain's *The Times, Guardian,* and *Daily Telegraph,* all of which are avidly read in virtually every corner of the United Kingdom. The national orientation of the British print media can be traced to the smaller size of the country and also to London's role as both the national capital and the largest cultural metropolis. The vastness of the United States and the existence of many large cities, such as New York, Los Angeles, and Chicago, effectively preclude a nationally united print medium in this country.

However, national distribution of the *New York Times,* the *Wall Street Journal, USA Today,* and the *Christian Science Monitor* does exist, and other newspapers, such as *The Washington Post* and the *Los Angeles Times,* have substantial influence from coast to coast. These six newspapers also have a pronounced effect on what the five major national **networks** (ABC, CBS, NBC, CNN, and Fox) broadcast on their evening news programs—or, in the case of CNN, air on cable around the clock. A major story that breaks in one of these papers is nearly guaranteed to be featured on one or more of the network news shows. These news shows are carried by hundreds of local stations—called **affiliates**—that are associated with the national networks and may choose to carry their programming. A **wire service,** such as the Associated Press (AP) (established in 1848), also nationalizes the news. Most newspapers subscribe to the service, which not only produces its own news stories but also puts on the wire major stories produced by other media outlets.

The national newspapers, wire services, and broadcast networks are supplemented by a number of national news magazines, whose subscribers number in the millions. *Time, Newsweek,* and *U.S. News & World Report* bring the week's news into focus and headline one event or trend for special treatment. Other news magazines stress commentary from an ideological viewpoint, including *The Nation* (left-wing), *The New Republic* (moderate-liberal), and *The National Review* (conservative). These last three publications have much smaller circulations, but because their readerships are composed of activists and opinion leaders, they have disproportionate influence.

In politics, as in every other field, the World Wide Web is truly the wave of the future. Already, web-based information has become standard fare for anyone interested in politics. Three web sites among the dozens now available are those of *The National Journal,* which includes its famous Hotline report (www.cloakroom.com); *The Washington Post,* whose site is widely considered the best political site on the web (www.washingtonpost.com); and an all-politics collaboration between CNN, *Time* magazine, and other media sources (www.cnn.com/ALLPOLITICS). Virtually every major newspaper, opinion magazine, and news magazine now has a site, as well as all the television networks, which endlessly offer not only the pieces that appear on the evening news, but also additional commentary and information too lengthy to include on the original thirty-minute broadcast.

Table 15.2   Younger Americans: Turned On by Information, Off by News

	18–29 %	30–49 %	50–64 %	65+ %
Like having so many information sources to choose from	77	70	64	52
Enjoy keeping up with the news a lot	33	48	59	68

Many people wonder if the media is cutting into its own subscription revenues, since it is not feasible to charge for the use of a public site associated with a newspaper or TV network. Interestingly, there is very little evidence that this is happening. By and large, the people who use media web sites are highly informed voters who devour additional information about politics and government and use the web for updates and supplements to their traditional media services. Web sites thus appear to be building interest in traditional media rather than detracting from them. And as the current generation of computer-literate children and young people become adult voters, the web is likely to become the primary means by which America informs itself about politics and government on a regular and current basis.

Web Exploration
What does it mean for a television station or a newspaper to have a website? To see which newspapers, magazines, and networks have a web presence, and how that coverage differs from or complements its standard coverage, go to www.awlonline.com/oconnor.

HOW THE MEDIA COVER POLITICIANS AND GOVERNMENT

Much of the media's attention is focused on our politicians and the day-to-day operations of our government. In this section we will discuss how the press covers the three constitutionally created branches of government (Congress, the president, and the courts), and show how the tenor of this coverage has changed since the Watergate scandal of the early 1970s.

Covering the Presidency

The three branches of the U.S. government—the executive, the legislative, and the judicial—are roughly equal in power and authority, but in the world of media coverage, the president is first among equals. All television cables lead to the White House, and a president can address the nation on all networks almost at will. On television, Congress and the courts appear to be divided and confused institutions—different segments contradicting others—whereas the commander-in-chief is in clear focus as chief of state and head of government. The situation is scarcely different in other democracies. In Great Britain, all media eyes are on No. 10 Downing Street, the office and residence of the prime minister.

Since Franklin D. Roosevelt's time, chief executives have used the presidential press conference to shape public opinion and explain their actions (see Figure 15.3). The

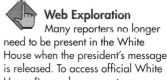

Web Exploration
Many reporters no longer need to be present in the White House when the president's message is released. To access official White House Press releases, go to www.awlonline.com/oconnor.

Figure 15.3 Presidential News Conferences, 1929–1996

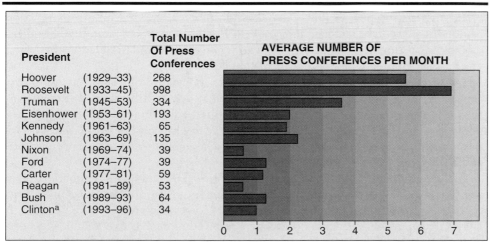

President		Total Number Of Press Conferences	AVERAGE NUMBER OF PRESS CONFERENCES PER MONTH
Hoover	(1929–33)	268	
Roosevelt	(1933–45)	998	
Truman	(1945–53)	334	
Eisenhower	(1953–61)	193	
Kennedy	(1961–63)	65	
Johnson	(1963–69)	135	
Nixon	(1969–74)	39	
Ford	(1974–77)	39	
Carter	(1977–81)	59	
Reagan	(1981–89)	53	
Bush	(1989–93)	64	
Clinton[a]	(1993–96)	34	

The modern president has less need to give frequent presidential news conferences than was the case in the past. Today, presidents prefer to give a limited number of well planned news conferences rather than make more regular appearances. The modern president relies on advisors and a press team to provide the media with daily briefings.

[a]As of December 31, 1996.

SOURCE: Adapted from Harold W. Stanley and Richard G. Niemi, *Vital Statistics on American Politics, 1997-1998 (6th ed.)*. (Washington, D.C.: Congressional Quarterly, Inc., 1998), Table 4-3, p.166.

Perhaps the most visible part of the national press corps is the group of correspondents who work at the White House. Every network, many large television stations, and virtually all big-city daily newspapers have at least one representative who works in the White House to cover the president and his chief advisers. Other media outlets representing foreign countries are also given access to the White House and are included in the presidential press corps.

White House reporters are usually restricted to the press room, where the president makes announcements and holds informal question-and-answer sessions. Although presidential appearances in the press room rarely occur more than once or twice a week, the president's news secretary appears daily to brief reporters on the chief executive's current schedule and activities. Frequently, the press secretary also makes announcements on behalf of the president (perhaps the chief executive's comments on just-released economic statistics, for example).

Formal presidential news conferences, often held in the East Room of the White House, are an elaborate production, especially if held during prime-time hours. All the networks carry them live and in full, and correspondents jockey to attract the president's attention. The best-known reporters are nearly guaranteed to be selected to ask a question, and these are prime opportunities for them and for the news organizations they represent. Over the years, many of the network's most prominent professionals have served on the White House beat, including CBS's Dan Rather and Lesley Stahl, NBC's Tom Brokaw, and ABC's Sam Donaldson.

It is not always easy for the president to have reporters literally underfoot. But the instantaneous access to the American people they give the president is essential to his work, and the scrutiny of the chief executive they offer the American people is vital to the voters as well.

presence of the press in the White House (see Highlight 15.2: The White House Press Corps) enables a president to appear even on very short notice and to televise live, interrupting regular programming. The White House's press-briefing room is a familiar sight on the evening news, not just because presidents use it so often, but also because the presidential press secretary has almost daily question-and-answer sessions there.

The press secretary's post has existed only since Herbert Hoover's administration (1929–1933), and the individual holding it is the president's main disseminator of information to the press. For this vital position, a number of presidents have chosen close aides who were very familiar with their thinking. For example, John F. Kennedy had Pierre Salinger (now an ABC News foreign correspondent), Lyndon B. Johnson had Bill Moyers (who now hosts many PBS documentaries), and Jimmy Carter chose his longtime Georgia associate Jody Powell. Probably the most famous recent presidential press secretary is James Brady, who was wounded and disabled in the March 1981 assassination attempt on President Ronald Reagan.

On any given day, presidents, their advisers, and their families do any number of things that might become news. In deciding what *does* become news, presidents and the press engage in a continuous "negotiation of news worthiness."[18] This negotiation occurs not only between the White House and the news media but within the two entities as well, and it involves "what get covered, who gets asked about a story, and how and for how long the story is covered."[19]

Finally, although the president receives the lion's share of the press's attention, political scientist Thomas Patterson suggests that much of this focus is unfavorable. Since the 1960s, press coverage of the president has become dramatically more negative. In fact, all three major presidential contenders received more negative than positive coverage in both 1992 and 1996. Patterson also finds that coverage of President Bush's handling of important national problems was almost solely negative.[20]

Covering Congress

Press coverage of Congress is very different from media coverage of the president. The size of the institution alone (535 members) and its decentralized nature (bicameralism, the committee system, and so on) make it difficult for the media to survey. Nevertheless, the congressional press corps has more than 3,000 members.[21] Most news organizations solve the size and decentralization problems by concentrating coverage on three groups of individuals. First, the leaders of both parties in both houses receive the lion's share of attention because only they can speak for a majority of their party's members. Usually the majority and minority leaders in each house and the Speaker of the House are the preferred spokespersons, but the whips also receive a substantial share of air time and column inches. Second, key committee chairs command center stage when subjects in their domain are newsworthy. Heads of the most prominent committees (such as Ways and Means or Armed Services) are guaranteed frequent coverage, but even the chairs and members of minor committees or subcommittees can achieve fame when the time and issue are right. Third, local newspapers and broadcast stations will normally devote some resources to covering their local senators and representatives, even when these legislators are junior and relatively lacking in influence. Most office holders, in turn, are mainly concerned with meeting the needs of their local media contingents, since these reporters are the ones who directly and regularly reach the voters in their home constituencies.

■ During the Clinton impeachment hearings C-SPAN provided extensive live Congressional coverage for cable viewers across the United States. (Photo courtesy: C-Span)

One other kind of congressional news coverage is worth noting: investigative-committee hearings. Occasionally, a sensational scandal leads to televised congressional committee hearings that transfix and electrify the nation. In the early 1950s, Senator Joseph R. McCarthy (R-Wisc.) held a series of hearings to expose and root out what he claimed were Communists in the State Department and other U.S. government agencies, as well as Hollywood's film industry. The senator's style of investigation, which involved many wild charges made without proof and the smearing and labeling of some innocent opponents as Communists, gave rise to the term *McCarthyism*.

The Watergate hearings of 1973 and 1974—which stemmed from White House efforts to eavesdrop on officials of the Democratic National Committee and then to cover up presidential involvement in the scheme—made heroes out of two committee chairs, Senator Sam Ervin (D-N.C.) and U.S. Representative Peter Rodino (D-N.J.). They uncovered many facts behind the Watergate scandal and then pursued the impeachment of President Richard M. Nixon. (Nixon resigned in August 1974, before the full House could vote on his impeachment.)

In 1987 the Iran-Contra hearings—set up to investigate a complicated Reagan-administration scheme in which arms were sold to Iran and the profits were then diverted to the anti-Communist Nicaraguan Contras—also created a popular hero. This time, however, the hero was not the committee chair but a witness, Lieutenant Colonel Oliver North, a White House aide deeply involved in the plot. North's boyish appeal and patriotic demeanor projected well on television, on which all the hearings were carried live (as were the McCarthy and Watergate hearings). North capitalized on his fame and in 1994 launched an unsuccessful campaign for a U.S. Senate seat from Virginia. In October 1991, the nation viewed another televised committee spectacle when Supreme Court nominee Clarence Thomas was accused of sexual harassment

More recently, throughout the latter months of 1995 and 1996, Whitewater hearings led by Senator Alfonse D'Amato (R-N.Y.) questioned the actions of President Clinton and Hillary Rodham Clinton in a failed investment venture while Clinton was Governor of Arkansas. On much the same subject, even more sensational hearings were

Impeaching the President and the Press

The year-long Clinton/Lewinsky scandal became one of the great media extravaganzas of all time—a mega-feeding frenzy to which every branch of the media devoted enormous time and space. To judge by most public opinion polls, the media dedicated too much attention to it, at the expense of policy issues in which the American public actually seemed more interested, such as the growing crisis is in the Balkans. Every cable station or network had its own impeachment logo, the most memorable of which was MSNBC's "The White House in Crisis." Coverage aired daily for months and required the media to manufacture crises even on days when there had been no substantive developments. The media were obliged to fill the airwaves with discussions between anchors, reporters, pundits, and politicians, and almost anyone with a political opinion received at least Andy Warhol's fifteen minutes of fame during the "crisis."

The climax of the impeachment scandal came in the Senate trial, in which the 100 U.S. senators had to decide for only the second time in history how to act on the House of Representatives' impeachment of the president and whether or not to oust him from his office in the middle of a term. This was by any measure a serious and legitimate news story, but at the same time, the disproportionate attention to the subject turned the affair into a media circus. Once again, almost anyone with an opinion was given time including random passers-by, who were asked for their thoughts on the President's behavior and the moral health of the nation.

Many in the media had predicted that the trial could last until May or June of 1999, though in the end it lasted only from mid-January to mid-February. The trial turned out to be relatively dignified, notwithstanding the media circus, and was taken seriously both by those participating and by the American public. The most gripping coverage was actually provided by C-SPAN, which simply allowed the public to see what was happening during the proceedings without the distractions of commentary.

After months of inattention by the media to other crucial issues (such as the Yugoslavian crisis, which finally did explode into war soon after the impeachment proceedings ended), the Clinton scandal finally drew to a close with the Senate's votes of acquittal on February 13. Though he retained his office, Clinton's presidency was severely damaged, not only by the charges themselves, but also by the media's revelation of significant troubles in his private life.

---

convened by the Senate under Tennessee Senator Fred Thompson in 1997 concerning the financing of President Clinton's 1996 reelection campaign. Though containing much sound and fury and a number of very serious charges, the hearings seemed to fizzle as the year wore on, as hard evidence was difficult to come by. Similar hearings were held on the House side headed by Representative Dan Burton (R-Ind.) in 1998. Burton was a highly controversial choice as chairman because of his staunchly anti-Clinton perspective and was not viewed as credibly as the moderate Thompson. Nonetheless, far more information was revealed, not only by his hearings, but by newspaper and television coverage surrounding his campaign finance hearings.

Coverage of Congress has been greatly expanded through use of the cable industry channel C-SPAN. C-SPAN1 and C-SPAN2 provide gavel-to-gavel coverage of House and Senate sessions as well as many committee hearings. For the first time, Americans can watch their representatives in action (or inaction, as the case may be), and do so twenty-four hours a day.

As with coverage of the president, press coverage of Congress is disproportionately negative. Much media attention given to the House and Senate focuses on conflict between members. Political scientists John Hibbing and Elizabeth Theiss-Morse believe that such reporting is at least partially responsible for the public's negative perceptions of Congress.[22]

Covering the Courts

The branch of government that is the most different, in press coverage as in many other respects, is the judicial branch. Cloaked in secrecy—because judicial deliberations and decision making are conducted in private—the courts receive scant coverage under most circumstances. However, a volatile or controversial issue, such as abortion, can change the usual type of coverage, especially when the Supreme Court is rendering the decision. Each network and major newspaper has one or more Supreme Court reporters, people who are usually well schooled in the law and whose instant analysis of court opinions interprets the decisions for the millions of people without legal training. Gradually, the admission of cameras into state and local courtrooms across the United States is offering people a more in-depth look at the operation of the judicial system. As yet, though, the Supreme Court does not permit televised proceedings. While the proceedings of the U.S. Supreme Court are conducted in public, the justices continue to resist attempts to have oral arguments televised. State courts, however, often allow television cameras in the courtroom. First the Palm Beach rape trial of William Kennedy Smith and then the O. J. Simpson trial attracted millions of viewers. The Simpson trial even spawned two new legal-oriented television programs: *Burden of Proof,* a CNN program hosted by Greta Van Sustern and Roger Cossack (who had served as commentators during the Simpson trial), and *Geraldo Live,* on CNBC. Court TV, which provides full televised coverage of many highly publicized trials, such as that of English nanny Louise Woodward, also draws significant viewership.

The work of Independent Counsel Kenneth Starr and the grand juries investigating Whitewater and the president's relationship with Monica Lewinsky also attracted the attention of the mass media, overshadowing the Pope's historic visit to Cuba in almost all media outlets. The operations of the federal and state courts, as well as the judges and attorneys who appear in them, are now regular fodder for media pundits and legal experts.

Watergate and the Era of Investigative Journalism

The Watergate scandal of the Nixon administration had the most profound impact of any modern event on the manner and substance of press conduct. In many respects Watergate began a chain reaction that today allows for intense scrutiny of public officials' private lives. Moreover, coupled with the civil rights movement and the Vietnam War, Watergate shifted the orientation of journalism away from mere description (providing an account of happenings) and toward prescription—helping to set the campaign's (and society's) agenda by focusing attention on the candidates' shortcomings as well as on certain social problems.

A new breed and a new generation of reporters were attracted to journalism, particularly to its investigative role. As a group they were idealistic, although aggressively mistrustful of authority, and they shared a contempt for "politics as usual." The Vietnam and Watergate generation dominates journalism today. They and their younger colleagues hold sway over most newsrooms, with two-thirds of all reporters now under the age of thirty-six and an ever-increasing number of editors and executives who had their start in journalism in the Watergate era.[23]

The Post-Watergate Era

A volatile mix of guilt and fear is at work in the post-Watergate press. The guilt stems from regret that experienced Washington reporters failed to detect the telltale signs of the Watergate scandal early on; that even after the story broke, most journalists underplayed the unfolding disaster until forced to take it more seriously by two young *Post* reporters; that over the years journalism's leading lights had become too close to the politicians they were supposed to check and therefore for too long failed to tell the public about dangerous excesses in the government. The press's ongoing fear is deep-seated and complements the guilt. Every political journalist is apprehensive about missing the next big story, of being left on the platform when the next scandal train leaves Union Station.

In the post-Watergate era, the sizable financial and personnel investments many major news organizations have made in investigative units

Web Exploration

Should television cameras be allowed in the courtroom, particularly the Supreme Court? To learn more about both sides of the debate, go to www.awlonline.com/oconnor.

■ An emotional Paula Jones addresses the media after her lawsuit against the President was dismissed in April 1998. (Photo courtesy: Eric Gay/AP/Wide World Photos)

ROOTS OF GOVERNMENT

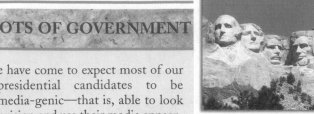

The Presidency in the Television Age

We have come to expect most of our presidential candidates to be media-genic—that is, able to look good on television and use their media appearance to achieve their political ends. From their hairstyles and suits to their televised personas, candidates aim to please the unblinking eye of the camera. But what of the period when television was first emerging as a mass medium? How did the presidency adapt to this strange and forbidding new medium?

Television first became a phenomenon for the mass public at the end of Harry Truman's presidency in the early 1950s. While historians now rate Truman as a near-great president—that is, among our top fifteen presidents—he was clearly not cut out for the cathode ray tube. He was not a gifted public speaker, and his looks were pedestrian. Had television been universal in those days, it is doubtful that Truman could have been elected without great difficulty. Democrat Truman was replaced by Republican Eisenhower, but while their policies and outlooks were very different, they shared the same aversion to television. Eisenhower was, if anything, an even worse public speaker than Truman. While the former World War II general had a dazzling smile that inspired Americans to like and trust him (thus the famous slogan, "I like Ike"), he was particularly inarticulate when delivering official speeches. Eisenhower's inad-

equacy in communicating with the American people may have been one reason why, despite his enormous personal popularity, he was unable to pass the presidency along to his chosen successor, Richard Nixon, in 1960.

Television ultimately had its inevitable effect upon politics in 1960. In that famous presidential campaign, John F. Kennedy clearly loved the television camera, and it loved him. His vigor (he pronounced it "vigah," with a Massachusetts accent); the Kennedy family touch football games; his beautiful wife; and his handsome young family all combined to give Kennedy an intangible but powerful media edge against the jowly Richard Nixon. In the famous televised Nixon-Kennedy debate, which probably tipped an extremely close election in JFK's favor, Kennedy's tanned and handsome visage was as much a part of his victory as any argument he employed. In contrast to television viewers, many radio listeners, judging the performance without visual aid, actually thought that Nixon had won the debate. Kennedy's time in office was brief, but he set the style that has dominated the presidency in the media ever since. All presidents have tried to live up to the Kennedy standard, some with more success than others, but it is difficult to imagine a talented but TV-phobic president like Truman or Eisenhower coming to the fore of the American political system again.

almost guarantee that greater attention will be given to scandals and that probably more of them—some real and some manufactured—will be uncovered.

The Character Issue in Media Coverage of Politicians.   Another clear consequence of Watergate has been the increasing emphasis by the press on the character of candidates. The issue of character has always been present in U.S. politics—George Washington was not made the nation's first president for his policy positions—but rarely if ever has character been such an issue as it has in elections from 1976 onward. (See Roots of Government: The Presidency in the Television Age.) Jimmy Carter's 1976 presidential campaign was characterized by moral posturing in the wake of Watergate. Edward M. Kennedy's 1980 presidential candidacy was destroyed in part by lingering character questions. The 1988 race witnessed an explosion of character concerns so forceful that several candidates (including Gary Hart) were badly scarred by it. And the 1992 contest for the White House became a tawdry debate about the alleged mistresses of Bill Clinton and George Bush.

The character issue may in part have been an outgrowth of the "new journalism" popularized by author Tom Wolfe in the 1970s.[24] Contending that conventional journalism was sterile and stripped of color, Wolfe and others argued for a reporting style that expanded the definition of news and, novel-like, highlighted all the personal details of the newsmaker. Then, too, reporters had witnessed the success of such books as Theodore H. White's *The Making of the President* series and Joe McGinniss's *The Selling of the President 1968*, which offered revealing, behind-the-scenes vignettes of the previous election's candidates.[25] Why not give readers and viewers this information before the election? the press reasoned. There was encouragement from academic quarters as well. "Look to character first" when evaluating and choosing among presidential candidates, wrote Duke University political science professor James David Barber in a widely circulated 1972 volume, *The Presidential Character* (see chapter 8).[26]

Communications scholar Roderick Hart believes that this shift in focus from issues to character is the result of the shift from newspaper to television news. Unlike print, television is a visual medium, which best portrays faces and images. As a result, voters who receive their political information from television are significantly more likely to rely on candidate traits (rather than issue positions) in casting their ballots than are voters who receive their political information primarily from newspapers.[27]

Whatever the precise historical origins of the character trend in reporting, it is undergirded by certain assumptions. First, the press sees that it has mainly replaced the political parties as the screening committee that winnows the field of candidates and filters out the weaker or more unlucky contenders. (This fact may be another reason to support the strengthening of the political parties. Politicians are in a much better position than the press to provide professional peer review of colleagues who are seeking the presidency.) Second, many journalists believe it necessary to tell people about any of a candidate's foibles that might affect his or her public performance. The press's third supposition is that it is giving the public what it wants and expects, more or less. Perhaps television has conditioned voters to think about the private lives of the rich and famous. The rules of television prominence now seem to apply to all celebrities equally, whether they reside in Hollywood or Washington. And, perhaps more important, scandal sells papers and attracts television viewers.

■ Led by law office employee Judy Smith, Monica Lewinsky weaves her way through the media to her attorney's Washington office. (Photo courtesy: Tyler Mallory/AP/Wide World Photos)

Loosening of the Libel Law.

Another factor permits the modern press to undertake character investigations. In the old days, a reporter would think twice about filing a story critical of a politician's character, and the editors probably would have killed the story had the reporter been foolish enough to do so. The reason? Fear of a libel suit. (Recall from chapter 5 that libel is published defamation of character that unjustly injures a person's reputation.) The first question editors would ask about even an ambiguous or suggestive phrase about a public official was, "If we're sued, can you prove beyond a doubt what you've written?"

Such inhibitions were ostensibly lifted in 1964, when the Supreme Court ruled in *New York Times Co. v. Sullivan*[28] that simply publishing a defamatory falsehood is not enough to justify a libel judgment. Henceforth a public official would have to prove "actual malice," a requirement extended three years later to all public figures, such as Hollywood stars and prominent athletes.[29] The Supreme Court declared that the First Amendment requires elected officials and candidates to prove that the publisher either believed the challenged statement was false or at least entertained serious doubts about its truth and acted recklessly in publishing it in the face of those doubts. The actual malice rule has made it very difficult for public figures to win libel cases.

Despite *Sullivan,* the threat of libel litigation (and its deterrent effect on the press) persists for at least two reasons. First, the *Sullivan* protections do little to reduce the expense of defending defamation claims. The monetary costs have increased enormously, as have the required commitments of reporters' and editors' time and energy. Small news organizations without the financial resources of a national network or the *New York Times* are sometimes reluctant to publish material that might invite a lawsuit because the litigation costs could threaten their existence. The second reason for the continuing libel threat is a cultural phenomenon of heightened sensitivity to the harm

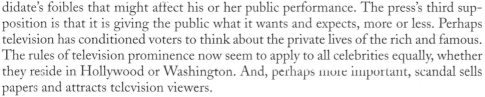

New York Times Co. v. Sullivan (1964):

Supreme Court decision ruling that simply publishing a defamatory falsehood is not enough to justify a libel judgment.

that words can do to an individual's emotional tranquility. As a result, politicians are often more inclined to sue their press adversaries, even when success is unlikely.

But high costs and the politicians' propensity to sue cut both ways. The overall number of libel suits filed in recent years has dropped because plaintiffs also incur hefty legal expenses, and—perhaps more important—they have despaired of winning. Some news outlets have added another disincentive by filing countersuits charging their antagonists with bringing frivolous or nuisance actions against them.

In practice, then, the loosening of libel law has provided journalists with a safer harbor from liability in their reporting on elected officials and candidates. Whether it has truly diminished press self-censorship, especially for financially less well-endowed media outlets, is a more difficult question to answer. However, at least for the wealthy newspapers and networks, the libel laws are no longer as severe a restraint on the press as they once were.

The Question of Bias.   Whenever the media break an unfavorable story about a politician, the politician usually counters with a cry of "biased reporting"—a claim that the press has told an untruth, has told only part of the truth, or has reported facts out of the complete context of the event. Who is right? Are the news media biased? The answer is simple and unavoidable: Of course they are. Journalists are fallible human beings who inevitably have values, preferences, and attitudes galore—some conscious, others subconscious, but all reflected at one time or another in the subjects selected for coverage or the slant of that coverage. Given that the press is biased, it is important to know in what ways it is biased and when and how the biases are shown.

Truth be told, most journalists lean to the left. First of all, those in the relatively small group of professional journalists (not many more than 100,000, compared with more than 4 million teachers in the United States) are drawn heavily from the ranks of highly educated social and political liberals, as a number of studies, some conducted by the media themselves, have shown.[30] Journalists are substantially Democratic in party affiliation and voting habits, progressive and antiestablishment in political orientation, and well to the left of the general public on most economic, foreign policy, and social issues (such as abortion, affirmative action, gay rights, and gun control). Second, dozens of the most influential reporters and executives entered (or reentered) journalism after stints of partisan involvement in campaigns or government, and a substantial majority worked for Democrats.[31]

Third, this liberal press bias does indeed show up frequently on screen and in print. A study of reporting on the abortion issue, for example, revealed a clear slant to the pro side on network television news, matching in many ways the reporters' own abortion-rights views.[32]

Conservative bias exists in the media as well. One example is the world of AM radio talk shows. Some studies have indicated that liberal programs actually enjoy more airtime than conservative ones, but there is no question that conservatives host by far the most popular shows, as exemplified by Rush Limbaugh, G. Gordon Liddy (of Watergate infamy), and Oliver North (of the Iran–Contra affair). These radio hosts are the political equivalent of "shock jocks." They strive for controversy and attack liberals (especially the Clinton family and administration) with ferocious and inflammatory rhetoric.

Of course, these conservative hosts are within their First Amendment rights, and their programs only exist because an audience exists to support them. The Limbaugh show, for example, attracts millions of listeners every day and is tremendously profitable. At the same time, others worry that these programs have a corrosive effect on political discourse and are simply unfair to their appointed targets. However, it must be said that these conservative organs provide some balance to the liberal orientation of much of the other media, especially in the evening news programs televised on the major networks and cable channels.

TRY IT!
Compare news coverage on a particular news story for evidence of political bias. Go to
www.awlonline.com/oconnor.

Other Sources of Bias.   From left to right, all of these media criticisms have some validity in different times and circumstances, in one media forum or another. But these critiques ignore some nonideological factors probably more essential to an understanding of press bias. Owing to competition and the reward structure of journalism, the deepest bias most political journalists have is the desire to get to the bottom of a good campaign story—which is usually negative news about a candidate. The fear of missing a good story, more than bias, leads all media outlets to develop the same headlines and to adopt the same slant.

A related nonideological bias is the effort to create a horse race where none exists. Newspeople, whose lives revolve around the current political scene, naturally want to add spice and drama, minimize their boredom, and increase their audience. Other human, not just partisan, biases are also at work. Whether the press likes or dislikes a candidate personally is often vital. Former Governor Bruce Babbitt and U.S. Representative Morris K. Udall, both wisecracking, straight-talking Arizona Democrats, were press favorites in their presidential bids (in 1988 and 1976, respectively), and both enjoyed favorable coverage. Richard M. Nixon, Jimmy Carter, and Gary Hart—all aloof politicians—were disliked by many reporters who covered them, and they suffered from a harsh and critical press. More recently, as House Speaker, Newt Gingrich was the favorite target of the press. Repeatedly, the stories newspaper editors decide to print about Gingrich when he was Speaker of the House cast him in a negative light. This treatment has contributed to his negative popularity ratings.

But does press bias affect election outcomes? Perhaps. Political scientist Eric Veblen shows that the net advantage that the *Manchester Union-Leader,* New Hampshire's most influential newspaper, provides its favored candidate can increase that candidate's vote share significantly. On the other hand, media darlings such as Bruce Babbitt and Morris Udall failed in their quest to become president, while those less popular with the media, such as Jimmy Carter and Richard Nixon, succeeded. Clearly, bias is not the be-all and end-all that critics on both the right and left often insist. Press tilt has a marginal to moderate effect, and it is but one piece in the media's new mosaic.[33]

■ Conservative talk-show host Rush Limbaugh became the symbol for the talk-radio phenomenon of the 1990s. In addition to his daily three-hour radio broadcast, Limbaugh also had a nightly syndicated television show. (Photo courtesy: Lennox McLendon/ AP/Wide World Photos)

THE MEDIA'S INFLUENCE ON THE PUBLIC

How much influence does the media have on the public? In most cases the press has surprisingly little effect. To put it bluntly, people tend to see what they want to see; that is, human beings will focus on parts of a report that reinforce their own attitudes and ignore parts that challenge their core beliefs. Most of us also selectively tune out and ignore reports that contradict our preferences in politics and other fields. Therefore, a committed Democrat will remember certain portions of a televised news program about a current campaign—primarily the parts that reinforce his or her own choice—and an equally committed Republican will recall very different sections of the report or remember the material in a way that supports the GOP position. In other words, most voters are not empty vessels into which the media can pour their own beliefs. This fact dramatically limits the ability of news organizations to sway public opinion.

And yet the news media do have some influence, called **media effects,** on public opinion. Let's examine how this is so.

First, reporting can sway people who are uncommitted and have no strong opinion in the first place. So, for example, the media has a greater influence on political

media effects:

The influence of news sources on public opinion.

independents than on strong partisans.[34] Indeed, many studies from the 1940s and 1950s, an era when partisanship was very strong, suggested that the media had no influence at all on public opinion. The last forty years, however, have seen the rapid decline in political partisanship,[35] thereby opening the door to greater media influence. On the other hand, the sort of politically unmotivated individual who is open to media effects is probably unlikely to vote in a given election, and therefore the media influence is of no particular consequence.

Second, the press has a much greater impact on topics far removed from the lives and experiences of its readers and viewers. News reports can probably shape public opinion about events in foreign countries fairly easily. Yet what the media say about domestic issues such as rising prices, neighborhood crime, or child rearing may have relatively little effect, because most citizens have personal experience of and well-formed ideas about these subjects.

Third, news organizations can help tell us what to think about, even if they cannot determine what we think. As mentioned earlier, the press often sets the agenda for government or a campaign by focusing on certain issues or concerns. For example, in the weeks following the Littleton, Colorado, school massacre in 1999, every national network devoted extensive coverage to the incident. And sure enough, concern about gun control, school safety, and cultural violence began to top the list of national problems considered most pressing by the public, as measured in opinion polls. Without the dramatic pictures and lavish attention that accompanied the shooting, it is doubtful that these issues would have risen so quickly to the forefront of the national agenda.

Thus, perhaps not so much in *how* they cover an event, but in *what* they choose to cover, the media make their effect felt. By deciding to focus on one event while ignoring another, the media can determine to a large extent the country's agenda, an awe-inspiring power.

The media's power to shape citizens' perceptions—though limited—can have important implications for the success of politicians. For example, voters' choice in presidential elections is often related to their assessments of the economy. In general, a healthy economy motivates voters to reelect the incumbent president, whereas a weak economy motivates voters to choose the challenger. Hence, if the media paints a consistently dismal picture of the economy, that picture may well hurt the incumbent president seeking reelection. In fact, political scientist Marc Hetherington convincingly shows that the media's relentlessly negative coverage of the economy in 1992 negatively shaped voters' retrospective assessments of the economy, which in turn helped lead to George Bush's defeat in the 1992 presidential election.[36]

HOW POLITICIANS USE THE MEDIA

President Clinton is an acknowledged master of media manipulation. Despite all of the negative coverage he has endured over his long political career, or perhaps because of it, Clinton knows how to push the right media buttons. For example, in his initiative to encourage better race relations, which he labeled a prime goal of his second term, President Clinton staged a series of town meetings and televised encounters among people of all colors. Most of these events were carefully stage managed and resulted in little frank talk, something experts in the field of race relations believe is a necessity if real progress is to be made. Yet reams of positive publicity resulted; so, at least from a public relations perspective, the race initiative could be termed a success. The president is not always the leader in getting the media to focus attention on a particular issue, however. Indeed, often the relationship is exactly the opposite—the president *reacts* to attention given to an issue by the news media. This seems to be especially true in foreign policy.[37]

Politics once again met policy on the day before President Clinton was scheduled to be impeached by the House of Representatives, when the president decided to launch the largest scale attack on Iraq since the Gulf War. While Clinton's military advisers urged this action, the timing was naturally highly suspicious to many on the Republican side of the aisle as well as in the press. Some went so far as to suggest that the president was following the script of a recent movie, *Wag the Dog,* in which a president attempts to detract attention from his sex scandal by starting a war. This was but the latest example of real-life politics imitating the art and entertainment of our time.

On a lighter note, Bill Clinton's most positive publicity in 1997 came when he decided to adopt a dog once his daughter Chelsea left for college at Stanford University. This became a major news focus for weeks, with the media highlighting each mane, insignificant detail during a "slow news" period. Incredibly, the dog received more coverage over a month's time than any major national issue, according to the Center for Media and Public Affairs. Journalists from the major news organizations understood full well that they were being manipulated by the Buddy "story." A president and his dog, however, was an irresistible human interest account, sure to increase ratings or sell newspapers.

On other occasions, candidates and their aides will go on background to give trusted newspersons juicy morsels of negative information about rivals. **On background**— meaning that none of the news can be attributed to the source—is one of several journalistic devices used to solicit and elicit information that might otherwise never come to light. **Deep background** is another such device; whereas background talks can be attributed to unnamed senior officials, deep background news must be completely unsourced, with the reporter giving the reader no hint about the origin of the information. An even more drastic form of obtaining information is the **off-the-record** discussion, in which nothing the official says may be printed. (If a reporter can obtain the same information elsewhere, however, he or she is free to publish it.) By contrast, in an **on-the-record** session, such as a formal press conference, every word an official utters can be printed—and used against that official. It is no wonder that office holders often prefer the nonpublishable alternatives!

Clearly, these rules are necessary for reporters to do their basic job—informing the public. But ironically, the same rules keep the press from fully informing their readers and viewers. Every public official knows that journalists are pledged to protect the confidentiality of their sources, and therefore the rules can sometimes be used to an official's own benefit.

GOVERNMENT REGULATION OF THE ELECTRONIC MEDIA

Not only do politicians manipulate the media, but the U.S. government also regulates the electronic component of the media. Unlike radio or television, the print media are exempt from most forms of government regulation, although even print media must not violate community standards for obscenity, for instance. There are two reasons for this unequal treatment. First, the airwaves used by the electronic media are considered public property; they are leased by the federal government to private broadcasters. Second, those airwaves are in limited supply, and without some regulation, the nation's many radio and television stations would interfere with one another's frequency signals. It was not, in fact, the federal government but rather private broadcasters, frustrated by the numerous instances in which signal jamming occurred, that initiated the call for government regulation in the early days of the electronic media. Newspapers, of course, are not subject to these technical considerations.

The first government regulation of the electronic media came in 1927, when Congress enacted the Federal Radio Act, which established the Federal Radio Commission (FRC) and declared the airwaves to be public property. In addition, the act required that all broadcasters be licensed by the FRC. In 1934 the Federal Communications Commission (FCC) replaced the FRC as the electronic media regulatory body. The FCC is composed of five members, of whom not more than three can be from the same political party. These members are selected by the president for five-year terms on an over-lapping basis. Because the FCC is shielded from direct, daily control by the president or Congress—although both have influence over the FCC commissioners—it is

■ The Clinton family, with dog Buddy, walking together as they depart Washington for a family vacation at Martha's Vineyard, Mass. This picture was taken August 18, 1998, the day after President Clinton admitted to an improper relationship with Monica Lewinsky. (Photo courtesy: Roberto Borea/AP/Wide World Photos)

on background:

A term for when sources are not included in a news story.

deep background:

Information gathered for news stories that must be completely unsourced.

off the record:

Term applied to information gathered for a news story that cannot be used at all.

on the record:

Term applied to information gathered for a news story that can be used and cited.

an independent regulatory agency (see chapter 9). In addition to regulating public and commercial radio and television, the FCC oversees telephone, telegraph, satellite, and foreign communications in the United States.

In 1996 Congress passed the sweeping Telecommunications Act, deregulating whole segments of the electronic media. The goal of the legislation was to break down the barriers required by federal and state laws and by the legal settlement that broke up the AT&T/Bell monopoly in 1984, which separated local phone service, long-distance service, and cable television service. The hope was that such deregulation and increased competition will create cheaper and better programming options for consumers and increase the global competitiveness of U.S. telecommunications firms. Under the new law, consumers might soon receive phone service from their cable provider, television programming from their local phone company, or local phone service from their long-distance phone provider. Besides more flexible service options, the legislation is expected to spur the development of new products and services such as unlimited movie selections, interactive television, and advanced computer networking that would permit more people to work from their homes.

The core of the new legislation is the federal preemption of state and local laws that grant monopolies to local telephone carriers. The seven "baby Bells," the regional phone companies that have been allowed to monopolize local telephone service since the 1984 breakup of AT&T, would be required to allow competitors to use their local networks. In return for opening their local networks to competition, the regional Bells would be allowed to enter the long-distance service market, from which they have been barred since the AT&T breakup.

There are also significant changes in the regulations for private ownership of broadcast stations. First, there is no longer a cap on how many FM and AM stations a single company can own. In the 1950s, under the 7-7-7 rule, companies were limited to seven each of television, AM, and FM stations that they could own throughout the nation. By the 1990s, however, this limit had been progressively raised to twelve television stations and twenty each of FM and AM stations. Despite eliminating the cap, there are still limits on how many stations any one firm can own in each market. The FCC will examine on a case-by-case basis whether an owner should be allowed to have two television stations in the same local market, which is currently prohibited.

The legislation has provoked criticism by civil libertarian groups that objected to provisions designed to curb "cyberpornography." The act would ban the dissemination of "indecent" material on the Internet and on-line services. Indecency is a very broad legal standard that includes use of profanity. While it has been applied to broadcasting in a limited way, it has not been used in recent years as a standard for written material. The act also requires all large-screen televisions to include built-in "V-chips" that permit parents to block objectionable material they do not wish their family to view.

Content Regulation

content regulation:

Governmental attempts to regulate the electronic media.

equal time rule:

The rule that requires broadcast stations to sell campaign air time equally to all candidates if they choose to sell it to any.

right-of-rebuttal rule:

A Federal Communications Commission regulation that people attacked on a radio or television broadcast be offered the opportunity to respond.

The government also subjects the electronic media to substantial **content regulation** that, again, does not apply to the print media. Charged with ensuring that the air waves "serve the public interest, convenience, and necessity," the FCC has attempted to promote equity in broadcasting. For example, the **equal time rule** requires that broadcast stations sell campaign air time equally to all candidates if they choose to sell it to any, which they are under no obligation to do. An exception to this rule is a political debate: Stations may exclude from this event less well-known and minor-party candidates.

Another noteworthy FCC regulation is the **right-of-rebuttal rule,** which requires that a person who is attacked on a radio or television station be offered the opportunity to respond. This rule was sanctioned judicially in the 1969 Supreme Court case *Red Lion Broadcasting Company* v. *FCC,* in which the Court ruled that Fred Cook, the author of a book on U.S. Senator Barry Goldwater (R-Ariz.) (the 1964 Republican nominee for president), must be afforded the chance to answer an attack on him aired by a Pennsylvania radio station.

GLOBAL POLITICS

Media Freedom

What role the media plays in politics is partly determined by how free it is. In 1999 Freedom House, an independent civil liberties organization, rated the degree of media freedom in 168 countries of the world. Using degree of government ownership of the media, pressures on media, and actual violations of media freedom as criteria, the organization rated countries on a 100-point scale. The lower the score, the freer the media is from government interference. Countries rated between 0 and 30 are considered to have free media, those between 31 and 60 partly free, and those between 61 and 100 not free.

The United States in this respect is in good company. All G-7 countries are considered to have free presses, although they vary in degree. The United States and German media are rated freest among the group. State restrictions on the media are highest in Italy and France, which are close to the partly free threshold.

Restrictions on the media vary among the cases. All G-7 countries have public media outlets, most of which are more visible and influential than National Public Radio or the Public Broadcasting Service are in the United States, but the degree of government editorial control varies. Japanese government agencies exercise informal restraints on the media by organizing press clubs, access to which is limited by the agencies themselves. The British, American, and German governments have passed legislation that makes certain kinds of media communications illegal (i.e., libel in Britain, Internet pornography in the

United States, and hate speech and Nazi propaganda in Germany).

Private-sector restraint of media freedom is not formally included in Freedom House's rating system, but the organization's descriptions of recent events in specific countries suggests it may also be a problem. Corporate ownership of media outlets in Italy and the United States is acknowledged as potentially restrictive because corporate-owned media outlets are tempted to try to suppress news that is critical of their owners. Freedom House reports on Canada, France, Germany, and Italy note recent attacks on journalists by members of private organizations in addition to government surveillance and arrest.

A free press is not confined to any specific part of the globe. Norway was rated the freest, with a score of 5. Nauru, in the South Pacific, was rated 6, followed by the Bahamas (7), and the Marshall Islands and New Zealand (8 each). Of 160 countries, 13, representing Europe, the Caribbean, and the South Pacific, were rated as having freer presses than the G-7 countries.

Freedom House Scores for Media Freedom in the Industrial Democracies

Country	Freedom House Numerical Score (1 = free media, 100 = not free media)	Freedom House Rating
Canada	16	Free
France	27	Free
Germany	13	Free
Italy	28	Free
Japan	19	Free
United Kingdom	20	Free
United States	13	Free

Source: Freedom House, *Press Freedom Worldwide.* http://freedomhouse.org/pls99/reports.html.

Perhaps the most controversial FCC regulation was the **fairness doctrine.** Implemented in 1949 and in effect until 1985, the fairness doctrine required broadcasters to be "fair" in their coverage of news events—that is, they had to cover the events adequately and present contrasting views on important public issues. Many broadcasters disliked this rule, however, claiming that fairness is simply too difficult to define and that the rule abridged their First Amendment freedoms. They also argued that it ultimately forced broadcasters to decrease coverage of controversial issues out of fear of a deluge of requests for air time from interest groups involved in each matter.

In a hotly debated 1985 decision, the FCC, without congressional consent, abolished the fairness doctrine, arguing that the growth of the electronic media in the United States during the preceding forty years had created enough diversity among the stations to render unnecessary the ordering of diversity within them. In 1986 a federal circuit court of appeals vindicated the FCC decision, holding that the FCC did not need congressional approval to abolish the rule. Seeking to counter the FCC's decision, Congress attempted to write the fairness doctrine into law, which, if successful, would

fairness doctrine:

Rule in effect from 1949 to 1985 requiring broadcasters to cover events adequately and to present contrasting views on important public issues.

have forced the FCC to implement it. Although both the House and the Senate passed the bill, President Reagan temporarily ended the controversy by vetoing it, citing his First Amendment concerns about government regulation of the news media.

The abolition of the fairness doctrine has by no means ended debate over its merit, however. Proponents, still trying to reinstate the doctrine, argue that its elimination results in a reduction of quality programming on public issues. In their view deregulation means more advertisements, soap operas, and situation comedies wasting airtime and leaving less room for public discourse on important matters. Opponents of the fairness doctrine, on the other hand, continue to call for decreased regulation, arguing that the electronic media should be as free as the print media—especially because the electronic media are now probably more competitive than are the print media.

Censorship

The media in the United States, while not free of government regulation, enjoy considerably more liberty than do their counterparts in Great Britain. One of the world's oldest democracies, Great Britain nonetheless owns that nation's main electronic medium, the British Broadcasting Company (BBC). And the BBC, along with the privately owned media, is subjected to unusually strict regulation on the publication of governmental secrets. For example, the sweeping Official Secrets Acts of 1911 makes it a criminal offense for a Briton to publish any facts, material or news collected in that person's capacity as a public minister or civil servant. The act was invoked most recently when the British government banned the publication of *Spy Catcher*, a 1987 novel written by Peter Wright, a former British intelligence officer, who undoubtedly collected much of the book's information while on the job.

In the United States, only government officials can be prosecuted for divulging classified information; no such law applies to journalists. Nor can the government, except under extremely rare and confined circumstances, impose prior restraints on the press—that is, the government cannot censor the press. This principle was clearly established in *New York Times* v. *United States* (1971).[38] In this case the Supreme Court ruled that the government could not prevent publication by the *New York Times* of the Pentagon Papers, classified government documents about the Vietnam War that had been stolen, photocopied, and sent to the *Times* and the *Washington Post* by Daniel Ellsberg, an antiwar activist. "Only a free and unrestrained press can effectively expose deception in the government," Justice Hugo Black wrote in a concurring opinion for the Court. "To find that the President has 'inherent power' to halt the publication of news by resort to the courts would wipe out the first Amendment."

To assist the media in determining what is and is not publishable, Great Britain provides a system called D-notice, which allows journalists to submit questionable material to a review committee before its publication. But D-notice has not quelled argument over media freedom in the United Kingdom. Indeed, the debate came to the fore during the 1982 Falkland Islands war between Great Britain and Argentina, when it centered on questions of how much information the public had a right to know and whether the media should remain neutral in covering a war in which the nation is involved. Once again, however, the British government prevailed in arguing for continued strict control of the media, declaring. "There can be sound military reasons for withholding the whole truth from the public domain, [or] for using the media to put out 'misinformation.'"[39]

Similar questions and arguments arose in he United States during the 1991 Persian Gulf War. Reporters were upset that the military was not forthcoming about events on and off the battlefield, while some Pentagon officials and many persons in the general public accused the press of telling the enemy too much in their dispatches. Unlike the case in Great Britain, however, the U.S. government had little recourse but to attempt to isolate offending reporters by keeping them away from the battlefield. Even this maneuver was highly controversial and very unpopular with news correspondents because it directly interfered with their job of reporting the news.

■ Political news coverage often involves "talking heads" in the studio and on the spot press conferences. On the left, Sam Donaldson and Cokie Roberts interview Tom Harkin and Pat Leahy, with commentator George Will on ABC's "This Week," one of the many political talk shows that celebrate the "talking heads." On the right, Helen Thomas (center) veteran UPI correspondent and dean of the White House press corps, looks on as Sam Donaldson questions White House Press Secretary Mike McCurry. (Photo courtesy: right, Susan Walsh/AP/Wide World Photos; left, ABC, Inc.)

Such arguments are an inevitable part of the landscape in a free society. Whatever their specific quarrels with the press, most Americans would probably prefer that the media tell them too much rather than not enough. Totalitarian societies have a tame journalism, after all, so press excesses may be the price of unbridled freedom. Without question, a free press is of incalculable value to a nation, as the recent revolution in the former Soviet Union has shown. The 1991 coup against then Soviet President Mikhail Gorbachev failed in part because the coup leaders could not smother the public's continued desire for freedom, stoked by the relatively uncensored television and print journalism that existed in the final years of Gorbachev's rule.

In the United States, freedom is secured mainly by the Constitution's basic guarantees and institutions. But freedom is also ensured by the thousands of independently owned and operated newspapers, magazines, and broadcast stations. The cacophony of media voices may often be off-key and harsh, but its very lack of orchestration enables us all to continue to sing the sweet song of freedom.

*C*ONTINUITY **and Change**

How TV Transformed our Politics

Whether one views television as good or evil, this technological marvel of the twentieth century has transformed all aspects of American society, especially government and politics. When televisions were first mass-produced in the late 1940s and early 1950s, television news was primitive. Broadcasts were limited to fifteen minutes or less, announcers simply read headlines from the Associated Press, and there were frequently no pictures or moving images of any sort used in the broadcast. The first half-hour broadcast appeared only in the early 1960s, hosted on CBS by anchor Walter Cronkite, and television remained very stilted and entirely respectful toward public figures.

As with American society, Vietnam and Watergate transformed television news coverage of politics from an entirely positive, passive, and boring project into an agent of change. The key broadcast in all of television's early years may have occurred in

1968, when Cronkite traveled to Vietnam after the Tet Offensive, in which North Vietnamese forces surprised Americans at home and abroad with widespread military offensives. Cronkite covered this crucial psychological setback and critically scrutinized President Lyndon B. Johnson's claim that there was "light at the end of the tunnel" (that is, a clear prospect of military and political success in Vietnam). Cronkite all but concluded that there was little hope for victory, and Johnson himself, sitting in the White House and watching Cronkite's report, turned to an aide and said, "We've lost the war, now that we've lost Walter Cronkite."

The phenomenal growth of cable television during the past three decades has given new competition to the major commercial television networks (ABC, CBS, NBC, and Fox). With over half of all U.S. households now wired for cable television, the networks' share of the national television audience has declined steadily. Today, fewer than six in every ten viewers are watching networks stations during prime-time hours, compared with the networks' near-monopoly thirty years ago. In addition to increased competition, the rise of cable television has brought with it a new breed of political talk show. Cable talk shows like *Larry King Live*, *Rivera Live*, *Hardball*, *Beltway Boys*, and *Capitol Gang* provide near-constant media scrutiny and commentary on the latest political events. While many of the cable news shows have come and gone in this highly competitive market, the fast-moving and combative format of these shows appears here to stay.

One of vital the differences between television's conventional role and its role in the future will undoubtedly be the growth of interactive systems—systems that allow two-way communication between the sender and the consumer. As computer and cable technologies merge in the future, interactive systems will permit viewers to immediately voice their opinions regarding breaking news and policy issues. Potentially, such arrangements could lead to televised town meetings on issues of general interest. (Both Ross Perot and Bill Clinton talked about holding electronic "town halls" in the future.) In a very real sense, not only does this technological development have the potential to change the way politics is covered in this country, but it might also actually help change the role citizenship—making television viewers more active political players in American democracy.

1. A recent trend in American media has been the concentration of commercial and cable television ownership into the hands of a relatively small number of corporate owners. Do you believe that this trend is likely to continue in the future and, if so, what are the implications for media coverage of politics?
2. Is the likely increased interactivity of the media in the future necessarily a positive trend? What are some of the negative consequences of injecting the public voice more directly into the political process? Do the potential benefits outweigh the likely costs?

Cast Your Vote. What role do you think media should play in the political process? To cast your vote, go to www.awlonline.com/oconnor.

SUMMARY

The simple words of the Constitution's First Amendment, that "Congress shall make no law . . . abridging the freedom of speech, or of the press," have shaped the American republic as much as or more than any others in the Constitution and its amendments. With the Constitution's sanction, as interpreted by the Supreme Court over two centuries, a vigorous and highly competitive press has emerged. In this chapter we examined the following topics:

1. THE AMERICAN PRESS OF YESTERYEAR

Journalism—the process and profession of collecting and disseminating the news—was introduced in America in 1690 with the publication of the nation's first newspaper. Until the mid- to late-1800s, when independent papers first appeared, newspapers were partisan; that is, they openly supported a particular party. In the twentieth century, first radio in the late 1920s and then television in the late 1940s revolutionized the transmission of political information, leading to more candidate-centered, entrepreneurial politics in the age of television.

2. THE CONTEMPORARY MEDIA SCENE

The modern media consist of print press (many thousands of daily and weekly newspapers, magazines, newsletters, and journals) and electronic media (television and radio stations and networks as well as computerized information services). In the United States the media are relatively uncontrolled and free to express many views, although that has not always been the case here and remains a problem in other countries.

3. HOW THE MEDIA COVER POLITICIANS AND GOVERNMENT

The media have shifted focus in recent years, first toward investigative journalism in the Watergate era and then toward character issues. While there are useful aspects to both kinds of coverage, excesses have occurred, especially unnecessary invasions of privacy and the publication and broadcast of unsubstantiated rumor.

4. THE MEDIA'S INFLUENCE ON THE PUBLIC

Studies have shown that by framing issues for debate and discussion, the media have clear and recognizable effects on voters. For example, people who are relatively uninformed about a topic can be more easily swayed by press coverage about that topic. However, in most cases the press has surprisingly little effect on people's views.

5. HOW POLITICIANS USE THE MEDIA

Politicians constantly try to manipulate and influence press coverage. One method many officials use is passing along tips (information) on an off-the-record basis in the hopes of currying favor or producing stories favorable to their interests. However regrettable the manipulation might be at times, it is an unavoidable part of the political process.

6. GOVERNMENT REGULATION OF THE ELECTRONIC MEDIA

The press is a business—big business, in the case of the networks and large newspapers—and as such it is regulated to some extent by the government. The government has gradually loosened its restrictions on the media. Officially, the Federal Communications Commission (FCC) licenses and regulates broadcasting stations, although in practice it has been quite willing to grant and renew licenses, and recently it has reduced its regulation of licensees. Additionally, cable transmission was first allowed on a widespread basis in the late 1970s, from whence it has grown into a large supplier of information. Finally, content regulations have loosened, with the courts using a narrow interpretation of libel. All of these trends toward deregulation were accelerated by the enactment of the Telecommunications Act of 1996, which further deregulated the communications landscape.

KEY TERMS

affiliates, p. 556
content regulation, p. 568
deep background, p.567
electronic media, p. 552
equal time rule, p. 568
fairness doctrine, p. 569
media effects, p. 565

muckraking, p. 551
network, p. 556
New York Times Co.
v. *Sullivan* (1964),
p. 563
off-the-record, p. 567
on background, p. 567

on-the-record, p. 567
print press, p. 552
right-of-rebuttal rule,
p. 568
wire service, p. 556
yellow journalism, p. 551

SELECTED READINGS

Arterton, F. Christopher. *Media Politics: The News Strategies of Presidential Campaigns.* Lexington, MA: Lexington Books, 1984.

Bartels, Larry A. "Message Received: The Political Impact of Media Exposure." *American Political Science Review* (June 1993).

Berkman, Ronald, and Laura W. Kitch. *Politics in the Media Age.* New York: McGraw-Hill, 1986.

Broder, David S. *Behind the Front Page.* New York: Simon & Schuster, 1987.

Cook, Timothy E. *Making Laws and Making News: Media Strategies in the U.S. House of Representatives.* Washington, DC: The Brookings Institution, 1989.

Crouse, Timothy. *The Boys on the Bus.* New York: Ballantine, 1973.

Entman, Robert M. *Democracy Without Citizens: Media and the Decay of American Politics.* New York: Oxford University Press, 1989.

Garment, Suzanne. *Scandal.* New York: Random House, 1991.

Graber, Doris A. *Mass Media and American Politics,* 5th ed. Washington, DC: CQ Press, 1996.

———. *Media Power in Politics,* 3rd ed. Washington, DC: CQ Press, 1992.

Grossman, Michael Baruch, and Martha Joynt Kumar. *Portraying the President: The White House and the News Media.* Baltimore: Johns Hopkins University Press, 1981.

Hamilton, John Maxwell. *Hold the Press: The Inside Story on Newspapers.* Baton Rouge: Louisiana State University Press, 1996.

Iyengar, Shanto, and Donald R. Kinder. *News That Matters.* Chicago: University of Chicago Press, 1987.

Kerbel, Matthew Robert. *Remote and Controlled: Media Politics in a Cynical Age.* Boulder, CO: Westview Press, 1995.

Kurtz, Howard. *Media Circus: The Trouble with America's Newspapers.* New York: Times Books, 1993.

Lichter, S. Robert, Stanley Rothman, and Linda S. Lichter. *The Media Elite.* Bethesda, MD: Adler & Adler, 1986.

Linsky, Martin. *Impact: How the Press Affects Federal Policymaking.* New York: Norton, 1986.

Patterson, Thomas E. *Out of Order.* New York: Vintage, 1993.

Press, Charles, and Kenneth VerBurg. *American Politicians and Journalists.* Glenview, IL: Scott, Foresman, 1988.

Ranney, Austin. *Channels of Power: The Impact of Television on American Politics.* New York: Basic Books, 1983.

Sabato, Larry J. *Feeding Frenzy: How Attack Journalism Has Transformed American Politics,* updated ed. New York: Macmillan/The Free Press, 1993.

Stephens, Mitchell. *A History of News: From the Drum to the Satellite.* New York: Viking, 1989.

West, Darrell M. *Air Wars: Television Advertising in Election Campaigns, 1952–1992.* Washington, DC: CQ Press, 1993.

Zaller, John. *The Nature and Origins of Mass Opinion.* Cambridge [England] and New York: Cambridge University Press, 1992.

NOTES

1. See Mitchell Stephens, *A History of News: From the Drum to the Satellite* (New York: Viking, 1989).

2. Charles Press and Kenneth VerBurg, *American Politicians and Journalists* (Glenview, IL: Scott, Foresman, 1988), 8–10.

3. See Merrill D. Peterson, *Thomas Jefferson and the New Nation* (New York: Oxford University Press, 1970), 185–87.

4. For a delightful rendition of this episode, see Shelley Ross, *Fall from Grace* (New York: Ballantine, 1988), chapter 12.

5. The name strictly derived from printing the comic strip "Yellow Kid" in color.

6. Doris A. Graber, *Mass Media and American Politics,* 3d ed. (Washington, DC: CQ Press, 1989), 12.

7. See Thomas C. Leonard, *The Power of the Press: The Birth of American Political Reporting* (New York: Oxford University Press, 1986), chapter 7.

8. Richard L. Rubin, *Press, Party, and Presidency* (New York: Norton, 1981), 38–39.

9. Stephen Bates, *If No News, Send Rumors* (New York: St. Martin's Press, 1989), 185.

10. Barbara Matusow, "Washington's Journalism Establishment," *The Washingtonian* 23 (February 1989): 94–101, 265–70.

11. See Eleanor Randolph, "Extra! Extra! Who Cares?" *The Washington Post* (April 1, 1990): C1, 4.

12. Sunday newspapers are exceptions to the trend. More than 100 new Sunday papers were created in the 1980s, and Sunday cir-

culation as a whole has increased 25 percent since 1970.

13. Harold W. Stanley and Richard G. Niemi, *Vital Statistics on American Politics* (Washington, DC: CQ Press, 1988), Table 2–8, 58.

14. See Evans Witt, "Here, There, and Everywhere: Where Americans Get Their News," *Public Opinion* 6 (August/September 1983): 45–48; and June O. Yum and Kathleen E. Kendall, "Sources of Political Information in a Presidential Primary Campaign," *Journalism Quarterly* 65 (Spring 1988): 148–51, 177.

15. This was the fundamental conclusion of Shanto Iyengar and Donald R. Kinder, *News That Matters* (Chicago: University of Chicago Press, 1987).

16. Matthew Baum and Samuel Kernell, "Has Cable Ended the Golden Age of Television?" *American Political Science Review* 93 (June 1999): 99–114.

17. Ben Bagdikan, *The Media Monopoly,* 4th ed. (Boston: Beacon Press, 1992).

18. Timothy E. Cook and Lyn Ragsdale, "The President and the Press: Negotiating Newsworthiness at the White House," in Michael Nelson, ed., *The Presidency and the Political System,* 5th ed. (Washington DC: Congressional Quarterly Press, 1998), 323.

19. Cook and Ragsdale, "The President and the Press," 326.

20. Thomas Patterson, *Out of Order* (New York: Vintage, 1994).

21. Harold W. Stanley and Richard G. Niemi, *Vital Statistics on American Politics,* 4th ed. (Washington, DC: CQ Press, 1994), 28.

22. John Hibbing and Elizabeth Theiss-Morse, *Congress as Public Enemy: Political Attitudes Toward American Political Institutions* (New York: Cambridge University Press, 1995).

23. American Society of Newspaper Editors, *The Changing Face of the Newsroom* (Washington, DC: ASNE, May 1989), 29.

24. See Tom Wolfe, *The New Journalism* (New York: Harper & Row, 1973), especially 9–32.

25. The first and best in White's series was *The Making of the President 1960* (New York: Atheneum, 1961). See also Joe McGinniss, *The Selling of the President 1968* (New York: Trident, 1969).

26. See James David Barber, *The Presidential Character* (Englewood Cliffs, NJ: Prentice Hall, 1972), 445.

27. Roderick Hart, *Seducing America: How Television Charms the Modern Voter* (New York: Oxford University Press, 1995).

28. 376 U.S. 254 (1964). See also Steven Pressman, "Libel Law: Finding the Right Balance," *Editorial Research Reports* 2 (August 18, 1989); 462–71.

29. *Curtis Publishing Co.* v. *Butts,* 388 U.S. 130 (1967); *Associated Press* v. *Walker,* 388 U.S. 130 (1967).

30. American Society of Newspaper Editors, "The Changing Face," 33; William Schneider and I. A. Lewis, "Views on the News," *Public Opinion* 8 (August/September 1985): 6–11, 58–59; and S. Robert Lichter, Stanley Rothman, and Linda S. Lichter, *The Media Elite* (Bethesda, MD: Adler & Adler, 1986).

31. See Dom Bonafede, "Crossing Over," *National Journal* 21 (January 14, 1989): 102; Richard Harwood, "Tainted Journalists," *The Washington Post* (December 4, 1988): L6; Charles Trueheart, "Trading Places: The Insiders Debate," *The Washington Post* (January 4, 1989): D1, 19; and Kirk Victor, "Slanted Views," *National Journal* 20 (June 4, 1988): 1512.

32. "*Roe* v. *Webster,*" *Media Monitor* 3 (October 1989): 1–6. See also David Shaw, "Abortion and the Media" (four-part series), *Los Angeles Times* (July 1, 1990). A1, 50–51, (July 2, 1990): A1, 20; (July 3, 1990): A1, 22–23; (July 4, 1990): A1, 28–29.

33. Eric Veblen, *The Manchester Union-Leader in New Hampshire Elections* (Hanover, NH: University of New England Press, 1975).

34. Shanto Iyengar and Donald Kinder, *News That Matters.* (Chicago: University of Chicago Press, 1987).

35. Martin P. Wattenberg, *The Decline of American Political Parties, 1952–1994* (Cambridge, MA: Harvard University Press, 1996).

36. Marc Hetherington, "The Media's Role in Forming Voters' National Economic Evaluations in 1992," *American Journal of Political Science* 40 (May 1996): 372–95.

37. George C. Edwards, III, and Dan Wood, "Who Influences Whom? The President, Congress, and the Media," *American Political Science Review* 93 (June 1999): 327–44.

38. 403 U.S. 713 (1971).

39. House of Commons, Defense Committee, *The Handling of the Press and Public Information During the Falklands Conflict* (London: Her Majesty's Stationery Office, 1982), x.

(Photo courtesy: Jim Sulley/The Image Works)

16

Interest Groups

- **What Are Interest Groups?**
- **The Roots and Development of American Interest Groups**
- **What Do Interest Groups Do?**
- **What Makes an Interest Group Successful?**

ow many offers for a new credit card at a "special introductory rate" did you get last year? If you are a traditional first-year college student, maybe not many But, by the end of your college career you will probably get between twenty-five and fifty. In all likelihood, promoters even had tables set up during your college orientation. Open an account, get a free airplane ticket, water bottle, or watch. In the past few years, credit card companies have extended credit to millions of unemployed college students. After a few years of heavy spending, many of them now don't have enough money to pay the credit card companies back. To remedy this, those same companies are frantically lobbying Congress to pass bankruptcy laws that will make it easier for them to collect the money charged by those who should not have been extended credit in the first place.

According to Senator Russ Feingold (D–Wisc.), bankruptcy reform "has become special-interest legislation" and campaign money is "a central component of the lobbying effort."[1] In 1998 the National Consumer Bankruptcy Coalition, an industry lobbying group with members like Visa and Mastercard as well as big banks and retailers, contributed more than $4.5 million to both political parties and candidates in addition to harder to track soft money contributions.[2] And their expenditures were especially well timed. For example, on the day that the House passed a bankruptcy reform bill in 1998 and sent it to the Senate, "Mastercard gave a $200,000 soft money contribution to the Republican Senatorial Committee." Later, during the month that the Judiciary Committee began debating the bill, coalition members contributed an additional $227,000 to the campaign coffers of key committee members.[3] These kinds of contributions are designed to reward friends in the legislature and to remind lawmakers about who can help them in the future.

interest group:

An organized group that tries to influence public policy.

Web Exploration
For more on the Christian Coalition of America, see www.awlonline.com/oconnor.

Web Exploration
For more on NOW, see www.awlonline.com/oconnor.

Web Exploration
For more on the NRA, see www.awlonline.com/oconnor.

Originally, most political scientists used the term "pressure group" because it best described what these groups did. Today most political scientists use the terms *interest group* or *organized interest*. In this book we use **interest group** as a generic term to describe the numerous organized groups that try to influence government policy. Thus, interest groups can be what we normally think of as organized interests as well as state and local governments, political action committees, and individual businesses and corporations. We also consider less formal groups as interest groups. Although these groups are more nebulous in form than interest groups traditionally studied by political scientists, they, too, engage in concerted action to influence government policy.

Multi-Issue Versus Single-Issue Interest Groups

Political scientists often talk of interest groups as single-issue or multi-issue. Many organizations, while founded around a single guiding principle such as the NAACP's interest in advancing the cause of civil rights, or the Christian Coalition's concern with Christian family values, are actually involved in a wide range of issue areas including education (school vouchers, prayer in school), television ratings, and abortion, and thus must divide some of its energies as it lobbies for varied policies in diverse forums. Similarly, the National Organization for Women (NOW) deals in issues of abortion and reproductive rights, affirmative action, economic equity, and lesbian rights, among others. Multi-issue groups often must have expertise in a wide array of areas and be prepared to work on the local, state, and national levels to advance their interests.

Single-issue groups differ from multi-issue groups in both the range and the intensity of their interests. Concentration on one area generally leads to greater zeal in a group's lobbying efforts. Probably the most visible single-issue groups today are those organized on either side of the abortion and gun control debates. Anti-abortion groups like Operation Rescue and pro-choice groups like the National Abortion and Reproductive Rights Action League (NARAL) are good examples of single-issue groups, as are the National Rifle Association (NRA) and Handgun Control, Inc. Today people singlemindedly pursue all kinds of interests. Drug- or AIDS-awareness groups, environmental groups, and anti–nuclear power groups, for example, can be classified as single-issue groups. Table 16.2 categorizes a number of prominent interest groups by their issue concentration.

Kinds of Organized Interests

Political scientists also categorize organized interests by the type of interest(s) they champion. The major types of organized interests are (1) economic interest groups; (2) public interest groups; and increasingly, (3) governmental units. Most of these groups lobby on behalf of their members and many hire D.C.-based lobbying firms to lead or supplement their efforts. (For a list of top lobbying firms, see Table 16.2)

Economic Interest Groups. Most groups have some sort of "economic" agenda, even if it only involves acquiring enough money in donations to pay the telephone bill or send out the next mailing. **Economic interest groups** are, however, a special type of interest group: Their primary purpose is to promote the economic interests of their members. Historically, business groups (including trade and professional groups), labor

■ Charlton Heston, the legendary actor, now serves as president of the National Rifle Association. (Photo courtesy: Eric Gay/AP/Wide World Photos)

Table 16.2 Profiles of Selected Interest Groups

Name (Founded)	Single- or Multi-Issue	Members	PAC	1997–98 Election Cycle PAC Donation
Economic Groups				
AFL–CIO (1886)	M	14.1 million	AFL–CIO PAC	$1.1 million
American Medical Association (AMA) (1847)	M	300,000	AMA PAC	$2.3 million
Association of Trial Lawyers of America (1946)	M	60,000	Association of Trial Lawyers of America PAC	$2.4 million
National Association of Manufacturers (NAM) (1895)	M	12,500	no	
Tobacco Institute (1958)	S	13 (cigarette companies)	yes	$75,000
U.S. Chamber of Commerce (1912)	M	180,000 companies	National Chamber Alliance for Politics	$10,900
Public Interest Groups				
American Association of Retired Persons (AARP) (1958)	M	32,000,000	no	
Amnesty International U.S.A. (1961)	S	386,000	no	
League of United Latin American Citizens (LULAC) (1929)	M	110,000	no	
National Abortion and Reproduction Rights Action League (NARAL) (1909)	S	450,000	NARAL PAC	$300,000
National Association for the Advancement of Colored People (NAACP) (1909)	M	500,000	no	
Human Rights Campaign (1980)	S	17,000	yes	$803,000
National Right to Life Committee (1973)	S	400,000	National Right to Life PAC	$107,000
Environmental Groups				
Environmental Defense Fund (EDF) (1967)	S	150,000	no	
Greenpeace USA (1971)	S	1,690,500 (1996)	no	
Sierra Club (1892)	S	550,000 (1996)	Sierra Club Political Committee	$237,000
Good Government Groups				
Common Cause (1970)	S	270,000	no	
Public Citizen, Inc. (1971)	M	100,000	no	

SOURCE: *Public Interest Profiles,* 1993–1994 (Washington, D.C.: Congressional Quarterly,1993); "Profiles of Interest Groups," *Health Line* (October 13, 1993); "Legal Times: Profiles of Interest Groups Part II," *Health Line* (October 14, 1993); NEXIS; and Center for Responsive Politics.

organizations (unions), and organizations representing the interests of farmers have been considered the "big three" of economic interest groups. The National Consumer Bankruptcy Coalition discussed in the chapter opening vignette is a good example of an economic interest group.

Groups that mobilize to protect particular economic interests generally are the most fully and effectively organized of all the types of interest groups.[13] They exist to make profits and to obtain economic benefits for their members. To achieve these goals, however, they often find that they must resort to political means rather than trust the operation of economic markets to produce outcomes favorable for their members.

Public Interest Groups. Political scientist Jeffrey M. Berry defines **public interest groups** as organizations "that seek a collective good, the achievement of which will not selectively and materially benefit the membership or activists of the organization."[14] Unlike economic interest groups, public interest groups do not tend to be particularly motivated by the desire to achieve goals that would benefit their members. As Berry notes, the public interest has many faces. In the past, for example, many Progressive era groups were created in the late 1800s and early 1900s to solve the varied problems of new immigrants and

economic interest group:

A group with the primary purpose of promoting the financial interests of its members.

public interest group:

An organization that seeks a collective good that will not selectively and materially benefit the members of the group.

the poor. Today civil and constitutional rights groups, environmental groups, good government groups such as Common Cause, peace groups, church groups, and groups that speak out for those who cannot (such as children, the mentally ill, or animals) are examples of public interest groups.

Governmental Units.   As discussed in chapter 3, state and local governments today are becoming strong organized interests as they lobby the federal government or even charitable foundations for money for a vast array of state and local programs. The Big Seven and state and local governments want to make certain that they get their fair share of federal dollars in the form of block grants or pork barrel projects. Most states retain lobbyists in Washington, D.C., to advance their interests or to keep them informed about legislation that could affect them. They want to make sure that they will get their share (if not more) of the federal budget designated to go back to the states in a variety of forms including money for roads, schools and poverty programs.

THE ROOTS AND DEVELOPMENT OF AMERICAN INTEREST GROUPS

Political scientists have long debated how and why interest groups arise, their nature, and their role in a democratic society. Do they contribute to the betterment of society, or are they an evil best controlled by government? From his days in the Virginia Assembly, James Madison knew that factions occurred in all political systems and that the struggle for influence and power among such groups was inevitable in the political process. This knowledge led him and the other Framers to tailor a governmental system of multiple pressure points to check and balance these factions, or what today we call interest groups, in the natural course of the political process. As we discuss in chapter 2, Madison and many of the other Framers were intent on creating a government of many levels—local, state, and national—with the national government consisting of three branches. It was their belief that this division of power would prevent any one individual or group of individuals from becoming too influential. They also believed that decentralizing power would neutralize the effect of special interests, who would not be able to spread their efforts throughout so many different levels of government. Thus the "mischief of faction" could be lessened. But, farsighted as they were, the Framers could not have envisioned the vast sums of money or technology that would be available to some interest groups.

Ironically, however, *The Federalist Papers* were a key component of one of the most skillful and successful examples of interest group activity in the history of this nation. If "the Federalists [themselves an interest group] had not been as shrewd in manipulation as they were sound in theory, their arguments could not have prevailed."[15]

As with the many different definitions of interest groups, a variety of sound reasons have been offered to explain why interest groups form. Generally, however, interest groups tend to arise in response to changes. These can be political or economic changes, changes in the population, technological changes, or even changes in society itself.

National Groups Emerge (1830–89)

Although all kinds of local groups proliferated throughout the colonies and in the new states, it was not until the 1830s, as communications networks improved, that the first groups national in scope began to emerge. Many of these first national groups were single-issue groups deeply rooted in the Christian religious revivalism that was sweeping the nation. Concern with humanitarian issues such as temperance (total abstinence from alcoholic beverages), peace, capital punishment, education, and, most important, slavery, led to the founding of numerous groups dedicated to solving these problems. Among the first of these groups was the American Anti-Slavery Society, founded in 1833 by William Lloyd Garrison.

After the Civil War, more groups were founded. For example, the Women's Christian Temperance Union (WCTU) was created in 1874 with the goal of outlawing the sale of liquor. Its members, many of them quite religious, believed that the consumption of alcohol was an evil injurious to family life because many men drank away their paychecks, leaving no money to feed or clothe their families. The WCTU's activities took conventional and nonconventional forms: organizing prayer groups, lobbying for prohibition legislation, conducting peaceful marches, and engaging in more violent protests that included destruction of saloons. Like the WCTU, the Grange was also formed during the period following the Civil War, as an educational society for farmers to teach them about the latest agricultural developments. Although its charter formally stated that the Grange was not to become involved in "politics," in 1876 it formulated a detailed plan to pressure Congress to enact legislation favorable to farmers.

Perhaps the most effective interest group of the day was the railroad industry. In a move that couldn't take place today because of its clear impropriety, the Central Pacific Railroad sent its own **lobbyist** to Washington, D.C., in 1861, where he eventually became the clerk (staff administrator) of the committees of both houses of Congress that were charged with overseeing regulation of the railroad industry. Subsequently, the Central Pacific Railroad (later called the Southern Pacific) received from Congress vast grants of lands along its route and large subsidized loans from the national government. The railroad became so important that it later went on to have nearly total political control of the California state legislature.

lobbyist:
Interest group representative who seeks to influence legislation that will benefit his or her organization through political persuasion.

After the Civil War, business interests began to play even larger roles in both state and national politics. A popular saying of the day noted that the Standard Oil Company did everything to the Pennsylvania legislature except refine it. Increasingly large trusts, monopolies, business combinations, and corporate conglomerations in the oil, steel, and sugar industries became sufficiently powerful to control many representatives in the state and national legislatures.

The Progressive Era (1890–1920)

By the 1890s, a profound change had occurred in the nation's political and social outlook. Rapid industrialization and an influx of immigrants created a host of problems, including crime, poverty, squalid and unsafe working conditions, widespread political corruption, and high prices caused by monopolistic business practices. Many Americans began to believe that new measures would be necessary to impose order on this growing chaos and to curb some of the more glaring problems brought on by industrialization and immigration. The political and social movement that grew out of these concerns was called the Progressive movement.

Not even the progressives themselves could agree on what the term "progressive" actually meant, but their desire for reform led to an explosion of all types of interest groups: single-issue, trade, labor, and the first public interest groups. Politically, the movement took the form of the Progressive Party, which sought on many fronts to limit or end the power of the industrialists' near-total control of the steel, oil, railroad, and other key industries.

In response to the pressure applied by progressive groups, the national government began to regulate business. Because businesses had a vested interest in keeping wages low and costs down, more business groups organized to consolidate their strength and to counter progressive moves. Not only did governments have to mediate progressive and business demands, but they also had to accommodate the role of organized labor which often allied itself with progressive groups against big business.

Organized Labor.   Although there were several early unsuccessful attempts to organize local labor groups into national unions, it was not until the creation of the American Federation of Labor (AFL) in 1886 that there was any real national union activity. The AFL for the first time brought skilled workers from several trades together into one stronger national organization. Its effectiveness in mobilizing for higher wages for workers triggered

Groups on both ends of the political spectrum historically have resorted to violence. Abolitionists, anti–nuclear power activists, anti-war activists, animal-rights advocates, and other groups on the "left" have broken laws, damaged property, and even injured or killed innocent bystanders. On the "right," groups such as Lambs of Christ (an anti-abortion group) and the Ku Klux Klan (KKK) have broken the laws and even hurt or killed people in the furtherance of their objectives. From the early 1900s until the 1960s, African Americans were routinely lynched by KKK members. Today some radical anti-abortion groups regularly block the entrances to abortion clinics; others active in the anti-abortion movement have taken credit for clinic bombings.

Other protest activities are less violent although still illegal. In 1998, for example, NAACP officials protested the lack of minority clerks at the U.S. Supreme Court and were arrested and removed from the steps of the Court.

Election Activities

In addition to trying to achieve their goals through the conventional and unconventional forms of lobbying and protest activity, many interest groups also become involved more directly in the electoral process.

Endorsements.   Many groups claim to be nonpartisan, that is, nonpolitical. Usually they try to have friends in both political parties to whom they can look for assistance and access. Some organizations, however, routinely endorse candidates for public office, pledging money, group support, and often even campaign volunteers. For example, at one time candidates in the Northeast fought for labor union endorsement, recognizing that their support would bring money, volunteers, and votes. In 1996, however, presidential candidate Bob Dole openly attacked teachers' unions in a speech as he accepted his party's nomination for president.

EMILY's List, a women's group (EMILY stands for "Early Money Is Like Yeast— it makes the dough rise"), not only endorses candidates, but contributes heavily to races. In 1998, Planned Parenthood broke with tradition and endorsed candidates for the first time. This pro-choice group believed the change of only three Senators could allow the Senate to override President Clinton's veto of anti-abortion restrictions. It is not unusual, moreover, for conservation or environmental groups to endorse candidates that they view as friends. Similarly, in 1998 the National Abortion Rights Action League (NARAL) concentrated its efforts on about sixty House and Senate races where candidates tried to minimize their actual opposition to abortion and downplay their stands on related issues.

Once groups become overly political, however, their tax-exempt status is jeopardized. Federal law precludes tax-exempt organizations from taking partisan positions. The Christian Coalition, for years claimed to be nonpartisan, although it was heavily involved in partisan elections. The Coalition uses score cards to evaluate candidates, and plays a key role in some elections. It does not, however, formally endorse candidates, although the FEC charged that it used money to promote the candidacies of specific candidates including George Bush and Sen. Jesse Helms (R-N.C.). In 1996 the Federal Election Commission (FEC) even brought suit against it for unlawful electioneering activities.[54]

Endorsements from some groups may be used by a candidate's opponent to attack a candidate. While labor union endorsements can add money to a candidate's campaign coffers, for example, they risk being labeled a "tool of the labor unions" by their opponents.

Rating the Candidates or Office Holders.   Many liberal and conservative ideological groups rate candidates to help their members (and the general public) evaluate the voting records of members of Congress. The American Conservative Union (conservative) and the Americans for Democratic Action (liberal)—two groups at ideological polar extremes—routinely rate candidates and members of Congress based on their votes on key issues of importance to the group, as illustrated in Table 16.5. So do groups including the ACLU, the Christian Coalition, and the League of Conservation Voters. These scores help voters to know more about their representatives' votes on issues that concern them.

Some groups target certain individuals and campaign against them to show their clout and to scare other elected officials into paying more attention to them. Beginning in 1970, for example, Environmental Action (EA) labeled twelve members of the House of Representatives "the dirty dozen" because of their votes against bills that the group believed were necessary to protect the environment. Over the years until its demise in 1996, EA's regular designation of many members of Congress with a similar label was widely publicized by the media and through direct-mail campaigns to voters interested in the environment. Through 1995 only seven members to earn EA's anti-environmental nickname were able to survive that dubious distinction in their bid to be reelected.

Creating Political Parties.
Another interest group strategy is to form a political party to publicize a cause and even possibly win a few public offices. In 1848 the Free Soil Party was formed to publicize the crusade against slavery; twenty years later the Prohibition Party was formed to try to ban the sale of alcoholic beverages. Similarly, in the early 1970s, the National Right-to-Life Party was formed to publicize the anti-abortion position, and it even ran its own candidate for president in 1976.

In 1995 many in the Ross Perot–founded group, United We Stand, established the Reform Party to highlight the group's goals, including government reform (in particular, passage of new campaign finance laws) and fiscal responsibility. Similarly, consumer advocate Ralph Nader was the 1996 nominee of the new Green Party, created to bring attention to environmental issues. Groups often see forming political parties as a way to draw attention to their legislative goals and to drive one of the major political parties to give their demands serious attention.

The effectiveness of an interest group in the election arena has often been overrated by members of the news media. In general, it is very difficult to assess the effect of a particular group's impact on any one election because of the number of other factors

Web Exploration
To examine the specific values and platforms of these new political parties, see
www.awlonline.com/oconnor.

Web Exploration
To learn more about the issue position of each of these interest groups, see
www.awlonline.com/oconnor.

Table 16.5   Interest Group Ratings of Selected Members of Congress, 1998*

Member	ACU	ACLU	ADA	AFL-CIO	CC	CoC	CFA	LCV
Senate								
Dianne Feinstein (D–Calif.)	4	83	90	57	10	61	86	100
Jesse Helms (R–N.C.)	100	25	0	14	100	88	14	0
Kay Bailey Hutchinson (R–Tex.)	88	20	0	0	91	100	29	0
Edward M. Kennedy (D–Mass.)	0	83	95	100	0	47	71	100
John McCain (R–Ariz.)	68	17	20	14	73	76	29	13
House								
Tom DeLay (R–Tex.)	96	6	0	0	100	100	33	10
Sheila Jackson-Lee (D–Tex.)	4	88	95	100	7	44	83	59
C.W. Bill Young (R–Fla.)	90	8	0	38	100	93	50	17

Key

ACU = American Conservative Union

ACLU = American Civil Liberties Union

ADA = Americans for Democratic Action

AFL–CIO = American Federation of Labor–Congress of Industrial Organizations

CC = Christian Coalition

CoC = Chamber of Commerce

CFA = Consumer Federation of America

LCV = League of Conservation Voters

*Members are rated on a scale from 1 to 100, with 1 being the lowest and 100 being the highest support of a particular group's policies.

present in any election or campaign. However, the one area in which interest groups do seem able to affect the outcome of elections directly is through a relatively new device called the political action committee.

Interest Groups and Political Action Committees.   Throughout most of history, powerful interests and individuals have often used their money to "buy" politicians or their votes. Even if outright bribery was not involved, huge corporate or other interest group donations certainly made some politicians look as if they were in the "pocket" of certain special interests. Congressional passage of the Federal Election Campaign Act began to change most of that. The 1971 act required candidates to disclose all campaign contributions and limited the amount of money that they could spend on media advertising.

In 1974, in the wake of the Watergate scandal (see chapter 8), amendments to the act made it more far-reaching by sharply limiting the amount of money any interest group could give to a candidate for federal office. However, the act also made it legal for corporations, labor unions, and interest groups to form what were termed **political action committees,** often referred to as **PACs,** which could make contributions to candidates for national elections. (See chapter 14 for more on this subject.)

Technically, a PAC is a political arm of a business, labor, trade, professional, or other interest group legally authorized to raise funds on a voluntary basis from employees or members in order to contribute to a political candidate or party. Even Generation X has its own PAC, X-PAC, to lobby for Social Security reform and other issues of concern to young voters. These monies have changed the face of U.S. elections. Unlike some contributions to interest groups, however, contributions to PACs are not tax deductible, and PACs generally don't have members who call legislators; instead, PACs have contributors who write checks specifically for the purpose of campaign donations. PAC money plays a significant role in the campaigns of many congressional incumbents, often averaging over half a House candidate's total campaign spending. PACs generally contribute to those who have helped them before and who serve on committees or subcommittees that routinely consider legislation of concern to that group.

> **political action committee (PAC):**
>
> A federally registered fund-raising committee that represents an interest group in the political process through campaign donations.

> **Web Exploration**
> To learn about X-PAC, see www.awlonline.com/oconnor.

WHAT MAKES AN INTEREST GROUP SUCCESSFUL?

Throughout our nation's history, all kinds of interests in society have organized to pressure the government for policy change. Some have been successful, and some have not E. E. Schattschneider once wrote, "Pressure politics is essentially the politics of small groups. . . . Pressure tactics are not remarkably successful in mobilizing general interests."[55] He was correct; historically, corporate interests often prevail over the concerns of public interest groups such as environmentalists.

All of the groups discussed in this chapter have one thing in common: They all want to shape the public agenda, whether by winning elections, maintaining the status quo, or obtaining favorable legislation or rulings from Congress, executive agencies, or the courts.[56] For powerful groups, simply making sure that certain issues never get discussed may be the goal. Gun manufacturers dread incidents such as Littleton, Colorado, because it propels the issue of gun regulation out of their hands. Similarly, the bank card companies profit when students and other consumers don't know about proposed changes in bankruptcy legislation that could hurt consumers. In contrast, those opposed to random stops of African-American drivers on the roads win when the issue becomes front-page news and law enforcement officials feel pressured to investigate, if not stop altogether, the discriminatory practice.

Groups often claim credit for "winning" legislation, court cases, or even elections individually or in coalition with other groups.[57] They also are successful when their leaders become elected officials or policy makers themselves. Each administration is often loaded with former group activists. In the Reagan administration, the Secretary of the Interior and the solicitor general were former leaders of the conservative public interest law firm, the Mountain States Legal Foundation. In the Clinton administration, Supreme Court appointee Ruth Bader Ginsburg was a former ACLU Board member and the Director of its Women's Rights Project.

Political scientists have studied several phenomena that contribute in varying degrees—individual and well as collectively—to particular groups' successes. These include (1) leaders and patrons, (2) adequate funding, and (3) a solid membership base.

1. Leaders and Patrons.

Interest group theorists such as Robert Salisbury frequently acknowledge the key role that leaders play in the formation, viability, and success of interest groups, a fact underscored in Highlight 16.1 "Perfect Patron?". Jack L. Walker contends that without what he terms **patrons** (those who often finance a group) few organizations could begin.[58]

patron:
Individual who finances an interest group.

Without the powerful pen of William Lloyd Garrison in the 1830s, who knows whether the abolitionist movement would have been as successful? Similarly, Frances Willard was the prime mover behind the WCTU, as were Marian Wright Edelman of the Children's Defense Fund in 1968, and the Reverend Jerry Falwell of the Moral Majority in the 1980s. Most successful groups, especially public interest groups, are led by charismatic individuals who devote most of their energies to "the cause." The role of an interest group leader is similar to that of an entrepreneur in the business world. As in the marketing of a new product, an interest group leader must have something attractive to offer to persuade members to join. Potential members of the group must be convinced that the benefits of joining outweigh the costs. Union members, for example, must be persuaded that the cost of their union dues will be offset by the union's winning higher wages for them.

2. Funding.

Funding is also crucial to all interest groups. Government, foundations, and wealthy individuals can serve as patrons providing crucial start-up funds for groups, especially public interest groups.

During the 1980s conservative groups for example, relied on the direct-mail skills of marketing wizard Richard Viguerie to raise monies for a variety of conservative causes. In the early 1990s, pro-choice groups appealed to supporters by requesting funds

---

HIGHLIGHT 16.1

Perfect Patron?

On August 24, 1994, billionaire Richard Mellon Scaife told those assembled at a luncheon on Nantucket, "We're going to get Clinton, and you'll be much happier because Al Gore will be president."[a] Well, Scaife was wrong, but the money he spent to "get" Clinton" underscores the powerful role that patrons can play in the political system. Not only did Scaife give $2.3 million to the conservative magazine the *American Spectator* to dig up negative information on Clinton and his associates, over the past forty years, he and members of his family have contributed $620 million in current dollars to conservative interest groups and causes.

Scaife's first foray into philanthropy was a 1962 contribution to the American Bar Association's Fund for Public Education, whose purpose was to educate against communism. Later he funded conservative research institutes at Stanford and Georgetown Universities and then became an important contributor to the conservative American Enterprise Institute. He also became a major contributor to the Heritage Foundation, which compiles a Directory of Public Policy Conservative Organizations. In 1998, it listed 300 groups; Richard Scaife has funded 111 of them; 76 in 1998."[b] Scaife has been particularly instrumental in providing support to conservative public interest law firms that were begun in part to counter the ACLU and environmental groups, and he is an important patron of the oldest and largest conservative public interest law firm, the Pacific Legal Foundation. The Southeastern Legal Foundation, another target of his largess, won the Supreme Court case barring the Census Bureau from using statistical sampling.

[a]This highlight draws heavily from Robert G. Kaiser and Ira Chinoy, "How Scaife's Money Powered a Movement," *Washington Post* (May 2, 1999): A1.
[b]Kaiser and Chinoy, "How Scaife's Money Powered a Movement."

to campaign for legislation in anticipation of the Supreme Court's reversal of *Roe* v. *Wade* (see Highlight 16.2: How Events Can Affect Interest Groups). When the Supreme Court did not overrule *Roe* in 1992, and Ruth Bader Ginsburg was appointed to the Supreme Court, contributions to pro-choice groups such as NARAL and Planned Parenthood dropped precipitously.

Similarly, after the school shootings at Littleton, Colorado, contributions to groups such as Handgun Control Inc. skyrocketed as new members joined and old members increased their contributions in the form of dues or other special contributions. Threats of rights lost or horrific disasters often provide the critical events that spur ordinary citizens, businesses, or trade associations to become involved in a particular group or coalition of groups, thereby adding to a particular group's treasury.

Other groups, particularly political action committees (PACs), measure their successes more directly, often by the number of candidates supported who won. The New Democratic Network, dedicated to electing centrist Democrats, for example, gave $1.4 million to thirty-four congressional candidates in 1998 and twenty-six won.[59] As highlighted in Figure 16.3, the tobacco companies enjoyed the same kind of success one election cycle earlier.

Tobacco companies contributed an estimated $11.3 million in the 1996 elections and received $50 billion in tax breaks as a result of congressional legislation. Similarly, the airlines individually and through several trade associations contributed $3.2 million. By 1997, they had won a 2.5 percent tax reduction on each ticket.[60]

3. Members. Alexis de Tocqueville, a French aristocrat and philosopher, toured the United States extensively during 1831 and 1832. A keen observer of American politics, he was very much impressed by the tendency of Americans to join groups in order to participate in the policy-making process. "Whenever at the head of some new undertaking you see government in France, or a man of rank in England, in the United States you will be sure to find an association,"[61] wrote de Tocqueville.

Figure 16.3 Contributions and Tax Breaks

A report by the public interest group Citizen Action shows significant associations between campaign contributions to U.S. Senators and Representatives to tax breaks in a 1996 tax and budget enactment.

Corporate Interest And Provision	Estimated Benefit	Contribution*
Tobacco companies: Proceeds from a 15 cent-per-pack cigarette tax increase would offset future costs of a national settlement of tobacco lawsuits.	$50 billion	$11.3 million
HMOs: Provision makes it easier for HMOs to tap into Medicare and Medicaid markets.	Not available	$8.9 million
Health insurance firms: Will be allowed to market high-deductible plans to Medicare recipients with medical savings accounts.	$4 billion	$3 million
Oil, energy, and natural resource firms: Alternative minimum tax (AMT) provision will exempt altogether companies with assets less than $5 million, and let larger companies pay at least 75% less AMT than they pay now.	$18 billion	$18.3 million
Big airlines: Air ticket taxes will be reduced from 10% to 7.5% per ticket. Also new $3 tax applied to each flight segment favors larger carriers by making smaller, multiple-stop airlines more expensive for consumers.	Not available	$3.2 million
Software companies: Tax exemption was enacted on all income earned from licensing, production, and distribution of software overseas.	$1.7 billion	$1.3 million

* Donations to all political parties and congressional candidates. The total for contributions exceeds $35 million because a few companies appear in more than one category.

SOURCE: *Washington Post*, August 22, 1997, A21. Ceci Connolly, Washington Post Staff Writer

The United States is still a nation of joiners. As a college student, think of the number of interest groups or voluntary associations to which you belong. It's likely that you belong to some kind of organized religion; to a political party; or to a college, or university social, civic, athletic, or academic group, at a bare minimum. You may also belong to a more general special-interest group, such as Greenpeace, People for the Ethical Treatment of Animals, the National Right-to-Life Committee, or Amnesty International.

Organizations are usually composed of three kinds of members. At the top are a relatively small number of leaders who devote most of their energies to the single group. The second tier of members is generally involved psychologically as well as organizationally. They are the workers of the group—they attend meetings, pay dues, and chair committees to see that things get done. In the bottom tier are the rank and file, members who don't actively participate. They pay their dues and call themselves group members, but they do little more. Most group members fall into this last category.

Political scientist E. E. Schattschneider has noted that the interest group system in the United States has a decidedly "upper-class bias," and he concluded that 90 percent of the population does not participate in an interest group, or what he called the pressure group, system.[62] Since the 1960s, survey data have revealed that group membership is drawn primarily from people with higher income and education levels.

Individuals who are wealthier can afford to belong to more organizations because they have more money and, often, more leisure time. Money and education are also associated with greater confidence that one's actions will bring results, a further incentive to devote time to organizing or supporting interest groups. As discussed in chapter 11, these elites are often more involved in politics and hold stronger opinions on many political issues.

People who do belong to groups often belong to more than one. Overlapping memberships can often affect the cohesiveness of a group. Imagine, for example, that you are an officer in the college Young Republicans. If you call a meeting, people may not attend because they have academic, athletic, or social obligations. Divided loyalties and multiple group memberships can often affect the success of a group, especially if any one group has too many members who simply fall into the dues-paying category.

Groups vary tremendously in their ability to enroll what are called potential members (see Table 16.6). Economist Mancur Olson, Jr., notes that all groups provide some **collective good**—that is, something of value, such as money, a tax write-off, a good feeling, or a better environment—that can't be withheld from a non–group member.[63] If one union member at a factory gets a raise, for example, all other workers at that factory will, too. Therefore those who don't join or work for the benefit of the group still reap the rewards of the group's activity. This phenomenon is called the **free rider** problem. Consequently, Olson asserts, potential members are unlikely to join a group because they realize that they will receive many of the benefits the group achieves regardless of their participation. Not only is it irrational for free riders to join any group, but the bigger the group, the greater the free rider problem. Thus groups need to provide a variety of other incentives to convince potential members to join. These can be newsletters, discounts, or simply a good feeling. Small groups, however, often have an organizational advantage because, in a small group such as the National Governor's Association, any individual's share of the collective good may be great enough to make it rational to join. Patrons, be they large foundations such as the Ford Foundation or individuals such as Jane Fonda, who pledged $500,000 from the Turner Foundation to the Georgia Campaign for Adolescent Pregnancy Prevention in 1995, often eliminate the free rider problem for public interest groups. They make the "costs" of joining minimal because they contribute much of the group's necessary financial support.[64]

collective good:

Something of value that cannot be withheld from a non–interest group member, for example, a tax write-off, a good feeling.

free rider:

A problem that occurs when those who don't join or work for the benefit of the group still reap the rewards of the group's activity.

Table 16.6   Potential *Versus* Actual Interest Groups

The goal of most groups is to mobilize all potential members. Often, that task is impossible. As Mancur Olson, Jr. points out, the larger the group, the more difficult it is to mobilize. To illustrate the potential versus actual membership phenomenon, here are several examples of groups and their potential memberships.

Population	Group	Number of Potential Members	Number of Actual Members
Governors	National Governor's Association	55	55 (includes territories)
Political Science Faculty	American Political Science Association	17,000	13,000
Physicians	American Medical Association (AMA)	548,000	300,000
Women	National Organization for Women (NOW)	127,000,000	500,000
African Americans	National Association for the Advancement of Colored People (NAACP)	30,600,000	500,000

*C*ONTINUITY and Change

A Nation of Joiners?

Interest groups long have been a factor in the course of American political history. Members of many discrete religious groups first settled in America seeking religious freedom. Later, after the Revolutionary War was fought and a new nation was created, political factions or groups—Federalists and Anti-Federalists—emerged with strong leaders and even publications clearly setting forth their goals and political philosophies.

When Alexis de Tocqueville toured the United States in the 1830s, he was struck by the tendency of Americans to join groups of all kinds. Interest groups, particularly labor and big business, also played a critical role in the development of the new nation, especially after the Civil War and into the Progressive Era.

The development of what some term the modern interest group society began in the 1960s with the development of myriad civil rights and public interest groups reminiscent of the kinds of interest group formation and activity that occurred during the Progressive movement. Environmental groups, of course, were a new interest group phenomenon, whose formation and successes in part spurred the development of new conservative groups and public interest law firms to counter their claims in the legislature, before executive agencies, and in the courts. In many ways, however, the power exerted by big business through trade associations, the hiring of professional lobbyists, and PACs is still quite reminiscent of the power it enjoyed just before and well into the Progressive movement.

By the year 2000, technology-based firms and corporations will contribute as much if not more to the economy than major U.S. car manufacturers. This new wealth will create with it new interests. In addition, the Internet is becoming an increasingly effective tool for grassroots mobilization for existing groups and may be usurping the role of patrons in the formation of new groups, whose start-up costs are now much lower. While Robert Putnam may be correct that people are no longer bowling in leagues, they are spending more and more time on the Internet.

1. What kinds of interest groups do you believe would be particularly amenable to start up on the Internet?
2. Will the research and conventional wisdom about organized interests and their effectiveness have to be rewritten in light of the growth of the Internet?

Cast Your Vote. In what ways will the Internet succeed as a mobilizing tool for interest groups ? In what ways will it fail? To cast your vote, go to www.awlonline.com/oconnor.

SUMMARY

Interest groups lie at the heart of the American social and political system. National groups first emerged in the 1830s. Since that time the type, nature, sophistication, and tactics of groups have changed dramatically. To that end we have made the following points:

1. WHAT ARE INTEREST GROUPS?

Those who study interest groups have offered a variety of definitions to explain what they are. Most definitions revolve around notions of "associations or groups of individuals" who "share" some sort of "common" "interest" or "attitude" and who try to "influence" or "engage in activity" to affect "governmental policies" or the people in "government." Political scientists find it helpful to categorize interest groups in several ways. They study multi-issue versus single-issue groups. They also examine economic, public interest and governmental units as participants in the interest group process.

2. THE ROOTS AND DEVELOPMENT OF AMERICAN INTEREST GROUPS

Interest groups, national in scope, did not begin to emerge until around the 1830s. Later, from 1890–1920, the Progressive movement emerged. The 1960s saw the rise of a wide variety of liberal interest groups. By the 1970s through the 1980s, legions of conservatives were moved to form new groups to counteract those efforts. Professional associations, too, became an active presence in Washington, D.C.

3. WHAT DO INTEREST GROUPS DO?

Interest groups often fill voids left by the major political parties and give Americans opportunities to make claims, as a group, on government. The most common activity of interest groups is lobbying, which takes many forms. Groups routinely pressure members of Congress and their staffs, the president and the bureaucracy, and the courts; they use a variety of techniques to educate and stimulate the public also to pressure key governmental decision makers. Interest groups also attempt to influence the outcome of elections; some even run their own candidates for office. Others rate elected officials to inform their members how particular legislators stand on issues of importance to them. Political action committees (PACs), a way for some groups to contribute money to candidates for office, are another method of gaining support from elected officials and ensuring that their "friends" stay in office. Reaction to public criticism of this influence led Congress to pass the first major lobbying reforms in fifty years.

4. WHAT MAKES AN INTEREST GROUP SUCCESSFUL?

Interest group success can be measured in a variety of ways including a group's ability to get its issues on the public agenda, winning key pieces of legislation in Congress or executive branch or judicial rulings, or backing successful candidates. Several factors contribute to interest group success including leaders and patrons, funding, and committed members.

KEY TERMS

collective good, p. 604
disturbance theory, p. 579
economic interest group,
p. 580
free rider, p. 604

interest group, p. 580
lobbying, p. 590
lobbyist, p. 583
patron, p. 601

political action committee
(PAC), p. 600
public interest group, p. 581
trade associations, p. 584

SELECTED READINGS

Berry, Jeffrey M. *The Interest Group Society*, 3d ed. New York: Longman, 1997

———. *Lobbying for the People: The Political Behavior of Public Interest Groups*. Princeton, NJ: Princeton University Press, 1977.

Cigler, Allan J., and Burdett A. Loomis, eds. *Interest Group Politics*, 5th ed. Washington, D C: CQ Press, 1998.

Herrnson, Paul S., Ronald G. Shaiko, and Clyde Wilcox. *The Interest Group Connection*. Chatham, NJ: Chatham House, 1998.

Kollman, Ken. *Outside Lobbying: Public Opinion and Interest Group Strategies*. Princeton: Princeton University Press, 1998.

McGlen, Nancy E., and Karen O'Connor. *Women, Politics and American Society.* 2d ed. Upper Saddle River, NJ: Prentice Hall, 1998.

Olson, Mancur, Jr. *The Logic of Collective Action: Public Good and the Theory of Groups.* Cambridge, MA: Harvard University Press, 1965.

Sabato, Larry J. *PAC Power: Inside the World of Political Action Committees.* New York: Norton, 1984.

Schlozman, Kay Lehman, and John T. Tierney. *Organized Interests and American Democracy.* New York: Harper & Row, 1986.

Truman, David B. *The Governmental Process: Political Interests and Public Opinion.* New York: Knopf, 1951.

Walker, Jack L., ed. *Interest Groups in America: Patrons, Professions and Social Movements.* Ann Arbor: University of Michigan Press, 1991.

Wilson, James Q. *Political Organizations.* Princeton: NJ, Princeton University Press, 1995.

Woliver, Laura. *From Outrage to Action: The Politics of Grassroots Dissent.* Urbana: University of Illinois Press, 1993.

Wolpe, Bruce C. and Bertram J. Levine. *Lobbying Congress: How the System Works,* 2d ed. Washington, DC: CQ Press, 1996.

NOTES

1. Russ Feingold, "Lobbyists' Rush for Bankruptcy Reform," *Washington Post* (June 7, 1999): A19.

2. Feingold, "Lobbyists' Rush."

3. Feingold, "Lobbyists' Rush."

4. Robert D. Putnam, "Bowing alone: America's Declining Social Capital" *Journal of Democracy* 6(1):65-665.

5. Richard Morin, "Who Says We're Not Joiners," quoting Everett Carll Ladd, *Washington Post* (May 2, 1999): B5.

6. Clive Thomas and Ronald Hrebenar, "Changing Patterns of Interest Group Activity: A Regional Perspective," in Mark Petracca, ed., *The Politics of Interests* (Boulder, CO: Westview Press, 1992), 4.

7. Graham Wilson, *Interest Groups in the United States* (New York: Oxford University Press, 1981), 4.

8. David B. Truman, *The Governmental Process: Political Interests and Public Opinion* (New York: Knopf, 1951), 33.

9. Robert H. Salisbury, "Interest Groups," in Fred I. Greenstein and Nelson W. Polsby, eds., *Handbook of Political Science*, vol. 4 (Reading, MA: Addison-Wesley, 1975), 175.

10. V. O. Key, Jr., *Politics, Parties and Pressure Groups* (New York: T. J. Crowell, 1942), 23.

11. Truman, *The Governmental Process*, chapter 16.

12. Salisbury, "An Exchange Theory of Interest Groups," 1–32.

13. Robert H. Salisbury, "An Exchange Theory of Interest Groups," *Midwest Journal of Political Science* 13 (1969): 1–32.

14. Jeffrey M. Berry, *Lobbying for the People: The Political Behavior of Public Interest Groups* (Princeton, NJ: Princeton University Press, 1977), 7.

15. Samuel Eliot Morrison and Henry Steel Commager, *The Growth of the American Republic* (New York: Oxford University Press, 1930), 163.

16. Quoted in Grant McConnell, "Lobbies and Pressure Groups," in Jack Greene, ed. *Encyclopedia of American Political History*, vol. 2 (New York: Macmillan, 1984), 768.

17. Lee Epstein, *Conservatives in Court* (Knoxville: University of Tennessee Press, 1985).

18. Jack L. Walker, "The Origins and Maintenance of Interest Groups in America," *American Political Science Review* 77 (June 1983). 390 406.

19. Peter Steinfels, "Moral Majority to Dissolve; Says Mission Accomplished," *New York Times* (June 12, 1989): A14.

20. Steve Goldstein, "The Christian Right Grows in Power," *Atlanta Journal* (November 11, 1994): A8.

21. Ralph Reed, *Contract with the American Family* (Nashville, TN: Moorings, 1995).

22. Richard S. Dunham, "Corporate America vs. the Religious Right?" *Business Week* (May 18, 1998): 46.

23. Thomas B. Edsall and Hanna Rosin, "Christian Coalition, Denied Tax-Exempt Status, Will Reorganize," *Washington Post* (June 11, 1999): A4.

24. Jill Lawrence and Jim Drinkard, "Christian Coalition Gains Momentum," *USA Today* (September 18, 1998): 6A.

25. Dunham, "Corporate America."

26. Dunham, "Corporate America."

27. David Mahood, *Interest Groups Participation in America: A New Intensity* (Englewood Cliffs, NJ: Prentice Hall, 1990), 23.

28. Bill McAllister, "Wisconsin Backers of Gingrich Terms Hill's Biggest Patrons," *Washington Post* (September 10. 1998): A19.

29. Quoted in Ronald J. Hrebenar and Ruth K. Scott, *Interest Group Politics in America*, 2d ed. (Englewood Cliffs, NJ: Prentice Hall, 1990), 263.

30. See Taylor E. Dark, *The Unions and the Democrats: An Enduring Alliance* (Ithaca, NY: ILR Press, 1999).

31. Remarks by John C. Sweeney, AFL-CIO President, November 4, 1998. http://www.aflcio.org/publ/speech98/sp1104.htm

32. Karen MacPherson, "Labor Claims Key Aid in Vote: 'Get Out the Vote' Effort Aided Workers' Allies, AFL-CIO Says," *Pittsburgh Post-Gazette* (November 5, 1998): A18.

33. Benjamin Radcliff and Martin Saiz, "Labor Organizations and Public Policy in the American States," *Journal of Politics* (February 1998): 121.

34. Radcliff and Saiz, "Labor Organizations and Public Policy."

35. Brenda Rios, "Big Blitz from TV to the Hill: A $100 Million Whirlwind of Spin Control," *Atlanta Journal* (July 22, 1994): A4.

36. Rios, "Big Blitz."

37. Rios, "Big Blitz."

38. Sam Loewenberg, "Now, The Tricky Part: Dividing Profits," *Legal Times* (May 31, 1999): 4.

39. Michael Wines, "For New Lobbyists, It's What They Know," *New York Times* (November 3, 1993): B14.

40. Quoted in Kay Lehman Schlozman and John T. Tierney, *Organized Interests and American Democracy* (New York: Harper & Row, 1986), 85.

41. Quoted in Norman J. Ornstein and Shirley Elder, *Interest Groups, Lobbying and Policy Making* (Washington, DC: CQ Press, 1978), 77.

42. Bill McAllister, "No Death of Lavish Lobbying in 1999," *Washington Post* (May 11, 1998): A19.

43. Thomas Cronin, *The State of the Presidency* (Boston: Little, Brown, 1975), 123.

44. Cronin, *The State of the Presidency.*

45. Some political scientists speak of "iron rectangles," reflecting the growing importance of a fourth party, the courts, in the lobbying process.

46. Clement E. Vose, "Litigation as a Form of Pressure Group Activity," *Annals* 319 (September 1958): 20–31.

47. Richard C. Cortner, "Strategies and Tactics of Litigation in Constitutional Cases," *Journal of Public Law* 17 (1968): 287.

48. Karen O'Connor, "Lobbying the Justices or Lobbying for Justice?" in Paul Herrnson, Ronald G. Shaiko and Clyde Wilcox, *The Interest Group Connection* (Chatham, NJ: Chatham House Publishers, 1998), 267–88.

49. Robert A. Goldberg, *Grassroots Resistance: Social movements in Twentieth Century America* (Belmont, CA: Wadsworth, 1991).

50. Jane Fritsch, "Sometimes, Lobbyists Strive to Keep Public in the Dark," *New York Times* (March 19, 1996): A1.

51. Joel Brinkley, "Cultivating the Grass Roots to Reap Legislative Benefits," *New York Times* (November 1, 1993): A1.

52. Michael E. Kanell, "News Lovers Offered Places for Opinions," *Atlanta Constitution* (February 11, 1998): E2.

53. Brinkley, "Cultivating the Grass Roots."

54. Thomas B. Edsall and Hanna Rosin, "Christian Coalition, Denied Tax-Exempt Status, Will Reorganize," *Washington Post* (June 11, 1999): A4.

55. E.E. Schattschneider, *The Semi-Sovereign People* (New York: Holt, Rinehart and Winston, 1960), p. 51.

56. Ken Kollman, *Outside Lobbying: Public Opinion and Interest Group Strategies* (Princeton, NJ: Princeton University Press, 1998) and Karen O'Connor, *Women's Organizations' Use of the Courts* (Lexington, MA: 1980).

57. Marie Hojnacki, "Interest Groups' Decisions to Join Alliances or Work Alone," *American Journal of Political Science* 41 (January 1997): 61–87.

58. Walker, "The Origins and Maintenance of Interest Groups in America."

59. Ceci Connolly, "New Democrat Dinner Is Record Fundraiser," *Washington Post* (February 14, 1999): A6.

60. Ceci Connolly, "Donors to Campaigns Fared Well in Budget," *Washington Post* (August 22, 1997): A20.

61. Alexis de Tocqueville, *Democracy in America*, vol. 1, trans. Phillips Bradley (New York: Knopf, Vintage Books, 1945; orig. published in 1835), 191.

62. E. E. Schattschneider, *The Semi-Sovereign People* (New York: Holt, Rinehart and Winston, 1960), 35.

63. Mancur Olson, Jr. *The Logic of Collective Action: Public Goods and the Theory of Groups* (Cambridge, MA: Harvard University Press, 1965).

64. Walker, "The Origins and Maintenance of Interest Groups," 390–406.

(Photo courtesy: Gatewood/The Image Works)

Social Welfare Policy

- **The Roots of Social Welfare Policy**
- **The Policy-Making Process**
- **Social Welfare Policies Today**

*W*elfare reform signed into law by President Clinton in 1996 reflected the popular view that America's welfare policies were "broken" and in need of repair. Sentiments were expressed that welfare inhibited initiative, helped in weakening the traditional family, and created a permanent underclass that replicated itself from generation to generation. A popular view of the time was that there was a need to reduce the level of government support and force people to work for their money. While this view of welfare gained credibility and helped produce the 1996 welfare reform, others maintained that the 1996 agreement went too far and was overly harsh. As a consequence, in 1997 Congress voted to reinstate Medicaid and Supplemental Security Income to some immigrants. This action was taken in conjunction with the landmark balanced-budget agreement. In 1998 the Senate voted to restore food stamps to a quarter of a million legal immigrants and refugees. This action eliminated what many analysts considered to be the most punitive aspects of the 1996 welfare reform. Possible negative implications of welfare reforms are perhaps best illustrated in the experience of the state of Idaho.

Idaho was a national leader in terms of limiting welfare payments and, in theory, eliminating disincentives to work. Between 1993 and 1997, the state succeeded in cutting its welfare rolls by 77 percent, the steepest cuts in the nation. In comparison, welfare rolls declined by an average of 31 percent in the United States as a whole. Even before the 1996 national welfare reform, Idaho was among the lowest three states in terms of per capita spending for children. It also had the dubious honor of having the highest proportions of abused or neglected children.

In the late 1990s, some cracks began to appear in local support for the state's spending priorities. Idaho's governor, Phil Batt, who initially backed Idaho's welfare policies and considered himself to be as conservative as any mainstream Republican, suggested in 1998 that the state may have been too harsh in the treatment of its children and the poor. The governor noted that food bank usage had increased and the poor seemed to have fared poorly. Many in Idaho, and elsewhere across the nation, who were removed from the welfare rolls were not necessarily lifted out of poverty.[1]

Social welfare policy is a term that designates a broad and varied range of government programs designed to provide people with protection against want and deprivation, to improve their health and physical well-being, to provide educational and employment training opportunities, and otherwise to enable them to lead more satisfactory, meaningful, and productive lives. In a nutshell, social welfare policies are intended to enhance the quality of life. They are meant to benefit all segments of society, but especially the less fortunate members, who often find it more difficult to provide for themselves and their families. More specifically, social welfare policies focus on such matters as public education, income security, medical care, sanitation and disease prevention, public housing, employment training, children's protective services, and improvements in human nutrition.

The issue of who is deserving and what they deserve is at the heart of the debate over social welfare programs. Over time, the focus of social welfare programs has expanded from providing minimal assistance to the destitute to helping the working poor attain a degree of security, to help them provide for their health, nutritional, income security, employment, and education needs.

In optimistic times, when political leaders expect the economic pie to continue expanding, the scope and generosity of social welfare programs are expected to grow. In the 1960s, for example, new programs provided food stamps and health care to meet two critical needs of the disadvantaged. The level of benefits for older programs like Social Security grew to keep pace with the cost of living.

Both Democrats and Republicans are loathe to increase taxes to support social programs, and the parties vie with one another in devising plans for cutting taxes. Republicans have led the way in proposing ways in which to cut social welfare spending as a step toward budget balancing. Democrats, sensing public dissatisfaction with endless streams of money going to programs that seem unable to get people off welfare and into jobs, have increasingly joined critics. Welfare fell under attack from both sides, and the full implication of reform is uncertain. For the minority of Americans who depend on these programs, and the even greater numbers who want them to be available if needed, tinkering with their design is unnerving.

Social welfare policy is clearly changing in the United States—almost daily. In order to enable you to follow its progress, in this chapter we explore the following issues:

- First, we will examine the history of social welfare policy, income security, and health insurance.
- Second, we will consider the nature of the *policy-making process* itself, presenting a model that provides a manageable way of dissecting the policy-making process and examining its components.
- Third, we will focus on the current state of *social welfare policy*.
- Fourth, we will examine *income security* programs to relieve economic dependency and poverty.
- Fifth, we will evaluate *medical care* programs.
- Sixth, we will devote substantial attention to the national government's involvement in *public education*.

Web Exploration
To understand how public policies are prioritized and analyzed, go to www.awlonline.com/oconnor.

THE ROOTS OF SOCIAL WELFARE POLICY

Most social welfare programs in the United States are largely a product of the twentieth century, although their origins can be traced far into the nation's past. As U.S. society became more urban and industrial, self-sufficiency declined and people became more interdependent and reliant on a vast system of production, distribution, and exchange. The Great Depression of the 1930s revealed both that hard work alone would not provide economic security for everyone and that the state governments and private charities lacked adequate resources to alleviate economic want and distress. Beginning with the Social Security Act of 1935, which we will describe below, a variety of national programs aimed at providing economic security have emerged.

Income Security

The Great Depression completely overwhelmed existing sources of assistance for the needy. In 1934 twenty-eight states had laws authorizing old-age assistance programs, but often these had closed down because of the lack of funding. Only ten states had fully functioning programs, and these typically paid pensions of less than $10 a month. At one extreme Indiana paid $4.50 a month, a princely sum compared to the 69 cents doled out monthly at the other extreme in North Dakota.

In accordance with the individualistic philosophy of President Herbert Hoover, the national government offered limited assistance to the needy during the Hoover administration (1929–33). The response of Franklin D. Roosevelt's New Deal (begun in 1933) took a very different tack. Initially, programs for direct cash assistance and work relief, such as the Works Progress Administration (WPA), were created to help the needy. Frequently derided as a "makework" program that paid for such activities as leaf raking, the WPA nevertheless helped many people weather the Great Depression.

The Roosevelt administration also designed permanent programs that would address the problems of income security and economic dependency. Roosevelt appointed the Committee on Economic Security to investigate the economic situation and make policy recommendations. Most of its proposals were subsequently endorsed by the President and enacted into law by Congress in 1935 as the **Social Security Act.**

The Social Security Act transformed public social welfare policy. The national government became the major contributor on a permanent and extensive basis in the income security area. Three major programs were put in place by the act: old age insurance (what we now call Social Security), public assistance for the needy, aged, blind, and families with dependent children (later, people with disabilities were added); and unemployment insurance (or compensation). Even though programs instituted as part of the Social Security Act have been modified (aid to families with dependent children no longer remained a federal guarantee in 1996 and states assumed greater responsibilities) and other income security programs have been added, these three programs formed the foundation for income security policies for decades.

National health insurance was considered when Social Security legislation was planned. Because of the strong opposition of the American Medical Association (AMA), which was the dominant force in American medicine, health insurance was omitted for fear that its inclusion would jeopardize adoption of the other Social Security programs. Health insurance remained on the policy back burner for several years.

National Health Insurance

In late 1945 President Harry S Truman put health insurance on the national policy agenda by calling for the enactment of compulsory national health insurance. Truman's advocacy touched off a titanic political struggle. The initial public reaction to compulsory health insurance was favorable: Of those who had heard of the proposal, 58 percent expressed approval in public opinion polls.[2] Support for the proposal came from many liberal and labor groups. In opposition were the AMA, drug manufacturers, private insurance companies, and conservatives—some of the same groups that oppose health care reform today. The AMA and its allies succeeded in stigmatizing compulsory health insurance as "socialized medicine," and by 1950 it was a dead issue.

Liberal political leaders did not lose interest in national health insurance. In 1958 a bill introduced in Congress covered only the hospital costs of elderly people receiving Social Security. The AMA again weighed in against this proposal; but by focusing on the aged, the proponents of health insurance changed the terms of the struggle. Strong support developed for providing medical assistance to the elderly, and in 1960

Social Security Act:

A 1935 law that established old age insurance (Social Security), assistance for the needy, children, and others; and unemployment insurance.

Congress passed legislation benefiting the needy aged. This provision, however, did not satisfy liberals and other supporters of a broader program. The issue was resolved by the 1964 elections, which produced sufficient votes in Congress to enact medical care legislation.

The Johnson administration proposed Medicare, which would provide hospital benefits for all aged people covered by Social Security. The Republicans countered with a plan for subsidized voluntary insurance that would cover major medical risks and physicians' services. The AMA sponsored a similar proposal. Representative Wilbur Mills (D–Ark.), chair of the House Ways and Means Committee (which had jurisdiction over the legislation), took hold of the policy process at this point. Wanting to put his own stamp on the legislation, he proposed combining the administration and Republican proposals and also adding an expanded program for the poor. This expanded proposal was enacted into law as Medicare and Medicaid, which we will examine later in the chapter.

Over the years, the national government's role in health care has grown tremendously. In 1965 the Medicaid program sought to bring health care to the nation's poor. The federal government is extensively involved not only in the provision of health care, through Medicaid and the U.S. Public Health Service, but also in the improvement of the health of all Americans. The Centers for Disease Control and Prevention (CDC), in particular, work to prevent disease.

Public health policies, for example, have been highly effective in reducing the incidence of infectious disease such as measles, infantile paralysis (poliomyelitis), and smallpox. A separate federal agency, the National Cancer Institute, has funded efforts to isolate causes of that killer and, in recent years, debate has surrounded the issue of whether Washington is doing enough to combat AIDS. Most Americans accept and support extensive government spending on medical research. Congress, in fact, often appropriates more money for medical research than the president recommends.

■ Representative Tom Davis 3d (R–Va.) at a 1996 rally on Capitol Hill supporting school vouchers for lower income parents. The House had passed a plan to use federal tax dollars to pay private school tuition for some low-income children in Washington. (Photo courtesy: J. Scott Applewhite/AP/Wide World Photos)

Public Education

Public education was almost the exclusive province of the state and local governments until well into the twentieth century. Even though some commentators and critics argue that education was one area the Framers intended to be reserved to the states by the Tenth Amendment, the national government has been involved in education since passage of the Northwest Ordinance in 1785. Moreover, constitutional justification for the national government's action on public education rests on a broad view of its delegated powers, such as taxing and spending for the general welfare. National financial aid for the public schools has been an agenda item from time to time during the twentieth century and has now become a permanent aspect of public school funding.

Beginning with the GI Bill, which paid for college for many World War II veterans, the federal government has helped students secure the funds needed to continue their educations beyond high school. Some programs, such as Pell Grants, have been targeted to students from poorer families. Loan guarantee programs have been available to students from a wider range of economic backgrounds. Loan guarantees are attractive because the federal government pays the interest on the loans as long as the recipient remains in school. The average student who takes advantage of this program owes $6,000, but there are indications that borrowing is increasing.[3]

Student loans have not been immune from the budget cutters. Both the Clinton administration in the 103rd Congress and Republicans in the 104th explored ways to reduce costs. Democrats urged having the government make the loans directly to students, replacing banks and private lenders. Republicans, eager to privatize as many functions as possible, objected to reducing the role of private lenders. The GOP also suggested allowing students to avoid interest payment while in school but requiring that they cover these costs on graduation. Members of both parties have been troubled by the high default rates of students who attend some proprietary vocational schools. There have been demands that tighter standards be developed to protect both students who may feel that they are not getting much training and the government that must pay off the loans for students who do not.

THE POLICY-MAKING PROCESS

Public policy is a purposive course of action followed by government in dealing with some problem or matter of concern.[4] Public policies are thus governmental policies, based on law; they are authoritative and binding on people. Individuals, groups, and even government agencies that do not comply with policies can be penalized through fines, loss of benefits, or even jail terms. As the phrase "course of action" implies, policies develop or unfold over time. They involve more than a legislative decision to enact a law or a presidential decision to issue an executive order. Also important is how the law or executive order is carried out. Whether a policy is vigorously enforced, enforced only in some instances, or not enforced at all helps determine its meaning and impact.

Political scientists and other social scientists have developed many theories and models of the formation of public policies. Some theories, such as elite theory and pluralist theory, focus on who dominates or controls the making of policy. As discussed in chapter 1, elite theorists contend that policy reflects the interests of a small, well-to-do segment of society. Pluralists, in contrast, argue that policy is the product of interaction and struggle among many groups and powerholders in society. Needless to say, these are markedly divergent theories that have provoked continuing intellectual conflict.

Who dominates or controls the formation of public policy is an important question, but we do not wrestle with it here. Rather, we present a widely used model (see Figure 17.1) of the policy-making process that views it as a sequence of stages or functional activities. Public policies do not just happen; rather, they are typically the products of such a predictable pattern of events. Models for analyzing the policy-making process do not always explain *why* public policies take the specific forms that they do, however. That depends on the political struggles over particular policies. Nor do models necessarily tell us *who* dominates or controls the formation of public policy. This model can be applied and used to analyze any of the issues discussed earlier in the book.

Despite the limitations of models, however, policy making frequently does follow the sequence of stages in Figure 17.1. Sometimes some of the stages may merge, such as the policy formulation and adoption stages. Another instance of stages merging occurs when administrative agencies like the Occupational Safety and Health Administration (OSHA) are forming policy through rule-making at the same time that they are implementing it. Finally, we need to recognize that what happens at one stage of the policy-making process affects action at later stages, and sometimes such action is done deliberately in anticipation of these effects. Thus particular provisions may be included in a law either to help or hinder its implementation, depending on the interests of the provisions' proponents.

Policy making typically is perceived as a process of sequential steps. For example, problems must first be recognized and defined. A problem that disturbs or distresses people gives rise to demands for relief, often through government action.

A *problem* that disturbs or distresses people gives rise to demands for relief, often through governmental action. Individual or group efforts are then made to get the problem placed on a governmental *agenda*. If successful, this step is followed by the *formulation* of alternatives for dealing with the problem. *Policy adoption* involves the formal enactment or approval of an alternative. *Budgeting* provides financial resources

public policy:
A purposive course of action followed by government in dealing with some problem or matter of concern.

Web Exploration
To see an overview of the legislative process for public policy, go to www.awlonline.com/oconnor.

Figure 17.1 Stages of the Public Policy Process

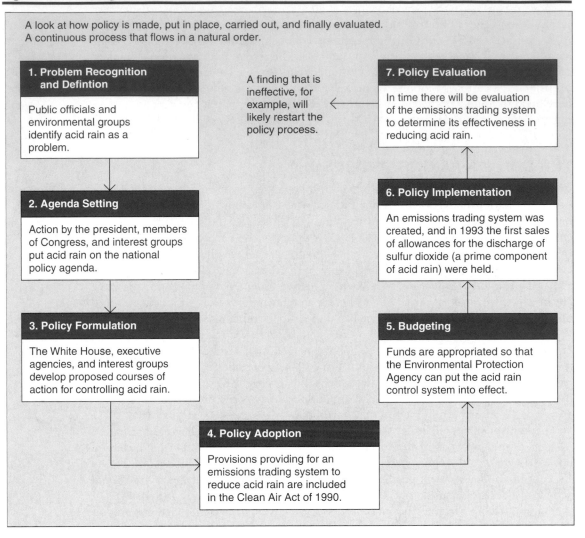

A look at how policy is made, put in place, carried out, and finally evaluated.
A continuous process that flows in a natural order.

1. Problem Recognition and Defintion

Public officials and environmental groups identify acid rain as a problem.

2. Agenda Setting

Action by the president, members of Congress, and interest groups put acid rain on the national policy agenda.

3. Policy Formulation

The White House, executive agencies, and interest groups develop proposed courses of action for controlling acid rain.

4. Policy Adoption

Provisions providing for an emissions trading system to reduce acid rain are included in the Clean Air Act of 1990.

5. Budgeting

Funds are appropriated so that the Environmental Protection Agency can put the acid rain control system into effect.

6. Policy Implementation

An emissions trading system was created, and in 1993 the first sales of allowances for the discharge of sulfur dioxide (a prime component of acid rain) were held.

7. Policy Evaluation

In time there will be evaluation of the emissions trading system to determine its effectiveness in reducing acid rain.

A finding that is ineffective, for example, will likely restart the policy process.

to carry out the approved alternative, which can now truly be called a "policy." *Policy implementation,* the actual administration or application of the policy to its targets, may then be followed by *policy evaluation* to determine the policy's actual accomplishments, consequences, or shortcomings. Evaluation may restart the policy process by identifying a new problem and touching off an attempt to modify or terminate the policy. With this overview in mind, let's now look in more detail at the various stages of the policy process or cycle.

Problem Recognition and Definition

A problem involves some condition or situation that causes distress or dissatisfaction or generates needs for which some kind of relief or corrective action is sought—often from the government (national, state, or local). At any given time, there are many conditions that disturb or distress people—polluted air, unsafe workplaces, earthquakes and hurricanes, too much or too little rain, the rising cost of medical care, the poor academic performance of high school students, too many handguns, too few "dedicated" public officials, or no prayers in the public schools. All disturbing conditions do not

■ "Rescue of Children from a Drunken Mother"—an artist's depiction of an early crusader for the Society for the Prevention of Cruelty to Children. (Photo courtesy: Corbis/Bettmann)

automatically become problems; some of them may be accepted as trivial, appropriate, inevitable, or beyond the control of government.

For a condition to become a problem, there must be some criterion—a standard or value—that leads people to believe that the condition does not have to be accepted or acquiesced to and, further, that it is something with which government can deal effectively and appropriately. Earthquakes, for example, are unlikely to become a policy problem because there is nothing that government can do about them directly. The consequences of earthquakes, the human distress and property destruction that they bring, are another matter. Their relief can be a focus of government action, as it was in the 1998 Florida fires, for which Congress appropriated several billion dollars for recovery activities. Conditions that at one time are accepted as appropriate and beyond government responsibility may at a later time be perceived as problems because of changes in public attitudes. Child abuse is illustrative of attitude change (see Roots of Government: Child Abuse as a Public Policy Problem).

Usually there is not a single agreed-on definition of a problem. Indeed, political struggle often occurs at this stage because how the problem is defined helps determine what sort of action is appropriate. If access to transportation for people with disabilities is defined as a transportation problem, then an acceptable solution is to provide the people with transportation by adapting the regular transportation system or by establishing other means of transport, such as a special van service. If access to transportation is defined as a civil rights problem, however, then people with disabilities are entitled to equal access to the regular transportation system. Solving a problem once defined as a civil right might require extensive and expensive alterations to make *all* public transport accessible to people with disabilities. After some wavering between these definitions in the 1980s, the national government appeared to be moving toward the transportation view of the problem. But congressional passage of the Americans with Disabilities Act forced a civil rights perspective on local governments by mandating that they make transportation accessible to the elderly and to all people with disabilities.

ROOTS OF GOVERNMENT

Child Abuse as a Public Policy Problem

Until the 1870s, reports Barbara J. Nelson, the maltreatment of children was of minimal concern to society. The disciplining of children, even when harsh, was usually viewed as a parental prerogative, except perhaps in instances of extreme brutality. Newspaper accounts of a gruesome instance of child beating in New York City in 1874 put the matter on the public agenda. In fact, some of the first efforts to protect children occurred under laws barring cruelty to animals! In the late 1800s, many large cities created units of the Society for the Prevention of Cruelty to Children modeled after the SPCA. In time, however, the problem receded from public view, although some protective activity for children continued.

Child abuse was rediscovered as a problem in the 1960s, a time of social activism and concern about people's rights. According to Professor Nelson, an article entitled "The Battered Child Syndrome," written by a physician and published in a leading medical journal, was the catalyst. Newspapers and popular magazines picked up the issue, and child abuse was again viewed as an urgent public problem. Between 1963 and 1967, all fifty state legislatures enacted laws requiring the reporting of child abuse. In 1974 Congress manifested its concern by passing the Child Abuse Prevention and Treatment Act, which requires the states to have child protection agencies. Since that time the problem of child abuse has continued to concern policy makers. In 1993 President Clinton signed the National Child Abuse Protection Act. This act establishes a national database to track child abusers in an effort to prevent their employment in child-care centers.

Child abuse again became a more highly publicized issue in the summer of 1998 as baseball player Mark McGwire captured Roger Maris's home run record. In 1997 McGwire announced that he would give $1 million a season during the life of his new three-year contract to start a foundation for sexually and physically abused children. McGwire hoped to build homes in Southern California and the St. Louis area to care for the abused. He apparently was motivated by a close friend who worked with abused children at Stuart House in Santa Monica, California.

Barbara J. Nelson, *Making an Issue of Child Abuse* (Chicago: University of Chicago Press, 1984), 1–17.

Henry Kempe, *et al.*, "The Battered Child Syndrome," *The Journal of The American Medical Association* 181 (July 7, 1962): 17–24.

Claire Smith, "McGwire Finds His Other Calling," nytimes.com.

Problems differ not only in terms of how they are defined, but also in terms of their tractability, that is, in terms of how easy they are to resolve. For instance, problems that affect large numbers of people or require widespread behavioral changes are more difficult to resolve. The Voting Rights Act of 1965, intended to ensure equal voting rights for African Americans, was easier to implement than was policy requiring desegregation of public schools. Only a small number of voting registrars were directly affected in the first instance; vast numbers of school officials, students, and parents were affected by the second instance. Tangible problems, such as low incomes or potholes in streets, often are more amenable to solutions than are more intangible problems, such as racism or sexism.

One additional point needs to be made. Public policies themselves are frequently viewed as problems or the causes of problems. Thus, for some people, gun control legislation is a solution to the handgun problem. To the National Rifle Association (NRA), however, any law that restricts gun ownership is a problem because of the NRA's view that such laws inappropriately restrict an individual's right to keep and bear arms. To conservatives legal access to abortion is a problem; whereas for many liberals laws restricting the right to abortion falls into the problem category.

Agenda Setting

Once a problem is recognized and defined, it must be brought to the attention of public officials and it must secure a place on an agenda.

Defining Agendas.   An **agenda** is a set of problems to which policy makers believe they should be attentive. Professors Roger W. Cobb and Charles D. Elder, experts in the study of agenda setting, have identified two basic agenda types: the systemic agenda and the governmental or institutional agenda.[5] The **systemic agenda** is essentially a dis-

agenda:
A set of problems to which policy makers believe they should be attentive.

systemic agenda:
All public issues that are viewed as requiring governmental attention; a discussion agenda.

cussion agenda; it comprises "all issues that are commonly perceived by the members of the political community as meriting public attention and as involving matters within the legitimate jurisdiction" of governments.[6] Every political community—national, state, and local—has a systemic agenda.

A **governmental** or **institutional agenda** includes only problems to which legislators or other public officials feel obliged to devote active and serious attention. Not all the problems that attract the attention of officials are likely to have been widely discussed by the general public, or even the "attentive" public—those who follow certain issues closely. Acid rain was a widely discussed public problem in the 1980s that was addressed by the Clean Air Act of 1990, but there was little public awareness of the Pollution Prevention Act, also adopted in 1990. This act set priorities for pollution control programs in an attempt to improve their effectiveness.

Problems or issues (an issue emerges when disagreement exists over what should be done about a problem) may move onto an institutional agenda, whether from the systemic agenda or elsewhere, in several ways. The congressional agenda represents issues that demand both legislative attention and official consideration. This agenda is the focus of the discussion here.

Getting on the Congressional Agenda. As discussed in chapter 8, the president is an important agenda-setter for Congress. In his State of the Union address, his budget, and special messages, the president presents Congress with a legislative program for its consideration.

■ The growing class struggle in nineteenth century America, as illustrated in William Balfour-Ker's graphic illustration *From the Depth*. Social welfare policy frequently deals with alleviating poverty. (Photo courtesy: General Research Division, The New York Public Library, Astor, Lenox and Tilden Foundations)

Much of Congress's time is spent deliberating presidential recommendations, although by no means does Congress always respond as the president might wish. Congress can be balky even when the president and congressional majorities come from the same party, as Bill Clinton discovered in his first year in the White House on such issues as homosexuals in the armed forces and tax increases. Clinton's problems multiplied in 1995 when Republicans with a markedly different agenda took control of both the House and the Senate. As Republicans, led by Speaker Newt Gingrich (R–Ga.), clashed with the president over key issues involving the size of the budget, annual deficits, and the very scope of federal responsibilities, government literally came to a halt when Congress and the president could not agree on a budget.

Interest groups are major actors and initiators in the **agenda-setting** process. Interest groups and their lobbyists frequently ask Congress to legislate on problems of special concern to them. Environmentalists, for instance, call for government action on such issues as global warming, the protection of wetlands, and the reduction of air pollution. Business groups may seek protection against foreign competitors, restrictions on product liability lawsuits, or government financial bailouts.

Problems may secure agenda status because of some crisis, natural disaster, or other extraordinary event. Coal mine explosions in the past put mining safety on the congressional agenda. When seven-year-old Jessica Dubroff's dream of becoming the youngest person to pilot a plane across the United States crashed in a Wyoming neighborhood, there were widespread calls for regulations on the age at which a person could take the controls of an aircraft. Some four years earlier, the massive oil spill in Prince William Sound in Alaska, caused when the supertanker *Exxon Valdez* ran aground, focused attention on ocean oil spills and led to enactment of the Oil Pollution Act of 1990. Such events trigger the interest of policy makers and the public.

governmental (institutional) agenda:

The changing list of issues to which governments believe they should address themselves.

agenda setting:

The constant process of forming the list of issues to be addressed by government.

■ In 1993 President Clinton signed the National Child Protection Act. The act, which establishes a national database to track child abusers, is the latest of several pieces of legislation passed over many years, as the problem of child abuse has waxed and waned on the public agenda. (Photo courtesy: Jeffrey Markowitz/Sygma)

Some problems and issues draw the attention of the news media and consequently gain agenda status, more salience, or both. Poignant television coverage was instrumental in putting hunger and starvation in Somalia during the early 1990s on both congressional and presidential agendas. The news media probably are more important in developing and sustaining interest in problems than in initially identifying them.

Individual private citizens, members of Congress, and other officials, acting as policy entrepreneurs, may push issues onto the congressional agenda. In the 1960s Ralph Nader's book *Unsafe at Any Speed* and Rachel Carson's *Silent Spring* brought motor vehicle safety and the misuse of pesticides, respectively, to the attention of Congress and many citizens. Representative Leonor Sullivan (D–Mo.) worked for a decade to secure the adoption in 1964 of a permanent food stamp program to help the needy. Senator Edmund Muskie (D–Maine) for many years was a leader in securing and shaping governmental action to protect the environment, as has been Vice President Al Gore. His book *Earth in the Balance,* written while he was a U.S. senator, was a wake-up call to many people about possible environmental disaster.

Finally, political changes may contribute to agenda setting. The landslide election of Democratic President Lyndon B. Johnson in 1964, along with strong, favorable Democratic majorities in Congress, made possible the enactment of a flood of Great Society legislation intended to mitigate social welfare problems such as poverty and inadequate medical care for the elderly and needy and to provide education for disadvantaged children. Similarly, the 1980 election of conservative Republican Ronald Reagan, who in his inaugural address asserted that "Government is not the solution; government is the problem," brought issues concerning the size and activities of government onto national policy agendas. His administration, however, had only limited success in cutting back the size of the government.[7]

It is useful to think of agenda setting as a competitive process. Congress, for instance, does not have the time or resources to take on all the problems and issues it is called on to handle. Whether because of their influence, skill in developing political support, or

Web Exploration
To understand how public policy laws are made, go to www.awlonline.com/oconnor.

presentation of more attractive issues, some players are more successful than others in steering items onto the agenda. Chance plays a small role in agenda setting, except in cases of accidents or natural disasters.

Policy Formulation

Policy formulation involves the crafting of appropriate and acceptable proposed courses of action to ameliorate or resolve public problems. It has both political and technical components. The political aspect of policy formulation encompasses determining generally what should be done to reduce acid rain, for example—whether standard setting and enforcement or emissions testing should be used. The technical facet involves correctly stating in specific language what one wants to authorize or accomplish, so as to adequately guide those who must implement policy and to prevent distortion of legislative intent. Political scientist Charles O. Jones suggests that formulation may take different forms:[8]

1. *Routine formulation* is "a repetitive and essentially changeless process of reformulating similar proposals within an issue area that is well established on the government agenda." For instance, the formulation of policy on agricultural price and income supports had not changed much in recent years until coming under attack from conservatives in 1995 and 1996.
2. In *analogous formulation* a new problem is handled by drawing on the experience of developing proposals for similar problems in the past. What has been done in the past to cope with the activities of terrorists? What has been done in other states to deal with child abuse or divorce law reform?
3. *Creative formulation* involves attempts to develop new or unprecedented proposals that represent a departure from existing practices and that will better resolve a problem. The people seeking to reform the welfare system, for example, have sought to

> **policy formulation:**
> The crafting of appropriate and acceptable proposed courses of action to ameliorate or resolve public problems.

■ The wreckage of the airplane in which Jessica Dubroff, her father, Lloyd, and instructor Joe Reid were killed, being loaded onto a trailer at the crash scene in Cheyenne, Wyoming. Some agenda setters hold that the seven-year-old would still be alive if federal regulations on pilot age had been stricter. (Photo courtesy: Ed Andrieski/AP Photo)

GLOBAL POLITICS

How Much Welfare Spending Is Too Much?

The American social welfare system is an anomaly in the developed world. Social welfare institutions in the United States are less extensive than in Europe and Canada in particular. The other G-7 countries have had national health care systems for decades. Germany maintains a private health insurance system in which the government provides insurance for those citizens who cannot afford regular coverage by a private company. Unlike the United States, however, all German citizens are covered by one or the other. Even Japan, with the lowest level of social welfare spending in the G-7, has a national health insurance system that includes free access to physicians and medical facilities.

Comprehensive welfare states have a relatively short history even in Europe. Germany pioneered social security in the late nineteenth century, created not by the social democratic left but by a conservative authoritarian government trying to keep workers satisfied. The big push for comprehensive welfare programs came after World War II, when practically all the governments of Western and Northern Europe and Canada established social security, unemployment insurance, health care, and other public programs. Japan's limited welfare state did not emerge until the 1960s. Despite the strains on public budgets that public welfare programs impose, polls continue to show that most Europeans support them. Reflecting the differences in political culture and public opinion noted in chapter 11, there is far less support in Europe and Canada than in the United States for significant privatization of key welfare programs.

As the table below suggests, aging populations will increasingly strain current social security policies in all G-7 countries. If anything, the point at which 18.5 percent of the national population is age 65 years or older (Florida's current situation) will come earlier in the other G-7 countries than it will here because their populations are aging more rapidly. In Italy, Germany, and Japan, the latter with the lowest social security expenditures in proportion to national income, nearly one-fifth of the total population will be retirement age almost immediately after the turn of the century.

SOURCES: *Japan 1997: An International Comparison* Tokyo. (Japan Institute for Social and Economic Affairs, 1997), 90; and Peter Peterson, "Grey Dawn: The Global Aging Crisis," *Foreign Affairs* 78 (January/February, 1999): 43–45.

Social Security Expenditures as a Percentage of GDP, 1993

Country	% of GDP	Year in Which Senior Population (%) Will Exceed Florida's
Canada	na	2021
France	30.9	2016
Germany	27.6	2006
Italy	25.8	2003
Japan	11.9	2005
United Kingdom	27.8	2016
United States	**21.3**	**2023**

develop innovative proposals that will provide care for the needy while preserving the incentive to work. This is a daunting task.

Policy formulation may be undertaken by various players in the policy process—the president and his aides, agency officials, specially appointed task forces and commissions, interest groups, private research organizations (or "think tanks"), and legislators and their staffs. The Bush administration's version of the Clean Air Act of 1990 was drafted by White House aides working with officials in the Environmental Protection Agency. In Congress, professional aides played a major role in drafting the detailed provisions of the law. Several competing alternatives may be formulated for a problem, such as was the case with welfare reform in 1996 (discussed later in this chapter).

The people engaged in formulation are usually looking down the road toward policy adoption. Particular provisions may be included or excluded from a proposal in an attempt to enhance its likelihood of adoption. To the extent that formulators think in this strategic manner, the formulation and adoption stages of the policy process often become muddled. Political feasibility is always on the mind of the wise policy formulators; they are more interested in getting action on a problem than in creating political issues.

Policy Adoption

Policy adoption involves the approval of a policy proposal by the people with requisite authority, such as a legislature or chief executive. This approval gives the policy legal force. Because most public policies in the United States are based on legislation, policy adoption frequently requires the building of majority coalitions necessary to secure the enactment of legislation.

In chapter 7 we discuss how power is diffused in Congress and how the legislative process comprises a number of roadblocks or obstacles—House subcommittee, House Committee, House Rules Committee, and so on—that a bill must successfully navigate before it becomes law. A majority is needed to clear a bill through each of these obstacles; hence, not one majority but a series of majorities are needed for congressional policy adoption. To secure the needed votes, a bill may be watered down or modified at each of these decision points. Or the bill may fail to win a majority at one of them and die, at least for the time being.

Much negotiation, bargaining, and compromise are entailed in the adoption of major legislation, such as the Tax Reform Act of 1986 or the Brady Bill. In some instances years or even decades may be needed to secure the enactment of legislation on a controversial matter. Federal aid to public education was considered by Congress off and on over several decades before finally winning approval in 1965. At other times, the approval process may move quickly. The Flag Protection Act, for example, was passed quickly by Congress after the Supreme Court ruled that a Texas statute banning flag burning was constitutional.[9] The Supreme Court, however, soon found that the new federal law was an unconstitutional violation of the First Amendment.[10]

The tortuous nature of congressional policy adoption has some important consequences. First, substantial periods of time may be required in order to pass complex legislation. Second, the legislation passed is often incremental, making only limited or marginal changes in existing policy. Third, legislation is frequently written in general or ambiguous language, as in the Clean Air Act. Necessary to reduce conflict over a law's adoption, such language may both provide considerable discretion to the people who implement the law and also leave them in doubt as to its intended purposes.

Not all policy adoption necessitates formation of majority coalitions. Presidential decision-making on foreign affairs, military actions, and other matters is often unilateral. Although the president has many aides and advisers and is bombarded with information and advice, the final decision rests with him. Ultimately, too, it is the president who decides whether to veto a bill passed by Congress. President Clinton's decision to intervene militarily in 1995 in Bosnia, for example, was ultimately his responsibility. Congress grudgingly acceded to the president's decision to help NATO enforce peace in the tattered remnants of Yugoslavia after he announced his intention to commit 20,000 American troops. Congress also agreed to the deployment of American troops to the Middle East in 1991 in response to the invasion of Kuwait by Iraqi leader Saddam Hussein. It should be noted that the president is much more likely to get his way with Congress on foreign than domestic policy issues. In the case of Bosnia, the Republican Congress let the president send troops even as a budget impasse was closing down parts of the federal government.

Budgeting

Most policies require money in order to be carried out; some policies, such as those involving income security (discussed later in this chapter), essentially involve the transfer of money from taxpayers to the government and back to individual beneficiaries. Funding for most policies and agencies is provided through the budgetary process (discussed in chapter 18). Whether a policy is well funded or poorly funded has a significant effect on its scope, impact, and effectiveness.

A policy can be nullified by an absence of funding or refusal to fund, which was the fate of the Noise Control Act. In 1981 the Reagan administration decided not to seek

policy adoption:
The approval of a policy proposal by the people with the requisite authority, such as a legislature.

Web Exploration
To learn more about how public policies are budgeted, go to www.awlonline.com/oconnor.

funds for the Office of Noise Abatement and Control, the unit within EPA that enforced the act. Because Congress followed the president's lead, this decision ended implementation of noise control policy.

Other policies or programs often suffer from inadequate funding. Thus the Occupational Safety and Health Administration (OSHA) can afford to inspect only a small fraction of the workplaces within its jurisdiction annually. Similarly, the Department of Housing and Urban Development has funds sufficient to provide rent subsidies only to approximately 20 percent of the eligible low-income families. When failure to adopt a budget in late 1995 caused a number of agencies to shut down operations, many functions, including most environmental enforcement, had to be suspended.

The budgetary process also gives the president and the Congress an opportunity to review the government's many policies and programs, to inquire into their administration, to appraise their value and effectiveness, and to exercise some influence on their conduct. Not all of the government's hundreds of programs are fully examined every year. But over a period of several years, most programs come under scrutiny. Some agencies, moreover, may come under sharp attack and experience cutbacks and restraints. In recent years, for example, conservatives in Congress have used the budget as a venue for attacking the activities of the National Endowment for the Arts (NEA). Charging that some of the projects funded by the Endowment are obscene or pornographic, they have sought to reduce funding for the NEA. Their actions have apparently made NEA officials more cautious in the funding of art projects.

In a given year, most agencies experience only limited or marginal changes in their funding. Still, budgeting is a vital part of the policy process that helps determine the impact and effectiveness of public policies. Having the potential to curb funding can be a powerful tool for congressional committee chairs.

Policy Implementation

policy implementation:

The process of carrying out public policy through governmental agencies and the courts.

Policy implementation refers to how public policies are carried out. Most public policies are implemented primarily by administrative agencies (see chapter 9). Some, however, are enforced in other ways. Product liability and product dating are two examples. Product liability laws are usually enforced by lawsuits initiated in the courts by injured consumers or their survivors. In contrast, state product-dating laws are implemented more by voluntary compliance when grocers take out-of-date products off their shelves or by consumers when they choose not to buy food products after the use dates stamped on them. The courts also get involved in implementation when they are called on to interpret the meaning of legislation, review the legality of agency rules and actions, and determine whether the administration of institutions such as prisons and mental hospitals conforms to legal and constitutional standards.

Administrative agencies may be authorized to use a number of techniques to implement the public policies within their jurisdictions. These techniques can be categorized as authority, incentive, capacity, and hortatory techniques, depending on the behavioral assumptions on which they are based.[11]

1. *Authoritative techniques* for policy implementation rest on the notion that people's actions must be directed or restrained by government in order to prevent or eliminate activities or products that are unsafe, unfair, evil, or immoral. Thus people who drive while intoxicated can, by law, have their driver's licenses revoked. On the federal level, consumer products must meet certain safety regulations and radio stations can have their broadcasting licenses revoked if they broadcast obscenities.

   Many governmental agencies have authority to issue rules and set standards to regulate such matters as meat and food processing, the discharge of pollutants into the environment, the healthfulness and safety of workplaces, and the safe operation of commercial airplanes. Compliance with these standards is determined by inspection and monitoring, and penalties may be imposed on people or companies that violate the rules and standards set forth in a particular policy. For example, under Title IX, the federal government can terminate funds to colleges or univer-

POLITICS NOW

Saving Social Security

In his 1999 State of the Union Address, President Bill Clinton presented a plan that would maintain the solvency of the Social Security trust fund until the year 2055. Estimates indicated that, in the absence of such a plan, the trust fund would begin depleting its assets in the year 2021 and that the fund would completely run out of money by the year 2032.

Demographics are clearly related to the anticipated deficiencies in the Social Security trust fund. At the inception of Social Security, life expectancy was considerably shorter than today, and therefore there were many more workers per retiree. For example, in 1950 there were sixteen workers for each Social Security beneficiary, in 1999 there were slightly more than three workers for every beneficiary, and by the second or third decade of the twenty-first century (when the baby boom generation is expected to retire) projections indicate that there will be only two people at work for each person receiving benefits. Unless changes are made, future generations of workers will be required to bear exceptionally heavy tax burdens to pay for the benefits of the large number of retirees.

Clinton's plan did not propose to change the tax rate placed on workers and employers (6.2 percent on wages below $72,600), nor would it alter the benefit structure. In essence, the Clinton proposal would use future budget surpluses to secure the Social Security trust fund. He proposed giving 62 percent of the budget surplus to the fund for a period of fifteen years. Roughly 25 percent of this money ($700 million) would be invested in the stock market; the rest of the money would be used to buy government bonds. One predicted consequence of bond purchases was that the national debt, as a proportion of the total economy, would fall from about 45 percent in 1999 to 10 percent in 2014, the lowest level since 1917.

Three advantages for Social Security were identified in the Clinton proposal. First, it was believed that the average return on stock investments over time would be higher than average returns on government bonds. It was estimated that over a period of 50 years (based upon long-term average returns on stock market investments), investing $700 million in stocks (instead of investing the money in government securities) would extend the life of the Social Security trust fund for five years. Second, all other things being equal, it was believed that paying down the national debt would lower interest rates and strengthen the overall economy. A stronger economy, in turn, would increase the pool of wages from which Social Security could draw. Third, interest payments on government bonds would be earmarked to the Social Security trust fund, enhancing its value.

Republicans criticized the Clinton plan on the basis of principle and economics, asserting that the president's proposal would give government officials too much control over private companies. They also argued that government control would lower returns on investments since political rather than financial factors would dominate decision making. Republicans were united on three basic points: (1) the government should not invest in the stock market, (2) the Social Security system should allow workers to personally invest some of the money they now pay in taxes, and (3) some of the surplus should be used to help Social Security but the rest of the surplus should be used for tax cuts. These points meshed with Republican preferences for individual rather than collective decision making.

Federal Reserve chairman Alan Greenspan also questioned the idea of investing government money in the stock market, asserting that it was tantamount to meddling in the free enterprise system. Furthermore, Greenspan stated that in the event deficits reappeared, Congress needed to explore other options, including an older retirement age, a reduction in the cost-of-living increase, and a less generous formula for calculating lifetime earnings.

David Rosenbaum, "Social Security: The Basics, With a Tally Sheet," www.nytimes.com.

Richard Stevenson, "Ideology Is Driving Battle Over the Competing Plans," www.nytimes.com.

Richard Stevenson, "Fed Chief Sees Hard Choices to Preserve Social Security," www.nytimes.com.

sities that discriminate against female students. This pattern of action is sometimes stigmatized as "command and control regulation" by its detractors, although in practice it often involves much education, bargaining, and persuasion in addition to the exercise of authority. In the case of Title IX, for instance, the Department of Education will try to negotiate with a school to bring it into compliance before funding is terminated.

2. *Incentive techniques* for policy implementation are based on the assumption that people are utility maximizers who act in their own best interest and must be provided with payoffs or financial inducements to get them to comply with public policies. Tax deductions may be given to encourage charitable giving, or grants awarded

to companies for the installation of pollution control equipment. Subsidies are given to farmers to make their production (or nonproduction) of wheat, cotton, and other commodities more profitable. Conversely, sanctions such as high taxes may be adopted to discourage the purchase and use of such products as tobacco or liquor, and pollution fees may be levied to reduce the discharge of pollutants by making this action more costly to businesses.

3. *Capacity techniques* provide people with information, education, training, or resources that will enable them to undertake desired activities. The assumption underlying the provision of these techniques is that people have the incentive or desire to do what is right but lack the capacity to act accordingly. Job training may enable able-bodied people to find employment, and accurate information on interest rates will enable people to protect themselves against interest-rate gouging. Financial assistance can help the needy acquire better housing and warmer winter coats and perhaps lead more comfortable lives.

4. *Hortatory techniques* encourage people to comply with policy by appealing to people's "better instincts" in an effort to get them to act in desired ways. In this instance the policy implementers assume that people decide how to act on the basis of their personal values and beliefs on matters such as right and wrong, equality, and justice. In the mid-1960s and late 1970s, the Johnson and Carter administrations, respectively, instituted voluntary (that is, there were no "punishments" for noncompliance) wage and price control programs to control inflation. Presidential appeals were made to individuals, labor unions, and businesses to avoid inflation-causing behavior. Hortatory techniques also include the use of highway signs that tell us "Don't Be a Litterbug" and "Don't Mess with Texas" to discourage littering. Slogans such as "Only You Can Prevent Forest Fires" are meant to encourage compliance with fire and safety regulations in national parks and forests.

The capacity of agencies to administer public policies effectively depends partly on whether the agencies are authorized to use appropriate implementation techniques. Many other factors also come into play, including the clarity and consistency of the policies' statutory mandates, adequacy of funding, political support, and the will and skill of agency personnel. There is no easy formula that will guarantee successful policy implementation; in practice, many policies only partially achieve their goals.

Policy Evaluation

policy evaluation:

The process of determining whether a course of action is achieving its intended goals.

Practitioners of **policy evaluation** are concerned with determining what a policy is actually accomplishing. They may also try to determine whether a policy is being fairly or efficiently administered. In the case of welfare programs, for instance, uncovering evidence of "waste, fraud, or abuse" in their administration has often been of more interest to official evaluators than whether the programs are meeting the needs of the poor.

Policy makers frequently make judgments on the effectiveness and necessity of particular policies and programs. These evaluations are often based mostly on anecdotal and fragmentary evidence rather than on solid facts and thorough analyses. Sometimes a program has been judged to be a good program simply because it is politically popular. In recent decades, however, policy evaluation has often taken a more rigorous, systematic, and objective form. Carefully designed studies or inquiries by social scientists and qualified investigators are undertaken to measure the societal impact of programs and to determine whether these programs are achieving their specified goals or objectives. The national executive departments and agencies often contain officials and units with responsibility for policy evaluation; so do state governments.

Policy evaluation may be conducted by a variety of players: congressional committees, through investigations and other oversight activities; presidential commissions; administrative agencies themselves; university researchers; private research organizations, such as the Brookings Institution and the American Enterprise Institute; and the General Accounting Office (GAO). The GAO, for example, originally created in 1921, is an important evaluator of public policies. Every year the GAO undertakes hundreds of studies of government agencies and programs either at the request of members of Congress or on its own initiative. The titles of three of its 1993 evaluations convey a notion of its work: *Pesticides: Pesticide Reregistration May Not Be Completed Until 2006; Energy Conservation: Appliance Standards and Labeling Programs Can Be Improved;* and *Federal Research: Super Collider Is Over Budget and Behind Schedule.* Subsequent congressional and agency actions may be guided by these studies.

Evaluation research and studies can stimulate attempts to modify or terminate policies and thus restart the policy process. Legislators and administrators may formulate and advocate amendments designed to correct problems or shortcomings in a policy. In 1988, for example, legislation was adopted to correct weaknesses in the enforcement of the Fair Housing Act of 1968, which banned discrimination in the sale or rental of most housing. However, some people may decide that the best alternative is simply to eliminate the policy. On occasion, policies are terminated; for example, through the Airline Deregulation Act of 1978, Congress eliminated the Civil Aeronautics Board and its program of economic regulation of commercial airlines. This action was taken on the assumption that competition in the marketplace would better protect the interests of airline users. On December 31, 1995, the Interstate Commerce Commission expired after more than a century of regulating railroads and other modes of transportation. The demise of programs is rare, however; more often, a troubled program is modified or allowed to limp along because it is doing something that some people strongly want done, even if the program is not doing it well.

SOCIAL WELFARE POLICIES TODAY

The remainder of this chapter focuses on three areas of **social welfare policy**—income security, health care, and public education—governmental programs designed to enhance or improve quality of life. Each area encompasses many complex policies and programs. While all levels of government (national, state, and local) are involved with the development and implementation of social welfare policies, we highlight the national government's role. The discussion in each of the three areas illustrates the expansion of national action as a consequence of dissatisfaction with what the state and local governments were doing. More recently, the tide has turned. President Clinton and Republican leaders have devised plans to give states greater control over public welfare and health care programs.

Income Security

Income security programs protect people against loss of income because of retirement, disability, unemployment, or death or absence of the family breadwinner. Although cases of total deprivation are now rare, many people are unable to provide a minimally decent standard of living for themselves and their families. They are poor in a relative if not an absolute sense. In 1998 a family of four with a gross yearly income of $13,656 or less was recognized as falling below the federal poverty line.

Income security programs fall into two general categories. *Social insurance* programs are **non-means-based programs** that provide cash assistance to qualified beneficiaries. **Means-tested programs** require that people must have incomes below specified levels to be eligible for benefits (see Table 17.1). Benefits of means-tested programs may come either as cash or in-kind benefits, such as food stamps.

In his book *Losing Ground*, policy analyst Charles Murray argues that, rather than helping the poor get on their feet, welfare programs encourage dependency.[12] He calls for the abolition of such programs. Even many who find Murray's prescription too harsh believe that the poor should do more to help themselves. Liberals, on the other hand, generally support income security programs; they believe that dependency results more from social causes than from personal shortcomings, such as laziness. But even liberals

Web Exploration
To learn about the research institutes and organizations that evaluate policies, go to www.awlonline.com/oconnor.

social welfare policy:
Governmental program designed to improve or enhance individual's quality of life.

non-means-based program:
Program such as Social Security where benefits are provided irrespective of the income or means of recipients.

means-tested program:
Income security program intended to assist those whose incomes fall below a designated level.

Table 17.1   Recipients of Social Insurance Programs

Program	Number of Recipients (Millions)	Percent of U.S. Population
Non-means-tested[*]		
Social Security (OASDI)	43.7	16.4
Medicare (hospital insurance)	37.3	14.0
Veterans' Benefits	2.7	1.0
State unemployment insurance	2.6	1.0
Means-tested		
Medicaid	36.1	13.6
Supplemental Security Income	6.6	2.5
Aid to Families with Dependent		
Children (AFDC)	13.4	5.1
Food Stamps	25.5	9.6
General Assistance	0.9	0.4

[*]"Means-tested" refers to the requirement of demonstrated financial need.

Note: OASDI and Supplemental Security Income numbers are as of December 1996, Medicare numbers are for 1995, Veterans' Benefits are as of September 1995, unemployment is an average for 1995, Medicaid numbers are for fiscal year 1996, AFDC numbers reflect average monthly numbers for 1995, Food Stamps reflect average numbers for 1996, General Assistance reflects average numbers for 1995.

SOURCE: Tables 3.C, 8.B, 9.F, 8.E, 9.G, 9.H1, 9.L1; *Social Security Bulletin, Annual Statistical Supplement,* 1997 (Washington, D.C.: U.S. Government Printing Office, 1997).

sometimes question the effectiveness of some income security programs and call for reforms that will help the poor become more self-sufficient.

Social Insurance: Non-Means-Based Programs.   Social insurance programs operate in a manner somewhat similar to private automobile or life insurance. Contributions are made by or on behalf of the prospective beneficiaries, their employers, or both. When a person becomes eligible for benefits, the monies are paid as a matter of right, regardless of how much wealth or unearned income (for example, from dividends and interest payments) the recipient has. (For Social Security, a limit is imposed on earned income. There is no means test.)

Old Age, Survivors, and Disability Insurance.   This program began as old age insurance, providing benefits only to retired workers. Its coverage was extended to survivors of covered workers in 1939 and to the permanently disabled in 1956. This is the program customarily called Social Security. It is not, as many people believe, a pension program that collects contributions from workers, invests them, and then returns them with interest to beneficiaries. Instead the current workers pay taxes that directly go toward providing benefits for retirees. A payroll tax of 7.65 percent on the first $62,700 of wages or salaries is paid by the employee and another 7.65 percent is paid by the employer into the Social Security trust fund. Nearly all employees and most of the self-employed (who pay a 15.3 percent tax) are now covered by Social Security. People earning less money pay a greater share of their income into the Social Security program than do workers earning more because earnings in excess of $62,700 are not subject to the payroll tax. The Social Security tax therefore is considered to be a regressive tax.

People are eligible to receive retirement benefits at age sixty-five. Individuals who opt to retire earlier, at age sixty-two, receive a reduced benefit. In the early 1990s, the average retired worker received about $700 a month. The maximum benefit in 1996 for a retired worker was $1,249 per month. An additional 50 percent was paid if the worker had a spouse. Social Security is the primary source of income for many retirees and

Web Exploration
To learn more about the most current Social Security benefits and statistics, go to
www.awlonline.com/oconnor.

keeps them from living in poverty. However, eligible people are entitled to Social Security benefits regardless of how much *unearned* income (for example, dividends and interest payments) they also receive. In 1996 there was a limit of $12,500 for persons aged sixty-five to sixty-nine, and $8,250 for those under the age of sixty-five on the annual *earned* income they can receive without a reduction in their benefits. A dollar of benefits is lost for every three dollars by which one exceeds that limit.

Expenditures for Social Security have greatly increased during the last couple of decades because the number of beneficiaries is growing, they are living longer, and benefit levels are rising. More than 40 million people, including some 3 million workers with disabilities, currently receive benefits. Social Security is by far the national government's largest entitlement program (see Figure 17.2).

■ The Great Depression, beginning in late 1929 and continuing throughout the 1930s, dramatically pointed out to average Americans the need for a broad social safety net and gave rise to a host of income, health, and finance legislation. (Photo courtesy: Corbis/Bettmann)

In the early 1980s, because of unstable economic conditions and a major increase in benefits, Social Security was in severe economic trouble. Benefits paid out were exceeding revenues, and the program's reserve fund was emptying, leading to fears that the programs would go broke. To solve this problem Democrats in Congress favored increasing Social Security taxes, while Republicans called for reduced benefits. Neither alternative drew much public support.

To lessen the political conflict surrounding the issue, President Ronald Reagan created the bipartisan National Commission on Social Security Reform. However, the commission was unable to reach agreement on a rescue plan. Consequently, in January 1983, a small group of White House officials, members of Congress, and private experts began negotiating a solution. After a few days of hard bargaining, they reached agreement on a bailout plan. Major components of the plan included higher Social Security taxes, reduced cost of living adjustments (COLAs) for retirement benefits, extension of Social Security coverage to all nonprofit organization employees and new federal workers, and taxation of the Social Security benefits of upper-income retirees. It was thought that this package would ensure the solvency of Social Security well into the twenty-first century.

The proposal was enacted into law in 1983 with minimal changes by Congress. As it turned out, the Social Security solvency program worked much better than expected in the short run. Annual revenues greatly exceeded benefit payments, thus swelling the size of the Social Security Trust Fund. In 1993 the fund had a $46.8 billion surplus. Despite this success it is expected to be insolvent by 2032 because the ratio of workers to retirees will decline as baby boomers hit retirement age (see Figure 17.2).[13] In anticipation of this problem, several members of Congress have called for a round of new reforms, including the removal of the Social Security Administration from the Department of Health and Human Services to make it an independent agency. (See Politics Now: Saving Social Security)

In 1998 Senator Daniel Patrick Moynihan of New York claimed that if the nation continued to treat the Social Security program as "the untouchable 'third rail' of American politics, the system could vanish."[14] For Moynihan, the threat to Social Security was real and he reminded citizens that Title IVA of the Social Security Act, Aid to Families with Dependent Children had recently been repealed, implying that it was not unthinkable to drastically alter the Social Security program.

In order to shore up Social Security, Moynihan proposed that workers should have the option of depositing up to 2 percent of their wages in a personal retirement account

Figure 17.2   Estimating Plunging Social Security Reserves

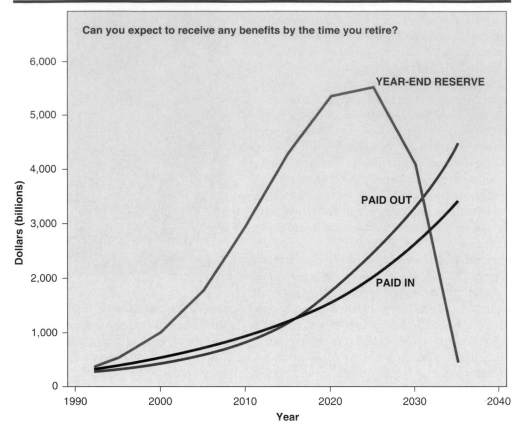

NOTE: The combined OASI and DI Trust Funds (Social Security) are estimated to become exhausted during 2035 under alternative II projections. For details see source.

SOURCE: U.S. Congress, House, House Committee on Ways and Means, "1992 Report of the Board of Trustees of the Federal Old-Age and Survivors Insurance and Disability Insurance Trust Funds," 102d Cong., 2d sess., April 2, 1992, 182.

which would complement but not replace the existing Social Security system. Senator Moynihan's plan also called for: an immediate payroll-tax cut from the current 12.4 percent to 10.4 percent; a 1 percentage point correction in cost-of-living adjustments for all indexed programs except Supplemental Security Income; an increase in the retirement age to sixty-eight by 2023, and to age seventy by 2073; taxing Social Security benefits to the same extent as private pensions; and extending Social Security coverage to newly hired employees in state and local positions.

Unemployment Insurance.   Financed by a payroll tax paid by employers, the unemployment insurance program pays benefits to covered workers who are unemployed through no fault of their own; for example, by being laid off during a recession. The Social Security Act provided that if a state set up a comparable program and levied a payroll tax for its support, most of the federal tax would be forgiven (not collected). The states were thus accorded a choice: either they could set up and administer an acceptable unemployment program, or they could let the national government handle the matter. Within a short time, all states had their own programs.

Unemployment insurance covers employers of four or more people, but not part-time or occasional workers. Benefits are paid to unemployed workers who have neither been fired nor quit their jobs and who are willing and able to accept suitable employment. State unemployment programs differ considerably in levels of benefits, length of benefit payment, and eligibility for benefits. In 1994 average weekly benefit payments, for example, ranged from $266 in Hawaii and $246 in New Jersey to $129 in Mississippi and $118 in Louisiana. The most generous programs exist in the northern industrial states, where labor unions are more powerful and influence the nature of these programs. Nationwide, only about half of the people counted as unemployed at any given time will be receiving benefits. (Figure 17.3 illustrates the variation among the states in unemployment rates.)

In recent years, during periods of economic slowdown, Congress has provided emergency unemployment benefits for long-term unemployed workers who have exhausted regular state-paid benefits. These emergency benefits are paid entirely by the national government and have extended the payment period from seven to twenty weeks, depending on the level of unemployment in each state.[15]

Social Insurance: Means-Tested Programs. Means-tested income security programs are intended to help the needy, that is, individuals or families whose incomes fall below specified levels, such as a percentage of the official poverty line. Included in this category are the Supplementary Security Income (SSI), Aid to Families with Dependent Children (AFDC), and Food Stamp programs (see Table 17.1).

■ "What a coincidence! My first Social Security check arrived along with my final student loan statement." (Copyright A. Bacall/Rothco Syndication. Reprinted with permission.)

Supplementary Security Income. This program began under the Social Security Act as a categorical grant-in-aid program to help the needy aged or blind. Financed jointly by the national and state governments from general revenues, the states played a major role in determining standards of eligibility and benefit levels. In 1950 Congress extended coverage to needy people who were permanently and totally disabled.

With the support of the Nixon administration, Congress reconfigured these programs into the Supplementary Security Income (SSI) programs in 1974. Primary funding for SSI is provided by the national government, which prescribes uniform benefit levels throughout the nation. To be eligible, beneficiaries can own only a limited amount of possessions. In 1997 monthly payments were about $360. The states may choose to supplement the federal benefits, and forty-eight states do. For years this program generated little controversy, as the modest benefits go to people who obviously cannot provide for themselves. In 1997 the federal government sent letters to immigrants who were not U.S. citizens informing them that they would be cut off from the Supplementary Security Income program. Changes in this program also impacted some children who were denied benefits as a consequence of tightened requirements for disability.

Aid to Families with Dependent Children (AFDC). In the early 1930s, nearly all states operating under the Social Security Act offered cash assistance to mothers (mostly widows) with dependent children. In 1950 Aid to Families with Dependent Children (AFDC) was broadened to include not only dependent children but also mothers themselves or other adults with whom dependent children were living.

Initially, AFDC was small because there were few unmarried mothers in 1935. The AFDC rolls have expanded greatly since 1960 because of the increasing numbers of children born to unwed mothers, the growing divorce rate, and the migration of poor people to cities, where they are more likely to apply for and be provided benefits. Now, most families covered by AFDC are headed by single mothers.

Figure 17.3 Low U.S. Unemployment Rates

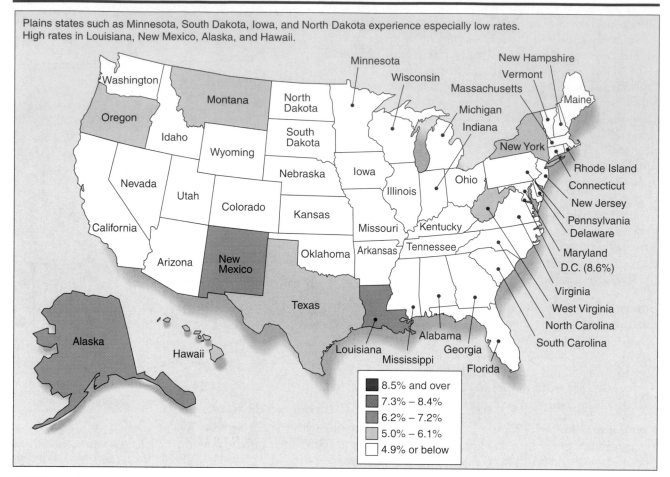

Plains states such as Minnesota, South Dakota, Iowa, and North Dakota experience especially low rates. High rates in Louisiana, New Mexico, Alaska, and Hawaii.

Legend:
- 8.5% and over
- 7.3% – 8.4%
- 6.2% – 7.2%
- 5.0% – 6.1%
- 4.9% or below

SOURCE: www.bls.gov/news.release/laus.t03.htm.

Because of its clientele, the AFDC program is the focus of much controversy and is frequently stigmatized as "welfare." Critics who point to the rising number of recipients claim that it encourages promiscuity and out-of-wedlock births and promotes dependency, which results in a permanent class of welfare families. Much effort has been expended by public officials to restrict the availability of aid, to ferret out fraud and abuse, and to hold down AFDC cost.

In 1988, with strong support from the National Governor's Association and the American Public Welfare Association, Congress passed legislation to reform AFDC. Titled the Family and Child Support Act, the law seeks to move people off welfare and into productive jobs. Each state must operate a Job Opportunities and Basic Skills (JOBS) program to provide education, training, and job experience for members of welfare families. Most adult welfare recipients are to be enrolled, with the states providing child care and other services necessary to permit participation. Funding for JOBS is shared by the national and state governments.

States are also required by the Family and Child Support Act to participate in the AFDC-UP program, which provides benefits for two-parent families in which the principal wage-earner is unemployed. A workfare provision included at the insistence of the Reagan administration requires one parent in a UP family to spend at least sixteen hours weekly in a work activity. Other provisions of the act call for stronger enforcement of

(Photo courtesy: Signe Wilken-
son/Cartoonists & Writers Syndicate.
Reprinted with permission.)

court orders for child support payments and greater efforts to establish paternity for children born out of wedlock.

The Family and Child Support Act represented significant reform of the welfare system. Because its provisions were phased in, it was not fully implemented until the early 1990s.[16] By early 1992, however, some 500,000 persons were participating in the act's education and training programs, a number that exceeded the required level of participation.[17] On the other hand, some states have difficulty providing welfare recipients with sufficient job and training opportunities.[18]

During the 1992 campaign, President Clinton pledged to "end welfare as we know it," and the Republican majority in the 104th Congress also moved to tackle the welfare problem. Sharply restricting access to AFDC was part of the Contract with America. To carry out this platform plank, congressional leaders sought to allow states greater latitude in providing welfare, thereby opening the way to end the entitlement status conferred by AFDC. Enactment of initial GOP proposals would have given states block grants and authority to determine eligibility standards although, with a few exceptions, recipients would not be able to collect payments for more than five years. Most teenage mothers would no longer be eligible for benefits and some bills would prohibit increasing assistance to families that had additional children while on welfare rolls. Copying from the welfare reforms advocated by Clinton, most adults on welfare would have to enroll in a job-training program within two years or find a job.

Reformers justify limiting the length of time that benefits can be collected as necessary to break the cycle of dependency from one generation to the next. They argue that by capping the benefits per family, they force welfare recipients to live in a world like that faced by workers who get no pay raise when they bring another child into the world. Senator Phil Gramm (R–Tex.), as a candidate for his party's presidential nomination in 1992, spoke against the status quo, calling AFDC "a system that subsidizes illegitimacy, which gives cash bonuses to people who have more and more children on welfare."[19]

Opponents warned that the victims of tougher standards will be blameless infants who face bleak futures even under the current program. Senator Edward M. Kennedy (D–Ma.) chided the GOP majority, claiming that "The Senate is on the brink of committing legislative child abuse."[20] Critics pointed out that proposed payments were so frugal that no rational mother would have children as a strategy to increase AFDC benefits. President Clinton, who found the Republican reforms too lacking in protections for the needy, vetoed the effort.

Then, in August 1996, President Clinton agreed to landmark legislation that swept away the New Deal covenant that guaranteed assistance to the poor. To secure the president's approval, Republicans backed away from turning the food stamp program into a block grant to the states and agreed to retain national standards for participating in the program. The nutrition program was changed, however, to exclude legal immigrants, the unemployed who do not have children at home, and convicted drug felons. Non-citizens were also cut off from the Supplemental Security Income program.

Presidential advisers divided sharply over whether the president should sign the legislation. President Clinton acknowledged that the bill was tougher than he would have preferred. It did, however, include some provisions that softened the blow. While states could tighten up the eligibility standards for welfare, they must continue to provide Medicaid for a year to families excluded from the program as a result of the new standards. Another provision promised to increase funding for child care facilities serving the poor.

The new bill abolished the Aid to Families with Dependent Children (AFDC) program, a program that had provided monthly cash benefits to millions of children. Consistent with anti-Washington sentiments of conservative politicians and the view that states should be able to experiment in order to forge workable social welfare policies, the AFDC program was replaced by a system of block grants. Significant features of the welfare plan included: (1) a requirement for single mothers with a child over five years of age to work within two years of receiving benefits; (2) a provision that unmarried mothers under the age of eighteen were required to live with an adult and attend school in order to receive welfare benefits; (3) a five-year lifetime limit for aid from block grants; (4) a requirement that mothers must provide information about a child's father in order to receive full welfare payments; (5) cutting off food stamps and Supplemental Security Income for legal immigrants; (6) cutting off cash welfare benefits and food stamps for convicted drug felons; and (7) limiting food stamps to three months in a three-year period for persons eighteen to fifty years old who are not raising children and not working.[21]

The welfare reform bill passed by an overwhelming margin once the president agreed to support it. Enactment allowed both the president and the Republican Congress to claim credit for reforming a policy area widely perceived by the public to be wasteful and ineffective. Moreover, by agreeing to this legislation, the president took away a campaign issue from 1996 GOP presidential nominee Bob Dole, who had hoped to castigate his Democratic opponent for failing to deliver on his 1992 pledge.

The welfare bill was hailed as the biggest shift in social policy since the Great Depression. It was criticized by liberals who wanted to protect the social safety net and praised by conservatives who believed that the welfare system inhibited initiative. The real debate over welfare policy revolved around contrasting views of its consequences. To some, welfare was simply a requirement for any modern, humane society. To others, welfare represented a mechanism that trapped people into a perpetual state of poverty and dependence. The results of this major overhaul are yet to be felt.

Earned Income Tax Credit Program (EITC).   Designed to help the working poor, this program was created in 1975 at the insistence of Senator Russell Long (D–La.). It helps the working poor by subsidizing their wages, and it also provides an incentive for people to go to work. Drawing extensive support from both Democrats and Republicans in Congress, the Earned Income Tax Credit is frequently described as being "pro-work and pro-family."

In 1997 the EITC provided an average credit of nearly $1,470 to almost 19 million workers and their families. For every dollar that a low-income worker earned up to a certain limit, he or she received between 7 cents and 40 cents as a tax credit. The intent

Web Exploration
For a progress report on welfare reform, go to www.awlonline.com/oconnor.

of the EITC was to enhance the value of working and encourage families to move from welfare to work.

Advocates of the EITC also claim that the program would enhance spending, which would in turn stimulate the economy. In addition to this stimulus, supporters of the EITC had two other objectives: (1) to increase work incentives among the welfare population, and (2) to refund indirectly part or all of the Social Security taxes paid by workers with low incomes. In theory, the EITC would serve to ease the regressive nature of the Social Security payroll tax.[22]

Food Stamp Program. The initial food stamp program (1939–43) was primarily an effort to expand domestic markets for farm commodities. Attempts to reestablish the program during the Eisenhower administration failed, but in 1961 a $381,000 pilot program began under the Kennedy administration. It was made permanent in 1964 and extended nationwide in 1974. Although strongly opposed by the Republicans in Congress, Democrats put together a majority coalition when urban members agreed to support a wheat and cotton price support program wanted by rural and Southern Democrats in return for their support of food stamps.

Initially, food stamp recipients had to pay cash for them, but this practice ceased in 1977. Benefiting poor and low-income families, the program has helped to combat hunger and reduce malnutrition. Food stamps went to more than 25.5 million beneficiaries in 1996 at a cost of $22.4 billion. The average participant received $73 worth of stamps per month. In 1995 families of four earning less than $1,642 per month qualified for food stamps.

Growth in the size of the food stamp program (in 1974 the cost of 12.9 million beneficiaries ran $2.8 billion) made this a target for Republican budget cutters. While 1995 House and Senate efforts differed on specifics, both sought to save more than $30 billion in projected food stamps costs over the seven years leading up to an anticipated balanced budget in 2002. Whether costs are reined in by capping appropriations, reducing benefits, or slowing cost-of-living increases, it appears likely that Republican-led efforts will reduce the high level of growth in this program.

The national government operates several other food programs for the needy. These programs include a special nutritional program for women, infants, and children (WIC); a school breakfast and lunch program; and an emergency food assistance program.

General Assistance. Some states and local governments, especially in the Northeast and Midwest, administer general assistance programs that assist poor people who are ineligible for AFDC or SSI. Persons who are physically able but not working may receive assistance, for instance. General assistance programs receive no support from the national government. Budgetary pressures have caused several states to cut back on their programs in recent years.

The Effectiveness of Income Security Programs. Many of the income security programs, including Social Security, Supplementary Security Income, and food stamps, are **entitlement programs.** That is, Congress sets eligibility criteria—such as age, income level, or unemployment—and those who meet the criteria are legally "entitled" to receive benefits. Moreover, unlike such programs as public housing, military construction, and space exploration, spending for entitlement programs is mandatory. Year after year, funds *must* be provided for them unless the laws creating the programs are changed. This feature of entitlement programs has made it quite difficult to control spending for them.

Poverty and economic dependency have not been eliminated by income security programs. Income security programs, however, have improved the lives of large numbers of people. Millions of elderly people in the United States would be living below the poverty line were it not for Social Security. Income security programs are basically alleviative rather than curative or remedial in their consequences. Poverty and economic

entitlement program:
Income security program to which all those meeting eligibility criteria are entitled.

dependency will not be eradicated so long as the conditions that give rise to them persist. There will probably always be people who are unable to provide adequately for themselves, whether because of old age, mental or physical disability, adverse economic conditions, or youth. A panoply of income security programs is a characteristic of all democratic industrial societies.

Health Care

Governments in the United States have long been active in the health field. Local governments began to establish public health departments in the first half of the nineteenth century and were followed by state health departments in the second half. Knowledge of the bacteriological causes of diseases and human ailments discovered in the late nineteenth and early twentieth centuries led to significant advances in improving public health. Public sanitation and clean water programs, pasteurization of milk, immunization programs, and other activities reduced greatly the incidence of infectious and communicable diseases. The increase in life expectancy at birth in the United States from forty-seven years in 1900 to seventy-five years in 1990 is mostly due to public health programs.

Beginning in 1798 with the establishment of the National Marine Service (NMS) for "the relief of sick and disabled seamen," which was the forerunner of the Public Health Service, the national government has provided health care for some segments of the population. Currently, many millions of people receive medical care through the medical branches of the armed forces, the hospitals and medical programs of the Department of Veterans Affairs, and the Indian Health Service. Billions of dollars are expended for the construction and operation of facilities and for the salaries of the doctors and other medical personnel making the government's medical business truly a big business.

Most medical research currently is financed by the national government, primarily through the National Institutes of Health (NIH). The National Cancer Institute, the National Heart, Lung, and Blood Institute, the National Institute of Allergy and Infectious Diseases, and the other NIH institutes and centers expend more than $10 billion annually on biomedical research. The research is conducted by NIH scientists and by scientists at universities, medical schools, and other research centers receiving NIH research grants.

The United States spends significant sums of money on public health, a larger proportion of its gross domestic product than most industrialized democracies. These proportions are shown in Table 17.2. Much of the money goes to the Medicare and Medicaid programs.

Medicare. **Medicare,** which covers persons receiving Social Security benefits, is administered by the Health Care Financing Administration in the Department of Health and Human Services. Medicare coverage has two components, Parts A and B. Benefits under Part A come to all Americans automatically at age sixty-five, when they qualify for Social Security. It covers hospitalization, some skilled nursing care, and home health services. Individuals have to pay about $700 in medical bills before they are eligible for Part A benefits. Medicare is financed by a

■ Activists rally at the State House in Boston, Massachusetts, in support of health care reform. (Photo courtesy: Marilyn Humphries/Impact Visuals)

payroll tax of 1.45 percent paid by both employees and employers on the total amount of one's wages or salary.

Part B, which is optional, covers payment for physicians' services, outpatient and diagnostic services, X-rays, and some other items not covered by Part A. Excluded from coverage are prescription drugs, eyeglasses, hearing aids, and dentures. This portion of the Medicare program is financed partly by monthly payments from beneficiaries and partly by general tax revenues. Almost all of the eligible people have opted for Part B coverage, which in 1996 cost $42.50 a month.

Medicare has become a costly program because people live longer, the elderly need more hospital and physicians' services, and medical care costs are rising rapidly. Attempts to limit or cap expenditures for the program have had only marginal effects. One attempt occurred in 1983, when Congress authorized use of the diagnosis related group (DRG) system, which pays a prescribed amount to a hospital for a given medical procedure or operation, regardless of the actual cost to the hospital. Previously, Medicare had compensated hospitals for "all reasonable costs." Hospitals responded by reducing the length of patient stays and otherwise economizing on medical care costs. They have also shifted the unreimbursed costs of Medicare patients that result from the application of the DRG system to privately insured patients, which increases the share of total medical costs paid by private insurance companies. Figure 17.4 shows the growth of Medicare expenditures between 1980 and 1996. Spending has grown exponentially in the Medicare program, partially fueled by larger numbers of enrollees. Spending increased from $37.5 billion in 1980 to $203.1 billion in 1996.

In 1989 the Congress turned its attention to the costs of physicians' services for Medicare patients. The Physician Payment Review Commission, which advises Congress on Medicare's physician reimbursement policies, recommended that payments to physicians be determined on the basis of the work involved in a given treatment plus geographical factors (whether service is provided in a large city or rural area, for instance) and other considerations.[23] Enacted into law by Congress, these physician-cost-control practices were put into effect in the mid-1990s.

Medicare does not cover long-term or catastrophic health care costs. Congress sought to remedy this situation in 1988 when, with the support of the Reagan administration, it passed the Catastrophic Health Care Act. This act provided elderly people with expanded hospital and physicians' benefits and limited nursing home and prescription drug coverage. These expenses were to be financed by a small monthly fee levied on all Medicare recipients and also by a tax paid by the more well-to-do among Medicare recipients. President Reagan had insisted that the elderly themselves had to pay for the program.

Many better-off elderly people quickly mobilized to protest the new law. Outraged elderly constituents bombarded members of Congress with letters, petitions, and telephone calls and accosted legislators at town meetings. Overwhelmed by this stampede of opposition from the wealthier elderly, Congress rushed to repeal the Catastrophic

Web Exploration
To learn more about the National Institutes of Health Funding and Scientific resources, go to www.awlonline.com/oconnor.

Medicare:

The federal program established in the Johnson administration that provides medical care to elderly Social Security recipients.

Table 17.2 Public Health Expenditures as a Percent of Gross Domestic Product, 1995, by Country

United States	6.6%	Germany	8.2%	New Zealand	5.4%
Australia	5.8%	Greece	4.4%	Norway	6.6%
Austria	5.9%	Iceland	6.9%	Portugal	5.0%
Belgium	7.0%	Ireland	5.1%	Spain	6.0%
Canada	6.9%	Italy	5.4%	Sweden	5.9%
Denmark	5.3%	Japan	5.7%	Switzerland	7.1%
Finland	5.8%	Luxembourg	6.5%	Turkey	2.6%
France	7.7%	Netherlands	6.8%	United Kingdom	5.9%

SOURCE: *Statistical Abstract of the United States 1997* (Washington, D.C.: U.S. Government Printing Office, 1997), 835.

Figure 17.4   Growth in Medicare Expenditures

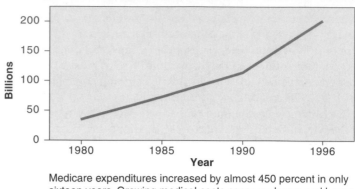

Medicare expenditures increased by almost 450 percent in only sixteen years. Growing medical costs consume larger and larger proportions of the federal budget.

SOURCE: *Statistical Abstract of the United States*, 1998 (Washingtion D.C.: Government Printing Office, 1998), 115.

Health Care Act in 1989. Although many of the wealthier elderly had private health insurance providing protection for themselves similar to that in the act, the poorer elderly were left with no protection.[24] Many people did not view this action as one of Congress's finer moments, but it demonstrated the power of well-funded, organized interest groups.

Medicaid:

An expansion of Medicare, this program subsidizes medical care for the poor.

Medicaid.   Enacted into law at the same time as Medicare, the **Medicaid** program provides comprehensive health care, including hospitalization, physicians service, prescription drugs, and long-term nursing home care (unlike Medicare) to all who qualify as needy under AFDC and SSI.

In 1986 Congress extended Medicaid coverage for pregnant women and children under age six in families with incomes of less than 133 percent of the official poverty level. The states were also accorded the option of extending coverage to all pregnant women and to all children under one year of age in families with incomes below 185 percent of the poverty level. By 1993 twenty-nine of the states had chosen to provide this coverage. In 1996 Medicaid served 36.1 million people at a cost of $121.7 billion. Most of the benefits paid out under the program went to the elderly. Nursing facility services, in-patient general hospital services, home health services, and prescription drugs represented major categories of spending within the Medicaid program.

Jointly financed by the national and state governments, the national government pays 50 to 79 percent of Medicaid costs on the basis of a formula based on average per capita income, which awards more financial support to poor than to wealthy states. Each state is responsible for the administration of its own program and sets specific standards of eligibility and benefit levels within the boundaries set by national guidelines. Nearly all needy people are covered by Medicaid in some states; in others only one-third or so of the needy are protected. Some states also award coverage to the "medically indigent," that is, to people who do not qualify for welfare but for whom large medical expenses would constitute a severe financial burden.

In fiscal year 1997, New York state spent $21.3 billion on more than 3 million Medicare recipients for an average of $6,771 per recipient. In contrast, California spent an average of $2,366 for its 4.9 million recipients, while states such as Arizona and Tennessee spent $466 and $2,074 respectively.[25]

While the average amount paid for by the states varies, the portion of state budgets going to Medicaid is similar—ever upward. From 1987 to 1994, the percentage of state budgets going to feed the insatiable Medicaid appetite almost doubled to 19.4 percent.[26]

Obviously, growth at that rate will drive other worthy projects out of state budgets and therefore cannot be sustained for long.

AIDS Funding. National government spending for AIDS research has expanded greatly, exceeding $1.5 billion in recent years. In the early 1980s, however, many public officials were disinclined to do much about AIDS, regarding it as a condition afflicting a narrow segment of the population. In part, at least, the decision to hold back on funding AIDS research reflected moralistic, antihomosexual sentiments.[27] Research scientists and advocates for the gay community, however, convinced policy makers that AIDS constituted a dire public health problem and that a major governmental response was required. Some critics now assert that too large a share (around one-sixth) of medical research dollars is being channeled into AIDS research, while others still believe that not enough is being done.

Funding for AIDS research produced notable benefits in the form of new drugs that were successful in slowing the spread of the human immunodeficiency virus (HIV). In the United States as well as other industrialized nations the AIDS death rate slowed dramatically. More HIV affected individuals were able to rise from their sick beds, return to active lives, and seek out protections against discrimination. In 1998 the Supreme Court ruled that the estimated 400,000 to 650,000 Americans infected with HIV but not sick enough to qualify as having AIDS were protected from discrimination by the 1990 Americans with Disabilities Act (ADA). Prior to the ruling in *Bragdon* v. *Abbott* the courts consistently held that the disability act only covered people with full-blown AIDS.

New Health Initiatives. The 1997 Balanced Budget Act (BBA) significantly influenced the nation's health care system. The BBA extended the life of the Medicare Trust Fund, strengthened preventive care, created more choice of plans, and permitted states to have greater flexibility in designing health programs. A major feature of the BBA provided funding for up to 5 million children in working families. Prior to the Balanced Budget Act, in 1996, the President and Congress enacted a bill, the Health Insurance Portability and Accountability Act (HIPAA), which helped people keep their health insurance when they changed jobs and limited the ability of insurers to deny coverage due to preexisting conditions.

The Clinton administration sought to improve preventive care, especially toward children and young adults. In another initiative, the Clinton administration attempted to curtail tobacco use by passing legislation that would discourage the marketing of cigarettes to young adults, provide the Food and Drug Administration (FDA) with authority to regulate tobacco products, reduce secondhand smoke, increase prices on cigarettes, and protect tobacco farmers. Clinton, however, was to learn that the political power of the tobacco industry (as the medical industry) was formidable and capable of frustrating legislation.

The Cost of Health Care. The costs of Medicare and Medicaid, which vastly exceed early estimates, have been major contributors to the ballooning costs of health care and the budget deficit. In 1997 national expenditures for Medicare were $190 billion and for Medicaid $101 billion, as indicated in Table 17.3. In 1997 the states collectively spent another $72 billion on Medicaid. If changes are not enacted, costs of these two programs will rise sharply over the next decade (see Figure 17.5).

Total health care expenditures in the United States have also soared in recent decades, growing from $27.1 billion in 1960 to $250.1 billion in 1980 to $884.2 billion in 1993.[28] A survey of business found that average health care benefits per employee stood at $3,821 in 1995.[29] In 1995 total health expenditures (public plus private) in the United States accounted for 14.2 percent of the nation's gross domestic product. This proportion of spending was higher than proportions found in other Western industrialized countries such as Germany (10.4 percent), France (9.8 percent), and the United

Web Exploration
For other health care policy initiatives and consumer health information, go to
www.awlonline.com/oconnor.

Table 17.3 The Rising Cost of Entitlement Programs: Government Spending on Automatic Pilot

The Biggest Entitlements in 1997 (in Billions)		Projections for 2003 (in Billions)	
1. Social Security	$366	1. Social Security	$472
2. Medicare	190	2. Medicare	256
3. Medicaid	101	3. Medicaid	143
4. Federal civilian retirement	42	4. Federal civilian retirement	54
5. Veterans' benefits and services	40	5. Veterans' benefits and services	47
6. Military retirement	30	6. Military retirement	36
7. Food stamps	28	7. Supplemental Security Income	32
8. Supplemental Security Income	27	8. Unemployment compensation	30
9. Earned Income Tax Credit	27	9. Food stamps	29
10. Unemployment compensation	21	10. Earned Income Tax Credit	27

SOURCE: *Budget of the United States Government for Fiscal Year 1999* (Washington, D.C.: U.S. Government Printing Office, 1998), 261–91.

Kingdom (6.9 percent). The government's health spending for Medicare, Medicaid, medical research, and other purposes amounted to 40 percent of total health spending.

A number of factors have contributed to the high and rising costs of health care. First, more people are living longer and are requiring costly and extensive care in their declining years. Second, the range and sophistication of diagnostic practices and therapeutic treatments, which are often quite expensive, have increased. Third, the expansion of private health insurance, along with Medicare and Medicaid, has reduced the direct costs of health care to most people and increased the demand for services. More people, in short, can afford needed care. They may also be less aware of the costs of care. Fourth, the costs of health care have also increased because of its higher quality and because labor costs have outpaced productivity in the provision of hospital care.[30] Fifth, U.S. medicine focuses less on preventing illnesses and more on curing them, which is more costly.

Public opinion polls indicate that the major cause of Americans' dissatisfaction with the health care system is its cost. While most people indicate that they are satisfied with the quality of health care services provided by physicians and hospitals, a substantial majority express dissatisfaction over the costs of health care.[31] There is, as a consequence, a strong belief in the need to improve the nation's health care system.

■ A crowded classroom at the Frey School in Edgewood, Texas. Lacking the funds to build new schools, many school districts face overcrowding. (Photo courtesy: Bob Daemmrich/ The Image Works)

Public Education

Historically, state and local governments funded public education. From the founding of the United States through the nineteenth century, local governments bore most of the responsibility. State government involvement has grown during the twentieth century and at present it is the largest source of public school funding. State education departments control curricula, textbook selection, graduation requirements, eligibility for extracurricular activity, and teacher and administrator certification. Nonetheless, local school districts, governed by appointed or elected boards, continue to control many daily operations of the public schools. The school districts are responsible, for example, for constructing and maintaining school build-

Figure 17.5   Rising Medicare and Medicaid Costs

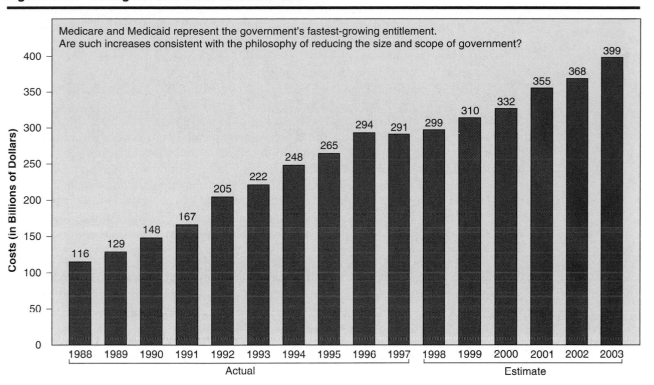

NOTE: Medicare and Medicaid are the government's fastest growing entitlements. Projected growth for the sum of both programs between 1997 and 2003 is 37 percent.

SOURCE: *United States Budget for Fiscal Year 1999* (Washington D.C.: US Government Printing Office, 1996), 261–291.

ings, hiring teachers, transporting students, operating school lunch programs, and designing educational programs. The balance between state and local funding responsibilities varies widely from state to state. In Hawaii, for example, local school systems bear little of the financial burden, while in New Hampshire localities pay the lion's share. Generally, the state shoulders more of the responsibility in the South, while the local school board has a greater voice in the Northeast.

The primary mission of American public schools once was to educate students, to provide them with reading, writing, and cognitive skills so that they could live more satisfactory and productive lives and become better citizens. This is still the primary mission of public schools, but they have also had many additional tasks loaded on them as parents and society increasingly view schools as a place to learn values and norms. As political scientist Thomas R. Dye portrays the situation:

> Today, schools are expected to do many things: resolve racial conflict and build an integrated society; inspire patriotism and good citizenship; provide values, aspirations, and a sense of identity to disadvantaged children; offer various forms of recreation and mass entertainment (football games, bands, choruses, majorettes, and the like); teach children to get along with others and adjust to group living; reduce the highway accident toll by teaching students to be good drivers; fight disease and ill health through physical education, health training, and even medical treatment; eliminate unemployment and poverty by teaching job skills; end malnutrition and hunger though school lunch and milk programs; produce scientists and other technicians to continue America's progress in science and technology; fight drug abuse and educate children about sex; and act as custodians for teenagers who have no interest in education but who are not permitted to work or roam the streets unsupervised.[32]

If there is some hyperbole in Dye's statement, most of it still rings true. Much is expected of the public schools, perhaps more than they can fairly be expected to deliver.

Many political issues are generated by the tasks that Dye lists, but we lack space here to examine them. Rather, we focus on another matter of fundamental importance—financing the public schools—especially as this involves federal financial aid to the public schools, a contentious political issue for many years.

In 1995 national, state, and local governments in the United States spent almost $287 billion on public (elementary and secondary) education (see Figure 17.6). Of this amount, 48 percent came from the state government, 45 percent from the local government, and 7 percent from the national government. There is much variation among states, and among school districts within states, on educational expenditures, as measured by spending on a per-student basis. Some states spend two or three times as much as other states according to this measure, but the proportion of funds supplied by each level of government remained the same in 1998.

Federal dollars are the smallest share of public school funding, but these dollars are still vital to school systems that are usually financially strapped and sometimes in dire need of additional revenue.

Federal Aid to Education.   The national government's participation in public education began with the Northwest Ordinance of 1787, which set aside one section of land in each township in the Northwest Territory (now the states of Ohio, Michigan, Indiana, Illinois, and Wisconsin) to support education.

In the two decades following World War II, the school-age population doubled. Classroom shortages became so severe that many urban schools operated on two shifts. At the same time technological knowledge was expanding rapidly, further challenging the adequacy of public education. Many people came to view federal financial assistance (more simply, federal aid) as a necessary part of the solution to the inadequacies of public education. Consequently, federal aid to education has been an item on the national policy agenda almost continually from the early 1950s.

Web Exploration
To learn about other educational policies, go to
www.awlonline.com/oconnor.

Figure 17.6   Sources of Public School Spending, 1995

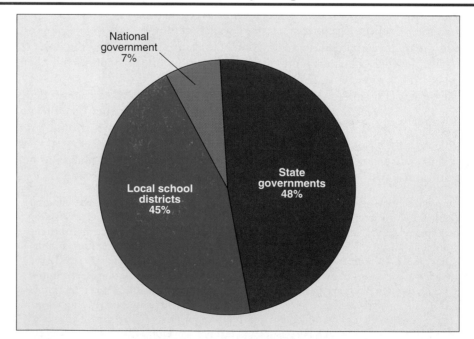

SOURCE: *Statistical Abstract of the United States*, 1998 (Washington D.C.: Government Printing Office, 1998).

In 1988 President George Bush and the nation's governors agreed to a program called Goals 2000 to improve the nation's schools. In 1994 Congress enacted the Goals 2000: Educate America Act to help all children achieve higher educational standards. For the first time, national standards were established (see Table 17.4: What High School Graduates Should Know), although compliance with these standards by the states is voluntary.

National legislation also sometimes imposes requirements on the public schools that are mandatory but not fully funded by the national government. An example is education for children with disabilities. Several million school-age children currently have disabilities that can range from mild physical disability to severe mental retardation. In the past many of the more handicapped children were excluded from the regular public school systems; some were enrolled in special state institutions, such as schools for the "deaf and dumb," as they were once called.

Beginning in the 1960s, the education of children with learning disabilities moved from the state to the national policy agenda. In 1975 Congress passed what is now called the Individuals with Disabilities Education Act to mandate that the states educate children with disabilities.[33] This law stated that every such child is entitled to a "free appropriate public education" provided through the regular public school system, which, for children with severe disabilities, can be a costly task. Because national funding covers only about one-fifth of the costs of educating children with disabilities, the states and local school districts bear the major costs of this unfunded federal mandate.

Inequality in Spending Among School Districts.   The revenues raised by most local school districts come almost entirely from property taxes. Because of substantial differences among districts in the value of the taxable property within their boundaries, some communities are able to generate much more revenue than others, even with lower tax rates. This variation is then reflected in spending disparities among schools when measured on a per-pupil basis. Within a given state some districts may spend more than twice as much per pupil as others. Many parents, educators, and public officials believe that such unequal spending results in significant disparities in the quality of the education that students receive.

Table 17.4 What High School Graduates Should Know

According to Goals 2000, some of the items high school graduates must know are:

Arts
- Know dances and dancers prior to the 20th century
- Identify historical sources of American musical theater
- Identify famous musicians

Math
- Know how to use a calculator
- Interpret tables, charts, graphs

Civics and Government
- Identify the Bill of Rights, Magna Carta, Declaration of Independence
- Explain the difference between a citizen and an alien
- Know the function of the U.N., NATO, Amnesty International

Geography
- Know how to use an atlas, a map, a globe
- Explain how war, famine, and disease play significant roles in human migration

Science
- Know what matter is
- Understand reproduction and heredity
- Define a cell

English
- Write clearly
- Know how to use a thesaurus

History
- Develop a position as to whether the Civil War was avoidable

SOURCE: From "The Multitudinous Rs," *Time,* April 4, 1994. © 1994 Time Inc. Reprinted by permission.

A challenge to inequality in education spending that arose out of the Texas public school system was decided in 1973 by the U.S. Supreme Court.[34] The five-justice majority ruled that the right to an education was not of such fundamental character that differences in per-pupil spending among districts violated the Fourteenth Amendment's equal protection clause. Although concerned about the inequalities in school funding, the Court held that this was a problem for the state governments to resolve.

Most conflicts concerning the quality of education that a state must provide have been solved through state administrative procedures. In some situations, however, disputes have ended up in the U.S. Supreme Court. In 1993, for example, the Court ruled that a school district must provide a sign language interpreter for a deaf child attending a Roman Catholic school.[35] In 1994, however, the U.S. Supreme Court ruled that a New York school district had gone too far to accommodate religious needs. The creation of a new school district to educate the special-needs children of the Satmar Hasidim, a strict Jewish sect, was found to violate the First Amendment's establishment clause.[36]

Since the early 1970s, school finance has been a priority item on the policy agendas in many states. In some states inequality in expenditures among districts has been held to violate the state constitution. In New Jersey, for instance, the state court practically forced the legislature to adopt an income tax to finance the schools.[37] School finance has been a volatile and vexing issue in many other states. Most people want good schools; paying for good schools, particularly if this requires raising taxes, stirs up much opposition in a time when "no new taxes" is a mantra with wide popular appeal.

Voucher Plans and Charter Schools.   Supporters of education vouchers believe that free market competition can improve the quality of American education by forcing underperforming schools to improve. In theory, if parents received vouchers for children to attend schools of their choice, the better-performing schools would grow and expand while the poorer performing schools close their doors. Free choice of schools would create greater efficiencies as parents "shop wisely" and send their children to better-performing schools. Opponents of vouchers argue that they would undermine public education.

In 1988 only a handful of active voucher programs could be found in Milwaukee and Cleveland, the nation's largest cities with the two largest programs serving low-income children. Cleveland's voucher program covered approximately 3,000 students, and Milwaukee's program served about 15,000 children. Both programs experienced moderate success as math and reading scores improved in each location. Partially in response to these successes, in 1998 voucher proposals were prepared for about half of the nation's fifty states. Voucher plans ran the gamut, ranging from bills introduced in state legislatures, to proposals for state constitutional amendments, to initiatives by local school boards.

Popular opinion, especially among minorities, seemed to fuel the drive for vouchers. Two national polls taken in 1997 found that blacks and Hispanics were more likely than whites to support these programs. In one survey, a Gallup poll found 72 percent of black respondents favored vouchers, compared to 48 percent of respondents in the general population. Another poll conducted by a Washington research group that specializes in black issues, the Joint Center for Political and Economic Research, discovered that support for vouchers ranged from 65 percent for Hispanic respondents to 56 percent for blacks and 47 percent for whites.[38] Support for vouchers also differed by age and income group. Vouchers received much stronger support among younger blacks (between the ages of twenty-six and thirty-five, 86 percent support) than blacks sixty-five years of age and older (19 percent support). Differences in support were also noted by income with 72 percent of poor blacks (income of $15,000 or less) supporting vouchers, compared to 50 percent support among blacks earning over $35,000.

Organized interests groups such as the National Association for the Advancement of Colored People (NAACP) and teachers unions, were in the forefront in their opposition to vouchers. Democratic politicians, in general, also voiced strong reservations about these plans. In 1998, President Clinton vetoed a bill that would have provided vouchers to selected poor children in Washington. It was the twenty-first veto of his presidency.[39]

In addition to vouchers, the concept of charter schools also gained support in the 1990s. Charter schools permit some institutions (those with charters) to operate beyond the reach of school boards. In theory, charter schools break the tight monopoly exercised by centralized school boards and allows students as well as parents to exercise choice. Costs for these schools are still paid by the taxpayer and charter schools are relatively free to choose what to teach, what to spend money on, and whom to hire.

In 1998, only six years after the first charter school was opened in Minneapolis, Minnesota, there were approximately 800 independent charter schools educating more than 165,000 students in twenty-three states and the District of Columbia. President Clinton endorsed the concept of charter schools calling for an increase in their number to 3,000 by the year 2000. Concerns about charter schools, however, were raised after a review of experiences in the states of Arizona and Michigan.

In 1998 Arizona and Michigan ran nearly half of the total number of charter schools in the nation. While a few charter schools in these states were noted for their exemplary performance, these high-performing schools were outnumbered by institutions perceived to be beset with problems as bad as, and in many cases worse than, traditional public schools. In Arizona private companies took advantage of the fact that the state only required high school students to attend school four hours a day. Companies ran two or three four-hour sessions in a day, often in rooms of commercial buildings without library facilities, and substituted self-paced computer instruction for regular teachers. Some courses only lasted a few weeks, typically there was no homework, and many students received credit for after school work. Private education companies typically targeted low achievers, truants, and discipline problems with promises of an easy route to graduation.[40]

Reducing Crime and Drug Abuse.   Education programs may have contributed to the dramatic reduction in crime rates in the 1990s. The Federal Bureau of Investigation (FBI) reported that the overall rate of serious crime had decreased by 4 percent in 1997, continuing six consecutive years of annual reductions in crime rates. In 1997 violent crimes declined by 5 percent, led by a 9 percent decrease in murders and robberies. The Northeast states led declines in virtually every category of crime. In New York City total number of crimes declined by 7 percent and murders declined by more than 20 percent. Experts attributed the declining crime rates to the aging of the population, tougher sentencing laws, a healthy economy, and increasing numbers of people in prison.[41] Three initiatives commonly cited for their contribution toward reducing crime include: shock incarceration programs, increased prison construction and the Drug Abuse Resistance Education (DARE) program.

President Clinton, Vice President Gore, and others endorsed the concept of boot camps or shock incarceration programs as an innovative method of instilling discipline, boosting self-esteem, teaching decency, and establishing respect for the law. In 1996 twenty-one states operated boot camps for juvenile offenders and thirty-seven states ran similar programs for adult inmates. The Louisiana program was typical of boot camp experiments. Participants in one Louisiana boot camp program engaged in activities such as daily work, drills, group counseling, drug education, and rehabilitation. After successful completion of this program, offenders were placed back into the community under intensive supervision. Restrictions were gradually relaxed if offenders successfully complied with mandates such as curfews and drug testing.

In 1999 it was reported that every week, on average, a new jail or prison was built to accommodate the influx of prisoners. Between 1985 and 1999 America's jail and prison population grew by 130 percent. Only Russia possessed a higher rate of incarceration, while the United States operated the largest penal system in terms of absolute numbers of inmates. Growth in the prison system correlated with declines in criminal behavior. This outcome was not cost free. Between 1989 and 1999 the federal corrections budget grew more than tenfold to about $4 billion. Spending to house inmates was also high at the state level. In California twenty-one prisons were opened between 1984 and 1999, accounting for a 60 percent increase in corrections spending. In addition to prison construction, corrections costs escalated as a consequence of more than doubling salaries

Web Exploration
To learn about recent policies aimed at curbing crime and drug abuse, go to
www.awlonline.com/oconnor.

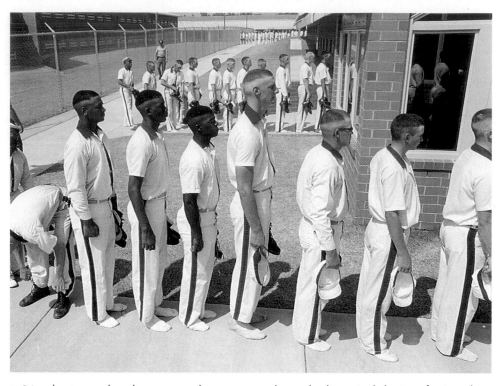

■ Prison boot camps have been promoted as a means to change the destructive behaviors of or juvenile offenders. Here prisoners at a camp in Forsyth, Georgia, line up outside their cellblocks (Photo courtesy: Mike Greenlar/Image Works)

for prison guards. While state corrections costs have escalated, other functional categories of spending did not fare as well. For example, there was virtually no growth in higher education spending during this time period. By 1999 salaries for prison guards in California surpassed that of first-year professors in the state's once acclaimed university system.[42]

Various programs have been implemented to reduce drug abuse among children and teens. The Drug Abuse Resistance Program, known as Project DARE, is probably the best known of these programs. Project DARE was developed in 1984 as a joint effort between the Los Angeles Police Department and the Los Angeles Unified School District. A seventeen-week curriculum was delivered primarily to fifth and sixth graders, with police officers conducting group discussions, engaging in role-playing, and encouraging parental involvement. By the early 1990s, the DARE program was hailed as a success and offered in over 450 cities throughout the United States.[43]

Recent studies on the effectiveness of the DARE program displayed mixed results. A 1998 study conducted by Dennis Rosenbaum, head of the Criminal Justice Department at the University of Illinois, found that participation in the DARE program did not produce declines in drug use. The study found that children in the suburbs who participated in DARE actually had higher levels of drug use than suburban kids who did not participate in the program. Other studies questioned the value of DARE; however, the program remained quite popular in the late 1990s. In 1997 DARE was being taught in 10,000 communities, with 250 and 300 new cities adopting the program annually.[44]

CONTINUITY and Change

Welfare Reform

It has been said that the poor will always be with us. History indicates that this appears to be true, yet in 1996 President Clinton sharply reduced the federal government's obligations to aid those in conditions of poverty. By eliminating the Aid to Families with Dependent Children (AFDC) program, Clinton effectively ended six decades of guaranteed help to the nation's poorest children. The new welfare legislation set time limits on payments to any family and gave states vast new powers to run their own welfare and work programs. This decentralization of power away from Washington represented the fulfillment of one of the most cherished goals of conservative politicians. For decades, leaders such as Richard Nixon, Ronald Reagan, and Newt Gingrich advocated that state and local governments should play a more prominent role in shaping and implementing public policy. Ironically, this goal was achieved on the watch of the Democratic president Bill Clinton.

The changes that were enacted in 1996 were profound from a number of perspectives. Perhaps most significant was the signal that it sent to recipients in regard to rights and privileges. The government appeared to be delivering the message that the welfare system would not serve as an open-ended right to the able-bodied poor. Welfare would be a privilege with eligibility to be determined by public sector officials. Changes in legislation ensured that the poor would have to make greater efforts to provide for themselves. The new goals of welfare would be to move recipients off the rolls and assist them in finding gainful employment. This in turn would reinforce the value of work and better enable the poor to achieve upward mobility.

By 1999 welfare reform was generally hailed as a success in that the numbers of recipients had declined markedly. Explanations for the decline in welfare rolls varied. Some analysts attributed the declining rolls to the robust economy and abundance of jobs for low-skilled workers. Others claimed that tougher monitoring of the program induced those who were not completely eligible to voluntarily drop out of the program. This standard of success (lower enrollments), however, was not universally embraced. A number of critics claimed that while the welfare rolls were declining, former recipients did not markedly improve their economic standing even though they were able to secure low-wage, full-time employment.

A number of questions remain in regard to welfare reform. What would happen to the poor if the economy goes into a recession? How large a safety net should be established? Who should qualify for such a safety net? What should be the overall responsibility of the government toward the poor? At what juncture could it be said that the government was not doing enough or doing too much in their efforts to assist the poor? Could state and local authorities address the issues of poverty in a more effective manner than the national government?

1. In what manner might the 1996 changes in welfare legislation prove to be beneficial to the nation as a whole? In what manner may the changes prove to be detrimental?
2. How might changes in welfare legislation alter incentives and the distribution of wealth in the nation?

Cast Your Vote. Is welfare reform good for America? To cast your vote, go to www.awlonline.com/oconnor.

SUMMARY

This chapter examined the policy-making process and social welfare policies. To that end, we made the following points:

1. THE ROOTS OF SOCIAL WELFARE POLICY

The origins of social welfare policy can be traced back to early initiatives in the nation's history. Only after the Great Depression, however, was a public-sector role in the delivery of social services broadly accepted. Programs initiated in the Great Depression became a model for greater public-sector responsibilities in the area of social welfare.

2. THE POLICY-MAKING PROCESS

The policy-making process can be viewed as a sequence of functional activities beginning with the identification and definition of public problems. Once identified, problems must get on the governmental agenda. Other stages of the process include policy formulation, policy adoption, budgeting for policies, policy implementation, and the evaluation of policy.

3. SOCIAL WELFARE POLICIES TODAY

Governments at all levels are involved in the policy process. The social welfare policies highlighted here are education, income security, and national health.

4. INCOME SECURITY

Income security programs to relieve economic dependency and poverty were mostly handled by state and local governments, albeit in minimal fashion, through the nineteenth century. Most income security programs generally take two forms: non-means-based programs and means-tested programs, which means that all people who meet eligibility criteria are automatically entitled to receive benefits.

5. MEDICAL CARE

Governments in the United States have a long history of involvement in the health of Americans. Most state and local governments have health departments, and the U.S. government has several public health and medical research divisions. Medicare and Medicaid are the two most prominent national programs. As the cost of health care has risen, however, new demands have been made to restrain the rate of growth in costs.

6. PUBLIC EDUCATION

Public education was the province of state and local governments through the nineteenth century. Through a variety of federal laws, Congress has attempted to improve educational standards, especially for disadvantaged students and also for people with disabilities. Today the national government provides a modest but vital share of the financing for public schools.

KEY TERMS

agenda, p. 618
agenda setting, p. 619
entitlement program,
p. 635
governmental (institu-
tional) agenda, p. 619
Medicaid, p. 638
Medicare, p. 637

means-tested program,
p. 627
non-means-based pro-
grams, p. 627
policy adoption, p. 623
policy evaluation, p. 623
policy formulation, p. 621

policy implementation,
p. 624
public policy, p. 615
Social Security Act, p. 613
social welfare policy,
p. 627
systemic agenda, p. 618

SELECTED READINGS

Aaron, Henry, ed. *The Problem That Won't Go Away: Reforming U.S. Health Care Financing.* Washington, DC: Brookings Institution, 1996.

Bierlein, Louann. *Controversial Issues in Education Policy.* Newbury Park, CA: Sage, 1993.

Chubb, John, and Terry Moe. *Politics, Markets and America's Schools.* Washington, DC: Brookings Institution, 1990.

Derthick, Martha. *Agency Under Stress: The Social Security Administration in American Government.* Washington, DC Brookings Institution, 1990.

Handler, Joel. *The Poverty of Welfare Reform.* New Haven, CT: Yale University Press, 1995.

Isaacs, Stephen, and James Knickman, eds. *To Improve Health and Health Care 1998–1999.* San Francisco: Jossey-Bass, 1998.

Lindbloom, Charles E., and Edward J. Woodhouse. *The Policy-Making Process,* 3d ed. Englewood Cliffs, NJ: Prentice Hall, 1993.

Mann, Thomas, and Norman Ornstein, eds. *Intensive Care: How Congress Shapes Health Policy.* Washington, DC: American Enterprise Institute and Brookings Institution, 1995.

Marmor, Theodore. *Understanding Health Care Reform.* New Haven, CT.: Yale University Press, 1994.

Mueller, Keith. *Health Care Policy in the United States.* Lincoln: University of Nebraska Press, 1993.

Norris, Donald F., and Lyke Thompson, eds. *The Politics of Welfare Reform.* Thousand Oaks, CA: Sage, 1995.

Olaskay, Marvin. *The Tragedy of American Compassion.* Washington, DC: Regnery Gateway, 1992.

Rushefsky, Mark, and Kant Patel. *Politics, Power and Policy Making: The Case of Health Care Reform in the 1990s.* Armonk, NY: M.E. Sharpe, 1998.

Sharp, Elaine. *The Dilemma of Drug Policy in the United States.* New York: Harper Collins, 1994.

Shilts, Randy. *And the Band Played On.* New York: St. Martin's Press, 1987.

Skocpol, Theda. *Social Policy in the United States: Future Possibilities in Historical Perspective.* Princeton, NJ: Princeton University Press, 1995.

Smith, David G. *Paying for Medicare: The Politics of Reform.* Chicago: Aldine, 1992.

Thompson, Frank, and John DiIulio, Jr. *Medicaid and Devolution: A View from the States.* Washington, DC: Brookings Institution Press, 1998.

Van Horn, Carl E., Donald C. Baumer, and William T. Gormley, Jr. *Politics and Public Policy,* 2d ed. Washington, DC: CQ Press, 1992.

Wilsford, David. *Doctors and the State: The Politics of Health Care in France and in the United States.* Durham, NC: Duke University Press, 1991.

NOTES

1. Lizette Alvarez, "In New Retreat, Senate Restores Food Stamps for Legal Immigrants," *The New York Times* (May 13, 1998): A1; Timothy Egan, "In Idaho, the Poor Fear They Will Go the Way of State's Democrats," *The New York Times* (April 16, 1998): A1, A12.

2. Paul Starr, *The Social Transformation of American Medicine* (New York: Basic Books, 1982), 282.

3. Alisa J. Rubin, "Parties Square Off Over Student Loans," *Congressional Quarterly Weekly Report* 35 (May 20, 1995): 1401.

4. James E. Anderson, *Public Policymaking: An Introduction*, 2d ed. (Boston: Houghton Mifflin, 1994), 5. This discussion draws on Anderson's study.

5. Roger W. Cobb and Charles D. Elder, *Participation in American Politics: The Dynamics of Agenda-Building*, 2d ed. (Baltimore: Johns Hopkins University Press, 1983), chapter 5.

6. Cobb and Elder, *Participation in American Politics*, 85.

7. Charles O. Jones, ed., *The Reagan Legacy: Promise and Performance* (Chatham, NJ: Chatham House, 1988). The essays in this volume examine several aspects of the Reagan administration.

8. Charles O. Jones, *An Introduction to the Study of Public Policy*, 3d ed. (Monterey, CA: Brooks/Cole, 1984), 87–89.

9. *Texas* v. *Johnson*, 492 U.S. 397 (1989).

10. *U.S.* v. *Eichman*, 496 U.S. 310 (1990).

11. This discussion draws on Anne Schneider and Helen Ingram, "Behavioral Assumptions of Policy Tools," *Journal of Politics*, 52 (May 1990): 510–29.

12. Charles Murray, *Losing Ground: American Social Policy, 1950–1980* (New York: Basic Books, 1984).

13. *Bondweek* (April 25, 1994), NEXIS.

14. Daniel Patrick Moynihan, "How to Preserve the Safety Net," *U.S. News & World Report* (April 20, 1998): 25.

15. *Congressional Quarterly Weekly Report* 51 (November 27, 1993): 3276.

16. *BNA Daily Labor Report* (March 16, 1994).

17. *Congressional Quarterly Weekly Report* 50 (March 28, 1992): 809–10.

18. *The New York Times* (May 5, 1993): C23.

19. Jeffrey L. Katz, "Uneasy Compromise Reached on Welfare Overhaul," *Congressional Quarterly Weekly Report* 53 (September 16, 1995): 2807.

20. Jeffrey L. Katz, "Senate Overhaul Plan Provides Road Map for Compromise," *Congressional Quarterly Weekly Report* 53 (September 23, 1995): 2911.

21. Steven G. Koven, Mack C. Shelley II, and Bert E. Swanson, *American Public Policy: The Contemporary Agenda* (Boston: Houghton Mifflin Company, 1998), 271.

22. Colin Campbell and William Pierce, *The Earned Income Credit* (Washington, D.C.: American Enterprise Institute, 1980).

23. *Congressional Quarterly Weekly Report* 47 (February 25, 1989): 588–89.

24. David Wilsford, *Doctors and the State: The Politics of Health Care in France and the United States* (Durham, NC: Duke University Press, 1991), 189–93.

25. Social Security Bulletin, *Annual Statistical Supplement, 1998* (Washington, D.C.: Government Printing Office, 1998).

26. Colette Fraley, "Republicans Are Standing Firm on Giving Medicaid to States," *Congressional Quarterly Weekly Report* 53 (September 23, 1995): 2901.

27. See Randy Shilts, *And the Band Played On* (New York: St. Martin's Press, 1987).

28. *Statistical Abstract of the United States, 1993* (Washington, D.C.: U.S. Government Printing Office, 1993), 92; and *The New York Times* (January 5, 1993): 1.

29. Andy Miller, "Health Benefits Cost Employees Just 2.1% More in '95 Survey Says," *Atlanta Journal* (January 30, 1996): D3.

30. Henry J. Aaron, *Serious and Unstable Condition: Financing America's Health Care* (Washington, D.C.: Brookings Institution, 1991), chapter 2.

31. Marilyn Werber Serafina, "Medicrunch," *National Journal* 27 (July 29, 1995): 1937.

32. Thomas R. Dye, *Politics in States and Communities*, 7th ed. (Englewood Cliffs, NJ: Prentice Hall, 1991), 411.

33. Erwin L. Levine and Elizabeth M. Wexler, *PL94-142: An Act of Congress* (New York: Macmillan, 1981).

34. *San Antonio Independent School District* v. *Rodriguez,* 411 U.S. 1 (1973).

35. *Zobrest* v. *Catalina Foothills School District,* 113 S. Ct. 2462 (1993).

36. *Board of Education of Kiriass Joel Village School District* v. *Grumet,* 114 S. Ct. 2481 (1994).

37. John J. Harrigan, *Policy and Politics in States and Communities,* 3d ed. (Glenview IL: Scott, Foresman, 1988), 300–1.

38. James Brooke, "Minorities Flock to Cause of Vouchers for Schools," *The New York Times* (December 27, 1997): A1.

39. *The New York Times* (May 21, 1998): A20.

40. Thomas Toch, "The New Education Bazaar," *U.S. News & World Report* (April 27, 1998): 35–46.

41. John Cushman Jr. "Serious Crime in U.S. Fell in 1997 for a 6th Year," *The New York Times* (May 18, 1998): A15.

42. Timothy Egan, "The War on Drugs Retreats, Still Taking Prisoners," www.nytimes.com.

43. Koven, Shelly, and Swanson, *American Public Policy,* 289–90.

44. www.ask.com.

(Photo courtesy: Adam Nadel/AP/Wide World Photos)

18

Economic Policy

- **The Roots of Government Intervention in the Economy**
- **Stabilizing the Economy**
- **The Economics of Regulating Environmental Pollution**

One image of the American economy of the 1990s is that of a rising tide that could not lift all boats. Some would believe that all Americans were prospering under the conditions of a booming stock market, low unemployment, and low inflation. Unfortunately, this was not the case. Between 1989 and 1996, earnings of the bottom 80 percent of the workforce flattened or declined while incomes of the rest rose substantially.[1] This pattern of a growing disparity in income was not new. In the early 1980s, earnings inequality had increased sharply. This pattern of income inequality, however, tapered off in the late 1980s only to reaccelerate in the 1990s. Increasingly, Americans operated in divergent economic universes.

To some Americans, economic conditions were never better. The Dow Jones average crossed the 11,000 mark in early 1999, rising more than 6,000 points since 1992. Corporate profits were robust and the number of millionaires as well as billionaires surged. Between 1980 and 1992, the average income of the top 1 percent of U.S. taxpayers rose 215 percent, America's wealthiest 1 percent (a group which controlled 21 percent of the nation's wealth in 1949) controlled 40 percent of the wealth in the 1990s. The wealthiest 10 percent of Americans controlled about two-thirds of the nation's wealth. To other Americans, however, times were not as rosy. Middle-income white-collar workers saw their jobs being downsized; relatively well paid blue-collar workers witnessed their jobs being eliminated as production moved to other nations where labor costs were significantly lower. Families at the middle and lower income levels witnessed the purchasing power of their incomes decline.

Various theories were presented in an effort to explain the growing disparities in income and wealth. For example, journalist Patrick Buchanan believes that America is fast becoming two nations with a new class of Americans (bankers, lawyers, diplomats, investors, lobbyists, academics, journalists, executives, professionals, high-tech entrepreneurs) prospering beyond their dreams, while another group of Americans ("sunset" industry workers producing goods such as cameras, shoes, radios, TVs, steel, autos, machine tools, and textiles) is being left behind. Jobs in these industries were increasingly locating in nations where workers were paid a fraction of their American counterparts.[2] Others discussed the political implications of growing disparities. For example, University of Texas economist James Galbraith claimed that the pay gap between good and bad jobs could undermine the sense of America as a nation of equals, threaten social solidarity, decrease stability, and ultimately transform the United States from a middle-class democracy into something more closely resembling an authoritarian quasi-democracy with an overclass, an underclass, and a hidden politics driven by money.[3]

The government and economy of the United States have always been interconnected. Traditionally, economic policies have been formulated with pragmatic goals in mind, such as assuring steady growth, low unemployment, decent wages, adequate incentives, and price stability. Government activities in the areas of ensuring order, protecting private property, enforcing contracts, providing a stable monetary system, maintaining a social safety net, granting corporate charters, and issuing patents all have contributed to the growth and vibrancy of the American economy. This economy is not only associated with great individual wealth but also with the sustenance of a large middle class. The size of this middle class of earners may be diminishing, yet in comparison to other nations it is still significant and contributes to the political stability of the United States. As we move into the twenty-first century, the creation of public policies that either enlarge or erode such an economic class will remain an important subject of controversy.

In this chapter, we deal somewhat selectively with public economic policies. In total, the chapter highlights the growth and impact of government intervention in the economy.

■ First, we will take a historical look at some of the major developments in *government intervention in the economy*—the kinds of interventions feared by Anti-Federalists.
■ Second, we will examine the government's role in *stabilizing the economy*, sometimes called "macroeconomic regulation."
■ Third, we will look at *regulation to control environmental pollution*, an important area of microeconomic regulation.
■ Fourth, we will look ahead at *ongoing proposals for balancing the federal budget.*

Web Exploration
To learn about the government bureau for economic analysis, go to www.awlonline.com/oconnor.

THE ROOTS OF GOVERNMENT INTERVENTION IN THE ECONOMY

During our nation's first century, most economic regulation was undertaken by states. The national government defined its role narrowly, although it did collect tariffs, fund public improvements, and regulate interstate commerce. Only with the perception that problems had outpaced the ability of states to provide adequate controls did Congress become active in setting national standards.

The Nineteenth Century

Although the U.S. economic system is a mixed free-enterprise system characterized by the private ownership of property, private enterprise, and marketplace competition, governments in the United States have always been deeply involved in the economy. The national government has long played an important role in fostering economic development through its tax, tariff, public lands disposal, and public works policies, and also through the creation of a national bank (see chapter 3). For much of the nineteenth century, however, national regulatory programs were few and were restricted to such topics as steamboat inspection and the regulation of trade with the Native American tribes.

The state governments, in comparison, were quite active in promoting and regulating private economic activity. They constructed such public works as the Erie Canal, built roads, and subsidized railroads to encourage trade within and among the states; they also carried on many licensing, inspection, and regulatory programs.

The experience of Pennsylvania is a case in point. Pennsylvania regulated such matters as creditor-debtor relations, labor relations, liquor traffic, and banks and insurance company activities. Inspection programs to guarantee the quality of products covered "such articles as flour, fish, beef, pork, hogslard, flaxseed, butter, biscuits, harness and leather, tobacco, shingles, potash and pearlash, staves, heading and lumber, ground black-oak bark, pickled fish, spiritous liquors, and gunpowder." Licenses were required for "innkeepers, peddlers, retailers of foreign goods, liquor merchants, brokers of vari-

ous kinds, wharfage pilots, and auction-
eers."[4] On the whole, the state governments
were capable of dealing adequately with the
small-scale and mostly agrarian economy of
early nineteenth-century America.

Following the Civil War, however, the
United States entered a period of rapid
economic growth. The rise of industrial
capitalism brought about extensive industrialization and the creation of large-scale
manufacturing enterprises. Many people
began working in factories for wages and
crowded into large cities. New problems
resulted from industrialization—industrial
accidents and disease, labor-management
conflict, unemployment, and the emergence of huge businesses that could exploit
workers and consumers. Another problem
was the loss of income by people because
of business cycles, which became more

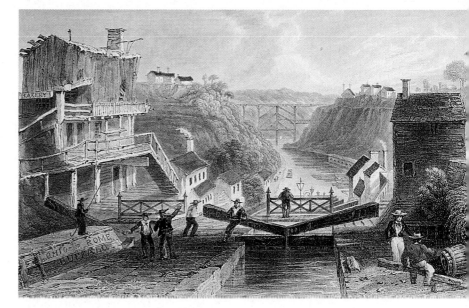

■ Public works projects such as the building of the Erie Canal spurred settlement and building throughout New York State. (Photo courtesy: Corbis/Bettmann)

severe in the new industrial society. **Business cycles** involve fluctuations between
growth and recession, or periods of "boom and bust," and seem an inherent part of
modern capitalist economies. During recessions many people lose their jobs, and a
low or even negative growth rate afflicts the economy.

Many people, disturbed by the problems resulting from industrialization, turned
to government for help. Because the states, with their limited jurisdictions, appeared
inadequate to cope with industrial problems, the national government was called on
to control these new forces. Businesses and conservatives, who had welcomed
national action to aid economic development in the early decades of the nineteenth
century, now proclaimed their faith in *laissez-faire*. Based on Adam Smith's *The
Wealth of Nations* (published in 1776), the doctrine of *laissez-faire* holds that governmental regulation of the economy is wrong and that the role of government
should be limited to the maintenance of order and justice, the conduct of foreign
affairs, and the provision of necessary public works such as roads or lighthouses,
which are not profitable for private persons to provide. Beyond that, individuals
should be left free to pursue their self-interest. In so doing, Smith held, people would
be guided by an "unseen hand" to promote the public welfare; that is, to provide consumers with a sufficient quantity of goods at reasonable prices. Competition and the
laws of supply and demand would control their behavior and ensure that self-interest did not get out of hand.

Although opposed to regulation of their activities, businesses did not shun other
forms of governmental intervention in the economy. They strongly supported tariffs
that provided protection from foreign competitors. Other favored policies included the
giveaway of public lands, subsidies for railroad construction, and the use of armed force
to put down strikes. Essentially, what businesses and their supporters wanted, and what
they thought of as *laissez-faire*, was an economic system and a set of governmental policies that would be congenial to the amassing of business profits.[5]

In time, because of pressures from small businesses, reformers in the cities, and the
Grangers and other powerful agrarian protest groups in the Midwest, the national government was impelled to action. In 1887, following nearly two decades of agitation,
Congress adopted the Interstate Commerce Act to regulate the railroads. The act, to
be enforced by the new Interstate Commerce Commission (ICC), required that railroad rates should be "just and reasonable."[6] The act also prohibited such practices as
pooling (rate agreements), rate discrimination, and charging more for a short haul than
for a long haul of goods.

business cycles:

Fluctuation between expansion and recession that is a part of modern capitalist economies.

laissez-faire:

A French term literally meaning "to allow to do, to leave alone." It is a hands-off governmental policy that is based on the belief that governmental regulation of the economy is wrong.

Web Exploration
To compare various busi-
ness cycle indicators, go to
www.awlonline.com/oconnor.

Three years later Congress dealt with the problem of "trusts," the name given to large-scale, monopolistic businesses that dominated many areas of production, including oil, sugar, whiskey, salt, cordage, and meatpacking. The Sherman Antitrust Act of 1890 is simple in its terms. Section 1 prohibits all restraints of trade, and section 2 prohibits all monopolization or attempts to monopolize. (Restraint of trade includes price-fixing, bid-rigging, and market allocation agreements; monopolization involves domination of a market by one company or a few companies.) The act was to be enforced by the Antitrust Division of the Department of Justice, which was empowered to sue violators in the federal courts. The Interstate Commerce Act and the Sherman Antitrust Act constitute the nineteenth- and early twentieth-century response of the national government to the new industrialization.

A modern manifestation of the Antitrust Act is found in the Department of Justice's lawsuit against the computer software company Microsoft, which began in October 1998. Among the competing corporations testifying against Microsoft were Intel, IBM Netscape Communications, America Online, Sun Microsystems, and Apple Computer. These companies portrayed the Microsoft corporation as a bullying monopolist. The government charged that Microsoft was guilty of illegally using its market power to impose restrictive contracts, engage in predatory pricing, stifle competition, and thwart the challenge that Internet software posed to the market position of Microsoft's Windows operating system. Attorneys general from nineteen states joined in the action of the federal government. The attorneys general stated that, should they win the case, they would not be satisfied with any remedy other than revamping the structure of the company. The court's antitrust remedies fell into two broad categories: conduct relief and structural relief. Conduct relief would limit Microsoft's ability to engage in anticompetitive activities. Structural relief, on the other hand, would mean breaking up the company into various units.[7]

Another area that turned to government intervention in the economy was agriculture. Agriculture was the largest sector of the economy throughout the nineteenth century. But as it shifted from subsistence farming to production for the market, farmers became more dependent on a vast system of distribution and exchange for their liveli-

THE BOSSES OF THE SENATE.

■ Here, a political cartoonist depicts how the U.S. government is perceived by some as being dominated by various trusts. (Photo courtesy: Corbis/Bettmann)

hoods. As this change occurred, and notwithstanding their storied individualism, farmers turned successfully to the national government for aid to improve their economic situation. The year 1862 was notably good for agriculture: It saw the establishment of the Department of Agriculture, which gained Cabinet status in 1889; the adoption of the Homestead Act, which gave 160 acres of public land in the West free to people willing to live on the land and improve it; and passage of the Morrill Land Grant Act, which subsidized the establishment of state colleges ("land grant schools") that offered instruction in the "agricultural and mechanical arts" (see chapter 3). Further intervention occurred in 1887, when the Hatch Act funded agriculture experiment stations in the various states to do basic and applied research. Other legislation provided regulatory programs to deal with such farm problems as pesticides, commodity standards, plant and insect pests, and the rail shipment of livestock. The expansion of farm programs continued in the early decades of the twentieth century. By the beginning of World War I, the Department of Agriculture had became a major regulatory agency.

The Progressive Era (1901–1917)

The Progressive movement drew much of its support from the middle class and sought to reform the political, economic, and social systems of U.S. society. Economically, there was a desire to bring corporate power fully under the control of government and make it more responsive to democratic ends. Progressive administrations under presidents Theodore Roosevelt and Woodrow Wilson strengthened regulatory programs to control railroads, business, and banking and to protect consumers. Several laws intended to make railroad regulation more effective were passed. Notable among these laws was the Hepburn Act (1906), which gave the Interstate Commerce Commission authority to set maximum reasonable rates for railroads. Strongly opposed by most of the railroads, the Hepburn Act helped make the ICC a more effective regulator.

Consumer protection legislation came in the form of the Pure Food and Drug Act and the Meat Inspection Act, both enacted in 1906. These statutes mark the beginning of consumer protection as a major task of the national government. The Meat Inspection Act was passed partly in response to publication of Upton Sinclair's novel *The Jungle*, which graphically portrayed the unsavory and unsanitary conditions in Chicago meatpacking plants. The food and drug law prohibited the adulteration and mislabeling of foods and drugs, which were common practices at this time.

In 1913 Congress passed the Federal Reserve Act. The act created the Federal Reserve System to regulate the national banking system and to provide for flexibility in the money supply in order to better meet commercial needs and to combat financial panics.

Passage of the Federal Trade Commission (FTC) Act and Clayton Act of 1914 strengthened antitrust policy. The FTC Act created the Federal Trade Commission and authorized it to prevent "unfair methods of competition." The commission also shared jurisdiction with the Department of Justice to enforce the Clayton Act, which prohibited a number of unfair business practices, such as price discrimination, exclusive dealing contracts, and corporate mergers that lessened competition. These statutes sought to prevent business from forming monopolies or trusts.

Throughout the nineteenth century, the revenue needs of the national government were adequately met by protective tariffs and a few excise taxes, such as those on alcoholic beverages. Indeed, in the late decades of the nineteenth century, the government was sometimes hard pressed to spend all of the funds generated by protective tariffs. Generous government pensions for Northern veterans of the Civil War and ample spending on internal infrastructure improvements helped absorb the available revenues.

As the national government's functions expanded in the early twentieth century, however, the government began to experience shortages of revenue. New sources of revenue became necessary, and the attention of public officials focused on the income tax as a way to raise money. In 1895, however, the Supreme Court had held that the income tax was a direct tax, which, according to the U.S. Constitution, had to be allocated among the states in proportion to their population.[8] This ruling made the income tax a political and administrative impossibility. Consequently, the Sixteenth Amendment to the Constitution, adopted in 1913, reversed that decision. The Sixteenth Amendment authorized the national government "to lay and collect taxes on incomes, from whatever source derived" without being apportioned among the states. Personal and corporate income taxes have since become the national government's major source of general revenues. They have also been a source of political controversy.

The Great Depression and the New Deal

The outbreak of World War I brought the Progressive era to an end. During the 1920s, under the conservative aegis of the Harding, Coolidge, and Hoover administrations, the expansion of national intervention in the economy was slowed almost to a halt.[9] Only a few new regulatory programs were adopted, including the Railway Labor Act and the Packers and Stockyards Act. The economy grew at a rapid pace, and many Americans thought that the resulting prosperity would last forever.

But "forever" came to an end on Thursday, October 27, 1929, when the stock market collapsed and the catastrophic worldwide economic decline known as the Great Depression set in. The initial response of the Hoover administration was to declare that the economy was fundamentally sound, a claim that few believed. Investors, business-people, and others lost confidence in the economy. Prices dropped, production declined, and unemployment rose. In the winter of 1932 to 1933, an estimated half of the labor force was unemployed. Many other people worked only part-time or at jobs below their skill levels. The economic distress produced by the Great Depression, which lasted for a decade, was unparalleled before or since that time.

There had been numerous financial panics and recessions before 1929, but none on the scale of the Great Depression had ever occurred. Although the Depression was worldwide in scope, the United States was especially hard hit. All sectors of the economy suffered—business, finance, labor, agriculture, and manufacturing. No economic group or social class was spared, although some fared better than others. Fully indus-trialized, the United States could no longer rely on subsistence agriculture as a refuge in times of economic decline.

Many intellectuals, economic experts, and disgruntled citizens viewed the Depres-sion as a massive institutional failure of the capitalist system. Whatever its shortcom-ings, such as substantial inequality in the distribution of wealth and income and the exploitation of some workers and farmers, no one had seriously questioned capitalism's productive capabilities before. When economic declines had occurred, it was accurately assumed that they would be short. Moreover, before the Depression, few people thought there was much that the government could do to prevent recessions or to stabilize the economy. These assumptions were now called into question.

Calling for a "New Deal" for the American people, Franklin D. Roosevelt over-whelmed Herbert Hoover and the Republican Party in the 1932 presidential election. Although Roosevelt's campaign speeches and declarations were often general and ambiguous, it was clear that he favored strong government action to relieve economic distress and to reform the capitalist economic system, while preserving its basic features through the processes of democratic government.

The Depression and the New Deal marked a major turning point in U.S. history in general and in U.S. economic history in particular. During the 1930s the *laissez-faire* state was replaced with the **interventionist state,** in which the government plays an active and extensive role in guiding and regulating the private economy. Until the 1930s, the national government's role in the economy was consistent with a broad interpretation of *laissez-faire* doctrine in that the government mostly provided a framework of rules within which the economy was left alone to operate. After the 1930s, however, that was no longer true. The New Deal established the national gov-ernment as a *major* regulator of private businesses, as a provider of social security (see

interventionist state:

Replaced the *laissez-faire* state as the government took an active role in guiding and regulating the private economy.

HIGHLIGHT 18.1

The WPA

The largest and most famous of the New Deal's job-creation programs was the WPA—the Works Progress Administration. Enacted in the midst of the Great Depression, the program's purpose was not simply to provide jobs for the unemployed—it was also intended to build public works, and this it did on a massive scale. What the WPA accomplished is staggering in its variety and magnitude. From 1935 to 1941, more than 600,000 miles of roads and streets were built or repaired, enough to encircle the world twenty-four times! Bridges were constructed or rebuilt, 116,000 of them; and nearly 600 airplane landing fields were constructed. More than 100,000 public libraries, schools, and other public buildings were erected. If only the *new* buildings were distributed evenly among the 3,000 counties in the United States, each county would have had about ten. WPA projects included draining swamps and repairing library books, teaching illiterate adults and serving school lunches, building stadiums and painting murals, and planting trees and harvesting oysters. The projects ranged from modest ones costing a

few hundred dollars to the building of major municipal airports and bridges, each of which cost tens of millions of dollars.

The WPA was not free of controversy and criticism. Some people objected in principle to the government's provision of jobs to so many people, and others complained that too much of the money was wasted on "make work" and used by politicians to reward their friends.

SOURCE: Donald S. Howard, *The WPA and Federal Relief Policy* (New York: Russell Sage Foundation, 1943).

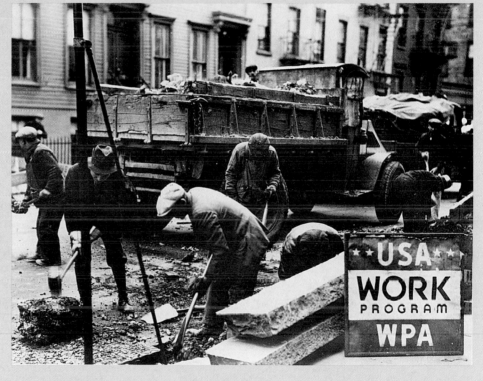

A construction project of the Works Progress Administration (WPA). This New Deal government program was created to provide jobs building roads, bridges, parks, and other public facilities. (Photo courtesy: Corbis/Bettmann)

chapter 17), and as ultimately responsible for maintaining a stable economy (see Highlight 18.1: The WPA).

Although the New Deal was not (and is not) without critics, most people today accept the notion that these areas of responsibility are properly within the scope of national governmental power. Specifically, *how* matters of Social Security and economic stability should be handled rather than *whether* they should be the province of the national government has been the basis for political conflict. Recently, however, Republicans have led a growing chorus of critics who argue that federal intervention is part of the problem and not the solution. These critics would replace Social Security with private retirement plans and allow the market a freer hand.

The New Deal brought about a number of reforms in almost every area, including finance, agriculture, labor, industry, and consumer protection.

Financial Reforms. The first actions of the New Deal were directed at reviving and reforming the nation's financial system (see Roots of Government: Regulation of Financial Markets and the Fed). Because of bad investments and poor management, many banks failed in the early 1930s. To restore confidence in the banks, the day after he was inaugurated, Roosevelt declared a bank holiday, closing all of the nation's banks. Then, on the basis of emergency legislation passed by Congress, only financially sound banks were permitted to reopen. Many unsound banks were closed for good and their depositors paid off.

The major New Deal banking laws were the Glass-Steagall Act (1933) and the Banking Act (1935). The Glass-Steagall Act required the separation of commercial and investment banking and set up the Federal Deposit Insurance Corporation (FDIC) to insure bank deposits, originally for $5,000 per account. Although it had long been opposed by conservatives, bank deposit insurance has now become an accepted feature of the U.S. banking system. The Banking Act reorganized the Federal Reserve System, removed the Secretary of the Treasury as an ex-officio member, and formally established the Open Market Committee (discussed later in this chapter).

Legislation was also passed to control other abuses in the stock markets. The Securities Act (1933) required that prospective investors be given full and accurate information about the stocks or securities being offered to them. The Securities Exchange Act (1934) created the Securities and Exchange Commission (SEC), an independent

 OOTS OF GOVERNMENT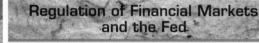

Regulation of Financial Markets and the Fed

Throughout the eighteenth and nineteenth centuries, the U.S. economy was plagued periodically by financial panics. Downturns in the business cycles were accompanied by runs on banks, widespread defaults on loans, bankruptcies of large enterprises, and sharp declines in stock prices. Panics, often preceded by speculative booms in real estate or securities, usually resulted when a spectacular failure caused a sudden, drastic reappraisal of business prospects. From 1790 to 1907, there were twenty-one panics or about one every six years. In 1914 Congress passed the Federal Reserve Act to regulate the currency and credit operations of banks in the United States, which had been manipulating financial markets. The law was designed to improve cooperation among the nation's banks and to decentralize financial control. As illustrated in Figure 18.2, it divided the United States into twelve districts with a Federal Reserve Bank in each.

In spite of these precautions, the stock market crash in October 1929 set off a succession of banking panics, with more than 9,000 bank failures between 1930 and 1933. The Federal Reserve Banks had no authority to prevent these disasters, to keep them from spreading, or to ease their effects.

Thus in 1933, Congress passed the Banking Act of 1933. It changed some of the ways in which Federal Reserve Banks worked and created the Federal Deposit Insurance Corporation. The objective of the act was to stabilize banking in the United States.

Today, the Federal Reserve System is empowered to create money to meet the seasonal needs of business and to counteract panic. In addition, the Federal Reserve imposed controls over bank reserves, accounting procedures, and management, produced a uniform currency, cleared checks and collections, and handled government finance. The Federal Reserve injects money into the financial system by purchasing government bonds. So when "the Fed" decides that the economy needs more money, it prints new money and promptly spends some (on bonds).

For all of its power and importance, the Federal Reserve System is a mysterious entity to most Americans. One observer has likened it to a religious institution, a characterization that, at first, seems bizarre, but that on closer examination reveals a bit of truth about the Fed. Housed in a dignified marble "temple" on Constitution Avenue in Washington, D.C., the "high priests" of monetary policy direct the economy in ways that are hidden from, and incomprehensible to, the average citizen. Their deliberations take place in secret. Their debates are conducted in the technical language of economics. Their powers to create money and to make it disappear inspire awe and fear. Such powers cannot be entrusted to ordinary "mortals" but must be exercised only by "priests" undefiled by "political considerations."

SOURCE: Quotation and paraphrasing from William Greider, *Secrets of the Temple: How the Federal Reserve Runs the Country* (New York: Simon & Schuster, 1987), chapter 2.

regulatory commission. The SEC was authorized to regulate the stock exchanges, to enforce the Securities Act, and to reduce the number of stocks bought on margin (that is, with borrowed money).

Agriculture.   The economic condition of U.S. agriculture, which had been weak even during the prosperous 1920s, became much worse with the Depression. The Agriculture Adjustment Act (AAA) of 1933 sought to boost farm income by restricting agriculture production in order to bring it into better balance with demand. Farmers who reduced their crop production in line with the program were eligible to receive cash payments and other benefits. In 1936, however, the Supreme Court held the AAA unconstitutional on the grounds that the national government lacked authority to regulate farming through any of its powers set out in Article I, section 8.[10] Congress quickly replaced the AAA with the Soil Conservation and Domestic Allotment Act, which paid farmers for taking land out of crop production and devoting it to soil conservation purposes. The crops taken out of production generally were those whose prices the AAA had been designed to increase. This ploy did not work very well to increase farm income.

In 1938 Congress adopted the second Agricultural Adjustment Act. The second AAA provided for subsidies to farmers raising crops such as corn, cotton, and wheat who grew no more than their allotted acreage. If two-thirds of the growers of a commodity voting in a referendum approved, then the allotments became mandatory, and farmers exceeding them were penalized. Direct payments and commodity loans were also available to participating farmers. In 1941 the Supreme Court upheld the constitutionality of the second AAA as an appropriate exercise of Congress's power to regulate interstate commerce.[11] The act, the foundation of the agricultural price support programs, has come under increasing attack from conservatives who claim that the program promotes inefficiency. Republicans, who took control of Congress in 1995, have sought to phase out crop supports as part of the effort to curb federal spending. In 1996 Congress passed a landmark agricultural bill with the aim of phasing out crop subsidies by the year 2002. The intent of the bill was to wean agriculture away from price supports and to make it more dependent upon the vagaries of the free market. Critics of the 1996 bill claimed that such a strategy would lead to overproduction and declining prices for some crops. By 1997 Congress was moving away from the intent of the landmark bill, appropriating significant sums of money to rescue farmers from bad weather, crop disease, and falling commodity prices.

Labor.   Organized labor had long been handicapped in its relationships with management by unfriendly public officials and hostile public policies. The fortunes of labor unions, which were strong supporters of the New Deal, improved significantly in 1935 when Congress passed the National Labor Relations Act. Better known as the Wagner Act after its sponsor, Senator Robert Wagner (D-N.Y.), this statute guaranteed workers' right to organize and bargain collectively through unions of their own choosing. A series of "unfair labor practices," such as discriminating against employees because of their union activities, was prohibited. The National Labor Relations Board (NLRB) was created to carry out the act and to conduct elections to determine which union, if any, employees wanted to represent them. Unions prospered under the protection provided by the Wagner Act.

The last major piece of New Deal economic legislation was the Fair Labor Standards Act (FLSA) of 1938. Intended to protect the interests of low-paid workers, the law set twenty-five cents an hour and forty-four hours per week as initial minimum standards. Within a few years, wages were to rise to forty cents per hour and hours to decline to forty per week. Not all employees were covered by the FLSA, however; farm workers, domestic workers, and fishermen, for example, were exempted. The act also banned child labor.

In 1996 Congress approved a two-step increase in the minimum wage. It was raised from $4.25 an hour, where it had been for the last five years, to $4.75. In September

TRY IT!
To access the most current labor and wages data for your state or region, go to www.awlonline.com/oconnor.

1997, it was raised again to $5.15. Controversy continues over whether minimum wage legislation creates employment by pricing some workers out of the labor market. Some economists argue that these workers, especially unskilled young people just entering the job market, would have jobs if they could be paid a lower wage. In 1998 House and Senate Democrats introduced bills to increase the minimum wage, but the proposals failed to make it to the floor for a vote. Figure 18.1 shows the growth of the minimum wage since its creation.

Industry Regulations.   Several industries were the subjects of new or expanded regulatory programs. The Federal Communications Commission (FCC), created in 1934 to replace the old Federal Radio Commission, was given extensive jurisdiction over the radio, telephone, and telegraph industries. The Civil Aeronautics Board (CAB) was put in place in 1938 to regulate the commercial aviation industry. The Motor Carrier Act of 1935 put the trucking industry under the jurisdiction of the Interstate Commerce Commission (ICC). Regulation of industries such as trucking and commercial aviation, like railroad regulation, extended to such matters as entry into the business, routes of service, and rates. To a substantial extent, government regulation, as a protector of the public interest, replaced competition in these industries. Supporters of these programs frequently spoke of a need to prevent destructive or excessive competition, as could occur among large numbers of trucking companies. Critics warned that limiting competition resulted in users having to pay more for the services.

Deregulation of the radio industry occurred with the landmark Telecommunications Act of 1996. This act allowed firms to own an unlimited number of stations nationwide, erasing the previous 40 station limit. The act also raised the previous 4 station limit per market to 8 stations. Following a pattern earlier established with airlines, trucking, and banking, deregulation predictably produced a consolidation within the industry. Regulation produced consolidation as a consequence of restricting competition through legislation. Deregulation also led to consolidation as the natural market forces enhanced the positions of the more efficient firms and drove the less efficient into bankruptcy. Radio station owners such as Jacor Communications went from possessing 50 stations in 1996 to 204 in 1998. The large media enterprise CBS owned 160 stations in 1998 and Capstar Broadcasting Partners owned 299. Ad revenues on radio in general grew 10 percent in 1997, cost savings were attained, and stock prices of sev-

Figure 18.1   Growth in the Minimum Wage Over Time.

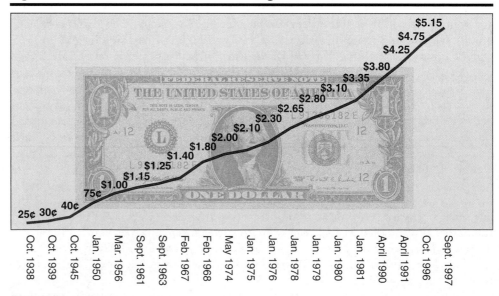

SOURCE: Associated Press.

eral companies specializing in radio climbed steadily. Negative consequences, however, could also be linked to deregulation and the resulting industry consolidation: it was estimated that between March 1996 and February 1998 the number of individual owners dropped 14 percent, minority ownership declined, and diversity of content suffered.

Consumer Protection.   Even though consumers as a group were poorly organized in the 1930s, a few laws were passed to help protect their interests. The Wheeler-Lea Act (1938) expanded the jurisdiction of the Federal Trade Commission (FTC) to include deceptive practices and false and misleading advertising. The act gave the FTC a clear mandate to engage in consumer protection.

The Pure Food, Drug, and Cosmetic Act (1938) represented an effort to plug some of the loopholes and remedy the shortcomings of the Pure Food and Drug Act of 1906. Cosmetic and therapeutic devices were added to foods and drugs as matters subject to government regulation. All traffic in foods that were injurious to health was banned. Also, factories producing foods, drugs, and cosmetics were brought under inspection by the Food and Drug Administration (FDA). Drugs and cosmetics had to bear informative labels relating to their use. Moreover, the marketing of any drug was prohibited until it had been tested and found safe when properly used. Most responsibility for enforcing the 1938 law was given to the Food and Drug Administration, which today is part of the Department of Health and Human Services.

Just as World War I brought down the curtain on the Progressive era, the war clouds gathering in Western Europe in the late 1930s diverted Americans' attention from domestic reform to international affairs and brought an end to the New Deal era. Many of the New Deal programs, however, became permanent parts of our public policy landscape. Moreover, the New Deal established the legitimacy and viability of national governmental intervention in the economy. Passive government was replaced with activist government, and the government in Washington became the people's primary source of solutions for economic problems.

The Post–World War II Era

In the two decades following the end of World War II, many areas of economic policy were fairly well settled and produced few major policy struggles. Transportation, finance and banking, agriculture, and consumer protection, for example, experienced little change. There were, however, some important policy developments in other areas. Here, we look at two of the most significant developments: the Employment Act and the Taft-Hartley Act.

The Employment Act.   As World War II neared its conclusion, policy planners and public officials began to worry that the conversion from a wartime to a peacetime economy would bring with it a new depression, as had happened after World War I. Officials in the administration of President Harry S. Truman and liberal and labor groups wanted to commit the national government to the use of fiscal policy (the government's taxing and spending policies) to create conditions providing full employment.[12] They backed a bill introduced in Congress by Senator James Murray (D-Mont.) to guarantee a "right to employment" to anyone willing and able to work. To accomplish this goal, Murray proposed that the president submit a "National Production and Employment Budget" to estimate the size of the labor force, the total national production needed to provide jobs for all, and the total investment required to provide that level of production. If the anticipated level of private investment was insufficient to achieve this level of production, then the national government would provide the additional investment and spending needed to reach the goal of full employment.

The Murray proposal ran into strong opposition from a conservative coalition of Republicans and Southern Democrats, egged on by many business groups. They feared that this bill would result in excessive government spending and control of the economy. Conservatives stressed the capacity of the private economy to provide jobs. What finally emerged from Congress as the Employment Act of 1946 was a substantially weakened version of the Murray bill. The declaration of policy in section 2 of the Employment Act states that "It is the continuing policy and responsibility of the federal government to use all practicable means consistent with its needs and obligations . . . to promote maximum employment, production and purchasing power."

Some policy machinery was established to carry out this policy. A Council of Economic Advisers (CEA), consisting of three professional economists and a small support staff, was created to advise the president on economic issues. The CEA later became quite influential in the Kennedy, Johnson, and Carter administrations. The president was directed to present an annual economic report to Congress. In this report the president analyzed current economic conditions and recommended a program for meeting the act's goals. Within Congress the Employment Act set up a Joint Economic Committee composed of ten senators and ten representatives to consider the president's economic report and to advise the two houses on its content and recommendations. The committee also holds hearings and commissions studies on economic policy. In all, the Joint Economic Committee has helped increase the "economic literacy" of Congress.

It is incorrect to dismiss the Employment Act as merely symbolic and without real impact. Its enactment reflected a high level of agreement among the members of Congress and provided a general direction for public policy makers. As economist Herbert Stein states, "It helped put an end to futile, tiresome, and meaningless debate between extremists and cleared the way for practical work to evolve a program" for stabilizing the economy and putting more people to work.[13] Since 1946 the national government has performed the role of overall manager of the economy.

The Taft-Hartley Act.   Business and conservative groups, which had stoutly opposed the Wagner Act in 1935, continued to be highly critical of it. When the Republican Party gained control of Congress following the 1946 elections, it got the opportunity to do something about its dissatisfaction with the Wagner Act and labor union power. Major strikes in the automobile, steel, meatpacking, railroad, and other industries in the months following the end of World War II had created negative public feelings toward unions. If organized labor and the Truman administration had been able to agree on moderate labor reform proposals, they might have been able to fend off the drastic changes in labor law contained in the Taft-Hartley act. They were not, however, and the conservative coalition favoring the act was strong enough to enact it into law in 1947 over Democratic President Harry S. Truman's veto.

Essentially, the Taft-Hartley Act sought to increase the power of management in collective bargaining by imposing a variety of restraints on labor unions while also strengthening management prerogatives. The act prohibited as unfair a number of union activities, such as featherbedding (requiring that extra employees be assigned to a job), jurisdictional strikes, and coercing employees to join a union. Unions were directed to file detailed reports on their finances and procedures with the Department of Labor. Employees of the national government were absolutely barred from striking. A procedure involving an eighty-day injunction against striking was authorized to help settle strikes that affected the "national health or safety." The closed shop arrangement, under which an employer agreed to hire only union members, was prohibited. A union shop, under which workers had to join the union (or at least pay union dues) within a designated time to retain their jobs, was permitted, except in states that had "right-to-work" laws. These laws, which now exist in about twenty states, provide that union membership or nonmembership cannot be a condition of employment. The result is an open shop. Labor union officials often called the Taft-Hartley Act a "slave labor" law.

Now, decades later, when labor unions have declined in membership and lost some of their political and economic strength, it is difficult to imagine the bitterness and intensity of the conflict that for years swirled around the Taft-Hartley Act. It injected government much more deeply into labor-management relations than did the Wagner Act. Conservatives who feared that the Full Employment Act would result in too much government control of the economy shed that concern when the control of labor unions was at stake. Sooner or later, everyone finds government programs of which he or she approves; this is one major reason for the growth and persistence of big government.

The Social Regulation Era

Economists and political scientists frequently distinguish between economic regulation and social regulation. **Economic regulation** focuses on such matters as control of entry into a business, prices or rates of charge, and service routes or areas. Regulation is usually tailored to the conditions of particular industries, such as railroads or stock exchanges. "Simply put, economic regulation places government in the driver's seat with respect to the economic direction and performance of the regulated industry."[14] In contrast, **social regulation** is concerned with such areas as the quality and safety of products and the conditions under which goods are produced and services rendered. Put another way, social regulation strives to protect and enhance the quality of life. Regulation of product safety by the Consumer Product Safety Commission is an example of social regulation. Professor Michael Reagan, noted authority in the study of regulation, makes a helpful distinction: "Social regulation can generally be differentiated from economic regulation by the former's concern with harm to our physical (and sometimes moral and aesthetic) well-being, rather than harm to our wallets."[15]

Most of the regulatory programs established through the 1950s fell into the category of economic regulation. From the mid-1960s to the mid-1970s, however, a huge wave of social regulatory legislation emanated from the national government on such topics as consumer protection, health and safety, and environmental protection. Congress enacted this legislation under its commerce clause authority.

Several major new regulatory agencies were set up to implement these new social regulations. These agencies include the Consumer Product Safety Commission, the Occupational Safety and Health Administration (OSHA), the Environmental Protection Agency (EPA), the Office of Surface Mining Reclamation and Enforcement, the Mining Enforcement and Safety Administration, and the National Transportation Safety Administration (see chapter 9). Most of these agencies have jurisdictions that cut across industry lines, in contrast to the industry-focused agencies born during the New Deal.

The social regulatory statutes took various forms. Some had specific targets and goals, such as the Egg Product Inspection Act and the Lead-Based Paint Poison Prevention Act. Others were quite lengthy and detailed, loaded with specific standards, deadlines, and instructions for the administering agency. Illustrative are the Clean Air Act of 1970 and Employee Retirement Income Security Act (intended to protect workers' pensions provided by private employers). Other statutes conferred broad substantive discretion on the implementing agency. Thus the Occupational Safety and Health Act guarantees workers a safe and healthful workplace, but it contains no health and safety standards with which workplaces must comply. These standards are set through rule-making proceedings conducted by the Occupational Safety and Health Administration, which also has responsibility for their enforcement.

As a consequence of this flood of social regulation, many industries that previously had had limited dealings with government now found government regulation to be of major importance in the conduct of their operations. A good example is the automobile industry, which previously had been lightly touched by antitrust, labor relations, and other general statutes. By the early 1970s, however, the quality of its products was heavily regulated by EPA motor vehicle emissions standards and federally mandated safety standards. The automobile companies found this experience both galling and expensive. The chemical industry found itself in much the same situation.

Four factors contributed to the surge of social regulation.[16] First, the late 1960s and early 1970s were a time of social activism; the consumer and environmental movements were at the peak of their influence. Public interest groups such as the Consumers Union, Common Cause, the Environmental Defense Fund, the Sierra Club, and Ralph Nader's

economic regulation:

Governmental regulation of business practices, industry rates, routes, or areas serviced by particular industries.

social regulation:

Governmental regulation of the quality and safety of products as well as the conditions under which goods and services are produced.

Web Exploration
To learn about current economic policy, go to
www.awlonline.com/oconnor.

■ The Lead-Based Paint Poison Prevention Act has led to redoubled efforts to test dwellings for lead paint, as this contractor is doing by taking samples. (Photo courtesy: Stephen Agricola/The Image Works)

numerous organizations were effective voices for consumer, environmental, and other programs (see chapter 16). Strong support also came from organized labor.

Second, the public had become much more aware of the dangers to health, safety, and the environment associated with various modern products. Unsafe products had always existed, but their numbers had been multiplied by modern technology. Products widely viewed as unsafe included the chemical DDT, cigarettes, leaded gasoline, poisonous household cleaners, the Chevrolet Corvair, spray cans, phosphates, vinyl chloride, lead-based paint, cyclamates, and some forms of intrauterine birth control devices such as the Dalkon Shield. Furthermore, add to this list the large quantities of toxic substances spewed into the air, dumped in streams and lakes, and buried in the ground. There was, noted one observer, "a level of public consciousness about environmental, consumer, and occupational hazards that appears to be of a different order of magnitude from public outrage over such issues during both the Progressive era and the New Deal."[17]

Third, members of Congress, aided and abetted by their professional staffs, saw the advocacy of social regulation as a way to gain visibility and national prominence and thus to enhance their election prospects. Some members became policy entrepreneurs. Senator Edmund Muskie (D–Me.), for example, took the lead on environmental issues, and Senator Warren Magnuson (D–Wash.) successfully pushed for a number of consumer protection laws.

Fourth, the presidents in office during most of this period—Lyndon B. Johnson and Richard M. Nixon, one a liberal, the other a pragmatic conservative—each gave support to the social regulation movement. For them, too, it was good politics to be in favor of health, safety, and environmental legislation. Also, in most instances, the direct costs to the government of this legislation were minimal.

Deregulation

Even before the wave of social regulation began to wane, deregulation emerged as an attractive political issue. Although this situation may seem paradoxical, there is a fairly simple explanation for what happened. The focus of the deregulation movement was on the economic regulatory programs for such industries as railroads, motor carriers, and commercial air transportation; most social regulatory programs continued to enjoy strong public support and were left largely alone by the deregulation movement.

Beginning in the 1950s and 1960s, economists, political scientists, and journalists began to point out defects in some of the economic regulatory programs.[18] They contended that regulation sometimes produced monopoly profits, discrimination in services, and inefficiency in the operation of regulated industries. Moreover, regulation often made it difficult for industries to compete on the basis of prices and also for new competitors to enter the market. For instance, no new major commercial airline was permitted to enter the industry after the Civil Aeronautics Board (CAB) began to regulate the industry in 1938. Consequently, consumers paid higher prices for airfares and had fewer choices than they would in a more competitive market. Regulated firms like the commercial airlines, on the other hand, were comfortable with the higher profits and less competitive rigors of their regulated markets. Critics contended that regulatory commissions like the CAB and the Interstate Commerce Commission were more responsive to the interests of the regulated firms than to the public interest.

For some time nothing changed in the regulatory arena, despite these criticisms. In the mid-1970s, however, President Gerald R. Ford decided to make deregulation a focal point of his administration. He saw regulation as one cause of the inflation that was then besetting the economy. Also, as a conservative Republican, he found deregulation consistent with his beliefs in less government and a free market. About this time Senator Edward M. Kennedy (D–Mass.) became chair of a subcommittee of the Senate Judiciary Committee. Wanting to use his new position and acting on the advice of his staff, he decided to hold hearings on airline deregulation. The combined actions of Ford and Kennedy put deregulation on the national policy agenda and got the deregulatory movement underway. Democrats and Republicans, liberals and conservatives, all found deregulation to be an appealing political issue.

Some of the many economists who favored deregulation were appointed to the regulatory commissions. Once on the commissions, they used the discretionary authority available to them to reduce the impact of regulation. This was done, for example, by economist Alfred Kahn, who was appointed chair of the CAB. Commission action of this sort both pressured and made it easier for Congress to act on deregulation. Economists also mustered a substantial body of empirical research showing that efficiency gains would flow from deregulation and, further, that deregulation would not have disruptive effects on the economy, as some opponents argued. Competition was depicted as a beneficent and effective regulator of the economy.[19]

Only one deregulation act was passed during the Ford administration. However, deregulation picked up momentum after Jimmy Carter became president in 1977. He made deregulation a high priority for his administration. Legislation that deregulated aspects of commercial airlines, railroads, motor carriers, and financial institutions was enacted during his term. Two additional deregulation laws were adopted in the early years of the first Reagan administration.

Deregulation usually involved a reduction in the entry, rate, and other controls imposed on an industry. The exception was the Airline Deregulation Act, which completely eliminated economic regulation of commercial airlines over several years. Although many new passenger carriers flocked into the industry when barriers to entry were first removed, they were unable to compete successfully with the existing major airlines. All of these new entrants have now disappeared. Indeed, so have some of the major airlines that were operating at the time of deregulation. Consequently there are now fewer major carriers than under the regulatory regime, although new airlines such as ValuJet (now called Airtran) try to compete by offering low fares. Competition has lowered some passenger rates, but the extent to which passengers have benefited from deregulation is in dispute because many routes have been abandoned and airline safety has been called into question in the wake of tragic crashes like ValuJet Flight 592 in the Everglades.

The deregulation of the savings and loan business, coupled with the failure of the Reagan administration adequately to enforce the remaining controls on savings and loans, led in time to a costly instance of deregulatory failure. Previously restricted to financing individual homes, deregulation took the lid off of what savings and loans could invest in. As a consequence of poor management, bad commercial investments, and corruption, hundreds of savings and loans, especially in Southwestern states, went bankrupt, sometimes to the tune of hundreds of millions of dollars or more.[20] After years of delay, during which the problem got worse, the Bush administration and Congress finally took action. The Financial Institutions Reform, Recovery, and Enforcement Act (1989) revamped the regulatory system for savings and loans, provided for the liquidation of insolvent associations, and bailed out their depositors. Expectations are that the total direct cost to taxpayers of the bailout will be $150 billion to $200 billion. With interest, it was estimated that the cost may approximate $500 billion.[21] Much of the cost of the bailout could have been avoided by more timely and effective action. What is surprising is that the public has accepted this financial debacle with minimal complaint or criticism.

In some policy areas, the pendulum has now completed its deregulatory swing. The broad consensus that made possible "pro-competitive" or economic deregulation does not exist for the field of social regulation. Strong support continues for regulation to protect consumers, workers, and the environment. In some areas in which deregulation occurred, there have been calls to "reregulate." This has occurred in the airline industry because of concern about its safety and domination by a small number of companies.

While congressional Republicans, in response to public outrage, have backed away from some of their ideas for weakening environmental regulations, they continue to call for less government involvement in a number of other areas. They have been particularly critical of affirmative action requirements designed to earmark a share of government contracts and public jobs for minorities.

In the following sections of this chapter, we take a detailed look at two areas of government regulation of economic activity, both of which are of much interest to most Americans. The first is macroeconomic regulation to influence the overall performance of the economy. The second is regulation to control environmental pollution.

STABILIZING THE ECONOMY

Until the early 1930s the prevailing view in the United States was that the country's economy was controlled by natural economic laws that could be disrupted but not improved on by the government. Fluctuations in the economy were accepted with a sense of inevitability. At a Conference on Unemployment sponsored by the national government in 1921, President Warren G. Harding stated the position of the government in his opening remarks: "There has been vast unemployment before and there will be again. There will be depression and inflation just as the tides ebb and flow. I would have little enthusiasm for any proposed remedy that seeks palliation or tonic from the Public Treasury."[22] At the time it was thought that the best things the government could do if a depression struck would be to increase taxes, cut spending, and balance the budget, or the situation might be made worse by a lack of public confidence in the government's financial condition. This was the tack taken by Herbert Hoover and, for a time, by Franklin D. Roosevelt during the early years of the Great Depression.

The policy change represented by the Employment Act of 1946, which committed the government to maintaining "maximum employment, production, and purchasing power," stemmed from a confluence of several factors.[23] First, the massive scale and persistence of the Great Depression refuted the notion that depressions were self-correcting. Second, new techniques of economic measurement and analysis enabled people to better understand the operation of the economy.

Third, the ideas of English economist John Maynard Keynes had gained acceptance and influence. In his *General Theory of Employment, Interests, and Money* (1936), Keynes argued that deficit spending by a government could supplement the total or aggregate demand for goods and services. Government spending would offset a decline in private spending and thus help maintain high levels of spending, production, and employment. During the New Deal, the national government engaged in limited deficit spending, which was sometimes referred to as "pump-priming," but it was not sufficient to bring economic recovery. Fourth, World War II brought with it a tremendous increase in government spending and large budget deficits. The economy expanded, production rose, and unemployment fell below 2 percent. The interaction of these factors contributed to the national government's assuming responsibility for maintaining economic stability.

Economic stability is often defined as a situation in which there is economic growth, a rising national income, high employment, and a steadiness in the general level of prices. Conversely, economic instability may involve inflation or recession. **Inflation** occurs when there is too much demand for the available supply of goods and services, with the consequence that general price levels rise as buyers compete for the available supply. Prices may also rise if large corporations and unions have sufficient economic power to push prices and wages above competitive levels. A **recession** involves a decline in the economy. Investment sags, production falls off, and unemployment increases.

The primary means available to government to maintain economic stability or, if one prefers, to combat instability are monetary and fiscal policy. Our attention now turns to a discussion of these concepts.

economic stability:

A situation in which there is economic growth, rising national income, high employment, and steadiness in the general level of prices.

inflation:

A rise in the general price levels of an economy.

recession:

A short-term decline in the economy that occurs as investment sags, production falls off, and unemployment increases.

Monetary Policy

Monetary policy, which is a form of macroeconomic regulation, involves regulating a nation's money supply and interest rates. A modern industrial economy operates on the basis of money, which is the medium through which nearly all income and all buying and selling transactions take place. When money is mentioned, most of us think of currency and coins, items we can feel, count, and carry in our pockets. But currency and coins are only a small portion of the nation's money supply. The term *money* also includes bank deposits and other financial assets. The Federal Reserve Board has three definitions of **money** based on this broader conception. *M1* (the first definition) includes currency, checking accounts, travelers checks, NOW accounts, and other checkable deposits. *M2* includes all of M1 plus savings and small time deposits and money market account balances. *M3* includes M2 plus large time deposits and institutional money market fund balances. The M2 definition is of the most concern to the Federal Reserve Board.

The Federal Reserve Board has responsibility for the formation and implementation of monetary policy because of its ability to control the credit-creating and lending activities of the nation's banks. When individuals and corporations deposit their money in financial institutions such as commercial banks (which accept deposits and make loans) and savings and loan associations (S&Ls), these deposits serve as the basis for loans to borrowers. In effect, the loaning of money creates new deposits or financial liabilities— new money that did not previously exist. But, we are getting ahead of our story. First, we'll look at the Federal Reserve System and its authority.

The Federal Reserve System. Created in 1913 to adjust the money supply to the needs of agriculture, commerce, and industry, the Federal Reserve System is comprised of the Federal Reserve Board (FRB) (formally, the Board of Governors of the Federal Reserve System; informally, "the Fed"), the Federal Open Market Committee, and the twelve Federal Reserve Banks in regions throughout the country (see Figure 18.2). The Fed represents a mixture of private interests and governmental authority.

The seven members of the Federal Reserve Board, who direct the system, are appointed by the president for fourteen-year, overlapping terms with the approval of the Senate. A member can be removed from office by the president for stated causes, but this has never occurred. One board member is designated by the president to serve as chair for a four-year term, which runs from the midpoint of one presidential term to the midpoint of the next to ensure economic stability during a change of administrations. Formally, the FRB has much independence from the executive branch, ostensibly so that monetary policy will not be influenced by political considerations. Defenders of the FRB's independent position assert that monetary policy is too important, complex, and technical to be under the day-to-day control of elected public officials, who might be inclined to make monetary decisions to advance their own short-term political interests (such as being reelected).

At the base of the Federal Reserve System are the twelve Federal Reserve Banks. These are "bankers' banks"; they are formally owned by the Federal Reserve System member banks in each region, and they do not do business with the public. A majority of the board of directors of each Federal Reserve Bank is elected by the commercial member banks in its region. The president of a Federal Reserve Bank is selected by its board of directors, not by the president of the United States.

The middle of the Federal Reserve System is occupied by the Federal Open Market Committee (FOMC). This committee consists of twelve members—all seven FRB members, plus five presidents from the Federal Reserve Banks. The representatives from the reserve banks rotate among the twelve regions, except for the New York Federal Reserve Bank. Because of its importance in the financial world, the New York Federal Reserve Bank is always represented on the FOMC.

The primary monetary policy tools are the setting of reserve requirements for member banks, control of the discount, and open market operations. Formally, authority to

monetary policy:
A form of government regulation in which the nation's money supply and interest rates are controlled.

money:
A system of exchange for goods and services that includes currency, coins, and bank deposits.

 Web Exploration
To learn more about regulation of financial markets via the Federal Reserve Board, go to
www.awlonline.com/oconnor.

Figure 18.2 Inside the Federal Reserve System

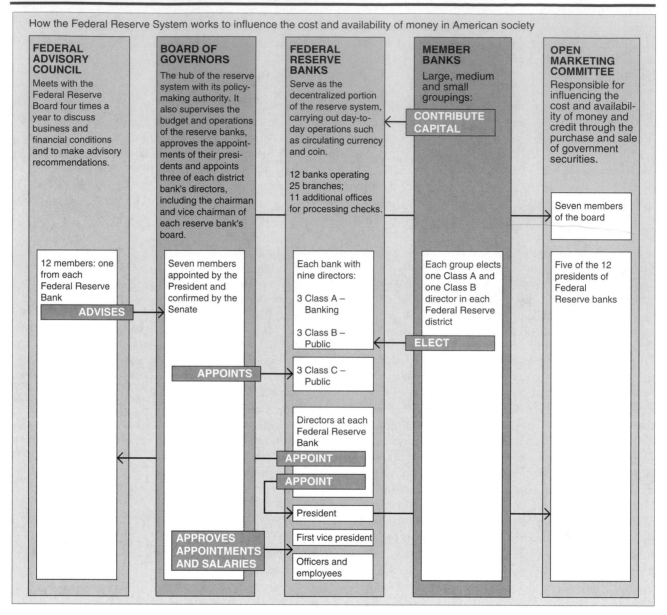

SOURCE: From Martin Maver, "Well Fed—or not? The Federal Reserve Faces a New Era While Raising Rates and Trying to Keep Independence," *Dallas Morning News* (May 22, 1994).

use these tools is allocated to the FRB, the Federal Reserve Bank boards of directors, and the FOMC, respectively. In actuality, however, all three are dominated by the FRB, which, in recent decades, has been under the sway of its chair. Arthur Burns and Paul Volcker (past chairs) and Alan Greenspan, the current chair, have been influential and respected policymakers. Much attention is given by public officials and the financial community to the utterances of the Fed's chair for clues to the future course of monetary policy.

Reserve requirements designate the portion of the banks' deposits that must be retained as backing for their loans. Raising the reserve requirement limits the capacity of banks to make new loans; lowering it enables them to expand their loans. Hypothetically, if the reserve requirement is 10 percent of deposits, banks can make more loans

reserve requirements:

Governmental requirements that a portion of member banks' deposits must be retained to back loans made.

■ Federal Reserve Board Chair Alan Greenspan gestures while addressing the National Association of Business Economists, October 7, 1998. Greenspan, who once bleakly cautioned stock investors not to get carried away, is now warning against undue pessimism. (Photo courtesy: Doug Mills/AP/Wide World Photos)

on a given amount of deposits than they can if the requirement is raised to 15 percent. When the FRB wants to increase the money supply in circulation, it can lower the reserve requirements; to reduce the money supply, it can raise the reserve requirement.

The **discount rate** is the rate of interest at which member banks can borrow money from their regional Federal Reserve Bank when they need additional reserves to support their loans. Raising the discount rate should discourage borrowing by banks to make loans and, in turn, will make loans more costly to people who want to borrow money. Conversely, lowering the discount rate should expand the money supply and encourage borrowing both by member banks and by people who want money to expand business and for other purposes. The assumption here is that what people do will be directly affected by whether interest rates are raised or lowered.

Open market operations involve the buying and selling of government securities by the FRB in the market, that is, wherever government securities are bought and sold. Government securities are interest-bearing bonds that are regularly bought and sold by investors in their quest for profits. When the FRB buys securities in the market, it ultimately pays for them by creating deposits for the sellers in the federal reserve banks. These deposits serve as additional reserves for commercial banks and enable them to expand their loans to borrowers. On the other hand, when the FRB sells government securities in the market, the buyers' payments for them are deducted from commercial banks, reserve accounts, reducing these reserves and thus the capacity of banks to lend money to their customers. As a rule of thumb, when the FRB buys securities, it expands the money supply; when the FRB sells securities, it restricts, or "tightens," the money supply. Open market operations are the tools the FRB uses most frequently because of their flexibility and direct impact.

Moral suasion refers to the capacity of the FRB to influence the actions of banks and other members of the financial community by suggestion, exhortation, and informal agreement. Because of its commanding position as a monetary policy maker, much attention and respect are given by the media, economists, and market observers to verbal signals about economic trends and conditions emitted by the FRB and its chair.

How the FRB uses these policy tools depends in part on how it perceives the state of the economy. (Ironically, we know more about the condition of the economy six months ago than about its current state because of lags in the availability of needed data.) If inflation appears to be the problem, then the Fed would likely restrict or tighten

discount rate:

The rate of interest at which member banks can borrow money from their regional Federal Reserve Bank.

open market operations:

The buying and selling of government securities by the Federal Reserve Bank in the securities market.

the money supply. The Fed could raise the reserve requirement and the discount rate and could sell government securities in the market. If a recession with rising unemployment appears to threaten the economy, then the FRB would probably act to loosen or expand the money supply in order to stimulate the economy. The Fed could lower the reserve and discount rates and could buy government securities in the market. In the early 1990s the Fed continually lowered interest rates to counteract a recession. Then, in early 1994, as the economy gained momentum, the FRB began to worry about inflation and acted several times to nudge up interest rates, somewhat to the consternation of Clinton administration officials.[24] In late 1995, in the wake of hints of an economic slowdown, interest rates dropped a few ticks. Such short-term actions are often characterized as "leaning against the wind."[25]

The President and the FRB.   Although the public generally holds the president responsible for maintaining a healthy economy, he does not really possess adequate constitutional or legal authority to meet this obligation. Responsibility for fiscal policy is shared with Congress, and the FRB is authorized by Congress to make monetary policy. In the area of monetary policy, presidential power is truly "the power to persuade." There are many informal contacts between the White House and the FRB, however, such as during periodic luncheon meetings, at which monetary policy is discussed. More formal meetings also take place. A group called the Quadriad, which consists of the secretary of the treasury, the director of the Office of Management and Budget, the chair of the Council of Economic Advisers, and the chair of the Federal Reserve Board, has met with varying frequency with the president since the time of the Kennedy administration. These meetings allow the president to express his views on monetary policy to the FRB. In turn, the FRB chair can convey some of his views on the economy to the administration. In all, there is quite a bit of contact and cooperation between the White House and the FRB. The result of this activity is that the monetary policy made by the FRB is customarily acceptable to the president, even if it is not precisely what he would prefer.[26]

Fiscal Policy

Fiscal policy involves the deliberate use of the national government's taxing and spending policies to influence the overall operation of the economy and maintain economic stability. Fiscal policy is formulated by the president and Congress and is conducted through the federal budget process. The powerful instruments of fiscal policy are budget surpluses and deficits. These are achieved by manipulating the overall or "aggregate" levels of revenue and expenditures.

According to standard fiscal policy theory, at some level of total or aggregate spending, the economy will operate at a full employment level. Total spending is the sum of consumer spending, private investment spending, and government spending. If consumer and business spending does not create demand sufficient to cause the economy to operate at full employment, then the government should make up the shortfall by increasing spending in excess of revenues. This was essentially what Keynes recommended that the national government should do during the Great Depression. If inflation is the problem confronting policy makers, then government can reduce demand for goods and services by reducing its expenditures and running a budget surplus.[27]

Discretionary fiscal policy involves deliberate decisions by the president and Congress to run budget surpluses or deficits. This can be done by increasing or decreasing spending while holding taxes constant; by increasing or cutting taxes while holding spending stable; or by some combination of changes in taxing and expenditure.

The first significant application of fiscal policy theory occurred in 1964. When John F. Kennedy, an activist president committed to getting the country "moving again," took office in 1961, he brought Keynesian economists to Washington as his economic advisers. These advisers believed that government action was needed to stimulate the economy in order to achieve full employment, and they were able to convince President Kennedy of this. The need, as they saw it, was for a budget deficit to add to aggre-

---

fiscal policy:

Federal government policies on taxes, spending and debt management, intended to promote the nation's macro-economic goals, particularly with respect to employment, price stability and growth.

 Web Exploration

To learn about current fiscal policy, go to
www.awlonline.com/oconnor.

gate demand. The problem was, however, that budget deficits were strongly opposed by many conservatives as bad public policy and perhaps even as immoral. Thinking strategically, President Kennedy's advisers decided that many conservatives and members of the business community would find deficits more palatable, or less objectionable, if they were achieved by cutting taxes rather than by increasing government spending. (Businesses had been complaining about high taxes.) Furthermore, a tax cut would increase private sector spending on goods and services. Higher government spending, on the other hand, would mean more spending on public goods and services and bigger government.

The result was the adoption of the Revenue Act of 1964, which reduced personal and corporate income tax rates. This variant of fiscal policy, which was more acceptable to the business community, has been labeled "commercial Keynesianism." The tax-cut stimulus contributed to the expansion of the economy through the remainder of the 1960s and reduced the unemployment rate to less than 4 percent, its lowest peacetime rate and what many people then considered to be full employment.[28]

In 1968 Congress enacted a tax increase at the urging of the Johnson administration in order to restrain inflation, which was stimulated by increased spending for Great Society programs and the Vietnam War. The tax increase contributed to a balanced budget in fiscal year 1969, the last time the budget was balanced until 1998. Tax changes were also used during the 1970s to stabilize the economy. Since the early 1980s, however, the government has incurred large annual budget deficits. These deficits can be viewed either as "neutralizing" fiscal policy, because they have politically foreclosed most major alterations in taxing and spending rates, or as a source of continuing stimulation to the economy.[29] Consequently, much of the burden of economic stabilization has been placed on FRB and monetary policy.

What we have discussed thus far is discretionary fiscal policy, so called because public officials must make overt decisions concerning its use. There are also some automatic stabilizers that have been built into the economy, whether intentionally or unintentionally, that operate without decisions by policy makers. These automatic stabilizers "act as buffers when the economy weakens by automatically reducing taxes and increasing government spending."[30] When the economy declines, for example, mandatory spending for such programs as unemployment insurance, food stamps, and Medicaid increases because eligibility for benefits depends on people's income or employment status. The tax system also acts as an automatic stabilizer. When the economy slows down and personal income and corporate profits decline, tax payments fall and help reduce the decline in after-tax incomes that would otherwise occur.[31] Conversely, when the economy revives, taxes begin to take a bigger bite out of incomes and thus help hold down spending. Although the automatic stabilizers are helpful in mitigating economic fluctuations, they are by themselves inadequate to stabilize the economy.

The Global Economy

As the world becomes smaller due to advances in transportation, communication, and transferrable technologies, the linkage between the United States and the rest of the world strengthens. International affairs play major roles in business decisions of American companies that wish to maximize their profits from reducing labor costs as well as expanding their markets. Free trade, in general, has had a beneficial impact on the U.S. economy. By 1999 the U.S. economy was enjoying more than eight years of uninterrupted growth, the third longest expansion in the nation's history. Reflecting this growth, the stock market soared by more than 300 percent between 1990 and 1999. (See Politics Now: Internet stocks: For Real or a Bubble.)

Consumer confidence was high, producing strong spending that pushed up corporate profits and stock prices. The downside of the strong consumer confidence was witnessed in savings levels that in 1997 declined to their lowest point since 1946. In the

POLITICS NOW

Internet Stocks: For Real or a Bubble?

In the late 1990s, almost any company associated with the Internet witnessed significant gains in their stock prices. For example, in January 1999 an initial public offering of the stock Marketwatch.com (a company that provides financial data to Internet sites) was offered to select investors for a price of $17 per share. When it opened for public trading on January 15, 1999, its price soared to $90 a share. Many Internet companies did not even record any profits, but that did not stop investors from bidding prices higher. Since profits were nonexistent, Wall Street reported stock prices in terms of the size of companies. For example, the stock Broadcast.com (a company that offered audio and video over the Internet) had a market value in early 1999 at $2.33 billion, or $9.3 billion for each of its 250 employees. Yahoo stock had an evaluation of $35 million per employee and eBay auction site was valued at $61 million per employee. These prices caused some analysts to predict a correction at a future date. A few government officials worried that the increased volatility of stocks combined with elevated price levels was reminiscent of the stock market before the historic crash of 1929. Political leaders since that time have tried to ensure greater stability in the economy through regulatory bodies such as the Securities and Exchange Commission. A sharp sell-off of stocks could have devastating impacts on present workers as well as retirees who have their pensions invested in the equities market.

In the late 1990s, Internet stocks reported spectacular price gains in a relatively short period of time. Amazon.com, an online shopping site, was trading at approximately $240 a share in the middle of December 1998. In less than a month the price of the stock rose past $400 a share and split. The company eBay saw its stock price rise from $18 to over $300 in a period of four months. The dollar amount of money pouring into Internet stocks was significant. In 1999 the market value of the company America Online exceeded that of General Motors.

As a consequence of these trends, analysts began to question whether Internet stock prices reflected true values or were merely speculative "bubbles" that could quickly burst and plunge the nation into a severe recession. Alan Greenspan, chairman of the Federal Reserve Board, noted that some of the small Internet companies would succeed and may even justify higher prices. However, he believed that the vast majority of Internet companies would in all likelihood fail. He compared buying Internet stocks to playing the lottery, viewing the entire Internet craze as another example of people's willingness to bet on a long shot. For centuries, according to Greenspan, Americans have been willing to pay more for lottery tickets than their chances of winning justified. The Internet stocks represented the latest manifestation of this phenomenon.

Some Wall Street observers warned that speculators may be inflating the value of Internet companies. They claimed that while there may be solid prospects in some Internet companies, investors' willingness to buy anything with a "dot com" moniker had made it difficult to distinguish solid prospects from companies simply trying to cash in on the Internet mania. Many companies did indeed cash in on the craze. In 1998 initial public offerings of Internet companies rose an average of 119 percent. Some companies such as Theglobe.com (rising 606 percent in its first day of trading) experienced more spectacular increases. Internet stocks recorded robust gains in late 1998 after reports of healthy Christmas sales over the net. Internet stock prices experienced high levels of volatility in early 1999 with sharp gains and sell-offs.

SOURCES: David Barboza, "Anything.com Likely to Be Hottest Issue in Class of 1999," www.nytimes.com. Kenneth Gilpin, "The Bubbles Must Burst, If They're Real Bubbles," www.nytimes.com. Edward Wyatt and David Barboza, "Internet Stocks Falter, Causing Wider Worries," www.nytimes.com.

1980s personal savings averaged 7.2 percent of disposable income, yet declined to 3.8 percent in 1997.

The stock market advance of the 1990s was impressive; but many believed that it could not last forever, noting that in the 1920s (between October 1923 and September 1929) the Dow Jones Industrial Average increased by 345 percent before its infamous crash. Some hazards to the American economy were cited by economists in the late 1990s. These dangers included: potential wage inflation, higher interest rates brought about to control inflation, an overvalued stock market, and Asia's economic crisis.[32]

The impact of the Asian crisis to the American economy remained an enigma. Early in 1998 the Federal Reserve Board welcomed the effects of the Asian crisis, believing that it would reduce the price of imports and that lower-cost imports would contain inflation. Later in the year, however, the Fed began to express concerns over rising levels of inventories of American goods, the impact of weaker Asian currencies on American exports, and the health of Asian banks. Individual corporations such as the Boeing Company (the world's largest aircraft manufacturer) and agricultural giant Cargill, Inc., contended that their exports would suffer as a consequence of the Asian crisis or what was being termed the "Asian flu." In order to contain the effects of this "flu," large corporations such as Boeing and Cargill pressured Congress to provide an additional $18 billion of funds to the International Monetary Fund (IMF) in order to assist troubled Asian economies and prevent a loss of American exports. Free-market conservatives in Congress argued that American corporations as well as American banks (threatened by the prospect of bad loans in Asia) should be disciplined by the vagaries of the marketplace and that it was not the responsibility of American taxpayers to protect profit margins of large corporations.[33]

One obvious impact of the Asian economic crisis was a worsening of the nation's trade deficit. Trade balances worsened in 1998 due to weaker overseas economies (making it more difficult for foreigners to purchase American goods), currency devaluations (making American goods more expensive to foreigners), and increased imports (currency devaluation also leads to lower priced foreign products and greater demand for them). In 1998 the Asian economic picture was bleak. Japan remained in recession, South Korea's unemployment rate tripled in less than one year, Indonesia was in chaos, forcing the resignation of its longstanding ruler, and China's rate of economic growth was slowing. The Institute of International Finance, a research group funded by private banks, reported in 1998 the following one year declines in gross domestic product: Indonesia (-12.5 percent), Malaysia (-2 percent), South Korea (-5 percent) and Thailand (-7 percent).[34] By 1999 the Asian economies were beginning to recover. It was anticipated that the recovery would lead to higher sales of American products in these nations. This outcome, however, could put pressure on the Federal Reserve Board to raise interest rates in an effort to prevent the return of inflation.

Web Exploration
To learn about economic policy briefs from the international community, go to
www.awlonline.com/oconnor.

The Budgetary Process

The Budget and Accounting Act of 1921 gave the president authority to prepare an annual budget and submit it to Congress for approval. A staff agency now called the Office of Management and Budget (OMB) was created to assist the president and handle the details of budget preparation (see also chapter 8). The budget runs for a single fiscal year, now beginning on October 1 of one calendar year and running through September 30 of the following calendar year. The fiscal year takes its name from the calendar year in which it ends; thus the time period from October 1, 1997, through September 30, 1998, is designated fiscal year (FY) 1998. An overview of where the federal government gets its money and how the money is spent is presented in Figure 18.3.

The president sends his budget to Congress in January or February of each year. Work on the budget within the executive branch will have begun nine or ten months earlier, however (see Table 18.1). Acting in accordance with presidential decision on the general structure of the budget, the OMB provides the various departments and agencies with instructions and guidance on presidential priorities to help them in preparing their budget requests. The departments and agencies then proceed to develop their detailed funding requests. Each agency believes in the value and necessity of its set of programs and seeks to expand or at least maintain its budget. The OMB's role, on the other hand, is to put together a budget that reflects the president's preferences and priorities. Consequently, agency budget requests are frequently modified and revised downward by the OMB. Agencies that are aggrieved by OMB reductions may try to appeal these decisions to the president. If this happens, the president usually agrees with the OMB. During the early years of the Reagan administration, this traditional "bottom-up" process of preparing the budget, in which the agencies' requests shape the budget, was replaced by a "top-down" process. In "top-down" budgeting, directives from the president and the OMB dominate the budgetary process.[35]

Web Exploration
To compare the current fiscal budget with budgets from prior years, go to
www.awlonline.com/oconnor.

Figure 18.3 Receipts and Outlays of the Federal Government

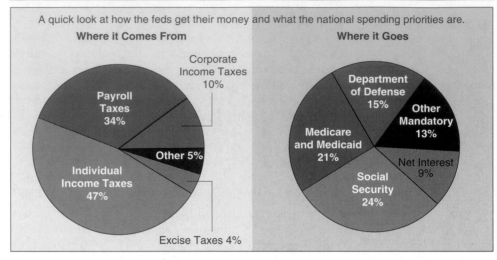

NOTE: Because of rounding, estimates do not total 100%.
SOURCE: *Budget of the United States Government, Fiscal Year 2000* (Washington D.C.: Government Printing Office, 1999), Table 2-1, Table 2-2.

Article I of the Constitution provides that "no money shall be drawn from the Treasury, but in consequence of appropriations made by law." Congress and its legislative committees (such as the committees on Resources, Education and Educational Opportunities, and National Security) may authorize that money be spent on programs, but it is Congress *and* the appropriations committees in each chamber that actually provide the funding needed to carry out these programs. The appropriations committees often deny some, and once in a while all, of the funding authorized by the legislative committees. Consequently, the legislative committees sometimes have resorted to backdoor spending—authorizing agencies to borrow money from the Treasury or creating entitlement programs that make funding mandatory in order to circumvent the appropriations committees.[36]

Conflicts often develop between Congress and the president over both the details of the budget and its overall dimensions, such as the size of the deficit, the balance between military and domestic spending, or international agreements affecting domestic economics. Uncertainty also arises over the political feasibility of funding very specific initiatives. Throughout the 1980s there was conflict between the Democrats in Congress, who favored more domestic spending and less military spending, and President Ronald Reagan and his administration, whose spending preferences leaned in the opposite direction. In 1993 the Clinton administration touched off a titanic partisan political struggle in Congress with its budget deficit-reduction plan involving a combination of spending cuts and tax increases. Drawing almost unanimous opposition from the Republicans in Congress and also from some conservative Democrats, the Clinton proposal was passed by Vice President Albert Gore Jr.'s tie-breaking vote in the Senate and by a margin of two votes in the House.[37] The Clinton administration, moreover, had to make many deals with members of Congress in order to secure the votes needed to adopt its budget proposal.

The 1993 congressional-presidential struggle was a love fest compared to the 1995–96 stalemate. Under the leadership of Speaker Newt Gingrich, the first Republican congressional majority in generations devised a plan to balance the budget in seven years. While President Clinton also professed a desire to eliminate annual deficits, he and Congress clashed over strategies and over what standard to apply to decide if the budget was likely to balance. Republicans favored sharper cuts in the rate at which

Table 18.1 The Federal Budget Process

First Monday in February	Congress receives the president's budget.
February 15	Congressional Budget Office (CBO) reports to the Budget Committees on fiscal policy and budget priorities, including an analysis of the president's budget.
February 25	Congressional committees submit views and estimates on spending to the Budget Committee.
April 1	Budget committees report concurrent resolution on the budget, which sets a total for budget outlays, an estimate of expenditures for major budget categories, and the recommended level of revenues. This resolution acts as an agenda for the remainder of the budgetary process.
April 15	Congress completes action on concurrent resolution on the budget.
May 15	Annual appropriations bills may be considered in the House.
June 10	House Appropriations Committee completes action on regular appropriations bills.
June 15	Congress completes action on reconciliation legislation, bringing budget totals into conformity with established ceilings.
June 30	House completes action on all appropriations bills.
October 1	The new fiscal year begins.

SOURCE: Adapted from Howard E. Shuman, *Politics and the Budget,* 3d ed. (Englewood Cliffs, NJ: Prentice Hall, 1992), 67.

Medicare, Medicaid, and various welfare and education programs would grow. Some of the savings from these cuts would be used to fund a tax cut. As negotiations struggled along, the president came to embrace most of the primary goals of the GOP. The Clinton administration, however, preferred less drastic cuts in the rate at which Medicare and other programs grew and also a less generous tax cut.

Since no one proposed that a balanced budget be achieved immediately, all sides relied on projections for the amounts to be raised in taxes and to be spent through the year 2002. President Clinton and his congressional allies preferred to use the more optimistic projections of his OMB, while Republicans relied on the more conservative estimates developed by the Congressional Budget Office.

President Clinton vetoed appropriations bills for FY 1996 designed to start the government down the road toward a Republican-style balanced budget. Despite widespread consensus among many partisanly neutral economists that something had to be done to curb federal health-care expenditures—and the sooner the better—President Clinton found that in late 1995 his public approval ratings rose as he flayed Congress for imperiling health care for the elderly. When a president who had never achieved broad-based popularity, and who was worried about reelection, confronted a congressional majority that believed that it had been sent to Washington to balance the budget, it was little wonder that agreement proved to be elusive. Both president and Congress believed that they were doing not just what was popular, but what was morally correct.

As with other legislation, appropriations bills passed by Congress need the president's approval to become law. Conventional wisdom once held that appropriations bills were "veto proof" because they provided the funds necessary to keep the government in operation. However, Presidents Richard M. Nixon and Gerald R. Ford both vetoed appropriations bills that they called "budget-busting" and inflationary because more funds were appropriated for some programs than the presidents wanted. These bills were later enacted into law after appropriations were reduced in an effort to meet presidential preferences. In 1995 and 1996, Bill Clinton vetoed appropriations bills that he believed cut social programs too severely.

The struggle between president and Congress ultimately closed parts of the government for extended periods in late 1995 and early 1996. When public opinion polls showed that Americans resented the shutdown and blamed Republicans, Congress relented and funded government programs for the rest of fiscal year 1996 at levels acceptable

■ A tourist in Washington, D.C., peers into the National Air and Space Museum, closed because of the 1995 federal shutdown. (Photo courtesy: Jay Mallin/Impact Visuals)

to President Clinton. As detailed in the previous chapter, a major restructuring of welfare programs was enacted in the summer of 1996.

The use of the budget as a part of fiscal policy to counteract fluctuations in the economy is handicapped by the fact that planning begins roughly a year and a half before the beginning of the fiscal year in which it is to take effect. Once a budget is adopted, it takes time to implement its provisions. Add to this the difficulty of predicting the future state of the economy and one discovers that the budget—which embodies changes in taxing and spending rates—is a rather blunt instrument for manipulating the economy.

For many years the budgetary process was a fragmented and disjointed operation. Appropriations and revenue decisions were considered separately by different committees. For purposes of congressional consideration and enactment, the president's budget was (and still is) divided into thirteen appropriations bills, each of which was handled by a different subcommittee of the House Appropriations Committee, where the most intensive examinations were accorded to budget requests. Each of the bills was also considered separately in the Senate Appropriations Committee. One by one the thirteen appropriations bills were eventually enacted into law. This disjointed process created two problems. First, it was difficult to establish spending priorities between domestic and military programs or among the many domestic programs. Second, the determination of total revenues and expenditures and, consequently, the size of the budget surplus or deficit was accidental, something that simply happened rather than being planned.

To provide itself with more control over the budget process, Congress initiated and enacted the Budget and Impoundment Control Act of 1974. The act establishes a budget process that includes setting overall levels of revenues and expenditures, the size of the budget surplus or deficit, and priorities among different "functional" areas (for example, national defense, transportation, agriculture, foreign aid, and health). New budget committees were established in the House and Senate to perform these tasks. The Congressional Budget Office (CBO), a professional staff of technical experts, was created to assist the budget committees and to provide members of Congress with their own source of budgetary information so they would be more independent of OMB.

The budget committees hold hearings on the president's proposed budget, soliciting advice from the OMB and CBO, executive agencies, and other members of Congress. The committees then formulate a concurrent budget resolution that set targets for overall levels of revenues and spending, and ceilings for each functional area in the budget. The budget resolution is supposed to be completed by April 15, although this deadline is often missed. Once the concurrent budget resolution is adopted (it does not require the president's approval), the House and Senate appropriations committees and their subcommittees are expected to act within its limits when making their decisions on the details of appropriations requests by various agencies. In most years reconciliation legislation is necessary to ensure that the revenue and spending targets in the budget resolution are actually met. The reconciliation process requires the taxation and legislative committees to propose changes in existing tax laws and entitlement programs, such as Medicare and food stamps. Typically, these changes involve cutting spending, although increasing taxes is an alternative. The budget committees then consolidate these proposed changes into a single reconciliation bill, which must be passed by both houses. Unlike the budget resolution, which is an internal congressional matter, the rec-

Figure 18.4   Entitlements and Discretionary Spending (in billions of dollars)

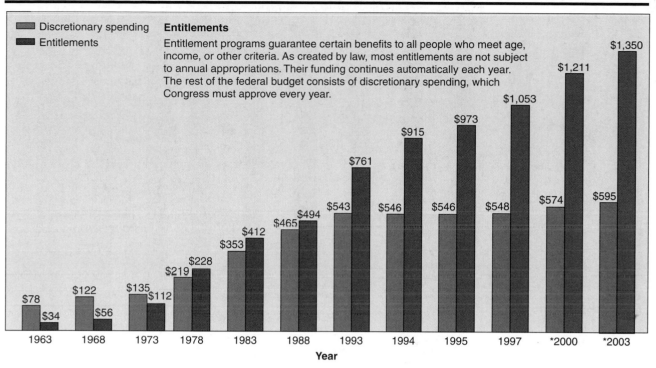

*Projections

SOURCE: *United States Budget for Fiscal Year* (Washington D.C.: Government Printing Office, various years).

onciliation bill requires presidential approval. Reconciliation legislation makes permanent changes in the laws involving the affected policies and programs. For instance, taxes may be increased or the benefits available under an entitlement program may be lowered.[38] Overall growth in both entitlements and discretionary spending are shown in Figure 18.4.

Legislative action on all appropriations bills is supposed to be completed by October 1, the start of the fiscal year. It is rare, however, for all appropriations bills to emerge from Congress by this date. For programs still unfunded at the start of the fiscal year, Congress can pass a continuing resolution, which authorizes agencies to continue operating on the basis of last year's appropriation until their new budget is approved. This procedure can cause some uncertainty in agency operations and when, as in 1995, president and Congress cannot agree, some programs may actually be shut down until terms for a continuing resolution can be worked out.

The budget process put into place in 1974 was intended to make the national budgetary process more rational, comprehensive, and coherent. To some extent it has done that. It has also compelled members of Congress to consider the overall dimensions of the budget and to directly confront the deficit. It has not, however, prompted Congress to balance the budget.

The Deficit and the Debt

Large annual budget deficits and a rapidly growing national debt (which is the cumulation of the annual budget deficits) have characterized government finance since the early 1980s. Several factors have contributed to this situation: a severe recession in the early 1980s; the large tax cut enacted in 1981; sharply increased spending for national defense during the 1980s; and continuously expanding spending on such

Table 18.2 National Government Finances, Selected Years, 1940–2003 (billions of current dollars)

Year	Receipts	Outlays	Surplus or Deficit	Year	Receipts	Outlays	Surplus or Deficit
1940	6.5	9.5	−2.9	1990	1031.3	1252.7	−221.4
1945	45.2	92.7	−47.6	1991	1054.3	1323.8	−269.5
1950	39.4	42.6	−3.1	1992	1090.5	1380.9	−290.4
1955	65.5	68.4	−3.0	1993	1153.5	1408.2	−254.7
1960	92.5	92.2	0.3	1994	1257.7	1460.9	−203.1
1965	116.8	118.2	−1.4	1995	1346.4	1538.9	−192.5
1970	192.8	195.6	−2.8	1996	1453.0	1560.0	−107.0
1975	279.1	332.3	−53.2	1997	1579.3	1601.2	−21.9
1980	517.1	590.9	−72.7	1998	1721.8	1652.6	69.2
1985	734.1	946.4	−212.3	1999*	1806.3	1727.1	79.3
1988	909.0	1064.1	−155.2	2000*	1883.0	1765.7	117.3
1989	990.7	1143.2	−152.5	2003*	2075.0	1893.0	141.3

*Estimates

**Surpluses beginning in year 1998 are assigned to the category "Reserve Pending Social Security Reform"

SOURCE: *Budget of the United States Government Fiscal Year 2000* (Washington, D.C.: U.S. Government Printing Office, 1999), 366;
Budget of the United States Government Fiscal Year 1998 (Washington, D.C.: U.S. Government Printing Office, 1997).

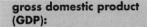

gross domestic product (GDP):

The total market value of all goods and services produced in a country during a year.

entitlement programs as Social Security, Medicare, and Medicaid.[39] National budget deficits, which rarely exceeded $60 billion before 1980 and usually were much less than that, averaged $150 billion during the decade of the 1980s (see Table 18.2). These dollar figures have increased in part because of inflation. One way to control for inflation when comparing budget deficits is to view the deficits as a percentage of **gross domestic product (GDP).** GDP is the total market value of all goods and services produced in the United States during a year. During the 1960s the budget deficit typically was less than 1 percent of GDP, compared with between 3 percent and 5 percent of GDP during the 1980s. This comparison also reveals a major increase in absolute budget deficit levels.

The national debt tripled during the 1980s. Standing at $909 billion in 1980, it soared beyond $2.87 trillion in 1989. By 1996, the national debt was nearly $5 trillion. Measured against GDP, the national debt increased from 34 to 55 percent of GDP during the 1980s (see Figure 18.5). Interest payments on the national debt accounted for about 14 percent of the national budget in 1999. But while the national debt has grown, so has the value of the national government's assets—including land, buildings, military installations, and equipment. According to one calculation, the government's assets approximately equaled its liabilities in 1960; by 1980 assets exceeded liabilities by $279 billion.[40] But a massive selloff of assets is highly unlikely.

Since peaking at $290 billion in 1992, deficits have declined each year, dropping to a level of $22 billion in 1997. Debt held by the public peaked at 50.2 percent of gross domestic product in 1993 and fell to 44.3 percent in 1998. The Omnibus Budget Reconciliation Act (OBRA) of 1993 helped to reduce the deficit, as did economic growth that exceeded most expectations. Total income tax receipts rose nearly 25 percent from 1992 to 1995, despite predictions of some economists that higher taxes enacted in the 1993 act would actually produce less revenues.

Gramm-Rudman-Hollings Act.   Strong partisan conflict and policy differences between the Democrats in Congress and the president during the Reagan administration over the size and composition of the budget made reduction of the budget deficit impossible through conventional budgetary procedures. The alarming size of the deficits and public concern over them pushed Congress into taking extraordinary action in 1985. Called "a bad idea whose time had come," the Balanced Budget and Emergency

Web Exploration

To compare the federal budget with the national debt, go to
www.awlonline.com/oconnor.

Figure 18.5   The National Debt as a Percentage of GDP, 1940–1998

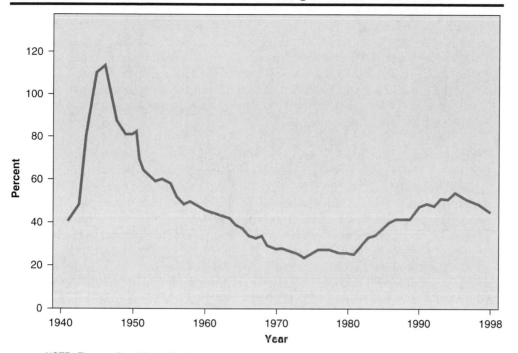

NOTE: Figures reflect debt held by the public and do not include debt held by federal government accounts.
SOURCES: 1940–1992: Office of Management and Budget, *Budget Baselines, Historical Data, and Alternatives for the Future* (Washington D.C.: U.S. Government Printing Office, 1993), 1346. 1993–1998: Office of Management and Budget, *Budget of the U.S. Government, Fiscal Year 2000* (Washington D.C.: U.S. Government Printing Office, 1999), 110. Statistical Abstracts of the United States (Washington D.C.: U.S. Government Printing Office, 1995), 333.

Deficit Reduction Act created a procedure for automatic deficit reduction. As mentioned in chapter 8, this act is better known as the Gramm-Rudman-Hollings Act after its three Senate sponsors—Phil Gramm (R–Tex.), Warren Rudman (R–N.H.), and Ernest Hollings (D–S.C.). There were three basic components to the act:

1. Budget deficit goals of $171.9 billion and $144 billion were set for 1986 and 1987. After that, the deficit goal would be lowered annually by $36 million decrements until it reached zero in 1991.
2. Several programs were exempted from automatic budget cuts, including Social Security, Medicaid, veterans' benefits, food stamps, Aid to Families with Dependent Children, child nutrition, and interest on the national debt.
3. If at the beginning of a fiscal year the deficit target was not met, then, by a process called sequestration (Congress seems to like these clumsy terms), automatic, across-the-board budget cuts, divided equally between nonexempt domestic and military programs, would be levied, sufficient to meet the deficit target.

In 1987 Congress and the Reagan administration were confronted with the need to reduce the deficit by $45 billion in order to meet the Gramm-Rudman-Hollings Act target. Most members of Congress found this disagreeable, as did the Reagan administration because of the required military spending cuts that would be required. Consequently, the act was amended to revise the budget deficit targets and make them easier to meet. The zero target date then became 1993, a year that, in reality, saw a deficit of $254.7 billion.

The Gramm-Rudman-Hollings Act did not accomplish much deficit reduction, although arguably budget deficits might have been larger had the act not been in effect. In this sense the act may have imposed some restraint. It was, however, possible for

Congress to avoid the requirements of the act. Deficit targets set by Congress can be altered by Congress, as they were in 1987.[41]

With the passage of legislation in 1996 and its implementation in 1997, President Clinton acquired the authority to cancel specific items in spending and taxing bills. This line-item veto authority represented a rare yielding of congressional power. In the infamous *Contract With America*, Speaker of the House Newt Gingrich called for giving the president, Republican or Democrat, "the authority to cut wasteful pork-barrel spending." Nevertheless, the U.S. Supreme Court quickly found the line item veto unconstitutional.

Budget Compromises.   In August 1997 a historic budget agreement was signed by President Clinton, with House Speaker Newt Gingrich at his side, balancing the federal budget by 2002 and cutting federal income taxes for the first time since 1981. The agreement ended a period of acrimonious conflict between the president and Congress over the budget. Tensions escalated following the election of 1994, when the Republican party gained control of Congress. The newly elected Republicans in the House of Representatives quickly canceled money that had been approved for fiscal year 1995 and declared President Clinton's 1996 budget "dead on arrival." In a direct attack on the Democratic party's priorities, money was withheld from programs such as housing, job training, and water projects. This initiated a period of intense conflict between the executive and legislative branches of government.

Early conflict represented a prelude to the more intense 1996 budget controversies. Under the leadership of a new chair of the House Budget Committee, John Kasich (R—Ohio), the House Budget Committee approved a plan that would cut $1 trillion in spending over seven years (to balance the budget by 2002), reduce taxes by $353, increase defense spending modestly, and abolish the departments of Commerce, Education and Energy, along with fourteen other agencies. Republicans were elated by the prospect of balancing the budget for the first time since 1969.

Clinton initially supported the Republican budgetary goals of reducing the scope of government, balancing the budget, cutting taxes, and reducing entitlements. He endorsed these aims on a national television appearance in June 1995 yet failed to reach consensus with Congressional Republicans. Confrontation over the budget led to heated rhetoric, confrontation, and government shutdown. By April 1996 the conflict ended as Clinton signed into law six appropriations bills.[42]

By the following year, President Clinton and the Republican Congress seemed to be weary of budgetary politics that characterized earlier struggles. Both sides came to realize that they could be badly damaged from the political fallout of budget deliberations. In 1997 the timing seemed right for budgetary compromise with President Clinton and the Republican Congress ready to strike a deal. According to Treasury Secretary Robert Rubin, the 1997 budget agreement was a "win-win" situation with elements in the compromise that each side treasured.[43] Republican Senator William Roth asserted that the GOP clearly received something of value, since balancing the budget and cutting taxes were Republican ideas. Enacted programs that were favored by Republicans included: a tax credit of $500 a child to help families (a program strongly supported by the Christian Coalition), cuts in capital gain taxes, reductions in inheritance taxes, medical savings accounts, and changes in Medicare. Democratic initiatives that were adopted in the 1997 bill included: a $1,500 Hope scholarship (tax credit of $1,500 for the first two years of college), health insurance for about half of the nation's uninsured children, and the elimination of limits on disability payments to legal immigrants.

In an odd twist to the 1997 budget compromise, Republicans praised Democratic programs that they had derided only a few months ago and Democrats applauded programs that were cherished by the Republican party. Clinton declared that the $500 a child tax credit (long sought by the Christian Coalition and "crown jewel" of the 1994 Contract With America) was his own way to help a "wide range of middle-class parents." Representative Bill Archer, the chairman of the House Ways and Means Com-

property may occur from pollution. Natural curiosities may be damaged, and scenic vistas may be obscured. In the 1980s air pollution often made it impossible to see across the Grand Canyon. Because Americans seem health conscious, the effects of pollution on human health often attract the greatest attention from policy makers.

Environmental Policy Making

Pollution control is the responsibility of government operating through the policy process. The market, which works through competition and the price system, is unable to deal satisfactorily with the problem of pollution. As economists tell us, pollution is an *externality,* or a *social cost* of industrial activity. This is so because, in the nature of things, air and water are "free" or public goods. Industries can dispose of wastes (pollutants) at low or no cost by emitting them into the air or dumping them into nearby bodies of water.

Consequently, the costs of waste disposal are borne by the people adversely affected by the wastes, for example, by people who breathe the air or use the water. Because the costs of waste disposal do not need to be considered in determining the prices of products, industries can sell—and consumers can buy—products at lower prices. A business has no incentive to clean up its pollutants because this action would drive up its expenses and thus the prices it charges. Moreover, if a business did clean up its pollutants, this would put it at an economic disadvantage with competitors who chose not to withstand the costs of pollution reduction. Consequently, in the absence of government action, control of pollution is unlikely to occur.

The organized groups supporting environmental protection have greatly increased in number, membership size, technical skill, and political sophistication since the early 1970s. Such well-known groups as the Wilderness Society, the Sierra Club, the National Wildlife Federation, the Environmental Defense Fund, and the Natural Resources Defense Council constitute the core of the environmental movement. They are flanked on the left by more radical groups, such as Earth First! and Greenpeace, who take direct action to protect the environment.[47] On the right, the Nature Conservancy works through the marketplace, buying land valuable for natural resource protection and thus removing it from business use. These and other environmental groups have been major forces pushing Congress to enact new environmental legislation and to strengthen existing laws. During the years of the Reagan administration, which was skeptical toward environmental and pollution control programs, environmental groups thrived.

Environmental groups have also benefited from strong public opinion in support of pollution control. Conflict over pollution control legislation typically becomes a struggle between liberal environmental groups and conservative business groups allied with labor groups who favor fewer or less-costly pollution controls. Pollution controls are often quite costly and, on the basis of the principle that "the polluter pays," most of the financial and other costs of complying with them fall initially on the business community. Often the costs can be passed on to consumers in the form of higher prices. Thus Bush administration officials estimated that the costs of complying with the Clean Air Act of 1990 would run more than $20 billion annually.[48] Pollution controls, by increasing the costs of doing business, may also discourage economic growth and job creation, or so it is frequently argued. Environmental groups want the strongest legislation possible. Business and economic development groups usually do not oppose all controls; rather, they favor controls that will be less stringent, intrusive, and costly to business. This is a politically more viable policy position than total opposition. As one would expect, resulting legislation usually reflects compromise between the environmental and business perspectives. An exception was the Clean Air Act of 1970, which called for a 90 percent reduction in automobile emissions and strong controls on industrial pollution. Driven by exceptionally strong public support for environmental protection, which was highlighted by the first Earth Day (April 22, 1970), this legislation became stronger as it moved through Congress.[49]

mittee, stated that Clinton's pet program, the $1,500 Hope Scholarship program, "tells young people that education is not only a virtue but that we, through the tax code, will help reduce the cost of it."[44]

As the case with most legislation, the budget compromise was both praised and condemned. Liberals claimed that the budget deal had abandoned the poor and provided too much help for the wealthy. Some conservatives claimed that the deal undermined welfare reform. A few Democrats asserted that the budget bill was overdue as a vehicle for bringing their party back to the center of the political spectrum. Representative Charles Rangel (D–N.Y.) stated that "we have now shattered the myth that we, as Democrats, are spending Democrats and taxing Democrats, because we have come forward in support of the President's package."[45] Clinton argued that the era of the "New Democrat" had arrived, that the tax and spend image of liberal Democrats was an anachronism, and that the party should embrace the tenets of fiscal conservatism. Smaller government, tax relief, and sharply focused spending priorities became the new buzzwords of the Democratic Party.[46]

The budget surplus that emerged in 1998 was also a testament to legislation that was passed during the Clinton administration in 1993 and 1997. It is somewhat ironic that in retrospect Ronald Reagan may be remembered as the propagator of a huge budget deficit while Clinton's greatest legacy may be the elimination of deficits and the creation of budget surpluses.

Many predicted that 1998 would produce a budget surplus even though President Clinton's ability to cut pork barrel programs had been severely constrained by the Supreme Court. Although President Clinton could no longer cut spending by use of

GLOBAL POLITICS — Economic Policy in a Globalizing Economy

As the G-7 enter the new century, issues of the global economy pose challenges for their economic growth. Traditionally, economic policy making has been seen as a largely domestic activity, a perspective reflected in this chapter. Increasingly, however, how nations fare economically is influenced by what happens beyond their borders.

The clearest case of this is occurring in the European Union, of which the European partners below are members. In 1999, France, Italy, and Germany joined eight other EU members in creating a single European currency, the Euro, to go into full effect in 2002 (Britain is staying out of the Euro for the time being). Joining the Euro has forced the member country governments to give up control over key areas of domestic policy making, including regulation of the domestic money supply, interest rates, and government debt. Not surprisingly, given the progressive unification of their economies, the European G-7 countries' dependence on trade, especially with each other, is relatively high (about one-fifth of total national economic production).

Canada's dependence on trade is the highest in the G-7. This reflects in no small part that country's economic interdependence with the United States, which has increased as a result of the establishment of North American Free Trade Agreement. Comparing trade dependence in the United States with Canada suggests just how large the former's economic presence north of the border is.

Finally, despite the ongoing trade friction between Japan and the United States in the last decade, the economy of neither is as dependent on trade as those of the other G-7 countries. This suggests that the governments of these two countries are, at least in some ways, better able to regulate their economies in spite of events outside their borders.

Dependence on Foreign Trade in the G-7, 1995

Country	Imports as % of GDP	Exports as % of GDP
Canada	29.6	33.8
France	17.7	18.5
Germany	18.4	21.1
Italy	16.5	18.5
Japan	6.6	8.6
United Kingdom	25.1	22.9
United States	**10.6**	**8.1**

Source: *Japan 1997: An International Comparison,* 1997, p. 54.

■ Dealing with toxic waste is an expensive process. (Photo courtesy: Stephen Ferry/The Image Works)

the line-item veto, he predicted in May of 1998 that a surplus of approximately $39 billion would accrue for the fiscal year. The Congressional Budget Office later estimated that the surplus would reach $63 billion while Wall Street analysts estimated that the surplus would range from $75 billion to $100 billion.

THE ECONOMICS OF REGULATING ENVIRONMENTAL POLLUTION

A large number and variety of the national government's economic policies entail some sort of direct control of or restriction on private economic activity. These economic regulatory policies are variously intended to prevent or mitigate actions and conditions regarded as unfair, undesirable, unhealthy, or immoral. Collectively, they comprise an extensive framework of rules governing the conduct of private (and occasionally public) economic activity. Here, we focus on one important segment of this web of regulatory policies—regulation of environmental activity to protect the public health and the national environment.

Until the late 1960s, the national government was only minimally involved in the control of environmental pollution. The national government had long been concerned with the conservation of natural resources and the management of public lands—national forests, national parks, and grazing lands in the Western states. However, air and water pollution were seen as matters for the state and local governments to handle, if they so chose. But few states opted to do this—indeed, many states did little or nothing to control pollution in the pre–World War II decades of the twentieth century. Pollution was not perceived as a problem, partly because the environment had considerable capacity to absorb wastes without great harm to people. Also, the volume of pollution was lower than it would become in later years.

Population growth, increased urbanization, industrialization, and the extensive production and use of chemicals after World War II changed this situation. In the course of the 1960s, the problem of environmental pollution became a prominent item on the national political agenda. Because of strong public concern about environmental pollution it continues to have that status.

Pollution involves the discharge into the environment of harmful and noxious substances—chemicals, human and animal waste, and other contaminants—that prevent or interfere with desired human uses of the air, water, and soil. Chemicals discharged into streams, for example, make them unsafe as sources of drinking water or for recreational purposes. (The fish often don't fare too well, either.) Because this definition of pollution hinges on *human* use (which is not limited to consumption of environmental resources), it implies that desirable levels of environmental quality will depend on preferred uses. Thus the quality of water that should be maintained in a given river depends on whether it is to be used as a source of drinking water or for fishing and swimming, transportation, or waste disposal. Much cleaner water is required for the river if it is used as a source of drinking water than primarily as a medium of transportation. The levels of water quality required for particular uses can be scientifically determined (although in practice scientists often disagree); whether a particular level of quality *should* be sought is a political issue over which various prospective users of our hypothetical river disagree.

Pollution interferes with human uses of the environment in various ways. Pollution may make the air unsafe to breathe, especially for people with respiratory ailments, or water unsafe to drink. Bodies of water may become unsafe or uninhabitable for fish populations for human consumption. Lake Erie, for example, became nearly a "dead" body of water in the 1970s because of industrial pollution. Damage to forest, crops, and

Since 1970 Congress has enacted a large volume of pollution control legislation intended to help clean up the nation's air and water and to regulate the disposal of hazardous and toxic wastes. A brief summary of the major laws is presented here.[50]

- *Clean Air Act.* This statute directs the Environmental Protection Agency (discussed in the next section) to set standards for motor vehicle emissions, ambient air quality, hazardous air pollutants, and new sources of pollution; to prevent significant deterioration of air quality in clean air areas; to reduce stratospheric ozone depletion; and to control acid rain through an emissions trading system.
- *Clean Water Act.* This law creates a federal grant program to help finance sewage treatment plant construction, authorizes technological standards to reduce water pollution, and establishes programs to control non-point source pollution, such as runoff from parking lots and livestock feedlots.
- *Safe Drinking Water Act.* This act provides for drinking water standards to protect public health, the regulation of underground waste injection, and control of water contaminants.
- *Toxic Substances Control Act.* This act authorizes testing of chemicals and regulation of their use in order to protect health and the environment.
- *Resource Conservation and Recovery Act.* This statute provides a cradle-to-grave system of regulation for hazardous substances and waste, as well as a control program for underground storage tanks, such as those at gasoline stations.
- *Comprehensive Environmental Response, Compensation, and Liability Act.* Commonly referred to as Superfund, this statute creates a fund from taxes levied on polluters to pay the costs of cleaning up abandoned hazardous waste sites.
- *Federal Insecticide, Fungicide, and Rodenticide Act.* This statute calls for EPA registration and regulation of the use of pesticides.
- *National Environmental Policy Act.* This act requires agencies taking actions that will have a major impact on the environment to prepare environmental impact statements (EISs), which are subject to review by the EPA.
- *Pollution Prevention Act.* This act stipulates that the prevention of pollution shall be an EPA priority and authorizes actions for reducing the sources of pollution.
- *Omnibus Parks and Public Lands Management Act.* This bill contained more than 100 parks and land initiatives, including preservation of the Presidio in San Francisco and purchase of land in Sterling Forest along the New York–New Jersey border.

Responsibility for the implementation of these laws rests primarily with the Environmental Protection Agency, to which we now turn.

The Environmental Protection Agency

The Environmental Protection Agency (EPA) was created in 1970 by Congress at the urging of President Richard M. Nixon. A number of environmental programs previously located in five executive departments were vested in the EPA, which is an independent agency (that is, the agency is located outside of the executive departments) that reports directly to the president. The EPA administrator is appointed by the president, with the approval of the Senate. The EPA consolidated responsibility for water pollution, air pollution, solid waste management, radiation control, and hazardous and toxic substance control.

The EPA is the nation's largest regulatory agency, issuing permits, establishing and overseeing environmental standards, and enforcing relevant federal statutes and rules. In 1998 it had approximately 17,000 employees located in Washington and in ten regional offices throughout the country. Its annual budget for operations was around $7.3 billion dollars. The EPA's budget has not grown proportionately as the duties assigned to it have multiplied in recent years. Liberal environmental groups advocate more resources to enforce environmental regulations. Conservative groups say that too much money is spent on these issues and business should not be subjected to so many regulations.

2. STABILIZING THE ECONOMY

The national government continues to shape monetary policy by regulating the nation's money supply and interest rates. Monetary policy is controlled by the Federal Reserve Board. Fiscal policy, which involves the deliberate use of the national government's taxing and spending policies, is another tool of the national government and involves the president and Congress setting the national budget. Although the budget is initially suggested by the president, Congress has constitutional authority over the process.

3. THE ECONOMICS OF REGULATING ENVIRONMENTAL POLLUTION

The environment is one area in which the national government has used its economic regulatory powers to alter business practices. Conflicts over environmental regulation frequently pit the business community against environmental groups. The Environmental Protection Agency (EPA), which was created as an independent agency, is the nation's largest regulatory agency.

KEY TERMS

business cycles, p. 655
discount rate, p. 671
economic regulation, p. 665
economic stability, p. 668
fiscal policy, p. 672
gross domestic product (GDP), p. 680

inflation, p. 668
interventionist state, p. 658
laissez-faire, p. 655
monetary policy, p. 669
money, p. 669
open market operations, p. 671

recession, p. 668
reserve requirements, p. 670
social regulation, p. 665

SELECTED READINGS

Bryner, Gary C. *Blue Skies, Green Politics: The Clean Air Act of 1990.* Washington, D.C.: CQ Press, 1993.

Conlan, Timothy J., Margaret T. Wrightson, and David R. Beam. *Taxing Choices: The Politics of Tax Reform.* Washington, D.C.: CQ Press, 1990.

Derthick, Martha, and Paul J. Quirk. *The Politics of Deregulation.* Washington, D.C.: Brookings Institution, 1985.

Eisner, Marc Allen. *Regulatory Politics in Transition.* Baltimore: Johns Hopkins University Press, 1993.

Gold, Steven D., ed. *The Fiscal Crisis of the States.* Washington, D.C.: Georgetown University Press, 1995.

Harr, Johnathan. *A Civil Action.* New York: Random House, 1995.

Keech, William. *Economic Politics: The Costs of Democracy.* Cambridge: Cambridge University Press, 1995.

Kettl, Donald F. *Deficit Politics: Public Budgeting in Its Institutional and Historical Context.* New York: Macmillan, 1992.

Krugman, Paul. *The Age of Diminished Expectations.* Cambridge, MA: The MIT Press, 1994.

Rosenbaum, Walter A. *Environmental Politics and Policy,* 2d ed. Washington, D.C.: CQ Press, 1991.

Switzer, Jacqueline Vaughn. *Environmental Politics: Domestic and Global Dimension.* New York: St. Martin's, 1994.

Wilson, James Q., ed. *The Politics of Regulation.* New York: Basic Books, 1980.

Woolley, John T. *Monetary Politics: The Federal Reserve and the Politics of Monetary Policy.* London: Cambridge University Press, 1984.

Young, James Harvey. *Pure Food: Securing the Federal Food and Drugs Act of 1906.* Princeton, NJ: Princeton University Press, 1990.

NOTES

1. Jared Bernstein and Lawrence Mishel, "Has Wage Inequality Stopped Growing?" *Monthly Labor Review* (December 1997): 3–16.

2. Patrick Buchanan, *The Great Betrayal: How American Sovereignty and Social Justice Are Being Sacrificed to the Gods of the Global Economy* (Boston: Little, Brown, 1998), 14.

3. James Galbraith, *Created Unequal: The Crisis in American Pay* (New York: Free Press, 1998).

4. Louis Hartz, *Economic Policy and Democratic Thought: Pennsylvania 1776–1860* (Cambridge, MA: Harvard University Press, 1948).

5. Howard R. Smith, *Government and Business* (New York: Ronald Press, 1958), 99.

6. After 108 years of operation, the ICC expired at the end of 1995 as part of the effort by congressional Republicans to reduce federal regulations and allow market forces more freedom in which to operate.

7. Joel Brinkley, "19 States Seek an Overhaul of Microsoft," www.nytimes.com; Steve Lohr, "The Prosecution Almost Rests," www.nytimes.com.

8. *Pollock* v. *Farmers' Loan and Trust Co.* 158 U.S. 429 (1895).

9. This discussion of the New Deal draws on Louis M. Hacker and Helene S. Zahler, *The United States in the 20th Century* (New York: Appleton-Century-Crofts, 1952); and William E. Leuchtenburg, *Franklin D. Roosevelt and the New Deal* (New York: Harper & Row, 1963).

10. *U.S.* v. *Butler,* 297 U.S. 1 (1936).

11. *Wickard* v. *Filburn,* 317 U.S. 111 (1942).

12. Stephen A. Bailey, *Congress Makes a Law: The Story Behind the Employment Act of 1946* (New York: Columbia University Press, 1951).

13. Herbert Stein, *The Fiscal Revolution in America* (Chicago: University of Chicago Press, 1969), 204.

14. Larry N. Gerston, Cynthia Fraleigh, and Robert Schwab, *The Deregulated Society* (Pacific Grove, CA: Brooks/Cole, 1988), 27.

15. Michael Reagan, *Regulation: The Politics of Policy* (Boston: Little, Brown, 1987), 86.

16. Gerston, Fraleigh, and Schwab, *The Deregulated Society,* 32–34.

17. David Vogel, "The 'New' Social Regulation in Historical and Comparative Perspective," in Thomas K. McCraw, ed., *Regulation in Perspective* (Cambridge, MA: Harvard University Press, 1981), 160.

18. A leading study is Martha Derthick and Paul J. Quirk, *The Politics of Deregulation* (Washington, D.C.: Brookings Institution, 1985).

19. Derthick and Quirk, *The Politics of Deregulation,* chapters 1, 2; Dorothy Robyn, *Braking the Special Interests: Trucking Deregulation and the Politics of Policy Reform* (Chicago: University of Chicago Press, 1987), chapter 4.

20. Martin Mayer, *The Greatest-Ever Bank Robbery: The Collapse of the Savings and Loan Industry* (New York: Scribner's, 1990).

21. L. William Seidman, *Full Faith and Credit: The Great S&L Debacle and Other Washington Sagas* (New York: Times Books, 1993). Seidman was in charge of the Resolution Trust Corporation during the early years of the S&L bailout.

22. Quoted in Robert A. Gordon, *Economic Instability and Growth: The American Record* (New York: Harper & Row, 1974), 22.

23. The following discussion draws on James E. Anderson, David W. Brady, Charles S. Bullock III, and Joseph Stewart Jr., *Public Policy and Politics in America,* 2d ed. (Monterey, CA: Brooks/Cole, 1984), chapter 2.

24. *Time* (March 7, 1994): 42.

25. William Greider, *Secrets of the Temple: How the Federal Reserve Runs the Country* (New York: Simon & Schuster, 1987), chapter 10.

26. This is the conclusion reached by John T. Woolley, *Monetary Politics: The Federal Reserve and the Politics of Monetary Policy* (New York: Cambridge University Press, 1984).

27. Anderson, *et al., Public Policy and Politics in America,* 38–40.

28. James D. Savage, *Balanced Budgets and American Politics* (Ithaca, NY: Cornell University Press, 1988), 176–79.

29. Herbert Stein, *Presidential Economics: The Making of Economic Policy from Roosevelt to Reagan and Beyond* (New York: Simon & Schuster, 1984), 290–91.

30. *Annual Report of the Council of Economic Advisers, 1993* (Washington, D.C.: Government Printing Office, 1993), 108.

31. *Annual Report of the Council of Economic Advisers, 1993,* 109.

32. Robert Samuelson, "Why We're All Married to the Market," *Newsweek* (April 27, 1998): 47–50.

33. David Sanger, "Fed Lets Rates Stand, Fearing Effect on Asia," *The New York Times* (May 20, 1998): A1, C9; David Hosansky, "Battle Over IMF Funding Looms as Business Steps Up Pressure," *Congressional Quarterly Weekly Report* (February 14, 1998): 377.

34. Robert Samuelson, "It's Still a Depression," *Newsweek* (May 18, 1998): 53.

35. This discussion of budgeting draws on James E. Anderson, *Public Policymaking: An Introduction,* 2d ed. (Boston: Houghton Mifflin, 1994), chapter 5.

36. Donald F. Kettl, *Deficit Politics: Public Budgeting in Its Institutional and Historical Context* (New York: Macmillan, 1992), 140–1.

37. *Congressional Quarterly Weekly Report* (August 7, 1993): 2122–29.

38. John Cranford, *Budgeting for America,* 2d ed. (Washington, D.C.: CQ Press, 1989), 197–98.

39. Paul E. Peterson, "The New Politics of Deficits," in John E. Chubb and Paul E. Peterson, eds., *The New Direction in American Politics* (Washington, D.C.: The Brookings Institution, 1985), chapter 13.

40. Robert Eisner and Paul J. Peiper, "A New View of the Federal Debt and Budget Deficits," *American Economic Review* 74 (March 1994): 23.

41. This discussion is based on *Budget of the United States, Fiscal Year 1995: Analytical Perspectives* (Washington, D.C.: Government Printing Office, 1994), 423–24.

42. *Congressional Quarterly Weekly Report* (May 3, 1997): 1002–4.

43. David Clymer, "Taxes Cut, Credit Taken," *The New York Times* (July 30, 1997): A1, A15.

44. Steven G. Koven, *Public Budgeting in the United States: The cultural and Ideological Setting* (Washington, D.C.: Georgetown University Press, 1999), 77.

45. Koven, *Public Budgeting in the United States: The Cultural and Ideological Setting,* 75.

46. Koven, *Public Budgeting in the United States: The Cultural and Ideological Setting,* 76.

47. Rick Scarce, *Eco-Warriors: Understanding the Radical Environmental Movement* (Chicago: Noble Press, 1990).

48. Richard E. Cohen, *Washington at Work: Back Rooms and Clean Air* (New York: Macmillan, 1992).

49. Charles O. Jones, *Clean Air: The Policies and Politics of Pollution Control* (Pittsburgh: University of Pittsburgh Press, 1975).

50. This listing relies partly on Walter A. Rosenbaum, "The Clenched Fist and the Open Hand: Into the 1990s at EPA," in Norman J. Vig and Michael E. Kraft, eds., *Environmental Policy in the 1990s,* 2d ed. (Washington D.C.: CQ Press, 1994), 126–27.

51. Kent E. Portney, *Controversial Issues in Environmental Policy: Science vs. Economics vs. Politics* (Newbury Park, CA: Sage Publications, 1992), 17–19. The quotation is on 49.

52. Walter A. Rosenbaum, *Environmental Politics and Policy,* 2d ed. (Washington, D.C.: CQ Press, 1991), 214.

53. *Congressional Quarterly Weekly Report* (February 5, 1994): 239–40.

54. Gary C. Bryner, *Blue Skies, Green Politics: The Clean Air Act of 1990* (Washington, D.C.: CQ Press, 1993), 68.

55. James L. Regens and Robert W. Rycroft, *The Acid Rain Controversy* (Pittsburgh: University of Pittsburgh Press, 1988), 45–47.

56. See Charles L. Schultze, *The Public Use of Private Interest* (Washington, D.C.: The Brookings Institution, 1977).

57. Allan Freedman, "Republicans Concede Missteps in Effort to Rewrite Rules," *Congressional Quarterly* 53 (December 2, 1995): 3646.

58. See, for example, Margaret Kriz, "The Green Card," *National Journal* 27 (September 16, 1995): 2265.

59. Timothy, Egan, "Dreams of Fields: The New Politics of Urban Sprawl," *New York Times* (November 15, 1998): Section 4, 1, 3.

(Photo courtesy: 5958/Liaison Agency)

Foreign and Military Policy

- **Pursuing Power and Plenty**
- **Grand Strategy**
- **The Roots of U.S. Foreign and Military Policy**
- **The United States Becomes a World Leader**
- **The Machinery of Modern Foreign Policy Making**
- **Challenges to Presidential Power in Foreign and Military Policy**

he personal stories from thousands of ethnic Albanian refugees streaming out of Kosovo in the spring of 1999 shared a similar theme. Ordered out of their homes by Serbian forces, often accompanied by beatings, mass murder, rape, and other acts of violence designed to terrorize and intimidate, they sought safety in neighboring Albania, Macedonia, and even the more independent Yugoslav republic of Montenegro. The policy of "ethnic cleansing" engaged in by Serbian police, military, and paramilitary forces was so effective that, by March 1999, the United Nations High Commissioner for Refugees reported 333,000 ethnic Albanian Kosovars had been displaced from their homes.[1]

A U.S.-led bombing campaign by the North Atlantic Treaty Organization (NATO) later in March only increased the pace of Serbia's ethnic cleansing in the Yugoslav province of Kosovo, creating hundreds of thousands more refugees. Instead of meeting to celebrate its fiftieth anniversary and recent expansion to nineteen members, NATO convened in April for a summit on its Kosovo operations.

The bombing campaign against Serbia marked several firsts for NATO. For the first time in its history, NATO began an offensive military operation outside the boundaries of its members. Moreover, the primary interest in protecting the rights of the ethnic Albanian Kosovars, with whom NATO members had few ties, led some pundits to describe the NATO bombing campaign as the first "humanitarian" war, aimed at preserving the basic human rights of an oppressed population rather than promoting more traditional political, military, or economic goals.

Acceptance of the need to intervene within a state for humanitarian reasons had grown, however, after widespread ethnic violence in Bosnia, Rwanda, Somalia, and elsewhere. Furthermore, many European members of NATO believed how they responded to the Kosovo crisis would indicate whether they could build a more stable and secure Europe in the next century based on common conceptions of human rights.

*T*he Clinton administration found a mixed reaction in Congress to America's leading role in the NATO bombing campaign to stop Serbian aggression in Kosovo. Many members of Congress argued that the air campaign would not bring Serbian leader Slobodan Milosevic to accept NATO demands regarding a more autonomous Kosovo. Many claimed that defending ethnic Albanian Kosovars, while morally admirable, was not a vital national interest. Others stated that the air campaign could not succeed without ground troops, or without an escalation that would involve Russia and other countries.

Effective alternatives to bombing were hard to identify, however. Although UN-sponsored economic sanctions had helped bring about the Dayton Peace Accord, which ended similar aggression in Bosnia, it was unclear whether economic sanctions could have done anything to halt the ethnic cleansing practices in Kosovo and the consequent flow of refugees. The United States often turned to economic sanctions to enforce its foreign policy interests but in some cases discovered that inflexible sanctions could work against other national interests, such as trade. In 1998 reliance on economic sanctions as a first rather than last resort brought sufficient complaints from U.S. industry to foster a bipartisan effort for sanction-reform legislation.[2] Thus, the United States continually balances its world leader role with economic concerns at home.

Web Exploration
To learn more about NATO's peacekeeping operations in Kosovo, go to www.awlonline.com/oconnor.

PURSUING POWER AND PLENTY

The concern about the use of costly economic sanctions reflects the changing views on the relationship between the economy and U.S. national security. During the Cold War, strengthening U.S. military capabilities overrode most other national security interests. As the Cold War drew to an end, however, the importance of other goals, especially economic and diplomatic strength, became clearer. The president outlines the balance of national security interests in an annual report to Congress. The 1998 report describes the three core objectives of U.S. strategy as follows:

- To enhance our security with effective diplomacy and with military forces that are ready to fight and win.
- To bolster America's economic prosperity.
- To promote democracy abroad.[3]

The report suggests that the "health of the international economy directly affects our security, just as stability enhances the prospects for prosperity. Prosperity ensures that we are able to sustain our military forces, foreign initiatives and global influence."[4] Compared with previous administrations, President Clinton increased the emphasis on improving U.S. economic strength, especially through increasing U.S. exports, as the foundations for long-term national security.

In this chapter we expand on these themes as we look at the following issues:

- First, we will review the concept of *grand strategy* in foreign policy, and what kind of priorities governments adopt.
- Second, we will examine *the roots of modern U.S. foreign and military policy* by seeing how policy evolved as America slowly became a world power.
- Third, we will focus on *the expanding global role of the United States* by studying U.S. policies during the Cold War.
- Fourth, we will discuss *the machinery of modern foreign policy* by examining the role of various departments and agencies in shaping policy and the key role of the president.
- Fifth, we will explore the *challenges to the president's power* by seeing how Congress, the press, the public, and the bureaucracy place limits on the president.

Not everyone believes in this same balance of national interests. When President Clinton traveled to China in June 1998, the trip was subject to considerable criticism on the basis of Chinese religious policies, its treatment of Tibet and Taiwan, its trade practices, and other policies. Despite the potential economic costs, for example, the chair of the Senate Foreign Relations Committee, Jesse Helms (R–N.C.), held hearings on

POLITICS NOW

China as Partner, China as Rival

When NATO missiles hit the embassy of the People's Republic of China (PRC) in Belgrade in April 1999, killing three Chinese journalists and wounding more than a dozen embassy personnel, tens of thousands of demonstrators in Beijing, Shanghai, and elsewhere in China expressed their deep anger against the United States and NATO actions in Yugoslavia. Tacitly encouraged by the Chinese government and the government-controlled media, which did not report U.S. and NATO apologies for several days and had pictured ethnic Albanian refugees as fleeing from the bombing, angry mobs threw bricks, paint bombs, and firebombs at the U.S. embassy and consulate buildings. U.S. Ambassador James Sasser and his staff, trapped in the embassy compound for four days, began destroying sensitive documents in case the mob broke through the ranks of the Chinese police. If anything, however, the response of the PRC strengthened the position of those who see China as a rival rather than a partner of the United States in the twenty-first century.

Since 1978 the PRC has moved toward a more market-oriented economy. Its gross domestic product (GDP) has doubled almost every eight years, persisting even when most other nations in East Asia have undergone a substantial financial crisis in recent years. The PRC is now a major trading partner of the United States. It exported more than $71 billion to the United States in 1998, making it a top-ten U.S. trading partner. The United States, however, exported slightly less than $14 billion to the PRC, an imbalance leading the U.S. government and many U.S. industries, especially in high technology sectors, to seek new ways to increase U.S. exports. Clinton administration officials, for example, hoped to finish negotiating the accession of the PRC into the World Trade Organization (WTO) in time for the April 1999 visit of PRC Premier Zhu Rongji to the United States. The terms of the PRC's entry into the WTO could open many market opportunities for U.S. businesses. Domestic politics on both sides of the Pacific, however, prevented an agreement during the summit, although the negotiations made considerable progress before the embassy bombing.

Frequent revelations about the loss of classified strategic information to the PRC also fueled the anti-China mood in Congress well into 1999. Most recently, the Cox Committee, for example, detailed transfers of sensitive technology in the Reagan, Bush, and Clinton administrations, while another congressional committee found that U.S. satellite transfers had probably enhanced PRC missile capabilities. Investigations into espionage related to a 1980s transfer of the design of the W-88 nuclear warhead at the Los Alamos National Laboratory also indicated that the key computer codes, including the design and test results of the entire U.S. nuclear arsenal, were placed on a nonsecured computer system. Concerns also arose over the access foreign nationals, including foreign graduate students, had to nuclear secrets at the various national laboratories. Then it appeared that China had acquired satellite radar technology from the United States in 1997 that they could use to identify the wakes of submarines underwater, making the U.S. fleet of submarines capable of launching strategic nuclear missiles more vulnerable.

U.S. policy on the export of commercial satellites and satellite technology remains a particular point of contention. Caught between a global shortage of reliable, low-cost launch vehicles and the increasing demand for commercial satellites, the Bush and Clinton administrations routinely granted a waiver under U.S. export regulations to allow U.S. satellite manufacturers and telecommunications companies to use Chinese Long March launch vehicles to put their satellites in orbit, which would produce many billions of dollars of revenue for U.S. industry. All the satellites went to China in sealed containers, under observation by U.S. Defense Department guards, with only U.S. personnel mounting them on the launchers.

In February 1996, however, a Chinese rocket with a $200 million satellite owned by Loral Space and Communications exploded shortly after takeoff, killing or wounding dozens of people in a village near the Xichang Satellite Launch Center. When Loral and Hughes Electronics employees released a review of the launch failure to Chinese authorities without getting the required approval of the U.S. State Department first, a criminal investigation followed, while Loral, whose chair was a major donor to the Democratic Party, continued to seek presidential waivers for more satellite launches. When the Clinton administration expedited a waiver for Loral in February 1998, in spite of the ongoing criminal investigation, many in Congress criticized the administration waiver policy. Several members of Congress who made these critiques however, were in an awkward position. In the early 1990s, they had also written to support routine waivers for satellite exports as a means of helping industry in their districts or states. In the meantime, the administration has continued to approve the export of some satellite items. Despite these tensions, Clinton administration officials repeatedly noted the cooperation the PRC had shown on key strategic issues, especially its support for U.S. initiatives with North Korea and Pakistan, the Comprehensive Test Ban Treaty, and other nuclear nonproliferation concerns.

Web Exploration

To learn more about U.S.–China relations from the perspective of the U.S. State Department and the Chinese Ministry of Foreign Affairs, go to www.awlonline.com/oconnor.

whether the Clinton administration had been lax in imposing sanctions against China. Senator Helms argued that the United States should sanction China for its role in proliferating missiles and nuclear and chemical weapons technology to Pakistan, Iran, and elsewhere (see Politics Now: China as Partner, China as Rival).

Regional security, if not global peace, seems increasingly threatened by conflicts old and new in the aftermath of the Cold War. Ethnic, political, racial, and religious violence has hit Kosovo, the Sudan, Sri Lanka, Mexico, and dozens of other countries. Territorial disputes between states in the South China Sea, in Kashmir, and many other places threaten to destabilize whole regions. The development of nuclear, chemical, or biological weapons (and the means to deliver them) by Iraq, Iran, North Korea, Libya, and more than thirty other countries, and the use of weapons of mass destruction by terrorists, criminal gangs, and other nongovernmental groups, such as Aum Shinrikyo in Japan, has increased the risk that the United States will face more adversaries with such weapons than ever before.

Even if one accepts that economic concerns are of primary importance to U.S. national security, it's not clear what policies the United States should adopt. Many House members, for example, view the North American Free Trade Agreement (NAFTA) as a threat to U.S. sovereignty and the U.S. national economy.

The new World Trade Organization, which manages multilateral negotiations to reduce barriers to trade and settle trade disputes between nations, has drawn particular wrath from those who favor isolationist or unilateralist strategies. In contrast many Democrats and Republicans alike see free trade policies and free trade agreements as essential to U.S. economic growth.

The arguments over the relative importance of economics and military security or what kind of foreign economic policy is appropriate for the United States are not new.

For hundreds of years, governments have struggled with how to pursue both power and plenty.[5] From 1500 to 1800, mercantilism dominated the beliefs and actions of most policy makers around the world. Mercantilists advocated policies to limit imports to achieve a trade surplus (more exports than imports). Similarly, modern critics of U.S. trade policy point to the sustained and large overall U.S. trade deficit. For the first time in many years, U.S. exports of goods and services declined from about $643 billion to roughly $635 billion in 1998. In contrast, imports to the United States rose sharply from $870 billion to nearly $914 billion, producing an enormous trade deficit of around $279 billion. The lingering Asian financial crisis accounts for much of this change. The value of U.S. exports to virtually every country in the region except China continued to decline in 1998, as the slowdown in East Asian economies reduced the demand for imported goods. At the same time, the strength of the U.S. economy attracted even more exports from the troubled industries of the region. Opponents to the increasing globalization of the U.S. economy point to the growing trade deficit as a reason to increase protectionism. Many have pushed the Clinton administration to limit steel imports and to take a strong stance in conflicts with the European Union over exports of bananas by U.S. companies.

A revolution of ideas began with the publication of Adam Smith's attack on mercantilism, *The Wealth of Nations,* in 1776. Smith demonstrated how barriers to international trade hurt rather than helped a nation's economy (Smith made exceptions for trade barriers that protected the military might of a nation or temporarily helped avoid economic injury to a large number of workers). These ideas of free trade, much like the notions of political liberty that drove Americans to contest British rule, became the basis for classical and modern trade theory on which many, if not most, countries base their trade policies. Most U.S. free trade advocates point out that U.S. exporters are now highly competitive, unlike a few years ago, and that the high trade deficit is a function of the U.S. economy growing much more rapidly than most of our major trading partners, particularly Japan and Germany in recent years. Free trade advocates argue that adopting protectionist policies would merely invite other countries to raise barriers on U.S. exports. From this perspective, Joseph Gorman, CEO of TRW, argues that "protectionism now would be little short of insane."[6]

GRAND STRATEGY

During the Cold War, the United States focused almost exclusively on balancing the military threat posed by the Soviet Union. With the end of the Cold War, the Soviet military threat is no longer a plausible rationale for public policy. For the first time in more than four decades, Americans are engaging in a wide-ranging debate about grand strategy. **Grand strategy** refers to the choices a government makes to balance and apply economic, military, diplomatic, and other national resources to preserve the nation's people and territory.[7] Grand strategy need not be planned, public, or explicit, but it often is in the United States. It is

■ Former Olympic ice skater Midori Ito pauses after lighting the Olympic Flame at the XVIII Olympic Winter Games in Nagao, Japan. The flame is one of the many powerful symbols of international unity that transcend nationalism found at the Olympic games. (Photo courtesy: Eric Draper/AP/Wide World Photos)

also often controversial as when the Department of Defense considered a new proposal for its defense policy guidance early in the first Clinton administration. The draft plan called on the United States to deter "potential competitors from even aspiring to a larger regional or global role," including current allies like Japan or members of the European Union.[8] When the plan was leaked to the press, the harsh public response helped the Pentagon drop the goal of seeking and preserving U.S. global dominance. Instead, the United States has sought to work with Japan and the European Union to shoulder more responsibility and burden for regional peace and security. The choices associated with grand strategy, about NAFTA and NATO, about foreign investment in the United States and military intervention in Kosovo, about all aspects of foreign and military policy, help define who we are, both to ourselves and to the rest of the world.

In their own form of grand strategy, John Jay and other Federalists argued that the United States could avoid being a battleground in European power struggles only if it were united. The Federalist views on the importance of national unity derive from the emergence of the **nation-state,** where, ideally, all of the people would share the same nationality and govern themselves. This form of political organization is based on the idea that one government should have sole authority over a well-defined territory. Though often associated with ethnicity and other common characteristics, nationality does not depend solely on shared racial, ethnic, religious, or linguistic ties, particularly in countries like the United States. Instead, nationality stems from a shared belief that a people have a common identity and destiny and, often, a common historical experience. By appealing to this sense of common nationality or nationalism, governments can support large military forces and sustain other costs to defend their interests. These national interests include preserving the nation's territorial boundaries, maintaining a relatively sovereign (independent) form of government, and promoting economic prosperity.

Nation-states range in size and resources from micro-states, such as Grenada, Monaco, and Tuvalu, to superpowers like the United States and the former Soviet Union. Though nation-states are still the most powerful type of political organization in international relations, the Framers of the Constitution could not have foreseen that other kinds of political organizations would become increasingly important in world affairs. Not until 1815, for example, did countries create the first **international governmental organization (IGO)** (an organization formed by three or more countries, with regular meetings and a permanent staff).[9] Similarly, few international non-governmental organizations (INGOs) existed in 1787. Now tens of thousands of INGOs, from Amnesty International to Greenpeace to the International Olympic

grand strategy:

The choices a government makes to balance and apply economic, military, diplomatic, and other national resources to preserve the nation's people and territory.

nation-state:

Ideally, a country where all the people share one nationality and govern themselves. This form of political organization is based on the idea that one government should have sole authority over a well-defined territory.

international governmental organization (IGO):

An organization formed by three or more countries, with regular meetings and a permanent staff.

Web Exploration
To learn more about IGOs, INGOs, and other international bodies, such as Amnesty International, Greenpeace International, and the International Olympic Committee, go to www.awlonline.com/oconnor.

Committee, influence many aspects of our daily lives as well as world affairs. In addition, the twentieth century witnessed an unprecedented growth in transnational economic organizations, such as multinational corporations, which some suggest will transcend nation-states in importance.[10]

International power—that is, the power of any one organization relative to another—depends on the issue involved. Japan, for example, has more power in international trade and aid issues than in military security issues. International power also varies over time. Even though the collapse of the Soviet Union increased the relative military power of the United States in the 1990s, many scholars argue that the overall power of the United States has been in decline since the early 1970s, similar to the rise and fall of other great powers over the last four centuries. As noted historian Paul Kennedy contends, the United States

> cannot avoid confronting the two great tests which challenge the longevity of every major power that occupies the "number one" position in world affairs: whether . . . it can preserve a reasonable balance between the nation's perceived defense requirements and the means it possesses to maintain those commitments; and whether . . . it can preserve the technological and economic bases of its power from relative erosion in the face of ever-shifting patterns of global production.[11]

These challenges emerge in every era but are most difficult when key political, social, technological, or economic changes have taken place either at home or abroad. Japan and Germany, for example, have had lengthy debates in the 1990s about whether their militaries should participate in U.N. peacekeeping operations, given their troubled histories of military aggression. Until the late 1980s and the emergence of the North American Free Trade Agreement (NAFTA), most Mexican governments had tried to restrict U.S. trade and investment in the Mexican economy. While Mexico relied on the military strength of its northern neighbor to deter any external military threat, formal ties with the U.S. military were limited. Until recently, for example, no U.S. secretary of defense had ever even gone to Mexico to meet with the head of the Mexican defense forces. Each nation, weak or strong, large or small, new or old, must answer these challenges.

THE ROOTS OF U.S. FOREIGN AND MILITARY POLICY

In its early years, the United States was a weak country on the margins of international affairs. Historically, weak states often depend on more powerful countries for security. The Atlantic Ocean and other physical barriers to the projection of European power in the Americas and abundant natural and human resources meant that the United States had another option: It could choose not to be involved in European affairs. To understand the origins of U.S. foreign and military policy, we must examine both the pre-constitutional era and the Constitution itself.

The Pre-Constitutional Era

John Adams, under the direction of the Continental Congress, developed a *Plan of Treaties* in 1776 that outlined many of the primary themes of early U.S. foreign policy.[12] Adams called for greater freedom of trade between nations without political or military ties. This echoed the views of Thomas Paine, who argued in *Common Sense* that independence was the only way to avoid entanglements.

The struggle for independence made foreign aid and military assistance an unavoidable requirement. The French gave substantial military and economic assistance to the newborn United States only because France was locked in a conflict with the British for global power at that time. With the Franco-American Treaty of 1778, the United States joined in a military alliance with France. The United States sought similar alliances with other European powers, but this proved to be its only military alliance with a European power until the twentieth century.

GLOBAL POLITICS   American Power in the World

Military and foreign aid are two conventional ways of measuring a nation-state's power in the international system. These two measures suggest the changes that are taking place in the structure of American power in the post–Cold War world.

By the criteria below, the United States remains the preeminent power, at this moment the one superpower, in the world. American military spending dwarfs that of the G-7 partners as well as that of other powerful states in the international system. Canada, France, and Britain can be called middle powers, capable of using military power in regional conflicts but unable to project military force worldwide in the manner the United States can. Germany and Japan, despite respectable military expenditures, have been hesitant to use their militaries for anything but national defense, strictly defined, because of the legacy of World War II. Even China, which is emerging as a potential rival to American power in East Asia, spent only about as much as Germany did in 1996.

American influence in the international aid community has declined in the last decade. Japan surpassed the United States as the largest donor of bilateral aid in 1989. In the early 1990s, as a result of congressional Republican majorities hostile to the foreign aid program and intent on cutting budget deficits, foreign aid budgets were lower than France's and Germany's as well. Even in 1997, the United States spent less than one-tenth of one percent of GNP on foreign aid. The United States thus appears to have become a foreign aid middle power. Despite lower spending levels, however, the United States still retains influence in the international debate over the uses of foreign aid, championing greater private sector involvement in what have long been government economic development efforts in the developing countries.

Comparative Military and Foreign Aid Expenditures

Country	Military Expenditures $millions, 1996	Foreign Aid $millions, 1997
Canada	9,590	2,045
France	40,260	6,307
Germany	35,100	5,827
Italy	17,840	1,266
Japan	42,400	9,358
United Kingdom	29,840	3,433
United States	**259,050**	**6,878**

SOURCE: MILEX Monitor, http://bicc.uni-bonn.de/milex/Updated April 4, 1999: Development Assistance Committee, *Development Cooperation: Efforts and Policies of the Members of the Development Assistance Committee, 1998 Report* (Paris: OECD, 1998) 96.

The Constitution

The Framers generally agreed that the republic's foreign policy was important but limited—its tasks were to keep the United States out of European affairs and to keep European countries out of U.S. affairs. The institutional framework for foreign and defense policy is laid out in the Constitution. Making and implementing foreign policy is a power clearly given to the federal government rather than to the states, although the states had an important function in creating state militia.

Scholars agree that the Framers intended to divide responsibility between Congress and the president in foreign affairs. Although the office of the president combines the powers of head of state (with the authority to appoint and receive ambassadors, sign treaties, and otherwise represent the United States in dealings with other countries) and head of government (with the responsibility for overseeing the daily affairs of making and executing public policy), the power of the president was not to be comparable to the greater power of the monarchs of the time. The Framers gave Congress the power to fund the army and navy and declare war; as commander-in-chief—that is, having constitutional power over all combined U.S. armed forces—the president leads the nation's military forces. Congress got the power to regulate commerce with foreign nations; the president got authority to negotiate and sign the treaties that govern such commerce (although for such treaties to become valid, two-thirds of the Senate is constitutionally required to ratify them). The president appoints ambassadors and other key foreign and military officials; the Senate grants advice and consent on these appointments.

Additionally, many powers not enumerated in the Constitution generally are accorded to the national government. In the wake of the U.S. victory in the Spanish-American War, for example, the United States acquired colonies in the Philippines and elsewhere in 1898. This went against the anticolonial principles of many Americans, and many claimed the United States government had no right to acquire territory. In a series of U.S. Supreme Court cases, collectively called the Insular cases, the Justices affirmed the right of the national government to take new territories and to create new forms of government for those territories.[13] In many other instances, through the doctrines of implied and inherent powers, the president and Congress have often gone beyond the powers specifically outlined in the Constitution.

The Early History of U.S. Military and Foreign Policy

The pre-constitutional desire for a limited foreign and defense policy carried over to the new republic. When the first Congress of the new United States eventually met in 1789, it authorized an army, but only at a maximum strength of 840. Most of the nation's military strength was decentralized in the form of state militia. Similarly, the Tariff Act of 1789 imposed low duties on imports (the Constitution bars taxes on exports), helping to keep trade relatively free from government interference.

The first important treaty entered into by the new United States regularized relations with Great Britain. The treaty, generally referred to as the *Jay's Treaty* after its chief negotiator, John Jay, helped settle disputes between Great Britain and the United States over the boundaries of the new nation, debts incurred during the war, and commerce between the two nations. Bitterness in the aftermath of the Revolutionary War led some members of Congress to oppose the treaty.

In 1796 George Washington, in his last public statement as president, discussed the dangers of divisive party politics and warned strongly against foreign entanglements. In his Farewell Address (written with Alexander Hamilton), Washington suggested that it be "our true policy to steer clear of permanent alliances with any portion of the foreign world." Washington believed that U.S. democracy and economic prosperity, two key national interests, depended not on complete isolation, but on keeping free of European politics.

From 1804 Great Britain began to adopt rules of the sea that worsened Anglo-American relations, especially the right to search any ship for deserting sailors. After one incident in June 1807, mobs gathered and demanded that President Jefferson seek war on Great Britain. Instead, Jefferson tried peaceful measures, negotiating the return of three of four sailors and arranging compensation (the fourth had been hanged). The British would not, however, renounce their right to search ships for deserting sailors. In December 1807 the United States passed the Embargo Act, stopping U.S. ships from leaving the country for any port in another country without approval by the federal government. Jefferson and Secretary of State James Madison believed that the European powers relied so much on U.S. shipping and raw materials that the Embargo Act would force the Europeans to change their policies and respect the rights of Americans at sea.

The Embargo Act proved very costly. Not only did European policies fail to change, but U.S. exports also fell by 80 percent, harming economic interests in virtually every region except those bordering Canada (since overland trade was not prohibited). With as many as 100,000 people out of work and inflation climbing in the depression created by the Embargo Act, dissatisfaction with the act allowed the Federalist Party to make noticeable gains in the election of 1808. In April 1809 an exchange of diplomatic notes between U.S. Secretary of State Robert Smith and David Erskine, the British minister in Washington, settled some of the disputes temporarily. The Erskine agreement, as this was called, became the first important **executive agreement**, a government-to-government accord entered into by the United States and binding only on the current administration.

Continued deterioration of Anglo-American relations led Great Britain and the United States to fight each other in the War of 1812. While peace talks began even

executive agreement:

A formal agreement entered into by the executive branches of different countries. These agreements do not require the advice and consent of the U.S. Senate.

before the first battles, the war ended only when the British decided to concentrate on defeating Napoleon. The British agreed to abide by the borders, treaty obligations, and other conditions in existence before the war, signing the Treaty of Ghent in December 1814 (the Battle of New Orleans was fought after the signing of the peace treaty). With the defeat of Napoleon in the summer of 1815, the British ceased the practice of impressment, and Anglo-American tensions eased. Great Britain and the United States also experimented with a new form of diplomacy by committing themselves to a process to settle future disputes by consultation and binding arbitration rather than military conflict.

For U.S. industries, however, global peace meant increased competition at home and abroad. Both before and immediately after the War of 1812, the U.S. government relied on the two key commercial principles in the Treaty Plan of 1776 in trade negotiations with other countries: *reciprocity* and *unconditional most-favored-nation (MFN)* status. Reciprocity meant a policy of national treatment, where U.S. traders would receive the same treatment as a national of another country. In practice, unconditional MFN status meant that U.S. exports would face the lowest **tariffs** (taxes on imports) offered to any other country. These principles were in line with the free trade and low tariffs advocated by Adam Smith's *The Wealth of Nations*.

As early as 1791, Alexander Hamilton, in the *Report on Manufactures*, had urged Congress to take action to protect some domestic industries from foreign competition. In 1816 the United States took the crucial step of adopting protectionist tariffs instead of simply using tariffs to raise money for the federal government. By this time Henry Clay urged an "American system" of trade protection, which came into full force in 1824. Overall, Congress and the president proved very receptive to demands for economic protection, and high tariffs—usually from 20 percent to 30 percent of the value of the import, but with some individual tariffs as high as 100 percent—became the norm for the next 120 years.[14] High tariffs, however, discouraged U.S. exports, since other countries kept their tariffs on U.S. goods high in retaliation for most of this period. For most of the years before the Civil War, the United States imported more than it exported, and the volume of trade declined steadily through 1830. Although trade increased after 1830, international trade grew at a rate slower than that of trade within the United States.

The Monroe Doctrine

The limited capacity of the U.S. government to provide military or foreign economic assistance helps explain its response to the revolutions in the 1820s that helped most Latin American countries gain their independence. President James Monroe threatened action if European powers attempted to recolonize the region and if the Russians extended their presence on the western coast of North America. In an annual message to Congress in December 1823, Monroe declared that it would be dangerous to American peace and safety for European states to attempt to extend their system to the Western hemisphere. This approach to hemispheric relations became known as the **Monroe Doctrine.**

Although tough sounding, the Monroe Doctrine was more preference than policy. Great Britain also aimed to keep other European powers out of the Western hemisphere to preserve British commercial interests. The difference between British and U.S. policy was that the incomparable British navy could enforce Britain's policy. In fact, the British expanded their limited colonial presence in Latin America several times after 1823 without U.S. policy makers invoking the doctrine.

The United States as an Emerging Power

At this time U.S. foreign policy dealt mainly with events in the Western hemisphere or with trade policy. Military activity was mainly within or on the borders of the United States, such as hostile relations with Canada during and following the War of 1812,

tariffs:

Taxes on imports, used to raise government revenue and to protect domestic industry.

Monroe Doctrine:

President James Monroe's 1823 pledge that the United States would oppose attempts by European states to extend their political control over the Western hemisphere.

■ A cartoon depicting President Theodore Roosevelt's support of building the Panama Canal to strengthen the U.S. naval presence in the world. (Photo courtesy: Corbis/Bettmann)

manifest destiny:

A popular theory during the U.S. expansion westward that it was a divinely mandated obligation to expand across North America to the Pacific Ocean.

hostile relations with Spain over Florida, war with Mexico in 1846, war with the seceding confederate states between 1861 and 1865, and wars in the South and West with Chief Tecumseh's confederacy and other Native American nations (Creeks, Seminoles, Sioux, Comanches, Apaches) that resisted expansion into their territory. During the Civil War (1861–65), the Confederacy even tried to bring the European powers into the war. The lack of a substantial confederate victory on Northern soil, the growing industrial and military might of the Union forces, and antislavery sentiment in Great Britain and elsewhere all thwarted Southern efforts to involve the Europeans in the conflict.

Eventually, the country stretched from the Atlantic to the Pacific. In particular, the defeat of Mexico in 1848 brought California under U.S. control. Some called this **manifest destiny,** a divinely mandated obligation to expand across North America to the Pacific Ocean and "overspread the continent allotted by Providence for the free development of our yearly multiplying millions."[15] The Pacific did not stop the westward expansion of the United States. Soon after the British forced the Chinese to open their markets to British goods, U.S. officials negotiated a commercial treaty with China and sought to keep any single European power from restricting U.S. trade with China. In 1852 and 1854, Commodore Matthew C. Perry took the East India Squadron of the U.S. navy into Japanese waters and opened Japan to Western interests.

For the last half of the century, Americans reached no consensus on the appropriate role for the United States in global affairs. Both major political parties were generally against acquiring colonies but were divided on such issues as free trade and military intervention, and no one party regularly controlled all branches of government during the period. The United States did take Midway, the Hawaiian islands, and the Samoan islands to protect its interests in the Pacific, but these actions heightened the debate about how to use U.S. power.

The belief in manifest destiny did not prepare the U.S. public for the revolution in the Philippines against U.S. rule in 1899. The United States sent nearly 200,000 troops to the islands over the next three years. When the fighting ceased in 1902, tens of thousands of Filipinos had died, along with 5,000 Americans. The atrocities committed on both sides dampened U.S. enthusiasm for foreign adventures. Nonetheless, the Spanish-American War propelled the United States from a regional to a world power (see Figure 19.1). A war hero with an expansionist vision of the U.S. global role, Theodore Roosevelt, became president. As president, Roosevelt supported the construction of the Panama Canal to make it easier for the U.S. navy to operate in two oceans. He also received the newly created Nobel Peace Prize for his efforts to end the Russo-Japanese War of 1904–05 and the Franco-German crisis over Morocco in 1905.

Foreign Trade and Aid Policy at the Turn of the Century

Debate between Democrats and Republicans grew as the high tariff rates occasionally created surpluses in government revenue (few wanted the government to have too much money) and as the European countries began to adopt lower tariffs and other free trade policies. The Democrats and Republicans made the tariff a major election issue throughout the 1880s, but the Republican victory in 1888 ensured the continuation of high tariffs. The 57 percent average rate of the Dingley Tariff Act of 1897 raised tariffs to a new high. They would remain high until Democratic electoral victories in 1912.[16]

From the Civil War on, the United States became increasingly self-sufficient. Self-sufficiency, coupled with high tariffs, reduced the relative demand for imported goods. At the same time, U.S. agriculture became more mechanized and U.S. industry more productive as many European states, particularly England, had greatly reduced their tariffs. This meant that U.S. goods became relatively cheaper to other countries and thus much more competitive on the world market. After 1895 the United States exported more than it imported for all but a few of the next seventy-five years.

Figure 19.1   The United States Emerges as a World Power

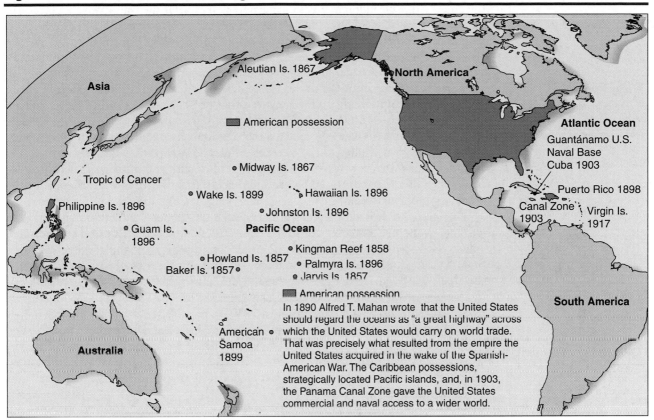

In 1890 Alfred T. Mahan wrote that the United States should regard the oceans as "a great highway" across which the United States would carry on world trade. That was precisely what resulted from the empire the United States acquired in the wake of the Spanish-American War. The Caribbean possessions, strategically located Pacific islands, and, in 1903, the Panama Canal Zone gave the United States commercial and naval access to a wider world.

SOURCE: James A. Henretta, *America's History Volume II*, Worth Publishers, 1999.

The late nineteenth century witnessed the rise of thousands of extremely wealthy business tycoons, some through ruthless means. A few, such as John D. Rockefeller and Andrew Carnegie, believed their fortunes brought responsibility as well as power, and they created charitable foundations to aid society, mainly in the United States but also overseas. Though the U.S. government provided no aid, these tycoons helped found new private institutions to assist the international community, such as the Carnegie Endowment for International Peace and the World Peace Foundation.

World War I

When World War I broke out in Europe in 1914, it was politically expedient for a nation of immigrants to stay out of the war because choosing sides would inevitably anger one group or another. President Woodrow Wilson ran for a second term in 1916 on the slogan "He kept us out of war," yet world events pressed the United States to enter the conflict. Especially disturbing was the German policy of "unrestricted" submarine warfare, which meant that U.S. ships carrying cargo to Great Britain would be sunk even though the United States had declared itself neutral.

Talking of a "war to end all wars," Wilson took the United States into its first great European conflict. Troops and aid from the United States began to arrive just when the human and material resources of its main allies, Britain and France, were nearly exhausted. Almost 5 million Americans served in the armed forces during the war. The newly created Food Administration, under Herbert Hoover (who had run a successful campaign to provide relief to Belgium early in the war), dramatically increased food production to supply the United States and its allies. The United States also provided the allies with $11 billion in loans during and shortly after the war. Even though it had entered the war late, the United States, by intervening militarily and economically, helped make possible the defeat of the German and Austro-Hungarian empires.

Wilson put great faith in an international organization that would be formed after the war to keep the peace. He was instrumental in writing the document that set up the **League of Nations**—the first IGO dedicated to preserving global peace. Wilson was so absorbed in foreign policy, however, that he neglected to build support for the League at home. He was a Democratic president facing a Senate controlled by Republicans, and he had not courted them by devices such as including a senator among the U.S. delegates to the Versailles Peace Conference. Many senators found membership in the new world body incompatible with the principles of U.S. independence. The Senate refused to give the necessary two-thirds vote to approve the ratification of the treaty.

The United States returned to a policy of high tariffs and a limited role in the international economy soon after the war. The destruction of Europe during the war provided relative benefits to the U.S. economy. As a source of credit and goods, the United States became the leading country of the world, and new technologies and cheap energy sustained this boom. In the 1920s a Republican-controlled Congress began raising tariffs to protect U.S. industry, especially manufacturers that had prospered during the war from reduced European competition. In 1930, in response to demands by U.S. industry for protection from foreign competition, Congress passed a very high tariff, called the Smoot-Hawley Tariff Act after its congressional sponsors. As many people had predicted, other countries responded by raising their tariffs and world trade declined rapidly. By 1932, the middle of the Great Depression, trade was at only about one-third of its former level.[17]

Many Americans thought that U.S. national interests were best served by keeping out of foreign political or economic affairs **(isolationism)** and by acting alone (unilateralism), often without consulting friendly governments. The Great Depression began to change this view. Not only did it create a better understanding of the links between the U.S. and foreign economies, but leaders later attributed the rise of Adolf Hitler and other rulers bent on world domination to the economic turmoil of the times. Without the power of the United States to support it, a weak League of Nations also meant that the world community had little chance of preserving the peace.

The desire to stay out of European affairs persisted throughout the 1930s in many quarters in the United States, particularly Congress. There, American isolationists passed a series of Neutrality Acts to keep President Franklin D. Roosevelt, other officials, or private citizens from involving the country in foreign conflicts. Through its immigration policy, the United States also prevented many refugees fleeing from persecution in Europe and Asia from entering the country, although many scientists fleeing European oppression did arrive in the 1930s and later played an important role in developing U.S. military and nuclear power.

THE UNITED STATES BECOMES A WORLD LEADER

The world found itself at war again in 1939. By not acting sooner to deter foreign aggression and foster global prosperity, the United States found that its grand strategy of isolationism, unilateralism, and strict neutrality failed to keep it out of a major war. The influence of American isolationists crumbled in December 1941, when the Japanese attacked U.S. territory by bombing Pearl Harbor in Hawaii and Germany declared war on the United States.

President Franklin D. Roosevelt quickly mobilized the U.S. economy for war. Increased spending for war materials helped boost U.S. industry out of its slow recovery from the Great Depression. Through its Lend-Lease program, by which Congress gave the president the authority to lend or lease any equipment to any country whose defense he believed necessary to the defense of the United States, the country provided

---

League of Nations:

Created in the peace treaty that ended World War I, it was the first IGO dedicated to preserving global peace; superseded by the United Nations.

Isolationism:

Grand strategy designed to keep a nation out of foreign political or economic affairs; dominated U.S. foreign policy until World War II.

Web Exploration
To see the reach and worldwide involvement of the United Nations, go to
www.awlonline.com/oconnor.

its allies with the weapons, equipment, and supplies necessary to wage war against the Axis powers (Germany, Italy, and Japan).

Even before the end of World War II, the United States and fifty-one of its allies created a new international governmental organization, the **United Nations.** Its purpose was to guarantee the security of member nations when attacked and to promote economic, physical, and social well-being around the world. This guarantee depended on the cooperation of the five great powers that worked together to defeat the Axis powers—China, France, Great Britain, the Soviet Union, and the United States; these nations held the only permanent seats on the new United Nations Security Council. The search for peace became even more important with the development of a weapon of immense destructive power, the atomic bomb, which the United States had dropped on Hiroshima and Nagasaki in August 1945 to help end the war with Japan.

As the war ended, the allies also created new international economic organizations to encourage trade, which many people believed would lead to both greater prosperity and peace. To stabilize exchange rates among various currencies, the allies established the **International Monetary Fund (IMF),** which fixed the price of currencies in terms of the United States dollar and the price of gold. To provide funds for large-scale projects in an effort to help heal the war-torn economies of Europe and Japan, the allies started the International Bank for Reconstruction and Development, better known as the **World Bank.** Finally, to lower trade barriers, the allies hoped to create an International Trade Organization, but fears that the organization would threaten control over the national economy led the U.S. Congress to reject these efforts until the creation of the World Trade Organization in 1995. Instead, the allies began work on the **General Agreement on Tariffs and Trade (GATT),** a set of agreements that brought about a substantial reduction in tariff levels. This included lowering U.S. tariffs, which permitted greater access to the large U.S. market.

U.S. participation in these institutions indicated a shift in grand strategy toward **multilateralism,** that is, a belief that foreign policy actions should be taken in cooperation with other states after extensive consultation. To many, sustaining economic recovery seemed as important as any military measures in preserving U.S. national security. At the end of the war, moreover, the United States accounted for about half of the world's total economic product and world trade. With promises of peace and cooperation in the air, the U.S. Army's size dropped from more than eight million at the close of World War II to less than one million by 1947. The United States, however, still had nuclear weapons and the most technologically advanced land, sea, and air forces.

The Origins of the Cold War

Cooperation between the United States and the Soviet Union, critical to peace after the war, quickly eroded. The leader of the Soviet Union, Joseph Stalin, seemed willing to do anything to make the countries of Central Europe Communist. In the eastern Mediterranean, particularly Greece and Turkey, the British had maintained a sphere of influence (an area dominated although not directly controlled by a country) before World War II. A crisis erupted when the British, weakened financially by the war, no longer believed they could counter Communist aggression in the region. They asked the United States to assume support for these countries. In a flurry of activity, the State Department, in a period of fifteen weeks in early 1947, devised a set of policies that turned the United States into a global power.

The Republican chair of the Senate Foreign Relations Committee, Arthur Vandenberg of Michigan, was sympathetic to this policy shift but remembered how Republicans—Vandenberg himself among them—had resisted President Roosevelt's attempts to end isolationism before World War II. Senator Vandenberg and others counseled President Harry S Truman to "scare hell out of the country" in order to win support for global policies. Truman did, in a 1947 speech to both houses of Congress that laid out the policy known as the **Truman Doctrine,** a policy of containment of Soviet expansion. In a key passage, Truman stated, "It must be the policy of the United States to

United Nations:

IGO created shortly before the end of World War II to guarantee the security of member nations when attacked, and to promote economic, physical, and social well-being around the world.

International Monetary Fund (IMF): —WORLD BANK

An IGO created shortly before the end of World War II designed to stabilize international financial relations through a system of fixed exchange rates.

World Bank:

Originally designed to provide loans for large economic projects in Western Europe's efforts to recover from the devastation of World War II; now the major multilateral lender for development projects in poor countries.

General Agreement on Tariffs and Trade (GATT):

Devised shortly after World War II as an interim measure until a World Trade Organization could be created, multilateral trade negotiations conducted under the GATT helped lower tariff and other trade barriers substantially.

multilateralism:

The foreign policy practice that actions should be taken in cooperation with other states after extensive consultation.

Web Exploration
To learn about the specific workings of the IMF and the World Bank, go to
www.awlonline.com/oconnor.

Truman Doctrine:

President Truman's 1947 strategy to provide U.S. military and economic assistance to Greece and Turkey to contain Soviet expansion.

■ During much of the Cold War, the United States and the Soviet Union carried on testing of nuclear weapons. The rapid expansion of nuclear arsenals resulted in a stalemate position known as Mutually Assured Destruction (MAD), whereby a first strike by either superpower would result in a devastating counterstrike. (Photo courtesy: National Archives [374-ANT-30-18-DPY-30-10])

support free peoples who are resisting attempted subjugation by armed minorities or by outside pressures."[18] The speech helped create an ideological consensus that cut across all parties and justified participation in world events—the consensus of anticommunism. It also created the belief that national security was something Americans needed to worry about even when the world was at peace and even when there were no apparent direct military threats to the United States.

The Marshall Plan, NATO, and Containment

Truman got Congress to approve the European Recovery Program, often called the **Marshall Plan** (Secretary of State George C. Marshall proposed the idea in a Harvard commencement speech). In a break with tradition, the Marshall Plan provided a massive transfer of aid from the United States mainly to Western Europe. In its first year alone, 1948–49, the Marshall Plan sent the West Europeans more than $6 billion. At that time that amounted to 10 percent of the entire federal budget, 4.1 percent of the gross domestic product, and 2.8 percent of the gross national product, comparable to more than $100 billion today. The plan succeeded in rebuilding the basis for strong economies in Western Europe, which in turn prevented Communist parties from winning control of governments in the region.

For the first time, the United States joined a political and military alliance in peacetime. The North Atlantic Treaty, signed in 1949, provided that a military attack against any of the signatories (Belgium, Canada, Denmark, France, Great Britain, Iceland, Italy, Luxembourg, the Netherlands, Norway, Portugal, and the United States) would be considered an attack against all of them. The following year treaty members created the **North Atlantic Treaty Organization (NATO),** a regional defense alliance, to implement the treaty (see Figure 19.2). Even though the United States was not at war and was not directly threatened by any hostile state, hundreds of thousands of U.S. troops were moved to Europe. Though many crises occurred in Europe after the creation of NATO, the organization deterred large-scale war in Europe until the collapse of the former Yugoslavia in the 1990s.

Marshall Plan:

The European Recovery Program, named after Secretary of State George C. Marshall, which provided a massive transfer of aid from the United States to Western Europe in the years after World War II.

North Atlantic Treaty Organization (NATO):

A political and military regional defense alliance created in 1950 to implement the North Atlantic Treaty of 1949; the first peace-time military alliance made by the United States.

Figure 19.2   The Cold War in Europe

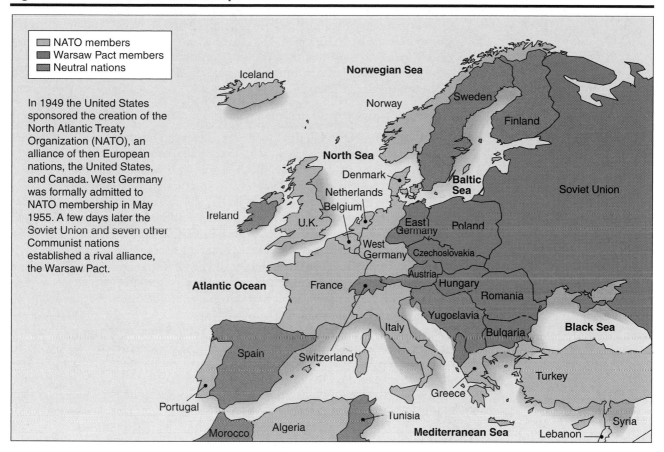

NATO members
Warsaw Pact members
Neutral nations

In 1949 the United States sponsored the creation of the North Atlantic Treaty Organization (NATO), an alliance of then European nations, the United States, and Canada. West Germany was formally admitted to NATO membership in May 1955. A few days later the Soviet Union and seven other Communist nations established a rival alliance, the Warsaw Pact.

Across the globe, Truman soon confronted a new crisis in Asia. After World War II, Korea had been partitioned into two zones, the one in the north occupied by Soviet troops, the one in the south by U.S. troops. Disagreements between the United States and the Soviet Union prevented reunification and led instead to the creation of separate states. Then, in June 1950, North Korea invaded South Korea. The United States was taken by surprise, but after brief consideration Truman decided to commit U.S. forces, through United Nations auspices, to help South Korea resist. The United States was able to get support for its action from the United Nations only because the Soviets were not attending Security Council meetings in protest (Security Council resolutions require unanimous approval of all permanent members present). U.S. troops did not stop the North Koreans in the first weeks, but the tide of the war reversed after a dramatic amphibious landing staged by the U.S. commander General Douglas MacArthur at the port city of Inchon. The tide of war reversed again when Chinese troops intervened in force on North Korea's behalf in November 1950. After months of indecisive fighting, the warring parties agreed to a truce, dividing the peninsula nearly in half by a demilitarized zone for the next five decades.

The Marshall Plan, NATO, and U.S. actions in Korea are examples of the grand strategy of **containment.** Based on the observations of a U.S. diplomat, George Kennan, the United States sought to contain Soviet Communism. Kennan argued that if the allies could stop the spread of Communism, the nature of the Soviet leadership and its political system would collapse. In practice this meant surrounding the Soviet Union with U.S. or Allied military forces in an effort to deter the Red Army, and deny or delay Soviet access to many Western goods and technologies through restrictions on trade and investment. This strategy was criticized by the left as too hostile (because the military deployments would provoke the Soviets) and by the right as too soft (because the

containment:

A strategy to oppose any further expansion of Soviet power, particularly in Western Europe and East Asia, by surrounding the Soviet Union with U.S. or Allied military forces.

United States did not roll back Communism in Eastern Europe and China). Much of the strategy was clarified in a complete review of U.S. foreign and defense policy conducted by the president's National Security Council (NSC). NSC Study number 68 (NSC-68), completed in 1950, maintained that the security of the United States was linked closely with the security of the Western, democratic world. With some modifications, the grand strategy of containment became the framework of U.S. foreign and military policy until the 1990s.

The Cold War Era

In retrospect, containment did limit Communist expansion in Europe until the Soviet Union collapsed as Kennan theorized. More important, containment did not lead to another world war. The political and military stability provided by the policy of containment and the economic stability promoted by international economic institutions, such as the IMF, the World Bank, and the GATT, allowed the Western allies (particularly the NATO members and Japan) to focus on economic development. The rapid recovery of Western Europe resulted in a spectacular round of global economic prosperity. Between 1950 and 1973, world trade grew at unprecedented rates in every year but one. Private U.S. investment overseas, mainly in Western Europe, and foreign investment in the United States increased dramatically after 1950. Finally, the gross national product (GNP) of the United States in constant dollar terms expanded in all but seven years between 1948 and 1990.

The grand strategy of containment raised the importance of the military in the United States. In 1940, the last year before the United States entered World War II, federal expenditures on defense were equal to 17.5 percent of the total federal budget and only 1.7 percent of the U.S. gross domestic product (GDP). In contrast, between 1947 and 1987, U.S. defense expenditures averaged 39.9 percent of the budget and 7.7 percent of GDP. Also, in contrast to efforts to curb arms sales before World War II, after the war the United States became the major supplier of arms to the rest of the Western world. As President Eisenhower noted in his last public address, the United States now had a vast "military-industrial complex" that made the military and defense industries a dominant factor in U.S. politics, with the "potential for the disastrous rise of misplaced power."

After the Soviet Union exploded its own atomic bomb in 1949, both sides began to build nuclear arsenals. Although the United States maintained a significant advantage in the early years, both sides eventually had enough nuclear weapons to absorb an attack by the other and launch a devastating nuclear strike in retaliation. This situation, known as **mutually assured destruction (MAD),** deterred each side from attacking the other.[19] As the dangers of nuclear war became clearer after the Cuban Missile Crisis (the United States-Soviet Union confrontation in 1962 over attempts to install Soviet ballistic missiles in Cuba), both sides began efforts to agree on limits to the size of their own nuclear forces through negotiations and treaties, culminating in the Strategic Arms Reduction Treaties (START I and START II). Under the START treaties and related agreements, as modified by the end of the Cold War, Belarus, Kazakhstan, and Ukraine sent the nuclear weapons on their soil to Russia, and Russia and the United States agreed to cut their strategic nuclear weapons in half.[20]

By the late 1960s, leaders in the Soviet Union and the United States agreed to cooperate to stop the proliferation of nuclear weapons to other countries. The most important feature of that cooperation was the negotiation of the Nuclear Non-Proliferation Treaty (NPT), which 186 states had signed by 1998. The NPT strikes a bargain between the nuclear weapons states, especially the United States and the Soviet Union (now Russia) and the non-nuclear weapons states. Nuclear weapons states promise not to help other countries get nuclear weapons and work to reduce the size of their nuclear arsenals, while the non-nuclear states promise not to acquire nuclear weapons. Originally, the NPT aimed at limiting proliferation among industrialized states, especially Germany and Japan, but after the first Indian test of a nuclear device in 1974, the sig-

mutually assured destruction (MAD):

The situation where one nation could absorb a nuclear strike by another and have sufficient nuclear forces to launch a devastating retaliatory strike; seen as a means of deterring nuclear war.

natories became more concerned with the aspirations of developing countries. In the early 1990s, both China and France signed the NPT, joining the United States, Russia, and the United Kingdom as the five nuclear weapons states recognized by the treaty. Among the many consequences of the NPT, for example, the International Atomic Energy Agency (IAEA) monitors over 1,000 installations to safeguard nuclear materials from diversion into military programs. Despite a 1995 agreement to extend the NPT indefinitely, the 1998 nuclear tests by India and Pakistan, neither of whom are signatories to the NPT, and the efforts to acquire nuclear weapons by Iraq and North Korea, both of whom are signatories, highlight some of the many challenges to the nuclear nonproliferation regime the United States and the Soviet Union crafted during the Cold War.

Web Exploration
For further information on the activities of the IAEA, go to www.awlonline.com/oconnor.

Containment was less clear on defining the appropriate role for the United States in wars of "national liberation," such as Vietnam.[21] With little information on the nature of the Vietnam conflict, such as the relative independence of the Vietnamese Communist movement from Soviet or Chinese control or the history of U.S. involvement in the region, Congress and the public were easily deceived on the extent and consequences of U.S. involvement by more than one administration. Perhaps the worst instance was the degree to which the Johnson administration misled Congress in order to pass the Gulf of Tonkin Resolution, which originally authorized a massive commitment of U.S. forces to support a series of anticommunist—though not democratic—governments in South Vietnam.

U.S. forces left South Vietnam in 1973, but the 57,000 dead and 300,000 injured, the unpopularity of the war at home, and the failure to build a truly democratic government in Vietnam, created a much longer legacy. In the 1960s many U.S. political leaders believed that appeasing Hitler rather than confronting him years earlier helped cause World War II. Just as this idea framed the debate about U.S. intervention in Vietnam, many current leaders see Vietnam as a lesson on the limits of U.S. military power today. In the days following the death of several U.S. soldiers in Somalia in 1993, for example, many members of Congress echoed the sentiment of Representative Jim Ramstad (R–Minn.), who warned, "The president better get his foreign policy act together before Somalia becomes another Vietnam."[22] In addition to its impact on political leaders, the Vietnam experience had a significant impact on public opinion. In the late 1940s through the 1960s, about a fourth of all Americans thought that the United States should stay out of world affairs. Since the early 1970s, however, this view has been shared by about a third of all Americans.[23]

Containment also said little about an appropriate foreign economic policy for the United States once Europe and Japan recovered from World War II. Though originally seeking a policy of "trade, not aid," President Eisenhower began to assist countries in Asia and elsewhere in response to an expansion of Soviet assistance programs. Encouraged by U.S. success in rebuilding Europe in the early 1950s, President John F. Kennedy saw U.S. foreign aid and assistance programs and international economic institutions as means of transforming poor countries in Africa, Asia, and Latin America into prosperous, anticommunist nations. The United States, together with other wealthy countries, however, did not offer programs as large as the Marshall Plan for problems that turned out to be much more difficult to solve.

Foreign assistance programs today take many forms, including low-interest loans, free food or weapons, and outright grants-in-aid. Often, direct aid to another country is tied to that country's promises to purchase goods from the donor. One reason for the success of multilateral lending institutions, such as the International Development Agency of the World Bank, is the demand for aid without such strings attached.

Most U.S. assistance loans and grants are made by the U.S. Agency for International Development. Although for most of the last four decades the United States has made the largest foreign aid contributions (in dollar amounts) of any country, the total aid is typically around one-half of one percent of the federal budget, much less than that given by many other rich countries. Despite this fact, since 1973 most polls indicate that 70

percent or more of Americans believe that the United States spends too much on foreign aid, though younger Americans are slightly less critical of these policies.[24]

Of the roughly $78 billion distributed by the U.S. Agency for International Development or its predecessors between 1962 and 1989, much went to governments threatened by Communist forces, as in El Salvador, Korea, Pakistan, the Philippines, South Vietnam, and Turkey. The two countries receiving the most aid were Israel and Egypt, because of their roles in the Middle East conflict. Diplomatic and military policies, however, are not the only determinant of U.S. aid. Substantial sums of money and supplies have gone for humanitarian and economic development purposes to countries in the Third World.

After the Cold War, U.S. foreign aid programs have had to meet many new challenges, such as assisting the formerly Communist states in their transition to democracy and a market economy. The U.S. Department of Defense also took greater

■ Many Americans continue to visit the Vietnam War Memorial in Washington, D.C. to grieve for those in the U.S. military who gave their lives during the conflict in Southeast Asia. (Photo courtesy: Bachman/The Image Works)

interest in disaster and humanitarian relief efforts, as well as new kinds of peacekeeping efforts. Many in Congress, however, oppose the current direction of U.S. foreign assistance programs. Senate Foreign Relations Committee Chair Jesse Helms (R–N.C.) eventually pressured the Clinton administration to integrate the lead agency administering U.S. foreign aid programs, the U.S. Agency for International Development (AID), along with the Arms Control and Disarmament Agency (ACDA), into the State Department in 1999. In return Congress approved the first real increase in the U.S. foreign aid budget in many years, increasing the budget for the programs run by the revised AID to around $7.2 billion in 1999. Many members of Congress want to restrict access to U.S. aid by family planning agencies that furnish abortions. Providing a wide range of services, not just abortions, these private agencies play a central role in population control worldwide, so many other members of Congress oppose these efforts to restrict funding.

Opposition to U.S. foreign assistance policies has had a wider impact on U.S. foreign aid and foreign relations. For many years, critics have argued that the U.S. share of U.N. costs are too high and that many U.N. programs suffer from mismanagement, so Congress has limited appropriations for U.N. activities. After the U.N. came under the leadership of new Secretary-General Kofi Annan, Congress agreed to pay about half of the $1.5 billion owed by the United States. In 1997, however, this agreement collapsed in the debate about the use of funds for family planning and the U.S. continued in arrears, owing far more than any other country. In recognition of these continuing financial woes, Ted Turner, the founder of CNN, made an unprecedented pledge to donate $1 billion over ten years to various U.N. programs.

By the 1970s global economic conditions had changed dramatically from the years immediately after World War II, affecting the relative influence of the United States in determining global economic activities. Japan and some of the countries of the **European Union (EU)** greatly improved their economic strength and technological capacity, enhancing their role on the world stage. By the 1990s, for example, Japan's program of Official Development Assistance (ODA) made that country, not the United States, the world leader in foreign aid contributions. The establishment of the new European currency, the euro, promises to challenge the U.S. dollar as the dominant currency for international trade and finance.

European Union (EU):

The union that joins most of the countries of Western Europe in their efforts to develop common economic, social, and foreign policies; successor to the European Communities.

In the early 1970s the global economy suffered its first major depression in three decades. Many people in the United States began to complain that nontariff barriers to trade used by other governments were hurting U.S. exports, while the U.S. market was relatively open. As a result, support for U.S. free trade policies began to decline. The U.S. trade deficit, particularly with Japan and Germany, increased steadily. Some wondered if Japan would eventually overtake the United States as the world's largest and richest economy.

By 1998 not only had the Japanese economic bubble burst, but almost every country in Asia faced a financial crisis that undermined nearly two decades of rapid economic growth in the region and even toppled the Indonesian government. While most of these countries relied on export-led economic growth, mostly based on trade with the United States, continued investment in questionable projects undermined confidence in these economies and their national currencies.

One key element of postwar economic recovery was the stability of the U.S. dollar, with the values of most currencies fixed to the value of gold and the dollar (called the fixed exchange-rate system). Through the International Monetary Fund (IMF), the dollar had become the global currency, with large deposits of U.S. dollars overseas. This meant that the U.S. government lost some capacity to influence inflation and interest rates through its control over its own money supply. In 1971 President Richard M. Nixon abandoned fixed exchange rates. This led to the current system where the value of the U.S. dollar and other major currencies depends on what people are willing to pay for them (called a **floating exchange rate**). When the value of the dollar increases, it helps attract foreign investment to the United States but often worsens the U.S. trade deficit considerably as the price of U.S. goods increases in the local currency of the other countries.

Finally, many Third World countries now viewed the United States and other rich, industrialized countries as economic adversaries and called for the creation of a new world economic order. In 1960 some of these countries joined together in a cartel known as the Organization of Petroleum Exporting Countries (OPEC). They gained influence in the global economy by raising the price of oil during much of the 1970s. Although the success of OPEC proved to be an exception compared with other efforts by Third World countries to control the supply or price of raw commodities, it symbolized Third World dissatisfaction with the global economy.[25]

The United States and the other key industrial powers have tried to coordinate their trade, investment, and monetary policies more closely since the 1970s. The leaders of seven countries—Canada, France, Germany, Great Britain, Italy, Japan, and the United States—now hold annual summits to discuss political and economic issues of mutual concern. Recently, Russian leaders have become involved in these now Group of Eight (G-8) discussions. Substantial disagreements exist within the G-8, and many people fear that the world is dividing into three competing economic blocs—East Asia, Europe, and North America. Taken together, these problems have diminished support in the United States for a grand strategy that includes freer trade and open economic policies.

THE MACHINERY OF MODERN FOREIGN POLICY MAKING

In *Federalist No. 8* John Jay noted that "it is the nature of war to increase the executive at the expense of the legislative authority." As the likelihood of international conflict became clearer in the 1930s, Congress granted the president broad authority to act in foreign affairs and specifically to allow the president to prohibit arms shipments to participants in foreign wars. In *United States* v. *Curtiss-Wright Export Corporation* (1936), the U.S. Supreme Court upheld the right of the Congress to grant this authority.[26] While referring to an isolationist strategy, in this ruling the U.S. Supreme Court

---

Web Exploration
To learn more about the EU or Japanese aid programs, go to www.awlonline.com/oconnor.

floating exchange rate:
When the value of a national currency depends on what people are willing to pay for it in other currencies, usually in U.S. dollars, English pounds, or German marks.

National Security Acts of 1947 and 1949:

The acts that unified the armed services and created the modern U.S. security establishment, including the National Security Council and the Central Intelligence Agency.

recognized the primary importance of the president in foreign policy and affirmed that the national government did not share power over foreign relations with the states. This marked the first time that the Supreme Court formally recognized the concept of inherent powers of the national government in foreign affairs.

Both World War II and the Cold War helped secure the central role of the president in the U.S. foreign policy-making process. Congress supported a larger role for the United States in global military affairs with the **National Security Acts of 1947 and 1949.** These acts consolidated the army, the navy, and the new air force into one department under civilian leadership, now known as the Department of Defense. The legislation also set up two new organizations: (1) the Central Intelligence Agency (CIA), which would collect and analyze the information deemed necessary to meet national security threats, and (2) the National Security Council (NSC), made up of the president, the vice president, the secretaries of state and defense, the chair of the Joint Chiefs of Staff, and the director of Central Intelligence. The NSC, along with the newly created post of assistant to the president for National Security Affairs (the national security adviser), would advise the president on foreign and military affairs.

The National Security Council, the National Economic Council, and the Central Intelligence Agency.

The modern policy-making process differs sharply from the process the United States followed in the past. The president now commands a vast military-industrial complex supported by a large foreign policy and intelligence network. The NSC, set up to institutionalize the system by which the U.S. government had conducted World War II, began to coordinate a wide range of foreign policy issues, such as dealing with the fall of the Shah of Iran or negotiating a new canal treaty with Panama. In addition to collecting intelligence information in the Cold War against the Soviet Union, the CIA ran covert (secret) operations to alter political outcomes in many countries.[27] At times, these secret operations undermined broader U.S. objectives by supporting assassinations, corruption, and other scandalous activities. In the 1970s Congress intensely criticized the CIA and mandated changes in procedures to provide more oversight over its covert actions. In the early 1990s, the end of the Cold War, the penetration of the CIA by foreign spy agencies, and other scandals again raised congressional interest in reforming the CIA. Consequently, Congress formed a special commission to consider how to reform the CIA in 1995. Since the end of the Cold War, the CIA has attempted to become more transparent in its activities. One indicator of this new openness is the CIA's Electronic Documents Release Center on the Internet.

In most critical military and foreign policy matters, direction is provided by the president with advice from the members of the NSC, the national security adviser, and the NSC staff, with input from other executive departments and agencies as the president desires. For foreign economic policy, President Bill Clinton created a National Economic Council (NEC) with a role parallel to the NSC's influence on security policy. The inner core of the NEC includes a presidential adviser who chairs the council; the secretaries of labor, treasury, and commerce; the director of the Office of Management and Budget; the U.S. trade representative; and the head of the Council of Economic Advisers. The NSC and the NEC work together, and even share staff on a number of issues, including trade. They also work with the Domestic Policy Council on some noneconomic issues.

Each president has an individual management style, and the precise pattern of foreign policy making differs for each administration as a result.[28] President Eisenhower, for example, wanted very formal lines of authority and divisions of responsibility. Presidents Clinton and Kennedy preferred a collegial management style, relying on *ad hoc* working groups. President Nixon changed from a collegial style to a more formal NSC over time. These styles affect the roles of the national security adviser in each administration.

The State and Defense Departments.

In addition to providing information and advice through the NSC, the departments of state and defense have primary responsibility for implementing foreign and military policy. One reflection of the global nature of U.S.

Web Exploration
For more about the CIA Electronic Documents Release Center, go to www.awlonline.com/oconnor.

Web Exploration
For more about the National Security Council, go to www.awlonline.com/oconnor.

Web Exploration
For more about the National Economic Council, go to www.awlonline.com/oconnor.

interests is the 162 countries served by U.S. embassies and consulates under the direction of the State Department. The 22,000 State Department personnel gather information on foreign political, economic, social, and military situations, represent the United States in international negotiations and international organizations, and provide a range of basic services such as processing passport and visa applications. In addition to foreign service officers and other members of the State Department, many other departments and agencies may have personnel stationed overseas. Typically, an ambassador, the personal representative of the president to the head of government of another country (or a group of countries or an international organization), serves as the leader of all U.S. officials stationed in that country, even if they are not members of the State Department. From their main offices in the Foggy Bottom section of Washington, most of the few thousand State Department officials are responsible for either specific issues or specific countries.

The State Department undertook several significant changes in 1999. As noted earlier in this chapter, it has absorbed two formerly independent federal agencies, the Agency for International Development (AID) and the Arms Control and Disarmament Agency (ACDA). Counting supplemental budgets, funding for foreign affairs programs directed through the State Department will be more than $21 billion in the year 2000, in no small measure because of its new responsibilities and efforts to make U.S. embassies more secure in light of persistent terrorist actions, such as the bombing of the U.S. embassy buildings in Kenya and Tanzania in 1998.

The Defense Department, with its far-flung system of bases and military units, provides the forces to conduct military operations. With the end of the Cold War, the United States has cut its military dramatically, from about 2.2 million personnel in 1987 to roughly 1.4 million in 1998. At the same time, the Defense Department has increased its efforts to use high technology to bring about fundamental changes in how the military completes its missions, a process known as the Revolution in Military Affairs (RMA). The Defense Department must also handle many new kinds of missions, from humanitarian relief for Iraqi Kurds through Operation Provide Comfort to disaster relief in the wake of Hurricane Fran to preparing for a possible terrorist attack using chemical or biological weapons on major cities in the United States. The U.S. has large overseas military forces in Western Europe, the Middle East, and the Pacific (see Figure 19.3).[29] In Europe U.S. armed forces play a key role in the military structure of NATO, the major military organization in the region. The very nature of NATO has begun to change in recent years, with its participation in operations like the Implementation Force (IFOR) in Bosnia and the air campaign in Yugoslavia. Most importantly, in January 1994 NATO members called on most European states to join in a Partnership for Peace. Despite substantial opposition from domestic and allied leaders that deemed it too costly or antagonistic toward Russia (and very vocal opposition from Russian leaders), the Clinton administration got NATO members to amend the treaty and enlarge the organization to include Poland, Hungary, and the Czech Republic in February 1998. In East Asia and the Pacific, the United States maintains about 100,000 personnel, mainly in South Korea and Japan. Clinton administration officials considered reducing these numbers, but rejected this option when many leaders in the region expressed their need for a U.S. military presence to preserve regional stability. The Japan–U.S. Security Treaty provides the key link in U.S. defense efforts in Asia. In 1997 the two countries agreed to enhance their defense cooperation in several ways, including greater support from Japanese defense forces for operations in areas surrounding Japan. With encouragement from the United States, these new guidelines for cooperation represented another shift in Japanese policy to expand its responsibilities in supporting regional stability.

The United States also maintains one of the world's most potent nuclear forces. In recent years the United States and the states of the former Soviet Union have started to eliminate many of their nuclear warheads and the missiles and bombers to deliver them. Nonetheless, the limits reached through START I and START II still mean that the United States and Russia each have far more nuclear weapons than any other country. If fully implemented by 2003, START II, which the Senate ratified in January 1996,

Web Exploration
To learn more about the mission, organization, and activities of the State Department, go to www.awlonline.com/oconnor.

Figure 19.3 Nominal U.S. Overseas Presence

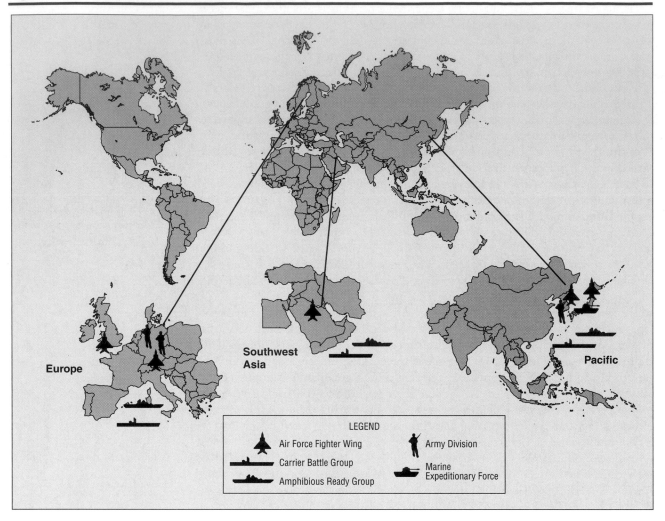

NOTE: 1. Boundary representations are not necessarily authoritative
      2. Varies according to national deployment schemes

SOURCE: U.S. Department of Defense, *1998 Annual Defense Report*, Washington, D.C.: U.S. Government Printing Office, 1998.

still would allow each side to have as many as 3,500 nuclear warheads on strategic vehicles (missiles and bombers). To put this in perspective, estimates suggest the next largest nuclear arsenal is France's 525 warheads (which it is reducing) and China's 435 warheads (which it is modernizing).

Civilian control over the armed forces has been one of the most sacred foundations for preserving the U.S. Constitution. Under the Secretary of Defense and other appointed civilian officials, the Defense Department directs U.S. forces from its main offices in the Pentagon, across the Potomac from the District of Columbia. With thousands of officials overseeing its massive operations, the Defense Department is among the most influential federal bureaucracies. While defense spending has declined with the end of the Cold War, it still accounted for nearly one-fifth of the federal government budgets during the mid-1990s.

The presence of tens of thousands of U.S. military personnel overseas causes some tension with the host nations, and not just from the noise made by low-flying planes or the damage of tanks to local fields. Members of Congress often questioned the costs of maintaining troops in Europe, even at the height of the Cold War. The United States removed most of its forces from the Philippines in recent years as disputes over the cost of maintaining the forces increased. Isolated instances of outrageous conduct by military personnel can damage relations as well. Three U.S. servicemen in Okinawa, for example, were convicted of raping a twelve-year-old Japanese girl in 1995. The furor raised by Japanese citizens caused both governments to promise to reduce U.S. military operations and presence on the island.

■ A U.S. soldier in the Bosnia peacekeeping force looks on as Bosnia citizens make their way to supervised municipal elections. (Photo courtesy: Tomislav

Presidential Primacy in Foreign Affairs

Compared with domestic policy, Congress and interest groups generally have a relatively smaller role in making foreign and military policy than does the president. Their role in foreign economic and military funding policies is somewhat larger, but not as large as their role in purely domestic policies. This occurs because the nature of foreign and military policy differs from the nature of domestic policy in ways that reinforce the power of the president.

Alexander Hamilton, in *Federalist No. 75,* recognized that foreign policy was different from domestic policy because it required:

1. Accurate and comprehensive knowledge of foreign politics
2. A steady and systematic adherence to the same views
3. A nice and uniform sensibility to national character
4. Decision, secrecy, and despatch [sic]

On each point, the office of the president has an advantage over Congress. Perhaps the most important source of power is the president's greater access to and control over information (see Roots of Government: Communication Technology and Foreign Policy). In domestic politics, many people, including those in the Congress, the media, and interest groups, often have important information that bears on policy decisions. When dealing with foreign affairs, however, the president has exclusive sources of information—diplomats working for the State Department, military attachés working for the Defense Department, agents controlled by the CIA, and technical means (such as satellites) controlled by the CIA and the National Security Agency (the NSA, which is in charge of electronic intelligence gathering). Private citizens, companies, interest groups, even Congress cannot balance the president's information with their own on issues such as the number of Soviet missiles in Cuba or the extent of Iraq's nuclear weapons program. Even the main source of information available to the president's critics, the news media, is dominated by the president (see chapter 15).

The president's authority is enhanced by the aura of secret information available to the nation's chief executive: diplomatic cables, CIA reports, NSA intercepts. Sometimes, to win points in debates against rivals, the president will declassify secret information. Virtually any other citizen could be prosecuted for revealing classified material, but the president may do so freely. In the 1980 election campaign, for

Web Exploration
To learn about current news on military operations around the globe, go to
www.awlonline.com/oconnor.

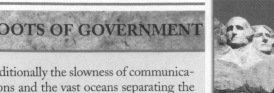
example, President Jimmy Carter, under attack from Republican opponents for neglecting U.S. defenses, authorized his secretary of defense to reveal that the United States had been developing a plane that would be invisible to radar, which became the B-2 Stealth bomber.

CHALLENGES TO PRESIDENTIAL POWER IN FOREIGN AND MILITARY POLICY

The president is powerful but not omnipotent in the field of foreign policy. International factors place limits on the power of the president. The foreign and military policy of the United States is often criticized as simply a reaction to the policies of other countries. In addition, all presidents face domestic constraints on their power from Congress, the bureaucracy, the media, and the public as well.

Congress

Web Exploration
To learn about key Congressional committees in military and foreign affairs, go to
www.awlonline.com/oconnor.

The most consistent restraint on presidential power in foreign affairs comes from Congress.[30] The Constitution gives a lesser role to Congress in foreign affairs than in domestic affairs, but much of the modern-day power of the president comes from broad authority granted to the executive through legislation, not through the Constitution. Congress also exercises its oversight powers on the foreign policy and military activities of the president and the executive branch. In this sense Congress has more power in holding the administration accountable for its foreign policy than legislatures in parliamentary systems, where members of the parliamentary majority also serve as government ministers. The British Parliament, for example, required a court inquiry and an independent investigation (the Scott Report) to find out that the administration misled it about approval of British exports of weapons-related goods to Iraqi military programs in the 1980s, whereas Congress (and the courts) were active in uncovering the extent of U.S. involvement in Iraqi military programs.

Congressional Leadership.   Normally the president proposes a foreign policy and Congress accepts, modifies, or rejects it. Congress also has the power to develop and implement policy. When the Soviet Union launched Sputnik, the first artificial Earth satellite, in 1957, President Dwight D. Eisenhower did not treat it as a serious threat to U.S. security. Other prominent Americans, however, were worried. With no proposal of action from the president, under the guidance of Senate Majority Leader Lyndon B. Johnson, the Preparedness Subcommittee of the Senate Armed Services Committee held hearings on the threat posed by Soviet space potential. Determining that there was indeed a threat, Congress set up the National Aeronautics and Space Administration (NASA) to run a U.S. space program and the National Defense Education Act to provide funding for science and foreign language education. Although technically civilian programs, these were seen at the time as very much a part of U.S. defense policy.

Congressional Oversight.   Congressional oversight is a relatively new check on the president's power to set foreign and military policy. During and after World War II, weapons became more and more complex, and Congress was willing to defer to presidential recommendations and military advice on what weapons the country needed. But in 1969 Congress for the first time challenged a president on a major defense expenditure. President Richard M. Nixon proposed a nationwide system of radar and interceptor missiles to defend against incoming missiles, known at the time as Anti-Ballistic Missiles (ABMs). The Senate, relying on expert testimony by Defense Department officials who had actually tried to develop such systems and believed they would not work, came within a single vote of turning down Nixon's request. Since 1969 the U.S. public has become accustomed to congressional scrutiny of weapon development and deployment. Particularly after a 1998 report on the missile threats facing the United States, for example, many in Congress have called for the development of a new Ballistic Missile Defense (BMD) system.

Treaties and Executive Agreements.   The Constitution gives the Senate explicit power to approve treaties. Even though the Senate has rejected treaties outright only sixteen times in U.S. history, the power is effective because presidents try to avoid direct defeats or filibusters. Until the Senate reached a compromise in the spring of 1996, Senator Helms, chair of the Senate Foreign Relations Committee, kept the Senate from considering ratification of the Chemical Weapons Convention (CWC), as he opposed the treaty as unverifiable. The CWC requires the destruction of all existing chemical weapons and bans the production, stockpiling, transfer, and use of chemical weapons by its signatories. Further, it restricts trade in many chemicals with nonsignatories, including chemicals that have military applications but wide commercial uses as well, which could have a significant impact on the chemical industry. The Senate barely ratified the CWC in time to make the United States a charter member of the new Organization for the Prohibition of Chemical Weapons (OPCW) in March 1997 and did not pass the necessary implementing legislation until 1998.

Congress also restrains presidential authority to negotiate treaties. In the case of trade treaties, several presidents have requested that Congress consider these treaties with limited amendments so that the bargains struck during negotiations will not come unglued. Congressional opposition to additional "fast-track" legislation, for example, undermined Clinton administration efforts to expand the **North American Free Trade Agreement (NAFTA)** to include Chile and other countries in the Western hemisphere.

As noted in chapter 8, presidents can avoid the treaty process altogether by using executive agreements and have done so more and more frequently since World War II, as illustrated in Table 19.1. Senate ratification is not required for an executive agreement, and prior to the Case Act of 1972, the president did not even have to inform Congress of the texts of these accords. Normally, presidents use executive agreements for routine business matters, such as purchasing and running embassies. But sometimes executive agreements have important policy implications. Several executive agreements

Web Exploration
For an unclassified version of the report of the commission to assess the ballistic missile threat to the United States, go to
www.awlonline.com/oconnor.

Web Exploration
For a world map of states that have ratified the Chemical Weapons Convention, go to
www.awlonline.com/oconnor.

North American Free Trade Agreement (NAFTA):

A treaty that promotes the free movement of goods and services between Canada, Mexico, and the United States.

Table 19.1 Treaties and Executive Agreements Concluded by the United States, 1789–1998

Years	Number of Treaties	Number of Executive Agreements
1789–1839	60	27
1839–1889	215	238
1889–1929	382	763
1930–1932	49	41
1933–1944 (F. Roosevelt)	131	369
1945–1952 (Truman)	132	1,324
1953–1960 (Eisenhower)	89	1,834
1961–1963 (Kennedy)	36	813
1964–1968 (L. Johnson)	67	1,083
1969–1974 (Nixon)	93	1,317
1975–1976 (Ford)	26	666
1977–1980 (Carter)	79	1,476
1981–1988 (Reagan)	125	2,840
1989–1992 (Bush)	67	1,371
1993–1998 (Clinton)	161	1,628

Note: Number of treaties includes those concluded during the indicated span of years. Some of these treaties did not receive the consent of the U.S. Senate. Varying definitions of what comprises an executive agreement and their entry-into-force date make the above numbers approximate.

SOURCES: Harold W. Stanley and Richard E. Niemi, eds. *Vital Statistics on American Politics, 1997–1998 (6th ed.)* (Washington, D.C.: Congressional Quarterly, 1998), 327. Clinton data provided by Treaties Office, Department of State.

that established U.S. military bases overseas in such countries as Spain and the Philippines, for example, had the effect of allying the United States with these countries.

Appointments.   As head of state and government, the president appoints ambassadors and other persons involved in the formation and implementation of foreign and defense policy. The Constitution gives the Senate the right to provide advice and consent on these posts. As in the domestic arena, important political appointees for foreign and defense policy frequently have close connections to Congress. A key link in President Ronald Reagan's foreign policy was the appointment of Richard Perle as assistant secretary of defense. A proponent of a strong anti-Soviet policy, Perle worked for many years as a staff adviser to conservative Senator Henry "Scoop" Jackson (D–Wash.), and his knowledge of Congress, the issue area, and President Reagan's policy aims made Perle a powerful figure.

Senators can put a hold on the confirmation process of some foreign policy positions to express concern about an issue as well as about the appointee (see chapter 7). Senator Jesse Helms (R–N.C.) used the hold privilege in 1994 to delay the appointment of political scientist Robert Pastor as ambassador to Panama. Helms distrusted Pastor's role in the Carter administration policy toward Nicaragua's formerly Marxist government. A similar result awaited William Weld, the Republican governor of Massachusetts, whom President Clinton nominated as ambassador to Mexico in 1997. Senator Helms, concerned over the governor's position on the medical use of marijuana, simply refused to hold hearings on Governor Weld, effectively derailing the nomination.

Appropriations.   Congress has a key role in shaping foreign and defense policy through its power to appropriate funds. Congress, for example, usually appropriates more funds for the Defense Department than requested by the Clinton administration, usually earmarking the increase for buying more weapons. In Fiscal Year 1999, Congress authorized $262.6 billion to the Defense Department. At slightly more than $267 billion for Fiscal Year 2000, Congress seems likely to press the White House to increase its budget request, especially in light of the Kosovo operation.[31]

Congress can even influence when and where the U.S. fights through its control of the budget. The power to go to war is shared between the executive and legislative branches of government, but the power to appropriate funds belongs to the legislature alone. Congress has been cautious about applying this power. In 1996 the House voted to cut off funding for the deployment of 20,000 U.S. troops as part of the 60,000-strong NATO Implementation Force in Bosnia. As failure to contribute these troops would scuttle the Dayton peace plan before it got started, the Senate rejected the cutoff. Instead, the Senate agreed to support efforts to fulfill U.S. obligations but did not use the word "approve" in its resolution.

In 1982 Congress used its appropriation power to limit U.S. involvement in Nicaragua. In 1979 an insurrection led by guerrillas named after an earlier Nicaraguan hero, Augusto Sandino, helped the Sandinistas to come to power. Because the Sandinistas received aid from Cuba and the Soviet Union, those opposing them—known as counterrevolutionaries, or Contras—found that the Reagan administration was willing to aid them. Many people in the United States opposed funding the Contras, and after much debate, Congress decided to cut appropriations. The Contras continued to receive supplies of weapons, however. In 1986 it was revealed that the supplies had been paid for with funds solicited from foreign states and from private individuals and with proceeds from arms deals with the Khomeini regime in Iran in which members of the Reagan administration participated.

The War Powers Act. Nicaragua was not the first instance when the executive branch supported military action against the will of Congress. With the Gulf of Tonkin Resolution in 1964, Congress had given broad authority to President Lyndon B. Johnson to conduct military operations in Vietnam. As support for the war dwindled, members of Congress became frustrated with their failure to influence policy on Vietnam. In 1973 Congress tried to prevent future interventions overseas without congressional approval by passing the **War Powers Act** (see Highlight 19.1: The War Powers Act). Under the act the president can deploy troops to hostile situations overseas only for a sixty-day period in peace-time (which could be extended for an extra thirty days to permit withdrawal) unless Congress explicitly gives its approval for a longer period. Under the act, the president could respond to an emergency, such as rescue of endangered Americans abroad, but not engage in a prolonged struggle without congressional approval.

The War Powers Act continues to be an issue in the struggle for control of foreign policy between the president and Congress. When first passed, it was vetoed by President Richard M. Nixon. Congress overrode the veto in March 1973, but Nixon called the act unconstitutional and said he was not bound by it. No issue arose to test the competing claims before Nixon was forced to resign in 1974, but such issues did arise under his successors.

The first serious test of the War Powers Act came under President Ronald Reagan. In 1982 Reagan ordered Marines into Lebanon as part of a peacekeeping mission. Because the troops were not in combat, Congress did not object. But after a year, the Marines came under increasing fire from various factions in Lebanon's civil war. Although Marines were being killed, Congress was slow to invoke the War Powers Act. In the midst of a drawn-out debate over U.S. involvement in Lebanon, a Lebanese terrorist drove an explosive-filled truck into the Marine barracks in Beirut, killing 241 service personnel. Shortly thereafter, all Marines were withdrawn on the president's initiative. In this and subsequent actions, presidents have usually complied with parts of the War Powers Act, especially the requirements for notifying key members of Congress.

When Iraq invaded Kuwait on August 2, 1990, President George Bush had to build domestic support for the U.S. response. Congressional attempts to restrain the

War Powers Act:

A law passed near the end of the Vietnam War to limit the powers of the president to engage U.S. military forces in combat abroad without congressional consent.

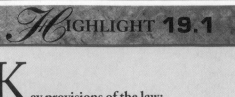

Key provisions of the law:

*   The president must consult Congress "in every possible instance" before committing military forces to imminent or probable combat overseas and must report any such mission to Congress within forty-eight hours.
*   Military forces must be brought home within sixty days unless Congress either declares war, otherwise approves of the mission, or extends the withdrawal deadline.

Proposals made in 1988 and 1993 by Senator Sam Nunn (D-Ga.):

*   Set up a "permanent consultative body" of House and Senate leaders and key committee chairs to meet regularly with the president on foreign policy issues.
*   Once military forces are committed overseas, Congress can force their withdrawal only by passing spe-

cific legislation. Congress can also pass legislation approving of the mission.
*   Spending of federal funds contrary to congressional legislation, such as an order to withdraw troops, would be prohibited.

H.J.RES.42 (the "War Powers Amendments Act") introduced by representative Peter DeFazio (D-Or.) on March 24, 1999:

*   Although related to concerns about the U. S. role in Kosovo, the resolution is just the latest of many recent efforts to add restrictions to the President's war powers;
*   Limits the President's right to use of force overseas to cases where Congress has declared war or specifically authorized the use of force, where foreign powers have attacked the United States or U.S. forces, or for evacuations.

SOURCE: http://thomas.loc.gov.

president could be circumvented in the short run, but a lengthy war would require substantial funds. Iraq was a more formidable opponent than either Panama or Nicaragua had been, and the United States would require several months of preparation before any serious military campaign could be undertaken. During the preparatory period, Congress tried to force the issue, with the Senate holding hearings on the war.

Bush was reluctant to ask for a resolution of support until he was certain it would pass, and Congress was reluctant to act until asked. But as the January 15, 1991, deadline for Iraq to leave Kuwait—agreed to by the United Nations—approached, members of Congress took the initiative in pressing for a debate. As the date of debate neared, the Bush administration began to focus discussion on Iraqi efforts to obtain nuclear, chemical, and biological weapons (and the missiles to deliver them) as well as on the aggression in Kuwait and the atrocious human rights record of the Hussein regime.

Congress avoided a direct declaration of war by debating instead a resolution authorizing the use of U.S. armed forces to carry out a U.N. resolution (which had itself only suggested that armed force could be used but had not called for it). Congress sidestepped the issue of war powers by stating that the resolution was "consistent with" (as opposed to "pursuant to") the War Powers Act, which did not mean the president accepted the act.

After several days of serious debate, legislators voted for the resolution by a substantial margin (250 to 183) in the House and a narrow margin (52 to 47) in the Senate. Members of Congress closed ranks once the vote was taken: The Democrats who had opposed the resolution declared that they too would support the president. Some Middle East experts suggested that Saddam Hussein, the ruler of Iraq, had misread the U.S. constitutional process and assumed the debate meant that he faced a divided and therefore irresolute opponent. In fact, building the necessary political coalitions to gain congressional and public support strengthens U.S. commitment to specific policies once they are adopted.

The Bureaucracy

Another major check on the foreign policy and military powers of the president comes from inside the executive branch. While not as powerful as bureaucrats in Japan, where the career officers in the Ministry of International Trade and Industry (MITI), the Ministry of Foreign Affairs, and other government agencies determine most foreign policies no matter who is prime minister, the U.S. federal bureaucracy wields power since it implements presidential decisions and Congressional mandates. Without full support of career bureaucrats, who usually have expert knowledge of the issues and procedures, policy decisions and actions can be ignored or delayed, and information can be leaked to Congress or the media to raise issues on the political agenda or to embarrass the president. Since many bureaucrats have strong ties to Congress or interest groups such as the defense industries, their loyalties may be divided.

Information.   The president has access to a broader range of information than any other public official or private individual in the United States, but rarely is this information received in the form of raw data. Even presidents who are "policy wonks" (people who immerse themselves in the numerous details of policy), such as Jimmy Carter and Bill Clinton, cannot filter the huge amount of information that comes in every day. By the time the president gets information from the CIA, the State Department, and other sources, it has usually gone through a few levels of bureaucratic screening. During the early years of the Cold War, for example, air force intelligence sources consistently argued that the Soviet Union had more long-range bombers than the CIA estimated. Not surprisingly, the more Soviet long-range bombers there were, the more funding air force officials could demand to meet the increased Soviet threat.

Implementation.   Once the president makes a foreign or military policy decision, the bureaucracy must act. As with many large organizations, however, federal bureaucracies can develop a culture of values that make implementation of presidential orders difficult. Decisions to integrate blacks and women into the U.S. military were resisted by many career military personnel, and incidents of racial and gender discrimination persisted long after the original orders. Female officers, for example, were assaulted or harassed by male navy and marine pilots at the 1991 Tailhook Association meeting in Las Vegas. As a result of subsequent investigations, the navy undertook a program to more fully address these issues. More recently, President Bill Clinton's interest in ending discrimination against homosexuals in the military was opposed by so many career military personnel (as well as many members of Congress and the public) that he compromised to develop a "don't ask, don't tell" policy regarding sexual orientation.

The News Media

Along with Congress and the bureaucracy, the press provides some check on presidential power in foreign and military affairs. In some countries most news media are government owned and operated, limiting the capacity to hold a government accountable for its actions. Government control of the media in the former Soviet Union and a policy of secrecy regarding airline crashes and other disasters that might damage the image of the Communist government, for example, meant that news of the Chernobyl nuclear reactor accident was hidden from the public and neighboring countries for some time, further endangering lives and property. As Soviet leader Gorbachev relaxed restrictions on the press with the policy of *glasnost* to make the Communist Party and government more accountable, media coverage of government excesses contributed to the sharp drop in public legitimacy of Communist rule.

Investigation.   During World War II and the early Cold War years, the U.S. press tended to support the president. As a rule, editors assumed that government statements

■ Gay rights in the military proved to be one of the most contentions issues of Bill Clinton's first presidential term. Clinton sought equal rights and full participation for gays in the armed forces, but in the face of
strong congressional opposition was forced to compromise with the "don't ask, don't tell" policy that still
outraged many gays and conservatives alike. (Photo courtesy: Porter Gifford/Liaison Agency)

were true and printed them as unquestioned fact. In the mid-1960s, however, the press's
role as a prop for foreign policy began to change.

As U.S. involvement in Vietnam grew, the press increasingly challenged statements
issued by government officials. The daily military briefing in Vietnam became known
among the media as "the Five O'Clock Follies" for its lack of candor. The press examined in great detail the differences between what administrations claimed and the reality of the battlefield. Beginning with the live coverage of parts of the Foreign Relations
Committee hearings on the Vietnam War in February 1966, dissent became a regular
feature of television coverage as well. From 1966 on, about 20 percent of all Vietnam
coverage (on CBS television, for which data are available) concerned various forms of
domestic controversy.[32]

In the years since, the news media have not been uniformly hostile to the president.
During the Persian Gulf War in 1991, some critics suggested that the press too willingly accepted the government's version of events. The glowing initial reports of the
success of the Patriot antimissile missiles in downing Iraqi SCUD missiles proved highly
inaccurate upon investigation after the war.

The fact that the media discussed their own shortcomings suggests that the country
will not return to the innocent days of the past. The mass media were very critical of
the Clinton administration's foreign policy regarding Bosnia, Haiti, Somalia, and Cuba.
President Clinton's first secretary of defense, Les Aspin, resigned partly as a result of
the criticism. President Clinton complained that the press ignored the administration's
foreign policy successes with the former Soviet Union on proliferation, with the European Union with the General Agreement on Tariffs and Trade, and in the Middle East.
In March 1998, for example, President Clinton made the most extensive trip to Africa
by a U.S. president, visiting twelve countries. Long-planned, the trip demonstrated U.S.
interest and highlighted democratic and economic reform on the continent. Although

■ President Clinton holds a joint news conference in Cape Town with South African President Nelson Mandela. During his six nation tour of Africa, President Clinton tried to keep the media focus on issues related to Africa rather than U.S. domestic political affairs. (Photo courtesy: Greg Gibson/AP/Wide World Photos)

well received in Africa, administration officials had difficulty getting the U.S. media to focus on the trip rather than on stories about President Clinton and Monica Lewinsky that had emerged early in the year.

Agenda Setting. The media can put issues on the foreign policy agenda. The problem of famine in the 1980s in East Africa, especially in Ethiopia, was well known to aid agencies such as CARE and OXFAM, and to government officials. It did not become a major issue in U.S. politics until television crews broadcast stories on the subject, complete with pictures of the dead and dying, into American living rooms. Countless reports about atrocities in Bosnia raised calls for action by the president, although long, brutal civil wars in many other parts of the world, such as the Sudan, remain virtually unknown to most of the U.S. public. Such complex issues as increasing international trade or reducing Third World debt that take time to explain and offer little opportunity for startling footage receive less attention than do stories about war and disaster, even though their ultimate impact may be much more significant to the average citizen.

Television and online news accounts of the refugee crisis in Kosovo clearly pushed NATO to intervene by mobilizing public concern in the West. Where reports of Serbian ethnic cleansing atrocities and the ensuing refugee crisis were delayed or not broadcast, such as in Russia or China, the public generally opposed NATO bombing operations, as they mainly relied on Serbian broadcasts. Inside Yugoslavia, the largely state-controlled media broadcast no reports on Serbian ethnic cleansing policies, nor did the government allow foreign journalists access to Kosovo to check reports of atrocities. It is less clear what impact news on the Internet has had on these conflicts, although the wide availability of these news sources may in the long run undermine government efforts to restrict or bias the flow of information.

The Public

The division of U.S. public opinion on general dimensions of foreign policy also constrains the president. Many scholars argue that public opinion has two dimensions, militarism/nonmilitarism and isolationism/internationalism, creating four basic opinion groups.[33] Others argue that a third dimension, unilateralism/multilateralism (essentially the difference between acting alone and acting in concert with other countries), is also important. Although the public is not equally divided among different opinion groups, U.S. foreign policies usually have to appeal across these dimensions to two or more groups in order to achieve widespread popular support. At the same time, the existence of these various dimensions means that almost every U.S. foreign policy will have a core group of opponents who are likely to try to limit the impact of the policy.

A crisis in foreign policy generally leads to a rise in a president's popularity, although the increase is often temporary, as noted in chapter 8. Support for leaders in other democracies follows this pattern too. The Falkland Islands war in 1982 between Great Britain and Argentina greatly increased the popularity of Prime Minister Margaret Thatcher, whose popularity had slipped because of a slumping domestic economy. The British victory in the Falklands provided her with a theme that she used to gain a victory in the general election the following year. But British prime ministers can (within limits) call for elections when they think they will win. President George Bush, by contrast, could not take advantage of his exceptionally high popularity in the wake of the Persian Gulf War to win reelection. Instead, he had to wait until his constitutionally ordained four-year cycle was completed, by which time the country was in a recession that contributed to Bush's defeat.

Elections.   Harry S Truman completed President Franklin D. Roosevelt's unexpired term and then won election in 1948 in his own right. He was eligible to run again in 1952, but his popularity was very low. The issue that made Truman so unpopular was one of foreign and military policy, the Korean War. Truman committed the United States to fight on behalf of South Korea in 1950, but the war stalemated by 1952, with about 250,000 U.S. troops committed to combat on the Korean peninsula and deaths approaching what would be their final total of 34,000. Popular dissatisfaction with the no-win war was very high. Sensing sure defeat, Truman withdrew from the race. The voters chose as president a popular military leader and hero from World War II, General Dwight D. Eisenhower, who helped bring an end to the fighting by agreeing to a truce with North Korea in 1953.

Similarly, in 1968 Lyndon B. Johnson decided not to run for a second term, in large part because of the unpopularity of his policy of escalating the war in Vietnam. A surprisingly strong showing for peace candidate Senator Eugene McCarthy (D–Minn.) in the New Hampshire primary suggested to Johnson that although he would probably win his party's nomination, he might not win the election.

Electoral control on the president's power is exercised in only the crudest of ways and only at set intervals—every fourth year when an election is held. Even then, the voters can approve or disapprove of an existing policy, but they can send no clear message for an alternative policy. In 1952 Eisenhower was elected on a vague promise to end the war in Korea. With such a promise, he was as free to end the war by introducing nuclear weapons (which he did not) as he was by negotiating a truce (which he did). In a similar vein, Richard M. Nixon succeeded Lyndon B. Johnson without having made clear what he would do to end the war in Vietnam other than to say "I have a plan" to end the war.

Public Opinion.   As revealed in Figure 19.4, the U.S. public is much more interested in what goes on at home. Since the 1960s Americans have considered domestic problems to be much more important than foreign ones. Yet even when it is not an election year, or Congress is not exerting pressure, or foreign policy is not the subject of media attention, public opinion is likely to be on the president's mind when examining foreign policy.

Figure 19.4   The Most Important Problem: Domestic or Foreign, 1947–1998

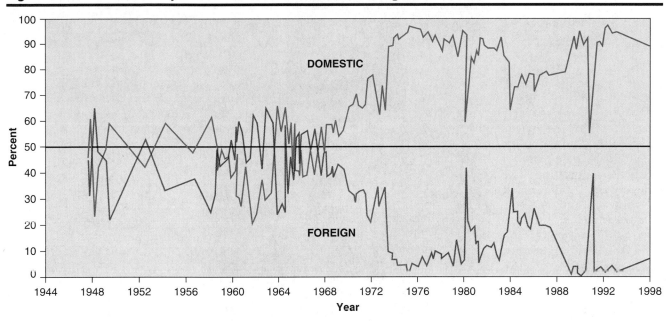

NOTE: Typical Question: "What do you think is the most important problem facing this country today?"

SOURCE. Harold W. Stanley and Richard G. Niemi, eds. *Vital Statistics on American Politics*. 1997–1998 (Washington, D. C. Congressional Quarterly, 1998). Reprinted by permission. Updates from the Roper Polls.

President Ronald Reagan's standing in the Gallup public opinion polls in the later years of his administration was higher than that of any of his recent colleagues. Yet Reagan and his advisers found themselves restrained by their perceptions of what the public would tolerate. Shortly after taking office, Reagan emphasized the need to help the right-wing Central American government of El Salvador fight leftist insurgents. The White House saw El Salvador as an issue that would generate even more support for Reagan, playing as it did on themes of anticommunism and national security. Yet to the White House's surprise, Reagan's standing in the public opinion polls began to go down. The president's advisers determined that their problem was that the conflict in El Salvador was being portrayed as another Vietnam. Advisers quickly stopped mentioning El Salvador. Reagan's ratings in the polls went back up. As other presidents had learned, the president could influence what went on the public's agenda but not the opinions the public would form.

Public Action.   Foreign and military policies do not consist only of government action. Without the public taking action that supports these policies, they are not likely to be effective. Widespread resistance to the draft during the Vietnam War made it much more difficult to reach the personnel levels desired by the military and helped move the U.S. military toward an all-volunteer force. In the 1990s the Bush and Clinton administrations tried to increase U.S. private investment in Russia with little impact because many Americans are simply reluctant to invest there, given Russia's highly uncertain political and economic environment.

Direct action by the public can often lead to a change in foreign policy (see Highlight 19.2: Individuals, Celebrities, and Landmines). Two planes carrying members of the anti-Castro group Brothers to the Rescue were shot down by the Cuban military in February 1996. The group began by helping families with relatives in Cuba, a problem that was magnified by the most recent exodus of Cuban refugees to the United States. By 1996 changes in Clinton administration policy (and in Cuba) made contact with relatives easier for family members, and U.S.–Cuban relations appeared to be warming. Many saw

HIGHLIGHT 19.2

Individuals, Celebrities, and Landmines

Cheap and easy to deploy, many fighting forces routinely use mines to defend a frontier; deny opponents the use of a road, and many other purposes. Often these landmines remain active long after the fighting has ceased, posing a significant threat to the safety of the civilian population. The U.N. currently estimates that 110 million antipersonnel landmines lay in about seventy countries. The magnitude and horror of this problem sparked a grassroots effort to ban landmines. From the inception of the International Campaign to Ban Landmines (ICBL) in 1991, the efforts of many individuals, especially Jody Williams, the coordinator of the ICBL, led to a new treaty to ban antipersonnel mines signed by more than 120 countries by mid-1998.

The campaign received a major boost in 1996 when Diana, Princess of Wales, joined in the effort, going to places most effected by land mines, comforting victims and

bringing the issue to the attention of millions. When Princess Diana died in a car crash in August 1997, sorrow often turned into commitments to support her charitable interests, including the effort to ban mines. Only a few nations remain opposed to the landmine convention. The United States, for example, would like an exception for its use of mines in Korea, where they protect the relatively smaller number of U.S. and South Korean forces from the large army of North Korea. The United States has also made substantial contributions to demining operations and limited its use of mines in military operations in response to the issue.

■ Diana, the late Princess of Wales, visits one of the most densely mined areas of Angola. Princess Diana raised public awareness about the long-term problems with landmines, which pushed many governments to support a new international convention against their use. (Photo courtesy: Giovanni Diffidenti/AP/Wide World Photos)

these changes as helping Castro stay in power, and called for harsher restrictions. After the downing of the two planes, Congress passed the Helms–Burton Act, which, among other things, imposed sanctions on some non-U.S. companies investing in Cuba. President Clinton reluctantly agreed to support the act, despite the considerable difficulties this produced with Canada, the European Union, and other countries. To reduce these problems, President Clinton began to waive the sanctions. Although Castro retained a strong hold on power, by 1999 U.S.-Cuban relations improved sufficiently for the Baltimore Orioles to go to Havana to play the Cuban national baseball team, and for the Cuban team to play in Baltimore. The teams split the series, each losing at home.

State and local governments do play some role in foreign and military policy. Border states make compacts with local governments in Canada and Mexico on a variety of issues, particularly in the area of transportation. State and local governments court overseas investors by offering tax breaks and other incentives. State governments promote home-grown products in the global market, most maintaining at least one office in Europe or Asia. Local activists join or work with international nongovernmental organizations that may oppose the president on issues ranging from the environment (Greenpeace, for example) or sports (such as the International Olympic Committee). Even in military affairs, the president faces potential opposition from state and local

Web Exploration
To see instances of state government activities, go to www.awlonline.com/oconnor.

government officials. In the 1980s some state governors argued that their national guard units could not be used overseas without their approval, in order to keep the units from being used to support Reagan administration initiatives in Central America.

The authority of the president in foreign and military policy is constrained by Congress, the federal bureaucracy, the media, and citizens expressing their will. Yet each of these restraints on presidential authority is imperfect. In part this imperfection comes from certain advantages bestowed on the president by the Constitution. One restraint is that the president combines the roles of head of government and head of state. Unlike the British system, where the monarch serves as head of state and the prime minister serves as head of government, the United States Constitution puts both of these functions in the hands of the president. This union has the effect of making the president not just a political actor but also the symbol of the nation. Another advantage is that the president (along with a hand-picked vice president) is the only official elected by the nation as a whole. It is not surprising, then, that Congress, the media, and the American people look to the president as a national leader. One senator summarized the prevailing view after a foreign policy vote: "In foreign policy initiatives, there should be a presumption in favor of supporting the President of the United States."[34]

Building a New Grand Strategy

The anticommunist consensus that dominated U.S. grand strategy for four decades from World War II to the late 1980s had some desirable results even for people who did not always share in its approach. Without that consensus, for example, it is unlikely the Congress would ever have appropriated money for foreign aid in the quantities that it did. The large burden of the Marshall Plan was justified primarily in the name of strengthening Europe against Communism. With the fading of the threat that provoked the consensus, old programs need new justification. Some people still advocate providing foreign aid for humanitarian reasons. But they must prevail against many others who want to use the money for domestic purposes—sheltering the homeless, rescuing savings institutions, or just reducing the deficit.

Only at rare times in history, such as at the end of World War II, does one country have sufficient power to shape the world largely to its own desires. The last few years of the 1990s, however, may be the best chance for many decades to use the relative power of the United States to define a new vision of the world.[35] Some suggest, with the end of the Cold War, the United States once again attained a pinnacle of power and could and should take unilateral action to achieve its ends. Others believe that the demise of Soviet Communism meant the "end of history," with no serious political and economic differences remaining between the major powers. This would mean that any crisis would be settled by collaboration, probably through the United Nations.

Both of these views appear to offer false hope. While leadership demands unilateral action at times, the United States (or any other country) has little hope of forging effective policy toward peace in Bosnia, trade restrictions on China, the use of products that destroy the ozone layer, or almost any other international issue, without widespread multilateral support. Similarly, the ideological clash with Communism was never the only cause of international conflicts. Nationalism, economic self-interest, calls for governments based on the most narrow-minded versions of Islamic or Asian values, and many other ideas or identities will cause conflicts in the next century.

The Lack of Consensus

In the absence of a consensus on the grand strategy of the United States, foreign policy issues have become partisan issues, provoking debates between Republicans and Democrats, liberals and conservatives. Some partisanship in foreign policy has always been present, of course, but there has been a perceptible increase as the Cold War has waned. Although controversial and costly, the objective of anticommunism gave U.S. foreign policy a consistent direction for more than forty years. Without anticommunism as a guide, debate on the direction of U.S. foreign policy has become more partisan.

In June 1989, for example, television audiences around the world watched in horror as the Chinese government used tanks to crush prodemocracy demonstrators in Tiananmen Square. Some members of Congress indicated their outrage at the Chinese government by calling for Chinese students already in the United States on student visas to be able to extend their stays. President George Bush, who was the U.S. envoy to China during the Ford administration, thought this action would anger the Chinese government. The resulting debate in Congress, the votes in Congress to allow the students to stay, the veto by the president, and finally the failed attempt to override the veto went almost completely along party lines.

Without the guidance of the anticommunist consensus, debates on the procedure of U.S. foreign and military policy making increased as well. Presidents have dispatched U.S. forces on more than 200 occasions when combat was very likely or did occur, including the situations in Korea, Vietnam, and more recently Somalia. When these deployments became unpopular, Congress tried to stop them, using legislative devices such as the War Powers Act or bill amendments that curtail specific foreign policy activities. Presidents at the time called these efforts an unconstitutional meddling in their authority.

President Jimmy Carter tried to build a new grand strategy based on support for human rights, much as the United States had formed a domestic consensus in support of civil rights. Proponents argued that this would align U.S. policy against both Communists, such as the Soviets, and non-Communist dictators, such as the Shah of Iran. Opponents argued that U.S. policy should not be based on ideal principles and that the battle against Communism sometimes required helping nondemocratic leaders. President Ronald Reagan tried to rebuild the anticommunist consensus by identifying the Soviet Union as an "evil empire" and supporting less-than-democratic forces in struggles against Communists in Angola, Nicaragua, and elsewhere.

The invasion of Kuwait in 1990 spurred President Bush to call for a "new world order." In a speech to the United Nations, Bush suggested that the United States and the other major powers could create a global order in which they would share responsibility for preserving freedom, justice, the rule of law, and protection of the rights of the weak, in which the United Nations would play an important institutional role through its peacekeeping activities.[36] While noble sentiments in the effort to defeat Iraq, this approach proved less effective in settling problems in Somalia and Bosnia and seemed to have little to do with the troubles in the international economy.

The lack of consensus has played a role in the Kosovo crisis. Before NATO had completed two months of the bombing campaign, members of Congress had managed to defeat a measure to approve the use of a full range of military options, including the use of ground troops, indicate their disapproval of the air campaign, but also agree not to require the end of the operation. President Clinton defined stopping the humanitarian tragedy in Kosovo as a vital U.S. interest, and the NATO bombing campaign challenged many current international norms and rules on intervention.

Challenges for the United States in the Next Century

Despite the apparent success of the Persian Gulf War, the United States faces many challenges that require a coherent grand strategy, beyond Kosovo and the Balkans. Poverty, food shortages, and economic collapse in many parts of the world are so severe that they may threaten U.S. security. Similarly, civil wars and political oppression in one country often disrupt life in other countries through the spread of terrorism or the influx of refugees. Rising economic tensions among the United States, the European Union, Japan, and the other emerging industrial nations of the Pacific Rim, however, suggest that economic policy issues, more than global or regional war, will dominate the agenda of international politics into the next century.

Public opinion polls suggest that the most important long-range foreign policy objectives should be, in order, protecting American jobs, the nonproliferation of weapons of mass destruction, securing adequate energy supplies, improving the global environment, and reducing the trade deficit.[37] Much lower on the list is protecting human rights in other countries, strengthening the United Nations, helping U.S. businesses overseas, improving Third World living standards, promoting democracy abroad, and protecting weaker nations. Public opinion on many foreign policy issues varies considerably over time, such as protecting U.S. foreign imports. In contrast foreign policy is often fairly stable. On trade issues, for example, all recent U.S. presidents have declared their support for free trade. In finalizing the Uruguay Round trade talks in 1993, President Bill Clinton concluded negotiations begun under President Ronald Reagan with the other members of the GATT to decrease tariffs generally and liberalize nontariff barriers to trade in agriculture and the service industries, among others. These nearly global negotiations also led to the creation of the **World Trade Organization (WTO),** which replaced the GATT institutions on January 1, 1995, to oversee and promote freer trade and settle trade disputes.

Though the Clinton administration has emphasized that international trade helps create jobs in the United States, the promised benefits of free trade, especially in the short term, contend with the real economic costs of trade. As foreign imports put pressure on U.S. business, Congress slowly began recapturing trade policy from the president. A major milestone was the 1988 Omnibus Trade and Competitiveness Act, which limited presidential discretion in making trade policy. It imposed mandatory requirements for retaliation under Section 301 of the act, for example, against countries that maintained substantial barriers to trade and whose exports greatly exceeded their imports from the United States. Through the mandatory provisions of Section 301, Congress attempted to gain more control over U.S. trade policy. Because Congress responds readily to economic interests (such as automobile producers), the president develops a coherent national policy on trade only with difficulty.[38]

To address these concerns, President Clinton has been more willing to threaten to use economic sanctions, as in the trade negotiations between then U.S. Trade Representative Mickey Kantor and then Japanese Minister of International Trade and Industry Ryutaro Hashimoto (who later became Prime Minister of Japan in part because of his views that Japan should get tougher in its negotiations with the United States) over autos and auto parts. The administration also sought to increase U.S. exports to $1.2 trillion by the year 2000 by easing restrictions on trade and providing more incentives and assistance to promote U.S. trade. The administration, for example, adopted the "Big Emerging Markets (BEMs)" strategy, where the United States would help U.S. companies expand their exports to Argentina, Brazil, Mexico, the countries in ASEAN (the Association of Southeast Asian Nations), the Chinese economic zone (the People's Republic of China, Taiwan, and Hong Kong), India, South Korea, Poland, Turkey, and South Africa.

Many found the emphasis on economic relations overplayed in the first years of the first Clinton administration, particularly in Asia. In part, this came from the desire to see military spending fit into a coherent post–Cold War foreign policy strategy. With the decline of the Soviet military threats, many expected a "peace dividend" in the shape of major cuts in defense spending. When faced with an impending cut in the military budget, presidents look to the impact on key electoral states and members of Congress look at the effect on their districts—and just about every congressional district benefits from defense spending. Even members of Congress conspicuous for their vocal opposition to the vague concept of military spending fight to retain military bases that provide jobs for their constituents.

More important are choices about the scope of the threat facing the United States. In 1993 then Secretary of Defense Les Aspin identified four major threats to U.S. national security, in a **bottom-up review** of the mission and needs of the Defense Department:

1. The proliferation of weapons of mass destruction, such as nuclear bombs, and the means to deliver those weapons.

World Trade Organization:
The IGO created in 1995 that manages multilateral negotiations to reduce barriers to trade and settle trade disputes between nations.

Web Exploration
To learn more about the World Trade Organization, go to www.awlonline.com/oconnor.

bottom-up review:
Post–Cold War review of U.S. defense forces and policies.

2. Regional conflicts in the Middle East, Korea, and elsewhere.
3. The emergence of antidemocratic forces in Russia.
4. The erosion of U.S. economic strength.[39]

In the May 1997 Report on the Quadrennial Defense Review, the Defense Department built upon these themes. One of its most alarming conclusions was that the increase in the relative U.S. military and economic power in the 1990s actually meant that the United States faced a greater chance of attack by chemical, biological, or other unconventional weapons as adversaries recognized the preponderance of U.S. power.

A critical decision in the bottom-up review was that the United States needed sufficient military forces to conduct Desert Shield/Desert Storm–type operations against two "rogue nations" at the same time. Currently, the United States sees Iraq, Iran, Libya, North Korea, and possibly Syria as rogue nations, while Defense Department scenarios picture a number of other states, such as China or India, as prospective problem states. In calling for forces to fight two conflicts like the Gulf War at about the same time, the United States requires most of the advanced conventional forces it used to face the old Soviet threat. In addition, proposed withdrawals of U.S. military forces from Asia and the Pacific were met with considerable alarm. Many countries feared a smaller U.S. military presence would promote an arms race and military adventures by other states in the region, so the Clinton administration promised to maintain current levels of its forces in the region. Together, this means that the "peace dividend" is peace, not a huge decline in the U.S. defense budget.

Wholly new international issues that challenge U.S. policy makers have emerged in foreign affairs. The dramatic international impact of the Russian nuclear accident at Chernobyl and the discovery of a large hole in the ozone layer of the earth's atmosphere that appears to be related to the use of chlorofluorocarbons (CFCs) and other gases are two incidents in a growing understanding of the importance of international environmental threats to the security of the United States. In a provocative 1989 article, Jessica Tuchman Matthews argued for a broader definition of national security "to include resource, environmental, and demographic issues."[40] To some extent, United States, participation in the 1992 United Nations Conference on Environment and Development, signing the 1993 Convention on Biological Diversity, bilateral aid for sustaining tropical forests, and other policies indicate that these issues are becoming part of a new definition of U.S. national security. Critics suggest, however, that in some instances environmental activists are trying to use the legitimacy associated with national security to advance their cause when in fact many environmental issues pose no real threat to U.S. security. Nonetheless, the threat of global climate modification and the loss of the ozone layer appear to pose direct threats to U.S. security, while other environmental problems, such as ocean pollution, overpopulation, and the loss of biodiversity are indirect but real threats to national security.

In early December 1997, the countries party to the U.N. Framework Convention on Global Climate Change met in Kyoto, Japan, to create a new treaty protocol to reduce the emission of greenhouse gases that contribute to global warming. Under the Kyoto Protocol, which largely follows U.S. proposals, the European Union, Japan, and the United States agreed to cut the emission of six greenhouse gases by 2012 by 6 to 8 percent below their 1990 emissions. Countries that emit high levels of greenhouse gases can also trade emis-

■ Stealth aircraft are one example of how the United States uses technology to project power to protect its global interests. (Photo courtesy: Randy Jolly/The Image Works)

■ U.S. Secretary of State Madeleine Albright places a wreath at the site of the 1998 bomb blast at the U.S. Embassy in Nairobi, Kenya. After this terrorist attack, with its hundreds of casualties, including many Kenyan bystanders, the State Department redoubled its efforts to make its embassies less vulnerable. (Photo courtesy: John McConnico/AP/Wide World Photos)

sion rights with countries that produce low levels of greenhouse gases (mainly in the Third World) to meet this commitment. An anticipated precondition of this trade, however, is that both sides to the bargain will commit to reducing their greenhouse emissions.[41]

Implementing the protocol has met resistance from business and from Congress. Many analysts contend that the bulk of the costs of meeting the reduction in greenhouse gases will come from improved energy efficiency. Nonetheless, the White House estimates that the treaty would impose about $100 on average for each household in the next decade, while at least one study sponsored by businesses that oppose the treaty contend it could cost more than $1,200 per family.[42] Other critics of the Kyoto Protocol contend that it will not reduce global emissions as it does little to constrain emissions from newly industrialized countries, such as China or India. In any case, environmental challenges, including global warming, will continue to move closer to the top of the foreign policy agenda during the next decade.

Officials at the U.S. Department of Defense and elsewhere have become convinced that U.S. military forces, and the U.S. homeland, will come under assault by other weapons of mass destruction besides nuclear weapons (although nuclear proliferation remains an important concern). They believe that the dominance of U.S. conventional armed forces will motivate adversaries to adopt an asymmetrical response—that is, use nuclear, chemical, or biological weapons. The extensive use of chemical weapons by Saddam Hussein during the Iran-Iraq war (and against the Kurdish people in Iraq), and the chemical attack on the Tokyo subway system by a religious cult, moved governments to develop an international means to limit the spread of chemical weapons. As the Cold War drew to a close, the United States and the Soviet Union (later Russia) also agreed to abandon chemical weapons and to open their chemical facilities to international inspections, without which no meaningful arms control was possible.

Even the use of cyberspace, the seemingly borderless world of the Internet and modern telecommunications systems, raises new national security concerns. The Department of Defense is already exploring measures (and countermeasures) to combat computer viruses and other electronic or physical threats to the information network that are crucial economic and military systems. The export of common encryption programs, for example, threatens the government's capability to gather intelligence on terrorists, inter-

Web Exploration
To learn more about critical infrastructure issues, go to www.awlonline.com/oconnor.

national criminal organizations, and rogue states. In the last several years, for example, Department of Defense or defense-related computer systems have suffered tens of thousands of attempted penetrations. One such action apparently damaged communications with U.S. forces in Somalia for an entire day. These threats prompted the formulation of Presidential Decision Directive 63 in 1998, which requires the government to develop a national plan to defend the United States against cyberwarfare. Under the Critical Infrastructure Assurance Office (CIAO), the federal government is planning to invest over $1 billion to protect the services on which we all depend, such as energy and telecommunications.

Potentially the most profound change in international relations, however, came with little fanfare with the creation of a world court to prosecute international war crimes and crimes against humanity. In a diplomatic reversal for the United States, 120 nations voted to give this court strong enforcement powers, with twenty-one nations abstaining and Israel, China, Libya, Iraq, Qatar, Yemen, and the United States voting no. Under this system an independent prosecutor could bring charges directly to the court, without going through the U.N. Security Council or other steps that might allow countries to block prosecution. Even more important, the prosecutor can charge crimes and the court can hear cases involving countries that have not signed the treaty, in effect giving the court universal jurisdiction. The United States opposed the treaty, fearing a spate of frivolous prosecutions against U.S. soldiers, given the extensive U.S. military presence abroad. One possible consequence: Senator Jesse Helms argued that the United States should require all formal U.S. defense relationships, such as NATO, the Japan–U.S. Security Treaty, even U.S. participation in the U.N., be rewritten with promises by our allies not to make such charges against U.S. personnel engaged in legitimate operations.

ℭONTINUITY and Change

Changing Foreign and Military Policy

The United States has redefined its role in world affairs several times since gaining independence from the British. President George Washington sought to keep the new, and relatively weak, nation out of the conflicts between more established European powers. Even the nineteenth century Monroe Doctrine, by which the United States sought to keep European powers from intervening in the Western Hemisphere, depended heavily on the British Navy for enforcement, as the United States had a limited capacity to project military power. As its military and commercial power increased, however, U.S. grand strategy changed as well. Although the concept of manifest destiny became hotly debated, by the end of the 19th century the United States had become a major exporter, had fought and defeated Spain, had acquired several territories in the Caribbean and the Pacific, and otherwise become deeply engaged in world politics. With its entry into World War I, U.S. grand strategy had done a turnabout, from keeping European troops out of the United States to putting U.S. troops in Europe.

By the end of World War I, the old European great power system had come to an end. President Woodrow Wilson helped create a League of Nations to replace this system, but the United States adopted a strategy of isolationism from world affairs and did not join the League. Without support from the United States, which had emerged from the war as the leading economic power, the League failed as the foundation for a new world order, and Europe and Asia soon fell into an outbreak of economic recession and racist nationalism that led to World War II. Even before the end of that war, the United States began to forge a new grand strategy that would integrate it with multilateral political and economic organizations, especially the United Nations system. As the deep divisions of the Cold War emerged, instead of withdrawing, the United States developed an unprecedented set of permanent military or political alliances with nations in Asia, Europe, and South America. Through the Marshall Plan, the Truman Doctrine, and other policies, the United States became the leader of the Western world.

Since the end of the Cold War, the United States has struggled with defining a new vision of the world and the U.S. role in it. The Clinton administration developed the principles of engagement and enlargement to guide its grand strategy. Engagement means that the United States will not retreat into isolationism as it did after World War I, but instead take measures to provide leadership in international economic, military and political affairs. As opposed to containment, the grand strategy of the Cold War, engagement implies that the United States will rely primarily on negotiation and cooperation rather than confrontation and conflict, although it will use force when needed. Enlargement often serves as the objective of engagement policies, as it means that the United States should promote democracy, open markets, and other Western political, economic, and social values around the world. In practice, engagement and enlargement meant the Partnership for Peace and NATO expansion, efforts designed to integrate the formerly Communist states of Eastern Europe and the old Soviet Union into Western security structures. It has meant dialogue with North Korea over their nuclear weapons program in return for economic and political incentives that will reduce their isolation from the world community.

Enlargement rests on the evidence that liberal market democracies do not fight wars with one another.* By promoting open markets and democratic politics abroad, particularly in Russia, the United States, in theory, will reduce the number of potential military threats it might face. This broad strategic objective, however, tells us very little about how to achieve it. China, India, and Russia, for instance, each pose different problems for U.S. grand strategy in the next century. China, with an increasingly liberal economy and an improving human rights record, is still communist. India, the most populous democracy in the world, has an insular market economy dominated by the state, with little room for open economic policies. Together, they challenge the United States to develop meaningful engagement policies for countries with sharply different world views than the United States but are neither friends nor foes. The vast economic and political problems in Russia, in contrast, challenge the United States to find appropriate policies that will help countries make the transition to democracy and open markets without falling into anarchy or authoritarianism.

The relative economic, military, and political resources of the United States have varied considerably over the last two centuries, and these changes have had a major impact on U.S. grand strategy in the future.

1. How will changes in the U.S. and world economy, such as the growth of the Internet globalization, affect U.S. grand strategy in the next century?
2. What impact might new threats, such as greater access to the technologies of biological, chemical, and nuclear weapons by terrorists or global warming, have on international relations if all states are democratic market economies?

Cast Your Vote. What should be the U.S. grand strategy as we enter the twenty-first century? To cast your vote, go to www.awlonline.com/oconnor.

---

*See, for example, Bruce Russett, *Grasping the Democratic Peace: Principles for a Post-Cold War World* (Princeton, NJ: Princeton University Press, 1993).

SUMMARY

Foreign and military policies differ in significant ways from other components of U.S. government. Their history has not been one of continuous development. To demonstrate that development, this chapter has made the following points:

1. PURSUING POWER AND PLENTY

Recent annual reports from the president on U.S. national security strategy identify three core objectives for the United States. These are that the United States must exercise prudent diplomacy and maintain a strong and effective military; bolster American prosperity; and promote democracy around the world. Not everyone agrees on the means to achieve these objectives nor their proper balance.

2. GRAND STRATEGY

Every government tries to develop a grand strategy that enhances its prospects for power and plenty. Federalists and the Framers believed that a strong national government was the key to assuring a strong nation. To this end, after winning a war of national liberation, with crucial support from France, Americans withdrew behind their two-ocean moat.

3. THE ROOTS OF U.S. FOREIGN AND MILITARY POLICY

For more than a century, foreign and military policy played—with occasional exceptions—only a minor part in American life. George Washington's warnings against foreign entanglements were heeded. As U.S. economic interests grew, it became more difficult for the United States to stay out of wars without risking its sovereignty and security. Despite prolonged attempts to regain its relative isolation after intervening in World War I, the United States was unable to avoid participating in World War II.

4. THE UNITED STATES BECOMES A WORLD LEADER

During World War II and the years of the Cold War, foreign and military policy began to dominate the political agenda. Defense spending went from a small fraction of the federal budget to one of its biggest components, even during peacetime. Global affairs went from a peripheral issue of concern only to specialists to the focus of presidential attention and public debate.

5. THE MACHINERY OF MODERN FOREIGN POLICY MAKING

The complex balances found in many other parts of the U.S. system are absent in the machinery of foreign and military policies. One branch of government, the executive (and one individual in that branch, the president), predominates. The predominance of the president has given rise to criticism of an imperial presidency, but debate about the content and the process of foreign and military policy has been inhibited by fears of endangering national security.

6. CHALLENGES TO PRESIDENTIAL POWER IN FOREIGN AND MILITARY POLICY

The countervailing forces in the Congress, the bureaucracy, the news media, and the public play an important role in limiting the power of the president. Other components of U.S. government, such as the judicial branch and the state and local levels, play almost no role at all.

KEY TERMS

bottom-up review, p. 733
containment, p. 711
European Union (EU)
p. 714
executive agreement,
p. 704
floating exchange rate,
p. 715
General Agreement on
Tariffs and Trade
(GATT), p. 709
grand strategy, p. 701
international governmental organization (IGO),
p. 701

International Monetary
Fund (IMF), p. 709
isolationism, p. 708
League of Nations, p. 708
manifest destiny, p. 706
Marshall Plan, p. 710
Monroe Doctrine, p. 705
multilateralism, p. 709
mutually assured destruction (MAD), p. 712
nation-state, p. 701
National Security Acts of
1947 and 1949, p. 716

North American Free
Trade Agreement
(NAFTA), p. 721
North Atlantic Treaty
Organization (NATO),
p. 710
tariffs, p. 705
Truman Doctrine, p. 709
United Nations, p. 709
War Powers Act, p. 723
World Bank, p. 709
World Trade Organization, p. 733

SELECTED READINGS

Allison, Graham F., and Philip Zelikow. *Essence of Decision: Explaining the Cuban Missile Crisis*, 2d ed. New York: Addison-Wesley, 1999.

Ambrose, Stephen. *Rise to Globalism*, 6th ed. New York: Penguin, 1991.

Barnet, Richard J. *The Rockets' Red Glare When America Goes to War: The Presidents and the People*. New York: Simon and Schuster, 1990.

Beck, Robert, Anthony Clark Arend, and Robert Vander Lugt, eds. *International Rules: Approaches from International Law and International Relations*. New York, NY: Oxford University Press, 1996.

Doyle, Michael, and G. John Ikenberry, eds. *New Thinking in International Relations Theory*. Boulder, CO: Westview Press, 1997.

Eckes, Alfred E., Jr. *Opening America's Market: U.S. Foreign Trade Policy Since 1776*. Chapel Hill: University of North Carolina Press, 1995.

Falk, Richard A. *Law in an Emerging Global village: A Post-Westphalian Perspective*. New York: Transnational Publishers, 1998.

Haass, Richard N., ed. *Economic Sanctions and American Diplomacy*. Washington, DC: Council on Foreign Relations, 1998.

Halberstam, David. *The Best and the Brightest*. New York: Random House, 1972.

Karnes, Margaret P., and Karen A. Mingst. *The United States and Multilateral Institutions*. New York: Routledge, 1992.

Kennan, George. *American Diplomacy 1900–1950*. Chicago: University of Chicago Press, 1951.

Kissinger, Henry. *Diplomacy*. New York: Simon & Schuster, 1994.

Klare, Michael. *Rogue States and Nuclear Outlaws: America's Search for a New Foreign Policy*. New York: Hill and Wang, 1995.

McGlen, Nancy E., and Meredith Reid Sarkees. *Women in Foreign Policy*. New York: Routledge, 1993.

Milner, Helen. *Interests, Institutions and Information*. Princeton, NJ: Princeton University Press, 1997.

Mueller, John E. *War, Presidents and Public Opinion*. New York: Wiley, 1973.

Ripley, Randall B., and James M. Lindsay, eds. *Congress Resurgent: Foreign and Defense Policy on Capitol Hill*. Ann Arbor: University of Michigan Press, 1993.

Rosecrance, Richard, and Arthur A. Stein, eds. *The Domestic Bases of Grand Strategy*. Ithaca: Cornell University Press, 1993.

Sagan, Scott and Kenneth Waltz. *The Spread of Nuclear Weapons: A Debate*. New York, NY: W. W. Norton, 1995.

Schlesinger, Arthur. *The Imperial Presidency*. Boston: Houghton Mifflin, 1989.

NOTES

1. Philip Shenon, "A State Department Report Documents Kosovo Abuses," *New York Times* (May 11, 1999): A12.

2. Bill Carey, "Commerce Officials Fight Back on Export Policies." *New Technology Week* 28 (July 13, 1998): 12.

3. Executive Office of the President, *A National Security Strategy for a New Century* (Washington, D.C.: The White House, October 1998) (available online at http://www.whitehouse.gov/WH/EOP/NSC/html/documents/mssr.pdf).

4. Executive Office of the President, *A New National Security Strategy for a New Century*, 5.

5. Jacob Viner, "Power *vs.* Plenty as Objectives of Foreign Policy in the Seventeenth and Eighteenth Centuries," *World Politics* 1 (1948): 1–29.

6. Ben Belton and Bill Montague, "Gains Boost Economy: U.S. Trade Scenario Better Than 10 Years Ago," *USA Today* (February 29, 1996): 1B.

7. Richard Rosecrance and Arthur A. Stein, "Beyond Realism: The Study of Grand Strategy," in Richard Rosecrance and Arthur A. Stein, eds., *The Domestic Bases of Grand Strategy* (Ithaca: Cornell University Press, 1993), 1–21.

8. Barton Gellman, "Keeping the U.S. First: Pentagon Would Preclude a Rival Superpower," *The Washington Post* (March 11, 1992): A1.

9. Harold K. Jacobson, William M. Reisinger, and Todd Mathers, "National Engagements in Governmental Organizations," *American Political Science Review*, 80 (March 1986): 141–59.

10. Raymond Vernon, *Sovereignty at Bay* (New York: Basic Books, 1971).

11. Paul Kennedy, *The Rise and Fall of the Great Powers: Economic Change and Military Conflict from 1500 to 2000* (New York: Vintage Books, 1989), 514.

12. Howard Jones, *The Course of American Democracy*, vol. 2, 2d ed. (Chicago: Dorsey Press, 1988), 6–8.

13. See, for example, *DeLima* v. *Bidwell*, 182 U.S. 1 (1901) and *Dooley* v. *United States*, 182 U.S. 222 (1901).

14. Alfred E. Eckes, Jr., *Opening America's Market: U.S. Foreign Trade Policy Since 1776* (Chapel Hill: University of North Carolina Press, 1995).

15. John L. O'Sullivan, writing in 1845, quoted in Julius W. Pratt, "The Ideology of American Expansion," in Avery Craven, ed., *Essays in Honor of William E. Dodd* (Chicago: University of Chicago Press, 1935), 343–44.

16. John A. C. Conybeare, "Voting for Protection: An Electoral Model of Tariff Policy," *International Organization* 45 (Winter 1991): 57–81.

17. Charles P. Kindleberger, *The World in Depression, 1929–1939* (Berkeley: University of California Press, 1986).

18. Henry Steel Commager, *Documents of American History*, 7th ed. (New York: Appleton-Century-Crofts, 1963), 525.

19. Richard Smoke, *National Security and the Nuclear Dilemma* (Reading, MA: Addison-Wesley, 1984).

20. See "START Supplement," *Arms Control Today* 21 (November 1991) and "START II Supplement," *Arms Control Today* 23 (January/February 1993).

21. Stanley Karnow, *Vietnam, A History: The First Complete Account of Vietnam at War* (New York: Viking Press, 1983).

22. "U.S. Boosts Forces in Somalia," *Star Tribune* (October 5, 1993): 1A.

23. William O. Chittick, Keith R. Billingsley, and Rick Travis, "A Three-Dimensional Model of American Foreign Policy Beliefs," *International Studies Quarterly* 39 (September 1995): 313–31.

24. Susan A. MacManus, *Young v. Old: Generational Combat in the 21st Century* (Boulder, CO: Westview, 1995), 216.

25. Stephen D. Krasner, *Structural Conflict: The Third World Against Global Liberalism* (Berkeley: University of California Press, 1985).

26. 299 U.S. 304 (1936).

27. Loch K. Johnson, *America's Secret Power: The CIA in a Democratic Society* (New York: Oxford University Press, 1989).

28. Alexander L. George, *Presidential Decision-making in Foreign Policy: The Effective Use of*

Information and Advice (Boulder, CO: Westview, 1980).

29. William S. Cohen, Secretary of Defense, *Annual Report to the President and the Congress 1998*, Washington, DC: USGPO, 1998. Also known as the *Annual Defense Report*. For the *1998 Annual Defense Report* by the Secretary of Defense, see http://www.dtic.mil/execsec/adr98/index.html.

30. James M. Lindsay, "Congress, Foreign Policy, and the New Institutionalism," *International Studies Quarterly* 38 (June 1994): 281–304.

31. William S. Cohen, Secretary of Defense, *Annual Report to the President and the Congress* (Washington, DC: Department of Defense, 1999), Table 16, available at http://www.dtic.mil/execsec/adr_intro.html.

32. Daniel Hallin, *The "Uncensored War"* (Berkeley: University of California Press, 1989), 192.

33. Eugene R. Wittkopf, "On the Foreign Policy Beliefs of the American People: A Critique and Some Evidence," *International Studies Quarterly*, 30 (December 1986): 425–55.

34. Steven V. Roberts, "Senate, 52–48, Supports Reagan on AWACs Sale to Saudis," *The New York Times* (October 29, 1981): A4

35. Charles Krauthammer, "The Unipolar Movement," *Foreign Affairs* 70 (Winter, 1990–91): 23–33.

36. *Congressional Quarterly Almanac* (1990): 731.

37. MacManus, *Young v. Old*, 236.

38. See, for example, E. E. Schattschneider, *Politics, Pressures, and the Tariff* (New York: Prentice, 1935) or Robert Pastor, *Congress and the Politics of U.S. Foreign Economic Policy* (Berkeley: University of California Press, 1980).

39. Frank Oliveri, "DoD Mulls 1997 Bottom-Up Review," *Defense News* (September 11, 1995).

40. Jessica Tuchman Matthews, "Redefining Security," *Foreign Affairs* 68 (Spring 1989): 162–77.

41. For a U.S. government factsheet on the Kyoto Protocol, see http://www.epa.gov/globalwarming/actions/global/uo/kyoto-docfc-011598.html.

42. Bruce Alpert, "Warming Pact Called Job Buster; Study Is Wrong White House Says," *The Times-Picayune* (June 10, 1998): C1.

THE DECLARATION OF INDEPENDENCE

In Congress, July 4, 1776

The Unanimous Declaration of the Thirteen United States of America

When in the Course of human events it becomes necessary for one people to dissolve the political bands which have connected them with another, and to assume, among the powers of the earth, the separate and equal station to which the Laws of Nature and of Nature's God entitle them, a decent respect to the opinions of mankind requires that they should declare the causes which impel them to the separation.

We hold these truths to be self-evident, that all men are created equal, that they are endowed by their Creator with certain unalienable Rights, that among these are Life, Liberty and the pursuit of Happiness. That to secure these rights, Governments are instituted among Men, deriving their just powers from the consent of the governed. That whenever any Form of Government becomes destructive of these ends, it is the Right of the People to alter or to abolish it, and to institute new Government, laying its foundation on such principles and organizing its powers in such form, as to them shall seem most likely to effect their Safety and Happiness. Prudence, indeed, will dictate that Governments long established should not be changed for light and transient causes; and accordingly all experience hath shewn that mankind are more disposed to suffer, while evils are sufferable, than to right themselves by abolishing the forms to which they are accustomed. But when a long train of abuses and usurpations, pursuing invariably the same Object evinces a design to reduce them under absolute Despotism, it is their right, it is their duty, to throw off such Government, and to provide new Guards for their future security.—Such has been the patient sufferance of these Colonies; and such is now the necessity which constrains them to alter their former Systems of Government. The history of the present King of Great Britain is a history of repeated injuries and usurpations, all having in direct object the establishment of an absolute Tyranny over these States. To prove this, let Facts be submitted to a candid world.

He has refused his Assent to Laws, the most wholesome and necessary for the public good.

He has forbidden his Governors to pass Laws of immediate and pressing importance, unless suspended in their operation till his Assent should be obtained; and when so suspended, he has utterly neglected to attend to them.

He has refused to pass other Laws for the accommodation of large districts of people, unless those people would relinquish the right of Representation in the Legislature, a right inestimable to them and formidable to tyrants only.

He has called together legislative bodies at places unusual, uncomfortable, and distant from the depository of their Public Records, for the sole purpose of fatiguing them into compliance with his measures.

He has dissolved Representative Houses repeatedly, for opposing with manly firmness his invasions on the rights of the people.

He has refused for a long time, after such dissolutions, to cause others to be elected; whereby the Legislative Powers, incapable of Annihilation, have returned to the People at large for their exercise, the State remaining in the mean time exposed to all the dangers of invasion from without, and convulsions within.

He has endeavored to prevent the population of these States; for that purpose obstructing the Laws of Naturalization of Foreigners; refusing to pass others to encourage their migration hither, and raising the conditions of new Appropriations of Lands.

He has obstructed the Administration of Justice, by refusing his Assent to Laws for establishing Judiciary powers.

He has made Judges dependent on his Will alone, for the tenure of their offices, and the amount and payment of their salaries.

He has erected a multitude of New Offices, and sent hither swarms of Officers to harass our people, and eat out their substance.

He has kept among us, in times of peace, Standing Armies without the Consent of our legislatures.

He has affected to render the Military independent of and superior to the Civil power.

He has combined with others to subject us to a jurisdiction foreign to our constitution, and unacknowledged by our laws, giving his Assent to their Acts of pretended Legislation:

For quartering large bodies of armed troops among us:

For protecting them, by a mock Trial, from punishment for any Murders which they should commit on the Inhabitants of these States:

For cutting off our Trade with all parts of the world:

For imposing Taxes on us without our Consent:

For depriving us in many cases, of the benefits of Trial by Jury:

For transporting us beyond Seas to be tried for pretended offences:

For abolishing the free System of English Laws in a neighboring Province, establishing therein an Arbitrary government, and enlarging its Boundaries so as to render it at once an example and fit instrument for introducing the same absolute rule into these Colonies:

For taking away our Charters, abolishing our most valuable Laws, and altering fundamentally the Forms of our Governments:

For suspending our own Legislatures, and declaring themselves invested with power to legislate for us in all cases whatsoever.

He has abdicated Government here, by declaring us out of his Protection and waging War against us.

He has plundered our seas, ravaged our Coasts, burnt out towns, and destroyed the lives of our people.

He is at this time transporting large Armies of foreign Mercenaries to compleat the works of death, desolation and tyranny, already begun with circumstances of Cruelty and perfidy scarcely paralleled in the most barbarous ages, and totally unworthy the Head of a civilized nation.

He has constrained our fellow Citizens taken Captive on the high Seas to bear Arms against their Country, to become the executioners of their friends and Brethren, or to fall themselves by their Hands.

He has excited domestic insurrections amongst us, and has endeavored to bring on the inhabitants of our frontiers, the merciless Indian Savages, whose known rule of warfare, is an undistinguished destruction of all ages, sexes and conditions.

In every stage of these Oppressions We have Petitioned for Redress in the most humble terms: Our repeated Petitions have been answered only by repeated injury: A Prince, whose character is thus marked by every act which may define a Tyrant, is unfit to be the ruler of a free people.

Nor have We been wanting in attention to our British brethren. We have warned them from time to time of attempts by their legislature to extend an unwarrantable jurisdiction over us. We have reminded them of the circumstances of our emigration and settlement here. We have appealed to their native justice and magnanimity; and we have conjured them by the ties of our common kindred to disavow these usurpations, which would inevitably interrupt our connections and correspondence. They too have been deaf to the voice of justice and consanguinity. We must, therefore, acquiesce in the necessity, which denounces our Separation, and hold them, as we hold the rest of mankind, Enemies in War, in Peace Friends.

We, therefore, the Representatives of the United States of America, in General Congress, Assembled, appealing to the Supreme Judge of the world for the rectitude of our intentions, do, in the Name, and by Authority of the good People of these Colonies, solemnly publish and declare, That these United Colonies are, and of Right ought to be Free and Independent States; that they are Absolved from all Allegiance to the British Crown, and that all political connection between them and the State of Great Britain, is and ought to be totally dissolved: and that as Free and Independent States, they have full power to levy War, conclude Peace, contract Alliances, establish Commerce, and to do all other Acts and Things which Independent States may of right do. And for the support of this Declaration, with a firm reliance on the protection of divine Providence, we mutually pledge to each other our Lives, our Fortunes and our sacred Honor.

JOHN HANCOCK,
Attest.

CHARLES THOMSON,
Secretary.

NEW HAMPSHIRE
Josiah Bartlett,
Wm. Whipple,
Matthew Thornton.

MASSACHUSETTS BAY
Saml. Adams,
John Adams,
Robt. Treat Paine,
Elbridge Gerry.

RHODE ISLAND
Step. Hopkins,
William Ellery.

CONNECTICUT
Roger Sherman,
Samuel Huntington,
Wm. Williams,
Oliver Wolcott.

NEW YORK
Wm. Floyd,
Phil. Livingston,
Frans. Lewis,
Lewis Morris

NEW JERSEY
Richd. Stockton,
J. Witherspoon,
Fras. Hopkinson,
John Hart,
Abra. Clark.

PENNSYLVANIA
Robt. Morris,
Benjamin Rush,
Benjamin Franklin,
John Morton,
Geo. Clymer,
Jas. Smith,
Geo. Taylor,
James Wilson,
Geo. Ross.

DELAWARE
Caesar Rodney,
Geo. Read,
Tho. McKean.

MARYLAND
Samuel Chase,
Wm. Paca,
Thos. Stone,
Charles Caroll
of Carollton.

VIRGINIA
George Wythe,
Richard Henry Lee,
Th. Jefferson,
Benjamin Harrison,
Thos. Nelson, jr.,
Francis Lightfoot Lee,
Carter Braxton.

NORTH CAROLINA
Wm. Hooper,
Joseph Hewes,
John Penn.

SOUTH CAROLINA
Edward Rutledge,
Thos. Heyward, Junr.,
Thomas Lynch, jnr.,
Arthur Middleton.

GEORGIA
Button Gwinnett,
Lyman Hall,
Geo. Walton.

APPENDIX II

THE CONSTITUTION OF THE UNITED STATES OF AMERICA

W e the People of the United States, in Order to form a more perfect Union, establish Justice, insure domestic Tranquility, provide for the common defence, promote the general Welfare, and secure the Blessings of Liberty to ourselves and our Posterity, do ordain and establish this Constitution for the United States of America.

ARTICLE I

SECTION 1. All legislative Powers herein granted shall be vested in a Congress of the United States, which shall consist of a Senate and House of Representatives.

SECTION 2. The House of Representatives shall be composed of Members chosen every second Year by the People of the several States, and the Electors in each State shall have the Qualifications requisite for Electors of the most numerous Branch of the State Legislature.

No person shall be a Representative who shall not have attained to the Age of twenty five Years, and been seven Years a Citizen of the United States, and who shall not, when elected, be an Inhabitant of that State in which he shall be chosen.

Representatives and direct Taxes shall be apportioned among the several States which may be included within this Union, according to their respective Numbers which shall be determined by adding to the whole Number of free Persons, including those bound to Service for a Term of Years, and excluding Indians not taxed, three fifths of all other Persons. The actual Enumeration shall be made within three Years after the first Meeting of the Congress of the United States, and within every subsequent Term ten Years, in such Manner as they shall by Law direct. The Number of Representatives shall not exceed one for every thirty Thousand, but each State shall have at Least one Representative; and until such enumeration shall be made, the State of New Hampshire shall be entitled to chuse three, Massachusetts eight, Rhode-Island and Providence Plantations one, Connecticut five, New-York six, New Jersey four, Pennsylvania eight, Delaware one, Maryland six, Virginia ten, North Carolina five, South Carolina five, and Georgia three.

When vacancies happen in the Representation from any State, the Executive Authority thereof shall issue Writs of Election to fill such Vacancies.

The House of Representatives shall chuse their speaker and other Officers; and shall have the sole Power of Impeachment.

SECTION 3. The Senate of the United States shall be composed of two Senators from each State chosen by the Legislature thereof, for six Years; and each Senator shall have one Vote.

Immediately after they shall be assembled in Consequence of the first Election, they shall be divided as equally as may be into three Classes. The Seats of the Senators of the first Class shall be vacated at the Expiration of the second year, of the second Class at the Expiration of the fourth Year, and of the third Class at the Expiration of the sixth Year, so that one third may be chosen every second Year and if Vacancies happen by Resignation, or otherwise, during the Recess of the Legislature of any State, the Executive thereof may make temporary Appointments until the next Meeting of the Legislature, which shall then fill such Vacancies.

No Person shall be a Senator who shall not have attained to the Age of thirty Years, and been nine Years a Citizen of the United States, and who shall not, when elected, be an Inhabitant of that State for which he shall be chosen.

The Vice President of the United States shall be President of the Senate, but shall have no Vote, unless they be equally divided.

The Senate shall chuse their other Officers, and also a President pro tempore, in the Absence of the Vice President, or when he shall exercise the Office of President of the United States.

The Senate shall have the sole Power to try all Impeachments. When sitting for that Purpose, they shall be on Oath or Affirmation. When the President of the United States is tried, the Chief Justice shall preside: And no Person shall be convicted without the Concurrence of two thirds of the Members present.

Judgment in Cases of Impeachment shall not extend further than to removal from Office, and disqualification to hold and enjoy any Office of honor, Trust or Profit under the United States; but the Party convicted shall nevertheless be liable and subject to Indictment, Trial, Judgment and Punishment, according to Law.

SECTION 4. The Times, Places and Manner of holding Elections for Senators and Representatives, shall be prescribed in each State by the Legislature thereof; but the Congress may at any time by law make or alter such Regulations, except as to the Places of chusing Senators.

The Congress shall assemble at least once in every Year, and such Meeting shall be on the first Monday in December, unless they shall by Law appoint a different Day.

SECTION 5. Each House shall be the Judge of the Elections, Returns and Qualifications of its own Members, and a Majority of each shall constitute a Quorum to do Business; but a smaller Number may adjourn from day to day, and may be authorized to compel the Attendance of absent Members, in such Manner, and under such Penalties as each House may provide.

Each House may determine the Rules of its Proceedings, punish its Members for disorderly Behaviour, and with the Concurrence of two thirds, expel a Member.

Each House shall keep a journal of its Proceedings, and from time to time publish the same, excepting such Parts as may in their judgment require Secrecy; and the Yeas and Nays of the Members of either House on any question shall, at the Desire of one fifth of those present, be entered on the Journal.

Neither House, during the Session of Congress, shall, without the Consent of the other, adjourn for more than three days, nor to any other Place than that in which the two Houses shall be sitting.

SECTION 6. The Senators and Representatives shall receive a Compensation for their Services, to be ascertained by Law, and paid out of the Treasury of the United States. They shall in all Cases, except Treason, Felony and Breach of the Peace, be privileged from Arrest during their Attendance at the Session of their respective Houses, and in going to and returning from the same; and for any Speech or Debate in either House, they shall not be questioned in any other Place.

No Senator or Representative shall, during the Time for which he was elected, be appointed to any civil Office under the Authority of the United States, which shall have been created, or the Emoluments whereof shall have been encreased during such time; and no Person holding any Office under the United States, shall be a Member of either House during his Continuance in Office.

SECTION 7. All Bills for raising Revenue shall originate in the House of Representatives; but the Senate may propose or concur with Amendments as on other Bills.

Every Bill which shall have passed the House of Representatives and the Senate, shall, before it become a Law, be presented to the President of the United States; If he approves he shall sign it, but if not he shall return it, with his Objections to that House in which it shall have originated, who shall enter the Objections at large on their journal, and proceed to reconsider it. If after such Reconsideration two thirds of that House shall agree to pass the Bill, it shall be sent, together with the Objections, to the other House, by which it shall likewise be reconsidered, and if approved by two thirds of that House, it shall become a Law. But in all such Cases the Votes of both Houses shall be determined by Yeas and Nays, and the Names of the Persons voting for and against the Bill shall be entered on the Journal of each House respectively. If any Bill shall not be returned by the President within ten Days (Sundays excepted) after it shall have been presented to him, the Same shall be a Law, in like Manner as if he had signed it, unless the Congress by their Adjournment prevent its Return, in which Case it shall not be a Law.

Every Order, Resolution, or Vote to which the Concurrence of the Senate and House of Representatives may be necessary (except on a question of Adjournment) shall be presented to the President of the United States; and before the Same shall take Effect, shall be approved by him, or being disapproved by him, shall be repassed by two thirds of the Senate and House of Representatives, according to the Rules and Limitations prescribed in the Case of a Bill.

SECTION 8. The Congress shall have Power To lay and collect Taxes, Duties, Imposts and Excises, to pay the Debts and provide for the common Defence and general Welfare of the United States; but all Duties, Imposts and Excises shall be uniform throughout the United States;

To borrow Money on the credit of the United States;

To regulate Commerce with foreign Nations, and among the several States, and with the Indian Tribes;

To establish a uniform Rule of Naturalization, and uniform Laws on the subject of Bankruptcies throughout the United States;

To coin Money, regulate the Value thereof, and of foreign Coin, and fix the Standard of Weights and Measures;

To provide for the Punishment of counterfeiting the Securities and current Coin of the United States;

To establish Post Offices and post Roads;

To promote the Progress of Science and useful Arts, by securing for limited Times to Authors and Inventors the exclusive Right to their respective Writings and Discoveries;

To constitute Tribunals inferior to the supreme Court;

To define and punish Piracies and Felonies committed on the high Seas, and Offences against the Law of Nations;

To declare War, grant Letters of Marque and Reprisal, and make Rules concerning Captures on Land and Water;

To raise and support Armies, but no Appropriation of Money to that Use shall be for a longer Term than two Years;

To provide and maintain a Navy;

To make Rules for the Government and Regulation of the land and naval Forces;

To provide for calling forth the Militia to execute the Laws of the Union, suppress Insurrections and repel Invasions;

To provide for organizing, arming, and disciplining, the Militia, and for governing such Part of them as may be employed in the Service of the United States, reserving to the States respectively, the Appointment of the Officers, and the Authority of training the Militia according to the discipline prescribed by Congress;

To exercise exclusive Legislation in all Cases whatsoever, over such District (not exceeding ten Miles square) as may, by Cession of particular States, and the Acceptance of Congress, become the Seat of the Government of the United States, and to exercise like Authority over all Places purchased by the Consent of the Legislature of the State in which the Same shall be for the Erection of Forts, Magazines, Arsenals, dock-Yards, and other needful Buildings;—And

To make all Laws which shall be necessary and proper for carrying into Execution the foregoing Powers, and all other Powers vested by this Constitution in the Government of the United States, or in any Department or Officer thereof.

SECTION 9. The Migration or Importation of such Persons as any of the States now existing shall think proper to admit, shall not be prohibited by the Congress prior to the Year one thousand eight hundred and eight, but a Tax or duty may be imposed on such Importation, not exceeding ten dollars for each Person.

The Privilege of the Writ of Habeas Corpus shall not be suspended, unless when in Cases of Rebellion or Invasion the public Safety may require it.

No Bill of Attainder or ex post facto Law shall be passed.

No Capitation, or other direct, Tax shall be laid, unless in Proportion to the Census or Enumeration herein before directed to be taken.

No Tax or Duty shall be laid on Articles exported from any State.

No Preference shall be given by any Regulation of Commerce or Revenue to the Ports of one State over those of another; nor shall Vessels bound to, or from, one State, be obliged to enter, clear, or pay Duties in another.

No Money shall be drawn from the Treasury, but in Consequence of Appropriations made by Law; and a regular Statement and Account of the Receipts and Expenditures of all public Money shall be published from time to time.

No Title of Nobility shall be granted by the United States: And no Person holding any Office of Profit or Trust under them, shall, without the Consent of the Congress, accept of any present, Emolument, Office, or Title, of any kind whatever, from any King, Prince, or foreign State.

SECTION 10. No state shall enter into any Treaty, Alliance, or Confederation; grant Letters of Marque and Reprisal; coin Money; emit Bills of Credit; make any Thing but gold and silver Coin a Tender in Payment of Debts; pass any Bill of Attainder, ex post facto Law, or Law impairing the Obligation of Contracts, or grant any Title of Nobility.

No State shall, without the Consent of the Congress, lay any Imposts or Duties on Imports or Exports, except what may be absolutely necessary for executing its inspection Laws: and the net Produce of all Duties and Imposts, laid by any State on Imports or Exports, shall be for the Use of the Treasury of the United States, and all such Laws shall be subject to the Revision and Controul of the Congress.

No State shall, without the Consent of Congress, lay any Duty of Tonnage, keep Troops, or Ships of War in time of Peace, enter into any Agreement or Compact with another State, or with a foreign Power, or engage in War, unless actually invaded, or in such imminent Danger as will not admit of delay.

ARTICLE II

SECTION 1. The executive Power shall be vested in a President of the United States of America. He shall hold his Office during the Term of four Years, and, together with the Vice President, chosen for the same Term, be elected as follows.

Each State shall appoint, in such Manner as the Legislature thereof may direct, a Number of Electors, equal to the whole Number of Senators and Representatives to which the State may be entitled in the Congress; but no Senator or Representative, or Person holding an Office of Trust of Profit under the United States, shall be appointed an Elector.

The Electors shall meet in their respective States, and vote by Ballot for two Persons, of whom one at least shall not be an Inhabitant of the same State with themselves. And they shall make a List of all the Persons voted for, and, of the Number of Votes for each; which List they shall sign and certify, and transmit sealed to the Seat of the Government of the United States, directed to the President of the Senate. The President of the Senate shall, in the Presence of the Senate and House of Representatives, open all the Certificates, and the Votes shall then be counted. The Person having the greatest Number of Votes shall be the President, if such Number be a Majority of the whole Number of Electors appointed; and if there be more than one who have such Majority, and have an equal Number of Votes, then the House of Representatives shall immediately chuse by Ballot one of them for President; and if no Person have a Majority, then from the five highest on the List the said House shall in like Manner chuse the President. But in chusing the President, the Votes shall be taken by States, the Representation from each State having one Vote; A quorum for this Purpose shall consist of a Member or Members from two thirds of the States, and a Majority of all the States shall be necessary to a Choice. In every Case, after the Choice of the President, the Person having the greatest Number of Votes of the Electors shall be the Vice President. But if there should remain two or more who have equal Votes, the Senate shall chuse from them by Ballot the Vice President.

The Congress may determine the Time of chusing the Electors, and the Day on which they shall give their Votes; which Day shall be the same throughout the United States.

No Person except a natural born Citizen, or a Citizen of the United States, at the time of the Adoption of this Constitution, shall be eligible to the Office of President; neither shall any Person be eligible to that Office who shall not have attained to the Age of thirty five Years, and been fourteen Years a Resident within the United States.

In Case of the Removal of the President from Office, or of his Death, Resignation, or Inability to discharge the Powers and Duties of the said Office, the Same shall devolve on the Vice President, and the Congress may by Law provide for the Case of Removal, Death, Resignation or Inability, both of the President and Vice President, declaring what Officer shall then act as President, and such Officer shall act accordingly, until the Disability be removed, or a President shall be elected.

The President shall, at stated Times, receive for his Services, a Compensation, which shall neither be encreased nor diminished during the Period for which he shall have been elected, and he shall not receive within that Period any other Emolument from the United States, or any of them.

Before he enter on the Execution of his Office, he shall take the following Oath or Affirmation—"I do solemnly swear (or affirm) that I will faithfully execute the Office of President of the United States, and will to the best of my Ability, preserve, protect and defend the Constitution of the United States."

Section 2. The President shall be Commander in Chief of the Army, and Navy of the United States, and of the Militia of the several States, when called into the actual Service of the United States; he may require the Opinion, in writing, of the principal Officer in each of the executive Departments, upon any Subject relating to the Duties of their respective Offices, and he shall have Power to grant Reprieves and Pardons for Offences against the United States, except in Cases of Impeachment.

He shall have Power, by and with the Advice and Consent of the Senate, to make Treaties, provided two thirds of the Senators present concur; and he shall nominate, and by and with the Advice and Consent of the Senate, shall appoint Ambassadors, other public Ministers and Consuls, Judges of the supreme Court, and all other Officers of the United States, whose Appointments are not herein otherwise provided for, and which shall be established by Law: but the Congress may by Law vest the Appointment of such inferior Officers, as they think proper, in the President alone, in the Courts of Law, or in the Heads of Departments.

The President shall have Power to fill up all Vacancies that may happen during the Recess of the Senate, by granting Commissions which shall expire at the end of their next Session.

Section 3. He shall from time to time give to the Congress Information of the State of the Union, and recommend to their Consideration such Measures as he shall judge necessary and expedient; he may, on extraordinary Occasions, convene both Houses, or either of them, and in Case of Disagreement between them, with Respect to the Time of Adjournment, he may adjourn them to such Time as he shall think proper; he shall receive Ambassadors and other public Ministers; he shall take Care that the Laws be faithfully executed, and shall Commission all the Officers of the United States.

Section 4. The President, Vice President and all civil Officers of the United States, shall be removed from Office on Impeachment for, and Conviction of, Treason, Bribery, or other high Crimes and Misdemeanors.

ARTICLE III

Section 1. The judicial Power of the United States, shall be vested in one supreme Court, and in such inferior Courts as the Congress may from time to time ordain and establish. The Judges, both of the supreme and inferior Courts, shall hold their Offices during good Behaviour, and shall, at stated Times, receive for their Services, a Compensation, which shall not be diminished during their Continuance in Office.

Section 2. The judicial Power shall extend to all Cases, in Law and Equity, arising under this Constitution, the Laws of the United States, and Treaties made, or which shall be made, under their Authority;—to all Cases affecting Ambassadors, other public Ministers and Consuls;—to all Cases of admiralty and maritime Jurisdiction;—to Controversies to which the United States shall be a Party;—to Controversies between two or more States;—between a State and Citizens of another State;—between Citizens of different States,—between Citizens of the same State claiming Lands under Grants of different States,—and between a State, or the Citizens thereof, and foreign States, Citizens of Subjects.

In all Cases affecting Ambassadors, other public Ministers and Consuls, and those in which a State shall be Party, the supreme Court shall have original Jurisdiction. In all the other Cases before mentioned, the supreme Court shall have appellate Jurisdiction, both as to Law and Fact, with such Exceptions, and under such Regulations as the Congress shall make.

The Trial of all Crimes, except in Cases of Impeachment, shall be by Jury; and such Trial shall be held in the State where the said Crimes shall have been committed; but when not committed within any State, the Trial shall be at such Place or Places as the Congress may by Law have directed.

Section 3. Treason against the United States, shall consist only in levying War against them, or in adhering to their Enemies, giving them Aid and Comfort. No Person shall be convicted of Treason unless on the Testimony of two Witnesses to the same overt Act, or on Confession in open Court.

The Congress shall have Power to declare the Punishment of Treason, but no Attainder of Treason shall work Corruption of Blood, or Forfeiture except during the Life of the Person attainted.

ARTICLE IV

Section 1. Full Faith and Credit shall be given in each State to the public Acts, Records, and judicial Proceedings of every other State. And the Congress may by general Laws prescribe the Manner in which such Acts, Records and Proceedings shall be proved, and the Effect thereof.

Section 2. The Citizens of each State shall be entitled to all Privileges and Immunities of Citizens in the several States.

A Person charged in any State with Treason, Felony, or other Crime, who shall flee from Justice, and be found in another State, shall on Demand of the executive Authority of the State from which he fled, be delivered up, to be removed to the State having Jurisdiction of the Crime.

No Person held to Service or Labour in one State under the Laws thereof, escaping into another, shall, in Consequence of any Law or Regulation therein, be discharged from such Service or Labour, but shall be delivered up on Claim of the Party to whom such Service or Labour may be due.

SECTION 3. New States may be admitted by the Congress into this Union; but no new State shall be formed or erected within the Jurisdiction of any other State; nor any State be formed by the Junction of two or more States, or Parts of States, without the Consent of the Legislatures of the States concerned as well as of the Congress.

The Congress shall have Power to dispose of and make all needful Rules and Regulations respecting the Territory or other Property belonging to the United States; and nothing in this Constitution shall be so construed as to Prejudice any Claims of the United States, or of any particular State.

SECTION 4. The United States shall guarantee to every State in this Union a Republican Form of Government, and shall protect each of them against Invasion, and on Application of the Legislature, or of the Executive (when the Legislature cannot be convened) against domestic Violence.

ARTICLE V

The Congress, whenever two thirds of both Houses shall deem it necessary, shall propose Amendments to this Constitution, or, on the Application of the Legislatures of two thirds of the several States, shall call a Convention for proposing Amendments, which, in either Case, shall be valid to all Intents and Purposes, as Part of this Constitution, when ratified by the Legislatures of three fourths of the several States, or by Conventions in three fourths thereof, as the one or the other Mode of Ratification may be proposed by the Congress; Provided that no Amendment which may be made prior to the Year One thousand eight hundred and eight shall in any Manner affect the first and fourth Clauses in the Ninth Section of the first Article; and that no State, without its Consent, shall be deprived of its equal Suffrage in the Senate.

ARTICLE VI

All Debts contracted and Engagements entered into, before the Adoption of this Constitution, shall be as valid against the United States under this Constitution, as under the Confederation.

This Constitution, and the laws of the United States which shall be made in Pursuance thereof; and all Treaties made, or which shall be made, under the Authority of the United States, shall be the supreme Law of the Land; and the Judges in every State shall be bound thereby, any Thing in the Constitution or Laws of any State to the Contrary notwithstanding.

The Senators and Representatives before mentioned, and the Members of the several State Legislatures, and all executive and judicial Officers, both of the United States and of the several States, shall be bound by Oath or Affirmation, to support this Constitution; but no religious Test shall ever be required as a Qualification to any Office or public Trust under the United States.

ARTICLE VII

The Ratification of the Conventions of nine States, shall be sufficient for the Establishment of this Constitution between the States so ratifying the Same.

Done in Convention by the Unanimous Consent of the States present the Seventeenth Day of September in the Year of our Lord one thousand seven hundred and Eighty seven and of the Independence of the United States of America the Twelfth. IN WITNESS whereof we have hereunto subscribed our Names,

Go. WASHINGTON,
Presid't. and deputy from Virginia

Attest
WILLIAM JACKSON,
Secretary.

DELAWARE
Geo. Read,
Gunning Bedford jun,
John Dickinson,
Richard Basset,
Jaco. Broom.

MASSACHUSETTS BAY
Nathaniel Gorham,
Rufus King.

CONNECTICUT
Wm. Saml. Johnson,
Roger Sherman.

NEW YORK
Alexander Hamilton.

NEW JERSEY
Wi. Livingston,
David Brearley,
Wm. Paterson,
Jona. Dayton.

PENNSYLVANIA
B. Franklin,
Thomas Mifflin,
Robt. Morris,
Geo. Clymer,
Thos. FitzSimons,
Jared Ingersoll,
James Wilson,
Gouv. Morris

NEW HAMPSHIRE
John Langdon,
Nicholas Gilman.

MARYLAND
James McHenry,
Dan of St. Thos. Jenifer,
Danl. Carroll.

VIRGINIA
John Blair,
James Madison, Jr..

NORTH CAROLINA
Wm. Blount,
Richd. Dobbs Spaight,
Hu. Williamson.

SOUTH CAROLINA
J. Rutledge,
Charles Cotesworth Pinckney,
Charles Pinckney.
Pierce Butler

GEORGIA
William Few,
Abr. Baldwin

Articles in addition to, and amendment of the Constitution of the United States of America, proposed by Congress and ratified by the Legislatures of the several states, pursuant to the Fifth Article of the original Constitution.

(The first ten amendments were passed by Congress on September 25, 1789, and were ratified on December 15, 1791.)

AMENDMENT I

Congress shall make no law respecting an establishment of religion, or prohibiting the free exercise thereof; or abridging the freedom of speech, or of the press; or the right of the people peaceably to assemble, and to petition the Government for a redress of grievances.

AMENDMENT II

A well regulated Militia, being necessary to the security of a free State, the right of the people to keep and bear Arms, shall not be infringed.

AMENDMENT III

No Soldier shall, in time of peace be quartered in any house, without the consent of the Owner, nor in time of war, but in a manner to be prescribed by law.

AMENDMENT IV

The right of the people to be secure in their persons, houses, papers, and effects, against unreasonable searches and seizures, shall not be violated, and no warrants shall issue, but upon probable cause, supported by Oath or affirmation, and particularly describing the place to be searched, and the persons or things to be seized.

AMENDMENT V

No person shall be held to answer for a capital, or otherwise infamous crime, unless on a presentment or indictment of a Grand Jury, except in cases arising in the land or naval forces, or in the Militia, when in actual service in time of War or public danger; nor shall any person be subject for the same offence to be twice put in jeopardy of life or limb; nor shall be compelled in any criminal case to be a witness against himself, nor be deprived of life, liberty, or property, without due process of law; nor shall private property be taken for public use, without just compensation.

AMENDMENT VI

In all criminal prosecutions, the accused shall enjoy the right to a speedy and public trial, by an impartial jury of the State and district wherein the crime shall have been committed, which district shall have been previously ascertained by law, and to be informed of the nature and cause of the accusation; to be confronted with the witnesses against him; to have compulsory process for obtaining witnesses in his favor, and to have the assistance of counsel for his defence.

AMENDMENT VII

In Suits at common law, where the value in controversy shall exceed twenty dollars, the right of trial by jury shall be preserved, and no fact tried by a jury, shall be otherwise re-examined in any Court of the United States, than according to the rules of the common law.

AMENDMENT VIII

Excessive bail shall not be required, nor excessive fines imposed, nor cruel and unusual punishments inflicted.

AMENDMENT IX

The enumeration in the Constitution, of certain rights, shall not be construed to deny or disparage others retained by the people.

AMENDMENT X

The powers not delegated to the United States by the Constitution, nor prohibited by it to the States, are reserved to the States respectively, or to the people.

AMENDMENT XI *(Ratified on February 7, 1795)*

The Judicial power of the United States shall not be construed to extend to any suit in law or equity, commenced or prosecuted against one of the United States by Citizens of another State, or by Citizens or Subjects of any Foreign State.

AMENDMENT XII *(Ratified on June 15, 1804)*

The Electors shall meet in their respective states, and vote by ballot for President and Vice-President, one of whom, at least, shall not be an inhabitant of the same state with themselves; they shall name in their ballots the person voted for as President, and in distinct ballots the person voted for as Vice-President, and they shall make distinct lists of all persons voted for as President, and of all persons voted for as Vice-President, and of the number of votes for each, which lists they shall sign and certify, and transmit sealed to the seat of the government of the United States, directed to the President of the Senate;—The President of the Senate shall, in the presence of the Senate and House of Representatives, open all the certificates and the votes shall then be counted;—The person having the greatest number of votes for President, shall be the President, if such number be a majority of the whole number of Electors appointed; and if no person have such majority; then from the persons having the highest numbers not exceeding three on the list of those voted for as President, the House of Representatives shall choose immediately, by ballot, the President. But in choosing the President, the votes shall be taken by states, the representation from each state having one vote; a quorum for this purpose shall consist of a member or members from two-thirds of the states, and a majority of all the states shall be necessary to a choice. And if the House of Representatives shall not choose a President whenever the right of choice shall devolve upon them, before the fourth day of March next following, then the Vice-President shall act as President, as in the case of the death or other constitutional disability of the President.—The person having the greatest number of votes as Vice-President, shall be the Vice-President, if such number be a majority of the whole number of Electors appointed, and if no person have a majority, then from the two highest numbers on the list, the Senate shall choose the Vice-President; a quorum for the purpose shall consist of two-thirds of the whole number of Senators, and a majority of the whole number shall be necessary to a choice. But no person constitutionally ineligible to the office of President shall be eligible to that of Vice-President of the United States.

AMENDMENT XIII *(Ratified on December 6, 1865)*

SECTION 1. Neither slavery nor involuntary servitude, except as a punishment for crime whereof the party shall have been duly convicted, shall exist within the United States, or any place subject to their jurisdiction.

SECTION 2. Congress shall have power to enforce this article by appropriate legislation.

AMENDMENT XIV *(Ratified on July 9, 1868)*

SECTION 1. All persons born or naturalized in the United States, and subject to the jurisdiction thereof, are citizens of the United States and of the State wherein they reside. No State shall make or enforce any law which shall abridge the privileges or immunities of citizens of the United States; nor shall any State deprive any person of life, liberty, or property, without due process of law; nor deny to any person within its jurisdiction the equal protection of the laws.

SECTION 2. Representatives shall be apportioned among the several States according to their respective numbers, counting the whole number of persons in each State, excluding Indians not taxed. But when the right to vote at any election for the choice of electors for President and Vice President of the United States, Representatives in Congress, the Executive and Judicial officers of a State, or the members of the Legislature thereof, is denied to any of the male inhabitants of such State, being twenty-one years of age, and citizens of the United States, or in any way abridged, except for participation in rebellion, or other crime, the basis of representation therein shall be reduced in the proportion which the number of such male citizens shall bear to the whole number of male citizens twenty-one years of age in such State.

SECTION 3. No person shall be a Senator or Representative in Congress, or elector of President and Vice President, or hold any office, civil or military, under the United States, or under any State, who, having previously taken an oath, as a member of Congress, or as an officer of the United States, or as a member of any State legislature, or as an executive or judicial officer of any State, to support the Constitution of the United States, shall have engaged in insurrection or rebellion against the same, or given aid or comfort to the enemies thereof. But Congress may by a vote of two-thirds of each House, remove such disability.

SECTION 4. The validity of the public debt of the United States, authorized by law, including debts incurred for payment of pensions and bounties for services in suppressing insurrection or rebellion, shall not be questioned. But neither the United States nor any State shall assume or pay any debt or obligation incurred in aid of insurrection or rebellion against the United States, or any claim for the loss or emancipation of any slave, but all such debts, obligations and claims shall be held illegal and void.

SECTION 5. The Congress shall have power to enforce, by appropriate legislation, the provisions of this article.

AMENDMENT XV *(Ratified on February 3, 1870)*

SECTION 1. The right of citizens of the United States to vote shall not be denied or abridged by the United States or by any State on account of race, color, or previous condition of servitude.

SECTION 2. The Congress shall have power to enforce this article by appropriate legislation.

AMENDMENT XVI *(Ratified on February 3, 1913)*

The Congress shall have power to lay and collect taxes on incomes, from whatever source derived, without apportionment among the several States, and without regard to any census or enumeration.

AMENDMENT XVII *(Ratified on April 8, 1913)*

The Senate of the United States shall be composed of two Senators from each State, elected by the people thereof, for six years; and each Senator shall have one vote. The electors in each State shall have the qualifications requisite for electors of the most numerous branch of the State legislatures.

When vacancies happen in the representation of any State in the Senate, the executive authority of such State shall issue writs of election to fill such vacancies: Provided, That the legislature of any State may empower the executive thereof to make temporary appointments until the people fill the vacancies by election as the legislature may direct.

This amendment shall not be so construed as to affect the election or term of any Senator chosen before it becomes valid as part of the Constitution.

AMENDMENT XVIII *(Ratified on January 16, 1919)*

SECTION 1. After one year from the ratification of this article the manufacture, sale, or transportation of intoxicating liquors within, the importation thereof into, or the exportation thereof from the United States and all territory subject to the jurisdiction thereof for beverage purposes is hereby prohibited.

SECTION 2. The Congress and the several States shall have concurrent power to enforce this article by appropriate legislation.

SECTION 3. This article shall be inoperative unless it shall have been ratified as an amendment to the Constitution by the legislatures of the several States, as provided in the Constitution, within seven years from the date of the submission hereof to the States by the Congress.

AMENDMENT XIX *(Ratified on August 18, 1920)*

The right of citizens of the United States to vote shall not be denied or abridged by the United States or by any State on account of sex.

Congress shall have power to enforce this article by appropriate legislation.

AMENDMENT XX *(Ratified on February 6, 1933)*

SECTION 1. The terms of the President and Vice President shall end at noon on the 20th day of January, and the terms of Senators and Representatives at noon on the 3d day of January, of the years in which such terms would have ended if this article had not been ratified; and the terms of their successors shall then begin.

SECTION 2. The Congress shall assemble at least once in every year, and such meeting shall begin at noon on the 3d day of January, unless they shall by law appoint a different day.

SECTION 3. If, at the time fixed for the beginning of the term of the President, the President elect shall have died, the Vice President elect shall become President. If a President shall not have been chosen before the time fixed for the beginning of his term, or if the President elect shall have failed to qualify, then the Vice President elect shall act as President until a President shall have qualified; and the Congress may by law provide for the case wherein neither a President elect nor a Vice President elect shall have qualified, declaring who shall then act as President, or the manner in which one who is to act shall be selected, and such person shall act accordingly until a President or Vice President shall have qualified.

SECTION 4. The Congress may by law provide for the case of the death of any of the persons from whom the House of Representatives may choose a President whenever the rights of choice shall have devolved upon them, and for the case of the death of any of the persons from whom the Senate may choose a Vice President whenever the right of choice shall have devolved upon them.

SECTION 5. Sections 1 and 2 shall take effect on the 15th day of October following the ratification of this article.

SECTION 6. This article shall be inoperative unless it shall have been ratified as an amendment to the Constitution by the legislatures of three-fourths of the several States within seven years from the date of its submission.

AMENDMENT XXI *(Ratified on December 5, 1933)*

SECTION 1. The eighteenth article of amendment to the Constitution of the United States is hereby repealed.

SECTION 2. The transportation or importation into any State, Territory, or possession of the United States for delivery or use therein of intoxicating liquors, in violation of the laws thereof, is hereby prohibited.

SECTION 3. This article shall be inoperative unless it shall have been ratified as an amendment to the Constitution by conventions in the several States, as provided in the Constitution, within seven years from the date of the submission hereof to the States by the Congress.

AMENDMENT XXII *(Ratified on February 27, 1951)*

No person shall be elected to the office of the President more than twice, and no person who has held the office of President, or acted as President, for more than two years of a term to which some other person was elected President shall be elected to the office of the President more than once. But this Article shall not apply to any person holding the office of President when this Article was proposed by the Congress, and shall not prevent any person who may be holding the office of President, or acting as President, during the term within which this Article becomes operative from holding the office of President or acting as President during the remainder of such term.

AMENDMENT XXIII *(Ratified on March 29, 1961)*

SECTION 1. The District constituting the seat of Government of the United States shall appoint in such manner as the Congress may direct:

A number of electors of President and Vice President equal to the whole number of Senators and Representatives in Congress to which the District would be entitled if it were a State, but in no event more than the least populous State; they shall be in addition to those appointed by the States, but they shall be considered, for the purposes of the election of President and Vice President, to be electors appointed by a State; and they shall meet in the District and perform such duties as provided by the twelfth article of amendment.

SECTION 2. The Congress shall have power to enforce this article by appropriate legislation.

AMENDMENT XXIV *(Ratified on January 23, 1964)*

SECTION 1. The right of citizens of the United States to vote in any primary or other election for President or Vice President, for electors for President or Vice President, or for Senator or Representative in Congress, shall not be denied or abridged by the United States or any State by reason of failure to pay any poll tax or other tax.

SECTION 2. The Congress shall have power to enforce this article by appropriate legislation.

AMENDMENT XXV *(Ratified on February 10, 1967)*

SECTION 1. In case of the removal of the President from office or of his death or resignation, the Vice President shall become President.

SECTION 2. Whenever there is a vacancy in the office of the Vice President, the President shall nominate a Vice President who shall take office upon confirmation by a majority vote of both Houses of Congress.

SECTION 3. Whenever the President transmits to the President pro tempore of the Senate and the Speaker of the House of Representatives his written declaration that he is unable to discharge the powers and duties of his office, and until he transmits to them a written declaration to the contrary, such powers and duties shall be discharged by the Vice President as Acting President.

SECTION 4. Whenever the Vice President and a majority of either the principal officers of the executive departments or of such other body as Congress may by law provide, transmit to the President pro tempore of the Senate and the Speaker of the House of Representatives their written declaration that the President is unable to discharge the powers and duties of his office, the Vice President shall immediately assume the powers and duties of the office as Acting President.

Thereafter, when the President transmits to the President pro tempore of the Senate and the Speaker of the House of Representatives his written declaration that no inability exists, he shall resume the powers and duties of his office unless the Vice President and a majority of either the principal officers of the executive department or of such other body as Congress may by law provide, transmit within four days to the President pro tempore of the Senate and the Speaker of the House of Representatives their written declaration that the President is unable to discharge the powers and duties of his office. Thereupon Congress shall decide the issue, assembling within forty-eight hours for that purpose if not in session. If the Congress, within twenty-one days after receipt of the latter written declaration, or, if Congress is not in session, within twenty-one days after Congress is required to assemble, determines by two-thirds vote of both Houses that the President is unable to discharge the powers and duties of his office, the Vice President shall continue to discharge the same as Acting President; otherwise, the President shall resume the powers and duties of his office.

AMENDMENT XXVI *(Ratified on July 1, 1971)*

SECTION 1. The right of citizens of the United States, who are eighteen years of age or older, to vote shall not be denied or abridged by the United States or by any State on account of age.

SECTION 2. The Congress shall have power to enforce this article by appropriate legislation.

AMENDMENT XXVII *(Ratified on May 7, 1992)*

No law varying the compensation for the services of Senators and Representatives shall take effect until an election of Representatives shall have intervened.

and from the influence of these on the sentiments and views of the respective proprietors, ensues a division of the society into different interests and parties.

The latent causes of faction are thus sown in the nature of man; and we see them every where brought into different degrees of activity, according to the different circumstances of civil society. A zeal for different opinions concerning religion, concerning Government and many other points, as well of speculation as of practice; an attachment to different leaders ambitiously contending for pre-eminence and power; or to persons of other descriptions whose fortunes have been interesting to the human passions, have in turn divided mankind into parties, inflamed them with mutual animosity, and rendered them much more disposed to vex and oppress each other, than to cooperate for their common good. So strong is this propensity of mankind to fall into mutual animosities, that where no substantial occasion presents itself, the most frivolous and fanciful distinctions have been sufficient to kindle their unfriendly passions, and excite their most violent conflicts. But the most common and durable source of factions, has been the various and unequal distribution of property. Those who hold, and those who are without property, have ever formed distinct interests in society. Those who are creditors, and those who are debtors, fall under a like discrimination. A landed interest, a manufacturing interest, a mercantile interest, a monied interest, with many lesser interests, grow up of necessity in civilized nations, and divide them into different classes, actuated by different sentiments and views. The regulation of these various and interfering interests forms the principal task of modern Legislation, and involves the spirit of party and faction in the necessary and ordinary operations of Government.

No man is allowed to be a judge in his own cause; because his interest would certainly bias his judgment, and, not improbably, corrupt his integrity. With equal, nay with greater reason, a body of men, are unfit to be both judges and parties, at the same time; yet, what are many of the most important acts of legislation, but so many judicial determinations, not indeed concerning the rights of single persons, but concerning the rights of large bodies of citizens, and what are the different classes of legislators, but advocates and parties to the causes which they determine? Is a law proposed concerning private debts? It is a question to which the creditors are parties on one side, and the debtors on the other. Justice ought to hold the balance between them. Yet the parties are and must be themselves the judges; and the most numerous party, or, in other words, the most powerful faction must be expected to prevail. Shall domestic manufactures be encouraged, and in what degree, by restrictions on foreign manufactures? are questions which would be differently decided by the landed and the manufacturing classes; and probably by neither, with a sole regard to justice and the public good. The apportionment of taxes on the various descriptions of property, is an act which seems to require the most exact impartiality; yet, there is perhaps no legislative act in which greater opportunity and temptation are given to a predominant party, to trample on the rules of justice. Every shilling with which they over-burden the in-ferior number, is a shilling saved to their own pockets.

It is in vain to say, that enlightened statesmen will be able to adjust these clashing interests, and render them all subservient to the public good. Enlightened statesmen will not always be at the helm: Nor, in many cases, can such an adjustment be made at all, without taking into view indirect and remote considerations, which will rarely prevail over the immediate interest which one party may find in disregarding the rights of another, or the good of the whole.

The inference to which we are brought, is, that the *causes* of faction cannot be removed; and that relief is only to be sought in the means of controlling its *effects*.

If a faction consists of less than a majority, relief is supplied by the republican principle, which enables the majority to defeat its sinister views by regular vote: It may clog the administration, it may convulse the society; but it will be unable to execute and mask its violence under the forms of the Constitution. When a majority is included in a faction, the form of popular government on the other hand enables it to sacrifice to its ruling passion or interest, both the public good and the rights of other citizens. To secure the public good, and private rights, against the danger of such a faction, and at the same time to preserve the spirit and the form of popular government, is then the great object to which our enquiries are directed: Let me add that it is the great desideratum, by which alone this form of government can be rescued from the opprobrium under which it has so long labored, and be recommended to the esteem and adoption of mankind.

By what means is this object attainable? Evidently by one of two only. Either the existence of the same passion or interest in a majority at the same time, must be prevented; or the majority, having such co-existent passion or interest, must be rendered, by their number and local situation, unable to concert and carry into effect schemes of oppression. If the impulse and the opportunity be suffered to coincide, we well know that neither moral nor religious motives can be relied on as an adequate control. They are not found to be such on the injustice and violence of individuals, and lose their efficacy in proportion to the number combined together; that is, in proportion as their efficacy becomes needful.

From this view of the subject, it may be concluded, that a pure Democracy, by which I mean, a Society, consisting of a small number of citizens, who assemble and administer the Government in person, can admit of no cure for the mischiefs of faction. A common passion or interest will, in almost every case, be felt by a majority of the whole; a communication and concert results from the form of Government itself; and there is nothing to check the inducements to sacrifice the weaker party, or an obnoxious individual. Hence it is, that such Democracies have ever been spectacles of turbulence and contention; have ever been found incompatible with personal security, or the rights of property; and have in general been as short in their lives, as they have been violent in their deaths. Theoretic politicians, who have patronized this species of Government, have erroneously supposed, that by reducing mankind to a perfect equality in their political rights, they would, at the same time, be perfectly equalized and assimilated in their possessions, their opinions, and their passions.

A republic, by which I mean a government in which the scheme of representation takes place, opens a different prospect, and promises the cure for which we are seeking. Let us examine the points in which it varies from pure democracy, and we shall comprehend both the nature of the cure and the efficacy which it must derive from the union.

The two great points of difference, between a democracy and a republic, are, first, the delegation of the government, in the latter, to a small number of citizens, elected by the rest; secondly, the greater number of citizens, and greater sphere of country, over which the latter may be extended.

The effect of the first difference is, on the one hand, to refine and enlarge the public views, by passing them through the medium of a chosen body of citizens, whose wisdom may best discern the true interest of their country, and whose patriotism and love of justice, will be least likely to sacrifice it to temporary or partial considerations. Under such a regulation, it may well happen, that the public voice, pronounced by the representatives of the people, will be more consonant to the public good, than if pronounced by the people themselves, convened for the purpose. On the other hand the effect may be inverted. Men of factious tempers, of local prejudices, or of sinister designs, may by intrigue, by corruption, or by other means, first obtain the suffrages, and then betray the interest of the people. The question resulting is, whether small or extensive republics are most favorable to the election of proper guardians of the public weal, and it is clearly decided in favor of the latter by two obvious considerations.

In the first place, it is to be remarked that, however small the republic may be, the representatives must be raised to a certain number, in order to guard against the cabals of a few; and that however large it may be, they must be limited to a certain number, in order to guard against the confusion of a multitude. Hence, the number of representatives in the two cases not being in proportion to that of the constituents, and being proportionally greatest in the small republic, it follows, that if the proportion of fit characters be not less in the large than in the small republic, the former will present a greater option, and consequently a greater probability of a fit choice.

In the next place, as each Representative will be chosen by a greater number of citizens in the large than in the small Republic, it will be more difficult for unworthy candidates to practise with success the vicious arts, by which elections are too often carried; and the suffrages of the people being more free, will be more likely to center on men who possess the most attractive merit, and the most diffusive and established characters.

It must be confessed, that in this, as in most other cases, there is a mean, on both sides of which inconveniences will be found to lie. By enlarging too much the number of electors, you render the representatives too little acquainted with all their local circumstances and lesser interests; as by reducing it too much, you render him unduly attached to these, and too little fit to comprehend and pursue great and national objects. The Federal Constitution forms a happy combination in this respect; the great and aggregate interests being referred to the national, the local and particular, to the state legislatures.

The other point of difference is, the greater number of citizens and extent of territory which may be brought within the compass of Republican, than of Democratic Government; and it is this circumstance principally which renders factious combinations less to be dreaded in the former, than in the latter. The smaller the society, the fewer probably will be the distinct parties and interests composing it; the fewer the distinct parties and interests, the more frequently will a majority be found of the same party; and the smaller the number of individuals composing a majority, and the smaller the compass within which they are placed, the more easily will they concert and execute their plans of oppression. Extend the sphere, and you take in a greater variety of parties and interests; you make it less probable that a majority of the whole will have a common motive to invade the rights of other citizens; or if such a common motive exists, it will be more difficult for all who feel it to discover their own strength, and to act in unison with each other. Besides other impediments, it may be remarked, that where there is a consciousness of unjust or dishonorable purposes, communication is always checked by distrust, in proportion to the number whose concurrence is necessary.

Hence it clearly appears, that the same advantage, which a Republic has over a Democracy, in controlling the effects of faction, is enjoyed by a large over a small Republic—is enjoyed by the Union over the States composing it. Does this advantage consist in the substitution of Representatives, whose enlightened views and virtuous sentiments render them superior to local prejudices, and to schemes of injustice? It will not be denied, that the Representation of the Union will be most likely to possess these requisite endowments. Does it consist in the greater security afforded by a greater variety of parties, against the event of any one party being able to outnumber and oppress the rest? In an equal degree does the increased variety of parties, comprised within the Union, increase this security? Does it, in fine, consist in the greater obstacles opposed to the concert and accomplishment of the secret wishes of an unjust and interested majority? Here, again, the extent of the Union gives it the most palpable advantage.

The influence of factious leaders may kindle a flame within their particular States, but will be unable to spread a general conflagration through the other States: a religious sect, may degenerate into a political faction in a part of the Confederacy but the variety of sects dispersed over the entire face of it, must secure the national Councils against any danger from that source: a rage for paper money, for an abolition of debts, for an equal division of property, or for any other improper or wicked project, will be less apt to pervade the whole body of the Union, than a particular member of it; in the same proportion as such a malady is more likely to taint a particular county or district, than an entire State.

In the extent and proper structure of the Union, therefore, we behold a Republican remedy for the diseases most incident to Republican Government. And according to the degree of pleasure and pride, we feel in being Republicans, ought to be our zeal in cherishing the spirit, and supporting the character of Federalists.

PUBLIUS

see it particularly displayed in all the subordinate distributions of power; where the constant aim is to divide and arrange the several offices in such a manner as that each may be a check on the other; that the private interest of every individual, may be a sentinel over the public rights. These inventions of prudence cannot be less requisite in the distribution of the supreme powers of the state.

But it is not possible to give to each department an equal power of self defense. In republican government the legislative authority, necessarily, predominates. The remedy for this inconveniency is, to divide the legislature into different branches; and to render them by different modes of election, and different principles of action, as little connected with each other, as the nature of their common functions, and their common dependence on the society, will admit. It may even be necessary to guard against dangerous encroachments by still further precautions. As the weight of the legislative authority requires that it should be thus divided, the weakness of the executive may require, on the other hand, that it should be fortified. An absolute negative, on the legislature, appears at first view to be the natural defense with which the executive magistrate should be armed. But perhaps it would be neither altogether safe, nor alone sufficient. On ordinary occasions, it might not be exerted with the requisite firmness; and on extraordinary occasions, it might be prefidiously abused. May not this defect of an absolute negative be supplied, by some qualified connection between this weaker department, and the weaker branch of the stronger department, by which the latter may be led to support the constitutional rights of the former, without being too much detached from the rights of its own department?

If the principles on which these observations are founded be just, as I persuade myself they are, and they be applied as a criterion, to the several state constitutions, and to the federal constitution, it will be found, that if the latter does not perfectly correspond with them, the former are infinitely less able to bear such a test.

There are moreover two considerations particularly applicable to the federal system of America, which place that system in a very interesting point of view.

First. In a single republic, all the power surrendered by the people, is submitted to the administration of a single government; and usurpations are guarded against by a division of the government into distinct and separate departments. In the compound republic of America, the power surrendered by the people, is first divided between two distinct governments, and then the portion allotted to each, subdivided among distinct and separate departments. Hence a double security arises to the rights of the people. The different governments will control each other; at the same time that each will be controlled by itself.

Second. It is of great importance in a republic, not only to guard the society against the oppression of its rulers; but to guard one part of the society against the injustice of the other part. Different interests necessarily exist in different classes of citizens. If a majority be united by a common interest, the rights of the minority will be insecure. There are but two methods of providing against this evil: The one by creating a will in the community independent of the majority, that is, of the society itself, the other by comprehending in the society so many separate descriptions of citizens, as will render an unjust combination of a majority of the whole, very improbable, if not impracticable. The first method prevails in all governments possessing an hereditary or self appointed authority. This at best is but a precarious security; because a power independent of the society may as well espouse the unjust views of the major, as the rightful interests, of the minor party, and may possibly be turned against both parties. The second method will be exemplified in the federal republic of the United States. While all authority in it will be derived from and dependent on the society, the society itself will be broken into so many parts, interests and classes of citizens, that the rights of individuals or of the minority, will be in little danger from interested combinations of the majority. In a free government, the security for civil rights must be the same as for religious rights. It consists in the one case in the multiplicity of interests, and in the other, in the multiplicity of sects. The degree of security in both cases will depend on the number of interests and sects; and this may be presumed to depend on the extent of country and number of people comprehended under the same government. This view of the subject must particularly recommend a proper federal system to all the sincere and considerate friends of republican government: Since it shows that in exact proportion as the territory of the union may be formed into more circumscribed confederacies or states, oppressive combinations of a majority will be facilitated, the best security under the republican form, for the rights of every class of citizens, will be diminished; and consequently, the stability and independence of some member of the government, the only other security, must be proportionally increased. Justice is the end of government. It is the end of civil society. It ever has been, and ever will be pursued, until it be obtained, or until liberty be lost in the pursuit. In a society under the forms of which the stronger faction can readily unite and oppress the weaker, anarchy may as truly be said to reign, as in a state of nature where the weaker individual is not secured against the violence of the stronger: And as in the latter state even the stronger individuals are prompted by the uncertainty of their condition, to submit to a government which may protect the weak as well as themselves: So in the former state, will the more powerful factions or parties be gradually induced by a like motive, to wish for a government which will protect all parties, the weaker as well as the more powerful. It can be little doubted, that if the state of Rhode Island was separated from the confederacy, and left to itself, the insecurity of rights under the popular form of government within such narrow limits, would be displayed by such reiterated oppressions of factious majorities, that some power altogether independent of the people would soon be called for by the voice of the very factions whose misrule had proved the necessity of it. In the extended republic of the United States, and among the great variety of interests, parties and sects which it embraces, a coalition of a majority of the whole society could seldom take place on any other principles than those of justice and the general good; and there being thus less danger to a minor from the will of the major party, there must be less pretext also, to provide for the security of the former, by introducing into the government a will not dependent on the latter; or in other words, a will independent of the society itself. It is no less certain than it is important, notwithstanding the contrary opinions which have been entertained, that the larger the society, provided it lie within a practicable sphere, the more duly capable it will be of self government. And happily for the *republican cause,* the practicable sphere may be carried to a very great extent, by a judicious modification and mixture of the *federal principle.*

PUBLIUS

APPENDIX V

PRESIDENTS, CONGRESSES, AND CHIEF JUSTICES: 1789–1997

Term	President and Vice President	Party of President	Congress	Majority Party		Chief Justice of the United States
				House	Senate	
1789–1797	**George Washington** John Adams	None	1st 2d 3d 4th	(N/A) (N/A) (N/A) (N/A)	(N/A) (N/A) (N/A) (N/A)	John Jay (1789–1795) John Rutledge (1795) Oliver Ellsworth (1796–1800)
1797–1801	**John Adams** Thomas Jefferson	Federalist	5th 6th	(N/A) Fed	(N/A) Fed	Oliver Ellsworth (1796–1800) John Marshall (1801–1835)
1801–1809	**Thomas Jefferson** Aaron Burr (1801–1805) George Clinton (1805–1809)	Democratic-Republican	7th 8th 9th 10th	Dem-Rep Dem-Rep Dem-Rep Dem-Rep	Dem-Rep Dem-Rep Dem-Rep Dem-Rep	John Marshall (1801–1835)
1809–1817	**James Madison** George Clinton (1809–1812)[a] Elbridge Gerry (1813–1814)[a]	Democratic-Republican	11th 12th 13th 14th	Dem-Rep Dem-Rep Dem-Rep Dem-Rep	Dem-Rep Dem-Rep Dem-Rep Dem-Rep	John Marshall (1801–1835)
1817–1825	**James Monroe** Daniel D. Tompkins	Democratic-Republican	15th 16th 17th 18th	Dem-Rep Dem-Rep Dem-Rep Dem-Rep	Dem-Rep Dem-Rep Dem-Rep Dem-Rep	John Marshall (1801–1835)
1825–1829	**John Quincy Adams** John C. Calhoun	National-Republican	19th 20th	Nat'l Rep Dem	Nat'l Rep Dem	John Marshall (1801–1835)
1829–1837	**Andrew Jackson** John C. Calhoun (1829–1832)[b] Martin Van Buren (1833–1837)	Democrat	21st 22d 23d 24th	Dem Dem Dem Dem	Dem Dem Dem Dem	John Marshall (1801–1835) Roger B. Taney (1836–1864)
1837–1841	**Martin Van Buren** Richard M. Johnson	Democrat	25th 26th	Dem Dem	Dem Dem	Roger B. Taney (1836–1864)
1841	**William H. Harrison**[a] John Tyler (1841)	Whig				Roger B. Taney (1836–1864)
1841–1845	**John Tyler** (VP vacant)	Whig	27th 28th	Whig Dem	Whig Whig	Roger B. Taney (1836–1864)
1845–1849	**James K. Polk** George M. Dallas	Democrat	29th 30th	Dem Whig	Dem Dem	Roger B. Taney (1836–1864)
1849–1850	**Zachary Taylor**[a] Millard Fillmore	Whig	31st	Dem	Dem	Roger B. Taney (1836–1864)

Term	President and Vice President	Party of President	Congress	Majority Party		Chief Justice of the United States
				House	Senate	
1850–1853	**Millard Fillmore** (VP vacant)	Whig	32d	Dem	Dem	Roger B. Taney (1836–1864)
1853–1857	**Franklin Pierce** William R.D. King (1853)[a]	Democrat	33d 34th	Dem Rep	Dem Dem	Roger B. Taney (1836–1864)
1857–1861	**James Buchanan** John C. Breckinridge	Democrat	35th 36th	Dem Rep	Dem Dem	Roger B. Taney (1836–1864)
1861–1865	**Abraham Lincoln**[a] Hannibal Hamlin (1861–1865) Andrew Johnson (1865)	Republican	37th 38th 38th	Rep Rep Rep	Rep Rep Rep	Roger B. Taney (1836–1864) Salmon P. Chase (1864–1873)
1865–1869	**Andrew Johnson** (VP vacant)	Republican	39th 40th	Union Rep	Union Rep	Salmon P. Chase (1864–1873)
1869–1877	**Ulysses S. Grant** Schuyler Colfax (1869–1873) Henry Wilson (1873–1875)[a]	Republican	41st 42d 43d 44th	Rep Rep Rep Dem	Rep Rep Rep Rep	Salmon P. Chase (1864–1873) Morrison R. Waite (1874–1888)
1877–1881	**Rutherford B. Hayes** William A. Wheeler	Republican	45th 46th	Dem Dem	Rep Dem	Morrison R. Waite (1874–1888)
1881	**James A. Garfield**[a] Chester A. Arthur	Republican	47th	Rep	Rep	Morrison R. Waite (1874–1888)
1881–1885	**Chester A. Arthur** (VP vacant)	Republican	48th	Dem	Rep	Morrison R. Waite (1874–1888)
1885–1889	**Grover Cleveland** Thomas A. Hendricks (1885)[a]	Democrat	49th 50th	Dem Dem	Rep Rep	Morrison R. Waite (1874–1888) Melville W. Fuller (1888–1910)
1889–1893	**Benjamin Harrison** Levi P. Morton	Republican	51st 52d	Rep Dem	Rep Rep	Melville W. Fuller (1888–1910)
1893–1897	**Grover Cleveland** Adlai E. Stevenson	Democrat	53d 54th	Dem Rep	Dem Rep	Melville W. Fuller (1888–1910)
1897–1901	**William McKinley**[a] Garret A. Hobart (1897–1899)[a] Theodore Roosevelt (1901)	Republican	55th 56th	Rep Rep	Rep Rep	Melville W. Fuller (1888–1910)
1901–1909	**Theodore Roosevelt** (VP vacant, 1901–1905) Charles W. Fairbanks (1905–1909)	Republican	57th 58th 59th 60th	Rep Rep Rep Rep	Rep Rep Rep Rep	Melville W. Fuller (1888–1910)
1909–1913	**William Howard Taft** James S. Sherman (1909–1912)[a]	Republican	61st 62d	Rep Dem	Rep Rep	Melville W. Fuller (1888–1910) Edward D. White (1910–1921)
1913–1921	**Woodrow Wilson** Thomas R. Marshall	Democrat	63d 64th 65th 66th	Dem Dem Dem Rep	Dem Dem Dem Rep	Edward D. White (1910–1921)
1921–1923	**Warren G. Harding**[a] Calvin Coolidge	Republican	67th	Rep	Rep	William Howard Taft (1921–1930)
1923–1929	**Calvin Coolidge** (VP vacant, 1923–1925) Charles G. Dawes (1925–1929)	Republican	68th 69th 70th	Rep Rep Rep	Rep Rep Rep	William Howard Taft (1921–1930)
1929–1933	**Herbert Hoover** Charles Curtis	Republican	71st 72d	Rep Dem	Rep Rep	William Howard Taft (1921–1930) Charles Evans Hughes (1930–1941)

Term	President and Vice President	Party of President	Congress	Majority Party		Chief Justice of the United States
				House	Senate	
1933–1945	**Franklin D. Roosevelt**[a] John N. Garner (1933–1941) Henry A. Wallace (1941–1945) Harry S Truman (1945)	Democrat	73d 74th 75th 76th 77th 78th	Dem Dem Dem Dem Dem Dem	Dem Dem Dem Dem Dem Dem	Charles Evans Hughes (1930–1941) Harlan F. Stone (1941–1946)
1945–1953	**Harry S Truman** (VP vacant, 1945–1949) Alben W. Barkley (1949–1953)	Democrat	79th 80th 81st 82d	Dem Rep Dem Dem	Dem Rep Dem Dem	Harlan F. Stone (1941–1946) Frederick M. Vinson (1946–1953)
1953–1961	**Dwight D. Eisenhower** Richard M. Nixon	Republican	83d 84th 85th 86th	Rep Dem Dem Dem	Rep Dem Dem Dem	Frederick M. Vinson (1946–1953) Earl Warren (1953–1969)
1961–1963	**John F. Kennedy**[a] Lyndon B. Johnson (1961–1963)	Democrat	87th	Dem	Dem	Earl Warren (1953–1969)
1963–1969	**Lyndon B. Johnson** (VP vacant, 1963–1965) Hubert H. Humphrey (1965–1969)	Democrat	88th 89th 90th	Dem Dem Dem	Dem Dem Dem	Earl Warren (1953–1969)
1969–1974	**Richard M. Nixon**[c] Spiro T. Agnew (1969–1973)[b] Gerald R. Ford (1973–1974)[d]	Republican	91st 92d	Dem Dem	Dem Dem	Earl Warren (1953–1969) Warren E. Burger (1969–1986)
1974–1977	**Gerald R. Ford** Nelson A. Rockefeller	Republican	93d 94th	Dem Dem	Dem Dem	Warren E. Burger (1969–1986)
1977–1981	**Jimmy Carter** Walter Mondale	Democrat	95th 96th	Dem Dem	Dem Dem	Warren E. Burger (1969–1986)
1981–1989	**Ronald Reagan** George Bush	Republican	97th 98th 99th 100th	Dem Dem Dem Dem	Rep Rep Rep Dem	Warren E. Burger (1969–1986) William H. Rehnquist (1986–)
1989–1993	**George Bush** J. Danforth Quayle	Republican	101st 102d	Dem Dem	Dem Dem	William H. Rehnquist (1986–)
1993–1999	**William J. Clinton** Albert Gore Jr.	Democrat	103d 104th 105th 106th	Dem Rep Rep Rep	Dem Rep Rep Rep	William H. Rehnquist (1986–)

[a]Died in office.
[b]Resigned from the vice presidency.
[c]Resigned from the presidency.
[d]Appointed vice president.

MAJOR SUPREME COURT CASES

- **Brown v. Board of Education (1954):** U.S. Supreme Court decision holding that school segregation is inherently unconstitutional because it violates the Fourteenth Amendment's guarantee of equal protection; marked the end of legal segregation in the United States.

- **Civil Rights Cases (1875):** Name attached to five cases brought under the Civil Rights Act of 1875. In 1883 the Supreme Court decided that discrimination in a variety of public accommodations, including theaters, hotels, and railroads, could not be prohibited by the act because it was private and not state discrimination.

- **Gibbons v. Ogden (1824):** The Court upheld broad congressional power over interstate commerce.

- **Immigration and Naturalization Service v. Chadha (1983):** Legislative veto ruled unconstitutional by the Supreme Court.

- **Marbury v. Madison (1803):** Supreme Court case in which the Court first asserted the power of judicial review in finding that a congressional statute extending the Court's original jurisdiction was unconstitutional.

- **McCulloch v. Maryland (1819):** Supreme Court upheld the power of the national government and denied the right of a state to tax the bank. The Court's broad interpretation of the necessary and proper clause paved the way for later rulings upholding expansive federal powers.

- **Miranda v. Arizona (1966):** The Fifth Amendment requires that individuals arrested for a crime must be advised of their right to remain silent and to have counsel present.

- **New York Times Co. v. Sullivan (1964):** Supreme Court decision ruling that simply publishing a defamatory falsehood is not enough to justify a libel judgment. "Actual malice" must be proved to support a finding of libel against a public figure.

- **Plessy v. Ferguson (1896):** *Plessy* challenged a Louisiana statute requiring that railroads provide separate accommodations for blacks and whites. The Court found that separate but equal accommodations did not violate the equal protection clause of the Fourteenth Amendment.

- **Roe v. Wade (1973):** The Supreme Court found that a woman's right to an abortion was protected by the right to privacy that could be implied from specific guarantees found in the Bill of Rights and the Fourteenth Amendment.

- **United States v. Nixon (1974):** There is no constitutional absolute executive privilege that would allow a president to refuse to comply with a court order to produce information needed in a criminal trial.

GLOSSARY

administrative adjudication: A quasi-judicial process in which a bureaucratic agency settles disputes between two parties in a manner similar to the way courts resolve disputes.

administrative discretion: The ability of bureaucrats to make choices concerning the best way to implement congressional intentions.

advisory referendum: A process in which voters cast nonbinding ballots on an issue or proposal.

affiliates: Local television stations that carry the programming of a national network.

affirmative action: A policy or program designed to redress prior discrimination.

agenda setting: The constant process of forming the list of issues to be addressed by government.

agenda: A set of problems to which policy makers believe they should be attentive.

amicus curiae: "Friend of the court"; a third party to a lawsuit who files a legal brief for the purpose of raising additional points of view in an attempt to influence a court's decision.

Anti-Federalists: Those who favored strong state governments and a weak national government; opposed the ratification of the U.S. Constitution.

appellate court: Courts that generally review only findings of law made by lower courts.

appellate jurisdiction: The power vested in an appellate court to review and/or revise the decision of a lower court.

aristocracy: A system of government in which control is based on rule of the highest.

Articles of Confederation: The compact among the thirteen original states that was the basis of their government. Written in 1776, the Articles were not ratified by all the states until 1781.

articles of impeachment: The specific charges brought against a president or a federal judge by the House of Representatives.

at-large election: Election in which candidates for office must compete throughout the jurisdiction as a whole.

bicameral legislature: A legislature divided into two houses; the U.S. Congress and every state legislature are bicameral (except Nebraska, which is unicameral).

bill of attainder: A law declaring an act illegal without a judicial trial.

Bill of Rights: The first ten amendments to the U.S. Constitution guaranteeing specific rights and liberties.

bill: A proposed law.

Black Codes: Laws denying most legal rights to newly freed slaves; passed by Southern states following the Civil War.

blanket primary: A primary in which voters may cast ballots in either party's primary (but not both) on an office-by-office basis.

block grant: Broad grant with few strings attached given to states by the federal government for specified activities, such as secondary education or health services.

bottom-up review: Post–Cold War review of U.S. defense forces and policies.

brief: A document containing the collected legal written arguments in a case filed with a court by a party prior to a hearing or trial.

bureaucracy: A set of complex hierarchical departments, agencies, commissions, and their staffs that exist to help the president carry out his constitutionally mandated charge to enforce the laws of the nation.

business cycles: Fluctuation between expansion and recession that is a part of modern capitalist economies.

Cabinet: The formal body of presidential advisers who head the fourteen departments Presidents often add others to this body of formal advisers.

campaign manager: The individual who travels with the candidate and coordinates the many different aspects of the campaign.

candidate debates: Forums in which political candidates face each other to discuss their platforms, records, and character.

capitalism: The economic system that favors private control of business and minimal governmental regulation of private industry.

casework: The process of solving constituents' problems dealing with the bureaucracy.

categorical grant: Grant for which Congress appropriates funds for a specific purpose.

charter: A document that, like a constitution, specifies the basic policies, procedures, and institutions of a municipality.

checks and balances: A governmental structure that gives each of the three branches of government some degree of oversight and control over the actions of the others.

city council: The legislature in a city government.

civil liberties: The personal rights and freedoms that the federal government cannot abridge by law, constitution, or judicial interpretation.

civil rights: Refers to the positive acts governments take to protect individuals against arbitrary or discriminatory treatment by governments or individuals based on categories such as race, sex, national origin, age, or sexual orientation.

Civil Rights Act of 1964: Legislation passed by Congress to outlaw segregation in public facilities and racial discrimination in employment, education, and voting; created the Equal Employment Opportunity Commission.

civil service laws: These acts removed the staffing of the bureaucracy from political parties and created a professional bureaucracy filled through competition.

civil service system: The system created by civil service laws by which many appointments to the federal bureaucracy are made.

clear and present danger test: Used by the Supreme Court to draw the line between protected and unprotected speech; the Court looks to see if there is an imminent danger that illegal action would occur in response to the contested speech.

clientele agency: Executive department directed by law to foster and promote the interests of a specific segment or group in the U.S. population (such as the Department of Education).

closed primary: A primary election in which only a party's registered voters are eligible to vote.

coalition: A group of interests or organizations that join forces for the purpose of electing public officials.

coattail effect: The tendency of lesser-known or weaker candidates lower on the ballot to profit in an election by the presence on the party's ticket of a more popular candidate.

collective good: Something of value that cannot be withheld from a noninterest group member, for example, a tax write-off, a good feeling.

commission: Form of local government in which several officials are elected to top positions which have both legislative and executive responsibilities.

Committees of Correspondence: Organizations in each of the American colonies created to keep colonists abreast of developments with the British; served as powerful molders of public opinion against the British.

common law: Traditions of society that are for the most part unwritten but based on the aggregation of rulings and interpretations of judges beginning in thirteenth-century England.

compact: A formal, legal agreement between a state and a tribe.

concurrent powers: Powers shared by the national and state governments.

confederation: Type of government in which the national government derives its powers from the states; a league of independent states.

conference committee: Joint committee created to iron out differences between Senate and House versions of a specific piece of legislation.

congressionalist: A view of the president's role in the law-making process that holds Article II's provision that the president should ensure "faithful execution of the laws" should be read as an injunction against substituting presidential authority for legislative intent.

congressional review: The process by which Congress can nullify an executive branch regulation by a resolution jointly passed in both Houses within sixty days of announcement of the regulation and accepted by the president.

conservative: One thought to believe that a government is best that governs least and that big government can only infringe on individual, personal, and economic rights.

constitutional court: Federal courts specifically created by the U.S. Constitution or by Congress pursuant to its authority in Article III.

containment: A strategy to oppose any further expansion of Soviet power, particularly in Western Europe and East Asia, by surrounding the Soviet Union with U.S. or Allied military forces.

content regulation: Governmental attempts to regulate the electronic media.

Contract with America: Campaign pledge signed by most Republican candidates in 1994 to guide their legislative agenda.

contrast ad: Ad that compares the records and proposals of the candidates, with a bias toward the sponsor.

cooperative federalism: A term used to characterize the relationship between the national and state governments that began with the New Deal.

county: A geographic district created within a state with a government that has general responsibilities for land, welfare, environment, and, where appropriate, rural service policies.

critical election: An election that signals a party realignment through voter polarization around new issues.

D

Declaration of Independence: Document drafted by Thomas Jefferson in 1776 that proclaimed the right of the American colonies to separate from Great Britain.

de facto **discrimination:** Racial discrimination that results from practice (such as housing patterns or other social factors) rather than the law.

deep background: Information gathered for news stories that must be completely unsourced.

de jure **discrimination:** Racial segregation that is a direct result of law or official policy.

delegate: Role played by elected representatives who vote the way their constituents would want them to, regardless of their own opinions.

deliberative poll: A new type of poll to bring a representative sample of people together to discuss and debate political issues in order to provide considered policy suggestions to lawmakers.

democracy: A system of government that gives power to the people, whether directly or through their elected representatives.

department: A major administrative unit with responsibility for a broad area of government operations. Departmental status usually indicates a permanent national interest in that particular governmental function, such as Defense, Health, or Agriculture.

direct (popular) referendum: A process in which voters can veto a bill recently passed in the legislature by placing the issue on a ballot and expressing disapproval.

direct democracy: A system of government in which members of the polity meet to discuss all policy decisions and then agree to abide by majority rule.

direct incitement test: The advocacy of illegal action is protected by the First Amendment unless imminent action is intended and likely to occur.

direct initiative: A process in which voters can place a proposal on a ballot and enact it into law without involving the legislature or the governor.

direct mailer: A professional who supervises a political campaign's direct-mail fundraising strategies.

direct primary: The selection of party candidates through the ballots of qualified voters rather than at party nomination conventions.

discharge petition: Petition that gives a majority of the House of Representatives the authority to bring an issue to the floor in the face of committee inaction.

discount rate: The rate of interest at which member banks can borrow money from their regional Federal Reserve Bank.

district-based election: Election in which candidates run for an office that represents only the voters of a specific district within the jurisdiction.

disturbance theory: The theory offered by political scientist David B. Truman that posits that interest groups form in part to counteract the efforts of other groups.

domestic dependent nation: A type of sovereignty that makes an Indian tribe in the United States outside the authority of state governments but reliant on the federal government for the definition of tribal authority.

dual federalism: The belief that having separate and equally powerful levels of government is the best arrangement.

dualist theory: The theory claiming that there has always been an underlying binary party nature to U.S. politics.

due process clause: Clause contained in the Fifth and Fourteenth Amendments. Over the years, it has been construed to guarantee to individuals a variety of rights ranging from economic liberty to criminal procedural rights to protection from arbitrary governmental action.

due process rights: Procedural guarantees provided by the Fourth, Fifth, Sixth, and Eighth amendments for those accused of crimes.

E

economic interest group: A group with the primary purpose of promoting the financial interests of its members.

economic regulation: Governmental regulation of business practices, industry rates, routes, or areas serviced by particular industries.

economic stability: A situation in which there is economic growth, rising national income, high employment, and steadiness in the general level of prices.

elastic clause: A name given to the "necessary and proper clause" found in the final paragraph of Article I, section 8, of the U.S. Constitution. It gives Congress the authority to pass all laws "necessary and proper" to carry out the enumerated powers specified in the Constitution.

elector: Member of the electoral college chosen by methods determined in each state.

electoral college: Representatives of each state who cast the final ballots that actually elect a president.

electorate: Citizens eligible to vote.

electronic media: The newest form of broadcast media, including television, radio, cable, and the Internet.

engagement: A policy that says the United States will take the lead in international political and economic affairs, largely through constructive dialogue, but also by securing regional and global peace.

enlargement: A policy that says the United States will promote democracy, open markets, and other Western political, economic, and social values around the world.entitlement program: Income security program to which all those meeting eligibility criteria are entitled.

entitlement program: Income security program to which all those meeting eligibility criteria are entitled.

enumerated powers: Seventeen specific powers granted to Congress under Article I, section 8, of the U.S. Constitution; these powers include taxation, coinage of money, regulation of commerce, and the authority to provide for a national defense.

Equal Employment Opportunity Commission: Federal agency created to enforce the Civil Rights Act of 1964, which forbids discrimination on the basis of race, creed, national origin, religion, or sex in hiring, promotion, or firing.

equal protection clause: Section of the Fourteenth Amendment that guarantees that all citizens receive "equal protection of the laws"; has been used to bar discrimination against blacks and women.

equal time rule: The rule that requires broadcast stations to sell campaign air time equally to all candidates if they choose to sell it to any.

establishment clause: The first clause in the First Amendment. It prohibits the national government from establishing a national religion.

European Union (EU): The union that joins most of the countries of Western Europe in their efforts to develop common economic, social, and foreign policies; successor to the European Communities.

exclusionary rule: Judicially created rule that prohibits police from using illegally seized evidence at trial.

executive agreement: A formal agreement entered into by the executive branches of different countries. These agreements do not require the advice and consent of the Senate.

Executive Office of the President (EOP): Establishment created in 1939 to help the president oversee the bureaucracy.

executive order: Presidential directive to an agency that provides the basis for carrying out laws or for establishing new policies.

exit poll: Poll conducted at selected polling places on Election Day.

ex post facto law: Law passed after the fact, thereby making previously legal activity illegal and subject to current penalty; prohibited by the U.S. Constitution.

fairness doctrine: Rule in effect from 1949 to 1985 requiring broadcasters to cover events adequately and to present contrasting views on important public issues.

Federal Employees Political Activities Act: 1993 liberalization of Hatch Act. Federal employees are now allowed to run for office in nonpartisan elections and to contribute money to campaigns in partisan elections.

federal system: Plan of government created in the U.S. Constitution in which power is divided between the national government and the state governments and in which independent states are government.

federalism: The philosophy that describes the governmental system created by the Framers; see also federal system.

Federalists: Those who favored a stronger national government and supported the proposed U.S. Constitution; later became the first U.S. political party.

The Federalist Papers: A series of eighty-five political papers written by John Jay, Alexander Hamilton, and James Madison in support of ratification of the U.S. Constitution.

Fifteenth Amendment: One of the three Civil War amendments, specifically enfranchises blacks.

filibuster: A formal way of halting action on a bill by means of long speeches or unlimited debate in the Senate.

finance chair: A volunteer who coordinates the fundraising efforts for the campaign.

First Continental Congress: Meeting held in Philadelphia from September 5 to October 26, 1774, in which fifty-six delegates (from every colony except Georgia) adopted a resolution that opposed the Coercive Acts.

fiscal policy: Federal government policies on taxes, spending and debt management, intended to promote the nation's macroeconomic goals, particularly with respect to employment, price stability and growth.

floating exchange rate: When the value of a national currency depends on what people are willing to pay for it in other currencies, usually in U.S. dollars, English pounds, or German marks.

Fourteenth Amendment: One of the three Civil War amendments; guarantees equal protection and due process of laws to all U.S. citizens.

franchise: The right to vote.

free exercise clause: The second clause of the First Amendment. It prohibits the U.S. government from interfering with a citizen's right to practice his or her religion.

free market economy: The economic system in which the "invisible hand" of the market regulates prices, wages, product mix, and so on.

free media: Coverage of a candidate's campaign by the news media.

free rider: A problem that occurs when those who don't join or work for the benefit of the group still reap the rewards of the group's activity.

front-loading: The tendency of states to choose an early date on the primary calendar.

gender gap: The tendency for women to vote for candidates of the Democratic Party.

General Agreement on Tariffs and Trade (GATT): Devised shortly after World War II as an interim measure until a World Trade Organization could be created, multilateral trade negotiations conducted under the GATT helped lower tariff and other trade barriers substantially.

general election campaign: That part of a political campaign following a primary election, aimed at winning a general election.

general election: Election in which voters decide which candidates will actually fill elective public offices.

gerrymandering: The legislative process through which the majority party in each statehouse tries to assure that the maximum number of representatives from its political party can be elected to Congress through the redrawing of legislative districts.

get-out-the-vote (GOTV): A push at the end of a political campaign to encourage supporters to go to the polls.

government corporation: Business set up and created by Congress that performs functions that could be provided by private businesses (such as the U.S. Postal Service).

governmental (institutional) agenda: The changing list of issues to which governments believe they should address themselves.

governmental party: The office holders and candidates who run under a political party's banner.

governor: Chief elected executive in state government.

grand strategy: The choices a government makes to balance and apply economic, military, diplomatic, and other national resources to preserve the nation's people and territory.

grandfather clause: Statute that allowed only those whose grandfathers had voted before Reconstruction to vote unless they passed a wealth or literacy test.

Great Compromise: A decision made during the Philadelphia Convention to give each state the same number of representatives in the Senate regardless of size; representation in the House was determined by population.

gross domestic product (GDP): The total market value of all goods and services produced in a country during a year.

hard money: Legally specified and limited contributions that are clearly regulated by the Federal Election Campaign Act and by the Federal Election Commission.

Hatch Act: Laws enacted in 1939 to prohibit civil servants from taking activist roles in partisan campaigns. This act prohibited federal employees from making political contributions, working for a particular party, or campaigning for a particular candidate.

hold: A tactic by which a senator asks to be informed before a particular bill is brought to the floor. In effect, this stops the bill from coming to the floor until the "hold" is removed.

impeachment: Actual bringing of charges against a public official; not the hearings or trial on those charges.

impeachment: The power delegated to the House of Representatives in the Constitution to charge the president, vice president, or other "civil officers," including federal judges, with "Treason, Bribery, or other high Crimes and Misdemeanors." This is the first step in the constitutional process of removing such government officials from office.

implementation: The process by which a law or policy is put into operation by the bureaucracy.

implied power: A power derived from an enumerated power and the necessary and proper clause. These powers are not stated specifically but are considered to be reasonably implied through the exercise of delegated powers.

incorporation doctrine: Principle in which the Supreme Court has held that most, but not all, of the specific guarantees in the Bill of Rights limit state and local governments by making those guarantees applicable to the states through the due process clause of the Fourteenth Amendment.

incumbency: The condition of already holding elected office.

incumbency effect: The fact that being in office helps a person stay in office because of a variety of benefits which go with the position.

independent executive agency: Governmental unit that closely resembles Cabinet departments, these have narrower areas of responsibility (such as the Central Intelligence Agency), and are not part of any Cabinet departments.

independent regulatory commission: An agency created by Congress that is generally concerned with a specific aspect of the economy.

indirect (representative) democracy: A system of government that gives citizens the opportunity to vote for representatives who will work on their behalf.

indirect initiative: A process in which the legislature places a proposal on a ballot and allows voters to enact it into law, without involving the governor or further action by the legislature.

inflation: A rise in the general price levels of an economy.

in forma pauperis: Literally, "in the form of a pauper"; a way for an indigent or poor person to appeal a case to the U.S. Supreme Court.

inherent powers: Powers of the president that can be derived or inferred from specific powers in the Constitution.

initiative: A process that allows citizens to propose legislation and submit it to the state electorate for popular vote.

inoculation advertising: Advertising that attempts to counteract an anticipated attack from the opposition before the attack is even launched.

interest group: An organized group that tries to influence public policy.

intergovernmental lobby: The pressure group or groups that are created when state and local governments hire lobbyists to lobby the national government.

international governmental organization (IGO): An organization formed by three or more countries, with regular meetings and a permanent staff.

International Monetary Fund (IMF): An IGO created shortly before the end of World War II designed to stabilize international financial relations through a system of fixed exchange rates.

interventionist state: Replaced the *laissez-faire* state as the government took an active role in guiding and regulating the private economy.

iron triangle: The relatively stable relationship and pattern of interaction that occur among an agency, interest groups, and congressional committees or subcommittees.

isolationism: Grand strategy designed to keep a nation out of foreign political or economic affairs; dominated U.S. foreign policy until World War II.

issue network: A term used to describe the loose and informal set of relationships that exist among a large number of actors who work in broad policy areas.

issue-oriented politics: Politics that focuses on specific issues rather than on party, candidate, or other loyalties.

Jim Crow laws: Laws enacted by Southern states that discriminated against blacks by creating "whites only" schools, theaters, hotels, and other public accommodations.

judicial activism: A philosophy of judicial decision-making that argues judges should use their power broadly to further justice, especially in the areas of equality and personal liberty.

judicial implementation: Refers to how and whether judicial decisions are translated into actual public policies affecting more than the immediate parties to a lawsuit.

judicial restraint: A philosophy of judicial decision-making that argues courts should allow the decisions of other branches of government to stand, even when they offend a judge's own sense of principles.

judicial review: The authority of a court to review the acts of the legislature, the executive, or states to determine their constitutionality; enunciated by Chief Justice John Marshall in *Marbury* v. *Madison* (1803).

Judiciary Act of 1789: Established the basic three-tiered structure of the federal court system.

jurisdiction: Authority vested in a particular court to hear and decide the issues in any particular case.

L

laissez-faire: A French term literally meaning "to allow to do, to leave alone." It is a hands-off governmental policy that is based on the belief that governmental regulation of the economy is wrong.

League of Nations: Created in the peace treaty that ended World War I, it was the first IGO dedicated to preserving global peace; superseded by the United Nations.

legislative courts: Courts established by Congress for specialized purposes, such as the Court of Military Appeals.

legislative veto: A procedure by which one or both houses of Congress can disallow an act of the president or executive agency by a simple majority vote; ruled unconstitutional by the Supreme Court.

Lemon test: The Court devised tests designed to measure the constitutionality of state laws that appear to further a religion.

libel: False statements or statements tending to call someone's reputation into disrepute.

liberal: One considered to favor extensive governmental involvement in the economy and the provision of social services and to take an activist role in protecting the rights of women, the elderly, minorities, and the environment.

libertarian: One who favors a free market economy and no governmental interference in personal liberties.

line-item veto: The authority of a chief executive to delete part of a spending bill passed by the legislature that involves taxing and/or spending. The legislature may override a veto, usually with a two-thirds majority of each chamber.

lobbying: The activities of groups and organizations that seek to influence legislation and persuade political leaders to support a group's position.

lobbyist: Interest group representative who seeks to influence legislation that will benefit his or her organization through political persuasion.

Louisiana Purchase: The 1803 land purchase authorized by Thomas Jefferson, which expanded the size of the United States dramatically and expanded the concept of inherent powers.

M

machine: A party organization that recruits its members with tangible incentives and is characterized by a high degree of control over member activity.

majority leader: The elected leader of the party controlling the most seats in the U.S. House of Representatives or the Senate; is second in authority to the Speaker of the House and in the Senate is regarded as its most powerful member.

majority party: The political party in each house of Congress with the most members.

majority rule: The central premise of direct democracy in which only policies that collectively garner the support of a majority of voters will be made into law.

manager: A professional executive hired by a city council or county board to manage daily operations and to recommend policy changes.

mandate: A command, indicated by an electorate's votes, for the elected officials to carry out their platforms.

mandates: National laws that direct states or local governments to comply with federal rules or regulations (such as clean air or water standards) under threat of civil or criminal penalties or as a condition of receipt of any federal grants.

manifest destiny: A popular theory during the U.S. expansion westward that it was a divinely mandated obligation to expand across North America to the Pacific Ocean.

margin of error: A measure of the accuracy of a public opinion poll.

Marshall Plan: The European Recovery Program, named after Secretary of State George C. Marshall, which provided a massive transfer of aid from the United States to Western Europe in the years after World War II.

matching funds: Donations to presidential campaigns from the federal government that are determined by the amount of private funds a qualifying candidate raises.

mayor: Chief elected executive of a city.

means-tested program: Income security program intended to assist those whose incomes fall below a designated level.

media campaign: That part of a political campaign waged in the broadcast and print media.

media consultant: A professional who produces political candidates' television, radio, and print advertisements.

media effects: The influence of news sources on public opinion.

Medicaid: An expansion of Medicare, this program subsidizes medical care for the poor.

Medicare: The federal program established in the Johnson administration that provides medical care to elderly Social Security recipients.

mercantile system: A system that binds trade and its administration to the national government.

merit system: The system by which federal civil service jobs are classified into grades or levels to which appointments are made on the basis of performance on competitive examinations.

minority leader: The elected leader of the party with the second highest number of elected representatives in either the House or the Senate.

minority party: Party with the second most members in either house of Congress.

Miranda **rights:** Statements that must be made by the police informing a suspect of his or her constitutional rights protected by the Fifth Amendment, including the right to an attorney provided by the court if the suspect cannot afford one.

monarchy: A form of government in which power is vested in hereditary kings and queens.

monetary policy: A form of government regulation in which the nation's money supply and interest rates are controlled.

money: A system of exchange for goods and services that includes currency, coins, and bank deposits.

Monroe Doctrine: President James Monroe's 1823 pledge that the United States would oppose attempts by European states to extend their political control over the Western hemisphere.

muckraking: A form of newspaper publishing, in vogue in the early twentieth century, concerned with reforming government and business conduct.

multilateralism: The foreign policy practice that actions should be taken in cooperation with other states after extensive consultation.

municipality: A government with general responsibilities that is created in response to

the emergence of relatively densely populated areas.

mutually assured destruction (MAD): The situation where one nation could absorb a nuclear strike by another and have sufficient nuclear forces to launch a devastating retaliatory strike; seen as a means of deterring nuclear war.

N

nation-state: Ideally, a country where the people share one nationality and govern themselves. This form of political organization is based on the idea that one government should have sole authority over a well-defined territory.

national convention: A party conclave (meeting) held in the presidential election year for the purposes of nominating a presidential and vice-presidential ticket and adopting a platform.

national party platform: A statement of the general and specific philosophy and policy goals of a political party, usually promulgated at the national convention.

National Security Acts of 1947 and 1949: The acts that unified the armed services and created the modern U.S. security establishment, including the National Security Council and the Central Intelligence Agency.

natural law: A doctrine that society should be governed by certain ethical principles that are part of nature and, as such, can be understood by reason.

necessary and proper clause: A name given to the clause found in the final paragraph of Article I, section 8 of the U.S. Constitution giving Congress the authority to pass all laws "necessary and proper" to carry out the enumerated powers specified in the Constitution; the "elastic" clause.

negative ad: Advertising on behalf of a candidate that attacks the opponent's platform or character.

network: An association of broadcast stations (radio or television) that share programming through a financial arrangement.

New Deal: The name given to the program of "Relief, Recovery, Reform" begun by President Franklin D. Roosevelt, in 1933 designed to bring the United States out of the Great Depression.

New Jersey Plan: A framework for the Constitution proposed by a group of small states; its key points were a one-house legislature with one vote for each state, a multiperson "executive," the establishment of the acts of Congress as the "supreme law" of the land, and a supreme judiciary with limited power.

nomination campaign: That part of a political campaign aimed at winning a primary election.

non-means-based program: Program such as Social Security where benefits are provided irrespective of the income or means of recipients.

nonpartisan election: A contest in which candidates run without formal identification or association with a political party.

North American Free Trade Agreement (NAFTA): A treaty that promotes the free movement of goods and services between Canada, Mexico, and the United States.

North Atlantic Treaty Organization (NATO): A political and military regional defense alliance created in 1950 to implement the North Atlantic Treaty of 1949; the first peace-time military alliance made by the United States.

off the record: Term applied to information gathered for a news story that cannot be used at all.

off-year election: Election that takes place in the middle of a presidential term.

oligarchy: A form of government in which the right to participate is always conditioned on the possession of wealth, social status, military position, or achievement.

on background: A term for when sources are not included in a news story.

on the record: Term applied to information gathered for a news story that can be used and cited.

one-partyism: A political system in which one party dominates and wins virtually all contests.

open market operations: The buying and selling of government securities by the Federal Reserve Bank in the securities market.

open primary: A primary in which party members, independents, and sometimes members of the other party are allowed to vote.

organizational campaign: That part of a political campaign involved in fund raising, literature distribution, and all other activities not directly involving the candidate.

organizational party: The workers and activists who staff the party's formal organization.

original jurisdiction: The jurisdiction of courts that hear a case first, usually in trial. Courts determine the facts of a case under their original jurisdiction.

oversight: Congressional review of the activities of an agency, department, or office.

package or general veto: The authority of a chief executive to void an entire bill that has been passed by the legislature. This veto applies to all bills, whether or not they have tax-

ing or spending components, and the legislature may override this veto, usually with a two-thirds majority of each chamber.

paid media: Political advertisements purchased for a candidate's campaign.

pardon: The restoration of all rights and privileges of citizenship to a specific individual charged or convicted of a crime.

party caucus: A formal gathering of all party members.

party identification: A citizen's personal affinity for a political party, usually expressed by his or her tendency to vote for the candidates of that party.

party realignment: A shifting of party coalition groupings in the electorate that remains in place for several elections.

party-in-the-electorate: The voters who consider themselves to be allied or associated with the party.

patron: Individual who finances an interest group.

patronage: Jobs, grants, or other special favors that are given as rewards to friends and political allies for their support.

Pendleton Act: Reform measure that created the Civil Service Commission to administer a partial merit system. It classified the federal service by grades to which appointments were made based on the results of a competitive examination. It made it illegal for political appointees to be required to contribute to a particular political party.

personal campaign: That part of a political campaign concerned with presenting the candidate's public image.

personal liberty: A key characteristic of U.S. democracy. Initially meaning freedom from governmental interference, today it includes demands for freedom to engage in a variety of practices free from governmental discrimination.

pocket veto: If Congress adjourns during the ten days the president has to consider a bill passed by both houses of Congress, without the president's signature, the bill is considered vetoed.

policy adoption: The approval of a policy proposal by the people with the requisite authority, such as a legislature.

policy evaluation: The process of determining whether a course of action is achieving its intended goals.

policy formulation: The crafting of appropriate and acceptable proposed courses of action to ameliorate or resolve public problems.

policy implementation: The process of carrying out public policy through governmental agencies and the courts.

political action committee (PAC): A federally registered fund-raising committee that

represents an interest group in the political process through campaign donations.

political consultant: Professional who manages campaigns and political advertisements for political candidates.

political culture: Attitudes toward the political system and its various parts, and attitudes toward the role of the self in the system.

political ideology: An individual's coherent set of values and beliefs about the purpose and scope of government.

political party: A group of office holders, candidates, activists, and voters who identify with a group label and seek to elect to public office individuals who run under that label.

political socialization: The process through which an individual acquires particular political orientations; the learning process by which people acquire their political beliefs and values.

politico: Role played by elected representatives who act as trustees or as delegates, depending on the issue.

politics: The process by which policy decisions are made.

pollster: A professional who takes public opinion surveys that guide political campaigns.

popular consent: The idea that governments must draw their powers from the consent of the governed.

popular sovereignty: The right of the majority to govern themselves.

pork barrel: Legislation that allows representatives to "bring home the bacon" to their districts in the form of public works programs, military bases, or other programs designed to benefit their districts directly.

positive ad: Advertising on behalf of a candidate that stresses the candidate's qualifications, family, and issue positions, without reference to the opponent.

precedent: Prior judicial decision that serves as a rule for settling subsequent cases of a similar nature.

preemption: A concept derived from the Constitution's supremacy clause that allows the national government to override or preempt state or local actions in certain areas.

presidentialist: One who believes that Article II's grant of executive power is a broad grant of authority and power allowing a president wide discretionary powers.

primary election: Election in which voters decide which of the candidates within a party will represent the party in the general election.

print press: The traditional form of mass media, comprising newspapers, magazines, and journals.

prior restraint: Judicial doctrine stating that the government cannot prohibit speech or publication before the fact.

privacy: The right to be let alone; a judicially created doctrine encompassing an individual's decision to use birth control or secure an abortion.

proportional representation: The practice of awarding legislative seats in proportion to the number of votes received.

prospective judgment: A voter's evaluation of a candidate based on what he or she pledges to do about an issue if elected.

public funds: Donations from the general tax revenues to the campaigns of qualifying presidential candidates.

public interest group: An organization that seeks a collective good that will not selectively and materially benefit the members of the group.

public opinion poll: Interviews or surveys with a sample of citizens that are used to estimate public opinion of the entire population.

public opinion: What the public thinks about a particular issue or set of issues at any point in time.

public policy: A purposive course of action followed by government in dealing with some problem or matter of concern.

R

random sampling: A method of selection that gives each potential voter or adult the same chance of being selected.

recall: Removal of an incumbent from office by popular vote.

recession: A short-term decline in the economy that occurs as investment sags, production falls off, and unemployment increases.

redistricting: The redrawing of congressional districts to reflect increases or decreases in seats allotted to the states, as well as population shifts within a state.

referendum: A procedure whereby the state legislature submits proposed legislation to the state's voters for approval.

regional primary: A proposed system in which the country would be divided into five or six geographic areas and all states in each region would hold their presidential primary elections on the same day.

regulation: Rule that governs the operation of a particular government program and has the force of law.

republic: A government rooted in the consent of the governed; a representative or indirect democracy.

reservation land: Land designated in a treaty that is under the authority of an Indian nation and is exempt from most state laws and taxes.

reserve (or police) powers: Powers reserved to the states by the Tenth Amendment that lie at the foundation of a state's right to legislate for the public health and welfare of its citizens.

reserve requirement: Governmental requirements that a portion of member banks' deposits must be retained to back loans made.

retrospective judgment: A voter's evaluation of the performance of the party in power.

right-of-rebuttal rule: A Federal Communications Commission regulation that people attacked on a radio or television broadcast be offered the opportunity to respond.

rule making: A quasi-legislative administrative process that has the characteristics of a legislative act.

Rule of Four: At least four justices of the Supreme Court must vote to consider a case before it can be heard.

runoff primary: A second primary election between the two candidates receiving the greatest number of votes in the first primary.

S

sampling error: A measure of the accuracy of a public opinion poll.

Second Continental Congress: Meeting that convened in Philadelphia on May 10, 1775, at which it was decided that an army should be raised and George Washington of Virginia was named commander-in-chief.

secular realignment: The gradual rearrangement of party coalitions, based more on demographic shifts than on shocks to the political system.

selective incorporation: A judicial doctrine whereby most but not all of the protections found in the Bill of Rights are made applicable to the states via the Fourteenth Amendment.

separation of powers: A way of dividing power among three branches of government in which members of the House of Representatives, members of the Senate, the president, and the federal courts are selected by and responsible to different constituencies.

Shays's Rebellion: A 1786 rebellion in which an army of 1,500 disgruntled and angry farmers led by Daniel Shays marched to Springfield, Massachusetts, and forcibly restrained the state court from foreclosing on their farms.

slander: Untrue spoken statements that defame the character of a person.

social contract theory: The belief that people are free and equal by God-given right and that this in turn requires that all people give their consent to be governed; espoused by John Locke and influential in the writing of the Declaration of Independence.

social regulation: Governmental regulation of the quality and safety of products as well as the conditions under which goods and services are produced.

Social Security Act: A 1935 law that established old age insurance (Social Security), as-

sistance for the needy, children, and others; and unemployment insurance.

social welfare policy: Governmental program designed to improve or enhance individuals' quality of life.

soft money: The virtually unregulated money funneled by individuals and political committees through state and local parties.

solicitor general: The fourth-ranking member of the Justice Department; responsible for handling all appeals on behalf of the U.S. government to the Supreme Court.

Speaker of the House: The only officer of the House of Representatives specifically mentioned in the Constitution; elected at the beginning of each new Congress by the entire House; traditionally a member of the majority party.

special district: A local government that is responsible for a particular function, such as K-12 education, water, sewerage, or parks.

spoils system: The firing of public-office holders of a defeated political party and their replacement with loyalists of the newly elected party.

spot ad: Television advertising on behalf of a candidate that is broadcast in sixty-, thirty-, or ten-second duration.

Stamp Act Congress: Meeting of representatives of nine of the thirteen colonies held in New York City in 1765, during which representatives drafted a document to send to the king listing how their rights had been violated.

standing committee: Committee to which proposed bills are referred.

stare decisis: In court rulings, a reliance on past decisions or precedents to formulate decisions in new cases.

stewardship theory: The theory that holds that Article II confers on the president the power *and* the duty to take whatever actions are deemed necessary in the national interest, unless prohibited by the Constitution or by law.

stratified sampling: A variation of random sampling; census data are used to divide a country into four sampling regions. Sets of counties and standard metropolitan statistical areas are then randomly selected in proportion to the total national population.

straw poll: Unscientific survey used to gauge public opinion on a variety of issues and policies.

strict constructionist: An approach to constitutional interpretation that emphasizes the Framers' initial intentions.

strict scrutiny: A heightened standard of review used by the Supreme Court to determine the constitutional validity of a challenged practice.

suffrage movement: Term used to refer to the drive for votes for women that took place in the United States from 1890 to 1920.

superdelegate: Delegate slot to the Democratic Party's national convention that is reserved for an elected party official.

supremacy clause: Portion of Article IV of the U.S. Constitution that mandates that national law is supreme to (that is, supersedes) all other laws passed by the states or by any other subdivision of government.

suspect classification: Category or class, such as race, that triggers the highest standard of scrutiny from the Supreme Court.

symbolic speech: Symbols, signs, and other methods of expression generally also considered to be protected by the First Amendment.

systemic agenda: All public issues that are viewed as requiring governmental attention; a discussion agenda.

Taftian theory: The theory that holds that the president is limited by the specific grants of executive power found in the Constitution.

tariffs: Taxes on imports, used to raise government revenue and to protect domestic industry.

term limits: Restrictions that exist in some states concerning how long an individual may serve in state and/or local elected offices.

third-partyism: The tendency of third parties to arise with some regularity in a nominally two-party system.

Thirteenth Amendment: One of the three Civil War amendments; specifically bans slavery in the United States.

Three-Fifths Compromise: Agreement reached at the Constitutional Convention stipulating that each slave was to be counted as three-fifths of a person for purposes of determining population for representation in the U.S. House of Representatives.

ticket-split: To vote for candidates of different parties for various offices in the same election.

tracking poll: Continuous surveys that enables a campaign to chart its daily rise or fall.

trade association: A group that represents specific industries.

trial court: Court of original jurisdiction where cases begin.

Truman Doctrine: President Truman's 1947 strategy to provide U.S. military and economic assistance to Greece and Turkey to contain Soviet expansion.

trust land: Land owned by an Indian nation and designated by the federal Bureau of Indian Affairs as exempt from most state laws and taxes.

trustee: Role played by elected representatives who listen to constituents' opinions and then use their best judgment to make final decisions.

turnout: The proportion of the voting-age public that votes.

unit rule: A traditional party practice under which the majority of a state delegation can force the minority to vote for its candidate.

United Nations: IGO created shortly before the end of World War II to guarantee the security of member nations when attacked, and to promote economic, physical, and social well-being around the world.

veto power: The formal, constitutional authority of the president to reject bills passed by both houses of Congress thus preventing their becoming law without further congressional action.

Virginia Plan: The first general plan for the Constitution, proposed by James Madison. Its key points were a bicameral legislature, an executive chosen by the legislature, and a judiciary also named by the legislature.

voter canvass: The process by which a campaign gets in touch with individual voters: either by door-to-door solicitation or by telephone.

𝒲

War Powers Act: A law passed near the end of the Vietnam War to limit the powers of the president to engage U.S. military forces in combat abroad without congressional consent.

Watergate: Term used to describe the events and scandal resulting from a break-in at the Democratic National Committee headquarters in 1972 and the subsequent coverup of White House involvement.

whip: One of several representatives who keep close contact with all members and take "nose counts" on key votes, prepare summaries of bills, and in general act as communications links within the party.

wire service: An electronic delivery of news gathered by the news services' correspondents and sent to all member news media organizations.

World Bank: Originally designed to provide loans for large economic projects in Western Europe's efforts to recover from the devastation of World War II; now the major multilateral lender for development projects in poor countries.

World Trade Organization: The IGO created in 1995 that manages multilateral negotiations to reduce barriers to trade and settle trade disputes between nations.

writ of certiorari: A formal document issued from the Supreme Court to a lower federal or state court that calls up a case.

𝒴

yellow journalism: A form of newspaper publishing in vogue in the late nineteenth century that featured pictures, comics, color, and sensationalized, oversimplified news coverage.

O

P